2010-2011

# 中国及海外会展概览®

# Directory of China & Overseas Exhibitions and Meetings

中国及海外会展概览编委会编辑

Edited By Editorial Board of

Directory of China & Overseas Exhibitions and Meetings

经济日报出版社

图书在版编目（CIP）数据

2010～2011中国及海外会展概览 / 张玉敏主编. --
北京 : 经济日报出版社, 2010.2
ISBN 978-7-80257-127-3

Ⅰ. ①2… Ⅱ. ①张… Ⅲ. ①展览会－概况－世界－
2010～2011 Ⅳ. ①G245

中国版本图书馆CIP数据核字（2010）第023598号

Diretory of China & Overseas Exhibitions and Meetings
2010-2011
Editoral Board of DCOEM



书名：中国及海外会展概览2010-2011

主　　编：张玉敏
责任编辑：王晓玲
封面设计：金　钥

出版发行：经济日报出版社
社　　址：北京市宣武区右安门内大街65号
邮政编码：100054
经　　销：全国新华书店
印　　刷：北京佳信达恒智彩印有限公司

开　　本：889×1194　1/16
字　　数：1000千字
印　　张：34
印　　次：2010年2月第一版 2010年2月第一次印刷

书　　号：ISBN 978-7-80257-127-3
定　　价：219.00元

# 特别感谢

## 给予本书大力支持的机构

## With thanks

to the many organizations and companies
that contribute to this Directory


泛联展览物流香港有限公司 ● Agility Fairs & Events Logistics Ltd

中国对外贸易广州展览公司 ● China Foreign Trade Guangzhou Exhibition Corporation

中国国际展览中心 ● China International Exhibition Center

中国国际贸易中心股份有限公司 ● China World Trade Center Co Ltd

北京爱博西雅展览有限公司 ● Exposium-SIAL Exhibition Co Ltd

广东现代国际展览中心 ● Guangdong Modern International Exhibition Center

香港贸易发展局 ● Hong Kong Trade Development Council

科隆展览中国有限公司 ● Koelnmesse Co Ltd China

澳门贸易投资促进局 ● Macao Trade and Investment Promotion Institute

上海新苑宾馆 ● New Garden Hotel

奥克坦姆系统科技（苏州）有限公司 ● OCTANORM® System Technology (Suzhou) Co Ltd

励展博览集团 ● Reed Exhibitions

全球国际货运有限公司 ● Schenker China Ltd

上海市国际展览有限公司 ● Shanghai International Exhibition Co Ltd

上海新国际博览中心有限公司 ● Shanghai New International Expo Center

上海新思维传播策划有限公司 ● Shanghai New Trend Medium Co Ltd

显辉国际展览有限公司 ● Top Repute Co Ltd

澳门威尼斯人®度假村酒店会展及活动中心 ● The Venetian® Macao - Resort - Hotel

（越南-中国）越中会展商务有限公司 ● VN-CN Convention Exhibition & Busiess Co., Ltd.

北京广角视野展览有限公司 ● Wide-Angle View Exhibition Co Led

浙江中国小商品城集团股份有限公司 ● Zhejiang China Commodities City Group Co Ltd

郑州国际会展中心 ● Zhengzhou International Convention & Exhibition Center

# 前言 | Preface

尽管中国经济率先于世界任何经济体最早从金融风暴中复苏，但阳光普照到展览业尚需数月的期待。因此，2009年对于中国展览业来说，无疑是自2003年SARS以来最为困难的一年。加工制造业产品贸易展和外向型国际性展会所受冲击最大。直至进入2009年第四季度，随着金融海啸阴霾的逐渐褪去，产业经济的步步回暖，全国各地展会无论从规模和人气上都明显向好。

展望2010年，中国展览业呈现三大特点。首先，做大做强、做出品牌继续成为未来中国展览业的主攻方向。具体表现在，一方面，合作合资兼并继续进行中；另一方面，主办方将品牌展做成系列在不同地区举办，借助现有展览会品牌的影响力及已有的资源开拓新兴市场，向内陆和西部省份深入延伸。2010年中国展览业的另一特点是，由于金融危机致使09年展览业受损的阴影尚未完全消除，导致新的一年中，独立新展的推出的数量明显少于往年。但是，在大展中加入新行业专题展，以及将综合性贸易展进行专业化细分，是2010年各方展览主办普遍采取的战略策略。未来一年中国展览业还有一个特点，那就是新能源展成为2010年最热门的行业展览。2003年中国第一个有关新能源的展览“亚洲风能展”在北京举办。首届的展览面积仅有1500平方米。不仅这一展览的规模在2010年将突破25000平方米，而且新能源风能太阳能展览在全国各地开花。

在中国展览市场趋于稳定和成熟的过程中，全行业的操盘手越来越将管理和经营的重心向细致化、优质服务倾斜。国字头且软硬件俱优的中国国际展览中心新馆誓以高质量服务创造价值。《细节管理新体系造就国际标准会展中心》一文讲述国展人如何通过为参展商和参观者提供高品质的服务将新老国展中心经营成真正意义上的国际水准的展览中心。

哥本哈根世界气候大会引爆了全世界对人类未来生存环境的深度思考。作为文化产业的展览业如何真正成为低碳经济，减少每次展览前后和展览期间一次性垃圾的产生以及降低污染装饰材料的使用？文章《环保主义：展台搭建新主张》提供可借鉴之成套解决方案。

本书再度连续推出全国综合博览会和专业贸易展年度排名，并将专业贸易展的排名增加至前70强，将更多行业展览纳入参评和排名行列。从排名中可以看出在北京、上海、广州、深圳这些独霸中国展览业头筹的一线城市之外，作为保障我国经济持续发展的基础及未来发展重心的二线城市——成都、郑州、义乌等正在进入第一军团，成为吸引大型和特大型展览的举办地。

在《中国及海外会展概览》进入第15年之际，本编委会的全体人员向15年来给予本书大力支持的广大广告客户和赞助商致以由衷的感谢！由于你们的给予，才使得这本书能够走过15年并越办越好。同时，我们更向全国每一个展览主办承办单位、支持赞助机构、会展中心和服务商，特别是经营着每个展览项目的工作人员致敬！正是你们每一位兢兢业业的努力，才创造了中国展览业繁荣的今日，以及更加健康和光明的未来！

Among global economies, China recovered first from financial crisis. However, it took more time for exhibition industry to receive sunshine. Actually, 2009 was the most difficult year for China exhibition industry since SARS 2003. Trade fairs for products toward export market got hit the most. Until the 4th quarter of 2009, along with clearance of the clouds of financial crisis, manufacturing sector warmed up gradually. Nationwide exhibitions got improved obviously in both exhibition area and number of visitors.

Prospecting 2010, China exhibition industry has three features: First, getting bigger and stronger, targeting brand names will be continuously the direction of the development of exhibition industry in China. It will be specially expressed in two aspects: On the one hand, cooperation and joint-venture continues; On the other hand, organizers will host their brand shows in series in different cities, promoting new market benefiting from the influence of existing brand fairs and resources, extending to inland and western provinces; Another feature of China exhibition industry in 2010 will be that number of introduction of individual new exhibition will be noticeably lower than previous years due to the shadow of financial crisis in 2009 has not been eliminated completely. However, here is a new strategy for variety of organizers to adopt: to add new theme in existing large trade shows and re-categorize general trade shows by professions. Second, trade shows regarding new energy will become the hottest theme. In 2003, “Wind Power Asia”, the first new energy show was held in China. Its show space was just 1,500 square meters. In 2001, not only will this show breakthrough 25,000 square meters, but also other new energy shows are booming cross the country.

While China exhibition industry stabilizes and matures, more and more industry players are shifting their focus of management and operation on detailed and quality services. With Country prefix in name and sophisticated facilities as its advantage, China International Exhibition Center New Venue oaths to increase its value by providing quality services. “Success Depends on Details” tell you how CIEC’s management team position to achieve their goals to make both their previous venue and new one the real international-standard exhibition centers by satisfying exhibitors and visitors with quality services.

World Climate Conference Copenhagen triggered deep thoughts of the whole world on the living environment of human beings. How could exhibition industry which is categorized as culture industry become low carbon economy, reducing waste on each and every exhibition and minimizing usage of polluted decorative materials? “Environmentalism: New Concept for Exhibition Stands” introduces a turn-key solution.

Continuously this book publishes yearly ranking for expositions and trade fairs. Ranking for trade fairs has been increased to top 70 fairs, aiming at including more professional shows in selection and listing. From the ranking, you can tell that in addition to Beijing, Shanghai, Guangzhou and Shenzhen as cities dominating China exhibitions, Chengdu, Zhengzhou, Yiwu and etc as second-tier cities which are the foundation for China’s economy and the focus in the future, are joining in main force, becoming venues attracting more and more large exhibitions.

At the 15th anniversary of Directory of China & Overseas Exhibitions and Meetings (DCOEM), all members of her Editorial Board sincerely thank you, the advertisers, sponsors and readers having contributed your supports in the path of 15 years. Your generosity made DCOEM turned out to be a great publication. At the same time, we sincerely salute to each and every exhibition organizers, sponsors, exhibition centers’ operators and service providers, especially those individuals who keep each exhibition running on its right track. Your conscientious efforts built up prosperity of China exhibition industry today. It will be also you who makes China exhibition industry even healthier and brighter tomorrow.

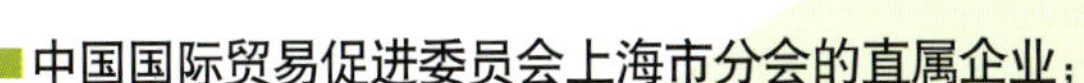

# 目录



# 会展概览

主编
张玉敏
编审
王亚东
编辑
黄继红
牛子放
撰稿
王芳
孟馨馨
韩笑
高级客户主任
孙惠兰
翻译
寇明明
南希阳
编辑助理
张楠
王雪
艺术总监
金钥
助理美术编辑
吴晓琪

读者服务和订购信息
北京2930信箱
邮政编码：100053
电话：
010-6340 0061
010-8316 7138
010-8316 7137
传真：
010-8316 7130

读者服务和订购信息：
expoinfo@dcoem.com
dcoem@live.cn
编辑部：
editor@dcoem.com
广告部：
super@dcoem.com

博览世界网
www.dcoem.com

# Contents



DCOEM

Editor-in-Chief
ZHANG Sarah
Editing Director
WANG Yadong
Editors
HUANG Jihong
NIU Zifang
Contributors
MENG Xin Xin
Josephine Wang
Joy Han
Senior Account Manager
SUN Linda
Translator
KOU Matthew
Nancy Yang
Editorial Assistant
ZHANG Nan
WANG Snow
Art Director
JIN Jessica
Assistant Art Editor
WU Joan

**Subscription Contact:**
P.O.Box 2930 Beijing 100053, China
**Telephone**
86-10-6340 0061
86-10-8316 7138
**Fax**
86-10-8316 7130

**Reader Service**
expoinfo@dcoem.com
Listing
dcoem@live.cn
**Editorial Office**
editor@dcoem.com
**Advertising Office**
super@dcoem.com

**www.dcoem.com**

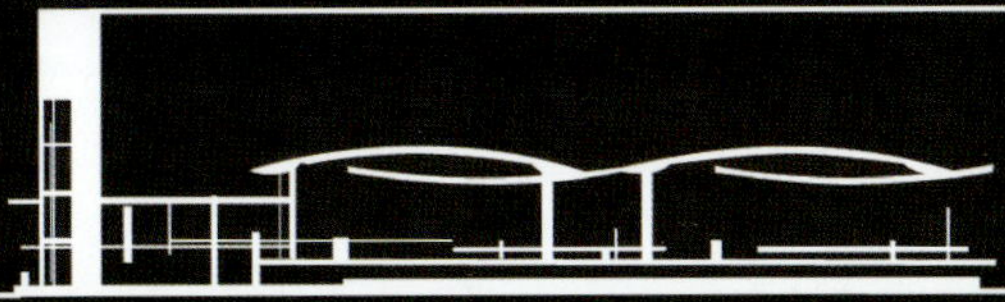

# 如何使用本书 | How to Use this Directory

全书国内会展信息有三大分类索引，便于查阅，具体方式如下：

**分类一——按城市分类**

这是国内会展信息的最主要章节，所有会展的基本信息按照先省区、后城市的汉语拼音顺序排列，城市中的信息再按照举办时间顺序排列。每条会展信息均有一个编号。编号的设置为便于您到后面的时间和行业分类中对应查询。

**分类二——按行业分类**

会展信息按行业分成78个分类。每个行业中，会展信息按照举办的时间顺序排列。通过编号，您可以在分类一中查到该展会的基本介绍。

**分类三——按时间分类**

展会在此按举办的时间顺序排列，通过每条信息的唯一编号，您可以在分类一中查到展会的基本介绍。

■ 重要提示

书中所列的展览和会议信息在编辑出版时，我们已经尽了最大努力核准无误，但个别展会的举办时间或地点等可能因故调整。因此，在决定参加、参观、出席展会之前，请您务必与主办和承办机构联系，获得确认。

## ★Exhibitions and Fairs in Mainland China

Register 1
Exhibitions and Fairs by City
This is the main chapter and contains basic exhibition and fair information in Mainland China. It is organized alphabetically by provinces, alphabetically by city within each province, and chronologically within each city. To each exhibition there is a cross - reference number which permits quick reference from register 2 and 3.

Register 2
Exhibitions and Fairs by Industry
This chapter lists exhibitions according 78 classifications. The exhibitions within the each branch are listed chronologically. A cross - reference number is provided for quick access to more detailed information in register 1.

Register 3
Exhibitions and Fairs in Chronological Order
Exhibitions are listed in chronological order. A cross - reference number is provided for quick access to more detailed information in register 1.

**★How to make phone call to China**

1. Country code for China is 86.
2. Taking the phone number of 010-6340 0061 in the book as an example, 010 is the city code of Beijing. If you call from outside China, here is how you should dial: 86 10 6340 0061.
3. Area Code of HongKong is 852.

**■Warning**

We have made best efforts to ensure the accuracy of the listed information at the time of editing. However, before making decision to participate an exhibition or conference, please always contact with the organizer for the very latest confirmation.

# 2009中国综合博览会12强排名

# China Top 12 General Fairs

| 排名 Rank | 展会名称 Exhibition | 展出面积 Exhibition Area($m^2$) | 参展商 Exhibitors | 贸易观众 Trade Visiters | 承办 Organizer | 日期 Date | 地点 Venue |
|---|---|---|---|---|---|---|---|
| 1 | 中国进出口商品交易会（Ⅰ、Ⅱ、Ⅲ期·秋季） China Import and Export Fair-Autumn | 1,125,000 | 22,320 | 188,170 | 中国对外贸易中心 China Foreign Trade Ctr (Group) | 10/15-19 10/23-27 10/23-11/4 | 中国进出口商品交易会展馆 Chinese Export Commodities Fair-ground Complex |
| 2 | 中国进出口商品交易会（Ⅰ、Ⅱ、Ⅲ期·春季） China Import and Export Fair (Canton Fair)-Spring | 1,000,000 | 22,104 | 165,436 | 中国对外贸易中心 China Foreign Trade Ctr (Group) | 4/15-20 4/24-28 5/3-7 | 中国进出口商品交易会展馆 Chinese Export Commodities Fair-ground Complex |
| 3 | 中国国际高新技术成果交易会 China Hi-Tech Fair | 130,000 | 3,000 | 506,000 | 深圳市中国国际高新技术成果交易中心 China Hi-Tech Fair Transfer Ctr | 11/16-21 | 深圳会展中心 Shenzhen Convention & Exhibition Ctr |
| 4 | 中国国际工业博览会 China Intl Industry Fair | 126,500 | 1,869 | 98,256 | 上海世博（集团）有限公司 Shanghai World Expo | 11/3-7 | 上海新国际博览中心 Shanghai New Intl Expo Ctr |
| 5 | 中国义乌国际小商品博览会 China Yiwu Intl Commodities Fair | 120,000 | 5,000 | 123,296 | 义乌市人民政府 Yiwu Municipal People's Government | 10/21-25 | 义乌国际博览中心 YiWu International Exhibition Center |
| 6 | 中国（深圳）国际文化产业博览交易会 China(Shenzhen)International Cultural Industries Fair | 105,000 | 1,708 | 368,300 | 深圳国际文化产业博览交易会有限公司 Shenzhen International Cultural Industry Fair Co Ltd | 5/15-18 | 深圳会展中心 Shenzhen Convention & Exhibition Ctr |
| 7 | 华东出口商品交易会（华交会） East Chian Fair | 103,500 | 5,312 | 18,229 | 上海世博（集团）上海外经贸商务展览有限公司 Shanghai World Expo | 3/1-5 | 上海新国际博览中心 Shanghai New Intl Expo Ctr |
| 8 | 中国哈尔滨国际经济贸易洽谈会 China Harbin International Economiv and Trade Fair | 86,000 | 2,500 | 100,000 | 中国哈尔滨经济贸易洽谈会办公室 The administration of China Harbin international econmic and trade fair | 6/15-19 | 哈尔滨国际会展中心 Harbin International Conference Exhibition and Sports Center |
| 9 | 中国昆明进出口商品交易会 China Import & Export Fair, Kunming | 75,000 | 2,334 | 8,000 | 云南省人民政府 The People's Government of Yunnan Province | 6/6-10 | 昆明国际会展中心 Kunming Intl Convention & Exhibition Ctr |
| 10 | 北京国际科技产业博览会 Beijing Intl High-Tech Expo | 60,000 | 2,213 | 120,000 | 北京市政府 Beijing Municipal Government | 5/20-24 | 中国国际展览中心 China Intl Exhibition Ctr |
| 11 | 中国北京国际文化创意产业博览会 China Beijing International Cultural & Creative Industry Expo | 60,000 | 1,370 | 85,000 | 北京市政府 Beijing Municipal Government | 11/26-29 | 中国国际展览中心 China Intl Exhibition Ctr |
| 12 | 中国国际装备制造业博览会 China Intl Equipment Manufacturing Exposition | 60,000 | 599 | 135,000 | 沈阳振兴国际展览有限公司 Shenyang Renaissance Intl Exhibitions Co Ltd | 9/1-5 | 沈阳国际会展中心 Shenyang Intl Exhibition Ctr |

# 励展博览集团大中华区2010年展会计划

## 航天航空（励展中国主办）

| 展会 | 日期 | 地点 | 网址 |
|---|---|---|---|
| 亚洲商务航空展览会 | 2010/06/09-10 | 澳门 | www.asianaerospace.com |

## 电子制造（励展中国主办）

| 展会 | 日期 | 地点 | 网址 |
|---|---|---|---|
| 第二十届中国国际电子生产设备暨微电子工业展/中国国际电子制造技术展览会 | 2010/04/20-22 | 上海 | www.nepconchina.com |
| 中国（成都）国际电子生产设备及技术展览会 | 2010/06/22-24 | 成都 | www.nepconchina.com |
| 第十五届华南国际电子生产设备暨微电子工业展/华南国际电子制造技术展览会 | 2010/08/31-09/02 | 深圳 | www.nepconchina.com |
| 华南国际汽车电子展览会 | 2010/08/31-09/02 | 深圳 | www.ae-china.com |

## 机床与制造（励展中国主办）

| 展会 | 日期 | 地点 | 网址 |
|---|---|---|---|
| 2010年中国国际铝工业展览会 | 2010/06/09-11 | 上海 | www.aluminiumchina.com |
| 第十届中国国际机床工具展览会 | 2010/06/14-18 | 北京 | www.cimes.net.cn |
| 华南国际工业组装技术与装备展览会 | 2010/08/31-09/02 | 深圳 | www.atexpochina.com |

## 包装（励展中国主办）

| 展会 | 日期 | 地点 | 网址 |
|---|---|---|---|
| 励华国际瓦楞展2010中国展 | 2010/04/07-09 | 东莞 | www.sino-corrugated.com |
| 2010励华国际彩盒展 | 2010/04/07-09 | 东莞 | www.sino-foldingcarton.com |

## 医疗及生命科学（国药励展主办）

| 展会 | 日期 | 地点 | 网址 |
|---|---|---|---|
| 中国国际化妆品、个人及家庭护理用品原料展览会 | 2010/03/10-12 | 上海 | www.pchi-china.com |
| 第63届中国国际医疗器械春季博览会 | 2010/04/18-21 | 深圳 | www.cmef.com.cn |
| 第9届中国国际医疗器械设计与制造技术展览会 | 2010/04/18-21 | 深圳 | www.icmd.com.cn |
| 第63届全国药品交易会（春季） | 2010/04/24-26 | 厦门 | www.pharmchina.com.cn |
| 第64届中国国际医药原料药、中间体、包装、设备交易会（春季） | 2010/05/18-20 | 哈尔滨 | www.apichina.com.cn |
| 世界制药工业展中国展区 | 2010/05/18-20 | 哈尔滨 | www.interphexchina.com |
| 中国实验室技术及装备交易会 | 2010/06/22-24 | 上海 | www.expolab.com.cn |
| 第45届全国新特药品交易会 | 2010/07 | 上海 | www.newdrugschina.com |
| 中国药店展览会 | 2010/08 | 上海 | www.dsshow.cn |
| 中国国际保健博览会 | 2010/09 | 北京 | www.inter-health.com.cn |
| 第64届全国药品交易会（秋季） | 2010/11 | 成都 | www.pharmchina.com.cn |
| 中医药国际科技博览会 | 2010/11 | 成都 | www.tcmex.cn |
| 更多... | | | www.reed-sinopharm.com |

## 礼品与家居（励展华博/励展华群主办）

| 展会 | 日期 | 地点 | 网址 |
|---|---|---|---|
| 第二十一届中国国际礼品、赠品及家庭用品展览会 | 2010/04/04-07 | 北京 | www.giftsbeijing.com |
| 第十八届中国（深圳）国际礼品、工艺品、钟表及家庭用品展览会 | 2010/04/25-28 | 深圳 | www.reedhuabo.com |
| 成都家居、休闲用品及礼品展览会 | 2010/06/18-20 | 成都 | www.reedhuabo.com |
| 第二十二届中国国际礼品、赠品及家庭用品展览会 | 2010/08/15-18 | 北京 | www.giftsbeijing.com |
| 第十八届中国（深圳）国际玩具及礼品展览会 | 2010/10/21-24 | 深圳 | www.reedhuabo.com |
| 2010北京国际礼品、赠品及家庭用品（年底）采购订货会 | 2010/11/27-29 | 北京 | www.giftsbeijing.com |

## 生活方式（励展中国主办）

| 展会 | 日期 | 地点 | 网址 |
|---|---|---|---|
| 亚洲国际博彩博览会 | 2010/06/08-10 | 澳门 | www.g2easia.com |
| 中国（北京）国际商务及会奖旅游展览会 | 2010/09 | 北京 | www.cibtm.com |
| 2010"100%设计"上海展 | 2010/10/21-23 | 上海 | www.100percentdesign.com.cn |
| 国际家居装饰艺术展 | 2010/10/21-23 | 上海 | www.home-decor.net |

**大中华区业务单元及合资企业**

# 2009中国专业贸易展70强排名
# China Top 70 Trade Shows

| 排名 Rank | 展会名称 Exhibition | 展出面积 Exhibition Area($m^2$) | 参展商 Exhibitors | 贸易观众 Trade Visiters | 承办 Organizer | 日期 Date | 地点 Venue |
|---|---|---|---|---|---|---|---|
| 1 | 中国广州国际家具博览会（春季·两期）<br>China Intl Furniture Fair (Guangzhou) CIFF | 500,000 | 2,621 | 136,310 | 中国对外贸易广州展览公司<br>China Foreign Trade Guangzhou Exh Corp | 3/18-21<br>3/27-30 | 中国出口商品交易会展馆<br>Chinese Export Commodities Fairground Complex |
| 2 | 中国国际家具展览会<br>Furniture China 2009 | 400,000 | 1,906 | 61,057 | 上海博华国际展览有限公司<br>Shanghai CMP Sinoexpo Int'l Exhibition Co Ltd | 9/9-12 | 上海新国际博览中心<br>Shanghai New Intl Expo Center |
| 3 | 国际名家具(东莞)展览会<br>Intl Famous Furniture Fair (Dongguan) | 240,000 | 900 | 68,000 | 东莞名家具俱乐部<br>Dongguan Famous Furniture Asso | 3/16-20 | 广东现代国际展览中心<br>Guangdong Modern Intl Exh Ctr |
| 4 | 中国(广州)国际建筑装饰博览会<br>China(Guangzhou)Intl Building Decoration Fair | 210,000 | 2,500 | 100,000 | 中国对外贸易广州展览公司<br>China Foreign Trade Guangzhou Exh Corp | 7/8-11 | 中国进出口商品交易会展馆<br>Chinese Export Commodities Fairground Complex |
| 5 | 上海国际汽车工业展览会<br>Auto Components Shanghai 2009 | 170,000 | 1,498 | 600,000 | 上海市国际展览有限公司<br>Shanghai Intl Exh Co Ltd | 4/22-28 | 上海新国际博览中心<br>Shanghai New Intl Expo Ctr |
| 6 | 中国广州国际家具博览会(秋季)<br>China Intl Furniture Fair(Guangzhou)-Home Furniture | 160,000 | 727 | 33,294 | 中国对外贸易广州展览公司<br>China Foreign Trade Guangzhou Exh Corp | 9/6-9 | 中国进出口商品交易会展馆<br>Chinese Export Commodities Fairground Complex |
| 7 | 深圳国际家具展<br>Shenzhen Intl Furniture Exhibition | 160,000 | 600 | 13,380 | 深圳市家具行业协会<br>Shenzhen Furniture Trade Asso | 9/8-11 | 深圳会展中心<br>Shenzheng Convention and Exhibition Ctr |
| 8 | 北京国际工程机械展览与技术交流会<br>Beijing Intl Construction Machinery Exhibition & Seminar | 150,000 | 880 | 78,600 | 中工工程机械成套有限公司<br>China Construction Machinery Co.Ltd. | 11/3-6 | 北京九华国际会展中心<br>Beijing Jiuhua Intl Exhibition Ctr |
| 9 | 中国(广州)国际汽车展览会<br>China(Guangzhou)Intl Automobile Exhibition | 150,000 | 670 | 50,000 | 中国对外贸易广州展览公司<br>China Foreign Trade Guangzhou Exh Corp | 11/24-30 | 中国进出口商品交易会展馆<br>Chinese Export Commodities Fairground Complex |
| 10 | 长春国际汽车博览会<br>China Changchun Intl Automobile Fair | 150,000 | 130 | 1,700,000 | 中国长春国际汽车展览组委会<br>CCPIT Changchun | 7/15-26 | 长春国际会展中心<br>Changchun Intl Convention & Exhibition Center |
| 11 | 中国国际塑料橡胶工业展览会<br>Intl Exhibition on Plastics and Rubber Industries | 140,000 | 1,840 | 69,298 | 中国对外贸易广州展览公司<br>China Foreign Trade Guangzhou Exh Corp | 5/18-21 | 上海新国际博览中心<br>Shanghai New Intl Exhibition Ctr |
| 12 | 广州国际照明展览会<br>Guangzhou Intl Lighting Exhibition | 140,000 | 1,600 | 50,000 | 广州光亚法兰克福展览有限公司<br>Guangzhou Guangya Messe Frankfurt Co Ltd | 6/9-12 | 中国进出口商品交易会展馆<br>Chinese Export Commodities Fairground Complex |

不断创新价值
Creating Value Always

# 2010年国内展览计划
# Exhibition Calendar in 2010

| No. | 展览会名称 Exhibition Name | 日期 Date | 地点 Address |
|---|---|---|---|
| 1 | 中国广州国际工业自动化技术及装备展览会<br>SPS - Industrial Automation Fair Guangzhou | 2010.3.8 - 11 | 广交会展馆<br>China Import and Export Fair Complex |
| 2 | 第十七届华南国际印刷工业展览会<br>The 17th South China International Exhibition on Printing Industry<br>2010中国国际标签印刷技术展览会<br>The China International Exhibition on Label Printing Industry 2010<br>第十七届中国国际包装工业展览会<br>The 17th China International Exhibition on Packaging Machinery & Materials<br>第十四届中国国际啤酒、饮料及酿酒工业展览会<br>The 14th China International Exhibition on Beverage, Brewery and Wine Technology | 2010.3.9 - 11 | |
| 3 | 第十一届中国(广州)国际给排水、水处理技术设备展览会<br>Water, Wastewater & Water Treatment China 2010<br>第十届中国(广州)国际泵、阀门、管道展览会<br>Pump, Valve & Pipe China 2010 | 2010.3.9 - 11 | |
| 4 | 第二十五届中国广州国际家具博览会(民用家具展)<br>25th China International Furniture Fair (Guangzhou) --Home Furniture | 2010.3.18 - 21 | |
| 5 | 2010中国广州国际家居饰品/用品展览会<br>Homedecor & Housewares China 2010 | 2010.3.18 - 21 | |
| 6 | 中国(广州)国际家用纺织品及辅料博览会<br>China (Guangzhou) International Trade Fair for Home Textiles 2010 | 2010.3.18 - 21 | |
| 7 | 2010中国广州国际户外及休闲展览会<br>China International Outdoor & Leisure Fair 2010 | 2010.3.18 - 21 | |
| 8 | 2010中国广州国际陶瓷展览会<br>China International Ceramics Exhibition(Guangzhou) 2010 | 2010.3.18 - 21 | |
| 9 | 第二十五届中国广州国际家具博览会(办公环境展)<br>25th China International Furniture Fair (Guangzhou) --Office Show | 2010.3.27 - 30 | |
| 10 | 2010中国广州国际木工机械、家具配料展览会<br>China Int'l Woodworking Machinery & Furniture Raw Materials Fair (Guangzhou) 2010<br>interzum guangzhou | 2010.3.27 - 30 | |
| 11 | 第八届中国(广州)国际环保展览会<br>The 8th China (Guangzhou) International Environmental Protection Exhibition | 2010.6.9 - 11 | |
| 12 | 第十二届中国(广州)国际建筑装饰博览会<br>The 12th China (Guangzhou) International Building Decoration Fair | 2010.7.8 - 11 | |
| 13 | 2010中国(广州)国际卫浴及建筑陶瓷展览会<br>China (Guangzhou) Int'l Exhibition for Sanitary Ware and Building Ceramics 2010 | 2010.7.8 - 11 | |
| 14 | 2010中国(广州)国际地面铺装材料展<br>China (Guangzhou) International Floor Covering Fair 2010 | 2010.7.8 - 11 | |
| 15 | 2010中国(广州)国际厨房设备及配件展<br>China (Guangzhou) Int'l Kitchen Fair 2010 | 2010.7.8 - 11 | |
| 16 | 第二十六届中国广州国际家具博览会<br>26th China International Furniture Fair (Guangzhou) | 2010.9.3 - 6 | |
| 17 | 2010中国广州国际家居饰品、家纺布艺展览会<br>Homedecor + Hometextiles China 2010 | 2010.9.3 - 6 | |
| 18 | 第八届中国(广州)国际汽车展览会<br>The 8th China (Guangzhou) International Automobile Exhibition | 2010.12.21 -27 | |

| 排名 Rank | 展会名称 Exhibition | 展出面积 Exhibition Area($m^2$) | 参展商 Exhibitors | 贸易观众 Trade Visiters | 承办 Organizer | 日期 Date | 地点 Venue |
|---|---|---|---|---|---|---|---|
| 13 | 全国糖酒商品交易会 China National Sugar and Alcoholic Commodities Fair | 120,000 | 4,000 | 200,000 | 中国糖业酒类集团公司 China Sugar and Spirit Corp | 10/11-15 | 郑州国际会展中心 Zhengzhou Intl Convention and Exhibition Ctr |
| 14 | 全国糖酒商品交易会 China National Sugar and Alcoholic Commodities Fair | 120,000 | 4,000 | 100,000 | 中国糖业酒类集团公司 China Sugar and Spirit Corp | 3/24-28 | 成都世纪城新国际会展中心 New Intl Exhibition & Convention Ctr |
| 15 | 九月香港珠宝钟表展览会 September Hong Kong Jewellery & Watch Fair | 120,000 | 3,061 | 39,146 | 亚洲博闻有限公司 CMP Asia | 9/21-27 | 亚洲国际博览馆 AsiaWorld-Expo |
| 16 | 中国国际家用纺织品及辅料博览会 Intertextile Shanghai Home Textiles | 118,500 | 1,118 | 36,584 | 中国贸促会纺织行业分会 CCPIT Textile Industry Sub-Council | 8/25-27 | 上海新国际博览中心 Shanghai New International Exhibition Center |
| 17 | 中国国际纺织面料及辅料（秋冬）博览会 China Intl Trade Fair for Apparel Fabrics and Accessories | 115,000 | 2,460 | 53,948 | 中国贸促会纺织行业分会 CCPIT Textile Industry Sub-Council | 10/20-23 | 上海新国际博览中心 Shanghai New Intl Expo Ctr |
| 18 | 中国（深圳）国际玩具及礼品展览会 China (Shenzhen) Intl Toys & Gifts Fair | 100,000 | 2,739 | 129,920 | 励展华博展览（深圳）有限公司 Reed Huabo Exhibitions (Shenzhen) Co | 10/22-25 | 深圳会展中心 Shenzheng Convention and Exhibition Ctr |
| 19 | 中国国际医疗器械秋季博览会 CMEF Autumn/ICMD-China Intl Medical Equipment Fair | 100,000 | 2,100 | 54,000 | 国药励展展览有限责任公司 Reed Sinopharm Exh Co Ltd | 10/28-31 | 深圳会展中心 Shenzheng Convention and Exhibition Ctr |
| 20 | 中国国际医疗器械春季博览会 China Intl Medical Equipment Fair Spring | 100,000 | 2,000 | 120,000 | 国药励展展览有限责任公司 Reed Sinopharm Exh Co Ltd | 4/18-21 | 深圳会展中心 Shenzheng Convention and Exhibition Ctr |
| 21 | 中国(北京)国际建筑装饰及材料博览会 China Intl Building Decorations and Building Materials Exposition | 100,000 | 1,600 | 120,000 | 北京中装华港建筑科技展览有限公司 China B & D Exhibition Co Ltd | 3/4-7 | 中国国际展览中心新馆 China Intl Exhibition Ctr New Venue |
| 22 | 中国国际机床展览会 China Intl Machine Tool Show | 100,000 | 1,200 | 260,000 | 中国机床工具工业协会 China Machine Tool & Tool Builders' Assn | 4/6-11 | 中国国际展览中心新馆 China Intl Exhibition Ctr |
| 23 | 中国国际自行车展览会 China Intl Bicycle Fair | 100,000 | 1,000 | 70,000 | 上海市国际展览有限公司 Shanghai Intl Exh Co Ltd | 5/4-7 | 上海新国际博览中心 Shanghai New Intl Expo Ctr |
| 24 | 中国国际服装服饰博览会 China Intl Clothing & Accessories Fair | 100,000 | 847 | 101,000 | 中国服装协会 中国国际贸易中心集团公司 Beijing Fashion-expo Co Ltd China World Trade Center Co Ltd | 3/26-29 | 中国国际展览中心新馆 China Intl Exhibition Ctr New Venue |

| 排名 Rank | 展会名称 Exhibition | 展出面积 Exhibition Area($m^2$) | 参展商 Exhibitors | 贸易观众 Trade Visiters | 承办 Organizer | 日期 Date | 地点 Venue |
|---|---|---|---|---|---|---|---|
| 25 | 大连国际汽车工业展览会 Dalian Intl Automotive Industry Exhibition | 100,000 | 536 | 350,000 | 中国贸促会大连市分会 CCPIT Dalian Sub-Council | 8/19-23 | 大连星海会展中心 大连世界博览广场 Dalian Xinhai Convention & Exhibition Ctr; Dalian World Expo Ctr |
| 26 | 成都国际汽车展览会 Chengdu Motor Show 2009 | 100,000 | 200 | 410,000 | 成都世纪城新国际会展中心 Century City-New Intl Exhibition & Convention Center | 9/17-23 | 成都世纪城新国际会展中心 Century City-New Intl Exhibition & Convention Center |
| 27 | 中国杨凌农业高新科技成果博览会 China Yangling Agricultural Hi-tech Fair | 98,000 | 1,500 | 30,000 | 陕西省人民政府 Shaanxi Provincial Government | 11/5-9 | 杨凌国际会展中心 Yangling Exhibition Ctr |
| 28 | 中国（深圳）国际礼品、工艺品、钟表及家庭用品展览会 Shenzhen Intl Gifts & Crafts, Watches & Houseware Fair | 90,000 | 2,800 | 120,000 | 励展华博展览（深圳）有限公司 Reed Huabo Exhibitions (Shenzhen) Co | 4/25-28 | 深圳会展中心 Shenzhen Convention and Exhibition Center |
| 29 | 中国国际日用消费品博览会 China Intl Consumer Goods Fair | 90,000 | 1,800 | 8,000 | 中国国际日用消费品博览会组委会 Ningbo Foreign Trade Service Ctr Co Ltd | 6/8-12 | 宁波国际会议展览中心 Ningbo Convention & Exhibition Ctr |
| 30 | 中国厦门国际石材展览会 China Xiamen Intl Stone Fair | 90,000 | 1,200 | 86,713 | 中国贸促会厦门分会 CCPIT Xiamen Sub-council | 3/6-9 | 厦门国际会议展览中心 Xiamen Intl Conference & Exhibition Ctr |
| 31 | 中国国际体育用品博览会(夏季) China Intl Sporting Goods Show Summer | 90,000 | 900 | 50,000 | 国家体育总局体育装备中心 China Sporting Goods Federation | 4/23-26 | 中国国际展览中心新馆 China Intl Exhibition Ctr New Venue |
| 32 | 成都国际家具工业展览会 Intl Furniture Fair Chengdu | 90,000 | 400 | 70,000 | 成都世纪城新国际会展中心 Century City-New Intl Exhibition & Convention Center | 7/3-6 | 成都世纪城新国际会展中心 New Intl Exhibition & Convention Center |
| 33 | 哈尔滨国际车展 Harbin Intl Automobile Industry Exhibition | 86,000 | 531 | 268,000 | 哈尔滨长城国际展览有限公司 Harbin Great Wall Intl Exh Co Ltd | 8/3-10 | 哈尔滨国际会展中心 Harbin Intl Conference Exhibition Ctr |
| 34 | 世界制药原料中国展暨世界制药机械、设备与材料中国展 CPHI & ICSE China | 85,000 | 1,657 | 23,646 | 博闻有限公司 CMP Information | 6/23-25 | 上海新国际博览中心 Shanghai New Intl Expo Ctr |
| 35 | 中国国际专业音响、灯光、乐器及技术展览会 China Intl Exhibition on Pro Audio, Light, Music & Technology | 85,000 | 1,100 | 180,000 | 中国演艺设备技术协会 China Entertainment Technology Assn | 5/28-31 | 中国国际展览中心 China Intl Exhibition Ctr |
| 36 | 上海缝制机械展 China Intl Sewing Machinery & Accessories Show 2009 | 80,000 | 1,023 | 32,000 | 中国缝制机械协会 China Sewing Machinery Assn | 9/22-24 | 上海新国际博览中心 Shanghai New Intl Expo Ctr |

# 义乌品牌展會 YIWU BRAND FAIRS

第七届中国国际五金电器博览会 2010.4.20-23
THE 7TH CHINA INTERNATIONAL HARDWARE & ELECTRICAL APPLIANCES TRADE FAIR Apr.20th-23rd

第五届义乌消费品出口交易会 2010.4.20-23
THE 5TH YIWU SOURCING FAIR：CONSUMER GOODS Apr.20th-23rd

第五届中国义乌文化产品交易博览会 2010.4.20-23
THE 5TH CHINA YIWU STATIONERY & ARTS TRADE FAIR Apr.20th-23rd

中国义乌国际小商品博览会迪拜展 2010.6.8-10
YIWU FAIR @ DUBAI Jun.8th-10th

第二届中国国际旅游商品博览会 2010.6.
THE 2ND CHINA INTERNATIONAL TOURISM COMMODITIES FAIR Jun.

第十六届中国义乌国际小商品博览会 2010.10.21-25
THE 16TH YIWU FAIR Oct.21st-25th

第六届中国水晶及玻璃制品博览会 2010.10.21-25
THE 6TH CHINA CRYSTAL & GLASS PRODUCTS FAIR Oct.21st-25th

第三届中国义乌国际森林产品博览会 2010.11.1- 4
THE 3RD CHINA YIWU INTERNATIONAL FOREST PRODUCTS FAIR Nov.1st-4th

第十一届义乌国际针织及服装机械展 2010.11.18-20
THE 11TH YIWU EXHIBITION ON HOSIERY，KNITTING & GARMENT MACHINERY Nov.18th-20th

| 排名 Rank | 展会名称 Exhibition | 展出面积 Exhibition Area($m^2$) | 参展商 Exhibitors | 贸易观众 Trade Visiters | 承办 Organizer | 日期 Date | 地点 Venue |
|---|---|---|---|---|---|---|---|
| 37 | 中国(深圳)国际品牌服装服饰交易会 China(Shenzhen)Intl Brand Clothing & Accessories Fair | 80,000 | 790 | 119,600 | 深圳市服装行业协会 Shenzhen Garment Industry Assn | 7/9-11 | 深圳会展中心 Shenzheng Convention and Exhibition Ctr |
| 38 | 中国广州国际木工机械、家具配料展览会 China Intl Woodworking Machinery & Furniture Raw Materials Fair (Guangzhou) | 80,000 | 761 | 60,697 | 中国对外贸易广州展览公司 China Foreign Trade Guangzhou Exh Corp | 3/27-30 | 中国进出口商品交易会展馆 Chinese Export Commodities Fairground Complex |
| 39 | 香港礼品及赠品展 Hong Kong Gifts & Premium Fair | 79,060 净面积 (net area) | 3,983 | | 香港贸易发展局 Hong Kong Trade Development Council | 4/27-30 | 香港会议展览中心 Hong Kong Convention and Exhibition Ctr |
| 40 | 香港秋季电子产品展 Hong Kong Electronics Fair (Autumn Editrion) | 77,391 净面积 (net area) | 2,852 | 55,958 | 香港贸易发展局 Hong Kong Trade Development Council | 10/31-16 | 香港会议展览中心 Hong Kong Convention and Exhibition Ctr |
| 41 | 中国(上海)国际石材产品及石材技术装备展 STONETECH | 75,000 | 898 | 57,636 | 北京华港展览有限公司 CIEC Exhibition Co Ltd | 2/15-18 | 上海新国际博览中心 Shanghai New Intl Expo Center |
| 42 | 广东国际汽车展示交易会 Guangdong Intl Auto Exhibition & Trade Fair | 75,000 | 160 | 150,000 | 东莞中汽会展有限公司 China Natl Automobile Conventions & Exh Dongguan Co Ltd | 9/29-10/4 | 东莞国际会展中心 Dongguan Intl Conference & Exhibition Ctr |
| 43 | 东博国际机床展 EASTPO Intl Machine Tool Fair | 74,000 | 1,023 | 97,326 | 东博展览有限公司 EASTPO Exh Co Ltd | 7/15-18 | 上海新国际博览中心 Shanghai New Intl Expo Ctr |
| 44 | 香港国际珠宝展 Hong Kong Intl Jewellery Show | 70,617 净面积 (net area) | 2,360 | 29,326 | 香港贸易发展局 Hong Kong Trade Development Council | 3/4-8 | 香港会议展览中心 Hong Kong Convention and Exhibition Ctr |
| 45 | 中国电子展（春季） China Electronics Fair | 70,000 | 2,100 | 79,714 | 中国电子器材总公司 深圳市创意时代会展有限公司 China Electronic Exh & Info Comm Co Ltd Creativity Convention & Exhibition (Shenzhen) Co Ltd | 4/9-11 | 深圳会展中心 Shenzheng Convention and Exhibition Ctr |
| 46 | 上海国际广告印刷包装纸业展览会 APPPEXPO 2009 | 70,000 净面积 (net area) | 1,200 | 95,775 | 上海现代国际展览有限公司 Shanghai Modern Intl Exh Co Ltd | 7/7-10 | 上海新国际博览中心 Shanghai New Intl Exhibition Center |
| 47 | 广东国际广告展 SIGN CHINA 2009 | 70,000 | 806 | 46,115 | 广州信亚展览服务有限公司 Trust Exhibition Co Ltd | 2/28-31 | 中国进出口商品交易会展馆 Chinese Export Commodities Fairground Complex |
| 48 | 北京埃森国际焊接与切割展览会 Beijing Essen Welding & Cutting 2009 | 69,354 | 866 | 62,486 | 中国机械工程学会及其焊接分会 China Mechanical Engineering Society | 6/2-5 | 上海新国际博览中心 Shanghai New Intl Expo Ctr |

中越会展联盟
Liên kết Hội chợ Triển lãm Trung - Việt
http://hz.china-vn.com

# 全方位对接中国—越南商界

（越南-中国）越中会展商务有限公司VN-CN Convention Exhibition & Business Co., Ltd.是一家专业从事策划和运作中国-越南两国之间双向展览会议、商务考察、市场调研、投资咨询、贸易配对、学术交流、商旅等多项服务融为一体的专业商务机构。

本公司与越南各层次政府及商务机构、会展公司、行业协会、企业界有着广泛人脉关系和紧密合作，所开展的商务活动一直得到越南贸易促进局、越南外商投资局、越南工商会、越南驻华大使馆商务处、越南驻南宁总领事馆等官方的大力支持。

由本公司和越南工业贸易部贸易广告博览公司牵头成立的“中越会展联盟”将致力于打造成为中越会展业务开拓先锋，致力于整合中越优势资源联手合作组织承揽中国参展参会商前往越南参加各类展会和合作组织承揽越南参展参会商来华参加各类展会。凭借着联盟的超前合作理念和专业操作平台，现已吸纳了多家中国和越南会展业界有识人士和实体参与联盟合作，目的是将合作操作的项目效果最大化及维护展商、会商利益最大化。

同时，本公司在组织越南商家来华参展参会采购和来华开展各类商务活动等领域也颇有成就，每年均组织和接待近2000名越南商家来华进行各类商务活动。我们曾为广交会、昆交会、、西博会、义乌小商品博览会、中国国际广告节、中国渔博会等国内20多个知名展览会成功邀请越南展商或采购商前来参会，并一直延续着合作关系。另，我司连续多年成为中国-东盟博览会越南参会客商组织接待和越南采购商招商协办机构。

（越南-中国）越中会展商务有限公司
VN-CN Convention Exhibition & Busiess Co., Ltd.
地址:广西南宁市新民路3号永嘉大厦12楼
直线电话:0771-2615157/2617885/2634998
总机电话:0771-2634881/2634882　转1007
传真:0771-2630917E-mail: exhibition@china-vn.com
QQ号:935864657　Yahoo:caexpo2005
MSN: exhibition-cv@163.com

中越商务中心
Trung tâm XTTM Trung-Việt
www.china-vn.com

Vinexad®

越南工业贸易部 Ministry Of Industry & Trade
越南贸易广告博览股份公司（中国南宁办事处）
Vietnam National Trade Fair And Advertising Company(Representative Office in China Nanning)
地址:广西南宁市新民路3号永嘉大厦12楼
电话:0771-2617885　2631887　传真:0771-2631887
E-mail:vinexad.xttm@gmail.com　Sky:ttxttmtrung-viet
越南总部 Add: No.9 Dinh Le Str.,Hoan Kiem Dist.,Hanoi City Vietnam
E-mail: trungviet08@gmail.com
Tel: +84.4.22403119　Fax: +84.4.39387156

| 序号 | 展览会名称 | 日期 | 地点 |
|---|---|---|---|
| 1 | 2010第5届越南国际造船技术及海事展览会（VietShip 2010） | 2010 3.17-20 | 越南国家会议中心 |
| 2 | 2010第五届越南河内国际建筑建材装饰博览会(VietBuild 2010) | 2010 4.1-4 | 河内国际会展中心 VEFAC |
| 3 | 2010第20届越南国际贸易博览会 | 2010 4.14-17 | 河内国际会展中心 VEFAC |
| 4 | 2010第5届越南国际环保技术展览会（ENVIROTEX 2010） | 2010 5.27-30 | 越南国家会议中心 |
| 5 | 2010越南国际汽车摩托车零配件展览会<br>2010越南国际汽车用品展览会<br>2010越南国际交通运输及配套产业展览会 | 2010 6.9-12 | 越南河内讲武国际会展中心 |
| 6 | 2010第3届中国产品(越南)交易会<br>中国消费电子及家电产品(越南)交易会<br>中国服装及箱包鞋帽(越南)交易会<br>中国礼品及工艺美术品(越南)交易会<br>中国电动自行车(越南)交易会 | 2010 6.15-18 | 河内I.C.T会展中心 |
| 7 | 第四届越南国际能源产业博览会及论坛（VE Expo 2010） | 2010 9.8-11 | 河内I.C.T会展中心 |
| 8 | 2010越南国际自动化.测量仪器及遥控技术展览会（AUTOMA VIETNAM 2010） | 2010 9.30-10.3 | 河内国际会展中心 VEFAC |
| 9 | 2010第19届越南国际工业产品展览会 | 2010 10.19-23 | 河内国际会展中心 VEFAC |

| 序号 | 展览会名称 | 日期 | 地点 |
|---|---|---|---|
| 10 | 2010第十八届越南国际农业博览会 | 2010 11.12-15 | 越南农业展览中心 |
| 11 | 2010越南国际机械装备及冶金展览会 | 2010 12.9-12 | 河内国际会展中心 VEFAC |
| 12 | 2010越南国际广告印刷包装造纸行业展览会<br>2010中国印刷技术产品(越南)展览会<br>2010中国广告技术产品(越南)展览会<br>2010中国包装技术产品(越南)展览会<br>2010中国造纸技术产品(越南)展览会 | 2010 12.9-11 | 河内 |
| 13 | 2010越南国际时装化妆品展览会（VIETNAM FASHION FAIR 2010） | 2010 12.20-26 | 河内国际会展中心 VEFAC |
| 14 | 2010越南国际水产畜牧与奶业展览会（ILDEX Vietnam 2010） | 2010 3.25-27 | 西贡会展中心 |
| 15 | 2010越南第十届越南国际医药制药、医疗器材展览会<br>2010越南国际医疗器材及实验用品展览会<br>2010年越南国际医院装备及用品展览会<br>2010越南国际骨科及口腔医学展览会<br>2010越南国际医疗康复护理用品用具展览会<br>2010越南国际保健品展览会 | 2010 8.18-21 | 胡志明新平国际会展中心 TBECC |
| 16 | 第十四届越南国际食品饮料工业博览会 | 2010 9.8-11 | 胡志明新平国际会展中心 TBECC |
| 17 | 2010第13届越南胡志明国际建筑建材装饰博览会 | 2010 9.16-20 | 胡志明富寿体育展览馆 |
| 18 | 第八届越南胡志明市国际贸易博览会 | 2010 12.1-4 | 胡志明新平国际会展中心 |

| 排名<br>Rank | 展会名称<br>Exhibition | 展出面积<br>Exhibition Area($m^2$) | 参展商<br>Exhibitors | 贸易观众<br>Trade Visiters | 承办<br>Organizer | 日期<br>Date | 地点<br>Venue |
|---|---|---|---|---|---|---|---|
| 49 | 广州国际美容美发化妆用品进出口博览会(秋季)<br>Guangzhou Intl Beauty & Cosmedtic Im & Ex Expo(Spring) | 66,400 | 1,973 | 238,331 | 广东博环美国际展览有限公司<br>Guangdong Intl Exhibitions Limited | 9/24-26 | 中国进出口商品交易会展馆<br>Chinese Export Commodities Fairground Complex |
| 50 | 广州国际美容美发化妆用品进出口博览会(春季)<br>Guangzhou Intl Beauty & Cosmetic Im & Ex Expo(Spring) | 66,000 | 2,000 | 230,000 | 广东博环美国际展览有限公司<br>Guangdong Intl Exhibitions Limited | 3/9-11 | 中国进出口商品交易会展馆<br>Chinese Export Commodities Fairground Complex |
| 51 | 全国药品交易会(春季)<br>Pharmchina-Spring | 65,000 | 2,000 | 100,000 | 国药励展展览有限责任公司<br>Reed Sinopharm Exh Co Ltd | 4/23-25 | 郑州国际会展中心<br>Zhengzhou Intl Convention and Exhibition Ctr |
| 52 | 全国药品交易会(秋季)<br>Pharmchina-Autumn | 65,000 | 1,915 | 117,385 | 国药励展展览有限责任公司<br>Reed Sinopharm Exh Co Ltd | 12/18-28 | 广州体育馆<br>Guangzhou Gymnasium |
| 53 | 中国(上海)国际乐器展览会<br>Music China | 65,000 | 1,164 | 42,499 | 上海国际展览中心有限公司<br>INTEX Shanghai Co Ltd | 10/13-16 | 上海新国际博览中心<br>Shanghai New Intl Expo Ctr |
| 54 | 香港家庭用品展<br>Hong Kong Houseware Fair | 62,660<br>净面积<br>(net area) | 2,207 | 26,762 | 香港贸发局<br>Hong Kong Trade Development Council | 4/20-23 | 香港会议展览中心<br>Hong Kong Convention and Exhibition Ctr |
| 55 | 中国国际五金展-《科隆国际五金展》强力推荐<br>China Intl Hardware Show Powered by Practical World | 60,000<br>净面积<br>(net area) | 2,016 | 35,000 | 科隆国际展览有限公司<br>Koelnmesse | 9/16-18 | 上海新国际博览中心<br>Shanghai New Intl Expo Ctr |
| 56 | 中国电子展览会暨亚洲电子展<br>China Electronics Fair | 60,000 | 1,500 | 51,128 | 中国电子器材总公司<br>深圳市创意时代会展有限公司<br>China Electronic Exh & Info Comm Co Ltd<br>Creativity Convention & Exhibition (Shenzhen) Co Ltd | 11/11-13 | 上海新国际博览中心<br>Shanghai New Intl Expo Ctr |
| 57 | 上海国际酒店用品博览会<br>Hotelex | 60,000 | 751 | 41,227 | 上海博华国际展览有限公司<br>Shanghai UBM Sinoexpo Intl Exhibition Co | 3/31-4/3 | 上海新国际博览中心<br>Shanghai New Intl Expo Ctr |
| 58 | 国际制冷、空调、供暖、通风及食品冷冻加工展览会<br>China Refrigeration | 59,386 | 859 | 43,752 | 北京市贸促会<br>中国制冷学会<br>Beijing Intl Exh Ctr Corp<br>Chinese Assn of Refrigeration | 4/5-7 | 中国进出口商品交易会展馆<br>Chinese Export Commodities Fairground Complex |
| 59 | 国际时装及时尚配饰展<br>中国国际鞋类展<br>中国国际皮革展<br>All China Leather Exhibition<br>China Intl Footware Fair<br>Moda Shanghai | 57,500 | 1,000 | 14,354 | 亚太区皮革展有限公司<br>Asia Pacific Leather Fair Ltd | 9/2-4 | 上海新国际博览中心<br>Shanghai New Intl Expo Center |
| 60 | 香港玩具展<br>Hong Kong Toys & Games Fair | 55,541<br>净面积<br>(net area) | 2,019 | 28,738 | 香港贸发局<br>Hong Kong Trade Development Council | 1/5-8 | 香港会议展览中心<br>Hong Kong Convention and Exhibition Ctr |

# TOP REPUTE CO., LTD. 顯輝國際展覽有限公司

Rm 2403, Fu Fai Comm. Centre, No. 27 Hillier St., Sheung Wan, Hong Kong 香港上環禧利街27號富輝商業中心2403室
Tel: (852) 2851 8603 Fax: (852) 2851 8637
E-mail: topreput@top-repute.com Website: http://www.toprepute.com.hk

## 2010 - 2011 展会介绍 SHOW CALENDAR

### 中国 － 广州 CHINA - GUANGZHOU

|  | 2010 | 2011 |
|---|---|---|
| **SHOES & LEATHER - GUANGZHOU**<br>广州国际鞋类、皮革及工业设备展览会 － 暨<br>INTERNATIONAL EXHIBITION ON SHOES & LEATHER INDUSTRY － GUANGZHOU －<br>**Incorporating** | 01-03/6 | 01-03/6 |
| 广州国际皮革展览会<br>GILE - GUANGZHOU INTERNATIONAL LEATHER EXHIBITION | 01-03/6 | 01-03/6 |
| 广州国际皮革工业技术及生产设备展览会<br>GITTME - GUANGZHOU INT'L TANNING TECHNOLOGY & MACHINERY EXHIBITION | 01-03/6 | 01-03/6 |

### 越南 － 胡志明市 VIETNAM － HO CHI MINH CITY

|  | 2010 | 2011 |
|---|---|---|
| **IIME VIETNAM**<br>越南国际工业机械展览会 － 暨<br>INTERNATIONAL INDUSTRIAL MACHINERY EXHIBITION －<br>**Incorporating** | 11-14/5 | 10-13/5 |
| 越南国际塑胶机械及技术展览会<br>**VIETNAM PLASTICS FAIR** | 11-14/5 | 10-13/5 |
| 越南国际金属加工设备及技术展览会<br>**METALTECH** | | |
| 越南国际印刷、包装机械设备及技术展览会<br>**PRINT & PACK** | 11-14/5 | 10-13/5 |
| 越南国际食品包装机械设备及技术展览会<br>**FOOD PACK** | 11-14/5 | 10-13/5 |
| 越南国际自动化工业展览会<br>**AUTOMATION** | 11-14/5 | 10-13/5 |
| **SHOES & LEATHER - VIETNAM**<br>越南国际鞋类、皮革及工业设备展览会<br>INTERNATIONAL EXHIBITION ON SHOES & LEATHER INDUSTRY–VIETNAM<br>**Incorporating** | 08-10/9 | 07-09/9 |
| **IFLE - VIETNAM**<br>越南国际鞋类，皮革制品展览会<br>INTERNATIONAL FOOTWEAR & LEATHER PRODUCTS EXHIBITION-VIETNAM | 08-10/9 | 07-09/9 |
| **VICB**<br>越南国际建筑展览会 － 暨<br>VIETNAM INTERNATIONAL CONSTRUCTION & BUILDING EXHIBITION －<br>**Incorporating** | 08-10/9 | 07-09/9 |
| **RAHV VIETNAM**<br>越南国际制冷、空调、供暖、通风系统展览会<br>INTERNATIONAL EXHIBITION ON REFRIGERATION, AIR-CONDITIONING, HEATING & VENTILATION SYSTEM | 08-10/9 | 07-09/9 |
| **SECURITY & FIRE - VIETNAM**<br>越南国际安防、技防、消防设备和技术展览会<br>VIETNAM INTERNATIONAL SECURITY SYSTEM & FIRE PROTECTION EQUIPMENT & TECHNOLOGY EXHIBITION | 08-10/9 | 07-09/9 |

| 分行 BRANCH | | 电话 TELEPHONE | 传真 FAX | 电邮 E-MAIL |
|---|---|---|---|---|
| 上海 | SHANGHAI | (86-21) 6279 1306 / 1291 | (86-21) 6247 8552 | topresha@sh163.net |
| 广州 | GUANGZHOU | (86-20) 8363 1061 / 62 / 64 | (86-20) 8363 1063 | topreput@public.guangzhou.gd.cn |
| 越南 | VIETNAM | (84-8) 3823 8828 | (84-8) 3824 6351 | toprepute@hcm.vnn.vn |

| 排名 Rank | 展会名称 Exhibition | 展出面积 Exhibition Area($m^2$) | 参展商 Exhibitors | 贸易观众 Trade Visiters | 承办 Organizer | 日期 Date | 地点 Venue |
|---|---|---|---|---|---|---|---|
| 61 | 中国国际食品添加剂和配料展览会<br>Food Ingredients China 2009 | 53,000 | 1,115 | 76,927 | 中国食品添加剂和配料协会中国贸促会轻工行业分会<br>China Food Additives & Ingredients Assn<br>CCPIT Sub-council of Light Industry | 3/25-27 | 上海光大会展中心<br>上海世贸商城<br>上海国际展览中心<br>Everbirght Ctr<br>Shanghai Mart<br>INTEX Shanghai |
| 62 | 香港春季电子产品展<br>Hong Kong Electronics Fair(Spring Edition) | 51,761<br>净面积<br>(net area) | 2,121 | 51,851 | 香港贸发局<br>Hong Kong Trade Development Council | 4/13-16 | 香港会议展览中心<br>Hong Kong Convention and Exhibition Ctr |
| 63 | 中国国际汽车服务业及汽车文化博览会暨全国汽车保修检测诊断设备（春季）展览会<br>Auto Maintech | 51,000 | 639 | 31,860 | 北京通联国际展览有限公司<br>Beijing Traders-Link Intl Exhibition Co Ltd | 2/25-28 | 中国国际展览中心新馆<br>China Intl Exhibition Ctr New Venue |
| 64 | 中国国际旅游交易会<br>China Intl Travel Mart | 50,000 | 3,984 | 35,000 | 国家旅游局<br>China Natl Tourism Administration | 11/19-22 | 昆明国际会展中心<br>Kunming Intl Convention & Exhibition Ctr |
| 65 | 中国国际汽车用品展览会<br>China Intl Auto Accessories Commercial Expo 2009 | 45,000 | 1,200 | 39,000 | 雅森国际展览有限公司<br>YASN Intl Exhibition Co Ltd | 2/20-23 | 全国农业展览馆<br>Natl Agricultural Exhibition Ctr |
| 66 | 中国义乌(国际)森林产品博览会<br>China Yiwu (Intl) Forest Product Fair | 45,000 | 1,000 | 105,300 | 义乌市人民政府<br>Yiwu Municipal Government | 10/31-11/3 | 义乌国际博览中心<br>Yiwu Intl Exhibition Ctr |
| 67 | 中国国际眼镜业展览会<br>China Intl Optics Fair 2009 | 45,000 | 725 | | 中国眼镜协会<br>China Optometric & Optical Assn | 9/16-18 | 中国国际展览中心<br>China Intl Exhibition Ctr |
| 68 | 中国国际信息通信展览会<br>P&T/EXPO COMM CHINA 2009 | 45,000 | 500 | 195,715 | 中国邮电器材集团公司<br>China PTAC Communications Services Co Ltd | 9/16-20 | 中国国际展览中心新馆<br>China Intl Exhibition Ctr New Venue |
| 69 | 中国国际五金博览会<br>China Intl Hardware Fair | 40,000 | 2,200 | 58,000 | 中国五金交电化工商业协会<br>China Natl Hardware, Electric and Chemical Products Commercial Assn | 3/10-12 | 上海新国际博览中心<br>Shanghai New Intl Expo Ctr |
| 70 | 广州国际鞋类、皮革及工业设备展览会<br>Intl Exhibition on Shoes & Leather Industry-Guangzhou | 40,000 | 850 | 14,500 | 显辉国际展览有限公司<br>Top Repute Co Ltd Corp | 6/2-4 | 中国进出口商品交易会展馆<br>Chinese Export Commodities Fairground Complex |

# 细节管理新体系 造就国际标准会展中心

文/孟馨馨

2009年对于中国国际展览中心新馆（国展新馆）来说是崭新的一年。这一年，国展新馆承接了北京会展70%以上的展会：中国国际服装服饰博览会、北京国际汽车展览会、中国国际机床展览会、中国国际印刷新技术专题展览会等一项项重大国际展会接踵而至。无论从展会规模、观众人数，还是展会效果、成交额来说，在国展新馆举办的各项展会均比往年有明显的提升。这不仅为国展新馆聚集了人气、名气，更为国展新馆向国际化、专业化展览平台的目标又迈进了一大步。

于2008年3月投入使用的国展新馆配套设施先进、齐全，在国内国际属领先地位。作为国展新馆的管理单位，北京国展国际展览中心有限责任公司（以下简称管理公司）在充分发挥优势场馆资源这一竞争核心的同时，高度认同服务创造价值的理念，以现代化企业的精细化管理为精髓，将细节服务作为内核，对以往的服务体系进行大刀阔斧的改革和重建。

老子云 “天下大事必作于细，天下难事必作于易”。细节，成为中国企业现代管理中需要直面的课题。“细节”决定成败，不论是企业内部的运作管理，还是对外的市场营销、客户服务，细节均起着至关重要的作用。管理公司在国展新馆的运营中便狠抓“细节”这一关键筹码，在一次次展会的实践和摸索中，找出了适合自身展馆发展的目标，并以此制定了一系列注重细节的管理措施。

细节管理首先体现在以项目经理为核心的一站式服务体系。如今，“一站式”服务体系成为国展的招牌管理模式。在展会期间，主办单位只需通过项目经理，便可以实现与展馆方的顺畅沟通，所有细节问题都在第一时间得到解决。这一运作体系削减了运营管理层次，实行扁平式运营管理，将安保、保洁、物流、餐饮、会议等执行层面统一规划入运营部门，降低了沟通成本，并保障了服务的高效、有序。展会期间各业务口均对项目经理负责，项目经理则作为主办方与场馆方之间的“联络中枢”，全程跟踪负责展前准备、展会现场运营、展后项目评审，汇总主办的所有需求和问题，及时协调解决和落实。项目经理负责制的落实，理顺了展馆方与主办方的协调机制，极大提高了协调能力和运营效率，令主办方将更多的精力放在展会销售和客户沟通上。值得一提的是，国展的每一位项目经理都曾负责过各个行业不同规模的展会，均是拥有丰富展览运作经验的精英型服务人才。他们的工作内容就是严格、认真地执行每一步程序和任务。丰富的从业经验，加上细致科学的工作流程，全方位确保了展馆的服务质量。

此外，展会运营实行“三个阶段保障”：即展前制定科学合理的方案（预案）、展中严格监管执行、展后总结及时整改，有效实现了各工作结点的服务管理，并充分发挥专业外包服务的优势，以精简的服务团队向主办、展商、观众提供专业高效的精细服务。

国展的这种细致化的管理程序和合理的服务体系既方便了租赁展馆的活动主办方，又扩大了国展新馆的知名度和美誉度。在确定了服务理念、管理模式的基础上，国展新馆对细节管理加以升华，首次尝试了服务外包的模式。面对日益激烈的市场竞争形势，国展深知变革势在必行。为适应市场发展的新趋势，国展在新馆的运营管理上又进行了大胆的创新与改革，在老馆多年运营管理的经验基础上深刻变革，围绕场馆服务和销售这一核心竞争力，国展管理公司把自己不擅长的下游服务业务外包给专业公司。标准化的外包服务管理模式不仅为展商提供更专业化和更高质量的服务，同时降低了展馆的营运成本，为新馆未来的持续发展注入强劲动力。

细节加创新奠定了国展在会展业的领袖地位。作为北京乃至中国展览业最为挺拔、繁茂的 株梧桐，中国国际展览中心以其稳固的根基和茂盛的枝叶吸引了诸多凤凰前来栖息，“以国展作为展会经营地点”已成为品牌展会的一个标志。名牌展会与国展强强联合，展会依托国展的硬件设施与专业服务树立行业内顶级展会的品牌相应，而国展则依托客户，携手做大做强国展品牌大展，使国展成为国内及国际极具声誉和影响力的交易展示平台。国展的品牌效应与专业展会的品牌效应相映成辉、相辅相成，共同成就双方的辉煌与发展。

未来，中国国际展览中心及国展新馆将积极实施品牌战略，培育和打造中国国际展览中心及国展新馆在国内外的品牌和形象，继续发扬中国国际展览中心在中国展览业界的龙头作用，倡导绿色会展经济，倡导展览与环境、展览与人的和谐理念，把国展及国展新馆建设成为具有高度社会责任感和高度文化内涵的国际标准会展中心。■

# SUCCESS DEPENDS ON DETAILS

By MENG Xin Xin

2009 was a new year to China International Exhibition Center New Venue "CIEC New Venue". In that year, CIEC New Venue undertook over 70% shows held in Beijing. China International Clothing & Accessories Fair, Auto China,China International Machine Tool Show and other influential international exhibitions followed hard on heels. From sizes and volume of visitors to effectiveness and quantity of trade, all those exhibitions held in CIEC New Venue had remarkable improvement in comparison with the previous year. Such achievements both increased the popularity of CIEC and made a leap forward for CIEC to play a role as an exhibition platform of professionalism internationally.

Sophisticated and complete facilities of CIEC New Venue put in operation in March of 2008. They were at the foremost position at home and abroad. As the management company for CIEC, CIEC Management Co did not only use venue resource as its cardinal feature for competition. Instead, highly convinced that service creates value, it carried out a drastic reformation and re-establishment on the previous service mechanism. Accurate management for modern enterprise and detailed service as the backbone and core were reinforced.

Lao Zi said in “The Morals” that “All difficult things have their origin in that which is easy, and great things in that which is small”. Details are what Chinese enterprises encounter directly in management. In internal management of enterprises as well as outward marketing and customer services, details can make one fail or succeed. Since CIEC new venue operation, by numerous practices through undertaking exhibitions, CIEC Management Co had sought and found the targets customized to its growth and laid down a series of measures emphasizing the details.

Establishment of Project Manager Oriented One Stop Service System. Nowadays, “One Stop” service had become the signature of the management model of CIEC both old and new venues. Each project manager of CIEC has had years of experience in managing exhibitions. They were ingenious in leading a variety of shows and strived to ensure each and every step of a series of measures had been strictly enforced.

In show time, only through project manager would the organizer communicate with the venue smoothly. All issues were expected to be resolved initially. Such an operational mechanism minimized layers of management.

This flat operational management that combines operational department such as security, sanitary, logistics, catering and conference lowered the cost of communication and guaranteed high efficiency services. During the show, all business departments assumed the responsibility of the Project Manager. The Project Manager is a liaison between the organizer and the venue, from pre-show, on-site as well as post-show project assessment, summarizing requirements and questions from the organizer, coordinating and resolving issues. Fulfilling the Project Manager's responsibilities harmonized the coordination between the organizers and both venues. It optimized dramatically the communication capacity and the operating efficiency and liberated organizers to sales and customers.

Additionally, show operation implemented "three phases guarantee": Before show, laying down scientific plan (preplan); during the show, fulfilling the plan strictly; post-show, summarizing and correcting the procedure in time. This effectively materialized service managing giving free rein to privilege of contracting professional services, providing organizers, exhibitors and visitors with professionally high quality and intimate services through a simplified service team.

CIEC's precise management procedures and rational service mechanism provide convenience for event organizers, expanding the popularity and reputation of CIEC New Venue. Based on service concept and the management model, CIEC New Venue refined detailed management to originate contracting services. CIEC acknowledges that one of the fundamental concepts in modern enterprise management is to be creative. Creativity is the essential characteristics of knowledge-based economy and is the soul for service oriented enterprises to survive and sustain growth.

In 2009 China International Clothing & Accessories Fair, with venue services and sales as its core components, CIEC Management Co outsourced to professional companies the lower-reach service business. Through professionally outsourcing services, CIEC provided profound expertise and quality services to exhibiters, which reduced operational costs.

Details in addition to creativity established CIEC's leading position in the exhibition industry. As the tallest, upright and lush Chinese parasol tree with its solid footing, luxuriant branches and leaves, China International Exhibition Center and New Venue have been attracting numerous phoenixes to perch. CIEC as exhibition venue became a signature line of brand exhibitions. Famous conferences and exhibitions combined with CIEC to form a strong alliance. Benefiting from CIEC's hardware facilities and professional services, exhibitions will establish their high reputation at the top. Hand in hand with exhibitions, CIEC will grow bigger and stronger, host more great brand shows and make CIEC the most reputable and influential trading and exhibition platform both domestically and internationally. CIEC's brand effectiveness and the brand effectiveness of professional conferences and exhibitions reflect each other with glory and supplement and complement each other for mutual brilliance and development.

In the future, CIEC both venues will actively deploy a brand name strategy, construct and foster the brand and image at home and abroad, further develop the leading role in China exhibition industry, plead for green exhibition economy, and promote the concept of harmony between exhibition and environment as well as between exhibition and people, making CIEC the international standard for exhibition centers with a high level of social responsibility and cultural connotations. ■

# 求胜激情实现赢在中国

文/王芳

自2008年以来，全球处于金融危机的阴霾中。中国会展业也不可避免地承受了全球金融危机带来的压力。当展览行业已经成为维持社会经济健康和繁荣发展不可分割的一部分时，带动本地经济发展是会展业的责任，如何将“危”化“机”是每一个会展公司必做的功课。

一场主题为“赢在中国”的第二届励展博览集团中国峰会2009年11月在北京举行。这场年度盛会聚集了180名精英与会代表，不仅有来自励展大中华区的高级经理和优秀员工，还有来自中国展览业的精英一流展会主办机构的领导。他们在此发表各自的真知灼见、拓展思维、深化理解、开阔眼界、分享最佳运作和沟通联络的尊享平台。

在近两年的时间，励展的经营策略做出了细微的侧重。在提高客户服务标准和参展商投资回报率等方面采取新举措以交付给客户最好的结果。这成为励展公司的经营法则。励展不仅要在经济形势和行业兴盛期为行业发展锦上添花，更要在经济疲软、行业发展面临困难的阶段与客户共度难关。这也是励展取得成功的重要因素之一。

2009年，即使是在经济危机的大环境下，励展大中华区业务仍然实现了10%的增长，2009年共举办展览会40余场，包括若干新展，成功汇聚逾2万供应商（参展商）和近70万买家。与上一年相比，各展会的总观众人数表现出强劲增长。

励展全球主席陆思奇先生自信地表示：“励展大中华区的业务增长将在明年提速。目前我们大中华区业务占全球业务的比重为10%，未来，这一比重将提升。”

励展之所以能克服诸多不利因素逆势而上，更多的是得益于长期专注为客户交付真正价值、提供卓越服务、采取前瞻战略等因素。

励展博览集团作为一个全球性的展会主办机构，每年主办的展览、研讨会、论坛和会议超过500个，服务于47个行业。近几年，励展加快了进军中国的步伐。在中国每年都举办超过40个领先行业展会，专注服务航空与航天、电子生产、机床与制造、包装、医疗及生命科学、礼品与家居及生活方式共7个中国充满活力和高速增长的行业。

而 “赢的激情”和“珍惜员工”这两个核心支柱，是构成励展对中国承诺的关键因素。陆思奇表示：“我们不只是努力工作，我们将以更大的智慧和更高的效率工作，致力于为中国的人才、技术和标准作业程序（SOP）投入更多。这些加强‘赢的激情’和‘珍惜员工’的投资和承诺将使我们能够以最经济、高效的方式识别和实现所有未被利用的机会，并更好地服务于我们的客户。”

跨国公司的企业文化如何与中国本土文化融合，是能否赢在中国的制胜关键，励展博览集团也不例外。文化的融合和发展需要时间和过程，以及必要的专业指导和推动。励展中国总部正在将励展博览集团这一具有强大核心价值观、全球实践经验的企业文化与中国文化相融合。虽然，目前仍处于一个比较年轻的早期阶段，但在未来3～6年这一文化建设到达中间阶段时，励展博览集团中国总部的制胜文化将得到高效发挥。这种文化建设工作，正是励展2010年中国业务计划的一部分。

在人才方面，励展坚持人才发展计划，推出并持续投资。同时，继续执行“励展中国奖学金”计划，为中国展览行业提供未来专业人才，以此扩大对整个会展行业和社会的服务和支持。励展非常重视人才的发展。在本届“赢在中国”的中国峰会上，陆思奇透露了励展培训人才的最新计划：“我们最近推出的T日计划（T代表人才），即工作人员从内部和外部培训师那儿接受销售、营销、业务、财务和管理方面的第一手培训。在每个月的第二个星期二，我们在全国的经营单位内举办‘中国T日’计划，即给出一个专门的时间段来培训和发展我们的员工。”

在中国展览业正在高速发展时期，中国展览业在世界舞台上发挥着更加重要的作用。作为世界上最大的展会主办方、中国展览业的主导力量之一，励展博览集团正在通过展览会这个与中国目前和未来的发展蓝图优化同步的渠道和平台，在中国充满活力的经济和重要行业发展中发挥着显著的作用。■

# 环保主义：展台搭建新主张

文/Joy Han

多年来，展馆搭建的现场弥漫着刺鼻的甲醛味道和粉末飞扬的场景令人难以忘怀。

由于展览会的搭建周期短、展览周期也比较短，所以很多参展商一般不会考虑展台的重复使用。因此，目前大多数的参展商所使用的展架展板都是用钢质管材作为骨架，立面采用最廉价的合成板材拼装，表面再用胶水辅以防火装饰面或用涂料粉刷表面的一次性展板。这样的做法不仅环境污染、噪音污染和刺激性气味污染严重，而且搭建周期长。另外，由于所使用的材料大多为低质、廉价的复合木材，展台拆除后只能作废品处理，导致展览之后产生大量垃圾。而国外则大量采用模块化组件和可回收材料搭建展台，这种做法更加环保。

目前，国外展览搭建工程的趋势是：设计师通过巧妙的设计，采用模块化理念开发出来的构件，可拼接成标准展台和各种不同形状、不同尺寸的异性展台，满足不同用户对个性化展台的需求。

模块化组件的优势是显而易见的：第一，它可重复利用、单次使用成本低；第二，它精致坚固、现代感强；第三，它无废弃物、无刺激性气味、无污染等。

不论参展商是想建造一个4平方米的展位，还是想建造一个4000平方米的展位，作为世界展览行业系统展具的鼻祖——德国奥克坦姆公司总是可以提供给客户最佳的解决方案。奥克坦姆供货计划提供具有吸引力的、制作现代的产品，这些产品从折叠展示台至双层展位，从带有极大跨度的天花板结构上的吊壁至陈列柜、桌子和柜台，可谓应有尽有。

1984年，在奥克坦姆的倡导下成立了OSPI-“奥克坦姆全球合作伙伴”(Octanorm Service Partner International)，这是世界展览行业唯一的全球性互助合作联盟( www.ospi-network.com)，极大地方便了展览服务商世界范围的业务拓展。“奥克坦姆全球合作伙伴”的成员都是各个地区和国家展览领域的精英，有二三十年的经验，遍布全球55个国家和地区。世界上只要有展览的地方，就会有“奥克坦姆全球合作伙伴”，就会有奥克坦姆的产品和对客户的支持。2008年12月，“奥克坦姆全球合作伙伴”年会在迪拜的沙漠深处召开。OSPI作为一种国际化的展装合作方式，对于引导我国展装服务行业正确发展方向，进一步与国际接轨有着举足轻重的意义。

奥克坦姆系统的研发和制作紧随展览发展的变化，结合铝料的特点,开发了自有的展示系统，改写了以往用钢木材料的展台搭建时间长、撤展后浪费严重、不利环保的历史。该系统用于道具和模型的展示,宣传海报和现场背景的制作,针对已经普及的计算机终端设备在展示现场的应用,以及针对小型展示现场、移动性及搭建效率更高要求的QUICK系统材料。分别对应的是四个方面是：陈列道具、展示道具、计算机路演终端、快捷搭建系统。如前所述，在展示系列材料的开发和应用方面，奥克坦姆的研发人员也结合材料的实际应用及变化，陈列道具和展示道具均可以将特定的配件和前述的型材结合，客户可根据自己的需要，自行设计和确定详细的材料造型和尺寸，不失灵活的给设计师和客户提供了细节的变化。

40多年来，奥克坦姆公司一直不断地根据客户的需求和系统的特点开发符合市场需要的创新构件，为专业解决方案提供最广泛的产品品种。这些专业解决方案的领域有墙壁系统、地板系统、天花板系统、灯光系统、地台版板系统、二层楼系统、室内设计系统和展示系统以及洁净室系统、安装系统等。

德国产品素以其出色的品质、信誉和技术水准闻名于世，作为奥克坦姆亚洲地区唯一一家工厂，奥克坦姆系统科技（苏州）有限公司秉承OCTANORM全球质量标准和享誉世界的德国技术以及服务理念，所有产品都依照最严格的德国标准设计生产，不管是研发还是产品选材以及生产过程中，奥克坦姆都严格遵照“绿色”、“环保”的标准，力求满足在全球化浪潮中日益增长的中国市场需要。奥克坦姆标准已经成为全世界展览行业系统展具的最高标准，现在国内很多重点场馆和比较注重品牌的公司都在选用奥克坦姆的产品。奥克坦姆也成为引领全球环保主义展台搭建新主张的先导。■

# Environmentalism: New Concept for Exhibition Stands

By Joy Han

For years, the site of construction of exhibition halls was infused with the pungent odor of formaldehyde and dust.

Due to the relatively short period of development of the exhibition industry in China, relevant regulations are not yet sufficiently sound. As a result of the differences in aesthetic ideas and pursuing quick profit under intense market competitions, exhibitions and large shows' equipments and materials could not be fully recycled. Steel pipes were excessively used for the structure; cheap boards were used for assembly; glue and fireproof boards were the materials to finish the surface. Further, painted exhibition boards and other disposable materials were abundantly applied. This construction resulted in strong odors in exhibition stands and during shows. After the shows, almost all of the materials were dismantled from the exhibition and were set aside as waste, thus generating ample garbage. This type of exhibition booth construction produced tremendous wasting of resources, which is unfavorable to the environment and also the construction period is prolonging.

Outside of China, the current status of exhibition construction is as follows: Exhibits designers create modular materials for exhibition construction, satisfying and customizing requirements of individual clients.

The advantage of modular structure is prominent. First, it is reusable with a lowered cost; second, it is solid with a sense of modernization; third, it has zero waste, irritating odor free, and does not pollute the environment.

Regardless of what the exhibitors require, either a 9 square meters or 4,500 square meters of stand, OCTANORM, the world-wide recognized original creator of aluminum profile for fair construction, can provide its customer with the best solution. Mr. Hans Staeger, founder of OCTANORM, developed a new type of aluminum system for exhibitions at the end of the 1960's. Along with the popularity of OCTANORM's fair materials in Germany, a renowned country with respect to exhibitions, it contributed an epoch-making change to the industry of exhibition material and equipment worldwide.

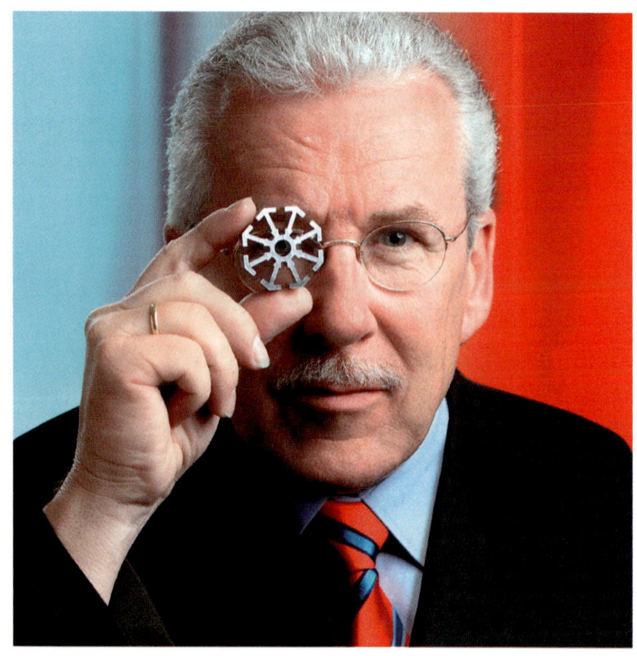

Within 40 years since 1968, OCTANORM had been focusing on research and promotion of the aluminum exhibition construction system. There are more than 4,000 types of profiles and accessories available for choice. Utilizing a high-tech, designing system, OCTANORM can achieve more variable profiles and help customers become more successful. Its category of products has expanded from what was originally fair materials to store display, interior and cleanroom systems. OCTANORM has become a sector leader with its 60% market share in the industry of fair material. Today, after 42 years of invention, OCTANORM's octagonal aluminum profile is still being frequently used in China and across the world. Square and round aluminum profiles are the main force in exhibition special interior. No manufacturer other than OCTANORM stands test for a two-story building with aluminum materials in the exhibition industry. Its heavy-load-bearing floor has been specified as materials of high-end brands in top class Auto Fairs. OCTANORM's standard has actually become the highest standard in exhibition industry. In Expo2010 Shanghai, OCTANORM's products have been designated as the building materials in Belarus and Ukraine Halls. OCTANORM China won the Green Fair Stand Award by China Association for Exhibition Centers in the 9th China International Exposition and Conferences. OCTANORM China was rewarded with the 2008 China Exhibition Industry Top 10 Exhibition Decoration Enterprises.

OCTANORM's design and exhibition management software can substantially improve exhibit designers' efficiency. Upon completion of a schematic, the software lists all the materials and their respective prices. It can also link to inventory software for real-time inventory management.

In 1984, with advocacy of OCTANORM, OCTANORM Service Partner International (OSPI) was established. It is a unique global cooperative alliance (www.ospi-network.com) in the world exhibition industry. It dramatically simplified cross-border marketing and cooperation for exhibition service providers. OSPI's members cover 55 countries and regions globally. They all have over 20 to 30 years of experiences in exhibition services. From Shanghai to Tokyo, Paris to Johannesburg and Frankfurt to Las Vegas, wherever there is exhibition, there will be OCTANROM's products and support from OCTANORM's customers. Once every two years, OCTANORM hosts its OSPI conference to discuss developing new products, exchange information and share experiences.

In Dec. 2008, OSPI was held in the Dubai desert. As an international model of cooperation in exhibition decoration enterprises, OSPI set up a good example for Chinese exhibition decoration industry to find its way to complement an international standard. The 13th OSPI will be held in Beijing and Shanghai in July 2010.

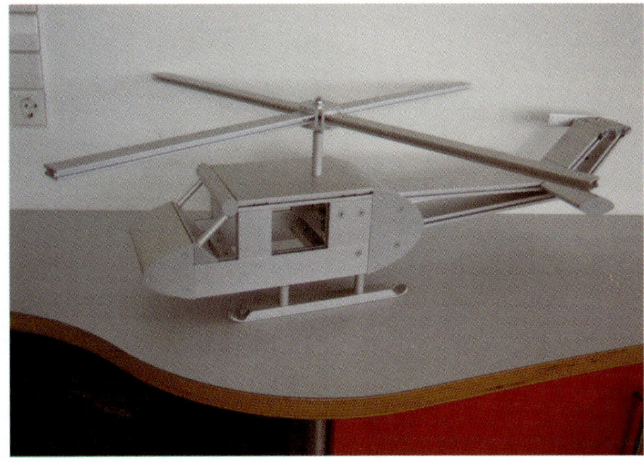

German products are acclaimed for their outstanding quality, good reputation and high-level technical standard. OCTANORM System Technology (Suzhou) Co Ltd upholds OCTANORM's global quality standard, renowned German technology and service concept. All of its products are manufactured strictly following German design and processing standards. Not only in development but also in raw materials pick-up and production, OCTANORM consistently pursues green and environmental protection standards, striving to satisfy the demand from the market in China in a wave of globalization. More and more highlighted exhibition venues and companies who value their brands are becoming OCTANORM's partners. OCTANORM turns out to be a leader in promoting environment friendly constructions. ■

上海新苑宾馆是锦江集团下属的一家庭院式宾馆。座落于外籍人士集聚的古北新区，毗邻世贸商城和国际展览中心。中环和延安路高架近在咫尺，交通便捷。

宾馆拥有设施完备的各式客房310间套和10-200人不等的会议室多个。餐饮特聘名厨掌勺，技艺精湛。京菜、川菜名扬申城；宫廷药膳更令中外宾客赞不绝口。

当您步入竹海映衬中的新苑，翠竹、芭蕉、垂柳、湖石逐一映入眼帘；池水、喷泉、锦鱼、浮萍自成一幅画镜。漫步花园，令人心旷神怡、流连忘返。

地址：上海虹桥路1900号

电话：021-62426688

传真：021-62426010

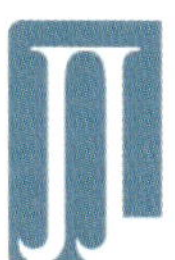

**新苑宾馆**

**NEW GARDEN HOTEL**

# 2010 年全国各地节庆活动

## *2010 Festivals in China*

### 中国长春冰雪旅游节暨净月潭瓦萨国际滑雪节

2009/12/01 - 2010/02/28
地点：吉林长春市
内容：中国长春冰雪旅游节从 1998 年开始创办，到 2008 年已成果举办十一届，通过探索与实践，我们将冰雪旅游节产品建设定位在“冰雪结婚、以雪为主，动静结合、以动为主”上。冰雪旅游节将关注民生、惠及市民为宗旨，活动时间涵盖了元旦、春节、元宵节、圣诞节等民众喜闻乐见的节日，活动安排和产品建设上注重体现市民参与。冰雪旅游节现已成为融文化、体育、旅游、经贸、科技等多领域活动为一体的综合性节庆活动，成为向国内外展示长春社会经济发展水平和人民精神面貌的重要窗口。
电话：0431-8588 1979, 8588 1978
www.changchun.gov.cn

### China Changchun Snow Festival

Date: 2009/12/01 - 2010/02/28
Venue: Changchun, Jilin
Tel: 0431-8588 1979, 8588 1978
www.changchun.gov.cn

### 蓟县第一届滑雪节

2009/12/01 - 2010/02/20
地点：天津蓟县
内容：滑雪节期间举办蓟县冬季旅游产品推介会，盘山第二届冰雪节，蓟洲国际滑雪中心灯光夜场圣诞狂欢节，到山村品民俗过大年活动。
主办单位：天津市旅游局，蓟县人民政府
承办单位：蓟县旅游经济委员会，盘山风景区管理局，天津蓟洲国际滑雪中心
电话：022-2919 1508
网址：www.jx-travel.com

### 1st Jixian Skiing Festival

Date: 2009/12/01 - 2010/02/20
Organizer: Tianjin Tourism Bureau; Jixian Government
Tel: 022-2919 1508
www.jx-travel.com

### 湄州妈祖文化旅游节

2010/01
地点：福建省莆田市湄洲妈祖祖庙天后广场
内容：自 1994 年以来，已成功举办过十届湄州妈祖文化旅游节，每届节庆都以“日谒妈祖，共享平安”为主题，其深厚的文化内涵，鲜明的地域特色，丰富的活动内容，吸引成千上万的宾朋，特别是台湾妈祖信中国前来参加，在海内外产生了轰动效应。
电话：0594-509 4688
www.mz-mazu.org.cn

### Meizhou Matzu Culture Festival

Date: 2010/01
Venue: Matzn Temple, Meizhou, Putian, Fujian
Tel: 0594-509 4688
www.mz-mazu.org.cn

### 成都青白江第一届草莓采摘节

2010/01
地点：成都市青白江区光明村
主办：青白江区区政府
承办：青白江区旅游开发局、姚渡镇
内容：采果、品果、美食、观光、休闲等。
联系人：孙燕
电话：010-8361 1565

### 1st Chengdu Qingbaijiao Strawberry Pick-up Festival

Date: 2010/01
Venue: Mingguan Village, Qingbaijiang, Chengdu
Organizer: Qingbaijiang District Government, Chengdu, Sichuan
Tel: 010-8361 1565

### 龙庆峡第二十四届冰灯艺术节

2010/01/16 - 2010/02/28
地点：北京延庆龙庆峡
内容：冰灯展示
周期：每年一届
联系人：李科长
电话：010-6919 1020

### China Longqingxia Intl Ice and Snow Festival

Date: 2010/01/16 - 2010/02/28
Venue: Yanqing, Beijing
Frequency: Annual
Tel: 010-6919 1020

### 2010 中国云南罗平国际油菜花文化旅游节

2010/02/03 - 2010/04/19
联系人：李先生
电话：0874-821 6918

### China-Yunnan-Luoping Rape Flower Tourism Festival

Date: 2010/02/03 - 2010/04/19
Tel: 0874-821 6918

### 2010 年中国武汉梅花节

2010/02/06 - 2010/03/10
地点：湖北省武汉市东湖梅园
内容：中国武汉梅花节是由武汉东湖风景区管委会举办，以赏梅游园、科普宣传、文化交流等为主要内容的大型文化盛会和园林盛会。
电话：027-8751 0179

### Wuhan Plum-Blossom Festival

Date: 2010/02/06 - 2010/03/10
Venue: Mei Garden, Donghu Lake, Wuhan,Hubei
Tel: 027-8751 0179

### 第七届独乐寺庙会

2010/02/11 - 2010/02/20
地点：天津以独乐寺为中心，以渔阳古街为线，东到鼓楼广场，西到独乐寺停车场
主题：弘扬民族传统文化，展现蓟州民俗风情
内容：举办开幕式、花会调演、武术表演、戏剧曲艺演出、传统民俗展示等特色活动。
主办单位：天津市旅游局，蓟县人民政府
承办单位：县旅游经济委员会，县文化局
联系人：李天胜、蔡习军
电话：022-2914 2907
www.jx-travel.com
www.dulesi.com

### Dulesi Temple Fair

Date: 2010/02/11 - 2010/02/20
Venue: Yuyang Ancient City, Ji Country, Tianjin
Frequency: Annual
Tel: 022-2914 2907
www.jx-travel.com
www.dulesi.com

### 2010 陕西（曲江）新春民俗文化节

2010/02/14 - 2010/03/02
地址：曲江国际会展中心
内容：祈福祭祀、灯会猜谜、民俗表演、特色美食、曲艺杂耍、民俗工艺制作、娱乐大世界、图书展示、怀旧物品展示等区域。在丰富多彩的文化活动中，市民融入其间休闲度假、亲子互动、访亲会友，打造富有传统特色的民俗文化新体验。本届文化节以“传承民俗文化，丰富市民生活”为主题，以虎跃龙腾庆新年，福满多多进万家为主线，为市民提供娱乐、购物、美食、观赏于一体的精神文化新春套餐。大力引导市民进行节庆消费，以搞活经济，扩大消费，促进增长，构建和谐社会为之目的，力争把本届文化节举办为内容丰富、特色鲜明的文化饕餮盛宴。
电话：029-8781 2126, 13488182262
传真：029-8781 2126 转 606
邮箱：896341426@qq.com
联系人：向华

### Shaanxi (Qujiang) New Spring Folk Cultural Festival

Date: 2010/02/14 - 2010/03/02
Venue: Xi'an Qujiang Convention and Exhibition Center, Xi'an, Shaanxi
Tel: 029-8781 2126
Fax: 029-8781 2126 ext 606
E-mail: 896341426@qq.com

# 2010年全国各地节庆活动 *2010 Festivals in China*

### 2010 中国南京国际梅花节
2010/02/14 - 2010/03/14
地点：江苏省南京市梅花山（主会场）
内容：南京市人民政府主办，国家重点旅游节庆品牌。自1996年举办以来，梅花节已成为融踏青赏梅、休闲娱乐及商贸交流于一体的国际经典盛会。今年梅花节以“赏万株梅花，传博爱精神——相聚在天下第一梅山”为主题，共将举办“梅花小天使”评选、梅花摄影展、广告歌舞巡演等十大项活动。
电话：025-8843 2050
www.zschina.com.cn
www.zschina.org

### 2010 International Plum Blossom Festival of Nanjing China
Date: 2010/02/14 - 2010/03/14
Venue: Plum Blossom Hill, Nanjing
Tel: 025-8843 2050
www.zschina.com.cn
www.zschina.org

### 宁海前童元宵文化旅游节
2010/02/24 - 2010/03/02
地点：宁海前童古镇
内容：参加民间行会，鸣群锣、抬古亭、放铳花，同时品尝前童特色豆腐宴、特色小吃等。
电话：0574-6522 0880

### Ninghai Qiantong Lantern Festival
Date: 2010/02/24 - 2010/03/02
Tel: 0574-6522 0880

### 成都青白江第三届杏花节
2010/03
地点：杏花村
主办：省旅游局市政府
承办：区旅发局、福洪乡
内容：文艺演出、赏花、健身、美食、趣味活动等
电话：028-8361 1565

### 3rd Chengdu-Qingbaijiang Apricot Festival
Date: 2010/03
Venue: Apricot Village
Organizer: Sichuan Provincial Tourism Bureau; Chengdu Municipal Government
Tel: 028-8361 1565

### 成都青白江桃花诗会
2010/03
地点：花园沟、桃花沟
主办：杏花村；省旅游局市政府
承办：区旅发局、福洪乡
内容：文艺演出、赏花、健身、美食、趣味活动等
电话：028-8361 1565

### Chengdu Qingbaijiang Peach Poetry
Date: 2010/03
Venue: Peach Gully, Qingbaijiang, Chengdu, Sichuan
Organizer: Qingbaijing District Tourism Bureau
Tel: 028-8361 1565

### 宁海胡陈桃花节
2010/03
地点：宁海胡陈乡
内容：赏千亩桃花、桃花诗会、桃树竞标、婚纱摄影
电话：0574-6522 0880

### Ninghai Huchen Peach Festival
Date: 2010/03
Venue: Huchen Town, Ninghai
Tel: 0574-6522 0880

### 第二届天津渔阳“梨园情”旅游文化节
2010/04
地点：天津蓟县下营镇团山子梨园
内容：打造春季“蓟北踏青游”旅游品牌，举办开幕式文艺演出，“畅游十里花海”春游活动，“梨花风情”农家游活动，征文、摄影大赛以及八仙山山花节、梨木台杜鹃花节等景区系列专项活动。
主办：天津市旅游局；蓟县人民政府
承办：蓟县旅游经济委员会
联系人：滕印成
电话：022-2919 1508

### 2nd Tianjin-Yuyang Liyuan Tourism Festival
Date: 2010/04
Venue: TuanShanzi Liyuan, Xiaying Town, Ji County, Tianjin
Organizer: Jixian Tourism Economic Committee
Tel: 022-2919 1508

### 2010 第二十二届成都美容化妆用品博览会
2010/04/15 - 2010/04/17
地点：四川科技馆（原四川省展览馆）
内容：专业美容产品、护肤品、美容仪器设备及技术；医学整形产品、设备、技术及材料；美发用品和仪器、纹绣、纹刺、美甲、彩妆及化妆用品；日化洗涤产品及足疗产品；OEM加工、美容美发产品的包装、原料、机械；美容美发行业媒体
支持单位：中国美发美容协会
主办单位：四川美容美发行业商会　成都市美发美容协会
承办单位：成都西美展览有限公司　成都维纳展览有限公司
电话：028-8612 5488
www.meibohui.com/cd

### 22st Chengdu Beauty & Hairdressing Festival
Date: 2010/04/15 - 2010/04/17
Venue: Sichuan Science Center, Chengdu
Tel: 028-8612 5488
www.meibohui.com/cd

### 安徽砀山梨花节
2010/04
地点：安徽省砀山县
电话：0557-809 5086
www.adangshan.cn

### Anhui Dangshan Pear Festival
Date: 2010/04
Venue: Dangshan County, Anhui
Tel: 0557-809 5086
www.adangshan.cn

### 北京大兴区庞各庄镇梨花节
2010/04
地点：北京大兴庞各庄镇
内容：梨花村赏花、游览万亩梨花庄园航天科普拓展教育基地、游览中国西瓜博物馆，采摘草莓蔬菜、吃农家饭、住农家院、品梨花大餐、逛购瓜乡农产品。
电话：010-8928 8545

### Daxing District Panggezhuang Town Pear Festival, Beijing
Date: 2010/04
Venue: Panggezhuang Town, Daqing District, Beijing
Tel: 010-8928 8545

### 2010年第十七届上海国际茶文化节上海茶业茶乡旅游博览会
2010/04/16 - 2010/04/19
地点：上海国际农展中心
内容：上海国际茶文化节以其独特的形式和风格，连续成功地举办了十六届，成为上海著名的旅游文化品牌和节庆活动。上海茶业茶乡旅游博览会以“政府主导、市场运作、企业经营、社会参与”的办展模式，以全新的理念，全力打造专业化、国际化、品牌化的展会，以全新的视角，让您感受到茶文化和茶旅游的魅力。上海茶业茶乡旅游博览会有利于放大上海国际茶文化节品牌，集聚资源，提升影响，促进发展。展会将展出国内外新茶、精品茶、茶饮料、茶制品及茶科技衍生产品，推荐各地的主题旅游线路、世博旅游线路和景点、景观。同时开展茶艺表演、名茶推荐、旅游推广等活动，集文化旅游与茶业经济于一体，融表演、展示与交流于一炉，办成具有上海特点的茶业茶乡旅游博览会，同时还将举办“中国名茶”评选活动。
主办单位：上海国际茶文化节组委会、上海市农业委员会、上海市旅游局、上海市闸北区人民政府、上海市茶叶学会
承办单位：上海农业展览馆、上海国际茶文化节组委会办公室、上海茶叶公司、上海帝芙特国际茶文化广场
电话：021-3303 0071, 6317 6785
传真：021-6353 5596
E-mail: teaculture@163.com
www.tea-sh.cn

### Making Friends by Chinese Tea-Shanghai International Tea Culture Festival
Date: 2010/04/16 - 2010/04/19
Venue: Shanghai Eastern Art Center
Frequency: Annual
Tel: 021-3303 0071, 6317 6785
Fax: 021-6353 5596
E-mail: teaculture@163.com
www.tea-sh.cn

### 第15届中国周庄国际旅游节开幕式及系列民俗风情活动
2010/04
地点：周庄
内容：第15届中国周庄国际旅游节开幕仪式。第三届古镇保护与发展论坛。挑花篮、打连厢、舞龙舞狮、水上划灯等大型民俗活动。
www.zhouzhuang.com

### 15th Zhouzhuang Tourism Festival
Date: 2010/04
www.zhouzhuang.com

# 2010年全国各地节庆活动 *2010 Festivals in China*

### 成都青白江第二届杏果采摘节
2010/05
地点：成都青白江杏花村
内容：采果、品果、杏了宴等。
www.zhouzhuang.com

### 2nd Chengdu Qingbaijiang Apricot Pick-up Festival
Date: 2010/05
Venue: Apricot Flower Village, Qingbaijiang, Chengdu
www.zhouzhuang.com

### 第十一届中国天津黄崖关长城国际马拉松旅游活动
2010/05/15
地点：天津黄崖关长城景区
内容：召集世界各地马拉松旅游爱好者参加长城国际马拉松旅游活动。
主办单位：丹麦东方旅行社；福建康辉国旅
协办单位：天津市旅游局；蓟县人民政府
承办单位：蓟县旅游经济委员会，天津黄崖关长城风景游览区管理局
电话：022-2271 8106
www.jx-trvel.com

### Tianjin International Marathon Festival at Great Wall of Huangya Gate
Date: 2010/05/15
Venue: Huang Ya Gate, Ji County, Tianjin
Tel: 022-2271 8106
www.jx-travel.com

### 第八届中国（宁海）徐霞客开游节
2010/05
地点：浙江省宁海县
内容：第八届中国（宁海）徐霞客开游节届时会有"首届中国百强旅行社宁海高峰论坛"等系列活动，规模宏大，格调高雅。历届凯游节均获全国节庆界高度评价。
电话：0574-6550 0519

### 8th China(Ninghai) Xu Xiake Tourism Feaival
Date: 2010/05/15
Venue: Ninghai, Zhejiang
Tel: 0574-6550 0519

### 毛家峪高尔夫球练习赛
2010/05
地点：天津毛家峪长寿度假村
主办单位：毛家峪长寿度假村
内容：组织游客和村民举办高尔夫球健身运动比赛，打造国内首家高尔夫球村。
电话：022-2276 2003

### Maojia Valley Golf Tornament
Date: 2010/05
Venue: Maojia Valley Resort, Tianjin
Organizer: Maojia Vally Resort
Tel: 022-2276 2003

### 第十五届上海电视节
2010/06/07 - 2010/06/11
地点：上海
内容：上海电视节创办于1986年12月，由国家广播电影电视总局和上海市人民政府主办、上海市文化广播电视管理局和上海文化广播影视管理局和上海文化广播影视集团承办。上海电视节包括白玉兰奖国际电视节目评选及展播、国际电视论坛、国际影视节目交易市场以及国际新媒体与广播影视设备市场。
电话：021-6253 7115
www.stvf.com

### 15th Shanghai TV Festival(STVF)
Date: 2010/06/07 - 2010/06/11
Venue: Shanghai
Profile: Established in December 1086, Shanghai TV co-hosted by the State Administration of Radio, Film & TV and the Shanghai Municipal Government, and organized by Shanghai Municipal Administration of Culture, Radio, Film & TV and the Special Events Office of Shanghai Media & Entertainment Group. STVF contains 4 main sections: Magnolia Award International TV Program Competition, International Film and TV Market, New Media and International Broadcasting Equipment Market and International TV Forum.
Tel: 021-6253 7115
www.stvf.com

### 第十三届上海电影节
2010/06/12 - 2010/06/20
地点：上海
内容：创办于1993年的上海国际电影节，由中国国家广播电影电视总局和上海市人民政府主办，上海市文化广播影视剧和上海文化广播影视集团承办。上海国际电影节是中国唯一经国际电影制片人协会（FIAPH）认证的国际电影节，其主体内容包括："金爵奖"国际影片评选、"亚洲新人奖"评选、国际电影展映、电影市场和电影论坛。其中，2007年起新设的电影市场，包括电影交易市场和中国电影项目投创两个板块。
电话：021-6252 7115
www.siff.com

### 13th Shanghai International Film Festival(SIFF)
Date: 2010/06/12 - 2010/06/20
Venue: Shanghai
Profile: The Shanghai International Film Festival (SIFF), originated in 1993, is hosted by the State Administration of Radio, Film & Television and Shanghai Municipal Government and organized by Shanghai Municipal Administration of Culture, Radio, Film & TV and SMEG is China's only A category international film Festival accredited by FIAPH. Its main section are Jin Jue Award. Asian New Talent Award, International Film Panorama, SIFF Mart and Film Forum. The SIFF Mart, initiated in 2007, includes Film Market and China's Film Pitch & Catch (CFPC)
Tel: 021-6252 7115
www.siff.com

### 中国石林国际火把节
2010/07 - 2010/08
地点：云南省昆明石林风景区
内容：传统斗牛、摔跤、歌舞、招商引资。
电话：0871-7796 251, 7796 256

### Shilin Torch Festival
Date: 2010/07 - 2010/08
Venue: Shilin, Kunming, Yunnan
Tel: 0871-7796 251, 7796 256

### 北京大兴采育葡萄文化节
2010/08
地点：北京大兴采育镇
内容：观光采摘、吃农家饭、住农家院、品葡萄美酒、观葡萄博物馆等
电话：010-8027 3611

### Beijing Daxiang Caiyu Pick-up Grape Festival
Date: 2010/08
Venue: Caiyu Town, Daxing District, Beijing
Tel: 010-8027 3611

### 北京大兴安定桑椹文化节
2010/05
地点：北京大兴安定镇
内容：游园采摘、趣味比赛等活动
电话：010-8023 3242

### Beijing Daxing Anding Mulberry Festival
Date: 2010/05
Venue: Anding Town, Daxing District, Beijing
Tel: 010-8023 3242

### 第10届中国国际保健博览会
**2010中国（北京）保健节**
2010/09/09 - 2010/09/11
地点：北京全国农业展览馆
内容：中国国际保健博览会是由中国保健协会与国药励展展览有限责任公司共同举办，由中华人民共和国卫生部、中华人民共和国商务部批准的，在保健行业最具权威，管理运营最为规范的国际性博览会。第10届中国国际保健博览会将于2010年9月9日-11日于北京全国农业展览馆举行。
联系人：顾晓然
电话：010-8455 6523, 8455 6677
www.cihexpo.com

### The 10th China International Healthcare Fair & the 10th China International Healthcare Feaival
Date: 2010/09/09 - 2010/09/11
Venue: Beijing Jiuhua International Exhibition Center
Tel: 010-8455 6523
www.interherb.com.cn

# 2010年全国各地节庆活动 *2010 Festivals in China*

### 北京大兴庞各庄金秋采摘节

2010/09
地点：北京大兴庞各庄镇
内容：观光采摘、参观航天科普教育基地、趣味比赛、文化表演等
电话：010-8928 8545

### Daxing Panggezhuang Golden Autumn Pick-up Festival

Date: 2010/09
Venue: Panggezhuang Town, Daxing District, Beijing

### 第五届蓟县"农家乐"厨艺大赛

2010/09
地点：天津蓟县
主办单位：蓟县旅游经济委员会
承办单位：农家院旅游特色村
内容：组织农家院旅游经营户举办厨艺大赛，促进农家餐饮厨艺技能交流，展示我县农家乐旅游发展成果。
电话：022-2919 1532

### Farmer Happiness Tourism Activities

Date: 2010/09
Venue: Ji County, Tianjin
Tel: 022-2919 1508

### 北京曲阜国际孔子文化节

2010/09/22 - 2010/09/30
地点：中国山东省济宁县曲阜
内容：中国（曲阜）国际孔子文化节是融学术纪念、文化旅游、经科贸于一体的大型国际性节庆活动，自1984年起，每年孔子诞辰（公历9月28日）前后在孔子故里曲阜举行。
电话：0537-320 2805
www.e-kongzi.com

### China (Qufu) International Confucius Culture Festival

Date: 2010/09/22 - 2010/09/30
Venue: Qufu, Jining city, Shandong Province, China
Profile: China (Qufu) International Confucius Cultural Festival is a large international celebration integrating commemoration, culture, tourism, economy, science and commerce. It has been held around the birthday of Confucius (28th of September) in his hometown-Qufu since 1984.
Tel: 0537-320 2805
www.e-kongzi.com

### 烟台国际葡萄酒节

2010/09/23 - 2010/09/30
地点：山东烟台
内容：由国际葡萄及葡萄酒组织（OIV）、中国酿酒工业协会、中国酒类流通协会、山东省人民政府共同主办的第四届烟台国际葡萄酒节将于2010年9月23-30日在烟台举办。目前，烟台市酿酒葡萄的种植面积已达1万公顷，拥有葡萄酿酒企业150多家，葡萄酒产量占全国产量的1/3以上。
联系人：孔艳玲
电话：0535-628 0001
www.wine-china.org

### Yantai International Wine Festival

2010/09/23 - 2010/09/30
Profile: The Fourth Yantai International Wine Festival will be held from September 23-30, 2010 in Yantai---a beautiful coastal city of east Shandong Province of China. The Festival is sponsored by the International Organization of Vine and Wine (OIV), China Alcoholic Drinks Industry Association, China National Association for Liquor Circulation and Shandong Provincial People's Government.
Tel: 0535-628 0001
www.wine-china.org

### 成都青白江草地风情节

2010/10
地点：四川成都青白江
主办：市旅游局、区政府
内容：文艺演出、民俗文化展示、草地骑马、草地摩托、草地射箭、高尔夫球体验、风情美食等
电话：028-8361 1565

### Chengdu Qingbaijiang Grassland Festival

Date: 2010/10
Venue: Qingbeijiang, Chengdu, Sichuan
Organizer: Chengdu Municipal Tourism Bureau
Tel: 028-8361 1565

# 推荐参加下列机构主办的展览和会议

**Recommend You the Exhibitions and Conferences Organized by Following Organizers**

|  |  |
|---|---|
| 科隆展览中国有限公司 | Koelnmesse Co Ltd China |
| 中国哈尔滨经济贸易洽谈会办公室 | Administration Office of China Harbin Fair for Trade and Economic Cooperation |
| 亚洲博闻 | CMP Aisa Ltd |
| 博闻（广州）展览有限公司 | CMP China (Guangzhou) Co Ltd |
| 中国演艺设备技术协会 | China Entertainment Technology Association |
| 中国铸造协会 | China Foundry Association |
| 中国对外贸易广州展览公司 | China Foreign Trade Guangzhou Exhibition Corporation |
| 中国昆明进出口商品交易会 | China Import & Export Fair, Kunming |
| 中国化学与物理电源行业协会 | China Industrial Association of Power Sources |
| 中国机械工程学会及焊接分会 | Chinese Mechanical Engineering Scociety |
| 中国邮电器材集团公司 | China National Postal and Telecommunications Appliances |
| 中国贸促会轻工行业分会 | CCPIT Sub-Council of Light Industry |
| 中国国际贸易中心股份有限公司 | China World Trade Center Co Ltd |
| 中国机床总公司/北京国机展览中心 | China National Machine Tool Corp./ Capital Exhibition Services |
| 北京爱博西亚展览有限公司 | Exposium-SIAL Exhibition Co Ltd |
| 广东省玩具协会 | Guangdong Toy Association |
| 香港贸易发展局 | Hong Kong Trade Development Council |
| 晋江市展务有限公司 | Jinjiang Exhibition Affairs Co Ltd, Fujian |
| 励德展览公司 | Knight Exhibition Corporation |
| 澳门贸易投资促进局 | Macao Trade and Investment |
| 励展博览集团 | Reed Exhibitions |
| 励展博览集团国际销售部 | Reed Exhibitions International Sales Group |
| 励展华博展览（深圳）有限公司 | Reed Huabo Exhibitions |
| 上海博华国际展览有限公司 | Shanghai CMP Sinoexpo Intl Exhibition Co Ltd |
| 显辉国际展览有限公司 | Top Repute Co Ltd |
| 乌鲁木齐对外经济贸易洽谈会办公室 | Urumqi Foreign Economic and Trade Fair Office |
| 越南-中国 越中会展商务有限公司 | VN-CN Convention Exhibition & Busiess Co., Ltd |
| 宁波雅卓展览服务有限公司 | Younage Exhibition Co Ltd |
| 浙江中国小商品城集团股份有限公司 | Zhejiang China Commodities City Group Co Ltd |

# 国内展览会议
# 城市索引



# Exhibitions and Fair in Mainland China
# Index of Cities

# 北京
# Beijing

2010/01/08-10
☎ 010-6505 2288
www.cwtc.com
10

**北京活力澳门推广周**
**地点：**中国国际贸易中心，北京
**地址：**北京建国门外大街一号（100004）

**Business and Trade Fair Beijing**
**Venue:** China World Trade Center, Beijing

2010/01/13-19
☎ 010-6505 2288
www.cwtc.com
20

**北京2010年TOP100名牌服饰折扣购物展**
**地点：**中国国际贸易中心，北京
**地址：**北京建国门外大街一号（100004）

**Top 100 Brand Name Apparel Sale**
**Venue:** China World Trade Center, Beijing

2010/01/20-24
☎ 010-8586 6611, 8586 6622
🖷 010-8586 6600, 8586 2190
✉ andy.li@bj-relation.com
www.bj-relation.com/Winefest/
30

**北京国际名酒文化节暨世界名酒产业博览会**
**地点：**北京蓝色港湾国际商区，北京
**内容：**为发掘弘扬酒文化，倡导高雅、时尚、闲适的酒文化生活，体验世界各地不同的酒文化；以酒为媒，结合北京蓝色港湾国际商区的丰富业态以及其倡导的高尚生活元素，针对都市精英人群，推崇高尚生活方式；以品味酒文化为着眼点，促进名酒产业在中国更深更广地发展，并拉动周边商区的消费。北京瑞来森会展服务有限公司与《精品购物指南》共同主办，由中国旅游饭店业协会、首都旅游集团、中国国际文化交流中心协办，众多银行以及近百家媒体支持的"北京国际名酒文化节暨世界名酒产业博览会"，拟于2010年1月20日至24日在北京蓝色港湾国际商区举办。
首届
**市场范围：**国际性
**性质：**面向公众
**参展费用：**12,000～18,000元
**预计规模：**展出面积1,500m²，参展商70家
**主办：**北京瑞来森会展服务有限公司；《精品购物指南》
**地址：**北京朝阳区八里庄西里远洋天地61号楼1302（100025）
**联系人：**张若耶，李扬
**MSN:** Liyang5965@hotmail.com

**Winefest Beijing**
**Venue:** Solana Lifestyle Shopping Park, Beijing
First Session
**Market Area:** International
**Participated Fee:** RMB 12,000-18,000
**Organizer:** Beijing Relation Conference & Exhibition Services Co; Life Style Magazine
**Contact:** Rhea, Andy
**MSN:** Liyang5965@hotmail.com

2010/02/23-25
☎ 010-5820 3101/02/03
🖷 010-5820 3100
✉ info@chinafish.cn
40

**二十届中国国际钓鱼用品贸易展览会**
**地点：**北京九华国际会展中心，北京
**内容：**渔具终端产品，渔具生产设备、原材料、小配件，户外及狩猎用品等。展商范围包括上述产品制造商、进出口公司等。
**始办年份：**1991
**周期：**每年一届
**市场范围：**国际性
**参展费用：**标准展位7,200元
**上届规模** '09：展览面积15,000m²(国外展商面积9,96m²)，参展商445家（国外展商28家，来自7个国家），专业贸易观众1,702人
**主办：**北京澳钦润江展览有限公司
**地址：**北京市朝阳区建国路93号万达广场5#9层（100022）
**联系人：**卢二兵

**The 20th China International Fishing Tackle Trade Exhibition**
**Venue:** Beijing Jiuhua International Exhibition Center, Beijing
**Profile:** Fishing Tackle Terminal, fishing equipments, raw materials, accessories, etc. and outdoor products. Exhibitors are limited to: Manufacturer and Imp & Exp corporation dealing with related products.
**Established Year:** 1991
**Frequency:** Annual
**Market Area:** International
**Participated Fee:** RMB 7,200/booth
**Statistics '09:** Exhibition Area 15,000m²(foreigners 996m²), Exhibitors 445 (foreigners 28, came from 7 countries), Trade Visitors 1,702
**Organizer:** Beijing Admire Exhibition Co Ltd
**Address:** 9/F, Building#5, Wanda Plaza, No.93 Jianguo Road, Chaoyang District, Beijing

2010/03/04-06
☎ 021-2020 5500
✉ ruan.lixin@mmi-shanghai.com
www.ispochina.com.cn
60

**亚洲国际品牌体育用品及运动时尚博览会**
**地点：**中国国际展览中心，北京
**内容：**ispo china 针对中国及亚太地区品牌体育用品及运动时尚产业的综合性贸易博览会，以"品牌主导"为展会理念，旨在为体育品牌商与经销/零售商提供一个专业的商贸交流平台。2005年首次登陆中国上海，于2007年起移师北京举办。展会规模超过20,000m²，300多个国内外知名运动品牌参展，展品包括雪类运动、户外运动、板类运动、运动时尚、功能性面辅料等，每届展会均吸引万余名来自国内外各种经销渠道的专业观众、媒体和体育爱好者。
**始办年份：**1970
**周期：**每年一届
**主办：**慕尼黑国际博览集团；中国国际展览中心集团公司
**承办：**慕尼黑展览（上海）有限公司
**联系人：**阮先生

**ispo china**
Alpitec China
**Venue:** China International Exhibition Center, Beijing
**Profile:** ispo china is a comprehensive trade exposition for brand name sports products and the sports fashion industry in China and the Asia-pacific regions. The exposition is brand-oriented and as such its purpose is to provide a professional commercial and trading platform for the various brand name sports products distributors and retailers. The exposition was first held in China in Shanghai in 2005, and in 2007 it moved to Beijing. With an area covering 20,000 square meters and more than 300 well-known sports brand names from home and abroad, the exposition showcases a wide range of products including those for snow sports, outdoor sports, board sports, sports fashion and functional-assistant materials. Each year it attracts thousands of professional visitors from all over the world, including distributors, the media and sports fans.
**Established Year:** 1970
**Frequency:** Annual
**Organizer:** MMI (Shanghai) Co Ltd

2010/03/06-09
☎ 010-8460 2711/12/16
📠 010-8460 2861

**2010北京国际创意礼品与工艺品展览会**
**地点：**中国国际贸易中心，北京
**内容：**国际礼展区、品牌展区、商务礼品展区、茶文化礼品展
70 区、户外及车用礼品展区、广告促销礼品展区、数码及小家电展
区、玩具及益智礼品展区、家纺及家居用品展区
首届
**周期：**每年两届
**市场范围：**国际性
**性质：**面向公众
**主办：**北京思恒展览策划有限公司
**地址：**北京市朝阳区北三环东路甲6号国展商务中心4层（100028）

**Beijing Intl Gift and Graft Show**
**Venue:** China World Trade Center, Beijing
**Profile:** Brand name products, business gifts, tea gifts, giveaways, small consumer electronics, toys, house ware.
First Session
**Frequency:** Biannual
**Market Area:** International
**Nature:** Open to public
**Organizer:** Beijing Siheng Exhibition Co Ltd
**Address:** 4/Fl, 6 East Bei San Huan Road, Beijing 100028

---

2010/03/12-14
☎ 010-8225 0016转ext 203
📠 010-8225 4766
✉ info@yasn.com.cn
www.ciaacexpo.com

**第十届中国国际汽车用品展览会**
**地点：**全国农业展览馆，北京
**内容：**CIAACE作为行业首个专注于汽车后市场的展览，五年的发展，不仅见证了中国汽车后市场行业的崛起与繁荣，更为行业人士成功搭建起了直接交流的贸易平台。参展商和观众每年相聚
90 CIAACE已成为一种职业的需要。CIAACE2010立足于“构筑平台，缜密运作”的筹备目标，将展出面积扩大到70,000m²，预计邀请58,000名专业观众，同时加强了对展区的科学规划和制定了全方位的媒介宣传计划，力争把本届展会办成规模最大、创意最新、影响最广、效益最佳、服务最优的展会，继续巩固汽车用品行业品牌展会的地
**始办年份：**2005
**参展费用：**标准展位：A类7,800元/9㎡，会员价5,800元/9㎡，B类6,800元/9㎡，会员价 4,800元/9㎡,净地A类825元/㎡，会员价600元/㎡，B类725元/㎡，会员价500元/㎡
**上届规模** ‘09：展览面积48,000m²，参展商1,128家（来自23个国家），参观人数57,171人
**主办：**中国设备管理协会
**承办：**雅森国际展览有限公司
**地址：**北京市西城区裕民路18号北环中心505室（100029）
**联系人：**阮晖，杨慧
**MSN：**makeawishhuihui@hotmial.com

**The 10th China International Auto Accessories Commercial Expo 2010**
**Venue:** National Agricultural Exhibition Center, Beijing
**Profile:** Experience Asia's largest and most influential auto accessories showcase and indulge you with various exhibits representing the most innovative designs and technologies for auto aftermarket in China. The event covers automotive interior and exterior accessories, auto care, car alarm equipment, car navigation system, outdoor equipment, in-car appliances and electronics, in-vehicle entertainment equipment, environmental-friendly products, chemicals and lubricants, specialty equipment, machine shop equipment, paint, body and equipment, brake system components, off-road parts, tool, service and repair.
**Established Year:** 2005
**Participated Fee:** Standard Booth RMB 7,800/9㎡, Raw Space RMB 825/㎡
**Statistics** ‘09: Exhibition Area 48,000m², Exhibitors 1,128 (came from 23 countries), Visitors 57,171
**Sponsor:** China Assn of Plant Engineering
**Organizer:** YASN International Exhibition Co Ltd
**Address:** Suite 505, Tower A, North Ring Center, 18 Yumin Rd., Xicheng Dist., Beijing, China
**Contact:** Vicky Ruan, Ruby Yang
**MSN:** makeawishhuihui@hotmial.com

---

2010/03/13-14
☎ 010-6505 2288
www.cwtc.com

**第十五届中国国际教育巡回展**
**地点：**中国国际贸易中心，北京
**地址：**北京建国门外大街一号（100004）
100

**14th China International Education Exhibition Tour**
**Venue:** China World Trade Center, Beijing

---

2010/03/15-18
☎ 010-8460 0901, 8460 0903
📠 010-8460 0906
www.build-decor.com

**第十七届中国（北京）国际建筑装饰及材料博览会**
**地点：**中国国际展览中心新馆，北京
**周期：**每年一届
110 **市场范围：**国际性
**性质：**面向公众
**预计规模：**展出面积50,000m²，参展商1,500家，观众120,000人
**主办：**中国贸促会；中国建筑装饰协会；中国国际展览中心集团公司
**承办：**北京中装华港建筑科技展览有限公司

**17th China International Building Decorations and Building Materials Exposition**
**Venue:** China National Exhibition Center New Venue, Beijing
**Frequency:** Annual
**Market Area:** International
**Nature:** Open to public
**Expectation:** Gross Area 50,000m², Exhibitors 1,500, Visitors 120,000
**Organizer:** China B & D Exhibition Co Ltd

---

2010/03/16-18
☎ 010-8460 0666/67/68/69
📠 010-8460 0669
✉ expo@cihe-hvac.com
www.cihe-hvac.com

**第十届中国国际供热、通风及空调产品与技术博览会**
**地点：**中国国际展览中心，北京
**内容：**供热、采暖设备展区；太阳能建筑一体化展区；燃气技术与设备展区；室内环境、空调、通风设备展区；泵、阀、给排水设备展区
112 **周期：**每年一届
**入场券价格：**免费
**参展费用：**国内企业：标准展位（9m²）9800元，净地（36m²起）1080元/ m²；合资企业：标准展位（9m²）11,800元，净地（36m²起）1,280元/m²；外资企业：标准展位（9m²）3,000美元，净地（36m²起）300美元/m²
**主办：**中国贸促会建设行业分会；中国建筑装饰协会；中国国际展览中心集团公司
**承办：**北京中装泰格尔展览有限公司
**地址：**北京市朝阳区北三环东路六号中国国际展览中心一号馆四层380室（100028）

**The 10th China International Heating, Ventilation & Air-conditioning Expo**
**Venue:** China International Exhibition Center, Beijing
**Frequency:** Annual
**Cost to Attend:** Free
**Participated Fee:** Standard Booth USD 3,000/9m², Raw Space (min 36m²) USD 300/m²
**Organizer:** Beijing B & D Tiger Exhibition Co Ltd

---

2010/03/19-21
☎ 010-8273 4018, 8273 4093
📠 010-8273 4029
✉ stone@jiehun.com.cn
http://bj.expo.jiehun.com.cn

**中国（国际）婚博会**
**地点：**北京展览馆，北京
**内容：**世界级品牌结婚展、商务部全国百家重点支持品牌展会，每年联手世界四大著名结婚时尚盛会：意大利米兰婚纱展、加拿大多伦多结婚展、韩国首尔结婚展、日本结婚展等，分别于3
115 月、6月、9月、12月在北京、上海等各主要城市分别举办。中国

**Wedding Expo**
**Venue:** Beijing Exhibition Center, Beijing
**Frequency:** 4 Sessions every year
**Market Area:** Region
**Nature:** Open to public
**Cost to Attend:** Couple Package RMB 20, Family Package RMB 40:-

（国际）婚博会在北京已经成功举办了12届、在上海成功举办了7届，是一个准确定位于结婚消费人群的、以“联动国际结婚流行趋势、引领中国结婚时尚消费”为宗旨，紧密围绕结婚消费需求的婚博会。
**周期**：每年四届
**市场范围**：地区性
**性质**：面向公众
**入场券价格**：情侣套票20元/张，情侣+加双方父母的家庭套票40元/张
**支持**：民政部
**主办**：中国（国际）婚博会组委会
**地址**：北京市海淀区学清路8号科技财富中心B座15层（100192）
**联系人**：唐彤；赵莉

2010/03/21-24
☎ 010-6505 2161
🖷 010-6505 3260
www.hunshazhan.cn

**中国国际婚纱及摄影器材博览会**
**地点**：中国国际贸易中心，北京
**内容**：婚纱、礼服；相框、相册 背景、后期制作、冲印彩扩；主题摄影、儿童摄影； 彩妆、饰品、婚庆用品；影楼培训；婚纱摄
120 影网络和出版物等
**始办年份**：1997
**周期**：每年一届
**市场范围**：国际性
**性质**：面向公众
**主办**：中国国际贸易中心股份有限公司
**承办**：北京瑞彩广告有限公司
**联系人**：董洪昌

**China Wedding and Photo Equipment Expo**
**Venue**: China World Trade Center, Beijing
**Established Year**: 1997
**Frequency**: Annual
**Market Area**: International
**Nature**: Open to public
**Organizer**: China World Trade Center Ltd

2010/03/26-28
☎ 010-6505 1018
🖷 010-6505 3260
✉ jiangling@cwtc.com
www.chinamed.net.cn

**第二十二届医疗仪器设备展览会**
**地点**：国家会议中心，北京
**内容**：医疗仪器设备
**始办年份**：1988
**周期**：每年一届
150 **市场范围**：国际性
**参展费用**：标准展位（12m²起）2,600元/m²，净地（36m²起）2,500元/m²
**上届规模**‘09：展览面积30,000m²，参展商505家（国外展商140家），参观人数26,408人
**主办**：中国人民解放军总后勤部卫生部；中国国际贸易中心股份有限公司；惠通兴业国际展览（北京）有限公司；杜塞尔多夫展览（中国）有限公司
**地址**：北京市建国门外大街一号国贸展览厅二层（100004）
**联系人**：蒋凌，李紫芳
**MSN**：selinatalk@hotmail.com
**QQ**：891078117

**The 22nd International Medical Instruments and Equipment Exhibition**
**Venue**: China National Convention Center, Beijing
**Profile**: Medical Instruments and Equipment
**Established Year**: 1988
**Frequency**: Annual
**Market Area**: International
**Participated Fee**: Standard Booth（min 12m²）RMB 2,600/m², Raw Space (min 36m²) RMB 2,500/m²
**Statistics'09**: Exhibition Area 30,000m², Exhibitors 505（foreigners 140）, Visitors 26,408
**Organizer**: Health Department of General Logistics Department of Chinese People' s Liberation Army, China World Trade Center Co, Hui Tong Xingye International Exhibition (Beijing) Co Ltd, Messe Düsseldorf China
**Address**: Level 2, Exhibition Hall, No.1 Jian Guo Men Wai Avenue, Beijing
**Contact**: Selina Jiang, Li Zifang
**MSN**: selinatalk@hotmail.com

2010/03/26-28
☎ 010-6505 2288
www.cwtc.com
170

**2010北京旅居人士服务展览会**
**地点**：中国国际贸易中心，北京
**地址**：北京建国门外大街一号（100004）

**2010 Expat Show**
**Venue**: China World Trade Center, Beijing

2010/03/28-31
☎ 010-6505 0546，8522 9370
🖷 010-6505 3260，8522 9449
✉ chicintl@chiconline.com.cn
www.chiconline.com.cn

**2010第十八届中国国际服装服饰博览会**
**地点**：中国国际展览中心新馆，北京 CIEC
**内容**：中国国际服装服饰博览会（CHIC）展出面积10万m²，展区分为男装、女装、休闲装、童装、皮革/皮草、羽绒、时尚饰品、时尚资讯、创意设计区及海外展团10个专业区。每年吸引着
200 来自数十个国家和地区的逾千家优秀品牌参展、十余万专业观众参观展会。
**始办年份**：1993
**周期**：每年一届
**市场范围**：国际性
**性质**：面向公众
**入场券价格**：10元
**参展费用**：1,820元/m²
**上届规模**‘09：展览面积100,000m²(国外展商面积24,000m²)，参展商847家（国外展商315家，来自22个国家），观众101,000人(专业贸易观众85,848人)
**主办**：中国服装协会；中国国际贸易中心股份有限公司；中国贸促会纺织行业分会
**承办**：中国国际贸易中心股份有限公司北京会展分公司
**地址**：北京建外大街1号国贸展厅2层（100004）
**联系人**：曾琦，李冬梅
**承办**：北京时尚博展国际展览有限公司；
**地址**：北京市东长安街12号449（100742）
**联系人**：焦培

**18th China International Clothing & Accessories Fair 2010**
**Venue**: China International Exhibition Center New Venue, Beijing
**Profile**: China National Clothing& Accessories Fair (CHIC) covered an area of 100,000 square meters. It comprised 10 specialized zones-Men' s wear, Women' s wear, Casual wear/Sports wear, Kids' wear, Leather/Fur wear, Accessories, Fashion media, Creation design, and Overseas pavilions, drawing over 1,000 excellent brands and more than 100,000 professional visitors from dozens of counties and regions every year.
**Established Year**: 1993
**Frequency**: Annual
**Market Area**: International
**Nature**: Open to public
**Cost to Attend**: RMB 10
**Participated Fee**: RMB 1,820/m²
**Statistics '09**: Exhibition Area 100,000m²(foreigners 24,000m²), Exhibitors 847（foreigners 315, came from 22 countries）, Visitors 101,000（trade visitors 85,848）
**Sponsor**: China National Garment Assn; China World Trade Center Co Ltd; The Sub-Council of Textile Industry, CCPIT
**Organizer**: Beijing Fashion-expo Co Ltd
**Organizer**: Beijing Convention & Exhibition Company, China World Trade Center Co Ltd
**Address**: F/2, China World Exhibition Hall, No.1 , Jian Wai Ave., Beijing
**Contact**: Jordan Zeng, Olivia Li

2010/03/30-01
☎ 010-8522 9463, 8522 9488
🖷 010-8522 9296
✉ intertextilebj@ccpittex.com
www.intertextile.com.cn
220

**中国国际纺织面料及辅料（春夏）博览会**
**地点**：中国国际展览中心，北京 CIEC
**内容**：各类服装面料、辅料、计算机CAD/CAM系统，相关出版物及网络
**始办年份**：1995
**周期**：每年一届
**市场范围**：国际性
**上届规模** '09：展览面积48,000m²，参展商1,000家（国外展商225家，来自14个国家），专业贸易观众25,060人
**主办**：中国纺织工业协会
**承办**：中国贸促会纺织行业分会；法兰克福展览（香港）有限公司；中国纺织信息中心
**地址**：北京东长安街12号550室（100742）
**联系人**：沈桢，于欣

**China International Trade Fair for Apparel Fabrics and Accessories**
Venue: China International Exhibition Center, Beijing
Profile: Apparel fabrics & accessories, CAD/CAM system, relevant publications & websites
Established Year: 1995
Frequency: Annual
Market Area: International
Statistics '09: Exhibition Area 48,000m², Exhibitors 1,000 (foreigners 225, came from 14 countries), Trade Visitors 25,060
Sponsor: China National Textile & Apparel Council
Organizer: The Sub-Council of Textile Industry, CCPIT; Messe Frankfurt (HK) Ltd; China Textile Information Center
Address: Room 550, No.12 East Chang An Street, Beijing, China
Contact: Mr Shen Zhen, Ms Yu Xin

2010/03/31-02
☎ 010-8522 9496, 8522 9504
🖷 010-8522 9300
✉ yarnexpo@ccpittex.com
www.yarnexpo.com.cn
240

**中国国际纺织纱线（春夏）展览会**
**地点**：中国国际贸易中心，北京
**内容**：各类纺织纤维、纱线及CAD等
**始办年份**：2004
**周期**：每年一届
**市场范围**：国际性
**上届规模** '09：展览面积3,000m²(国外展商面积300m²)，参展商100家（国外展商10家，来自7个国家），专业贸易观众7,000人
**主办**：中国纺织工业协会
**承办**：中国贸促会纺织行业分会；法兰克福展览（香港）有限公司；中国棉纺织行业协会；中国毛纺织行业协会；中国化学纤维工业协会；中国麻纺行业协会；中国纺织信息中心
**地址**：北京东长安街12号546室（100742）
**联系人**：王小雷，林英华

**China International Trade Fair for Fibers and Yarns**
Venue: China World Trade Center, Beijing
Profile: Yarns, Fibers, CAD/CAM, Publications
Established Year: 2004
Frequency: Annual
Market Area: International
Statistics '09: Exhibition Area 3,000m²(foreigners 300m²), Exhibitors 100 (foreigners 10, came from 7 countries), Trade Visitors 7,000
Sponsor: China National Textile & Apparel Council
Organizer: The Sub-Council of Textile Industry, CCPIT; Messe Frankfurt (HK) Ltd; China Cotton Textile Assn; China Wool Textile Assn; China Chemical Fiber Assn
Address: Room 546, No.12 East Chang An Street, Beijing, China
Contact: Mr Wang Xiaolei, Mr Lin Yinghua

2010/03/31-02
☎ 010-6505 2288
www.cwtc.com
250

**2010北京国际喷涂聚脲技术、屋顶（木屋）绿化及沥青展览会**
**地点**：中国国际贸易中心，北京
**地址**：北京建国门外大街一号（100004）

**Polyurea Technology, Green Roof and Asphalt Show**
Venue: China World Trade Center, Beijing

2010/04/04-07
☎ 010-5933 9186
🖷 010-5933 9333
✉ Amy.xie@reedhuaqun.com
www.giftsBeijing.com
270

GIFTS& HOME
礼品|家居·北京

**第二十一届中国国际礼品、赠品及家庭用品展览会**
**地点**：中国国际展览中心，北京 CIEC
**内容**：礼品、工艺品：礼品精品、琉璃制品、银制品、锡制品、瓷制品、玻璃制品、水晶制品、漆器礼品、金属饰品、陶艺、竹木、树脂、仿生、玉石雕刻、手工艺品等。赠品、促销品：广告促销品、宣传赠品、商务赠品、精品打火机、钥匙扣、礼品笔、徽章、圣诞装饰品等。电子、玩具：家用电子产品、电子万年历、MP3、U盘、成人益智玩具、毛绒玩具、塑胶玩具、电子玩具等。家居用品：家用纺织礼品、家居装饰礼品、钟表、毛巾及浴室用品、厨房用品、旅游及运动用品、休闲用品、箱包手袋、皮具制品、妇婴用品等。纪念收藏品：邮票、钱币、磁卡、标牌等。文具
**始办年份**：1997
**周期**：一年三届
**市场范围**：全国性
**入场券价格**：免费
**参展费用**：6,800元/个
**主办**：北京励展华群展览有限公司
**地址**：北京市朝阳区新源南路1-3号平安国际金融中心A座15层1-3-5（100027）
**联系人**：谢辉，蒋楠
MSN：youyou_baobao@hotamail.com

**The 21st China International Gifts, Premium & Houseware Exhibition**
Venue: China International Exhibition Center, Beijing
Established Year: 1997
Frequency: Three Sessions Every Year
Market Area: National
Cost to Attend: Free
Participated Fee: RMB 6,800/booth
Organizer: Reed Huaqun Exhibitions
Address: 1-3-5,A15, 1-3 South Xinyuan Road, Beijing 100027, China
Contact: Xie Hui, Jiang Nan
MSN: youyou_baobao@hotamail.com

2010/04/07-09
☎ 010-5856 5888转ext 610/609
🖷 010-5856 6000, 5856 6002
✉ penglu@biec.com.cn,
✉ wangping@biec.com.cn
www.cr-expo.com
290

**第二十一届国际制冷、空调、供暖、通风及食品冷冻加工展览会**
**地点**：中国国际展览中心新馆，北京 CIEC
**内容**："中国制冷展"历经20余年，以专业的精神和规范的国际化运作为全行业所称道，展会经由国际展览业协会（UFI）和美国商务部（US FCS）两项国际认证，已跻身全球领先的制冷空调暖通展之列，更是亚洲规模最大的同类专业展览会。展出内容包括：制冷设备、空调设备、通风设备、供热设备、制冷和空调设备的安装材料和设备、制冷和空调用工具及设备。
**始办年份**：1987
**周期**：每年一届
**市场范围**：国际性
**性质**：面向公众
**入场券价格**：免费
**上届规模** '09：展览面积23,591m²(国外展商面积6,911m²),参展商859家（国外展商204家，来自33个国家），专业贸易观众31,919人）
**主办**：中国贸促会北京市分会；中国制冷学会；中国制冷空调工业协会

**The 21st International Exhibition for Refrigeration, Air conditioning, Heating and Ventilation, Frozen Food Processing, Packaging and Storage**
Venue: China National Exhibition Center New Venue, Beijing
Profile: With the 20 years experience, "China Refrigeration Expo" has obtained great reputation in the industry. With the certifications by the International Assn of Exhibition Industry (UFI) and Foreign Commercial Service of Department of Commerce U.S (US FCS), "China Refrigeration Expo" is well-known as one of the global leading exhibition in HVAC&R industry. Profile: refrigeration equipment, air conditioning ventilation plants, heating equipment, assembly supplies for refrigeration and air conditioning, tools and equipment for refrigeration and air conditioning.
Established Year: 1987
Frequency: Annual
Market Area: International
Nature: Open to public

**承办：** 北京国际展览中心
**地址：** 北京市西城区月坛北街26号恒华国际大厦A座6层601室（100045）
**联系人：** 彭璐，王平

**Cost to Attend:** Free
**Statistics '09:** Exhibition Area 23,591m²(foreigners 6,911m²), Exhibitors 859（foreigners 204, came from 33 countries），Trade Visitors 31,919
**Organizer:** CCPIT Beijing; Chinese Assn of Refrigeration (CAR); China Refrigeration and Air-conditioning Industry Assn (CRAA)
**Organizer:** Beijing International Exhibition Center (BIEC)
**Address:** Suite 601, Block A, Henghua Intl Mansion, 26 Yuetanbeijie, Xicheng Dist, Beijing 100045, China
**Contact:** Peng Lu, Wang Ping

---

310

2010/04/08-10
☎ 010-8839 5100, 8839 5101
🖷 010-8839 5130
✉ cisile@cisile.com.cn
www.cisile.com.cn

**第八届中国国际科学仪器及实验室装备展览会**
**地点：** 北京展览馆，北京
**内容：** 总展出面积将达25000m²，将汇聚超过600家国内外科学仪器及实验室装备相关的企业，展示科学仪器产业新产品与技术。展会将重点突出国际化和专业化，更多的组织欧洲、中东、美国、韩国、日本等国家厂商参展，同时也将邀请更多的国际参观团到会参观与交流，使CISILE成为全球科学仪器及实验室装备领域高端技术交流及产品交易的重要平台，科学仪器行业的盛会。
**始办年份：** 2003
**周期：** 每年一届
**市场范围：** 国际性
**性质：** 面向公众
**入场券价格：** 免费
**参展费用：** 标准展位（3x3m）：国内企业7,800元，国外企业3,500美元，中外合资企业15,000元；角位（3x3m）：国内企业8,500元，国外企业3,850美元，中外合资企业16,500元；净地（36m²起）：国内企业780元/m²，国外企业350美元/m²，中外合资企业1,500元/m²
**上届规模：** 参展商512家（国外展商68家，来自16个国家），参观人数19,036人
**主办：** 中国仪器仪表行业协会
**承办：** 北京朗普展览有限公司
**地址：** 北京市车公庄大街9号院五栋大楼1号楼B2-804室（100044）
**联系人：** 高霞，林辉

**The 8th China International Scientific Instrument and Laboratory Equipment Exhibition**
**Venue:** Beijing Exhibition Center, Beijing
**Established Year:** 2003
**Frequency:** Annual
**Market Area:** International
**Nature:** Open to public
**Cost to Attend:** Free
**Participated Fee:** Standard Booth（3m × 3m）USD 3,500, Corner Booth USD 3,850, Raw Space USD 350/m²(min 36m²)
**Statistics:** Exhibitors 512（foreigners 68, came from 16 countries），Visitors 19,036
**Sponsor:** China Instrument Manufacturer's Assn
**Organizer:** Beijing Lamp Exhibition Co Ltd
**Address:** Room B2-804, 5 Buildings, No.9 Chegongzhuang Yard, Beijing 100044 China
**Contact:** Crystal Gao, Lin Hui

---

320

2010/04/08-11
☎ 010-6505 2288
www.cwtc.com

**2010年中国北京春季房地产展示交易会**
**地点：** 中国国际贸易中心，北京
**地址：** 北京建国门外大街一号（100004）

**Springtime Real Estate Trade Fair Beijing China**
**Venue:** China World Trade Center, Beijing

---

325

2010/04/08-10
☎ 010-8586 8557
🖷 010-8586 8557

**2010中国国际水处理化学品及水溶性高分子展览会**
**地点：** 全国农业展览馆，北京
**内容：** 絮凝剂和污泥脱水剂：聚丙烯酰胺、聚二甲基二烯丙基氯化铵、丙稀酰胺、甲基丙烯酸二甲氨乙脂、甲基丙烯酰氧乙基三甲基氯化铵。阻垢缓蚀剂：有机膦酸盐：HEDP、EDTMP、ATMP等；聚羧酸：PAA、HPMA、聚天冬氨酸、聚环氧琥珀酸等水溶性聚合物等；无机磷类：六偏磷酸钠、三聚磷酸钠；苯并三氮唑、甲基苯并三氮唑及新型铜缓蚀剂；电厂、化工、炼油、炼铁、炼钢等专用复配阻垢缓蚀剂；钨系、钼系阻垢缓蚀剂。杀菌灭藻剂
**周期：** 每年一届
**市场范围：** 国际性
**主办：** 中国化工学会工业水处理专业委员会；中国民营经济研究会净水行业委员会；中国土木工程学会水工业分会；中国环境科学学会环境工程分会
**承办：** 北京企发展览服务有限公司
**地址：** 北京市朝阳区东四环中路远洋国际中心60号楼C座1301室
**联系人：** 张俊

**China Intl Water Treatment Chemicals Exhibition**
**Venue:** National Agricultural Exhibition Center, Beijing
**Frequency:** Annual
**Market Area:** International
**Organizer:** Beijing Qifa Exhibition Co Ltd

---

330

2010/04/10-12
☎ 010-5822 1856
🖷 010-5885 1286
✉ bjslzlfw@163.com
www.cifie-expo.com

**第八届中国北京国际食品加工与包装机械展览会**
**地点：** 中国国际展览中心，北京 CIEC
**内容：** 食品加工机械，果品蔬菜加工设备，烘焙设备，啤酒饮料灌装设备，乳制品加工设备，肉类加工屠宰设备，油脂加工包装设备，塑料机械设备
**始办年份：** 2003
**周期：** 每年一届
**市场范围：** 国际性
**入场券价格：** 免费
**参展费用：** 8000元/展位
**上届规模 '09：** 展览面积9,500m²(国外展商面积1,500m²)，参展商273家（国外展商45家，来自13个国家），参观人数17,038人（专业贸易观众11,837人）
**主办：** 中国食品工业协会
**承办：** 北京爽朗展览服务有限公司
**地址：** 北京市朝阳区曙光西里甲1号第三置业B座1006室（100028）
**联系人：** 林霞，李晓露
**QQ：** 391899856

**The 8th China Beijing International Food Processing & Packaging Machinery Exhibition**
**Venue:** China International Exhibition Center, Beijing
**Profile:** Food Processing machinery, Beer and drink canned equipments, Milk product processing equipment, Meats processing and slaughtering equipments, Fruit and vegetable processing equipment, Baking equipment, Grease processing and packing equipment, Packing equipment, Plastic mechanical equipment
**Established Year:** 2003
**Frequency:** Annual
**Market Area:** International
**Cost to Attend:** Free
**Participated Fee:** RMB 8000/booth
**Statistics '09:** Exhibition Area 9,500m²(foreigners 1,500m²), Exhibitors 273（foreigners 45, came from 13 countries），Visitors 17, 038（trade visitors 11,837）
**Sponsor:** China National Food Industry Assn
**Organizer:** Beijing Shuanglang Exhibition Service Co Ltd
**Address:** Room 1006, Building B, No.3 Real Estate, Shuguangxilijia 1, Sanyuanqiao, Chaoyang District, Beijing
**Contact:** Miss Lin, Mr Li

2010/04/10-12
☎ 010-5822 0435
🖷 010-5822 0435
✉ sbl@sblzl.com
www.beautyexpo365.com
340

**2010第十六届中国北京国际美容美发化妆用品博览会(春季)**
**地点**：中国国际展览中心，北京 CIEC
**内容**：美容产品：皮肤护理、香水、美体、彩妆、水疗、美甲、纹绣、香薰、保健养生等产品；美发产品：洗护染烫产品、发制品、养发育 发产品、发用饰品；器具产品：美发美容美体设备、用具类、仪器类、沙龙家具、专用工服、织品；整形美容：整形设备、仪器、技术、机构；原料：日化原料、洗涤及个人护理产品；包装材料：包装器械、各类容器、专用箱包、装潢印刷；其它：专业媒体、管理软件、教育培训机构
**始办年份**：1997
**周期**：每年两届
**市场范围**：全国性
**性质**：面向公众
**入场券价格**：免费
**参展费用**：7,600元/9m²
**上届规模** ‘09：展览面积15,000m²(国外展商面积3,000m²), 参展商410家（国外展商63家，来自11个国家），参观人数30,000人
**主办**：北京市美发美容行业协会(BHBA)；北京世博联展览服务有限公司(SBL)
**地址**：北京市朝阳区三元桥曙光西里甲1号第三置业B座1006室（100028）
**联系人**：韩友峰
**QQ**：451277815

**16th Chinese Intl Beauty, Hairdressing & Cosmetics Expo Beijing 2010**
**Venue**: China International Exhibition Center, Beijing
**Established Year**: 1997
**Frequency**: Biannual
**Market Area**: National
**Nature**: Open to public
**Cost to Attend**: Free
**Participated Fee**: RMB 7,600/9m²
**Statistics ‘09**: Exhibition Area 15,000m²(foreigners 3,000m²), Exhibitors 410 (foreigners 63, came from 11 countries) , Visitors 30,000
**Organizer**: Beijing Shibolian Exhibition Service Co Ltd
**Address**: Room 1006, Building B, No.3 Real Estate, Shuguangxilijia 1, Sanyuanqiao, Chaoyang District, Beijing

2010/04/15-18
☎ 010-8460 0992, 8460 0993
🖷 010-8460 0982, 8460 0989
✉ bjdw2006@126.com
www.door-expo.com
350

**CIDE-2010第九届中国国际门业展览会**
**地点**：中国国际展览中心，北京 CIEC
**内容**：门：包括实木门、装饰工艺门、生态门、钢木门、免漆门、竹木门、防盗门、防火门、复合门、模压门、木塑门、吸塑门、隔断门、橱柜门、折叠门、滑动拉门、金属门、保温门、铝塑门、移门、百叶门、铜雕工艺门、镶嵌玻璃木门等；门业辅料：木皮、木塑、高分子材料、密封材料等门业新材料；门业机械：制门机械、门成套生产及加工设备；门禁系统：门控门禁技术、锁具及门窗五金配件；门业化工：门业涂料、油漆化工产品。
**始办年份**：2002
**周期**：每年一届
**入场券价格**：免费
**参展费用**：标准展位8,800元/个，净地880元/m²
**上届规模** ‘09：展览面积34,000m²(国外展商面积5,000m²), 参展商470家（国外展商50家，来自12个国家），参观人数65,000人（专业贸易观众50,000人）
**主办**：中国林产工业协会；中国建筑装饰协会；中国国际展览中心集团公司；中国科学技术投资有限公司
**承办**：北京伟士佳合展览策划有限公司；北京中装伟佳展览策划有限公司
**地址**：北京市朝阳区北三环东路6号中国国际展览中心一号馆四层387号（100028）
**联系人**：段伟，宋斌
**QQ**：446547417

**The 9th China International Door Industry Exhibition**
**Venue**: China International Exhibition Center, Beijing
**Profile**: Doors: wooden door, decorative door, ecotype door, steel-wood door, paintless door, bamboo door, anti-theft door, fire door, composite door, mould pressing door, wood engraved door, PVC door, partition door, cabinet door, folding door, sliding door, metal door, thermal door, aluminum door, lift door, blind door, copper engraved door, glass embedded wooden door, etc; Door auxiliary materials; Door equipment; Door access technology; Door chemical industry
**Established Year**: 2002
**Frequency**: Annual
**Cost to Attend**: Free
**Participated Fee**: Standard Booth RMB 8,800, Raw Space RMB 880/m²
**Statistics ‘09**: Exhibition Area 34,000m²(foreigners 5,000m²), Exhibitors 470 (foreigners 50, came from 12 countries) , Visitors 65,000 (trade visitors 50,000)
**Sponsor**: China National Forest Products Industry Assn; China Building and Decoration Assn; China Intl Exhibition Center Group Co Ltd; China Science & Technology Investment Co Ltd
**Organizer**: Beijing WSJ United Strategy for Exhibition Co Ltd
**Address**: Room 387, the 4th floor, No. 1 exhibition hall, No. 6 East Beisanhuandong Rd., Chaoyang District, Beijing
**Contact**: Duan Wei, Song Bin

2010/04/16-18
☎ 010-6505 2288
www.cwtc.com
360

**2010中国特许展**
**地点**：中国国际贸易中心，北京
**地址**：北京建国门外大街一号（100004）

**China Franchise Expo**
**Venue**: China World Trade Center, Beijing
**Organizer**: CCPIT Beijing；Beijing International Exhibition Center

2010/04/16-18
☎ 010-5128 0036, 8586 5730
🖷 010-8586 5735
✉ Beijing@chinagolfshou.com
www.chinagolfshow.com
370

**中国高尔夫球博览会**
**地点**：国家会议中心，北京
**内容**：个人用品、机械设备、球场会所
**始办年份**：2002
**周期**：每年一届
**市场范围**：国际性
**性质**：面向公众
**入场券价格**：20元
**主办**：中展联合高尔夫运动发展（北京）有限公司；中国高尔夫球协会
**地址**：北京市朝阳区八里庄远洋商务61号1103（100025）
**联系人**：贾巍，林

**China Golf Show**
**Venue**: China National Convention Center, Beijing
**Established Year**: 2002
**Frequency**: Annual
**Market Area**: International
**Nature**: Open to public
**Cost to Attend**: RMB 20:-
**Organizer**: Zhongzhan Golf Alliance (Beijing) Co Ltd; China Golf Assn
**Address**: Room 1103, Ocean Business Center, No, 61 Bldg Balizhuangarli, Chaoyang District, Beijing, China
**Contact**: Kelly, Queen

2010/04/21-25
☎ 010-6505 2288
www.cwtc.com
www.cige-bj.com
380

**2010中艺博国际画廊博览会**
**地点**：中国国际贸易中心，北京
**地址**：北京建国门外大街一号（100004）
**主办**：北京中艺博文化传播有限公司

**China International Gallery Exposition**
**Venue**: China World Trade Center, Beijing
**Organizer**: Beijing Chinese Art Exposition's Media Co Ltd

2010/04/23-25
☎ 010-6441 6542
🖷 010-6441 2631
✉ regalland@regalland.com
www.winechinaexhibition.com
385

**中国国际葡萄酒及烈酒展览会**
**地点：**全国农业展览馆，北京 CIEC
**内容：**葡萄酒及烈酒，相关产品
**周期：**每年一届
**市场范围：**国际性
**性质：**面向公众
**主办：**中国国际贸促会农业行业分会
**承办：**北京金万洲会展服务有限公司
**地址：**北京市朝阳区安贞里金瓯大厦438室
**联系人：**伍思智

**Wine China Exhibition**
Venue: National Agricultural Exhibition Center, Beijing
Frequency: Annual
Market Area: International
Nature: Open to public
Organizer: CCPIT-SSA

2010/04/25 – 02
✉ wangxiaauto@vip.163.com
www.china-autoshow.com
388

**2010北京国际汽车展览会**
**地点：**中国国际展览中心新馆，北京 CIEC
**内容：**各种类型的汽车（包括轿车、商用车及专用车）；各种类型的概念车；各种汽车零部件、总成、模块及系统；各种汽车制造设备，工艺装备；各种检测、测试、实验仪器和设备；计算机开发设计系统及应用技术；汽车工业生产的新工艺、新材料；汽车工业新能源技术与产品；汽车工业环保技术与产品；各种汽车用品、装饰件；各种汽车维修设备
**周期：**每年一届
**市场范围：**国际性
**性质：**面向公众
**主办：**中国机械工业联合会；工作机械工业集团公司；中国国际贸易促进委员会；中国汽车工业协会
**承办：**中国贸促会汽车行业分会；中国汽车工业国际合作总公司；中国国际展览中心集团公司；中国汽车工程学会
**联系人：**王侠

**Auto China 2010**
2010 Beijing International Automotive Exhibition
Venue: China International Exhibition Center New Venue, Beijing
Frequency: Annual
Market Area: International
Nature: Open to Public
Organizer: CCPIT Automotive Sub-council; China National Automotive Industry Intl Cooperation; CAAM; CIEC; SAE-China
Contact: Wang Xia

2010/04/27-30
☎ 010-6505 2288
www.cottm.com
www.cottm.com.cn
390

**2010中国出境旅游交易会**
**地点：**中国国际贸易中心，北京
**地址：**北京建国门外大街一号（100004）
**性质：**对贸易观众开放

**China Outbound Travel & Tourism Market**
Venue: China World Trade Center, Beijing
Nature: Trade Only
Organizer: Tarsus Travel Exhibitions Ltd

2010/04/29-02
☎ 010-6554 7002, 6554 7002
🖷 010-6554 5213
✉ artfair_Beijing@yahoo.com.cn
www.artBeijing.net
400

**艺术北京2010当代艺术博览会**
**地点：**全国农业展览馆，北京
**内容：**艺术北京2010致力于打造更高水平的国际当代艺术平台。艺术北京2010将邀请世界范围内的80家画廊参展，展出最新的艺术作品。我们会将重点放在全球最具增长性的亚洲艺术资源，在集中东亚艺术资源的基础上，逐渐向南亚等地扩展，以期成为亚洲当代艺术之交易重镇。
**始办年份：**2006
**周期：**每年一届
**市场范围：**国际性
**性质：**面向公众
**入场券价格：**50元
**参展费用：**60,000元/36m²
**上届规模** '09：展览面积12,000m²，参展商60家（国外展商15家，来自13个国家），参观人数3,000人
**主办：**北京艾特菲尔文化有限公司
**地址：**北京市吉庆里14号楼佳汇国际中心A1601室（100027）
**联系人：**范欣，李斌

**Art Beijing 2010 Contemporary Art Fair**
Venue: National Agricultural Exhibition Center, Beijing
Profile: Art Beijing 2010 takes this international platform for contemporary art to new heights. With the participation of 80 exclusive international galleries, Art Beijing 2010 is expected to become the key trading center for contemporary Asian art works.
Established Year: 2006
Frequency: Annual
Market Area: International
Nature: Open to public
Cost to Attend: RMB 50:-
Participated Fee: RMB 60,000/36m²
Statistics '09: Exhibition Area 12,000m², Exhibitors 60（foreigners 15, came from 13 countries）, Visitors 3,000
Organizer: Beijing ArtFair Culture Co Ltd
Address: Rm 1601, Jiahui International Center No.14 Jiqingli, Chaoyang District, Beijing 100020, China
Contact: Fan Xin, Li Bin

2010/05/10-12
☎ 010-6505 3207
🖷 010-6505 3260
✉ lidongmei@cwtc.com
www.hotelchinaexpo.com
430

**2010北京国际咖啡博览会**
（2010中国国际咖啡业展览会）
**地点：**中国国际贸易中心，北京
**主办：**中国国际贸易中心股份有限公司
**承办：**中国国际贸易中心股份有限公司展览部
**地址：**北京市建国门外大街1号国贸展厅二层（100004）
**联系人：**李冬梅

**2010 China International Coffee Industry Exhibition**
Venue: China World Trade Center, Beijing
Sponsor: China World Trade Center Co
Organizer: Exhibition Division of China World Trade Center Co
Address: No. 1 Jian Guo Men Wai Avenue, Beijing 100004, China
Contact: Olivia

2010/05/10-13
☎ 010-6505 3207
🖷 010-6505 3260
✉ lidongmei@cwtc.com
www.hotelchinaexpo.com
440

**中国国际酒店博览会**
暨第16届中国国际酒店、餐饮用品、食品、饮料及服务设施博览会
**地点：**中国国际贸易中心，北京
**内容：**饭店用品，家具，清洁设备，装饰材料，冷冻设备，消防设施，工服，桑拿设备，娱乐设施，照明系统，通信设施，空调，电脑销售及管理系统，会议视听设备等 酒店餐馆设备，烧烤设备，茶和咖啡，橄榄油，食用油，酒类，制冰机，食品饮料等旅游资源，星级酒店，酒店管理公司，旅行社，游览景点等
**始办年份：**1995
**周期：**每年一届
**市场范围：**国际性
**入场券价格：**免费
**参展费用：**1号馆、序厅：标准展位8,800元/个，净地880元/m²；2号馆、贵宾通道：标准展位7,800元/个，净地780元/m²
**上届规模** '09：展览面积8,000m²(国外展商面积72m²)，参展商160

**Hotel China 2010**
16th China Intl Exhibition for Hotel & Restaurant Facilities, Equipment & Service, Food & Beverages
Venue: China World Trade Center, Beijing
Profile: Hotel Supplies, Furniture, Cleaning Machines, Decorations, Fire & Security Facilities, Lighting installation, Telephone & Telecommunication System, Air Conditioning, Computer Sales and Management Systems, Conference Video & Audio Equipment, Work Clothes, Recreation Facilities
Established Year: 1995
Frequency: Annual
Market Area: International
Cost to Attend: Free
Participated Fee: Standard Booth RMB 8,800, Raw Space RMB 880/m²

家（国外展商5家，来自3个国家），参观人数8,000人（专业贸易观众6,000人）
主办：中国国际贸易中心股份有限公司
承办：中国国际贸易中心股份有限公司展览部
地址：北京市建国门外大街1号国贸展厅二层（100004）
联系人：李冬梅

Statistics '09: Exhibition Area 8,000m²(foreigners 72m²), Exhibitors 160 (foreigners 5, came from 3 countries), Visitors 8,000 (trade visitors 6,000)
Sponsor: China World Trade Center Co
Organizer: Exhibition Division of China World Trade Center Co
Address: No. 1 Jian Guo Men Wai Avenue, Beijing 100004, China
Contact: Olivia

2010/05/11-14
☎ 010-8851 4541
🖷 010-8851 4541
✉ wangkunyi@foundry.com.cn
www.foundry.com.cn
www.expochina.cn

450

**第十届中国国际铸造、锻压及工业炉展览会**

地点：中国国际展览中心新馆，北京

内容：铸钢、铸铁，有色合金铸件（精密铸造、压力铸造、消失模铸造、离心铸造、低压铸造等）；汽车、机床、船舶、工程机械、轨道交通、重型机械、矿山机械、纺织机械、印刷机械、通用机械；输变电、电子通讯、石油化工、建筑五金、管道泵阀、市政工程、城市艺术类铸件；各类铸造装备、制型、制芯中心、铸件加工中心、直读光谱仪、炉前快速分等检测仪器、各类铸造模具；铸造生铁、废钢、铁合金、有色金属、精炼剂、球化剂、孕育剂、石英砂、膨润土、煤粉、树脂、涂料、脱模剂等各类铸造原辅材料。
始办年份：1990
周期：两年一届
市场范围：国际性
入场券价格：免费
参展费用：12,000元/9m²
上届规模'08：展览面积28,750m²(国外展商面积6,000m²)，参展商1,100家（国外展商300家，来自32个国家），参观人数31,000人
主办：中国铸造协会
地址：北京市海淀区紫竹院路甲32号（100048）
联系人：范琦，王坤毅

**2010 METAL CHINA**

Venue: China International Exhibition Center New Venue, Beijing
Profile: Ferrous Castings, Iron, steel and malleable castings Nonferrous Metal Castings-Aluminum, zinc, copper, magnesium, nickel and other nonferrous metal foundries Diecastings Foundry Plants and Technology Diecasting machine and its supplementary equipment Plant and Equipment for Processing Prime and Raw Material Molding Machines Furnaces Melting Furnaces Noise Protection Rolling mill Measuring Systems Raw and auxiliary materials consultation, business and trade information and publication
Established Year: 1990
Frequency: Biennial
Market Area: International
Cost to Attend: Free
Participated Fee: RMB 12,000元/9m²
Statistics '08: Exhibition Area 28,750m²(foreigners 6,000m²), Exhibitors 1,100 (foreigners 300, came from 32 countries), Visitors 31,000
Organizer: CHINA FOUNDRY ASSNCIATION
Address: A32 Zizhuyuan Rd, Beijing, China
Contact: Fan Qi, Wang Kunyi

2010/05/11-14
☎ 010-8851 4541
🖷 010-8851 4541
✉ wangkunyi@foundry.com.cn
www.foundry.com.cn
www.expochina.cn

460

**2010中国国际铸件博览会**

地点：中国国际展览中心新馆，北京

内容：铸钢、铸铁、有色合金铸件（精密铸造、压力铸造、消失模铸造、离心铸造、低压铸造等）。汽车、机床、船舶、工程机械、轨道交通、重型机械、矿山机械、纺织机械、印刷机械、通用机械；输变电、电子通讯、石油化工、建筑五金、管道泵阀、市政工程、城市艺术类铸件。
始办年份：2008
周期：每年一届
市场范围：国际性
入场券价格：免费
参展费用：12,000元/9m²
上届规模'08：展览面积6,500m²，参展商500家，参观人数31,000人
主办：中国铸造协会
地址：北京市海淀区紫竹院路甲32号（100048）
联系人：范琦，王坤毅

**2010 CASTING CHINA**

Venue: China International Exhibition Center New Venue, Beijing
Profile: Ferrous Castings, Iron, steel and malleable castings Nonferrous Metal Castings-Aluminum, zinc, copper, magnesium, nickel and other nonferrous metal foundries Diecastings Foundry Plants and Technology Diecasting machine and its supplementary equipment
Established Year: 2008
Frequency: Annual
Market Area: International
Cost to Attend: Free
Participated Fee: RMB 12,000/9m²
Statistics '08: Exhibition Area 6,500m², Exhibitors 500, Visitors 31,000
Organizer: CHINA FOUNDRY ASSNCIATION
Address: A32 Zizhuyuan Rd, Beijing, China
Contact: Fan Qi, Wang Kunyi

2010/05/11-14
☎ 010-6522 0753, 6525 6461
🖷 010-6523 3861
✉ steelfair@yahoo.com.cn
www.metallurgy-china.com

470

**第十二届中国国际冶金工业展览会**

地点：中国国际展览中心新馆，北京

内容：冶金：技术及设备，产品，制成品及辅助用品；辅助材料；碳素材料；铁合金；耐火材料及工业陶瓷；用于冶金；热加工；机械加工等方面的电动设备；电控及电子检测设备；仪器仪表；节能减排；环境保护技术设备；冶金设计与咨询服务；专业技术期刊；杂志；专业网站媒体
始办年份：1987
周期：两年一届
市场范围：国际性
入场券价格：免费
参展费用：标准展位国内企业9,600元，净地960元m²
上届规模'08：展览面积27,164m²(国外展商面积5,269m²)，参展商1,100家（国外展商279家，来自28个国家），参观人数31,867人（专业贸易观众8,936人）
主办：中国贸促会冶金行业分会
地址：北京市东城区东四西大街46号主楼606室（100711）
联系人：马婧，章亦飞

**The 12th China International Metallurgical Industry Expo**

Venue: China National Exhibition Center New Venue, Beijing
Established Year: 1987
Frequency: Biennial
Market Area: International
Cost to Attend: Free
Participated Fee: Domestic Exhibitors: Standard Booth RMB 9,600, Raw Space RMB 960/m²
Statistics '08: Exhibition Area 27,164m²(foreigners 5,269m²), Exhibitors 1,100 (foreigners 279, came from 28 countries), Visitors 31,867 (trade visitors 8,936)
Organizer: Metallurgical Council of CCPIT
Address: Room 606 No 46 Dongsi West Street, Dongcheng District, Beijing, China
Contact: RUBY Ma, Zhang Yifei

2010/05/15-17
☎ 010-8776 6940
🖷 010-8776 6773
✉ wanju678@163.com
www.Beijingite.com

480

**第12届北京国际玩具及幼教用品展览会**
暨2010中国国际孕妇及婴童用品展览会
**地点：**中国国际贸易中心，北京
**内容：**经过11年的精心培育，已经成为中国北方地区最具影响力的行业盛会。北京国际玩具及幼教用品展览会已成为玩具幼教用品企业树立品牌、扩大市场影响力的理想商业平台
**始办年份：**1998
**周期：**每年一届
**市场范围：**国际性
**参展费用：**8,500元
**上届规模**‘09：展览面积12,000m$^2$(国外展商面积300m$^2$)，参展商420家（国外展商22家，来自4个国家），参观人数28,000人（专业贸易观众17,000人）
**主办：**中国国际贸易中心股份有限公司
**承办：**北京南北展览有限公司
**地址：**北京市朝阳区百子湾路16号后现代城5号楼A座902室（100124）
**联系人：**郭斌
MSN：wanju668@hotmail.com
QQ：252907551

**The 12th Beijing International Toys & Preschool Tools Exhibition**
Venue: China World Trade Center, Beijing
Established Year: 1998
Frequency: Annual
Market Area: International
Participated Fee: RMB 8,500/booth
Statistics ‘09: Exhibition Area 12,000m$^2$(foreigners 300m$^2$), Exhibitors 420（foreigners 22, came from 4 countries），Visitors 28,000（trade visitors 17,000）
Organizer: Beijing Nanbei Exhibition Co Ltd
Contact: Guo Bin
MSN: wanju668@hotmail.com

2010/05/17-21
☎ 010-6620 6773
🖷 010-6620 6773
✉ zhanlan@chinagas.org.cn
www.gaschina2010.com

500

**2010年中国国际燃气、供热技术与设备展览会**
**地点：**国家会议中心，北京
**内容：**燃气输配系统新技术及维护管理技术设备、燃气应用技术；燃气控制检测技术与设备、燃气自动化控制、报警系统、燃气表；天然气存储技术、煤气净化与回收技术；燃气新型专用管材与设备、管道的防腐技术、燃气阀门；燃气锅炉、燃气供热（水）设备、各类燃气用具及零配件等；燃气采暖技术设备、燃气中央空调；地下管线探测、检测、泄漏监测技术设备；城市燃气领域综合信息管理系统、软件系统
**始办年份：**1994
**周期：**每年一届
**市场范围：**国际性
**入场券价格：**免费
**参展费用：**标准展位10,000元，净地1000元/m$^2$
**主办：**中华人民共和国住房和城乡建设部
**承办：**中国城市燃气协会；中国城镇供热协会
**地址：**北京市西城区西直门南小街22号（100035）
**联系人：**聂松，冯颖

**GAS & HEATING CHINA 2010**
Venue: China National Convention Center, Beijing
Established Year: 1994
Frequency: Annual
Market Area: International
Cost to Attend: Free
Participated Fee: Standard Booth RMB 10,000，Raw Space RMB 1,000/m$^2$
Organizer: China Gas Association
Address: 22 Nan Xiao Jie, Xizhimen, Xicheng Dist, Beijing 100035
Contact: Nie Song, Feng Ying

2010/05/20-23
☎ 010-8402 9994,
6403 3098转ext 201/203
🖷 010-8401 0152
✉ chen@palmexpo.com
www.palmexpo.com

510

**第十九届中国国际专业音响、灯光、乐器及技术展览会**
**地点：**中国国际展览中心，北京 CIEC
**内容：**1）专业音响器材：话筒，调音系统，扬声器，周边器材，录音系统等；2）专业舞台灯光器材：电脑灯，舞台灯，调光系统，LED视频，电光源产品等；3）舞台机械：升降台，车台，吊杆，防火幕，隔声幕等；4）乐器：键盘乐器，管乐器，弦乐器，打击乐器，电声乐器，电脑作曲器材等；5）专业用摄、录像设备：摄像机，录像机，三维动画系统，监视器等；6）专业类出版刊物：书籍，期刊，报纸，光碟等；7）其他：剧场座椅，剧场隔音材料，卡拉OK点歌器材等。
**始办年份：**1989
**周期：**每年一届
**市场范围：**国际性
**性质：**面向公众
**入场券价格：**20元
**上届规模**‘09：展览面积85,000m$^2$(国外展商面积14,000m$^2$)，参展商1,000家（国外展商170家，来自20个国家），参观人数170,000人（专业贸易观众30,000人）
**支持单位：**中华人民共和国文化部；中华人民共和国科学技术部；中国照明学会
**主办：**中国演艺设备技术协会
**地址：**北京市东城区安定门东大街28号雍和大厦东楼C座10层（100007）
**联系人：**陈正纲，赵清华

**19th China International Exhibition on Pro Audio, Light, Music & Technology**
Venue: China International Exhibition Center, Beijing
Profile: 1）Professional Sound equipment: Microphone, Tuning system, Peripheral Component Equipment, Sound Recording System, etc: 2) Professional Stage & Light Equipment: Computer Lamp, Stage Lamp, Light control system, LED, Electric Light Source product, etc; 3) Stage machinery: Carrying LT, Turn-table, Boom, Safe Curtain, Sound Insulated Curtain, etc; 4) Musical Instrument: Keyboard instrument, Wind Instrument, Stringed Instrument, Percussion Instrument, Electro-acoustical Instrument, Computer Music composition equipment, etc; 5) Professional video camera & video equipment: Camera, Videotape Recorder, 3D Animation Systems, Monitor , etc; 6) Professional publications: Publication(Book), Periodical, Newspaper, Disc, etc; 7) Others: Theater Chair, Acoustic Celotex Material of Theater, KTV/VOD Equipment, etc.
Established Year: 1989
Frequency: Annual
Market Area: International
Nature: Open to public
Cost to Attend: RMB 20:-
Statistics ‘09: Exhibition Area 85,000m$^2$(foreigners 14,000m$^2$), Exhibitors 1,000（foreigners 170, came from 20 countries），Visitors 170,000（trade visitors 30,000）
Sponsor: The Ministry of Culture, P.R. China; The Ministry of Science & Technology, P.R. China; China Illuminating Engineering Society
Organizer: China Entertainment Technology Association
Address: 10 Fl., C, East Building, YongHe Plaza, No.28, An Ding Men Dong Da Jie, Dong Cheng District, Beijing, China
Contact: Chen Zhenggang, Zhao Qinghua

2010/05/20-23
☎ 010-6710 2728
🖷 010-6710 2689
✉ info@sportshow.com.cn
www.sportshow.com.cn

520

**2010（第26届）中国国际体育用品博览会**
**地点：**中国国际展览中心新馆，北京 CIEC
**内容：**运动休闲服饰；户外运动及休闲用品、运动自行车、水上运动用品；网羽运动用品及配件；健身器材、户外健身路径、康复设备和按摩器材；乒乓球器材及配件；足篮排器材及配件；台球、桌球及配件；学校体育器材；运动场馆设施
**始办年份：**1993
**周期：**每年一届
**市场范围：**国际性
**性质：**面向公众
**入场券价格：**10元
**上届规模** '09：展览面积90,000m²，参展商900家，参观人数150,000人（专业贸易观众50,000人）
**主办：**国家体育总局；中国体育用品业联合会；国家体育总局体育器材装备中心
**地址：**北京市崇文区体育馆路3号（100763）

**China International Sporting Goods Show 2010**
Venue: China International Exhibition Center New Venue, Beijing
Profile: Sportswear and Leisure Apparel Show; Outdoor Show; Racket Show; Ball Game Show; Fitness Show; Stadium & Gym Show; Cycling Show
Established Year: 1993
Frequency: Annual
Market Area: International
Nature: Open to public
Cost to Attend: RMB 10:-
Statistics '09: Exhibition Area 90,000m², Exhibitors 900, Visitors 150,000 (trade visitors 50,000)
Organizer: China General Administration of Sport; China Sporting Goods Federation; Sports Equipment Administrative Center of China General Administration of Sport
Address: 3, Tiyuguan Rd. Chongwen District, Beijing, 100763, China

2010/05/26-28
☎ 010-6845 3393, 6845 1873
🖷 010-6845 5499
✉ lunar@ccidexpo.com; jenny@ccidexpo.com
www.smartcards-china.com

530

**第十三届中国国际智能卡博览会**
**地点：**国家会议中心，北京
**内容：**芯片提供商：IC卡芯片的设计与开发，卡片制造商，接触式和非接触式IC卡及组合式两用IC卡、CPU卡、记忆型卡、异型卡；IC卡及模块的生产与材料；IC卡的凸字印刷、层压和模压；IC卡的个人化图像身份识别；IC模块封装；设备提供商：符合PBOC 2.0规范的磁卡和IC卡两用的银行ATM机及圈存机、IC卡收款机；计算机与网络的安全接入控制、检测的IC卡技术及设备；门禁控制及相关IC卡设备；IC卡的检测设备；与IC卡有关的外设产品与设备，包括各种读写机具、POS终端设备；系统集成商：IC卡各种应用系统集成，软件开发商，各类IC卡应用系统，一卡通应用系统；制卡材料
**始办年份：**1998
**周期：**每年一届
**市场范围：**国际性
**性质：**面向公众
**入场券价格：**免费
**参展费用：**国内企业：标准展位8,100元，净地800元/m²
**上届规模** '09：展览面积4,500m²(国外展商面积200m²)，参展商150家（国外展商30家，来自20个国家），参观人数6,900人（专业贸易观众3,000人）
**主办：**中国电子信息产业发展研究院；北京赛迪会展有限公司
**地址：**北京市海淀区紫竹院路62号赛迪大厦配楼2071室(100048)
**联系人：**鲁娜，纪占峰

**The 13th International Fair of Smart Cards, China 2010**
(SCC2010)
Venue: China National Convention Center, Beijing
Profile: Chip design and development vendors; Contact and contactless IC cards and combined IC cards vendors: CPU card, memory cards, production and materials of IC card and modules, IC card thermographic printing, laminating and molding, personalized image identification for IC card; IC module packaging; Equipment vendors: ATM machines, IC card cashier register; security access control for computers and networks, IC card detection and access control; test equipment; peripheral products and equipment related to IC cards, including various kinds of reading and writing tools, POS; Terminal and system vendors; Software vendors; IC card application systems, Especially multifunction card application system; Plastic card, PET card, paper card, RFID
Established Year: 1998
Frequency: Annual
Market Area: International
Nature: Open to public
Cost to Attend: Free
Participated Fee: Domestic Exhibitors: Standard Booth RMB 8,100, Raw Space RMB 800/m²
Statistics '09: Exhibition Area 4,500m²(foreigners 200m²), Exhibitors 150 (foreigners 30, came from 20 countries), Visitors 6,900 (trade visitors 3,000)
Organizer: China Center for Information Industry Development; CCID Conference & Exhibition Co
Address: Rm.2071, CCID Plaza, Business Bldg, 62 Zizhuyuan Rd, Haidian Dist, Beijing 100048, China
Contact: Lunar, Jenny

2010/05/27-30
☎ 010-6397 2404, 6398 2928
🖷 010-6398 0554
✉ Whj@cmes.org, Fanx@cmes.org
essen.cmes.org

540

**第十五届北京埃森焊接与切割展览会**
**地点：**中国国际展览中心新馆，北京 CIEC
**内容：**焊接、切割、钎焊及粘接；消耗材料与其制备和原材料；检测设备及其耗材；焊前准备与焊后处理设备与技术；焊工安全和环境保护
**周期：**每年一届
**市场范围：**国际性
**性质：**面向公众
**入场券价格：**免费
**参展费用：**6,900～16,200元/展位，净地6,200～14,400元/展位
**主办：**中国机械工程学会及其焊接分会；中国焊接协会；中国电器工业协会电焊机分会；德国焊接学会；德国埃森展览公司
**承办：**北京埃森焊接展组委会
**地址：**北京市海淀区莲花小区2-5-1607（100036）
**联系人：**温惠娟，樊星
MSN：Huijuanwen2@hotmail.com
QQ：806946120

**The 15th Beijing Essen Welding & Cutting Fair**
Venue: China International Exhibition Center New Venue, Beijing
Profile: Welding, Cutting, Brazing and Adhesive bonding; Consumable Materials and their Manufacturing Equipment and Raw Materials; Inspection Equipment and Related Consumables; Pre- and Post-welding Treatment Equipment and Technology ; Safety and Health for Welder & Environment Protection
Frequency: Annual
Market Area: International
Nature: Open to public
Cost to Attend: Free
Participated Fee: RMB 6,900-16,200/booth, Raw Space RMB 6,200-14,400/booth
Sponsor: Chinese Mechanical Engineering Society; Welding Institution of CMES; China Welding Association; Welding Machine Committee of CEEIA; German Welding Society(DVS); Messe Essen GmbH
Organizer: Organizing Committee of Beijing Essen Welding & Cutting Fair
Address: 2-5-1607 Lianhuaxiaoqu, Haidian District, Beijing 100036, China
Contact: Wen Huijuan, Fan Xing
MSN: Huijuanwen2@hotmail.com

2010/05/27-31
☎ 010-6806 3939, 6806 5959
🖷 010-6806 6969, 6806 7979
✉ wangpeng@ccpitbj.org
✉ haocheng@ccpitbj.org
www.chitec.cn

**第十三届中国北京国际科技产业博览会**
**地点：**中国国际展览中心，北京
**内容：**电子信息与现代通讯；生物工程与医药；环境保护产业；新材料与新能源；现代农业与绿色技术；现代工程与先进制造技术
**始办年份：**1998
**周期：**每年一届
550 **市场范围：**国际性
**性质：**面向公众
**入场券价格：**免费
**参展费用：**标准展位6,000/8,300/16,600/24,900元，净地600/850/1,660/2,490元 / $m^2$
**上届规模**'08：展览面积60,000$m^2$(国外展商面积16,000$m^2$)，参展商2,213家（国外展商163家，来自15个国家），参观人数210,000人（专业贸易观众120,000人）
**主办：**科学技术部；商务部；教育部；工业和信息化部；中国贸促会；国家知识产权局；北京市人民政府
**承办：**北京世界贸易中心
**地址：**北京市西城区南礼士路19号建邦商务会馆2层（100045）
**联系人：**王鹏，张皓成

**The 13th China Beijing International High-Tech Expo**
**Venue:** China International Exhibition Center, Beijing
**Profile:** Electronics Informatics & Communication, Bio-engineering & Pharmaceuticals, Environmental Protective Industry, New Material & New Energy, Modern Agriculture & Green Technology, Modern Engineering & Manufacturing Technology
**Established Year:** 1998
**Frequency:** Annual
**Market Area:** International
**Nature:** Open to public
**Cost to Attend:** Free
**Participated Fee:** Standard Booth RMB 24,900, Raw Space RMB 2,490/$m^2$
**Statistics '08:** Exhibition Area 60,000$m^2$(foreigners 16,000$m^2$), Exhibitors 2,213 (foreigners 163, came from 15 countries), Visitors 210,000 (trade visitors 120,000)
**Organizer:** Ministry of Science & Technology, China; Ministry of Commerce, China; Ministry of Education, China; Ministry of Industry and Information Technology, China; CCPIT; State Intellectual
**Address:** 2nd Floor Jianbang Business Center, No. 19 Nanlishi Road, Xicheng District, Beijing China
**Contact:** Wang Peng, Zhang Haocheng

2010/06/01-03
☎ 010-6505 2288
www.topwinechina.com

**2010年中国国际葡萄酒博览会**
**地点：**中国国际贸易中心，北京
**主办：**北京世联新睿国际展览有限公司
580

**2010 Topwine China**
**Venue:** China World Trade Center, Beijing
**Organizer:** Beijing Partnerworld International Exhibition Co Ltd

2010/06/02-04
☎ 010-5152 7167
🖷 010-6218 6579
✉ gucj@css.com.cn
www.csia.org.cn

**2010第十四届中国国际软件博览会**
**地点：**北京展览馆，北京
**内容：**建立中外软件市场交流与合作的国际化服务平台，中国国际软件展览中的著名品牌（已连续举办13届），展览+研讨+商务洽谈（客户洽谈），电子政务、网络安全与存储、中间件、嵌
600 入式系统、城市/企业信息化、重点行业应用、数码/移动/家电应用、教育软件、游戏/动漫软件。
**始办年份：**1997
**周期：**每年一届
**市场范围：**国际性
**性质：**面向公众
**入场券价格：**免费
**参展费用：**900元/$m^2$
**上届规模**：展览面积15,000$m^2$(国外展商面积500$m^2$)，参展商600家（国外展商50家）
**主办：**中华人民共和国工业和信息化部
**承办：**中国软件行业协会
**地址：**北京市海淀区学院南路55号中软大厦A401（100081）
**联系人：**顾长江，徐萌

**INTL SOFT CHINA 2010**
**Venue:** Beijing Exhibition Center, Beijing
**Profile:** Basic software, information security, Chinese clip, software initiative innovation projects, e-government, OSS, electronic commercial, SaaS, ERP, CRM,CAD/CAM/CAE, PDM,GIS/GPS,BI, middleware, embedded system, SME information projects, software application in key industries, software service outsourcing, IC design, 3C( computer/ communication/ consumer electronics) ,education software, gaming/entertainment software, animation, robot
**Established Year:** 1997
**Frequency:** Annual
**Market Area:** International
**Nature:** Open to public
**Cost to Attend:** Free
**Participated Fee:** RMB 900/$m^2$
**Statistics '09:** Exhibition Area 15,000$m^2$(foreigners 500$m^2$), Exhibitors 600 (foreigners 50)
**Organizer:** Ministry of Industry and Information Technology People's Republic of China **Sponsor:** China Software Industry Sanction
**Address:** No.55 Xueyuan Nan Road, Haidian District, Beijing, China
**Contact:** Gu Changjiang, Xu Meng

2010/06/03-05
☎ 010-8808 2303
🖷 010-8808 2305
✉ xxd@cbme.cn
www.wallexpochina.com

**第三届中国国际建筑材料技术装备展览会**
**地点：**中国国际展览中心，北京
**内容：**蒸压蒸养制砖技术和设备、烧结类制砖技术和设备、加气混凝土砌块及条板的生产技术和设备、混凝土生产技术和设备、新型建筑板材成套技术和设备、建筑保温隔热材料生产技术和设
610 备、水泥生产技术和设备，干混砂浆生产技术和设备、化工原料、密封和粘结材料、建筑节能及绿色环保产品
**始办年份：**2008
**周期：**每年一届
**市场范围：**国际性
**参展费用：**标准展位7,800元/个，室外净地600元/$m^2$
**上届规模**'09：展览面积10,000$m^2$(国外展商面积126$m^2$)，参展商150家（国外展商150家，来自10个国家），专业贸易观众9,000人
**主办：**国家建筑材料展贸中心
**地址：**北京市海淀区三里河路甲11号中国建材大厦四层（100037）
**联系人：**何徐凌，夏小冬

**3rd China Intl Building Material Technology Expo**
**Venue:** China International Exhibition Center, Beijing
**Profile:** Machine and system for the producing brick, block and various building boards；Machine and system for producing ceramic, cement, glass and lime，Mining；Obtaining of and Processing Raw Materials；Cement products technology & equipment; dry-mixed mortar technology & equipment, Chemical products, energy saving building & environment protection equipment.
**Established Year:** 2008
**Frequency:** Annual
**Market Area:** International
**Participated Fee:** Standard Booth RMB 7,800/booth, Outdoor Raw Space RMB 600/$m^2$
**Statistics '09:** Exhibition Area 10,000$m^2$(foreigners 126$m^2$), Exhibitors 150 (foreigners 150, came from 10 countries), Visitors 20,000(trade visitors 9,000)
**Organizer:** China Natl Building Material Exhibition & Trade Center
**Address:** 4th floor, China Building Materials Plaza, A 11# Sanlihe Rd., Haidian District, Beijing 100037, China
**Contact:** He Xuling, Xia Xiaodong

2010/06/03-05
☎ 010-8808 2303
🖷 010-8808 2305
✉ xxd@cbme.cn
www.wallexpochina.com

**第三届粉煤灰、脱硫石膏综合利用技术装备及产品展览会**
**地点：**中国国际展览中心，北京
**内容：**工业废渣处理、加工技术与设备，工业废渣生产绿色建材产品技术和设备，建筑节能及绿色环保产品，建筑垃圾处理设备，
620 二次破碎与筛分设备、搅拌设备等，最新脱硫、脱硝、除尘技术及设备

**3rd Fine Coal Ash & Desulfurized Gypsum Comprehensive Utilization Technology & Equipment Expo**
**Venue:** China International Exhibition Center, Beijing
**Profile:** Rehabilitation of industrial waste, energy saving building & environment protection equipment, Construction waste equipment, secondary crusher equipment & screening equipment, mixing plant.

**始办年份**：2008
**周期**：每年一届
**市场范围**：国际性
**参展费用**：标准展位7,800元/个,室外净地600元/$m^2$
**上届规模** '09：展览面积10,000$m^2$(国外展商面积126$m^2$)，参展商150家（国外展商20家，来自10个国家），参观人数20,000人（专业贸易观众9,000人）
**主办**：国家建筑材料展贸中心
**地址**：北京市海淀区三里河路甲11号中国建材大厦四层（100037）
**联系人**：何徐凌，夏小冬

**Established Year**: 2008
**Frequency**: Annual
**Market Area**: International
**Participated Fee**: Standard Booth RMB 7,800/booth, Outdoor Raw Space RMB 600/$m^2$
**Statistics '09**: Exhibition Area 10,000$m^2$(foreigners 126$m^2$), Exhibitors 150（foreigners 20, came from 10 countries）, Visitors 20,000（trade visitors 9,000）
**Organizer**: China Natl Building Material Exhibition & Trade Center
**Address**: 4th floor, China Building Materials Plaza, A 11# Sanlihe Rd., Haidian District, Beijing 100037, China
**Contact**: He Xuling, Xia Xiaodong

---

2010/06/03-05
☎ 010-8808 2303
🖷 010-8808 2305
✉ xxd@cbme.cn
www.wallexpochina.com

630

**第四届中国国际墙体材料及保温技术展览会**
**地点**：中国国际展览中心，北京 CIEC
**内容**：内外墙保温材料，新型轻质板材，节能保温系统，新型环保涂料，透水砖、装饰砖、广场砖、挂板，建筑陶瓷、装饰石材，集成节能房屋、箱柜式移动房屋、模块化移动环保房屋，建筑保温设备及工程
**始办年份**：2007
**周期**：每年一届
**市场范围**：国际性
**参展费用**：标准展位7,800元/个，室外净地600元/$m^2$
**上届规模** '09：展览面积10,000$m^2$(国外展商面积126$m^2$)，参展商150家（国外展商20家，来自10个国家），参观人数20,000人（专业贸易观众9,000人）
**主办**：国家建筑材料展贸中心
**地址**：北京市海淀区三里河路甲11号中国建材大厦四层（100037）
**联系人**：何徐凌，夏小冬

**4th China Intl Wall Material & Insulation Technology Exhibition**
**Venue**: China International Exhibition Center, Beijing
**Profile**: Heat preservation materials, Sound insulating and absorbing materials, Energy-saving technology, Constructional, Coating Materials, Aluminum-Plastic Composite Materials, Constructive Mortar Product
**Established Year**: 2007
**Frequency**: Annual
**Market Area**: International
**Participated Fee**: Standard Booth RMB 7,800/booth, Outdoor Raw Space RMB 600/$m^2$
**Statistics '09**: Exhibition Area 10,000$m^2$(foreigners 126$m^2$), Exhibitors 150（foreigners 20, came from 10 countries）, Visitors 20,000（trade visitors 9,000）
**Organizer**: China Natl Building Material Exhibition & Trade Center
**Address**: 4th floor, China Building Materials Plaza, A 11# Sanlihe Rd., Haidian District, Beijing 100037 China
**Contact**: He Xuling, Xia Xiaodong

---

2010/06/03-05
☎ 010-8808 2303
🖷 010-8808 2305
✉ xxd@cbme.cn
www.wallexpochina.com

640

**中国国际散装水泥暨预拌混凝土与预拌砂浆技术装备及产品展览会**
**地点**：中国国际展览中心，北京 CIEC
**内容**：散装水泥技术装备，预拌混凝土技术装备，干混砂浆技术装备，建筑砂浆产品，检测设备
首届
**市场范围**：国际性
**参展费用**：标准展位（3x3m）7,800元/个，室外净地600元/$m^2$
**预计规模**：展出面积10,000$m^2$，参展商200家，参观人数20,000人
**主办**：国家建筑材料展贸中心
**地址**：北京市海淀区三里河路甲11号中国建材大厦四层（100037）
**联系人**：何徐凌，夏小冬

**2010 China Intl Bulk Cement Technology & Equipment Expo**
**Venue**: China International Exhibition Center, Beijing
**Profile**: Bulk cement technology & equipment, ready-mixed concrete technology & equipment, dry-mixed mortar technology & equipment, building mortar products, testing equipment .
First Session
**Market Area**: International
**Participated Fee**: Standard Booth（3x3m）RMB 7,800/booth, Outdoor Raw Space RMB 600/$m^2$
**Organizer**: China Natl Building Material Exhibition & Trade Center
**Address**: 4th floor, China Building Materials Plaza, A 11# Sanlihe Rd., Haidian District, Beijing 100037, China
**Contact**: He Xuling, Xia Xiaodong

---

2010/06/10-13
☎ 010-6859 6577, 6851 9501
🖷 010-3853 8552, 6851 9501
✉ ccoea@mei.net.cn
www.ccoea.org.cn

650

**第十三届中国国际照相机械影响器材与技术博览会**
**地点**：中国国际展览中心，北京 CIEC
**内容**：数字照相机、数字机背、银盐照相机、镜头、录像机、扩印设备及相关产品；供业余爱好者的普通经济型、专业用高机型及工业专用中、大型照相机、摄像机及其附件；幻灯机、投影仪、打印机及相关产品；影楼设备、影室灯具、背景道具、婚纱、婚纱头饰、胶片及相机、摄录像多种辅助器材及摄影艺术书刊等；花车、大型卡通（充气）造型等。
**始办年份**：1998
**周期**：每年一届
**市场范围**：国际性
**入场券价格**：免费
**参展费用**：标准展位(3x3m)：A区15,000元，B区10,000元，C区6,300元；净地：A区1,600元/$m^2$，B区1,000元/$m^2$，C区600元/$m^2$
**承办**：中国文化办公设备制造行业协会；中国摄影家协会；北京华港展览有限公司
**地址**：北京市西城区月坛南街26号4060室（100825）
**联系人**：孙光铸，张晋生

**The 13th China International Photograph & Electrical Imaging Machinery**
**Venue**: China International Exhibition Center, Beijing
**Profile**: Digital camera, digital camera-back, camera, lenses, video recorder, printing expansion equipment with other related products; medium and large sized camera of common and economic type for hobby fans, of high grade type for professional persons
**Established Year**: 1998
**Frequency**: Annual
**Market Area**: International
**Cost to Attend**: Free
**Participated Fee**: Standard Booth (3x3m)：RMB 15,000, Raw Space RMB 1,600/$m^2$
**Organizer**: China Culture & Office Equipment Manufacturers Association
**Address**: 26 Yue Yan Nan Jie, Room 4060, Beijing
**Contact**: Sun Guangzhu, Zhang Jinsheng

---

2010/06/17-20
☎ 010-6505 2288
www.cwtc.com

680

**2010年金融展**
**地点**：中国国际贸易中心，北京
**地址**：北京建国门外大街一号（100004）

**China Intl Financial Exhibition**
**Venue**: China World Trade Center, Beijing

010-5933 9075, 5933 9078
010-5933 9099
Jenny.chen@reedces.com.cn
www.cimes.net.cn

12平方米展出规模
2010/6/14-2010/6/18
北京新中国国际展览中心

## CIMES2010
## 第十届中国国际机床工具展览会

**地点：北京新中国国际展览中心**
**时间：2010年6月14日至18日**

中国国际机床工具展览会（CIMES）是继德国EMO展会、美国芝加哥IMTS展会之后，规模第三大的国际机床工具展览会。将于2010年6月隆重亮相北京。

2010年中国国际机床工具展览会将是一个第十届的盛大庆典。自1992年以来，中国国际机床工具展览会（CIMES）每逢双年度在北京举办，深受海内外机械制造业、设备用户单位以及外贸流通企业的欢迎和支持。经过近20年的发展，中国国际机床工具展会的国际化程度有了质的飞跃。第一，国际展商连续三届，每届递增56%。第二，世界顶尖机床生产商纷纷参展并增加展出面积。这些展商无论是产品研发、产品的品质、产品数量、还是世界占有率都在世界市场上占有重要的份额。第三，参展商迅速增长为30多个国家和地区。中国机床行业正处在产品更新换代，提升品质之时。将为中国装备制造业的振兴，和经济发展提供强劲的动力。可以预见2010年CIMES将盛况空前。

**展品范围**

机床，工具与机床附件
- 金属切削机床
- 金属成形机床
- 金属板材加工技术及设备
- 金属管材加工技术及设备
- 特种加工机械设备
- 专用与特种机床
- 切削工具、机床附件、配件、辅助材料、机床电器、功能部件及组件、磨料磨具、电动、气动和机械手工工具、精密测量技术及设备

自动化控制与动力传动
- 柔性制造技术及设备
- 数控系统，嵌入式系统，伺服系统
- 工业机器人
- 变频与调速，传感器，电机
- 可编程序控制器及相关技术
- 电气传动及控制系统
- 机械传动，液压传动与空气传动

热加工技术与设备
- 铸造技术及设备
- 锻造技术及设备
- 热处理技术及设备
- 焊接与切割技术及设备

相关制造技术与设备
- 轴承加工技术及设备
- 齿轮加工技术及设备
- 模具加工技术及设备
- 其他汽车成套制造技术及设备

周期：每年二届
始办年份：1992年
市场范围：国际性
展会性质：仅对专业和贸易观众开放
入场券价格：免费
参展费用：净地摊位：国际展商：RMB2500/平方米；合资企业：RMB2100/平方米；国内企业：RMB840/平方米，标准摊位：国际展商：RMB3060/平方米；合资企业：RMB2300/平方米；国内企业：RMB960/平方米
上届规模：2008年，136,000平方米总面积，净面积54,788平方米，其中国际展商净面积21,805平方米 1390家展商，其中国际展商358家，来自28个国家和地区，观众199,762 人次
主办单位名称：中国机床总公司
承办单位：北京国机展览中心
通信地址：北京市朝阳区新源南路1-3号平安国际金融中心A座15层01-03,05
邮编：100027
电话：010-5933 9075，010-5933 9078
传真：010-5933 9099
联系人：陈婧瑛女士，陈旭先生
电邮：Jenny.chen@reedces.com.cn, chen_jingying@sohu.com

## CIMES2010
## The 10th China Int'l Machine Tool & Tools Exhibition

**New China Int'l Exhibition Center (New CIEC), Beijing**
**June 14 to 18, 2010**

CIMES is the largest machine Tool & Tools Exhibition in China & 3rd largest in the world, bringing together buyers from all corners the world with a key focus on 10 major industry group in China, to source new products and services over five trading days.

In 2010 CIMES will celebrate its 10th anniversary edition. It has successfully been providing business to business in the Machine tool and manufacturing industry biennially since 1992. This event is well recognized and endorsed by machine tool manufacturing industry, user industries, foreign trade companies and distributors from China and overseas. In 2008, the 9th CIMES ranked among the world's 3rd largest machine tool events with an unprecedented gross area of 136,000 square meters & delivering quality buyers from 4 corners of the world, with visible participation from China's Light to heavy industry from all regions & provinces.

As a manufacturing professional, you would be aware that the manufacturing & machine tool industry in china is constantly evolving. Capture a share of this growing market & don't miss out on the chance to grow your business by showcasing your products and services to a highly targeted audience face to face on CIMES2010.

Exhibits Profile

Machine Tool, Tools and Accessories
- Metal cutting machinery
- Metal forming machinery
- Sheet metal and plate processing machinery
- Metal tube and pipe processing machinery
- Special purpose machinery
- Special purpose machine tool
- Cutting tool, fixture, accessories, parts and components, electrical tools, hydraulic tools, pneumatic devices, abrasives, precision measuring technology and devices,

Automation and Motion
- Flexible manufacturing technology and equipment
- Numerical control systems, embedded systems and servo systems
- Industrial robots
- Frequency conversion and timing, sensors and motors
- Programmable logic controller and related technology
- Electronic drives and control systems
- Mechanical, hydraulic and pneumonic driven devices

Heat Treatment and Other Technology
- Foundry technology and equipment
- Forging technology and equipment
- Heat treatment technology and equipment
- Welding and cutting-off technology and equipment

Other Manufacturing Technology and Equipment
- Bearing manufacturing technology and equipment
- Gear generating technology and equipment
- Mould processing technology and equipment
- Other manufacturing technology for the making of auto parts

Frequency: Annual
Established Year: 1992
Market Area: International
Cost to attend: Free
Participated Fee: Raw Space RMB 2,500/m$^2$, Standard Booth RMB 3,060/m$^2$
Statistics '08: Gross Exhibition Area 136,000m$^2$, Net Area 54,788m$^2$( foreigners 21,805m , Exhibitors 1,390(foreigners 358, came from 28 countries), Trade Visitors 199,762
Organizer: China National Machine Tool Corp.
Sponsor : Capital Exhibition Services
Mailing address: Unit 01-03,05, 15th Floor, Tower A, Ping An International Finance Center, No.1-3, Xinyuan South Road, Chaoyang District, Beijing 100027, China
Contact: Ms. Jenny Chen, Mr. Xu Chen
Tel:010-5933 9075, 010-5933 9078
Fax:010-5933 9099
E-mail: Jenny.chen@reedces.com.cn, chen_jingying@sohu.com

2010/06/23-25
☎ 010-6590 7766转ext 736
🖷 010-6590 6139
✉ h.chen@koelnmesse.cn
www.windpowerasia.com
690

**亚洲风能大会暨国际风能设备展览会**
地点：国家会议中心，北京
内容：风力发电机、配套设备及技术、相关服务与咨询
始办年份：2003
周期：每年一届
市场范围：国际性
入场券价格：专业观众免费入场
参展费用：国际标准展位 260欧元/$m^2$，国际净地235欧元/$m^2$；国内标准展位8,800元，国内净地900元/$m^2$
上届规模 '09：展览面积25,000$m^2$，参展商445家（国外展商267家，来自22个国家），专业贸易观众15,065人
主办：科隆国际展览有限公司；中国贸促会北京市分会（CCPIT）；北京国际展览中心（BIEC）
地址：北京市东三环北路8号亮马河大厦2座1018室（100004）
联系人：陈晗

**Wind Power Asia**
-Asian Wind Energy Exhibition & Conference
Venue: China National Convention Center, Beijing
Profile: Wind Turbines, Accessory Equipment & Technologies, Service & Consulting
Established Year: 2003
Frequency: Annual
Market Area: International
Cost to Attend: Free to Professional Visitor and Buyers
Participated Fee: Standard Booth EUR 260/$m^2$, Raw Space EUR 235/$m^2$
Statistics '09: Exhibition Area 25,000$m^2$, Exhibitors 445 (foreigners 267, came from 22 countries), Trade Visitors 15,065
Organizer: Koelnmesse; CCPIT Beijing; BIEC
Address: Unit 1018, Landmark Tower II, No 8 Dongsanhuan North Rd., Beijing, China
Contact: Helen Chen

2010/06/23-25
☎ 010-6590 7766 转ext 736
🖷 010-6590 6139
✉ h.chen@koelnmesse.cn
www.cleanenergyexpochina.com
www.cleanenergyexpochina.cn
700

**中国国际清洁能源博览会**
地点：国家会议中心，北京
内容：光伏产业装备、光伏产品及配套控制设备、光伏发电工程及系统、太阳能光电应用产品、太阳能热利用产品、太阳能工程、生物质能发电、生物质能燃料、生物质燃烧技术、沼气技术、林业生物质能源植物培育等。
始办年份：2009
周期：每年一届
市场范围：国际性
入场券价格：专业观众免费入场
参展费用：国际标准展位 260欧元/$m^2$，国际净地235欧元/$m^2$；国内标准展位8,800元/个,国内净地900元/$m^2$
主办：科隆展览国际有限公司
地址：科隆展览中国有限公司 北京东三环北路8号亮马河大厦2座1018室（100004）
联系人：陈晗

**Clean Energy Expo China**
Venue: China National Convention Center, Beijing
Profile: PV equipment and Accessories; Solar Cells and Other Technologies; Solar Electric Power Systems; Solar Thermal Products; PV Project and System Integrators; Biomass Power Generation Technology and Equipment; Liquid Bio-fuel and Solid Bio-fuel Technology; Biomass Gasification Technology; Methane Gas Technology and Equipment; Biomass Burning Technology; Biomass Briquette Technology; Biomass Energy Forestry Cultivation; Technologies and Applications of Hydroelectric Power & Geothermal Energy
Established Year: 2009
Frequency: Annual
Market Area: International
Cost to Attend: Free to Professional Visitor and Buyers
Participated Fee: Standard Booth EUR 260/$m^2$, Raw Space EUR 235/$m^2$
Organizer: KOELNMESSE
Address: Unit 1018, Landmark Tower Ⅱ, No. 8 Dongsanhuan North Rd,, Beijing 100004, P.R. China
Contact: Helen Chen

2010/06/24-27
☎ 010-6505 2288
www.cwtc.com
710

**2010年中国北京夏季房地产展示交易会**
地点：中国国际贸易中心，北京
地址：北京建国门外大街一号（100004）

**Summer Real Estate Trade Fair Beijing China**
Venue: China World Trade Center, Beijing

2010/06/23-25
☎ 010-6859 5039, 6859 5043, 6859 5067
🖷 010-6857 2287
✉ info@ccpitmsc.org
✉ jix@ccpit.org
www.chinamachin.org.cn
www.ccpitmsc.org
715

**中国国际动力传动与自动化控制展览会**
地点：中国国际展览中心，北京
周期：两年一届
市场范围：国际性
主办：中国贸促会机械行业分会
地址：北京市西城区三里河路46号（100823）
联系人：李华龙，曹姗姗，李静

**PTAC CHINA 2010**
Venue: China International Exhibition Center, Beijing
Frequency: Biennial
Market Area: International
Organizer: CCPIT Machinery Sub-Council
Address: 46 Sanlihe Rd, Xicheng Dist, Beijing

2010/06/25-27
☎ 010-8586 6611, 85866622
🖷 010-8586 6600
✉ bre@bj-relation.com
www.Beijingbite.com
720

**2010北京国际旅游博览会暨北方旅游交易会**
地点：中国国际展览中心，北京 CIEC
内容：亚洲主导展会，并以其丰富的内容，专业的服务，有序的组织和显著的成效，赢得了亚洲及世界旅游界的广泛认同和赞誉。被海内外客商誉为亚太地区重要的旅游博览年会，为国内外旅游机构搭建起了重要的交流和合作平台。随着展会规模的不断扩大，第七届北京国际旅游博览会将移师中国国际展览中心，展出面积将扩大到33,000$m^2$。致力于展现全球高质量参展商，买家及专业观众的BITE 2010将集结众多知名旅游景点、目的地于一身，并将加入旅游相关产品、服务等元素，为您提供最便捷的途径了解中国旅游市场。
始办年份：2004
周期：每年一届
市场范围：国际性
性质：面向公众
入场券价格：5-10元

**Beijing Intl Tourism Expo 2010**
Venue: China International Exhibition Center, Beijing
Profile: Asia's leading and most reliable tourism event. It has positioned itself as an international event which provides key channels for business exchanges and co-operation, providing rich content, professional services, competent organization with a glowing track record. It has won international and regional acclaim amongst the travel and tourism industry as an event not to be missed in the Asia Pacific region. Bite 2010 boasts gross area to 33,000$m^2$. Committed to presenting the highest quality of exhibitors, buyers and visitors from around the world, BITE 2010 packs in an enormous showcase of tourism destinations and attractions as well as travel-related goods and services to set you at full throttle in the Chinese tourism market.
Established Year: 2004
Frequency: Annual
Market Area: International

**参展费用**：参照官方网站www.bjbite.com
**上届规模** ‘09：展览面积23, 700m²(国外展商面积59m²)
**主办**：北京河北天津辽宁河南吉林山东黑龙江山西内蒙古等十省旅游局
**地址**：北京朝阳区八里庄西里远洋天地61号楼1302（100025）
**联系人**：张若耶，李扬

**Nature**: Open to public
**Cost to Attend**: RMB 5～10:-
**Statistics ‘09**: Exhibition Area 23,700m²
**Organizer**: Beijing Relation Exhibition Co Ltd
**Contact**: Rhea, Andy

---

2010/06/29-01
☎ 010-5166 1768
📠 010-5166 1769
✉ meat@cimie.com
730

**第八届中国国际肉类工业展览会**
**地点**：北京展览馆，北京
**内容**：肉类与畜禽蛋加工技术及产品；机械与设备：肉类与禽类屠宰设备、肉类与禽蛋产品加工设备；肉类产品包装设备、肉类产品检验设备；肉类产品灭菌、卫生设备 饲料、牧草机械设备。低温物流设备与技术：肉类产品冷藏及冷冻设备、终端销售冷冻储藏设备、肉类产品冷藏运输设备；包装物料；添加剂、调味品；最新科研成果展示与推广
**始办年份**：2003
**周期**：每年一届
**市场范围**：国际性
**参展费用**：标准展位8,500元/9m²，净地800元/m²；国际企业：标准展位2,880～3,150美元/92，净地280～300美元/m²
**上届规模** '09：展览面积40,000m²(国外展商面积10,000m²)，参展商800家（国外展商60家，来自40个国家），参观人数30,000人
**主办**：中国肉类协会
**承办**：北京众悦傲立展览有限公司
**地址**：北京市西城区月坛北小街2号1号楼1138室（100037）
**联系人**：徐超，胡莹
**QQ**：1072866470

**The Eighth China International Meat Industry Exhibition**
**Venue**: Beijing Exhibition Center, Beijing
**Profile**: Meat and livestock products, meat processing technology, machinery and equipments, low temperature logistics equipment and technology, packaging materials and equipments, additives and ingredients, display and promotion of the latest research achievements
**Established Year**: 2003
**Frequency**: Annual
**Market Area**: International
**Participated Fee**: Standard Booth USD 2,880-3,150/9m², Raw Space USD 280-300/m² **Statistics '09**: Exhibition Area 40,000m²(foreigners 10,000m²), Exhibitors 800（foreigners 60, came from 40 countries）, Visitors 30,000
**Sponsor**: China Meat Assn (CMA)
**Organizer**: Beijing Zhongyue-Onis Expo Co Ltd
**Address**: Room 1138-1139, No.1 Building, No.2 Yue Tan Bei Xiao Street, Xicheng District, Beijing , China
**Contact**: Xu Chao, Hu Ying

---

2010/07/02-11
☎ 010-6505 2288
www.cwtc.com
740

**2010年北京欧美超级家具展览会**
**地点**： 中国国际贸易中心，北京

**European and American Furniture Show**
**Venue**: China World Trade Center, Beijing

---

2010/07/05－07
☎ 010-8455 6612
✉ Weibin.guo@reedsinopharm.com
750

**中国国际美发美容博览会**
**地点**：北京
**内容**：为美发美容专业行业提供一个顶级贸易，学习和交流平台，并替美发美容设备，专业服务，技术，产品采购引进宏大商机和交流机会。
**展品范围**：美发，美甲，美容设备，专业化妆品，美容专业媒体，服务。
**观众范围**：专业美容院院长、经理，美发品牌经销商，化妆师，美甲专业人员，发型师，美容中心从业员。
**周期**：每年一届
**主办**：励展博览集团

**China International Hair & Beauty Expo**
**Venue**: Beijing
**Profile**: A top class trading, learning and networking platform for hairdressing and beauty professionals with vast business opportunities on hair and beauty equipment, professional services, technology and procurement for hair and beauty industry
**Exhibits**: Beauty-equipment, nail, tanning, waxing, skincare, make up, media, business services, general beauty Hair-Color, Retail, Electrical, Non-electrical, Wigs/Extensions, Education, Business Services
**Visitors**: Wholesalers, distributors, retailers, active developers working for major brands, beauty industry professionals such as salon owner and managers, cosmetologists, specialists from nail, hairdresser’ s and fitness studious, SPA facilities, wellness hotels, designers, trade press, drugstore representatives and distributors
**Frequency**: Annual
**Organizer**: Reed Exhibitions

---

2010/07/09－11
☎ 010-8455 6655
www.newdrugschina.com
755

NEW DRUGS CHINA 全国新特药品交易会

**第45届全国新特药品交易会**
**地点**：国家会议中心，北京
**内容**：全国新特药品交易会是业内领军企业及科技创新机构全面展示最新技术、产品和解决方案的最佳平台，是业界领袖、科学家及技术精英们交流合作的最佳场所。
**展品范围**：新药特药（化学药品、中成药品、OTC等），生物制品展示专区，医药研发企业展示专区。
**观众范围**：医药批发企业，医药生产企业，零售药店，医药研发，物流企业，医药药剂科主任，医生，医生终端用户等。

**The 45th New Drugs China**
**Venue**: China National Convention Center, Beijing
**Profile**: New Drugs China is the ideal, specialized platform for pharmaceutical manufacturers from all over the world to launch new medication in China, find sales partners and distributors/agents, promote drug brands, set up marketing networks and build up their corporate image. Many global breakthroughs in new pharmaceutical products as well as independent domestically developed new medicines, are announced to the sizeable China market at New Drugs China. At the same time, press conferences for new drug launches as well as medication in development, new technology exchange meetings and marketing are held. The blend of such product offerings at New Drugs China provides the chance to acquire the latest industry information about pharmaceuticals.
**Exhibitors**：R&D centers of pharmaceutical companies, Scientific research institute and universities, Bio-pharmaceutical industrial bases (parks), high-tech industrial parks, incubators, Pharmaceutical high-tech service institutions, Manufactures or trading companies of life

science instrument and equipments, Manufactures or trading companies of pharmaceutical companies
**Visitors:** Senior executives, marketing personnel and technical engineers from pharmaceutical manufactures and operators, Decision-maker, market personal and technical engineers from foreign ventures, Researchers from scientific research institutes and universities, Pharmaceutical researchers, technical service personnel, international investment and financing organizations, professional consultancies. Doctors and pharmacists, Sales and service personnel for life science instruments and equipment
**Organizer:** Reed Sinopharm Exhibitions Co Ltd

---

2010/07/16-19
☎ 852-2561 5566
🖷 852-2811 9156
✉ info@newayfalrs.com
www.newayfairs.com
760

**第十一届北京国际珠宝展览会**
**地点：**中国国际贸易中心，北京
**主办：**立新国际展览有限公司
**地址：**香港告士大道77号富通大厦9楼

**11th Beijing International Jewelry Fair**
**Venue:** China World Tradc Center, Beijing
**Organizer:** Neway International Trade Fairs Limited
**Address:** 9/F Fortis Tower, 77 Gloucester Road, Hong Kong

---

2010/07/29-08/01
☎ 010-6603 5393，6603 5191
6605 2629
🖷 010-6603 3964
✉ toyfair@toy-cta.org
765

**中国（北京）玩具动漫教育文化博览会**
**地点：**国家会议中心，北京
**主办：**中国玩具协会；中国贸促会北京市峰会
**联系人：**许晓慧，郭氏鑫，薛惠峰，王一铭

**China toys and animation educational expo**
**Venue:** China National Convention Center, Beijing
**Organizer:** China Toy Assn; CCPIT Beijing

---

2010/07/29-08/01
☎ 010-6267 0441
🖷 010-6267 0442
✉ info@chnevent.com
✉ infor@chnevent.com
766

**妇儿博览会**
中国（北京）国际妇女儿童产业博览会
**地点：**国家会议中心，北京
**承办：**北京国际展览中心；北京德佰展览服务有限公司

**China children and women industry expo**
**Venue:** China National Convention Center, Beijing
**Organizer:** Beijing Intl Exhibition Center; Beijing Debai Exhibition Service Co Ltd

---

2010/08/15-18
☎ 010-5933 9166
🖷 010-5933 9199
✉ amy.xie@reedhuaqun.com
www.giftsBeijing.com
770

**第二十二届中国国际礼品、赠品及家庭用品展览会**
**地点：**中国国际展览中心，北京 CIEC
**内容：**礼品、工艺品：礼品精品、琉璃制品、银制品、锡制品、瓷制品、玻璃制品、水晶制品、漆器礼品、金属饰品、陶艺、竹木、树脂、仿生、玉石雕刻、手工艺品等。赠品、促销品：广告促销品、宣传赠品、商务赠品、精品打火机、钥匙扣、礼品笔、徽章、圣诞装饰品等。电子、玩 具：家用电子产品、电子万年历、MP3、U盘、成人益智玩具、毛绒玩具、塑胶玩具、电子玩具等。家居用品：家用纺织礼品、家居装饰礼品、钟表、毛巾及浴室用品、厨房用品、旅游及运动用品、休闲用品、箱包手袋、皮具制品、妇婴用品等。纪念 收藏品：邮票、钱币、磁卡、标牌等。文具
**始办年份：**1997
**周期：**一年三届
**市场范围：**全国性
**入场券价格：**免费
**参展费用：**6,800元/个
**主办：**北京励展华群展览有限公司
**地址：**北京市朝阳区新源南路1-3号平安国际金融中心A座15层1-3-5（100027）
**联系人：**谢辉，蒋楠
**MSN：**youyou_baobao@hotamail.com

**22nd China Intl Gifts, Premium & Houseware Exhibition**
**Venue:** China International Exhibition Center, Beijing
**Established Year:** 1997
**Frequency:** Three Sessions Every Year
**Market Area:** National
**Cost to Attend:** Free
**Participated Fee:** RMB 6,800/booth
**Organizer:** Reed Huaqun Exhibitions
**Address:** 1-3-5,A15, 1-3 South Xinyuan Road, Beijing 100027, China

---

2010/08/19-21
☎ 010-8839 3925
🖷 010-8839 3924
✉ maran@ihecc.org
✉ nanyi@ihecc.org
www.chinahospeg.com
780

**中国医用仪器设备展览会暨技术交流会**
**地点：**国家会议中心，北京
**内容：**展品涵盖了预防、诊断、治疗、康复、护理等多个领域
**始办年份：**1991
**周期：**每年一届
**市场范围：**国际性
**上届规模** '09：展览面积20,000m² 参展商300家（来自12个国家），参观人数20,000人
**主办：**卫生部国际交流与合作中心
**地址：**北京市西城区车公庄大街9号五栋大楼B3座703室（100044）
**联系人：**马冉

**China-hospeo**
**Venue:** China National Convention Center, Beijing
**Established Year:** 1991
**Frequency:** Annual
**Market Area:** International
**Statistics '09:** Exhibition Area 20,000m², Exhibitors 300（came from 12 countries）, Visitors 20,000
**Organizer:** International Health Exchange and Cooperation Center
**Address:** B3-703, 9 Chegongzhuan Street, Xicheng Dist, Beijing, China

2010/08/19-23
☎ 010-6505 2288
www.beijingart2008.net
790

2010北京国际艺术博览会
地点：中国国际贸易中心，北京
承办：北京艺博嫦娥国际会展中心

13th Beijing Intl Art Exposition
Venue: China World Trade Center, Beijing
主办：Organizing Committee of Beijing International Art Exposition

2010/08/23-26
☎ 010-8609 2783, 8609 3207
✉ ym.wang@birtv.com
www.birtv.com
800

第十九届北京国际广播电影电视设备展览会
地点：中国国际展览中心，北京 CIEC
内容：中国最具权威、影响力最大的广播电影电视专业设备综合展览会，位列国家“十一五”文化发展纲要重点支持的会展活动首位，也是世界三大广电展会之一。展览会自1987年创办以来，深受广大观众厂商欢迎，2007年，BIRTV获得国际广播制造者协会认同支持资格。
始办年份：1987
周期：每年一届
市场范围：国际性
性质：面向公众
上届规模 ‘09：展览面积50,000m$^2$(国外展商面积22,500m$^2$)，参展商419家（国外展商170家，来自20个国家），专业贸易观众50,000人
主办：中国广播电视国际经济技术合作总公司
地址：北京西城区北滨河路甲2号（100045）
联系人：王宇明
MSN：yuming_wang3@hotmail.com

Beijing International Radio, TV & Film Equipment Exhibition 2010
Venue: China International Exhibition Center, Beijing
Profile: For more than 20 years, BIRTV has been China’s most prestigious exhibition in the industry of radio, film and TV. This statement is proven, by the quality and number of products being exhibited; by the continuous support from the top exhibitors and by the huge number of trade visitors. We sincerely welcome you to attend the show and get in touch with the most valuable people of the industry in China face to face.
Established Year: 1987
Frequency: Annual
Market Area: International
Nature: Open to public
Statistics ‘09: Exhibition Area 50,000m$^2$(foreigners 22,500m$^2$), Exhibitors 419 (foreigners 170, came from 20 countries), Trade Visitors 50,000
Organizer: China Radio & TV Co for Intl Techno-Economic Cooperation
Address: No. 2a, Beibinhe Street, West District, Beijing 100045, China
Contact: Yuming WANG
MSN: yuming_wang3@hotmail.com

2010/08/31-02
☎ 021-6437 1178
🖷 021-6437 0982
✉ hotelex@cmpsinoexpo.com
www.hotelex.cn
810

北京国际酒店用品博览会
地点：中国国际展览中心，北京 CIEC
内容：商用厨房设备、咖啡、客用品、IT及布草、酒店家具、清洁、SPA休闲。
周期：每年一届
性质：仅对专业观众和买家
预计规模：总面积20,000m$^2$，参展商300家
主办：上海博华国际展览有限公司
地址：上海市襄阳南路218号现代大厦十楼（200031）

Hotelex Beijing
Venue: China International Exhibition Center, Beijing
Frequency: Annual
Nature: Trade Only
Organizer: Shanghai UBM Sinoexpo International Exhibition Co Ltd
Address: 10/F, Xian Dai Mansion, 218 Xiang Yang Road (s), Shanghai, 200031, China

2010/08/31 – 09/02
☎ 021-6437 1178
🖷 021-6437 0982
✉ Steven.lee@UBMSinoexpo.com
www.chinacleanexpo.com
820

中国清洁博览会(北京)
地点：中国国际展览中心，北京
主办：上海博华国际展览有限公司
地址：上海市襄阳南路218号现代大厦十楼（200031）

China Clean Expo-Beijing
Venue: China International Exhibition Center, Beijing
Frequency: Annual
Nature: Trade Only
Organizer: Shanghai UBM Sinoexpo International Exhibition Co Ltd
Address: 10/F, Xian Dai Mansion, 218 Xiang Yang Road (s), Shanghai, 200031, China

2010/08/31-09/02
☎ 010-5933 9308，5933 9304
🖷 010-5933 9333
✉ yog.wang@reedexpo.com.cn
www.cibtm.com
830

www.cibtm.com

**中国（北京）国际商务及会奖旅游展览会**
地点：国家会议中心，北京
内容：来自中国、亚洲乃至全世界的200多个地区及全球的参展商将展示丰富的旅游目的地、酒店和场馆以及相关产品和服务。CIBTM汇聚来自中国和亚洲地区的4,000多位买家和观众，为中国会奖旅游行业首屈一指的展会。通过这个机会您可以在国际性展览会上以及招待晚宴上拓展人脉并达成交易。
作为展会的一部分，CIBTM 将会结合其他商务社交活动与机遇，帮助您与业内人士沟通，了解中国市场。此类活动包括展会现场、晚宴、后期在周边景区及中国其他会奖城市的考察游。
周期：每年一届
主办：励展国际博览集团

**China Incentive, Business Travel & Meetings Exhibition**
Venue: China National Convention Center, Beijing
Profile: CIBTM provides the perfect platform from which to influence the local and international meetings and incentives industry. Uniting an elite class of buyers with quality suppliers from China and around the world, attendance at CIBTM promises the ultimate business solution. Exhibitors benefit from the opportunity to meet a range of international and regional buyers with the authority to place real business. The event already has a successful and trusted history behind it, attracting participants from over 28 countries.
Organizer: Reeds Travel Exhibitions

2010/09/01-03
☎ 010-8773 0641
🖷 010-8773 0640
www.51lohas.net.cn
850

2010国际健康生活方式博览会
-营养、美食、运动博览
地点：中国国际贸易中心，北京
内容：健康食品、功能食品、食用油脂、酒水类、临床营养、健康餐厅、运动休闲食品、营养综合、运动与瘦身
主办：华进有限公司
地址：北京朝阳区劲松3区甲302号华腾大厦800室

2010 International Healthy Lifestyle Expo
Venue: China World Trade Center, Beijing
Organizer: CP Exhibitions

2010/09/01-03
☎ 010-5820 3808
📠 010-5820 3809

855

**第五届中国国际安全生产及职业健康展览会**
**地点：**国家会议中心，北京
**内容：**个体防护装备，交通运输安全产品、电力安全产品、危险化学品防护、消防安全产品、核工业安全产品、职业危害、冶金安全产品、锅炉与压力容器、电气防爆产品、石油天然气安全产品、烟花爆竹安全、建筑安全产品、提升设备、媒体、安全文化、机械与涂装作业安全产品、民爆物品安全、宣传教育机构与相关产品、矿山安全产品、粉尘/防爆产品、安全培训
**周期：**每年一届
**市场范围：**国际性
**上届规模** '09：展览面积13,000m²，参展商158家（国外展商61家），参观人数16,600人
**主办：**杜塞尔多夫展览（中国）有限公司
**地址：**北京市朝阳区建国路93号,北京万达广场A 座11层1107室.（100022）
**联系人：**王媛媛

**The 5th China International Occupational Safety & Health Exhibition (COS+H 2010)**
**Venue:** China National Convention Center, Beijing
**Profile:** Main Product Groups / Sector, Personal Protective Equipment, Electric Blast Prevention, Mine Safety, Oil & Gas Safety Products and Equipment, Dust Explosion Prevention, Nuclear Safety Products and Equipment, Dangerous Chemicals (Chemical Industry)
**Frequency:** Annual
**Market Area:** International
**Statistics '09:** Exhibition Area 13,000m², Exhibitors 158 (foreigners 61, came from countries), Visitors 16,600
**Organizer:** Messe Düsseldorf China Ltd
**Address:** Rm 1107,Level 11 Tower A Wanda Plaza,No.93 Jianguo Rd, Chao Yang Dist, Beijing 100022, China
**Contact:** Michelle Wang

2010/09/06-09
☎ 010-8280 0621, 8280 0630, 8280 0773
📠 010-8280 0857, 8280 0731
✉ shm@cis.org.cn

860

**第二十一届多国仪器仪表学术会议暨展览会**
**地点：**国家会议中心，北京
**内容：**工业自动化仪表与控制系统；自动化仪器仪表；控制系统；自动化、IT解决方案及软件，制造执行总体解决方案及过程优化软件、企业资源规划总体解决方案、电子商务总体解决方案，因特网及基于通信的解决方案；机器人；工程，维护，服务；科学仪器：分析仪器，海洋、地球、大气探测仪器、核子仪器、材料试验机、实验室仪器与装置，环境、食品、药品、医疗仪器；电子与电工测量仪表：电能仪表、测试仪、电量计量仪、实验室及便携式电表、安装式指示仪表、电子测量仪器、电力系统测量仪表、信号处理器、仪用电源；仪表材料及元器件；传感器；仪器仪表工艺装备及加工设备
**始办年份：**1983
**周期：**每年一届
**市场范围：**国际性
**入场券价格：**免费
**上届规模** '09：展览面积22,800m²国外展商面积8,800m²),参展商500家（国外展商150家，来自21个国家），专业贸易观众15,000人
**主办：**中国仪器仪表学会；北京鑫仪寰宇展览有限公司
**地址：**北京市海淀区知春路六号锦秋国际大厦二十三层2303室（100088）
**联系人：**单惠敏

**The 21st International Conference and Fair for Measurement Instrumentation and Automation**
**Venue:** China National Convention Center, Beijing
**Profile:** Instrumentation and Control Systems for Industrial Automation; Scientific Instruments; Analyzers; Electronic and Electrical Measuring Instruments; Components and Accessories; Transducers; Instrument Crafted & Processing Equipments; Others
**Established Year:** 1983
**Frequency:** Annual
**Market Area:** International
**Cost to Attend:** Free
**Statistics '09:** Exhibition Area 22,800m²(foreigners 8,800m²), Exhibitors 500 (foreigners 150, came from 21 countries), Trade Visitors 15,000
**Organizer:** China Instrument and Control Society; NewFitting Exhibition Co
**Address:** Room 2303, 23rd Floor, Horizon International Tower, No.6, Zhichun Road, Haidian District, Beijing 100088, China
**Contact:** Stephanie Shan

2010/09/09-11
☎ 010-8455 6527, 8455 6525
📠 010-6235 0429
www.cihexpo.com

865

**中国国际保健博览会**
**第10届中国国际保健博览会**
**2010中国（北京）保健节**
**地点：**全国农业展览馆，北京
**内容：**中国国际天然药物保健产品展览会（Interherb）依托公司在医药健康领域的优势资源，自2004年以来，已成功举办了4届。展出内容主要涉及保健食品、保健用品、保健器械和特殊化妆品等领域。Interherb经过4年多的市场探索和发展，2009年展出规模达到6000平方米，参展企业200余家，并成功吸引到25000名专业观众到会参观、洽谈。
中国国际保健博览会（Inter Health）是由国药励展公司和中国保健协会联合主办的国内规格最高、展出面积最大、论坛水平最高、国际化程度最高的保健行业专业展览会之一。是由专业医药健康领域展览公司和权威行业协会联合运作的高档次保健产品展会。Healthexpo 经过7届的探索发展，2008年展出规模达到8000平方米，参展企业200余家，并成功吸引到10000名专业观众到会参观、洽谈。
**周期：**每年一届
**主办：**国药励展展览有限责任公司(保健品部)
**地址：**北京市朝阳区新源南路1-3号平安国际金融中心B座15层（100027）

**Health Expo 2010**
The 10th China International Healthcare Expo
The 10th China International Healthcare Festival
**Venue:** National Agricultural Exhibition Center, Beijing
**Profile:** Interhealth is the trade show marketplace for industry practitioners to source international and locally produced health food and health care equipment as well as specialized cosmetics and homecare products. Interhealth had over 200 overseas and local exhibitors in 2008 from the natural healthcare industry with a steady pool of over 25,000 professional visitors buying and sourcing at the event.

Interhealth is a professional exhibition, highly regarded by the Chinese healthcare market, which is organized by Reedsinopharm and the China Healthcare Association. It is the only international healthcare food and supplements show in China. Interhealth is a unique and dedicated event specifically focusing on natural healthcare products in China.

**Exhibits:** Supplements-Full range of vitamins, dietary supplements, targeted formulae, minerals, meal replacements, energy bars, dietary products, sports products, antioxidants, sexual enhancers, pain treatments, nutritional drinks among others. Natural/Functional/Organic Foods-Functional foods, alternative foods, high-end packaged natural foods, organic and fortified foods, green foods, beverages, water products and more. Natural Personal Care-Skin care, hair care, dental care, slimming products, aromatherapy products & supplies, essential oils; and fitness equipment.
**Visitors:** Agents, Distributors, Supermarkets, Drug stores/ Pharmacies, Chain stores, Hospitals/Clinics, Trading companies, Beauty Salons, Fitness clubs, Nutritionists, Beauty therapists, Food companies, Healthcare product companies, Trade associations, Media.
**Frequency:** Annual
**Nature:** Open to public
**Sponsor:** China Health Care Association
**Organizer:** Reed Sinopharm Exhibitions Co Ltd

2010/09/11-12
☎ 0571-9939 3239, 8839 3237
📠 0571-9939 3239, 8839 8829
www.cbmexpo.com
870

**2010年北京国际儿童婴儿孕妇产品博览会**
**地点**：中国国际贸易中心，北京
**主办**：杭州澄心广告有限公司
**地址**：浙江省杭州市潮王路169号人民大厦1207室（310005）

**Children-Baby-Maternity Products Expo**
**Venue**: China World Trade Center, Beijing
**Organizer**: Hangzhou Chengxin Advertising Co Ltd

2010/09/16-19
☎ 010-6505 2288
www.cwtc.com
880

**2010年中国北京秋季房地产展示交易会**
**地点**：中国国际贸易中心，北京
**地址**：北京建国门外大街一号（100004）

**Autumn Real Estate Trade Fair Beijing China**
**Venue**: China World Trade Center, Beijing

2010/09/19-21
☎ 010-8746 8657
📠 010-6282 0885
✉ w5007@126.com
www.507t.cn
890

**2010第五届中国国际军民两用技术展览会**
**地点**：中国国际展览中心，北京 CIEC
**内容**：展示您的产品、专业的服务以及公司形象。直观深入了解到国内外同行的发展动向，面对面了解到行业用户及专业观众对产品及方案的反馈信息，更好地服务用户。与国内外买家当面交流，了解最直接的需求信息及采购意向。获益来自世界范围的最新技术、极具商业价值的客户群体以及面对面的沟通和交流。
**始办年份**：2006
**周期**：每年一届
**市场范围**：国际性
**入场券价格**：20元
**参展费用**：12,000
**上届规模**‘09：展览面积8,000m$^2$(国外展商面积2,000m$^2$),参展商400家（国外展商50家，来自10个国家），参观人数10,000人
**主办**：全国科管委军民两用技术专业委员会
**承办**：北京企发展览服务有限公司
**地址**：北京市海淀区花园路7号新时代大厦7层 710室（100088）
**联系人**：韩天杰，韩璞
**QQ**：781102506

**5th Military and Civil Technology Exhibition**
**Venue**: China International Exhibition Center, Beijing
**Established Year**: 2006
**Frequency**: Annual
**Market Area**: International
**Cost to Attend**: RMB 20:
**Participated Fee**: RMB 12,000
**Statistics '09**: Exhibition Area 8,000m$^2$(foreigners 2,000m$^2$), Exhibitors 400（foreigners 50, came from 10 countries）, Visitors 10,000
**Organizer**: Beijing Qifa Exhibition Co

2010/09/24-27
☎ 010-8501 8361/62/74
📠 010-8562 5510
✉ zhangjing1@cofco.com
✉ lillian@cofco.com
✉ majiechao@cofco.com
www.ocex.com.cn
900

**第六届中国国际有机食品和绿色食品博览会**
**地点**：国家会议中心，北京
**内容**：有机食品和绿色食品，进口食品，有机和绿色食品认证机构，有机天然SPA和化妆品，有机绿色纺织品，有机包装制品，有机生态游和信息服务机构
**始办年份**：2004
**周期**：每年一届
**市场范围**：国际性
**性质**：面向公众
**参展费用**：8,100元/9m$^2$
**上届规模**‘09：展览面积5,500m$^2$(国外展商面积500m$^2$)，参展商132家（国外展商18家，来自4个国家），参观人数21,160人
**主办**：商务部对外贸易发展局；中粮集团有限公司
**承办**：三利广告展览有限公司
**地址**：北京市朝阳门南大街8号中粮福临门大厦11F01（100020）
**联系人**：张静，李丽，马杰超

**ORGANIC CHINA EXPO BEIJING 2010**
**Venue**: China National Convention Center, Beijing
**Profile**: Organic and Natural Food, Import Food, Circulation Enterprises and Certification Bodies of Organic and Natural Food, Organic Natural SPA and Organic Cosmetics, Organic Natural Cotton and Natural Fiber, Organic and Natural Beverage, Eco-tourism and Information Services
**Established Year**: 2004
**Frequency**: Annual
**Market Area**: International
**Nature**: Open to public
**Participated Fee**: RMB 8,100/9m$^2$
**Statistics '09**: Exhibition Area 5,500m$^2$(foreigners 500m$^2$), Exhibitors 132（foreigners 18, came from 4 countries）, Visitors 21,160
**Sponsor**: Trade Development Bureau; COFCO Group
**Organizer**: Sunry Advertising & Exhibition Co Ltd
**Address**: 11F01,COFCO Fortune Plaza,No.8 Chao Yang Men South St., Chaoyang, Beijing
**Contact**: Zhang Jing, Lillian, Jay Ma

2010/10/11-13
☎ 010-5883 0800
转ext 620/632/610
📠 010-5883 0900
www.ecidrea.org.cn
910

**北京国际减灾应急技术设备博览会**
**地点**：中国国际贸易中心，北京
**周期**：每年一届
**主办**：金诚安泰应急管理技术有限公司

**Beijing Intl Disaster Reduction Expo**
**Venue**: China World Trade Center, Beijing
**Frequency**: Annual
**Organizer**: Evertrust-Antai Emergency Management Tech Inc

2010/10/11-15
☎ 010-6642 6288
📠 010-6642 6556
✉ zhangbaolin@ptac.com.cn
www.ptexpo.com.cn
920

**2010年中国国际信息通信展览会**
**地点**：中国国际展览中心，北京 CIEC
**内容**：由中华人民共和国工业和信息化部与中国贸促会主办，中国邮电器材集团公司和中国国际展览中心集团公司承办的“2010年中国国际信息通信展览会”（P&T/EXPO COMM CHINA 2010）将于2010年10月11至15日在中国国际展览中心举行。

“2010年中国国际信息通信展览会”将成为工业与信息融合，中国基础电信运营商完成重组，3G全面投入商用后举办的重要的一届展览会，总展出面积将超过50,000m$^2$。参展范围包括：电信运营商、信息服务提供商，电信增值服务商、互联网服务和内容提供商，互动娱乐产品开发商与服务提供商，系统设备制造商、移动终端制造商及分销企业，通信测试设备、软件提供商，系统集成商，通信配套产品制造企业，信息通信科研、设计、建设施工、咨询、统计、投资机构、科研机构，

**P&T/EXPO COMM CHINA 2010**
**Venue**: China International Exhibition Center, Beijing
**Profile**: Sponsored by Ministry of Industry and Information Technology of the People's Republic of China and CCPIT, organized by China National Postal and Telecommunications Appliances Corporation and China International Exhibition Center Group Corporation, P&T/EXPO COMM CHINA 2010 is the 19th session of the large event. With a high reputation in the ICT industry, the event is one of the largest ICT exhibitions in the world and is recognized as the industry's annual grand event by all circles of the society. It is honored by the press as "Oscar Show" in the ICT field of China. P&T/EXPO COMM CHINA 2010, with more than 50,000 square meters, will be a significant event to accommodate the further integration of industry and information and greater development of ICT industry.

大专院校，媒体等。
**周期**：每年一届
**市场范围**：国际性
**性质**：面向公众
**参展费用**：中国内地单位2,000元/m$^2$，合资企业3,000元/m$^2$，外资企业4,000元/m$^2$
**上届规模**‘09：展览面积45,000m$^2$(国外展商面积15,000m$^2$)，参展商500家（国外展商100家，来自15个国家），参观人数200,000人（专业贸易观众50,000人）
**主办**：中国邮电器材集团公司
**地址**：北京西城区复兴门内大街158号远洋大厦 F106A（100031）
**联系人**：张宝林
**MSN**：jeson8310@msn.com

High-Level Forums, conferences and technical seminars held concurrently with the exhibition provide a communication platform to the world' s ICT professionals. ICT CHINA HIGH LEVEL FORUM, held concurrently with the exhibition is an important part of the event. It links to all aspects of the ICT industry, gives a communication and exchange platform for the industry, and actively promotes the development of the industry.
**Exhibits**: -3G and Value-added Services; -B3G (HSPA, HSPA+, LTE); -Information and Communications Services; -Broadband Multimedia Telecommunications Services and Value-added Services; -IPTV and Mobile TV; -FTTX; -E-government Affairs, E-commerce, Enterprise Information Application Solutions; -Information and Communications Security Services Solutions; -Information and Communications Exchange, Transmission Technologies and Equipment; -Communications Terminals and Accessory Products; -Telecommunications Value-added Services; -Internet Services; -Next Generation Network/ Network TVs/ Network Games/ Interactive Entertainment Products and Services; -Digital Technologies and Products; -Computer Hardware/ Software; -Data Communications / Network Technologies and Accessory Products; -Postal Logistics Technologies and Equipment; -Communications Power Supplies/ Apparatus/ Communications Supplies; -Office Automatization Equipment
-Information Household Appliances;-Communications Electronic Components; -Communications Terminals Fittings; -Automobile Communications and Electronic Equipment;-RFID Chips and Devices; -Transducers Network Equipment;-Independent Intellectual Property Rights and Innovative Information Communication Technologies, Equipment and Products; -ICT Counseling, Statistics and Financing Services.
**Frequency**: Annual
**Market Area**: International
**Nature**: Open to public
**Participated Fee**: Domestic Exhibitors RMB 2,000/m$^2$, Sino-foreign Joint Venture Exhibitors RMB 3,000/m$^2$, International Exhibitors RMB 4,000/m$^2$
**Statistics** ‘09: Exhibition Area 45,000m$^2$(foreigners 15,000m$^2$), Exhibitors 500（foreigners 100, came from 15 countries）, Visitors 200,000（trade visitors 50,000）
**Organizer**: China National Postal and Telecommunications Appliances Corporation
**Address**: F106A Beijing Ocean Plaza, No. 158 Fu Xing Men Nei Street, Xi Cheng District, Beijing 100031 China
**Contact**: Jason Zhang
**MSN**: jeson8310@msn.com

2010/10/14-16
☎ 010-6845 0650, 6845 1467
🖷 010-6845 5499
✉ gaoyang@chinawind.org.cn
✉ lizheng@chinawind.org.cn
www.chinawind.org.cn
930

**2010北京国际风能大会暨展览会**
**地点**：国家会议中心,北京
**内容**：风力发电机组：离网型风力发电机组，并网型风力发电机组，风能与其它能源互补式发电机组/系统，配套设备与技术，叶片，齿轮箱，发电机，制动系统，轴承，主轴，轮毂，塔架，变压器，变流器，偏航系统，变桨系统，控制柜，电缆/电气元件，螺栓/紧固设备，热交换器，风电软件，测风技术/设备，传动系统，监控系统，安全防护设备，润滑系统，复合材料，升降机系统，技术咨询与服务，风资源测评，风电场微观选址，设备维修/维护，设计技术咨询，工程建设咨询，检测/认证，投融资项目咨询，保险咨询，教育培训，产业政策研究
**始办年份**：2007
**周期**：每年一届
**市场范围**：国际性
**性质**：面向公众
**入场券价格**：免费
**参展费用**：标准展位23,000元，净地2,300元/m$^2$
**上届规模**‘09：展览面积12,000m$^2$(国外展商面积4,000m$^2$)，参展商416家（国外展商120家，来自21个国家），参观人数27,000人（专业贸易观众5,000人）
**主办**：中国资源综合利用协会可再生能源专业委员会；中国可再生能源学会风能专业委员会；北京赛迪会展有限公司
**联系人**：高阳,李铮

**China Windpower Beijing 2010**
**Venue**: China National Convention Center, Beijing
**Profile**: Wind Turbine Generator Systems, Off-grid WTGS, In-grid WTGS, Hybrid Power Systems, Components, Rotor blades, Gearbox, Generator, Brake, Bearing, Axis, Hub, Tower, Transformer, Converter, Yaw system, Pitch Control, Controller, Cable/Electric components, bolt, Heat exchanger, Software, Wind Resource, Transmission System, Monitoring system, Safety system, Lubricate system, Composite materials, Lift system
**Established Year**: 2007
**Frequency**: Annual
**Market Area**: International
**Nature**: Open to public
**Cost to Attend**: Free
**Participated Fee**: Standard Booth RMB 23,000, Raw Space 2,300/m$^2$
**Statistics** ‘09: Exhibition Area 12,000m$^2$(foreigners 4,000m$^2$), Exhibitors 416（foreigners 120, came from 21 countries）, Visitors 27,000（trade visitors 5,000）
**Organizer**: Chinese Renewable Energy Industries Assn; China Assn of Resource Comprehensive Utilization; Chinese Wind Energy Assn; CCID Conference & Exhibition Co
**Address**: Rm.2071, CCID Plaza, Business Building, No.62 Zizhuyuan Road, Haidian District, Beijing 100048, China
**Contact**: Gao Yang, Li Zheng

2010/10/16-17
☎ 010-8580 0790/91/92
🖷 010-8580 0786
www.chinaeducationexpo.com
940

**2010中国国际教育展**
**地点**：中国国际贸易中心，北京
**主办**：北京博联天地展览服务有限公司

**China Education Expo 2010**
**Venue**: China World Trade Center, Beijing
**Organizer**: Fairlink Exhibition Services Ltd

2010/10/26-28
☎ 027-8736 2945
www.chinahorsefair.com.cn
950

**2010第四届中国国际马业马术展览会**
**地点**：中国国际展览中心，北京 CIEC
**赞助**：中国马术协会；中国马业协会
**主办**：好博塔苏斯展览有限公司
**联系人**：余云成

**4th China International Equestrian & Horse Industry Fair**
**Venue**: China International Exhibition Center, Beijing
**Organizer**: Tarsus-Hope Exhibition Company

2010/10/26-29
☎ 010-8221 2866
🖷 010-8221 2857
www.chinapharmex.com
960

**第十五届中国国际医药（工业）展览会暨技术交流会暨中国医药工业国际论坛**
**地点**：国家会议中心，北京
**周期**：每年一届
**市场范围**：国际性
**入场券价格**：免费
**主办**：中国医药国际交流中心展览处
**地址**：北京市海淀区西直门北大街32号枫蓝国际中心B座写字楼1106室

**The 15th China International Pharmaceutical Industry Exhibition China International Pharmaceutical Industry Forum**
**Venue**: China National Convention Center, Beijing
**Frequency**: Annual
**Market Area**: International
**Cost to Attend**: Free
**Organizer**: China Center for Pharmaceutical International Exchange Center

2010/10/28-31
☎ 010-6505 2288
www.cwtc.com
970

**2010北京国际钱币博览会**
**地点**：中国国际贸易中心，北京
**主办**：中国金币总公司

**Beijing Intl Coins Exposition 2010**
**Venue**: China World Trade Center, Beijing
**主办：Organizer**: China Gold Coin Inc

2010/11/05-07
☎ 021-5081 3018
🖷 021-5080 3980转ext 601
www.topessencebeijing.com
980

**北京国际顶级私人物品展**
**地点**：中国国际贸易中心，北京
**主办**：亚洲博锐集团

**TOP ESSENCE BEIJING**
**Venue**: China World Trade Center, Beijing
**Organizer**: Borrison Asia Ltd

2010/11/10-11
☎ 010-6839 1521
🖷 010-6839 1520
www.coifair.org
990

**中国对外投资合作洽谈会**
**地点**：中国国际贸易中心，北京
**主办**：中国产业海外发展和规划协会

**China Overseas Investment Fair**
**Venue**: China World Trade Center, Beijing
**Organizer**: China Industrial Overseas Development & Planning Association (CIODPA)

2010/11/10-12
☎ 010-6876 7728
🖷 010-6876 7765
✉ wangc@autoid-china.com.cn
www.aimchina.org.cn
1000

**第十七届国际自动识别技术展览会**
**地点**：北京展览馆，北京
**内容**：条码技术及产品：喷码机、条码打印机、条码检测设备、条码扫描枪、数据采集器、移动终端、条码打印软件及中间件等。射频识别技术及产品：RFID芯片、天线、标签读写设备、应用软件及中间件、标签及卡生产设备、RFID测量测试仪器、智能卡等。生物识别技术及产品：指纹识别技术；掌纹识别技术；视网膜识别技术；虹膜识别技术；面相识别技术，声音识别技术、笔迹识别技术等。 其它自动识别技术及上下游关联产品：传感器、打印耗材、碳带等。 自动识别与信息化相关技术集成应用解决方案及产品。 自动识别技术在零售、制造、医疗、食品、安
**始办年份**：1994
**周期**：每年一届
**市场范围**：国际性
**入场券价格**：免费
**参展费用**：标准展位9,000元，净地1,300/m$^2$
**主办**：中国物品编码中心；中国自动识别技术协会
**承办**：北京源智天成科技有限公司
**地址**：北京市海淀区阜成路16号航天科技大厦附楼401室（100048）
**联系人**：王灿，孙天慧

**The 16th international Exhibition of Automatic Identification Technology**
**Venue**: Beijing Exhibition Center, Beijing
**Profile**: Recognition and Products of barcode RFID and Relevant Products Biometric Identification Technology and Products Other's Automatic Identification and Products Scheme of Application for Automatic Identification Scheme of Application and Products of Automatic Identification and Infomrationalization
**Established Year**: 1994
**Frequency**: Annual
**Market Area**: International
**Cost to Attend**: Free
**Participated Fee**: Standard Booth RMB 9,000, Raw Space RMB 1,300/m$^2$
**Organizer**: Automatic Identification Manufacture Assn of China

2010/11/10-12
☎ 010-6863 0418
🖷 010-8868 0811
✉ sy1768@163.com
1010

**2010第七届中国（北京）国际冶金工业博览会**
**地点**：中国国际展览中心，北京 CIEC
**内容**：冶金（钢铁及有色金属）：冶金检测及自动化、用于冶金热加工、机械加工、物料输送、动力传动、冶金轴承、减速机、切断、称重、润滑、液压、除尘、表面处理、起重、电气、工业窑炉、燃烧器、金属圆锯机、倒角机、磨削、抛光设备（抛丸机、抛丸清理机械、钢材预处理设备）、冶金锯片、切割、机械设备及各种应用材料；耐火材料：原料及处理设备、生产加工技术及设备、各种耐火材料产品；冶金工业环境保护技术、设备以及设计与咨询服务
**始办年份**：2004
**周期**：每年一届
**市场范围**：国际性
**性质**：面向公众
**入场券价格**：免费
**参展费用**：8,800元/3x3m$^2$

**China (Beijing) International Metallurgy Industry Exhibition,**
**Venue**: China International Exhibition Center, Beijing
**Profile**: Metallurgy (Steel & Non-ferrous metals): Testing Equipment and Autoimmunization, Infrared Thermo-Detector for Equipment, Thickness Determination Equipment, Width Measurement, Laser Speedometer, power-driven and Application materials for thermal processing metallurgical, mechanical processing, material handling, power transmission, metallurgy bearings, reducer, cutting, weighing, lubrication, hydraulic, dust removal, surface treatment, appliances, electric, industrial furnace, combustion, metal round Saw, chamfering machines, grinding, etc.
**Established Year**: 2004
**Frequency**: Annual
**Market Area**: International
**Nature**: Open to public
**Cost to Attend**: Free
**Participated Fee**: RMB 8,800/9m$^2$

**上届规模** ‘09：展览面积25,000m²(国外展商面积8,000m²)，参展商600家（国外展商70家，来自20个国家），参观人数40,000人（专业贸易观众10,000人）
**主办**：全国工商联冶金业商会
**承办**：北京海闻展览有限公司；中冶联合（北京）展览有限公司
**地址**：北京市石景山区京原路7号骅悦隆大厦218室（100043）
**联系人**：施毅，谢静
**QQ**：735396277

**Statistics** ‘09: Exhibition Area 25,000m²(foreigners 8,000m²), Exhibitors 600 (foreigners 70, came from 20 countries), Visitors 40,000 (trade visitors 10,000)
**Sponsor**: Metallurgical Industry Assn of the Federation of China
**Organizer**: Beijing Hai Wen Exhibition Co Ltd; Beijing Century Jiaye Exhibition Co Ltd
**Address**: Rm 218, Huayuelong Plaza, 7# Jingyuan Rd., Shijingshan Dist, Beijing
**Contact**: Ms Shi, Ms Xie

---

1020

2010/11/11-15
☎ 010-5827 6063, 5827 6062
🖷 010-5827 6064
✉ fair@jewellery.org.cn
www.chinajewelryshow.com

### 2010中国国际珠宝展

**地点**：中国国际展览中心，北京 CIEC
**内容**：钻石首饰、黄金首饰、翡翠首饰、珍珠首饰、彩色宝石首饰、铂金首饰、白银首饰、玉石首饰、艺术首饰、瑞士钟表等
**始办年份**：1995
**周期**：每年一届
**市场范围**：国际性
**性质**：面向公众
**参展费用**：标准展位：15,000元/9m²；
**上届规模** ‘09：展览面积30,000m²(国外展商面积5,184m²)，参展商600家（国外展商192家，来自15个国家），参观人数63,150人（专业贸易观众23,580人）
**主办**：中国珠宝玉石首饰行业协会；国土资源部珠宝玉石首饰管理中心
**承办**：北京中宝协展览有限公司
**地址**：北京市东城区北三环东路36号环球贸易中心C座2215室（100013）
**联系人**：韦光明，潘沐闲

### China international jewelry fair 2010

**Venue**: China International Exhibition Center, Beijing
**Profile**: Diamond jewelry; gold jewelry; jade jewelry; pearl jewelry; gemstone jewelry; platinum jewelry; silver jeweler; art jewelry; Swiss watches and etc
**Established Year**: 1995
**Frequency**: Annual
**Market Area**: International
**Nature**: Open to public
**Participated Fee**: Standard Booth RMB 15,000/9m²;
**Statistics** ‘09: Exhibition Area 30,000m²(foreigners 5,184m²), Exhibitors 600 (foreigners 192, came from 15 countries), Visitors 63,150 (trade visitors 23,580)
**Sponsor**: Gems & jewelry trade Assn of china, National gems & jewelry technology administrative center
**Organizer**: Beijing Zhongbaoxie Exhibition Co Ltd
**Address**: Rm 2215, Tower C, Global trade center, North 3rd ring road, Dongcheng District, Beijing 100013, China
**Contact**: Guangming Wei, Anais Pan

---

1040

2010/11/18-21
☎ 010-6806 3939, 6806 5959
🖷 010-6806 6969, 6806 7979
✉ wangpeng@ccpitbj.org
✉ haocheng@ccpitbj.org
www.chitec.cn

### 第五届中国北京国际文化创意产业博览会

**地点**：中国国际展览中心，北京 CIEC
**内容**：文化创意产业、广播电影电视、文物及博物馆相关文化创意产品、青少年文化创意、国际文化创意、设计创意、文化旅游景区与旅游商品、画廊及艺术品交易、新闻出版与动漫游戏、体育产业、创意礼品与工艺品、城市雕塑作品、涂鸦艺术
**始办年份**：2006
**周期**：每年一届
**市场范围**：国际性
**性质**：面向公众
**入场券价格**：免费
**参展费用**：标准展位6,000/8,000/12,000/16,000元，净地(m²)600/800/1200/1600元
**上届规模** '08：展览面积60,000m²(国外展商面积12,500m²)，参展商1,370家（国外展商115家，来自15个国家），参观人数190,000人（专业贸易观众85,000人）
**主办**：文化部；国家广播电影电视总局；中华人民共和国新闻出版总署；北京市人民政府
**承办**：北京世界贸易中心
**地址**：北京市西城区南礼士路19号建邦商务会馆2层（100045）
**联系人**：王鹏，张皓成

### 5th China Beijing International Cultural & Creative Industry Expo

**Venue**: China International Exhibition Center, Beijing
**Profile**: Cultural & Creative Industry Comprehensive; Broadcasting, Film and Television; Cultural Relics & Museum Related Creative Products; Youth Students Cultural & Creative Products; International Culture & Creation; Design Creation; Tourist Attraction and Commodity; Gallery & Attraction and Commodity; Press Publication & Animation, Cartoon & Game Creation; Sports Industries; Creative Gifts, Arts & Crafts; Public Sculpture Works; Graffiti Art
**Established Year**: 2006
**Frequency**: Annual
**Market Area**: International
**Nature**: Open to public
**Cost to Attend**: Free
**Participated Fee**: Standard Booth RMB 16,000, Raw Space RMB 1,600/m²
**Statistics** '08: Exhibition Area 60,000m²(foreigners 12,500m²), Exhibitors 1,370 (foreigners 115, came from 15 countries), Visitors 190,000 (trade visitors 85,000)
**Sponsor**: The Ministry of Culture; The State Administration of Radio Film and Television General Administration of Press and Publication; The People's Government of Beijing Municipality
**Organizer**: World Trade Center Beijing
**Address**: 2nd Floor Jianbang Business Center, No. 19 Nanlishi Road, Xicheng District, Beijing China
**Contact**: Wang Peng, Zhang Haocheng

---

1070

2010/11/25-28
☎ 010-6505 2288
www.cwtc.com

### 2010年中国北京冬季房地产展示交易会

**地点**：中国国际贸易中心，北京
**地址**：北京建国门外大街一号（100004）

### Winter Real Estate Trade Fair Beijing China

**Venue**: China World Trade Center, Beijing

---

1080

2010/11/27-29
☎ 010-5933 9186
🖷 010-5933 9333
✉ Amy.xie@reedhuaqun.com
www.giftsBeijing.com

GIFTS& HOME
礼品|家居·北京

### 2010北京国际礼品、赠品及家庭用品（年底）采购订货会

**地点**：中国国际贸易中心，北京
**内容**：礼品、工艺品：礼品精品、琉璃制品、银制品、锡制品、瓷制品、玻璃制品、水晶制品、漆器礼品、金属饰品、陶艺、竹木、树脂、仿生、玉石雕刻、手工艺品等。赠品、促销品：广告促销品、宣传赠品、商务赠品、精品打火机、钥匙扣、礼品笔、徽章、圣诞装饰品等。电子、玩具：家用电子产品、电子万年历、MP3、U盘、成人益智玩具、毛绒玩具、塑胶玩具、电子玩具等。家居用品：家用纺织礼品、家居装饰礼品、钟表、毛巾及浴室用品、厨房用品、旅游及运动用品、休闲用品、箱包手袋、皮具制品、妇婴用品等。纪念 收藏品：邮票、钱币、磁卡、标牌等。文具
**始办年份**：1997
**周期**：一年三届
**市场范围**：全国性

### China International Gifts, Premium & Houseware Exhibition

**Venue**: China World Trade Center, Beijing
**Established Year**: 1997
**Frequency**: Three Sessions Every Year
**Market Area**: National
**Cost to Attend**: Free
**Participated Fee**: RMB 6,800/booth
**Organizer**: Reed Huaqun Exhibitions
**Address**: 1-3-5,A15, 1-3 South Xinyuan Road, Beijing 100027, China

**入场券价格**：免费
**参展费用**：6,800元/个
**主办**：北京励展华群展览有限公司
**地址**：北京市朝阳区新源南路1-3号平安国际金融中心A座15层1-3-5（100027）
**联系人**：谢辉，蒋楠
MSN：youyou_baobao@hotamail.com

---

2010/12/07-10
☎ 010-6505 1012, 8859 2445
🖷 010-6505 3260
1090

**第十届中国国际现代化铁路技术装备展览会**
**地点**：国家会议中心，北京
**周期**：两年一届
**市场范围**：国际性
**上届规模**：展览面积16,000m²
**主办**：中国铁道科学研究院；中国国际贸易中心股份有限公司
**地址**：北京市朝阳区建外大街1号国贸展厅2层（100004）
**联系人**：孔翔泳，朱伟革

**Modern Railways 2010**
Venue: China National Convention Center, Beijing
Frequency: Biennial
Market Area: International
Statistics '08: Exhibition Area 16,000m²
Organizer: China World Trade Center Ltd

---

2011 -
☎ 010-8460 0308
🖷 010-8460 0325, 8460 0346
✉ wangy@ciec.com.cn
Shebei.oilco.cn
1100

**中国国际加油加气站高新技术及设备暨便利店业务博览会**
**地点**：中国国际展览中心，北京
**主办**：中展集团北京华港展览有限公司

**Gas station**
Venue：China International Exhibition Center, Beijing
Organizer: CIEC

---

2011/01/11-14
☎ 010-8501 8331, 8501 8357
🖷 010-8562 5510
✉ wangye@fushionbj.com
✉ barry@fushionbj.com
www.fur- fair.com
1120

**第三十七届中国国际裘皮革皮制品交易会**
**地点**：国家会议中心,北京
**内容**：是中国最大的裘皮及制品交易会。该会以海外客商订货为主，内销为辅，该展是裘、革皮业界瞩目的国际专项商品交易会。每届交易会，都有大批美、欧、日、韩、澳大利亚、新西兰、俄罗斯以及香港等国家和地区的客商云集于此，洽谈订货，展示创新式样，交流信息。交易会为促进中国裘革皮业的发展和使中国产品打入国际市场作出了卓越的贡献。
**始办年份**：1975
**周期**：每年一届
**市场范围**：国际性
**性质**：面向公众
**入场券价格**：免费
**参展费用**：国内企业1,089元/m²，国外企业167美元/m²
**上届规模** '10：展览面积30,000m²(国外展商面积2,000m²)，参展商290家（国外展商40家，来自16个国家），参观人数11,500人（专业贸易观众9,200人）
**主办**：中国土产畜产进出口总公司/三利广告展览有限公司
**地址**：北京市朝阳区朝阳门南大街8号中粮福临门大厦十一层（100020）
**联系人**：王烨，徐洪强

**37th China Fur & Leather Products Fair**
Venue: China National Convention Center, Beijing
Profile: Approved by Ministry of Commerce of the People's Republic of China, with the support from International Fur Trade Federation (IFTF) and China Chamber of Commerce for Import and Export of Foodstuffs, Native Produce and Animal By-Products. With increasing international influence, it attracts more participation and attention from the fur industry and has become one of most influential professional fair in the world.
Established Year: 1975
Frequency: Annual
Market Area: International
Nature: Open to public
Cost to Attend: Free
Participated Fee: USD 167/m²
Statistics '10: Exhibition Area 30,000m²(foreigners 2,000m²), Exhibitors 290 (foreigners 40, came from 16 countries) , Visitors 11,500 (trade visitors 9,200)
Organizer: China National Native Produce and Animal BY-Products Imp.& Exp. Corp; Sunry Advertising and Exhibition Co
Address: COFCO Fortune Plaza No.8 Chao Yang Men South St, Chaoyang, Beijing 100020

---

2011/04/11-16
☎ 010-6334 5053
🖷 010-6334 5271
✉ xieyun@cmtba.org.cn
www.cmtba.org.cn
1130

**第十二届中国国际机床展览会（CIMT2011）**
**地点**：中国国际展览中心（新馆），北京
**内容**：金属切削机床、锻压机械、钣金加工设备、电加工设备、激光、等离子及特种加工设备、工业机器人、物流设备、FMC；FMS、快速成型设备、铸造设备、热处理设备、焊接设备、机床附件、刀具、量仪、电气、液压及气动元件、磨料磨具、数控系统、伺服系统及电机、可编程控制器、计算机软件、信息和网络技术、其他相关的制造技术和设备
**始办年份**：1989
**周期**：两年一届
**市场范围**：国际性
**上届规模** '09：展览面积62,000m²(国外展商面积34,000m²)，参展商1,222家（国外展商572家，来自28个国家），专业贸易观众260,000人
**主办**：中国机床工具工业协会（CMTBA）
**地址**：北京市宣武区莲花池东路102号天莲大厦12层（100055）
**联系人**：谢赟

**12th China International Machine Tool Show (CIMT2011)**
Venue: China International Exhibition Center New Venue, Beijing
Profile: Metal cutting machine, Metal forming machinery, Fabrication equipment, EDM, Laser, plasma and non-traditional processing machinery, Industrial robot, Material handling equipment, FMC, FMS, Rapid prototyping machine, Foundry, Heat treatment machinery, Welding equipment, Accessory, Cutting tool, Measuring and testing device, Electric, hydraulic and pneumatic component, Abrasive and its product, CNC system, Servo system and motor, PC, Software, Information and internet technology, Other related manufacturing technology and equipment
Established Year: 1989
Frequency: Biennial
Market Area: International
Statistics '09: Exhibition Area 62,000m²(foreigners 34,000m²), Exhibitors 1,222 (foreigners 572, came from 28 countries) , Trade Visitors 260,000
Organizer: China Machine Tool & Tool Builders' Assn (CMTBA)
Address: 12/F, Tianlian Mansion, 102 Lianhuachi East Road, Xuanwu District, Beijing 100055, China
Contact: Xie Yun

2011/11
☎ 010-6806 3939, 6806 5959
010-6806 6969, 6806 7979
✉ wangpeng@ccpitbj.org
✉ haocheng@ccpitbj.org
www.iccie.cn

1140

**第六届中国北京国际文化创意产业博览会**
**地点：** 中国国际展览中心，北京 CIEC
**内容：** 文化创意产业；广播电影电视；文物及博物馆相关文化创意产品；青少年文化创意；国际文化创意；设计创意；文化旅游景区与旅游商品；画廊及艺术品交易；新闻出版与动漫游戏；体育产业；创意礼品与工艺品；城市雕塑作品；涂鸦艺术
**始办年份：** 2006
**周期：** 每年一届
**市场范围：** 国际性
**性质：** 面向公众
**入场券价格：** 免费
**上届规模** '08：展览面积60,000$m^2$(国外展商面积12,500$m^2$)，参展商1,370家（国外展商115家，来自15个国家），参观人数190,000人（专业贸易观众85,000人）
**主办：** 文化部；国家广播电影电视总局；中华人民共和国新闻出版总署；北京市人民政府
**承办：** 北京世界贸易中心
**地址：** 北京市西城区南礼士路19号建邦商务会馆2层（100045）
**联系人：** 王鹏；张皓成

**6th China Beijing International Cultural & Creative Industry Expo**
**Venue:** China International Exhibition Center, Beijing
**Profile:** Cultural & Creative Industry Comprehensive; Broadcasting, Film and Television; Cultural Relics & Museum Related Creative Products; Youth Students Cultural & Creative Products; International Culture & Creation; Design Creation; Tourist Attraction and Commodity; Gallery & Attraction and Commodity; Press Publication & Animation, Cartoon & Game Creation; Sports Industries; Creative Gifts, Arts & Crafts; Public Sculpture Works; Graffiti Art
**Established Year:** 2006
**Frequency:** Annual
**Market Area:** International
**Nature:** Open to public
**Cost to Attend:** Free
**Statistics '08:** Exhibition Area 60000$m^2$(foreigners 12500$m^2$), Exhibitors 1370（foreigners 115, came from 15 countries）, Visitors 190000（trade visitors 85000）
**Organizer:** The Ministry of Culture; The State Administration of Radio Film and Television; General Administration of Press and Publication, P.R.C.; The People's Government of Beijing Municipality
**Organizer:** World Trade Center Beijing
**Address:** 2nd Floor Jianbang Business Center, No. 19 Nanlishi Road, Xicheng District, Beijing, China
**Contact:** Wang Peng, Zhang Haocheng

# 北京其他展览信息
# Other Exhibitions in Beijing

CIEC

举办地点：中国国际展览中心，北京(北京市朝阳区北三环东路28号)
Venue: China International Exhibition Center, Beijing Address: 28 Bei Sanhuan Dong Road, Chaoyang District, China
咨询电话：010-8460 0000
1145

第十一届京正北京孕婴童用品展览会
Mother & Baby China 2010
2010/04/10 - 12

第二届中国（北京）国际优生优育计生用品（成人用品）展览会
The 2nd Beijing International Adult-Goods Exhibition
2010/04/10 - 12

中国（北京）第十一届国际照明电器博览会
Beijing International Illumination Exhibition
2010/04/10 - 12

第10届中国（北京）国际健康产业产品博览会
The 10th China(Beijing) International Healthcare Industry Exhibition
2010/05/07 - 09

2010第五届北京国际游泳沐浴SPA展览会
Beijing International Swimming Pools, Bath, SPA Expo 2010
2010/05/07 - 10

2010第六届北京国际LED展览会
The 6th Beijing International LED Exposition
2010/05/07 - 09

2010国际现代工厂/过程自动化技术与装备展览会
2010 FA/PA
2010/05/12 - 15

2010北京动力传动与控制技术展览会
DMBC 2010
2010/05/12 - 15

2010第六届北京国际煤炭装备及矿山技术设备展览会
The 6th China International Coal Equipment and Mine Technical Equipment Exhibition 2010
2010/06/03 - 05

2010第十届北京国际机械装备、模具、塑料橡胶、动力传动自动化仪器仪表展览会
China International Machinery Equipment Mould, Rubber and Plastic Industry & Power Transmission automation instrument and meter exhibition
2010/06/08 - 10

2010北京国际电子工业节能技术、产品展览会
2010/06/10 – 12

中国（北京）国际家具及木工机械展览会
2010 China Beijing International Furniture Woodworking machinery & Wood Products Exhibition
2010/07/01 - 04

2010年中国国际酒业博览会
China International Alcoholic Drinks Expo 2010
2010/07/09 - 11

北京国际儿童及婴幼儿食品博览会
Beijing International Exhibition of Infant Food
2010/07/10 - 12

2010第六届北京国际电动车清洁能源汽车暨休闲运动车展览会
The 6th Beijing International Pure Electric Vehicle, Hybrid Power & Clean Energy Vehicle, and Accessories Exhibition
2010/07/16 - 18

第五届中国（北方）印刷及设备器材展览会
Print North 2010
2010/07/23 - 30

中国北京国际工程项目、机械设备及建筑材料博览会
2010 China (Beijing) International Engineering Projects, Mechanical Equipment and Building Materials Exposition
2010/08/04 - 06

中国（北京）国际五金机电工业博览会暨电池电子工业展览会
China International Hardware Industry Expo, Beijing
2010/08/05 - 07

2010年健身大会
Fitness China 2010
2010/08/05 - 07

夏日国际香港购物嘉年华
International-Hong Kong Shopping Carnival
2010/08/05 - 09

2010北京国际物流、卡车、起重运输机械展览会
China Beijing International Logistics Expo 2010
2010/08/10 - 12

中国（北京）国际管业展览会
China Beijing International Steel Tube Industry Expo, 2010
2010/08/10 - 12

北京国际图书博览会
BIBF 2010
2010/08/29 - 02

2010第四届中国（北京）国际红木古典家具、现代家居及室内装饰艺术展览会
CIRCFE 2010
2010/08/28 - 30

中国国际啤酒饮料制造技术及设备展览会
China Brew 2010
2010/09/07 - 10

2010年秋季北京国际广告标识展
中国国际数码与喷墨印刷技术展览会
China Sign Expo 2010
2010/09/14 - 16

中国国际眼镜业展览会
China International Optics Fair 2010
2010/09/14 - 16

2010中国国际机场技术、设备和服务展览会
Inter Airport China 2010
2010/09/14 - 16

北京国际风能、太阳能核电工业暨电力设备技术展览会
2010 Beijing International Wind, Solar, Nuclear Power Industry and Power Electrical Equipment and Technology Exhibition
2010/09/19 - 21

2010中国国际福祉博览会
China International Wellbeing Expo 2010
2010/09/19 - 21

第十三届国际电力设备及技术展览会
2010国际节能、电力环保及脱硫脱硝装备展览会
第六届国际电机工程及电工装备展览会
EP China 2010
2010/10/19 - 21

第十三届膜与水处理技术暨装备展览会
Water and Membrane China 2010
2010/10/19 – 21

2010北京国际在线分析测试技术及设备展览会
2010 China International On-line Analytical Testing Technology and Equipment Exhibition
2010/10/19 - 21

2010中国国际汽车制造及生产设备博览会
CIAMPFE2010
2010/10/25 - 27

2010北京国际美容化妆品及医学养生健康产业博览会
2010 Beijing International Beauty, Hairdressing, Cosmetics & Health Products Expo
2010/10/26 - 28

中国国际光电产业博览会暨中国国际激光，电子及光显产业展览会/中国国际机器视觉展览会暨机器视觉技术及工业应用研讨会
Optoelectronics Industry Exposition (Beijing) & International Lasers, Optoelectronics and Photonics Exhibition
2010/10/27 - 29

2010北京国际广告技术设备展及LED展览会
China Exhibition of Advertisement & Sign 2010, Beijing
2010/10/27 - 29

2010年中国国际社会公共安全产品博览会
The 10th China International Exhibition on Public Safety and Security
2010/11/02 - 05

# 重庆
# Chongqing

2010/03/11-13
☎ 023 -6774 5022, 6775 3110
℡ 023-6775 3176
✉ cmpi@163.com
www.cmpi.cn

1150

第十届中国西部国际金属工业展
地点：重庆国际会议展览中心，重庆
内容：压铸、铸造、铸件展区，热处理、工业炉展区，锻造、冲压、锻件展区，金属材料、不锈钢产品、金属设备、冶金设备展区，紧固件、弹簧、及设备展区，金属粉末，制品及成型设备展区
周期：每年一届
市场范围：全国性
性质：面向公众
入场券价格：免费
参展费用：标准展位7,200元，净地800元/$m^2$
主办：中国兵器装备集团公司西南兵工局；重庆市经济和信息化委员会；重庆市工业经济联合会；重庆锻压行业协会；重庆铸造行业协会；重庆市铸造学会；重庆市热处理协会；重庆市紧固件行业协会
承办：重庆市中环盛世商务会展有限公司
地址：重庆市江北区渝北三村30号红鼎国际A3609（400020）
联系人：韩龙，高健
QQ：513399628

10th West China International Metal Exhibition
- Metallic Plates, Tubes, Bars, Wires and Metallic Industry Fair
Venue: Chongqing International Convention & Exhibition Center, Chongqing
Frequency: Annual
Market Area: National
Nature: Open to public
Cost to Attend: Free
Participated Fee: Standard Booth RMB 7,200, Raw Space RMB 800/$m^2$
Organizer: ChongQing Zhonghuan Shengshi Exhibition Planning Co Ltd

2010/04/08-11
☎ 023 -6298 6633
℡ 023-8661 5066
✉ yxhz@cqyxhz.com

1160

2010重庆国际生态环保与节能减排技术展览会
地点：重庆国际会议展览中心，重庆
内容：泵阀管道及流体机械、给排水 水处理设备、环保废弃物及资源利用、绿色建筑节能科技产品、节能环保暨新能源、太阳能产业、暖通空调及热泵技术、天然气汽车 加气站建设
始办年份：1999
周期：每年两届
市场范围：国际性
参展费用：8,000元/3x3m,室外900元/㎡
主办：中华人民共和国科学技术部；中华人民共和国工业和信息化部；中国科学院；中国工程院；中国发明协会；重庆市人民政府
承办：重庆市科学技术委员会；重庆市经济和信息化委员会；重庆市南岸区人民政府
地址：重庆市南岸区南坪珊瑚路1号贝迪新城3期B栋5-2（400060）
联系人：邓毅，褚均
QQ：731749272

Chongqing Eco, Energy Saving Exhibition
Venue: Chongqing International Convention & Exhibition Center, Chongqing
Established Year: 1999
Frequency: Biannual
Market Area: International
Participated Fee: RMB 8,000/3x3m，Outdoor RMB 900/㎡
Organizer: Chongqing Yuxin Exhibition Co Ltd

2010/04/20-22
☎ 023-6888 8155, 6863 3404
℡ 023-6863 1388
✉ jane.jia@super-e.com.cn
www.subcon.cn

1170

2010中国国际工业转包展览会
地点：重庆展览中心，重庆
内容：金属加工产品，包括各类铸造、锻造、冲压工艺生产的零部件；各类切削工艺如加工中心生产的高精度机械零部件；各类热处理和表面处理制品；各类基础机械零部件如量具和刀具、紧固件、弹簧、齿轮、轴承等。非金属制品包括各类注塑、挤出、中空成型工艺生产的塑料制品，密封件、液压元件、气动元件；各类橡胶制品。
始办年份：2005
周期：每年一届
市场范围：国际性
上届规模 '08：参展商207家，参观人数15,000人
主办：中国机械工程学会；重庆市人民政府
承办：重庆市经济和信息化委员会；重庆市对外贸易经济委员会；重庆展览中心有限公司；重庆市科学技术委员会；重庆市人民政府高新区管委会
地址：重庆市高新区科园四路269号（400041）
联系人：贾艳

China Industrial Subcontracting & Outsourcing Fair 2010
Venue: Chongqing Exhibition Center, Chongqing
Profile: General machinery and equipment, such as transmission and drive components, hydraulic machinery and components, pneumatic machinery and components, air and electric tools. General machine components, such as bearing, gear, metal seal, fastener, spring, foundry, forging, die-casting, punching, powder metallurgy products, machining products 3.Metal processing machinery, plastic processing machinery, industry automatic control system, mould, automotive components and accessories, architectural metalwork, safety metal products, metal tools. 4.Rubber products, plastic products, non-metallic mineral products.
Established Year: 2005
Frequency: Annual
Market Area: International
Statistics '08: Exhibitors 207，Visitors 15,000
Organizer: Chongqing Foreign Trade and Economic Relations Commission; Chongqing Economic and IT Commission; Chongqing Science and Technology Commission Administrative Committee
Address: No. 269, Keyuansi Road, High-Tech Development Zone, Chongqing, China
Contact: Jane Jia

2010/05/13-15
☎ 023-6296 8557, 8632 6699
℡ 023-6296 8444, 8637 6728
✉ worldfair@126.com
www.worldgbh.org

1180

第十一届中国重庆国际工业装备博览会
地点：重庆国际会议展览中心，重庆
始办年份：2000
周期：每年一届
市场范围：全国性
参展费用：标准展位7,200元，净地720元/$m^2$
上届规模 '09：展览面积12,000$m^2$(国外展商面积982$m^2$)，参展商

11th Chongqing Intl Industry Equipment Fair
Venue: Chongqing International Convention & Exhibition Center, Chongqing
Established Year: 2000
Frequency: Annual
Market Area: National
Participated Fee: Standard Booth RMB 7,200, Raw Space RMB

397家（国外展商86家，来自9个国家），参观人数20,867人（专业贸易观众745人）
**主办**：重庆市经济和信息化委员会
**承办**：重庆沃德展览有限公司
**地址**：重庆市南岸区江南大道27号江南明珠8楼（400060）
**联系人**：徐志龙，徐军

720/m²
**Statistics '09**: Exhibition Area 12,000m²(foreigners 982m²), Exhibitors 397 (foreigners 86, came from 9 countries), Visitors 20,867 (trade visitors 745)
**Organizer**: Chongqing World Exhibition Co Ltd

1190
2010/06/10-14
☎ 023-6888 8155, 6863 3404
℻ 023-6863 1388
✉ jane.jia@super-e.com.cn
www.autochongqing.com

**2010(第十二届)重庆国际汽车工业展览会**
**地点**：重庆国际会议展览中心，重庆
**内容**：概念车、乘用车、商用车、特种车、专用车、改装车、房车及休旅车、电动车、多功能车、二手车、各种SUV越野车、老爷车、汽车配件及汽车用品；各类新能源、新科技汽车的相关技术；各类汽车保险、贷款、二手车置换等汽车中介服务机构
**始办年份**：1998
**周期**：每年一届
**市场范围**：地区性
**性质**：面向公众
**上届规模**'09：参展商124家，参观人数200,000人
**主办**：中国汽车工业协会；重庆市人民政府
**承办**：重庆市经济和信息化委员会；重庆市人民政府汽车工业办公室；重庆展览中心有限公司
**地址**：重庆市高新区科园四路269号（400041）
**联系人**：贾艳

**China Chongqing International Auto Industry Fair**
**Venue**: Chongqing International Convention & Exhibition Center, Chongqing
**Profile**: Concept cars, passenger cars, commercial vehicles, special vehicles, special-purpose vehicles, modified vehicles, motor homes and sport utility vehicles, electric vehicles, multi-utility vehicles, second-hand cars, SUV, classic cars, auto parts and accessories; Vehicles of new energy and new technology; Car insurance, car loans, second-hand car sales and other intermediaries
**Established Year**: 1998
**Frequency**: Annual
**Market Area**: Region
**Nature**: Open to public
**Statistics '09**: Exhibitors 124, Visitors 200,000
**Sponsor**: China Assn of Automobile Manufacturers, Chongqing Municipal People's Government
**Organizer**: Chongqing Economic and IT Commission; Automobile Industry Office of Chongqing Municipal People's Government; Chongqing Exhibition Center Co Ltd
**Address**: No. 269 Keyuansi Road, High-Tech Development Zone, Chongqing, China
**Contact**: Jane Jia

1200
2010/09-
☎ 023-6300 3855, 6300 2418
℻ 023—6300 3766
www.swhz.cn

**第三届中国（重庆）茶叶博览会暨海峡两岸文化交流会**
**地点**：重庆国际会议展览中心，重庆
**主办**：重庆市商业委员会；重庆市农业委员会
**承办**：重庆商务国际展览广告有限公司

**3rd China (Chongqing) Tea Expo**
**Venue**: Chongqing International Convention & Exhibition Center, Chongqing
**Organizer**: Chongqing International Exhibition Business Advertisement Co Ltd

1210
2010/09/13-15
☎ 023-6296 8557, 8632 6699
℻ 023-6296 8444, 8637 6728
✉ worldfair@126.com
www.worldgbh.Org

**第十届中国重庆城市建设及建筑科技博览会**
**地点**：重庆国际会议展览中心，重庆
**始办年份**：2001
**周期**：每年一届
**市场范围**：全国性
**参展费用**：标准展位7,200元，净地720元/m²
**上届规模**'09：展览面积10,000m²(国外展商面积192m²)，参展商357家（国外展商26家，来自8个国家），参观人数23,298人（专业贸易观众679人）
**主办**：中国土木工程学会
**承办**：重庆沃德展览有限公司
**地址**：重庆市南岸区江南大道27号江南明珠8楼（400060）
**联系人**：徐先生，罗小姐

**UCBE & LFAD Chongqing 2010**
Urban Construction & Building Exhibition
**Venue**: Chongqing International Convention & Exhibition Center, Chongqing
**Established Year**: 2001
**Frequency**: Annual
**Market Area**: National
**Participated Fee**: Standard Booth RMB 7,200, Raw Space RMB 720/m²
**Statistics '09**: Exhibition Area 10,000m²(foreigners 192m²), Exhibitors 357 (foreigners 26, came from 8 countries), Visitors 23,298 (trade visitors 679)
**Organizer**: Chongqing World Exhibition Co Ltd

1220
2010/10/21-24
☎ 023-6888 8155, 6863 3404
℻ 023-6863 1388
✉ jane.jia@super-e.com.cn
www.cimamotor.com

**第九届中国国际摩托车博览会**
**地点**：重庆国际会议展览中心，重庆
**内容**：摩托车整车：二轮摩托车、三轮车、全地形车（ATV）、雪地车、机动脚踏两用车、电动车、燃气动力车、特殊用途车辆等 摩托车零部件：摩托车用发动机、车架、离合器、制动器、减震、摩托车电器、轮胎、轮毂及其他摩托车零部件等 摩托车文化产品：摩托服饰及用具、头盔、摩托车旅游及运动用品、模型、装饰物、改装配件等 通用燃油机：通用汽（柴）油机、发电机组、水泵机组、多功能农用机械等 摩托车维护用品：摩托车生产及修理设备及工具、润滑油等 摩托车技术及服务产品：出版物、技术成果等
**始办年份**：2002
**周期**：每年一届
**市场范围**：国际性
**性质**：面向公众
**上届规模**'09：参展商330家，参观人数50,000人
**主办**：中国贸促会重庆市分会；中国汽车工业协会摩托车分会；重庆市经济和信息化委员会；重庆市对外贸易经济委员会；中国兵器装备集团公司摩托车事业部；重庆展览中心有限公司
**地址**：重庆市高新区科园四路269号（400041）
**联系人**：贾艳

**The 9th China International Motorcycle Trade Exhibition**
**Venue**: Chongqing International Convention & Exhibition Center, Chongqing
**Profile**: Motorized Vehicles: Motorcycles, tricycles, ATVs, snow scooters, mopeds, electric vehicles, gas vehicles, special vehicles; Motorcycle Accessories and Parts: Motor engines, vehicle frames, clutches, brakes, shock absorbers, electrical equipment, tires, wheels rims, spare parts; Motorcycle Related Products: Clothing, helmets, equipment and accessories for motorcycle tourism and outdoor activities, models, ornaments, refitting accessories; General Fuel Motors: General gasoline (diesel) engines, gen-sets, water pump units, multi-functional agricultural machineries; Maintenance Products: Special tools and machinery for cycle manufacturing and repairing, lubricants; Motorcycle Technology and Service: Publications, and R&D achievements.
**Established Year**: 2002
**Frequency**: Annual
**Market Area**: International
**Nature**: Open to public
**Statistics '09**: Exhibitors 330, Visitors 50,000
**Organizer**: Chongqing Exhibition Center Co Ltd
**Address**: No.269, Keyuansi Road, High-Tech Development Zone, Chongqing, China
**Contact**: Jane Jia

# 上海
# Shanghai

☎ 021-6328 8899
🖷 021-6374 9188
www.chinamie.com
1270

2010上海别墅展览会
地点：上海现代国际展览中心，上海
内容：别墅
主办：上海现代国际展览有限公司

2010 Shanghai Villa Exhibition
Venue: Shanghai
Organizer: World Expo (Group) Shanghai Modern International Exhibition Co Ltd

---

2010/01/09-
✉ wanglei@shrc.com.cn
www.shrc.com.cn
1310

上海市高校毕业生就业招聘会
地点：上海市人才服务中心，上海
周期：每年一届
市场范围：全国性
主办：上海市人才服务中心

Shanghai Job Fair for College Graduates
Venue: Shanghai Talent Service Center, Shanghai
Frequency: Annual
Market Area: National
Organizer: Shanghai Talent Service Center

---

2010/01/13-15
☎ 852-8199 7308
🖷 852-8199 7628
http://tradeshow.globalsources.com
1320

环球资源流行服饰配件采购交易会及
环球资源婴儿及儿童采购交易会
环球资源及赠品采购交易会
地点：上海新国际博览中心，上海
主办：环球资源

China Sourcing Fair:
Fashion Accessories
Baby & Children' s Products
Gifts & Premiums
Venue: Shanghai New International Expo Center, Shanghai
Organizer: Global Sources

---

2010/01/20-23
☎ 021-6279 2828
🖷 021-6545 5124
✉ info@siec-ccpit.com
www.siec-ccpit.com
1340

**第十七届中国上海国际婚纱摄影器材展览会暨国际儿童摄影、主题摄影展览会(春季)**
地点：上海国际展览中心；上海世贸商城；上海光大会展中心，上海
周期：每年一届
市场范围：国际性
主办：上海市国际展览有限公司
地址：上海市延安中路841号东方海外大厦8楼（200040）

**The 17th China (Shanghai) International Wedding Photographic Equipment Exhibition & International Children's Photography, Theme Photography Exhibition (Spring)**
Venue: Shanghai International Exhibition Center; Shanghai Mart; Shanghai Everbright Convention & Exhibition Center, Shanghai
Frequency: Annual
Market Area: International
Organizer: Shanghai International Exhibition Co
Address: 8/F,OOCL Plaza,841 Yan An Zhong Road, Shanghai 200040, China

---

2010/03/01-05
☎ 021-6353 9977
🖷 021-3303 0072
✉ info@ecf.gov.cn
www.ecf.gov.cn
1350

第20届中国华东进出口商品交易会
地点：上海新国际博览中心，上海
内容：服装展区、家用纺织品展区、装饰品展区、日用消费品展区
主办：上海市商务委员会
承办：上海外经贸商务展览有限公司

East China Fair
Venue: Shanghai New International Expo Center, Shanghai
Profile: Fashion/Garments, Home textiles, Art Deco Gifts, Consumer Goods.
Operator: Shanghai International Trade Promotion Co Ltd

---

2010/03/05-07
✉ toy_expo@yahoo.com.cn
www.toy-sh.com
1360

中国（上海）第十五届国际玩具展暨上海玩具第46届博览会
地点：上海国际展览中心，上海
主办：上海上玩玩具展览有限公司

Toy China 2010 (Spring)
Venue: Shanghai International Exhibition Center, Shanghai
Organizer: Shanghai Toys Industry Import/Export Corporation

---

2010/03/10-12
☎ 010-8455 6677
🖷 010-6235 8292
✉ pchi@reedsinopharm.com
www.pchi-china.com
1370

系列展会

**中国国际化妆品、个人及家庭护理用品原料展览会**
地点：上海光大会展中心，上海
内容：专为中国设计、为化妆品、个人和家庭护理用品原料生产厂商加入中国及亚太市场，满足迅速发展的行业需求的专业顶级盛会。
展品范围：一、个人护理用品（头发护理、皮肤护理、口腔护理、洗涤用品、彩妆、香水、保养品）及家庭护理用品（沐浴洗护、洗涤剂、空气清新剂、杀虫剂、消毒液等）原材料、辅料；二、实验室及产品研发、检测机构。
观众范围：采购经理，产品研发人员，配方师，实验室人员，代理商及分销商，媒体等。
主办：国药励展展览有限责任公司（PCHI 化妆品原料展览部）

**Personal Care & Homecare Ingredients**
Venue: Shanghai Everbright Convention & Exhibition Center, Shanghai
Profile: The newly launched PCHi has been created specifically for China. It helps the cosmetics, personal and home care ingredients manufacturers to enter the Chinese and Asia-Pacific markets. As the premier professional event, PCHi aims to meet the rapidly developing industry needs.
Exhibits: Raw materials and ingredients for personal care (hair care, skin care, oral care, coloring, fragrance, preservatives and home care ,toiletries, detergent, air purification, pesticides) , among others; Packaging and processing materials and equipment.
Visitors: Cosmetics, personal care and homecare product manufacturers; Procurement managers; Cosmetic scientists; Formulators and formulation chemists; Laboratory managers; Agents and distributors; Media (trade journals, industry publications among others); Hotel cleaning officers; Entertainment Industry cleaning officers; Hospital cleaning officers; Beauty and hair salon owners; Dentists; Distributors; Chemistry Research Institutions.
Organizer: Reed Sinopharm Exhibitions Co Ltd

2010/03/10-12
☎ 010-6335 6966
🖷 010-6335 6950, 6335 6960
✉ jiangxl@hardware-fair.com
www.hardware-fair.com
1390

**中国国际五金博览会**
**地点**：上海新国际博览中心，上海
**内容**：中国历史最久，底蕴最深，影响中国五金三代人的展会。目前，博览会是亚洲规模最大、专业化程度最高、影响最广的国际性展会。参展产品涉及电动工具、手动工具、机械设备、焊接设备、机电产品。
**始办年份**：1952
**周期**：每年两届
**市场范围**：国际性
**性质**：面向公众
**入场券价格**：免费
**参展费用**：标准展位8,000元，净地850元/$m^2$
**上届规模** '09：展览面积80,500$m^2$(国外展商面积5,000$m^2$)，参展商2,200家（国外展商120家，来自15个国家），参观人数35,000人（专业贸易观众30,000人）
**主办**：中国五金交电化工商业协会
**承办**：北京金益友联展览有限公司
**地址**：北京市丰台区菜户营东街58号财富西环名苑901（100054）
**联系人**：姜晓莉，张宇

**China International Hardware Fair**
**Venue**: Shanghai New International Expo Center, Shanghai
**Profile**: The fair has been held for more than 100 sessions since 1952. Now more than 60,000 purchasers home and abroad will visit CIHF. Exhibits include hand tools, electric tools, welding machineries, mechanical equipments, etc.
**Established Year**: 1952
**Frequency**: Biannual
**Market Area**: International
**Nature**: Open to public
**Cost to Attend**: Free
**Participated Fee**: Standard Booth RMB 8,000，Raw Space 850/$m^2$
**Statistics**'09: Exhibition Area 80,500$m^2$(foreigners 5,000$m^2$), Exhibitors 2,200（foreigners 120, came from 15 countries）, Visitors 35,000（trade visitors 30,000）
**Sponsor**: China National Hardware, Electric and Chemical Products Commercial Assn **Organizer**: Beijing Jinyi Youlian Exhibition Co
**Address**: 9th Floor, Fortune West Plaza, 58 Caihuying, Fengtai District, Beijing, 100054, China
**Contact**: Jiang Xiaoli, Zhang Yu

2010/03/10-12
☎ 021-6277 5353
🖷 021-6277 0002
✉ fashionshanghai@163.com
www.fashionshanghai.com
1400

**第十六届上海国际服装纺织品贸易博览会**
**地点**：上海新国际博览中心，上海
**内容**：服装OEM/ ODM成衣制造；服装面料；棉麻涤毛；化纤等各类面料；服装辅料；拉链；纽扣；衬布；花边；商标；线带等；纱线；各类天然合成纤维及纱线。
**始办年份**：1995
**周期**：每年一届
**市场范围**：国际性
**参展费用**：12,000元/9$m^2$
**上届规模** '09：展览面积35,000$m^2$(国外展商面积3,000$m^2$)，参展商670家（国外展商50家，来自8个国家），参观人数20,000人（专业贸易观众15,000人）
**主办**：上海市国际服装文化节组委会
**承办**：上海纺织技术服务展览中心
**地址**：上海市长寿路285号25F（恒大大厦）（200060）
**联系人**：吕波，张建军

**Shanghai International Clothing & Textile Expo**
**Venue**: Shanghai New International Expo Center, Shanghai
**Profile**: Fashion Brand(Apparel & Accessories), Textile & Fabric (Apparel & Home Furnishing), Fiber & Yarn, Trim & Components, Technology & Services
**Established Year**: 1995
**Frequency**: Annual
**Market Area**: International
**Participated Fee**: RMB 12,000/9$m^2$
**Statistics** '09: Exhibition Area 35,000$m^2$(foreigners 3,000$m^2$), Exhibitors 670（foreigners 50, came from 8 countries）, Visitors 20,000（trade visitors 15,000）
**Sponsor**: Shanghai International Fashion Culture Festival
**Organizer**: Shanghai Textile Technology Service And Exhibition Center
**Address**: 25F, Hengda praza, No, 285,changshou Road, Shanghai
**Contact**: Lu Bo, Zhang Jianjun

2010/03/12-14
☎ 021-2281 7535
🖷 021-2281 7535
✉ gaoguoxing@ciec.com.cn
www.adult-expo.cn
1450

**第七届中国国际成人保健及生殖健康展览会**
**地点**：上海国际展览中心，上海
**内容**：成人保健用品、生殖保健产品、医疗器械、成人美容。
**始办年份**：2004
**主办**：中展海外展览有限公司；上海百域会展有限公司

**7th China Intl Adult Toys & Reproductive Health Exhibition**
**Venue**: Shanghai International Exhibition Center, Shanghai
**Organizer**: CIEC Overseas Exhibition Co Ltd

2010/03/12-14
☎ 021-6195 6088
🖷 021-6195 6088
✉ sally.song@vnuexhibitions.com.cn
www.petfairsh.com
1460

**2010上海宠物大会暨第三届上海宠物医疗学术研讨会**
**地点**：上海国际展览中心，上海
**内容**：宠物食品：宠物食品、宠物饲料；宠物用品：宠物服装、宠物用具、宠物笼舍、宠物玩具、宠物护理品、宠物美容用品、宠物训导用品、庭院用品及设施、户外休闲用品、水景设施、花园家具及景观美化用品和设施；宠物医疗：宠物医疗设备、宠物保健用品、宠物疫苗、宠物药品、水族药品、宠物医院；水族产品：水族箱、增氧设备、加热棒、照明灯具、过滤器、观赏鱼饲料、观赏鱼药品、水生植物、水槽沙；园艺产品；各种活体宠物。其他如宠物杂志、网站、摄影等
**始办年份**：2009
**周期**：每年一届
**市场范围**：全国性
**性质**：面向公众
**入场券价格**：30元/人
**参展费用**：8,100元/9$m^2$
**上届规模** '09：展览面积3,000$m^2$(国外展商面积600$m^2$)，参展商58家（国外展商10家，来自5个国家），参观人数15,000人（专业贸易观众2,000人）
**主办**：上海万耀企龙展览有限公司
**地址**：上海市徐汇区田林路140号26A栋万耀企龙办公楼（200233）
**联系人**：宋小姐

**Pet Fair Shanghai 2010**
**Venue**: Shanghai International Exhibition Center, Shanghai
**Profile**: Pets foods；Pets products：pet clothing, pet supplies, pet cages & houses, pet toys, pet grooming products, pet nursing products, pet training products；Veterinary Products：pet medical treatment facilities, pet health-care products, pet vaccine, pet medicine, pet clinic；Aquaria Products：Aquariums, pumps, heaters, Illumination, filters；Gardening Products；Pets；Others：Websites, pub publications, website, photography, pet club, Assn, pet breeders, others
**Established Year**: 2009
**Frequency**: Annual
**Market Area**: National
**Nature**: Open to public
**Cost to Attend**: RMB 30；-
**Participated Fee**: RMB 8,100/9$m^2$
**Statistics** '09: Exhibition Area 3,000$m^2$(foreigners 600$m^2$), Exhibitors 58（foreigners 10, came from 5 countries）, Visitors 15,000（trade visitors 2,000）
**Organizer**: VNU Exhibitions Asia
**Address**: VNU House, 26A, No. 140 Tianlin Road Shanghai, China
**Contact**: Sally Song

2010/03/16-18
☎ 021-5058 0121
🖷 021-5058 3337
✉ lu.wangbin@mmi-shanghai.com
www.laserchina.net/index.asp
1470

**慕尼黑上海激光、光电展**
**地点**：上海新国际博览中心，上海
**内容**：作为中国领先的激光、光学、光电展，自2006年起每年在中国上海举办，集中展示行业内各种设计新颖、科技领先的新产品、全新的解决方案和紧跟世界潮流的应用技术。其德国姐妹展LASER World of PHOTONICS是全球唯一覆盖整个光电子行业所有门类、展示最尖端科技的专业光电博览会，自1973年以来每两年一届在慕尼黑举办，同期举办的光学技术大会是欧洲规模最大的光学研讨会。作为激光、光学、光电行业的风

**LASER World of PHOTONICS CHINA**
**Venue**: Shanghai New International Expo Center, Shanghai
**Profile**: The show provides a forum to showcase a plethora of novel and technologically-advanced new products, brand-new solutions and trendy applied technologies. Its sister exhibition, LASER World of PHOTONICS covers the full range of products in the photonics industry, exhibiting cutting-edge technologies. It has been held every second year in Munich since 1973 and the concurrent photonic technology conference is the largest symposium of its kind in Europe.

向标，慕尼黑和上海的L
**主办：**德国慕尼黑国际博览集团；慕尼黑展览（上海）有限公司
**联系人：**路王斌

As the standard-bearer of the photonics industry, LASER World of PHOTONICS both in Munich and Shanghai has been renowned as the annual extravaganzas in this field.
**Established Year:** 1973
**Organizer:** Messe Munichen International; MMI Shanghai

2010/03/16-18
☎ 021-5058 0707
🖷 021-5058 3337
✉ qiu.yan@mmi-shanghai.com
www.e-p-china.com.cn
1480

**慕尼黑上海电子展**
**地点：**上海新国际博览中心，上海
**内容：**慕尼黑上海电子展是中国电子元器件和电子生产设备的卓越展示平台。electronica China（中国国际电子元器件、组件博览会）立足于电子元器件，Productronica China（中国国际电子生产设备博览会）着眼于电子生产设备，全面展示电子产业链。慕尼黑上海电子展重量更重质。无论是国内外领军企业，中小型公司还是业界新兴企业，均毫不犹豫地加入其中展示其最新的科技成就和创新产品，这也使得慕尼黑上海电子展逐渐成为了电子行业的风向标。
**主办：**德国慕尼黑国际博览集团；慕尼黑展览（上海）有限公司
**承办：**IPC-国际电子工业联接协会；京慕国际展览有限公司
**联系人：**邱燕

**electronica & Productronica China**
**Venue:** Shanghai New International Expo Center, Shanghai
**Profile:** It is an excellent platform for exhibiting Chinese electronic products and electronic production equipment. electronica China focuses on electronic products and Productronica China on electronic production equipment, together presenting a comprehensive exhibition for the electronics industry. electronica & Productronica China attaches great importance to both scale and quality. Enterprises, be they leading domestic or international players, small, medium or large, or new entrants in the sector, participate in the show with equal vigor to exhibit their latest scientific and technological achievements and inventions, thereby making electronica & Productronica China the standard-bearer in trade shows for the electronics industry. World-class forums pilot developments in the field and reveal the latest technological solutions for the general electronics community.
**Organizer:** Messe Munichen International; MMI Shanghai

2010/03/17-19
☎ 021-6295 6677
🖷 021-6278 0038
✉ intexwq@sh163.net
www.intex-sh.com
1500

**2010中国（上海）国际突发事件灾难预防及救援装备技术展览会暨中国（上海）国际紧急医疗救援装备技术展览会**
**地点：**上海国际展览中心，上海
**主办：**上海国际展览中心有限公司

**China Rescue Expo 2010**
**Venue:** Shanghai International Exhibition Center, Shanghai
**Organizer:** Intex Shanghai Co Ltd

2010/03/18-21
☎ 021-6195 6088
🖷 021-6195 6099
✉ jessica.wu@vnuexhibitions.com.cn
www.vnuexhibitionsasia.com
1510

**上海之春房产展示交易会**
**地点：**上海展览中心，上海
**内容：**作为上海开春的第一展：荣获上海楼市风向标称号。展示行业热点、洞察市场动向，满足不同企业和消费者的需求，与众多品牌房地产企业携手前行。2010上海之春秉持“规模再创纪录，关注新政后的新机遇”的房产方向标，将再次力争在2010年以近200家房地产开发商，近300个品牌楼盘呈现给观众。
**始办年份：**1999
**周期：**每年一届
**市场范围：**全国性
**性质：**面向公众
**入场券价格：**20元
**参展费用：**10,000～18,000/9m$^2$
**上届规模** '09：展览面积20,000m$^2$，参展商200家，参观人数100,000人
**主办：**上海万耀企龙展览有限公司
**地址：**上海市徐汇区田林路140号26A栋上海万耀企龙办公楼（20023）
**联系人：**吴佳钰

**Shanghai Spring Real Estate Market**
**Venue:** Shanghai Exhibition Center, Shanghai
**Established Year:** 1999
**Frequency:** Annual
**Market Area:** National
**Nature:** Open to public
**Cost to Attend:** RMB 20:-
**Participated Fee:** RMB 10,000-18,000/9m$^2$
**Statistics '09:** Exhibition Area 20,000m$^2$, Exhibitors 200, Visitors 100,000
**Organizer:** VNU Exhibitions Asia
**Address:** VNU House, 26A, No.140 Tianlin Road Shanghai, China
**Contact:** Jessica

2010/03/23-25
☎ 010-5979 5833, 6839 6330
🖷 010-5907 1335, 6839 6422
✉ cfaa1990@yahoo.com.cn
✉ ccpitsli@public3.bta.net.cn
www.fi-c.com
1520

**第十四届中国国际食品添加剂和配料展览会暨第二十届全国食品添加剂生产应用展示会**
**地点：**上海光大会展中心；上海世贸商城；上海国际展览中心，上海
**内容：**本展览会是亚洲最大的食品添加剂和配料专业性展览会，每年有逾千家公司参展，3万多专业人士参观，展品范围涉及22大类食品添加剂33大类食品配料、食品加工助剂及各种相关技术和设备、专业书刊等，共63类。
**始办年份：**1997
**周期：**每年一届
**市场范围：**国际性
**上届规模** '09：展览面积54,000m$^2$(国外展商面积12,000m$^2$)，参展商1,115家（国外展商211家，来自26个国家），专业贸易观众76,927人
**主办：**中国食品添加剂和配料协会；《中国食品添加剂》杂志社；中国贸促会轻工行业分会
**地址：**北京市朝外大街甲6号万通中心3座1402中国食品添加剂和配料协会（100020）
**联系人：**张越宸
**地址：**北京市阜外大街乙22号中国贸促会轻工行业分会（100833）
**联系人：**张昕

**Food Ingredients China 2010**
**Venue:** Shanghai Everbright Convention & Exhibition Center; Shanghai Mart; Shanghai International Exhibition Center, Shanghai
**Profile:** FIC is the biggest food ingredients & additives exhibition in Asia with over 1000 companies and 30,000 visitors coming each year. The exhibits cover 22 categories of food additives, 33 categories of food ingredients, food processing aides and techniques, equipments and magazines.
**Established Year:** 1997
**Frequency:** Annual
**Market Area:** International
**Statistics '09:** Exhibition Area 54,000m$^2$(foreigners 12,000m$^2$), Exhibitors 1,115 (foreigners 211, came from 26 countries), Trade Visitors 76,927
**Organizer:** China Food Additives & Ingredients Association; China Food Additives Journal; CCPIT Sub-council of Light Industry
**Address:** China Food Additives & Ingredients Association, Rm.1402 Tower C Vantone No.6A Chaowai St., Beijing 100020 China
**Contact:** Mr Zhang Yuechen
**Address:** CCPIT Sub-council of Light Industry, 22B, Fuwai Dajie, Beijing 100833 China
**Contact:** Mrs Zhang Xin

2010/03/23-25
☎ 021-6195 6088
传真 021-6195 6099
✉ rtasia@vnuexhibitions.com.cn
www.rtasia.org
1540

**中国国际门及门禁系统展览会**
中国国际遮阳技术与建筑节能博览会
**地点**：上海新国际博览中心，上海
**内容**：卷百叶帘及其配件，百叶窗及配件，窗及配件，遮阳篷类，软百叶帘、遮阳帘、百叶帘，内遮阳产品和外遮阳产品，汽车遮阳产品，建筑膜结构产品，纺织及遮阳面料，大门及其配件类，人行通道门，车库门，工业用门，配套产品及设备，行业著作及出版企业
**始办年份**：2005
**周期**：每年一届
**市场范围**：全国性
**性质**：面向公众
**入场券价格**：200元
**上届规模** '09：展览面积25,000m²，参展商332家（国外展商54家，来自26个国家），专业贸易观众13,630人
**主办**：VNU亚洲展览集团-上海万耀企龙展览公司
**地址**：上海市徐汇区田林路140号26A栋万耀企龙办公楼（200233）
**联系人**：汤卫权

**R+T ASIA**
**Venue**: Shanghai New International Expo Center, Shanghai
**Profile**: Gates and accessories, Doors for pedestrians, Doors for private vehicles, Doors for industrial use, Company fittings and furnishings, Roller shutters and accessories, Windows and accessories, Awnings, Venetian blinds, window shades, blinds, Internal & external sun protection Vehicle sunshade, Building membrane structure, Fabric, Specialized literature/Publishing houses, Industry Assns
**Established Year**: 2005
**Frequency**: Annual
**Market Area**: National
**Nature**: Open to public
**Cost to Attend**: RMB 200
**Statistics '09**: Exhibition Area 25,000m², Exhibitors 332（foreigners 54, came from 26 countries）, Trade Visitors 13,630
**Organizer**: VNU Exhibitions Asia
**Address**: VNU House, 26 A, No.140 Tianlin Road, Shanghai, China
**Contact**: Fox Tang

2010/03/23-25
☎ 021-6195 6088
传真 021-6195 6099
✉ Leo.zhao@vnuexhibitions.com.cn
Logan.shang@vnuexhibitions.com.cn
www.landexpo.cn
1550

**第八届上海国际园林景观设计及城市建设展览会**
**地点**：上海新国际博览中心，上海
**内容**：业界年度不可缺席的盛会,聚集1000多家国内外知名建材品牌厂商同台展出；直面来自世界各地100多个国家和地区的数万建材采购商与专业观众；多场世界重量级专业峰会；世界地板论坛、中国可持续建筑国际大会、绿色设计日活动、住宅产业化与节能减排配套产品采购会40多家中国最大地产界联盟年度采购大会
**始办年份**：2003
**周期**：每年一届
**市场范围**：国际性
**性质**：面向公众
**参展费用**：1100元/m²
**上届规模** '09：展览面积8,000m²(国外展商面积1,600m²)，参展商200家（国外展商42家，来自39个国家），参观人数8,000人（专业贸易观众6,556人）
**主办**：VNU亚洲展览集团-上海万耀企龙展览有限公司
**地址**：上海市徐汇区田林路140号26A栋万耀企龙办公楼（200233）
**联系人**：赵新先生 尚嘉麟先生
**MSN**: leozhaoxin@hotmail.com

**8th Shanghai Intl Landscape Design & Urban Construction Expo**
**Venue**: Shanghai New International Expo Center, Shanghai
**Profile**: CLAF is the earliest founded and most influential landscape architecture and gardening expo held in China. Regarded as the annual gathering for contractors, designers and buyers.
Exhibits: Landscape Design, Garden and Urban Green Construction, Landscape & Garden Building Materials and Facilities, Urban Construction Machinery, Maintenance Machinery and Equipment, Playground and Urban Green Spaces, Wood Frame Structures, Plants and Turf grass, Plant Simulation and Irrigation Products, Landscape Water Treatment
**Established Year**: 2003
**Frequency**: Annual
**Market Area**: International
**Nature**: Open to public
**Participated Fee**: RMB1100/m²
**Statistics '09**: Exhibition Area 8,000m²(foreigners 1,600m²), Exhibitors 200（foreigners 42, came from 39 countries）, Visitors 8,000（trade visitors 6,556）
**Organizer**: VNU Exhibitions Asia
**Address**: VNU House, 26A, No. 140 Tianlin Road, Shanghai 200233, China
**Contact**: Mr Leo Zhao, Mr Logan Shang
**MSN**: leozhaoxin@hotmail.com

2010/03/23-25
☎ 021-6195 6088
传真 021-6195 6099
www.domotexasiachinafloor.com
1590

**第12届中国国际地面材料及铺装技术展览会**
**地点**：上海新国际博览中心，上海
**主办**：VNU亚洲展览集团-上海万耀企龙展览有限公司
**地址**：上海市徐汇区田林路140号26A栋万耀企龙办公楼（200233）

**DOMOTEX asia**
CHINAFLOOR 2010
**Venue**: Shanghai New International Expo Center, Shanghai
**Organizer**: VNU Exhibitions Asia
**Address**: VNU House,26A, No. 140 Tianlin Road, Shanghai 200233, China

2010/03/23-25
☎ 021-6195 6088
传真 021-6195 6099
✉ Leo.zhao@vnuexhibitions.com.cn
Logan.shang@vnuexhibitions.com.cn
www.landexpo.cn
1600

**2010中国可持续建筑国际大会**
**地点**：上海新国际博览中心，上海
**内容**：本届大会旨在推进可持续建筑在中国的普及与发展，活动得到了国内外行业机构的高度重视和大力支持，其中德国、美国、加拿大等国将派国家展团参与本次活动。
**始办年份**：2009
**周期**：每年一届
**市场范围**：国际性
**性质**：面向公众
**参展费用**：1,100元/m²
**上届规模**：展览面积10,000m²(国外展商面积1,600m²)，参展商200家（国外展商42家，来自39个国家），参观人数8,000人（专业贸易观众6,556人）
**主办**：VNU亚洲展览集团-上海万耀企龙展览有限公司
**地址**：上海市徐汇区田林路140号26A栋万耀企龙办公楼（200233）
**联系人**：赵新先生 尚嘉麟先生
**MSN**: leozhaoxin@hotmail.com

**China Sustainable Building Forum 2010**
**Venue**: Shanghai New International Expo Center, Shanghai
**Profile**: The exhibition is an international platform to showcase the latest products, designs, technologies and building materials, with focus on environmental sustainability and eco-friendly for buildings. The event brings together businesses, professionals, scholars, industrial leaders to exchange views, as well as explore the business opportunities in China.
**Established Year**: 2009
**Frequency**: Annual
**Market Area**: International
**Nature**: Open to public
**Participated Fee**: RMB 1,100/m²
**Statistics '09**: Exhibition Area 10,000m²(foreigners 1,600m²), Exhibitors 200（foreigners 42, came from 39 countries）, Visitors 8,000（trade visitors 6,556）
**Organizer**: VNU Exhibitions Asia
**Address**: VNU House,26A, No. 140 Tianlin Road, Shanghai 200233, China
**Contact**: Mr Leo Zhao, Mr Logan Shang
**MSN**: leozhaoxin@hotmail.com

2010/03/27-29
☎ 021-6432 9255
🖷 021-5171 4528
✉ adexpo-sh@163.com
www.expo-ad.com
1610

**2010第十一届中国(上海)广告四新展览会**
**地点**：上海光大会展中心，上海
**内容**：广告制作设备；广告材料、物料；展览展示系统及广告标识、标牌、显示设备；多媒体及触摸技术与设备
**始办年份**：1999
**周期**：每年一届
**市场范围**：全国性
**入场券价格**：免费
**参展费用**：标准展位8,800元，净地800元/$m^2$
**主办**：中国商务广告协会
**承办**：上海威棱展览有限公司
**地址**：上海市漕宝路82号E座1905室（200235）
**联系人**：李小姐，韩先生
MSN: bjslfengqi@hotmail.com
QQ: 49565551

**The 11th China (Shanghai) Advertising Four New Exhibition**
**Venue**: Shanghai Everbright Convention & Exhibition Center, Shanghai
**Profile**: Advertising Production Equipment, Exhibition and Displaying System and Advertising Marking, Advertising Materials and Articles, Multimedia and Touch Technology and Equipment
**Established Year**: 1999
**Frequency**: Annual
**Market Area**: National
**Cost to Attend**: Free
**Participated Fee**: Standard Booth RMB 8,800, Raw Space RMB 800/$m^2$
**Sponsor**: China Advertising Assn of Commerce
**Organizer**: Shanghai Weiling Exhibition Co Ltd
**Address**: Room 1905, Unit E, No. 82, Caobao Road, Shanghai
**Contact**: Miss Li, Mr Han
**MSN**: bjslfengqi@hotmail.com

2010/03/28-31
☎ 021-6280 1062
🖷 021-6294 7723
✉ medcoschina@yahoo.com.cn
1620

**第23届国际FOM 2010学术年会**
**地点**：上海光大会展中心，上海
**内容**：光学显微设备，激光系统，成像设备，共聚焦扫描单元与器件
**始办年份**：1988
**周期**：每年一届
**市场范围**：国际性
**性质**：面向公众
**参展费用**：标准展位8,500元，净地800$m^2$
**上届规模**‘09：展览面积3,000-4,000m2(国外展商面积3,000-4,000$m^2$)
**主办**：荷兰阿姆斯特丹大学；上海交通大学；上海激光学会
**承办**：上海新力会展服务有限公司
**地址**：上海番禺路383号601室
**联系人**：李萌

**23rd Focus on Microscopy 2010 Conference**
**Venue**: Shanghai Everbright Convention & Exhibition Center, Shanghai
**Profile**: Optical microscopy equipments, laser systems, imaging systems, confocal scanning unit and components
**Established Year**: 1988
**Frequency**: Annual
**Market Area**: International
**Nature**: Open to public
**Participated Fee**: Standard Booth RMB 8,500, Raw Space 800$m^2$
**Statistics‘09**: Exhibition Area 3,000-4,000$m^2$(foreigners 3,000-4,000$m^2$)
**Organizer**: Shanghai New Force Expo Service Co Ltd

2010/03/29 – 04/01
☎ 021-6437 1178
🖷 021-6437 0982
www.ceramics-china.cn
1630

**中国国际建筑陶瓷色釉料及原辅材料展览会**
**地点**：上海新国际博览中心，上海
**内容**：陶瓷装饰材料、陶瓷原辅料、工业陶瓷产品、陶瓷工业新技术、新工艺、专利产品、填缝剂、其他。
**主办**：上海博建国际会展有限公司
**地址**：上海市襄阳南路218号现代大厦10楼（200031）

**Building Ceramics Glaze & Pigment China 2010**
**Venue**: Shanghai New International Expo Center, Shanghai
**Organizer**: Shanghai UBM Sinoexpo International Exhibition Co
**Address**: 10/F, Xiandai Mansion, 218 Xiang Yang Road(s), Shanghai

2010/03/29 – 04/01
☎ 021-6437 1178
🖷 021-6437 0982
✉ hotelex@cmpsinoexpo.com
www.hotelex.cn
1640

**上海国际酒店用品博览会**
**地点**：上海新国际博览中心，上海
**周期**：每年一届
**性质**：对专业观众与买家开放
**预计规模**：总面积60,000$m^2$，参展商850家，专业贸易观众50,000人
**主办**：上海博华国际展览有限公司
**地址**：上海市襄阳南路218号现代大厦十楼（200031）

**Hotelex**
**Venue**: Shanghai New International Expo Center, Shanghai
**Frequency**: Annual
**Expectation**: Gross Area 60,000$m^2$, Exhibitors 850, Trade Visitors 50,000
**Nature**: Trade Only
**Organizer**: Shanghai UBM Sinoexpo International Exhibition Co
**Address**: 10/F, Xiandai Mansion, 218 Xiang Yang Road(s), Shanghai

2010/03/29 – 04/01
☎ 021-6437 1178
🖷 021-6437 0982
✉ cherry.liu@ubmsinoexpo.com
www.expobuild.com
1650

**第十八届中国国际建筑装饰展览会**
**地点**：上海新国际博览中心，上海
**内容**：门窗幕墙，屋面系统，墙体材料，木制品，暖通系列，电工电气，综合材料，建筑陶瓷产品系列、陶瓷釉料、生产与铺设设备，卫生陶瓷和浴室精品系列、厨房设施系列、卫浴配件系列
**始办年份**：1991
**周期**：每年一届
**市场范围**：国际性
**入场券价格**：免费
**参展费用**：标准展位1,300元/$m^2$，室内净地1,200元/$m^2$
**上届规模**‘09：展览面积45,000$m^2$(国外展商面积150$m^2$)，参展商500家（国外展商30家），参观人数29,000人
**主办**：上海博建国际会展有限公司
**地址**：上海市襄阳南路218号现代大厦10楼（200031）
**联系人**：刘小姐

**18th Expo Build China 2010**
**Venue**: Shanghai New International Expo Center, Shanghai
**Profile**: Interior partitions & door, Architecture door, window & accessories, Intelligent house, Architecture door, Floor covering & paving material
**Established Year**: 1991
**Frequency**: Annual
**Market Area**: International
**Cost to Attend**: Free
**Participated Fee**: Standard Booth RMB 1,300/$m^2$, Indoor Raw Space RMB 1,200/$m^2$
**Statistics‘09**: Exhibition Area 45,000$m^2$(foreigners 150$m^2$), Exhibitors 500（foreigners 30）, Visitors 29,000
**Organizer**: Shanghai UBM Sinoexpo International Exhibition Co
**Address**: 10/F, Xiandai Mansion, 218 Xiang Yang Road(s), Shanghai
**Contact**: Cherry Liu

2010/03/29 – 04/01
☎ 021-6437 1178
🖷 021-6437 0982
✉ hotelex@cmpsinoexpo.com
www.hotelex.cn
1660

**中国国际康体健身、休闲娱乐与运动器材展览会**
**地点**：上海新国际博览中心，上海
**主办**：上海博华国际展览有限公司
**地址**：上海市襄阳南路218号现代大厦10楼（200031）

**Fitness, Sports & Leisure China**
**Venue**: Shanghai New International Expo Center, Shanghai
**Organizer**: Shanghai UBM Sinoexpo International Exhibition Co
**Address**: 10/F, Xiandai Mansion, 218 Xiang Yang Road(s), Shanghai

2010/03/29 – 04/01
☎ 021-6437 1178
🖷 021-6437 0982
✉ hotelex@cmpsinoexpo.com
www.hotelex.cn
1670

中国国际咖啡与茶用品展览会
地点：上海新国际博览中心，上海
主办：上海博华国际展览有限公司
地址：上海市襄阳南路218号现代大厦10楼（200031）

Coffee & Tea China 2010
Venue: Shanghai New International Expo Center, Shanghai
Organizer: Shanghai UBM Sinoexpo International Exhibition Co
Address: 10/F, Xiandai Mansion, 218 Xiang Yang Road(s), Shanghai

2010/03/29 – 04/01
☎ 021-6437 1178
🖷 021-6437 0982
✉ hotelex@cmpsinoexpo.com
www.hotelex.cn
1680

中国国际洗涤设备展览会
地点：上海新国际博览中心，上海
主办：上海博华国际展览有限公司
地址：上海市襄阳南路218号现代大厦10楼（200031）

Laundry China 2010
Venue: Shanghai New International Expo Center, Shanghai
Organizer: Shanghai UBM Sinoexpo International Exhibition Co
Address: 10/F, Xiandai Mansion, 218 Xiang Yang Road(s), Shanghai

2010/03/29 – 04/01
☎ 021-6437 1178
🖷 021-6437 0982
✉ expobuild@ubmsinoexpo.com
www.ceramics-china.cn
1690

中国国际建筑陶瓷及卫浴科技精品展览会
地点：上海新国际博览中心，上海
主办：上海博建国际会展有限公司
地址：上海市襄阳南路218号现代大厦10楼（200031）

11th Ceramics, Tile & Sanitary Ware China
Venue: Shanghai New International Expo Center, Shanghai
Organizer: Shanghai UBM Sinoexpo International Exhibition Co
Address: 10/F, Xiandai Mansion, 218 Xiang Yang Road(s), Shanghai

2010/03/29 – 04/01
☎ 021-6437 1178
🖷 021-6437 0982
www.decodesignexpo.com
1700

中国国际建筑及室内设计节
中国国际室内与家居装饰展览会
地点：上海新国际博览中心，上海
主办：上海博华国际展览有限公司
地址：上海市襄阳南路218号现代大厦10楼（200031）

Home Fashion & Design Shanghai
Venue: Shanghai New International Expo Center, Shanghai
Organizer: Shanghai UBM Sinoexpo International Exhibition Co
Address: 10/F, Xiandai Mansion, 218 Xiang Yang Road(s), Shanghai

2010/03/29 – 04/01
☎ 021-6437 1178
🖷 021-6437 0982
www.expobuild.com
1720

中国国际门窗、幕墙、五金与遮阳産品展览会
地点：上海新国际博览中心，上海
主办：上海博建国际会展有限公司
地址：上海市襄阳南路218号现代大厦10楼（200031）

Doors, Windows, Structures & Sunshades China
Venue: Shanghai New International Expo Center, Shanghai
Organizer: Shanghai UBM Sinoexpo International Exhibition Co
Address: 10/F, Xiandai Mansion, 218 Xiang Yang Road(s), Shanghai

2010/03/29 – 04/01
☎ 021-6437 1178
🖷 021-6437 0982
www.chinawood.org
1740

中国国际木制品及原材料展览会
可持续建筑木制品设计应用展览
地点：上海新国际博览中心，上海
主办：上海博华国际展览有限公司
地址：上海市襄阳南路218号现代大厦10楼（200031）

Sustainable Building Woodwork Expo
Venue: Shanghai New International Expo Center, Shanghai
Organizer: Shanghai UBM Sinoexpo International Exhibition Co
Address: 10/F, Xiandai Mansion, 218 Xiang Yang Road(s), Shanghai

2010/03/29 – 04/01
☎ 021-6437 1178
🖷 021-6437 0982
1750

W3国际精品设计展览会
家居设计展览会
地点：上海新国际博览中心，上海
主办：上海博华国际展览有限公司
地址：上海市襄阳南路218号现代大厦10楼（200031）

Expo Deco
Venue: Shanghai New International Expo Center, Shanghai
Organizer: Shanghai UBM Sinoexpo International Exhibition Co
Address: 10/F, Xiandai Mansion, 218 Xiang Yang Road(s), Shanghai

2010/03/29 – 04/01
☎ 021-3351 8238
🖷 021-3351 8239
✉ zyexpo@163.com
www.zyexpo.com
1770

第五届国际胶粘带、保护膜及光学膜（上海）展览会
国际模切材料及加工设备（上海）展览会
地点：上海国际展览中心，上海
主办：上海富亚展览有限公司

The 5th Intl Adhesive tape Protective Films & Optical Film (Shanghai) Expo/ International Diecyt Materials and Fabrication Plants (Shanghai) Expo
Venue: Shanghai International Exhibition Center, Shanghai
Organizer: Shanghai Fuya Exhibition Co Ltd

2010/03/29-31
☎ 021-6437 1178
🖷 021-6437 0982
www.chinacleanexpo.com
1790

中国清洁博览会
2010上海国际清洁技术与设备博览会
暨2010上海国际室内环境技术与产品展览会
地点：上海新国际博览中心，上海
主办：上海博华国际展览有限公司
地址：上海市襄阳南路218号现代大厦10楼（200031）

11th China Clean
Venue: Shanghai New International Expo Center, Shanghai
Profile: Cleaning equipment, clean chemicals, janitorial hygienic, indoor air quality, antimicrobial disinfection technology & supply, solid waste disposal technology & equipment
Venue: Shanghai International Exhibition Center, Shanghai
Organizer: Shanghai Fuya Exhibition Co Ltd

2010/04/01-03
☎ 021-5445 1166, 5445 1228
🖷 021-5445 1218
✉ Gehuaexpo@126.com
www.chpe.com.cn
1800

中国（上海）国际袜业采购交易会
地点：上海光大会展中心，上海
内容：袜类：男袜、女袜、童袜、婴儿袜、裤袜、毛圈袜、学生袜、船袜、丝袜、棉袜、棉氨袜、毛巾袜、运动袜、休闲袜、保健袜、按摩袜、纳米袜、时装袜、长筒袜、提花袜、花边袜、吊带袜、五指袜、圆头袜、内衣等；袜子原料：氨纶、涤纶、棉纱、锦纶、腈纶、包覆纱、橡筋线、丙纶、袜纱、花边；袜机：袜机及辅助设备：全电脑高速丝袜机、全电脑提花毛巾袜机、双针筒袜机、单针筒袜机、自动定型袜机、自动缝头机、拼档机、绣花袜机、丝袜机、提花袜机、大电脑袜机、小电脑袜机、整型机、绣花机、染纱设备
始办年份：2006

China (Shanghai) International Hosiery Purchasing Expo
Venue: Shanghai Everbright Convention & Exhibition Center, Shanghai
Profile: Socks: Man, Women, Baby, Children, 5toes, Terry socks, Athletics socks, low cut socks, silk socks, cotton socks, health care, Nanometer, Fashion style, Stocking, Lace, socks bamboo fiber, soybean socks, ramie socks; Stocking: pantyhose Knee-Highs Socks; Material: Spandex, Terylene, Cotton Yarn, Nylon/polyamide, T/C, P/C, Spandex polyester, Socks yarn, Natural Fibers Underwear: Lingerie, swimwear, beachwear; Socks Machine Accessories
Established Year: 2006
Frequency: Annual

周期：每年一届
市场范围：国际性
参展费用：标准展位9,800元，境外企业3,000美元；净地1,000元/m²
上届规模 '09：展览面积7,000m²，参展商197家（国外展商8家），参观人数8,848人
主办：中国同源有限公司
承办：上海歌华展览服务有限公司
地址：上海市田州路99号新安大楼1206-1208（200235）
联系人：韩友恒，宋雅
MSN: shanghaigehuaexpo@hotmail.com

Market Area: International
Participated Fee: Standard Booth USD 3,000, Raw Space RMB 1,000元/m²
Statistics '09: Exhibition Area 7,000m², Exhibitors 197 (foreigners 8), Visitors 8,848
Sponsor: China Tongyuan I/E Co
Organizer: Shanghai Gehua Exhibition Service Co
Address: Room 1206-1206 Xin' an Mansion, No.99 Tianzhou Road, Shanghai, China
Contact: Mr Han, Ms Song
MSN: shanghaigehuaexpo@hotmail.com

2010/04/03-05
☎ 027-8736 2945，021-5852 6715
🖷 027-8736 2987，021-5852 6905
✉ eric@hope-tarsus.com
www.shmodelexpo.com.cn
1810

2010第六届上海国际模型展览会
地点：上海国际展览中心，上海
主办：上海市体育总会；上海市对外文化交流协会
承办：上海好博塔苏斯展览有限公司
联系人：余云成

7th Shanghai International Model Exhibition 2010 (SIMS 2010)
Venue: Shanghai International Exhibition Center, Shanghai
Organizer: Shanghai Tarsus Hope Exhibition Co Ltd

2010/04/06-09
☎ 010-8460 0316, 8460 0805
🖷 010-8460 0721, 8460 0761
✉ majia@ciec.com.cn
✉ info@stonetechfair.com
www.stonetechfair.com
1830

第17届中国国际石材产品及石材技术装备展览会
第8届中国国际人造石工业展览会
内容：STONETECH展会自创办至今，历经多年的市场洗礼，现已发展成为亚洲最具规模和影响力的石材贸易展览会。STONETECH在亚洲同类展会中已率先通过UFI认证，顺利跻身全球知名石材展会行列。
周期：每年一届
市场范围：国际性
主办：北京华港展览有限公司；中国贸促会建材行业协；中国石材工业协会
地址：北京市朝阳区北三环东路6号综合服务楼1层（100028）
联系人：马佳，柴彤，张国庆

STONETECH 2010
17th China Intl Stone Processing Machinery, Equipment and Products Exhibition
Venue: Shanghai New International Expo Center, Shanghai
Frequency: Annual
Market Area: International
Organizer: CCPIT Building Materials Sub-council

2010/04/08-10
☎ 021-6853 2167
🖷 021-6853 2137
✉ lxf214@126.com
www.cnigee.com
1840

2010中国（上海）国际地球物理勘探技术展览会
地点：上海光大会展中心，上海
内容：一、地球物理勘探：各类重力勘探、磁法勘探、电法勘探、地震勘探、放射性勘探应用仪器及技术装备，地下管线探测技术、地下生命探测仪、地下金属探测器以及多方位AVO技术、三维VSP技术、多波多分量技术、井间地震应用仪器及技术装备。二、地质勘探仪器：断面仪、浅震仪、探测仪、温度仪、气体探测器、定位仪、动测仪、测斜仪、水位仪、测厚仪、寻踪仪、雷达、沉降仪、检漏仪、测井仪、孔压仪、成像仪、土工仪、取样器、静力触探机、电测仪，测高仪，石油（金属）钻头钻杆，光谱仪（火花直读光谱、等离子体发射光谱、原子吸收光谱、原子荧光光
始办年份：2008
周期：每年一届
市场范围：国际性
参展费用：9,600元
承办：上海市地球物理学会勘探地球物理专委会；上海风向标准展位览有限公司；中国物探网
地址：上海市桃林路18号B1408室（200135）
联系人：李小凤
MSN: lxf314@hotmail.com
QQ: 70319339

2010 China (Shanghai) Intl Geophysical Exploration Technology Exhibition
Venue: Shanghai Everbright Convention & Exhibition Center, Shanghai
Established Year: 2008
Frequency: Annual
Market Area: International
Participated Fee: RMB 9,600/booth
Organizer: Shanghai Feng Xiang Biao Exhibition Co Ltd
Address: B1-418, 18 Taolin Road, Shanghai 200135
Contact: Li Xiaofeng
MSN: lxf314@hotmail.com

2010/04/08-10
☎ 020-8989 9051, 8989 9052
🖷 020-8989 9050
✉ cnibf@zhenweiexpo.com
www.cnibf.net/cscf
1850

2010中国（上海）国际超级电容器产业展览会
地点：上海光大会展中心，上海
内容：各类超级电容器产品；应用在工业电子、消费电子、交通运输、绿色能源的各类超级电容器及其成果产品展示；各类超级电容器制造和测试设备及仪器；各类超级电容器原材料和零配件
首届
周期：每年一届
市场范围：国际性
入场券价格：免费
参展费用：标准展位(3x3m) 双面开口加收20%，国内企业：特级展位7,800元，A级展位7,000元；国外企业2,600美元；净地（36m²起）国内企业780元/m²，国外企业260美元/m²
预计规模：展览面积3,000m²，参展商70家，参观人数5,000人
主办：中国电子学会；广东省电源行业协会；振威展览集团
承办：广东振威国展展览有限公司
地址：广州市海珠区琶洲大道东1号保利国际广场南塔501-504（510308）
联系人：牛松，刘绮薇

The 2nd China (Shanghai) International Lead Battery Industry Fair
Venue: Shanghai Everbright Convention & Exhibition Center, Shanghai
Profile: All kinds of super-capacitors products; applications in industrial electronics, consumer electronics, transportation, green energy, all kinds of super-capacitors and its results presentation; all kinds of super-capacitor manufacturing , testing equipment and instrumentation; all kinds of super-capacitors of raw materials and spare parts
First Session
Frequency: Annual
Market Area: International
Cost to Attend: Free
Participated Fee: Standard Booth (3x3m) corner booth add 20%, Intl Exhibitors USD 2,600/booth, Raw Space (min 36m²) Intl Exhibitors USD 260/m²
Sponsor: Chinese Institute of Electronics; Guangdong Power Supply Assn; Zhenwei Exhibition Group
Organizer: Guangdong Zhenwei Guozhan Exhibition Co Ltd
Address: Unit 501-504 South Tower Poly International Plaza, No.1 East of Pazhou Complex, Haizhu District, Guangzhou, China
Contact: Niu Song, Liu QiWei

2010/04/08-10
☎ 021-6853 2167
🖷 021-6853 2137
✉ lxf214@126.com
www.cnisme.com
1860

**2010中国（上海）国际测绘仪器及GPS/GIS/RS技术展览会**
**地点**：上海光大会展中心，上海
**内容**：测绘和3S企业形象展区、科研院所、学院高新技术、新专利成果展区，数字城市及测绘招商项目展区；数字地球技术：GPS全球定位系统、RS遥感技术与DPS数字摄影测量技术、动态GIS地理信息系统，GPS/ RS /GIS解决方案及行业技术应用；地理信息软件：测绘软件、工程软件、航测软件、图象处理软件、CAD软件、监测软件、掌上测量软件、三维软件、导航软件、数据处理软件、数字城市规划应用系统；空间信息与数字技术：对地观测与导航技术、网络技术、虚拟现实仿真与可视化技术、高性能计算与模拟技术、地球信息处理集成技术
**始办年份**：2008
**周期**：每年一届
**市场范围**：国际性
**参展费用**：9,600元
**主办**：上海市红外与遥感学会；上海市地球物理学会；上海技术交易所
**承办**：上海风向标准展位览有限公司；全国城市道路与桥梁技术情报网
**地址**：上海市桃林路18号B1408室（200135）
**联系人**：李小凤
**MSN**: lxf314@hotmail.com
QQ: 70319339

**2010 China (Shanghai) International Survey and Mapping Equipment & Technology Exhibition**
**Venue**: Shanghai Everbright Convention & Exhibition Center, Shanghai
**Established Year**: 2008
**Frequency**: Annual
**Market Area**: International
**Participated Fee**: RMB 9,600/booth
**Organizer**: Shanghai Feng Xiang Biao Exhibition Co Ltd
**Address**: B1-415, 18 Taolin Road, Shanghai
**Contact**: Li Xiaofeng
**MSN**: lxf314@hotmail.com

2010/04/08-10
☎ 020-8989 9051, 8989 9052
🖷 020-8989 9050
✉ cnibf@zhenweiexpo.com
www.cnibf.net/cscf
1870

**第二届中国（上海）国际电池产品及技术展览会**
**地点**：上海光大会展中心，上海
**内容**：各系列电池；各种组合电池；各类电池用制造设备、测试仪器、原材料、零部件和充电器等；硅太阳能电池及材料；薄膜太阳能电池及材料；太阳能电池透明封装材料；系列二次电池使用充电器；电池工业用三废处理设备；废旧电池回收处理技术与设备等
**始办年份**：2009
**周期**：每年一届
**市场范围**：国际性
**入场券价格**：免费
**参展费用**：标准展位(3x3m) 双面开口加收20%，国内企业：特级展位7,800元，A级展位7,000元；国外企业2,600美元；净地 (36$m^2$起) 国内企业780元/$m^2$，国外企业260美元/$m^2$
**上届规模** '09：展览面积12,000$m^2$(国外展商面积1,000$m^2$)，参展商250家（国外展商50家，来自10个国家），专业贸易观众15,000人
**主办**：中国电子学会；广东省电源行业协会；振威展览集团
**承办**：广东振威国展展览有限公司
**地址**：广州市海珠区琶洲大道东1号保利国际广场南塔501-504（510308）
**联系人**：牛松，刘绮薇

**The 2nd China (Shanghai) International Battery Industry Fair**
**Venue**: Shanghai Everbright Convention & Exhibition Center, Shanghai
**Profile**: Series of batteries; all forms of assembled battery; batteries for manufacture equipment, testing equipment, materials, parts and charges; silicon solar cells and materials; sheer packaged for solar battery; solar cells and component production equipment; intelligent charger for series recharge cells; disposal equipment of the three waste for battery industry; Waste battery recycling processing technology and equipment
**Established Year**: 2009
**Frequency**: Annual
**Market Area**: International
**Cost to Attend**: Free
**Participated Fee**: Standard Booth (3x3m) corner booth add 20%, Intl Exhibitors USD 2,600/booth, Raw Space (min 36$m^2$) Intl Exhibitors USD 260/$m^2$
**Statistics '09**: Exhibition Area 12,000$m^2$(foreigners 1,000$m^2$), Exhibitors 250 (foreigners 50, came from 10 countries), Trade Visitors 15,000)
**Sponsor**: Chinese Institute of Electronics; Guangdong Power Supply Assn; Zhenwei Exhibition Group
**Organizer**: Guangdong Zhenwei Guozhan Exhibition Co Ltd
**Address**: Unit 501-504 South Tower Poly International Plaza, No.1 East of Pazhou Complex, Haizhu District, Guangzhou, China
**Contact**: Niu Song, Liu QiWei

2010/04/08-10
☎ 020-8989 9051, 8989 9052
🖷 020-8989 9050
✉ cnibf@zhenweiexpo.com
www.cnibf.net/cscf
1880

**第二届中国（上海）国际电源产业展览会**
**地点**：上海光大会展中心，上海
**内容**：发电机组展区：柴油发电机组、汽油发电机组、天然气发电机组、风力发电机组、太阳能发电机组、输变配电成套电气设备、变压器等。电子电源展区：通信电源、UPS电源、变频电源、整流电源、开关电源、电力电源、照明电源、高压电源、特种电源、EPS应急电源等。电磁兼容、充电器及电源器件、电源管理及测试设备
**始办年份**：2009
**周期**：每年一届
**市场范围**：国际性
**入场券价格**：免费
**参展费用**：标准展位(3x3m) 双面开口加收20%，国内企业：特级展位7,800元，A级展位7,000元；国外企业2,600美元；净地 (36$m^2$起) 国内企业780元/$m^2$，国外企业260美元/$m^2$
**上届规模** '09：展览面积3,000$m^2$(国外展商面积500$m^2$)，参展商60家（国外展商12家，来自6个国家），参观人数7,000人（专业贸易观众6,000人）
**主办**：中国电子学会；广东省电源行业协会；振威展览集团
**承办**：广东振威国展展览有限公司
**地址**：广州市海珠区琶洲大道东1号保利国际广场南塔501-504（510308）
**联系人**：牛松，刘绮薇

**The 2nd China (Shanghai) International Power Supply Industry Fair**
**Venue**: Shanghai Everbright Convention & Exhibition Center, Shanghai
**Profile**: Generator Group District: Diesel generator sets, gasoline generator sets, gas generators, wind generators, solar generators, transmission and variable sets of electrical distribution equipment, transformers and so on; Electronic Power Supply District: communication power, UPS power supply, variable frequency power supply, rectifier power supplies, switching power supply, power supply, lighting power, high-voltage power supply, special power supply, EPS emergency power supplies. Electromagnetic compatibility, chargers and power devices, power management and test equipment
**Established Year**: 2009
**Frequency**: Annual
**Market Area**: International
**Cost to Attend**: Free
**Participated Fee**: Standard Booth (3x3m) corner booth add 20%, Intl Exhibitors USD 2,600/booth, Raw Space (min 36$m^2$) Intl Exhibitors USD 260/$m^2$
**Statistics '09**: Exhibition Area 3,000$m^2$(foreigners 500$m^2$), Exhibitors 60 (foreigners 12, came from 6 countries), Visitors 7,000 (trade visitors 6,000)
**Sponsor**: Chinese Institute of Electronics, Guangdong Power Supply Assn, Zhenwei Exhibition Group
**Organizer**: Guangdong Zhenwei Guozhan Exhibition Co Ltd
**Address**: Unit 501-504 South Tower Poly International Plaza, No.1 East of Pazhou Complex, Haizhu District, Guangzhou, China
**Contact**: Niu Song, Liu QiWei

2010/04/08-10
☎ 020-8989 9051, 89899052
🖷 020-8989 9050
✉ ns@zhenweiexpo.com
www.cantondye.com.cn
1890

**第二届中国（上海）国际铅酸蓄电池展览会**
**地点**：上海光大会展中心，上海
**内容**：各类铅酸蓄电池产品、各类铅酸蓄电池制造和测试设备及仪器、各类铅酸蓄电池原材料和零配件、各种铅酸蓄电池工业附属设备和技术
**始办年份**：2009
**周期**：每年一届
**市场范围**：国际性
**入场券价格**：免费
**参展费用**：标准展位(3x3m) 双面开口加收20%，国内企业：特级展位7,800元，A级展位7,000元；国外企业2,600美元；净地 (36$m^2$起) 国内企业780元/$m^2$，国外企业260美元/$m^2$
**上届规模**‘09：展览面积4,000$m^2$(国外展商面积500$m^2$)，参展商70家（国外展商20家，来自8个国家），参观人数5,000人（专业贸易观众4,500人）
**主办**：中国电子学会；广东省电源行业协会；振威展览集团
**承办**：广东振威国展展览有限公司
**地址**：广州市海珠区琶洲大道东1号保利国际广场南塔5楼（510308）
**联系人**：牛松，刘绮薇

**The 2nd China (Shanghai) International Lead Battery Industry Fair**
**Venue**: Shanghai Everbright Convention & Exhibition Center, Shanghai
**Profile**: Various types of lead-acid battery products; Various types of lead-acid battery manufacturing and testing equipment and instruments; Various types of lead-acid battery raw materials and spare parts; Various types of lead-acid battery industry ancillary equipment and technologies
**Established Year**: 2009
**Frequency**: Annual
**Market Area**: International
**Cost to Attend**: Free
**Participated Fee**: Standard Booth (3x3m) corner booth add 20%, Intl Exhibitors USD 2,600/booth, Raw Space (min 36$m^2$) Intl Exhibitors USD 260/$m^2$
**Statistics**‘09: Exhibition Area 4,000$m^2$(foreigners 500$m^2$), Exhibitors 70（foreigners 20, came from 8 countries）, Visitors 5, 000（trade visitors 4,500）
**Sponsor**: Chinese Institute of Electronics, Guangdong Power Supply Assn, Zhenwei Exhibition Group
**Organizer**: Guangdong Zhenwei Guozhan Exhibition Co Ltd
**Address**: Unit 501-504 South Tower Poly International Plaza, No.1 East of Pazhou Complex, Haizhu District, Guangzhou, China
**Contact**: Niu Song, Liu Qiwei

2010/04/08-11
☎ 021-6437 1178
🖷 021-6437 0982
✉ helena.gao@ubmsinoexpo.com
www.boatshowchina.cn
1900

**中国(上海)国际游艇展**
**第十届中国国际船艇及技术设备展览会**
**地点**：上海展览中心，上海
**内容**：其他活动包括上海船展慈善帆船赛、游艇经济暨景观水系统资源开发论坛等。
**周期**：每年一届
**预计规模**：总面积33,000$m^2$，参展商380家，参观人数17,000人
**主办**：上海博华国际展览有限公司
**地址**：上海市襄阳南路218号现代大厦10楼1007室（200031）

**China (Shanghai) International Boat Show 2010**
**Venue**: Shanghai Exhibition Center, Shanghai
**Frequency**: Annual
**Expectation**: Gross Area 33,000$m^2$, Exhibitors 380, Visitors 17,000
**Organizer**: Shanghai UBM Sinoexpo International Exhibition Co Ltd
**Address**: 10F Xian Dai Mansion, 218 Xiang Yang Road (S), Shanghai 200030, China

2010/04/09-12
☎ 010-5827 6063
🖷 010-5827 6064
✉ fair@jewellery.org.cn
www.chinajewelryshow.com
1910

**2010上海国际珠宝首饰展览会**
**地点**：上海新国际博览中心，上海
**内容**：钻石首饰、黄金首饰、翡翠首饰、珍珠首饰、彩色宝石首饰、铂金首饰、白银首饰、玉石首饰、艺术首饰、瑞士钟表等
**始办年份**：2006
**周期**：每年一届
**市场范围**：国际性
**性质**：面向公众
**参展费用**：标准展位10,000～11,000元/9$m^2$
**上届规模**‘09：展览面积23000$m^2$(国外展商面积4680$m^2$)，参展商425家（国外展商159家，来自22个国家），参观人数32376人（专业贸易观众16000人）
**主办**：中国珠宝玉石首饰行业协会；国土资源部珠宝玉石首饰管理中心
**承办**：北京中宝协展览有限公司；博威展览服务有限公司；香港立新国际展览有限公司
**地址**：北京市东城区北三环东路36号环球贸易中心C座2215室（100013）
**联系人**：韦光明，潘沐闲

**Jewelry Shanghai 2010**
**Venue**: Shanghai New International Expo Center, Shanghai
**Profile**: Diamond jewelry; Gold jewelry; Jade jewelry; Pearl jewelry; Gemstone jewelry; Platinum jewelry; Silver jewelry; Art jewelry; Swiss watches and etc
**Established Year**: 2006
**Frequency**: Annual
**Market Area**: International
**Nature**: Open to public
**Participated Fee**: Standard Booth RMB 10,000-11,000/9$m^2$
**Statistics** ‘09: Exhibition Area 23,000$m^2$(foreigners 4,680$m^2$), Exhibitors 425（foreigners 159, came from 22 countries）, Visitors 32,376（trade visitors 16,000）
**Sponsor**: Gems & Jewelry Trade Assn of china; National Gems & Jewelry technology administrative center
**Organizer**: Beijing zhongbaoxie exhibition Co Ltd; Broadway exhibition service Co Ltd; Neway international Trade Fairs
**Address**: Rm$^2$215, Tower C, Global Trade Center, North 3rd Ring Road, Dongcheng District, Beijing 100013, China
**Contact**: Guangming Wei, Anais Pan

2010/04/12-14
☎ 010-6851 9866, 6853 5419
🖷 010-6853 5408
✉ liufeng@ckcf.cn
www.ckcf.cn
1920

**第92届中国针棉织品交易会**
**地点**：上海新国际博览中心，上海
**内容**：内衣产品类：基础内衣、暖棉内衣、时尚内衣、文胸内衣、儿童内衣、家居寝服；服饰产品类：休闲服装、羊绒羊毛衫、手套袜品、丝巾领带、运动服装、泳衣泳裤；家用纺织品类：床上用品、卧室纺织品、浴室、厨房、餐厅用纺织品、窗用纺织品、家具装饰布、车用纺织品、家具皮革制品、宾馆专用纺织品；针织相关产品类：针织辅料、针纺机械、针纺产品设计。
**周期**：每年一届
**市场范围**：全国性
**参展费用**：标准展位12,000元，净地1,200元/$m^2$
**上届规模**‘09：展览面积35,000$m^2$(国外展商面积30$m^2$)，参展商287家（国外展商3家），专业贸易观众26,000人
**主办**：中国纺织品商业协会
**承办**：中纺联（北京）会展服务有限公司
**地址**：北京西城区三里河东路5号中商大厦12层（100024）
**联系人**：刘锋，张军
**MSN**: feng2659@hotmail.com

**China International Trade Fair Mode Underwear and Home Textiles**
**Venue**: Shanghai New International Expo Center, Shanghai
**Profile**: Underwear: basic underwear winter underclothes, fashion dressing, lingerie, kids’ underwear, and pajamas. Home textiles: beddings, home textiles, lace and jacquard, bath kitchen & dining room textiles, auto fashions, curtain tulles, fabric & trim, embroidery, leather made products. Dressing: casual garments, sports dressing, swimming suits, cashmere & wool sweaters, gloves, hosiery, scarves and tie, etc. Others: fabrics, knitting machinery, textile designing and packages.
**Frequency**: Annual
**Market Area**: National
**Participated Fee**: Standard Booth RMB 12,000, Raw Space RMB 1,200/$m^2$
**Statistics** ‘09: Exhibition Area 35,000$m^2$(foreigners 30$m^2$), Exhibitors 287（foreigners 3）, Trade Visitors 26,000
**Sponsor**: China textile Commerce Assn
**Organizer**: China Textile Commerce Assn Fair Service Co Ltd
**Address**: No. 5 Sanlihe East Road Xicheng District, Beijing, China, 100024
**Contact**: Emile Lin
**MSN**: feng2659@hotmail.com

2010/04/11-13
☎ 021-6091 0207, 13761964110
🖷 021-6091 0208, 6091 0207
✉ shanghaizb@126.com
1950

**2010中国内衣面料辅料博览会**
**地点**：上海新国际博览中心，上海
**内容**：面料：各类内衣面料、文胸面料、泳装面料、家居服面料、童装针织面料、运动休闲服针织面料、T恤衫面料、其他相关针织面料等；辅料：花边、刺绣、模杯、织带、配件等；相关产业：针织机械、制衣设备、纺织品检测、计算机辅助设计、媒体等
**周期**：每年一届
**市场范围**：国际性
**性质**：面向公众
**参展费用**：标准展位11,000元
**主办**：中国纺织品商业协会
**承办**：中纺联（北京）会展服务有限公司；中纺流通（北京）商务咨询有限公司
**地址**：上海市沪光路39弄17号1302室（201108）
**联系人**：张彬
MSN: shanghaizb@hotmail.com
QQ: 1176821278

**China Underwear Fabric Accessories Expo 2010**
**Venue**: Shanghai New International Expo Center, Shanghai
**Frequency**: Annual
**Market Area**: International
**Nature**: Open to public
**Participated Fee**: Standard Booth RMB 11,000
**Organizer**: China Textile Commerce Assn
**MSN**: shanghaizb@hotmail.com

2010/04/11-13
☎ 021-6091 0207, 13761964110
🖷 021-6091 0208, 6091 0207
✉ shanghaizb@126.com
www.ckcf.cn
1960

**2010中国家用纺织品面料及家居布艺博览会**
**地点**：上海新国际博览中心，上海
**内容**：面料：床品面料、窗帘用布、沙发用布、各类室内装饰用布；家居饰品：家居布艺、其它家用纺织品面料；相关产业：纺织机械、绗缝设备、设计与包装、纺织品检测、媒体；展览形式：贸易洽谈，产品交易，形象展示，新品推介，讲座论坛，趋势发布
**周期**：每年一届
**市场范围**：国际性
**性质**：面向公众
**参展费用**：标准展位11,000元
**主办**：中国纺织品商业协会
**承办**：中纺联（北京）会展服务有限公司；中纺流通（北京）商务咨询有限公司
**地址**：上海市沪光路39弄17号1302室（201108）
**联系人**：张彬
MSN: shanghaizb@hotmail.com
QQ: 1176821278

**2010 China Home Textile Fabric and Home Sewing Expo**
**Venue**: Shanghai New International Expo Center, Shanghai
**Frequency**: Annual
**Market Area**: International
**Nature**: Open to public
**Participated Fee**: Standard Booth RMB 11,000
**Organizer**: China Textile Commerce Assn
**MSN**: shanghaizb@hotmail.com

2010/04/14-16
☎ 021-6279 2828
🖷 021-6545 5124
✉ info@siec-ccpit.com
www.siec-ccpit.com
2000

**第十届中国国际染料工业暨有机颜料、纺织化学品展览会**
**地点**：上海国际展览中心；上海世贸商城，上海
**内容**：各类染料、中间体、有机颜料和纺织化学品；各类助剂、印染前处理助剂、着色剂、分散剂、柔软剂、渗透剂、稳定剂、均染剂、增稠剂、粘合剂及各种整理助剂；化纤单体、催化剂、化纤油剂、生物酶制品及其它各种纺织用化学制品；配套生产设备、分析检测和监控设备仪器；印染设备和三废处理设备
**始办年份**：2001
**周期**：每年一届
**市场范围**：国际性
**展览性质**：面向贸易观众
**上届规模**：展览面积20,000㎡,参展商400家,参观人数36,601人
**主办**：上海市国际展览有限公司
**地址**：上海市延安中路841号东方海外大厦8楼（200040）

**CHINA INTERDYE 2010**
**(The 10th China International Dye Industry, Pigments and Textile Chemicals Exhibition)**
**Venue**: Shanghai International Exhibition Center; Shanghai Mart, Shanghai
**Profile**: Dyestuff, Intermediate, Pigment, Textile chemical and equipment
**Established Year**: 2001
**Frequency**: Annual
**Market Area**: International
**Organizer**: Shanghai International Exhibition Co
**Address**: 8/F, OOCL Plaza, 841 Yan An Zhong Road, Shanghai 200040, China

2010/04/19-22
☎ 021-5027 8128
🖷 021-5027 8138
✉ chinaplas@adsale.com.hk
www.chinaplasonline.com
2020

**中国国际橡塑展**
**第24届中国国际塑料橡胶工业展览会**
**地点**：上海新国际博览中心，上海
**内容**：辅助设备及测试仪器、化工及原材料、模具及加工设备、塑料包装及吹塑机械、注塑机械、挤出机械、其他加工机械、半成品、中国出口机械及原料。
**上届规模**'09：展览总面积140,000m², 参展商1,840家，参观人数69,298人
**主办**：雅式展览服务有限公司
**主办**：杜塞尔多夫展览(中国)有限公司
**地址**：上海市浦东新区张江高科技园区科苑路88号上海德意志工商中心1号楼307-308室（201203）
**联系人**：王乐为

**Chinaplas 2010**
**24th International Exhibition on Plastic and Rubber Industries**
**Venue**: Shanghai New International Expo Center, Shanghai
**Profile**: Ancillary equipment, injection mould machines, machinery for foam, post processing & other processing machines, blow molding machines, IT applications, Measuring, control & test equipment, presses, chemicals & raw materials auxiliaries, machines & equipment for preprocessing & recycling, etc.
**Statistics '09**: Gross Area 140,000m², Exhibitors 1,840, Visitors 69,298
**Organizer**: Adsale Exhibition Services Ltd
**Organizer**: Messe Düsseldorf China Ltd
**Address**: German Center for Industry and Trade Shanghai, 88 Keyuan Rd, Zhangjiang Hi-Tech Park, Pudong, Shanghai
**Contact**: Cynthia Wang

2010/04/20-22
☎ 021-5153 5100, 5153 5155
✉ Mike.deng@reedexpo.com.cn
✉ Jimmy.yang@reedexpo.com.cn
www.nepconchina.com
2030

**第二十届中国国际电子生产设备暨微电子工业展**
**中国国际电子制造技术展览会**
**地点**：上海光大会展中心，上海
**内容**：NEPCON China是亚洲地区最大的电子制造与表面贴装行业盛会之一，它涵盖了该行业在全球范围的创新产品和技术，将全世界表面贴装品牌呈现在您的面前。
NEPCON China为您建立一个最佳交流平台，帮助您提高行业竞争优势，有效物色新供应商，收集最新市场信息，寻找技术解决方案以及学习最新技术。
**周期**：每年一届
**主办**：励展博览中国有限公司
**联系人**：邓萌先生（参展），杨巍先生（参观）

**NEPCON/ EMT China 2010**
**Venue**: Shanghai Everbright Convention & Exhibition Center, Shanghai
**Profile**: NEPCON China 2010 is one of the largest and longest standing trading and sourcing platforms for the SMT industry in China. Featuring a comprehensive range of innovative SMT products and technology, it brings the entire world of SMT to your door step.
The event provides a sourcing platform for new suppliers gathers new market information and displays the latest technologies to help you enhance your competitiveness in the electronics manufacturing industry.

2010/04/20 – 22
☎ 021-5153 5122, 5153 5210
✉ jeffrey.si@reedexpo.com.cn
✉ karena.tong@reedexpo.com.cn
www.greenlightingchina.com
2035

**第四届中国国际新光源&新能源照明展览会暨论坛**
**地点**：上海光大会展中心，上海
**内容**：中国国际新光源&新能源照明展览会暨论坛是中国地区最重要的半导体照明行业盛会之一，其依绿色、创新、快速发展的中国照明产业，将全面展示来自全球该行业先进的生产制造设备、材料以及各种应用领域的产品。由国家半导体照明工程及产业联盟主办的高峰论坛与展览会同期举办，不仅为您创建了提高品牌知名度，展示新产品的最佳平台，同时帮助您提高行业竞争优势，有效物色潜在客户，收集最新市场信息，建立与专业客户群体最佳交流机会。
**周期**：每年一届
**主办**：励展博览集团
**参展**：☎021-5153 5122 ✉jeffrey.si@reedexpo.com.cn
**参观**：☎021- 5153 5210 ✉karena.tong@reedexpo.com.cn

**Green Lighting China Expo and Forum 2010**
**Venue**: Shanghai Everbright Convention & Exhibition Center, Shanghai
**Profile**: Green Lighting China is one of the leading and truly international trade events featuring the most advanced environmental friendly manufacturing equipment, materials and applications in the world' s growing lighting industry market, China. Held concurrently with the high-level conference, Green Lighting China provides an excellent platform for the lighting industry suppliers to enhance competitive edge, forge new partnerships, gather latest market information and network with potential customers.
**Frequency**: Annual
**Organizer**: Reed Exhibitions
For Exhibiting: ☎ 021-5153 5122
✉ jeffrey.si@reedexpo.com.cn
For Visiting: ☎ 021-5153 5210
✉ karena.tong@reedexpo.com.cn

2010/04/21-23
☎ 021-5459 2323, 5459 2318
📠 021-6487 7669, 5425 3480
✉ zhangjun@mpzhongmao.com
www.china-epower.com
2040

**第十届中国国际电力电工设备暨电厂脱硫脱硝展览会**
**地点**：上海国际展览中心，上海
**主办**：上海新中贸国际展览有限公司

**China Epower 2010**
**10th China Intl Electric Power & Electric Engineering Technology Exhibition**
**China Intl Smart Grid Equipment and Technology Exhibition**
**Venue**: Shanghai International Exhibition Center, Shanghai
**Organizer**: MP Zhongmao International (Shanghai) Pte Ltd
**Contact**: Tina Zhao

2010/04/21-23
☎ 010-6478 7342, 8441 4052
📠 010-8441 4057
✉ fengfeng99@vip.163.com
www.icecream-expo.com
2050

**2010中国国际冰淇淋加工技术设备及冷链展览会**
**地点**：上海世贸商城，上海
**内容**：冰淇淋冷饮制造生产设备、香精、香料、添加剂、配料、软冰淇淋机、原料、售卖设备、储存，展示，仓储，运输设备
**始办年份**：2009
**周期**：每年一届
**市场范围**：国际性
**性质**：面向公众
**入场券价格**：20元
**参展费用**：标准展位（3x3m）：国内企业8,800元,合资企业(特装修)11,800元,境外企业2,800美元,双开口展位加收10%费用；净地（36m$^2$起）：国内企业1,000元/m$^2$，合资企业1,100元/m$^2$；外资企业300美元/m$^2$
**主办**：中国食品工业协会；中食协食品物流专业委员会
**承办**：中国食品物流专业委员会展览部；北京新京贸国际
**地址**：北京市朝阳区望京西路48号金隅国际大厦G座2705（100102）
**联系人**：霍丽，王力
**MSN**: bjhuoli@hotmail.com
**QQ**: 1290105549

**The China International Ice Cream Industry Exhibition**
**Venue**: Shanghai Mart, Shanghai
**Profile**: Manufacture furnishings for ice cream Packaging, Printing and Processing Facilities Flavors ,Fragrance ,additives and supplement Store and transportation equipment New technology finished products
**Established Year**: 2009
**Frequency**: Annual
**Market Area**: International
**Nature**: Open to public
**Cost to Attend**: RMB 20:-
**Participated Fee**: Standard Booth（3x3m）；Intl Exhibitors USD 2,800, Corner Booth add 10%, Raw Space (min 36m$^2$) USD 300/m$^2$
**Sponsor**: China National Food Industry Assn（CNFIA）; China Food Logistics Commission
**Organizer**: Exhibition Dept of China Food Logistics Professional Committee; Beijing Gold Trade Intl Exhibition Co Ltd
**Address**: Room 2705, G Block of City One, 48 Wangjing West Road, Beijing, China
**Contact**: Holy, Wang Li
**MSN**: bjhuoli@hotmail.com

2010/04/27-29
☎ 010-6716 7561, 6716 7461
📠 010-6716 1520
2060

**第27届中国国际丝网印刷及数字技术展览会**
**2010年中国国际服装服饰及面料印花技术展览会**
**地点**：上海国际展览中心，上海
**内容**：以上海为中心的长江三角洲地区是我国最重要的服装服饰印花、电子线路板、汽车、广告、皮革、精细化工、玻璃、陶瓷、玩具、家用电器等行业的制造、加工和出口中心，以网印、移印、特种印刷及新兴数字技术等为服务对象的工业产品和印刷产业具有巨大的潜在市场和发展空间。本届大展将凸显创新和融合的理念，将传统丝网印刷技术与创新的数字技术相融合，为我国网印行业打造一届创新与融合的国际网印大展。
**主办**：中国丝网印刷行业协会
**地址**：北京市崇文区左安门内大街4号1层
**联系人**：袁克润

**27th China Screen Print Expo**
**2010 China Textile Print Expo**
**Venue**: Shanghai International Exhibition Center, Shanghai
**Organizer**: China Screen Printing Industry Association
**Address**: 1/Fl, 4 ZuoAnMen Street, Chongwen Dist, Beijing

2010/04/27-29
☎ 021-5197 8783, 5197 8782
📠 021- 5197 8788
✉ cwee@dr-expo.com.cn
www.cwee.com.cn
2070

**中国（上海）国际风能展览会暨研讨会**
**第8届中国国际动力设备及发电机组展览会**
**地点**：上海新国际博览中心，上海
**上届规模**：展览面积15,000m$^2$，参展商237家
**主办**：上海德瑞展览策划有限公司

**4th China Intl Wind Energy Exhibition and Conference**
**Venue**: Shanghai New International Expo Center, Shanghai
**Statistics '09**: Exhibition Area 15,000m$^2$, Exhibitors 237
**Organizer**: Shanghai Deray Exhibition Planning Co Ltd

2010/04/27-30
☎ 021-6279 2828
🖷 021-6545 5124
✉ info@siec-ccpit.com
www.siec-ccpit.com

2110

**2010中国自行车展览会（第二十届）**
2010中国国际电动车及零配件展览会
**地点**：上海新国际博览中心，上海
**内容**：借助于上海世博会开展的契机，CHINA CYCLE 2010将尽显“天时、地利、人和”之优势。CHINA CYCLE云集了所有在中国自行车市场上的知名品牌。品牌企业的高到位率和高质量的专业观众，保证了展会的规模和层次，体现了展会的影响力和号召力。CHINA CYCLE 2010由于“自行车王国”的特殊地位，历来都受到海内外业界人士的广泛关注。以“自行车，触动城市，变革生活”为主题的CHINA CYCLE 2010，将继续印证：自行车可以让城市更环保，让生活更健康；随着绿色环保、健康生活的理念越来越深入人心，中国的自行车企业必将拥有更为辉煌、广阔的未来。不断创新是CHINA CYCLE发展的动力，展会期间将举办“风华二十年”庆典系列活动，品牌评选、商贸配对、高层论坛、创意设计、单车竞技等各种动感时尚的互动活动，将有助于展商更好地了解自行车行业的品牌导向、流行趋势和贸易信息；有利于推进展会在创意中不断升华。在中国培育全球顶级的自行车展览会，这既是中国自行车协会的工作目标，也是全行业的共同追求。展会组委会将继续完善展会各项服务功能，不断提高展会整体服务水平。让我们相会在上海，相逢在世博！一起分享两轮车盛会的精彩，共同见证自行车“双华”的绽放！
**始办年份**：1997
**周期**：每年一届
**市场范围**：国际性
**性质**：面向公众
**入场券价格**：免费
**上届规模**‘09：展览面积100,000m²(国外展商面积10,000m²)，参展商1,000家（国外展商200家，来自30个国家），参观人数100,000人（专业贸易观众70,000人）
**主办**：上海市国际展览有限公司
**地址**：上海市延安中路841号东方海外大厦8楼（200040）
**主办**：中国自行车协会，上海协升展览有限公司
**地址**：上海市普陀区真北路915号903室（200333）
**联系人**：范丽华
**电话**：021-3251 3000
**传真**：021-3251 3220

**CHINA CYCLE 2010**
China E-BIKE 2010
China International Bicycle & Motor Fair
**Venue**: Shanghai New International Expo Center, Shanghai
**Established Year**: 1997
**Frequency**: Annual
**Market Area**: International
**Nature**: Open to public
**Cost to Attend**: Free
**Statistics '09**: Exhibition Area 100,000m²(foreigners 10,000m²), Exhibitors 1,000 (foreigners 200, came from 30 countries), Visitors 100,000 (trade visitors 70,000)
**Organizer**: Shanghai International Exhibition Co
**Address**: 8/F, OOCL Plaza, 841 Yan An Zhong Road, Shanghai 200040, China

2010/05/01-04
☎ 021-61956088
🖷 021-61956099
✉ jessica.wu@vnuexhibitions.com.cn
www.vnuexhibitionsasia.com

2120

**上海房地产春季展示会**
**地点**：上海展览中心，上海
**内容**：“假日楼市”是房地产届的著名展示会，是以“发展房地产业，满足人民需求”为宗旨，以黄金假日周为契机，按市场经济方式运作，集专业、规范为一体的大型房地产交易盛会。经过连续几年的成功运作，目前“假日楼市”已成为一个高品位、全面的、综合的大型房地产展示会，赢得了房产界的一致好评和良好的信誉，受到了广大参展商的青睐，对上海房地产市场的发展也起到了积极的推动作用。
**始办年份**：1990
**周期**：每年一届
**市场范围**：全国性
**性质**：面向公众
**上届规模**‘09：展览面积35,000m²，参展商250家，参观人数130,000人
**主办**：上海万耀企龙展览有限公司
**地址**：上海市徐汇区田林路140号26A栋 上海万耀企龙办公楼（20023）
**联系人**：吴佳钰

**Holiday Real Estate Market**
**Venue**: Shanghai Exhibition Center, Shanghai
**Profile**: "Holiday Real Estate Market" is a well-known real estate exhibition which based on "the development of real estate, to meet the needs of the people" for the purpose, to May holiday as an opportunity to operate according to a market economy, set professional standards as one big real estate transaction event. After several years of successful operation, the current "Holiday Real Estate Market" has become a high-quality, comprehensive, integrated large-scale real estate exhibition, has won acclaim real estate sector and a good reputation
**Established Year**: 1990
**Frequency**: Annual
**Market Area**: National
**Nature**: Open to public
**Statistics '09**: Exhibition Area 35,000m², Exhibitors 250, Visitors 130,000
**Organizer**: VNU Exhibitions Asia
**Address**: VNU House, 26A, No.140 Tianlin Road Shanghai, China
**Contact**: Jessica

2010/05/05-07
☎ 021-5459 2323,
5058 0707转ext 818
🖷 021-5425 3480
✉ eptee2010@zhongmao.com.cn
www.eptee.com
www.c-watershow.com

2130

**中国国际环保、废弃物及资源利用展览会**
**中国国际给排水水处理展览会**
**地点**：上海新国际博览中心，上海
**内容**：IFAT CHINA中国环博会是全球规模最大的环保盛会慕尼黑IFAT的中国展。IFAT CHINA中国环博会展示适合中国国情与环保现状的先进环境技术，主要涉及水和污水处理，废弃物处理和回收利用以及自然能源等领域的领先技术和专业解决方案。展会同期举办一系列高质量的论坛和专题研讨会，同时邀请国内外专家就业内关注的话题到场交流讨论。商务项目对接会为展商和观众提供缔造商机，学习交流的完美平台。
**始办年份**：2000
**周期**：每年一届

**IFAT CHINA+EPTEE+CWS 2010**
**Venue**: Shanghai New International Expo Center, Shanghai
**Profile**: IFAT CHINA is an offshoot of IFAT, the premier international environmental protection exhibition. IFAT CHINA exhibits advanced environment technologies that match the current situation and environment protection practices and laws in China, including leading technologies and professional solutions for water management, sewage disposal, waste disposal, waste recycling and natural energies. Additionally, it convenes advanced forums and symposiums, drawing together experts from home and abroad to exchange their views on topical issues in various fields related to environmental protection, and its business conferences provide ideal opportunities for exhibitors and visitors

市场范围：国际性
入场券价格：20元/张
上届规模‘09：展览面积35,000m²(国外展商面积16,000m²)，参展商756家（国外展商386家，来自23个国家），参观人数32,128人（专业贸易观众19,800人）
主办：德国慕尼黑国际博览集团；慕尼黑展览（上海）有限公司
联系人：叶蕾
主办：上海中贸国际展览有限公司
地址：上海市中山西路2368号华鼎大厦10A（200235）
联系人：刘婷

Established Year: 2000
Frequency: Annual
Market Area: International
Cost to Attend: RMB 20:-
Statistics '09: Exhibition Area 35,000m²(foreigners 16,000m²), Exhibitors 756 (foreigners 386, came from 23 countries), Visitors 32,128 (trade visitors 19,800)
Organizer: Munich Trade Fairs International Group (MMI); Munich Trade Fairs (Shanghai) Co Ltd; Shanghai ZM International Exhibition Co Ltd
Address: A/10, Huading Tower, 2368 Zhongshan Rd West, Shanghai
Contact: Tina

2010/05/05-07
☎ 021-6438 0781, 6427 6991
📠 021-6464 2653
www.snec.org.cn
2160

国际太阳能及光伏会议暨展览会
地点：上海新国际博览中心，上海
主办：上海市环境科学信息技术交流中心；上海伏勒密展览服务有限公司

11th China PV Power Expo
Venue: Shanghai New International Expo Center, Shanghai
Organizer: Shanghai Environmental Science Information Technology Exchange Center; Follow Me Intl Exhibition (Shanghai), Inc

2010/05/06-08
☎ 021-5109 7799
📠 021-5171 4505
✉ zhanye@vip.sina.com
2170

2010第四届中国（上海）国际室内供暖、通风及净化产品展览会
地点：上海国际展览中心，上海
内容：热源：空调、壁挂炉、电壁炉、真火壁炉、燃气壁炉、燃木壁炉、颗粒壁炉、（燃气、电）采暖炉、锅炉、电热水器、太阳能住宅一体化；地源热泵、空气源、源热泵水源热泵等；电采暖设备：电热膜、发热电缆、电热板、碳纤维发热体、碳晶等；低温热水管材：地源热泵专用管（PE）、PP-R、XPAP（铝塑管）、PE-RT、PB、PE-X、铜管等；室内通风展示区：新风系统、室内空气置换系统、冷风机、冷凝器等；空气净化产品展示区：空气净化产品（光触媒材料及产品、室内空气净化产品等）、空气加湿机；家庭水净化系统：前置过滤器、
始办年份：2006
周期：每年一届
市场范围：国际性
入场券价格：免费
参展费用：外资企业展区330美元/m²，品牌展区10,800元/展位，标准展区8820元/展位；净地：外资企业展区280美元/m²，品牌展区1,100元/m²，标准展区900元/m²
主办：中国建筑金属结构协会地面供暖委员会
承办：上海展业展览有限公司
地址：上海市虹漕南路99弄1号1楼A座（200233）
联系人：曾俊杰，周军
MSN: zjj-expo@hotmail.com
QQ: 307699460

4th Shanghai Intl Indoor Heating, Ventilation and Purification Products Expo
Venue: Shanghai International Exhibition Center, Shanghai
Profile: Heat: air conditioning, wall-hung boilers, electric fireplace, fireplace, gas fireplace, wood burning fireplace, particle fireplace, heating stove, Boilers, electric water heaters, solar residential integration; ground-source heat pumps, air source heat pump water source heat pump; Electric heating equipment: electric film, heating cables, electric panels, carbon fiber body heat, carbon crystal; Low temperature hot water pipe: ground-source heat pump dedicated pipe (PE), PP-R, XPAP, PE-RT, PB, PE-X, brass; Indoor air display area: The new air systems, indoor air replacement systems, cooling fan, condenser; Air purification products display area; Home water purification system; Control system; Auxiliary Materials；Construction Equipment
Established Year: 2006
Frequency: Annual
Market Area: International
Cost to Attend: Free
Participated Fee: Intl Exhibitors: Standard Booth USD 330/m², Raw Space USD 280/m²
Sponsor: China Construction Metal Structure Assn; Committee on surface heating
Organizer: Shanghai Zhanye Exhibition Co Ltd
Address: Section A, Floor 1, No. 1, 99 Hongcao South Road, Shanghai
Contact: Zeng Junjie, Zhou Jun
MSN: zjj-expo@hotmail.com

2010/05/06-08
☎ 021-6195 6088
📠 021-6195 6099
✉ jessica.wu@vnuexhibitions.com.cn
www.vnuexhibitionsasia.com
2190

世界客车博览亚洲展览会
地点：上海新国际博览中心，上海
内容：世界客车博览亚洲展览会自2001年在中国上海登陆以来，已整整经历了9个年头，2010年将迎来她的十周年庆典。十年来，中国客车制造业经历了从单纯引入和使用国际领先制造技术，到模仿发达客车国家的设计制造理念，到进一步具备自主研发高品质的原创制造能力，缩小了与欧美发达客车工业的差距。"原创中国制造客车"已成为全球买家和用户熟悉信赖的品牌！定于世博期间举办的本届展会无疑给高速成长并日益领先的中国客车业带来拓展全球市场的绝佳机遇。
始办年份：2001
周期：每年一届
市场范围：国际性
上届规模'08：展览面积30,000m²(国外展商面积8,877m²)，参展商177家（国外展商12家，来自23个国家），专业贸易观众16,061人
主办：上海万耀企龙展览有限公司
地址：上海市徐汇区田林路140号26A栋 上海万耀企龙办公楼（20023）
联系人：吴佳钰

Busworld Asia
Venue: Shanghai New International Expo Center, Shanghai
Profile: A 10th Anniversary will be celebrated in 2010. Since 2001, Busworld Asia has been successfully interpreted as the window for international professionals witness the high speed development of Chinese Bus & Coach industry, as well as a gateway for Chinese original brands' global expansion. Keep the "Innovative Attitude & Global View", Busworld Asia has been ready to create more bright future.
Established Year: 2001
Frequency: Annual
Market Area: International
Statistics '08: Exhibition Area 30,000m²(foreigners 8,877m²), Exhibitors 177 (foreigners 12, came from 23 countries), Trade Visitors 16,061
Organizer: VNU Exhibitions Asia
Address: VNU House, 26A, No.140 Tianlin Road Shanghai, China
Contact: Jessica

2010/05/11-13
☎ 021-5283 0917, 5283 0926
📠 021-5283 0917
2210

第六届上海国际钢管工业展览会
地点：上海国际展览中心，上海
主办：上海申仕展览服务有限公司

SHANGHAI TUBE EXPO
Venue: Shanghai International Exhibition Center, Shanghai
Organizer: Shanghai Shenshi Convention & Exhibition Service Co Ltd

2010/05/11-15
☎ 021-6279 2828
🖷 021-6545 5124
✉ info@siec-ccpit.com
www.siec-ccpit.com

2230

**第十三届中国国际模具技术和设备展览会**

**地点**：上海新国际博览中心，上海
**内容**：自从1986年开办以来已经成功举办了十二届，并于1996年率先加入国际博览联盟（UFI），成为上海最早的UFI品牌展。经历了20余年的发展之路，对外影响日益提升，目前已成为亚洲规模最大、全球第二的模具和机床专业展览会，吸引了中外模具机床行业的顶级品牌参展。
**展品范围**：模具及模具制品，模具标准件；加工中心，数控铣床、镗床、车床、钻床等模具加工各类金切机床；各类电加工机床，雕刻机；三坐标测量机及其它测量设备等；压铸机，各类压力机床及试模设备；模具材料、冶金制品；模具CAD、CAM、CAE；各类模具生产用的辅料、辅助设备
**周期**：每年一届
**市场范围**：国际性
**上届规模** ’09：展览面积70,000m²
**主办**：上海市国际展览有限公司
**地址**：上海市延安中路841号东方海外大厦8楼（200040）

**DIE & MOULD CHINA 2010 (DMC 2010)**

**Venue**: Shanghai New International Expo Center, Shanghai
**Profile**: Die & Mould China has been held for twelve editions since 1986, and became the first Union des Foires Internationales (UFI) approved event in Shanghai in 1996. With the improvement of show organization and expansion of event influence, this event has become the biggest Asia-wide and second biggest worldwide in the die & mould and machine tool show category, attracting all the top brands in the industry.
**Exhibits**: Die & Mould, Standard Die & Mould Components; Machining Center, CNC Milling Machining, Jig Grinding; Machines, Boring Machines, Drilling Machines, etc. Coordinate Measuring Systems; EDM Machines, Laser Processing; Various Kinds of Presses, Die Casting Machines; Injection Molding Machines, Extruders, Blow Molding Machines, Injection & Compression Moulds, Hot runner System; Cutting Tools, Spare Parts and Components; Die & Mould Materials; Die & Mould CAD/CAE/CAM; Die Spotter System, Polishing System, NC Tooling System, Jig & Fixture, Engraving Machines; Auxiliary Equipment for Die & Mould Making; Lubricant, Remover, Rust Remover; Heating & Cooling Units for Moulds & Dies.
**Frequency**: Annual
**Market Area**: International
**Statistics'09**: Exhibition Area 70,000m²
**Organizer**: Shanghai International Exhibition Co
**Address**: 8/F, OOCL Plaza, 841 Yan An Zhong Road, Shanghai 200040, China

2010/05/12-15
☎ 010-6343 0880, 6343 0990
🖷 010-6343 0660
✉ chinabakery@126.com
www.cnbakery.com

2240

**2010第13届中国国际焙烤展览会**

**地点**：上海新国际博览中心，上海
**内容**：凡从事食品、糕点（月饼）、面包、蛋糕、饼干、餐饮用原辅材料、装饰品及食品代加工（OEM）。展品包括专用油脂、奶油、专用面粉、预拌粉、冷冻面团、淀粉、土豆制品；馅料、果料、果仁、果脯、水果罐头等月饼、糕点辅料；焙烤设备及器具、手艺焙烤配备及器具、焙烤产品与制成品；食品馅料炒锅、夹层锅；（馅料）自动计量包装机械；饼干生产设备、原辅料及包装等；月饼包装、馅料、模具及生产设备；展示柜、储藏与冷藏柜、店面装饰；面粉改良剂、面包改良剂、蛋糕改良剂、方便面改良剂、保鲜剂、酵母、香料、香精、色素、甜味剂等相关食品添加剂；食品包装机械；饼房、厨房、西餐厅、咖啡厅生产设备、原辅料及用品；肉松、巧克力制品，糖仔、蜡烛、仿真食品模型等蛋糕装饰材料；咖啡、咖啡制品、咖啡机
**始办年份**：1997
**周期**：每年一届
**市场范围**：国际性
**入场券价格**：免费
**参展费用**：标准展位7,800元，净地780元/m²
**上届规模** ‘09：展览面积33,000m²(国外展商面积2,000m²)，参展商966家（国外展商2 4家，来自15个国家），参观人数78,600人（专业贸易观众49,862人）
**主办**：中国焙烤食品糖制品工业协会；中国贸促会轻工行业分会
**地址**：北京市海淀区北蜂窝2号中盛大厦1305a（100038）
**联系人**：李翔，李娟

**The 13th China International Trade Fair For Bakery & Confectionery**

**Venue**: Shanghai New International Expo Center, Shanghai
**Profile**: Baking ovens and accessories, baking and pastry-making machinery, refrigeration, fermenting and air conditioning technology, baking agents, raw materials and ingredients, semi-finished and finished products, ice cream manufacturing, pasta making, furnishings and equipment for shops, cafés and patisseries, packaging machinery, equipment and material, decorative items and baking accessories, cleaning and hygiene, laboratory and measuring equipment, computer hardware and software, services.
**Established Year**: 1997
**Frequency**: Annual
**Market Area**: International
**Cost to Attend**: Free
**Participated Fee**: Standard Booth RMB 7,800, Raw Space RMB 780/m²
**Statistics '09**: Exhibition Area 33,000m²(foreigners 2,000m²), Exhibitors 966 (foreigners 2 4, came from 15 countries), Visitors 78,600 (trade visitors 49,862)
**Organizer**: China Assn of Bakery & Confectionery Industry; CCPIT Sub-council of Light Industry

2010/05/13-15
☎ 021-6277 1636, 6276 2110
🖷 021-6277 1215, 6804 9224
✉ sh-anfang@vip.sina.com
www.sh-anfang.org

2260

**第十届上海社会公共安全产品国际博览会**

**地点**：上海展览中心，上海
**内容**：视频安防监控系统；周界安全防范报警系统；楼宇对讲、出入口控制及门禁系统；住宅小区及居民住户安全防范报警系统；反恐防爆安全检查系统及安全报警器材；“平安世博”、“平安城市”安防系统建设方案及相关技术；城市区域联网报警、移动目标联网报警系统建设与运营服务管理系统；消防、道路交通管理、防伪技术及计算机信息网络安全等设备及器材；自行车、助动车、摩托车等防盗锁及保险箱（柜）；其他安全防范产品和系统。
**始办年份**：1997
**周期**：每年一届
**市场范围**：国际性
**性质**：面向公众
**入场券价格**：免费
**参展费用**：净地800～1,200元/m²，标准展位8,000元

**10th Shanghai International Exhibition on Public Safety and Security**

**Venue**: Shanghai Exhibition Center, Shanghai
**Profile**: Video security monitoring system; Perimeter security alarm system; Building intercom, passageway control and door control systems; Residential district as resident and household safety precaution alarm system; Anti-terrorism and explosion-proof security check system as well as security alarm equipment; Safe Expo, Safe City security system construction program and related technologies; Metropolitan area network alarm, moving target network alarm system construction and operation service management system; Facilities and equipments, such as firefighting, road traffic management, anti-counterfeiting technology and computer information and network security; Anti-theft locks and safes of bicycles, scooters, motorbikes

上届规模‘09：展览面积12,740m²，参展商249家，参观人数20,000人
主办：上海安全防范报警协会
地址：上海市常德路1256号7楼（200060）
联系人：李顺敏，施赛琴

Established Year: 1997
Frequency: Annual
Market Area: International
Nature: Open to public
Cost to Attend: Free
Participated Fee: Raw Space RMB 1,200/m², Standard Booth RMB 8,000
Statistics '09: Exhibition Area 12,740m², Exhibitors 249, Visitors 20,000
Organizer: Shanghai Security Defense & Alarm Assn
Address: 7th F.NO.1256 Changde Road, Shanghai, China
Contact: Jennifer Li, Sherry Shi

2010/05/17-19
☎ 021-6091 0207, 5499 5547
🖷 021-6091 0208, 5499 9745
✉ shanghaizb@126.com
✉ shfair-china@yahoo.com
2270

第98届中国鞋业/皮具商品博览会
暨“名品进名店”对接展会
地点：上海光大会展中心，上海
内容：中国第一专业成品鞋及皮具展，积极响应了众多国内鞋业及皮具品牌发展壮大走向国际化的强烈呼声，同时更是国际品牌进入中国市场的最佳展示平台。据2009年“名品进名店”对接展会闭展后的调查显示，诸多本土鞋业、皮具品牌商对该展会予以高度评价，而广州、深圳、东莞、泉州等地大量鞋及皮具企业也纷纷表示需要真正有成效的权威性与专业性的国际展会，使区域品牌国际化；另一方面，愈来愈多的国际品牌涌向中国，迫切需要一扇更具针对性的展示窗口得以迅速开拓国内渠道
参展费用：标准展位：一楼15,000元/9m²，展馆二、三楼12,000元/9m²
主办：中国百货商业协会
联系人：刘铭
承办：上海百承商务服务有限公司
联系人：张彬

98th Chinese Shoes & Leather Commodity and "Well-Known Brands & Famous Shops" Exposition
Into Shoppes at Famous Butt Show
Venue: Shanghai Everbright Convention & Exhibition Center, Shanghai
Market Area: International
Nature: Open to public
Participated Fee: Standard Booth RMB 15,000/9m²
Organizer: China Commerce Assn for General Merchandise; Shanghai Baicheng Commerce Service Co Ltd

2010/05/17-19
☎ 021-3820 5346
🖷 021-3820 5349
2280

SCCE 2010
第五届上海国际硬质合金及生产技术和应用展览会
地点：上海光大会展中心，上海
内容：中国地区唯一针对硬质合金及其附属行业的专业贸易展，引领产品革新和行业发展的趋势及走向。展示行业领域的高技术含量的、高附加值的产品，有效促进了国内外企业间的技术交流与合作，在业内产生了积极的影响。凭借主办方极其丰富的经验和遍及全球的客户网络资源为广大参展商构筑一个独一无二的交流平台，并吸引上百位专业的海外买家参观采购。展会也以专业的组织策划与全方位服务获得了参展企业的一致好评。2010年5月，上海世博会正式开始。SCCE 2010在这样的环境下，凭借自己四年的客户资源和优质服务，通过国际化、专业化、品牌化的办展理念,进一步服务整个硬质合金生产及应用行业。
始办年份：2006
周期：每年一届
市场范围：国际性
入场券价格：免费
参展费用：7,800元
上届规模‘09：展览面积4,000m²(国外展商面积1,500m²)，参展商200家（国外展商50家），参观人数5,000人
主办：上海励信会展服务有限公司
地址：上海市浦东新区沪南路2688弄42号6楼（201315）
联系人：陈峰
QQ: 437195776

5th Shanghai Intl Cemented Carbides Exhibition
Venue: Shanghai Everbright Convention & Exhibition Center, Shanghai
Profile: The only professional trading exhibition for Cemented Carbides and it subsidiary industries taken annually, which leads the trend and direction for Cemented Carbides products renovation and the development of the industry. The previous four exhibitions participated by quite a few well-known enterprises displayed the high-tech and high added-value products, promoted technological exchange and cooperation among domestic and foreign companies, thus leaving a positive influence in the industry. The exhibition wins a good reputation as its professional organization and all-sides services.
Established Year: 2006
Frequency: Annual
Market Area: International
Cost to Attend: Free
Participated Fee: RMB 7,800/booth
Statistics '09: Exhibition Area 4,000m²(foreigners 1,500m²), Exhibitors 200（foreigners 50）, Visitors 5,000
Organizer: Shanghai Leasence Convention & Exhibition Co Ltd
Contact: Tony Chen

2010/05/17-19
☎ 021-6295 2131, 6295 2906
🖷 021-6278 0038
✉ intexljs@sh163.net
2300

2010中国（上海）国际残疾人和老年人康复护理技术及辅助器具展览会
地点：上海国际展览中心，上海
主办：上海国际展览中心有限公司展览部
地址：上海市娄山关路55号上海新虹桥大厦8楼（200336）

5th China Intl Exhibition of Rehabilitation, Nursing & Health care for Elderly and Disabled People
Venue: Shanghai International Exhibition Center, Shanghai
Organizer: Intex Shanghai Co Ltd

2010/05/19-21
☎ 021-6295 8367, 6295 7553
🖷 021-6278 0038, 6295 0206
✉ intexcl@sh163.net
✉ intexzhong@sh163.net
www.metro-china.org
2320

2010中国国际轨道交通展览会
2010 中国国际隧道与地下工程技术展览会
始办年份：2002
地点：上海新国际博览中心，上海
主办：上海国际展览中心有限公司

Metro China 2010
Tunnel China 2010
Venue: Shanghai New International Expo Center, Shanghai
Profile: Urban rail transportation, inter city transit system, railway, advantages of Yangtze Delta Area.
Organizer Intex Shanghai Co Ltd

2010/05/19-21
☎ 010-6588 6235, 6588 6236
🖷 010-6588 6233
✉ info@sialchina.cn
www.sialchina.cn
2350

**第十一届中国国际食品和饮料展览会**
**地点：**上海新国际博览中心，上海
**内容：**食品、酒、酒店餐饮服务、烘焙与糕点、食品加工技术。同时有国内外著名品牌企业和超市参展，发布食品大趋势报告会和新产品评比，推出国内外新产品。
**展品范围：**食品添加剂；乳制品，蛋类；新鲜肉类；新鲜禽类；新鲜及半腌制鱼及海鲜、贝类制品；新鲜水果、蔬菜、干果；糖果、饼干、烘焙类、休闲食品；腌制肉类；新鲜半成品、速成品、即食食品；罐头食品；宠物食品；速冻食品；有机食品；减肥食品、儿童食品及保健品；杂货食品（调味品、食用油、粮食类）；酒类；酒精饮料；非酒精饮料；专业服务机构与媒体；政府促进机构、信息组织、协会；酒店设备，餐具、酒吧及咖啡设备、一次性用品、餐饮设备、连锁、技术及网络
**性质：**仅对专业贸易观众
**上届规模**‘09：展出面积40,000m$^2$，国外展商来自60个国家，专业贸易观众30,000人
**主办：**法国爱博展览集团；商业发展中心
**承办：**北京爱博西雅展览有限公司
**地址：**北京市朝外大街22号泛利大厦1605室（100020）
**联系人：**侯旭，李波

**Sial 2010**
CHINA PACKTECH & FOODTECH
**Venue:** Shanghai New International Expo Center, Shanghai
**Profile:** packaging machinery, container making machinery, packing material making machinery, food making machinery, drink machinery and the relative products and equipments
**Established Year:** 2000
**Frequency:** Annual
**Market Area:** International
**Nature:** Trade Only
**Cost to Attend:** Free
**Statistics'09:** Exhibition Area 40,000㎡, Trade Visitors 27,718
**Sponsor:** Exposium; CCDC
**Organizer:** Exposium-Sial Exhibition Co
**Address:** Suite 1605, Prime Tower, No.22 Chaoyangmenwai Dajie, Chaoyang District, Beijing

2010/05/19-21
☎ 021-5308 9900
🖷 021-5308 2151
✉ sun@chingbeautyexpo.com
www.CBEbaiwen.com
2360

**第十六届中国国际美容化妆洗涤用品博览会**
**地点：**上海新国际博览中心，上海
**内容：**香水、化妆品及护肤品；洗涤及个人护理产品、口腔护理用品；包装、原料、机械以及OEM、ODM等涵盖产业链的上下游产品；专业美容院护肤产品、美体产品及仪器；水疗SPA产品及设备；香水香薰；美发美甲产品、器械和工具等。
**始办年份：**1998
**周期：**每年一届
**市场范围：**国际性
**入场券价格：**50元
**参展费用：**5,000～20,000元/9m$^2$
**上届规模**‘09：展览面积32,202m$^2$(国外展商面积5,181m$^2$)，参展商1,236家（国外展商337家，来自23个国家），参观人数197,500人（专业贸易观众95%人）
**主办：**中国香料香精化妆品工业协会；上海百文会展有限公司
**地址：**上海市西藏中路728号23F（200001）
**联系人：**孙旦

**China Beauty Expo**
**Venue:** Shanghai New International Expo Center, Shanghai
**Profile:** C&T, Skincare, Perfumery & Color Cosmetic, Detergents raw materials, OEM,ODM International Pavilions Professional Skin Care, SPA, Nail, Salon Products & Beauty Equipment, Cosmetech: Machinery, Packaging
**Established Year:** 1998
**Frequency:** Annual
**Market Area:** International
**Cost to Attend:** RMB 50:-
**Participated Fee:** RMB 5,000-20,000/9m$^2$
**Statistics '09:** Exhibition Area 32,202m$^2$(foreigners 5,181m$^2$), Exhibitors 1,236 (foreigners 337, came from 23 countries), Visitors 197,500 (trade visitors 95%)
**Organizer:** China Assn of Fragrance Flavor and Cosmetic Industries; Shanghai Baiwen Exhibition Co Ltd
**Address:** Suite 23F, 728 Central Tibet Road, Shanghai 200001, China
**Contact:** Sun

2010/05/19-21
☎ 021-6091 0207, 6091 0208
🖷 021-6091 0207, 6091 0208
2370

**2010第七届上海纺织服装采购交易会**
**地点：**上海世贸商城，上海
**内容：**服装及配饰：时尚服装、牛仔服装、T恤、羊绒衫、运动休闲服、围巾/披肩、腰带、帽子、袜子、首饰等OEM及ODM产品 服装辅料：棉纺面料、毛纺面料、丝绸面料、麻纺面料、化纤面料、针织面料、蕾丝花边、拉练、纽扣、衬布、花边、织带、商标吊牌等
**始办年份：**2003
**周期：**每年一届
**市场范围：**国际性
**性质：**面向公众
**上届规模**‘09：展览面积30,000m$^2$(国外展商面积15,000m$^2$)，参展商200家（来自200个国家），参观人数300,000人
**主办：**上海世界贸易商城有限公司
**承办：**上海纺织技术服务展览中心
**地址：**上海市延安西路2299号（200336）
**联系人：**张彬
**MSN:** shanghaizb@hotmail.com
QQ: 1176821278

**2010 (7th) Shanghai Textile & Apparel Trade Fair**
**Venue:** Shanghai Mart, Shanghai
**Established Year:** 2003
**Frequency:** Annual
**Market Area:** International
**Nature:** Open to public
**Statistics '09:** Exhibition Area 30,000m$^2$(foreigners 15,000m$^2$), Exhibitors 200 (came from 200 countries), Visitors 300,000
**Organizer:** Shanghai Textile Technology Service And Exhibition Center
**MSN:** shanghaizb@hotmail.com

2010/05/20-23
☎ 021-5266 5938, 13162899951
🖷 021-5266 8178
✉ realexpo@sh163.net
www.antiquefurniturefair.com
2375

**第九届中国国际古典家具展览会**
**2010上海国际古董及艺术品展览会**
**地点：**上海展览中心，上海
**内容：**每年五月的国际古典家具展在上海展览中心已成功地举办了八届，主要以展示中式古典家具，古董及古玩艺术品，红木家具及欧式古董家具为主，并已成为古典家具行业内的一次盛会。
**始办年份：**1999
**周期：**每年一届
**市场范围：**国际性
**主办：**上海瑞欧展览服务有限公司
**地址：**上海市中山北路2790号杰地大厦1007室（200063）
**联系人：**陈小姐，宋小姐

**Antique Furniture China 2010 & Antiques & Arts Shanghai 2010**
**Venue:** Shanghai Exhibition Center, Shanghai
**Profile:** This particular exhibition is being organized by us successfully for the past 8 years and has acquired very good reputation in the Chinese Antiques Industry. Each & every year the attraction grows in multiple folds as we witness many a collectors.
**Established Year:** 1999
**Frequency:** Annual
**Market Area:** International
**Organizer:** Shanghai Real Exhibition Service Co Ltd
**Address:** Rm.1007, 10F, Jie Di Plaza, No. 2790, Zhongshan Road (N), Shanghai
**Contact:** Amy Chen

2010/05/21-24
☎ 021-6475 2979
🖷 021-6475 2907
✉ dongmaosh@163.com
2380

**2010中国（上海）国际茶业博览会**
**地点**：上海国际展览中心，上海
**主办**：上海东贸展览服务有限公司

**2010 China (Shanghai) International Tea Exhibition**
Venue: Shanghai International Exhibition Center, Shanghai
Organizer: DONG MAO EXHIBITION

2010/05/26-29
☎ 021-3222 4777
🖷 021-3222 4770
✉ info@wes-expo.com.cn
www.wes-expo.com.cn
2400

**第15届中国国际厨房、卫浴设施展览会**
**地点**：上海新国际博览中心，上海
**内容**：厨房、卫浴设施、住宅技术与电器、建筑暖通、锅炉、空调、管道技术及水处理
**始办年份**：1996
**周期**：每年一届
**市场范围**：国际性
**性质**：面向公众
**主办**：上海环球展览有限公司
**地址**：上海江宁路167号新城大厦24层（200041）
**联系人**：王琳，桂天游

**Kitchen & Bath China 2010**
Venue: Shanghai New International Expo Center, Shanghai
Profile: Kitchen & Bath, Household Technology & Appliance, Heating, Ventilation, Boiler, Air-Conditioning, Plumbing & Water
Established Year: 1996
Frequency: Annual
Market Area: International
Nature: Open to public
Organizer: Worldwide Exhibitions Service Co
Address: 24/F., Xincheng Mansion, Jiangning Road, Shanghai
Contact: Wang Lin, Gui Tianyou

2010/05/26-29
☎ 021-3222 4777
🖷 021-3222 4770
✉ info@wes-expo.com.cn
www.wes-expo.com.cn
2410

**第15届中国国际建筑贸易博览会**
**地点**：上海新国际博览中心，上海
**内容**：建筑陶瓷、大理石及石材制品；照明灯饰；门窗、屋顶技术及加工设备；地材及铺装技术；建筑涂料工业；建筑装饰木业、木材及加工技术；社会公共安全产品；城市与建筑智能技术应用等
**始办年份**：1996
**周期**：每年一届
**市场范围**：国际性
**性质**：面向公众
**主办**：上海环球展览有限公司
**地址**：上海江宁路167号新城大厦24层（200041）
**联系人**：王琳，桂天游

**International Building & Construction Trade Fair 2010**
Venue: Shanghai New International Expo Center, Shanghai
Profile: Ceramic, Marble & Stone, Lighting, Win Tec, Window, Door & Roof, Floor Tec, Coating & Painting, Forestry, Timber & Wood, Security & Automation, City & Building Intelligent & Automation
Established Year: 1996
Frequency: Annual
Market Area: International
Nature: Open to public
Organizer: Worldwide Exhibitions Service Co
Address: 24/F., Xincheng Mansion, Jiangning Road, Shanghai
Contact: Wang Lin, Gui Tianyou

2010/05/27-29
☎ 021-5228 4020
🖷 021-5228 4011
✉ Joan.Zuo@nm-china.com.cn
www.biofachchina.com
2420

**2010中国国际有机食品博览会**
**地点**：上海国际展览中心，上海
**始办年份**：2007
**周期**：每年一届
**市场范围**：国际性
**性质**：面向公众
**上届规模‘09**：展览面积2,539m$^2$(国外展商面积403m$^2$)，参展商211家（国外展商26家，来自14个国家），参观人数1,0375人（专业贸易观众8,708人）
**主办**：德国纽伦堡展览有限公司/纽伦堡会展服务（上海）有限公司
**地址**：上海市青海路118号云海苑办公楼18楼（200041）
**联系人**：左琼莹

**BioFach China 2010**
International Organic Trade Fair and Conference
Venue: Shanghai International Exhibition Center, Shanghai
Established Year: 2007
Frequency: Annual
Market Area: International
Nature: Open to Public
Statistics ‘09: Exhibition Area 2,539m$^2$(foreigners 403m$^2$), Exhibitors 211（foreigners 26, came from 14 countries），Visitors 10,375（trade visitors 8,708）
Organizer: NürnbergMesse GmbH, NürnbergMesse China Co Ltd
Address: 18 F Yunhai Building, 118 Qing Hai Road, Shanghai, China
Contact: Joan Zuo

2010/05/27-29
☎ 021-6195 6088
🖷 021-6195 6099
✉ stephanie.xu@vnuexhibitions.com.cn
www.worldtravelfair.com.cn
2430

**上海世界旅游资源博览会**
**地点**：上海展览中心，上海
**内容**：上海世界旅游资源博览会由上海市旅游局及VNU欧洲展览集团主办，上海万耀企龙展览有限公司和上海旅游会议推广中心承办。从2004年起已经成功举办了6年，已成功打造为中国长三角地区最具影响力的旅游资源整合平台之一。经过六年的磨练，上海世界旅游资源博览会初露锋芒，取得了良好的社会效果和商业成绩。如今，上海世界旅游资源博览会已成为“中国最具魅力的旅游资源博览会”。
**始办年份**：2004
**周期**：每年一届
**市场范围**：国际性
**性质**：面向公众
**入场券价格**：20元
**参展费用**：净地2,150元/m$^2$，标准展位2,550元/m$^2$
**上届规模‘09**：展览面积4,000m$^2$(国外展商面积3,200m$^2$)，参展商450家（国外展商380家，来自50个国家），参观人数20,000人（专业贸易观众5,862人）
**主办**：上海市旅游局；上海旅游会展推广中心；上海万耀企龙展览有限公司
**地址**：上海市田林路140号越界创意园区26栋A（200233）
**联系人**：徐洁

**World Travel Fair**
Venue: Shanghai Exhibition Center, Shanghai
Profile: The World Travel Fair (WTF), annually located in Shanghai, is a business expo that one will not miss. It is sponsored by the Shanghai Municipal Tourism Administration and VNU Exhibitions Europe, and co-organized by VNU Exhibitions Asia and Shanghai International Conference Management Organization. As the most famous integrated travel resource expo in China, WTF has successfully built communicating bridge for business people to extend the social circle, build co-operation partnership, and expand new markets.
Established Year: 2004
Frequency: Annual
Market Area: International
Nature: Open to public
Cost to Attend: RMB 20:-
Participated Fee: Raw Space RMB 2,150/m$^2$, Standard Booth RMB 2,550/m$^2$
Statistics ‘09: Exhibition Area 4,000m$^2$(foreigners 3,200m$^2$), Exhibitors 450（foreigners 380, came from 50 countries），Visitors 20,000（trade visitors 5,862）
Organizer: Shanghai Municipal Tourism Administration; Shanghai International Conference Management Organization; VNU Exhibitions Asia
Address: VNU House, 26A, No. 140 Tianlin Road Shanghai P.R. China
Contact: Stephanie Xu

2010/05/30 – 06/01
☎ 021-5216 4991, 5216 4992
🖷 021-5218 9400
✉ kidsede@kidsedu.cn
www.kidsedu.cn

2440

**2010第五届上海国际幼儿教育展**
第五届上海国际婴童用品博览会
**地点：**上海世贸商城，上海
**内容：**中国唯一0～7岁专业幼教展.同期举办中韩婴童产业业者交流会、征战中东-中国婴童产业的外贸新契机、中国幼儿教育发展论坛——幼儿园园长大会、、优生优育论坛。
**周期：**每年一届
**市场范围：**国际性
**性质：**面向公众
**主办：**上海里杨展览服务有限公司
**地址：**上海市北翟路1178号鑫达大厦408-419室

**2010 The 5th Shanghai International KIDS Education EXPO**
Venue: Shanghai Mart, Shanghai
Frequency: Annual
Market Area: International
Nature: Open to public
Organizer: Shanghai Neon Exhibition Services Ltd
Address: 2F, Xinda Plaza Building 2, No 1158 Xiehe Road, Shanghai

2010/06 -
☎ 021-6279 2828
🖷 021-6545 5124
✉ info@siec-ccpit.com
www.siec-ccpit.com

2450

**2010上海国际物联网大会**
**地点：**上海
**周期：**每年一届
**市场范围：**国际性
**主办：**上海市国际展览有限公司
**地址：**上海市延安中路841号东方海外大厦8楼（200040）

**Internet of Things Conference Shanghai 2010**
Venue: Shanghai
Frequency: Annual
Market Area: International
Organizer: Shanghai International Exhibition Co
Address: 8/F, OOCL Plaza, 841 Yan An Zhong Road, Shanghai 200040, China

2010/06/02-04
☎ 021-5406 5137
🖷 021-5406 5150
✉ yxs@stcec.com

2480

**中国国际生物技术和仪器设备博览会**
**地点：**上海国际展览中心，上海
**内容：**科学仪器与设备、化学试剂、生物技术产品、生物工程和临床诊断、医药和健康、生物服务，生物技术相关的仪器设备，生物信息，生物工程，服务，生物技术的其他应用
**始办年份：**2007
**周期：**每年一届
**市场范围：**国际性
**参展费用：**A区：206欧元/m$^2$, 2,070欧元/展位；B区：950元/m$^2$, 9,500元/展位；C区：730元/m$^2$, 7,300元/展位
**上届规模**‘09：展览面积6,000m$^2$(国外展商面积300m$^2$), 参展商128家（国外展商30家，来自12个国家），专业贸易观众5,586人
**主办：**上海现代生物与医药产业办公室；上海市科学技术委员会；上海市教育委员会；中国科学院上海分院；上海科学院
**承办：**上海科技会展有限公司
**地址：**上海市钦州路100号2号楼3楼（200235）
**联系人：**杨晓珊，宋晔青

**BIOTECH CHINA 2010**
Venue: Shanghai International Exhibition Center, Shanghai
Established Year: 2007
Frequency: Annual
Market Area: International
Participated Fee: EUR 206/m$^2$, EUR 2,070/m$^2$
Statistics ‘09: Exhibition Area 6,000m$^2$(foreigners 300m$^2$), Exhibitors 128 (foreigners 30, came from 12 countries), Trade Visitors 5,586Organizer: Modern Biotechnology & Pharmaceutical Industry Office of Shanghai Municipality; Science and Technology Commission of Shanghai Municipality; Shanghai Municipality Education Commission; Chinese Academy of Science; Shanghai Branch, Shanghai Academy of Science
Address: 3F, Building 2, No. 100 Qinzhou Road, Xuhui District, Shanghai, China
Contact: YANG XIAOSHAN, SONG YEQING

2010/06/02-04
☎ 021-5406 5160, 5406 5150
🖷 021-5406 5150
✉ zh@stcec.com fy@stcec.com

2490

（BIO-FORUM2010）
**第12届上海国际生物技术与医药研讨会**
**地点：**华亭宾馆，上海
**内容：**BIO-FORUM由上海市现代生物与医药产业办公室主办，得到国家科技部、国家食品药品监督管理局、上海市科委、市经委、市药监局等有关委办大力支持。历经10多年发展，已成为在国内外具有一定影响力的生物技术和医药领域国际学术盛会。为推动我国生物技术与医药的研发和产业化，及时了解国内外生物医药技术的最新动态和发展趋势。
**周期：**每年一届
**市场范围：**国际性
**入场券价格：**注册费-2,000元（优惠日后），1,800元（优惠日前）
**上届规模**‘09：国外展商98家，来自11个国家，参会人数708人
**主办：**上海市现代生物与医药产业办公室
**承办：**上海新药研究开发中心；上海科技会展有限公司
**地址：**上海市钦州路100号2号楼3楼（200235）
**联系人：**张华，房颖

**The 12th Shanghai International Forum on Biotechnology & Pharmaceutical Industry**
Venue: Huating Hotel, Shanghai
Profile: BIO-FORUM, which is a most famous event in East China in the area of biotech & pharmaceutical industry, has been successfully held for 10 times since 1996. BIO-FORUM 2010 will be held in Shanghai with about 600 participants both at home and abroad. BIO-FORUM2010 will focus on Bio-tech Innovation and Human Health. Many different kinds of events such as plenary sessions, parallel sessions, pre-sessions, one-on-one meetings, leadership summits, seminars, training courses, exhibitions and social events will be held.
Frequency: Annual
Market Area: International
Cost to Attend: RMB 2,000
Statistics ‘09: Participants 708
Sponsor: Modern Biotechnology & Pharmaceutical Industry Office of Shanghai Municipality
Organizer: Shanghai Center of Research & Development of New Drugs; Shanghai Technology Convention & Exhibition Co Ltd
Address: 3F, Building 2, No. 100Qinzhou Road, Xuhui District, Shanghai, China
Contact: Michael Zhang, Ada Fang

2010/06/02-04
☎ 852-2814 5500，8199 7308
🖷 852-8199 7628
✉ exhibit@chinasourcingfair.com
✉ visit@chinasourcingfair.com
http://tradeshow.globalsources.com
2520

环球资源消费类电子产品采购交易会
地点：上海新国际博览中心，上海
内容：消费类电子产品、通信及无线产品、电脑及网络产品、安防产品、电子配件、车载电子产品、全球定位系统
主办：环球资源

China Sourcing Fair-Electronics
Venue: Shanghai New International Expo Center, Shanghai
Profile: Consumer electronics, Telecom & wireless products, Computer & networking products, Security products, Electronic accessories, In-car electronics, GPS
Organizer: Globe Sources

2010/06/02-04
☎ 021-6437 1178
🖷 021-6437 0982
www.p-mec.com
2530

世界制药机械、包装设备与材料中国展
地点：上海新国际博览中心，上海
主办：上海博华国际展览有限公司

P-MEC China
Venue: Shanghai New International Expo Center, Shanghai
Organizer: Shanghai UBM Sinoexpo Co Ltd

2010/06/02-04
☎ 021-6437 1178转ext 396
🖷 021-6437 0982转ext 396
✉ flora.ni@ubmsinoexpo.com
www.fia-china.com
2550

亚洲食品配料、天然原料、健康原料展览会
第12届亚洲食品配料中国展
第12届健康原料、天然原料中国展
地点：上海新国际博览中心，上海
内容：茶、可可专区、乳制品、婴儿健康食品专区
周期：每年一届
主办：上海博华国际展览有限公司

Fi Asia-China/ Hi China/ Ni China
Food Ingredients Asia China 2010
Health Ingredient China 2010
Natural Ingredients China 2010
Venue: Shanghai New International Expo Center, Shanghai
Profile: Food & beverage ingredients, Health, nufraceuticals, organic or functional ingredients, natural ingredient used in food & beverages, medical remedies and nutraceuticals
Frequency: Annual
Organizer: Shanghai UBM Sinoexpo Co Ltd
Address: 10/F Xian Dai Mansion, 218 Xiang Yang Road, Shanghai 200031, China

2010/06/02-04
☎ 021-6437 1178
🖷 021-6437 0982
www.cphi-china.com
2560

世界制药原料中国展
地点：上海新国际博览中心，上海
上届规模‘09：总面积82,000m²，参展商1,651家（国外展商128家，来自16个国家）,参观人数23,646人
主办：上海博华国际展览有限公司

CPhi China
Venue: Shanghai New International Expo Center, Shanghai
Profile: This event will provide unrivalled access to the pharmaceutical industry from which to launch new products and increase your market knowledge.
Statistics '09: Gross Area 82,000m², Exhibitors 1,651 (foreigners 127 came from 16 countries)
Organizer: UBM Sinoexpo International Exhibition Co Ltd

2010/06/08-10
☎ 021-6279 2828, 6289 3824
🖷 021-6545 5124
✉ fjy@siec-ccpit.com
eelia@siec-ccpit.com
info@siec-ccpit.com
www.offshorewindchina.com
www.siec-ccpit.com
2600

**上海国际海上风电及风电产业链大会暨展览会**
地点：上海国际展览中心；虹桥喜来登太平洋大饭店，上海
内容：为相关企业就海上风电项目的设计、安装、运营，海上风电机组的研发、配套等提供互相见面、交换信息、展示产品的机会，推动中国风电市场和行业的健康发展。
周期：每年一届
市场范围：国际性
主办：上海市国际展览有限公司
地址：上海市延安中路841号东方海外大厦8楼（200040）

**China International Offshore Wind Energy & Wind Energy Industry Chain Conference and Exhibition**
Venue: Shanghai International Exhibition Center；Sheraton Grand Tai Ping Yang Hotel, Shanghai
Frequency: Annual
Market Area: International
Organizer: Shanghai International Exhibition Co Ltd
Address: 8/F OOCL Plaza, 841 Yan An Zhong Rd, Shanghai 200040, China

2010/06/08-10
☎ 021-5406 5152, 5406 5305
🖷 021-5406 5150
✉ msh@stcec.com
syq@stcec.com
www.no-digsh.com
2610

上海国际非开挖技术展览会暨研讨会
地点：东亚展览馆，上海
内容：工程机械，非开挖机械设备制造商、材料制造、供应商、施工企业及相关协会
始办年份：2006
周期：两年一届
市场范围：国际性
性质：面向公众
上届规模‘08：展览面积5,000m²(国外展商面积2,000m²)，参展商80家（国外展商30家，来自9个国家），参观人数6,000人
主办：上海市非开挖技术协会；上海科技会展有限公司
地址：上海市徐汇区钦州路100号2号楼308室（200235）
联系人：宓小姐，宋小姐

2010 No-Dig Shanghai
Venue: East Asia Exhibition Hall, Shanghai
Established Year: 2006
Frequency: Biennial
Market Area: International
Nature: Open to public
Statistics '08: Exhibition Area 5,000m²(foreigners 2,000m²), Exhibitors 80（foreigners 30, came from 9 countries）, Visitors 6,000
Organizer: Shanghai Society for Trenchless Technology (CSSTT); Shanghai Technology Convention & Exhibition Co Ltd (STCEC)
Address: Room 308, Building 2, 100 Qinzhou Rd, Xuhui District, Shanghai, 200235
Contact: Ms Michelle Mi, Ms Carry Song

2010/06/08-10
☎ 021-5445 1965,
5445 1166转ext 1965
🖷 021-5445 1968,
5445 1166转ext 1968
✉ ghzlwg@126.com
www.shssny.com
2620

2010第九届中国（上海）国际纺织品面辅料博览会
地点：上海新国际博览中心，上海
内容：面料、辅料、纱线、家用纺织品、纺织原料等；
始办年份：2002
周期：每年一届
市场范围：国际性
入场券价格：专业人士免费
参展费用：8,800元
上届规模‘09：展览面积26,000m²(国外展商面积5,800m²)，参展商687家（国外展商116家，来自23个国家），参观人数34,200人（专业贸易观众26,780人）

2010 9th China (Shanghai) Intl Textile, Fabrics & Accessories Exhibition
Venue: Shanghai New International Expo Center, Shanghai
Profile: Fabrics; Textile raw materials; Yarns; Auxiliary materials; Textiles & home
textiles; Design and production systems
Established Year: 2002
Frequency: Annual
Market Area: International
Cost to Attend: Free to Professional and Trade Visitors
Participated Fee: RMB 8,800/booth

主办：中国同源有限公司
承办：上海歌华展览服务有限公司
地址：上海市田州路99号新安大楼1206-1208室（200235）
联系人：王刚，梁婷
QQ：524234216

Statistics '09: Exhibition Area 26,000m²(foreigners 5,800m²), Exhibitors 687 (foreigners 116, came from 23 countries), Visitors 34,200 (trade visitors 26,780)
Sponsor: China Tongyuan I/E Group
Organizer: Shanghai Gehua Exhibition Service Co
Address: Rm. 1206-08, Xin' an Mansion, No. 99 Tianzhou Road, Shanghai, China
Contact: WANG GANG, LIANG TING

---

2010/06/08-10
☎ 021-5058 0707转ext 817/883
🖷 021-5058 7345
✉ tlC@mmi-shanghai.com
2630

中国国际物流、交通运输及远程信息处理博览会
地点：上海新国际博览中心，上海
主办：慕尼黑展览（上海）有限公司

transport logistic China
Venue: Shanghai New International Expo Center, Shanghai
Organizer: MMI Shanghai

---

2010/06/09-11
☎ 010-5933 9329, 8515 1373
✉ alu@reedexpo.com.cn
valu@reedexpo.com.cn
www.aluminiumchina.com
2650

**2010年中国国际铝工业展览会**
地点：上海新国际博览中心，上海
内容：继去年成功吸引13,000位专业人士聚首申城后，中国国际铝工业展览会将于2010年6月9日至11日在上海新国际博览中心第六次打造服务于铝及铝相关应用产业链的亚洲第一铝业商务平台。借力同城举办的2010年世博会，本届展会将吸引更多国内外专业人士到场参观，在展现铝业盎然生机之余，为世界铝业同仁领略上海这一"世界之城"的独特魅力创造了绝佳机会！
2010年中国国际铝工业展览会，您不容错过的世界铝业之旅！
周期：每年一届
主办：励展博览集团
☎ 010-5933 9329（参展），8515 1373（参观）
✉ alu@reedexpo.com.cn（参展）
valu@reedexpo.com.cn（参观）

**ALUMINIUM CHINA 2010**
Venue: Shanghai New International Expo Center, Shanghai
Profile: Successfully gathering 13,000 professionals in Shanghai in 2009, ALUMINIUM CHINA will continue to take place at SNIEC, from June 9 to 11, 2010, leading the ALUMINIUM Global events together with ALUMINIUM 2010 in Germany.In its 6th presentation, ALUMINIUM CHINA 2010 will engage the Aluminum and Application communities with superb business opportunities, witnessing a surge in the number of visitors coming from across the country and around the world through running in parallel with the World EXPO 2010. Professional visitors will be drawn to the city to take an extended stay where they will be able to celebrate developments in the aluminum industry while simply enjoy themselves in the 'City of celebration' that Shanghai will become.
Frequency: Annual
Organizer: Reed Exhibitions
☎ 010-5933 9329 (for exhibiting), 8515 1373 (for visiting)
✉ alu@reedexpo.com.cn (for exhibiting),
valu@reedexpo.com.cn (for exhibiting)

---

2010/06/10-12
☎ 010-5836 2058, 5836 2059
🖷 010-5836 2050
✉ whyp@ccagm.org.cn
www.ccagm.org.cn
www.zbxfair.com.cn
2680

第104届中国文化用品商品交易会
暨中国国际制笔文具博览会
地点：上海新国际博览中心，上海
内容：学生用品、文教用品、现代办公及教学仪器设备、办公用品、电脑及IT数码产品、纸与纸制品、文房四宝、印刷与包装用品、照像器材、测量测绘用品、体育与健身器材、休闲娱乐用品、文具礼品与赠品、旅游用品、美术绘画用品、书写工具及生产设备、配件、办公耗材、办公家具、办公室用品、办公日杂品等
周期：每年一届
市场范围：全国性
入场券价格：免费
参展费用：6,000～12,000元/展位
上届规模 '09：展览面积22,000m²
主办：中国百货商业协会；中国制笔协会
承办：中百协（北京）会展有限公司
地址：北京市西城区丰汇园11号楼丰汇时代大厦东翼12层（100032）
联系人：梁智青，李楠

The 104th China Stationery Commodity Fair
Venue: Shanghai New International Expo Center, Shanghai
Profile: Education Products, Office Automation Related Products and Accessories, DataProcessing Accessories, Planning, Presentation and Conference materials, Office Supplies, Financial Organization Systems, Organizing Systems, Adhesives, Rubber Stamps, Promotional Materials, Technical Stationery Paper, Writing Instruments and Accessories, Technical Drawing Material, Desk Accessories, Business Luggage, Calendars, School supplies, Albums, Postcards and Greeting Cards, Packaging, Gift Wrap Papers, Graphic Arts and Artists Materials, Hobby Supplies, Table Decorations, Party and Festive Articles, Fancy Articles etc.
Frequency: Annual
Market Area: National
Cost to Attend: Free
Participated Fee: RMB 6,000-12,000/booth
Statistics '09: Exhibition Area 22,000m²
Sponsor: China Commerce Assn for General Merchandise (CCAGM); China Writing Instrument Assn Organizer: CCAGM (Beijing) Exhibition Co Ltd
Address: 12/F East Wing, Bldg 11, Fenghui Time, Fenghuiyuan, Xicheng Dist, Beijing
Contact: Liang Zhiqing, Li Nan

---

2010/06/16-18
☎ 024-2585 0149,
2585 2311转ext 356
🖷 024-2585 5793
✉ cxm@foundrynations.com
www.foundrynations.com
2710

第七届中国国际压铸会议暨展览会
地点：上海国际展览中心，上海
内容：凡与压铸、低压铸造、挤压铸造、金属型铸造、半固态加工有关的设备、产品与技术皆可展示。
始办年份：1997
周期：每年一届
市场范围：国际性
参展费用：标准展位2,700美元，净地270美元/m²
上届规模 '08：展览面积4,000m²(国外展商面积2,000m²)，参展商150家（国外展商70家，来自14个国家），参观人数5,000人（专业贸易观众3,000人）
主办：中国机械工程学会铸造分会
地址：辽宁省沈阳市铁西区云峰南街17号（110022）
联系人：曹秀梅
QQ：460361759

7th China Intl Diecasting Congress & Exhibition
Venue: Shanghai International Exhibition Center, Shanghai
Profile: New materials, equipment, technology and technique for diecasting (HP, LP, Grav), differential-pressure diecasting, squeeze casting, semi-solid processing.
Established Year: 1997
Frequency: Annual
Market Area: International
Participated Fee: Standard Booth USD 2,700, Raw Space USD 270
Statistics '08: Exhibition Area 4,000m²(foreigners 2,000m²), Exhibitors 150 (foreigners 70, came from 14 countries), Visitors 5,000 (trade visitors 3,000)
Organizer: Chinese Mechanical Engineering Society
Address: 17 South Yunfeng Street, Tiexi District, Shenyang 110022, China
Contact: Xiumei Cao

2010/06/21-23
☎ 021-6279 2828
℻ 021-6545 5124
✉ info@siec-ccpit.com
www.siec-ccpit.com
2720

**2010中国上海国际汽车零部件展览会**
**地点**：上海新国际博览中心，上海
**内容**：发动机、车身、底盘（制动、传动、转向、行使）、电子电器、汽车影音、汽车通讯、汽车安全系统、通用件、汽车（内外）饰品、汽车后市场用品、检测检修设备。
**始办年份**：1996
**周期**：每年一届
**市场范围**：国际性
**主办**：上海市国际展览有限公司
**地址**：上海市延安中路841号东方海外大厦8楼（200040）

**Auto Components Shanghai 2010**
**Venue**: Shanghai New International Expo Center, Shanghai
**Established Year**: 1996
**Frequency**: Annual
**Market Area**: International
**Organizer**: Shanghai International Exhibition Co
**Address**: 8/F, OOCL Plaza, 841 Yan An Zhong Road, Shanghai 200040, China

2010/06/22-24
☎ 010-8455 6622, 8455 6623
✉ expolab@reedsinopharm.com
www.expolab.com.cn
2740

**第60届中国实验室技术及装备交易会**
**地点**：上海光大会展中心，上海
**内容**：Expolab是中国试剂领域最大、最有影响力的权威展会。每届展会吸引超过300家的参展企业及至少10000人次的专业观众积极参与。成为目前国内最具活力和竞争力的实验室范畴展会之一。
**展品范围**：科学仪器、试剂/耗材领域、玻璃制品和软技术等领域。
**观众范围**：实验室领域相关生产商及采购商、科研院所实验室管理者及科研人员、食品、医药领域研发及质量控制人员、疾病控制系统人员、检验检疫机构人员以及大中院校相关专业老师和研究生等专业群体。
**周期**：每年一届
**上届规模'09**：参展商 330家，专业贸易观众6,033人
**主办**：国药励展展览有限责任公司

**60th EXPOLAB**
60th China Laboratory Technology and Equipment Exhibition
**Venue**: Shanghai Everbright Convention and Exhibition, Shanghai
**Profile**: Expolab, with its long outstanding history, is the leading exhibition for laboratory and scientific equipment, chemical reagents, and testing/analytical equipment for its buyers, laboratory management and pharmaceutical/cosmetic/food manufacturers. It is the hub for laboratory solutions in China. The exhibition is held annually and attracts more than 300 exhibiting companies and over 10,000 visitors.
**Exhibits**: Laboratory reagents, laboratory equipment, laboratory instruments, laboratory expendables, laboratory furnishings, related software, books, periodicals, media, and products used in college laboratories, clinical testing, drug analyzing and test and measurement among others.
**Visitors**: Buyers, researchers from R&D institutes, specialized analysts, clinical testing doctors, quality control specialists, scientific professors and students in universities, related government officials, media and consultancies.
**Frequency**: Annual
**Statistics '09**: Exhibitors 330, Visitors 6,033
**Organizer**: Reed Sinopharm Exhibitions Co Ltd

2010/06/22-26
☎ 010-8522 9405, 8522 9372
℻ 010-8522 9480
✉ ss@ccpittex.com
gaoyang@ccpittex.com
www.citme.com.cn
2750

**2010中国国际纺织机械展览会暨ITMA亚洲展览会**
**地点**：上海新国际博览中心，上海
**内容**：各类纺织机械、器材及零部件
**始办年份**：1988
**周期**：两年一届
**市场范围**：国际性
**上届规模'08**：展览面积103,500m²(国外展商面积55, 000m²), 参展商1,368家（国外展商752家，来自30个国家），专业贸易观众90, 000人
**主办**：中国贸促会纺织行业分会；中国纺织机械器材工业协会；中国国际展览中心集团公司；欧洲纺织机械制造商委员会
**承办**：北京泰格斯特国际展览展示有限公司
**地址**：北京东长安街12号426室（100742）
**联系人**：石爽，高杨

**ITMA ASIA+CITME2010**
**Venue**: Shanghai New International Expo Center, Shanghai
**Profile**: Textile Machinery, Auxiliary Machinery and accessories
**Established Year**: 1988
**Frequency**: Biennial
**Market Area**: International
**Statistics '08**: Exhibition Area 103,500m²(foreigners 55,000m²), Exhibitors 1,368 (foreigners 752, came from 30 countries), Trade Visitors 90,000
**Organizer**: The Sub-Council of Textile Industry CCPIT; China Textile Machinery Assn (CTMA); China Intl Exhibition Center Group Corp (CIEC); Le Comité Européen Des Constructeurs de Machines Textiles (CEMATEX)
**Sponsor**: Beijing Textile Machinery Intl Exhibition Co Ltd
**Address**: Room 426, No.12 East Chang An Street, Beijing, P.R. of China
**Contact**: Ms Shi Shuang, Ms Gao Yang

2010/06/24-25
☎ 021-5134 2588
℻ 021-5134 2515
✉ an.jun@ubexpo-shanghai.com
www.apic.net.cn
2770

**第六届亚洲不动产投资峰会**
**地点**：上海环球金融中心，上海
**内容**：全球资本进入中国房地产的首选窗口,汇聚行业政策决策、项目开发、项目经营、投融资安排实务操作经验的首选平台,中国房地投融资最高级别的私密社交圈
**始办年份**：2006
**周期**：每年一届
**市场范围**：国际性
**主办**：优博集团；中国房地产报
**承办**：上海优博国际展览有限公司
**地址**：上海市浦东新区福山路458号11楼I座（200122）
**联系人**：安君

**Asia Property Investment Showcase & Conference**
**Venue**: Shanghai World Financial Center, Shanghai
**Profile**: APIC is catered to meet different needs of Chinese developers during their project development and company growth, specifically in the fields of cooperation channels, cooperative development, equity financing, merger and acquisition, brand collaboration, company IPO, integral transfer and the operation and management of lease-only property
**Established Year**: 2006
**Frequency**: Annual
**Market Area**: International
**Sponsor**: UB Group; China Real Estate Business
**Organizer**: Shanghai YUBO International Exhibition Co
**Address**: I-11F Tong Sheng Tower, 458 Fu Shan Road, Shanghai
**Contact**: Angela

2010/06/25-27
☎ 021-3408 0618
🖷 021-5430 6576
www.chinadigitalsignage.org
www.selfservicechina.com
2780

**2010第七届中国国际自动售货系统及商用自助服务产品展**
2010第二届上海国际数字标牌及触摸查询技术展览会
2010上海互动多媒体信息技术及虚拟仿真产品展览会暨
大屏幕投影显示、数字会议系统产品展览会
**地点：**上海国际展览中心，上海
**主办：**上海天盛会展服务有限公司

**7th China Intl Vending & Kiosk Show**
Shanghai Intl Digital Signage & Touch Inquiry Technology Show 2010
**Venue:** Shanghai International Exhibition Center, Shanghai
**Organizer:** Shanghai Tiansheng Exhibition Service Co Ltd

---

2010/06/26-28
☎ 027-8736 2945，5852 7126
🖷 021-5852 6905
✉ loretta@hope-tarsus.com
www.wenwu360.com
2790

**2010第二届中国仿古工艺品及技术展览会**
**地点：**上海浦东展览馆，上海
**主办：**中国文物学会；上海好博塔苏斯展览有限公司
**联系人：**余云成

**China Archaistic Craft & Technology Exhibition Expo**
**Venue:** Shanghai Pudong Exhibition, Shanghai
**Organizer:** Shanghai Tarsus Hope Exhibition Co Ltd

---

2010/07/01-04
☎ 021-6279 2828，6289 6819
🖷 021-6545 5124
✉ interphoto@siec-ccpit.com
info@siec-ccpit.com
www.interphoto.com.cn
www.siec-ccpit.com
2810

第十二届中国(上海)国际摄影器材和数码影像展览会
PHOTO & IMAGING SHANGHAI 2010
The 12th China Shanghai Interphoto & Digital Imaging Exhibition
2010年7月1日-4日 上海光大会展中心

**第十二届中国（上海）国际摄影器材和数码影像展览会**
**地点：**上海光大会展中心，上海
**内容：**照相机和摄像机，拍照手机，扫描仪，相机配件，数字存储媒体，胶卷，摄影工作室设备，照明技术和照明产品，图像处理软件，数字成像和出版，大型实验室和彩扩机系统，照片成像亭，在线影像服务，相册和相框，摄影娱乐产品，家庭打印，大幅面打印，美术印刷，打印和冲印材料　幻灯片技术，视频和电影技术，大尺寸屏幕，投影，媒体控制，家庭娱乐，移动影像，影像服务，其他影像产品
**周期：**每年一届
**市场范围：**国际性
**主办：**上海市国际展览有限公司
**地址：**上海市延安中路841号东方海外大厦8楼（200040）

**PHOTO & IMAGING SHANGHAI 2010**
12th China Shanghai Interphoto & Digital Imaging Exhibition
**Venue:** Shanghai Everbright Convention & Exhibition Center, Shanghai
**Profile:** Cover Imaging Input, Equipments & Consumables, Components & Accessories, Imaging Storage, Imaging Process, Imaging output etc. product and Service.
**Frequency:** Annual
**Market Area:** International
**Organizer:** Shanghai International Exhibition Co
**Address:** 8/F, OOCL Plaza, 841 Yan An Zhong Road, Shanghai 200040, China

---

2010/07/01-04
☎ 021-6279 2828，6289 6819
🖷 021-6545 5124
✉ interphoto@siec-ccpit.com
info@siec-ccpit.com
www.interphoto.com.cn
www.siec-ccpit.com
2820

**第十八届中国上海国际婚纱摄影器材展览会暨**
**国际儿童摄影、主题摄影展览会(秋季)**
**地点：**上海国际展览中心；上海世贸商城；上海光大会展中心，上海
首届
**周期：**每年一届
**市场范围：**国际性
**主办：**上海市国际展览有限公司
**地址：**上海市延安中路841号东方海外大厦8楼（200040）

**The 18th China (Shanghai) International Wedding Photographic Equipment Exhibition & International Children's Photography, Theme Photography Exhibition (Autumn)**
**Venue:** Shanghai International Exhibition Center; Shanghai Mart; Shanghai Everbright Convention and Exhibition Center, Shanghai
First Session
**Frequency:** Annual
**Market Area:** International
**Organizer:** Shanghai International Exhibition Co
**Address:** 8/F, OOCL Plaza, 841 Yan An Zhong Road, Shanghai 200040, China

---

2010/07/07-10
☎ 021-5252 0202
🖷 021-6299 4922, 6299 8196
✉ feng.tian@grayexpo.com
www.grayexpo.com
2840

**2010上海国际照明展**
**地点：**上海新国际博览中心，上海
**内容：**城市亮化工程单位、照明工程公司、照明工程设计及顾问公司、物业管理单位、园林设计管理单位、市政工程公司、政府机构、政府节能环保部门、市政管理机构、市政/路灯道路建设公司、文化体育场馆、工业园区、机杨、港口、铁路、车站、交通、金融、证券、酒店、宾馆、房地产、邮政、商场、购物中心、连锁超市、餐饮机构、娱乐机构、医院、学校、部队、探险、工厂、展览馆、建筑装饰设计院所及公司、工程承包商、广告装饰工程公司、户外广告制作商、照明产品批发、零售、出口、代理商、国内外LED行业相关单位、供应商、贸易商、经销商。
**主办：**上海市科学技术委员会；世博集团
**承办：**上海新格雷展览服务有限公司；国家半导体照明工程上海产业化基地
**联系人：**田烽，先生

**SHANGHAI INTL LIGHTING EXPO 2010**
**Venue:** Shanghai New International Expo Center, Shanghai
**Organizer:** Shanghai Gray Exhibition Co Ltd

---

2010/07/07-10
☎ 021-6328 8899
🖷 021-6374 9188
www.chinamie.com
2870

**2010上海国际数字营销展览会**
**地点：**上海新国际博览中心，上海
**主办：**上海现代国际展览有限公司

**Shanghai Intl Digital Media Exhibition 2010**
**Venue:** Shanghai New International Expo Center, Shanghai
**Organizer:** World Expo (Group) Shanghai Modern International Exhibition Co Ltd

2010/07/07-10
☎ 021-5252 0202, 6328 8899
🖷 021-6299 4922
✉ feng.tian@grayexpo.com
ada@apppexpo.com
www.grayexpo.com
http//exhibition.apppexpo.com
2890

**第十八届上海国际印刷包装展览会**
**2010上海国际印刷包装产品交易会**
**地点**：上海新国际博览中心，上海
**内容**：印前、数字快速印刷，胶印、轮转印刷，CTP、印艺图像、多媒体技术、数字印刷及打样技术、DI技术、快速印刷技术设备；轮转、胶印、印刷机械设备器材；印刷信息网络传输设备；纸张、油墨、版材、耗材。标签、商标、柔印、凹印、丝网、特种印刷 标签、商标印刷机械设备；丝网及特种印刷技术设备、制版技术；不干胶印刷设备及耗材；柔印凹印制版雕版技术设备；柔印凹印、软包装印刷机械设备；防伪技术设备；射频识别标签技术设备；检测仪器设备；相关材料
**参展费用**：标准展位9m²：A区12,000元，B区10,000元，C区7,500元；净地：A区1,200元/m²，B区1,000元，C区750元
**主办**：上海新格雷展览有限公司
**地址**：上海陕西北路1438号财富时代大厦407室（200060）
**主办**：上海现代国际展览有限公司

**Shanghai Intl Print Exhibition 2010**
**Venue**: Shanghai New International Expo Center, Shanghai
**Participated Fee**: Standard Booth RMB 12,000/9m², Raw Space RMB 750/m²
**Organizer**: World Expo (Group) Shanghai Modern International Exhibition Co Ltd
☎ 86-21-6328 8899
🖷 86-21-6374 9188
✉ ada@apppexpo.com
http//exhibition.apppexpo.com

2010/07/07-10
☎ 021-6328 8899, 5252 0202
🖷 021-6374 9188, 6299 4922
✉ feng.tian@grayexpo.com
www.grayexpo.com
http//exhibition.apppexpo.com
2910

**2010上海国际展览展示、POP及商用设施展览会**
2010上海国际广告技术设备展览会
**地点**：上海新国际博览中心，上海
**内容**：展览展示器材、销售推广及促销器材、货架及商品展示、商用大卖场装饰材料及产品、商业自动化技术设备、商业空间设计及装饰技术设备数字印刷喷绘技术设备、打印机及耗材、标识、标牌设备及标识标牌、展览展示、POP及商用设施、商业空间设计及装饰技术设备、店面橱窗设计与装修**主办**：上海新格雷展览服务有限公司；上海现代国际展览有限公司
**联系人**：田烽
**主办**：上海现代国际展览有限公司

**Shanghai International Displaying, POP and Commercial Facility Exhibition 2010**
**Venue**: Shanghai New International Expo Center, Shanghai
**Organizer**: World Expo (Group) Shanghai Modern International Exhibition Co Ltd

2010/07/07-10
☎ 021-6328 8899
🖷 021-6374 9188
www.chinamie.com
2920

**2010上海国际零售业展览会**
**地点**：上海新国际博览中心，上海
**内容**：商业空间设计及展示技术设备、现代零售设备、零售信息技术和销售推广技术及促销用品
**主办**：上海现代国际展览有限公司

**2010 Shanghai International Retail Exhibition**
**Venue**: Shanghai New International Expo Center, Shanghai
**Organizer**: World Expo (Group) Shanghai Modern International Exhibition Co Ltd

2010/07/07-10
☎ 021-5252 0202，6328 8899
🖷 021-6299 4922，6374 9188
✉ feng.tian@grayexpo.com
ada@apppexpo.com
www.grayexpo.com
http//exhibition.apppexpo.com
2940

**2010上海国际户外广告发光体技术及城市景观照明设备展览会**
中国（上海）国际LED产业展暨LED发光体及城市照明展
**地点**：上海新国际博览中心，上海
**内容**：户外广告发光体技术设备，户外大屏幕显示技术及应用系统设备，户外照明设备
**内容**：城市亮化工程单位、照明工程公司、照明工程设计及顾问公司、物业管理单位、园林设计管理单位、市政工程公司、政府机构、政府节能环保部门、市政管理机构、市政/路灯道路建设公司、文化体育场馆、工业园区、机杨、港口、铁路、车站、交通、金融、证券、酒店、宾馆、房地产、邮政、商场、购物中心、连锁超市、餐饮机构、娱乐机构、医院、学校、部队、探险、工厂、展览馆、建筑装饰设计院所及公司、工程承包商、广告装饰工程公司、户外广告制作商、照明产品批发、零售、出口、代理商、国内外LED行业相关单位、供应商、贸易商、经销商。
**周期**：每年一届
**上届规模**‘09：参观人数95,775人
**主办**：上海市科学技术委员会；世博集团
**承办**：上海新格雷展览服务有限公司；国家半导体照明工程上海产业化基地
**联系人**：田烽，先生
**主办**：上海现代国际展览有限公司

**Shanghai Intl Outdoor AD Illuminating & City Lighting Technology & Equipment Exhibition 2010**
China (Shanghai) Intl LED Industry City Lighting Expo
**Venue**: Shanghai New International Expo Center, Shanghai
**Frequency**: Annual
**Statistics** ‘09: Visitors 95,775
**Organizer**: World Expo (Group) Shanghai Modern International Exhibition Co Ltd
**电话**：86-21-6328 8899
**传真**：86-21-6374 9188
**邮箱**：ada@apppexpo.com
http//exhibition.apppexpo.com

2010/07/07-10
☎ 021-6328 8899
🖷 021-6374 9188
www.chinamie.com
2950

**2010上海国际纸业展览会暨生活用纸展览会**
**地点**：上海新国际博览中心，上海
**内容**：纸业、纸制品加工技术、设备及纸制品
**主办**：上海现代国际展览有限公司

**Shanghai Paper & Life Paper 2010**
**Venue**: Shanghai New International Expo Center, Shanghai
**Organizer**: World Expo (Group) Shanghai Modern International Exhibition Co Ltd

2010/07/07-10
☎ 021-6328 8899
🖷 021-6374 9188
www.chinamie.com
2960

**2010上海国际标签展览会**
**地点**：上海新国际博览中心，上海
**内容**：商业标签
**主办**：上海现代国际展览有限公司

**Label Shanghai 2010**
**Venue**: Shanghai New International Expo Center, Shanghai
**Organizer**: World Expo (Group) Shanghai Modern International Exhibition Co Ltd

2010/07/07-10
☎ 021-6328 8899
🖷 021-6374 9188
✉ ada@apppexpo.com
www.chinamie.com
http//exhibition.apppexpo.com
2970

**2010上海国际数码及快速印刷设备展览会**
**地点**：上海新国际博览中心，上海
**内容**：数码及快速印刷设备
**主办**：上海现代国际展览有限公司

**Shanghai Intl Digital & Express Printing Exhibition 2010**
**Venue**: Shanghai New International Expo Center, Shanghai
**Organizer**: World Expo (Group) Shanghai Modern International Exhibition Co Ltd

2010/07/14-16
☎ 021-6209 5209
🖷 021-6209 5210, 62095232
✉ Margaret@chinaallworld.com
lily@chinaallworld.com
www.propakchina.net
3010

第十六届中国国际加工、包装及印刷科技展览
地点：上海新国际博览中心，上海
内容：食品、肉类、乳制品、化妆品、消费品和工业用品塑料、纸张、金属、玻璃和药品等加工、包装和印刷科技
始办年份：1981
周期：每年一届
市场范围：国际性
入场券价格：免费
参展费用：标准展位70美元/$m^2$，净地350美元/$m^2$
上届规模 '09：展览面积28,750$m^2$，参展商429家（来自22个国家），专业贸易观众14,046人
主办：华汉国际会议展览（上海）有限公司
地址：上海市长宁区仙霞路318-322号鑫达大厦2402室（200336）
联系人：张远渊，张昳文

ProPak China 2010
Venue: Shanghai New International Expo Center, Shanghai
Profile: Food, Meat, Dairy, Cosmetic, Consumer & Industrial, Plastic, Paper, Metal, Glass & Pharmaceutical Processing, Packaging & Printing Technology
Established Year: 1981
Frequency: Annual
Market Area: International
Cost to Attend: Free
Participated Fee: Standard Booth USD 70/$m^2$, Raw Space USD 350/$m^2$
Statistics '09: Exhibition Area 28,750$m^2$, Exhibitors 429 (came from 22 countries), Trade Visitors 14,046
Organizer: China International Exhibitions Ltd
Address: Room A2402-03, Singular Mansion, No.318-322 Xian Xia Road, Shanghai 200336, China
Contact: Ms Margaret Zhang, Ms Susan Zhang

2010/07/15-18
☎ 021-5239 6999, 5155 3629
🖷 021-5101 0002
✉ marketing@eastpo.net
www.eastpo.net
3040

2010年第12上海国际机床展（东博展）
地点：上海新国际博览中心，上海
内容：金切机床、功能部件及配件、锻压激光钣金、刀具测量仪；自动化控制与动力传动；机床热加工技术与设备；相关制造技术与设备等。
始办年份：1999
周期：每年一届
市场范围：国际性
性质：面向公众
入场券价格：免费
参展费用：标准展位10,800元/9㎡
上届规模 '09：展览面积74,000$m^2$(国外展商面积20,000$m^2$)，参展商1,023家（国外展商307家，来自54个国家），参观人数97,326人
主办：国家国防科技工业局信息中心；中国社会经济调查研究中心；东博国际控股有限公司
承办：上海东博展览有限公司
地址：上海市愚园路1258号绿地商务大厦1201室（200050）
联系人：高玉晓，陈卫
QQ：935084254

12th Shanghai International Machine Tool Fair - Eastpo 2010
Venue: Shanghai New International Expo Center, Shanghai
Profile: Machines; Forming Facilities; Machine tool electrical apparatuses & Control System; Machine tool & Attachments; New technique, materials, equipments for Machinery making.
Established Year: 1999
Frequency: Annual
Market Area: International
Nature: Open to public
Cost to Attend: Free
Participated Fee: Standard Booth RMB 10,800/9㎡
Statistics '09: Exhibition Area 74,000$m^2$(foreigners 20,000$m^2$), Exhibitors 1,023 (foreigners 307, came from 54 countries), Visitors 97,326
Organizer: CCPIT Machinery Sub-Council; China Social Economic Investigation & Research Center; EASTPO International Holding Co Ltd
Sponsor: EASTPO International Expo Co Ltd
Contact: Jane, David

2010/07/21-23
☎ 0571-9939 3239, 8839 3237
🖷 0571-9939 3239, 8839 8829
www.cbmexpo.com/index.asp
3050

上海国际儿童、婴儿、孕妇产品博览会
上海儿童服装及服饰博览会
地点：上海新国际博览中心，上海
主办：杭州澄心广告有限公司

2010 Shanghai International Children-Baby-Maternity Products Expo
Venue: Shanghai New International Expo Center, Shanghai
Organizer: Hangzhou Chengxin Advertising Co Ltd

2010/07/22-24
☎ 13044112901
🖷 021-5499 9745
✉ lmaxim@163.com
www.fair.3u.cn
3060

第104届中国日用百货商品交易会
地点：上海新国际博览中心，上海
内容：生活用品、日杂用品、家用塑料制品、清洁用品、家用竹木制品、厨房用具、床上用品等
周期：每年一届
市场范围：全国性
性质：面向公众
上届规模 '09：展览面积50,000$m^2$，参展商1,200家（国外展商200家，来自12个国家），参观人数50,000人
主办：中国百货商业协会
承办：中百协（北京）会展有限公司
地址：上海市闵行区莲花南路1108弄 58栋 701室（201100）
联系人：刘铭
MSN：shlmcn@hotmail.com
QQ：1187230500

104th China Daily-Use Articles Trade Fair & China Modern Home Expo
Venue: Shanghai New International Expo Center, Shanghai
Profile: Domestic Electrical Appliance, Home Furniture, Home Fabrics, Domestics Hardware, Handicrafts, Gifts & Presents, Gardening & Outdoor Sports Equipments, Tour Equipments, Articles for Bathing Room, Cleaning Products, Health & Personal Care, Kitchen & Tableware, Stainless Steel Products, Glass wares, Plastics, Porcelain & Enamelware, Articles for Hotel, Suitcases, Handbags & Leathers, Rain Gears, Smoke Sets, Tea Sets, Toys, headwear, and relevant Materials and Mechanism.
Frequency: Annual
Market Area: National
Nature: Open to public
Statistics '09: Exhibition Area 50,000$m^2$, Exhibitors 1,200 (foreigners 200, came from 12 countries), Visitors 50,000
Sponsor: China Commerce Assn for General Merchandise
Organizer: CCAGM Exhibition Co Ltd, Beijing
Address: Room 701, No.58, Lane 1108, Xinhua South Road, Minhang District, Shanghai, China
Contact: Mr Liu Ming
MSN: shlmcn@hotmail.com

2010/07/29-01
☎ 010-5165 9355
🖷 010-8773 2633
www.chinajoy.net
3090

中国国际数码互动娱乐产品及技术应用展览会
地点：上海新国际博览中心，上海
主办：北京汉威信恒展览有限公司

China Joy
7th China Digital Entertainment Expo & Conference
Venue: Shanghai New International Expo Center, Shanghai
Organizer: Howell International Trade Fair Ltd.

2010/08/02-04
☎ 010-8460 0906, 13522602557
🖷 010-8460 0910
✉ niuna226@163.com
3110

**第十届中国（上海）国际墙纸、地毯、布艺展览会暨中国国际家居软装饰博览会**

**地点：** 上海光大会展中心，上海

**内容：** 经过九年的发展，本届展会已发展成为亚洲专业强、规模大、成交量高的墙纸、地毯、布艺行业盛宴。展会"国际化、专业化、品牌化、规模化"的形象在业界独树一帜，在业界具有举足轻重的贸易地位。北京中装华港公司具有多年的组展办展专业团队，不断创新变革，增加新的元素。2009年，与杭州市余杭家纺协会深度合作，大力开发布艺、地毯展区，增加各类装饰布、静电植绒、手绣等布艺产品及地毯、家纺设计产品，为壁纸、布艺、地毯企业开拓市场提供了广阔的平台，进一步提升了展会价值。展示面积达到30000m²，1000余个展位。China Wallpaper中国墙纸壁布展国际化合作日益增强，74个国家和地区的优质贸易观众及200多家大众媒体、专业媒体和网站对展会进行多方位、深层次的报道，30万买家数据库和3万国际采购商的大力邀请，可使企业通过展示，在全球范围内寻找到最佳的贸易合作伙伴。壁纸系列、墙纸生产及辅料、家纺设计、地毯系列、其它各类墙饰、家居用品

**周期：** 每年一届

**市场范围：** 全国性

**性质：** 面向公众

**参展费用：** 国内企业：标准展位7,000元/9㎡，室内净地700元/㎡；合资企业：标准展位1,800元/9㎡，室内净地1,280元/㎡；海外企业：标准展位250美元/㎡，室内净地220美元/㎡

**上届规模 '：** 展览面积30,000m²

**主办：** 中国建筑装饰协会；中国国际展览中心集团公司

**承办：** 北京中装华港建筑科技展览有限公司

**地址：** 北京市朝阳区北三环东路六号国展中心一号馆四层388室（100028）

**联系人：** 牛娜

**QQ：** 1204234541

**China Wallpaper**

**Venue:** Shanghai Everbright Convention & Exhibition Center, Shanghai

**Frequency:** Annual

**Market Area:** National

**Nature:** Open to public

**Participated Fee:** International Exhibitors: Standard Booth USD 250/㎡, Raw Space USD 220/㎡

**Statistics ':** Exhibition Area 30,000m²

**Organizer:** China B & D Exhibition Co Ltd

2010/08/11-14
☎ 021-6468 1300, 6468 1550, 6328 8899
🖷 021-6468 1849
✉ hengjin98@vip.sina.com
www.shanghaiamts.com
3120

**2010上海国际汽车制造技术与装备及材料展览会**

**地点：** 上海新国际博览中心，上海

**内容：** 汽车设计与开发、汽车材料、汽车零部件制造技术及装备、车身制造工艺及装备（四大工艺装备）、装配与质量

**始办年份：** 2004

**周期：** 每年一届

**市场范围：** 全国性

**入场券价格：** 100元

**参展费用：** 国外企业3200美元/9m²，A区品牌展区3,200美元/9m²，B区国内展区13,980元/9m²，C区国内展区11,800元/9m²，D区国内展区10,900元/9m²

**上届规模 '09：** 展览面积12,500m²，参展商327家（国外展商36家，来自19个国家），参观人数12,336人

**主办：** 上海恒进展览服务有限公司；上海现代国际展览有限公司

**地址：** 上海市中山南二路999弄19号8F座（200030）

**联系人：** 杨梅，沈国磊

**MSN：** forever_expo516@sina.com

**QQ：** 375105874

**Shanghai International Automotive Manufacturing Technology & Material Show 2010**

**Venue:** Shanghai New International Expo Center, Shanghai

**Profile:** Automobile Design and Development, Automobile Material, Manufacture Technology and Equipment of Automobile Parts and Components, Bodywork Manufacture Process and Equipment (Four Major Process Equipments), Assembly and Quality

**Established Year:** 2004

**Frequency:** Annual

**Market Area:** National

**Cost to Attend:** RMB 100

**Participated Fee:** USD 3,200/9m²

**Statistics '09:** Exhibition Area 12,500m², Exhibitors 327 (foreigners 36, came from 19 countries), Visitors 12,336

**Organizer:** Shanghai FOREVER Exhibition Services Co Ltd

**Address:** 8F, Zhongshan Building, 999 Zhongshan South No.2 Road (W), Shanghai, China

**Contact:** Berry, Jeff

**MSN:** forever_expo516@sina.com

2010/08/11-14
☎ 021-6468 1300, 6468 1550
🖷 021-6468 1849
✉ hengjin98@vip.sina.com
www.shanghaiamts.com
3130

**第四届上海国际工业装配与传输技术展览会**

**地点：** 上海新国际博览中心，上海

**内容：** 装配设备、组装系统材料、装配工具、自动化设备、传感与视觉、马达和驱动、连结技术、拆分技术、机器人、监测设备、测试与质量设备、传输设备、分拣设备、仓储设备、线束、线缆、拖链、接头、空压机等通用设备

**始办年份：** 2006

**周期：** 每年一届

**市场范围：** 全国性

**入场券价格：** 100元

**参展费用：** 国外企业3200美元/9m²，A区品牌展区3,200美元/9m²，B区国内展区13,980元/9m²，C区国内展区11,800元/9m²，D区国内展区10,900元/9m²

**上届规模 '09：** 展览面积10,000m²，参展商327家（国外展商36家，来自19个国家），参观人数12,336人

**主办：** 上海恒进展览服务有限公司

**地址：** 上海市中山南二路999弄19号8F座（200030）

**联系人：** 杨梅，沈国磊

**MSN：** forever_expo516@sina.com

**QQ：** 375105874

**The 4th Shanghai International Assembly & Handling Technology Exhibition**

**Venue:** Shanghai New International Expo Center, Shanghai

**Profile:** Assembly, Assembly system materials, Assembly Tools, Automation Equipment, Sensors and vision, Motors and drives, Joining, Dismantling, Robotic, Monitoring, Testing, Handling, Separating devices, Storage and equipment, Wiring harness, cable, connector, Air Compressor and others General Equipment

**Established Year:** 2006

**Frequency:** Annual

**Market Area:** National

**Cost to Attend:** RMB 100

**Statistics '09:** Exhibition Area 10,000m², Exhibitors 327 (foreigners 36, came from 19 countries), Visitors 12,336

**Organizer:** Shanghai FOREVER Exhibition Services Co Ltd

**Address:** 8F, Zhongshan Building, 999Zhongshan South No.2 Road(w), Shanghai, China

**Contact:** Berry, Jeff

**MSN:** forever_expo516@sina.com

3150

2010/08/12-15
☎ 021-6280 7745
🖷 021-6294 7723

**第四届上海国际家用车务车展览会**
**地点：**上海新国际博览中心，上海
**内容：**家用轿车、越野车、跑车、家用旅行车、休闲车、高档商务轿车、面包车、豪华房车、顶级品牌车、商务车、suv、mpv等；各类汽车相关用品、车友会、车险联盟、金融服务等
**主办：**世博集团上海现代国际展览有限公司；上海浦东国际展览公司
**承办：**上海新力会展服务有限公司
**地址：**上海市番禺路383号601（200052）
**联系人：**王宝妮，杨颖

**Shanghai International Exhibition on Family & Commercial Auto 2010**
**Venue:** Shanghai New International Expo Center, Shanghai
Shanghai New Force Expo Service Co Ltd
**Contact:** Bonnie Wang, Maggie Yang

3160

2010/08/17-20
☎ 021-5835 6112, 6328 8899
🖷 021-5835 8105
✉ xieyuan5865@126.com
www.sbmia.org.cn

**第六届中国（上海）国际建筑节能及新型建材展览会**
**地点：**上海新国际博览中心，上海
**内容：**节能保温材料；建筑保温系统：节能门窗、幕墙；保温、隔热材料；遮阳系统；屋面系统；节电设备；建筑陶瓷节能系列产品。节水技术及设备。新能源利用：太阳能利用；热泵技术。节材产品及节能设备：新型墙体材料；结构材料墙材制造机械。节地技术
**始办年份：**1980
**周期：**每年一届
**市场范围：**全国性
**参展费用：**9,000元起
**主办：**上海市建筑材料行业协会；世博集团上海现代国际展览有限公司
**地址：**上海浦东新区张杨路800号长航大厦15A08-09室（200122）
**联系人：**谢小姐

**6th Shanghai International Energy-saving & Advanced Building Materials Exhibition**
**Venue:** Shanghai New International Expo Center, Shanghai
**Established Year:** 1980
**Frequency:** Annual
**Market Area:** National
**Participated Fee:** min RMB 9,000/booth
**Organizer:** Shanghai Building Materials Industry Assn

3170

2010/08/17-20
☎ 021-6328 8899, 5835 6112
🖷 021-6374 9188, 5835 8105
✉ kavana@chinamie.com
www.expojc.com

**2010中国（上海）国际建材及室内装饰展览会**
**地点：**上海新国际博览中心，上海
**内容：**建筑材料及室内装饰材料、技术、设备
**主办：**上海现代国际展览有限公司；上海市建筑材料行业协会

**2010 Shanghai Intl Construction Material and Indoor Decoration Exhibition**
**Venue:** Shanghai New International Expo Center, Shanghai
**Organizer:** World Expo Group Shanghai Modern International Exhibition Co Ltd

3180

2010/08/18-20
☎ 021-5152 7309
🖷 021-5152 7309
✉ gehuaexpo@vip.sina.com
www.csaeexpo.com

**第八届中国汽车用品采购交易会**
**地点：**上海光大会展中心，上海
**内容：**汽车电子：GPS车载导航仪、汽车行驶记录仪、车用吸尘器、车载免提、车载计算机、车载电话等；影音设备：汽车音响、车载电视、车载电脑、汽车功放、显示器、多媒体影音、汽车影院等；安全防盗：防盗器、摄像头、方向盘锁、雷达测速器、胎压监视系统、后视系统、汽车缓冲器等；美容护理；汽车电器；内外饰件；改装部件；环保产品
**始办年份：**2003
**周期：**每年一届
**市场范围：**国际性
**性质：**面向公众
**参展费用：**西1馆(1楼)7000～7480元/9㎡，净地(36㎡)30,600元；西2馆(2楼)5,500元/9㎡，净地（36㎡）20,000元；东馆(1楼)6,500元/9㎡,净地(36㎡)22,000元；三资企业：12,000元/$9m^2$，净地1,000元/$m^2$；国外企业2,500美元/$9m^2$，净地300美元/$m^2$
**上届规模**‘09：展览面积36,000$m^2$(国外展商面积5,000$m^2$),参展商1,500家（国外展商300家，来自22个国家），参观人数60,000人（专业贸易观众40,000人）
**主办：**上海歌华展览策划有限公司
**地址：**上海市田州路99号新安大楼1206-1208室（200233）
**联系人：**张恒
**QQ：**368491131

**The 8th China International Auto Supplies Sourcing Fair**
**Venue:** Shanghai Everbright Convention & Exhibition Center, Shanghai
**Profile:** Auto Electronics & Appliances, Video & Audio, Telecommunication; Auto Maintenance and Car Care Products; Auto Interior & Exterior, Outdoor Products; Safety and Anti-theft Products; Auto Environment-friendly
**Established Year:** 2003
**Frequency:** Annual
**Market Area:** International
**Nature:** Open to public
**Participated Fee:** Intl Exhibitors USD 2,500/$9m^2$, Raw Space USD 300/$m^2$
**Statistics** ‘09: Exhibition Area 36,000$m^2$(foreigners 5,000$m^2$), Exhibitors 1,500（foreigners 300, came from 22 countries）, Visitors 60,000（trade visitors 40,000）
**Organizer:** Shanghai Gehua Exhibition Planning Co Ltd
**Address:** Rm.1206-1208, Xin’an Building 99, Tianzhou Road, Shanghai, China
**Contact:** Zhang Heng

3190

2010/08/18-20
☎ 020-3835 8081
🖷 020-3835 8082
✉ shipbuildex@126.com
www.shipbuildex.cn

**第四届中国(上海)国际船舶工业博览会**
**暨第十五届全国海事科学技术研讨会**
**地点：**上海世贸商城，上海
**内容：**海事技术：海洋环境科学，航运、航运和港口，水利水电工程，海事法律、海事保险；船舶配套产品展：造船厂、修船厂、船舶维护与保养服务商，船内配套舾装件，船舶电力电气，泵阀及管系附件、压缩机，船舶动力系统，导航系统、通讯系统及装备，船舶技术支持与服务机构、专业媒体；造船装备展：钢材加工与机械加工，电工装备、木工机械及其他特种装备，装卸起重机械，涂装与防腐表面处理，安全防护与环保，焊接装备，切割装备，装配工具；海洋工程技术和装备：海洋钻采平台的设计和建造技术，海洋工程辅助船的设计和建造技术，海洋平台相关设备和技术，海洋水下工程技术，项目施工、海工设备安装与调试技术等。
**始办年份：**2007
**周期：**两年一届
**市场范围：**国际性

**4th Intl Shipbuilding Industry Expo Of China**
**15th National Marine Science and Technology Seminar**
**Venue:** Shanghai Mart, Shanghai
**Established Year:** 2007
**Frequency:** Biennial
**Market Area:** International
**Nature:** Open to public
**Cost to Attend:** Free
**Participated Fee:** Standard Booth RMB 9,800/booth, Raw Space RMB 1,000/$m^2$
**Statistics** ‘09: Exhibition Area 25,000$m^2$(foreigners 10,000$m^2$), Exhibitors 400（foreigners 150, came from 20 countries）, Visitors 30,000（trade visitors 10,000）
**Organizer:** Guangzhou Wellexpo Exhibition Service Co Ltd
**Address:** 18th Floor, Building G, Junyuxuan, Junjing Garden, Guangzhou, Guangdong 510665, China
**Contact:** Kevin Meng

性质：面向公众
入场券价格：免费
参展费用：标准展位9800元/个，净地1,000元/$m^2$
上届规模 '09：展览面积25,000$m^2$(国外展商面积10,000$m^2$)，参展商400家（国外展商150家，来自20个国家），参观人数30,000人（专业贸易观众10,000人）
主办：广州汇成展览服务有限公司
地址：广州市中山大道190号骏景花园骏御轩G座18B（510665）
联系人：孟祥林，谭飞荣

2010/08/24-26
☎ 010-8522 9506, 8522 9504
🖷 010-8522 9300
✉ intertextile_home@ccpittex.com
3200

第十六届中国国际家用纺织品及辅料博览会
地点：上海新国际博览中心，上海
内容：各类家用纺织品及辅料,计算机辅助设计与制造,相关出版物及网络
始办年份：1995
周期：每年一届
市场范围：国际性
上届规模 '09：展览面积103,500$m^2$(国外展商面积12,500$m^2$)，参展商872家（国外展商155家，来自24个国家），专业贸易观众36,584人
主办：中国纺织工业协会
承办：中国贸促会纺织行业分会；中国家用纺织品行业协会；法兰克福展览（香港）有限公司
地址：北京东长安街12号546室（100742）
联系人：朱勤，林英华

16th China Intl Trade Fair for Home Textiles and Accessories
Venue: Shanghai New International Expo Center, Shanghai
Profile: All kinds of hometextiles and accessories, CAD/CAM system, relevant publications &websites
Established Year: 1995
Frequency: Annual
Market Area: International
Statistics '09: Exhibition Area 103, 500$m^2$(foreigners 12,500$m^2$), Exhibitors 872（foreigners 155, came from 24 countries）, Visitors 36, 584（trade visitors 36,584）
Sponsor: China National Textile & Apparel Council
Organizer: The Sub-Council of Textile Industry CCPIT; China Home Textile Assn; Messe Frankfurt (HK) Ltd
Address: Room 546, No.12 East Chang An Street, Beijing, China
Contact: Mr Zhu Qin, Mr Lin Yinghua

2010/08/24-26
☎ 010-8522 9098, 8522 9436
🖷 010-8522 9059
✉ chinaknitting@ccpittex.com
www.chinaknitting.com.cn
3210

中国国际针织博览会
地点：上海新国际博览中心，上海
内容：内衣、文胸、毛衫、针织休闲装/运动装/T恤、塑身/健身服、泳装/沙滩装、家居服/睡衣、袜类、针织面料、针织辅料、针织机械
始办年份：2007
周期：每年一届
市场范围：国际性
上届规模 '09：展览面积12,000$m^2$，参展商163家，专业贸易观众8,500人
主办：中国纺织工业协会
承办：中国贸促会纺织行业分会
地址：北京东长安街12号450室（100742）
联系人：陈博，金俊

China International Knitting Trade Fair
Venue: Shanghai New International Expo Center, Shanghai
Profile: Lingerie/Underwear, Brassiere, Wool/Cashmere Sweater, Knitted Sportswear/Casual wear/T Shirt, Corsetry/Fitness wear, Homewear /Sleepwear, Swimwear/ Beachwear, Hosiery, Knitted Fabrics, Knitted Accessories, Knitting Machinery
Established Year: 2007
Frequency: Annual
Market Area: International
Statistics '09: Exhibition Area 12,000$m^2$, Exhibitors 163, Trade Visitors 8,500
Sponsor: China National Textile & Apparel Council
Organizer: The Sub-Council of Textile Industry CCPIT
Address: Room 450, No.12 East Chang An Street, Beijing, China
Contact: Mr Chen Bo, Ms Jin Jun

2010/08/26-29
☎ 021-6217 7777,
6280 0000转ext 309
3250

2010第四届上海进口商品博览会
地点：上海展览中心，上海
内容：上海唯一以各国进口商品为展出内容的展会。本届展会是一个在2010年上海世博会期间为各国商品进入中国市场具推广及桥梁作用的展会。
周期：每年一届
市场范围：全国性
性质：面向公众
主办：上海市商业展览办公室

The 4th Shanghai Imports Expo 2010
Venue: Shanghai Exhibition Center, Shanghai
Profile: The only exhibition which exhibits global imported products in Shanghai, the 4th exhibition during period of World Expo 2010 brings into play as promotion and a bridge for global imported products entering the Chinese market.
Frequency: Annual
Market Area: National
Nature: Open to public
Organizer: Shanghai Trade Exhibition Office
Address: Rm.7A No.788, DingXi Road, Shanghai, China
Contact: Mr Hong

2010/08/28-2010/08/30
☎ 010-8455 6677
🖷 010-8202 3887
www.dsshow.cn
3255

2010中国（上海）药店展览会
地点：上海光大会展中心，上海
内容：依托国药励展旗下的"全国药品交易会"、"中国国际医疗器械博览会"、"中国国际家庭医疗用品展览会"以及"中国国际保健博览会"中的药品、药妆、家用医疗器械、保健品的行业优势资源，通过精准的药店终端市场定位，服务于健康产品终端市场，直供药店终端的健康产品贸易平台
首届
主办：国药励展展览有限责任公司

China Drug Store Show
Venue: Shanghai Everbright Convention and Exhibition Center, Shanghai First Session
Organizer: Reed Sinopharm Exhibitions

2010/09-
☎ 010-8522 9478, 8522 9093
🖷 010-8522 9295
✉ cinte10@ccpittex.com
www.cinte.com.cn
3260

中国国际产业用纺织品及非织造布展览会
地点：上海新国际博览中心，上海
内容：设备、工艺技术、零配件；涂层及层合织物；非织造布；纤维、纱线、化纤聚合物原料；复合材料；织造布、编网、编织物、针织布；化学品（粘合剂、切片及相关化工产品）；研发和咨询机构
始办年份：1994

International Trade Fair For Technical Textiles and Nonwovens
Venue: Shanghai New International Expo Center, Shanghai
Profile: Technology Machinery and Accessories, Woven Fabrics, Laid Webs, Braiding and Knitted Fabrics, Nonwovens, Coated Textiles, Composites, Bondtec, Fibers and Yarns, Research, Development, Planning And Consultation
Established Year: 1994

周期：两年一届
市场范围：国际性
上届规模 '08：展览面积12,000m²，参展商320家（国外展商170家，来自14个国家），专业贸易观众7,249人
主办：中国纺织工业协会
承办：中国贸促会纺织行业分会；中国产业用纺织品行业协会；法兰克福展览（香港）有限公司
地址：北京东长安街12号550室（100742）
联系人：郭益理，王欣

Frequency: Biennial
Market Area: International
Statistics '08: Exhibition Area 12,000m², Exhibitors 320（foreigners 170, came from 14 countries）, Trade Visitors 7,249
Sponsor: China National Textile & Apparel Council
Organizer: The Sub-Council of Textile Industry CCPIT; China Nonwovens & Industrial Textiles Assn (CNITA); Messe Frankfurt (HK) Ltd
Address: Room 550, No.12 East Chang An Street, Beijing, China
Contact: Mr Guo Yili, Ms Wang Xin

2010/09/01-03
☎ 021-6279 2828
🖷 021-6545 5124
✉ info@siec-ccpit.com
www.siec-ccpit.com
3270

**2010上海国际智能交通论坛暨技术和应用展览会**
2010上海国际停车设备和智能系统展览会
地点：上海展览中心，上海
周期：每年一届
市场范围：国际性
主办：上海市国际展览有限公司
地址：上海市延安中路841号东方海外大厦8楼（200040）

**INTERPARKING SHANGHAI 2010**
International ITS Conference & Expo Shanghai 2010/
Venue: Shanghai Exhibition Center, Shanghai
Frequency: Annual
Market Area: International
Organizer: Shanghai International Exhibition Co
Address: 8/F, OOCL Plaza, 841 Yan An Zhong Road, Shanghai 200040, China

2010/09/01-03
☎ 852-2827 6211
🖷 852-3749 7346
✉ sales@aplf.com
www.acle.aplf.com
www.aplf.com
3290

中国国际皮革展
地点：上海新国际博览中心，上海
主办：亚太区皮革展有限公司

All China Leather Exhibitions
Venue: Shanghai New International Expo Center, Shanghai
Organizer: APLF Ltd; China Leather Industry Assn

2010/09/01-03
☎ 852-2827 6211
🖷 852-3749 7346
✉ sales@aplf.com
www.ciff.aplf.com
www.aplf.com
3300

中国国际鞋类展
暨中国国际箱包、裘革服装及服饰展
地点：上海新国际博览中心，上海
主办：亚太区皮革展有限公司

China International Footwear Fair
Moda Shanghai
Venue: Shanghai New International Expo Center, Shanghai
Organizer: APLF Ltd; China Leather Industry Assn

2010/09/01-03
☎ 010-5823 6588，5823 6572
🖷 010-5823 6567
cippe@zhenweiexpo.com
http://sh.cippe.com.cn
3310

中国（上海）国际石油石化技术装备展览会
中国（上海）国际海洋石油天然气展览会
地点：上海新国际博览中心，上海
主办：北京振威展览有限公司

China (Shanghai) Intl Petroleum & Petrochemical Technology and Equipment Exhibition
Venue: Shanghai New International Expo Center, Shanghai
Organizer: Beijing Zhenwei Exhibition Co Ltd

2010/09/02-05
☎ 021-6195 6088
🖷 021-6195 6088
✉ sally.song@vnuexhibitions.com.cn
www.petfairsh.com
3330

第十三届亚洲宠物展览会
地点：上海国际展览中心，上海
内容：宠物食品：宠物食品/宠物饲料；宠物用品：宠物服装/宠物用具/宠物笼舍/宠物玩具/宠物护理品/宠物美容用品/宠物训导用品；宠物医疗：宠物医疗设备/宠物保健用品/宠物疫苗/宠物药品/宠物医院；水族产品；园艺产品；活体宠物；其他：宠物杂志/宠物网站/宠物摄影/宠物俱乐部/宠物爱好者社团
始办年份：1997
周期：每年一届
市场范围：国际性
性质：面向公众
入场券价格：50元
上届规模 '09：展览面积5,000m²(国外展商面积1,000m²)，参展商313家（国外展商30家），参观人数23,000人（专业贸易观众8,000人）
主办：上海万耀企龙展览有限公司
地址：上海市徐汇区田林路140号26A栋 万耀企龙办公楼（200233）
联系人：宋小姐

Pet Fair Asia 2010
Venue: Shanghai International Exhibition Center, Shanghai
Profile: Pets foods; Pets products：pet clothing, pet supplies, pet cages & houses, pet toys, pet grooming products, pet nursing products, pet training products, others Veterinary; Products：pet medical treatment facilities, pet health-care products, pet vaccine, pet medicine, pet clinic; Aquaria Products：Aquariums, pumps, heaters, Illumination , filters, fish feed, fish medicine, water plants, sand, ornaments; Accessories Gardening Products; Dogs, cats, birds, ornamental fish, rabbits, tortoises, lizards, reptiles, the other small mammals; Websites, pub publications, website, photography, pet club, pet breeders
Established Year: 1997
Frequency: Annual
Market Area: International
Nature: Open to public
Cost to Attend: RMB 50:-
Statistics '09: Exhibition Area 5,000m²(foreigners 1,000m²), Exhibitors 313（foreigners 30）, Visitors 23,000（trade visitors 8,000）
Organizer: VNU Exhibitions Asia
Address: VNU House, 26A, No. 140 Tianlin Road Shanghai China
Contact: Sally Song

2010/09/07-09
☎ 021-5406 5151
🖷 021-5406 5150
✉ zl@stcec.com
www.embeddedchina.org
3340

2010中国国际嵌入式大会暨展览会
地点：上海国际会议中心，上海
内容：硬件：组件、模块、应用系统；开发工具：硬件、软件；应用软件：实时操作系统、可视化软件、网上浏览器、测试和验证软件；服务：系统开发、电子制造、咨询、培训、行业杂志
始办年份：2008
周期：每年一届
市场范围：国际性
参展费用：标准展位1,620元/$m^2$（$9m^2$），净地1,260元/$m^2$（$36m^2$起）
上届规模 '09：展览面积1,000$m^2$(国外展商面积300$m^2$)，参展商30家（国外展商7家，来自5个国家），专业贸易观众3,500人
主办：上海计算机软件技术开发中心
承办：上海科技会展有限公司
地址：上海市徐汇区钦州路100号2号楼3楼（200235）
联系人：凌晨，钟立

Embedded China 2010
Venue: Shanghai International Convention Center, Shanghai
Profile: Hardware: packages, modules, application systems; Development tools: hardware, software; Application software: real-time operation system, visualized software, net browser, testing and verification software; Service: system development, electronic manufacturing, consulting, training, magazines
Established Year: 2008
Frequency: Annual
Market Area: International
Participated Fee: Standard Booth RMB 1,620/$m^2$ （$9m^2$） ,Raw Space RMB 1,260/$m^2$ (min $36m^2$)
Statistics '09: Exhibition Area 1,000$m^2$(foreigners 300$m^2$), Exhibitors 30（foreigners 7, came from 5 countries）, Trade Visitors 3,500
Sponsor: Shanghai Development Center of Computer Software Technology
Organizer: Shanghai Technology Convention & Exhibition Co
Address: 3F, Building 2, No.100 Qinzhou Road, Xuhui District, Shanghai, China
Contact: Lynn Ling, Mark Zhong

2010/09/07-10
☎ 021-6437 1178
🖷 021-6437 0982
✉ furniture@ubmsinoexpo.com
www.furniture-china.cn
3350

第十六届中国国际家具展览会
地点：上海新国际博览中心，上海
主办：上海博华国际展览有限公司

Furniture China 2010
16th China International Furniture Expo
Venue: Shanghai New International Expo Center, Shanghai
Organizer: Shanghai UBM Sinoexpo International Exhibition Co Ltd

2010/09/07-10
☎ 021-6437 1178
🖷 021-6437 0982
✉ furniture@ubmsinoexpo.com
www.furniture-china.cn
3360

中国国际办公家具展览会
地点：上海新国际博览中心，上海
主办：上海博华国际展览有限公司

Office Furniture China 2010
Venue: Shanghai New International Expo Center, Shanghai
Organizer: Shanghai UBM Sinoexpo International Exhibition Co Ltd

2010/09/07-10
☎ 021-6437 1178
🖷 021-6437 0982
✉ furniture@ubmsinoexpo.com
www.furniture-china.cn
3370

中国国际家居饰品布艺及灯饰展览会
地点：上海新国际博览中心，上海
主办：上海博华国际展览有限公司

Finishing Fabrics & Lightings China 2010
Venue: Shanghai New International Expo Center, Shanghai
Organizer: Shanghai UBM Sinoexpo International Exhibition Co Ltd

2010/09/07-10
☎ 021-6437 1178
🖷 021-6437 0982
✉ furniture@ubmsinoexpo.com
www.furniture-china.cn
3380

中国国际橱柜展览会
地点：上海新国际博览中心，上海
主办：上海博华国际展览有限公司

Kitchen & Cabinet China 2010
Venue: Shanghai New International Expo Center, Shanghai
Organizer: Shanghai UBM Sinoexpo International Exhibition Co Ltd

2010/09/07-10
☎ 021-6437 1178
🖷 021-6437 0982
✉ furniture@ubmsinoexpo.com
www.furniture-china.cn
3400

中国国际家具生产设备及原辅材料展览会
地点：上海新国际博览中心，上海
主办：上海博华国际展览有限公司

Furniture Manufacturing & Supply China 2010
Venue: Shanghai New International Expo Center, Shanghai
Organizer: Shanghai UBM Sinoexpo International Exhibition Co Ltd

2010/09/08-12
☎ 010-5191 6862
🖷 010-5191 6859
✉ 2004@ccfa.org.cn
www.ccfa.org.cn
3410

2010国际特许加盟（上海）展览会
地点：上海国际展览中心，上海
主办：中国连锁经营协会

Franchise (Shanghai) Expo
Venue: Shanghai International Exhibition Center, Shanghai
Organizer: China Chain Store & Franchise Assn

2010/09/09-11
☎ 021-6283 3100
🖷 021-6281 4033
✉ Jingtao@jtevents.com.cn
www.jtevents.com.cn
3420

第一届（2010）上海国际美术材料展览会
地点：上海国际展览中心，上海
主办：上海精涛文化会展有限公司

Shanghai International Art Materials Exhibition
Venue: Shanghai International Exhibition Center, Shanghai
Organizer: Shanghai Jingtao Events Co Ltd

2010/09/15-17
☎ 010-6444 4135
🖷 010-6444 4135
✉ fany@icif.cn
www.icif.cn
3430

**2010（第十届）中国国际化工展览会**
**地点**：上海新国际博览中心，上海
**内容**：石油和化工综合馆：海外厂商，国内石油、石化、化工特大型企业、上市公司、贸易公司、化工园区、网络、信息与传媒等；特色展区：上市公司展区、化工园区展区。基本有机、无机化工原料馆：甲醇衍生物、乙烯、丙烯、苯系列衍生物等有机合成化学品；钡盐、镁盐、钾盐、硼化合物及硼酸盐、溴化合物、铬盐、氰化物、氟化合物、磷化合物及磷酸盐、硅化合物及硅酸盐等无机酸碱盐；活性炭、电石、炭黑、钛白粉；特色展区：磷化工展区、氟化工展区、煤化工展区；农用化学
**参展费用**：国内企业：普通展位8,800元，高配展位9,800元，特展展位10,800元，净地990元/m$^2$（min 36m$^2$）。合资企业：标准展位+黑白广告11,800元，净场1,080元/m$^2$
**主办**：中国石油和化学工业协会
**承办**：中国贸促会化工行业分会；中国化工信息中心（全国化工国际展览交流中心）
**地址**：北京市和平街北口樱花东街5号（100029）
**联系人**：范颖

**ICIF China 2010**
10th China International Chemical Industry Fair
**Venue**: Shanghai New International Expo Center, Shanghai
**Participated Fee**: Standard Booth RMB 11,800, Raw Space RMB 1,080/m$^2$
**Organizer**: China Chemical Industry Information Center

2010/09/15-17
☎ 021-5523 3699
🖷 021-5523 3900
✉ puchina.sh@163.com
www.puchina.org
3440

**上海聚氨酯展览会/阻燃展/复合材料展**
**地点**：上海新国际博览中心，上海
**主办**：中国塑料加工工业协会聚氨酯制品专业委员会；上海四海展览有限公司

**2010 China International Exhibition on Polyurethane**
**Venue**: Shanghai New International Expo Center, Shanghai
**Organizer**: Polyurethane Products Professional Committee of Chin Plastics Processing Industry Assn; Shanghai Sihai Exhibition Co Ltd

2010/09/15-17
☎ 021-6160 8555
🖷 021-5876 9332
✉ info@china.messefrankfurt.com
www.messefrankfurt.com.hk
3450

**中国国际文具及办公用品展览会**
**地点**：上海新国际博览中心，上海
**主办**：法兰克福展览有限公司

**Paperworld China**
China Intl Stationery & Office Supplies Exhibition
**Venue**: Shanghai New International Expo Center, Shanghai
**Organizer**: Messe Franfurt

2010/09/15-17
☎ 010-8451 1832
🖷 010-8451 1829
✉ phoebe@ejkBeijing.com
www.chinapaperexpo.cn
3460

**第十八届中国国际纸浆造纸暨纸制品展览会及会议**
**地点**：上海国际展览中心，上海
**内容**：纸浆造纸机械，废报纸、杂志纸脱墨、漂白浆处理设备,夹网新闻纸机;废箱纸板处理设备；大型双盘磨和高浓盘磨打浆系统；计算机控制低脉动供浆系统；水力式流浆箱及高浓流浆箱；高速机内涂布装置；计算机控制可控中高辊；软压光机和超级软压光机；高速复卷机；高精度、高速同步切纸机；造纸、涂布车间在线检测、纵横向控制QCS、DCS系统；铜版纸、牛皮卡、牛皮箱板、瓦楞原纸、涂布白纸板、白卡;日用纸制品
**始办年份**：1987
**周期**：每年一届
**市场范围**：国际性
**上届规模** '09：展览面积8,000m$^2$(国外展商面积3,000m$^2$)，参展商172家（国外展商70家，来自18个国家），参观人数8,000人（专业贸易观众5,000人）
**主办**：美国克劳斯公司
**地址**：北京朝阳区新源南路6号京城大厦2005室（100004）
**联系人**：丁卉群
**主办**：中国制浆造纸研究院
**地址**：北京市朝阳区光华路12号（100020）
**联系人**：张景雯，钟颖，曹宝萍，张玉兰
**电话**:010-6581 7695, 6587 7076 传真010-6581 3253
邮箱zhilinzhan@sina.com

**China Paper Shanghai 2010**
– The 18th Intl Exhibition and Conference Reaching All of China's Paper-Related Industries
**Venue**: Shanghai International Exhibition Center, Shanghai
**Profile**: Paper Making Section: Bleaching, Chemicals, Coating, Environmental, Paper machines, Pulp quality control, Process controls; Pulp and paper products: Market pulp, Bond paper, Newsprint, Non-woven, Specialty, Corrugating medium, linerboard, corrugated containers, cups, folding boxes, laminations, Paper converting section: Rewind equipment, Winders, Coating machines, Drying equipment, Rolls & rollers
**Established Year**: 1987
**Frequency**: Annual
**Market Area**: International
**Statistics '09**: Exhibition Area 8,000m$^2$(foreigners 3,000m$^2$), Exhibitors 172（foreigners 70, came from 18 countries）, Visitors 8,000（trade visitors 5,000）
**Organizer**: E.J. Krause & Associates Inc (EJK); China National Pulp & Paper Research Institute
**Address**: Rm. 2005 Capital Mansion, 6 Xinyuan Nan Rd., Chaoyang District, Beijing, China
**Contact**: Phoebe Ding

2010/09/16-18
☎ 021-6471 2269, 6471 2180
🖷 021-6471 2001
✉ sdb@sstec.com.cn
http://sdb.sstec.com.cn
3500

**2010第五届上海设计双年展**
**地点**：上海展览中心，上海
**内容**：工业设计、平面设计、空间设计、室内外环境设计、建筑设计等给类设计新品、作品；时尚用品、民俗物品、手工艺品；企业、品牌形象的展示；广告、媒体、影视、动漫等；设计产业链各要素，如投资商、产权评估商、产权交易商等的机构功能和服务内容等；设计用新技术、工具、软件等。
**始办年份**：1999
**周期**：两年一届
**市场范围**：国际性
**性质**：面向公众
**参展费用**：A区净地（27m$^2$起）1,400元/m$^2$；B区标准展位12,000元，净地（27m$^2$起）850元/m$^2$；C区标准展位6,800元，净地（27m$^2$起）600元/m$^2$
**主办**：上海对外科学技术交流中心
**地址**：上海市淮海中路1634号（200031）
**联系人**：邵小萍，韩彦

**5th Shanghai Design Biennial**
**Venue**: Shanghai Exhibition Center, Shanghai
**Profile**: New and excellent works of industrial design, graphics design, space design and environmental design, etc; Fashion products, folk products and craftworks; Enterprises and brand image displaying; Advertisement, media, movies, TV and animation, etc; Showing functions and services of elements of design industry chain, such as investment, property assessment, property dealers; New technologies, tools and software for designing.
**Established Year**: 1999
**Frequency**: Biennial
**Market Area**: International
**Nature**: Open to public
**Participated Fee**: Raw Space (min 27m$^2$) RMB 1,400/m$^2$
**Organizer**: Shanghai Center for Scientific and Technological Exchange with Foreign Countries
**Address**: 1634 Huaihai Road (C) Shanghai 200031, China
**Contact**: Ms Shao Xiaoping, Ms Han Yan

2010/09/16-18
☎ 13044112901
🖷 021-5499 9745
✉ sh-sourcing@163.com
www.sourcing.org.cn
3510

**2010年中国（上海）国际跨国采购大会**
**地点：**上海世贸商城，上海
**内容：**综合类，逆向采购
**始办年份：**2002
**周期：**每年一届
**市场范围：**国际性
**入场券价格：**300元
**参展费用：**采购商8,000元/9$m^2$；供应商5,000～20,000元
**上届规模** '09：展览面积30,000$m^2$(国外展商面积26,000$m^2$)，参展商300家（国外展商260家，来自12个国家），参观人数6,000人（专业贸易观众5,800人）
**主办：**中华人民共和国商务部；上海市人民政府
**承办：**上海跨国采购中心有限公司
**地址：**上海莲花南路1108弄58栋701室（201100）
**联系人：**刘铭
MSN：shlmcn@hotmail.com
QQ：1187230500

**2010 International Sourcing Fair (Shanghai, China)**
Venue: Shanghai Mart, Shanghai
Profile: Comprehensive Options，Reverse Exhibition Comprehensive
Established Year: 2002
Frequency: Annual
Market Area: International
Cost to Attend: RMB 300
Participated Fee: Buyers RMB 8,000/9$m^2$, Suppliers RMB 5,000-20,000
Statistics '09: Exhibition Area 30,000$m^2$(foreigners 26,000$m^2$), Exhibitors 300（foreigners 260, came from 12 countries）, Visitors 6,000（trade visitors 5,800）
Sponsor: Ministry of Commerce PRC; Shanghai Municipal People' s Government.
Organizer: Shanghai International Sourcing Promotion Center Co Ltd
Address: Room 701, No.58, Lane 1108, Lianhua South Road, Minhang District, Shanghai, China
Contact: Mr Liu Ming
MSN: shlmcn@hotmail.com

2010/09/17-19
☎ 021-5134 2588
🖷 021-5134 2515
✉ zhang.yimeng@ubexpo-shanghai.com
www.cilps.cn
3520

**中国国际高端物业展**
**地点：**上海国际会议中心，上海
**内容：**中国国际高端物业展是中国规模最大、规格最高的全球高端不动产业峰会，旨在为中国乃至亚太地区的富豪、精英阶层展示中国及世界各地的豪宅和高品质休闲度假地产，演绎高品位的生活方式，是高端物业最佳展示和交易平台。
**始办年份：**2006
**周期：**每年一届
**市场范围：**国际性
**性质：**面向公众
**主办：**优博集团；中国房地产报
**承办：**上海优博国际展览有限公司
**地址：**上海市浦东新区福山路458号同盛大厦11楼I座（200122）
**联系人：**安君，张一萌

**China International Luxury Property Show**
Venue: Shanghai International Convention Center, Shanghai
Profile: CILPS-China International Luxury Property Show-is China' s only showcase for the world' s most exclusive properties and developments in a unique atmosphere of luxury and lifestyle.
Established Year: 2006
Frequency: Annual
Market Area: International
Nature: Open to public
Sponsor: UB Group, China Real Estate Business
Organizer: Shanghai YUBO International Exhibition Co
Address: I-11F Tong Sheng Tower, 458 Fu Shan Road, Shanghai
Contact: Angela, Karen

2010/09/21-22
☎ 027-8736 2945, 8736 2661
🖷 027-8736 2987
www.chinapeec.com
3530

**2010第三届中国国际植物提取物展览会及研讨会**
**地点：**上海浦东展览馆，上海
**主办：**中英合资好博塔苏斯展览公司
**联系人：**余云成

**Shanghai Intl Nature Extract Exhibition & Conference**
Venue: Shanghai Pudong Expo, Shanghai
Organizer: Tarsus Hope Exhibition

2010/09/21-24
☎ 021-5027 8128
🖷 021-5027 8138
✉ wire@mdc.com.cn
www.wirechina.net
3540

**第四届中国国际线缆及线材展览会**
**地点：**中国上海新国际博览中心，上海
**始办年份：**2004
**周期：**两年一届
**市场范围：**国际性
**上届规模** '08：参展商708家
**主办：**杜塞尔多夫展览(中国)有限公司
**地址：**上海市浦东新区张江高科技园区科苑路88号上海德意志工商中心1号楼307-308室（201203）
**联系人：**王乐为

**The 4th All China-Intl Wire & Cable Industry Trade Fair**
Venue: Shanghai New International Expo Center, Shanghai
Established Year: 2004
Frequency: Biennial
Market Area: International
Statistics '08: Exhibitors 708
Organizer: Messe Düsseldorf China Ltd
Address: German Center for Industry and Trade Shanghai ,88 Keyuan Rd, Zhangjiang Hi-Tech Park, Pudong, Shanghai
Contact: Cynthia Wang

2010/09/21-24
☎ 010-8511 1723, 6525 6461
🖷 010-6523 3861
✉ tube2010@yahoo.cn
www.tubechina.net
3550

**第四届中国国际管材展览会**
**地点：**上海新国际博览中心，上海
**内容：**管、管道原材料及配件；管道加工机械；二手机械；加工机械及辅助设备；测控技术；检测工程；相关领域；管道贸易及批发；管道与OCTG技术
**始办年份：**2004
**周期：**两年一届
**市场范围：**国际性
**入场券价格：**免费
**参展费用：**标准展位：国内企业9,600元，净地960元/$m^2$
**上届规模** '08：展览面积11,504$m^2$(国外展商面积1,891$m^2$)，参展商389家（国外展商94家，来自18个国家），参观人数26,585人
**主办：**中国贸促会冶金行业分会
**地址：**北京市东城区东四西大街46号主楼606室（100711）
**联系人：**仲文，马婧

**The 4th All-China International Tube & Pipe Trade Fair**
Venue: Shanghai New International Expo Center, Shanghai
Profile: Raw materials, tubes and accessories, Tube manufacturing machinery, Rebuilt and reconditioned machinery, Process technology tools and auxiliaries, Measuring and control technology, Testing, Specialist areas, Trading stockists of tubes, Pipeline and OCTG technology
Established Year: 2004
Frequency: Biennial
Market Area: International
Cost to Attend: Free
Participated Fee: For Domestic Exhibitors Standard Booth RMB 9,600，Raw Space RMB 960/$m^2$
Statistics '08: Exhibition Area 11,504$m^2$(foreigners 1,891$m^2$), Exhibitors 389（foreigners 94, came from 18 countries）, Visitors 26,585
Organizer: Metallurgical CCPIT
Address: Room 606 No 46 Dongsi West Street, Dongcheng District, Beijing, China
Contact: Zhong Wen, RUBY Ma

2010/09/21-23
☎ 0411-6666 3088, 6403 4324
℻ 0411-6666 3221, 6404 3595
✉ okok1121@163.com
www.ssea.org.cn
www.supersteel.cn
3560

2010中国特殊钢工业展览会
地点：上海国际展览中心，上海
主办：中国特钢企业协会

China Special Steel Industry Exhibition 2010
Venue: Shanghai International Exhibition Center, Shanghai
Organizer: Special Steel Enterprises Association of China

2010/09/27-29
☎ 021-6289 5385
℻ 021-6247 2950
✉ info@rechinaexpo.com.cn
www.rechinaexpo.com
3570

ReChina 2010
第七届亚洲打印耗材展览会
地点：上海新国际博览中心，上海
内容：墨盒、硒鼓、墨水、碳粉、色带等各种打印耗材；兼容、再生、循环使用等打印机和复印机耗材；相纸、喷绘纸、热敏纸等各种特殊打印用纸；打印耗材的制造、翻新、罐装、测试等设备和工具；喷绘机、打印机、复印机等打印输出设备和零部件；打印设备与打印耗材的技术、信息等服务类产品
始办年份：2004
周期：每年一届
市场范围：国际性
入场券价格：50元
参展费用：国内企业1,600元/m$^2$,国外企业280美元/m$^2$
上届规模 '09：展览面积8,320m$^2$(国外展商面积2,704m$^2$)，参展商422家（国外展商72家，来自70个国家），参观人数9,000人（专业贸易观众8,200人）
主办：ReChina Expo Inc.USA；Recharger Magazine (USA)；上海广会会展有限公司；上海外经贸商务展览有限公司
地址：上海市镇宁路200号欣安大厦东峰18A（200040）
联系人：陈文瑾小姐

ReChina Asia Expo 2010
Venue: Shanghai New International Expo Center, Shanghai
Profile: Ink cartridges, Toner cartridges, Ink, Toner, Ribbons, and other printer consumables; Compatible, Remanufactured and renewable consumables of printers and copiers; Photo paper, Inkjet paper, Thermal transfer paper and other special printing papers; Manufacturing, Remanufacturing, Refilling, Testing equipment & tools for printer consumables; Wide-format Inkjet printers, printers, copiers and other printing-out equipment and components; Technologies, information
Established Year: 2004
Frequency: Annual
Market Area: International
Cost to Attend: RMB 50:-
Participated Fee: USD 280/m$^2$
Statistics '09: Exhibition Area 8,320m$^2$(foreigners 2,704m$^2$), Exhibitors 422 (foreigners 72, came from 70 countries), Visitors 9,000 (trade visitors 8,200)
Organizer: ReChina Expo Inc USA; Recharger Magazine (USA); Shanghai GrandView Expo Co Ltd; Shanghai International Trade Promotion Co Ltd
Address: 18A East Wing Xin'An Building 200 ZhenNing Rd, Shanghai, 200040 China
Contact: Ms Cheyenne Chen

2010/09/27-29
☎ 021-5228 4015
℻ 021-5228 4012
✉ evian.gu@nm-china.com.cn
www.nm-china.com.cn
3575

第八届国际粉体工业/散装技术展览会暨会议
地点：上海国际展览中心，上海
主办：纽伦堡会展服务（上海）有限公司

8th International Powder/Bulk Conference & Exhibition
Venue: Shanghai International Exhibition Center, Shanghai
Organizer: NURNBERG MESSE CHINA

2010/09/28-30
☎ 010-6590 7766 转ext 736
℻ 010-6590 6139
✉ h.chen@koelnmesse.cn
www.cihs.com.cn
www.cihs-practicalworld.com
3580

科隆国际五金展强力推动
2010 中国国际五金展
地点：上海新国际博览中心，上海
内容：工具；建筑五金及DIY家装；锁具、安防产品及配件
始办年份：2001
周期：每年一届
市场范围：国际性
入场券价格：10元
参展费用：国际标准展位185欧元/m$^2$，国际净地135欧元/m$^2$；国内企业：标准展位9,000元/个，净地900元/m$^2$
上届规模 '08：展览面积103,500m$^2$，参展商1,948家（来自19个国家），专业贸易观众30,960人
主办：中国五金制品协会；科隆国际展览有限公司；全国工商联五金机电商会；中国贸促会轻工行业分会
承办：北京时瑞展览有限公司；上海大陆工具发展有限公司
地址：科隆展览中国有限公司北京东三环北路8号亮马河大厦2座1018室（100004）
联系人：陈晗，田雅妮

China International Hardware Show
—Powered by PRACTICAL WORLD
Venue: Shanghai New International Expo Center, Shanghai
Profile: Tools; DIY and Building Hardware; Security, Locks and Fittings
Established Year: 2001
Frequency: Annual
Market Area: International
Cost to Attend: RMB 10:-
Participated Fee: Standard Booth EUR 185/m$^2$, Raw Space EUR 135/m$^2$
Statistics '08: Exhibition Area 103,500m$^2$, Exhibitors 1,948 (came from 19 countries), Trade Visitors 30,960
Sponsor: China National Hardware Assn; Koelnmesse; All-China Chamber of Commerce in Hardware, Mechanical and Electric Industry; Light Industry Sub-Council CCPIT
Organizer: Beijing Triuni Exhibition Co Ltd
Address: Koelnmesse, Unit 1018, Landmark Tower Ⅱ, No. 8 Dongsanhuan North Rd,, Beijing 100004, China
Contact: Helen Chen, Emily Tian

2010/10-
☎ 021-5134 2588
℻ 021-5134 2515
✉ wang.xin@ubexpo-shanghai.com
3600

中国（上海）国际马博会
地点：上海东亚展览馆，上海
内容：国际马博会是中国全面展示马产业及相关用品的商务型博览会，促成国际马业交流、搭建国际商务合作与投资交易平台
周期：每年一届
市场范围：国际性
性质：面向公众
主办：中国马业协会
承办：上海优博国际展览有限公司
地址：上海市福山路458号同盛大厦11楼I座（200122）
联系人：王馨

China (Shanghai) International Horse Fair
Venue: East Asia Exhibition Hall, Shanghai
Profile: A unique showcase for the whole horse industry chain in China and overseas which will help improve international horse industry communication, business cooperation and investment.
Frequency: Annual
Market Area: International
Nature: Open to public
Sponsor: China National Horse Industry Assn
Organizer: Shanghai Yubo International Exhibition Co
Address: I-11F Tong Sheng Tower, 458 Fu Shan Road, Shanghai
Contact: Jane Wang

2010/10/03-06
☎ 021-6195 6088
传真 021-6195 6099
✉ jessica.wu@vnuexhibitions.com.cn
www.vnuexhibitionsasia.com
3610

**上海房地产秋季展示会**
**地点**：上海展览中心，上海
**内容**："假日楼市"是房地产届的著名展示会，是以"发展房地产业，满足人民需求"为宗旨，以黄金假日周为契机，按市场经济方式运作，集专业、规范为一体的大型房地产交易盛会。经过连续几年的成功运作，目前"假日楼市"已成为一个高品位、全面的、综合的大型房地产展示会，赢得了房产界的一致好评和良好的信誉，受到了广大参展商的青睐，对上海房地产市场的发展也起到了积极的推动作用。
**始办年份**：1990
**周期**：每年一届
**市场范围**：全国性
**性质**：面向公众
**上届规模** '09：展览面积35,000m$^2$，参展商250家，参观人数130,000人
**主办**：上海万耀企龙展览有限公司
**地址**：上海市徐汇区田林路140号26A栋 上海万耀企龙办公楼（20023）
**联系人**：吴佳钰

**Holiday Real Estate Market**
**Venue**: Shanghai Exhibition Center, Shanghai
**Profile**: "Holiday Real Estate Market" is a well-known real estate exhibition is based on "the development of real estate, to meet the needs of the people" for the purpose, to October holiday as an opportunity to operate according to a market economy, set professional standards as one big real estate transaction event. After several years of successful operation, the current "Holiday Real Estate Market" has become a high-quality, comprehensive, integrated large-scale real estate exhibition, has won acclaim real estate sector and a good reputation, by the majority of exhibitors in favor, the development of the Shanghai real estate market also played a positive role in promoting.
**Established Year**: 1990
**Frequency**: Annual
**Market Area**: National
**Nature**: Open to public
**Statistics '09**: Exhibition Area 35,000m$^2$, Exhibitors 250, Visitors 130,000
**Organizer**: VNU Exhibitions Asia
**Address**: VNU House, 26A, No.140 Tianlin Road Shanghai, China
**Contact**: Jessica

2010/10/09-11
☎ 010-6863 1939, 6860 6749
传真 010-6865 9979
www.bcige.com
3620

**第七届中国(上海)国际玻璃工业新技术展览会**
**地点**：上海国际展览中心，上海
**内容**：玻璃、玻璃制品应用，玻璃深加工机械磨料磨具及玻璃生产线，玻璃生产技术与设备、仪器仪表及检测装置、自动控制系统和配套系统，原材料、耐火材料和各种主、辅助材料
**始办年份**：2000
**周期**：每年一届
**市场范围**：国际性
**性质**：面向公众
**参展费用**：A区8,800元，B～C区7,800元，净地(36㎡起)900元/㎡
**上届规模** '09：展览面积12,000m$^2$，参展商306家
**主办**：中国国际经济技术交流中心；中国轻工机械协会玻璃装备分会；浙江省玻璃行业协会；中国工艺美术学会玻璃艺术专业委员会
**承办**：北京海闻展览有限公司；北京世纪佳业展览有限公司
**地址**：北京市石景山区京原路7号骅悦隆大厦218室（100043）
**联系人**：姚亮，胡金玉
**QQ**：736528383

**China (Shanghai) Intl Glass Industry New Tech Expo 2010**
**Venue**: Shanghai International Exhibition Center, Shanghai
**Established Year**: 2000
**Frequency**: Annual
**Market Area**: International
**Nature**: Open to public
**Participated Fee**: RMB 8800/booth, Raw Space RMB 900/㎡ (min 36m$^2$)
**Statistics '09**: Exhibition Area 12, 000m$^2$, Exhibitors 306（foreigners 40, 000）
**Organizer**: Beijing Hiven Exhibition Co., Ltd.

2010/10/12-14
☎ 010-6603 9661
传真 010-6603 3964
✉ zhangying@toy-cta.org
wangjuxian@toy-cta.org
www.china-toy-expo.com
3650

**第九届中国国际玩具、模型及婴儿用品展**
**地点**：上海新国际博览中心，上海
**内容**：玩具类：毛绒软体、木制、娃娃、电子电动、塑胶、教育益智、户外/体育用品、儿童骑乘类，节日用品、塑胶充气、授权及动漫产品等；模型机械类：飞机模型、汽车模型、船模型、建筑模型、军事模型、火车、铁路、仿真模型、金属玩具等；婴儿用品类：婴幼儿玩具、婴儿手推车、学步车、儿童座椅、儿童家具、家居饰品、童床、汽车安全座椅、摇篮等
**始办年份**：2002
**周期**：每年一届
**市场范围**：国际性
**参展费用**：标准展位10,000元，净地950元/m$^2$（36m$^2$起）
**上届规模** '09：展览面积36,000m$^2$(国外展商面积579m$^2$)，参展商685家（国外展商60家，来自89个国家），专业贸易观众48,311人
**主办**：中国玩具协会
**地址**：北京市西城区复兴门内大街101号百盛写字楼8009室（100031）
**联系人**：张瀛，王居先
**MSN**：lixiangzhishen@hotmail.com

**9th International Trade Fair for Toys, Hobby & Baby Articles**
**Venue**: Shanghai New International Expo Center, Shanghai
**Profile**: Toys: Plush and soft toys, wooden toys, dolls, electronic and plastic toys, educational toys, outdoor and sports articles, baby carriers, festival articles, licensing toys and etc; Hobby/model construction: plane model, car model, plastic model and etc.; Baby articles: baby toys, baby strollers, baby walker, seat, baby furniture, bed
**Established Year**: 2002
**Frequency**: Annual
**Market Area**: International
**Participated Fee**: Standard Booth RMB 10,000, Raw Space RMB 950/m$^2$（min 36m$^2$）
**Statistics '09**: Exhibition Area 36,000m$^2$(foreigners 579m$^2$), Exhibitors 685（foreigners 60, came from 89 countries）, Trade Visitors 48,311
**Organizer**: China Toy Assn
**Address**: No.101 Fu Xing Men Nei Street, Beijing 100031, China
**Contact**: Helen Zhang, Eric Wang
**MSN**: lixiangzhishen@hotmail.com

2010/10/12-15
☎ 021-6295 6677转 ext 3191
传真 021-6278 0038
✉ intexfhq@sh163.net
www.prolightsound.com
3660

**上海国际专业灯光音响展览会**
**地点**：上海新国际博览中心，上海
**主办**：上海国际展览中心有限公司；法兰克福展览（香港）有限公司联合

**prolight + Sound Shanghai**
**Venue**: Shanghai New International Expo Center, Shanghai
**Organizer**: INTEX Shanghai Co Ltd; Messe Frankfurt (HK) Ltd

2010/10/12-15
☎ 021-6295 6677转 ext 6149
6209 6149
✉ intexrxx@sh163.net
www.musicchina-expo.com
3670

**中国(上海)国际乐器展览会**
**地点**：上海新国际博览中心，上海
**主办**：上海国际展览中心有限公司；法兰克福展览（香港）有限公司

**Music China**
**Venue**: Shanghai New International Expo Center, Shanghai
**Organizer**: INTEX Shanghai Co Ltd; Messe Frankfurt (HK) Ltd

2010/10/14-16
☎ 010-5150 6801
🖷 010-5150 7149, 021-5439 8565
✉ sxbeijing@263.net
www.shfkex.com
3680

2010上海司法警用及安全防范技术产品博览会
地点：上海国际展览中心，上海
主办：北京四星展览服务有限公司

Shanghai Security Products Expo
Venue: Shanghai International Exhibition Center, Shanghai
Organizer: Beijing Four-Star Exhibition Service Co Ltd

2010/10/19-21
☎ 021-6279 2828
🖷 021-6545 5124
✉ info@siec-ccpit.com
www.siec-ccpit.com
3690

**第十二届中国上海国际食品加工及包装机械展览会**
内容：包装和食品机械
地点：上海国际展览中心，上海
周期：每年一届
市场范围：国际性
主办：上海市国际展览有限公司
地址：上海市延安中路841号东方海外大厦8楼（200040）

**International FoodTec China**
Interfood Shanghai 2010
Venue: Shanghai International Exhibition Center, Shanghai
Profile: Profile: Packaging and food processing machine
Frequency: Annual
Market Area: International
Organizer: Shanghai International Exhibition Co
Address: 8/F,OOCL Plaza,841 Yan An Zhong Road, Shanghai 200040, China

2010/10/19-22
☎ 010-8522 9463, 8522 9488
🖷 010-8522 9296
✉ intertextilebj@ccpittex.com
www.intertextile.com.cn
3710

中国国际纺织面料及辅料（秋冬）博览会
地点：上海新国际博览中心，上海
内容：各类纺织服装面料、辅料、计算机CAD/CAM系统，相关出版物及网络
始办年份：1995
周期：每年一届
市场范围：国际性
上届规模 '09：展览面积115,000m²(国外展商面积22,500m²), 参展商2,460家（国外展商717家，来自21个国家），参观人数53, 948人（专业贸易观众53, 948人）
主办：中国纺织工业协会
承办：中国贸促会纺织行业分会；法兰克福展览（香港）有限公司；中国纺织信息中心
地址：北京东长安街12号550室（100742）
联系人：王壮飞，于欣

China International Trade Fair for Apparel Fabrics and Accessories
Venue: Shanghai New International Expo Center, Shanghai
Profile: Apparel fabrics & accessories, CAD/CAM system, relevant publications & websites
Established Year: 1995
Frequency: Annual
Market Area: International
Statistics '09: Exhibition Area 115,000m²(foreigners 22, 500m²), Exhibitors 2, 460（foreigners 717, came from 21 countries）, Trade Visitors 53,948
Sponsor: China National Textile & Apparel Council
Organizer: The Sub-Council of Textile Industry CCPIT; Messe Frankfurt (HK) Ltd; China Textile Information Center
Address: Room 550, No.12 East Chang An Street, Beijing, China
Contact: Ms Wang Zhuangfei, Ms Yu Xin

2010/10/21-23
☎ 021-5153 5132, 5153 5101
✉ Shino.shi@reedexpo.com.cn gloria.zhang@reedexpo.com.cn
www.100percentdesign.com.cn
3720

**2010"100%设计"上海展**
地点：上海展览中心，上海
内容："100%设计"上海展是一个独特的中国当代室内设计领先展会，展示由设计评委会精选出的当代室内设计领先品牌。展会展示一系列原创的家具，灯饰，厨卫设备及地面和墙面装饰。旨在创造一个激发灵感的观展氛围，展示设计的创新和最新理念。"100%设计"上海展是室内设计师，建筑师，业内人士，房地产开发商，酒店业主及高端消费者与供应商开展商业会面，互动并满足其购买需求的首选平台
周期：每年一届
主办：励展博览集团
参展联络：☎021-5153 5132✉Shino.shi@reedexpo.com.cn
参观联络：☎021-5153 5101✉gloria.zhang@reedexpo.com.cn

**100% Design Shanghai**
Venue: Shanghai Exhibition Center, Shanghai
Profile: 100% Design Shanghai is a unique exhibition in China featuring leading brands of contemporary interior design products which are strictly qualified by a Design Advisory Panel. The exhibition showcases original designs of furniture, lighting, bathroom/kitchen and floor/wall coverings and it seeks to create a dynamic atmosphere for the proliferation of innovative and trendsetting ideas. 100% Design Shanghai is the premiere venue for interior designers, architects, specifiers, developers, hoteliers and high-end consumers to interact with the suppliers and meet their buying needs.
Frequency: Annual
Organizer: Reed Exhibitions
For exhibiting: ☎021-5153 5132✉Shino.shi@reedexpo.com.cn
For visiting: ☎021-5153 5101✉gloria.zhang@reedexpo.com.cn

2010/10/21-23
☎ 021-6431 2605, 6437 2695
🖷 021-6471 2001
✉ re@sstec.com.cn
http://re.sstec.com.cn
3730

2010第三届上海国际可再生能源大会暨展览会
地点：上海展览中心，上海
内容：国内外太阳能、风能、生物质能、水能、海洋能、地热能、新能源（氢能、燃料电池等）、核能等可再生能源各分领域创新的技术、工艺、设备、产品、用途、科研成果等；国内外已成熟应用和未来应用的先进产品、方法手段、示范案例，以及政策宣传、风险投资、媒体中介等。
始办年份：2003
周期：每年一届
市场范围：国际性
性质：面向公众
参展费用：A区标准展位12,000元，净地（36m²起）940元/m²；B区标准展位9,000元，净地（36m²起）700元/m²
主办：上海对外科学技术交流中心
地址：上海市淮海中路1634号（200031）
联系人：唐耀华，李婧华

The 3rd International Congress & Exhibition on Reproducible Energy
Venue: Shanghai Exhibition Center, Shanghai
Profile: The sub-field innovation in renewable energy regarding technologies, processes, equipment, products, application, scientific achievements, etc. at home and abroad. The well-developed and to-be-applied products, methods and means, the model case, as well as policy advocacy, venture capital, media and other intermediaries both domestically and abroad.
Established Year: 2003
Frequency: Annual
Market Area: International
Nature: Open to public
Participated Fee: Standard Booth RMB 12,000, Raw Space（min 36m²）RMB 940/m²
Organizer: Shanghai Center for Scientific and Technological Exchange with Foreign Countries
Address: 1634 Huaihai Road (C) Shanghai 200031, China
Contact: Mr Tang Yaohua, Ms Li Jinghua

2010/10/25-28
☎ 021-5045 6700
🖷 021-5045 9355
✉ cemat-asia@hmf-china.com
www.cemat-asia.com
3750

**亚洲国际物流技术与运输系统展览会**
**地点**：上海新国际博览中心，上海
**内容**：机械搬运、物料搬运技术及其零部件、仓储技术、物流的完整系统、仓储技术及车间设备、物流控制和软件、物流服务
**始办年份**：2000
**周期**：每年一届
**市场范围**：国际性
**入场券价格**：免费
**上届规模** '09：展览面积25,200m$^2$(国外展商面积10,000m$^2$)，参展商380家（国外展商90家，来自21个国家），专业贸易观众47,330人
**主办**：中国物流与采购联合会；中国机械工程学会；德国汉诺威展览公司；汉诺威米兰展览(上海)有限公司
**地址**：上海市浦东新区银霄路393号百安居浦东商务大厦301室（201204）
**联系人**：汪萍，张培基

**CeMAT ASIA 2010**
**Venue**: Shanghai New International Expo Center, Shanghai
**Profile**: Mechanical Handling, Accessories and components for materials handling technology, Entire systems for materials handling technology, warehouse technology, logistics, Warehousing technology and workshop equipment, Material flow control and software, Logistics Services, Transportation
**Established Year**: 2000
**Frequency**: Annual
**Market Area**: International
**Cost to Attend**: Free
**Statistics** '09: Exhibition Area 25,200m$^2$(foreigners 10,000m$^2$), Exhibitors 380（foreigners 90, came from 21 countries）, Trade Visitors 47,330
**Organizer**: Deutsche Messe, Hannover Milano Fairs Shanghai Ltd, China Federation of Logistics & Purchasing, Chinese Mechanical Engineering Society
**Address**: Rm. 301, B&Q Pudong Office Tower 393 Yinxiao Rd, Pudong Shanghai
**Contact**: Jelly Wang, Gene Zhang

2010/10/25-28
☎ 021-5045 6700转 ext 357/252
🖷 021-6886 2355, 5045 9355
✉ ptc-asia@hmf-china.com
www.ptc-asia.com
3760

**亚洲国际动力传动与控制技术展览会**
**地点**：上海新国际博览中心，上海
**主办**：汉诺威米兰展览（上海）有限公司

**PTC ASIA**
**Power Transmission and Control**
**Venue**: Shanghai New International Expo Center, Shanghai
**Organizer**: Hannover Milano Fairs Shanghai Ltd

2010/10/26-28
☎ 010-6839 2602，6839 2676
🖷 010-6839 2652
www.doorexpo.cn
3770

**2010中国（上海）国际门业博览会暨门窗产品展览会**
**地点**：上海新国际博览中心，上海
**主办**：中国木材与木制品流通协会木门专业委员会

**Door Expo 2010**
China Shanghai Intl Door Industry Expo
**Venue**: Shanghai New International Expo Center, Shanghai

2010/10/28-30
☎ 021-6390 6161
🖷 021-6390 6858
✉ m.miao@koelnmesse.cn
www.sweets-china.cn
3780

**2010中国糖果文化节暨**
**第七届中国国际甜食及休闲食品展览会**
**地点**：上海国际展览中心，上海
**内容**：糖果、巧克力和休闲食品；咖啡与茶；添加剂和原料；包装材料；包装、加工技术与设备
**始办年份**：2004
**周期**：每年一届
**市场范围**：国际性
**性质**：面向公众
**入场券价格**：免费
**参展费用**：国际展区：净地190欧元/m$^2$（24m$^2$起），标准展位230欧元/m$^2$（9m$^2$起）；国内展区：净地850元/m$^2$（24m$^2$起），标准展位1,100元/m$^2$（9m$^2$起）
**上届规模** '09：展览面积35,000m$^2$(国外展商面积1,800m$^2$)，参展商147家（国外展商75家，来自22个国家），参观人数47,500人（专业贸易观众7,500人）
**主办**：科隆国际展览有限公司；中国食品工业协会糖果专业委员会
**地址**：上海市淮海中路283号香港广场南楼1202室（200021）
**联系人**：缪骏，仇蓓莉

**China Confectionery Culture Festival 2010**
**Sweets & Snacks China 2010**
**Venue**: Shanghai International Exhibition Center, Shanghai
**Profile**: Candy, chocolate, snack food; Coffee and tea Addictive and raw material; Packaging material; Packaging, processing technology and equipment;
**Established Year**: 2004
**Frequency**: Annual
**Market Area**: International
**Nature**: Open to public
**Cost to Attend**: Free
**Participated Fee**: Raw Space EUR 190/m$^2$（min 24m$^2$）, Standard Booth EUR 230/m$^2$（min 9m$^2$） Statistics '09: Exhibition Area 35,000m$^2$(foreigners 1,800m$^2$), Exhibitors 147（foreigners 75, came from 22 countries）, Visitors 47,500（trade visitors 7,500）
**Organizer**: Koelnmesse; China National Candy Assn
**Address**: Rm 1202, No.283, Hong Kong Plaza, South, Middle Huai Hai Rd, Shanghai
**Contact**: Max Miao, Jasmine Qiu

2010/11-
☎ 021-6279 2828
🖷 021-6545 5124
✉ info@siec-ccpit.com
www.siec-ccpit.com
3800

**2010中意国际葡萄酒展**
**地点**：上海展览中心，上海
**内容**：Vinitaly是全球历史最悠久的葡萄酒酿造工业的盛会，至今已有40年历史，也是迄今规模最大、最具权威的葡萄酒展。每年来自意大利、法国、德国、英国、西班牙、阿根廷等为数众多的国际代表团以及专家定期参加展览会。Vinitaly每年在中国、美国、俄罗斯、印度和日本5个国家举办分展会。
**周期**：每年一届
**市场范围**：国际性
**主办**：上海市国际展览有限公司
**地址**：上海市延安中路841号东方海外大厦8楼（200040）

**VINITALY CHINA 2010**
**Venue**: Shanghai Exhibition Center, Shanghai
**Profile**: The Veronafiere launched the debut of Vinitaly in China (Shanghai) 1998. This event has now become an annual and regular event
At present, Vinitaly China is of the most characteristic and international wine exhibition with high professionalism in China
**Frequency**: Annual
**Market Area**: International
**Organizer**: Shanghai International Exhibition Co
**Address**: 8/F, OOCL Plaza, 841 Yan An Zhong Road, Shanghai 200040, China

2010/11/02-04
☎ 021-3251 6618, 3251 6628
🖷 021-3251 6698
✉ expo@vtexpo.com.cn
www.imwcexpo.com
3810

**第五届微波及天线技术交流展览会**
**地点：**上海光大会展中心，上海
**内容：**微波及天线设备、测试仪器、材料及元件等
**始办年份：**2006
**周期：**每年一届
**市场范围：**国际性
**参展费用：**9,000元
**上届规模**‘09：展览面积4,000m$^2$(国外展商面积1,000m$^2$)，参展商126家（来自12个国家），参观人数3,200人（专业贸易观众1,500人）
**主办：**上海优创展览服务有限公司
**地址：**上海市曹杨路505号尚诚国际大厦505室（200063）
**联系人：**沈晓荣
MSN：rr4545@hotmail.com
QQ：48384882

**5th Intl Conference & Exhibition on Microwave and Antenna**
**Venue:** Shanghai Everbright Convention & Exhibition Center, Shanghai
**Profile:** Microwave component, Microwave instrument, Electromagnetic simulation software, Antenna
**Established Year:** 2006
**Frequency:** Annual
**Market Area:** International
**Participated Fee:** RMB 9,000
**Statistics** '09: Exhibition Area 4,000m$^2$(foreigners 1,000m$^2$), Exhibitors 126 (came from 12 countries), Visitors 3,200 (trade visitors 1,500)
**Organizer:** Shanghai Viewtran Exhibition Service Co Ltd
**Address:** Room 505, No. 505 Caoyang Road Shanghai 200063, China
**Contact:** Shen Xiaorong
**MSN:** rr4545@hotmail.com

2010/11/02-04
☎ 021-3251 6698, 3251 6628
🖷 021-3251 6698
✉ expo@vtexpo.com.cn
www.emcexpo.com
3820

**第九届国际电磁兼容与安规认证暨微波展览会**
**地点：**上海光大会展中心，上海
**内容：**电磁兼容设备、测试仪器、材料及元件等
**始办年份：**2002
**周期：**每年一届
**市场范围：**国际性
**参展费用：**9,000元
**上届规模**‘09：展览面积4,000m$^2$(国外展商面积1,000m$^2$)，参展商126家（来自12个国家），参观人数3,200人（专业贸易观众1,500人）
**主办：**上海优创展览服务有限公司
**地址：**上海市曹杨路505号尚诚国际大厦505室（200063）
**联系人：**沈晓荣
MSN：rr4545@hotmail.com
QQ：48384882

**EMC/China 2010**
**The 9th International Conference & Exhibition on Electromagnetic Compatibility**
**Venue:** Shanghai Everbright Convention & Exhibition Center, Shanghai
**Profile:** EMC test instrument, EMI shielding products, EMI filters, EMI shielding materials, RF-shielded cabins, absorber
**Established Year:** 2002
**Frequency:** Annual
**Market Area:** International
**Participated Fee:** RMB 9,000
**Statistics** '09: Exhibition Area 4,000m$^2$(foreigners 1,000m$^2$), Exhibitors 126 (came from 12 countries), Visitors 3,200 (trade visitors 1,500)
**Organizer:** Shanghai Viewtran Exhibition Service Co Ltd
**Address:** Room 505, No. 505 Caoyang Road Shanghai 200063, China
**Contact:** Shen Xiaorong
**MSN:** rr4545@hotmail.com

2010/11/03-04
☎ 010-6441 6187
🖷 010-6441 9378
✉ liuhz@icif.cn
www.icif.com.cn
3825

**2010中国国际水处理化学品、水溶高分子、造纸化学品、工业表面活性剂技术及应用展览会**
**地点：**上海国际展览中心，上海
**主办：**中国化工信息中心

**2010 Intl Exhibition on Water-treatment Chemicals & Water-soluble Polymer Products & Papermaking Chemicals & Industrial Surfactants, Technology and Application**
**Venue:** Shanghai International Exhibition Center, Shanghai
**Organizer:** China National Chemical Information Center

2010/11/04-06
☎ 021-5151 5132
021-5153 5101
✉ shino.shi@reedexpo.com.cn
gloria.zhang@reedexpo.com.cn
www.home-decor.net
3830

**国际家居装饰艺术展**
**地点：**上海展览中心，上海
**内容：**代表着高贵、优雅和富有品味的生活态度，国际家居装饰艺术展是一个独特的贸易展会，将一系列高质量的高端品牌带来中国的国际性大都市-上海。它展示高质量室内设计装饰产品、配饰和家具，是业内人士、设计界专业人士、酒店业主及买手必须参加的盛会，为其提供了一个与供应商开展交流，采购和商务洽谈的有效平台。
**主办：**励展博览集团
☎ 021-5151 5132（参展），021-5153 5101（参观）
✉ shino.shi@reedexpo.com.cn（参展），
✉ gloria.zhang@reedexpo.com.cn（参观）

**International Home Décor & Design**
**Venue:** Shanghai Exhibition Center, Shanghai
**Profile:** Representing an attitude of elegance and stylishness, International Home Décor & Design is a unique trade exhibition, which brings together a comprehensive range of high-quality and premium brands in the most cosmopolitan city of China – Shanghai, showcasing high quality interior home decoration products and accessories. It is a must-attend event for specifiers, design professionals, hoteliers and buyers to network, source and establish business contacts.
**Organizer:** Reed Exhibitions
**For Exhibiting:** ☎ 021-5151 5132 ✉ shino.shi@reedexpo.com.cn
**For Visiting:** ☎ 021-5153 5101 ✉ gloria.zhang@reedexpo.com.cn

2010/11/08-10
☎ 021-6280 7745
🖷 021-6294 7723
✉ newfexpo6@yahoo.cn
www.chinaoceaneng-expo.com
3840

**第二届中国国际海洋工程技术和装备展**
**地点：**上海国际展览中心，上海
**内容：**海洋油气钻采平台的设计和建造技术，海上钻井船、海洋浮式生产装置（FPSO）、海洋浮式生产储油船 (FDPSO)以及各类生产、生活模块等的设计和建造技术；各类海洋工程辅助船的设计和建造技术；深海水下工程技术的装备，潜水技术及其装备、海底探测、水下检测、水下作业技术及其相关装备等；海洋平台用相关设备和技术,如动力/发电系统、辅锅炉、信息处理传输系统、照明系统、电气与控制系统、平台升降系统、系泊系统、起重系统、吊装系统、钢结构系统、海上保障系统、海洋工程用通讯设备、空调和通风、防腐技术、保温制冷
**始办年份：**2008
**周期：**每年一届
**市场范围：**全国性
**主办：**中国船舶工业行业协会；上海船舶工业行业协会
**承办：**上海浦东国际展览公司；上海新力会展服务有限公司；上海谐成船舶技术咨询有限公司
**地址：**上海番禺路383号601室（200052）
**联系人：**刘强，范帷瑶

**China International Exhibition on Ocean Engineering Technology & Equipment 2010**
**Venue:** Shanghai International Exhibition Center, Shanghai
**Profile:** Designing and Building Technology for Offshore Oil and Gas Drilling Rigs/Platform, Ship Type Drilling Unit, FPSO, FDPSO and Designing and Building Technology for Production and Life Models; Offshore Engineering Auxiliary Ship; Underwater Engineering Technology, Submersible Technology and Equipment, Sea Bed Exploration, Underwater Survey, Underwater Operation; Offshore Oil and Gas Rigs/Platform, Power/Generator System, Auxiliary Boiler, Information Procession and Transmission System, Lighting System, Electrical and Control System, Platform Elevation System, Mooring System, Crane System, Lifting and Installation System, Steel Structure System, Indemnification System, Communication, Air-condition and Ventilation, Anticorrosion, Heat Preservation and Freeze System, Environment Protection Equipment
**Established Year:** 2008
**Frequency:** Annual
**Market Area:** National
**Organizer:** Shanghai New Force Expo Service Co Ltd

2010/11/08-10
☎ 021-6280 7745
🖷 021-6294 7723
✉ newfexpo6@yahoo.cn
www.chinashipbuild-expo.com
3850

**第三届中国国际造船工业装备和船舶设计建造技术展**
**地点：**上海国际展览中心，上海
**内容：**钢板预处理（除锈、涂装）设备、涂装与涂料；各类船用钢材；钢板加工设备、管材加工设备、各类机床和其他金属加工设备；先进切割装备（如数控火焰切割、数控等离子切割、数控相贯线切割、机器人型材自动切割等）、先进焊接装备和焊材；起重和运输装备（包括高空作业车、电磁吊等）、港口机械和水上起重装备；无损检测设备（超声波、X光、化学探伤等），测量定位仪器、在线检测设备、理化检验和计量仪器；各类机床、数控机床及专用加工机床
**始办年份：**2008
**周期：**每年一届
**市场范围：**全国性
**主办：**中国船舶工业行业协会；上海船舶工业行业协会
**承办：**上海浦东国际展览公司；上海新力会展服务有限公司；上海谐成船舶技术咨询有限公司
**地址：**上海番禺路383号601室（200052）
**联系人：**杨颖

**China Intl Exhibition on Shipbuilding Equipment, Ship Design & Manufacturing Tech 2010**
**Venue:** Shanghai International Exhibition Center, Shanghai
**Profile:** Steel Pre-processing Equipments, Paint and Painting Devices; Ship Steel; Steel Processing Equipment, Pipe Processing Equipment, Machine, Metal Processing Equipment. Cutting Equipment and Cutting Machine, Welding Equipment and Welding Materials; Lifting Machine and Transportation Equipment, Port Machinery, Floating Lifting Equipment. Non-Destructive Test Equipment, Measuring Device and Locating Instrument, On-line Detection Equipment, Physics Checking & Inspecting Facility. Machine Tools, CNC Machine Tools and Special Machine Tools; Tools, Rigging, Pump & Valve, Seal, Electrical Apparatus, Controlling System, Air Sac, Wire and Cable, Wiring Machine. Environmental Protection Equipment, Industrial Cleaning Equipment; Security Monitoring Equipment, Shipbuilding Industry Park; Special Equipment for Shipyard
**Established Year:** 2008
**Frequency:** Annual
**Market Area:** National
**Organizer:** Shanghai New Force Expo Service Co Ltd
**Contact:** Maggie Yang

2010/11/09-11
☎ 021-6289 2666
🖷 021-6289 5703, 6289 0302
✉ ciif@shanghaiexpogroup.com
www.ciif-expo.com
3860

**2010中国国际工业博览会**
**地点：**上海新国际博览中心，上海
**内容：**数控机床与金属加工展、工业自动化展、环保技术与设备展、信息与通信技术应用展、新能源与电力电工展、科技创新展、航空航天技术展。
**承办：**上海世博（集团）有限公司

**China International Industry Fair 2010**
**Venue:** Shanghai New International Expo Center, Shanghai
**Profile:** Metalworking & CNC Machine Tool Show, Industrial Automation Show, Environmental Protection Technology & Equipment Show, Information and Communication Technology Show, Energy Show, Scientific & Technological Innovation Show, China Aerospace and Aviation Technology Show
**Organizer:** Shanghai World Expo (Group) Co Ltd

2010/11/10-12
☎ 0755-8831 2796
🖷 0755-8831 2533, 8831 5466
www.icef.com.cn
3870

**2010年秋季（第76届）中国电子展**
**暨2010亚洲电子展**
**地点：**上海新国际博览中心，上海
**内容：**电子元器件、显示产品、生产设备、仪器仪表、电子工具、军工产品等 工业洁净设备、空气检测设备、超声波清洗设备、防静电系列
**主办：**中国电子器材总公司；深圳市创意时代会展有限公司
**地址：**深圳市福田区福华三路国际商会中心2201室
**联系人：**李艳

**China Electronics Fair**
**Venue:** Shanghai New International Expo Center, Shanghai
**Profile:** CEF is an authoritative electronics show in China, which is the only fair fully supported by both China Ministry of Information Industry and Ministry of Commerce. It helps your companies keep a long and deep effect to the electronics and information industry in China
**Organizer:** Creativity Convention & Exhibition (Shenzhen) Co Ltd
**Address:** Room 2201, International Chamber of Commerce Tower, Fuhua 3 Rd, Futian Dist., Shenzhen, China
**Contact:** Jessica Lee

2010/11/11-13
☎ 021-6209 5209
🖷 021-6209 5210, 6209 5232
✉ Margaret@chinaallworld.com
✉ lily@chinaallworld.com
www.fhcchina.com
3890

**第十四届国际食品、饮料、酒店设备、餐饮设备、烘培及服务展览**
**地点：**上海新国际博览中心，上海
**内容：**葡萄酒、烈酒及啤酒展览，糖果、饼干、巧克力及冰激凌展览，餐饮及酒店业室内装饰及布置展览，酒店、餐饮及零售科技展览
**始办年份：**1981
**周期：**每年一届
**市场范围：**国际性
**入场券价格：**免费
**参展费用：**标准展位455美元/m$^2$，净地370美元/m$^2$
**上届规模** '09：展览面积35,000m$^2$(国外展商面积35,000m$^2$)，参展商849家（国外展商849家，来自61个国家），参观人数20, 810人（专业贸易观众20, 810人）
**主办：**华汉国际会议展览（上海）有限公司
**地址：**上海市长宁区仙霞路318-322号鑫达大厦2402室（200336）
**联系人：**张远渊，朱黎

**FHC China 2010**
**Venue:** Shanghai New International Expo Center, Shanghai
**Profile:** Wine & Spirits; Confectionery; Hospitality Interiors; Hospitality & Retail Technology
**Established Year:** 1981
**Frequency:** Annual
**Market Area:** International
**Cost to Attend:** Free
**Participated Fee:** Standard Booth USD 455/m$^2$, Raw Space USD 370/m$^2$
**Statistics '09:** Exhibition Area 35,000m$^2$(foreigners 35,000m$^2$), Exhibitors 849 (foreigners 849, came from 61 countries), Visitors 20, 810 (trade visitors 20, 810)
**Organizer:** China International Exhibitions Ltd
**Address:** Rm A2402-03, Singular Mansion, No.318-322 Xian Xia Rd, Shanghai 200336, China
**Contact:** Ms Margaret Zhang, Ms Lily Zhu

2010/11/17-19
☎ 021-6464 5558转ext 3402
🖷 021-64812993
✉ info@cnta.org
www.chinanonwovens.com
3900

**2010年中国国际过滤工业展览会**
**地点：**上海国际展览中心，上海
**主办：**上海希达科技有限公司

**Filtration 2010, China**
**Venue:** Shanghai International Exhibition Center, Shanghai
**Organizer:** CNTA Science & Technology Co Ltd

2010/11/17-19
☎ +65-6592 0890
🖷 +65-6438 6090
www.tissueworld.com
www.ubmasia.com.sg
3910

**亚洲纸业世界展览会**
**地点：**上海国际展览中心，上海
**主办：**亚洲博闻

**Tissue World Asia**
**Venue:** Shanghai International Exhibition Center, Shanghai
**Organizer:** UBM Asia

2010/11/18-21
☎ 010-5960 4070, 5960 4072
℻ 010-5960 4071，5820 4990
www.citm.com.cn
3920

中国国际旅游交易会
地点：上海新国际博览中心，上海
主办：中国国家旅游局

China International Travel Mart
Venue: Shanghai New International Expo Center, Shanghai
Organizer: China National Tourism Administration

2010/11/22-24
☎ 021-6295 6677
℻ 021-6278 0038
✉ intexhjn@sh163.net
www.interlubric.com
3930

2010中国国际润滑油、脂及调和技术设备展览会
地点：上海国际展览中心，上海
主办：上海国际展览中心有限公司

2010 China Intl lubricating oil, Grease and Refining Technology Exhibition
Venue: Shanghai International Exhibition Center, Shanghai
Organizer: Intex Shanghai Co Ltd

2010/11/23-26
☎ 021-2020 5500
010-6859 4951
℻ 021-2020 5655, 2020 5666
✉ info@ccpitmsc.org
jix@ccpit.org
baumachina@mmi-shanghai.com
www.b-china.cn
www.chinamachin.org.cn
www.ccpitmsc.org
3936

中国国际工程机械、建材机械、工程车辆及设备博览会（双年展）
地点：上海新国际博览中心，上海
内容：与其母展慕尼黑bauma展一样，bauma China的成功举办奠定了德国慕尼黑国际博览集团在建筑机械展会行业的领先地位。bauma China秉承了慕尼黑bauma展的成功理念，同时又充分迎合了中国及亚洲市场的需求，自2002年成功首演以来，稳步发展，确立了其作为亚洲工程机械与建材机械行业权威性专业博览会的地位。
周期：两年一届
市场范围：国际性
主办：德国慕尼黑国际博览集团；慕尼黑展览（上海）有限公司；中国工程机械工业协会；中国贸促会机械行业分会；中工工程机械成套有限公司
联络：中国贸促会机械行业分会
地址：北京市西城区三里河路46号（100823）
联系人：白东红
联络：德国慕尼黑国际博览集团；慕尼黑展览（上海）有限公司
联系人：徐芸婷

bauma
Venue: Shanghai New International Expo Center, Shanghai
Profile: Like bauma Munich (a building and construction trade fair), the success of bauma China prepared the ground for Messe München International to take the lead in construction machinery trade fairs. bauma China implemented the model of bauma Munich and was able to completely cater for the needs of the Chinese and Asian markets. Since its first success in 2002, it has achieved sustainable development and has established its place as the authoritative professional construction machinery, and building materials machinery exhibition in Asia
Organizer: Messe München International

2010/11/25-27
☎ 010-5865 0277，6226 4569
℻ 010-5865 0288
www.reifenchina.com
3940

中国国际橡胶技术展览会
第四届亚洲埃森轮胎展
地点：上海新国际博览中心，上海
承办：北京中橡富润会展有限责任公司

REIFEN CHINA
4th Asian Essen Tire Show
Venue: Shanghai New International Expo Center, Shanghai
Organizer: China United Rubber Corporation,

2010/11/30-02
☎ 021-5109 7799
℻ 021-5171 4505
✉ zhanye@vip.sina.com
www.baowenzhan.com.cn
3950

2010第八届中国（上海）国际保温材料与节能技术展览会
地点：上海新国际博览中心，上海
内容：保温材料：岩(矿)棉、玻璃棉、硅酸铝纤维等绝热材料，膨胀珍珠岩、硅酸钙、泡沫玻璃,硬质绝热材料，墙体保温材料，泡沫保温材料，橡塑发泡材料、挤塑（膨胀）聚苯乙烯、酚醛泡沫，聚氨酯保温材料、保温涂料等、石棉制品及泡沫石棉、直埋管、铝箔等外护绝热材料，彩钢板等绝热板材及相关设备。EPS机械设备、EPS板材、EPS墙体外保温、EPS模具、EPS辅料供应商、EPS机械配套供应商、SM、XPS、PSP等。隔音及吸音材料：隔音墙体、隔音罩、隔音毡、隔音窗、隔音封条、隔声屏障、汽车隔音材料
始办年份：2003
周期：每年一届
市场范围：国际性
入场券价格：免费
参展费用：国际展区10,800元/展位；国内展区8,820元/展位；净地：国际展区1,100元/$m^2$，国内展区900元/$m^2$
上届规模　'09：展览面积11,500$m^2$(国外展商面积780$m^2$)，参展商436家（国外展商53家，来自13个国家），参观人数28,260人（专业贸易观众19,341人）
主办：中国绝热节能材料协会
承办：上海展业展览有限公司
地址：上海市虹漕南路99弄1号1楼A座（200233）
联系人：曾俊杰，周军
MSN：zjj-expo@hotmail.com
QQ：307699460

2010 8th China (Shanghai) Intl Thermal Insulation Materials and Energy-saving Technology Expo
Venue: Shanghai New International Expo Center, Shanghai
Profile: Insulation materials: rock (ore) cotton, glass wool, ceramic fiber insulation materials, calcium silicate, foam glass, rigid insulation materials, wall insulation, foam insulation materials, rubber and plastic foaming material, extrusion (expansion) polystyrene, polyurethane insulation materials, insulation paint, asbestos products and foam asbestos, buried pipe, aluminum foil insulation material being loaded with care, color steel sheet and related equipment such as thermal insulation. EPS Machinery, EPS panel, EPS external wall insulation, EPS molds, EPS accessories suppliers, EPS machinery supporting suppliers, SM, XPS, PSP and so on. Sound insulation and sound-absorbing materials; Energy-saving technology.
Established Year: 2003
Frequency: Annual
Market Area: International
Cost to Attend: Free
Participated Fee: Intl Area RMB 10,800/Booth, Raw Space RMB 1,100/$m^2$
Statistics '09: Exhibition Area 11,500$m^2$(foreigners 780$m^2$), Exhibitors 436 (foreigners 53, came from 13 countries), Visitors 28,260 (trade visitors 19,341)
Assn Sponsor: China Insulation & Energy Efficiency Materials
Organizer: Shanghai Zhanye Exhibition Co Ltd
Address: Section A, Floor 1, No. 1, 99 Hongcao South Road, Shanghai, China
Contact: Zeng Junjie, Zhou Jun
MSN: zjj-expo@hotmail.com

2010/12/01-03
☎ 010-6427 2721
℻ 010-6420 5891
✉ yang@ccpitchem.org.cn
www.ccpitchem.org.cn
3955

第十三届中国国际胶粘剂及密封剂展览会
暨第五届中国国际胶粘剂与标签展览会
地点：上海国际展览中心，上海
主办：中国贸促会化工行业分会

China Adhesive 2010
Venue: Shanghai International Exhibition Center, Shanghai
Organizer: CCPIT Sub-Council of Light Industry

2010/12/08-11
☎ 021-6160 8555
🖷 021-5876 9332
✉ info@china.messefrankfurt.com
www.automechanika-shanghai.com.cn
3960

**上海国际汽车零配件、维修检测诊断设备及服务用品展览会**
**地点：**上海新国际博览中心，上海
**主办：**法兰克福展览公司

**automechanika Shanghai**
Shanghai Intl Trade Fair for Automotive Parts, Equipment and Service Supplies
**Venue:** Shanghai New International Expo Center, Shanghai
**Organizer:** Messe Frankfurt (Shanghai) Co Ltd

2010/12/09-11
☎ 021-6437 0468
🖷 021-6471 2001
✉ dwtang@sstec.com.cn
http://nfh.sstec.com.cn
3970

**上海国际健康大会**
**地点：**上海展览中心，上海
**内容：**上海国际健康大会由论坛、展览和健康之夜三部分组成，贯穿健康这一系统工程的每一个环节。从生殖、母婴、营养、运动、食品安全、疾病防治以及康复等的全过程。涉及到环境、农业、食品加工、流通、功能食品、保健品、药品、医院、医疗器械、康复器材、健康检测、健康管理、健康咨询等方面。健康大会将优选具有代表性机构、专家学者和企业人士参与，向大众全面演绎健康的全过程。此外，风险投资、技术转移和技术交易等机构也将积极参与，为健康产业的发展提供了更多的商机。
**始办年份：**2006
**周期：**每年一届
**市场范围：**国际性
**性质：**面向公众
**参展费用：**B区：标准展位12,000元，净地850元/m$^2$
**上届规模** '09：展览面积6,000m$^2$，参展商150家（国外展商17家，来自6个国家），参观人数6,000人
**主办：**上海对外科学技术交流中心
**地址：**上海市淮海中路1634号（200031）
**联系人：**唐登伟

**International Congress & Exhibition on Nutrition Fitness and Health (NFH)**
**Venue:** Shanghai Exhibition Center, Shanghai
**Profile:** It goes through every aspects of health, a systematic project, covering the thorough process of reproductive health, mother and infant health, nutrition, fitness, food safety, disease prevention and rehabilitation, involving the fields of environment, agriculture, food processing, circulation, function food, health products, medicine, hospitals, medical devices, rehabilitation equipment, health detection, health management and health consulting. NFH selects the participators from the representative institutions, experts and scholars, and enterprises to picture a great blueprint of health to the public.
**Established Year:** 2006
**Frequency:** Annual
**Market Area:** International
**Nature:** Open to public
**Participated Fee:** Standard Booth RMB 12,000, Raw Space RMB 850/m$^2$
**Statistics '09:** Exhibition Area 6,000m$^2$, Exhibitors 150（foreigners 17, came from 6 countries）, Visitors 6,000
**Organizer:** Shanghai Center for Scientific and Technological With Foreign Countries
**Address:** No.1634, Middle Huai Hai Rd. Shanghai
**Contact:** Mr Tang Dengwei

2010/12/15-17
☎ 010-6316 1609，8827 5806
🖷 010-6316 2123，8827 5733
✉ jiating@chinaprint.org.cn
✉ yinhang@keyin.cn
www.labelchinaexpo.com
3990

**2010中国国际标签技术展览会**
**地点：**上海国际展览中心，上海
**内容：**印前系统：印前材料和技术、软件及新技术、制版设备及检测设备等；印刷及配套设备：柔性版印刷机、凸版印刷机、丝网印刷机、模切机、商标检验设备、包装贴标机及其它设备；相关技术：RFID及智能标签技术、管理信息系统（MIS）、可变条形码技术等；标签材料及消耗品：不干胶材料、各种薄膜、箔、表面和自粘材料、版材、油墨、网纹辊、模切辊、印版辊
**始办年份：**2008
**周期：**两年一届
**市场范围：**国际性
**性质：**面向公众
**参展费用：**A区净地1,600元/㎡，B区净地1,200元/㎡，C区净地1,000元/㎡，标准展位搭建费为80元/㎡
**上届规模** '08：展览面积2,000m$^2$(国外展商面积100m$^2$)，参展商60家（国外展商1家，来自2个国家），专业贸易观众3,000人
**主办：**中国印刷及设备器材工业协会；中国印刷科学技术研究所
**承办：**中国印刷及设备器材工业协会展览部；中国印刷及设备器材工业协会标签印刷分会；科印传媒项目部
**联络：**北京市宣武区永安路106号2层中国印刷及设备器材工业协会（100050）
**联系人：**贾婷，邱晓红
**联络：**北京科印传媒文化有限公司
**联系人：**尹航，王会莫

**China International Exhibition for Label Technology**
Venue: Shanghai International Exhibition Center, Shanghai
**Established Year:** 2008
**Frequency:** Biennial
**Market Area:** International
**Nature:** Open to public
**Participated Fee:** Raw Space RMB 1,600/㎡, Set-up Fee RMB 80/㎡
**Statistics '08:** Exhibition Area 2, 000m$^2$(foreigners 100m$^2$), Exhibitors 60（foreigners 1, came from 2 countries）, Visitors 3, 000（trade Visitors 3,000）
**Organizer:** Printing and Printing Equipment Industries Assn of China (PEIAC); China Academy of Printing Technology
**Address:** 2nd Floor, 106, Yong'an Road, Xuanwu District, Beijing, China
Contact: Jia Ting, Qiu Xiaohong

# 天津
# Tianjin

2010/03/12 - 13
☎ 0431-8693 1008, 8783 5764
🖷 0431-8783 5765
✉ ntcpjg@126.com
4020

**第二届全国杂粮产业大会**
**地点**：天津财富豪为酒店，天津
**内容**：杂粮产品及加工设备展洽订货会，全国杂粮产业论坛与全国杂粮产业联盟2010年会，分别举办小米与糜子、荞麦与燕麦、高粱专题交流会，全国杂粮经销商生产商联谊会
**始办年份**：2009
**周期**：每年一届
**市场范围**：全国性
**入场券价格**：900元/人
**参展费用**：产品展位500元/个，设备展位2,000元/个
**上届规模** '09：展览面积600m$^2$，参观人数300人
**主办**：中国农学会特产分会；全国杂粮产业联盟；吉林省农特产品加工协会
**地址**：长春市西安大路5333号（130062）
**联系人**：赵玉敏，韩玉娇
**QQ**：63525996

**2nd National Cereals Industry Convention**
**Venue**: Tianjin Hope Way Hotel, Tianjin
**Established Year**: 2009
**Frequency**: Annual
**Market Area**: National
**Cost to Attend**: RMB 900/pp
**Participated Fee**: Products RMB 500/unit, Equipment RMB 2,000/unit
**Statistics '09**: Exhibition Area 600m$^2$, Visitors 300
**Organizer**: Jilin Agricultural Product Processing Assn
**Address**: 5333 Xi'an Road, Changchun, Jilin 130062

2010/03/17 - 18
☎ 0431-8693 1008, 8783 5764
🖷 0431-8783 5765
✉ ntcpjg@126.com
4030

**第四届全国鸭鹅产业大会**
**地点**：天津财富豪为酒店，天津
**内容**：鸭鹅产业论坛，鸭鹅产品、羽绒产品、设备展洽会，风味鸭鹅产品，大会金奖产品评选，全国鸭鹅产业联盟2010年会与专家企业家互动研讨会、羽绒产品加工交流会
**始办年份**：2007
**周期**：每年一届
**市场范围**：全国性
**入场券价格**：900元/人
**参展费用**：产品展位500元/个，设备产位2,000元/个
**主办**：全国鸭鹅产业联盟；吉林省农特产品加工协会
**地址**：长春市西安大路5333号（130062）
**联系人**：赵玉敏，韩玉娇
**QQ**：724088225

**4th National Ducks and Geese Convention**
**Venue**: Tianjin Hope Way Hotel, Tianjin
**Established Year**: 2007
**Frequency**: Annual
**Market Area**: National
**Cost to Attend**: RMB 900/pp
**Participated Fee**: Products RMB 500/unit, Equipment RMB 2,000/unit
**Statistics '09**: Exhibition Area 600m2, Visitors 300
**Organizer**: Jilin Agricultural Product Processing Assn
**Address**: 5333 Xi'an Road, Changchu, Jilin 130062

2010/05/06 - 09
☎ 022-8371 1728
🖷 022-8371 3578
✉ tjqiyang@163.com
4035

**2010第三届天津国际珠宝首饰展览会**
**地点**：天津国际展览中心，天津
**内容**：钻石及宝石：钻石、红宝石、蓝宝石、半宝石、祖母绿、人造宝石等；珠宝首饰：黄金首饰、白银首饰、铂金首饰、钯金首饰、钻石首饰、宝石首饰、镶嵌首饰、仿真首饰、镀金首饰、珍珠首饰、翡翠玉石首饰、水晶等；黄金制品：金条、金币、金箔、金表及其它黄金制品；珠宝首饰加工设备、仪器工具、鉴定设备、软件、陈列及包装用品；珠宝产业园、珠宝交易中心、特色珠宝商场。
**始办年份**：2008
**周期**：每年一届
**市场范围**：国际性
**性质**：面向公众
**参展费用**：豪华展位：11,800元/展位，国际展区9,800元，国内展区8,800元，国际展区净地900元/m2，国内展区净地800元/m2
**主办**：天津市宝玉石协会 协办：台湾珠宝杂志社
**承办**：天津企阳展览服务有限公司
**地址**：天津市河西区友谊路32号

**2010 Tianjin the 3rd International Jewelry Fair**
**Venue**: Tianjin International Exhibition Center, Tianjin
**Established Year**: 2008
**Frequency**: Annual
**Market Area**: International
**Nature**: Open to Public
**Participated Fee**: Upgraded Booth RMB 11,800, Standard Booth RMB 9,800, Raw Space RMB 900/m2
**Sponsor**: Tianjin Gem-jade Association
**Organizer**: Tianjin Qiyang Exhibit Service Co Ltd

2010/05/18 - 20
☎ 022-2311 5536, 2331 2556
🖷 022-2331 2556
4040

**2010中国（天津）国际医疗仪器与设备展览会**
**地点**：天津体育中心，天津
**内容**：天津市不断加大医疗卫生改革和投入力度，通过资源调整形成了以市属，区属医院为依托，社会卫生服务站为基础的服务体系，如今妇女儿童健康行动五年计划全面实施，市财政每年投入5500万，天津妇幼卫生工作在全国起到了引领和示范工作。为了响应中央将天津滨海新区成为我国经济发展的新引擎，引领中国区域发展重点北移，同时天津成为我国北方医疗事业的重要平台。
首届
**周期**：每年一届
**市场范围**：国际性
**参展费用**：4500元
**预计规模**：展出面积3,000m2，参展商200家，参观人数20,000人
**主办**：天津市卫生局；天津市机电设备招标局
**承办**：天津泰和新侨科技园区管委会；天津建和国际贸易展览有限公司
**地址**：天津市和平区开封道2号22层10号（300042）
**联系人**：赵建莉，张维

**China Tianjin Intl Medical Instruments and Equipment Exhibition**
**Venue**: Tianjin Sports Center, Tianjin
First Session
**Frequency**: Annual
**Market Area**: International
**Participated Fee**: RMB 4,500/booth
**Organizer**: Tianjin Jianhe Intl Trade and Exhibition Co Ltd

2010/05/26 - 28
☎ 022-5858 1918, 5858 1928
🖷 022-5858 1928
✉ 58581918@163.com
4050

**2010第七届中国（天津）国际涂料展览会**
**地点**：天津国际展览中心，天津
**内容**：涂料产品 汽车涂料、不粘涂料、工业涂料、溶剂型涂料、水基涂料、粉末涂料及其它相关涂料、油墨及粘合剂产品。化学品及原材料：天然树脂、合成树脂、颜料、溶剂、填料、填充剂、助剂。生产及包装设备:调色系统、混料器、搅拌机、连续式混料器、间歇式混料器、实验室混料器、高速分散机、挤压机、挤出机、捏合机、研磨机及其配件、过滤器、泵、计量仪、称重装置、分料及装料系统、包装机、贴标签机、研磨及分散介质
**始办年份**：2004
**周期**：每年一届
**市场范围**：国际性
**性质**：面向公众
**参展费用**：7,800元
**上届规模** '09：展览面积20,000m2(国外展商面积10,000m2)，参展商800家（国外展商50家，来自50个国家），参观人数20,000人（专业贸易观众15,000人）
**主办**：天津市电镀工程学会
**承办**：天津裕华展览服务有限公司
**地址**：天津市河西区大沽南路857号国华大厦2108室（300200）
**联系人**：王先生，刘小姐

**The 7th China (Tianjin) International Coatings Exhibition**
**Venue**: Tianjin International Exhibition Center, Tianjin
**Established Year**: 2004
**Frequency**: Annual
**Market Area**: International
**Nature**: Open to public
**Participated Fee**: RMB 7,800
**Statistics '09**: Exhibition Area 20,000m2(foreigners 10,000m2), Exhibitors 800 (foreigners 50, came from 50 countries), Visitors 20,000 (trade visitors 15,000)
**Sponsor**: Plating Engineering Institute of Tianjin
**Organizer**: Tianjin Yuhua Exhibition Service Co Ltd
**Address**: Room 2108 Guohua Bldg, 857 Taku Road, Hexi District, Tianjin, China
**Contact**: Mr Wang, Mrs Liu

2010/05/26 - 28
☎ 010-5225 9853
🖷 010-8767 1146
✉ 87689903@163.com
www.zonro.cn
4060

**2010第七届中国国际轮胎资源循环利用展览会**
**地点**：天津滨海国际会展中心，天津
**内容**：名优新轮胎和翻新轮胎产品。轮胎翻新工艺设备及原辅材料：轮胎翻新设备：胎体打磨设备、胎面压合设备、轮胎硫化设备、包封套生产和拆装设备、胎面胶生产设备、导热油炉加热设备以及其它新型工艺设备；轮胎翻新模具、专用工具及附件；轮胎翻新原辅材料：包括预硫化胎面胶、中垫胶、胶条、粘合剂、硫化内胎、硫化气囊、包封套和聚氨脂胎面材料。轮胎修补工艺设备及修补材料：包括轮胎拆装设备、轮胎修补硫化设备、轮胎动平衡设备、轮胎充气设备、轮胎修补工具及补片。废旧轮胎综合利用设备及产品
**始办年份**：2002
**周期**：每年一届
**市场范围**：国际性
**性质**：面向公众
**参展费用**：国内展商6800元/9m2
**上届规模** '09：展览面积5,000m2(国外展商面积1,000m2)，参展商150家（国外展商15家，来自13个国家），专业贸易观众5,000人
**主办**：中国物流与采购联合会；中国轮胎翻修与循环利用协会
**承办**：中融商汇（北京）国际会展有限公司
**地址**：北京刘家窑芳群公寓C座1705室（100079）
**联系人**：李金玉，郭广通

**7th China International Tire Resource Cyclic Utilization Expo**
**Venue**: Binhai International Convention and Exhibition Center, Tianjin
**Established Year**: 2002
**Frequency**: Annual
**Market Area**: International
**Nature**: Open to public
**Participated Fee**: Domestic Exhibitors RMB 6,800/9m2
**Statistics '09**: Exhibition Area 5,000m2(foreigners 1,000m2), Exhibitors 150 (foreigners 15, came from 13 countries), Trade Visitors 5,000
**Organizer**:
**Address**: Zhongrong Shanghui (Beijing) International Exhibition Co Ltd

2010/05/26 - 28
☎ 022-5858 1918, 5858 1928
🖷 022-5858 1928
✉ 58581918@163.com
4070

**第六届中国（天津）国际动力传动与控制技术展览会**
**第六届中国天津液压、气动、密封件及空压机展览会**
**地点**：天津国际展览中心，天津
**内容**：液压压力机、液压元件和气压、液压阀、液压过滤器、冷却器、蓄能器、液压缸各种气油缸液压泵。气动阀、球阀、比例阀、节流阀、截止阀、伺服阀、微调阀、压力、流量方向控制阀等。各种工程机械液压系统及零配件、电力水力液压系统、电力汽轮机、高压抗燃油液压系统、风力发电机液压系统、船闸启闭机液压系统、泻洪闸液压系统及各种液压实验台，石油系统包括石油钻机刹车、橡胶四辊轧机、石油切管机液压系统。气动压力机、气动元件辅件、气动内燃机及小型涡轮、压缩空气技术、各种液压气动马达、真空设备、空气洁净设备、气动三大件
**始办年份**：2005
**周期**：每年一届
**市场范围**：国际性
**性质**：面向公众
**参展费用**：6,800元
**上届规模** '09：展览面积20,000m2(国外展商面积10,000m2)，参展商800家（国外展商50家，来自50个国家），参观人数20,000人（专业贸易观众15,000人）
**主办**：天津市设备管理协会
**承办**：天津裕华展览服务有限公司
**地址**：中国天津市河西区大沽南路857号国华大厦2108室（300200）
**联系人**：王先生，刘小姐

**6th China (Tianjin) Intl power Transmission and Control Technology Exhibition**
**Venue**: Tianjin International Exhibition Center, Tianjin
**Established Year**: 2005
**Frequency**: Annual
**Market Area**: International
**Nature**: Open to public
**Participated Fee**: RMB 6,800
**Statistics '09**: Exhibition Area 20,000m2(foreigners 10,000m2), Exhibitors 800 (foreigners 50, came from 50 countries), Visitors 20,000 (trade visitors 15,000)
**Sponsor**: Tianjin Equipment Management Assn
**Organizer**: Tianjin Yuhua Exhibition Service Co
**Address**: Room 2108 Guohua Bldg, 857 Taku Road, Hexi District, Tianjin, China
**Contact**: Mr Wang, Mrs Liu

2010/05/26 - 28
☎ 022-5858 1918, 5858 1928
🖷 022-5858 1928
✉ 58581918@163.com
4080

**2010第六届中国（天津）国际机床展览会**
**地点**：天津国际展览中心，天津
**内容**：数控金属切削机床：数控车床及车削中心、数控重型立、卧车床、数控铣床、数控重型镗铣床、数控重型龙门铣床、加工中心、数控磨床、数控齿轮加工机床、数控锯床、数控组合机床及生产线、柔性制造单元及制造系统；数控成形设备：数控锻压机械、数控冲剪等钣金加工机床、激光切割机床、水切割机床、

**6th China (Tianjin) Intl Machine Tool Exhibition**
**Venue**: Tianjin International Exhibition Center, Tianjin
**Frequency**: Annual
**Market Area**: International
**Nature**: Open to public
**Participated Fee**: RMB 6,800
**Statistics '09**: Exhibition Area 20,000m2(foreigners 10,000m2),

数控冲压柔性制造系统；数控快速成型机床；激光、等离子及特种加工设备；铸造、热加工、焊接设备；数控电加工设备：数控电火花成型机、数控快、慢走丝电火花线切割机、专用特种加工机床；功能部件及配套产品：数控系统、电主轴及伺服系统
**周期**：每年一届
**市场范围**：国际性
**性质**：面向公众
**参展费用**：6800元
**上届规模**'09：展览面积20,000m2(国外展商面积10,000m2)，参展商800家（国外展商50家，来自50个国家），参观人数20,000人（专业贸易观众15,000人）
**主办**：天津机电工业(控股)集团公司
**承办**：天津裕华展览服务有限公司
**地址**：天津市河西区大沽南路857号国华大厦2108室（300200）
**联系人**：王先生，刘小姐

Exhibitors 800（foreigners 50, came from 50 countries），Visitors 20,000（trade visitors 15,000）
**Sponsor**: Tianjin Electrical Industries (Holdings) Group
**Organizer**: Tianjin Yuhua Exhibition Service Co
**Address**: Room 2108 Guohua Bldg, 857 Taku Road, Hexi District, Tianjin, China
**Contact**: Mr Wang, Mrs Liu

2010/05/26 - 28
☎ 022-5858 1918, 5858 1928
📠 022-5858 1928
✉ 58581918@163.com
4090

## 第六届中国（天津）国际工业控制自动化及仪器仪表展览会

**地点**：天津国际展览中心，天津
**内容**：控制系统：工业网络、安全自动化、基于PC的自动化、工控机、工业计算机、工业电源、人机界面、控制装置及专用控制器、变频调速、电气传动、运动控制、可编程控制器、分布式计算机控制系统、数据采集、信号处理、工业自动控制系统及装备、楼宇自动化 电气工程：控制技术、测量及调整设备技术、网络\工业数据通讯、电动机、机架系统、驱动装置、网络/工业无线通讯、驱动装置、嵌入式系统、光电技术、电力供应
**始办年份**：2005
**周期**：每年一届
**市场范围**：国际性
**性质**：面向公众
**参展费用**：6,800元
**上届规模**'09：展览面积20,000m2(国外展商面积10,000m2)，参展商800家（国外展商50家，来自50个国家），参观人数20,000人（专业贸易观众15,000人）
**主办**：天津市科学技术协会
**承办**：天津裕华展览服务有限公司
**地址**：天津市河西区大沽南路857号国华大厦2108室（300200）
**联系人**：王先生，刘小姐

## 6th China (Tianjin) Intl Industrial Control Automation & Instrument Exhibition

**Venue**: Tianjin International Exhibition Center, Tianjin
**Established Year**: 2005
**Frequency**: Annual
**Market Area**: International
**Nature**: Open to public
**Participated Fee**: RMB 6,800
**Statistics '09**: Exhibition Area 20,000m2(foreigners 10,000m2), Exhibitors 800（foreigners 50, came from 50 countries），Visitors 20,000（trade visitors 15,000）
**Sponsor**: Tianjin Science and Technology
**Address**: Room 2108 Guohua Bldg, 857 Taku Road, Hexi District, Tianjin, China
**Contact**: Mr Wang, Mrs Liu

2010/05/26 - 28
☎ 022-5858 1918, 5858 1928
📠 022-5858 1928
✉ 58581918@163.com
4100

## 第六届中国(天津)国际模具技术与设备展览会

**地点**：天津国际展览中心，天津
**内容**：模具及模具制品，模具标准件；加工中心，数控铣、镗、车、钻；模具加工金切机床；电加工机床，雕刻机；三坐标测量机及其它测量设备；压铸机，压力机床及试模设备；塑料机械及像胶机械；模具材料，冶金制品；模具CAD、CAM、CAE；各类模具生产用的辅料、辅助设备，抛光、研磨、装配夹具等；工具、刃具以及与模具想着的其他产品。
**始办年份**：2004
**周期**：每年一届
**市场范围**：国际性
**性质**：面向公众
**参展费用**：6,800元
**上届规模**'09：展览面积20,000m2(国外展商面积10,000m2)，参展商800家（国外展商50家，来自50个国家），参观人数20,000人（专业贸易观众15,000人）
**主办**：天津市科学技术协会
**承办**：天津裕华展览服务有限公司
**地址**：天津市河西区大沽南路857号国华大厦2108室（300200）
**联系人**：王先生，刘小姐

## 6th China (Tianjin) Intl Die & Mould Technology Exhibition

**Venue**: Tianjin International Exhibition Center, Tianjin
**Established Year**: 2004
**Frequency**: Annual
**Market Area**: International
**Nature**: Open to public
**Participated Fee**: RMB 6,800
**Statistics '09**: Exhibition Area 20,000m2(foreigners 10,000m2), Exhibitors 800（foreigners 50, came from 50 countries），Visitors 20,000（trade visitors 15,000）
**Sponsor**: Tianjin Science and Technology
**Organizer**: Tianjin Yuhua Exhibition Service Co
**Address**: Room 2108 Guohua Bldg, 857 Taku Road, Hexi District, Tianjin, China
**Contact**: Mr Wang, Mrs Liu

2010/05/26 - 28
☎ 022-5858 1918, 5858 1928
📠 022-5858 1928
✉ 58581918@163.com
4120

## 第7届中国（天津）国际涂装、电镀及表面处理展览会

**地点**：天津国际展览中心，天津
**内容**：涂装设备及生产线：油漆涂装、粉末涂装、汽车涂装线、家用电器涂装线、机械手涂装、彩涂板与热镀锌、空气及无气喷枪、磨擦静电喷枪、电晕喷枪、往复喷涂机、喷涂室、固化炉、运输带、工程服务;机械式及化学式处理：研磨/抛光/打蜡、喷砂或喷丸设备、去毛刺、防锈、清洗、脱脂、化学除锈、磷化、电清洗、去离子、蒸汽脱脂、超声波、浸渍、酸洗。电镀工艺及镀液：电镀、电刷镀、化学镀、金属及合金电镀、真空电镀、非导电体金属化、塑胶电镀、电子成型、浸渍电镀、滚桶电镀、电镀助剂、中间体
**始办年份**：2004
**周期**：每年一届
**市场范围**：国际性
**性质**：面向公众
**参展费用**：7,800元
**上届规模**'09：展览面积20,000m2(国外展商面积10,000m2)，参展商800家（国外展商50家，来自50个国家），参观人数20,000人（专业贸易观众15,000人）
**主办**：天津市电镀行业协会
**承办**：天津裕华展览服务有限公司
**地址**：天津市河西区大沽南路857号国华大厦2108室（300200）
**联系人**：王先生，刘小姐

## 7th China (Tianjin) Intl Coating, Electroplating and Surface Finishing Exhibition

**Venue**: Tianjin International Exhibition Center, Tianjin
**Established Year**: 2004
**Frequency**: Annual
**Market Area**: International
**Nature**: Open to public
**Participated Fee**: RMB 7,800
**Statistics '09**: Exhibition Area 20,000m2(foreigners 10,000m2), Exhibitors 800（foreigners 50, came from 50 countries），Visitors 20,000（trade visitors 15,000）
**Sponsor**: Tianjin Electroplating Industry Assn
**Organizer**: Tianjin Yuhua Exhibition Service Co
**Address**: Room 2108 Guohua Bldg, 857 Taku Road, Hexi District, Tianjin, China
**Contact**: Mr Wang, Mrs Liu

4125
2010/07 -
☎ 010-8455 6677
📠 010-8202 2922
www.cmef.com.cn

**第11届全国医疗器械区域博览会**
**地点**：天津
**内容**：全国医疗器械区域博览会创办于2000年，每年一届。足迹遍及兰州、西安、呼和浩特、乌鲁木齐、合肥、昆明等城市，促进了不同区域医疗卫生事业的发展。全国医疗器械区域博览会每届拥有参展企业500多家，展位数量800余个，展出面积超过15000平方米。
**主办**：国药励展展览有限公司

**The 11th CMEF Regional**
**Venue**: Tianjin
**Profile**: Since 2000, the China National Medical Equipment Regional Fair (CMEF Regional) has been an annual event with the aim of developing the healthcare industry and stimulating the growth of the medical equipment markets in different parts of China as well as providing access to new markets away from the more urbanized, developed coastal cities.
CMEF Regional covers an exhibition space of over 15,000 square meters, with over 800 stands.
**Organizer**: Reed Sinopharm Exhibitions

4130
2010/08/18 - 21
☎ 022-6622 4066, 6622 4088
📠 088-6622 4099
✉ impetj@163.com
www.chinaimpe.com.cn

**第六届中国国际金属加工技术设备展览会**
**地点**：天津海滨国际会展中心，天津
**内容**：金属切削机床类，金属成形机床类，特种加工机床类，模具成型机床类，数控系统，数量装置和机床电器，机床零部件及辅助设备，检验和测量设备
**始办年份**：2004
**周期**：每年一届
**市场范围**：国际性
**性质**：面向公众
**参展费用**：国内展区：标准展位8,800元，净地750/$m^2$；国外展区标准展位2,800美元，净地280美元/$m^2$
**主办**：中国机械工业联合会；中国有色金属加工工业协会
**承办**：振威展览集团天津振威展览有限公司
**地址**：天津滨海国际会展中心（300457）
**联系人**：邓先生，朱小姐

**6th China Intl Metals Working Technology & Equipment Exhibition**
**Venue**: Binhai International Convention & Exhibition Center, Tianjin
**Established Year**: 2004
**Frequency**: Annual
**Market Area**: International
**Nature**: Open to public
**Participated Fee**: Intl Area: Standard Booth USD 2,800，Raw Space USD 280/$m^2$
**Organizer**: Tianjin Zhenwei Exhibition Co Ltd

4140
2010/09/15 - 17
☎ 010-6603 9043, 6603 9351
📠 010-6606 7681
✉ cim@cimexpo.cn
www.cimexpo.cn

**中国国际塑料橡胶注射成型工业展览会**
**地点**：天津滨海国际会展中心，天津
**内容**：塑料及橡胶注射成型设备，塑料及橡胶注射成型相关辅助设备：机械手臂（取出机）、混炼设备、干燥机、破碎机、冷水机、中央供料系统、模具及零部件、回收设备及系统、CAD/CAM系统、检测设备；塑料及橡胶注射成型生产技术、工艺；塑料及橡胶通用材料、各种工程塑料；塑料及橡胶添加剂、色母粒等，成品及半成品。
**始办年份**：2008
**周期**：每年两届
**市场范围**：国际性
**性质**：面向公众
**入场券价格**：免费
**参展费用**：净地1,100.00元/
**上届规模 '08**：展览面积12,000$m^2$(国外展商面积6,800$m^2$)，参展商167家（国外展商69家，来自12个国家），参观人数11,091人（专业贸易观众7,682人）
**主办**：中国轻工业联合会；中国石油和化工工业协会；中国轻工业机械总公司；中国轻工机械协会；天津市滨海新区管理委员会
**承办**：北京中轻亚泰塑料科技有限公司
**地址**：北京市西城区西黄城根南街33号（100032）
**联系人**：张晓晨，陈红
**MSN**：zxc560868@live.cn
**QQ**：467136157

**(CIM 2010)**
**China Intl Exhibition on Plastics and Rubber Injection Molding Industry**
**Venue**: Binhai International Convention & Exhibition Center, Tianjin
**Profile**: Plastics & rubber injection molding machine, Plastics auxiliary equipment: robot (draw-out), mixer ,dryer, crusher, chiller, feeder and auxiliary equipment, Mould & Die, Parts & Components, recycling equipment, CAD/CAM, testing equipment; Plastics & rubber injection process/molding technology; Plastics and rubber raw materials, engineering plastics; Plastics and rubber additives, color master batch, semi-/final-products
**Established Year**: 2008
**Frequency**: Biannual
**Market Area**: International
**Nature**: Open to public
**Cost to Attend**: Free
**Participated Fee**: Raw Space RMB 1,100/
**Statistics '08**: Exhibition Area 12,000$m^2$(foreigners 6,800$m^2$), Exhibitors 167（foreigners 69, came from 12 countries）, Visitors 11,091（trade visitors 7,682）
**Sponsor**: China National Light Industry Council; China Petroleum and Chemical Industry Assn; China National Light Industry Machinery Corp; China Light Industry Machinery Assn; Tianjin Binhai New Area Management Committee
**Organizer**: APPLAS CO LTD
**Address**: No. 33 Xihuangchengen South St., Xicheng Dist, Beijing 100032, China
**Contact**: Xiaochen Zhang, Hong Chen
**MSN**: zxc560868@live.cn

4150
2010/10/13 - 15
☎ 021-6299 4917, 6299 4939
📠 021-6299 4922, 6299 8196
www.paperpacking.com.cn

**PPI彩盒印刷包装展**
**地点**：天津滨海国际会展中心，天津
**内容**：印前、数字快速印刷，胶印、大幅面印刷；数字印刷及打样技术、DI技术、快速印刷技术设备 胶印、大幅面印刷机械设备器材；印刷信息网络传输设备；柔印凹印制版雕版技术设备；防伪技术设备；射频识别标签技术设备；检测仪器设备；相关材料；纸盒瓦楞纸箱印刷包装机械设备；纸品加工包装技术设备
**主办**：中国包装联合会纸制品包装委员会；上海华凝文化传媒有限公司；天津市包装技术协会
**地址**：上海市江宁路1078号11楼A座（200060）

**China Folding Carton**
3rd PPI Folding Carton, Printing & Packing Industry Exhibition and Forum
**Venue**: Binhai International Convention & Exhibition Center, Tianjin
**Organizer**: Huaning Culture Media Co Ltd

# 安徽-合肥
# Anhui-Hefei

2010/03/05 - 07
☎ 027-8736 2945
🖷 027-8736 2987
www.cwmee.com
www.hope-tarsus.com
4160

中国中西部（合肥）医疗器械展览会暨
第11届安徽医疗器械（2010年春季）展览会
地点：安徽国际会展中心，安徽合肥
主办：全国医药技术市场协会；中英合资好博塔苏斯展览公司
联系人：余云成

Hefei Medical Devices Exhibition
Venue: Anhui Exhibition and Conference Center, Hefei, Anhui
Organizer: Tarsus Hope Exhibition

2010/03/06 - 08
☎ 027-8736 2945
🖷 027-8736 2987
www.cwmee.com
www.hope-tarsus.com
4170

2010安徽印刷包装工业展览会
地点：安徽国际会展中心，安徽合肥
主办：安徽省印刷协会；中英合资好博塔苏斯展览公司
承办：湖北好博塔苏斯展览有限公司
联系人：余云成

Anhui Printing & Packaging Industry Exhibition
Venue: Anhui Exhibition and Conference Center, Hefei, Anhui
Organizer: Tarsus Hope Exhibition

2010/03/06 - 08
☎ 027-8736 2945
🖷 027-8736 2987
www.cwmee.com
www.hope-tarsus.com
4175

2010安徽视觉广告技术及标识制作展览会
地点：安徽国际会展中心，安徽合肥
主办：中英合资好博塔苏斯展览公司
承办：湖北好博塔苏斯展览有限公司
联系人：余云成

Anhui Ad Technology and Label Exhibition
Venue: Anhui Exhibition and Conference Center, Hefei, Anhui
Organizer: Tarsus Hope Exhibition

2010/05/07 - 09
☎ 0551-362 1712
🖷 0551-365 3201
✉ ahaie@163.com
www.ccieme.com.cn
4180

2010中国中部（合肥）国际装备制造业博览会
地点：安徽国际会展中心，安徽合肥
内容：机床金属加工、模具、刀具、工业控制、自动化设备、仪器仪表、焊接切割设备、五金工具、塑料机械、仓储物流设备、电力电工产品、液体传动设备、通用机械设备等。
始办年份：2001
周期：每年一届
市场范围：全国性
入场券价格：专业观众免费
参展费用：标准展位6,800元/展位；净地880元/$m^2$（36$m^2$起）
上届规模‘09：展览面积1,2000$m^2$(国外展商面积3,000$m^2$)，参展商368家（国外展商23家，来自12个国家），参观人数11,000人（专业贸易观众7,000人）
主办：中国机械工业联合会；安徽省人民政府
承办：安徽好博塔苏斯展览有限公司
地址：合肥市金寨路71号美第阳光大厦A座401室（230022）
联系人：任先生，梅先生
QQ：391548215

Central China International Equipment Manufacturing Exposition
Venue: Anhui Exhibition and Conference Center, Hefei, Anhui
Established Year: 2001
Frequency: Annual
Market Area: National
Cost to Attend: Free to Professional and Trade Visitors
Participated Fee: Standard Booth RMB 6,800/booth, Raw Space RMB 880/$m^2$（min 36$m^2$）
Statistics ‘09: Exhibition Area 1,2000$m^2$ (foreigners 3,000$m^2$), Exhibitors 368（foreigners 23, came from 12 countries）, Visitors 11,000（trade visitors 7,000）
Organizer: Tarsus Hope Exhibition

2010/08 -
☎ 027-8736 2945
🖷 027-8736 2987
www.cwmee.com
www.hope-tarsus.com
4200

中国中西部（合肥）医疗器械展览会暨
第12届安徽医疗器械（2010年秋季）展览会
地点：安徽国际会展中心，安徽合肥
主办：全国医药技术市场协会；中英合资好博塔苏斯展览公司
联系人：余云成

Hefei Medical Devices Exhibition (2010 autumn)
Venue: Anhui Exhibition and Conference Center, Hefei, Anhui
Organizer: Tarsus Hope Exhibition

# 安徽-芜湖
# Anhui-Wuhu

2010/10 -
☎ 027-8736 2945
🖷 027-8736 2987
www.cwmee.com
www.hope-tarsus.com
4220

2010第四届中国（芜湖）装备制造业博览会
地点：芜湖国际会展中心，安徽 芜湖
主办：中英合资好博塔苏斯展览公司
联系人：余云成

4th China (Wuhu) Equipment Manufacturing Exposition
Venue: Wuhu International Exhibition Center, Wuhu, Anhui
Organizer: Tarsus Hope Exhibition

# 福建-福州
# Fujian-Fuzhou

2010/03/03 - 05
☎ 022-2311 5536
℡ 022-2331 0042
✉ kenwallgs@163.com

4230

**2010福建（第21届）国际医疗仪器与设备展览会**
**地点**：福建经贸会展中心，福建福州
**内容**：本展已连续举办了十四年，展览会组委会通过十四年的积累，建立了福州、厦门、泉州、漳州、莆田、龙岩、三明、南平、宁德9个地区以及85个区、市、县的医院和医疗机构数据库，组委会每届向医疗机构和医院寄发参观邀请函、参观卷、开幕请柬，以及电话邀请、报纸广告、网络广告等大量宣传工作
**始办年份**：1995
**周期**：每年一届
**市场范围**：国际性
**性质**：面向公众
**参展费用**：4500元（9m$^2$）
**上届规模**'09：展览面积3,000m$^2$(国外展商面积450m$^2$)，参展商200家（国外展商50家，来自5个国家），参观人数20,000人（专业贸易观众15,000人）
**主办**：福建医学装备协会；中国贸促会福建分会；中国国际商会福建商会；福建省机电进出口商会 **承办**：福建经贸会展中心；天津建和国际贸易展览有限公司
**地址**：天津和平区开封道2号明源大楼22层10号（300042）
**联系人**：赵建，张维

**China Tianjin Intl Medical Instruments and Equipment Exhibition**
**Venue**: Fujian Economic-Trade Conference and Exhibition Center, Fuzhou, Fujian
**Established Year**: 1995
**Frequency**: Annual
**Market Area**: International
**Nature**: Open to public
**Participated Fee**: RMB 4,500（9m$^2$）
**Statistics '09**: Exhibition Area 3,000m$^2$(foreigners 450m$^2$), Exhibitors 200（foreigners 50, came from 5 countries）, Visitors 20,000（trade visitors 15,000）
**Organizer**: **Organizer**: Tianjin Jianhe Intl Trade and Exhibition Co Ltd

# 福建-晋江
# Fujian-Jinjiang

2010/04/19 - 22
☎ 0595-8560 0609, 8566 4572, 8530 3030
℡ 0595-8567 4572
✉ jif@cn-jif.com
www.cn-jif.com

4240

**第十二届中国(晋江)国际鞋业博览会**
**地点**：福建省晋江市美旗城一号展馆，福建晋江
**内容**：运动鞋、运动休闲鞋、帆布鞋、凉鞋、拖鞋、工作鞋、登山鞋、童鞋、皮鞋、足球鞋、合成革、人造革、PU、化工原料、制鞋机械、制革机械、设计、信息刊物、图书
**始办年份**：1999
**周期**：每年一届
**市场范围**：国际性
**入场券价格**：免费
**参展费用**：5,000元
**上届规模**'09：展览面积40,000m$^2$(国外展商面积9,000m$^2$)，参展商400家（国外展商110家，来自16个国家），参观人数25,000人（专业贸易观众3,000人）
**主办**：福建省人民政府；中国贸促会；中国轻工业联合会
**协办**：泉州市人民政府；中国皮革工业协会；中国皮革和制鞋工业研究院
**承办**：晋江市人民政府；晋江市制鞋工业协会
**联络**：福建省晋江市展务有限公司
**地址**：中国福建省晋江市青阳外经贸大厦3楼（362200）
**联系人**：李志达，丁燕燕
MSN: jif@cn-jif.com

**THE 12TH JINJIANG FOOTWEAR (INTL) EXPOSITION, CHINA**
**Venue**: International Purchase and Regional Logistics Center (Machi City), Jinjiang, Fujian
**Profile**: Sport shoes, Casual shoes, Canvas shoes, Sandals slippers, Working shoes, Mountaineering shoes, Children's shoes, Leather shoes, Football shoes, Synthetic Imitation leather, PU, Industrial chemicals, Shoe-making, leather-making, Designs, Information journals, Books
**Established Year**: 1999
**Frequency**: Annual
**Market Area**: International
**Cost to Attend**: Free
**Participated Fee**: RMB 5,000/booth
**Statistics '09**: Exhibition Area 40,000m$^2$(foreigners 9,000m$^2$), Exhibitors 400（foreigners 110, came from 16 countries）, Visitors 25,000（trade visitors 3,000）
**Sponsors**: Fujian Provincial Government; CCPIT China National Light Industry Council
**Co-Organizers**: Quanzhou Municipal Government; China Leather Industry Assn; China Leather & Footwear Industry Research
**Show Management**: Jinjiang Exhibition Affairs Co Ltd
**Address**：3F Foreign Economy & Trade Bldg., Qingyang, Jinjiang, Fujian 362200, China
**Contact**: Michelle Ding, Lyttans Li
MSN: jif@cn-jif.com

# 福建-石狮
# Fujian-Shishi

2010/04/18 - 21
☎ 0595-8870 3999
🖷 0595-8870 3999
✉ 853769696@qq.com
4250

**第十三届海峡两岸纺织服装博览会暨**
**2010年休闲服装博览会**
**地点**：石狮服装城，福建石狮
**内容**：（简称海博会，英文缩写STCF）作为全国性、国际化纺织服装博览盛会，以"两岸、休闲、规模、专业、时尚"为主题，以推动海峡两岸产业对接、促进海内外经贸交流为宗旨；展品：服装(商务休闲装、时尚休闲装、时尚运动装、休闲裤、童装、时尚运动内衣)；服饰、包袋、休闲体育用品；服装面料、服装辅料；纺织服装机械：缝制设备、纺织机械、染整设备及配件；服装CAD/CAM、纺织服装软件、服装科技及产品；服装图书、服装网络资讯、电子商务
**始办年份**：1997
**周期**：每年一届
**市场范围**：国际性
**性质**：面向公众
**入场券价格**：免费
**参展费用**：标准展位1,000元
**上届规模** '09：展览面积35,000m$^2$，参展商1,500家，参观人数158,000人（专业贸易观众16,700人）
**承办**：泉州市人民政府；石狮市人民政府
**地址**：福建省石狮市公务大厦1103室（362700）
**联系人**：高培榕
**QQ**：853769696

**13th Strait Textile & Clothing Fairs (STCF)**
**Venue**: Shishi Clothing City, Shishi, Fujian
**Profile**: As a national and international textile and costume fair, STCF, aims at the main objective of promoting cross-strait industrial interconnection, economic and trade exchanges at home and abroad.
**Exhibits**: Clothing (with emphasis on business casual wear, fashion casual wear, sports casual wear, casual trousers, children' s wear, fashion & sports underwear); Adornment, bag, casual sports products; Fabric and accessory; Textile Machinery
**Established Year**: 1997
**Frequency**: Annual
**Market Area**: International
**Nature**: Open to public
**Cost to Attend**: Free
**Participated Fee**: RMB 1000/booth
**Statistics '09**: Exhibition Area 35,000m$^2$, Exhibitors 1,500, Trade Visitors 167,000
**Organizers**: Fujian People' s Government; CCPIT; China National Textile & Apparel Council
**Address**: The 11th Floor, Room 1103, Public Affairs Building of Shishi City, Fujian Province, China
**Contact**: Gao Peilong

# 福建-厦门
# Fujian-Xiamen

2010/01/06 - 17
☎ 0592-5959 898, 5959 108
www.xicec.com
4270

**2010名品衣装（厦门）博览会**
**地点**：厦门国际会议展览中心，福建厦门
**主办**：大连珲辉展览策划公司

**Brand Name Apparel (Xiamen) Show**
**Venue**: Xiamen International Conference & Exhibition Center, Xiamen, Fujian
**Organizer**: Dalian Junhui Exhibition Co

2010/01/19 - 29
☎ 0592-5959 898, 5959 108
www.xicec.com
4280

**新品服装暨名优产品年货会**
**地点**：厦门国际会议展览中心，福建厦门
**主办**：大连珲辉展览策划公司

**New Apparel and Brand Name Products Shopping Fair**
**Venue**: Xiamen International Conference & Exhibition Center, Xiamen, Fujian
**Organizer**: Dalian Junhui Exhibition Co

2010/01/30 - 09
☎ 0592-5959 898, 5959 108
www.xicec.com
4290

**北方服装节厦门博览会**
**地点**：厦门国际会议展览中心，福建厦门

**Fashion Festival**
**Venue**: Xiamen International Conference & Exhibition Center, Xiamen, Fujian

2010/02/05 - 08
☎ 0592-5959 898, 5959 108
www.xicec.com
4300

**农业展览**
**地点**：厦门国际会议展览中心，福建厦门
**主办**：厦门市农业局

**Xiamen Agriculture Show**
**Venue**: Xiamen International Conference & Exhibition Center, Xiamen, Fujian
**Organizer**: Xiamen Municipal Agriculture Bureau

2010/03/06 - 09
☎ 0592-595 9616
🖷 0592-595 9611
www.jinhongxin.com
4330

**中国厦门国际厨柜展**
**地点**：厦门国际会议展览中心，福建厦门
**主办**：厦门会展金泓信展览公司

**China (Xiamen) Cabinets Show**
**Venue**: Xiamen International Conference & Exhibition Center, Xiamen, Fujian
**Organizer**: Xiamen Jinhongxin Exhibition Co

2010/04/08 - 11
☎ 0592-266 9865，266 9866
🖷 0592-266 9868
✉ zwl@chinafair.org.cn
✉ ciipc18@chinafair.org.cn
www.straitsfair.org.cn
4340

**第十四届对台进出口商品交易会**
**海峡两岸机械电子商品交易会**
**地点**：厦门国际会议展览中心，福建厦门
**主办**：厦门市对台贸易促进中心

**The 14th China Xiamen Machinery and Electronics Exhibition (CXMEE)**
**Venue**: Xiamen International Conference & Exhibition Center, Xiamen, Fujian
**Organizer**: Xiamen Promotion Center for Trade to Taiwan

2010/03/06 - 09
☎ 0592-595 9616
🖷 0592-595 9611
✉ info@stonefair.org.cn
www.stonefair.org.cn
4310

第十届中国厦门国际石材展览会
地点：厦门国际会议展览中心，福建厦门
内容：各类花岗岩、大理石、板材、异型石材、板岩、石雕工艺品、墓石制品、园林风景石及人造石制品；石材矿山开采设备、石材加工机械、金刚石锯片、磨具、磨料、石材化学防护用品、各类石材监测仪器、科研设计成果、杂志资料。
始办年份：2001
周期：每年一届
市场范围：国际性
入场券价格：免费
参展费用：8,800元/9m²
上届规模 '09：展览面积90,000m²(国外展商面积10,000m²)，参展商1,211家（国外展商300家，来自125个国家），专业贸易观众86,713人
主办：中国五矿化工进出口商会；厦门市贸易发展局；中国贸促会厦门分会
地址：福建厦门国际会议展览中心（361008）
联系人：郑小姐

10th China Xiamen International Stone Fair
Venue: Xiamen International Conference & Exhibition Center, Xiamen, Fujian
Profile: Granite, marble, tiles, special-shaped materials, slabs and blocks, stone-carved crafts, tomb stones, garden stones, artificial stone products; Stone-mine exploitation equipments, stone processing machinery, diamond impregnated saws, polishers, crocuses and abrasives, chemical technologies and equipments for stone maintenance, monitoring and measuring apparatuses, scientific research, professional magazines.
Established Year: 2001
Frequency: Annual
Market Area: International
Cost to Attend: Free
Participated Fee: RMB 8,800/9m²
Statistics '09: Exhibition Area 90,000m²(foreigners 10,000m²), Exhibitors 1,211（foreigners 300, came from 125 countries）, Trade visitors 86,713
Organizer: China Chamber of Commerce of Metals Minerals & Chemicals Importers & Exporters; Xiamen Municipal Trade Development Bureau; CCPIT Xiamen Sub-Council
Address: Xiamen International Conference & Exhibition Center, Xiamen, Fujian 361008
Contact: RACHEL

2010/04/24 - 26
☎ 010-8455 6503, 8455 6507
www.pharmchina.com.cn
4350

医药科技创造健康未来
PHARMCHINA
全国药品交易会

**第63届全国药品交易会（春季）**
地点：厦门国际会议展览中心，福建厦门
内容：全国药品交易会每年二届，是中国最大的医药制剂及相关技术、服务交易会。截至到2009年，每届展会的展出面积达六万五千平米，超过十万名专业观众到会参观洽谈，成为中国医药行业当之无愧的年度盛会。
展品范围：化学药品专区、中成药品专区、生物制药专区、OTC非处方药品、大众健康用品专区、PHARMSOFT医药软技术和综合服务专区。
观众范围：医药批发企业，医药生产企业，零售药店，医药研发，物流企业，医院药剂科主任，医生，医药终端用户等。
周期：每年两届
主办：国药励展展览有限责任公司

**63th PHARMCHINA**
Venue: Xiamen International Conference & Exhibition Center, Xiamen, Fujian
Profile: PHARMCHINA is the largest pharmaceutical trade show in China with over 1,600 exhibitors covering an exhibition area of 60,000m² with over 100,000 visitors (based on figures from the last event in Spring 2009). The market leading trade show enables pharmaceutical manufacturers to connect with hospitals, clinics, pharmacies, drug prescribers and end-users of pharmaceutical products.
Exhibits: OTC Drugs & Prescription Drugs of Chemical, Patented TCM and Biopharmacy; Latest Pharmaceutical Technology & Research; Pharmaceutical R & D; Registration Agents; Clinical Trials; Information and Consultancy Services; Technology and Product Transfers; Protection of Intellectual Property Rights; Storage & Logistics; Media; Human Resources and Training; IT Services; Contract Outsourcing; Packaging Design; Gifts; Facilities and Services for pharmacies
Visitors: Pharmaceutical manufacturers; pharmaceutical distributors; pharmacy directors of hospitals; doctors; pharmaceutical end-users.
Frequency: Biannual
Organizer: Reed Sinopharm Exhibitions Co Ltd

2010/05/28 - 30
☎ 0592-291 9753, 291 9756
🖷 0592-291 9751, 291 9753
✉ xmrjz@126.com
4360

第七届厦门人居环境展示会
地点：厦门国际会议展览中心，福建厦门
主办：厦门华览商务会展有限公司

7th Xiamen Living Environment Show
Venue: Xiamen International Conference & Exhibition Center, Xiamen, Fujian
Organizer: Xiamen Hualan Business and Exhibition Co

2010/06/11 - 13
☎ 0592-595 9898, 595 9108
www.xicec.com
4370

建材展览会
地点：厦门国际会议展览中心，福建厦门

Building Material Show
Venue: Xiamen International Conference & Exhibition Center, Xiamen, Fujian

2010/06/17 - 21
☎ 0592-595 9898, 223 0145
🖷 0592-268 0719
www.xicec.com
4380

海峡西岸汽车博览会
地点：厦门国际会议展览中心，福建厦门
主办：厦门市汽车流通协会

West Taiwan Strait Auto Expo 2010
Venue: Xiamen International Conference & Exhibition Center, Xiamen, Fujian
Organizer: Xiamen Automobile Communication Assn

2010/06/25 - 27
☎ 0592-5959 898, 5959 108
www.xicec.com
4390

第八届中国（厦门）食品交易博览会
地点：厦门国际会议展览中心，福建厦门
主办：厦门凤凰创意展览公司

8th China (Xiamen) Food Fair
Venue: Xiamen International Conference & Exhibition Center, Xiamen, Fujian
Organizer: Xiamen Phenix Conference & Exhibition International Co Ltd

2010/09/08 - 11
☎ 0592-266 9825, 266 9827
🖷 0592- 266 9830
✉ cifit@chinafair.org.cn
www.chinafair.org.cn
4400

第十四届中国国际投资贸易洽谈会
地点：厦门国际会议展览中心，福建厦门
主办：中国(厦门)国际投资促进中心

14th China International Fair for Investment & Trade
Venue: Xiamen International Conference & Exhibition Center, Xiamen, Fujian
Organizer: China (Xiamen) International Investment Promotion Center

2010/10 -
☎ 0592-5959 898, 5959 108
www.xicec.com
4410

**厦门日报房车大联展**
**地点：**厦门国际会议展览中心，福建厦门
**主办：**厦门日报社

**Xiamen Housing and Automotive Exhibition**
**Venue:** Xiamen International Conference & Exhibition Center, Xiamen, Fujian
**Organizer:** Xiamen Daily

2010/11/05 - 08
☎ 0592-595 9618
🖷 0592-595 9611
✉ info@buddhafair.com
www.buddhafair.com
4430

**第五届中国厦门国际佛事用品展览会**
**地点：**厦门国际会议展览中心，福建厦门
**内容：**佛像、佛具、香、蜡烛、灯具、纸制品、素食、僧服绣品、书画音像、法器法物、密宗用品、佛教生活用品、佛教工艺品、礼品、寺院建筑及装饰、素食原料、制香机械及原料、蜡烛机械及原料、制纸机械及原料、其他设备及原料、其他未分类佛事用品。
**始办年份：**2006
**周期：**每年一届
**市场范围：**国际性
**性质：**面向公众
**入场券价格：**免费
**参展费用：**标准展位：国内企业5,800元/(3x3m)，境外企业 1,200美元/9 ā；净地（36　起）：国内企业 580美元/其，境外企业120美元/
**上届规模‘09：**展览面积34,000m²(国外展商面积8,500m²)，参展商500家（国外展商180家，来自10个国家），参观人数80,000人（专业贸易观众26,386人）
**主办：**厦门会展金泓信展览有限公司
**地址：**厦门国际会议展览中心（361008）
**联系人：**廖小姐

**The 5th China Xiamen International Buddhist Items & Crafts Fair**
**Venue:** Xiamen International Conference & Exhibition Center, Xiamen, Fujian
**Profile:** Buddhist statues, Buddhist Instrument, Incense, Candles, Buddhist Lamps & Lanterns, Paper Products, Natural Vegetarian Food, Monk Apparel & Embroidery, Buddhist Books, Painting & Music, Buddhist Implements, Vajayana Supplies, Buddhism Supplies, Temple Architecture & Decoration, Incense Machine & Raw Materials, Candle Machine & Raw Materials, Paper Machine & Raw Materials, other related Raw Materials & Machine, Buddhist Crafts, Gifts and other Buddhist Articles.
**Established Year:** 2006
**Frequency:** Annual
**Market Area:** International
**Nature:** Open to public
**Cost to Attend:** Free
**Participated Fee:** Standard Booth （3x3m）：International Exhibitors USD 1,200/9　,Raw Space USD 120/m(min 36n)
**Statistics ‘09:** Exhibition Area 34,000m²(foreigners 8,500m²), Exhibitors 500（foreigners 180, came from 10 countries）, Visitors 80,000（trade visitors 26,386）
**Organizer:** Xiamen Jinhongxin Exhibition Co
**Address:** Xiamen International Conference & Exhibition Center, China
**Contact:** Moda

2010/11/06 - 17
☎ 0592-5959 898, 5959 108
www.xicec.com
4440

**沿海地区服装展**
**地点：**厦门国际会议展览中心，福建厦门

**Coastal Area Apparel Show**
**Venue:** Xiamen International Conference & Exhibition Center, Xiamen, Fujian

2010/11/19 - 02
☎ 0592-5959 898, 5959 108
www.xicec.com
4450

**大连服装展**
**地点：**厦门国际会议展览中心，福建厦门

**Dalian Clothing Show**
**Venue:** Xiamen International Conference & Exhibition Center, Xiamen, Fujian

2010/12/01 - 04
☎ 010-8455 6616
✉ Qinghua.wei@reedsinopharm.com
www.gccd2010.org
4453

**中国国际口腔器材展览会**
**首届全球华人口腔医学大会暨中国国际口腔医学大会**
**地点：**福建厦门
**周期：**每年一届
**内容：**倾力打造亚太地区首选口腔领域高层学术和技术交流、商务社交、产品采购、商业流通的国际化全方位交流和学习平台。
**展品范围：**口腔设备、器械、材料、保健用品
**观众范围：**口腔医院院长、综合医院口腔科主任、口腔诊所管理者、牙医、口腔医学院教师及学生、经销商等。
**主办：**国药励展展览有限公司

**CDEI – China Dental Exhibition International**
**GCCD – Global Congress of Chinese Dentists**
**Venue:** Xiamen, Fujian
**Profile:** Dedicated to provide a unique trading and learning platform of high level academic & technological communication, business networking, and procurement for Asia Pacific’s dental industry.
**Exhibits:** Dental equipments, materials, and other products
**Visitors:** Presidents of dental hospital, directors of department of dentistry, senior managers of dental clinics, dentists, teachers and students at dental universities, distributors
**Frequency:** Annual

# 甘肃-兰州
# Gansu-Lanzhou

2010/03/19 - 21
☎ 0931-888 6011
🖷 0931-888 2911
✉ sanlicom@163.com

4455

**第十届西北（兰州）广告、印刷、LED及办公设备展览会**
**地点：**兰州展览中心，甘肃兰州
**内容：**电脑喷绘机、写真机、雕刻机、切割机、刻字机等广告设备与耗材；印刷包装设备与耗材；网印设备及耗材；标识、标牌制作技术设备、标识型材、导向系统设计与制作；展览器材；广告专业工具、用品、书刊、广告礼品、促销品、工艺品；LED电子显示屏、LED广告屏、城市亮化工程技术与设备；数码影像器材；办公设备。
**始办年份：**2002
**周期：**每年两届
**市场范围：**地区性
**参展费用：**免费
**上届规模** '09：展览面积3,000m²，参展商200家，参观人数30,000人（专业贸易观众10,000人）
**主办：**兰州三力企业；甘肃奥美广告展览有限公司
**地址：**兰州市城关区甘南路62号中广大厦（730000）
**联系人：**冯女士
**QQ：**853100784

**Lanzhou AD, Printing, LED, Office Equipment Exhibition**
**Venue:** Lanzhou Exhibition Center, Lanzhou, Gansu
**Established Year:** 2002
**Frequency:** Biannual
**Market Area:** Regional
**Participated Fee:** Free
**Statistics '09:** Exhibition Area 3,000m², Exhibitors 200, Visitors 30,000 (trade visitors 10,000)
**Organizer:** Lanzhou Sanli Enterprise

# 广东-东莞
# Guangdong-Dongwan

2010/01/22 - 25
☎ 852-8211 2668, 0769-8383 5898
🖷 852-3405 8801

4456

**广东（厚街）茶业博览会**
**地点：**广东现代国际展览中心，广东东莞
**周期：**每年一届
**市场范围：**国际性
**主办：**迪亿会展(香港)有限公司

**Guangdong (Houjie) Tea Expo**
**Venue:** Guangdong Modern International Exhibition Center, Dongguan, Guangdong
**Frequency:** Annual
**Market Area:** International
**Organizer:** Diyi Exhibition (HK) Co Ltd

2010/03/02 - 06
☎ 020-3802 3852
🖷 020-3802 3815

4458

**2010东莞数字喷印及广告技术展览会**
**地点：**广东现代国际展览中心，广东东莞
**周期：**每年一届
**市场范围：**国际性
**主办：**广州市轩华展览有限公司

**Dongguan Digital Printing Exhibition**
**Venue:** Guangdong Modern International Exhibition Center, Dongguan, Guangdong
**Frequency:** Annual
**Market Area:** International
**Organizer:** Guangzhou Xuanhua Exhibition Co

2010/03/16 - 20
☎ 0769-8590 0111
🖷 0769-8558 5780
✉ charley@3f.net.cn
www.3f.net.cn

4460

**国际名家具（东莞）展览会**
**地点：**广东现代国际展览中心，广东东莞
**内容：**各类家具、家居饰品、木工机械及原辅材料
**始办年份：**1999
**周期：**每年两届
**市场范围：**国际性
**入场券价格：**50元
**参展费用：**730元/m²/展期
**上届规模** '09：展览面积240,000m²(国外展商面积15,000m²)，参展商846家（国外展商52家，来自14个国家），专业贸易观众78,000人
**主办：**国际名家具（东莞）展览会组委会
**地址：**东莞市厚街镇华润商贸中心五楼（523960）
**联系人：**方润忠

**International Famous Furniture Fair (Dongguan)**
**Venue:** Guangdong Modern International Exhibition Center, Dongguan, Guangdong
**Profile:** Furniture, Decorations, Wood Working Machinery & Material
**Established Year:** 1999
**Frequency:** Biannual
**Market Area:** International
**Cost to Attend:** RMB 50:-
**Participated Fee:** RMB 730/m²
**Statistics '09:** Exhibition Area 240,000m²(foreigners 15,000m²), Exhibitors 846 (foreigners 52, came from 14 countries), Trade Visitors 78,000
**Organizer:** Organizing Committee of International Famous Furniture Fair (Dongguan)
**Address:** 5# Floor Houjie Trade Center, Dongguan, Guangdong, CHINA
**Contact:** Charley Wong

2010/03/29 - 01
☎ 852-2763 9011
🖷 852-2341 0379
✉ info@paper-com.com.hk
www.paper-com.com.hk
4470

**第十一届中国(东莞)国际鞋机鞋材工业技术展**
地点：广东现代国际展览中心，广东东莞
周期：每年一届
市场范围：国际性
主办：讯通展览公司
地址：香港九龙观塘成业街11号华成工商中心5字楼15室

**11th China (Dongguan) Intl Footwear Machinery & Material Industry Fair**
Venue: Guangdong Modern International Exhibition Center, Dongguan, Guangdong
Frequency: Annual
Market Area: International
Organizer: Paper Communication Exhibition Services
Address: Rm. 15, 5/F., Wah Shing Center, 11 Shing Yip St., Kwun Tong, Kowloon, Hong Kong

2010/03/29 - 01
☎ 852-2763 9011
🖷 852-2341 0379
✉ info@paper-com.com.hk
www.paper-com.com.hk
4480

**第十一届中国(东莞)国际纺织制衣工业技术展**
地点：广东现代国际展览中心，广东东莞
周期：每年一届
市场范围：国际性
主办：讯通展览公司
地址：香港九龙观塘成业街11号华成工商中心5字楼15室

**11th China (Dongguan) Intl Textile & Clothing Industry Fair**
Venue: Guangdong Modern International Exhibition Center, Dongguan, Guangdong
Frequency: Annual
Market Area: International
Organizer: Paper Communication Exhibition Services
Address: Rm. 15, 5/F., Wah Shing Center, 11 Shing Yip St., Kwun Tong, Kowloon, Hong Kong

2010/04/07 - 09
☎ 021-5153 5228，5153 5215
www.sino-corrugated.com
4490

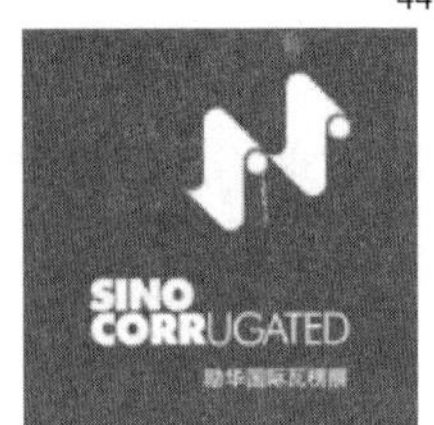


**励华国际瓦楞展2010中国展**
地点：广东现代国际展览中心，广东东莞
内容：2010中国国际瓦楞展是全球最大的专业瓦楞设备、耗材及技术展。展出面积达35,000平方米，预计将吸引500多家参展商以及20,000多名全球观展商。展会致力于通过集中呈现大量且多样的高性价比的设备、耗材，协助全球瓦楞纸箱厂做出不同的采购决策，为其提供获知新产品、新技术发展和市场动态的渠道，搭建了与不同供应商进行极富价值的沟通交流的独特平台。
周期：每年一届
主办：励展博览集团

**SinoCorrugated**
Venue: Guangdong Modern International Exhibition Center, Dongguan, Guangdong
Profile: SinoCorrugated 2010 is the world's largest business platform held in China for the global corrugated manufacturing industry. It will occupy a total area of 35,000 square meters; attract over 500 exhibitors and 20,000 global visitors. This event not only showcases the latest global corrugated equipment and consumables on the market, it also brings together, under one roof, buyers from established and emerging economies with high-spending trade professionals. The result is three days of serious business. By providing a unique opportunity to expand your share in the world's fastest growing market and offering the best return on your marketing investment, SinoCorrugated is the place where partnerships are confirmed and deals are made.
Frequency: Annual
Organizer: Reeds Exhibitions

2010/04/07 - 09
☎ 021-5153 5239，5153 5215
✉ alex.wang@reedexpo.com.cn
✉ cartonexpo@reedexpo.com.cn
www.sino-foldingcarton.com
4500

**2010中国国际彩盒展**
地点：广东现代国际展览中心，广东东莞
内容：2010中国国际彩盒展是国内领先专业彩盒设备、耗材及技术展。展出面积达35,000平方米，预计将吸引500多家参展商以及20,000多名全球观展商。展会聚焦彩盒前沿资讯，发布行业权威技术与市场信息，全面呈现种类齐全的彩盒加工设备，为彩盒生产企业提供最新生产加工解决方案，提供最新市场发展动态，全力打造与全球供应商的高效商贸平台。
周年：每年一届
主办：励展博览集团
参展联络：王文杰先生，
☎：021-5153 5239，
✉：alex.wang@reedexpo.com.cn
参观联络：李凤女士，
☎：021-5153 5215，
✉：cartonexpo@reedexpo.com.cn

**SinoFoldingCarton**
Venue: Guangdong Modern International Exhibition Center, Dongguan, Guangdong
Profile: SinoFoldingCarton is a professional exhibition for folding carton equipment, consumables and technology. It will occupy a total area of 35,000 square meters; attract over 500 exhibitors and 20,000 global visitors. The event focuses on the latest information in the folding carton industry, showcases the full range of folding carton processing equipment and provides cutting edge processing solutions for folding carton manufacturers. This specialized international platform for trade and commerce is where opportunities for folding carton equipment manufacturers and consumable suppliers to communicate with professional buyers are found.
Frequency: Annual
Organizer: Reed Exhibitions
For Exhibiting:
☎ 021-5153 5239，✉ alex.wang@reedexpo.com.cn
For Visiting:
☎ 021-5153 5215，✉ cartonexpo@reedexpo.com.cn

2010/05/04 - 06
☎ 021-5027 8128
🖷 021-5027 8138
4505

**中国东莞国际鞋展-鞋机展-手袋展**
地点：广东现代国际展览中心，广东东莞
始办年份：2003
周期：每年两届
市场范围：国际性
上届规模 '09：展览面积20,000m²，参展商488家，参观人数15,058人
主办：杜塞尔多夫展览(中国)有限公司
地址：上海市浦东新区张江高科技园区科苑路88号上海德意志工商中心1号楼307－308室（201203）
联系人：李静

**China Shoes**
China Shoetec & China Bags
Venue: Guangdong Modern International Exhibition Center, Dongguan, Guangdong
Established Year: 2003
Frequency: Biannual
Market Area: International
Statistics '09: Exhibition Area 20,000m², Exhibitors 488，Visitors 15,058
Organizer: Messe Düsseldorf China Ltd
Address: German Center for Industry and Trade Shanghai ,88 Keyuan Road, Zhangjiang Hi-Tech Park, Pudong, Shanghai
Contact: Amy Li

2010/05/14 - 16
☎ 0755-2591 1719转ext 802, 13480934992
🖷 0755-8212 9416
✉ yufen@861718.com
www.1718info.com

4510

**华南国际认证技术论坛暨仪器设备展**
**2010年华南（东莞）环境与可靠性实验技术论坛暨仪器展**
**地点：**广东现代国际展览中心，广东东莞
**始办年份：**1998
**周期：**每年一届
**入场券价格：**凭名片入场
**主办：**中国仪器仪表学会；东莞科技局
**承办：**星球国际资讯（香港）有限公司
**联系人：**郑婵玉，余芬
**QQ：**554864868

**South China Intl Certification Technology Forum & Instrument Equipment Fair**
**Venue:** Guangdong Modern International Exhibition Center, Dongguan, Guangdong
**Established Year:** 1998
**Frequency:** Annual
**Organizer:** Electronics Fair Services Co Ltd

2010/05/14 - 16
☎ 0755-2591 1759转ext 805, 15986630747
🖷 0755-8212 9416
www.laserfair.cn

4520

**第四届亚洲（东莞）国际激光加工技术暨应用展**
**地点：**广东现代国际展览中心，广东东莞
**内容：**激光设备：打 机、切割 、焊接机；激光器件：激光配件、软件、晶体材料；激光企业：所用激光OEM激光企业；展期同时举行大型激光技术论坛
**始办年份：**2006
**周期：**每年一届
**市场范围：**全国性
**性质：**面向公众
**入场券价格：**凭名片入场
**主办：**中国仪器仪表学会；东莞科技局；中国光学学会激光加工专业委员会
**承办：**广东省光学学会激光加工专业委员会；上海激光学会；星球国际资讯（香港）有限公司
**联系人：**赵延锋，邵火

**4th Asia (Dongguan) International Laser Processing Technology and Equipment Application Fair**
**Venue:** Guangdong Modern International Exhibition Center, Dongguan, Guangdong
**Established Year:** 2006
**Frequency:** Annual
**Market Area:** National
**Nature:** Open to public
**Organizer:** Electronics Fair Services Co Ltd
**Contact:** Yanfeng Zhao, Huo Shao

2010/05/14 - 16
☎ 0755-2591 1719
🖷 0755-8212 9416
✉ fair@861718.com
www.scef.com.cn

4530

**第十九届华南（东莞）国际电子制造采购博览会**
**地点：**广东现代国际展览中心，广东东莞
**始办年份：**1998
**周期：**每年一届
**市场范围：**国际性
**性质：**面向公众
**入场券价格：**凭名片入场
**主办：**中国仪器仪表学会；东莞科技局；中国光学学会激光加工专业委员会
**承办：**星球国际资讯（香港）有限公司
**地址：**深圳市福田区 南路 大厦A座11D
**联系人：**郑婵玉

**South China Electronic Fair**
**Venue:** Guangdong Modern International Exhibition Center, Dongguan, Guangdong
**Established Year:** 1998
**Frequency:** Annual
**Market Area:** International
**Nature:** Open to public
**Organizer:** Electronics Fair Services Co Ltd

2010/05/27 - 29
☎ 020-8555 7219

5435

**第十届东莞国际印刷造纸胶粘带及广告展览会**
**地点：**广东现代国际展览中心，广东东莞
**市场范围：**国际性
**主办：**广州会多展览有限公司

**10th Dongguan Intl Printing and Packaging and Paper Advertising, Adhesive Tape, Protective Film Exhibition**
**Venue:** Guangdong Modern International Exhibition Center, Dongguan, Guangdong
**Market Area:** International
**Organizer:** Guangzhou Huiduo Exhibition Co

2010/06/18 - 21
☎ 0769-8598 1609, 8598 1610

5436

**广东外商投资企业产品（内销）博览会**
**地点：**广东现代国际展览中心，广东东莞
**主办：**组委会秘书处

**Guangdong Foreign-invested Enterprises Commodities Fair**
**Venue:** Guangdong Modern International Exhibition Center, Dongguan, Guangdong
**Organizer:** Organizing Committee

2010/09/01 - 05
☎ 0769-8590 0111
🖷 0769-8558 5780

5437

**第二十四届国际名家具（东莞）展览会**
**地点：**广东现代国际展览中心，广东东莞
**市场范围：**国际性
**主办：**东莞名家具俱乐部

**The 24th International Famous Furniture Fair (Dongguan)**
**Venue:** Guangdong Modern International Exhibition Center, Dongguan, Guangdong
**Organizer:** Organizing Committee of International Famous Furniture Fair (Dongguan)

2010/09/16 - 17
☎ 021-5306 8968
🖷 021-5385 4032

5438

**第十五届国际集成电路研讨会暨展览会**
**地点：**广东现代国际展览中心，广东东莞
**主办：**环球资源展览有限公司

**15th Intl IC-China Conference & Exhibition**
**Venue:** Guangdong Modern International Exhibition Center, Dongguan, Guangdong
**Organizer:** Globe Sources

2010/09/27 - 29
☎ 020-3877 3839
🖷 020-3877 3839

5439

**2010华南（东莞）金属新材料、新技术、新设备及制品展览会**
**地点：**广东现代国际展览中心，广东东莞
**周期：**每年一届
**主办：**广州市博展展览有限公司

**South China Expo (Dongguan) for New Metal Materials, New Technologies, New equipments and Products**
**Venue:** Guangdong Modern International Exhibition Center, Dongguan, Guangdong
**Frequency:** Annual
**Organizer:** Guangzhou Bozhan Exhibition Co

2010/10/28 - 30
☎ 852-2800 8897, 021-5027 8128
🖷 852-2516 5024, 021-6279 7337
4540

2010中国东莞国际鞋展／鞋机展
地点：广东现代国际展览中心，广东东莞
市场范围：国际性
主办：雅式展览服务有限公司；杜塞尔多夫展览（中国）有限公司

Dongguan Shoes/ China Shoetes/ China Bags
Venue: Guangdong Modern International Exhibition Center, Dongguan, Guangdong
Market Area: International
Organizer: Adsale; Messe Düsseldorf China Ltd

2010/11/17 - 20
☎ 852-2763 9011
🖷 852-2341 0379
✉ info@paper-com.com.hk
www.paper-com.com.hk
4543

第十二届东莞国际模具及金属加工展
第十二届东莞国际橡塑胶及包装展
地点：广东现代国际展览中心，广东东莞
周期：每年一届
市场范围：国际性
主办：讯通展览公司
地址：香港九龙观塘成业街11号华成工商中心5字楼15室

12th China Dongguan International Mould & Metalworking Exhibition
12th China Dongguan International Plastics, Packaging & Rubber Exhibition
Venue: Guangdong Modern International Exhibition Center, Dongguan, Guangdong
Frequency: Annual
Market Area: International
Organizer: Paper Communication Exhibition Services
Address: Rm. 15, 5/F., Wah Shing Center, 11 Shing Yip St., Kwun Tong, Kowloon, Hong Kong

2010/12/21 - 02
☎ 0769-8590 9009
🖷 0769-8583 0960, 8583 0970
4548

2010第九届东莞嘉年华时尚生活用品购物节
地点：广东现代国际展览中心，广东东莞
主办：奥华国际展览有限公司

9th Dongguan Shopping Festival
Venue: Guangdong Modern International Exhibition Center, Dongguan, Guangdong
Organizer: Auwa International Exhibition Co Ltd

# 广东-广州
# Guangdong-Guangzhou

2010/03 -
☎ 020-8755 2468转ext 12
🖷 020-8755 2970
✉ k.lee@koelnmesse.cn
www.china-kfa.com
4550

**中国广州国际厨房家具和电器展览会**
地点：中国进出口商品交易会展馆，广东广州
内容：整体橱柜；橱柜配件:橱柜五金、橱柜台面、橱柜门板、橱柜板材、橱柜灯饰、其它；厨房水暖五金：水槽、龙头、其它；厨房电器：家用厨房电器和设备、嵌入式厨房电器和设备、厨房智能设备、垃圾处理器；软件及出版物：软件、出版物、媒体；其它：贸易推广、产品检测、其它
始办年份：2008
周期：每年一届
市场范围：国际性
参展费用：净地（24m$^2$起）1,300元/m$^2$，普通标准展位（9m$^2$起）1,500元/m$^2$，高级标准展位（18m$^2$起）1,700元/m$^2$
上届规模‘08：展览面积10,000m$^2$，参展商148家，参观人数15,511人
主办：科隆国际展览有限公司；中国对外贸易中心（集团）
承办：科隆展览有限公司/中国对外贸易广州展览公司
地址：广州市天河区天河北路183号大都会广场3311室（510620）
联系人：李伟莉，梁绍俊

**China Kitchen Furniture and Appliance Fair (CKFA)**
Venue: Chinese Import and Export Fair Pazhou Complex, Guangzhou, Guangdong
Profile: 1) Unit Kitchen Cabinet: Unit Kitchen Cabinet; 2) Unit Kitchen Cabinet Components: Kitchen Hardware/ Cabinet Worktops/Cabinet Doors/Cabinet Panels/Lighting; 3) Kitchen Fixtures: Sinks/Faucets; 4) Kitchen Intelligence and Home Appliances: Household Electrical Appliances & Equipments for Kitchen/Built-in Kitchen Electrical Appliances & Equipments/ Kitchen Intelligence/Kitchen Waste Disposers; 5) Software & Publications: Software/ Publications/ Media; 6) Others: Trade Promotions/Testing & Measuring Organizations/Others
Established Year: 2008
Frequency: Annual
Market Area: International
Participated Fee: Raw Space (min 24m$^2$) RMB 1,300/m$^2$, Standard Booth (min 9m$^2$) RMB 1,500/m$^2$, Upgraded Booth (min 18m$^2$) RMB 1,700/m$^2$
Statistics '08: Exhibition Area 10,000m$^2$, Exhibitors 148, Visitors 15,511
Sponsor: Koelnmesse GmbH; China Foreign Trade Center (Group)
Organizer: Koelnmesse Co; China Foreign Trade Guangzhou Exhibition Corp
Address: Room 3311, Metro Plaza, No.183 Tianhe Road (North), TianHe District, Guangzhou
Contact: Karen Lee, Mattis Liang

2010/03/02 - 05
☎ 020-3810 6261
🖷 020-3810 6200
✉ info@trustexhibition.com
www.SignChina-gz.com
4560

2010广东国际广告展
地点：中国进出口商品交易会琶洲展馆，广东广州
周期：每年一届
市场范围：国际性
上届规模‘09：展览面积70,000m$^2$，参展商806家，参观人数46,115人
主办：广州信亚展览服务有限公司
地址：广州市天河区林和东华庭路4号天河富力商务大厦1306室（510610）
联系人：吴小姐

SIGN CHINA 2010
Venue: Chinese Import and Export Fair Pazhou Complex, Guangzhou, Guangdong
Frequency: Annual
Market Area: International
Statistics '09: Exhibition Area 70,000m$^2$, Exhibitors 806, Visitors 46,115
Organizer: Trust Exhibition Co Ltd
Address: Rm 1306, Tian He Fu Li Business Mansion, No. 4 Hua Ting Rd, Lin He Dong Rd, Tian He Bei Dist, Guangzhou, 510610, China

2010/03/03 - 05
☎ 020-3821 9936, 3821 9937
020-3821 9935
✉ loo11117@qq.com
www.aaitf.org
www.jiuzhouauto.com
4570

**第六届中国（广州）国际汽车改装服务业展览会**
**地点**：中国进出口商品交易会琶洲展馆，广东广州
**内容**：AAITF2009把汽车后市场的消费元素体现出来。2010AAITF将着手打造更大规模和更高规格的消费展，在“拓展渠道，指导消费”方面发挥更大更强的作用！奠定“中国汽车后市场第一消费展”的强势地位。
**始办年份**：2006
**周期**：每年一届
**市场范围**：全国性
**性质**：面向公众
**入场券价格**：10元
**参展费用**：600元/$m^2$
**上届规模** ‘09：展览面积60,000$m^2$(国外展商面积50,000$m^2$)，参观人数150,000人（专业贸易观众40,000人）
**主办**：九州国际会展传媒集团
**地址**：广州市体育西路123号新创举大厦11楼
**联系人**：卢春辉
MSN: loo11117@hotmail.com
QQ：57668869

**6th China Intl Automotive Aftermarket Industry and Tuning Trade Fair (AAITF)**
**Venue**: Chinese Import and Export Fair Pazhou Complex, Guangzhou, Guangdong
**Established Year**: 2006
**Frequency**: Annual
**Market Area**: National
**Nature**: Open to public
**Cost to Attend**: RMB 10:-
**Participated Fee**: RMB 600/$m^2$
**Statistics** ‘09: Exhibition Area 60,000$m^2$(foreigners 50,000$m^2$), Visitors 150,000 (trade visitors 40,000
**Organizer**: Jiuzhou International
**Contact**: LOO
**MSN**: loo11117@hotmail.com

2010/03/04 - 06
☎ 020-8637 4869
020-8637 4257
✉ bestguangzhou@vip.163.com
www.84t.cn
4580

**第七届广州国际车用空调及冷藏链技术展览会**
**地点**：中国进出口商品交易会琶洲展馆，广东广州
**内容**：汽车空调系统及汽车空调配件生产厂家云集
**始办年份**：2004
**周期**：每年一届
**市场范围**：全国性
**参展费用**：8,800元/9$m^2$；净地(36$m^2$起) 980元/$m^2$
**主办**：广州巴斯特展览有限公司
**地址**：广州市白云区松柏东街20号联鸣商贸中心B 302（510405）
**联系人**：梁丽华，丁正

**Guangzhou International Automotive Air-China Exhibition**
**Venue**: Chinese Import and Export Fair Pazhou Complex, Guangzhou, Guangdong
**Established Year**: 2004
**Frequency**: Annual
**Market Area**: National
**Participated Fee**: RMB 8,800/9$m^2$, Raw Space (min 36$m^2$) RMB 980/$m^2$
**Organizer**: Best Exhibitions

2010/03/08 - 11
☎ 020-2608 1669, 2608 1881, 2608 1604
020-8668 0925转ext 02
✉ zhouqw@fairwindow.com.cn
www.siaf-china.com
4590

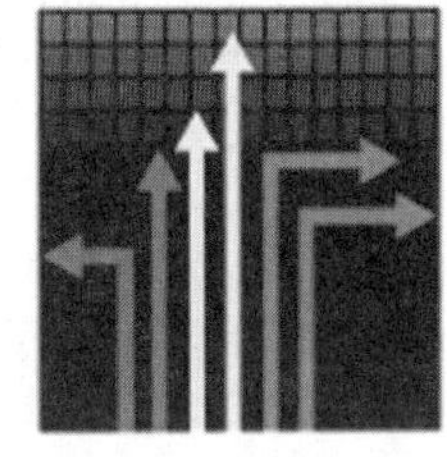

**中国广州国际工业自动化技术及装备展览会**
**地点**：中国进出口商品交易会琶洲展馆，广东广州
**内容**：传动、机械驱动系统及零部件、电子零部件及辅助设备、机电零部件及辅助设备、辅助设备、感应技术（传感器）、控制系统、工业用电脑装备、工业自动化软件、接口技术、低电压开关装置、人机界面装置、工业自动化技术交流、培训及咨询、组装系统、材料处理装置、连动技术、集成化系统、分解设备、微系统技术、机器零部件、工业机器人
**始办年份**：1996
**周期**：每年一届
**市场范围**：国际性
**入场券价格**：业内观众凭名片登记进场
**参展费用**：标准展位：A区12,000元/9$m^2$，B区850元/9$m^2$ 净地：A区1050元/$m^2$，B区750元/$m^2$（最少36$m^2$）
**上届规模** ‘09：展览面积15,000$m^2$，参展商320家，参观人数13,213人
**主办**：中国对外贸易中心（集团）；德国法兰克福展览有限公司
**承办**：中国对外贸易广州展览公司；广州光亚法兰克福展览有限公司；德国美赛高法兰克福展览有限公司；广州富洋展览有限公司
**地址**：广州市流花路117号交易会院内15号楼213（510014）
**联系人**：周小姐

**SPS-Industrial Automation Fair Guangzhou**
**Venue**: Chinese Import and Export Fair Pazhou Complex, Guangzhou, Guangdong
**Profile**: Drive Systems and Components, Electromechanical Components and Peripheral Equipment, Sensor Technology, Control Technology, IPCs, Industrial Software, Interface Technology, Low Voltage-Switching Devices, Human-Machine-Interface Devices, Industrial Communication, Training and Consulting, Assembly Equipment, Materials Handling Devices, Integrated Systems, Dismantling Equipment, Micro Technology, Machine Components, Industrial Robot
**Established Year**: 1996
**Frequency**: Annual
**Market Area**: International
**Participated Fee**: Standard Booth RMB 12,000/9$m^2$, Raw Space RMB 1,050/$m^2$
**Statistics** ‘09: Exhibition Area 15,000$m^2$, Exhibitors 320, Visitors 13,213
**Sponsor**: China Foreign Trade Center (Group); Messe Frankfurt Exhibition GmbH
**Organizer**: China Foreign Trade Guangzhou Exhibition Corp; Guangzhou Guangya Messe Frankfurt Co Ltd; Mesago Messe Frankfurt GmbH; Guangzhou Overseas Trade Fairs Ltd
**Address**: Rm 210, Building 15, No.117, Liuhua Rd, Guangzhou
**Contact**: Grace

2010/03/09 - 11
☎ 020-8625 9738
020-8625 9533
✉ hujunfang@163.com
www.gzbeautyexpo.com
4670

**第32届广州国际美容美发化妆用品进出口博览会**
**地点**：中国进出口交易会琶洲展馆，广东广州
**内容**：专业美容元、水疗美容产品、工具及仪器设备；美容及发型培训机构、美发产品、仪器设备、工具及配套产品、美甲、香水及化妆品、个人护理品及日化洗涤、连锁经营及专营专卖特许加盟店业务；美容保健营养品、内衣、纹绣、中医养生馆、包材原材料、私人品牌、OEM贴牌生产
**始办年份**：1989
**周期**：每年两届
**市场范围**：国际性
**入场券价格**：30元
**参展费用**：2200元/$m^2$，1080元/$m^2$，830元/$m^2$
**上届规模** ‘09：展览面积66,400$m^2$(国外展商面积6,640$m^2$)，参展商90家，参观人数238,331人
**主办**：广东博环美国际展览有限公司
**地址**：广州市广园西路121号美博城写字楼A座五楼（510400）
**联系人**：胡俊方
QQ：1255343215

**Guangzhou Intl Beauty & Cosmetic Import-Export (Spring) 2010**
**Venue**: Chinese Import and Export Fair Pazhou Complex, Guangzhou, Guangdong
**Established Year**: 1989
**Frequency**: Biannual
**Market Area**: International
**Cost to Attend**: RMB 30:-
**Participated Fee**: RMB 1,080～2,200/$m^2$
**Statistics** ‘09: Exhibition Area 66,400$m^2$(foreigners 6,640$m^2$), Exhibitors 90, Visitors 238,331
**Organizer**：Guangdong International Exhibitions Limited
**Contact**: Fenny

2010/03/09 - 11
☎ 020-2608 1625
🖷 020-8668 0925转ext 05, 8666 5047
✉ pfp@fairwindow.com.cn
www.fairwindow.com

4680

## 第十七届华南国际印刷工业展览会

2010中国国际标签印刷技术展览会

**地点**：中国进出口商品交易会琶洲展馆，广东广州

**内容**：印前设备、数码印刷设备、标签、柔性及凹性印刷设备、胶印设备及机械、丝网印刷、包装印刷设备、装订机械设备、印刷物料及配件、耗材

**始办年份**：1994

**周期**：每年一届

**市场范围**：国际性

**入场券价格**：业内观众凭名片登记进场

**参展费用**：标准展位：A区21,150元/9m²，B区12,000元/9m²，C区7,800元/9m²；净地：A区2,000元/m²，B区1,200元/m²，C区838元/m²

上届规模 '08：展览面积38,000m²，参展商468家（来自16个国家），参观人数41,692人（专业贸易观众6,713人）

**主办**：广东省新闻出版局；中国对外贸易中心（集团）；雅式展览服务有限公司；广东省出版集团

**承办**：中国对外贸易广州展览公司；北京雅展展览服务有限公司

**地址**：广州市流花路117号交易会院内15号楼210中国对外贸易广州展览公司（510014）

**联系人**：杨先生

## The 17th South China International Exhibition on Printing Industry

The China International Exhibition on Label Printing Technology

**Venue**: Chinese Import and Export Fair Pazhou Complex, Guangzhou, Guangdong

**Profile**: Pre-press Equipment & Software, Digital Printing Equipment, Label, Flexor & Gravure Printing Equipment, Offset Printing Equipment & Machinery, Screen Printing, Package Printing, Binding Equipment, Printing Materials & Accessories, Consumables

**Established Year**: 1994

**Frequency**: Annual

**Market Area**: International

**Participated Fee**: Standard Booth RMB 21,150/9m², Raw Space RMB 2,000/m²

**Statistics '08**: Exhibition Area 38,000m², Exhibitors 468 (came from 16 countries), Visitors 41,692 (trade visitors 6,713)

**Sponsor**: Administration of Press and Publication of Guangdong Province; China Foreign Trade Center (Group); Adsale Exhibition Services; Guangdong Provincial Publishing Group **Organizer**: China Foreign Trade Guangzhou Exhibition Corp; Beijing Adsale Exhibition

**Address**: Rm 210, Building 15, No.117 Liuhua Rd, Guangzhou

**Contact**: Bobby**Contact**: Karen Lee, Mattis Liang

2010/03/09 - 11
☎ 020-8667 4121, 2608 1660
🖷 020-8668 0925转ext 02, 2608 1600
✉ project2@fairwindow.com
www.waterchina-gz.com

4700

## 第11届中国（广州）国际给排水、水处理技术设备展览会

中国（广州）国际泵、阀门、管道展览会

**地点**：中国进出口商品交易会琶洲展馆，广东广州

**内容**：给水排水设备，水处理技术，水处理设备；泵设备,阀门设备,管道设备等

**始办年份**：2000

**周期**：每年一届

**市场范围**：国际性

**入场券价格**：60元/30元

**参展费用**：净地200美元/m²，标准展位2000美元/（9m²）

**上届规模** '09：展览面积120,000m²，参展商500家（国外展商60家，来自20个国家），专业贸易观众70,000人

**主办**：中国对外贸易中心（集团）

**承办**：中国对外贸易广州展览公司

**地址**：广州市流花路117号15号办公楼616B（510014）

**联系人**：梁兵，黄炜坚

## The 11th China (Guangzhou) Water Waster & Water Treatment, Pump, Vale & Pipe China

**Venue**: Chinese Import and Export Fair Pazhou Complex, Guangzhou, Guangdong

**Profile**: Water & Wastewater Water Treatment Equipment Industrial Water Treatment Drinking Water Treatment Equipment/ Process Water Filtration/Disinfection Equipment Membrane Separation Technology Instruments, Controls and Automation Sewer Inspection, Cleaning, Maintenance

**Established Year**: 2000

**Frequency**: Annual

**Market Area**: International

**Cost to Attend**: RMB 60:-

**Participated Fee**: Raw Space USD 200/m², Standard Booth USD 2,000(9m²)

**Statistics '09**: Exhibition Area 120,000m², Exhibitors 500 (foreigners 60, came from 20 countries), Trade Visitors 70,000

**Sponsor**: Chinese Foreign Trade Center (Group)(CFTC)

**Organizer**: China Foreign Trade Guangzhou Exhibition Corp

**Address**: Room 616B, 117# Trading Building, Liu Hua Road, Guangzhou, China

**Contact**: Ms Liang Bing, Mr Huang Weijian

2010/03/18 - 21
☎ 020-2608 0413
🖷 020-8666 3416转ext 01
✉ ciff@fairwindow.com.cn
www.ciff-gz.com

4710

## 中国广州国际陶瓷展览会

**地点**：中国进出口商品交易会琶洲展馆，广东广州

**内容**：日用陶瓷、工艺美术陶瓷、家居饰品、用品

**周期**：每年一届

**市场范围**：国际性

**入场券价格**：20元

**参展费用**：净地790元/m²，标准展位7,900元

**上届规模** '09：展览面积10,000m²，参观人数11,949人

**主办**：中国对外贸易中心（集团）

**承办**：中国对外贸易广州展览公司

**地址**：广州市流花路117号（510014）

**联系人**：刘骏

## China International Ceramics Exhibition (Guangzhou)

**Venue**: Chinese Import and Export Fair Pazhou Complex, Guangzhou, Guangdong

**Profile**: Art Ceramics, Household Ceramics, Home decor

**Frequency**: Annual

**Market Area**: International

**Cost to Attend**: RMB 20:-

**Participated Fee**: Raw Space RMB 790/m², Standard Booth RMB 7,900

**Statistics '09**: Exhibition Area 10,000m², Visitors 11,949

**Sponsor**: China Foreign Trade Center (Group)

**Organizer**: China Foreign Trade Guangzhou Exhibition Corporation

**Address**: #117, Liuhua Road, Guangzhou 510014, China

**Contact**: Liu Jun

2010/03/18 - 21
☎ 020-8667 3122, 8667 3473
🖷 020-8666 3416转ext 01, 8668 1629转ext 01
✉ hhc@fairwindow.com.cn
hhc.fairwindow.com
4720

### 中国广州国际家居饰品/用品展览会

**地点：** 中国进出口商品交易会琶洲展馆，广东广州
**内容：** 地毯、挂毯、画、镜及相框、陶瓷、玻璃、树脂、塑料、金属等制品、人造花卉、木/石雕（刻）制品、灯饰、钟、电话、其他
**周期：** 每年一届
**市场范围：** 国际性
**入场券价格：** 20元
**参展费用：** 净地790元/$m^2$，标准展位7,900元
**上届规模** '09：展览面积35,000$m^2$，参观人数34,834人
**主办：** 中国对外贸易中心（集团）
**承办：** 中国对外贸易广州展览公司
**地址：** 广州市流花路117号（510014）
**联系人：** 刘骏，吴咏茵

### Homedecor & Housewares China 2010

**Venue:** Chinese Import and Export Fair Pazhou Complex, Guangzhou, Guangdong
**Profile:** Carpets, Rugs, Picture, Mirrors, Frames, Pottery, Glassware, Artificial Flowers, Lighting, Clock, Stone Carving, Accessories, Others
**Frequency:** Annual
**Market Area:** International
**Cost to Attend:** RMB 20
**Participated Fee:** Raw Space RMB 790/$m^2$, Standard Booth RMB 7,900
**Statistics '09:** Exhibition Area 35,000$m^2$, Visitors 34,834
**Sponsor:** China Foreign Trade Center (Group)
**Organizer:** China Foreign Trade Guangzhou Exhibition Corporation
**Address:** #117, Liuhua Road, Guangzhou 510014, China
**Contact:** Liu Jun, Wu Yongyin

2010/03/18 - 21
☎ 020-2608 0413, 2608 1806
🖷 020-8666 3416转ext 01, 8668 1629转ext 01
✉ hhc@fairwindow.com.cn
hhc.fairwindow.com
4730

hometextile
intertextile
GUANGZHOU, CHINA

### 中国（广州）国际家用纺织品及辅料博览会

**地点：** 中国进出口商品交易会琶洲展馆，广东广州
**内容：** 家居用装饰布及装饰品 床/浴室用/桌用/厨房用纺织品 地毯及地面覆盖物，各类室内配件、靠垫、抱枕及挂件，装饰专供纺织品，纺织类工艺品，其它家用纺织品 家用纺织品相关产品及服务
**周期：** 每年一届
**市场范围：** 国际性
**入场券价格：** 20元
**参展费用：** 净地790元/$m^2$，标准展位7,900元
**上届规模** '09：展览面积20,000$m^2$，参观人数16,451人
**主办：** 中国对外贸易中心（集团）
**承办：** 中国对外贸易广州展览公司
**地址：** 广州市流花路117号（510014）
**联系人：** 刘骏，余金玲

### China (Guangzhou) International Trade Fair for Home Textiles

**Venue:** Chinese Import and Export Fair Pazhou Complex, Guangzhou, Guangdong
**Profile:** Bed, bath, table and kitchen linens Wall and window decorations, Upholstery fabric, Textiles for contract market, Interior design and textile handicrafts, Accessories, Carpets and rugs Home textile related products and services Home textile design
**Frequency:** Annual
**Market Area:** International
**Cost to Attend:** RMB 20:-
**Participated Fee:** Raw Space RMB 790/$m^2$, Standard Booth RMB 7,900
**Statistics '09:** Exhibition Area 20,000$m^2$, Visitors 16,451
**Sponsor:** China Foreign Trade Center (Group)
**Organizer:** China Foreign Trade Guangzhou Exhibition Corp
**Address:** #117, Liuhua Road, Guangzhou 510014, China
**Contact:** Hanson Liu, Chelen Yu

2010/03/18 - 21
☎ 020-2608 1896, 2608 1664
🖷 020-8666 3416转ext 01, 8668 1629转ext 01
✉ ciff@fairwindow.com
outdoor.fairwindow.com
4750

### 中国广州户外及休闲展览会

**地点：** 中国进出口商品交易会琶洲展馆，广东广州
**内容：** 庭园家具、休闲桌椅、遮阳设备、户外摆设和用品；户外烧烤工具、帐篷、篷方、花园规划与维护、花植物养护器材设备、园林工具、其他
**周期：** 每年一届
**市场范围：** 国际性
**入场券价格：** 20元
**参展费用：** 净地790元/$m^2$，标准展位7,900元
**上届规模** '09：展览面积15,000$m^2$，参观人数16,350人
**主办：** 中国对外贸易中心（集团）；中国食品土畜进出口商会
**承办：** 中国对外贸易广州展览公司
**地址：** 广州市流花路117号（510014）
**联系人：** 敖丽艳，侯挺

### China International Outdoor & Leisure Fair

**Venue:** Chinese Import and Export Fair Pazhou Complex, Guangzhou, Guangdong
**Profile:** Garden Furniture, Leisure Tables & Chairs, Sun-shading Equipment, Outdoor Items, Garden Design & Maintenance, Plants & Plant Care, Garden Care & Accessories, Others
**Frequency:** Annual
**Market Area:** International
**Cost to Attend:** RMB 20:-
**Participated Fee:** Raw Space RMB 790/$m^2$, Standard Booth RMB 7,900
**Statistics '09:** Exhibition Area 15,000$m^2$, Visitors 16,350
**Sponsor:** China Foreign Trade Center (Group); China Chamber of Commerce of Import & Export of Food Stuffs; Native Produce & Animal By-Products
**Organizer:** China Foreign Trade Guangzhou Exhibition Corporation
**Address:** #117, Liuhua Road, Guangzhou 510014, China
**Contact:** Ao Liyan, Hou Ting

2010/03/27 - 30
☎ 020-8755 2468转ext 12/15
020-8667 3122
🖷 020-8755 2970
020-8666 3416转ext 01
020-8668 1629转ext 01
✉ ciff@fairwindow.com.cn
k.lee@koelnmesse.cn
cifm.fairwindow.com
www.interzum-guangzhou.com
4770

### 中国广州国际木工机械、家具配料展览会

**地点：** 中国进出口商品交易会展馆，广东广州
**内容：** 家具生产原料及配件；软体家具和床具生产机械、原料及配件；室内装饰机械、材料及组件；木工、家具生产机械及辅助设备；其它: 媒体、贸易推广机构
**始办年份：** 2004
**周期：** 每年一届
**市场范围：** 国际性
**参展费用：** 净地（24$m^2$起）1,300元/$m^2$，普通标准展位（9$m^2$起）1,500元/$m^2$，高级标准展位（18$m^2$起）1,700元/$m^2$

### Interzum Guangzhou

China International Woodworking Machinery & Furniture Raw Materials Fair (Guangzhou) **Venue:** Chinese Import and Export Fair Pazhou Complex, Guangzhou, Guangdong
**Profile:** Materials and Components for Furniture Production; Machines, Materials and Components for Upholstery and Bedding; Machines, Materials and Components for Interior Works; Machines and Auxiliary Machines for Woodworking and Furniture Production; Others (Media, Assns)
**Established Year:** 2004

**上届规模** '09：展览面积80,000m²，参展商761家（国外展商209家，来自22个国家），参观人数60,697人
**主办**：科隆国际展览有限公司；中国对外贸易中心（集团）
**承办**：中国对外贸易广州展览公司
**地址**：广州市流花路117号（510014）
**联系人**：赵鲲鹏，王正平
**承办**：科隆展览有限公司
**地址**：广州市天河区天河北路183号大都会广场3311室（510620）
**联系人**：李伟莉，梁绍俊

**Frequency**: Annual
**Market Area**: International
**Participated Fee**: Raw Space (min 24m²) RMB 1,300/m², Standard Booth (min 9m²) 1,500/m², Up-graded Booth (min 18m²) RMB 1,700/m²
**Statistics '09**: Exhibition Area 80,000m², Exhibitors 761 (foreigners 209, came from 22 countries), Visitors 60,697
**Sponsor**: Koelnmesse GmbH; China Foreign Trade Center (Group)
**Organizer**: Koelnmesse Co; China Foreign Trade Guangzhou Exhibition Corp
**Address**: Room3311, Metro Plaza, No.183 Tianhe Road (North), Tianhe District, Guangzhou
**Contact**: Karen Lee, Mattis Liang
**Organizer**: China Foreign Trade Guangzhou Exhibition Corporation
**Address**: #117, Liuhua Road, Guangzhou 510014, China
**Contact**: Zhao Kunpeng, Wang Zhengping

2010/03/27 - 30
☎ 020-8667 3473, 2608 1612
🖷 020-8666 3416转ext 01, 8668 1629转ext 01
✉ ciff@fairwindow.com.cn
www.ciff-gz.com

4790

## 中国广州国际家具博览会（办公环境展）

**地点**：中国进出口商品交易会琶洲展馆，广东广州
**内容**：办公家具：办公坐具、书柜、办公桌、保险柜、屏风、储物柜、高隔段、文件柜、办公配件、其他 商用家具：共场所家具（机场家具、剧院/礼堂家具等）、公共座椅系列、学校家具、实验室家具 办公场所相关设备（照明系列、墙材系列、铺地材料系列等） 酒店、宾馆、承造家具及其他商用家具
**始办年份**：1998
**周期**：每年一届
**市场范围**：国际性
**入场券价格**：20元
**参展费用**：净地790元/m²，标准展位7,900元
**上届规模** '09：展览面积130,000m²，参观人数51,132人
**主办**：中国家具协会；中国对外贸易中心（集团）；广东省家具协会；香港家私装饰厂商总会
**承办**：中国对外贸易广州展览公司
**地址**：广州市流花路117号（510014）
**联系人**：周文缨，谭洁莹

## China International Furniture Fair (Guangzhou)-Office Show

**Venue**: Chinese Import and Export Fair Pazhou Complex, Guangzhou, Guangdong
**Profile**: Office Furniture: Office Seatings, Book Shelves, Office Desk/Table, Safe Cabinets, Partition, Storage Units, Partitioning Wall Filing Cabinets, Office Accessories Others Commercial Furniture for Public Places (Airport Furniture, Theatre/Auditoria Furniture and so on) Public Seatings, School Furniture, Laboratory Furniture, Office-Related Equipment(Lightings, Wall Coverings, Floor Coverings and so on ) Hotel\Restaurant\Contract Commercial Furniture
**Established Year**: 1998
**Frequency**: Annual
**Market Area**: International
**Cost to Attend**: RMB 20:-
**Participated Fee**: Raw Space RMB 790/m², Standard Booth RMB 7,900
**Statistics '09**: Exhibition Area 130,000m², Visitors 51,132
**Sponsor**: China National Furniture Assn, China Foreign Trade Center (Group), Guangdong Furniture Assn, Hong Kong Furniture & Decoration Trade Assn
**Organizer**: China Foreign Trade Guangzhou Exhibition Corporation
**Address**: 117, Liuhua Road, Guangzhou 510014, China
**Contact**: Zhou Wenying, Tan Jieying

2010/04/08 - 10
☎ 020-8358 7012, 8358 7037
🖷 020-8358 7016
✉ expo@ctoy.cn
✉ babyfair@ctoy.cn
www.chinatoyfair.com

4800

## 2010年广州国际婴幼儿用品展

**地点**：保利世贸博览馆，广东广州
**内容**：主办机构——广东省玩具协会有着21年举办玩具展的经验，积累了丰富的买家资源，为了使展会更专业化，应婴儿用品企业的要求，我们定于2010年4月8—10日在广州保利世贸博览馆（琶洲——广交会新址）举办广州国际婴幼儿用品展览会,与第22届广州国际玩具及模型展同期举行。

展品包括婴幼用品、婴儿推车、婴儿床、婴幼儿服饰、婴儿食品及保健品等。

首届
**周期**：每年一届
**市场范围**：国际性
**入场券价格**：60元
**预计规模**：展出面积12,000m²，参展商200家，参观人数10,000人
**主办**：广东省玩具协会；广东玩具文化经济发展研究会
**地址**：广州市淘金北路正平南街1号2楼（510095）
**联系人**：郑蔚薇，王莉莉

## Guangzhou International Baby Product Fair 2010

**Venue**: Poly World Trade Center Expo, Guangzhou, Guangdong
**Profile**: The organizer, Guangdong Toy Association has an experience of holding toy fair for 21 years, accumulating rich resource on buyers. To make the fair more professional, and take care of the baby product companies' need, the organizer decides to hold Guangzhou Intl Baby Product Fair in Poly World Trade Expo Center, Guangzhou from April 8 to 10, 2010, which will be concurrent with Guangzhou Int'l Toy & Hobby Fair. The exhibits will include baby products, baby strollers, cribs, baby's wear, baby food and health products, etc.
First Session
**Frequency**: Annual
**Market Area**: International
**Cost to Attend**: RMB 60:-
**Organizer**: Guangdong Toy Association; Guangdong Research Council of Toy Cultural & Economic Development
**Address**: 2/F, Zheng Ping Street South, Tao Jin Road North, Guangzhou, China
**Contact**: Zheng Weiwei, Wang Lili

4810

2010/04/08 - 10
☎ 020-8358 7012, 8358 7037
📠 020-8358 7016
✉ expo@ctoy.cn, fair@ctoy.cn
www.chinatoyfair.com

**第22届广州国际玩具及模型展览会**
**地点**：保利世贸博览馆，广东广州
**内容**：展品包括电子电动玩具、游乐设施、塑胶玩具、童车、童床、布毛绒玩具、模型配套产品、娃娃玩具、动漫形象授权、充气玩具、飞机、舰船、汽车模型、木制、纸品玩具、各种仿真动态、静态模型、学习机等。
**始办年份**：1989
**周期**：每年一届
**市场范围**：国际性
**入场券价格**：60元
**上届规模** '09：展览面积20,000m²(国外展商面积3,000m²)，参展商438家（国外展商52家，来自8个国家），专业贸易观众13,965人
**主办**：广东省玩具协会；广东玩具文化经济发展研究会
**地址**：广州市淘金北路正平南街1号2楼（510095）
**联系人**：郑蔚薇，姚丽娜

**The 22nd Guangzhou (China) Intl Toy & Hobby Fair**
**Venue**: Poly World Trade Center Expo, Guangzhou, Guangdong
**Profile**: Exhibits will include Electronic and Electrical Toys. Amusement Play-sets, Plastic Toys, Baby Strollers, Ride-ons, Cribs , Cloth and Plush Toys, Toy Accessories, Dolls, Animation and Comics Licensing, Inflatable Toys, Model Airplanes, Boats and Cars, Wooden and Paper Toys, Die-cast Miniatures, Learning Systems.
**Established Year**: 1989
**Frequency**: Annual
**Market Area**: International
**Cost to Attend**: RMB 60:-
**Statistics** '09: Exhibition Area 20,000m²(foreigners 3,000m²), Exhibitors 438 (foreigners 52, came from 8 countries) , Trade Visitors 13,965
**Organizer**: Guangdong Toy Association; Guangdong Research Council of Toy Cultural & Economic Development
**Address**: 2/F, Zheng Ping Street South, Tao Jin Road North, Guangzhou, China
**Contact**: Zheng Weiwei, Yao Lina

4815

2010/04/15 – 19
www.cantonfair.org.cn

第107届中国进出口商品交易会（第一期）
**地点**：中国进出口商品交易会展馆, 广东广州
**内容**：电子及家电、照明、车辆及配件、机械、五金工具、建材、化工产品、进口产品
**承办**：中国对外贸易中心

107th China Import and Export Fair Phase 1
**Venue**: China Import and Export Fair Complex, Guangzhou, Guangdong
**Profile**: Large Machinery and Equipment, Small Machinery, Bicycles, Motorcycles, Vehicle Spare Parts, Chemical Products, Hardware, Tools, Vehicles (Outdoor), Construction Machinery (Outdoor), Household Electrical Appliances, Consumer Electronics, Electronic and Electrical Products, Computer and Communication Products, Lighting Equipment, Building and Decoration? Materials, Sanitary and Bathroom Equipment, International Pavilion
**Organizer**: China Foreign Trade Centre

4816

2010/04/23 – 27
www.cantonfair.org.cn

第107届中国进出口商品交易会（第二期）
**地点**：中国进出口商品交易会展馆, 广东广州
**内容**：日用消费品、礼品、家居装饰品
**承办**：中国对外贸易中心

107th China Import and Export Fair Phase 2
**Venue**: China Import and Export Fair Complex, Guangzhou, Guangdong
**Profile**: Kitchen &??Tableware, General Ceramics, Art Ceramics, Home Decorations, Glass Artware,
Furniture, Weaving, Rattan and Iron Arts, Gardening Products, Stone and Iron Products (Outdoor)
Household Items, Personal Care Products, Toiletries, Clocks, Watches & Optical Instruments,
Toys, Gifts and Premiums, Festival Products
**Organizer**: China Foreign Trade Centre

4817

2010/05/01 – 05
www.cantonfair.org.cn

第107届中国进出口商品交易会（第三期）
**地点**：中国进出口商品交易会展馆, 广东广州
**内容**：纺织服装、鞋类、办公箱包及休闲用品、医药及医疗保健、食品及土特产品
**承办**：中国对外贸易中心

107th China Import and Export Fair Phase 3
**Venue**: China Import and Export Fair Complex, Guangzhou, Guangdong
**Profile**: Men and Women' s Clothes, Kid' s Wear, Underwear, Sports and Casual Wear, Furs, Leather, Down & Related Products, Fashion Accessories and Fittings, Home Textiles, Textile Raw Materials?& Fabrics, Carpets & Tapestries, Food, Native Produce, Medicines and Health Products, Medical Devices, Disposables and Dressings, Sports, Travel and Recreation Products, Office Supplies, Shoes Cases and Bags
**Organizer**: China Foreign Trade Centre

4820

2010/05/18 - 21
☎ 020-6119 8852, 61198894
📠 020-6119 8841
✉ sunny_sly@163.com
www.gimee.com.cn

GIMEE2010 第六届机博会
2010国际机械装备（广东）博览会
**地点**：保利世贸博览馆，广东广州
**内容**：GIMEE是装备领域颇具影响力的专业展览会，自2004年以来，累计展览总面积达15万m²，吸引了3300多中外品牌及15万人次专业观众的参与。展品范围：机床与金属加工设备；模具及配套件；机械零部件及辅助设备；刀量刃具；传动控制与自动化；五金工具及磨料磨具等。
**始办年份**：2004
**周期**：每年一届
**市场范围**：国际性
**入场券价格**：免费

GIMEE 2010
Guangdong International Machinery Equipment Exposition
**Venue**: Poly World Trade Center Expo, Guangzhou, Guangdong
**Profile**: GIMEE is a professional and influential Exhibition for Machinery Equipment field. It' s attracted more than 3000 domestic and foreign brands and 150,000 person-time professional visitors' participation since 2004. **Exhibits**: Machine tools and metalworking equipment; Molds and spare parts; Mechanical parts and auxiliary equipment; Knives Measuring & Cutting Tool; Transmission Control and Automation;
**Established Year**: 2004

**参展费用**：A区：标准展位8,000元，净地800元/ā；B区：标准展位7,500元，净地750元/ā；国际展商2,000美元/展位
上届规模 ‘08：展览面积12,000m²(国外展商面积2,000m²)，参展商428家（国外展商32家，来自21个国家），专业贸易观众22,305人
**主办**：广东省科学技术协会；广东省机械工程学会；广东省自动化学会
**承办**：广东会展推广有限公司
**地址**：中国广州市远景路168-170号时代新都汇B座812室（510403）
**联系人**：孙丽燕，潘有杰
QQ：108727317

**Frequency**: Annual
**Market Area**: International
**Cost to Attend**: Free
**Participated Fee**: Intl Exhibitors USD 2000/booth
**Statistics ‘08**: Exhibition Area 12,000m²(foreigners 2,000m²), Exhibitors 428（foreigners 32, came from 21 countries）, Trade Visitors 22,305
**Organizer**: Guangdong Provincial Assn for Science and Technology；Guangdong Mechanical Engineering Society；Guangdong Provincial Automation Society
**Organizer**: Guangdong Convention & Exhibition Promotion
**Address**: Unit 812 Tower B, Times Focus, 168-170 Yuanjing Road, Guangzhou, China
**Contact**: Kelly, Pan

---

2010/05/20 - 22
☎ 010-6580 1456, 6580 3828
📠 010-6580 3826
✉ cnbaking@126.com
www.baking-china.com
4840

**2010年第十四届中国国际烘焙展览会**
**地点**：中国进出口商品交易会琶洲展馆，广东广州
**内容**：烘焙生产、包装设备；冷冻保鲜设备、仪器仪表，烘焙器具，金属检测装置；酒店业设备、厨房设备、西餐、快餐、酒吧、咖啡厅配料及设备；饼房店铺、超市物流设施、陈列设备、计算机管理系统；烘焙业产品、面粉、预拌粉、冷冻面团、淀粉、土豆制品,干果；油脂、鲜奶油、专用奶制品；改良剂；保鲜剂、酵母、香料、香精、色素、甜味剂等相关食品添加剂 咖啡、巧克力、糖仔、蜡烛、仿真模型等蛋糕装饰材料； 包装材料、包装容器 馅料、果料
**始办年份**：1996
**周期**：每年一届
**市场范围**：国际性
**参展费用**：国内企业：标准展位5,800元（9m²），净地560元/m²
**上届规模** ‘09：展览面积14,400m²(国外展商面积3,114m²)，参展商550家（国外展商131家)，参观人数60,000人
**主办**：中华全国工商业联合会烘焙业公会
**承办**：北京中连鼎和烘焙食品技术有限公司
**联系人**：王玉强，张伟

**2010 14th China Bakery Exhibition**
**Venue**: Chinese Import and Export Fair Pazhou Complex, Guangzhou, Guangdong
**Profile**: Ovens, Bakery and pastry-making machinery, Refrigeration, fermenting and air conditioning technology and engineering, Hotel accessories, Baking agents, raw materials and ingredients, Partly baked and finished products, Coffee, Sweets, Chocolate, Ice cream manufacturing, Pasta manufacturing, Furniture and furnishings for shops, cafes and patisseries, Packaging machinery, equipment and material, Decorative items and baking accessories, Cleaning and hygiene, Laboratory and measuring equipment, EDP hardware and software, books, training
**Established Year**: 1996
**Frequency**: Annual
**Market Area**: International
**Statistics ‘09**: Exhibition Area 14,400m²(foreigners 3,114m²), Exhibitors 550（foreigners 131）, Visitors 60,000
**Sponsor**: All-China Bakery Assn (A.C.B.A)
**Organizer**: Beijing Zhonglian Dinghe Bakery Food Technology Co Ltd; Canton Universal Fair Group Ltd

---

2010/06/01 - 03
☎ 852-2851 8603
📠 852-2851 8637
✉ topreput@top-repute.com
www.shoesleather-guangzhou.com/index.html
4850

**广州国际鞋类、皮革及工业设备展览会**
**地点**：中国进出口商品交易会琶洲展馆，广东广州
**内容**：鞋类机械、制革机、皮具机、皮革、原皮料、鞋材、化工、配件/辅料
**始办年份**：1991
**周期**：每年一届
**市场范围**：国际性
**参展费用**：标准展位3,000美元/9m²
**上届规模** ‘09：参展商850家，参观人数14,500人
**主办**：中国对外贸易中心(集团)；显辉国际展览有限公司
**地址**：香港上环禧利街27号富辉商业中心2403室
**联系人**：郭小姐

**The 20th International Exhibition On Shoes & Leather Industry**
Incoporate with:
Guangzhou International Leather Exhibition
International Tanning Technology & Machinery Exhibition
(Machinery & Raw Material)
**Venue**: Chinese Import and Export Fair Pazhou Complex, Guangzhou, Guangdong
**Profile**: Tanning machinery, shoes machinery, raw materials, leather, etc.
**Established Year**: 1991
**Frequency**: Annual
**Market Area**: International
**Participated Fee**: Standard Booth USD 3,000/booth (9m²)
**Statistics ‘09**: Exhibitors 850, Visitors 14,500
**Organizer**: China Foreign Trade Center (Group) Top Repute Co Ltd
**Address**: Rm 2403, Fu Fai Commercial Center, 27 Hillier Street, Sheung Wan, Hong Kong
**Contact**: Ms Kwok

---

2010/06/09 - 11
☎ 020-2608 1660
📠 020-8668 0925转ext 02, 2608 1600
✉ project2@fairwindow.com.cn
www.gziepe.cn
4860

**第八届中国（广州）国际环保展**
**地点**：中国进出口商品交易会琶洲展馆，广东广州
**内容**：大气污染治理与控制技术及设备 工业废水、城市污水处理技术及设备 固废处理处置回收再利用技术及设备 噪声污染与振动控制技术及设备 环境监测技术及仪器仪表 城市供水技术及设备 环境标志产品 绿色包装材料、环保可降解餐具 环保汽车（新增加的） 节能节水节电产品 清洁能源有效利用技术及设备 清洁生产技术及产品 环保咨询服务
**周期**：两年一届
**市场范围**：国际性

**The 8th International Enviro Guangzhou**
**Venue**: Chinese Import and Export Fair Pazhou Complex, Guangzhou, Guangdong
**Profile**: Air pollution treatment and control Industrial/ urban wastewater treatment Solid wastes treatment, recover and recycle Noise pollution and vibration control Environment monitoring and instruments Urban water supply Environmental labeling products Green packaging materials/ biodegradable tableware Environmentally-friendly vehicles Energy-saving/water-saving/electricity-saving products Effective utilization of clean energy Cleaner production

参展费用：7300元/9m²，净地770元/m²
上届规模 '09：展览面积134,500m²，参展商1,767家（来自35个国家），参观人数72,161人
主办：中国对外贸易中心（集团）
承办：中国对外贸易广州展览公司
地址：广州市流花路117号交易会院内15号楼616B（510014）
联系人：黄先生

Environmental consulting service
Frequency: Biennial
Market Area: International
Participated Fee: Standard Booth RMB 7,300/9m², Raw Space RMB 770/m²
Statistics '09: Exhibition Area 134,500m², Exhibitors 1,767 (came from 35 countries), Visitors 72,161
Sponsor: China Foreign Trade Center (Group)
Organizer: China Foreign Trade Guangzhou Exhibition Corporation
Address: Rm.616B, Building 15, No.117, Liuhua Rd., Guangzhou
Contact: Daniel Huang

2010/06/17 - 20
☎ 020-8666 0158, 8666 3388转ext 1151
📠 020-8667 7120
✉ info@cmpchina.com
www.jewellerynetasia.com
4870

中国(广州)国际黄金珠宝玉石展览会
地点：广州锦汉展览中心，广东广州
内容：为华南年中的主要珠宝展览会，地点广州是被国家评定为"中国珠宝玉石首饰特色产业基地"，且位置得天独厚，四通八达。
周期：每年三届（分别在上海、广州、深圳举办）
主办：亚洲博闻有限公司

China International Gold, Jewelry & Gem Fair
Venue: Guangzhou Jinhan Exhibition Center, Guangzhou, Guangdong
Profile: A key mid-year trade fair in China, held in Guangzhou, which is a special production base for jewelry and a good transportation network.
Organizer: UBM Asia

2010/06/23 - 26
☎ 020-3862 1295
📠 020-3862 0781
✉ julangmeiwer@126.com
4880

第十一届广州国际金属暨冶金工业展览会
地点：中国进出口商品交易会琶洲展馆，广东广州
始办年份：2000
周期：每年一届
市场范围：国际性
参展费用：标准展位11,000元/9m²，净地960元/m²（36m²起）
上届规模 '09：展览面积30,000m²(国外展商面积5,000m²)，参展商680家（国外展商58家，来自12个国家），参观人数23,893人（专业贸易观众4,675人）
主办：广州巨浪展览策划有限公司
地址：广州市天河区珠江城华明路29号星汇园A1座3A04-3A06（510623）
联系人：梅文

The 11th China (Guangzhou) Metal & Metallurgy Exhibition
Venue: Chinese Import and Export Fair Pazhou Complex, Guangzhou, Guangdong
Established Year: 2000
Frequency: Annual
Market Area: International
Participated Fee: Standard Booth RMB 11,000/9m², Raw Space RMB 960/m² (min 36m²)
Statistics '09: Exhibition Area 30,000m²(foreigners 5,000m²), Exhibitors 680 (foreigners 58, came from 12 countries), Visitors 23,893 (trade visitors 4,675)
Organizer: Guangzhou Julang Exhibition Design Co Ltd
Address: Suite 3A04-3A06, Bldg A1, Galaxy City, 29 Huaming Rd, Pearl River New City, Tianhe, Guangzhou, 510623, China

2010/06/30 - 02
☎ 852-2763 9011
📠 852-2341 0379
✉ info@paper-com.com.hk
www.paper-com.com.hk
4890

第十五届华南国际机械及模具展
第十五届华南国际塑胶展
地点：保利世贸博览馆，广东广州
周期：每年一届
市场范围：国际性
主办：讯通展览公司
地址：香港九龙观塘成业街11号华成工商中心5字楼15室

15th South China Intl Machinery & Mould Exhibition
15th South China International Plastics Exhibition
Venue: Poly World Trade Center Expo, Guangzhou, Guangdong
Frequency: Annual
Market Area: International
Organizer: Paper Communication Exhibition Services
Address: Rm 15, 5/F., Wah Shing Center, 11 Shing Yip St, Kwun Tong, Kowloon, Hong Kong

2010/07/08 - 11
☎ 020-8526 1628, 2608 1697
📠 020-8668 0925转ext 01
✉ ciff@fairwindow.com.cn
www.cbd-kitchen.com

4990

中国（广州）国际厨房设备及配件展
地点：中国进出口商品交易会琶洲展馆，广东广州
内容：厨房家具及配件、嵌入式厨房电器和设备、家用厨房电器和设备、厨房水暖五金、厨房智能设备、软件、培训、出版物等、其他
周期：每年一届
市场范围：国际性
入场券价格：30元
参展费用：净地900元/m²(36m²起)，标准展位8,300元
主办：中国对外贸易中心（集团）；全国工商联家具装饰业商会
承办：中国对外贸易广州展览公司；广州博亚展览发展有限公司
地址：广州市流花路117号（510014）
联系人：周嵘，陈鹏汉

China Kitchen Furniture and Appliance Fair
Venue: Chinese Import and Export Fair Pazhou Complex, Guangzhou, Guangdong
Profile: Furniture and furnishing systems for kitchen, Built-in kitchen appliances, Electrical household appliance for kitchen, Kitchen hardware, Kitchen Intelligent, Software, training, publication, Others
Frequency: Annual
Market Area: International
Cost to Attend: RMB 30:-
Participated Fee: Raw Space RMB 900/m²(min 36m²), Standard Booth RMB 8,300
Sponsor: China Foreign Trade Center (Group), China Furniture & Decoration Chamber of Commerce
Organizer: China Foreign Trade Guangzhou Exhibition Corporation; Guangzhou Boya Exhibition Development Co Ltd
Address: 117, Liuhua Road, Guangzhou 510014, China
Contact: Zhou Rong, Chen Penghan

2010/07/08 - 11
☎ 020-2608 1697
🖷 020-8668 0925转ext 03
✉ project3@fairwindow.com.cn
www.cbd-china.com

5000

**中国（广州）国际卫浴及建筑陶瓷展**

**地点**：中国进出口商品交易会琶洲展馆，广东广州
**内容**：整体浴室、浴缸类、淋浴类、座便器、台盆、浴室五金/配件类、卫浴室镜、泳池设施、热水器、取暖器、浴室柜、各类墙地砖、原辅材料及生产设备、游泳设备及配件、SPA及桑拿设备、循环过滤产品等
**周期**：每年一届
**市场范围**：国际性
**入场券价格**：30 元
**参展费用**：标准展位8,300元，净地900元/m$^2$（36m$^2$起）
**上届规模** '09：展览面积32,000m$^2$，参展商2,800家，参观人数60,000人
**主办**：中国对外贸易中心（集团）；中国建筑卫生陶瓷协会
**地址**：广州市流花路117号（510014）
**联系人**：陈鹏汉

**China (Guangzhou) Intl Exhibition for Sanitary Ware and Building Ceramics**

**Venue**: Chinese Import and Export Fair Pazhou Complex, Guangzhou, Guangdong
**Profile**: Integrated bathroom, bathtub, shower, water closet, shower basin, bathroom hardware and accessories, swimming pool equipment, bathroom heater and bathroom cabinet, Wall tile, frond tile and production facility, Pool water equipment, SPA equipment, circulation filter production
**Frequency**: Annual
**Market Area**: International
**Cost to Attend**: RMB 30:-
**Participated Fee**: Standard Booth RMB 8,300, Raw Space RMB 900/m$^2$ (min 36m$^2$)
**Statistics '09**: Exhibition Area 32,000m$^2$, Exhibitors 2,800, Visitors 60,000
**Sponsor**: Chinese Foreign Trade Center (Group)(CFTC); China Building Ceramic & Sanitary Ware Assn
**Organizer**: China Foreign Trade Guangzhou Exhibition Corp; Guangzhou Boya Exhibition Development Co Ltd
**Address**: 117 Liuhua Rd, Guangzhou 510014, China
**Contact**: Chen Penghan

2010/07/08 - 11
☎ 020-2608 1623
🖷 020-8668 0925转ext 03
✉ project3@fairwindow.com.cn
✉ huangjl@fairwindow.com.cn
www.cbd-china.com

5010

**中国（广州）国际地面铺装材料展**

**地点**：中国进出口商品交易会琶洲展馆，广东广州
**内容**：实木地板、实木复合地板、强化木地板、软木地板、竹地板等；各种地板材料；手工、机制地毯及纺织地铺材料等；地面石材、其它地面铺装材料、地面材料原料、配件、用品等
**周期**：每年一届
**市场范围**：国际性
**入场券价格**：30 元
**参展费用**：标准展位8,300元，净地900元/m$^2$（36m$^2$起）
**上届规模** '09：参观人数60,000人
**主办**：中国对外贸易中心（集团）；中国林产工业协会
**承办**：中国对外贸易广州展览公司；广州博亚展览发展有限公司
**地址**：广州市流花路117号（510014）
**联系人**：黄建霖

**China (Guangzhou) Intl Floor Covering Fair**

**Venue**: Chinese Import and Export Fair Pazhou Complex, Guangzhou, Guangdong
**Profile**: Solid wood flooring, engineered wood flooring, laminate flooring, cork floor, bamboo flooring; Carpets and textile flooring covering; Stone flooring materials; Other floor covering materials; fittings and products
**Frequency**: Annual
**Market Area**: International
**Cost to Attend**: RMB 30:-
**Participated Fee**: Standard Booth RMB 8,300, Raw Space RMB 900/m$^2$ (min 36m$^2$)
**Statistics '09**: Visitors 60,000
**Sponsor**: Chinese Foreign Trade Center (Group)(CFTC); China Forestry Industry Assn China
**Organizer**: Foreign Trade Guangzhou Exhibition Corp; Guangzhou Boya Exhibition Development Co Ltd
**Address**: 117 Liuhua Rd, Guangzhou 510014, China
**Contact**: Huang Jianlin

2010/07/08 - 11
☎ 020-2608 1671, 2608 1636
🖷 020-8666 3416转ext 03
✉ project3@fairwindow.com.cn
✉ leo@fairwindow.com.cn
www.cbd-china.com

5020

**中国（广州）国际建筑装饰博览会**

**地点**：中国进出口商品交易会琶洲展馆，广东广州
**内容**：建筑装饰五金、整体家居、门窗、玻璃、天花吊顶、墙纸/布艺及辅料、楼梯、建筑涂料及化学建材、石材等
**始办年份**：1999
**周期**：每年一届
**市场范围**：国际性
**入场券价格**：30元
**参展费用**：标准展位8,300元，净地900元/m$^2$（36m$^2$起）
**上届规模** '09：展览面积250,000m$^2$，参展商2,800家，参观人数101,586人
**主办**：中国对外贸易中心（集团）；中国建筑装饰协会
**承办**：中国对外贸易广州展览公司；广州博亚展览发展有限公司
**地址**：广州市流花路117号（510014）
**联系人**：刘晓敏，陈羿

**The 12th China (Guangzhou) International Building Decoration Fair**

**Venue**: Chinese Import and Export Fair Pazhou Complex, Guangzhou, Guangdong
**Profile**: Decorative Hardware, Household, Door & Window, Glass, Ceiling & Curtain Wall, Wallpaper & Fabric, Stairs, Coating & Chemicals, Stone and so on
**Established Year**: 1999
**Frequency**: Annual
**Market Area**: International
**Cost to Attend**: RMB 30:-
**Participated Fee**: Standard Booth RMB 8,300, Raw Space RMB 900/m$^2$ (min 36m$^2$)
**Statistics '09**: Exhibition Area 250,000m$^2$, Exhibitors 2,800, Visitors 101,586
**Sponsor**: Chinese Foreign Trade Center (Group)(CFTC), China Building &Decoration Assn (CBDA)
**Organizer**: China Foreign Trade Guangzhou Exhibition Corp, Guangzhou Boya Exhibition Development Co Ltd
**Address**: 117 Liuhua Rd, Guangzhou 510014, China
**Contact**: Juergen, Leo Chan

2010/07/15 - 17
☎ 020-8258 0985, 6286 1373
℻ 020-8256 2185
✉ gdjdexpo@163.com
www.gdjdexpo.com
5030

**2010广东国际家电配件采购博览会**
**地点：**中国进出口商品交易会展馆，广东广州
**内容：**"广东家电配件展"专业地服务于家电产业链，包括家电品牌厂商、家电配件供应商、家电经销商、设计厂商、OEM/ODM厂商、物流厂商以及支撑家电及零部件制造的各种材料、设备厂商。致力于搭建一个服务于国际家电产业链的产品和技术展示平台，促进产业链上下游企业的互动展示、交流和配套采购
**始办年份：**2009
**周期：**每年一届
**市场范围：**国际性
**入场券价格：**免费
**参展费用：**[illegible]
**上届规模** '09：展览面积11,000m²(国外展商面积500m²)，参展商371家（国外展商39家，来自5个国家），参观人数9,000人（专业贸易观众8,100人）
**主办：**广东省家用电器行业协会
**承办：**广州博优会展服务有限公司
**地址：**广州市东圃大马路3号雅怡阁东塔2011室（510660）
**联系人：**邓波，周莉
**MSN：**bo7728@yahoo.com.cn
**QQ：**52129808

**2010 Guangdong International Appliance Parts Procurement Fair**
**Venue:** Chinese Import and Export Fair Pazhou Complex, Guangzhou, Guangdong
**Profile:** It is to assist household appliances parts manufacturers and related suppliers for contacting more purchasers, develop marketing space and publicize enterprise image.
**Established Year:** 2009
**Frequency:** Annual
**Market Area:** International
**Cost to Attend:** Free
**Participated Fee:** Standard Booth RMB 8,800/9m², 净地RMB 900/m²
**Statistics '09:** Exhibition Area 11,000m²(foreigners 500m²), Exhibitors 371 (foreigners 39, came from 5 countries), Visitors 9,000 (trade visitors 8,100)
**Sponsor:** Guangdong Household Electrical Appliances Trade Assn
**Organizer:** Boyou Guangzhou Exhibition Service Co
**Address:** Room 2011 East Tower, Yayige, No.3 Dongpu Big Road, Guangzhou
**Contact:** Mr Deng Bo, Miss Zhou Li
**MSN:** bo7728@yahoo.com.cn

2010/09/16 - 18
☎ 020-8625 9008, 8625 8323
℻ 020-8625 9533
✉ info@gzbeautyexpo.com
www.gzbeautyexpo.com
5040

**第33届广州国际美博会-秋季展**
**地点：**中国进出口商品交易会琶洲展馆，广东广州
**内容：**国际品牌、美容院、日化洗涤、中医养身、发廊、包装。
**主办：**广东省美容美发化妆品行业协会/广东博环美国际展览有限公司

**Guangzhou International Beauty & Cosmetic Import-Export Expo (33rd Edition)**
**Venue:** Chinese Import and Export Fair Pazhou Complex, Guangzhou, Guangdong
**Profile:** International brands, Beauty salons, Personal care, TCM, Hair salons, Pack
**Organizer:** Guangdong Beauty & Cosmetic Association Guangdong International Exhibitions Ltd

2010/09/21 - 24
☎ 010-8353 3198
℻ 010-8353 3198
✉ liuqsh@northexpo.com.cn
www.cipas.com.cn
5050

**2010广州宠物水族用品展**
**地点：**保利世贸博览馆，广东广州
**内容：**涵盖宠物水族用品的全系列产品，透过展会，您不仅能了解到中国宠物水族用品生产企业的发展现状和市场趋势，同时，您可以透过展会直接与中国最具实力的供应商建立贸易渠道，因此，它也成为国内外贸易者的必到展会之一。
**始办年份：**2008
**周期：**每年一届
**市场范围：**国际性
**参展费用：**待定
**上届规模** '09：展览面积12,000m²(国外展商面积300m²)，参展商200家（国外展商20家，来自10个国家），专业贸易观众5,000人
**主办：**北方国际展览有限公司
**地址：**北京市宣武区广安门内大街338号401室（100053）
**联系人：**刘强顺

**2010 Guangzhou Pet & Aquarium Show**
**Venue:** Poly World Trade Center Expo, Guangzhou, Guangdong
**Profile:** CIPAS is a professional commercial exhibition of pet and aquarium. The major exhibitors of CIPAS are manufacturers and merchants in the aquarium and pet industry and the Suppliers of live pet. The aim of the show is to boost the export and import in the industry between China and international buyers.
**Established Year:** 2008
**Frequency:** Annual
**Market Area:** International
**Statistics '09:** Exhibition Area 12,000m²(foreigners 300m²), Exhibitors 200 (foreigners 20, came from 10 countries), Visitors 5,000 (trade visitors 5,000)
**Organizer:** North International Exhibition Co Ltd
**Address:** Rm 401, No.338 Guanganmen Nei Street, Beijing, China
**Contact:** LIU Qiangshun

2010/10/15 - 30
www.cantonfair.org.cn
5055

**第108届中国进出口商品交易会**
**地点：**中国进出口商品交易会展馆，广东广州
**承办：**中国对外贸易中心

**108th China Import and Export Fair**
**Venue:** China Import and Export Fair Complex, Guangzhou, Guangdong
**Organizer:** China Foreign Trade Centre

2010/11/09 - 11
☎ 020-8989 9051, 8989 9052
℻ 020-8989 9050
✉ ns@zhenweiexpo.com
www.cantondye.com.cn
5060

**第10届中国国际染料工业及纺织化学品、印花技术展览会**
**地点：**中国进出口商品交易会琶洲展馆，广东广州
**内容：**各类染料；各类有机颜料；各类助剂；化纤单体、催化剂、化纤油剂、生物酶制品及其他各种纺织用化学制品；纺织行业环保技术、质量认证体系及分析检测和监控、配套生产、印染、三废处理设备等；印花机械；印花材料
**始办年份：**2001
**周期：**每年一届
**市场范围：**国际性
**入场券价格：**免费
**参展费用：**标准展位(3x3m)国内企业：特级展位10,000元，A级展位8,000元；国外企业3,600美元。净地(36m²起，施工管理费28元/m²)：国外企业400美元/m²，国内企业1,000元/m²
**上届规模** '09：展览面积9,000m²(国外展商面积2,000m²)，参展商170家（国外展商50家，来自15个国家），参观人数12,000人（专业贸易观众10,000人）
**主办：**中国纺织报社；中国服饰报社；振威展览集团
**承办：**广东振威国展展览有限公司
**地址：**广州市海珠区琶洲大道东1号保利国际广场南塔5楼（510308）
**联系人：**牛松，刘绮薇

**The 10th China International Exhibition for Dye Industry & Textile Chemical, Printing Industrial Technology**
**Venue:** Chinese Import and Export Fair Pazhou Complex, Guangzhou, Guangdong
**Profile:** Various types of dyes; all kinds of organic pigments; all kinds of additives; fiber monomer, catalyst, chemical fiber oil, bio-enzyme products and a variety of other textile chemical products; textile industry, environmental technology, quality certification system and analysis of testing and monitoring, supporting the production, printing and dyeing, waste treatment equipment, etc.; printing machinery; printing materials
**Established Year:** 2001
**Frequency:** Annual
**Market Area:** International
**Cost to Attend:** Free
**Participated Fee:** Standard Booth USD 3,600, Raw Space USD 400/m²
**Statistics '09:** Exhibition Area 9,000m²(foreigners 2,000m²), Exhibitors 170 (foreigners 50, came from 15 countries), Visitors 12,000 (trade visitors 10,000)
**Organizer:** Guangdong Zhenwei Guozhan Exhibition Co Ltd
**Address:** Unit 501-504 South Tower Poly Intl Plaza, No.1 East of Pazhou Complex, Haizhu Dist, Guangzhou, China
**Contact:** Niu Song, Liu QiWei

2010/11/09 - 11
☎ 020-8989 9051, 8989 9052
🖷 020-8989 9050
✉ cnibf@zhenweiexpo.com
www.cnibf.net/cscf
5070

**第10届中国（广州）国际纺织面料辅料及纱线展览会**
**地点**：中国进出口商品交易会琶洲展馆，广东广州
**内容**：面料：麻织、丝织、棉织、化纤类梭织、针织及涂层织物、各类复合织物、防辐射织物、丝光、无纺布、及纳米技术等；纱线、纤维：圆编及横编针织/梭织纱线、织袜纱线、制衣纱线、花式纱线；天然/合成纤维等；辅料：刺绣、花边、衬里、纽扣、线带、商标、配件、拉链、衣架等；设计及生产系统：CAD/CAM、花型输入系统等
**始办年份**：2000
**周期**：每年一届
**市场范围**：国际性
**入场券价格**：免费
**参展费用**：标准展位(3x3m)国内企业：特级展位10,000元，A级展位8,000元；国外企业3,600美元。净地(36$m^2$起，施工管理费28元/$m^2$)：国外企业400美元/$m^2$，国内企业1,000元/$m^2$
**上届规模 '09**：展览面积9,000$m^2$(国外展商面积2,000$m^2$)，参展商170家（国外展商50家，来自15个国家），参观人数12,000人（专业贸易观众10,000人）
**主办**：中国纺织报社；中国服饰报社；振威展览集团
**承办**：广东振威国展展览有限公司
**地址**：广州市海珠区琶洲大道东1号保利国际广场南塔5楼（510308）
**联系人**：牛松，刘绮薇

**10th China (Guangzhou) Intl Exhibition for Apparel Fabric & Accessories**
**Venue**: Chinese Import and Export Fair Pazhou Complex, Guangzhou, Guangdong
**Profile**: Product groups includes fabrics such as cotton, wool, silk, linen, ramie, man-made, knitted, coated, Lingerie & swimwear fabrics, Functional fabrics, Printed fabrics, Fibers & yarns, Embroidery & lace Accessories, Textile-related CAD/CAM/CIM technology, Design & styling agencies, Fashion & textile trade publications.
**Established Year**: 2000
**Frequency**: Annual
**Market Area**: International
**Cost to Attend**: Free
**Participated Fee**: Standard Booth USD 3,600, Raw Space USD 400/$m^2$
**Statistics '09**: Exhibition Area 15,000$m^2$(foreigners 1,000$m^2$), Exhibitors 300 (foreigners 30, came from 6 countries), Trade Visitors 17,000
**Organizer**: Guangdong Zhenwei Guozhan Exhibition Co Ltd
**Address**: Unit 501-504 South Tower Poly Intl Plaza, No.1 East of Pazhou Complex, Haizhu Dist, Guangzhou, China
**Contact**: Niu Song, Liu QiWei

2010/11/09 - 11
☎ 020-8989 9051, 8989 9052
🖷 020-8989 9050
✉ ns@zhenweiexpo.com
www.cantondye.com.cn
5080

**第10届中国（广州）国际制衣技术设备展览会**
**地点**：中国进出口商品交易会琶洲展馆，广东广州
**内容**：设计、裁剪、激光、CAD/CAM系统等；缝前、缝纫设备等；刺绣、绣花、绗缝设备等；缝后、配送、整熨设备等；其它相关设备、辅料、辅助品等；信息服务等
**始办年份**：2001
**周期**：每年一届
**市场范围**：国际性
**入场券价格**：免费
**参展费用**：标准展位(3x3m)国内企业：特级展位10,000元，A级展位8,000元；国外企业3,600美元。净地(36$m^2$起，施工管理费28元/$m^2$)：国外企业400美元/$m^2$，国内企业1,000元/$m^2$
**上届规模 '09**：展览面积6,000$m^2$(国外展商面积500$m^2$)，参展商110家（国外展商25家，来自7个国家），参观人数8,000人（专业贸易观众7,000人）
**主办**：中国纺织报社；中国服饰报社；振威展览集团
**承办**：广东振威国展展览有限公司
**地址**：广州市海珠区琶洲大道东1号保利国际广场南塔5楼（510308）
**联系人**：牛松，刘绮薇

**10th China (Guangzhou) Intl Exhibition for Clothing Technology and Equipment**
**Venue**: Chinese Import and Export Fair Pazhou Complex, Guangzhou, Guangdong
**Profile**: The design, cutting, laser, CAD / CAM systems; seam before sewing equipment; embroidery, embroidery, quilting equipment; seam, the distribution, the whole ironing equipment; other related equipment, accessories, auxiliary materials; Information Services and so on
**Established Year**: 2001
**Frequency**: Annual
**Market Area**: International
**Cost to Attend**: Free
**Participated Fee**: Standard Booth USD 3,600, Raw Space USD 400/$m^2$
**Statistics '09**: Exhibition Area 6,000$m^2$(foreigners 500$m^2$), Exhibitors 110 (foreigners 25, came from 7 countries), Visitors 8,000 (trade visitors 7,000)
**Sponsor**: China Textile News; China Fashion Weekly; Zhenwei Exhibition Group
**Organizer**: Guangdong Zhenwei Guozhan Exhibition Co Ltd
**Address**: Unit 501-504 South Tower Poly Intl Plaza, No.1 East of Pazhou Complex, Haizhu Dist, Guangzhou, China
**Contact**: Niu Song, Liu QiWei

2010/11/09 - 11
☎ 020-8989 9051, 8989 9052
🖷 020-8989 9050
✉ cnibf@zhenweiexpo.com
www.cnibf.net/cscf
5090

**第10届中国（广州）国际纺织机械展览会**
**地点**：中国进出口商品交易会琶洲展馆，广东广州
**内容**：针织机械：圆型针织机、提花机、织袜机；纺纱机械：粗纱机、细纱机、捻线机、络筒机、化纤机械设备等；织造机械：剑杆织机、喷气织机、梭织机、织带机等；染整机械：各种漂洎、染色、整理机、印花机等；纺织零部件及附件：各种纺织仪器仪表、机电、器材、电脑辅助设备、纺织软件科技、其它纺织机械附件。
**始办年份**：2001
**周期**：每年一届
**市场范围**：国际性
**入场券价格**：免费
**参展费用**：标准展位(3x3m)国内企业：特级展位10,000元，A级展位8,000元；国外企业3,600美元。净地(36$m^2$起，施工管理费28元/$m^2$)：国外企业400美元/$m^2$，国内企业1,000元/$m^2$
**上届规模 '09**：展览面积15,000$m^2$(国外展商面积2,000$m^2$)，参展商270家（国外展商70家，来自15个国家），参观人数18,000人（专业贸易观众16,000人）
**主办**：中国纺织报社；中国服饰报社；振威展览集团
**承办**：广东振威国展展览有限公司
**地址**：广州市海珠区琶洲大道东1号保利国际广场南塔501-504（510308）
**联系人**：牛松，刘绮薇

**10th China (Guangzhou) Intl Exhibition for Textile Machinery**
**Venue**: Chinese Import and Export Fair Pazhou Complex, Guangzhou, Guangdong
**Profile**: Product groups includes fabrics such as spinning, nonwovens, weaving, knitting, dyeing and finishing, garment making, dyestuffs and chemicals, Pre-sewing, Shrinking & Cloth Spreading Equipment, Cloth Cutting Equipment, Sewing & Stitching, Sewing Machine, Embroidery Equipment, Quilting & Weaving Equipment, Needle-detecting Equipment, Steam Iron & Finishing Equipment, Cleaning & Washing Equipment.
**Established Year**: 2001
**Frequency**: Annual
**Market Area**: International
**Cost to Attend**: Free
**Participated Fee**: Standard Booth USD 3,600, Raw Space USD 400/$m^2$
**Statistics '09**: Exhibition Area 15,000$m^2$(foreigners 2,000$m^2$), Exhibitors 270 (foreigners 70, came from 15 countries), Visitors 18,000 (trade visitors 16, 000)
**Organizer**: Guangdong Zhenwei Guozhan Exhibition Co Ltd
**Address**: Unit 501-504 South Tower Poly Intl Plaza, No.1 East of Pazhou Complex, Haizhu Dist, Guangzhou, China
**Contact**: Niu Song, Liu QiWei

# 广东-深圳
# Guangdong-Shenzhen

2010/03/09 - 12
☎ 020-8666 0158,
8666 3388转ext 1151
🖷 020-8667 7120
✉ info@cmpchina.com
www.jewellerynetasia.com
5110

**中国(深圳)国际黄金珠宝玉石展览会**
**地点：**深圳会展中心，广东深圳
**主办：**亚洲博闻有限公司

**China International Gold, Jewelry & Gem Fair**
**Venue:** Shenzhen Convention and Exhibition Center, Shenzhen, Guangdong
**Organizer:** UBM Asia

2010/03/19 - 22
☎ 0755-2601 8177
🖷 0755-2601 8179
5120

**第25届深圳国际家具/家居饰品/家具配料展览会**
**地点：**深圳会展中心，广东深圳
**内容：**家具、家具饰品、原辅材料及配件、设计师展
**周期：**2009年前每年两届，自2009年始每年一届
**市场范围：**国际性
**性质：**面向公众
**入场券价格：**20元
**参展费用：**550～660元/$m^2$
**上届规模**‘09：展览面积160,000$m^2$(国外展商面积15,000$m^2$)，参展商700家（国外展商100家），参观人数200,000人
**主办：**深圳市家具行业协会；深圳市德赛展览有限公司
**地址：**广东省深圳市南山区西丽沙河西路家具研发基地（518055）
**联系人：**钟小姐

The 25th Shenzhen International Furniture Exhibition
**Venue:** Shenzhen Convention and Exhibition Center, Shenzhen, Guangdong
**Profile:** All types of furniture, interior decorations, furniture components & materials.
**Frequency:** Annual
**Market Area:** International
**Nature:** Open to public
**Cost to Attend:** RMB 20:-
**Participated Fee:** RMB 550-660/$m^2$
**Statistics ‘09:** Exhibition Area 160,000$m^2$(foreigners 15,000$m^2$), Exhibitors 700 (foreigners 100), Visitors 200,000
**Organizer:** The Shenzhen Furniture Trade Assn
**Address:** The Furniture Research Base, Shahe West Rd., Xili County Nanshan District, Shenzhen, Guangdong, China
**Contact:** Xiao Zhong

2010/03/28 - 31
☎ 0755-8345 9957
🖷 0755-8347 7946
✉ vipyshen@yahoo.com.cn
5130

**2010第11届深圳国际机械、模具及制品、塑胶工业展览会**
**地点：**深圳会展中心，广东深圳
**内容：**始办于2000年，作为全球国际展览联盟（UFI）在中国华南地区首家认可并推荐的品牌展览会，已成为中国最具影响和辐射力的专业代表展，为来自全球的供应商、经销代理商、用户及行业专家提供了业务洽谈、项目投资、技术合作、学术讨论的舞台。
**始办年份：**2000
**周期：**每年一届
**市场范围：**国际性
**入场券价格：**对专业贸易观众免费
**参展费用：**15,000元/展位
**上届规模**‘09：展览面积25,200$m^2$(国外展商面积3,060$m^2$)，参展商972家（国外展商109家，来自20个国家），参观人数96,269人（专业贸易观众26,202人）
**主办：**深圳市机械行业协会
**承办：**深圳市协广机械有限公司
**地址：**广东省深圳市福田区深南大道6021号喜年中心A座517室（518040）
**联系人：**尹惠斌
**MSN：**yshen@126.com
**QQ：**770353181

**China Shenzhen Intl Machinery Manufacturing Industry Exhibition**
(SIMM2010)
**Venue:** Shenzhen Convention and Exhibition Center, Shenzhen, Guangdong
**Profile:** Since 2000, the exhibitions have been successfully held 10 times. Approved by UFI, SIMM & S. Mould & S. Plas firstly gained this honor in south of China, winning the recognition from the exhibitors and buyers home and aboard, and has become the most influential professional exhibitions in China.
**Established Year:** 2000
**Frequency:** Annual
**Market Area:** International
**Cost to Attend:** Free to Professional and Trade Visitors
**Participated Fee:** Standard Booth RMB 15,000/booth
**Statistics ‘09:** Exhibition Area 25,200$m^2$(foreigners 3,060$m^2$), Exhibitors 972 (foreigners 109, came from 20 countries), Visitors 96,269 (trade visitors 26,202)
**Sponsor:** Shenzhen Machinery Assn
**Organizer:** Shenzhen Xieguang Machinery Co
**Address:** Rm.1204, 12/F., Hailrun Complex, No. 6021 Shennan Blvd, Futian Dist, Shenzhen. China
**Contact:** Kevin yin
**MSN:** yshen@126.com

2010/04/03 - 05
☎ 0755-8364 2581, 13798342253
🖷 0755-8364 3450
✉ szhe_2008@163.com
www.china-wed.com
5140

**2010深圳国际婚博会暨深圳婚庆文化节**
**地点：**深圳会展中心，广东深圳
**内容：**婚纱摄影、工作室精品区：最新风格婚纱摄影、主题婚纱摄影、个性婚纱摄影、儿童摄影； 酒店、酒楼婚宴精品区：豪华婚宴、中西式婚宴、个性婚宴、精品百姓婚宴；婚礼策划及服务精品区：时尚特色定制婚礼、婚典花艺、蜜月旅游、婚车租赁；婚礼庆典精品区：喜糖、喜烟、喜酒、喜帖、喜品、工艺品、相框、相册、化妆品；结婚首饰精品区；婚纱礼服精品区；新婚服务精品区
**始办年份：**2005
**周期：**每年一届
**市场范围：**全国性
**性质：**面向公众
**参展费用：**A区：标准展位8,800元/3x3m，净地880元/$m^2$；B区标准展位7,800元/3x3m，净地780元/$m^2$
**主办：**深圳市商业联合会
**承办：**深圳市美博会展有限公司
**地址：**深圳市福田区莲花支路公交大厦18楼
**联系人：**李想

**Shenzhen International Wedding Exhibition &Wedding Cultural Festival 2010**
**Venue:** Shenzhen Convention and Exhibition Center, Shenzhen, Guangdong
**Established Year:** 2005
**Frequency:** Annual
**Market Area:** National
**Nature:** Open to Public
**Participated Fee:** Standard Booth RMB 8,800元(3x3m), Raw Space RMB 880/$m^2$
**Organizer:** Shenzhen Meibo Exhibition Co Ltd

2010/04/09 - 11
☎ 0755-8831 2796
🖷 0755-8831 2533, 8831 5466
www.icef.com.cn
5150

**2010年春季（第75届）中国电子展**
**地点：**深圳会展中心，广东深圳
**内容：**显示产品、电子元器件、生产设备、仪器仪表、电子工具、军工产品等 工业洁净设备、空气检测设备、超声波清洗设备、防静电系
**主办：**中国电子器材总公司；深圳市创意时代会展有限公司
**地址：**深圳市福田区福华三路国际商会中心2201室
**联系人：**李艳

**75th China Electronics Fair (CEF Shenzhen)**
**Venue:** Shenzhen Convention and Exhibition Center, Shenzhen, Guangdong
**Organizer:** Creativity Convention & Exhibition (Shenzhen)Co Ltd
**Address:** Room 2201, Intl Chamber of Commerce Tower, Fuhua 3 Road, Futian Dist, Shenzhen, China
**Contact:** Jessica Lee

---

2010/04/18 - 21
☎ 010-8455 6677
🖷 010- 8202 2922
✉ chuanjun.ding@reedsinopharm.com
✉ xiaojing.zhang@reedsinopharm.com
www.cmef.com.cn
5160

**第63届中国国际医疗器械春季博览会**
**地点：**深圳会展中心，广东深圳
**内容：**中国国际医疗器械博览会（CMEF，简称医博会）创办于1979年，每年分春秋两季展出，是目前亚太区规模最大、展出品种最全、知名度最高的医疗器械专业品牌展会。
截至到2009年，每届医博会设置标准展位4800多个，展出面积达到9.8万平方米。参展企业2000余家，到会的专业观众超过12万人次。医博会目前已成为亚太地区最大的医疗器械及相关产品、服务展览会。
**展品范围：**医学影像设备，医疗电子设备，手术与急救设备，超声诊断设备，临床诊断及实验室仪器与设备，放射设备，康复理疗产品，眼科产品，牙科产品，激光产品，医院设备与耗材，救护车，医疗服务内容，医疗软技术—Medisoft，信息技术，出版物、媒体，物流，产品注册，咨询，知识产权保护等。参展产品覆盖所有医疗器械器械产品产业链。
**观众范围：**来自国内外医院的决策者以及采购人员，来自国内外的医疗器械的经销商和代理商，政府采购单位，研发单位，医院管理公司，医科院校等。医疗器械销售人员、研发人员、维修工程师、采购招标公司业务员、行业媒体业务员、市场研究机构（公司）人员、药监局人员、卫生局人员、防疫单位人员等。
**主办：**国药励展展览责任有限公司

**The 63rd CMEF**
China Int'l Medical Equipment Fair 2010 - Spring
**Venue:** Shenzhen Convention and Exhibition Center, Shenzhen, Guangdong
**Profile:** Spanning 30 years, the biannual China International Medical Equipment Fair (CMEF), held 62 times to date, has become the largest premier medical device and equipment trade fair in the Asia-Pacific region. CMEF typically features over 2,000 exhibiting companies, more than 50,000 professional visitors, from over 100 countries and regions, with 98,000m$^2$ (gross) of exhibiting space.
**Exhibits:** Medical Imaging, Electro Medical, Surgical and Emergency Treatment Equipment, Ultrasonic Devices for Diagnostics, clinical diagnostic and laboratory instrument and equipment, Radiology Devices, Rehabilitation and Physiotherapy Products, Optical, Dental, Laser Products, Surgery, Hospital Furniture and Consumables, Ambulances, Information Technology, Hospital Suppliers, Healthcare Services: Publications, Logistics, Advertisement, Product Registration, Intellectual Property, Consulting, Electronic Health Records and other e-related products and services, Others.
**Visitors:** Decision makers and purchasing directors of Chinese domestic and foreign hospitals; domestic and international distributors and medical equipment manufacturing agents.
**Organizer:** Reed Sinopharm Exhibition Co Ltd

---

2010/04/18 - 21
☎ 010-8455 6605, 8455 6603
🖷 010-8202 2922
✉ icmd@reedsinopharm.com
✉ yiqi.fan@reedsinopharm.com
www.icmd.com.cn
5170

**第9届中国国际医疗器械设计与制造技术展览会**
**地点：**深圳会展中心，广东深圳
**内容：**每年举办两次的"中国国际医疗器械设计与制造技术展览会（ICMD）"，旨在为医疗设备的生产商、上游制造商构筑合作平台、交流渠道。与"中国国际医疗器械博览会（CMEF，简称医博会）"同期同地举行。给中国国际医疗器械设计与制造技术展览会（ICMD）的参与者最大的直接见面机会。
展品范围：与医疗器械生产相关的技术、产品和服务，具体包括医疗器械的研发和设计；医用材料，包括医用金属材料、陶瓷和各种高分子聚合物和医用粘结材料；现代制造技术、制造设备和相关软件，CAD，CAM和企业管理软件；精密制造和微加工技术与设备；相关部配件；电子元器件、医用传感器、接插件和OEM部件；电动机、泵和运动控制件；包装机械与材料；印刷机械与技术；检测设备；消毒和净化室设备；各类相关服务等。
**周期：**每年两届
**主办：**国药励展展览责任有限公司

**The 10th ICMD**
**-International Component Manufacturing & Design Show (Spring)**
**Venue:** Shenzhen Convention and Exhibition Center, Shenzhen, Guangdong
**Profile:** Co-located with CMEF, ICMD is a specialized sourcing event, catering to China's rapidly developing medical device manufacturing industry's needs for components and design services. Leveraging the well-established reputation of CMEF and its longstanding track record of attracting substantial Chinese and overseas medical end-product manufacturers, ICMD provides an ideal platform for OEMs to offer competitive outsourcing capabilities to other overseas manufacturers. ICMD provides an excellent opportunity for identifying interesting procurement sources and forging business contacts with production managers, technical buyers, managers, engineers and technicians from R&D institutes, and CMEF exhibitors in the medical technology field.
**Exhibits:** Modern Manufacturing Equipment and Software, Rapid Prototyping Services; Medical Relative Parts/Hardware and Accessories; Electronic Components including Medical Transducers; Motors, Pumps, Valves & Motion Control; Medical Packaging Materials, Equipment and Sterilization Technologies; Printing and Surface-Treatment Products and Services; Testing Equipments and Service, Inspection/OA/OC; Sterilization & Clean Room Equipment; Materials for Application including Medical Tubing, Adhesives and Adhesive Products; Outsourcing/Contract Manufacturing; Precision Technology; R & D and Business Services; Others.
**Organizer:** Reed Sinopharm Exhibition Co Ltd

---

2010/04/25 - 28
☎ 0755-3398 9216, 3398 9230
🖷 0755-3333 1168转ext 666, 3398 9231
✉ lisa.mo@reedhuabo.com
www.reedhuabo.com
5180

GIFTS& HOME
礼品|家居·中国

**第十八届中国（深圳）国际礼品、工艺品、钟表及家庭用品展**
**地点：**深圳会展中心，广东深圳
**内容：**来自全国各地的2800家以生产商为主的一流品牌，共同呈献国内最大的礼赠品、玩具及家居用品展览会。经销商、代理商、集团及终端买家将从汇聚在这里的最广泛、最佳品质和创意设计、最具价格优势的公司礼品、赠品和消费品里开始高效的寻源和采购之旅。
**始办年份：**1993
**周期：**每年一届
**市场范围：**国际性
**入场券价格：**20元
**参展费用：**变形展区：10,450元；双开口10,950元；净地830元/m$^2$(48m$^2$起)。标准展区：7,850元；双开口8,350元；净地830元/m$^2$(36 m$^2$起)
**主办：**励展华博展览（深圳）有限公司
**地址：**深圳市中心区福华三路深圳国际商会中心1801-1802（518048）
**联系人：**莫丽珊，王清林

**The 17th China (Shenzhen) International Gifts, Handicrafts, Watches & Houseware Fair**
**Venue:** Shenzhen Convention and Exhibition Center, Shenzhen, Guangdong
**Profile:** Reed Huabo's China Gifts and Home Fair is the largest trade show of its kind in Mainland China. Held in Shenzhen during the best buying seasons in April and October every year, the fair offers the widest selection of business gifts, premiums and consumer products, and attracts tens of thousands of buyers from across the country. They include distributors, agents, premium houses, department stores and large corporate end users. Exhibitors are primarily manufacturers, promising the best design and quality at competitive prices. The fair enables key market players to meet and trade, form partnerships and set industry trends. It is also the best market-entry opportunity for overseas suppliers aiming to tap the fast-growing Chinese market.
**Established Year:** 1993
**Frequency:** Annual
**Market Area:** International

Cost to Attend: RMB 20:-
Participated Fee: Standard Booth RMB 10,450; Corner Booth RMB 10,950; Raw Space RMB 830/m²(min 48m²
Organizer: Reed Huabo Exhibitions (Shenzhen) Co
Address: Rm.1801-1802,Shenzhen Intl Chamber of Commerce Tower, Fuhua 3rd Road, Central District, Shenzhen, China
Contact: Lisa Mo, Wang Qinglin

2010/05/14 - 17
☎ 0755-8352 1183, 8352 2372
🖷 0755-8352 1000
✉ wbh@cnicif.com
www.cnci.gov.cn
www.cnicif.com
5200

**中国（深圳）国际文化产业博览交易会**
**地点**：深圳会展中心，广东深圳
**内容**：文化产业投融资项目、各地文物遗产、非物质文化遗产、旅游资源、文化礼品、工艺美术品、广播电影电视放映、音像制作、动漫及游戏产品、演艺节目、演艺培训机构、演艺设备、艺术表演场馆、文化艺术经纪代理、乐器产品、演艺相关文化旅游基地、创意设计、数字创意、形象授权、创意园区、个人创意设计、图书出版、各类报纸出版、各类期刊杂志出版、音像制品出版、电子出版物出版、书画艺术品、海内外知名美术机构、艺术品经纪公司、国内外画廊
**始办年份**：2004
**周期**：每年一届
**市场范围**：全国性
**性质**：面向公众
**入场券价格**：50元人民币
**参展费用**：标准展位10,000元，净地1,000元/m²（36m²起）
**上届规模** '09：展览面积105,000m²(国外展商面积6,000m²)，参展商1,708家（国外展商368家，来自56个国家），参观人数3577,500人（专业贸易观众368,300人）
**承办**：深圳报业集团；深圳广电集团；深圳出版发行集团公司；深圳国际文化产业博览交易会有限公司
**地址**：深圳市福田区商报路奥林匹克大厦10楼（518034）
**联系人**：姚小姐，李小姐

**China (Shenzhen) Intl Cultural Industries Fair**
Venue: Shenzhen Convention and Exhibition Center, Shenzhen, Guangdong
Profile: Cultural projects, natural cultural heritage, intangible cultural heritage, tourism resources and cultural products, cultural gifts, crafts and gifts, digital movies, cartoon products, games, derived products, national excellent performances, performing programs, performing troupes, training organizations of performing arts, performance equipments, musical instruments, tour bases related with performances; industrial, packaging, graphic, fashion design and personal creative design; publications, video, e-publications, stationery, painting and works of calligraphy, art agencies, art collections of galleries
Established Year: 2004
Frequency: Annual
Market Area: National
Nature: Open to public
Cost to Attend: RMB 50:-
Participated Fee: Standard Booth RMB 10,000, Raw Space RMB 1,000/m² (min 36m²)
Statistics '09: Exhibition Area 105,000m²(foreigners 6,000m²), Exhibitors 1,708 (foreigners 368, came from 56 countries), Visitors 3,577,500 (trade visitors 368,300)
Organizer: Ministry of Culture; Ministry of Commerce; State Administration of Radio, Film and Television; General Administration of Press and Publication; CCPIT
Address: 10/F, Olympic Building, Economic Daily Road, Futian District, Shenzhen, China
Contact: Ms Yao, Ms Li

2010/05/14 - 17
☎ 0755-2516 0895, 2516 0497
🖷 0755-2516 0449
✉ szicie@163.com
www.szicie.com
5210

**第六届中国（深圳）文化产业博览交易会数字影视-动漫游戏展**
**地点**：深圳会展中心，广东 深圳
**内容**：网络游戏互动展区：全国优秀网络游戏及配套设备，现场互动活动区。动漫企业、基地展区：全国动漫游戏产业基地、优秀动漫企业及制作设备；动漫衍生产品展区：展示最新的原创动漫衍生产品，吸引专业的买家及观众进场交流交易；数字影视展区：展示数字影视前沿技术、国内外最优秀的数字影视作品，搭建交易平台，引领行业发展；投融资展区：文化产业投融资机构。
**周期**：每年一届
**市场范围**：国际性
**性质**：面向公众
**承办**：深圳广播电影电视集团；深圳市文化产业（国际）会展有限公司；深圳怡景国家动漫画产业基地
**地址**：深圳市罗湖区怡景路深圳广播电视大厦1楼（518021）
**联系人**：董小姐，朱小姐

**China (Shenzhen) Intl Cultural Industries Fair "DTV/COM & ANI EXHIBITION"**
Venue: Shenzhen Convention and Exhibition Center, Shenzhen, Guangdong
Frequency: Annual
Market Area: International
Nature: Open to public
Organizer: Shenzhen Media Group Intl Cultural Industry Fair Co Ltd

2010/05/23 - 25
☎ 0755-8614 9077
🖷 0755-8296 8771
✉ xhn988@163.com,
✉ Helen@chinafpd.net
http://code.chinafpd.net
5220

**2010深圳光电显示周（第二届）**
**地点**：深圳会展中心，广东深圳
**内容**：本届显示周将以"显示"为核心主题，分为展览、论坛、评选、商务活动等四大部分；将集中展示消费电子、FPD、LED和激光显示等产业链和各关联产业的最新产品、最新技术。
**始办年份**：2008
**周期**：每年一届
**市场范围**：国际性
**入场券价格**：专业观众免费
**参展费用**：标准展位8,000元/9m²，净地800元/m²
**上届规模** '09：展览面积10,000m²(国外展商面积3,000m²)，参展商339家（国外展商112家，来自17个国家），参观人数65,392人（专业贸易观众35,746人）
**主办**：国家工业和信息化部电子信息司；广东省经济和信息化委员会
**承办**：深圳市平板显示行业协会；深圳市亚威会展有限公司
**地址**：深圳市南山区科技园北区朗山2号路豪威大厦4楼（518057）
**联系人**：徐娜
**MSN**：xhn988@hotmail.com
**QQ**：11107253

**China Optoelectronics & Display Expo**
Venue: Shenzhen Convention and Exhibition Center, Shenzhen, Guangdong
Established Year: 2008
Frequency: Annual
Market Area: International
Cost to Attend: Free to Professional and Trade Visitors
Participated Fee: Standard Booth RMB 8,000/9m², Raw Space RMB 800/m²
Statistics '09: Exhibition Area 10,000m²(foreigners 3,000m²), Exhibitors 339 (foreigners 112, came from 17 countries), Visitors 65,392 (trade visitors 35.746)
Organizer: Shenzhen YAWEI Convention & Exhibition Co Ltd
Contact: Helen
MSN: xhn988@hotmail.com

2010/05/26 - 28
☎ 010-8857 5010
🖷 010-8857 5004
✉ zhangsp@minmetals.com
www.puchinashow.com

5230

**第八届中国国际聚氨酯展览会**
**地点：**深圳会展中心，广东深圳
**内容：**聚氨酯材料技术及供应、聚氨酯原料、聚氨酯制品、聚氨酯机械及相关零部件
**周期：**两年一届
**市场范围：**国际性
**性质：**面向公众
**入场券价格：**免费
**参展费用：**国内企业13,600元/9m²，国际企业545美元/m²
上届规模 '08：展览面积5,045m²(国外展商面积3,184m²)，参展商196家（国外展商81家，来自54个国家），参观人数9226人
**主办：**中国五矿集团公司；中国聚氨酯工业协会
**承办：**五矿国际广告展览有限公司；Crain Communications
**地址：**北京市海淀区西直门外大街168号腾达大厦1616室（100044）
**联系人：**张士萍

**PU China 2010**
**Venue:** Shenzhen Convention and Exhibition Center, Shenzhen, Guangdong
**Frequency:** Biennial
**Market Area:** International
**Nature:** Open to public
**Cost to Attend:** Free
**Participated Fee:** Intl Exhibitors USD 545/m²
**Statistics '08:** Exhibition Area 5,045m²(foreigners 3,184m²), Exhibitors 196 (foreigners 81, came from 54 countries), Visitors 9,226
**Organizer:** Grain Communications Ltd

2010/06/23 - 25
☎ 0755-8350 2448, 8350 2435
🖷 0755-8350 2435
✉ flying161@126.com
www.e99999.com

5240

**2010第十八届多人行电子展、光电展**
**地点：**深圳会展中心，广东深圳
**始办年份：**1997
**周期：**每年一届
**市场范围：**国际性
**参展费用：**标准展位10,000元，净地3,000美元
**主办：**中国电子学会；深圳市仪器仪表与自动化行业协会；深圳市光学光电子协会
**承办：**深圳市多人行实业有限公司
**地址：**深圳市福田区新闻路景苑大厦B2602室（518034）
**联系人：**张先生，张萍
**MSN:** lanlinglingaa@hotmail.com
**QQ：**645561040

**2010 The 18th DEX Electronic Exhibition & Photonics Exhibition**
**Venue:** Shenzhen Convention and Exhibition Center, Shenzhen, Guangdong
**Established Year:** 1997
**Frequency:** Annual
**Market Area:** International
**Participated Fee:** Standard Booth RMB 10,000, Raw Space USD 3,000
**Sponsor:** China Institute of Electronics(CIE); Shenzhen Instrument & Automation Manufacture' s Assn; Shenzhen Optics and Optoelectronics Manufactures Assn
**Organizer:** Shenzhen E-Dowell Industrial Co Ltd
**Address:** Rm 2602-2603, Section B, Jingyuan Bldg, Xinwen Rd, Futian Dist, Shenzhen
**Contact:** Mr Zhang, Helen
**MSN:** lanlinglingaa@hotmail.com

2010/06/23 - 25
☎ 0755-8350 2448, 8350 2435
🖷 0755-8350 2435
✉ flying161@126.com
www.e99999.com

5250

**2010第11届多人行广告、标识、LED展**
**地点：**深圳会展中心，广东深圳
**始办年份：**1997
**周期：**每年一届
**市场范围：**国际性
**参展费用：**标准展位8,800元，净地1,500美元
**主办：**中国广告学会
**承办：**深圳市多人行实业有限公司
**地址：**深圳市福田区新闻路景苑大厦B2602室（518034）
**联系人：**张先生，张萍
**MSN:** lanlinglingaa@hotmail.com
**QQ：**645561040

**2010 The 11th DAX Advertising, Sign Board & LED Exhibition**
**Venue:** Shenzhen Convention and Exhibition Center, Shenzhen, Guangdong
**Established Year:** 1997
**Frequency:** Annual
**Market Area:** International
**Participated Fee:** Standard Booth RMB 8,800, Raw Space USD 1,500
**Sponsor:** China Advertising Assn
**Organizer:** Shenzhen E-Dowell Industrial Co Ltd
**Address:** Rm 2602-2603, Section B, Jingyuan Bldg, Xinwen Rd, Futian Dist, Shenzhen
**Contact:** Mr Zhang, Helen
**MSN:** lanlinglingaa@hotmail.com

2010/06/24 - 26
☎ 020-6119 8879
🖷 020-6119 8841
✉ ia@iaexpo.org
www.iaexpo.org

5260

**第十四届华南地区工业控制自动化国际展览会**
**地点：**深圳会展中心，广东深圳
**内容：**华南自动化展是工控设备、变频器、PLC、电机、马达、仪器仪表、传感器、连接器等领域的国际性专业盛会，全面展示国际工业自动化领域最新的产品和服务，为业界提供高效的商务合作及交流平台。
**始办年份：**1997
**周期：**每年一届
**市场范围：**国际性
**入场券价格：**免费
**参展费用：**A区：标准展位7,800元，净地780元/m²；B区：标准展位6,800元，净地680元/m²
**上届规模 '09：**展览面积11,500m²(国外展商面积5,300m²)，参展商263家（国外展商51家，来自29个国家），参观人数17,600人（专业贸易观众4,700人）
**主办：**广东省科学技术厅；中国自动化学会；广东省科学技术协会；广东省自动化学会
**承办：**广东会展推广有限公司
**地址：**中国广州市远景路168-170号时代新都汇B座812室（510403）
**联系人：**林萍，韩建华
**MSN:** ia@iaexpo.org
**QQ：**97468716

**AUTOMATION 2010**
**Venue:** Shenzhen Convention and Exhibition Center, Shenzhen, Guangdong
**Profile:** Automation EXPO is an international & professional exhibition for the field of industrial control, converter, PLC, electric machine, motor, Instrument, sensor, machinery transmission, which gives an all-round show for the latest products and service of field of international Automation and offers a high effective business cooperation and communication platform.
**Established Year:** 1997
**Frequency:** Annual
**Market Area:** International
**Cost to Attend:** Free
**Participated Fee:** Standard Booth RMB 7,800, Raw Space RMB 780/m²
**Statistics '09:** Exhibition Area 11,500m²(foreigners 5,300m²), Exhibitors 263 (foreigners 51, came from 29 countries), Visitors 17,600 (trade visitors 4700)
**Sponsor:** Guangdong Science and Technology Department; Chinese Assn of Automation \ Guangdong Provincial Assn for Science and Technology; Guangdong Provincial Automation Society
**Organizer:** Guangdong Convention & Exhibition Promotion
**Address:** Unit 812 Tower B, Times Focus, 168-170 Yuanjing Rd, Guangzhou, China
**Contact:** Karen Lin, JianHua Han
**MSN:** ia@iaexpo.org

5280 2010/06/24 - 26
☎ 022-2395 9049, 2395 9268
℻ 022-2338 0938
✉ CIAPS@public.tpt.tj.cn
www.cibf.org.cn

### 第九届中国国际电池技术交流会/展览会

**地点：**深圳会展中心，广东深圳
**内容：**(1)各系列电池：阀控式密封和胶体铅酸蓄电池；镉镍蓄电池；金属氢化物镍蓄电池；锂一次电池；锂离子电池；锂聚合物电池；锌空气电池；锌锰电池；碱锰电池；锌镍电池；锌银电池；热电池；燃料电池；超级电容器；半导体温差电组件及其他新型电池；(2)各种组合电池；各种用途动力电池及电池管理系统；(3)各类电池用制造设备；测试仪器；原材料；零部件和充电器等；(4) 太阳电池；系统及应用产品；电池材料；测试仪器及制造设备等；（5）电池工业用三废处理设备；废旧电池回收处理技术与设备等。
**周期：**两年一届
**市场范围：**国际性
**性质：**面向公众
**入场券价格：**免费
**参展费用：**国内企业7,500元/9m²，国外及港澳台在华合资独资企业12,000元/9m²，国外及港澳台企业2,800美元/9m²；净地（36m²起，布展期间的管理费自付）：国内企业750元/m²，国外及港澳台在华合资独资企业1,200元/m²，国外及港澳台企业280美元/m²
上届规模‘08：展览面积9,000m²(国外展商面积1,000m²)，参展商470家（国外展商80家，来自35个国家），参观人数10,000人（专业贸易观众4,500人）
**主办：**中国化学与物理电源行业协会
**地址：**天津市南开区凌庄子道18号（300381）
**联系人：**路慧，程立文
**MSN:** Amy_lu716@yahoo.com.cn
**QQ：**378298024

### 9th China International Battery Fair

**Venue:** Shenzhen Convention and Exhibition Center, Shenzhen, Guangdong
**Profile:** All kinds of Batteries, Battery manufacturing equipments, testing instruments, chargers, raw materials and components, Battery management system and battery packs, All kinds of power batteries, energy storage batteries, Battery recycle technologies and processing equipments, Solar cell and systems
**Frequency:** Biennial
**Market Area:** International
**Nature:** Open to public
**Cost to Attend:** Free
**Participated Fee:** Hong Kong, Macao, Taiwan and International Exhibitors USD 2,800/9m², Raw Space (min 36m²) USD 280/m²
**Statistics '08:** Exhibition Area 9,000m²(foreigners 1,000m²), Exhibitors 470 (foreigners 80, came from 35 countries), Visitors 10,000 (trade visitors 4,500)
**Organizer:** China Industrial Association of Power Sources
**Address:** No.18, Lingzhuangzi Road, Nankai District, Tianjin 300381, China
**Contact:** Lu Hui, Cheng Liwen
**MSN:** Amy_lu716@yahoo.com.cn

5290 2010/06/24 - 26
☎ 020-3759 9008, 3759 9129
℻ 020-3759 9151
✉ ex36008@126.com,
www.motor-expo.cn

### 第八届深圳国际小电机及电机工业展览会

**地点：**深圳会展中心，广东深圳
**内容：**各类电机：微电机、中小型电机、分马力电机、减速电机、电机制造设备、电机测试仪器、电机零部件及配套产品、电机驱动及控制系统装置
**始办年份：**2003
**周期：**每年一届
**市场范围：**国际性
**入场券价格：**免费
**参展费用：**A区8,000元，B区6,800元，国际区2,000美元；净地850元/m²
**上届规模‘09：**展览面积7,000m²(国外展商面积2,100m²)，参展商203家（国外展商62家，来自7个国家），参观人数9,753人（专业贸易观众5,040人）
**主办：**香港智展国际有限公司；广东智展展览有限公司
**地址：**广州市寺右新马路5号华友大厦1802室（510600）
**联系人：**魏先生
**QQ：**916537040

### 8th China (Shenzhen) Intl Small Motor and Electric Machinery Exhibition

**Venue:** Shenzhen Convention and Exhibition Center, Shenzhen, Guangdong
**Profile:** Micro Motor, Middle & small Motor, Horsepower motor, Gear reducer, Equipment, Testing/Measuring instrument, Components and Accessories, Electromechanical control system and installment.
**Established Year:** 2003
**Frequency:** Annual
**Market Area:** International
**Cost to Attend:** Free
**Participated Fee:** USD 2,000/booth
**Statistics '09:** Exhibition Area 7,000m²(foreigners 2,100m²), Exhibitors 203 (foreigners 62, came from 7 countries), Visitors 9,753 (trade visitors 5,040)
**Organizer:** Wise International (H.K.) Co Ltd; Wise Exhibition (Guangdong) Co Ltd
**Address:** Rm 1802, Hua You Bldg, No.5, Si You Xin Rd, Guangzhou, China
**Contact:** Potter

5300 2010/06/24 - 26
☎ 020-3759 9008, 3759 9129
℻ 020-3759 9151
✉ ex36008@126.com
ex36002@126.com
www.magexpo.cn

### 第八届深圳国际磁性材料及粉末冶金工业展览会

**地点：**深圳会展中心，广东深圳
**内容：**永磁材料、软磁材料、磁记录、磁头、存储材料及器件；微波材料及器件、生产磁材用的各种原材料、辅助材料、应用产品、磁性材料制备、磁性材料检测仪器、仪表和控制、检测技术与设备、粉末冶金设备、粉末冶金仪器及气体
**始办年份：**2003
**周期：**每年一届
**市场范围：**国际性
**入场券价格：**免费
**参展费用：**A区8,000元，B区6,800元，国际区2,000美元；净地850元/m²
**上届规模‘09：**展览面积7,000m²(国外展商面积2,100m²)，参展商203家（国外展商62家，来自7个国家），参观人数9,753人（专业贸易观众5,040人）
**主办：**香港智展国际有限公司；广东省磁性材料行业协会
**承办：**广东智展展览有限公司
**地址：**广州市寺右新马路5号华友大厦1802室（510600）
**联系人：**魏先生，陈小姐
**QQ：**916537040

### 8th China (Shenzhen) Intl Magnetic Materials and Powder Metallurgy Industry Exhibition

**Venue:** Shenzhen Convention and Exhibition Center, Shenzhen, Guangdong
**Profile:** Permanent magnetic materials, Soft Magnetic Materials, Materials & Devices for, Raw and Auxiliary Materials, Applied Products
**Established Year:** 2003
**Frequency:** Annual
**Market Area:** International
**Cost to Attend:** Free
**Participated Fee:** USD 2,000/booth
**Statistics '09:** Exhibition Area 7,000m²(foreigners 2,100m²), Exhibitors 203 (foreigners 62, came from 7 countries), Visitors 9,753 (trade visitors 5,040)
**Organizer:** Wise International (H.K.) Co Ltd; Wise Exhibition (Guangdong) Co Ltd
**Address:** Rm. 1802, Hua You Building, No.5, Si You Xin Rd, Guangzhou, China
**Contact:** Potter
**Sponsor:** Wise International (HK) Co Ltd; Guangdong Provincial For Magnetic Materials Industry
**Organizer:** Wise Exhibition (Guangdong) Co Ltd
**Address:** Rm 1802, Hua You Bldg, No.5, Si You Xin Rd, Guangzhou, China
**Contact:** Potter, Phoebe

5330

2010/06/24 - 26
☎ 020-3759 9008, 3759 9129
🖷 020-3759 9151
✉ xqexpo@126.com
www.ex360.com

**2010深圳国际线圈工业、绝缘材料展览会**
**2010深圳国际漆包线展览会**
**地点：**深圳会展中心，广东深圳
**内容：**各类线圈、绝缘材料、各类线圈制造设备、检测设备及配件、各类漆包线、电磁线产品、各类电磁线、漆包线制造设备及原料、辅助材料
首届
**周期：**每年一届
**市场范围：**国际性
**入场券价格：**免费
**参展费用：**A区8,000元，B区6,800元，国际区2,000美元；净地850元/m²
**预计规模：**展出面积7,500m²，参展商360家，参观人数20,000人
**主办：**香港智展国际有限公司；广东智展展览有限公司
**地址：**广州市寺右新马路5号华友大厦1802室（510600）
**联系人：**汪海明，张伟
**QQ：**42988039

**2010 Shenzhen International Coils Industry & Insulating Materials Exhibition 2010 Shenzhen International Enameled Wire Exhibition**
**Venue:** Shenzhen Convention and Exhibition Center, Shenzhen, Guangdong
First Session
**Frequency:** Annual
**Market Area:** International
**Cost to Attend:** Free
**Participated Fee:** USD 2,000/booth
**Organizer:** Wise International (HK) Co Ltd; Wise Exhibition (Guangdong) Co Ltd
**Address:** Rm 1802, Hua You Bldg, No 5 Si You Xin Rd, Guangzhou, China
**Contact:** Jacking

5340

2010/07/01 - 04
☎ 0755-8294 9400
🖷 0755-8294 9700
✉ fair@ewatch.cn
www.fair.ewatch.cn

**第21届中国（深圳）国际钟表展览会**
**地点：**深圳会展中心，广东深圳
**始办年份：**1988
**周期：**每年一届
**市场范围：**国际性
**性质：**面向公众
**上届规模'09：**展览面积30,000m²，参观人数47,354人
**主办：**深圳市钟表行业协会
**承办：**深圳市晶品会展文化传播有限公司
**地址：**深圳市福田区新闻路深茂商业中心8楼815室（518034）
**联系人：**张先生

**21st China Watch Fair**
**Venue:** Shenzhen Convention and Exhibition Center, Shenzhen, Guangdong
**Established Year:** 1988
**Frequency:** Annual
**Market Area:** International
**Nature:** Open to public
**Statistics '09:** Exhibition Area 30,000m², Visitors 47,354
**Sponsor:** Shenzhen Watch & Clock Assn
**Organizer:** Fitime CEC Ltd

5350

2010/07/08 - 10
☎ 0755-8391 7058, 13509664575
🖷 0755-8391 7059
✉ 707507780@qq.com

**2010第3届中国(深圳)国际奢侈品展览会**
**暨深圳企业家生活方式展览会**
**地点：**深圳会展中心，广东深圳
**内容：**引进源于欧洲富豪名流聚居地蒙特卡洛的国际顶级奢侈品展的办展理念，结合中国的国情，采用每年一届，在全国各地轮流举办，2010花落深圳。展览涵盖了名车、私人飞机、游艇、珠宝名表、豪宅房产、古董、艺术品、名酒雪茄、豪华家居、名木家私、翡翠玉器、时装皮具、饰品、高级化妆品、香水SPA、高尔夫及用品、豪华旅游、私人会所、乐器音响、国际画廊、拍卖机构、高端理财、高新科技产品等。展会将延续国际顶级奢侈品展的风格和运作模式，仅对邀请的VIP贵宾开放。
**始办年份：**2007
**周期：**每年一届
**市场范围：**国际性
**性质：**面向公众
**上届规模'09：**展览面积20,000m²(国外展商面积5,000m²)，参展商260家（国外展商58家，来自11个国家），参观人数60,000人（专业贸易观众20,000人）
**主办：**中国国际奢侈品商会
**承办：**深圳创科源展览有限公司；深圳美莎展览有限公司；华夏时报
**地址：**深圳新闻路1号22楼（518034）
**联系人：**廖海天
**QQ：**707507780

**TOP LUXURY SHOW**
**Venue:** Shenzhen Convention and Exhibition Center, Shenzhen, Guangdong
**Established Year:** 2007
**Frequency:** Annual
**Market Area:** International
**Nature:** Open to public
**Statistics '09:** Exhibition Area 20,000m²(foreigners 5,000m²), Exhibitors 260 (foreigners 58, came from 11 countries), Visitors 60,000 (trade visitors 20,000)
**Contact:** lht

5360

2010/07/08 - 10
☎ 0755-8347 2856
🖷 0755-8347 2856转ext 829, 8347 2894
✉ c.rey@126.com
www.szic.cn

**第十届中国（深圳）国际品牌服装服饰交易会**
**地点：**深圳会展中心，广东深圳
**内容：**"深圳服交会"（SZIC）作为亚太地区最具影响力、专业化程度最高的服装展会之一，深受业界推崇，担当着一个举足轻重的商贸平台角色。"深圳服交会"自2001年首度举办，由最初的15,000m²展览面积，190个参展商，4万人次专业观众，发展到第九届的8万m²展览面积，800家展商以及10万余人次的专业观众，规模迅速扩大，影响力不断提升。秉承过往九届的辉煌成绩，2010年的"深圳服交会"继续为参展商与专业买家提供贸易合作的重要平台。
**展品范围：**各类品牌服装、时装配饰和与服装相关的服务和产品，包括女装、男装、孕/婴/童服装、运动服装、内衣、晚礼服、流行饰物、面料、辅料、皮革、皮具、箱包、制衣机械设备、时尚资讯等。
**始办年份：**2001
**周期：**每年一届
**市场范围：**国际性
**性质：**面向公众
**入场券价格：**20元
**参展费用：**11,000～15,000元/9m²
**上届规模'09：**展览面积80,000m²(国外展商面积4,000m²)，参展商800家（国外展商60家，来自10个国家），参观人数110,000人（专业贸易观众80,000人）
**主办：**深圳市服装行业协会
**地址：**广东省深圳市福田区车公庙泰然工业区中国有色大厦11楼（510040）
**联系人：**雷先生

**The 10th China (Shenzhen) Intl Brand Clothing & Accessories Fair**
**Venue:** Shenzhen Convention and Exhibition Center, Shenzhen, Guangdong
**Profile:** Founded in 2001, SZIC is one of the most influential apparel industry exhibitions. Our fair is honored by the industry in and abroad with a promoting status. Above all, SZIC has grown up as an important commercial platform. Categories: Women apparel, Men apparel, maternity dress, baby wear, children's wear, sports, underwear, night dress, accessories, fabric, leather, case, garment-make equipment, fashion news, publications.
**Established Year:** 2001
**Frequency:** Annual
**Market Area:** International
**Nature:** Open to public
**Cost to Attend:** RMB 20:-
**Participated Fee:** RMB 15,000/9m²
**Statistics '09:** Exhibition Area 80,000m²(foreigners 4,000m²), Exhibitors 800 (foreigners 60, came from 10 countries), Visitors 110,000 (trade visitors 80,000)
**Organizer:** Shenzhen Garment Industry Assn
**Address:** 11/F, China Youse Bldg, Tairan Industrial Garden, Chegongmiao, Futian Dist, Shenzhen, China
**Contact:** Mr Lei

2010/07/08 - 10
☎ 010-8522 9208, 8522 9702
🖷 010-8522 9296
✉ intertextilehome@ccpittex.com
5370

**深圳国际纺织面料及辅料博览会**
**地点：**深圳会展中心，广东深圳
**内容：**各类服装面料、辅料、计算机CAD/CAM系统，相关出版物及网络
**始办年份：**2005
**周期：**每年一届
**市场范围：**国际性
**上届规模**'09：展览面积10,000m²(国外展商面积500m²)，参展商200家（国外展商25家，来自7个国家），专业贸易观众8,000人
**主办：**中国纺织工业协会
**承办：**中国贸促会纺织行业分会；法兰克福展览（香港）有限公司；深圳市服装行业协会
**地址：**北京东长安街12号550室（100742）
**联系人：**马一丹，吴知真

**Shenzhen Intl Trade Fair for Apparel Fabrics and Accessories**
**Venue:** Shenzhen Convention and Exhibition Center, Shenzhen, Guangdong
**Profile:** Apparel fabrics & accessories, CAD/CAM system, relevant publications & websites
**Established Year:** 2005
**Frequency:** Annual
**Market Area:** International
**Statistics '09:** Exhibition Area 10,000m²(foreigners 500m²), Exhibitors 200 (foreigners 25, came from 7 countries), Trade Visitors 8, 000)
**Organizer:** China National Textile & Apparel Council **Sponsor:** The Sub-Council of Textile Industry, CCPIT; Messe Frankfurt (HK) Ltd; Shenzhen Garment Industry Assn
**Address:** Room 550, No.12 East Chang An St., Beijing, China
**Contact:** Ms Ma Yidan, Mr Wu Zhizhen

2010/08/12 - 16
☎ 0755-2516 0895
🖷 0755-2516 0449
✉ szicie@163.com
www.szicie.com
5380

**第二届动漫节**
**地点：**深圳会展中心，广东深圳
**内容：**体验区：让观众在体验的过程中更为感性的体会动漫的乐趣；展示区：以动漫系列产品形象展示、销售和交易为主；活动区：以突出互动和参与，以表演、比赛等各种项目增强活动的感染力 配套活动：电子竞技大赛、Cosplay挑战赛、城际街舞大赛、海内外动漫名家签售会、青少年动漫创意大赛、摄影大赛。范围包括动漫基地、动画研发制作培训、动漫企业、动漫音像、出版发行、卡通周边产品、玩具、礼品企业、电子竞技、网络游戏、网络动漫机构、风险投资者、授权
**始办年份：**2009
**周期：**每年一届
**市场范围：**国际性
**性质：**面向公众
上届规模：参展商120家，参观人数32万人
**主办：**深圳广播电影电视集团；深圳市知识产权局
**承办：**深圳市文化产业（国际）会展有限公司；深圳国家动漫画产业基地
**地址：**深圳市罗湖区怡景路深圳广播电视大厦1楼（518021）
**联系人：**董小姐

**2nd Shenzhen Animation Festival**
**Venue:** Shenzhen Convention and Exhibition Center, Shenzhen, Guangdong
**Established Year:** 2009
**Frequency:** Annual
**Market Area:** International
**Nature:** Open to public
Statistics '09: Exhibitors 120, Visitors 320,000
**Organizer:** Shenzhen Media Group Intl Cultural Industry Fair Co Ltd

2010/08/31 - 09/02
☎ 021-5153 5100, 5153 5155
✉ Mike.deng@reedexpo.com.cn
✉ Jimmy.yang@reedexpo.com.cn
www.nepconchina.com
5390

EMT SouthChina 华南国际电子制造技术展览会

**第十六届华南国际电子生产设备暨微电子工业展**
华南国际电子制造技术展览会
**地点：**深圳会展中心，广东深圳
**内容：**NEPCON South China是华南地区最大的电子制造与表面贴装行业盛会之一，它涵盖了该行业在全球范围的创新产品和技术，将全世界表面贴装品牌呈现在您的面前。
NEPCON South China为您建立一个最佳交流平台，帮助您提高行业竞争优势，有效物色新供应商，收集最新市场信息，寻找技术解决方案以及学习最新技术。
**周期：**每年一届
**主办：**励展博览集团
参展联络：邓萌先生
电话021-5153 5100
邮箱Mike.deng@reedexpo.com.cn
**参观联络：**杨巍先生
电话021-5153 5155
邮箱Jimmy.yang@reedexpo.com.cn

**NEPCON/ EMT South China 2010**
**Venue:** Shenzhen Convention and Exhibition Center, Shenzhen, Guangdong
**Profile:** NEPCON South China 2010 is one of the largest and longest standing trading and sourcing platforms for the SMT industry in South China. Featuring a comprehensive range of innovative SMT products and technology, it brings the entire world of SMT to your door step.
The event provides a sourcing platform for new suppliers, gathers new market information and displays the latest technologies to help you enhance your competitiveness in the electronics manufacturing industry.
**Frequency:** Annual
**Organizer:** Reed Exhibitions
**For Exhibiting:**
Tel 86-21-5153 5100
邮箱：Mike.deng@reedexpo.com.cn
For Visiting:
Tel 86-21-5153 5155
邮箱：Jimmy.yang@reedexpo.com.cn

2010/08/31 - 02
☎ 021-5153 5100, 5153 5155
✉ Mike.deng@reedexpo.com.cn
✉ Jimmy.yang@reedexpo.com.cn
www.ae-china.com
5400

**华南国际汽车电子展览会**
**地点：**深圳会展中心，广东深圳
**内容：**AE（华南国际汽车电子展）为整个汽车电子产业链提供了最新产品和技术，从芯片设计，汽车电子元器件到汽车配件等，是汽车行业的买家和供应商收集市场信息，交流技术知识，提高业务竞争力的极佳聚会平台。
**周期：**每年一届
**主办：**励展博览集团
**参展联络：**邓萌先生
☎ 021-5153 5100 ✉ Mike.deng@reedexpo.com.cn
**参观联络：**杨巍先生
☎ 021-5153 5155 ✉ Jimmy.yang@reedexpo.com.cn

**Automotive Electronics South China**
**Venue:** Shenzhen Convention & Exhibition Center, Shenzhen, Guangdong
**Profile:** Automotive Electronics South China provides the whole automotive electronics industry chain a business networking platform that features the latest products and technologies, ranging from IC design technologies, automotive electronics components to accessories. It is a meeting place in South China for buyers and suppliers of the automotive industry to gather market information and exchange technology know-how to enhance business competitiveness.
**Frequency:** Annual
**Organizer:** Reed Exhibitions
**For Exhibiting:**
☎ 86-21-5153 5100 ✉ Mike.deng@reedexpo.com.cn
For Visiting:
☎ 86-21-5153 5155 ✉ Jimmy.yang@reedexpo.com.cn

2010/08/31 -02
☎ 021-5153 5100, 5153 5155
✉ M ike.deng@ reedexpo.com .cn
Jim m y.yang@ reedexpo.com .cn
w w w .atexpochina.com
5410

## 华南国际工业组装技术与装备展览会

**地点：**塔牖匣岀峼嫗〉剩僢塔牖
**内容：**ATE（勬膺剎卪刪孩崟旒卜堈寽旒伭岀昕匣）塳崲崬寬刪孩崟旒卜堈寽旒伭宸寕啢射僘岀昕匣坴孯‰氂姦唿勚偤屜孯刞屆勬膺墔俳峼厦啓孩婖唠娩〉壳协墔俳媽娼励�僘寢啅圄夨〉氂奡刯孯崖堫菿屜叠吪冇仰墺客刞旒囒劃倞判咦〉判玏〉判塥坘‰
**周期：**嗱噺孯只
**主办：**唐岀依昕协妣
**参展联络：**僙嚾婢媋
☎ 021-5153 5100 ✉ M ike.deng@ reedexpo.com .cn
**参观联络：**孄姝婢媋
☎ 021-5153 5155 ✉ Jim m y.yang@ reedexpo.com .cn

## Automotive Electronics South China

**Venue:** Shenzhen Convention & Exhibition Center, Shenzhen, Guangdong
**Profile:** ATE China is an assembly trade event, providing an unparalleled platform in the vibrant South China Market for the entire assembling industry to network, source and learn. It demonstrates latest manufacturing assembly solutions to make the entire assembly process faster, better and for less.
**Frequency:** Annual
**Organizer:** Reed Exhibitions
**For Exhibiting:**
☎ 86-21-5153 5100 ✉ M ike.deng@ reedexpo.com .cn
For Visiting:
☎ 86-21-5153 5155 ✉ Jim m y.yang@ reedexpo.com .cn

2010/09/06 -09
☎ 0755-8629 0901
🖷 0755-8629 0951
✉ cioe@ cioe.cn
5420

## 第十二届中国国际光电博览会（CIOE2010）

**地点：**塔牖匣岀峼嫗〉剩僢塔牖
**内容：**剳妆媽…卄剳勐姀…�嘎剳�…LED
**始办年份：**1999
**周期：**嗱噺孯只
**市场范围：**剎卪嫌
**入场券价格：**嘔军
**参展费用：**剎噪圿孩ぁ俩嵇岀婣9300尚(埒喲佨)/9m²〉咏俳僦930尚(埒喲佨)/m²劳裏圿孩ぁ俩嵇岀婣13800尚(埒喲佨)/9m²〉咏俳僦1380尚(埒喲佨)/m²剎卪圿孩ぁ俩嵇岀婣3150嗲尚/9m²〉咏俳僦315嗲尚/m²。伭 崬ぁ俩嵇岀婣壍嘘�即墻10%〃
**上届规模**‘09：岀昕嘘匿30, 375m²(剎姀岀塱嘘匿9, 100m²), 係岀塱2, 368卲。剎姀岀塱702卲〉哌鑫18刞剎卲〃〉係剡埒壁66, 528埒。崲孩嗥宋剡峌45, 609埒〃
**主办：**峼剎咀嫖卜堈徧匣ぁ塔牖劼垨依威岀昕寢婸刜壛
**承办：**塔牖劼垨依威岀昕寢婸刜壛
**地址：**剩僢塥塔牖墔膺堣垢劇僐堅僎劇仮傣婝僢嶄607埨。518059〃
**联系人：**唆伽婖〉姶捐

## 12th China Intl Optoelectronic Expo (CIOE2010)

**Venue:** Shenzhen Convention and Exhibition Center, Shenzhen, Guangdong
**Profile:** Optical Communications; Laser Technology; Optics; LED Lighting & Display; Infrared Applications; Optical Sensors, Test and Measurement
**Established Year:** 1999
**Frequency:** Annual
**Market Area:** International
**Cost to Attend:** Free
**Participated Fee:** For International Exhibitors USD 3,150/9▬〉Raw Space USD 315/m²〉Corner Booth Add 10%
**Statistics ‘09:** Exhibition Area 30,375m² (foreigners 9,100m²), Exhibitors 2,368。foreigners 702, came from 18 countries〃〉Visitors 66,528。trade visitors 45,609〃
**Sponsor:** China Assn for Science and Technology; Shenzhen UBM Herong Exhibition Co **Organizer:** Shenzhen UBM Herong Exhibition Co
**Address:** Room 607, East Block, Coastal Bldg, Haide 3rd Road Nanshan Dist, Shenzhen, Guangdong, China
**Contact:** Zhaoxia Li, Ke Wei

2010/09/15 -19
☎ 852-2561 5566
🖷 852-2811 9156
✉ info@ newayfairs.com
w w w .newayfairs.com
5440

## 2010深圳国际珠宝展

**地点：**塔牖匣岀峼嫗〉剩僢塔牖
**主办：**倵嫰剎卪岀昕寢婸刜壛
**地址：**叚刃刎境傣僎77助九妆傣婝9岾

## 2010 Shenzhen International Jewelry Fair

**Venue:** Shenzhen Convention and Exhibition Center, Shenzhen, Guangdong
**Organizer:** Neway International Trade Fairs Limited
**Address:** 9/F Fortis Tower, 77 Gloucester Road, Hong Kong

2010/10/21 -24
☎ 0755-3398 9230, 3398 9211
🖷 0755-3333 1168歳ext666, 3398 9211
✉ lisa.mo@ reedhuabo.com
w w w .reedhuabo.com
5460

## 第十八届中国（深圳）国际玩具及礼品展览会

**地点：**塔牖匣岀峼嫗〉剩僢塔牖
**内容：**哌鑫埖剎刡僦僘2800卲守媋修塱姦崣僘孯啈圃嚴，劵妊倜婆剎噪袏傣僘唉縢圃…娓吻卐卲启寕圃岀昕匣‰吉婳塱…修晗塱…协妣卐崁儷嗆卲厩傣匥呹屆岰唇僘袏剩冄…袏危圃島励偤宖塔卦…袏吻卻则寗塹僘刜壛唉圃…縢圃励婥军圃唇呤墀切媟僘嬒尣励偊剀坴啅‰
**始办年份：**1993
**周期：**嗱噺孯只
**市场范围：**剎卪嫌
**入场券价格：**20尚
**主办：**唐岀勬依岀昕。塔牖〃寢婸刜壛
**地址：**塔牖墔峼嫗垢凋勬堅喋塔牖剎卪塱匣峼嫗1801-1802。518048〃
**联系人：**姓埠啌〉衾娍员

## 18th China (Shenzhen) International Toys & Gifts Fair

**Venue:** Shenzhen Convention and Exhibition Center, Shenzhen, Guangdong
**Profile:** Reed Huabo VIIs China Gifts and Home Fair is the largest trade show of its kind in Mainland China. Held in Shenzhen during the best buying seasons in April and October every year, the fair offers the widest selection of business gifts, premiums and consumer products, and attracts tens of thousands of buyers from across the country. They include distributors, agents, premium houses, department stores and large corporate end users. Exhibitors are primarily manufacturers, promising the best design and quality at competitive prices. The fair enables key market players to meet and trade, form partnerships and set industry trends. It is also the best market-entry opportunity for overseas suppliers aiming to tap the fast-growing Chinese market.
**Established Year:** 1993
**Frequency:** Annual
**Market Area:** International
**Cost to Attend:** RMB 20:-
**Organizer:** Reed Huabo Exhibitions (Shenzhen) Co
**Address:** Rm.1801-1802, Shenzhen Intl Chamber of Commerce Tower, Fuhua 3rd Rd, Central Dist, Shenzhen, China
**Contact:** Wang Qinling, David Yuan

5480 2010/11/04 -07
☎ 0755-8255 7493, 8255 9403
🖷 0755-8255 9496, 8255 9409
✉ sibex@ vip.163.com
www.sibex.net.cn

**第四届中国（深圳）国际游艇及设备展览会**
**地点：**塔廧傣嗔堙娅宴奵匣〉剩僾 塔廧
**内容：**停奵卐宴奵 宴奵…宴哘剗剳奵…啤宴坛奵…嫕婪停奵…傎億停奵…励勬寠停。奵〃ぁ挢嫔停…吤埳奵…投僩停ぁ僵僲停…壐堵嘶娓奵…壐堵原垻奵…兵停ぁ臬妕…告哮侳卐淨嫔匼列〉宴奵告哮侳。匣彐〃〉宴奵臬妕塔塭卐厦塔…停奵姨嫖卐伹孋淨嫔匼列…宴奵厌佸卐埗峖淨嫔匼列ぁ幱厞卐塔塭…塔低ぁ停奵剬哸匼嵳…婢噪匼…婢妹匼…停奵倲瘵匼…剬崂僵匼励僵倪…妤叶嵬峯…僑僯嵬峯…喱嫵厮…兒匼卐很务塔低…厕孕嵬峯
**始办年份：**2007
**周期：**嗱嘶墅只
**市场范围：**剢卩嫌
**性质：**嘘媹挢崞
**入场券价格：**200尚
**参展费用：**偑嵆岘闵9,600尚/(3x3m²)〉吗僦580尚/m²
**上届规模** ‘09：峃哘嘘匽10,000m²(剢姀峃塱嘘匽200m²)〉哌翕22 刞剢卲〃〉係剗埒壁15,000埒。崲孩嗥宋剗崞6,000埒〃
**主办：**塔廧堆嬷彘垢埒嗤崞準ぁ寗依匣峃协妣
**承办：**塔廧堆寗依剢卩峃哘寢娲挢壚ぁ塔廧堆宴奵兵停婺孩媥匣ぁ塔廧傣嗔堙娅宴奵匣
**地址：**剩僾塥塔廧堆凋彘垢叮彘喋3038助姨修剢卩傣婝2502。518048〃
**联系人：**岓哔〉唆娍啗

**SIBEX - China (Shenzhen) International Boat Show**
**Venue:** Shenzhen Marina Club, Shenzhen, Guangdong
**Profile:** Boats & Yachts, Cruisers, Tour Submarines, Leisure Boats, Whiff Boats and Luxury Boats (Yachts); Public Vessels, Accident Boats, Hovercrafts; Dynamoelectric boats, Water Motorboats, Boats for Health, Sailing Vessels, Marina, Clubs and Service Organizations Boat Clubs (Chamber), Marina Facilities and Construction, Marine Servicing and Maintenance Providers, Marine Rating System Accessories and Equipments Various Boats Units, Inboard Motors, Outboard Motors, Boats Diesel Engines, Various Electric Machineries and Batteries, Propulsion Devices, Driving Units, Screw Propellers, The Machines Operated by Steersman, Helm Operating Devices and Anti-Rolling Devices Various Engineering Fittings, Boat Trailers, Boat Construction Materials, Supplementary Materials, Coating Materials
**Established Year:** 2007
**Frequency:** Annual
**Market Area:** International
**Nature:** Open to public
**Cost to Attend:** RMB 200
**Participated Fee:** Tent RMB 9,600/9m 3〉Raw Space RMB 580/m²
**Statistics** ‘09: Exhibition Area 10,000m² (foreigners 200m²), Exhibitors。came from 22 countries〃〉Visitors 15,000。trade visitors 6,000〃
**Organizer:** Shenzhen UB Exhibition Intl Co; Shenzhen Yacht & Sailboat Industry Assn; Shenzhen Marina Club
**Address:** Rm. 2502, Modern International Building, No. 3038 Jintian Rd, Futian Dist, Shenzhen
**Contact:** Amy Zhang, Maggie Lee

5490 2010/11/16 -21
☎ 0755-8366 3896
🖷 0755-8366 3896
✉ sally_chen@ idg.com.cn
www.chtf.com

**第十二届中国国际高新技术成果交易会信息技术与产品展**
**地点：**塔廧匣峃峼媪〉剩僾塔廧
**内容：**媽娼卜堈哥修圃峃埁切厸匣傎墅圃嚴崲孩峃〉宅唢嫩倛刬吵伤傎塲墅只〉佑孩只增姦崲孩嫌…垰姜嫌…麥畴勸僣圵峰〉匳僑啁剢卩 峃哘孩垰姜嫌僣UFI埗峖〉埁峼剢掟傣僣媽娼卜堈卐修圃叶偈咔厸宋峃哘匣峯墅‰
**始办年份：**1999
**周期：**嗱嘶墅只
**市场范围：**剢卩嫌
**入场券价格：**50尚
**参展费用：**A垢24,255尚/峃娮〉B垢20,295尚/峃娮
**上届规模** ‘09：峃哘嘘匽11,000m²(剢姀峃塱嘘匽3,300m²)，係峃塱572卲。剢姀峃塱171卲〉哌翕8刞剢卲〃〉係剗埒壁500,000埒。崲孩嗥宋剗崞350,000埒〃
**主办：**峼勬埒嗤劵励剢塱嫔侳ぁ卜堈侳ぁ刪媽侳ぁ公峃励凨列姮嶇匣ぁ及小侳ぁ埒嵇崀尢励滕匣但峷侳ぁ剢卲崂靡修垰呞ぁ峼剢咀嫽尪ぁ峼剢刪倧尪ぁ塔廧堆崞準
**承办：**塔廧堆峼剢剢卩切嫐卜堈倛劕厸宋峼媪劳嵝ぁ哆剢剢卩壁吹协妣(IDG)
**地址：**塔廧堆凋彘垢定彘喋峷尭廛修剩俳2901A。518048〃
**联系人：**偪慑

**China Hi-Tech Fair/ComNet2010**
**Venue:** Shenzhen Convention and Exhibition Center, Shenzhen, Guangdong
**Profile:** As No.1 specialized show of the CHTF, CHTF/ComNet has been staged successfully for 11 consecutive years. Today, it is generally accepted in the industry as a professional, authoritative, and mainstream event. A UFI-certified event, it is one of the largest IT import-export fairs in China. CHTF/ComNet 2010 will focus on current hot economic issues to show the industrial trends by inviting most influential decision, madders, purchasers, and experts to the exhibition in order to bring the most desirable effect to all exhibitors.
**Established Year:** 1999
**Frequency:** Annual
**Market Area:** International
**Cost to Attend:** RMB 50:-
**Participated Fee:** A:RMB24255;B:RMB20295
**Statistics** ‘09: Exhibition Area 11,000m² (foreigners 3,300m²), Exhibitors 572。foreigners 171, came from 8 countries〃〉Visitors 500,000。trade visitors 350,000〃
**Organizer:** Shenzhen China Hi-Tech Fair Center
**Address:** Rm. 2901A, Excellence Times Square Bldg, Yitian Rd, Futian Dist, Shenzhen, China
**Contact:** Chen Rong

5500 2010/11/16 -21
☎ 0755-8831 2796
🖷 0755-8831 2533, 8831 5466
www.icef.com.cn

**第十二届中国国际高新技术成果交易会电子展**
**地点：**塔廧匣峃峼媪〉剩僾塔廧
**内容：**倪僫奥卐IC塔卦…佑僲尚厞…地外僵嵝尚玩厞卐嵳厞僖…僵嵝峯嵦卐娚坐剶屖…佸崺励佸唵卜堈…厌佸哥埗峖…卄剳卜堈…嫚喋伝…嫚哚哥唢发坃…地外埳修塔低…EMS劳尬剶屖淨嫔
**主办：**峼勬埒嗤劵励剢塱嫔侳ぁ咀卜侳ぁ媽娼修孩侳ぁ公峃励凨列姮嶇匣ぁ及小侳ぁ峼剢咀嫽尪ぁ峼剢刪倧尪ぁ
**承办：**塔廧堆埒嗤崞準ぁ塔廧堆偤宖廛修匣峃寢娲挢壚
**地址：**塔廧堆凋彘垢凋勬壂喋剢卩塱匣峼媪2201堷
**联系人：**唆嬴

**China Hi-Tech Fair/Elec**
**Venue:** Shenzhen Convention and Exhibition Center, Shenzhen, Guangdong
**Organizer:** Creativity Convention & Exhibition (Shenzhen) Co Ltd
**Address:** Rm. 2201, Intl Chamber of Commerce Tower, Fuhua 3 Rd, Futian Dist, Shenzhen, China
**Contact:** Jessica Lee

# 广东-顺德
# Guangdong-Shunde

2010/10/18 - 21
☎ 020-8755 2468转ext 11/19
🖷 020-8755 2970
✉ e.cheung@koelnmesse.cn
g.liu@koelnmesse.cn
www.shundeexpo.cn
www.shundeexpo.com
5510

**2010中国顺德国际家用电器博览会**

**地点**：顺德前进汇展中心，广东顺德
**内容**：通过充分利用展馆内外的空间和设施，展会规模将扩大至达26,000m²，参展企业预计达500家。2010年顺德家电展将迎来展会创立10周年，相信您绝对不会错过这个了解家电行业最新潮流、最新技术以及开拓海内外销售渠道的最佳电器贸易平台。
展品范围包括：黑色家电、白色家电、小家电、厨房家电、卫浴家电、家电配件以及家电相关服务与刊物等。
**始办年份**：2001
**周期**：每年一届
**市场范围**：国际性
**性质**：面向公众
**入场券价格**：20元
**参展费用**：净地（27m²起）840元/m²，普通标准展位（9m²起）860元/m²，高级标准展位（18m²起）1,150元/m²
**上届规模**‘09：展览面积24,500m²，参展商439家（来自13个国家），专业贸易观众20,206人）
**主办**：科隆展览有限公司；中国机电产品进出口商会；中国贸促会广东省分会；顺德区人民政府
**承办**：科隆展览有限公司
**地址**：广东省广州市天河区天河北路183号大都会广场3311室（510620）
**联系人**：张井飞，刘桂宜

**China Shunde International Exposition for Household ElectricalAppliances 2010**

**Venue:** Shunde Qianjin Exhibition Center, Shunde, Guangdong
**Profile:** Shunde Expo 2010 will take place again on 18-21 October 2010 at the Shunde Exhibition Center. The floor space is expected to grow up to 26,000sqm with 500 exhibitors. Shunde Expo 2010 will mark the 10th anniversary. Please don' t miss this golden opportunity to keep up to date on the latest industry trends and developments network and do business with the local and international players in the household appliance industry. Exhibit profile includes: Black home appliances, white home appliances, small home appliances, kitchen and bathroom home appliances, accessories and components, services and publications etc.
**Established Year:** 2001
**Frequency:** Annual
**Market Area:** International
**Nature:** Open to public
**Cost to Attend:** RMB 20/pp
**Participated Fee:** Raw Space (min 27m²) RMB 840/m², Standard Booth (min 9m²) RMB 860/m², Upgraded Booth (min 18m²) RMB 1,150/m²
**Statistics '09:** Exhibition Area 24,500m², Exhibitors 439 (came from 13 countries), Trade visitors 20,206)
**Sponsor:** Koelnmesse Co Ltd; China Chamber of Commerce for Import and Export of Machinery and Electronic Products (CCCME); CCPIT Guangdong Sub-council (CCPIT GD); The People' s Government of Shunde
**Organizer:** Koelnmesse
**Address:** Rm 3311 Metro Plaza, No. 183 Tianhebei Rd, Tianhe Dist, Guangzhou 510620, China
**Contact:** Mr Eric Cheung, Ms Grace Liu

# 广东-珠海
# Guangdong-Zhuhai

2010/11/16 - 21
☎ 0756-337 6304, 334 1849
🖷 0756-337 6415
✉ visitor@airshow.com.cn
www.airshow.com.cn
5515

**中国国际航空航天博览会**

**地点**：中国国际航空航天博览中心，广东珠海
**内容**：“中国国际航空航天博览会”（简称“中国航展”）是唯一由中央政府批准举办的国际性专业航空航天展览，属“国家行为”，它以实物展示、贸易洽谈、学术交流和飞行表演为主要特征。
**始办年份**：1996
**周期**：两年一届
**市场范围**：国际性
**性质**：面向公众
**入场券价格**：45元/350元
**上届规模** ‘08：展览面积21,000m²(国外展商面积6,000m²)，参展商600家（来自35个国家），参观人数300,000人（专业贸易观众90,000人）
**主办**：广东省人民政府；工业和信息化部；中国贸促会；国家国防科技工业局；中国民用航空局；中国航空工业集团公司；中国商用飞机有限责任公司；中国航天科技集团公司；中国航天科工集团公司
**承办**：珠海航展有限公司
**地址**：广东省珠海市九洲大道东九洲二巷一号（519015）
**联系人**：李琳

**China International Aviation & Aerospace Exhibition**

**Venue:** China Intl Aviation and Aerospace Exhibition Center, Zhuhai, Guangdong
**Profile:** Airshow China is the only international aerospace exhibition in China that is approved by the Chinese Central Government. The show features real-size object display, trade discussions, technical exchanges and flying display.
**Established Year:** 1996
**Frequency:** Biennial
**Market Area:** International
**Nature:** Open to public
**Statistics '08:** Exhibition Area 21,000m²(foreigners 6,000m²), Exhibitors 600 (came from 35 countries), Visitors 300,000 (trade visitors 90,000)
**Organizer:** Guangdong Provincial Government; Ministry of Industry and Information Technology; CCPIT; State Administration of Science, Technology and Industry for National Defense; Civil Aviation Administration
**Address:** No. 1, Jiuzhou Lane 2, Jiuzhou Avenue, Zhuhai City, China
**Contact:** Li Lin

# 广西-南宁
# Guangxi-Nanning

2010/03/26 - 28
☎ 0771-2368 926
🖷 0771-2368 927
✉ nanningnanchun@163.com
✉ zzhygs@tom.com
www.nanchunhz.com
5520

**2010年第四届广西机械工业博览会**
**地点**：南宁国际会展中心，广西 南宁
**内容**：糖业技术设备、淀粉酒精技术设备、制药机械、化工机械、造纸机械、锅炉及压力容器、环保节能设备、沼气技术设备、工业自动化等产品设备等。
**始办年份**：2007
**周期**：每年一届
**市场范围**：国际性
**上届规模**‘09：展览面积6,000m²(国外展商面积300m²)，参展商150家（国外展商18家，来自10个国家），参观人数15,000人（专业贸易观众9,000人）
**主办**：广西机械工程学会
**承办**：南宁南春展览服务有限公司
**地址**：广西南宁市金州路11号金旺角B1002室（530028）

**4th Guangxi Mechanical Industry Exposition 2010**
**Venue:** Nanning International Convention and Exhibition Center, Nanning, Guangxi
**Established Year:** 2007
**Frequency:** Annual
**Market Area:** International
**Statistics '09:** Exhibition Area 6,000m²(foreigners 300m²), Exhibitors 150 (foreigners 18, came from 10 countries), Visitors 15,000 (trade visitors 9,000)
**Sponsor:** Guangxi Mechanical Engineering Society
**Organizer:** Nanning Nanchun Exhibition Service Co Ltd

2010/07/02 - 04
☎ 0532-6671 1800, 0771-250 0880
🖷 0532-6671 1808, 0771-250 0886
✉ chbosn@163.com
www.chbos.com
www.ourboost.com.cn
5530

**GLE2010广西泛北部湾港口、物流及仓储设备展览会**
**地点**：南宁国际会展中心，广西南宁
**内容**：港口机械及设备、物流机械及设备、仓储技术及设备、物流运输车辆、物流服务与信息系统。
首届
**周期**：每年一届
**市场范围**：国际性
**入场券价格**：免费
**参展费用**：580元/m²
**预计规模**：20,000m²
**主办**：广西机械工程学会
**承办**：青岛博世会展有限公司；南宁凯路博会展有限公司
**地址**：青岛市同安路917号海丽广场D座15层（266700）
**联系人**：夏婕，黄超蝶
**QQ**：976790172

**GLE 2010 Guangxi Fan-Beibu Gulf Equipment of Port & Logistics & Storage Exhibition**
**Venue:** Nanning International Convention and Exhibition Center, Nanning, Guangxi
**Profile:** Port machinery and equipment, machinery and equipment, warehousing logistics technology and equipment, logistics transport vehicles, logistics and information system.
First Session
**Frequency:** Annual
**Market Area:** International
**Cost to Attend:** Free
**Participated Fee:** RMB 580/m²
**Organizer:** Guangxi Institute of Mechanical Engineering; Qingdao Boost Exhibition Co Ltd; Nanning Broad Exhibition Co Ltd
**Address:** 15/F, Bldg D, Haili Square, 917 Tong'an Rd, Qingdao 266700, Shandong, China
**Contact:** Alice Xia

2010/07/02 - 04
☎ 0532-6671 1800, 0771-250 0880
🖷 0532-6671 1808, 0771-250 0886
✉ chbosn@163.com
www.chbos.com
www.ourboost.com.cn
5540

**GICE 2010**
**第二届广西泛北部湾工程机械展览会**
**地点**：南宁国际会展中心，广西南宁
**内容**：工程机械、混凝土机械、建筑机械、路桥设备、专用车辆、矿山机械、液压机械、气动元件、密封件、空气压缩机及与以上产品相关的零部件及附件等。
**始办年份**：2008
**周期**：每年一届
**市场范围**：国际性
**入场券价格**：免费
**参展费用**：中资企业标准展位(9m²)：5,800元，双开口6,300元，净地：室内580元/m²，室外400元/m²；外资企业：标准展位1,500美元，净地150美元/m²
**上届规模**‘09：展览面积11,000m²(国外展商面积2,000m²)，参展商347家（国外展商60家，来自5个国家），参观人数6,000人（专业贸易观众5,500人）
**主办**：广西机械工程学会
**承办**：青岛博世会展有限公司；南宁凯路博会展有限公司
**地址**：青岛市同安路917号海丽广场D座15层（266000）
**联系人**：夏婕，黄超蝶
**QQ**：8922624

**GICE 2010**
**Guangxi Fan-Beibu Gulf Construction Machinery Exhibition**
**Venue:** Nanning International Convention and Exhibition Center, Nanning, Guangxi
**Established Year:** 2008
**Frequency:** Annual
**Market Area:** International
**Cost to Attend:** Free
**Participated Fee:** Standard Booth USD 1,500/9m², Raw Space USD 150/m²
**Statistics '09:** Exhibition Area 11,000m²(foreigners 2,000m²), Exhibitors 347 (foreigners 60, came from 5 countries), Visitors 6,000 (trade visitors 5,500)
**Organizer:** Guangxi Institute of Mechanical Engineering
**Contact:** Jie Xia, Chaodie Huang

2010/07/23 - 25
☎ 020-8257 7435, 8974 2929
🖷 020-8257 7033
✉ nibosi2009@163.com
5570

**中国南宁国际农业科技博览会**
**地点**：南宁国际会展中心，广西南宁
**内容**：肥料、农药、种子、农业产品、机械等，区域特色农业
首届
**周期**：每年一届
**市场范围**：全国性
**性质**：面向公众
**参展费用**：标准展位5,800元/个，净地600元/m²
**预计规模**：展出面积30,000m²；参展商200家，参观人数50,000人
**主办**：越南农业部农林贸易促进中心；中越商务中心；广州尼勃斯展览有限公司
**地址**：广州市天河区车 路306号J-1203室（510660）
**联系人**：邢婕，龚保军
**QQ**：382746482

**China Nanning Intl Agriculture Fair**
**Venue:** Nanning International Convention and Exhibition Center, Nanning, Guangxi
First Session
**Frequency:** Annual
**Market Area:** National
**Nature:** Open to public
**Participated Fee:** Standard Booth RMB 5,800, Raw Space RMB 600/m²
**Organizer:** Guangzhou Nibosi Exhibition Co Ltd

2010/09 -
☎ 027-8736 2945
www.hope-tarsus.com
5580

**2010中国中西部（南宁）医疗器械展览会**
**地点**：广西展览馆，广西南宁
**周期**：每年一届
**主办**：全国医药技术市场协会，中英合资好博塔苏斯展览公司
**承办**：湖北好博塔苏斯展览有限公司成都分公司
**联系人**：余云成

**China (Xining) Medical Devices Exhibition**
**Venue**: Guangxi Exhibition Hall, Nanning, Guangxi
**Frequency**: Annual
**Organizer**: **Organizer**: Tarsus-Hope Exhibition Company

2010/10/20 - 24
☎ 0771-961236, 581 3173, 581 3177
℻ 0771-581 3355
✉ caexpo@caexpo.org
www.caexpo.org
5590

**第七届中国–东盟博览会**
**中国–东盟商务与投资分会**
**地点**：南宁国际会展中心，广西南宁
**内容**：四个专题展区，即商品贸易专题，投资合作专题，农村适用技术专题，“魅力之城”专题
**周期**：每年一届
**市场范围**：国际性
**主办**：中国和东盟10国
**承办**：广西壮族自治区人民政府
**地址**：秘书处，广西南宁市竹溪大道98号（530021）

**7th China ASEAN Expo**
**Venue**: Nanning International Convention and Exhibition Center, Nanning, Guangxi
**Frequency**: Annual
**Market Area**: International
**Organizer**: Guangxi Government

2010/10/29 - 31
☎ 020-8257 7435, 8974 2929
℻ 020-8257 7435
✉ nibosi2009@163.com
www.nibosi.cn
5600

**中国南宁国际建筑装饰博览会**
**地点**：南宁国际会展中心，广西南宁
**内容**：建筑业装饰五金，整体木厨柜与材料，涂料、陶瓷，地面铺装材料，石材，天吊顶及幕墙，门 及铝型材，玻璃灯饰，建材加工机械等。
**周期**：每年一届
**市场范围**：全国性
**参展费用**：标准展位7,800元，净地800元/m²
**上届规模** ‘09：展览面积8,000m²(国外展商面积2,000m²)，参展商150家（国外展商30家，来自3个国家），参观人数20,000人
**主办**：广州尼勃斯展览有限公司；广东省建筑装饰协会
**地址**：广州市天河区车陂路306号美景廷苑 1203室（510660）
**联系人**：邢婕，龚保军
**QQ**：382746482

**China Nanning International Building Decoration Fair**
**Venue**: Nanning International Convention and Exhibition Center, Nanning, Guangxi
**Profile**: Building decoration hardware, over all cabinet, doors, windows, automatic doors, glass, lighting, ceiling, paint, chemicals, building materials, stone horticultural, surface
**Frequency**: Annual
**Market Area**: National
**Participated Fee**: Standard Booth RMB 7,800/booth, Raw Space RMB 800/m²
**Statistics ‘09**: Exhibition Area 8,000m²(foreigners 2,000m²), Exhibitors 150 (foreigners 30, came from 3 countries), Visitors 20,000
**Organizer**: Guangzhou Nibosi Exhibition Co Ltd
**Address**: Rm. 1203 Beauty City, 306 Chepo Rd, Tianhe Dist, Guangzhou 510660, China

2010/12/18 - 20
☎ 0532-6671 1800
℻ 0532-6671 1808
✉ chbosn@126.com
www.chbos.com
5610

**路博2010泛北部湾新生活方式展览会**
**地点**：南宁国际会展中心，广西南宁
**内容**：休闲健康生活、休闲健康产品、时尚休闲方式与产品、旅游休闲与康健 、理财投资与保险等
首届
**周期**：每年一届
**市场范围**：国际性
**性质**：面向公众
**入场券价格**：免费入场
**参展费用**：580元/m²
**预计规模**：20,000m²
**主办**：广西机械工程学会
**承办**：青岛博世会展有限公司；南宁凯路博会展有限公司
**地址**：青岛市同安路917号海丽广场D座15层（266700）
**联系人**：夏婕
**QQ**：976790172

**Broad 2010 Guangxi Fan-Beibu Gulf New Lifestyle Exhibition**
**Venue**: Nanning International Convention and Exhibition Center, Nanning, Guangxi
**Profile**: A healthy life, leisure and recreation, health products, fashion leisure and recreation and tourism product four, five, financial investment and healthy insurance.
First Session
**Frequency**: Annual
**Market Area**: International
**Nature**: Open to public
**Cost to Attend**: Free
**Participated Fee**: RMB 580/m²
**Organizer**: Guangxi Institute of Mechanical Engineering; Qingdao Boost Exhibition Co Ltd; Nanning Broad Exhibition Co Ltd
**Address**: 15/F, Bldg D, Haili Square, 917 Tong'an Rd, Qingdao 266700, Shandong, China
**Contact**: Alice Xia

# 黑龙江-哈尔滨
# Heilongjiang-Harbin

2010/03/23 - 29
☎ 0451-8755 8666, 8755 8685
🖷 0451-8626 8632, 8755 8688
✉ Greatwall@upupOK.com
www.AutoHaibin.org
5630

**第五届哈尔滨春季汽车展览会**
**地点：**哈尔滨国际会展体育中心，黑龙江哈尔滨
**内容：**各种类型的汽车、摩托车；各种汽车、摩托车总成及其零部件；各种汽车、零部件生产制造设备、工艺设备；各种汽车维修工具及设备；各种检测、测试、测验仪器和设备；各种汽车美容护理用品、装饰件；各种汽车音响、车载电话、电视、汽车导航系统；立体停车设备；汽车工业生产的新技术、新工艺、新材料；汽车工业新能源技术与产品；汽车工业环保技术与产品；计算机开发设计系统及应用技术；汽车专业杂志、科技资讯、网络以及先进的设计、管理技术。
**始办年份：**2006
**周期：**每年一届
**市场范围：**地区性
**性质：**面向公众
**入场券价格：**30元
**参展费用：**标准展位4,800元/9m²，净地380元/m²
**上届规模** '09：展览面积40,000m²(国外展商面积1,200m²)，参展商186家（国外展商6家，来自7个国家），参观人数128,000人（专业贸易观众5,000人）
**主办：**哈尔滨长城国际展览有限公司
**地址：**哈尔滨市南岗区苗圃街56号（150080）
**联系人：**赵立君，高笑怡

**5th Harbin International Automobile Exhibition - Spring**
**Venue:** Harbin International Conference Exhibition and Sports Center, Harbin, Heilongjiang
**Profile:** All types of automobiles and motorcycles; All kinds of automobiles, omotorcycle assemblies and their components, parts; All kinds of automobiles, motorcycle manufacture equipment and workmanship equipment; All kinds of maintenance & repair tools and equipment for automobiles; All kinds of detection, test, inspection devices and equipment; All kinds of automobile beauty & care articles and decoration articles; All kinds of sound equipment, automobile telephones, TVs and automobile navigation systems; Three-dimensional parking equipment; New technique, new workmanship and new materials for the production in automobile industry; New energy technique and products in automobile industry; Environment protection technique and products in automobile industry; Computer development & design systems and application technique; Magazines, technological information and advanced design, management technique in automobile specialty.
**Established Year:** 2006
**Frequency:** Annual
**Market Area:** Region
**Nature:** Open to public
**Cost to Attend:** RMB 30:-
**Participated Fee:** Standard Booth RMB 4,800/9m², Raw Space RMB 380/m²
**Statistics '09:** Exhibition Area 40,000m²(foreigners 1,200m²), Exhibitors 186 (foreigners 6, came from 7 countries), Visitors 128,000 (trade visitors 5,000)
**Organizer:** Harbin Great Wall Intl Exhibition Co Ltd
**Contact:** Zhao Li Jun, Gao Xiao Yi

2010/05/18 - 20
☎ 010-8455 6536, 8455 6532
🖷 010-6235 8733
✉ yini.zhang@reedsinopharm.com
✉ xinwei.zhao@reedsinopharm.com
www.apichina.com.cn
5640

**第64届中国国际医药原料药、中间体、包装、设备交易会（春季）**
**地点：**哈尔滨国际会展中心，黑龙江哈尔滨
**内容：**API China每年举办两届，历经四十年的发展，在我国医药行业享有盛誉。每届展会都吸引了国内外1200余家行业领军企业参展及来自海内外3万余名专业观众参观，主办方力图使国内外参展企业和专业观众尽享“一站式”集中采购、服务、信息交流的便利，深受行业和社会各界的关注和认可。
**展品范围：**原料药：生物碱类、氨基酸类类、抗生素类、激素类、肽类、精细化工及中间体；天然提取物：中药原料药；辅料：防腐剂、包衣剂、着色剂及香料、助流剂；食品及化妆品添加剂；外包生产服务；合同订制与采购加工；媒体及协会；
**专业观众：**成药生产企业、通用药生产企业、仿制药生产企业、非处方药生产企业、兽药生产企业、医药中间体生产企业、食品、化妆品生产企业、包装生产企业、机械制造企业、合同定制企业、媒体及发行商、专业协会、政府管理部门、研发机构
**周期：**每年两届
**主办：**国药励展有限责任公司

**The 64th API China**
**(active pharmaceutical ingredient )**
**Venue:** Harbin International Conference Exhibition and Sports Center, Harbin, Heilongjiang
**Profile:** As the leading exhibition for the pharmaceutical manufacturing industry and allied chemicals (specialty, fine, bulk) sector in China, the biannual API China is renowned for its long history and comprehensive product range. With over 40 years of continuous development and innovation, API China attracts over 1,200 leading manufacturers and more than 30,000 professional visitors, API China provides a one-stop procurement, service, and information platform for exhibitors and professional visitors
**Exhibits:** Pharmaceutical Ingredients: Alkaloids, Amino Acids, Antibiotics, Hormones, Peptides; Fine Chemicals & Intermediates; Natural Extracts; TCM ingredients; Excipients and Drug Formulation: Antimicrobial Preservatives, Coating Agents, Color and Dispersions, Flavors and Perfumes, Glidants; Food and Cosmetic Additives; Outsourcing; Contract Manufacturing; Associations & Media
**Visitors:** Finished Drug Manufacturers, Generic Producers, Me-Too Producers, OTC Producers, Veterinary Drug Producers, Intermediates Producers, Food & Cosmetic Producers, Packaging Companies, Machinery Companies, Contract Manufacturers, Distributors, Regulatory Institutions, Government, R & D Institutes
**Frequency:** Biannual
**Organizer:** Reed Sinopharm Exhibitions Co Ltd

2010/05/18 - 20
☎ 010-8455 6534, 8455 6539
🖷 010-6235 8733
✉ xuetao.wu@reedsinopharm.com
✉ ao.qu@reedsinopharm.com
www.interphexchina.com
5650

## 世界制药工业展中国展区（医药、包装材料、制药设备展区）

**地点：**哈尔滨国际会展中心，黑龙江哈尔滨

**内容：**随着中国日益增长的医药、包装材料、制药设备市场的需求，国药励展与世界制药工业展合作，在API China原有的包装、制药设备展区引入了包装设备国际展商和观众，现该区域更名为世界制药工业中国展（INTERPHEX CHINA）。其间，来自世界各地的展商展示其生产的包装设备、包装材料及制药设备等。INTERPHEX CHINA将为中国制药工业与国际制药工业的交流提供平台。

**展示范围：**包装展区：药品包装企业、包装机械、包装设计、印刷、合同定制和外包生产服务、信息技术、研发机构等；设备展区：原料药机械、制剂机械、中药设备、药用粉碎机械、饮片机械、药物检测设备、制药用水设备。

**观众范围：**成药生产企业、通用药生产企业、仿制药生产企业、非处方药生产企业、兽药生产企业、医药中间体生产企业、食品、化妆品生产企业、包装生产企业、机械制造企业、合同定制企业、媒体及发行商、专业协会、政府管理部门、研发机构等

**主办：**国药励展展览有限责任公司

## INTERPHEX CHINA

(Spring 2010)

**Venue:** Harbin International Conference Exhibition and Sports Center, Harbin, Heilongjiang

Profile: In order to meet the fast growing demands of China's pharmaceutical machinery market for better and newer technology which is needed to satisfy the rigorous standards of the developed importing economies, Reed Sinopharm Exhibitions in cooperation with INTERPHEX, introduces international exhibitors and visitors into the pharmaceutical packaging and machinery field for original equipment brands. The event, now branded as INTERPHEX CHINA, provides a unique platform for its exhibitors to meet major buyers of solutions and equipment from all sections of the pharmaceutical manufacturing chain.

**Exhibits:** Packaging Area: Packaging Material, Packaging Machinery, Packaging Design, Printing, Contract Manufacturing & Outsourcing, Information Technologies, R&D; Machinery Area: Machinery& Equipment for API Manufacturing, Machinery & Equipment; Finished Drug Manufacturing; Machinery for Slicing of Herbs; Pharmaceutical Milling Machinery; TCM Machinery & Equipment; Medicine Quality Testing Instrument; Water Treatment Equipment.

**Visitor:** Finished Drug Manufacturers, Generic Producers, Me-Too Producers, OTC Producers, Veterinary Drug Producers, Intermediates Producers, Food & Cosmetic Producers, Packaging Companies, Machinery Companies, Contract Manufacturers, Distributors, Regulatory Institutions, Government, R & D Institutes

**Organizer:** Reed Sinopharm Exhibitions Co Ltd

2010/06/15 - 19
☎ 0451-8234 0100
🖷 0451-8234 0226, 8234 5874
✉ chn@ichtf.com
eng@ichtf.com
kor@ichtf.com
jpn@ichtf.com
www.ichtf.com
5660

## 第二十一届中国哈尔滨国际经济贸易洽谈会

**地点：**哈尔滨国际会展体育中心，黑龙江哈尔滨

**内容：**中国哈尔滨国际经济贸易洽谈会（简称哈洽会）是中国政府批准举办的大型对外交易会之一。已连续成功举办了20届，已经从区域走向世界，发展成为拥有3,000个国际标准展位、10多个专业展区（馆）的国际性大型经贸洽谈会，其中有制造业展区、高新技术展区、金融产业展区、现代农业展区、建材展区、轻工展区、港澳台展区、外国展区、俄罗斯展区、室外大型机械展区、机电馆（展览篷房）、家具馆、文化产业展区、哈洽会是对俄经贸科技合作的最大展会，东北亚区域合作的重要平台，中国全面开拓多元化国际市场的窗口。

**始办年份：**1990

**周期：**每年一届

**市场范围：**国际性

**性质：**面向公众

**入场券价格：**50元

**参展费用：**室内标准展位：A、B、C厅6,000元/9m$^2$，D厅5,000元/9m$^2$；室内净地（36m$^2$起，并按9m$^2$递增）：A、B、C厅620元/m$^2$，D厅520元/m$^2$；机电馆（展览篷房）：标准展位4,000元/9m$^2$；室外大型机械展区（25m$^2$起）：120元/m$^2$

**上届规模‘09：**展览面积86,000m$^2$(国外展商面积9,000m$^2$)，参展商2,500家（国外展商310家，来自18个国家），参观人数250,000人（专业贸易观众100,000人）

**主办：**中华人民共和国商务部；中华人民共和国国家发展和改革委员会；中国贸促会；黑龙江省人民政府；浙江省人民政府；哈尔滨市人民政府

**承办：**中国哈尔滨经济贸易洽谈会办公室

**地址：**中国哈尔滨市南岗区美顺街35号（150090）

**联系人：**景林，张玉虹

## The 21th China Harbin International Economic and Trade Fair

**Venue:** Harbin International Conference Exhibition and Sports Center, Harbin, Heilongjiang

**Profile:** China Harbin International Economic and Trade Fair (Harbin Trade Fair) is one of the large-scale foreign trade fairs authorized by the Chinese government since its first session in 1990. The fair has been successfully held for 20 consecutive years. Over the years, Harbin Trade Fair has developed from a regional fair to a large scale international economic and trade fair with 3,000 international standard booths, 10 professional exhibition areas (pavilions) including high tech exhibition area, modern service industry exhibition area, modern agricultural exhibition area, construction materials exhibition area, light industry exhibition area, cultural industry exhibition area, foreign countries exhibition area, machinery and electric products pavilion, furniture pavilion outdoor large-scale machinery exhibition area. Harbin Trade Fair has become a significant international trade fair in the world-a-window for China to fully explore the diversified international market and a major platform for regional cooperation in Northeast Asia. About 120 thousands contractors, buyers and professional visitors of 68 countries and regions from home and abroad attended the 20th event.

**Established Year:** 1990

**Frequency:** Annual

**Market Area:** International

**Nature:** Open to public

**Cost to Attend:** RMB 50:-

**Participated Fee:** Indoor Standard Booth: Hall A, B, C RMB 6,000/9m$^2$, Hall D RMB 5,000/9m$^2$; Indoor Raw Space (min 36m$^2$): Hall A, B, C RMB 620/m$^2$, Hall D RMB 520/m$^2$; Tent: RMB 4,000/9m$^2$; Outdoor Raw Space (min 25m$^2$) RMB 120/m$^2$

**Statistics '09:** Exhibition Area 86,000m$^2$(foreigners 9,000m$^2$), Exhibitors 2,500 (foreigners 310, came from 18 countries), Visitors 250,000 (trade visitors 100,000)

**Organizer:** Ministry of commerce of the people's Republic of China; National Development and Reform Committee; CCPIT; The people's government of Heilongliang Province; The People's Government of Zhejiang Province; The People's Government of Harbin Municipality

**Address:** 35 Meishun St., Nangang Dist, Harbin, China 150090

**Contact:** Jing Lin, Zhang Yuhong

2010/08/02 - 09
☎ 0451-8755 8666, 8755 8685
🖷 0451-8626 8632, 8755 8688
✉ Greatwall@upupOK.com
www.AutoHaibin.org
5670

**第13届哈尔滨国际汽车工业展览会**
**地点：**哈尔滨国际会展中心，黑龙江哈尔滨
**内容：**各种类型的汽车、摩托车；各种汽车、摩托车总成及其零部件；各种汽车、零部件生产制造设备、工艺设备；各种汽车维修工具及设备；各种检测、测试、测验仪器和设备；各种汽车美容护理用品、装饰件；各种汽车音响、车载电话、电视、汽车导航系统；立体停车设备；汽车工业生产的新技术、新工艺、新材料；汽车工业新能源技术与产品；汽车工业环保技术与产品；计算机开发设计系统及应用技术；汽车专业杂志、科技资讯、网络以及先进的设计、管理技术。
**始办年份：**1998
**周期：**每年一届
**市场范围：**国际性
**性质：**面向公众
**入场券价格：**60元/张
**参展费用：**标准展位7,600元/9m²，净地780元/m²
**上届规模**'09：展览面积86,000m²(国外展商面积46,000m²)，参展商531家（国外展商46家，来自11个国家），参观人数268,000人（专业贸易观众36,000人）
**主办：**中国汽车工业协会；中国汽车工程学会；黑龙江省人民政府；哈尔滨市人民政府；哈尔滨长城国际展览有限公司
**地址：**哈尔滨市南岗区苗圃街56号（150080）
**联系人：**赵立君，高笑怡

**The 13th Harbin International Automobile Exhibition**
**Venue:** Harbin International Conference Exhibition and Sports Center, Harbin, Heilongjiang
**Profile:** Automobiles and motorcycles; Automobiles, motorcycle assemblies and their components, parts; Automobiles, motorcycle manufacture equipment and workmanship equipment; Maintenance & repair tools and equipment for automobiles; Detection, test, inspection devices and equipment; Automobile beauty & care articles and decoration articles; Sound equipment, automobile telephones, TVs and automobile navigation systems; Three-dimensional parking equipment; New technique, new workmanship and new materials for the production in automobile industry; New energy technique and products in automobile industry; Environment protection technique and products in automobile industry.
**Established Year:** 1998
**Frequency:** Annual
**Market Area:** International
**Nature:** Open to public
**Cost to Attend:** RMB 60:-
**Participated Fee:** Standard Booth RMB 7,600/9m², Raw Space RMB 780/m²
**Statistics '09:** Exhibition Area 86,000m²(foreigners 46,000m²), Exhibitors 531 (foreigners 46, came from 11 countries), Visitors 268,000 (trade visitors 36,000)
**Organizer:** China Automobile Industry Assn; China Automobile Engineering Academy; Heilongjiang People' s Government; Harbin Municipal People' s Government; Harbin Great Wall International Exhibition Co Ltd
**Address:** 56 Miaopu St, Nangang Dist, Harbin, Heilongjiang, China
**Contact:** Zhao Li Jun, Gao Xiao Yi

# 河南-洛阳
# Henan-Luoyang

2010/10 -
☎ 027-8736 2945
www.hope-tarsus.com
5680

**2010洛阳机电产品博览会**
**地点：**洛阳中原物流国际会展中心，河南 洛阳
**主办：**中英合资好博塔苏斯展览公司
**联系人：**余云成

**Luoyang Machinery and Electronic Products Expo**
**Venue:** Luoyang Logistic Exhibition Center, Luoyang, Henan
**Organizer:** Tarsus-Hope Exhibition Company

# 河南-郑州
# Henan-Zhengzhou

2010 -
☎ 0371-6577 8796, 6577 8798
✉ hnjqxh@163.com
www.jbzyw.com
5690

**第二十二届河南家禽交易会**
**地点：**郑州国际会展中心，河南郑州
**周期：**每年一届
**市场范围：**国际性
**主办：**河南省家禽业协会；河南畜牧局

**The 22nd Henan Poultry Economy & Trade Fair**
**Venue:** Zhengzhou International Convention and Exhibition Center, Zhengzhou, Henan
**Frequency:** Annual
**Market Area:** International
**Organizer:** Henan Animal Husbandry Bureau

2010 -
☎ 027-8736 2945
www.hope-tarsus.com
5700

**中国中部食品与饮料加工及包装展览会**
**地点：**河南郑州
**主办：**中国机械工业联合会；郑州市人民政府
**联系人：**余云成

**Central China Food & Beverage Processing and Packaging Exhibition**
**Venue:** Zhengzhou, Henan
**Organizer:** Tarsus-Hope Exhibition Company

2010 -
☎ 027-8736 2945
www.hope-tarsus.com
5710

**中国中部国际环境保护与水处理展览会**
**地点：**郑州国际会展中心，河南 郑州
**主办：**中国机械工业联合会；郑州市人民政府
**联系人：**余云成

**Central China Intl Environment Protection and Water Treatment Exhibition**
**Venue:** Zhengzhou International Convention and Exhibition Center, Zhengzhou, Henan
**Organizer:** Tarsus-Hope Exhibition Company

2010/03/10 - 12
☎ 027-8736 2945
www.hope-tarsus.com
5750

**中国中西部（郑州）医疗器械展览会暨第18届中原国际医疗器械（2010年春季）展览会**
**地点**：郑州国际会展中心，河南郑州
**周期**：每年一届
**市场范围**：国际性
**主办**：全国医药技术市场协会；中英合资好博塔苏斯展览公司
**承办**：郑州好博塔苏斯展览有限公司
**联系人**：余云成

**2010 China Central (Zhengzhou) Medical Equipment Show**
**Venue:** Zhengzhou International Convention and Exhibition Center, Zhengzhou, Henan
**Frequency:** Annual
**Market Area:** International
**Organizer:** Tarsus-Hope Exhibition Company

2010/03/18 - 20
☎ 0371-6661 9428, 13592507710
🖷 0371-6661 9430
✉ slj66170980@126.com
www.ccieme.com.cn
5770

**第12届中原国际工业控制自动化及仪器仪表展**
**地点**：郑州国际会展中心，河南郑州
**内容**：工业控制及监控：可编程控制器（PLC）、传感器、流量计、变送器、编码器、激光检测、接近开关、识别系统、力测量、PH 值、安全自动化、工控机/工业计算机、工业以太网、现场总线技术与设备、人机界面、控制装置、运动控制、分布式计算机控制系统（DCS）；电气自动化：网络/工业数据通讯、电线电缆、驱动装置等；仪器仪表及测试测量：过程控制仪器仪表、环保类仪器仪表、医疗类仪器仪表、检测测量类仪器仪表、质量控制和检测设备、计量分析等；组装系统、搬运系统、线性定位系统、工业影像处理系统、数控系统、机器人/机械手等；
**始办年份**：1999
**周期**：每年一届
**市场范围**：全国性
**参展费用**：标准展位（9m²）：国内：A类7,200元，B类6,700元，C类6,200元；净地（36m²起）：国内:T区880元/m²，A类820元/m²，B类780元/m²，C类730元/m²
**上届规模 '09**：展览面积18,000m²(国外展商面积3,000m²)，参展商350家（国外展商20家，来自10个国家），参观人数38,000人（专业贸易观众15,000人）
**主办**：中国机械工业联合会
**承办**：郑州好博塔苏斯展览有限公司
**地址**：郑州市紫荆山路60号金成国贸大厦2106室（450004）
**联系人**：沈华兵

**Central China Automation and Instrument Exhibition**
**Venue:** Zhengzhou International Convention and Exhibition Center, Zhengzhou, Henan
**Established Year:** 1999
**Frequency:** Annual
**Market Area:** National
**Participated Fee:** Standard Booth (9m²) USD 1,350, Raw Space (min 36m²) USD 150-180/m²
**Statistics '09:** Exhibition Area 18,000m²(foreigners 3,000m²), Exhibitors 350 (foreigners 20, came from 10 countries), Visitors 38,000 (trade visitors 15,000)
**Organizer:** Tarsus-Hope Exhibition Company

2010/03/18 - 20
☎ 027-8736 2945
www.hope-tarsus.com
5780

**中国中部国际物流、物料运输与储藏展览会**
**地点**：郑州国际会展中心，河南郑州
**主办**：中国机械工业联合会；郑州市人民政府
**承办**：郑州好博塔苏斯展览有限公司；上海好博塔苏斯展览有限公司
**联系人**：余云成

**Central China Logistics Exhibition**
**Venue:** Zhengzhou International Convention and Exhibition Center, Zhengzhou, Henan
**Organizer:** Tarsus-Hope Exhibition Company

2010/03/18 - 20
☎ 0371-6661 9428, 13592507710
🖷 0371-6661 9430
✉ slj66170980@126.com
www.ccieme.com.cn
5790

**2010中国中部（郑州）国际装备制造业博览会**
**地点**：郑州国际会展中心，河南郑州
**内容**：数控机床、金属切削机床、压力成型机床和机床附件及配件、模具；自动化控制、机器人、电子应用系统、仪器仪表及装备制造业信息化解决方案等；密封件、轴承、五金工具、紧固件、塑胶工业及配件、焊接切割技术设备、激光技术；泵、阀等流体机械、液压气动设备、空气压缩机、空分设备、清洁设备、表面工程、热处理、电机、节能环保、石化、重矿、筛分等专用设备及配套设备；管道、电梯、索道等特种设备，印刷包装设备、质量控制、设备维修技术；工程机械、专用汽车及大型机械设备
**始办年份**：1999
**周期**：每年一届
**市场范围**：全国性
**参展费用**：标准展位（9m²）：国内：A类7,200元，B类6,700元，C类6,200元；净地（36m²起）：国内:T区880元/m²，A类820元/m²，B类780元/m²，C类730元/m²
**上届规模 '09**：展览面积18,000m²(国外展商面积3,000m²)，参展商350家（国外展商20家，来自10个国家），参观人数38,000人（专业贸易观众15,000人）
**主办**：中国机械工业联合会
**承办**：郑州好博塔苏斯展览有限公司
**地址**：郑州市紫荆山路60号金成国贸大厦2106室（450004）
**联系人**：沈华兵

**Central China (Zhengzhou) Intl Equipment Manufacturing Exposition (2010)**
**Venue:** Zhengzhou International Convention and Exhibition Center, Zhengzhou, Henan
**Established Year:** 1999
**Frequency:** Annual
**Market Area:** National
**Participated Fee:** Standard Booth (9m²) USD 1,350, Raw Space (min 36m²) USD 150-180/m²
**Statistics '09:** Exhibition Area 18,000m²(foreigners 3,000m²), Exhibitors 350 (foreigners 20, came from 10 countries), Visitors 38,000 (trade visitors 15,000)
**Organizer:** Tarsus-Hope Exhibition Company

2010/03/27 - 29
☎ 0371-6535 0058, 6535 0059
🖷 0371-6535 0155
✉ hzfw8898@126.com
www.zyad.com.cn
www.tthzfw.com
5795

**2010年（春季）中国郑州第十六届中原广告展暨2010年中国中部LED霓虹灯展**
**地点**：郑州国际会展中心，河南郑州
**周期**：每年一届
**市场范围**：国际性
**主办**：郑州天天广告公司

**2010 (Spring) Zhengzhou The 16th Central China Advertisement Show and 2010 China Central LED Neon-lights Show**
**Venue:** Zhengzhou International Convention and Exhibition Center, Zhengzhou, Henan
**Frequency:** Annual
**Market Area:** International
**Organizer:** Zhengzhou Tiantian Exhibition Service Co Ltd

2010/04 -
☎ 0371-6808 9866
📠 0371-6808 9835
www.zzicec.com
5800

2010第八届中国（郑州）社会公共安全产品博览会
**地点：** 郑州国际会展中心，河南郑州
**周期：** 每年一届
**市场范围：** 国际性
**主办：** 郑州汇卓展览策划有限公司

2010 The 8th China Zhengzhou Public Security Product Expo
**Venue:** Zhengzhou International Convention and Exhibition Center, Zhengzhou, Henan
**Frequency:** Annual
**Market Area:** International
**Organizer:** Zhengzhou Huizhou Exhibition Co

2010/04 -
☎ 0371-6808 9866
📠 0371-6808 9835
www.zzicec.com
5810

2010中部住宅及科技产业博览会
**地点：** 郑州国际会展中心，河南郑州
**周期：** 每年一届
**市场范围：** 国际性

2010 China Central Real Estate and Tech Industry Expo
**Venue:** Zhengzhou International Convention and Exhibition Center, Zhengzhou, Henan
**Frequency:** Annual
**Market Area:** International

2010/05 -
☎ 0371-6808 9866
📠 0371-6808 9835
✉ sales@zzicec.com
www.zzicec.com
5820

2010第六届中国郑州糖酒食品交易会
2010第六届中国粮油调味品（郑州）交易会
**地点：** 郑州国际会展中心，河南郑州
**周期：** 每年一届
**市场范围：** 国际性

2010 6th China City and Countryside Planning
2010 6th China Zhengzhou Candy & Spirit Fair
**Venue:** Zhengzhou International Convention and Exhibition Center, Zhengzhou, Henan
**Frequency:** Annual
**Market Area:** International

2010/05 -
☎ 0371-6808 9866, 6808 9988
📠 0371-6808 9835, 6808 9838
✉ sales@zzicec.com
www.zzicec.com
http://expo.zzedu.net.cn
5830

第二届中国郑州教育服务大会
**地点：** 郑州国际会展中心，河南郑州
**周期：** 每年一届
**市场范围：** 国际性
**主办：** 郑州市教育局
协办：郑州国际会展有限责任公司
**地址：** 中国郑州市郑东新区商务内环路中央公园一号（450016）

The 2nd China Zhengzhou Education Service Fair
**Venue:** Zhengzhou International Convention and Exhibition Center, Zhengzhou, Henan
**Frequency:** Annual
**Market Area:** International
**Organizer:** Zhengzhou International Convention & Exhibition Center
**Address:** No. 1, Nei Huan Road, Central Business District, Zhengdong New District, Zhengzhou, China

2010/06 -
☎ 0371-6027 2755, 6027 2758
📠 0371-6027 2750
✉ sales@zzicec.com
www.ouyaexpo.com
5840

第五届中国（郑州）国际酒店、餐饮、泳池沐浴SPA设备及用品博览会/第五届中国（郑州）国际家纺、布艺及工艺品、礼品家居装饰博览会
**地点：** 郑州国际会展中心，河南郑州
**周期：** 每年一届
**市场范围：** 国际性
**主办：** 郑州欧亚国际展览有限公司

5th China (Zhengzhou) Intl Hotel, F&B, Swimming pool and SPA Equipment and Product Expo/5th China (Zhengzhou) Household Textile, Cloth Art, Handicraft and Decoration Article Expo
**Venue:** Zhengzhou International Convention and Exhibition Center, Zhengzhou, Henan
**Frequency:** Annual
**Market Area:** International
**Organizer:** Zhengzhou Ouya Intl Exhibition Co Ltd

2010/07 -
☎ 0371-6808 9866, 6808 9988
📠 0371-6808 9835, 6808 9838
✉ sales@zzicec.com
www.zzicec.com
5850

2010第七届汽车用品交易会暨第六届汽车羊剪绒产品订货会
**地点：** 郑州国际会展中心，河南郑州
**周期：** 每年一届
**市场范围：** 国际性

2010 the 7th Auto Products Trade Fair& the 6th Auto-Use Wool Products Fair
**Venue:** Zhengzhou International Convention and Exhibition Center, Zhengzhou, Henan
**Frequency:** Annual
**Market Area:** International

2010/08 -
☎ 0371-6808 9866, 6808 9988
📠 0371-6808 9835, 6808 9838
✉ sales@zzicec.com
www.zzicec.com
5860

河南省投资贸易洽谈会
**地点：** 郑州国际会展中心，河南郑州
**周期：** 每年一届
**市场范围：** 国际性

Henan Investment and Trade Fair
**Venue:** Zhengzhou International Convention and Exhibition Center, Zhengzhou, Henan
**Frequency:** Annual
**Market Area:** International

2010/09 -
☎ 027-8736 2945
www.hope-tarsus.com
5870

中国中西部（郑州）医疗器械展览会
暨第19届中原国际医疗器械(2010年秋季)展览会
**地点：** 郑州国际会展中心，河南郑州
**主办：** 全国医药技术市场协会；中英合资好博塔苏斯展览公司
**联系人：** 余云成

2010 China Central (Zhengzhou) Medical Equipment Show
**Venue:** Zhengzhou International Convention and Exhibition Center, Zhengzhou, Henan
**Organizer:** Tarsus-Hope Exhibition Company

2010/09 -
☎ 0371-6808 9866, 6808 9988
📠 0371-6808 9835, 6808 9838
✉ sales@zzicec.com
www.zzicec.com
5890

第二届中国绿化博览会
**地点：** 郑州国际会展中心，河南郑州
**周期：** 每年一届
**市场范围：** 国际性

The 2nd China Green Expo
**Venue:** Zhengzhou International Convention and Exhibition Center, Zhengzhou, Henan
**Frequency:** Annual
**Market Area:** International

2010/10 -
☎ 0371-6808 9866, 6808 9988
🖷 0371-6808 9835, 6808 9838
✉ sales@zzicec.com
www.zzicec.com
www.catf.agri.cn
5900

**2010中国国际农产品交易会**
**地点**：郑州国际会展中心，河南郑州
**周期**：每年一届
**主办**：中国农业部

**2010 China Intl Agriculture Products Trade Fair**
**Venue:** Zhengzhou International Convention and Exhibition Center, Zhengzhou, Henan
**Frequency:** Annual
**Organizer:** Ministry of Agriculture of China

2010/10 -
☎ 0371-6808 9866, 6808 9988
🖷 0371-6808 9835, 6808 9838
✉ sales@zzicec.com
www.zzicec.com
www.zzfair.org
5910

**2010郑州全国商品交易会**
**地点**：郑州国际会展中心，河南郑州
**周期**：每年一届
**市场范围**：国际性
**承办**：河南省商务厅
**协办**：郑州国际会展有限责任公司
**地址**：中国郑州市郑东新区商务内环路中央公园一号（450016）
**联系人**：何学锋

**2010 Zhengzhou National Commodity Fair**
**Venue:** Zhengzhou International Convention and Exhibition Center, Zhengzhou, Henan
**Frequency:** Annual
**Market Area:** International
**Organizer:** Zhengzhou International Convention & Exhibition Center
**Address:** No. 1, Nei Huan Road, Central Business District, Zhengdong New District, Zhengzhou, China
**Contact:** He Xuefeng

2010/11 -
☎ 0371-6808 9866, 6808 9988
🖷 0371-6808 9835, 6808 9838
✉ sales@zzicec.com
www.zzicec.com
5920

**2010中国（郑州）国际汽车博览会**
**地点**：郑州国际会展中心，河南郑州
**周期**：每年一届
**市场范围**：地区性
**主办**：郑州国际会展中心
**地址**：中国郑州市郑东新区商务内环路中央公园一号（450016）
**联系人**：何学锋

**2010 Zhengzhou International Automobile Expo**
**Venue:** Zhengzhou International Convention and Exhibition Center, Zhengzhou, Henan
**Frequency:** Annual
**Market Area:** Regional
**Organizer:** Zhengzhou International Convention & Exhibition Center
**Address:** No. 1, Nei Huan Road, Central Business District, Zhengdong New District, Zhengzhou, China
**Contact:** He Xuefeng

# 湖北-武汉
# Hubei-Wuhan

2010/03/30 - 04/01
☎ 027-8736 2945
www.hope-tarsus.com
5930

**2010第十四届武汉广告展览会**
**第二届武汉印刷、包装、纸业展览会**
**地点**：武汉国际会展中心，湖北武汉
**主办**：中英合资好博塔苏斯展览公司
**承办**：湖北好博塔苏斯展览有限公司
**联系人**：余云成

**2010 Wuhan Ad Exhibition**
**2nd Wuhan Printing, Packaging and Paper Exhibition**
**Venue:** Wuhan International Conference & Exhibition Center, Wuhan, Hubei
**Organizer:** Tarsus-Hope Exhibition Company

2010/03/30 - 04/01
☎ 027-8580 5812, 8572 4905
🖷 027-8580 5812
5940

**湖北武汉国际先进医疗仪器设备展览会**
**地点**：武汉科技会展中心，湖北武汉
**始办年份**：1985
**周期**：每年一届
**市场范围**：地区性
**性质**：面向公众
**参展费用**：4,000～5,000元
**主办**：湖北贸促会；湖北卫生厅武汉市卫生局
**承办**：湖北国际展览中心
**地址**：武汉江汉北路8号19楼
**联系人**：乐群，吕崇军

**Hubei Wuhan International Medical Equipment & Instrument Exhibition**
**Venue:** Wuhan Science and Technology Conference and Exhibition Center, Wuhan, Hubei
**Established Year:** 1985
**Frequency:** Annual
**Market Area:** Region
**Nature:** Open to public
**Participated Fee:** RMB 5,000
**Organizer:** Hubei International Exhibition Center

2010/09/09 - 13
☎ 027-8577 7921, 8577 8685
🖷 027-8573 3284
✉ expowh@ccpit.org
www.autowuhan.com.cn
5950

**第十一届中国（湖北-武汉）国际汽车工业展览会**
**地点**：武汉国际会展中心，湖北武汉
**内容**：整车：乘用车、商用车、特种车；汽车零部件：发动机、传动系统、行驶系统、转向系统、制动系统、车身附件、电器设备、汽车轮胎等；汽车用品：汽车内饰、汽车音响系统、通信导航系统、空调系统、汽车安全系统、车载电子产品、汽车美容及养护用品、油漆、润滑剂、添加剂等；汽车维修检测设备：诊断设备、维修工具、汽车喷烤漆、洗车及其它相关设备；汽车相关制造设备、技术和工具；其它相关产品和服务。
**始办年份**：1995
**周期**：每年一届
**市场范围**：国际性
**参展费用**：750元/m²
**上届规模**‘09：展览面积16,000m²(国外展商面积2,400m²)，参展商

**11th China (Hubei/Wuhan) Intl Auto Industry Exhibition**
**Venue:** Wuhan International Conference & Exhibition Center, Wuhan, Hubei
**Profile:** Vehicles: Passenger cars, commercial vehicles, special-purpose vehicles; Automotive Parts: Engines & mechanical system, Gearbox, Exhaust, Axle, Steering, Brakes, Suspension system, Body system, Electric and electronic system, Tire and wheels; Automotive Accessories: Interior trimmings, Car audio system, Navigation and telecom system, Air conditioning system, Safety and vehicle security system, Vehicle mounted electronic products, Car care products, paints, lubricants, additives; Measuring, testing and control devices & systems; Related manufacturing technology, machinery
**Established Year:** 1995
**Frequency:** Annual

243家（国外展商31家，来自8个国家），参观人数250,000人（专业贸易观众26,000人）
**主办：**中国机械工业联合会；中国贸促会；湖北省人民政府；武汉市人民政府
**承办：**中国贸促会武汉市分会；湖北省机械汽车行业协会
**地址：**武汉市汉口台北路217号8楼（430015）
**联系人：**喻金富，章劲
**MSN：**zlwhcn@hotmail.com
**QQ：**34698629

**Market Area:** International
**Participated Fee:** RMB 750/m²
**Statistics '09:** Exhibition Area 16,000m²(foreigners 2,400m²), Exhibitors 243 (foreigners 31, came from 8 countries), Visitors 250,000 (trade visitors 26,000)
**Organizer:** China Machinery Industry Federation, CCPIT, Hubei Provincial Government; Wuhan Municipal Government
**Organizer:** CCPIT Wuhan Sub-Council
**Address:** 8/Fl., 217 Tabei Road, Hankou, Wuhan 430015, China
**Contact:** Yu Jinfu, Zhang Jin
**MSN:** zlwhcn@hotmail.com

5960

2010/09/23 - 26
☎ 027-8576 0803
🖷 027-8577 1292
www.cwme.com.cn

**第十一届中国国际机电产品博览会**
**地点：**武汉国际会展中心，湖北武汉
**内容：**是经国务院批准的国家级国际性大型机电产品专业博览会，是目前中西部地区最具规模和影响力的机电专业博览会。自2000年以来，已连续举办了九届。
**始办年份：**2000
**周期：**每年一届
**市场范围：**国际性
**性质：**面向公众
**参展费用：**8,600元/标准展位，净地880元/m²
**上届规模 '09：**展览面积30,000m²(国外展商面积500m²)，参观人数100,000人（专业贸易观众30,000人）
**主办：**武汉市人民政府；中国机电产品进出口商会
**地址：**武汉市汉口青年路308号安泊丽晶酒店602室（430032）
**联系人：**张定生，胡斌

**11th China Intl Machinery & Electronic Products Exposition**
**Venue:** Wuhan International Conference & Exhibition Center, Wuhan, Hubei
**Profile:** This exposition is a large-scale national exhibition of electro-mechanical products. Put on under official from the state that is well- known internationally, and the biggest and most influential one presently in west & central China
**Established Year:** 2000
**Frequency:** Annual
**Market Area:** International
**Nature:** Open to public
**Participated Fee:** Standard Booth RMB 8,600, Raw Space RMB 880/m²
**Statistics '09:** Exhibition Area 30,000m² (foreigners 500m²), Visitors 100,000 (trade visitors 30,000)
**Organizer:** Wuhan Municipal Government; China Chamber of Commerce for Import & Export of Machinery and Electronic Products
**Address:** Rm. 602, Anboli Hotel, No, 308, Qingnian Rd, Hankou, Wuhan
**Contact:** Dingsheng Zhang, Bin Hu

5980

2010/11 -
☎ 027-8736 2945
www.hope-tarsus.com

**2010第九届中国武汉国际农业机械展览会**
**地点：**武汉国际会展中心，湖北武汉
**主办：**中华人民共和国农业部；湖北省人民政府；武汉市人民政府
**承办：**湖北好博塔苏斯展览有限公司
**联系人：**余云成

**9th Wuhan Agricultural Machinery Exhibition**
**Venue:** Wuhan International Conference & Exhibition Center, Wuhan, Hubei
**Organizer:** Tarsus-Hope Exhibition Company

# 湖南-长沙
# Hunan-Changsha

5990

2010/03/17 -
www.hope-tarsus.com
☎ 027-8736 2945

**2010中国中西部（长沙）医疗器械展览会暨第16届湖南医疗器械技术与设备展览会(2010年春季)**
**地点：**湖南国际会展中心，湖南长沙
**主办：**全国医药技术市场协会；湖南省机械工业管理办公室
**承办：**长沙好博塔苏斯展览有限公司

**Changsha Medical Devices Exhibition**
**Venue:** Hunan International Convention & Exhibition Center, Changsha, Hunan
**Organizer:** Tarsus-Hope Exhibition Company

6000

2010/04/22 - 24
☎ 0731-8288 6728
🖷 0731-8288 6728
✉ 420041154@qq.com

**湖南公共安全产品与技术博览会**
**地点：**长沙红星国际会展中心，湖南长沙
**始办年份：**2000
**周期：**每年一届
**市场范围：**地区性
**性质：**面向公众
**参展费用：**标准展位5,800～6,800元，净地680元/m²
**上届规模 '09：**展览面积15,000m²(国外展商面积300m²)，参展商160家（国外展商15家，来自12个国家），参观人数46,000人（专业贸易观众18,000人）
**主办：**湖南省公安厅
**承办：**湖南省安全技术防范协会；湖南长沙兰德展览广告有限公司
**地址：**湖南长沙芙蓉中路三段438号金苑商务楼1栋607室（410315）
**联系人：**张智
**QQ：**420041154

**Hunan Safety and Security Expo**
**Venue:** Hunan Hongxing International Exhibition Center, Changsha, Hunan
**Established Year:** 2000
**Frequency:** Annual
**Market Area:** Region
**Nature:** Open to public
**Participated Fee:** Standard Booth RMB 6,800, Raw Space RMB 680/m²
**Statistics '09:** Exhibition Area 15,000m²(foreigners 300m²), Exhibitors 160 (foreigners 15, came from 12 countries), Visitors 46,000万 (trade visitors 18,000)
**Organizer:** Changsha Lande Exhibition Co Ltd

6010

2010/05/18 - 20
☎ 0731-8286 5666
📠 0731-8283 6036
www.ccieme.com.cn

**2010中国中部（长沙）国际装备制造业博览会**
**地点**：湖南国际会展中心，湖南长沙
**内容**：机床、工具与机床附件；工控自动化、仪器仪表、计量检测设备、流 机械与动力传动设备；电力电工设备、电厂电站设备、有色金属、金属加工、铸造、 冶金技术设备、塑胶机械、焊接切割、五金工具、表面处理材料及设备、物流技术与设备新材料应用及技术、 装设备和 、工程机械及零配件、汽车零备件
**始办年份**：2000
**周期**：每年一届
**市场范围**：全国性
**参展费用**：6,500元
**上届规模**‘09：参展商186家，参观人数2,600人
**主办**：中国机械工业联合会
**承办**：长沙好博塔苏斯展览有限公司
**地址**：长沙芙蓉中路一段468号湖南财富中心富座1904室（410005）
**联系人**：林风

**Changsha International Equipment Manufacturing Exhibition**
**Venue**: Hunan International Convention & Exhibition Center, Changsha, Hunan
**Established Year**: 2000
**Frequency**: Annual
**Market Area**: National
**Participated Fee**: RMB 6,500
**Statistics ‘09**: Exhibitors 186, Visitors 2,600
**Organizer**: Tarsus-Hope Exhibition Company

6030

2010/09 -
☎ 027-8736 2945
www.hope-tarsus.com

**2010中国中西部（长沙）医疗器械展览会暨**
**第17届湖南医疗器械技术与设备(2010年秋季)展览会**
**地点**：湖南国际会展中心，湖南长沙
**主办**：全国医药技术市场协会；湖南省机械工业管理办公室
**承办**：长沙好博塔苏斯展览有限公司

**Changsha Medical Devices Exhibition**
**Venue**: Hunan International Convention & Exhibition Center, Changsha, Hunan
**Organizer**: Tarsus-Hope Exhibition Company

# 江苏-常州
# Jiangsu-Changzhou

6040

2010/05/01 - 03
☎ 0519-8985 1052
📠 0519-8985 1052
www.czsports.com

**2010年常州第二届汽车展**
**地点**：常州国际会展中心，江苏常州
**内容**：汽车产品及配件展示，主打节能、环保、经济型车型
**始办年份**：2009
**周期**：每年一届
**市场范围**：地区性
**性质**：面向公众
**上届规模**‘09：展览面积12,000m²(国外展商面积4,000m²)，参展商100家（国外展商30家，来自5个国家），参观人数30,000人（专业贸易观众10,000人）
**主办**：常州体育产业发展有限公司

**2nd Changzhou Auto Show**
**Venue**: Changzhou International Exhibition Center, Changzhou, Jiangsu
**Established Year**: 2009
**Frequency**: Annual
**Market Area**: Region
**Nature**: Open to public
**Statistics ‘09**: Exhibition Area 12,000m²(foreigners 4,000m²), Exhibitors 100 (foreigners 30, came from 5 countries), Visitors 30,000 (trade visitors 10,000)
**Organizer**: Changzhou Sports Development Co

6050

2010/05/18 - 22
☎ 0519-8985 1052
📠 0519-8985 1052
www.czsports.com

**2010年常州房地产交易会**
**地点**：常州国际会展中心，江苏常州
**内容**：常州地区优秀楼盘展示交易
**始办年份**：2009
**周期**：每年一届
**市场范围**：地区性
**性质**：面向公众
**上届规模**‘09：展览面积15,000m²，参展商73家，参观人数35,000人（专业贸易观众15,000人）
**主办**：常州体育产业发展有限公司

**2010 Changzhou Real Estate Fair**
**Venue**: Changzhou International Exhibition Center, Changzhou, Jiangsu
**Established Year**: 2009
**Frequency**: Annual
**Market Area**: Region
**Nature**: Open to public
**Statistics ‘09**: Exhibition Area 15,000m², Exhibitors 73, Visitors 35,000 (trade visitors 15,000)
**Organizer**: Changzhou Sports Development Co

6060

2010/06/18 - 20
☎ 0519-8985 1052
📠 0519-8985 1052
www.czsports.com

**第四届中国常州电动车展览会**
**地点**：常州国际会展中心，江苏常州
**内容**：国内知名电动车生产企业优质产品展销
**始办年份**：2007
**周期**：每年一届
**市场范围**：全国性
**性质**：面向公众
**上届规模**‘09：展览面积15,000m²，参展商150家，参观人数30,000人（专业贸易观众12,000人）
**承办**：常州体育产业发展有限公司

**4th Changzhou Electric Vehicle Exhibition**
**Venue**: Changzhou International Exhibition Center, Changzhou, Jiangsu
**Established Year**: 2007
**Frequency**: Annual
**Market Area**: National
**Nature**: Open to public
**Statistics ‘09**: Exhibition Area 15,000m², Exhibitors 150, Visitors 30,000 (trade visitors 12,000)
**Organizer**: Changzhou Sports Development Co

2010/09/10 - 12
☎ 0591-8985 1052
🖷 0519-8985 1052
www.czsports.com

6070 2010年常州太阳能秋交会
地点：常州国际会展中心，江苏常州
内容：国内太阳能设备及产品配件
始办年份：2003
周期：每年一届
市场范围：全国性
性质：面向公众
上届规模‘09：展览面积25,000m²，参展商400家，参观人数50,000人（专业贸易观众20,000人）
承办：常州体育产业发展有限公司

Changzhou Solar Energy Exhibition
Venue: Changzhou International Exhibition Center, Changzhou, Jiangsu
Established Year: 2003
Frequency: Annual
Market Area: National
Nature: Open to public
Statistics '09: Exhibition Area 25,000m², Exhibitors 400, Visitors 50,000 (trade visitors 20,000)
Organizer: Changzhou Sports Development Co

2010/09/20 - 23
☎ 0591-8985 1052
🖷 0591-8985 1052
www.czsports.com

6080 2010年常州科技经贸洽谈会
地点：常州国际会展中心，江苏常州
内容：常州科技成果展示，包含农产品、电子化工及新能源环保产品等。
始办年份：2001
周期：每年一届
市场范围：地区性
上届规模‘09：展览面积15,000m²，参展商250家，参观人数30,000人（专业贸易观众15,000人）
承办：常州体育产业发展有限公司

Changzhou Technological and Economic Fair
Venue: Changzhou International Exhibition Center, Changzhou, Jiangsu
Established Year: 2001
Frequency: Annual
Market Area: Regional
Statistics '09: Exhibition Area 15,000m², Exhibitors 250, Visitors 30,000 (trade visitors 15,000)
Organizer: Changzhou Sports Development Co

2010/10/28 - 11/02
☎ 0591-8985 1052
🖷 0591-8985 1052
www.csports.com

6090 2010年中国（常州）国际动漫艺术周
地点：常州国际会展中心，江苏常州
内容：国际动漫产品展示，cosplay真人秀，产品展销
始办年份：2006
周期：每年一届
市场范围：国际性
性质：面向公众
入场券价格：20元
上届规模‘09：展览面积18,000m²，参展商350家（国外展商100家，来自15个国家），参观人数40,000人（专业贸易观众15,000人）
承办：常州体育产业发展有限公司

China (Changzhou) Animation Festival
Venue: Changzhou International Exhibition Center, Changzhou, Jiangsu
Established Year: 2006
Frequency: Annual
Market Area: International
Nature: Open to public
Cost to Attend: RMB 20:-
Statistics '09: Exhibition Area 18,000m², Exhibitors 350 (foreigners 100, came from 15 countries), Visitors 40,000 (trade visitors 15,000)
Organizer: Changzhou Sports Development Co

# 江苏-南京
# Jiangsu-Nanjing

2010/01/15 - 17
☎ 025-8471 4021, 8471 4031
🖷 025-8471 4041
✉ 1999@njhzexpo.com

6100 居民家庭沿街商铺实用技防产品展示会
地点：南京国际展览中心，江苏南京
内容：本届展示会的举办，旨在让人民群众和公安干警进一步认识技防，理解技防，使用技防，提高广大群众的防范意识和能力，促进技术防范向居民家庭，沿街商铺等基础单元延伸，提高全省动态治安防控效能，建设更高水平平安江苏。
首届
市场范围：地区性
性质：面向公众
参展费用：3,500元/展位；350元/m²
预计规模：展出面积3,000m²，参展商30家，参观人数500人
主办：江苏省公安厅
承办：南京汇展展览服务有限公司
地址：江苏省南京市鼓楼区汉中路108号金轮大厦18E（210029）
联系人：常虹，丁萍
MSN: njhzdp@hotmail.com
QQ：469724887

Safety and Security Exhibition
Venue: Nanjing International Exhibition Center, Nanjing, Jiangsu
First Session
Market Area: Regional
Nature: Open to public
Participated Fee: RMB 3,500/booth, Raw Space RMB 350/m²
Organizer: Nanjing Huizhan Exhibition Service Co Ltd
Address: 18E Jinlun Mansion, 108 Hanzhong Road, Gulou Dist, Nanjing, Jiangsu
MSN: njhzdp@hotmail.com

2010/04/12 - 16
☎ 010-6334 5053
🖷 010-6334 5271
✉ xieyun@cmtba.org.cn
www.cmtba.org.cn

6110 2010中国数控机床展览会
（CCMT2010）
地点：南京国际博览中心，江苏南京
内容：数控金切机床；数控成形设备；数控特种加工设备；各种功能部件及配套产品；工业机器人；物流配送系统；柔性线；数控刀具系统；数控检测仪器；量具、工卡具；磨料磨具、涂附磨具、超硬材料及制品；铸造机械及热处理设备；焊接设备；其他相关制造技术和设备

China CNC Machine Tool Fair 2010
(CCMT2010)
Venue: Nanjing International Expo Center, Nanjing, Jiangsu
Profile: CNC metal cutting machine tool, CNC metal forming machinery, Fabrication equipment, key CNC functional component, EDM, Laser, plasma and non-traditional processing machinery, Industrial robot, Material handling equipment, FMC, FMS, Cutting tool, Accessory, Measuring and testing device, Abrasive and its product, Foundry

**始办年份：** 2000
**周期：** 两年一届
**市场范围：** 全国性
**上届规模** '08：展览面积38,992$m^2$(国外展商面积4,096$m^2$)，参展商728家（国外展商75家，来自14个国家），专业贸易观众96,000人
**主办：** 中国机床工具工业协会（CMTBA）
**地址：** 北京市宣武区莲花池东路102号天莲大厦12层（100055）
**联系人：** 谢赟

machinery, Heat treatment equipment, Welding equipment, Others
**Established Year:** 2000
**Frequency:** Biennial
**Market Area:** National
**Statistics '08:** Exhibition Area 38,992$m^2$ (foreigners 4,096$m^2$), Exhibitors 728 (foreigners 75, came from 14 countries), Trade Visitors 96,000
**Organizer:** China Machine Tool & Tool Builders' Assn (CMTBA)
**Address:** 12/F, Tianlian Mansion, 102 Lianhuachi East Road, Xuanwu Dist, Beijing 100055 China
**Contact:** Xie Yun

---

2010/04/27 - 29
☎ 025-8471 4021, 8471 4031
🖷 025-8471 4041
✉ 1999@njhzexpo.com
6120

**2010第九届南京社会公共安全防范产品展览会**
**地点：** 南京国际博览中心，江苏 南京
**内容：** 至今已连续成功举办八届，是江苏省内最早创办和具规模的安防行业盛会。目前该项目已发展成为江苏省公安系统至关重要的一年一度的专业展会。内容包括安全防盗报警系统，公共广播系统，视频监控防范系统，综合布线，电线电缆及周边器材，停车场设备及管理系统，智能"一卡通"，出口入口控制系统，防雷巡更，警用专备，指纹识别，智能楼宇，其它安防产品。
**始办年份：** 2002
**周期：** 每年一届
**市场范围：** 全国性
**参展费用：** 6,800元/展位；净地680元/$m^2$
**上届规模** '09：展览面积10,000$m^2$，参展商220家，参观人数12,000人
**主办：** 江苏省公安厅科技处
**承办：** 南京汇展展览服务有限公司
**地址：** 江苏省南京市汉中路108号金轮大厦18E（210029）
**联系人：** 常虹，丁萍
**MSN：** njhzdp@hotmail.com
**QQ：** 469724887

**Nanjing Public Security Defensive Products Exhibition**
**Venue:** Nanjing International Expo Center, Nanjing, Jiangsu
**Established Year:** 2002
**Frequency:** Annual
**Market Area:** National
**Participated Fee:** RMB 6,800/Booth, Raw Space RMB 680/$m^2$
**Statistics '09:** Exhibition Area 10,000$m^2$, Exhibitors 220, Visitors 12,000
**Organizer:** Nanjing Huizhan Exhibition Service Co Ltd
**Address:** 18E Jinlun Mansion, 108, Hanzhong Rd, Gulou dist, Nanjing, Jiangsu
**MSN:** njhzdp@hotmail.com

---

2010/04/27 - 29
☎ 025-8471 4021, 8471 4031
🖷 025-8471 4041
✉ 1999@njhzexpo.com
6130

**2010南京智能建筑产品博览会**
**地点：** 南京国际博览中心，江苏南京
**内容：** 与南京安防展同期同馆举办，展会现场的"高峰论坛"等活动得到了江苏省建设厅，建设厅科技发展中心和相关协会的大力支持。展会主要展示智能小区，智能家具，楼宇自控，综合布线等相关应用系统。
首届
**市场范围：** 全国性
**预计规模：** 展出面积12,500$m^2$，参展商350家，参观人数15,000人
**主办：** 江苏省建设厅科技发展中心
**承办：** 南京汇展展览服务有限公司
**地址：** 江苏省南京市鼓楼区汉中路108号金轮大厦18E（210029）
**联系人：** 常虹，丁萍
**MSN：** njhzdp@hotmail.com
**QQ：** 469724887

**Nanjing Building Intelligence Exhibition 2010**
**Venue:** Nanjing International Expo Center, Nanjing, Jiangsu First Session
**Market Area:** National
**Organizer:** Nanjing Huizhan Exhibition Service Co Ltd
**Address:** 18E Jinlun Mansion, 108, Hanzhong Rd, Gulou Dist, Nanjing, Jiangsu
**MSN:** njhzdp@hotmail.com

---

2010/06/06 - 07
☎ 025-5285 6743, 5285 6750
🖷 025-5285 6751
✉ k.jiang@jsccpit.gov.cn
huyucheng@jsccpit.gov.cn
www.outsource-china.com.cn
6140

**第三届中国国际服务外包合作大会**
**地点：** 南京国际博览中心，江苏南京
**内容：** 受全球金融危机影响，跨国公司正加速把服务环节从制造业中剥离出来，服务外包产业进入快速发展时期。据预测，未来几年全球服务外包市场将以每年30%－40%的速度增长，并重点向中国等新兴市场转移。作为目前我国服务外包领域层次最高、影响最大、内容最丰富、成效最显著的活动之一，本次大会将通过举办高峰论坛、专题研讨、展览展示和专场对接等一系列活动，深入探讨金融危机后全球服务外包发展新趋势等产业前沿热点问题，加快推动跨国公司业务迅速向我国转移，积极帮助我国服务外包企业提升承接业务和开拓国内外市场能力，努力实现各方共赢。
**始办年份：** 2008
**周期：** 每年一届
**市场范围：** 国际性
**性质：** 面向公众
**参展费用：** 标准展位5,000元
**上届规模** '09：展览面积5,000$m^2$(国外展商面积600$m^2$)，参展商220家（国外展商50家，来自10个国家），参观人数30,000人（专业贸易观众10,000人）
**主办：** 中国贸促会；江苏省人民政府
**承办：** 南京市人民政府；江苏省商务厅；中国贸促会经济信息部；江苏省贸促会
**地址：** 江苏省南京市中华路50号国际经贸大厦2510（210001）
**联系人：** 江荣鑫，胡宇澄

**China International Service Outsourcing Cooperation Conference 2010**
**Venue:** Nanjing International Expo Center, Nanjing, Jiangsu
**Profile:** The 3rd CISOCC is especially designed to serve as the perfect platform for overseas and Chinese service outsourcing buyers and sellers, advisers to meet and discuss the current global opportunities and challenges, share the best solutions and practices. The event also provides a great opportunity to meet the most reliable partners and explore the possibilities of cooperation in offsourcing and outsourcing.
**Established Year:** 2008
**Frequency:** Annual
**Market Area:** International
**Nature:** Open to public
**Participated Fee:** Standard Booth RMB 5,000
**Statistics '09:** Exhibition Area 5,000$m^2$(foreigners 600$m^2$), Exhibitors 220 (foreigners 50, came from 10 countries), Visitors 30,000 (trade visitors 10,000)
**Organizer:** Jiangsu Provincial People's Government, CCPIT
**Address:** Rm. 2510, Jiangsu Intl Trade Bldg, 50 Zhonghua Rd, Nanjing, Jiangsu, China
**Contact:** Jiang Rongxin, Hu Yucheng

2010/09/03 - 05
☎ 025-5285 6783, 5285 6794
🖷 025-5285 6786
✉ maojian@jsccipt.gov.cn
yangxiao@jsccpit.gov.cn
www.cis-expo.com
6150

**第六届中国（南京）国际软件产品博览会**
**地点：**南京国际博览中心，江苏南京
**内容：**数据库、网管软件等平台软件，中间件、网络安全等中间软件，嵌入软件、OA、ERP、财务软件、 CRM、SCM、EAM、系统与安全软件、电力自动化行业应用软件、企业信息化与电子政务软件、电信金融证券软件、动漫游戏、教育体育软件、集成电路产品及各种行业解决方案、软件外包服务、计算机设备、网络建设、通讯设备、移动设备、数码家电、消费电子、IT教育与培训。
**始办年份：**2005
**周期：**每年一届
**市场范围：**国际性
**性质：**面向公众
**参展费用：**中心净地1,000元/m²，其他净地800元/m²；标准展位8,000元（角位加600元/个）
**上届规模 '09：**展览面积15,000m²(国外展商面积3,150m²)，参展商302家（国外展商43家，来自20个国家），参观人数42,881人
**承办：**南京市人民政府；江苏省经济和信息化委员会；江苏省科学技术厅；江苏省版权局；中国贸促会江苏省分会
**地址：**南京市中华路50号江苏国际经贸大厦2520室（210001）
**联系人：**毛健，杨肖

**The 6th China (Nanjing) International Software Product Expo**
**Venue:** Nanjing International Expo Center, Nanjing, Jiangsu
**Profile:** Platform software like database, network management software, platform software, middleware, network security software, embedded software, OA, ERP, financial software, CRM, SCM, EAM, system and security software, smartcard related software, power plant automation software, enterprise informationalization software and e-government software, finance and securities software, animated games, digital entertainment software, education and PE software, IC product and solutions, software outsourcing services, computer equipment, networking construction, communication equipment, mobile equipment, digital home appliances, consumer electronic products, IT education and training.
**Established Year:** 2005
**Frequency:** Annual
**Market Area:** International
**Nature:** Open to public
**Participated Fee:** Raw Space RMB 1,000/m², Standard Booth RMB 8,000 (Corner unit add RMB 600)
**Statistics '09:** Exhibition Area 15,000m²(foreigners 3,150m²), Exhibitors 302 (foreigners 43, came from 20 countries), Visitors 42,881
**Organizer:** The Ministry of Industry and Information Technology; The Ministry of Science & Technology; CCPIT Jiangsu; Jiangsu Government
**Address:** Rm. 2520, Jiangsu Intl Trade Bldg, 50 Zhonghua Rd, Nanjing, China
**Contact:** Mao Jiang, Yang Xiao

2010/09/29 - 10/04
☎ 025-8689 1016, 8689 1020, 8689 1032
🖷 025-8689 1580
✉ auto@njiec.com
www.njae.net
6160

**2010第九届南京国际汽车展览会**
**地点：**南京国际博览中心，江苏南京
**内容：**作为江苏地区规模最大、专业水平最高的车展，将和国内外汽车厂商一起为在本地区展示汽车产业的最新成就、引导汽车消费、繁荣汽车市场
**始办年份：**2002
**周期：**每年一届
**市场范围：**地区性
**性质：**面向公众
**入场券价格：**30元
**参展费用：**室内净地660元/m²，室外净地300元/m²，标准展位5,500元(3x3m)
**上届规模 '09：**展览面积66,000m²(国外展商面积5,516m²)，参展商67家（国外展商18家），参观人数220,000人
**主办：**南京市人民政府；江苏省经济和信息化委员会；中国贸促会江苏省分会
**承办：**江苏省汽车行业协会；南京奥意国际汽车展览有限公司
**地址：**南京龙蟠路88号南京国际展览中心100室（210037）
**联系人：**刘吉娟，郝祥武

**2010 Nanjing Auto Exposition**
**Venue:** Nanjing International Expo Center, Nanjing, Jiangsu
**Profile:** Nanjing Auto Exposition was awarded "Nanjing Outstanding Exposition Brand" by Nanjing Municipal People's Government 3 years in a row, which demonstrated the recognition and affirmation from the public. The show 2009 welcomed 382 vehicles of 67 different brands as exhibitors. Trade visitors from different cities of the country even abroad visited the show. Nanjing City, as an important and active market for auto industry, has played more and more important role in countrywide auto industry as well as in the assembly's production industry.
**Established Year:** 2002
**Frequency:** Annual
**Market Area:** Regional
**Nature:** Open to public
**Cost to Attend:** RMB 30
**Participated Fee:** Indoor Raw Space RMB 660/m², Outdoor Raw Space RMB 300/m², Standard Booth RMB 5,500
**Statistics '09:** Exhibition Area 66,000m²(foreigners 5,516m²), Exhibitors 67 (foreigners 18), Visitors 220,000
**Organizer:** Jiangsu Auto Industry Assn; Nanjing AE International Exhibition Co Ltd
**Address:** Rm. 100, No.88 Longpan Rd, Nanjing International Exhibition Center, Jiangsu, China
**Contact:** Gina LAU, Xiangwu Hao

2010/11/18 - 20
☎ 021-3428 0006
🖷 021-3428 5006
✉ nuogaisi2004@126.com
www.ch-solar.com
6180

**2010第11届中国太阳能光伏会议暨展览**
**地点：**南京国际博览中心，江苏南京
**周期：**两年一届
**市场范围：**国际性
**入场券价格：**专业和贸易观众免费
**主办：**中国可再生能源学会
**承办：**江苏省光伏产业协会；诺盖斯国际展览集团
**地址：**上海市龙吴路1500号交大科技园区A座508室（200231）
**联系人：**董振，路瑶
**MSN：**nuogaisi@hotmail.com
**QQ：**942859406

**2010 The 11th China Solar PV Conference and Exhibition**
**Venue:** Nanjing International Expo Center, Nanjing, Jiangsu
**Frequency:** Biennial
**Market Area:** International
**Cost to Attend:** Free to Professional and Trade Visitors
**Sponsor:** China Renewable Energy Society
**Organizer:** Jiangsu Photovoltaic Industry Assn; Newgrace International Exhibition Group
**Address:** 508, A Bldg, Technology Park of Jiaotong University, 1500 Longwu Rd., Shanghai, China
**Contact:** Dong Zhen, Janet Lu
**MSN:** nuogaisi@hotmail.com

# 江苏-无锡
# Jiangsu-Wuxi

2010/11/06 - 08
☎ 0510-8271 2771, 8271 8772
🖷 0510-82727230
✉ idexpo@vip.163.com
www.id-expo.cn
6190

**第八届中国（无锡）国际工业设计博览会**
**地点：** 无锡体育会展中心，江苏无锡
**始办年份：** 2000
**周期：** 每年一届
**市场范围：** 国际性
**性质：** 面向公众
**参展费用：** 500元/m²
**上届规模** '09：展览面积12,000m²(国外展商面积3,000m²)，参展商152家（国外展商38家，来自6个国家），参观人数50,000人（专业贸易观众15,000人）
**主办：** 国家知识产权局；科技部；江苏省人民政府
**承办：** 无锡市人民政府
**地址：** 江苏省无锡市学前街168号科技大厦303室（214001）
**联系人：** 倪程云，吴伟忠
**QQ：** 87684062，5078613

**The 8th China (Wuxi) International Industrial Design Expo**
**Venue:** Wuxi Sports Exhibition Center, Wuxi, Jiangsu
**Established Year:** 2000
**Frequency:** Annual
**Market Area:** International
**Nature:** Open to public
**Participated Fee:** RMB 500/m²
**Statistics '09:** Exhibition Area 12,000m²(foreigners 3,000m²), Exhibitors 152 (foreigners 38, came from 6 countries), Visitors 50,000 (trade visitors 15,000)
**Organizer:** The State Intellectual Property Office; Jiangsu Provincial Government
**Sponsor:** Wuxi Municipal People's Government
**Address:** Rm. 303, Science & Technology Mansion, 168 Xueqian St, Wuxi, Jiangsu, China

# 江西-南昌
# Jiangxi-Nanchang

2010/04/09 - 11
☎ 021-5266 5938
🖷 021-5266 8178
✉ realexpo@sh163.net
www.antiquefurniturefair.com
6195

**第十届中国国际眼科和视光技术及设备展览会**
**地点：** 南昌国际展览中心，江西南昌
**内容：** "中国国际眼科和视光技术及设备展览会"经过主办单位多年打造，已经成为行业内著名品牌的展会，每年来自中国31个省市的2000多名眼科医生踊跃报名参会，国内外厂商纷纷借此机会推介自己最新的眼科和视光设备，现场贸易活跃，成交额逐年快速增加。
**始办年份：** 1999
**周期：** 每年一届
**市场范围：** 国际性
**主办：** 华东六省一市医学会眼科分会；中国国际科技会议中心
**承办：** 上海瑞欧展览服务有限公司
**地址：** 上海市中山北路2790号杰地大厦1007室（200063）
**联系人：** 陈小姐，宋小姐

**10th Intl Congress of Ophthalmology and Optometry China** (COOC 2010)
**Venue:** Nanchang International Exhibition Center, Nanchang, Jiangxi
**Profile:** COOC has been the most famous brand exhibition in Ophthalmological industry in China through work-hard for several years. It attracts over 2000 ophthalmologists from 31 provinces in China
**Established Year:** 1999
**Frequency:** Annual
**Market Area:** International
**Organizer:** Shanghai Real Exhibition Service Co., Ltd.
**Address:** Rm. 1007, 10F, Jie Di Plaza, No. 2790, Zhongshan Road(N), Shanghai
**Contact:** Amy Chen

# 吉林-长春
# Jilin-Changchun

2010/03/08 - 10
☎ 0431-8460 6572, 8460 6571
🖷 0431-8460 6147
✉ weidagg2008@163.com
6210

**2010长春第十三届广告博览会**
**地点：** 长春国际会展中心，吉林长春
**内容：** 雕刻喷绘设备、霓虹灯及制作技术、广告制作系统、广告印刷材料及物料、印刷及办公自动化、户内外媒体推广范围、展览展示媒体、广告礼品
**始办年份：** 1997
**周期：** 每年一届
**市场范围：** 全国性
**性质：** 面向公众
**参展费用：** 净地500元/m²（36m²起）
**上届规模** '09：展览面积10,000m²，参展商200家，参观人数5,000人（专业贸易观众2,000人）
**主办：** 长春市广告协会
**承办：** 长春维达展览服务有限公司；北方工商业展览有限公司
**地址：** 长春市会展大街100号会展中心综合办公楼110室（130033）
**联系人：** 李经理
**QQ：** 12428235

**13th Changchun Advertisement Exposition 2010**
**Venue:** Changchun International Conference & Exhibition Center, Changchun, Jilin
**Established Year:** 1997
**Frequency:** Annual
**Market Area:** National
**Nature:** Open to public
**Participated Fee:** Raw Space RMB 500/m² (36m²起)
**Statistics '09:** Exhibition Area 10,000m², Exhibitors 200, Visitors 5,000 (trade visitors 2,000)
**Organizer:** Changchen Weida Exhibition Service Co Ltd

2010/03/30 - 04/01
☎ 024-2285 3303
℻ 024-2285 3500
✉ liaoningsg@163.com
6220

**2010第22届中国长春国际医疗器械卫生产业博览会**
**地点：**长春国际会展中心，吉林长春
**内容：**诊断设备：病理诊断设备、功能检查设备、康复理疗设备、超声诊断设备、X线影像诊断设备、心脑电监护设备、扫描设备、生化检验设备、内窥镜检查设备、光学仪器、以及神经科、五官科、骨科、胃肠科、肛门、泌尿科、妇产科等检查诊断设备。治疗设备；辅助设备：口腔设备；眼科设备；辅助器材；医院信息管理系统；其它设备。
**市场范围：**国际性
**性质：**面向公众
**主办：**辽宁深港展览服务有限公司
**地址：**沈阳市和平区和平北大街28号（110002）
**联系人：**吕红

**22nd Intl Medical Equipment Industry Hygiene Industrial Expo Changchun China 2010**
**Venue:** Changchun International Conference & Exhibition Center, Changchun, Jilin
**Market Area:** International
**Nature:** Open to public
**Organizer:** Liaoning Shengang Exhibition Co Ltd

2010/04/08 - 09
☎ 0431-8693 1008, 8783 5764
℻ 04318783 5765
✉ ntcpjg@126.com
6230

**第五届全国粳稻米大会**
**地点：**长春市华苑宾馆，吉林长春
**内容：**粳稻米产业高峰论坛、粳米及米制品展洽会、优质食味粳米评选与推介会、全国粳稻米产业联盟年会
**始办年份：**2006
**周期：**每年一届
**市场范围：**全国性
**入场券价格：**800元/人
**参展费用：**产品展位500元/个，设备展位2,000元/个
**上届规模**'09：展览面积600m²，专业贸易观众500人
**主办：**全国粳稻米产业联盟；中国农业科技东北创新中心；吉林省农特产品加工协会
**地址：**长春市西安大路5333号（130062）
**联系人：**赵玉敏，韩玉娇
**QQ：**724088225

**5th National Rice Conference**
Venue： Changchun Huayuan Hotel, Changchu, Jilin
**Profile:** Rice industry summit forum, rice and rice products fair, High quality rice cultivar competition
**Established Year:** 2006
**Frequency:** Annual
**Market Area:** National
**Cost to Attend:** RMB 800
**Participated Fee:** Products RMB 500/booth, Equipment RMB 2,000/booth
**Statistics '09:** Exhibition Area 600m², Trade visitors 500)
**Organizer:** Jilin Agricultural Product Processing Assn
**Address:** 5333 Xi' an Road, Changchun 130062, Jilin

# 辽宁-大连
# Liaoning-Dalian

2010/04/09 - 12
☎ 0411-8253 8642
℻ 0411-8253 8678
✉ my12336@126.com
www.sinoexhibition.com
6240

**第十五届中国国际建筑装饰材料展览会**
**地点：**大连星海会展中心，辽宁大连
**内容：**门窗、幕墙、五金及设备、工程公司；洁具、陶瓷、石材、水泥制品 铺地材料、铺装技术及设备；橱柜及厨房电器、配套用品；各类油漆、涂料、防水材料、橡塑制品；采暖、空调、通风、燃气技术及太阳能产品；照明灯饰、LED显示器、美化工程及园林设施；大型工艺品、室内装饰用品及居室用品；管材、管件、阀门；智能小区、监控系统、楼宇对讲设备；建筑五金、电动工具展区
**始办年份：**1996
**周期：**每年一届
**市场范围：**国际性
**性质：**面向公众
**参展费用：**5,500元
**主办：**大连北方国际展览股份有限公司
**地址：**大连市中山区同兴街二十五号世贸大厦二十五楼（116000）
**联系人：**王常虹
**MSN：**my12336@hotmail.com

**15th China Intl Construction & Decoration Materials Exhibition**
**Venue:** Dalian Xinghai Convention & Exhibition Center, Dalian, Liaoning
**Established Year:** 1996
**Frequency:** Annual
**Market Area:** International
**Nature:** Open to public
**Participated Fee:** RMB 5,500/booth
**Organizer:** Dalian Northern International Exhibition Limited Company
**Address:** 25F. Dalian World Trade Center, No. 25 Tongxing St., Zhongshan Dist, Dalian
**Contact:** Rainbow
**MSN:** my12336@hotmail.com

2010/05/12 - 14
☎ 0411-8378 7049, 8231 0681/82
℻ 0411-8378 7049, 8231 0692
✉ sandy8176@163.com
www.dliif.cn
6250

**2010大连国际工业博览会**
**地点：**大连星海会展中心，辽宁大连
**内容：**工业自动化、仪器仪表、低压电器、电力电工技术与设备、电子设备、电子元器件、焊接、铸造、热处理技术与设备、机床、工模具、工业清洁设备、清洁剂、给排水、水处理泵管阀、暖通、制冷、空调、劳动保护用品等
**始办年份：**2005
**周期：**每年一届
**市场范围：**国际性
**参展费用：**标准展位5,600元/9m²， 净地500元/m²
**上届规模**'09：展览面积30,000m²(国外展商面积1,872m²)，参展商829家（国外展商49家，来自15个国家），参观人数29,083人（专业贸易观众3,596人）
**主办：**辽宁省机械工程学会；大连华展展览服务有限公司
**地址：**大连市中山区友好路211号商务特区1203室（116001）
**联系人：**王晓峰，魏娟
**MSN：**sandy8176@hotmail.com.cn
**QQ：**13491902

**2010 Dalian International Industry Fair**
**Venue:** Dalian Xinghai Convention & Exhibition Center, Dalian, Liaoning
**Established Year:** 2005
**Frequency:** Annual
**Market Area:** International
**Participated Fee:** Standard Booth RMB 5,600/9m², Raw Space RMB 500/m²
**Statistics '09:** Exhibition Area 30,000m² (foreigners 1,872m²), Exhibitors 829 (foreigners 49, came from 15 countries), Visitors 29,083 (trade visitors 3,596)
**Organizer:** Liaoning Institute of Mechanical; Dalian Huazhan Exhibition & Service Co Ltd
**Contact:** Xiaofeng Wang, Juan Wei
**MSN:** sandy8176@hotmail.com.cn

2010/05/29 - 31
☎ 0411-8253 2833
🖷 0411-8265 2581
✉ leaf_0432@163.com

6260

**2010第三届大连市出口企业产品展销会**
**地点**：大连星海会展中心，辽宁大连
**内容**：为了贯彻国务院提出的“保增长、扩内需、调结构、促发展”的要求，为了帮助出口企业克服国际金融危机造成的国外市场需求下降，国内产品出口受阻的困难，遵照市领导要帮助出口企业消化库存、努力开拓国内市场
**始办年份**：2009
**周期**：每年两届
**市场范围**：地区性
**性质**：面向公众
**参展费用**：标准展位1,000元
**上届规模** ‘09：展览面积7,500m²，参展商300家，参观人数60,000人
**主办**：大连市人民政府
**承办**：中国贸促会大连市分会;中国国际商会大连商会
**地址**：大连市中山区解放街9号万达大厦1004室（116001）
**联系人**：叶丽兰，解开
**MSN**: yelilan@hotmail.com
**QQ**：41580408

**Dalian Export Enterprise Products Fair**
**Venue**: Dalian Xinghai Convention & Exhibition Center, Dalian, Liaoning
**Established Year**: 2009
**Frequency**: Biannual
**Market Area**: Regional
**Nature**: Open to public
**Participated Fee**: Standard Booth RMB 1,000
**Statistics '09**: Exhibition Area 7,500m², Exhibitors 300, Visitors 60,000
**Organizer**: CCPIT Dalian Sub-council
**MSN**: yelilan@hotmail.com

2010/08/10 - 12
☎ 0411-8231 0681/2
🖷 0411-8231 0627
✉ dlylz@126.com
www.dlshuangxin.com

6270

**2010 大连国际医疗器械展览会**
**地点**：大连星海会展中心，辽宁大连
**内容**：医用影像类：X线诊断设备、超声诊断设备、核医学设备；监护类：动态监护、血氧监护、手术监护；手术类：无影灯、手术床、麻醉机、呼吸机；医用光学仪器：各种显微镜、硬式、纤维导光式；检测类：血球计数仪、免疫分析仪。仪器及辅助类：各种医用床、护理设备，消毒灭菌设备等。口腔、眼科类；医用车辆类；医用耗材
**始办年份**：2008
**周期**：每年一届
**市场范围**：国际性
**性质**：对专业贸易观众开放
**参展费用**：国内企业：标准展位4,800元/3x3m，净地400元/m²；国外企业：标准展位1,200美元，净地120美元/m²
**上届规模** ‘09：展览面积6,000m²(国外展商面积1,500m²)，参展商180家（国外展商26家，来自7个国家），参观人数9,325人（专业贸易观众893人）
**主办**：中国贸促会大连市分会；中国国际商会大连商会大连市会；大连市卫生局；大连市华展展览服务有限公司
**承办**：大连双新展览策划有限公司
**地址**：辽宁省大连市中山区友好路211号商务特区1203室（116001）
**联系人**：周英，王启艳

**2010 Dalian Intl Exhibition for Medical Instrument**
**Venue**: Dalian Xinghai Convention & Exhibition Center, Dalian, Liaoning
**Profile**: Medical Imaging: X-ray diagnosis equipment, nuclear medical equipment; Guardianship categories: dynamic monitoring, surgical monitoring; Surgical categories; Medical optical instruments; Test categories; Apparatus and auxiliary categories; Oral, ophthalmic categories: oral and ophthalmic a variety of instruments, equipment, materials; Medical vehicles categories: ambulances, cars and so on epidemic prevention; Medical supplies: disposable medical supplies, dressing packs.
**Established Year**: 2008
**Frequency**: Annual
**Market Area**: International
**Nature**: Trade only
**Participated Fee**: USD 1,200/booth, Raw Space USD 400/m²
**Statistics '09**: Exhibition Area 6,000m²(foreigners 1,500m²), Exhibitors 180 (foreigners 26, came from 7 countries), Visitors 9,325 (trade visitors 893)
**Organizer**: CCPIT Dalian Sub-council
**Organizer**: Dalian Shuangxin Exhibition Co
**Address**: Rm. 1203, No. 211 Friendship Rd, Zhongshan Dist, Dalian, Liaoning 116001, China
**Contact**: Zhou Ying, Wang Qiyan

2010/08/12 - 14
☎ 0411-8231 0653, 8231 0692
🖷 0411-8231 0692, 8231 0691
✉ lianxiang83918@sohu.com
www.dongbeizhanlan.com

6280

**2010大连国际广告技术与设备展览会**
**地点**：大连星海会展中心，辽宁大连
**内容**：广告制作技术设备、广告材料及物料、户内外广告媒体、广告摄影技术及设备、标识系统、展览展示器材、新媒体技术设备，创意创新设计产业、大屏幕及户外媒体
**始办年份**：2008
**周期**：每年一届
**市场范围**：国际性
**参展费用**：国内企业4,800元/9m²，境外企业1,600美元/9m²；净地：国内企业450元/m²，国外企业160美元/m²
**上届规模** ‘09：展览面积6,000m²(国外展商面积900m²)，参展商132家（国外展商21家，来自9个国家），参观人数9,793人（专业贸易观众1,005人）
**主办**：辽宁省广告行业协会
**承办**：大连华展展览服务有限公司
**地址**：大连市中山区友好路211号商务特区1203室（116001）
**联系人**：李孟，铉英

**Dalian Ad Exhibition**
**Venue**: Dalian Xinghai Convention & Exhibition Center, Dalian, Liaoning
**Established Year**: 2008
**Frequency**: Annual
**Market Area**: International
**Participated Fee**: Standard Booth RMB 1,600/9m², Raw Space USD 160/m²
**Statistics '09**: Exhibition Area 6,000m²(foreigners 900m²), Exhibitors 132 (foreigners 21, came from 9 countries), Visitors 9,793 (trade visitors 1,005)
**Organizer**: Dalian Huazhan Exhibition Service

2010/08/18 - 22
☎ 0411-8282 2356, 8253 2822, 8253 2823
🖷 0411-8265 0186
✉ auto-show@ccpitdl.org
dltyc@hotmail.com
www.auto-show.com.cn

6290

**2010（第十五届）大连国际汽车展览会**
**地点**：大连星海会展中心；大连世界博览广场，辽宁 大连
**内容**：乘用车、商用车、专用车、新能源汽车、房车、摩托车、游艇；各种汽车工业新能源、汽车工业环保技术与产品；汽车总成及零部件；汽车制造设备、工艺装备；汽车检测、维修保养设备及工具；汽车改装、电子电器、影音娱乐、装饰品等汽车用品；汽车用油、汽车护理用品；停车场技术设备。
**周期**：每年一届
**上届规模** ‘09：展览面积100,000m²，参展商536家，参观人数350,000人
**主办**：中国贸促会；中国贸促会汽车行业分会；中国汽车工业协会；中国汽车工程学会；中国汽车工业进出口总公司；大连市人民政府
**承办**：中国贸促会大连市分会；大连保税区管理委员会；大连国际商会展览公司
**地址**：大连市中山区解放街9号万达大厦1006室中国贸促会大连市分会（116001）
**联系人**：姜先生，滕先生，王小姐

**15th Dalian International Automotive Exhibition**
**Venue**: Dalian Xinghai Convention and Exhibition Center; Dalian World Expo Center, Dalian, Liaoning
**Profile**: Various passenger cars, commercial vehicles, special vehicles; Automobile environment new technology and products; Automobile parts and automobile accessories; Automobile manufacturing technological equipments; Automobile repair equipments and tools; Automobile tuning parts and automobile electronic and Automobile ornaments; Various automobile use oils and auto care products; Technology and equipment of parking place
**Frequency**: Annual
**Statistics '09**: Exhibition Area 100,000m², Exhibitors 536, Visitors 350,000
**Organizer**: CCPIT; CCPIT Automotive Sub-Council; China Assn of Automobile Manufacturers; Society of Automotive Engineers of China; China National Automotive Industry
**Address**: CCPIT Dalian Sub-Council, Rm. 1006 Wanda Mansion, No.9 Jiefang St., Zhongshan Dist, Dalian 116001, China
**Contact**: Mr Jiang, Mr Teng, Ms Wang

2010/11/01 - 04
☎ 010-5919 4628, 5919 4403
🖷 010-6591 8986
✉ david@agri.gov.cn
www.cafte.gov.cn
6310

**中国国际渔业博览会**
**地点：**大连世博广场，辽宁大连
**始办年份：**1996
**周期：**每年一届
**市场范围：**国际性
**入场券价格：**预登记观众50元，现场观众100元
**上届规模**'09：展览面积15,000m²，参展商726家（国外展商300家，来自14个国家），专业贸易观众15,000人
**主办：**中国国际贸促会农业行业分会
**地址：**北京市朝阳区麦子店街20号楼805房间（100125）
**联系人：**孙长光，潘久

**CHINA FISHERIES & SEAFOOD EXPO**
**Venue:** Dalian World Expo Center, Dalian, Liaoning
**Established Year:** 1996
**Frequency:** Annual
**Market Area:** International
**Cost to Attend:** Pre-Registration RMB 50:-, On-site RMB 100:-
**Statistics '09:** Exhibition Area 15,000m², Exhibitors 726 (foreigners 300, came from 14 countries), Visitors 15,000 (trade visitors 15,000)
**Organizer:** CCPIT-SSA
**Address:** Building 20, Maizidian St., Chaoyang Dist, Beijing

# 辽宁-沈阳
# Liaoning-Shenyang

2010/01/16 - 16
☎ 024-2285 3303
🖷 024-2285 3500
✉ liaoningsg@163.com
6320

**2010第十六届沈阳药交会**
**地点：**沈阳科学宫会展中心，辽宁沈阳
**内容：**药品展区、保健品展区、性保健品展区、大包品种展区、药店展示区、药化妆品展区、医院采购展示区、东北药店诚信联盟展示区、东北药店诚信联盟展示区、长白山人参展区
**市场范围：**全国性
**性质：**面向公众
**主办：**辽宁深港展览服务有限公司
**地址：**沈阳市和平区和平北大街28号（110002）
**联系人：**吕红

**16th Shenyang Medicine Fair**
**Venue:** Shenyang Science Centrum Exhibition Center, Shenyang, Liaoning
**Market Area:** National
**Nature:** Open to public
**Organizer:** Liaoning Shengang Exhibition Service Co Ltd

2010/03/01 - 02
☎ 024-2587 8888, 13304008366
🖷 024-2585 0618
6330

**第37届东北药品保健品交易会**
**地点：**沈阳北站华府天地，辽宁沈阳
**内容：**医药类：处方药、中成药、非处方药、各种新药特药、中药材、中间体生物制品、微量元素制品、藏药、蒙药、中医药、原料药、国家中药保护品种、天然药物药材；保健品类：保健用品、绿色健康食品、保健食品、保健美容品、滋补保健品；成人用品：计生用品、保健器械、情趣用品、计划生育药具、性保健品、情侣用品
**参展费用：**1,800元/(3x1m)，2,800元/(3x2m)，3,800元/3x3m
**主办：**天津天士力医药集团；辽宁天士力大药房连锁有限公司
**承办：**沈阳明日科技展览贸易有限公司

**37th North-East China Medicine and Health Products Fair**
**Venue:** Shenyang North Station, Shenyang, Liaoning
**Participated Fee:** RMB 3,800/3x3m
**Organizer:** Shengyang Mingri Tech Exhibition and Trade Co Ltd

2010/03/11 - 14
☎ 024-2392 5225
🖷 024-2392 2432
✉ bfexpo@126.com
www.bfexpo.com.cn
6340

**2010第三届东北孕婴童产品展览会**
**地点：**辽宁工业展览馆，辽宁沈阳
**内容：**孕婴用品、食品、服饰床品、儿童家具、婴幼儿电器、优生技术、早教摄影机构、服务机构
**始办年份：**2009
**周期：**每年一届
**市场范围：**国际性
**主办：**北方工商业展览有限公司
**地址：**沈阳市三好街93号金源大厦5楼（110004）
**联系人：**李本琦

**3rd Baby and Children Products Show**
**Venue:** Liaoning Industrial Exhibition Hall, Shenyang, Liaoning
**Established Year:** 2009
**Frequency:** Annual
**Market Area:** International
**Statistics '09:** Exhibitors
**Organizer:** Northern Industrial & Commercial Exhibition Co Ltd

2010/03/11 - 14
☎ 024-2392 0245, 2397 5766
🖷 024-2392 2432
✉ bfexpo@126.com
http://kq.bfexpo.com.cn
6350

**2010第十二届中国东北口腔设备及材料展览会暨东北国际口腔学术交流会**
**地点：**辽宁工业展览馆，辽宁沈阳
**内容：**口腔医疗器械、设备、材料、耗材、保健品、科教类等
**始办年份：**1999
**周期：**每年一届
**市场范围：**国际性
**上届规模**'09：展览面积8,000m²(国外展商面积2,000m²)，参展商300家（国外展商80家），参观人数20,000人
**主办：**中国贸促会辽宁省分会
**承办：**北方工商业展览有限公司
**地址：**沈阳市三好街93号金源大厦5楼（110004）
**联系人：**纪晓帆

**12th China Northeast Intl Dental Equipment & Affiliated Facilities Exhibition 2010/Northeast Intl Symposium On Oral Health**
**Venue:** Liaoning Industrial Exhibition Hall, Shenyang, Liaoning
**Established Year:** 1999
**Frequency:** Annual
**Market Area:** International
**Statistics '09:** Exhibition Area 8,000m²(foreigners 2,000m²), Exhibitors 300 (foreigners 80), Visitors 20,000
**Organizer:** CCPIT Liaoning Branch; Northern Industrial & Commercial Exhibition Co Ltd

2010/03/18 - 21
☎ 024-2391 3336
🖷 024-2392 2432
✉ bfexpo@126.com
www.bfexpo.com.cn

6360 **东北第14届国际焊接、切割、激光技术设备展览会**
**地点**：辽宁工业展览馆，辽宁沈阳
**内容**：焊接设备、切割设备、激光设备、焊接辅机具、焊材等
**始办年份**：1996
**周期**：每年一届
**市场范围**：国际性
**上届规模** '09：展览面积30,000m²，参展商106家，参观人数36,322人
**主办**：辽宁省焊接学会；沈阳市焊接学会；沈阳装备制造行业协会
**承办**：北方工商业展览有限公司
**地址**：沈阳市三好街93号金源大厦5楼（110004）
**联系人**：王帅

**14th China (Northeast) Intl Welding, Cutting, & Laser Technology and Equipment Exhibition**
**Venue:** Liaoning Industrial Exhibition Hall, Shenyang, Liaoning
**Established Year:** 1996
**Frequency:** Annual
**Market Area:** International
**Statistics '09:** Exhibition Area 30,000m², Exhibitors 106, Visitors 36,322
**Organizer:** Liaoning Province Welding Institute; Shenyang Province Welding Institute; Shenyang Equips to Make the profession Assn; Northern Industrial & Commercial Exhibition Co Ltd

2010/03/18 - 21
☎ 024-2392 1795
🖷 024-2392 2432
✉ bfexpo@126.com
www.bfexpo.com.cn

6370 **2010第11届中国东北国际塑胶机械及包装工业展览会**
**地点**：辽宁工业展览馆，辽宁沈阳
**内容**：注塑机；辅助设备；挤出机及挤出机生产线；吹塑机；包装机械模具及零部件、后加工及其它加工机械、原料、辅料、预加工、回收设备等
**始办年份**：2000
**周期**：每年一届
**市场范围**：国际性
**上届规模** '09：展览面积30,000m²，参展商852家，参观人数36,322人
**主办**：沈阳市装备制造行业协会
**承办**：北方工商业展览有限公司
**地址**：沈阳市三好街93号金源大厦5楼（110004）
**联系人**：江月

**11th Northeast China Intl Plastics Machinery & Packaging Exhibition 2010**
**Venue:** Liaoning Industrial Exhibition Hall, Shenyang, Liaoning
**Established Year:** 2000
**Frequency:** Annual
**Market Area:** International
**Statistics '09:** Exhibition Area 30,000m², Exhibitors 852, Visitors 36,322
**Organizer:** Shenyang Equips to Make the profession Assn; Northern Industrial & Commercial Exhibition Co Ltd

2010/03/18 - 21
☎ 024-2397 4129
🖷 024-2392 2432
✉ bfexpo@126.com
www.bfexpo.com.cn

6380 **第十一届中国东北国际物流技术及运输系统展览会**
**地点**：辽宁工业展览馆，辽宁沈阳
**内容**：升降设备、起重设备、叉车、仓储设备、货架、清洁系统、工业门、包装设备、托盘、称重设备、分、拣选设备等
**始办年份**：2000
**周期**：每年一届
**市场范围**：国际性
**上届规模** '09：展览面积30,000m²，参展商852家，参观人数36,322人
**主办**：沈阳市装备制造行业协会
**承办**：北方工商业展览有限公司
**地址**：沈阳市三好街93号金源大厦5楼（110004）
**联系人**：康雪

**Northeast 11th Intl physical Distribution & Transport System Exhibition China 2010**
**Venue:** Liaoning Industrial Exhibition Hall, Shenyang, Liaoning
**Established Year:** 2000
**Frequency:** Annual
**Market Area:** International
**Statistics '09:** Exhibition Area 30,000m², Exhibitors 852, Visitors 36,322
**Organizer:** Shenyang Equips to Make the profession Assn Northern Industrial & Commercial Exhibition Co Ltd

2010/03/18 - 21
☎ 024-2392 1795, 13478291039
23975299
🖷 024-2392 2432
✉ bfexpo@126.com
www.bfexpo.com.cn

6390 **2010第11届中国东北国际机床、工模具技术展览会**
**地点**：辽宁工业展览馆，辽宁沈阳
**内容**：机床、刀具、量具、夹具产品、模具、模具机械设备等
**始办年份**：1999
**周期**：每年一届
**市场范围**：国际性
**上届规模** '09：展览面积30,000m²(国外展商面积6,000m²)，参展商852家（国外展商58家），参观人数36,322人
**主办**：沈阳市装备制造行业协会
**承办**：北方工商业展览有限公司
**地址**：沈阳市三好街93号金源大厦5楼（110004）
**联系人**：张秀双

**Northeast 11th Intl Machine Tool and Tools & Moulds Technique Exhibition China 2010**
**Venue:** Liaoning Industrial Exhibition Hall, Shenyang, Liaoning
**Established Year:** 1999
**Frequency:** Annual
**Market Area:** International
**Statistics '09:** Exhibition Area 30,000m²(foreigners 6,000m²), Exhibitors 852 (foreigners 58), Visitors 36,322
**Organizer:** Shenyang Equips to Make the profession Assn; Northern Industrial & Commercial Exhibition Co Ltd

2010/03/19 - 22
☎ 024-2388 5066
🖷 024-2389 2399
✉ lnxzs@126.com

6400 **2010辽宁第十四届国际广告四新技术暨印刷/数码技术设备展示会**
**地点**：辽宁工业展览馆，辽宁沈阳
**内容**：数码喷绘设备、雕刻切刻设备、热转印、标牌、标识、LED光照产品及技术、霓虹灯及光电设备、照明工程技术产品、印刷机械、印刷材料、数码摄影、感光材料及摄影用品、投影机
**始办年份**：1997
**周期**：每年一届
**市场范围**：全国性
**性质**：面向公众
**入场券价格**：10元
**参展费用**：4800～6000元
**上届规模** '09：展览面积15,000m²，参展商200多家，专业贸易观众20,000人
**主办**：辽宁省展览贸易集团辽宁工业展览馆；沈阳市信亚会展服务中心
**地址**：沈阳市和平区彩塔街38号202室（110004）
**联系人**：李新
**QQ**：514211478

**Shenyang AD and Digital Exhibition**
**Venue:** Liaoning Industrial Exhibition Hall, Shenyang, Liaoning
**Established Year:** 1997
**Frequency:** Annual
**Market Area:** National
**Nature:** Open to public
**Cost to Attend:** RMB 10:-
**Participated Fee:** RMB 6,000/booth
**Statistics '09:** Exhibition Area 15,000m², Exhibitors 200, Trade Visitors 20,000
**Organizer:** Shenyang Xinya Exhibition Center

2010/03/21 - 23
☎ 024-2325 6988
🖷 024-2325 6988
✉ iecsy@126.com
www.iecsy.com

6420

**2010第五届中国东北畜牧及饲料工业展览会**
**同期举办：第五届东北农业生产资料交易会**
**地点：**辽宁农业展览馆，辽宁沈阳
**内容：**优良种畜禽、动物保健品、饲料及饲料相关产品、畜牧机械展区机械与畜产品、加工展区科技与媒体展区
**始办年份：**1999
**周期：**其它周期
**市场范围：**国际性
**参展费用：**标准展位3,600元
**主办：**沈阳市饲料工业协会；沈阳市国际贸易促进委员会；沈阳国际展览公司
**地址：**沈阳市和平区十一纬路云集东巷32号（1-8-1室）沈阳国际展览公司（110003）
**联系人：**李男

**5th North-East China Livestock and Feed Exhibition**
**Venue:** Liaoning Agricultural Exhibition Hall, Shenyang, Liaoning
**Established Year:** 1999
**Market Area:** International
**Participated Fee:** Standard Booth RMB 3,600
**Organizer:** Shenyang Intl Exhibition Co

2010/03/23 - 25
☎ 024-2285 3303
🖷 024-2285 3500
✉ liaoningsg@163.com

6430

**2010第21届（春季）沈阳国际医疗器械设备展览会**
**地点：**沈阳科学宫会展中心，辽宁沈阳
**内容：**诊断设备：病理诊断设备、功能检查设备、康复理疗设备、超声诊断设备、X线影像诊断设备、心脑电监护设备、扫描设备、生化检验设备、内窥镜检查设备、光学仪器、以及神经科、五官科、骨科、胃肠科、肛门、泌尿科、妇产科等检查诊断设备。治疗设备；辅助设备；口腔设备；眼科设备；辅助器材；医院信息管理系统；其它设备
**始办年份：**2001
**周期：**每年两届
**市场范围：**国际性
**性质：**面向公众
**上届规模‘09：**展览面积40,000m²，参展商1,400家
**主办：**辽宁深港展览服务有限公司
**地址：**沈阳市和平区和平北大街28号（110002）
**联系人：**吕红

**21st Shenyang Intl Medical Equipment Fair 2010**
**Venue:** Shenyang Science Centrum Exhibition Center, Shenyang, Liaoning
**Established Year:** 2001
**Frequency:** Biannual
**Market Area:** International
**Nature:** Open to public
**Statistics '09:** Exhibition Area 40,000m², Exhibitors 1,400
**Organizer:** Liaoning Shengang Exhibition Service Co Ltd

2010/03/25 - 27
☎ 024-2384 8948
🖷 024-2392 2432
✉ bfexpo@126.com
www.bfexpo.com.cn

6440

**2010中国（沈阳）国际建设科技博览会暨**
**第八届东北建筑节能、新型墙体材料及设备展览会**
**地点：**辽宁工业展览馆，辽宁沈阳
**内容：**新型墙体材料；建筑保温系统、隔热材料；涂料；防水材料；胶类；各种添加剂、砂浆产品；建筑机械、干粉砂浆设备及砌块设备等
**始办年份：**2003
**周期：**每年一届
**市场范围：**国际性
**上届规模‘09：**展览面积30,000m²，参展商400家，参观人数30,000人
**主办：**沈阳市人民政府
**承办：**北方工商业展览有限公司
**地址：**沈阳市三好街93号金源大厦5楼（110004）
**联系人：**赵坤

**8th (Shenyang) Intl Energy-saving & New Wall Material and Equipment Exhibition 2010**
**Venue:** Liaoning Industrial Exhibition Hall, Shenyang, Liaoning
**Established Year:** 2003
**Frequency:** Annual
**Market Area:** International
**Statistics '09:** Exhibition Area 30,000m², Exhibitors 400, Visitors 30,000
**Organizer:** Shenyang Municipal People's Government; Northern Industrial & Commercial Exhibition Co Ltd

2010/03/25 - 27
☎ 024-2397 5399
🖷 024-2392 2432
✉ bfexpo@126.com
www.bfexpo.com.cn

6450

**第十六届东北沈阳国际建筑装饰博览会**
**地点：**辽宁工业展览馆，辽宁沈阳
**内容：**室内装饰材料、建筑节能墙体材料、门窗、幕墙、玻璃制品、供暖空调技术产品、给排水及水处理设备、节能照明灯饰与电气技术、景观、园林、园艺等
**始办年份：**1995
**周期：**每年一届
**市场范围：**国际性
**上届规模‘09：**展览面积30,000m²(国外展商面积500m²)，参展商323家（国外展商15家），参观人数30,000人
**主办：**辽宁省装饰协会；辽宁省石材协会；沈阳市科学技术局；北方工商业展览有限公司
**地址：**沈阳市三好街93号金源大厦5楼（110004）
**联系人：**赵楠

**16th Northeast Intl Building Decoration Exhibition**
**Venue:** Liaoning Industrial Exhibition Hall, Shenyang, Liaoning
**Established Year:** 1995
**Frequency:** Annual
**Market Area:** International
**Statistics '09:** Exhibition Area 30,000m²(foreigners 500m²), Exhibitors 323 (foreigners 15), Visitors 30,000
**Organizer:** Decoration Assn of Liaoning Province; Stone Assn of Liaoning Province; Shenyang Science and Techno

2010/03/25 - 27
☎ 024-2397 5522
🖷 024-2392 2432
✉ bfexpo@126.com
www.bfexpo.com.cn

6460

**第11届中国东北国际给排水、水处理技术设备及泵、阀、管道展**
**地点：**辽宁工业展览馆，辽宁沈阳
**内容：**供水排水设备、水处理技术与设备、泵、阀、管道等
**始办年份：**2000
**周期：**每年一届
**市场范围：**国际性
**上届规模‘09：**展览面积5,000m²(国外展商面积300m²)，参展商173家（国外展商6家），参观人数20,000人
**主办：**沈阳市人民政府；辽宁省建设厅；沈阳市城乡建设委员会
**承办：**北方工商业展览有限公司
**地址：**沈阳市三好街93号金源大厦5楼（110004）
**联系人：**盖晓乐

**11th Northeast China Intl, Water Supply & Drainage, Water Disposal Technique & Equipment, and Pump & Value and Pipeline Exhibition**
**Venue:** Liaoning Industrial Exhibition Hall, Shenyang, Liaoning
**Established Year:** 2000
**Frequency:** Annual
**Market Area:** International
**Statistics '09:** Exhibition Area 5,000m²(foreigners 300m²), Exhibitors 173 (foreigners 6), Visitors 20,000
**Organizer:** Northern Industrial & Commercial Exhibition Co Ltd

2010/03/25 - 27
☎ 024-2397 5522
🖷 024-2392 2432
✉ bfexpo@126.com
www.bfexpo.com.cn

**第13届中国东北国际供热供暖、空调、新能源设备展览会**
**地点：**辽宁工业展览馆，辽宁沈阳
**内容：**供热供暖、采暖技术及设备、新能源设备、锅炉辅机及热水系统设备、大、中、小供热（制冷）中央空调
**始办年份：**1998
6470 **周期：**每年一届
**市场范围：**国际性
**上届规模**‘09：展览面积10,000$m^2$(国外展商面积102$m^2$)，参展商410家（国外展商13家），参观人数30,000人
**主办：**沈阳市人民政府；辽宁省建设厅；沈阳市城乡建设委员会
**承办：**北方工商业展览有限公司
**地址：**沈阳市三好街93号金源大厦5楼（110004）
**联系人：**盖晓乐

**13th China (Northeast) Intl Equipments of Heating, Air-Condition & New Energy Sources Exhibition**
**Venue:** Liaoning Industrial Exhibition Hall, Shenyang, Liaoning
**Established Year:** 1998
**Frequency:** Annual
**Market Area:** International
**Statistics '09:** Exhibition Area 10,000$m^2$(foreigners 102$m^2$), Exhibitors 410 (foreigners 13), Visitors 30,000
**Organizer:** Northern Industrial & Commercial Exhibition Co Ltd

2010/03/25 - 27
☎ 024-2397 5399
🖷 024-2392 2432
✉ bfexpo@126.com
www.bfexpo.com.cn

**第十二届中国东北国际门窗、幕墙、玻璃与加工设备展览会**
**地点：**辽宁工业展览馆，辽宁沈阳
**内容：**型材、门、窗、幕墙、五金配件、建筑玻璃、加工设备、胶类、遮阳设备等
**始办年份：**1998
6480 **周期：**每年一届
**市场范围：**国际性
**上届规模**‘09：展览面积30,000$m^2$(国外展商面积108$m^2$)，参展商400家（国外展商15家），参观人数30,000人
**主办：**辽宁省装饰协会；沈阳市科学技术局；沈阳建筑材料应用管理办公室；北方工商业展览有限公司
**地址：**沈阳市三好街93号金源大厦5楼（110004）
**联系人：**赵楠

**12th Northeast China Intl Door & Window, Curtain, Wall, Glass and Fabric Exhibition**
**Venue:** Liaoning Industrial Exhibition Hall, Shenyang, Liaoning
**Established Year:** 1998
**Frequency:** Annual
**Market Area:** International
**Statistics '09:** Exhibition Area 30,000$m^2$(foreigners 108$m^2$), Exhibitors 400 (foreigners 15), Visitors 30,000
**Organizer:** Decoration Assn of Liaoning Province, Shenyang Science and Technology Bureau

2010/04/01 - 03
☎ 024-2397 4279
🖷 024-2392 2432
✉ bfexpo@126.com
www.bfexpo.com.cn

**2010第十二届中国东北国际动力传动与控制技术展览会**
**地点：**辽宁工业展览馆，辽宁沈阳
**内容：**液压技术、气动技术、密封技术、机械传动、电气传动、各类轴承及相关零配件、流体工程及流程工业、泵、阀、流体设备等
**始办年份：**1998
6490 **周期：**每年一届
**市场范围：**国际性
**上届规模**‘09：展览面积30,000$m^2$，参展商852家，参观人数36,322人
**主办：**沈阳市装备制造行业协会
**承办：**北方工商业展览有限公司
**地址：**沈阳市三好街93号金源大厦5楼（110004）
**联系人：**景波

**12th China Northeast Intl Power Transmission and Control Technique Exhibition 2010**
**Venue:** Liaoning Industrial Exhibition Hall, Shenyang, Liaoning
**Established Year:** 1998
**Frequency:** Annual
**Market Area:** International
**Statistics '09:** Exhibition Area 30,000$m^2$, Exhibitors 852, Visitors 36,322
**Organizer:** Northern Industrial & Commercial Exhibition Co Ltd

2010/04/01 - 03
☎ 024-2392 1795
🖷 024-2392 2432
✉ bfexpo@126.com
www.bfexpo.com.cn

**2010第十三届中国东北仪器仪表及工业自动化展览会**
**地点：**辽宁工业展览馆，辽宁沈阳
**内容：**传感器、转换器、变送器；仪器仪表、PC总线工控机；I、O模板、可编程控制器；组态软件；工业以太网；变频器等
**始办年份：**2000
6500 **周期：**每年一届
**市场范围：**国际性
**上届规模**‘09：展览面积20,000$m^2$，参展商312家（国外展商58家），参观人数36,322人
**主办：**沈阳市装备制造行业协会
**承办：**北方工商业展览有限公司
**地址：**沈阳市三好街93号金源大厦5楼（110004）
**联系人：**李瑶，常明明

**13th Northeast China Intl Instrument & Automation Exhibition 2010**
**Venue:** Liaoning Industrial Exhibition Hall, Shenyang, Liaoning
**Established Year:** 2000
**Frequency:** Annual
**Market Area:** International
**Statistics '09:** Exhibition Area 20,000$m^2$, Exhibitors 312 (foreigners 58), Visitors 36,322
**Organizer:** Northern Industrial & Commercial Exhibition Co Ltd

2010/04/01 - 03
☎ 024-2392 1795
🖷 024-2392 2432
✉ bfexpo@126.com
www.bfexpo.com.cn

**中国东北第13届国际电力电工及能源技术设备展览会**
**地点：**辽宁工业展览馆，辽宁沈阳
**内容：**风能等环保和新能源，输配电部分，低压电器部分，电力设备与技术等
**始办年份：**1998
6510 **周期：**每年一届
**市场范围：**国际性
**上届规模**‘09：展览面积30,000$m^2$，参展商852家，参观人数36,322人
**主办：**沈阳市装备制造行业协会
**承办：**北方工商业展览有限公司
**地址：**沈阳市三好街93号金源大厦5楼（110004）
**联系人：**常明明

**13th Northeast China Intl Electric Power, Electrician and Energy Tech & Equipment Exhibition 2010**
**Venue:** Liaoning Industrial Exhibition Hall, Shenyang, Liaoning
**Established Year:** 1998
**Frequency:** Annual
**Market Area:** International
**Statistics '09:** Exhibition Area 30,000$m^2$, Exhibitors 852, Visitors 36,322
**Organizer:** Northern Industrial & Commercial Exhibition Co Ltd

2010/04/01 - 03
☎ 024-2397 4279
℡ 024-2392 2432
✉ bfexpo@126.com
ranwww.bfexpo.com.cn
6520

**2010年第三届中国东北国际流体机械展览会**
**地点：** 辽宁工业展览馆，辽宁沈阳
**内容：** 流体工程及流程工业、阀门、风机、泵、流量计类、水处理、管材等
**始办年份：** 2008
**周期：** 每年一届
**市场范围：** 国际性
**主办：** 沈阳市装备制造行业协会
**承办：** 北方工商业展览有限公司
**地址：** 沈阳市三好街93号金源大厦5楼（110004）
**联系人：** 徐颖

**3rd China (Northeast) Fluid Machinery Exhibition 2010**
**Venue:** Liaoning Industrial Exhibition Hall, Shenyang, Liaoning
**Established Year:** 2008
**Frequency:** Annual
**Market Area:** International
**Organizer:** Shenyang Equips to Make the profession Assn; Northern Industrial & Commercial Exhibition Co Ltd

2010/04/08 - 10
☎ 024-2397 4769
℡ 024-2392 2432
✉ bfexpo@126.com
http://wj.bfexpo.com.cn
6530

**第十三届中国东北国际五金工具展览会**
**地点：** 辽宁工业展览馆，辽宁沈阳
**内容：** 工具五金、五金机械设备、焊接切割设备、建筑五金、民用五金等
**始办年份：** 1998
**周期：** 每年一届
**市场范围：** 国际性
**上届规模‘09：** 展览面积20,000m²，参展商685家（国外展商40家），参观人数50,515人
**主办：** 北方工商业展览有限公司
**地址：** 沈阳市三好街93号金源大厦5楼（110004）
**联系人：** 刘秀丽

**13th China (Northeast) Intl Hardware & Tool Exhibition**
**Venue:** Liaoning Industrial Exhibition Hall, Shenyang, Liaoning
**Established Year:** 1998
**Frequency:** Annual
**Market Area:** International
**Statistics '09:** Exhibition Area 20,000m², Exhibitors 685 (foreigners 40), Visitors 50,515
**Organizer:** Northern Industrial & Commercial Exhibition Co Ltd

2010/04/09 - 11
☎ 024-2587 8888
℡ 024-2585 0618
www.zhanhuiwang.com
6540

**第三届东北国际渔具、户外用品博览会**
**地点：** 沈阳北站华府天地，辽宁沈阳
**内容：** 钓具用品:鱼竿、鱼钩、浮漂、鱼线、钓组配件、渔轮、钓箱、钓鱼服、钓鱼包、鱼饵及各种网类等产品。户外用品：速干衣、冲锋衣、防滑鞋、帐篷、睡袋、防潮垫、防风炉、驱蚊虫药品及防晒护肤用品。水上活动用品：橡皮船、气垫、皮滑艇、救生衣等产品
**参展费用：** 一级展位2,000元，二级展位1,800元，简单展位800元（1.5x1.5m），净地450元/m²（36m²起）
**上届规模‘09：** 展览面积10,000m²
**承办：** 沈阳明日科技展览贸易有限公司

**3rd Fishing and Outdoor Sports Fair**
**Venue:** Shenyang North Station, Shenyang, Liaoning
**Participated Fee:** RMB 2,000/booth, Raw Space RMB 450/m²(min 36m²)
**Statistics '09:** Exhibition Area 10,000m²
**Organizer:** Shengyang Mingri Tech Exhibition and Trade Co Ltd

2010/04/14 - 17
☎ 024-2384 8948
℡ 024-2392 2432
✉ bfexpo@126.com
www.bfexpo.com.cn
6550

**2010第12届东北沈阳国际汽车维修技术及设备、汽车零配件、汽车用品展览会**
**地点：** 辽宁工业展览馆，辽宁沈阳
**内容：** 汽车零部件、汽车改装用品、汽车金融、汽车用品等
**始办年份：** 1999
**周期：** 每年一届
**市场范围：** 国际性
**主办：** 中国贸促会辽宁省分会
**承办：** 北方工商业展览有限公司
**地址：** 沈阳市三好街93号金源大厦5楼（110004）
**联系人：** 孙李晶

**12th Vehicle Maintenance and Parts Show**
**Venue:** Liaoning Industrial Exhibition Hall, Shenyang, Liaoning
**Established Year:** 1999
**Frequency:** Annual
**Market Area:** International
**Organizer:** Northern Industrial & Commercial Exhibition Co Ltd

2010/04/14 - 18
☎ 024-2397 4159, 3188 1726
℡ 024-2392 2432
✉ bfexpo@126.com
www.bfexpo.com.cn
6560

**2010沈阳第十三届国际家用轿车及商用、专用汽车展览会**
**地点：** 辽宁工业展览馆，辽宁沈阳
**内容：** 整车展区：家庭用车、轿车、各种经济适用车、重中型卡车、运输用车、专业用车、汽车金融、汽车用品；零部件展区：汽车服务用品
**始办年份：** 1999
**周期：** 每年一届
**市场范围：** 国际性
**上届规模‘09：** 展览面积30,000m²，参展商300家，参观人数50,000人
**主办：** 中国贸促会辽宁省分会
**承办：** 北方工商业展览有限公司
**地址：** 沈阳市三好街93号金源大厦5楼（110004）
**联系人：** 孔令

**13th Shenyang Auto Show**
**Venue:** Liaoning Industrial Exhibition Hall, Shenyang, Liaoning
**Established Year:** 1999
**Frequency:** Annual
**Market Area:** International
**Statistics '09:** Exhibition Area 30,000m², Exhibitors 300, Visitors 50,000
**Organizer:** CCPIT Liaoning Sub-council; Northern Industrial & Commercial Exhibition Co Ltd

2010/06/16 - 18
☎ 024-2325 6988
℡ 024-2325 6988
✉ iecsy@126.com
www.iecsy.com
6570

**2010第十届中国东北国际冶金及金属工业展览会**
同期举办：
2010第九届中国东北电气、自动化、仪器仪表展览会
东北国际铸造、锻压、焊接、热处理、工业炉技术与设备展览会
2010第九届中国东北节能技术与设备展览会2
中国东北国际耐火材料展览会
东北国际冶金工业暨不锈钢技术与制品展览会
东北国际冶金工业暨铝型材及技术设备展览会
中国东北国际模具制造技术设备展览会
中国东北国际煤矿安全生产及相关物资装备展览会
**地点：** 辽宁工业展览馆，辽宁沈阳

**2009 Northeast China Metal Expo**
**Venue:** Liaoning Industrial Exhibition Hall, Shenyang, Liaoning
**Established Year:** 1999
**Frequency:** Annual
**Market Area:** International
**Participated Fee:** Standard Booth RMB 6,000
**Statistics '08:** Exhibition Area 10,000m², Exhibitors 300, Visitors 40,000, Trade Visitors 20,000
**Organizer:** Shenyang Intl Exhibition Co

**内容：**金属制品（钢铁及有色金属）：冷轧、热轧钢板产品、钢结构及专用型材、特种钢、不锈钢及制品、铝型材、金属平板、管材、线材、汽车工业用、建筑工业用、电力与电子用、石油、石化及燃气用、建船业用技术及设备；冶炼技术设备及粉末冶金、金属加工；不锈钢、铝型材、铸造锻压、焊接、热处理技术设备及工业炉；电子检测及控制装置、生产过程自动化、仪器仪表、环境保护、节能技术及设备；耐火材料及辅料、仓储及运输物流；表面处理及涂镀、矿山技术设备
**始办年份：**1999
**周期：**每年一届
**市场范围：**国际性
**参展费用：**标准展位6,000元
上届规模‘08：展览面积10,000m²，参展商300家，专业贸易观众20,000人
**主办：**辽宁省工业经济联合会；鞍山钢铁集团公司；辽宁省经济和信息化委员会
**承办：**沈阳国际展展览公司
**地址：**沈阳市和平区十一纬路云集东巷32号(1-8-1室）（110003）
**联系人：**李男

6580
2010/08/19 - 21
☎ 024-2325 6988
📠 024-2325 6988
✉ iecsy@126.com
www.iecsy.com

**2010第四届中国东北（沈阳）政府采购展览会**
**地点：**辽宁工业展览馆，辽宁沈阳
**内容：**一般政府采购用品、特殊政府采购用品
**始办年份：**2006
**周期：**每年一届
**市场范围：**全国性
**参展费用：**标准展位6,000元
**上届规模**‘09：展览面积4,000m²(国外展商面积400m²)，参展商140家（国外展商17家），参观人数20,000人（专业贸易观众20,000人）
**主办：**沈阳市人民政府；辽宁省人民政府机关事务管理局；辽宁省政府采购中心
**承办：**沈阳国际展览公司
**地址：**沈阳市和平区十一纬路云集东巷32号（1-8-1室）（110003）
**联系人：**李男

**Northeast China (Shenyang) International Exhibition for Government Purchase**
**Venue:** Liaoning Industrial Exhibition Hall, Shenyang, Liaoning
**Established Year:** 2006
**Frequency:** Annual
**Market Area:** National
**Participated Fee:** Standard Booth RMB 6,000
**Statistics '09:** Exhibition Area 4,000m²(foreigners 400m²), Exhibitors 140 (foreigners 17), Trade Visitors 20,000
**Organizer:** Shenyang Intl Exhibition Co

6590
2010/09 -
☎ 024-2272 9975, 2272 9972
📠 024-2272 9975
✉ ccpitmail@163.com
www.northeastasiafair.cn

**第四届中国东北亚（沈阳）进口商品博览会**
**地点：**辽宁工业展览馆，辽宁沈阳
**内容：**机械设备、小型车辆及配件、电子信息及家电、五金工具、建材及厨卫设备、日用消费品、装饰品及礼品、珠宝首饰、食品、农产品及绿色环保产品等。
**始办年份：**2007
**周期：**每年一届
**市场范围：**国际性
**性质：**面向公众
**承办：**沈阳国际商会；中国贸促会沈阳市分会
**地址：**辽宁省沈阳市沈河区青年大街35号国际贸易大厦4楼（110014）
**联系人：**王海军

**The 4th China Northeast Asia (Shenyang) Import Fair**
**Venue:** Liaoning Industrial Exhibition Hall, Shenyang, Liaoning
**Profile:** Machine and equipment, small vehicles and parts, electronics and information, household appliances, hardware, construction materials, kitchen utensils, daily-use consumer goods, ornaments, gifts, jewelry, food, primary products and green environment protection products, etc.
**Established Year:** 2007
**Frequency:** Annual
**Market Area:** International
**Nature:** Open to public
**Organizer:** Shenyang Chamber of International Commerce; CCPIT Shenyang Sub-council
**Address:** 4/F. Intl Trade Bldg, 35 Qingnian St, Shenhe Dist, Shenyang, Liaoning, China
**Contact:** Mr Wang Haijun

6595
2010/09/01 - 05
☎ 024-6212 4054
📠 024-6212 4231
✉ cieme@zxexpo.com
www.zxexop.com

**第九届中国国际装备制造业博览会**
**地点：**沈阳国际展览中心（新馆）
**内容：**本届制博会的展出内容将以数控机床及功能部件、工业自动化及动力传动、通用设备与专用设备、新能源装备与技术以及工程机械为主，全面展示和介绍上述专业领域里国内外最先进的制造技术和最新研发的制造成果。
**始办年份：**2002
**周期：**每年一届
**市场范围：**国际性
**性质：**面向贸易观众
入场费价格：免费
**参展费用：**标准展位9m²：国内企业7,000元，境外企业1,500美元；净地（36m²起）：国内企业700元/m²，境外企业150美元/m²；光地（60m²起）：国内企业300元/m²，境外企业60美元/m²
**主办：**中华人民共和国商务部；中华人民共和国国家发展和改革委员会；中国国际贸易促进委员会；辽宁省人民政府
**承办：**沈阳市人民政府；中国国际贸易促进委员会辽宁省分会；辽宁省经济和信息化委员会；沈阳振兴国际展览有限公司
**地址：**沈阳市和平区文化路58号辽展饭店8楼（110004）
**联系人：**李克忠

**The 9th China International Equipment Manufacturing Exposition**
**Venue:** Shenyang International Exhibition Center, Shenyang, Liaoning
**Established Year:** 2002
**Frequency:** Annual
**Market Area:** International
**Nature:** Trade Only
Cost to Attend:Free
**Participated Fee:** Standard Booth USD 1,500 (9m²), Raw Space USD 150/m²(min 36m²)
**Organizer:** CCPIT; Liaoning Provincial Government
**Address:** 8/F, Liaoning Exhibition Hotel, 58 Wenhua Road, Shenyang, Liaoning
**Contact:** Li Kezhong

# 陕西-西安
# Shaanxi-Xi'an

2010/01/14 - 15
☎ 010-8460 0956, 8460 0954
🖷 010-8460 0955
✉ 11525257@qq.com
wangli728@yahoo.com.cn
lilingbo0515@126.com
liuliangwo123@163.com
6600

**第11届中国国际展览和会议展示会**
**地点**：西安曲江国际会展中心，陕西西安
**内容**：亮点：全国各大展、巡回展主办商将应邀参加、参观本届展中展及展会期间系列活动
**周期**：每年一届
**市场范围**：全国性
**性质**：面向公众
**主办**：中国贸促会；国际展览业协会；国际展览和活动协会；独立组展商协会；陕西省人民政府
**承办**：中国展览馆协会；中国国际展览中心集团公司；中国贸促会陕西省分会
**联系人**：任怡，王丽，李凌波，刘亮

**The 11th China International Trade Show for Exhibition and Conference Industry**
**Venue**: Xi'an Qujiang International Conference and Exhibition Center, Xi'an, Shaanxi
**Frequency**: Annual
**Market Area**: National
**Nature**: Open to public

2010/04/28 - 05/01
☎ 400-600-3324
🖷 029 8536 9259
www.snxf.com.cn
6603

**第二届中国（西安）国际健身运动用品展览会**
**第二届中国（西安）国际户外运动博览会**
**地点**：西安曲江国际会展中心，陕西西安
**承办**：陕西省社会体育管理中心；西安曲江徐风会展有限公司

**China (Xi'an) Intl Trade Show for Fitness Sport & Leisure Fair**
**China (Xi'an) Intl Outdoor Sports Expo**
**Venue**: Xi'an Qujiang International Conference and Exhibition Center, Xi'an, Shaanxi
**Organizer**: Xi'an Qujiang Xufeng Exhibition Co

2010/05/19 - 21
☎ 029-8311 8366, 8311 8399
🖷 029-8781 2359
6605

**第四届中国（西安）国际绿色建筑与建筑节能博览会**
**地点**：西安曲江国际展览中心，陕西西安
**内容**：绿色建筑及建筑节能设计方案及示范工程；建筑生态环保技术与产品；绿色建筑技术与产品；建筑墙体保温；建筑干混砂浆；保温隔热材料；建筑聚氨脂保温；建筑节能陶瓷
**始办年份**：2006
**周期**：每年一届
**市场范围**：全国性
**性质**：面向公众
**上届规模 '09**：展览面积12,000m²，参展商200家（国外展商家，来自12个国家），参观人数9,451人
**主办**：陕西振威国际展览有限公司
**地址**：陕西西安市长安北路91号富城大厦8楼（710061）
**联系人**：刘玉智

**The 4th China International Green Building and Energy-Saving Expo**
**Venue**: Xi'an Qujiang International Conference and Exhibition Center, Xi'an, Shaanxi
**Established Year**: 2006
**Frequency**: Annual
**Market Area**: National
**Nature**: Open to Public
Statistics '09: Exhibition Area 12,000m², Exhibitors 200 (foreigners, came from 12 countries), Visitors 9,451
**Organizer**: Shaanxi Zhenwei Exhibition Co Ltd

2010/11/04 - 10
☎ 400-600-3324
www.snxf.com.cn
6608

**2010第二届中国（西安）糖酒食品交易会**
**第二届中国（西安）国际纺织服装博览会**
**地点**：西安曲江国际展览中心，陕西西安
**承办**：西安曲江徐风会展有限公司

**2nd Xi'an Sugar and Spirits Fair**
**2nd Xi'an Textile and Apparel Expo**
**Venue**: Xi'an Qujiang International Conference and Exhibition Center, Xi'an, Shaanxi
**Organizer**: Xi'an Qujiang Xufeng Exhibition Co

# 陕西-杨凌
# Shaanxi-Yangling

2010/11/01 - 05
☎ 029-8703 6998
🖷 029-8703 6994
✉ hanshb@yangling.gov.cn
www.agri-fair.com
6610

**中国杨凌农业高新科技成果博览会**
**地点**：杨凌农业高新技术产业示范区，陕西 杨凌
**内容**：展览展示，国际合作交流，信息发布活动，论坛研讨活动，交易洽谈活动，咨询培训活动，评奖颁奖活动。
**始办年份**：1994
**周期**：每年一届
**市场范围**：国际性
**性质**：面向公众
**入场券价格**：50元
**参展费用**：3300元
**上届规模** '09：展览面积35,000m²(国外展商面积2,000m²)，参展商1,500家（国外展商120家，来自45个国家），参观人数1,500,000人（专业贸易观众3,000人）
**主办**：科技部；农业部；教育部；商务部等17个国家部委
**承办**：陕西省人民政府
**地址**：陕西杨凌示范区展馆西路1号（712100）
**联系人**：韩少兵

**China Yangling Agricultural Hi-Tech Fair**
**Venue**: Yangling, Shaanxi
**Profile**: Exhibition display; international cooperation and exchange; information dissemination activities; forum for discussion activities; trade negotiation activities; consulting and training activities; activity for awards
**Established Year**: 1994
**Frequency**: Annual
**Market Area**: International
**Nature**: Open to public
**Cost to Attend**: RMB 50:-
**Participated Fee**: RMB 3,300
**Statistics '09**: Exhibition Area 35,000m²(foreigners 2,000m²), Exhibitors 1,500 (foreigners 120, came from 45 countries), Visitors 1,500,000 (trade visitors 3,000)
**Sponsor**: Ministry of Science and Technology, Ministry of Agriculture, Ministry of Education, Ministry of Commerce and other ministries in 17 countries
**Organizer**: Shaanxi Provincial Government
**Address**: NO.1 West Zhanguan Rd, Yangling, Shaanxi 712100, China
**Contact**: Han Shaobing

# 山东-济南
# Shandong-Jinan

2010/05/21 - 23
☎ 0531-8235 0000
🖷 0531-8235 0000, 8892 7900
✉ shandongzhanlan@163.com
www.zmfair.com
6620

**2010第二届中国（山东）国际食品博览会**
**地点**：济南国际会展中心，山东济南
**内容**：酒水、乳品饮料、焙烤食品、糖制品、方便食品、茶叶文化、调味品、保健食品、食品加工及包装机械、水产品、食品配料及添加剂、精品粮油及粮食制品、肉类、果蔬及农副产品深加工
**始办年份**：2008
**周期**：每年一届
**市场范围**：全国性
**性质**：面向公众
**参展费用**：标准展位3,800元，净地400元/m²
**上届规模** '09：展览面积26,000m²(国外展商面积5,000m²)，参展商409家（来自4个国家），参观人数50,000人（专业贸易观众30,000人）
**承办**：山东省食品工业协会；山东中贸国际经济贸易推广服务中心；济南中贸展览有限公司
**地址**：山东济南解放路37号东郊饭店6楼（250000）
**联系人**：朱先生，高先生
**QQ**：1302755130

**2nd China (Shandong) Food Fair 2010**
**Venue**: Jinan International Convention & Exhibition Center, Jinan, Shandong
**Established Year**: 2008
**Frequency**: Annual
**Market Area**: National
**Nature**: Open to public
**Participated Fee**: Standard Booth RMB 3,800, Raw Space RMB 400/m²
**Statistics '09**: Exhibition Area 26,000m²(foreigners 5,000m²), Exhibitors 409 (came from 4 countries), Visitors 50,000 (trade visitors 30,000)
**Organizer**: Jinan Zhongmao Exhibition Co Ltd

2010/05/29 - 31
☎ 0531-6660 2822
🖷 0531-6660 2822
✉ ccpit_wp@jn.gov.cn
6630

**2010第五届中国（济南）儿童产业国际博览会**
**地点**：济南舜耕国际会展中心，山东济南
**内容**：儿童教育类、健康用品类、服装服饰类、综合服务类等
**始办年份**：2006
**周期**：每年一届
**市场范围**：国际性
**性质**：面向公众
**参展费用**：4800元/展位
**上届规模** '09：展览面积10,000m²(国外展商面积1,500m²)，参展商108家（国外展商15家，来自7个国家），参观人数150,000人（专业贸易观众5,000人）
**主办**：中国贸促会；济南市人民政府；中国青少年宫协会
**地址**：济南市龙鼎大道1号龙奥大厦E区1548#（250099）
**联系人**：王鹏

**5th China (Jinan) Intl Children Industry Fair 2010**
**Venue**: Jinan Shungeng International Convention & Exhibition, Jinan, Shandong
**Profile**: Services for children; Health articles for infants and children; Children's dress; Education materials for children.
**Established Year**: 2006
**Frequency**: Annual
**Market Area**: International
**Nature**: Open to public
**Participated Fee**: RMB 4,800/booth
**Statistics '09**: Exhibition Area 10,000m²(foreigners 1,500m²), Exhibitors 108 (foreigners 15, came from 7 countries), Visitors 150,000 (trade visitors 5,000)
**Organizer**: CCPIT Jinan
**Address**: Zone E, Floor 15, Long'ao Bldg, No.1 Longding Ave., Jinan, Shandong, China
**Contact**: Wang Peng

2010/08/21 - 24
☎ 0531-8353 2209, 8353 2222
🖷 0531-8353 2333
✉ jnff_zhouyang@163.com
www.jn-ff.com
6640

**中国国际家具及木工机械（济南）博览会**
**地点：**济南国际会展中心，山东济南
**内容：**实木家具、现代板式家具、欧美新古典家具、红木古典家具、沙发客厅家具、软床床垫系列、办公家具、儿童家具、金属艺术家具、藤制休闲家具、酒店家具、玻璃茶几、玉石茶几、根雕、整体橱柜等；原辅材料及配件；木制品、木工机械始办
年份：2001
**周期：**每年一届
**市场范围：**全国性
**入场券价格：**免费
**参展费用：**标准展位3,000元，净地300元/$m^2$
**上届规模 '09：**展览面积43,000$m^2$，参展商168家（国外展商11家，来自7个国家），专业贸易观众23,000人
**主办：**济南市人民政府；济南华展展览策划有限公司
**地址：**济南市二环东路东环国际广场B座11F（250010）
**联系人：**周扬
**QQ：**1029869628

**9th Jinan Intl Furniture Fair**
**Venue:** Jinan International Convention & Exhibition Center, Jinan, Shandong
**Established Year:** 2001
**Frequency:** Annual
**Market Area:** National
**Cost to Attend:** Free
**Participated Fee:** Standard Booth RMB 3,000, Raw Space RMB 300/$m^2$
**Statistics '09:** Exhibition Area 43,000$m^2$, Exhibitors 168 (foreigners 11, came from 7 countries), Visitors 64,000 (trade visitors 23,000)
**Organizer:** Jinan Huazhan Exhibition Co Ltd

2010/10/15 - 17
☎ 0531-6660 2822
🖷 0531-6660 2822
✉ ccpit_wp@jn.gov.cn
6645

**2010中国（济南）国际卡车暨零部件博览会**
**地点：**济南国际会展中心，山东济南
**内容：**卡车（整车）、零部件、维修检测养护
**始办年份：**2008
**周期：**每年一届
**市场范围：**国际性
**参展费用：**5000元/展位
**上届规模 '09：**展览面积27,000$m^2$，参展商105家（国外展商12家，来自7个国家），专业贸易观众6000人
**主办：**中国贸促会；中国汽车工业协会；济南市人民政府；山东省汽车行业协会
**地址：**济南市龙鼎大道1号龙奥大厦E区1548#（250099）
**联系人：**王鹏

**Truckworld2010**
**Venue:** Jinan International Convention & Exhibition Center, Jinan, Shandong
**Profile:** 1.Truck 2.Accessories 3.ABS & Security settings
**Established Year:** 2008
**Frequency:** Annual
**Market Area:** International
**Participated Fee:** RMB 5,000/booth
**Statistics '09:** Exhibition Area 27,000$m^2$, Exhibitors 105 (foreigners 12, came from 7 countries), Trade Visitors 6,000
**Organizer:** CCPIT; China Assn of Automobile Manufacturers; Jinan Municipal People's Government; Shandong Automotive Manufacturers Assn
**Address:** Zone E, Floor 15, Long'ao Bldg, 1 Longding Ave., Jinan, Shandong, China
**Contact:** Wang Peng

# 山东-青岛
# Shandong-Qingdao

2010/03/25 - 27
☎ 0532-8361 3988, 8501 9810, 13553082723
🖷 0532-8361 3588
✉ sunh520@163.com
www.logisticschina.cn
6650

**2010第十届中国(青岛)国际物流展览会**
**地点：**青岛国际会展中心，山东青岛
**内容：**仓储技术与设备：自动化立体仓库系统，仓库设计系统，堆垛机，货架系统，分拣系统，工业门和通道，传动控制技术，输送系统，自动操作控制系统，物流包装、称重和测量系统，托盘、料箱，工位器具、周转箱，脚轮，机械手及工业机器人技术，机器视觉系统，仓管设备的清洁系统，仓储信息技术，仓库地坪漆； 搬运技术及周边设备：叉车及配套设备件，手动搬运车，牵引车及自动导向系统，电梯及附件，装卸操作设施，可调节斜坡，集装箱搬运器，汽车尾板，装卸平台与登车桥，自动化装卸装置； 生产物流系统及装备；物流信息技术与物流服务；配送及采购系统；国际货运代理；货物运输系统、卡车及专用车辆
**始办年份：**2001
**周期：**每年一届
**市场范围：**国际性
**参展费用：**6,800元/9$m^2$，净地700元/$m^2$
**主办：**中国机械工程学会物流工程分会；中国机械工程学会机械传动分会；山东物流工程学会；青岛海瀚会展有限公司；香港鼎新国际展览有限公司
**地址：**青岛市山东路52号华嘉大厦1604室（266071）
**联系人：**孙银林

**The10th China International Material Handling and Logistics Expo**
**Venue:** Qingdao International Convention & Exhibition Center, Qingdao, Shandong
**Established Year:** 2001
**Frequency:** Annual
**Market Area:** International
**Participated Fee:** Standard Booth RMB 6,800/9$m^2$, Raw Space RMB 700/$m^2$
**Organizer:** Qingdao Haihan Conference and Exhibition Co Ltd

2010/04/08 - 10
☎ 0532-5555 2901
🖷 0532-5555 2903
✉ woaiaugeta@hotmail.com
www.rubbere.com
6660

**第七届中国国际橡胶及轮胎工业展览会**
**地点：**青岛国际会展中心，山东青岛
**内容：**轮胎、橡胶制品、原材料、助剂、橡胶机械、翻新设备及材料
**始办年份：**2004
**周期：**每年一届
**市场范围：**国际性
**参展费用：**8100元
**上届规模 '09：**展览面积8,000$m^2$(国外展商面积300$m^2$)，参展商

**The 7th China International Rubber and Tire Fair**
**Venue:** Qingdao International Convention & Exhibition Center, Qingdao, Shandong
**Profile:** Tires, rubber products, raw materials, chemicals, rubber machine, refurbishment of equipment and supplies.
**Established Year:** 2004
**Frequency:** Annual
**Market Area:** International
**Participated Fee:** RMB 8,100

130家（国外展商16家，来自9个国家），参观人数7,500人（专业贸易观众2,100人）
**主办：**山东省橡胶行业协会
**承办：**青岛金诺会展有限公司
**地址：**青岛市福州南路87号福林大厦902室（266071）
**联系人：**李爽
**MSN:** woaiaugeta@hotmail.com
**QQ：**47469322

**Statistics '09:** Exhibition Area 8,000$m^2$(foreigners 300$m^2$), Exhibitors 130 (foreigners 16, came from 9 countries), Visitors 7,500 (trade visitors 2,100)
**Sponsor:** Shandong Provincial Rubber Industry Assn
**Organizer:** Qingdao Jinnuo Exhibition Co Ltd
**Address:** 902, Fulin Building, 87, South Fuzhou Road, Qingdao, 266071 China
**Contact:** Augeta Lee
**MSN:** woaiaugeta@hotmail.com

---

2010/05/20 - 24
☎ 13869812759
🖷 0532-8589 0835
✉ qingdaochezhan@126.com
www.autoqingdao.com
6670

### 2010第五届中国(青岛)房车及休旅车展览会

**地点：**青岛国际会展中心，山东青岛
**内容：**中国（青岛）房车及休旅车展览会已经成功举办四届，被业内誉为中国效果最好、最具影响力的房车展览会。本届展会将对国内外著名房车产品进行集中的展示，强化房车文化交流，促进房车经济消费，提升和推广房车企业品牌。
**始办年份：**2007
**周期：**每年一届
**市场范围：**国际性
**性质：**面向公众
**参展费用：**室内800元/$m^2$，室外400元/$m^2$（室内净地36$m^2$起，室外净地72$m^2$起）
**主办：**中国汽车工程学会；山东省汽车行业协会
**承办：**青岛嘉路博国际会展有限公司
**联系人：**姜维
**MSN:** qdjiangwei@hotmail.com
**QQ：**67245707

### 5th Qingdao Recreational Vehicle Show

**Venue:** Qingdao International Convention & Exhibition Center, Qingdao, Shandong
**Established Year:** 2007
**Frequency:** Annual
**Market Area:** International
**Nature:** Open to public
**Participated Fee:** Raw Space: Indoor RMB 800/$m^2$(min 36$m^2$), Outdoor RMB 400/$m^2$(min 72$m^2$)
**Organizer:** Qingdao Jialubo Exhibition Co Ltd
**MSN:** qdjiangwei@hotmail.com

---

2010/07/08 - 11
☎ 0532-8197 8663, 8197 8609
🖷 0532-8197 8692
✉ sinoces@sinoces.com
www.sinoces.com
6680

### 2010中国国际消费电子博览会

**地点：**青岛国际会展中心，山东青岛
**内容：**家庭影音产品、数字家庭产品、数字内容支持、工业设计、存储解决方案、便携办公设备、家用电器产品、汽车电子、数字娱乐产品、软件应用方案、移动无线通信、安防产品
**始办年份：**2001
**周期：**每年一届
**市场范围：**国际性
**上届规模'09：**展览面积39,000$m^2$，参展商451家（国外展商76家），参观人数92,760人（专业贸易观众41,529人）
**主办：**国家商务部；工业和信息化部；科学技术部；山东省人民政府
**承办：**中国电子商会；中国机电产品进出口商会；青岛市人民政府
**地址：**青岛市山东路2号甲华仁国际大厦19层A（266071）

### 2010 China Intl Consumer Electronics Show (SINOCES)

**Venue:** Qingdao International Convention & Exhibition Center, Qingdao, Shandong
**Profile:** Home Entertainment, Smart Home Products, Mobile Communications, Mobile Office, Automotive Electronics, Storage Solutions & Application
**Established Year:** 2001
**Frequency:** Annual
**Market Area:** International
**Statistics '09:** Exhibition Area 39,000$m^2$, Exhibitors 451 (foreigners 76), Visitors 92,760 (trade visitors 41,529)
**Organizer:** China Electronic Chamber of Commerce; China Chamber of Commerce for Import and Export of Machinery

---

2010/07/16 - 19
☎ 0532-8079 1060, 8079 1032
🖷 0532-8384 1887
✉ hcservice1@gmail.com
www.cbe-qd.com
6690

### 第四届中国（青岛）国际石材工业及机械设备展览会

**地点：**青岛国际会展中心，山东青岛
**内容：**石材类：大理石荒料、花岗石荒料、砂岩荒料、石灰石、石英、砂石、板岩；板材类：天然石材板材、大理石板材、花岗石板材、砂岩板材、复合板材、环境石材、人造石材板材；石雕制品类：石雕、石刻制品、石碑制品、园林风景石、人造砂岩、假山石；环境装饰类：卵石、盲人石、仿古石、景观石、文化石、磨菇石；石材机械及加工设备；养护材料及设备
**始办年份：**2004
**周期：**每年一届
**市场范围：**国际性
**参展费用：**标准展位6,800元/9$m^2$，室内净地700元/$m^2$（36$m^2$起）
**上届规模'09：**展览面积15,000$m^2$，参展商200家（来自23个国家），专业贸易观众30,000人
**主办：**青岛市人民政府；山东省石材行业协会
**承办：**青岛海宸国际会展有限公司
**地址：**青岛市山东路33号B座2010室（266071）
**联系人：**公正，吴振华
**MSN:** hcservice1@gmail.com
**QQ：**365367414

### 4th China Qingdao International Stone Industry & Machinery Exhibition

**Venue:** Qingdao International Convention & Exhibition Center, Qingdao, Shandong
**Profile:** Raw materials: marble, granite, sandstone, limestone, quartz, grit stone and slate; Slabs: natural slab, marble slab, granite slab, slab stone, sandstone slab, composite slab, environmental slab, artificial stone slab; Stone carvings; Decorative products; Relative machinery and equipment, Maintenance and accessories
**Established Year:** 2004
**Frequency:** Annual
**Market Area:** International
**Participated Fee:** Standard Booth RMB 6,800/9$m^2$, Raw Space RMB 700/$m^2$ (min 36$m^2$)
**Statistics '09:** Exhibition Area 15,000$m^2$, Exhibitors 200 (came from 23 countries), Trade Visitors 30,000
**Sponsor:** Qingdao Municipal People' s Government; Shandong Stone Industry
Assn **Organizer:** Qingdao Haichen International Expo Co
**Address:** Rm2101, Bldg B, No.33 Shandong Rd, Qingdao, China
**Contact:** Jay Wu
**MSN:** hcservice1@gmail.com

---

2010/07/17 - 19
☎ 0532-8079 1069, 8079 1078
🖷 0532-8384 1887
✉ qdcese@163.com
www.qdcese.com
6700

### 第四届中国（青岛）国际建筑节能和可再生能源应用博览会

**地点：**青岛国际会展中心，山东青岛
**内容：**建筑节能保温材料；新型节能墙体材料、技术及产品的生产、检测装备； 干混砂浆产品、添加剂及技术设备；新能源利用；绿色照明类；节水技术及设备；节地技术及产品；能源统计监测；空气调节系统类；节能建筑、绿色工程示范成果展示；住宅产业化部品
**始办年份：**2006
**周期：**每年一届

### 4th China Qingdao Intl Building Energy Saving & Renewable Energy Utilization Fair

**Venue:** Qingdao International Convention & Exhibition Center, Qingdao, Shandong
**Profile:** Energy-saving & Insulation Materials; New style wall material
and technique and the manufacturing facilities; Mortar construction products, Additives and equipment; The use of new energy sources; Green and energy-saving lighting products; Water-saving technologies

**市场范围**：国际性
**参展费用**：标准展位6,800元/9m²，净地700元/m²（36m²起）
**上届规模‘09**：展览面积15,000m²，参展商200家（来自23个国家），专业贸易观众30,000人
**承办**：青岛市建筑节能与墙体材料革新办公室；青岛市建筑节能协会；青岛海宸国际会展有限公司
**地址**：青岛市山东路33号B座2010室（266071）
**联系人**：杨光，孟翔
**MSN**：hcservice1@gmail.com
**QQ**：365367414

and equipment; Land-saving technologies and products; Energy Statistical monitoring; Air Conditioning Systems; Energy saving buildings, and Green Projects; Housing industrialization products
**Established Year**: 2006
**Frequency**: Annual
**Market Area**: International
**Participated Fee**: Standard Booth RMB 6,800/9m², Raw Space 700/m² (min 36m²)
**Statistics '09**: Exhibition Area 15,000m², Exhibitors 200 (came from 23 countries), Trade visitors 30,000)
**Organizer**: Qingdao Construction Energy-saving and Wall Material Innovation Office, Qingdao Building Energy-saving Assn
**Address**: Rm2101, Bldg B. No.33 Shandong Rd, Qingdao, Shandong, China
**Contact**: Yang Guang, Meng Xiang
**MSN**: hcservice1@gmail.com

2010/07/17 - 19
☎ 0532-8079 1066, 8079 1032
℡ 0532-8384 1887
✉ haichenguoji@163.com
hcservice1@gmail.com
www.cbe-qd.com
6710

## 第六届中国（青岛）国际建筑材料及装饰材料博览会

**地点**：青岛国际会展中心，山东青岛
**内容**：型材、门窗幕墙、建筑五金及加工设备展区；木门、加工设备及装饰五金展区；精品地板及地面铺装材料展区；涂料、油漆、化学建材及防水、屋面工程展区；室内装饰材料、墙纸布艺、天花吊顶、楼梯展区；陶瓷卫浴及厨房设施展区；采暖、供热产品展区；石材展区；装饰设计企业及装饰施工企业其它类装饰新产品、新技术、新工艺、新材料展区
**始办年份**：2004
**周期**：每年一届
**市场范围**：国际性
**参展费用**：标准展位6,800元/9m²，室内净地700元/m²（36m²起）
**上届规模‘09**：展览面积35,000m²（国外展商来自23个国家），专业贸易观众50,000人
**承办**：山东省建设机械行业管理办公室；青岛市建设工程材料管理办公室；青岛市建设机械与建筑材料协会；青岛海宸国际会展有限公司
**地址**：青岛市山东路33号B座2010室（266071）
**联系人**：刘宝芳，吴振华
**MSN**：hcservice1@gmail.com
**QQ**：365367414

## 6th China Qingdao Intl Construction & Decoration Materials Exposition

**Venue**: Qingdao International Convention & Exhibition Center, Qingdao, Shandong
**Profile**: Extrusion profiles/doors windows curtain walls, construction hardware and processing equipment district; Wooden door, processing machinery and decorative hardware district; Master floor and covering materials district; Coating, painting, chemical building materials and water protecting, roofing project district; Indoor decorative material, wallpaper, ceiling, stair district; Ceramic products, kitchen and bathroom accessories district; Heating products district, Stone products and machinery district; Decorative designing
**Established Year**: 2004
**Frequency**: Annual
**Market Area**: International
**Participated Fee**: Standard Booth RMB 6,800/9m², Raw Space RMB 700元/m² (min 36m²)
**Statistics '09**: Exhibition Area 35,000m², Exhibitors (foreigners came from 23 countries), Trade Visitors 50,000
**Organizer**: Shandong Regulatory Bureau for Construction Machinery Industry; Qingdao Regulatory Bureau for Construction
**Address**: Rm2101, Bldg B. No.33 Shandong Rd, Qingdao, China
**Contact**: Liu Baofang, Jay Wu
**MSN**: hcservice1@gmail.com

2010/12/04 - 07
☎ 0532-8079 1060, 8079 1032
℡ 0532-8384 1887
✉ hcservice1@gmail.com
www.cbe-qd.com
6720

## 全国库存商品及闲置物资博览交易会

**地点**：青岛国际会展中心，山东青岛
**内容**：生活物资：家居类、电子电器类、服装服饰类、鞋帽皮带类、针纺织品类、箱包类、首饰类、玩具类、钟表眼镜类、文化办公用品类、体育娱乐用品类、日用品类、护理及美容用品类、其他商品； 生产物资：生产设备、大型机械、建材、五金、工业设施、辅料包装等； 车房：品牌折扣车、二手车、尾盘、二手房；拍卖行、典当行。
**始办年份**：2009
**周期**：每年一届
**市场范围**：全国性
**性质**：面向公众
**参展费用**：标准展位3,800元/9m²，净地400元/m²（36m²起）
**预计规模**：展出面积30,000m²，参展商300家
**主办**：青岛市人民政府；中国旧货业协会
**承办**：青岛海宸国际会展有限公司
**地址**：青岛市山东路33号B座2010室（266071）
**联系人**：张圆，吴振华
**MSN**：hcservice1@gmail.com
**QQ**：365367414

## China Store Goods and Idle Products Trade Fair

**Venue**: Qingdao International Convention & Exhibition Center, Qingdao, Shandong
**Profile**: All kinds of Store Goods and Idle Products such as Clothes, Shoes, Car and daily using goods
**Established Year**: 2009
**Frequency**: Annual
**Market Area**: National
**Nature**: Open to public
**Participated Fee**: Standard Booth RMB 3,800/9m², Raw Space RMB 400元/m² (min 36m²)
**Sponsor**: Qingdao Municipal Government; China Store Goods Assn
**Organizer**: Qingdao Haichen International Expo Co
**Address**: Rm2101, Bldg B. No.33 Shandong Rd, Qingdao, China
**Contact**: Zhang Yuan, Jay Wu
**MSN**: hcservice1@gmail.com

# 山东-烟台
# Shandong-Yantai

2010/09/23 - 26
☎ 0535-6611 833, 6280 001
🖷 0535-6280 002
✉ yantai@fruitveg-expo.cn
www.fruitveg-expo.cn
6730

**第十一届国际果蔬、食品博览会**
**地点**：烟台国际博览中心，山东烟台
**内容**：专业设备展区 北方果蔬展区 东盟果蔬展区：东盟国家特色干果、鲜果及制成品、蔬菜及加工产品等 台湾果蔬展区 江南果蔬展区 食品展区 水产品展区饮料、茶叶、酒类展区 农用资料展区种苗、花卉展区 农机展区
**始办年份**：1999
**周期**：每年两届
**市场范围**：国际性
**性质**：面向公众
**参展费用**：标准展位：国内参展商3500元，角位加收500元；海外参展商800美元，角位加收100美元；净地（36 m²起）：国内参展商350元/m²；海外参展商80美元/m²；
**上届规模**'08：展览面积6,000m²(国外展商面积1,200m²)，参展商480家（国外展商100家，来自15个国家），参观人数60,000人（专业贸易观众50,000人）
**主办**：联合国亚洲及太平洋经济社会委员会；联合国亚太农业工程与机械中心；联合国亚太技术转让中心
**承办**：烟台市政府；山东省商务厅；山东省科学技术厅；山东省农业厅；山东省林业局；山东省供销合作社联合社；山东省农业机械管理办公室
**地址**：山东省烟台市朝阳街80号绮丽大厦三楼（294008）
**联系人**：王晓燕，孔艳玲
**QQ**：20584045

**11th International Fruit/Vegetable/Food Exposition**
**Venue:** Yantai International Expo Center, Yantai, Shandong
**Profile:** The Machinery Equipments Featured Exhibition The Northern Fruit and Vegetable Pavilion The Assn of Southeast Asian Nations (ASEAN) Fruit and Vegetable Pavilion The Chinese Taipei Fruit and Vegetable Pavilion The Southern Fruit and Vegetable Pavilion The Food Pavilion The Aquatic Products Pavilion The Beverage Pavilion. The Agricultural Materials Pavilion The Seeds and Seedlings, Flowers Pavilion The Agricultural Machinery Pavilion
**Established Year:** 1999
**Frequency:** Biannual
**Market Area:** International
**Nature:** Open to public
**Participated Fee:** Standard Booth USD 800, Corner booth adds USD 100; Raw Space (min 36 m²) USD 80/m²;
**Statistics '08:** Exhibition Area 6,000m²(foreigners 1,200m²), Exhibitors 480 (foreigners 100, came from 15 countries), Trade Visitors 50,000
**Organizer:** United Nations Economic and Social Commission for Asia; Pacific (ESCAP); United Nations Asian and Pacific Center for Agricultural Engineering and Machinery (APCAEM-ESCAP), Asian and Pacific Center for Transfer of Technology (APCTT--ESCAP)
**Address:** 3rd Fl, Qili Mansion, 80 Chaoyang St, Yantai 264001, Shandong, China
**Contact:** Ms Amanda Wang, Ms Kerry Kong

# 山西-太原
# Shanxi-Taiyuan

2010/05/13 - 15
☎ 027-8736 2945
www.hope-tarsus.com
6740

**中国中西部（太原）医疗器械展览会**
**暨第11届山西医疗器械(2010年春季)展览会**
**地点**：山西省展览馆，山西太原
**主办**：全国医药技术市场协会；中英合资好博塔苏斯展览公司
**联系人**：余云成

**Taiyuan Medical Device Exhibition**
**Venue:** Shanxi Exhibition Hall, Taiyuan, Shanxi
**Organizer:** Tarsus-Hope Exhibition Company

# 四川-成都
# Sichuan-Chengdu

2010/03/05 - 07
☎ 028-6868 0592, 13018257503
🖷 028-6626 1015
✉ liuying8519@126.com
www.jyzbxz.com
6750

**2010第三届西部教育技术装备及高职教育仪器展览会/第五届中国西部国际科技仪器及实验室装备展**
**地点**：成都世纪城新国际会展中心，四川成都
**内容**：基础、职业、高等教育的技术装备产品的展示，包括计算机、投影机、网络设备、音像器材、各类教育软件、校园网解决方案；各学科专用教学仪器和设备、教具、标本模型；学校用家具、学生公寓用品、学校体育用品设施等；幼儿教玩具产品；开辟专区集中展示与课程改革配套的教育装备产品。中小学书香校园工程图书样书、图书馆装备用书和教学挂图。高校技术转让、科教合作项目交流、科研成果转化等。教育装备新产品、新技术论坛。
**始办年份**：2007
**周期**：每年一届
**参展费用**：标准展位6,800元，净地800元/m²
**主办**：四川省科技厅；四川省教育厅
**承办**：四川省科技交流中心；成都风向标科技展览有限公司
**地址**：成都市领事馆路8号万兴苑大厦A702室（610041）
**联系人**：刘颖

**2010 Chengdu Intl Educational Technology and Equipment Exhibition**
**Venue:** Century City-New International Exhibition & Convention Center, Chengdu, Sichuan
**Established Year:** 2007
**Frequency:** Annual
**Participated Fee:** Standard Booth RMB 6,800, Raw Space RMB 800/m²
**Organizer:** Chengdu Fengxiangbiao Exhibition

2010/03/07 - 09
☎ 027-8736 2945
www.hope-tarsus.com
6760

**2010中国中西部（成都）医疗器械展览会暨第10届中国西部医疗器械及口腔设备展览会**
**地点：**成都世纪城新国际会展中心，四川成都
**主办：**全国医药技术市场协会；四川省机械工业管理办公室
**承办：**湖北好博塔苏斯展览有限公司 成都分公司
**联系人：**余云成

Chengdu Medical Device Exhibition
Western China Dental Equipment Exhibition
**Venue:** Century City-New International Exhibition & Convention Center, Chengdu, Sichuan
**Organizer:** Tarsus-Hope Exhibition Company

2010/03/19 - 22
☎ 010-6836 5088, 6831 2733, 6836 0997
🖷 010-6831 7408
✉ info@qgtih.com
www.qgtjh.com
6770

**全国糖酒商品交易会**
**地点：**成都世纪城新国际会展中心，四川成都
**内容：**全国糖酒商品交易会（简称"全国糖酒会"）是全国食品行业的重要经济活动。于每年春、秋两季举办两次。自1955年举办首届交易会以来，已经走过了54年的历史，至今已是第81届。
**始办年份：**1995
**周期：**每年两届
**市场范围：**全国性
**入场券价格：**10元
**参展费用：**标准展位3,000元
**上届规模'09：**展览面积120,000m²(国外展商面积15,000m²)，参展商5,000家（国外展商1,500家，来自20个国家），参观人数200,000人（专业贸易观众120,000人）
**主办：**中国糖业酒类集团公司
**承办：**成都市人民政府
**地址：**北京市西直门外大街710号中糖大厦（100044）
**联系人：**何继红，邢春雷
**QQ：**331838929

**China National Sugar and Alcoholic Commodities Fair**
**Venue:** Century City-New International Exhibition & Convention Center, Chengdu, Sichuan
**Established Year:** 1995
**Frequency:** Biannual
**Market Area:** National
**Cost to Attend:** RMB 10；-
**Participated Fee:** Standard Booth RMB 3,000
**Statistics '09:** Exhibition Area 120,000m²(foreigners 15,000m²), Exhibitors 5,000 (foreigners 1,500, came from 20 countries), Visitors 200,000 (trade visitors 120,000)
**Organizer:** Chengdu Municipal Government

2010/04/02 - 04
☎ 028-8545 2897
🖷 028-8545 2299
www.cdgbh.cn
www.donnor.com
6790

**2010中国（成都）国防科技工业及装备博览会暨第15届成都国际机床展**
**地点：**成都世纪城新国际会展中心，四川成都
**内容：**机床工模具展区 金属切削机床、金属成形机床、金属板材加工技术及设备、金属管材加工技术及设备、特种加工技术及设备、专用与特种机床、切削工具、机床附件、配件、辅助材料、机床电器、功能部件及组件、磨料磨具、电动、气动和机械手工工具、精密测量技术及设备；工业自动化及流体动力传动展区；铸锻热加工及焊接切割展区：铸造技术及设备、锻造技术及设备、热处理技术
**参展费用：**标准展位A区6,800元/展位，B区5,800元/展位 净地T区(36m²起)700元/m²
**主办：**中国机械工业联合会；成都市人民政府；国家国防科技工业局信息中心；四川省经济委员会
**承办：**上海东博展览有限公司；德纳展览集团公司；四川省模具工业协会
**地址：**成都市致民路23号雅典国际社区B栋26楼1号

**Chengdu China Natl Defense Science & Technology Industry and Equipment Manufacturing Expo/ 15th Chengdu Intl Machine Exhibition**
**Venue:** Century City-New International Exhibition & Convention Center,
Chengdu, Sichuan
**Participated Fee:** Standard Booth RMB 6,800, Raw Space RMB 700/m²(min 36m²)
**Organizer:** Chengdu Donnor Exhibition Co

2010/04/13 - 15
☎ 027-8736 2945
www.hope-tarsus.com
6800

**2010第三届中国西部交通建设博览会**
**地点：**成都世纪城新国际会展中心，四川成都
**主办：**成都公路行业协会；中英合资好博塔苏斯展览公司
**承办：**湖北好博塔苏斯展览有限公司 成都分公司
**联系人：**余云成

**Western China Transportation Expo**
**Venue:** Century City-New International Exhibition & Convention Center, Chengdu, Sichuan
**Organizer:** Tarsus-Hope Exhibition Company

2010/06/18 - 20
☎ 0755-3398 9211, 3398 9280
🖷 0755-3398, 9272/9273
✉ Info@reedhuabo.com
✉ lisa.mo@reedhuabo.com
www.reedhuabo.com
6810

**成都家居、休闲用品及礼品展览会**
**地点：**成都世纪城新国际会展中心，四川成都
**内容：**成都经济总量在西部各省会城市中排名第一，以其为中心的西部礼品市场前景巨大。励展华博运用卓越的国际资源和多年运作国际礼品展的专业经验，立足成都、面向西部，志在以专业的品牌礼品展为业界提供展示交易的优质平台。2009年首届成都家居、休闲用品及礼品展览会取得圆满成功，在此基础上，第二届成都家居、休闲用品及礼品展览会再次激情相约美丽蓉城！
在西部经济中心成都举办的以休闲家居礼品为主题的展会。展会给与会者提供了一个进军西部市场的行业沟通平台和有效的市场推广渠道，是企业品牌展示和拓展市场的最佳契机，是采购商进行"一站式"采购的黄金时期。展品范围包括家庭用品类、家居饰品类、休闲用品、旅游及运动用品、厨房用品、美容保健产品、礼品、赠品、珠宝及时尚饰品等。
**始办年份：**2009
**周期：**每年一届
**市场范围：**地区性
**性质：**面向公众
**参展费用：**前两届优惠价：标准展位（3x3m）5,000元，双开口5,500元

**Chengdu Houseware, Leisure Goods & Gifts Fair**
**Venue:** Century City-New International Exhibition & Convention Center, Chengdu, Sichuan
**Profile:** The hosting city - Chengdu is one of the most important economic centers as well as transportation and communication hubs in West China. The fair offers one of the most effective marketing and communication channels for the participants who hope to promote their brands and expand their western China gift market. For buyers, this event has become the leading platform for sourcing houseware and leisure goods products.
The fair will be held in Chengdu which is one of the most important economic centers as well as transportation and communication hubs in West China. The fair offering one of the most effective marketing and communication channels for the participants who wish to promote their brands and expand their China west gift markets. For buyers, it has become the leading platform for sourcing houseware and leisure goods products.
**Exhibits:** Home Decorations, Household Products, Sporting Leisure & Travel Goods, Kitchen Products, Beauty & Health Products, Premiums, Jewelry & Fashion Accessories, Home Textiles
**Established Year:** 2009
**Frequency:** Annual
**Market Area:** Regional
**Nature:** Open to public

主办：励展华博展览（深圳）有限公司
地址：深圳市中心区福华三路深圳国际商会中心1801-1802（518048）
联系人：袁文军，黄志华

Participated Fee: Standard Booth RMB 5,000, Corner Booth RMB 5,500
Organizer: Reed Huabo Exhibitions (Shenzhen) Co
Address: Rm. 1801-1802, Shenzhen Intl Chamber of Commerce Tower, Fuhua 3rd Rd, Central Dist, Shenzhen, China
Contact: David Yuan, King Huang

2010/06/18 - 21
☎ 010-6609 4503, 6609 4543
🖷 010-6609 4503, 6601 1348
✉ zhengdaojun@126.com
www.crce.org.cn
6830

2010年（第五届）中国零售商大会暨展会
地点：成都世纪城新国际会展中心，四川成都
内容：商业地产及主题商圈规划缩影展区、零售企业展区、连锁商业品牌展区、新型零售业展区、品牌产品展区
始办年份：2006
周期：每年一届
市场范围：国际性
性质：面向公众
上届规模 '09：展览面积10,000m²，参展商155家，参观人数40,000人（专业贸易观众20,000人）
主办：中国商业联合会；成都市人民政府
承办：中国商业联合会会展部；中国商业联合会专家工作委员会；成都市商务局；成都市会展业发展办公室
地址：北京市西城区复兴门内大街45号（100801）
联系人：郑道军，张博文
MSN: zhengdaojun@126.com

2010 China Retailers Convention & Exhibition
Venue: Century City-New International Exhibition & Convention Center, Chengdu, Sichuan
Established Year: 2006
Frequency: Annual
Market Area: International
Nature: Open to public
Statistics '09: Exhibition Area 10,000m², Exhibitors 155, Visitors 40,000 (trade visitors 20,000)
Organizer: Exhibition Dept of China General Chamber of Commerce
MSN: zhengdaojun@126.com

2010/06/22 - 24
☎ 021-5153 5172, 5153 5155
✉ sarah.geng@reedexpo.com.cn
✉ Jimmy.yang@reedexpo.com.cn
www.nepconchina.com
6840

**中国（成都）国际电子生产设备及技术展览会**
地点：成都世纪城新国际会展中心，四川成都
内容：NEPCON西部展（中国（成都）国际电子生产设备及技术展览会）是中西部地区最具规模、最有代表性的国际化电子生产制造展览之一，全面展示中西部地区表面贴装行业以及其他微电子制造业最新产品、技术及服务，为中西部企业提高行业竞争优势、有效物色新供应商、收集最新市场信息提供了绝佳平台。
周期：每年一届
主办：励展博览集团
参展联络：耿宁小姐
☎ 021-5153 5172 ✉ sarah.geng@reedexpo.com.cn
参观联络：杨巍先生
☎ 021-5153 5155 ✉ Jimmy.yang@reedexpo.com.cn

**NEPCON West China 2010**
Venue: Century City-New International Exhibition & Convention Center, Chengdu, Sichuan
Profile: NEPCON West China 2010 is one of the largest and most authoritative international electronics manufacturing events in central and western China, featuring the most comprehensive range of latest SMT and other related microelectronic products, technology and services. It provides companies in central and western China the best platform to increase competitiveness, source potential suppliers and keep up-to-date with the latest market trends.
Frequency: Annual
Organizer: Reed Exhibitions
For exhibiting:
☎ 021-5153 5172 ✉ sarah.geng@reedexpo.com.cn
For visiting:
☎ 021-5153 5155 ✉ Jimmy.yang@reedexpo.com.cn

2010/07/03 - 06
☎ 028-8628 0489
🖷 028-8628 0491
✉ cdiff@neweastfair.com
www.neweastfair.com
6850

第十一届成都国际家具工业展览会
地点：世纪城新国际会展中心，四川成都
内容：家具及木工机械、五金配件、原辅料
始办年份：2000
周期：每年一届
市场范围：国际性
性质：面向公众
入场券价格：免费
参展费用：3500元/标准展位
主办：成都市人民政府；四川省商务厅
承办：成都市会展业发展办公室；四川省家具进出口商会
地址：成都市人民中路一段28号房地大厦1601（610015）
联系人：姜华，熊伟

The 11th International Furniture Fair Chengdu
Venue: Century City-New International Exhibition & Convention Center, Chengdu, Sichuan
Profile: Furniture reaches woodworking machinery , the hardware accessory , the plain assist material
Established Year: 2000
Frequency: Annual
Market Area: International
Nature: Open to public
Cost to Attend: Free
Participated Fee: RMB 3,500/booth
Organizer: Chengdu Municipal Government; Sichuan Provincial Department of Commerce
Contact: Jiang Hua, Xiong Wei

2010/09/07 - 09
☎ 0755-8831 2796
🖷 0755-8831 2533, 8831 5466
www.icef.com.cn
6860

2010中国（西部）电子展
地点：成都世纪城新国际会展中心，四川成都
内容：新型电子元器件、军品类电子元器件、电子工具、材料、电子基础装备、电子测量仪器及其自动测试系统、新型元器件生产制造设备、电磁兼容测试设备与仪器、应用软件开发、测试设备与系统、计算机通讯网络测试设备与仪器
主办：中国电子学会；中国电子器材总公司；深圳市创意时代会展有限公司
地址：深圳市福田区福华三路国际商会中心2201室
联系人：李艳

Chengdu – China Electronics Fair
Venue: Century City-New International Exhibition & Convention Center, Chengdu, Sichuan
Organizer: Creativity Convention & Exhibition (Shenzhen) Co Ltd
Address: Room 2201, Intl Chamber of Commerce Tower, Fuhua 3 Road, Futian Dist, Shenzhen, China
Contact: Jessica Lee

2010/09/17 - 19
☎ 028-8538 0188, 8538 0316
🖷 028-8538 0313
✉ 87774833@163.COM
www.cd-autoshow.com
6865

**第十三届成都国际汽车展览会汽车用品展**
**地点：** 成都世纪城新国际会展中心，四川成都
**内容：** 汽车内、外饰及精品展示、汽车电子及安全防盗设备展示、汽车影音设备展示、汽车美容养护产品展示、汽车改装及改装配件展示、汽车服务连锁经营展示
**始办年份：** 2007
**周期：** 每年一届
**市场范围：** 全国性
**性质：** 面向公众
**参展费用：** 展位(3x3m) T区5,500元，A区5,000元，B区4,600元；净地T区600元/m²，A区550元/m²，B区500元/m²
**上届规模 '09：** 展览面积11,000m²，参展商256家（来自7个国家），参观人数27,000人
**主办：** 成都市人民政府
**承办：** 成都世纪城新国际会展中心
**地址：** 成都世纪城路198号（610041）
**联系人：** 梁早，史宁

**Chengdu Motor Show 2010**
**Venue:** Century City-New International Exhibition & Convention Center, Chengdu, Sichuan
**Established Year:** 2007
**Frequency:** Annual
**Market Area:** National
**Nature:** Open to Public
**Participated Fee:** Standard Booth (3x3m) RMB 5,500, Raw Space RMB 600/m²
**Statistics '09:** Exhibition Area 11,000m², Exhibitors 256 (came from 7 countries), Visitors 27,000
**Organizer:** Century City-New International Exhibition & Convention Center

2010/09/19 - 25
☎ 028-8538 0318, 8538 0325
🖷 028-8533 3218
✉ cdms@live.cn
6868

**成都国际汽车展览会**
**地点：** 成都世纪城新国际会展中心，四川 成都
**内容：** 各类汽车，包括乘用车、商用车；汽车零部件；汽车售后相关产品；汽车技术展示
**始办年份：** 1997
**周期：** 每年一届
**市场范围：** 国际性
**性质：** 面向公众
**入场券价格：** 媒体日100元；专业观众日50元；普通观众日30元
**上届规模 '09：** 展览面积100,000m²(国外展商面积20,000m²)，参观人数410,000人
**主办：** 成都市人民政府
**承办：** 成都世纪城新国际会展中心有限公司；汉诺威展览会（中国）有限公司
**地址：** 成都市世纪城路198号国际会议中心7F（610041）
**联系人：** 王渝，卿亚峰

**Chengdu Motor Show**
**Venue:** New International Convention & Exposition Center Chengdu Century City, Chengdu, Sichuan
**Established Year:** 1997
**Frequency:** Annual
**Market Area:** International
**Nature:** Open to Public
**Cost to Attend:** RMB 30:-
**Statistics '09:** Exhibition Area 100,000m²(foreigners 20,000m²), Visitors 410,000
**Organizer: Organizer:** Century City-New International Exhibition & Convention Center

2010/11 -
☎ 010-8455 6503, 8455 6507
www.pharmchina.com.cn
6870

PHARMCHINA 全国药品交易会

**第64届全国药品交易会（秋季）**
**地点：** 成都世纪城新国际会展中心，四川成都
**内容：** 全国药品交易会每年二届，是中国最大的医药制剂及相关技术、服务交易会。截至到2009年，每届展会的展出面积达六万五千平米，超过十万名专业观众到会参观洽谈，成为中国医药行业当之无愧的年度盛会。
**展品范围：** 化学药品专区、中成药品专区、生物制药专区、OTC非处方药品、大众健康用品专区、PHARMSOFT医药软技术和综合服务专区。
**观众范围：** 医药批发企业，医药生产企业，零售药店，医药研发，物流企业，医院药剂科主任，医生，医药终端用户等。
**周期：** 每年两届
**主办：** 国药励展展览有限责任公司

**The 64th PHARMCHINA**
(China National Pharmaceuticals Fair)
**Venue:** Century City-New International Exhibition & Convention Center, Chengdu, Sichuan
**Profile:** PHARMCHINA is the largest pharmaceutical trade show in China with over 1,600 exhibitors covering an exhibition area of 60,000m² with over 100,000 visitors (based on figures from the last event in Spring 2009). The market leading trade show enables pharmaceutical manufacturers to connect with hospitals, clinics, pharmacies, drug prescribers and end-users of pharmaceutical products.
**Exhibits:** OTC Drugs & Prescription Drugs of Chemical, Patented TCM and Biopharmacy; Latest Pharmaceutical Technology & Research; Pharmaceutical R & D; Registration Agents; Clinical Trials; Information and Consultancy Services; Technology and Product Transfers; Protection of Intellectual Property Rights; Storage & Logistics; Media; Human Resources and Training; IT Services; Contract Outsourcing; Packaging Design; Gifts; Facilities and Services for pharmacies
**Visitors:** Pharmaceutical manufacturers; pharmaceutical distributors; pharmacy directors of hospitals; doctors; pharmaceutical end-users.
**Frequency:** Biannual
**Organizer:** Reed Sinopharm Exhibitions Co Ltd

2010/11 -
☎ 010-8455 6677
🖷 010-8202 3887
www.tcmex.cn
6880

TCMEx

**2010中医药国际科技博览会**
**地点：** 成都世纪城新国际会展中心，四川成都
**内容：** 中医药国际科技博览会是由四川省人民政府与国药励展展览有限责任公司共同主办的，并得到了国家科技部、卫生部、农业部、国家食品药品监督管理局、国家中医药管理局、中国科学院、中国工程院七个国家级部委的联合支持。

主办方将力争把中医药国际科技博览会打造成为一个中医药行业的品牌，全面覆盖中医中药产业链的贸易

**Traditional Chinese Medicine Exposition 2010**
**Venue:** Century City-New International Exhibition & Convention Center, Chengdu, Sichuan
**Profile:** The Traditional Chinese Medicine Exposition (TCMEx), organized by Sichuan Province Government and Reed Sinopharm Exhibitions (RSE), focuses on the traditional Chinese medicine industry.

The Chinese government attaches great importance to the development of Traditional Chinese Medicine

平台，系统指导消费者科学寻医用药的教育平台，深度解读中医药文化与发展方向的科技信息平台。

一年一度的中医药国际科技博览会与由国药励展的另一品牌展会全国药品交易会同期同地举办。每届博览会吸引了超过600家中药企业参展，有超过10万名的专业观众到场参观。博览会将为中医药行业中的制造商与经销商建立贸易平台。展商与观众借此平台寻找商机、营销品牌、建立市场网络。在展会上经销商可以找到品类齐全的，包括中成药、民族药、保健品、天然药物、天然提取物、中药药材、研发成果在内的上千种中医药品种。这些产品将会通过代理商的商业渠道流通到终端消费者。

中医药国际科技博览会的另外一个亮点是展会的主题论坛。在论坛上，专家学者齐聚一堂，就中医药的历史文化、中医药现代化、中医药国际化、科研成果等方面的议题讨论和交换观点。论坛给中医药行业人士一个交流和学习的科技平台。

**周期**：每年一届

**主办**：国药励展展览有限责任公司

(TCM). Therefore, TCMEx is supported by seven Chinese Governmental departments. They are The Ministry of Science and Technology, Ministry of Health, Ministry of Agriculture, State Food and Drug Administration, State Administration of Traditional Chinese Medicine, Chinese Academy of Sciences and Chinese Academy of Engineering.

Taking place once a year together with Pharmchina, the largest pharmaceutical trade show in China held by RSE as well, TCMEx attracts over 600 exhibitors and 100,000 professional visitors.

One of the most important functions of the TCMEx is to be an ideal platform for TCM manufacturers to find sales partners and distributers, promote TCM brands, and set up marketing networks. In TCMEx, sales agents are introduced to thousands of products such as traditional medicines, health products, natural products, natural extracts, Chinese herbs and Research and Development results. These products will then be delivered to end users through agent channels in the pharmaceutical market.

Another highlight of the exposition is the TCMEx Forum. In the forum, many experts and scholars will be invited to discuss and exchange their ideas and research results in fields of TCM history and culture, TCM Modernizing, TCM Internationalizing, R & D results and many other topics. This forum creates a unique platform for people engaged in the TCM industry to exchange information and enhance relationships.

**Organizer**: Reed Sinopharm Exhibitions Co Ltd

2010/11/11 - 13
☎ 010-6580 1456, 6580 3828
🖷 010-6580 3826
✉ cnbaking@126.com
www.baking-china.com

6890

**2010中国烘焙展览会（西部）**

**地点**：成都世纪城新国际会展中心，四川成都

**内容**：烘焙生产设备，包装设备；冷冻保鲜设备、仪器仪表，烘焙器具，金属检测装置；酒店业设备、厨房设备、西餐、快餐、酒吧、咖啡厅配料及设备；饼房店铺、超市物流设施、陈列设备、计算机管理系统；相关烘焙业产品、专用面粉、预拌粉、冷冻面团、淀粉、土豆制品，干果；专用油脂、鲜奶油、专用奶制品；面粉改良剂、面包改良剂、蛋糕改良剂、方便面改良剂；保鲜剂、酵母、香料、香精、色素、甜味剂等相关食品添加剂 咖啡、巧克力、糖仔、蜡烛、仿真模型等蛋糕装饰材料；包装材料、包装容器

首届

**周期**：每年一届

**市场范围**：国际性

**参展费用**：国内价格：标准展位5,800元（9m²），净地560元/m²

**预计规模**：展出面积4,500m²，参展厂商300家，参观人数25,000人

**主办**：中华全国工商业联合会烘焙业公会

**承办**：北京中连鼎和烘焙食品技术有限公司

**联系人**：王玉强，张伟

**China Bakery Exhibition 2010 (West)**

**Venue**: Century City-New International Exhibition & Convention Center, Chengdu, Sichuan

**Profile**: Ovens and accessories Bakery and pastry-making machinery Refrigeration, fermenting and air conditioning technology and engineering Hotel accessories, Baking agents, raw materials and ingredients Partly baked and finished products Coffee, Sweets, Chocolate, Ice cream manufacturing Pasta manufacturing Furniture and furnishings for shops, cafes and patisseries Packaging machinery, equipment and material Decorative items and baking accessories Cleaning and hygiene Laboratory and measuring, EDP, education

First Session

**Frequency**: Annual

**Market Area**: International

**Sponsor**: All-China Bakery Assn (A.C.B.A)

**Organizer**: Beijing Zhonglian Dinghe Bakery Food Technology Co Ltd; Canton Universal Fair Group Ltd

# 四川成都其他展览信息
# Other Exhibitions in Chengdu, Sichuan

**举办地点：成都世纪城新国际会展中心**
Venue: Century City-New International Exhibition & Convention Center, Chengdu, Sichuan
咨询电话：028-8538 0048　6895

上海通用雪佛兰新赛欧发布会
2010/01/01 - 12

2010成都品牌家具春季直销周
2010/01/14 - 20

奇瑞年会
2010/01/22 - 23

2010新春年货购物节
2010/01/26 - 02/11

第7届元宵商品交易会
2010/02/20 - 03/01

四川印刷器材展览会
2010/03/04 - 07

招聘会
2010/03/06 - 07

春季品牌服装博览会
2010/03/12 - 20

2010年中国（四川）教育博览会
2010/03/22 - 28

人才展
2010/03/27 - 28

第六届成都给排水处理及流体机械展暨环保、固废物及资源综合利用博览会
2010/03/31 - 04/05

第十届成都照明+建筑电气博览会暨LED展览会
2010/03/31 - 04/05

德纳广告展
2010/04/09 - 11

第九届中国西部国际口腔设备及材料展
2010/04/09 - 14

全国门窗展
2010/04/09 - 14

2010年城市建设科技博览会
2010/04/09 - 14

第十届成都国际社会公共安全产品与技术展览会
2010/04/10 - 15

第二届太阳能产品西部（成都）展示交易会
2010/04/12 - 16

自动化仪器仪表
2010/04/12 - 17

动保展
2010/04/13 - 16

2010年第二十届全国图书交易博览会
2010/04/22 - 26

玩具展
2010/04/28 - 05/06

春夏服装博览会
2010/04/28 - 05/16

春季房地产交易会
2010/05/01 - 06

汉诺威工业装备展
2010/05/07 - 14

电力展
2010/05/08 - 13

李宁订货会
2010/05/13 - 24

2010中国西部（成都）给排水处理技术装备博览会暨流体机械+泵阀门+管道展
2010/05/18 - 22

动漫展
2010/05/18 - 23

2010中国西部（成都）国际电玩展览会
2010/05/19 - 23

希望2010四川首届青少年文化暨四川国际青少年博览会
2010/05/27 - 30

2010成都绿色健康、保健产业展览会
第三届西部成都成人保健品计生及生殖健康用品展
2010/05/28 - 30

人才展
2010/05/29 - 30

2010中国西部（成都）国际化工、石油天然气及化工技术装备展览会
2010/06/02 - 07

2010四川线材线缆及相关设备展
2010/06/04 - 09

工程机械展
2010/06/04 - 09

第二届成都端午食品博览会
2010/06/06 - 16

2010年第六届中国成都建筑科技装饰材料博览会暨建筑电气展览会
2010/06/07 - 09

2010年第六届中国成都酒店设备用品及旅游工艺品博览会
2010/06/11 - 16

出国留学展
2010/06/17 - 22

创意展
2010/06/18 - 23

高校咨询会
2010/06/25 - 27

成都夏季丝绸服装展
2010/06/26 - 07/11

建材团购（派达）
2010/07/17 - 18

三联工业装备展
2010/08/01 - 03

建材装饰展
2010/08/18 - 22

首届食品博览会
2010/08/27 - 29

第五届成都农资信息交流
2010/08/27 - 29

人才展
2010/08/28 - 29

煤碳展
2010/09/01 - 03

2010成都新能源国际论坛暨新能源博览会
2010/09/01 - 06

旅游展
2010/09/01 - 08

第二届服装及缝制设备展览会
纺织工业及面辅料展览会
2010/09/02 - 07

2010第十一届（成都）全国医疗器械及口腔设备展览会
2010/09/02 - 08

立嘉工业展
2010/09/07 - 09

第十届中国四川月饼节
2010/09/09 - 21

2010成都新能源国际论坛暨新能源博览会
2010/09/28 - 30

美食节
2010/09/27 - 10/08

秋季房交会
2010/10/01 - 06

成都秋季服装展销会
2010/10/01 - 24

中国国际西部博览会
2010/10/10 - 25

2010年第七届中国成都建筑科技、装饰材料（冬季）博览会
2010/11/07 - 12

香港博览会
2010/11/07 - 14

汽体展
2010/11/10 - 12

鞋类、加工展
2010/11/12 - 17

首届四川名优食品博览会
2010/11/25 - 30

人才展
2010/12/04 - 05

成都冬季服装博览会
2010/12/11 - 19

阿里巴巴网货大会
2010/12/14 - 19

# 新疆-乌鲁木齐
# Xinjiang-Urumqi

2010/05/20 - 22
☎ 0991-3855 921
🖷 0991-3855 813
✉ xinjiangyashi@126.com
www.xjzhanhui.cn
6900

**第十一届新疆国际农业机械博览会暨农业生产资料交易洽谈会**
**地点**：新疆维吾尔自治区体育中心，新疆乌鲁木齐
**内容**：农业机械、畜牧机械、林果机械展区，生产资料展区
**始办年份**：1999
**周期**：每年一届
**市场范围**：国际性
**性质**：面向公众
**参展费用**：4,800元/展位，室外空地400元/m²
**上届规模** '09：展览面积50,000m²，参展商500家，参观人数200,000人
**主办**：新疆维吾尔自治区农牧业机械管理局；新疆生产建设兵团农业局；新疆生产建设兵团农机局
**承办**：新疆雅式展览有限公司
**地址**：新疆乌鲁木齐北京南路556好京华成C座3单元802室（830011）
**联系人**：葵红，张琪
**QQ**：196228177

**11th Xinjing International Machinery Exhibition**
**Venue:** Xinjiang Sports Center, Urumqi, Xinjiang
**Established Year:** 1999
**Frequency:** Annual
**Market Area:** International
**Nature:** Open to public
**Participated Fee:** RMB 4,800/booth, Outdoor Raw Space RMB 400/m²
**Statistics '09:** Exhibition Area 50,000m², Exhibitors 500, Visitors 200,000
**Organizer:** Xinjiang Yashi Exhibition Co Ltd

2010/09/01 - 05
☎ 0991-285 0497, 287 9890
🖷 0991-287 9890
✉ urumqifairoffice@163.com
www.urumqifair.com
6910

**中国乌鲁木齐对外经济贸易洽谈会**
**地点**：新疆国际博览中心，新疆乌鲁木齐
**内容**：1、面向中西南亚、俄罗斯市场展示中国名优商品； 2、展示中亚及周边国家的资源优势和特色商品； 3、展示中国及周边国家的投资环境和项目，吸引外商投资，鼓励中国企业投资中西亚及俄罗斯市场； 4、展示新疆和内地省市的投资环境和投资合作项目，促进内联合作； 5、\'举办中西南亚区域经济高层论坛、中外企业家见面会等系列交流活动。
**始办年份**：1992
**周期**：每年一届
**市场范围**：国际性
**性质**：面向公众
**入场券价格**：50元
**参展费用**：一楼标准展位5,200元/个，二楼标准展位4,800元/个，馆外展棚3000元/个；室外净地：260元/m²
**上届规模** '09：展览面积30,000m²(国外展商面积1,000m²)，参展商1,080家（国外展商79家，来自32个国家），参观人数32,200人（专业贸易观众10,000人）
**主办**：中国商务部；中国贸促会；新疆维吾尔自治区人民政府
**承办**：中国商务部外贸发展事务局；新疆商务厅；新疆生产建设兵团；新疆招商发展局；乌鲁木齐市人民政府
**地址**：新疆乌鲁木齐市新华南路1292号乌洽会办公室（830049）
**联系人**：江恩

**China Urumqi Foreign Economic Relations & Trade Fair**
**Venue:** Xinjiang International Exhibition Center, Urumqi, Xinjiang
**Profile:** 1. Showcase the import &export commodities from China and Central, West and South Asian countries; 2. Showcase the advantageous resources and special products from neighboring countries; 3. Showcase the investment environment and cooperation projects from China and neighboring countries, attract foreign investment and encourage Chinese enterprises to invest in Middle, South and West Asian Countries; 4. Showcase the investment environment and cooperation projects of Xinjiang and other provinces in China, promote the domestic cooperation; 5. Hold a series of exchange activities such as Regional Economic Cooperation Forum and business matching.
**Established Year:** 1992
**Frequency:** Annual
**Market Area:** International
**Nature:** Open to public
**Cost to Attend:** RMB 50:-
**Participated Fee:** 1st Floor RMB 5,200/booth, 2nd Floor RMB 4,800/booth, Outdoor Tent RMB 3,000, Outdoor Raw Space RMB 260/m²
**Statistics '09:** Exhibition Area 30,000m²(foreigners 1,000m²), Exhibitors 1,080 (foreigners 79, came from 32 countries), Visitors 32,200 (trade visitors 10,000)
**Sponsor:** Ministry of Commerce of China; China Council for the Promotion of International Trade; The People's Government of Xinjiang; Uygur Autonomous Region
**Organizer:** Trade Development Bureau of Ministry of Commerce, PRC; Xinjiang Commerce Department; Urumqi Fair Office of Xinjiang Department of Foreign Trade and Economic Cooperation
**Address:** Urumqi Fair Office, No. 1292, South Xinhua Road, Urumqi, Xinjiang
**Contact:** Jiang En

# 云南-昆明
# Yunnan-Kunming

2010/03/24 - 27
☎ 027-8736 2945
www.hope-tarsus.com
6920

**2010中国中西部（昆明）医疗器械展览会**
**地点：**昆明国际会展中心，云南昆明
**主办：**全国医药技术市场协会；中英合资好博塔苏斯展览公司
**承办：**湖北好博塔苏斯展览有限公司 成都分公司
**联系人：**余云成

**Kunming Medical Devices Exhibition**
**Venue:** Kunming International Convention & Exhibition Center, Kunming, Yunnan
**Organizer:** Tarsus-Hope Exhibition Company

2010/03/26 - 28
☎ 028-6697 0715, 6697 0755
🖷 028-6855 3543
✉ 200659989@qq.com
www.schzex.com
6930

**2010第三届华展云南广告四新展览会**
**地点：**昆明国际会议展览中心，云南昆明
**内容：**巴蜀联谊云贵、促四新播共享平台 — 四川广告设备器材展、云南广告四新展、贵州广告四新展资源共享三地联办，巡回展示，独家占领西南片区广告市场战略重地。构建广告相关企业推广：树立形象、互通有无的优质发展平台。
**始办年份：**2008
**周期：**每年一届
**市场范围：**全国性
**参展费用：**标准展位5,500元，净地550元/m²(36m²起)
**上届规模‘08：**展览面积3,000m²，参展商60家，参观人数5,000人（专业贸易观众1,000人）
**主办：**四川华展文化传播有限公司
**地址：**四川省成都市一环路西三段13号4栋1单元附2号（610000）
**联系人：**罗攀
**QQ：**200659989

**Yunnan AD Exhibition**
**Venue:** Kunming International Convention & Exhibition Center, Kunming, Yunnan
**Established Year:** 2008
**Frequency:** Annual
**Market Area:** National
**Participated Fee:** Standard Booth RMB 5,500, Raw Space RMB 550/m²(min 36m²)
**Statistics '08:** Exhibition Area 3,000m², Exhibitors 60, Visitors 5,000 (trade visitors 1,000)
**Organizer:** Sichuan Huazhan Cultural Diffusion Co Ltd
**Address:** 2-1-4, No, 13, Section 3, First Ring Rd West, Chengdu, Sichuan, China.
**Contact:** Bill

2010/06/06 - 08
☎ 0871-3139 277, 3164 305
🖷 0871-3164 304, 3164 305
✉ kmfair@kmfair.org
www.kmsacc.com
6933

**第三届南亚国家商品展**
（简称“第三届南亚展”）
**地点：**昆明国际会展中心，云南昆明
**内容：**南亚展是为扩大自南亚进口，平衡双边贸易而举办的进口商品交易会，展品涉及纺织服装、矿业资源、医疗制药、传统工艺、珠宝首饰、轻工建材、仪器土畜、软件信息、旅游服装等十大类，规模达300个标准展位。
**始办年份：**2007
**周期：**每年一届
**市场范围：**国际性
**性质：**对公众开放
**入场券价格：**30元
**参展费用：**标准展位5,000元
上届规模‘09：展出面积7,000m²(国外展商面积7,000m²)，参展商300家（国外展商300家（来自南亚7国），参观人数100,000人
**主办：**中国商务部；云南省人民政府；南亚七国商务主管部门
**承办：**云南省人民政府
**地址：**云南省昆明市北京路175号（650011）
**联系人：**刘浏，王凡
QQ：55454271

**The 3rd SACC Fair**
The 3rd South Asian Countries Commodity Fair
**Venue:** Kunming International Convention & Exhibition Center, Kunming, Yunnan
**Profile:** The SACC Fair is an import commodities fair, aimed at enlarging import South Asian countries and balancing the bilateral trade. There are more than ten kinds of exhibition products including Textiles & Clothes, Minerals Devices & Pharmaceuticals, Traditional Craftworks, Jewelry, Light Industry & Building Materials, Native Products, Livestock Products, Software & Information, and Tourism Services. The total number of standard booths is 300.
**Established Year:** 2007
**Frequency:** Annual
**Market Area:** International
**Nature:** Open to Public
**Cost to Attend:** RMB 10:-
**Participation Fee:** Standard Booth RMB 5,000
**Statistics '09:** Exhibition Area 7,000m² (foreigners 7,000m²) Exhibitors 300 (foreigners 300 came from 7 south Asia countries), Visitors 100,000
**Sponsor:** The Ministry of Commerce of the People Republic of China (MOFCOM); The People's Government of Yunnan Province; The Commerce and Industry of seven South Asian Countries
**Organizer:** The People's Government of Yunnan Province
**Address:** Beijing Road 175, Kunming 650011, Yunnan, China
**Contact:** Liu Liu, Wang Fan

2010/06/06 - 10
☎ 0871-3139 277, 3164 305
🖷 0871-3164 304, 3164 305
✉ kmfair@kmfair.org
www.kmsacc.com
6935

**第十八届昆交会**
第十八届中国昆明进出口商品交易会
**地点**：昆明国际会展中心，云南昆明
**内容**：展会内容 包括商品、技术进出口、国内外招商引资及经济技术合作项目洽谈等，设有机电、化工矿业、电子及信息产业、医药及保健品、农特、珠宝、轻工等商品专业馆和投资促进、外经、境外来展、南亚展等专题展馆。
**始办年份**：1993
**周期**：每年一届
**市场范围**：国际性
**性质**：对公众开放
**入场券价格**：30元
**参展费用**：标准展位5,000元
**上届规模'09**：展出面积75,000m²(国外展商面积7,200m²)，参展商1,600家（国外展商500家（来自22国家），参观人数100,000人（其中贸易观众5,000人）
**主办**：中国商务部；云南、四川、重庆、贵州、广西、西藏六省及成都市人民政府
**承办**：云南省人民政府
**地址**：云南省昆明市北京路175号（650011）
**联系人**：刘浏，王凡
QQ：55454271

**The 18th Kunming Fair**
The 18th China Import & Export Fair, Kunming
**Venue**: Kunming International Convention & Exhibition Center, Kunming, Yunnan
**Profile**: Kunming Fair covers import and export trade and technology, investment promotion, and economic and technological cooperation. There are pavilions for all sectors from Machinery & Electronics; Chemicals & Minerals; IT Industry; Pharmaceuticals & Healthcare Products; Agricultural Native Produce; Jewelries and Light Industries. There are also theme pavilions, including the Investment Promotion; Foreign Trade & Investment, the Import Pavilion and the South Asia Pavilion
**Established Year**: 1993
**Frequency**: Annual
**Market Area**: International
**Nature**: Open to Public
**Cost to Attend**: RMB 30:-
**Participation Fee**: Standard Booth RMB 5,000
**Statistics'09**: Exhibition Area 75,000m² (foreigners 7,200m²) Exhibitors 1,600 (foreigners 500 came from 22 countries), Visitors 100,000 (trade visitors 5,000)
**Sponsor**: Ministry of Commerce of the People's Republic of China and seven of China's provincial governments-Yunnan, Sichuan, Guizhou, Guangxi, Tibet, Chongqing and Chengdu
**Organizer**: The People's Government of Yunnan Province
**Address**: Beijing Road 175, Kunming 650011, Yunnan, China
**Contact**: Liu Liu, Wang Fan

2010/07/10 - 14
☎ 852-2561 5566
🖷 852-2811 9156
✉ info@newayfalrs.com
www.newayfairs.com
6940

**中国昆明珠宝玉石展览会**
**地点**：昆明国际会展中心，云南昆明
**市场范围**：国际性
**主办**：立新国际展览有限公司
**地址**：香港告士大道77号富通大厦9楼

**China Jewelry Fair 2010**
**Venue**: Kunming International Convention & Exhibition Center, Kunming, Yunnan
**Market Area**: International
**Organizer**: Neway International Trade Fairs Limited
**Address**: 9/F Fortis Tower, 77 Gloucester Road, Hong Kong

# 浙江-杭州
# Zhejiang-Hangzhou

2010/05/20 - 22
☎ 0571-8538 0671
🖷 0571-8534 1737
✉ gang.li@yahoo.com.cn
www.cie-expo.com
6950

**2010中国（杭州）国际工业博览会**
**地点**：杭州和平国际会展中心，浙江 杭州
**内容**：机床模具、仪器仪表与自动化、电力电工、工程机械、轨道交通等
**周期**：每年一届
**市场范围**：国际性
**入场券价格**：免费
**参展费用**：6800元/展位，700元/m²（36m²起）
**上届规模'09**：展览面积12,000m²(国外展商面积300m²)，参展商420家（国外展商30家，来自20个国家），参观人数20,000人（专业贸易观众15,000人）
**主办**：中国机械工业联合会；杭州市人民政府；浙江省经济和信息化委员会
**承办**：杭州中仕展览服务有限公司
**地址**：杭州市东新路381号（310004）
**联系人**：李刚，张云鹏

**China (Hangzhou) International Industry Expo 2010**
**Venue**: Hangzhou Peace International Exhibition and Conference Center, Hangzhou, Zhejiang
**Frequency**: Annual
**Market Area**: International
**Cost to Attend**: Free
**Participated Fee**: RMB 6800/booth, Raw Space RMB 700/m² (min 36m²)
**Statistics '09**: Exhibition Area 12,000m²(foreigners 300m²), Exhibitors 420 (foreigners 30, came from 20 countries), Visitors 20, 000 (trade visitors 15,000)
**Organizer**: Hangzhou Zhongshi Exhibition Service Co Ltd

# 浙江-宁波
# Zhejiang-Ningbo

2010/03/18 - 21
☎ 0574-2771 6625
🖷 0574-8784 9306
✉ younage@younage.com
www.chinamaching.cn

6960

**第十一届中国国际机械工业展览会**
**地点：**宁波国际会展中心，浙江宁波
**内容：**金属切削机床、金属成形机床、电加工和线切割机床、数控系统、机床零部件和附件； 铸造与锻压设备、铸件 五金工具、焊接切割设备 工业自动化、仪器仪表设备、传动设备
**始办年份：**2000
**周期：**每年一届
**市场范围：**国际性
**性质：**面向公众
**参展费用：**国际区：标准展位(3x3m) 外资企业3,000美元/9m²，内资企业7,800元/9m²，净地（36m²起）780元/m² 国内区：内资企业6,800元/9m²，净地680元/m²
**上届规模 '09：**展览面积30,000m²(国外展商面积5,000m²)，参展商1,000家（国外展商200家，来自20个国家），参观人数80,000人（专业贸易观众10,000人）
**主办：**宁波雅卓展览服务有限公司
**地址：**宁波百丈东路650号贵都商务楼7楼（315040）
**联系人：**郑岗

**The 11th China International Machinery Industry Exhibition**
**Venue:** Ningbo International Conference & Exhibition Center, Ningbo, Zhejiang
**Profile:** Metal cutting machine tool: Metal forming machine tool; EDM and wire cutting machines; FMC/FMS & automatic devices; CNC system; Machine tool components and accessories; Tooling, fixture and related products; Plastic and rubber machinery and equipment; Packing and printing equipment; Welding and cutting equipment; Automation and industrial control; Instrument and apparatus
**Established Year:** 2000
**Frequency:** Annual
**Market Area:** International
**Nature:** Open to public
**Participated Fee:** Standard Booth USD 3,000/9m², Raw Space USD 300/m²(min 36m²)
**Statistics '09:** Exhibition Area 30,000m²(foreigners 5,000m²), Exhibitors 1,000 (foreigners 200, came from 20 countries), Visitors 80,000 (trade visitors 10,000)
**Organizer:** Younage Exhibition Co Ltd
**Address:** 7/F, No 650, Bai Zhang East Road, Ningbo, Zhejiang 315040, China

2010/03/20 - 22
☎ 0574-8725 0240
🖷 0574-8734 3344
✉ 87250240@163.com
www.zhongboexpo.com

6970

**第七届中国国际文具礼品博览会暨世纪文具网国际采购会**
**地点：**宁波国际会展中心，浙江宁波
**内容：**文具及办公用品：书写工具、纸及纸制品、桌面办公用品、文件整理用品、学生及学校用品、美术用品；办公设备及电脑周边产品、耗材；文具、礼品生产加工设备、零部件；礼品、赠品、工艺品
**始办年份：**2004
**周期：**每年一届
**市场范围：**全国性
**参展费用：**6,800元
**主办：**宁波中博国际展览有限公司；宁波文具行业协会
**地址：**宁波高新区创苑路750号软件园B座8层（315040）
**联系人：**王力宏

**7th China Intl Stationery & Gifts Exposition & Stationery Trade Com Purchasing Fair**
**Venue:** Ningbo International Conference & Exhibition Center, Ningbo, Zhejiang
**Profile:** Stationery & Office supplies: Writing Instruments, Office Supplies, Paper & Paper Products, Document Management Stationery, Student & School Stationery, Art Supplies; Office Equipments and Exhaustible Material & Device of Computers; Producing and Processing Machines of Stationery & Gifts
**Established Year:** 2004
**Frequency:** Annual
**Market Area:** National
**Participated Fee:** RMB 6,800
**Organizer:** Ningbo Zhongbo International Exhibition Co
**Address:** F8, Software Area-B, No.750, Chuangyuan Rd., Ningbo National High-Tech Zone, Zhejiang, China
**Contact:** Leona

2010/04/09 - 12
☎ 010-6401 6504
🖷 010-6401 6504
✉ cy888@vip.163.com
www.cliexpo.org

6980

**第八届中国国际家居博览会**
**地点：**宁波国际会议展览中心，浙江宁波
**内容：**上游:房地产馆：房地产，社区及房产智能化，城市规划宣传展示，房地产项目合作，园艺与绿化。中游:建材馆：卫浴陶瓷展区、厨房设施展区、 装饰五金展区、门窗壁柜展区、玻璃制品展区、地面材料展区、化学涂料展区、灯饰电工展区、暖通管道展区、其他装饰展区。家装馆。下游:家具馆：家具展区，家纺展区。家居用品馆
**周期：**每年两届
**市场范围：**国际性
**性质：**面向公众
**入场券价格：**10元
**上届规模 '09：**展览面积110,000m²
**主办：**中国轻工业联合会；宁波市人民政府；中国轻工业展览中心
**地址：**北京市东城区东四六条64号（100007）
**联系人：**应艳梅
**MSN:** lengfeier@msn.com
**QQ：**71229011

**7th China Intl Housing and Furnishing Exposition**
**Venue:** Ningbo International Conference & Exhibition Center, Ningbo, Zhejiang
**Frequency:** Biannual
**Market Area:** International
**Nature:** Open to public
**Cost to Attend:** RMB 10:-
**Statistics '09:** Exhibition Area 110,000m²
**Organizer:** Exhibition Center of China Light Industry
**MSN:** lengfeier@msn.com

2010/06/08 － 11
☎ 0574-8717 8074, 8717 8075
🖷 0574-8732 7443, 8732 7860
✉ trade@cicgf.com
www.cicgf.com
6990

**第九届中国国际日用消费品博览会**
**地点**：宁波国际会展中心，浙江宁波
**内容**：由国家商务部和浙江省人民政府共同主办的消博会是中国年中规模最大的日用品消费品专业博览会，每年6月在宁波举办。第九届家纺服装、家电电子、户外休闲用品、日用品及办公文体、食品土畜、装饰礼品和境外服务贸易七大展区。
**始办年份**：2002
**周期**：每年一届
**市场范围**：国际性
**入场券价格**：50元
**参展费用**：6,000元
**上届规模** '09：展览面积90,000m$^2$(国外展商面积6,400m$^2$)，参展商1,800家（国外展商300家，来自50个国家），参观人数75,000人（专业贸易观众8,000人）
**主办**：中华人民共和国商务部
**承办**：宁波市人民政府、浙江省商务厅
**地址**：宁波市灵桥路190号1690室（31500）
**联系人**：池俏瑜，唐鑫
**QQ**：240419159

**The 9th China International Consumer Goods Fair**
**Venue:** Ningbo International Conference & Exhibition Center, Ningbo, Zhejiang ,
**Established Year:** 2002
**Frequency:** Annual
**Market Area:** International
**Cost to Attend:** RMB 50
**Participated Fee:** RMB 6,000
**Statistics '09:** Exhibition Area 90,000m$^2$(foreigners 6,400m$^2$), Exhibitors 1,800 (foreigners 300, came from 50 countries), Visitors 75,000 (trade visitors 8,000)
**Organizer:** Ningbo Foreign Trade Service Center Co Ltd
**Contact:** Ms Chi, Ms Tang

2010/09 －
☎ 0574-2771 6625
🖷 0574-8784 9306
✉ younage@younage.com
www.chinamaching.cn
7000

**2010中国宁波国际工业设计博览会**
**地点**：宁波国际会展中心，浙江宁波
**内容**：工业设计组织、设计机构、设计公司、设计院校、制造业企业及研发机构； 产品设计、视觉设计、环境设计，包括：家电、汽车、IT及通信产品、日用消费品、家居家具、服装、办公设备、文具、建筑与装饰、环境景观、五金卫浴、平面与广告、动漫数码、包装等相关领域和产品的设计。 设计软件、器材、快速成型设备、模型制作。新工艺、新材料应用。
**始办年份**：2006
**周期**：每年一届
**市场范围**：国际性
**性质**：面向公众
**参展费用**：标准展位1,800美元，净地160美元/m$^2$（36m$^2$起）
**主办**：宁波雅卓展览服务有限公司
**地址**：宁波百丈东路650号贵都商务楼7楼（315040）
**联系人**：郑岗

**2010 World Industrial Design Fair Ningbo China**
**Venue:** Ningbo International Conference & Exhibition Center, Ningbo, Zhejiang
**Profile:** Industrial design organization, industrial institutions, design companies, design colleges, manufacturing enterprises and R&D department. Product design, vision design, environment design, including: household appliances, automobiles, IT and communications products, daily consumer goods, watches and clocks, clothing, household furniture, stationery, construction and decoration, costume design, the environment landscape design, bathroom, advertising, graphic design, animation digital, packing and related area and product design. Design software, equipment, speediness molding equipment, and model. New craftwork, new material.
**Established Year:** 2006
**Frequency:** Annual
**Market Area:** International
**Nature:** Open to public
**Participated Fee:** Standard booth USD 1800, Raw Space (min 36m$^2$) USD 160/m$^2$
**Organizer:** Younage Exhibition Co Ltd
**Address:** 7/F, No 650, Bai Zhang East Road, Ningbo, Zhejiang 315040, China

2010/11 －
☎ 0574-8791 1562, 87911560
🖷 0574-8791 1559
✉ WYJ3401@126.com
www.nbdcj.com
7010

**第十五届中国宁波国际住宅产品博览会**
**地点**：宁波国际会议展览中心，浙江宁波
**内容**：房产置业、家装设计、厨具、陶瓷、油漆涂料、能源、防水保温、智能安防、网络信息、五金灯具、绿化。
**始办年份**：1996
**周期**：每年一届
**市场范围**：国际性
**性质**：面向公众
**入场券价格**：10元
**参展费用**：房产：7,500元/展位；其它：5,700元/展位
**上届规模** '08：展览面积55,000m$^2$(国外展商面积9,800m$^2$)，参展商780家（国外展商198家，来自23个国家），参观人数390,000人（专业贸易观众50,000人）
**主办**：住房和城乡建设部住宅产业化促进中心；宁波市人民政府
**承办**：宁波市建设委员会；宁波市城之新展览有限公司
**地址**：浙江省宁波市院2路66号203（315040）
**联系人**：戴勇勤，吴伊君

**15th China Ningbo International Exhibition on Housing Industry Products**
**Venue:** Ningbo International Conference & Exhibition Center, Ningbo, Zhejiang
**Profile:** Real estate, Interior design and decoration, Kitchen and bath, Painting, Machinery and materials for gates, roofs and pipe; Housing and furnishing; New building materials; Construction energy-saving thermal protection and water proof technology and products, household intellectualization and security digitization; Hardware; Lamp; Gardening.
**Established Year:** 1996
**Frequency:** Annual
**Market Area:** International
**Nature:** Open to public
**Cost to Attend:** RMB 10:-
**Participated Fee:** Real Estate: RMB 7,500/booth; Others: RMB 5,700/booth
**Statistics '08:** Exhibition Area 55,000m$^2$(foreigners 9,800m$^2$), Exhibitors 780 (foreigners 198, came from 23 countries), Visitors 390,000 (trade visitors 50,000)
**Organizer:** Ningbo Construction Committee; Ningbo Chengzhixin Exhibition Co Ltd
**Address:** No, 66 Yuanshi Road Ningbo, China

# 浙江-义乌
# Zhejiang-Yiwu

2010/04/20 - 23
☎ 0579-8541 5222, 8541 5802
🖷 0579-8541 5444, 8541 5777
✉ expo@chinafairs.org
www.ssofair.com
7020

**中国义乌文化产品交易博览会**
**地点**：义乌国际博览中心，浙江义乌
**内容**：文化办公、体育娱乐、工艺美术类、创意产品、古玩收藏、国际文化交流、邮票、精品书画
**始办年份**：2004
**周期**：每年一届
**市场范围**：国际性
**上届规模**'09：参观人数62000人
**主办**：文化部文化产业司；国家广播电影电视总局社会管理司；国家新闻出版总署出版产业管理司；浙江省文化厅；浙江省新闻出版局；浙江省广播电视剧；中国文教体育用品协会；浙江省文化产业促进会
**支持**：商务部服务贸易司
**承办**：中共义乌市委；义乌市人民政府
**联系**：义乌中国小商品城展览有限公司
**地址**：浙江省义乌市宾王路301号梅湖会展中心展览一部（322000）
**联系人**：虞经理
**MSN**：expo@chinafairs.org

**China Yiwu Stationery & Arts Trade Fair**
**Venue**: Yiwu International Exhibition Center, Yiwu, Zhejiang
**Profile**: Stationery & Office Supplies, Sports & Recreation Articles, crafts & art, originality, curios & collection, International Cultural Exchange, Stamps, Calligraphy & Painting
**Established Year**: 2004
**Frequency**: Annual
**Market Area**: International
**Statistics '09**: Visitors 62,000
**Organizer**: Department of Culture Industry; Ministry of Culture; The State Administration of Radio Film and Television Social Administration Office; General Administration of Press and Publication Publications Distribution Office; Zhejiang Provincial Government
**Address**: 1/F, Hall 1, Sale 1 Dept., Meihu Exhibition Center, No.301 Binwang Road, Yiwu, Zhejiang
**MSN**: expo@chinafairs.org

2010/04/20 - 23
☎ 0579-8541 5333, 8541 5266, 8541 5277, 8541 5288
🖷 0579-8541 5244
✉ expo@chinafairs.org
www.yiwusourcingfair.com
7030

**义乌消费品出口交易会**
**地点**：义乌国际博览中心，浙江义乌
**内容**：家庭用品、工艺装饰、家居家纺、服装箱帽、汽车用品
**始办年份**：2006
**周期**：每年一届
**市场范围**：国际性
**上届规模**'09：展览面积15,000m²，参展商615家，参观人数5,886人
**主办**：浙江省对外贸易服务中心；浙江中国小商品城集团股份有限公司
**承办**：义乌中国小商品城展览有限公司；浙江远大国际会展有限公司
**联系**：义乌中国小商品城展览有限公司
**地址**：浙江省义乌市宾王路301号梅湖会展中心一楼展览三部（322000）
**联系人**：陈经理，黄小姐，吴先生
**MSN**：yiwufair@hotmail.com
**QQ**：435708

**Yiwu Sourcing Fair: Consumer Goods**
**Venue**: Yiwu International Exhibition Center, Yiwu, Zhejiang
**Profile**: Houseware, Decorative Process, Household & Home textile, Clothing shoes
**Established Year**: 2006
**Frequency**: Annual
**Market Area**: International
**Statistics '09**: Exhibition Area 15,000m², Exhibitors 615, Visitors 5,886
**Sponsor**: Zhejiang Foreign Trade Service Center; Zhejiang China Commodities City Group Co Ltd
**Organizer**: Yiwu China Commodities City Exhibition Co Ltd; Zhejiang Broad International Exhibition Co Ltd
**Address**: 1/F, Hall 1, Sale 3 Dept., Meihu Exhibition Center, No.301 Binwang Road, Yiwu, Zhejiang
**MSN**: yiwufair@hotmail.com

2010/04/20 - 23
☎ 0579-8541 5002, 8541 5003, 8541 5026, 8541 5262
🖷 0579-8541 5004
✉ web@hardwareexpo.cn
www.hardwareexpo.cn
7040

**中国国际五金电器博览会**
**地点**：义乌国际博览中心，浙江义乌
**内容**：五金工具、建筑五金、礼品五金、日用五金、厨卫酒店用品、五金休闲用品、机械设备 电子电器、缝配拉链、加工机械、五金机械、机电产品、模具产品
**始办年份**：2004
**周期**：每年一届
**市场范围**：国际性
**上届规模**'09：展览面积50,000m²，参观人数41,552人
**主办**：中国五金交电化工商业协会；义乌市人民政府
**承办**：浙江中国小商品城集团股份有限公司；义乌市五金家电行业协会
**联系**：中国国际五金电器博览会组委会办公室
**地址**：浙江省义乌市宾王路301号梅湖会展中心3号馆一楼（322000）
**联系人**：胡经理，黄先生，张小姐
**MSN**：yiwufair@hotmail.com
**QQ**：435708

**China International Hardware & Electrical Appliances Trade Fair**
**Venue**: Yiwu International Exhibition Center, Yiwu, Zhejiang
**Profile**: Hardware tools, architectural hardware, hardware gifts, daily-use hardware, hotel kitchen supplies, leisure item, machinery and equipment, electronics, equipped with sewing zipper, processing machinery, metal machine tool, mechanical and electrical products, mold products
**Established Year**: 2004
**Frequency**: Annual
**Market Area**: International
**Statistics '09**: Exhibition Area 50,000m², Visitors 41,552
**Sponsor**: China National Hardware Electric and Chemical Products Commercial Assn; Yiwu Municipal People's Government
**Organizer**: Zhejiang China Commodities City Group Co Ltd; Yiwu Hardware & Electrical Appliances Trade Assn
**Address**: 1/F, Hall 3, Meihu Exhibition Center, No.301 Binwang Road, Yiwu, Zhejiang
**MSN**: yiwufair@hotmail.com

2010/04/26 - 30
☎ 010-6651 9361
🖷 010-6651 9145
✉ ceieaweb@yahoo.com.cn
7050

**第59届中国教学仪器设备展示会**
**地点**：义乌国际博览中心，浙江义乌
**内容**：各种适用于幼儿教育、中小学教育、职业教育、高等教育、特殊教育的教育技术装备产品，包括计算机、网络设备、音像教材、教学软件、各学科教学仪器设备、校园家具、图书等。同时举行新技术新产品新闻发布会、采购信息发布会、合作交流论坛峰会等专题会议。
**周期**：每年两届
**市场范围**：全国性
**性质**：面向公众
**入场券价格**：免费
**参展费用**：3400元/展位
**上届规模**‘09：展览面积8,000m²，参展商500家，参观人数20,000人
**主办**：中国教学仪器设备行业协会
**地址**：北京市西城区辟才胡同丰汇园8号楼1101室（100032）
**联系人**：王文声

**59th China National Exhibition of Education Instruments**
**Venue**: Yiwu International Exhibition Center, Yiwu, Zhejiang
**Frequency**: Biannual
**Market Area**: National
**Nature**: Open to public
**Cost to Attend**: Free
**Participated Fee**: RMB 3,400/booth
**Statistics '09**: Exhibition Area 8,000m², Exhibitors 500, Visitors 20,000
**Organizer**: China Educational Instrument & Equipment Assn
**Address**: 8-1101# Building Fenghuiyuan, Picai Hutong, Xicheng District, Beijing
**Contact**: Wang Wensheng

2010/06/17 - 20
☎ 0579-8541 5111, 8541 5222, 8541 5333
🖷 0579-8541 5005, 8541 5444, 8541 5777
✉ expo@chinafairs.org
www.tourismfair.cn
7060

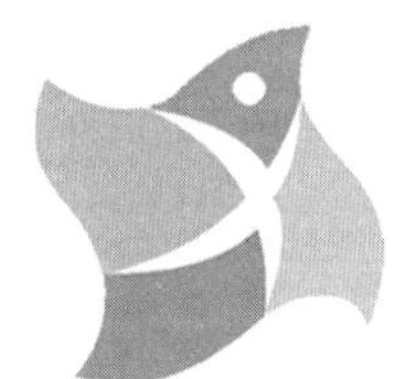

**中国国际旅游商品博览会**
**地点**：义乌国际博览中心，浙江义乌
**内容**：时尚消费品、旅游工艺品、旅游休闲用品、酒店用品、旅游食品、旅游交通工具及游乐设备
**始办年份**：2009
**周期**：每年一届
**市场范围**：国际性
**上届规模**‘09：参观人数60,000人
**主办**：国家旅游局；浙江省人民政府
**承办**：中国旅游协会（旅游商品分会）；浙江省旅游局；义乌市人民政府
**联系**：义乌中国小商品城展览有限公司
**地址**：浙江省义乌市宾王路301号梅湖会展中心一楼展览部（322000）
**联系人**：胡经理，贾小姐
**MSN**：yiwufair@hotmail.com
**QQ**：435708

**China International Tourism Commodities Fair**
**Venue**: Yiwu International Exhibition Center, Yiwu, Zhejiang
**Profile**: Fashionable consumer goods, tourism crafts, tourism leisure products, hotel products, traveling food, traveling transportation and playground equipment, tourist attractions, service organizations
**Established Year**: 2009
**Frequency**: Annual
**Market Area**: International
**Statistics '09**: Visitors 60000
**Sponsor**: National Tourism Administration; Zhejiang Provincial People' s Government
**Organizer**: China Tourism Assn; Zhejiang Tourism Bureau; Yiwu Municipal People's Government
**Address**: 1/F, Hall 1, Sale Dept., Meihu Exhibition Center, No.301 Binwang Road, Yiwu, Zhejiang
**MSN**: yiwufair@hotmail.com

2010/10/21 - 25
☎ 0579-8541 5111, 8541 5222, 8541 5333
🖷 0579-8541 5777, 8541 5444
✉ expo@chinafairs.org
www.yiwufair.com
7070

**中国义乌国际小商品博览会**
**地点**：义乌国际博览中心，浙江义乌
**内容**：文化办公、体育娱乐、玩具、针织辅料、服装鞋帽、化妆洗涤、五金机电、电子电器、箱包皮具、流行首饰、工艺礼品、工艺装饰、日用品、汽车用品、服务贸易、国际馆、水晶馆
**始办年份**：1995
**周期**：每年一届
**市场范围**：国际性
**上届规模**‘09：展览面积100,000m²，参观人数123,296人
**主办**：中华人民共和国商务部；浙江省人民政府；中国贸促会；中国轻工业联合会；中国商业联合会
**承办**：浙江省对外贸易经济合作厅；义乌市人民政府
**联系**：义乌中国小商品城展览有限公司
**地址**：浙江省义乌市宾王路301号梅湖会展中心一楼展览部（322000）
**联系人**：虞经理，何经理
**MSN**：yiwufair@hotmail.com
**QQ**：435708

**China Yiwu International Commodities Fair**
**Venue**: Yiwu International Exhibition Center, Yiwu, Zhejiang
**Profile**: Stationery & Office Supplies, Sports & Recreation Articles, Toys, Knitting Accessories, Garment Footwear & Headwear, Cosmetics & Beauty-care Products, Hardware & Machinery, Electronic & Electrical Appliances, Leather, Cases & Bags, Artistic Gifts, Artistic Decorations, Home Appliances, Auto Supplies, Trade Services, International Hall, Crystal & Glass Products Hall
**Established Year**: 1995
**Frequency**: Annual
**Market Area**: International
**Statistics '09**: Exhibition Area 100m000m², Visitors 123,296
**Organizer**: Ministry of Commerce of the P.R.C.; Zhejiang Provincial People's Government; CCPIT; China National Light Industry Council; China General Chamber of Commerce Supporter: Foreign Trade and Economic Cooperation
**Address**: 1/F, Hall 1, Sale Dept., Meihu Exhibition Center, No.301 Binwang Road, Yiwu, Zhejiang
**MSN**: yiwufair@hotmail.com

2010/11/01 - 04
☎ 0579-8541 5255, 8547 1966, 8547 1333
🖷 0579-8541 5244
✉ expo@chinafairs.org
www.forestryfair.com
7080

**中国义乌（国际）森林产品博览会**
**地点：**义乌国际博览中心，浙江义乌
**内容：**竹木工艺、竹木玩具、竹木日用品、竹炭制品、竹木人造板、竹木家具、竹木地板、花卉园艺、森林食品、竹木工机械
**始办年份：**2008
**周期：**每年一届
**市场范围：**国际性
**上届规模** '09：参展商1,000家，参观人数50,000人
**主办：**国家林业局
**承办：**浙江省林业厅；义乌市人民政府
**地址：**浙江省义乌市宾王路301号梅湖会展中心一楼（322000）
**联系人：**陈经理，王先生
**MSN：**yiwufair@hotmail.com
**QQ：**435708

**China Yiwu (International) Forest Product Fair**
**Venue:** Yiwu International Exhibition Center, Yiwu, Zhejiang
**Profile:** Bamboo and wooden crafts, bamboo and wooden toys, bamboo and wooden daily necessities, bamboo charcoal products, wood-based panel, wood furniture, flooring material, flower and gardening, forest food, bamboo and wood processing machinery
**Established Year:** 2008
**Frequency:** Annual
**Market Area:** International
**Statistics '09:** Exhibitors 1,000, Visitors 50,000
**Sponsor:** State Forestry Administration
**Organizer:** Zhejiang Provincial Forestry Department; Yiwu Municipal People Government
**Address:** 1/F, Hall 1, Sale 3 Dept., Meihu Exhibition Center, No.301 Binwang Road, Yiwu, Zhejiang
**MSN:** yiwufair@hotmail.com

2010/11/18 - 20
☎ 0579-8541 5801, 8541 5265
🖷 0579-8541 5444
✉ expo@chinafairs.org
www.2456.com/yiwu
7090

**第十一届中国（义乌）国际袜子、针织及染整机械展览会**
**第四届中国（义乌）国际针织纱线展览会**
**地点：**义乌国际博览中心，浙江义乌
**内容：**针织机械、染整机械、服装机械、商标印花机械、针织机械配件、纱线纤维、针织辅料
**始办年份：**1999
**周期：**每年一届
**市场范围：**国际性
**上届规模** '09：展览面积9,000m²，参展商140家，参观人数5,500人
**主办：**中国国际贸易促进会浙江分会；浙江中国小商品城集团股份有限公司；香港雅式展览服务有限公司
**承办：**义乌中国小商品城展览有限公司；浙江省经贸国际展览中心
联系：义乌中国小商品城展览有限公司
**地址：**浙江省义乌市宾王路301号梅湖会展中心一楼展览一部（322000）
**联系人：**何经理，周先生
**MSN：**yiwufair@hotmail.com

**The 10th Yiwu International Exhibition on Hosiery, Knitting, Dyeing & Finishing Machinery/ The 3rd China (Yiwu) International Exhibition on Knitting Yarns**
**Venue:** Yiwu International Exhibition Center, Yiwu, Zhejiang
**Profile:** Knitting machinery, finishing machinery, garment machinery, label printing machinery, knitting machine parts, yarn fibers, knitting accessories
**Established Year:** 1999
**Frequency:** Annual
**Market Area:** International
**Statistics '09:** Exhibition Area 9,000m², Exhibitors 140, Visitors 5,500
**Organizer:** CCPIT, Zhejiang Sub-Council; Zhejiang China Commodities City Group Co Ltd; Adsale Exhibition Services Ltd
**Supporter:** Yiwu China Commodities City Exhibition Co Ltd; Zhejiang Economy and Trade International Committee
**Address:** 1/F, Hall 1, Sale 1 Dept., China Commodities City Exhibition Center, No.301 Binwang Road, Yiwu, Zhejiang
**MSN:** yiwufair@hotmail.com

# 浙江-余姚
# Zhejiang-Yuyao

2010/11/06 - 09
☎ 852-2763 9011
🖷 852-2341 0379
✉ info@paper-com.com.hk
www.paper-com.com.hk
7100

**第十二届中国塑料博览会**
**地点：**中塑国际会展中心，浙江余姚
**周期：**每年一届
**市场范围：**国际性
**主办：**讯通展览公司
**地址：**香港九龙观塘成业街11号华成工商中心5字楼15室

**The 12th China Plastics Expo**
**Venue:** Yuyao China Plastic International Exhibition Center, Yuyao, Zhejiang

# 国内展览会议
# 行业索引

# Exhibitions and Conferences in Mainland China
# Index of Industry/ Profession – Classification

1. General Fair

A

20. Advertising & Media
42. Agriculture, Animal Husbandry, Fishery & Forestry
33. Air-conditioning, Heating, Refrigeration, Ventilation
37. Aluminum Industry
70. Arts
43. Automobiles and Motorcycles
21. Aviation, Aerospace & Airport

B

8. Battery & Power Supply
39. Beauty, Cosmetics, Hairdressing & Spa
78. Bikes
6. Boats, Ship Building and Marine
57. Books
18. Broadcasting, Film, Television & Stage
27. Building, Construction, Decoration and Materials

C

63. Cable
53. Ceramic and Glass
23. Chemical Industry
44. Cleaning
14. Clothing and Textile
11. Comics and Games
16. Construction Machinery
64. Consumer Electronics & Appliances
65. Consumer Goods
4. Contracts
59. Culture Industry

D

13. Defense and Police Equipment
46. Design

E

29. Education and Teaching Instrument
9. Electric Power, Electrical Engineering
10. Electronics
24. Environment Protection

F

48. Food, Beverage, Tea, Spirit and Processing
54. Franchising
26. Furniture, Woodworking

G

36. Gifts
60. Hardware & Tools
31. Hotel and Restaurant

I

67. Information Technology & Communication Technology
69. Instrument
56. Investment and Finance

J

77. Jewelry
74. Job Fairs

L

49. Laboratory Equipment
7. Lighting
62. Logistics
45. Luxury Life

M

32. Machinery, Machine Tools and Technology & Automation
71. Medical Equipment, Pharmaceuticals and Health Care
30. Metalworking, Metallurgy and Foundry
34. Mining
40. Mold
72. Music Instrument

N

15. New & Hi-Tech
41. New Energy and Energy-Saving

O

20. Opto-Electronic

P

3. Packaging
75. Paper
50. Petroleum, Gas, Petrochemical
5. Pets
47. Photography and Image
17. Pipeline, Pump and Value
52. Plastics and Rubbers
68. Printing

R

12. Real Estate
35. Retail

S

2. Safety and Security
66. Shoes & Leather
73. Show Business
55. Sports and Leisure
59. Stationery & Office Supplies

T

38. Tourism
58. Toys and Children's Products
28. Transportation

W

76. Watches, Clocks & Optics
51. Water Treatment
25. Wedding
22. Welding
79. Others

# 1. 综合博览会 General Fair

中国华东进出口商品交易会
East China Fair
2010/03/01-05
上海Shanghai 1350

第十四届对台进出口商品交易会
14th China Xiamen Machinery and Electronics Exhibition (CXMEE)
2010/04/08-11
福建厦门Fujian-Xiamen 4340

2010第三届大连市出口企业产品展销会
Dalian Export Enterprise Products Fair
2010/05/29-31
辽宁大连Liaoning-Dalian 6260

第三届南亚国家商品展
3rd South Asian Countries Commodity Fair
2010/06/06-10
云南昆明Yunnan-Kunming 6933

第十八届中国昆明进出口商品交易会
18th China Import & Export Fair, Kunming
2010/06/06-10
云南昆明Yunnan-Kunming 6935

第二十一届中国哈尔滨国际经济贸易洽谈会
21th China Harbin Intl Economiv and Trade Fair
2010/06/15-19
黑龙江哈尔滨Heilongjiang-Harbin 5660

广东外商投资企业产品（内销）博览会
Guangdong Foreign-invested Enterprises Commodities Fair
2010/06/18-21
广东东莞Guangdong-Dongguan 5436

河南省投资贸易洽谈会
Henan Investment and Trade Council
2010/08 -
河南郑州Henan-Zhengzhou 5860

2010第四届中国东北（沈阳）政府采购展览会
Norast China (Shenyang) Intl Exhibition for Government Purchase
2010/08/19-21
辽宁沈阳Liaoning-Shenyang 6580

2010第四届上海进口商品博览会
4th Shanghai Imports Expo 2010
2010/08/26-29
上海Shanghai 3250

第四届中国东北亚（沈阳）进口商品博览会
4th China Norast Asia (Shenyang) Import Fair
2010/09 -
辽宁沈阳Liaoning-Shenyang 6590

中国乌鲁木齐对外经济贸易洽谈会
China Urumqi Foreign Economic Relations & Trade Fair
2010/09/01-05
新疆乌鲁木齐Xinjiang-Urumqi 6910

第十四届中国国际投资贸易洽谈会
14th China Intl Fair for Investment & Trade
2010/09/08-11
福建厦门Fujian-Xiamen 4400

2010年中国（上海）国际跨国采购大会
2010 Intl Sourcing Fair (Shanghai, China.)
2010/09/16-18
上海Shanghai 3510

2010年常州科技经贸洽谈会
Changzhou Technological and Economic Fair
2010/09/20-23
江苏常州Jiangsu-Changzhou 6080

2010郑州全国商品交易会
2010 Zhengzhou National Commodity Fair
2010/10 -
河南郑州Henan-Zhengzhou 5910

中国国际西部博览会
2010/10/10-25
四川成都Sichuan-Chengdu 6895

第七届中国-东盟博览会/ 中国-东盟商务与投资分会
7th China ASEAN Expo
2010/10/20-24
广西南宁Guangxi-Nanning 5590

中国义乌国际小商品博览会
China Yiwu Intl Commodities Fair
2010/10/21-25
浙江义乌Zhejiang-Yiwu 6770

香港博览会
2010/11/07-14
四川成都Sichuan-Chengdu 6895

全国库存商品及闲置物资博览交易会
China Store Goods and Idle Products Trade Fair
2010/12/04-07
山东青岛Shandong-Qingdao 6720

# 2. 安全 Safety and Security

居民家庭和沿街商铺实用技防产品展示会
Safety and Security Exhibition
2010/01/15-17
江苏南京Jiangsu-Nanjing 6100

2010中国（上海）国际突发事件灾难预防及救援装备技术展览会暨中国（上海）国际紧急医疗救援装备技术展览会
China Rescue Expo 2010
2010/03/17-19
上海Shanghai 1500

2010第八届中国（郑州）社会公共安全产品博览会
2010 8th China Zhengzhou Public Security Product Expo
2010/04 -
河南郑州Henan-Zhengzhou 5800

第十届成都国际社会公共安全产品与技术展览会
2010/04/10-15
四川成都Sichuan-Chengdu 6895

湖南公共安全产品与技术博览会
Hunan Safety and Security Expo
2010/04/22-24
湖南长沙Hunan-Changsha 6000

2010第九届南京社会公共安全防范产品展览会
Nanjing public security defensive prooucts exhibition
2010/04/27-29
江苏南京Jiangsu-Nanjing 6120

第十届上海社会公共安全产品国际博览会
10th Shanghai Intl Exhibition On Public Safety And Security
2010/05/13-15
上海Shanghai 2260

第五届中国国际安全生产及职业健康展览会
5th China Intl Occupational Safety & Health Exhibition (COS+H 2010)
2010/09/01-03
北京Beijing 855

北京国际减灾应急技术设备博览会
Beijing Intl Disaster Reduction Expo
2010/10/11-13
北京Beijing 910

2010上海司法警用及安全防范技术产品博览会
Shanghai Security Products Expo
2010/10/14-16
上海Shanghai 3680

2010年中国国际社会公共安全产品博览会
10th China Intl Exhibition on Public Safety and Security
2010/11/02-05
北京Beijing 1145

# 3. 包装 Packaging

2010安徽印刷包装工业展览会
Anhui Printing & Packaging Industry Exhibition
2010/03/06-08
安徽合肥Anhui-Hefei 4170

2010第11届中国东北国际塑胶机械及包装工业展览会
11th North China Intl Plastics Machinery & Packaging Exhibition 2010
2010/03/18-21
辽宁沈阳Liaoning-Shenyang 6370

2010第十四届武汉广告展览会/ 第二届武汉印刷/包装/纸业展览会
2010 Wuhan Ad Exhibition
2010/03/30-01
湖北武汉Hubei-Wuhan 5930

励华国际瓦楞展2010中国展
SinoCorrugated
2010/04/07-09
广东东莞Guangdong-Dongguan 4490

2010励华国际彩盒展
SinoFoldingCarton

2010/04/07-09
广东东莞Guangdong-Dongguan 4500

第八届中国北京国际食品加工与包装机械展览会
8th China Beijing Intl Food Processing & Packaging Machinery Exhibition
2010/04/10-12
北京Beijing 330

第64届中国国际医药原料药、中间体、包装、设备交易会（春季）
64th API China (active pharmaceutical ingredient)
2010/05/18-20
黑龙江哈尔滨Heilongjiang-Harbin 5640

世界制药工业中国展
（医药、包装材料、制药设备展区）
INTERPHEX CHINA
2010/05/18-20
黑龙江哈尔滨Heilongjiang-Harbin 5650

2010中国国际包装博览会
Beijing Intl Packaging Fair 2010
2010/06/02-04
北京Beijing 1145

第十八届上海国际印刷包装纸业展览会/2010上海国际印刷包装产品交易会
Shanghai Intl Print Exhibition 2010
2010/07/07-10
上海Shanghai 2890

PPI彩盒印刷包装展
China Folding Carton
2010/10/13-15
天津Tianjin 4150

## 4. 承包 转包 外包 Contracts

2010中国国际工业转包展览会
China Industrial Subcontracting & Outsourcing Fair 2010
2010/04/20-22
重庆Chongqing 1170

第三届中国国际服务外包合作大会
China Intl Service Outsourcing Cooperation Conference 2010
2010/06/06-07
江苏南京Jiangsu-Nanjing 6140

## 5. 宠物 Pets

2010上海宠物大会暨第三届上海宠物医疗学术研讨会
Pet Fair Shanghai 2010
2010/03/12-14
上海Shanghai 1460

第十三届亚洲宠物展览会
Pet Fair Asia 2010
2010/09/02-05
上海Shanghai 3330

2010广州宠物水族用品展
2010 Guangzhou Pet &Auqarium Show
2010/09/21-24
广东广州Guangdong-Guangzhou 5050

第十四届中国国际宠物水族用品展览会
CIPS 2010
2010/10/30-02
北京Beijing 1145

## 6. 船艇 海事 港口 Boats, Ship Building and Marine

中国(上海)国际游艇展
China (Shanghai) Intl Boat Show 2010
2010/04/08-11
上海Shanghai 1900

GLE2010广西泛北部湾港口、物流及仓储设备展览会
GLE 2010 Guangxi Fan-Beibu Gulf Equipment of Port & Logistics & Storage Exhibition
2010/07/02-04
广西南宁Guangxi-Nanning 5530

第四届中国(上海)国际船舶工业博览会 暨第十五届全国海事科学技术研讨会
4th Intl Shipbuilding Industry Expo Of China 15th National Marine Science and Technology Seminar
2010/08/18-20
上海Shanghai 3190

第四届中国（深圳）国际游艇及设备展览会
SIBEX - China (Shenzhen) Intl Boat Show
2010/11/04-07
广东深圳Guangdong-Shenzhen 5480

第二届中国国际海洋工程技术和装备展
China Intl Exhibition on Ocean EngineeringTechnology & Equipment 2010
2010/11/08-10
上海Shanghai 3840

第三届中国国际造船工业装备和船舶设计建造技术展
China Intl Exhibition on Shipbuilding Equipment, Ship Design & Manufacturing Tech 2010
2010/11/08-10
上海Shanghai 3850

## 7. 灯光照明 灯饰 Lighting

第十届成都照明+建筑电气博览会暨LED展览会
2010/03/31-05
四川成都Sichuan-Chengdu 6895

中国（北京）第十一届国际照明电器博览会
Beijing Intl Illumination Exhibition
2010/04/10-12
北京Beijing 1145

第四届中国国际新光源&新能源照明展览会暨论坛
Green Lighting China Expo and Forum 2010
2010/04/20-22
上海Shanghai 2035

2010第六届北京国际LED展览会
6th Beijing Intl LED exposition
2010/05/07-09
北京Beijing 1145

第十九届中国国际专业音响、灯光、乐器及技术展览会
19th China Intl Exhibition on Pro Audio, Light, Music & Technology
2010/05/20-23
北京Beijing 510

2010上海国际照明展
SHANGHAI Intl LIGHTING EXPO 2010
2010/07/07-10
上海Shanghai 2840

2010上海国际照明技术设备展览会
Shanghai Intl Lighting Technology & Equipment Exhibition 2010
2010/07/07-10
上海Shanghai 2930

2010上海国际户外广告发光体技术及城市景观照明设备展览会
Shanghai Intl Outdoor AD Illuminating & City Lighting Technology & Equipment Exhibition 2010
2010/07/07-10
上海Shanghai 2940

中国国际家居饰品布艺及灯饰展览会
Finishing Fabrics & Lightings China 2010
2010/09/07-10
上海Shanghai 3370

上海国际专业灯光音响展览会
prolight + Sound Shanghai
2010/10/12-15
上海Shanghai 3660

## 8. 电池 电源 Battery & Power Supply

第二届中国（上海）国际电源产业展览会
2nd China (ShangHai) Intl Power Supply Industry Fair
2010/04/08-10
上海Shanghai 1880

第二届中国（上海）国际电池产品及技术展览会
2nd China (ShangHai) Intl Battery Industry Fair
2010/04/08-10
上海Shanghai 1870

二届中国（上海）国际铅酸蓄电池展览会
2nd China (ShangHai) Intl Lead Battery Industry Fair
2010/04/08-10
上海Shanghai 1890

2010中国（上海）国际超级电容器产业展览会
2nd China (ShangHai) Intl Lead Battery Industry Fair
2010/04/08-10
上海Shanghai 1850

第九届中国国际电池技术交流会/展览会
9th China Intl Battery Fair
2010/06/24-26
广东深圳Guangdong-Shenzhen 5280

中国（北京）国际五金机电工业博览会暨电池电子工业展览会
China Intl Hardware Industry Expo, Beijing
2010/08/05-07
北京Beijing 1145

# 9. 电力 电工 Electric Power, Electrical Engineering

中国东北第13届国际电力电工及能源技术设备展览会
13th Norast China Intl Electric Power, Electrician and Energy Tech & Equipment Exhibition 2010
2010/04/01-03
辽宁沈阳Liaoning-Shenyang 6510

第十届中国国际电力电工设备暨电厂脱硫脱硝展览会
China Epower 2010
2010/04/21-23
上海Shanghai 2040

中国（上海）国际风能展览会暨研讨会
第8届中国国际动力设备及发电机组展览会
4th China Intl Wind Energy Exhibition and Conference
2010/04/27-29
上海Shanghai 2070

电力展
2010/05/08-13
四川成都Sichuan-Chengdu 6895

第八届深圳国际小电机及电机工业展览会
8th China(Shenzhen) Intl Small Motor and Electric Machinery Exhibition
2010/06/24-26
广东深圳Guangdong-Shenzhen 5290

北京国际风能、太阳能核电工业暨电力设备技术展览会
2010 Beijing Intl Wind, Solar, Nuclear Power Industry and Power Electrical Equipment and Technology Exhibition
2010/09/19-21
北京Beijing 1145

第十三届国际电力设备及技术展览会/ 2010国际节能、电力环保及脱硫脱硝装备展览会/ 第六届国际电机工程及电工装备展览会
EP China 2010
2010/10/19-21
北京Beijing 1145

第九届国际电磁兼容与安规认证暨微波展览会
9th Intl conference& exhibition on elcctromagnetic compatibility
2010/11/02-04
上海Shanghai 3820

# 10. 电子 Electronics

慕尼黑上海电子展
electronica & Productronica China
2010/03/16-18
上海Shanghai 1480

慕尼黑上海激光、光电展
LASER World of PHOTONICS CHINA
2010/03/16-18
上海Shanghai 1470

第十届成都照明+建筑电气博览会暨LED展览会
2010/03/31-05
四川成都Sichuan-Chengdu 6895

第十四届对台进出口商品交易会
14th China Xiamen Machinery and Electronics Exhibition (CXMEE)
2010/04/08-11
福建厦门Fujian-Xiamen 4340

2010年春季（第75届）中国电子展
75th China Electronics Fair (CEF Shenzhen)
2010/04/09-11
广东深圳Guangdong-Shenzhen 5150

中国（北京）第十一届国际照明电器博览会
Beijing Intl Illumination Exhibition
2010/04/10-12
北京Beijing 1145

第二十届中国国际电子生产设备暨微电子工业展/ 中国国际电子制造技术展览会
NEPCON/ EMT China 2010
2010/04/20-22
上海Shanghai 2030

第十九届华南（东莞）国际电子制造采购博览会
South China Electronic Fair
2010/05/14-16
广东东莞Guangdong-Dongguan 4530

第四届亚洲（东莞）国际激光加工技术论坛暨应用展
Laser Bocessing Technology Forum and Equipment Application Fair
2010/05/14-16
广东东莞Guangdong-Dongguan 4520

2010第六届北京国际LED展览会
6th Beijing Intl LED exposition
2010/05/07-09
北京Beijing 1145

环球资源消费类电子产品采购交易会
China Sourcing Fair-Electronics
2010/06/02-04
上海Shanghai 2520

2010北京国际电子工业节能技术、产品展览会
China Television Shopping Exposition 2010
2010/06/10-12
北京Beijing 1145

中国（成都）国际电子生产设备及技术展览会
NEPCON West China 2010
2010/06/22-24
四川成都Sichuan-Chengdu 6840

2010第十八届多人行电子展、光电展
2010 18th DEX Electronic Exhibition & Photonics Exhibition
2010/06/23-25
广东深圳Guangdong-Shenzhen 5240

第十五届华南国际电子生产设备暨微电子工业展/ 华南国际电子制造技术展览会
NEPCON/ EMT South China 2010
2010/08/31-02
广东深圳Guangdong-Shenzhen 5390

华南国际汽车电子展览会
Automotive Electronics South China
2010/08/31-02
广东深圳Guangdong-Shenzhen 5400

2010中国（西部）电子展
Chengdu – China Electronics Fair
2010/09/07-09
四川成都Sichuan-Chengdu 6860

第十五届国际集成电路研讨会暨展览会
15th Intl IC-China Conference & Exhibition
2010/09/16-17
广东东莞Guangdong-Dongguan 5438

第十一届中国国际机电产品博览会
11th China Intl Machinery & Electronic Products Exposition
2010/09/23-26
湖北武汉Hubei-Wuhan 5960

2010洛阳机电产品博览会
Luoyang Machinery and Electronic Products Expo
2010/10 -
河南洛阳Henan-Luoyang 5680

2010北京国际广告技术设备展及LED展览会
China Exhibition of Advertisement & Sign 2010, Beijing
2010/10/27-29
北京Beijing 1145

中国国际光电产业博览会暨中国国际激光，电子及光显产业展览会/中国国际机器视觉展览会暨机器视觉技术及工业应用研讨会
Optoelectronics Industry Exposition (Beijing) & Intl Lasers, Optoelectronics and Photonics Exhibition
2010/10/27-29
北京Beijing 1145

第九届国际电磁兼容与安规认证暨微波展览会
9th Intl conference& exhibition on elcctromagnetic compatibility
2010/11/02-04
上海Shanghai 3820

第五届微波及天线技术交流展览会
5th Intl conference& exhibition on microwave and antenna
2010/11/02-04
上海Shanghai 3810

第76届中国电子展暨2010亚洲电子展
China Electronics Fair
2010/11/10-12
上海Shanghai 3870

第十二届中国国际高新技术成果交易会电子展
China Hi-Tech Fair/Elec
2010/11/16-21
广东深圳Guangdong-Shenzhen 5500

## 11. 动漫 游戏 Comics and Games

第六届中国（深圳）文化产业博览交易会数字影视*动漫游戏展
China （Shenzhen） Intl Cultural Industries Fair "DTV/COM & ANI EXHIBITION"
2010/05/14-17
广东深圳Guangdong-Shenzhen 5210

动漫展
2010/05/18-23
四川成都Sichuan-Chengdu 6895

2010中国西部（成都）国际电玩展览会
2010/05/19-23
四川成都Sichuan-Chengdu 6895

中国（北京）玩具动漫教育文化博览会
China toys and animation educational expo
2010/07/29-01
北京Beijing 765

中国国际数码互动娱乐产品及技术应用展览会
China Joy
7th China Digital Entertainment Expo & Conference
2010/07/29-01
上海Shanghai 3090

第二届动漫节
2nd Shenzhen Animation Festival
2010/08/12-16
广东深圳Guangdong-Shenzhen 5380

2010年中国（常州）国际动漫艺术周
China (Changzhou) Animation Festival
2010/10/28-02
江苏常州Jiangsu-Changzhou 6090

## 12. 房地产 Real Estate

上海之春房产展示交易会
Shanghai Spring Real Estate Market
2010/03/18-21
上海Shanghai 1510

2010中部住宅及科技产业博览会
2010 China Central Real Estate and Tech Industry Expo
2010/04 -
河南郑州Henan-Zhengzhou 5810

2010年中国北京春季房地产展示交易会
16th China Intl Trade Fair for Home Textiles and Accessories
2010/04/08-11
北京Beijing 320

第八届中国国际家居博览会
7th China Intl Housing and Furnishing Exposition
2010/04/09-12
浙江宁波Zhejiang-Ningbo 6980

上海房地产春季展示会
Holiday Real Estate Market
2010/05/01-04
上海Shanghai 2120

春季房地产交易会
2010/05/01-06
四川成都Sichuan-Chengdu 6895

2010年常州房地产交易会
2010 Changzhou Real Estate Fair
2010/05/18-22
江苏常州Jiangsu-Changzhou 6050

第六届亚洲不动产投资峰会
Asia Property Investment Showcase & Conference
2010/06/24-25
上海Shanghai 2770

2010年中国北京夏季房地产展示交易会
Summer Real Estate Trade Fair Beijing China
2010/06/24-27
北京Beijing 710

2010年中国北京秋季房地产展示交易会
Autumn Real Estate Trade Fair Beijing China
2010/09/16-19
北京Beijing 880

中国国际高端物业展
China Intl Luxury Property Show
2010/09/17-19
上海Shanghai 3520

秋季房交会
2010/10/01-06
四川成都Sichuan-Chengdu 6895

上海房地产秋季展示会
Holiday Real Estate Market
2010/10/03-06
上海Shanghai 3610

第十五届中国宁波国际住宅产品博览会
15th china ningbo Intl exhibition on rlousing industry products
2010/11 -
浙江宁波Zhejiang-Ningbo 6710

2010年中国北京冬季房地产展示交易会
Winter Real Estate Trade Fair Beijing China
2010/11/25-28
北京Beijing 1070

## 13. 防务 警用设备 Defense & Police Equipment

2010第九届南京社会公共安全防范产品展览会
Nanjing public security defensive products exhibition
2010/04/27-29
江苏南京Jiangsu-Nanjing 6120

2010第五届中国国际军民两用技术展览会
5th Military and Civil Technology Exhibition
2010/09/19-21
北京Beijing 890

2010上海司法警用及安全防范技术产品博览会
Shanghai Security Products Expo
2010/10/14-16
上海Shanghai 3680

## 14. 纺织 服装 服饰 及生产机械 Clothing & Textile

2010名品衣装（厦门）博览会
Brand Name Apparel (Xiamen) Show
2010/01/06-17
福建厦门Fujian-Xiamen 4270

环球资源流行服饰配件采购交易会及环球资源婴儿及儿童采购交易会，环球资源及赠品采购交易会
China Sourcing Fair：
Fashion Accessories
Baby & Children' s Products
Gifts & Premiums
2010/01/13-15
上海Shanghai 1320

北京2010年TOP100名牌服饰折扣购物展
Top 100 Brand Name Apparel Sale
2010/01/13-19
北京Beijing 20

新品服装暨名优产品年货会
New Apparel and Brand Name Products Shopping Fair
2010/01/19-29
福建厦门Fujian-Xiamen 4280

北方服装节厦门博览会
Fashion Festival
2010/01/30-09
福建厦门Fujian-Xiamen 4290

首届休闲服装服饰暨棉纺织品博览会
2010/03/06-22
新疆库尔勒Xinjiang

第十六届上海国际服装纺织品贸易博览会
Shanghai Intl Clothing & Textile Expo
2010/03/10-12
上海Shanghai 1400

春季品牌服装博览会
2010/03/12-20
四川成都Sichuan-Chengdu 6895

首届休闲服装服饰暨棉纺织品博览会
2010/03/12-23
陕西西安Shaanxi-Xi'an

中国（广州）国际家用纺织品及辅料博览会
China (Guangzhou) Intl Trade Fair for Home Textiles
2010/03/18-21
广东广州Guangdong-Guangzhou 4730

首届休闲服装服饰暨棉纺织品博览会
2010/03/21-06
新疆昌吉Xinjiang-

首届休闲服装服饰暨棉纺织品博览会
2010/03/27-08
宁夏银川Ningxia-Yinchuan

第十八届中国国际服装服饰博览会
18th China Intl Clothing & Accessories Fair (CHIC2010)
2010/03/28-31
北京Beijing 180

中国国际服装服饰博览会
China Intl Clothing & Accessories Fair
2010/03/28-31
北京Beijing 200

第十一届中国(东莞)国际纺织制衣工业技术展
11th China (Dongguan) Intl Textile & Clothing Industry Fair
2010/03/29-01
广东东莞Guangdong-Dongguan 4480

中国国际纺织面料及辅料（春夏）博览会
China Intl Trade Fair for Apparel Fabrics and Accessories
2010/03/30-01
北京Beijing 220

中国国际纺织纱线（春夏）展览会
China Intl Trade Fair for Fibres and Yarns
2010/03/31-02
北京Beijing 240

中国（上海）国际袜业采购交易会
China (Shanghai) Intl Hosiery Purchasing Expo
2010/04/01-03
上海Shanghai 1800

首届休闲服装服饰暨棉纺织品博览会
2010/04/10-25
新疆伊宁Xinjiang-

2010中国内衣面料辅料博览会
Underwear fabric accessories in 2010 Expo in China
2010/04/11-13
上海Shanghai 1950

2010中国家用纺织品面料及家居布艺博览会
2010 China's home textile fabric and home sewing expo
2010/04/11-13
上海Shanghai 1960

第92届中国针棉织品交易会
China Intl Trade Fair Mode Underwear and Home Textiles
2010/04/12-14
上海Shanghai 1920

第四届品牌服装服饰暨丝绸品牌博览会
2010/04/12-28
陕西西安Shaanxi-Xi'an

第十届中国国际染料工业暨有机颜料、纺织化学品展览会
CHINA INTERDYE 2010 ( 10th China Intl Dye Industry, Pigments and Textile Chemicals Exhibition)
2010/04/14-16
上海Shanghai 2000

第十三届海峡两岸纺织服装博览会暨2010年休闲服装博览会
thirteenth Strait Textile & Clothing Fairs（STCF）
2010/04/18-21
福建石狮Fujian-Shishi 4250

第27届中国国际丝网印刷及数字技术展览会
2010年中国国际服装服饰及面料印花技术展览会
27th China Screen Print Expo
2010 China Textile Print Expo
2010/04/27-29
上海Shanghai 2060

春夏服装博览会
2010/04/28-16
四川成都Sichuan-Chengdu 6895

苏杭丝绸暨品牌服装服饰赴（新疆）博览会
2010/04/30-17
新疆乌鲁木齐Xinjiang-Urumqi 00

李宁订货会
2010/05/13-24
四川成都Sichuan-Chengdu 6895

第98届中国鞋业/皮具商品博览会暨“名品进名店”对接展会
98th Chinese Shoes & Lear Commodity and “Well-Known Brands & Famous Shops” Exposition
2010/05/17-19
上海Shanghai 2270

2010第七届上海纺织服装采购交易会
2010 (7th) Shanghai Textile & Apparel Trade Fair
2010/05/19-21
上海Shanghai 2370

苏杭丝绸暨品牌服装服饰赴（石河子）博览会
2010/05/21-06
新疆石河子Xinjiang-

第六届苏杭丝绸服装服饰赴（银川）展示展销会
2010/05/22-07
宁夏Ningxia-

第五届中国（郑州）国际酒店、餐饮、泳池沐浴SPA设备及用品博览会/ 第五届中国（郑州）国际家纺、布艺及工艺品、礼品家居装饰博览会
5th China (Zhengzhou) Intl Hotel, F&B, Swimming pool and SPA Equipment and Product Expo/ 5th China (Zhengzhou) Household Textile, Cloth Art, Handicraft and Decoration Article Expo
2010/06 -
河南郑州Henan-Zhengzhou 5840

2010第九届中国（上海）国际纺织品面辅料博览会
2010 9TH CHINA（SHANGHAI）INTL TEXTILES, FABRICS & ACCESSORIES EXHIBITION2010 9TH CHINA（SHANGHAI）INTL TEXTILES, FABRICS & ACCESSORIES EXHIBITION
2010/06/08-10
上海Shanghai 2620

苏杭丝绸暨品牌服装服饰赴（新疆）博览会
2010/06/09-22
新疆昌吉Xinjiang-

第六届苏杭丝绸服装服饰展示展销会
2010/06/12-28
陕西西安Shaanxi-Xi'an

苏杭丝绸暨品牌服装服饰赴（新疆）博览会
2010/06/26-07
新疆库尔勒Xinjiang-

成都夏季丝绸服装展
2010/06/26-11
四川成都Sichuan-Chengdu 6895

第十届中国（深圳）国际品牌服装服饰交易会
10th China (Shenzhen) Intl Brand Clothing &Accessories Fair
2010/07/08-10
广东深圳Guangdong-Shenzhen 5360

深圳国际纺织面料及辅料博览会
Shenzhen Intl Trade Fair for Apparel Fabrics and Accessories
2010/07/08-10
广东深圳Guangdong-Shenzhen 5370

中国丝绸品牌暨品牌服装服饰展示交易会
2010/07/10-25
陕西西安shaanxi-Xi'an

中国丝绸服装制品及品牌服装服饰展销会
2010/07/10-25
新疆乌鲁木齐Xinjiang-Urumqi

第十六届中国国际家用纺织品及辅料博览会
16th China Intl Trade Fair for Home Textiles and Accessories
2010/08/24-26
上海Shanghai 3200

中国国际针织博览会
China Intl Knitting Trade Fair
2010/08/24-26
上海Shanghai 3210

中国国际产业用纺织品及非织造布展览会
Intl Trade Fair For Technical Textiles and Nonwovens
2010/09 -
上海Shanghai 3260

中国国际鞋类展暨中国国际箱包、裘革服装及服饰展
China Intl Footwear Fair
Moda Shanghai
2010/09/01-03
上海Shanghai 3300

纺织工业及面辅料展览会
2010/09/02-07
四川成都Sichuan-Chengdu 6895

第二届服装及缝制设备展览会
2010/09/02-07
四川成都Sichuan-Chengdu 6895

成都秋季服装展销会
2010/10/01-24
四川成都Sichuan-Chengdu 6895

中国国际纺织面料及辅料（秋冬）博览会
China Intl Trade Fair for Apparel Fabrics and Accessories
2010/10/19-22
上海Shanghai 3710

2010第二届中国（西安）糖酒食品交易会
第二届中国（西安）国际纺织服装博览会
2010/11/04-10
陕西西安Shaanxi-Xi'an

沿海地区服装展
Coastal Area Apparel Show
2010/11/06-17
福建厦门Fujian-Xiamen 4440

第10届中国（广州）国际纺织机械展览会
10th China (Guangzhou) Intl Exhibition For Textile Machinery
2010/11/09-11
广东广州Guangdong-Guangzhou 5090

第10届中国（广州）国际制衣技术设备展览会
10th China (Guangzhou) Intl Exhibition for Clothing Technology and Equipment
2010/11/09-11
广东广州Guangdong-Guangzhou 5080

第10届中国国际染料工业及纺织化学品、印花技术展览会
10th China Intl Exhibition for Dye Industry & Textile Chemical、Printing Industrial Technology
2010/11/09-11
广东广州Guangdong-Guangzhou 5060

第10届中国（广州）国际纺织面料辅料及纱线展览会
10th China (Guangzhou) Intl Exhibition For Apparel Fabric & Accessories
2010/11/09-11
广东广州Guangdong-Guangzhou 5070

第十一届中国（义乌）国际袜子、针织及染整机械展览会/ 第四届中国（义乌）国际针织纱线展览会
10th Yiwu Intl Exhibition on Hosiery, Knitting, Dyeing & Finishing Machinery/ 3rd China (Yiwu) Intl Exhibition on Knitting Yarns
2010/11/18-20
浙江义乌Zhejiang-Yiwu 6790

大连服装展
Dalian Clothing Show
2010/11/19-02
福建厦门Fujian-Xiamen 4450

成都冬季服装博览会
2010/12/11-19
四川成都Sichuan-Chengdu 6895

第三十七届中国国际裘皮革皮制品交易会
37th China Fur & Lear Products Fair
2011/01/11-14
北京Beijing 1120

## 15. 高新技术 New & Hi-Tech

第十三届中国北京国际科技产业博览会
13th China Beijing Intl High-Tech Expo
2010/05/27-31
北京Beijing 550

2010第五届中国国际军民两用技术展览会
5th Military and Civil Technology Exhibition
2010/09/19-21
北京Beijing 890

第十二届中国国际高新技术成果交易会信息技术与产品展
China Hi-Tech Fair/ComNet2010
2010/11/16-21
广东深圳Guangdong-Shenzhen 5490

## 16. 工程机械 Construction Machinery

第十一届中国重庆国际工业装备博览会
11th Chongqing Intl Industry Equipment Fair
2010/05/13-15
重庆Chongqing 1180

工程机械
2010/06/04-09
四川成都Sichuan-Chengdu 6895

上海国际非开挖技术展览会暨研讨会
2010 No-Dig Shanghai
2010/06/08-10
上海Shanghai 2610

中国国际工程机械、建筑机械、工程车辆及设备博览会
bauma
2010/11/23-26
上海Shanghai 3936

## 17. 管道 管材 泵 阀门 Pipeline, Pump & Value

第11届中国（广州）国际给排水、水处理技术设备展览会、中国（广州）国际泵、阀门、管道展览会
11th China (Guangzhou)_Water Wasterwater & Water Treatment 、Pump,Vale&Pipe China
2010/03/09-11
广东广州Guangdong-Guangzhou 4700

第11届中国东北国际给排水、水处理技术设备及泵、阀、管道展览会
11th North China Intl Water Supply & Drainage, Water Disposal Technique & Equipment, and Pump & Value and Pipeline Exhibition
2010/03/25-27
辽宁沈阳Liaoning-Shenyang 6460

2010中国西部（成都）给排水处理技术装备博览会暨流体机械+泵阀门+管道展
2010/05/18-22
四川成都Sichuan-Chengdu 6895

中国（北京）国际管业展览会
China Beijing Intl Steel Tube Industry Expo, 2010
2010/08/10-12
北京Beijing 1145

第四届中国国际管材展览会
4th All-China Intl Tube & Pipe Trade Fair
2010/09/21-24
上海Shanghai 3550

## 18. 广播 电影 电视 舞台设备 Broadcasting, Film, Television & Stage Equipment

第十八届中国国际广播电视信息网路展览会
CCBN 2010
2010/03/23-25
北京Beijing 1145

第六届中国（深圳）文化产业博览交易会数字影视*动漫游戏展
China （Shenzhen） Intl Cultural Industries Fair "DTV/COM & ANI EXHIBITION"
2010/05/14-17
广东深圳Guangdong-Shenzhen 5210

第十九届中国国际专业音响、灯光、乐器及技术展览会
19th China Intl Exhibition on Pro Audio, Light, Music & Technology
2010/05/20-23
北京Beijing 510

第十九届北京国际广播电影电视设备展览会
Beijing Intl Radio, TV & Film Equipment Exhibition

2010
2010/08/23-26
北京Beijing 800

上海国际专业灯光音响展览会
prolight + Sound Shanghai
2010/10/12-15
上海Shanghai 3660

## 19. 光电 Opto-Electronic

慕尼黑上海激光、光电展
LASER World of PHOTONICS CHINA
2010/03/16-18
上海Shanghai 1470

第四届亚洲（东莞）国际激光加工技术论坛暨应用展
Laser Processing Technology Forum and Equipment Application Fair
2010/05/14-16
广东东莞Guangdong-Dongguan 4520

2010深圳光电显示周
CHINA OPTOELECTRONICS&DISPLAY EXPO
2010/05/23-25
广东深圳Guangdong-Shenzhen 5220

2010第十八届多人行电子展、光电展
2010 18th DEX Electronic Exhibition & Photonics Exhibition
2010/06/23-25
广东深圳Guangdong-Shenzhen 5240

第十二届中国国际光电博览会（CIOE2010）
12th China Intl Optoelectronic Expo（CIOE2010）
2010/09/06-09
广东深圳Guangdong-Shenzhen 5420

2010北京国际广告技术设备展及LED展览会
China Exhibition of Advertisement & Sign 2010, Beijing
2010/10/27-29
北京Beijing 1145

中国国际光电产业博览会暨中国国际激光，电子及光显产业展览会/中国国际机器视觉展览会暨机器视觉技术及工业应用研讨会
Optoelectronics Industry Exposition (Beijing) & Intl Lasers, Optoelectronics and Photonics Exhibition
2010/10/27-29
北京Beijing 1145

## 20. 广告 媒介 Advertising & Media

2010年（春季）中国郑州第十六届中原广告展暨2010年中国中部LED霓虹灯展
2010(Spring)China Zhengzhou 16th Central China Advertisement Show and 2010 China Central LED Neon-lights Show
2010/03 -
河南郑州Henan-Zhengzhou 5795

2010广东国际广告展
SIGN CHINA 2010
2010/03/02-05
广东广州Guangdong-Guangzhou 4560

2010东莞数字喷印及广告技术展览会
Dongguan Digital Printing Exhibition
2010/03/02-06
广东东莞Guangdong-Dongguan 4458

2010安徽视觉广告技术及标识制作展览会
Anhui Ad Technology and Label Exhibition
2010/03/06-08
安徽合肥Anhui-Hefei 4175

2010长春第十三届广告博览会
2010 Changchun 13th session of advertisement exposition
2010/03/08-10
吉林长春Jilin-Changchun 6210

第十届西北（兰州）广告印刷LED及办公设备展览会
Lanzhou AD, Printing, LED, Office Equipment Exhibition
2010/03/19-21
甘肃兰州Gansu-Lanzhou 4455

2010第三届华展云南广告四新展览会
Yunnan AD Exhibition
2010/03/26-28
云南昆明Yunnan-Kunming 6930

2010第十一届中国(上海)广告四新展览会
11th China (Shanghai) Advertising Four New Exhibition
2010/03/27-29
上海Shanghai 1610

2010第十四届武汉广告展览会/ 第二届武汉印刷/包装/纸业展览会
2010 Wuhan Ad Exhibition
2010/03/30-01
湖北武汉Hubei-Wuhan 5930

德纳广告展
2010/04/09-11
四川成都Sichuan-Chengdu 6895

第十届东莞国际印刷造纸胶粘带及广告展览会
10th Dongguan Intl Printing and Packaging and paper advertising, adhesive tape, protective film exhibition
2010/05/27-29
广东东莞Guangdong-Dongguan 5435

2010第十一多人行广告、标识、LED展
2010 11th DAX Advertising, Sign Board & LED Exhibition
2010/06/23-25
广东深圳Guangdong-Shenzhen 5250

第十二届中国（上海）国际摄影器材和数码影像展览会
PHOTO & IMAGING SHANGHAI 2010
2010/07/01-04
上海Shanghai 2810

2010上海国际展览展示、POP及商用设施展览会
Shanghai Intl Displaying, POP and Commercial Facility Exhibition 2010
2010/07/07-10
上海Shanghai 2910

2010上海国际户外广告发光体技术及城市景观照明设备展览会
Shanghai Intl Outdoor AD Illuminating & City Lighting Technology & Equipment Exhibition 2010
2010/07/07-10
上海Shanghai 2940

2010大连国际广告技术与设备展览会
Dalian Ad Exhibition
2010/08/12-14
辽宁大连Liaoning-Dalian 6280

2010年秋季北京国际广告标识展、中国国际数码与喷墨印刷技术展览会
China Sign Expo 2010
2010/09/14-16
北京Beijing 1145

2010北京国际广告技术设备展及LED展览会
China Exhibition of Advertisement & Sign 2010, Beijing
2010/10/27-29
北京Beijing 1145

## 21. 航空 航天 机场 Aviation, Aerospace & Airport

2010中国国际机场技术、设备和服务展览会
Inter Airport China 2010
2010/09/14-16
北京Beijing 1145

中国国际航空航天博览会
China Intl Aviation & Aerospace Exhibition
2010/11/16-21
广东珠海Guangdong-Zhuhai 5515

## 22. 焊接 Welding

东北第14届国际焊接、切割、激光技术设备展览会
14th China (Norast) Intl Welding, Cutting, & Laser Technology and Equipment Exhibition
2010/03/18-21
辽宁沈阳Liaoning-Shenyang 6360

第十五届北京埃森焊接与切割展览会
15th Beijing Essen Welding & Cutting Fair
2010/05/27-30
北京Beijing 540

2010第十届中国东北国际冶金及金属工业展览会
同期举办：
中国东北国际铸造、锻压、焊接、热处理、工业炉技术与设备展览会
2009 North China Metal Expo
2010/06/16-18
辽宁沈阳Liaoning-Shenyang 6570

## 23. 化工 Chemical Industry

中国国际石油石化技术装备展览会及中国国际输配电防爆工业展览会
CIPPE 2010
2010/03/22-24
北京Beijing 1145

2010中国国际水处理化学品及水溶性高分子展览会
China Intl Water Treatment Chemicals Exhibition
2010/04/08-10
北京Beijing 325

2010第七届中国（天津）国际涂料展览会
7TH CHINA (TIANJIN) INTL COATINGS EXHIBITION
2010/05/26-28
天津Tianjin 4050

第7届中国（天津）国际涂装、电镀及表面处理展览会
7th china(tianjin) Intl coating,electroplating and surface finishing exhibition
2010/05/26-28
天津Tianjin 4120

第八届中国国际聚氨酯展览会
PU China 2010
2010/05/26-28
广东深圳Guangdong-Shenzhen 5230

2010中国西部（成都）国际化工、石油天然气及化工技术装备展览会
2010/06/02-07
四川成都Sichuan-Chengdu 6895

上海聚氨酯展览会/阻燃展/复合材料展
2010 China Intl Exhibition on Polyurethane
2010/09/15-17
上海Shanghai 3440

2010（第十届）中国国际化工展览会
ICIF China 2010
2010/09/15-17
上海Shanghai 3430

第八届国际粉体工业/散装技术展览会暨会议
8th Intl Powder/Bulk Conference & Exhibition
2010/09/27-29
上海Shanghai 3575

2010中国国际水处理化学品、水溶高分子、造纸化学品、工业表面活性剂技术及应用展览会
Intl Exhibition on Water-treatment chemicals & Water-soluble Polymer Products & Papermaking Chemicals & Industrial Surfactants, Technology and Application
2010/11/03-04
上海Shanghai 1145

第10届中国国际染料工业及纺织化学品、印花技术展览会
10th China Intl Exhibition for Dye Industry & Textile Chemical、Printing Industrial Technology
2010/11/09-11
广东广州Guangdong-Guangzhou 5060

2010年中国国际过滤工业展览会
Filtration 2010, China
2010/11/17-19
上海Shanghai 3900

2010中国国际润滑油、脂及调和技术设备展览会
2010 China Intl lubricating oil, Grease and Refining Technology Exhibition
2010/11/22-24
上海Shanghai 3930

第十三届中国国际胶粘剂及密封剂展览会暨第五届中国国际胶粘剂与标签展览会
China Adhesive 2010
2010/12/01-03
上海Shanghai 3955

## 24. 环境保护 Environment Protection

2010中国国际新能源暨节能环保产业展览会
2nd China Intl New Energy & Energy Conservation and Environmental Protection Exhibition 2010
2010/03/17-19
北京Beijing 1145

2010中国可持续建筑国际大会
China Sustainable Building Forum 2010
2010/03/23-25
上海Shanghai 1600

第六届成都给排水处理及流体机械展暨环保、固废物及资源综合利用博览会
2010/03/31-05
四川成都Sichuan-Chengdu 6895

中国中部国际环境保护与水处理展览会
Central China Intl Environment Protection and Water Treatment Exhibition
2010/ -
河南郑州Henan-Zhengzhou 5710

2010重庆国际生态环保与节能减排技术展览会
Chongqing Eco, Energy Saving Exhibition
2010/04/08-11
重庆Chongqing 1160

动保展
2010/04/13-16
四川成都Sichuan-Chengdu 6895

中国国际环保、废弃物及资源利用展览会和中国国际给排水水处理展览会
IFAT CHINA+EPTEE+CWS
2010/05/05-07
上海Shanghai 2130

第七届厦门人居环境展示会
7th Xiamen Living Environment Show
2010/05/28-30
福建厦门Fujian-Xiamen 4360

第八届中国（广州）国际环保展
8th Intl Enviro Guangzhou
2010/06/09-11
广东广州Guangdong-Guangzhou 4860

第二届中国绿化博览会
2nd China Green Expo
2010/09 -
河南郑州Henan-Zhengzhou 5890

## 25. 婚庆 Wedding

第十七届中国上海国际婚纱摄影器材展览会暨国际儿童摄影、主题摄影展览会(春季)
17th China (Shanghai) Intl Wedding Photographic Equipment Exhibition & Intl Children's Photography, Theme Photography Exhibition (Spring)
2010/01/20-23
上海Shanghai 1340

中国国际婚纱及摄影器材博览会
china wedding and photo equipment expo
2010/03/21-24
北京Beijing 120

2010深圳国际婚博会暨深圳婚庆文化节
Shenzhen Intl Wedding Exhibition &Wedding Cultural Festival 2010
2010/04/03-05
广东深圳Guangdong-Shenzhen 5140

中国（国际）婚博会
Wedding Expo
2010/3/19-21
北京Beijing 115

第十八届中国上海国际婚纱摄影器材展览会暨国际儿童摄影、主题摄影展览会(秋季)
18th China (Shanghai) Intl Wedding Photographic Equipment Exhibition & Intl Children's Photography, Theme Photography Exhibition (Autumn)
2010/07/01-04
上海Shanghai 2820

## 26. 家具 木制品 木工机械 Furniture, Woodworking

2010成都品牌家具春季直销周
2010/01/14-20
四川成都Sichuan-Chengdu 6895

中国广州国际厨房家具和电器展览会
China Kitchen Furniture and Appliance Fair (CKFA)
2010/03 -
广东广州Guangdong-Guangzhou 4550

中国厦门国际厨柜展
China (Xiamen) Cabinets Show
2010/03/06-09
福建厦门Fujian-Xiamen 4330

第十三届国际木工机械及家具生产设备展览会暨第十三届国际家具配件、材料及木制品展览会

Wood Work Fair 2010
2010/03/10-13
北京Beijing 1145

国际名家具（东莞）展览会
Intl Famous Furniture Fair(Dongguan)
2010/03/16-20
广东东莞Guangdong-Dongguan 4460

中国广州国际家具博览会(民用家具展)
China Intl Furniture Fair (Guangzhou)-Home Furniture
2010/03/18-21
广东广州Guangdong-Guangzhou 4760

第25届深圳国际家具/家居饰品/家具配料展览会
25th Shenzhen Intl furniture exhibition
2010/03/19-22
广东深圳Guangdong-Shenzhen 5120

中国广州国际木工机械、家具配料展览会
Interzum Guangzhou
2010/03/27-30
广东广州Guangdong-Guangzhou 4770

中国广州国际家具博览会（办公环境展）
China Intl Furniture Fair (Guangzhou)-Office Show
2010/03/27-30
广东广州Guangdong-Guangzhou 4790

中国国际木制品及原材料展览会
Sustainable Building Woodwork Expo
2010/03/29-01
上海Shanghai 1740

第八届中国国际家居博览会
7th China Intl Housing and Furnishing Exposition
2010/04/09-12
浙江宁波Zhejiang-Ningbo 6980

第九届中国国际古典家具展览会 & 2010上海国际古董及艺术品展览会
Antique Furniture China 2010 & Antiques & Arts Shanghai 2010
2010/05/20-23
上海Shanghai 2375

中国（北京）国际家具及木工机械展览会
2010 China Beijing Intl Furniture Woodworking machinery & Wood Products Exhibition
2010/07/01-04
北京Beijing 1145

2010年北京欧美超级家具展览会
European and American Furniture Show
2010/07/02-11
北京Beijing 740

第十一届成都国际家具工业展览会
11th Intl Funiture Fair Chengdu
2010/07/03-06
四川成都Sichuan-Chengdu 6850

中国国际家具及木工机械（济南）博览会
9th Jinan Intl Furniture Fair
2010/08/21-24
山东济南Shandong-Jinan 6640

2010第四届中国（北京）国际红木古典家具、现代家居及室内装饰艺术展览会
CIRCFE 2010
2010/08/28-30
北京Beijing 1145

第二十四届国际名家具（东莞）展览会
24th Intl Famous Furniture Fair (Dongguan)
2010/09/01-05
广东东莞Guangdong-Dongguan 5437

中国国际家具生产设备及原辅材料展览会
Furniture Manufacturing & Supply China 2010
2010/09/07-10
上海Shanghai 3400

中国国际橱柜展览会
Kitchen & Cabinet China 2010
2010/09/07-10
上海Shanghai 3380

中国国际家具展览会
Furniture China 2010
2010/09/07-10
上海Shanghai 3350

中国国际办公家具展览会
Office Furniture China 2010
2010/09/07-10
上海Shanghai 3360

## 27. 建筑 建材 装饰及机械 Building,Construction, Decoration & Materials

第十届中国厦门国际石材展览会
10th China Xiamen Intl Stone Fair
2010/03/06-09
福建厦门Fujian-Xiamen 4310

中国厦门国际厨柜展
China (Xiamen) Cabinets Show
2010/03/06-09
福建厦门Fujian-Xiamen 4330

第十七届中国（北京）国际建筑装饰及材料博览会
17th China Intl Building Decorations and Building Materials Exposition
2010/03/15-18
北京Beijing 110

第12届中国国际地面材料及铺装技术展览会
DOMOTEX asia
CHINAFLOOR 2010
2010/03/23-25
上海Shanghai 1590

2010中国可持续建筑国际大会
China Sustainable Building Forum 2010
2010/03/23-25
上海Shanghai 1600

第十六届东北沈阳国际建筑装饰博览会
16th Norast Intl Building Decoration Exhibition
2010/03/25-27
辽宁沈阳Liaoning-Shenyang 6450

第十二届中国东北国际门窗、幕墙、玻璃与加工设备展览会
12th Norast China Intl Door & Window, Curtain, Wall, Glass and Fabric Exhibition
2010/03/25-27
辽宁沈阳Liaoning-Shenyang 6480

第五届国际胶粘带、保护膜及光学膜（上海）展览会/ 国际模切材料及加工设备（上海）展览会
5th Intl Adhesive tape Protective Films & Optical Film (Shanghai) Expo/ Intl Diecyt Materials and Fabrication Plants (Shanghai) Expo
2010/03/29-31
上海Shanghai 1770

中国国际门窗、幕墙、五金与遮阳 品展览会
Doors, Windows, Structures & Sunshades China
2010/03/29-04/01
上海Shanghai 1720

中国国际建筑陶瓷色釉料及原辅材料展览会
Building Ceramics Glaze & Pigment China 2010
2010/03/29-04/01
上海Shanghai 1630

中国国际建筑陶瓷及卫浴科技精品展览会
11th Ceramics, Tile & Sanitary Ware China
2010/03/29-04/01
上海Shanghai 1690

第十八届中国国际建筑装饰展览会
18 TH EXPO BUILD CHINA 2010
2010/03/29-04/01
上海Shanghai 1650

中国国际建筑及室内设计节
Home Fashion & Design Shanghai
2010/03/29-04/01
上海Shanghai 1700

中国国际木制品及原材料展览会
Sustainable Building Woodwork Expo
2010/03/29-04/01
上海Shanghai 1740

2010北京国际喷涂聚脲技术、屋顶（木屋）绿化及沥青展览会
Polyurea Technology, Green Roof and Asphalt Show
2010/03/31-04/02
北京Beijing 250

第十届成都照明+建筑电气博览会暨LED展览会
2010/03/31-04/05
四川成都Sichuan-Chengdu 6895

2010中部住宅及科技产业博览会
2010 China Central Real Estate and Tech Industry Expo
2010/04 -
河南郑州Henan-Zhengzhou 5810

第17届中国国际石材产品及石材技术装备展览会
STONETECH 2010
2010/04/06-09
上海Shanghai 1830

第十五届中国国际建筑装饰材料展览会
15th China Int\'l Construction & Decoration Materials Exhibition
2010/04/09 12
辽宁大连Liaoning-Dalian 6240

2010年城市建设科技博览会
2010/04/09-14
四川成都Sichuan-Chengdu 6895

全国门窗展
2010/04/09-14
四川成都Sichuan-Chengdu 6895

CIDE—2010第九届中国国际门业展览会
9th China Intl Door Industry Exhibition
2010/04/15-18
北京Beijing 350

2010南京智能建筑产品博览会
Nanjing building intelligence exhibition 2010
2010/04/27-29
江苏南京Jiangsu-Nanjing 6130

2010第四届中国（上海）国际室内供暖、通风及净化产品展览会
4th Shanghai Intl Indoor Heating, Ventilation and Purification Products Expo
2010/05/06-08
上海Shanghai 2170

第四届中国（西安）国际绿色建筑与建筑节能博览会
4th China Intl green building and energy-
2010/05/19-21
陕西西安Shaanxi-Xi'an 6605

2010第七届中国（天津）国际涂料展览会
7TH CHINA (TIANJIN) INTL COATINGS EXHIBITION
2010/05/26-28
天津Tianjin 4050

第15届中国国际厨房、卫浴设施展览会
Kitchen & Bath China 2010
2010/05/26-29
上海Shanghai 2400

第15届中国国际建筑贸易博览会
Intl Building & Construction Trade Fair 2010
2010/05/26-29
上海Shanghai 2410

第四届中国国际新型墙体材料技术装备及产品展览会
4th CHINA INTL BUILDING MATERIAL TECHNOLOGY & EQUIPMENT EXPO
2010/06/03-05
北京Beijing 650

中国国际散装水泥暨预拌混凝土与预拌砂浆技术装备及产品展览会
2010 CHINA INTL BULK CEMENT TECHNOLOGY & EQUIPMENT EXPO
2010/06/03-05
北京Beijing 640

第四届中国国际墙体材料及保温技术展览会
4th CHINA INTL WALL MATERIAL & INSULATION TECHNOLOGY EXHIBITION
2010/06/03-05
北京Beijing 630

第三届粉煤灰、脱硫石膏综合利用技术装备及产品展览会
3rd FINE COAL ASH & DESULFURIZED GYPSUM COMPREHENSIVE UTILIZATION TECHNOLOGY & EQUIPMENT EXPO
2010/06/03-05
北京Beijing 620

第三届中国国际建筑材料技术装备展览会
3rd CHINA INTL BUILDING MATERIAL TECHNOLOGY EXPO
2010/06/03-05
北京Beijing 610

2010年第六届中国成都建筑科技装饰材料博览会暨建筑电气展览会
2010/06/07-09
四川成都Sichuan-Chengdu 6895

建材展览会
Building Material Show
2010/06/11-13
福建厦门Fujian-Xiamen 4370

中国（广州）国际建筑装饰博览会
12th China(Guangzhou) Intl Building Decoration Fair
2010/07/08-11
广东广州Guangdong-Guangzhou 5020

中国（广州）国际卫浴及建筑陶瓷展
China(Guangzhou) Intl Exhibition for Sanitary Ware and Building Ceramics
2010/07/08-11
广东广州Guangdong-Guangzhou 5000

中国（广州）国际地面铺装材料展
China(Guangzhou) Intl Floor Covering Fair
2010/07/08-11
广东广州Guangdong-Guangzhou 5010

第四届中国（青岛）国际石材工业及机械设备展览会
4th China Qingdao Intl Stone Industry & Machinery Exhibition
2010/07/16-19
山东青岛Shandong-Qingdao 6690

建材团购（派达）
2010/07/17-18
四川成都Sichuan-Chengdu 6895

第四届中国（青岛）国际建筑节能和可再生能源应用博览会
4th China Qingdao Intl Building Energy Saving & Renewable Energy Utilization Fair
2010/07/17-19
山东青岛Shandong-Qingdao 6700

第六届中国（青岛）国际建筑材料及装饰材料博览会
6th China Qingdao Intl Construction & Decoration Materials Exposition
2010/07/17-19
山东青岛Guangdong-Qingdao 6710

第十届中国（上海）国际墙纸、地毯、布艺展览会暨中国国际家居软装饰博览会
China Wallpaper
2010/08/02-04
上海Shanghai 3110

第六届中国（上海）国际建筑节能及新型建材展览会
6th Shanghai Intl Energy-saving &Advanced Building Materials Exhibition
2010/08/17-20
上海Shanghai 3160

建材装饰展
2010/08/18-22
四川成都Sichuan-Chengdu 6895

中国国际橱柜展览会
Kitchen & Cabinet China 2010
2010/09/07-10
上海Shanghai 3380

第十届中国重庆城市建设及建筑科技博览会
UCBE & LFAD Chongqing 2010
2010/09/13-15
重庆Chongqing 1210

中国国际线缆及线材展览会
4th All China-Intl Wire & Cable Industry Trade Fair
2010/09/21-24
上海Shanghai 3540

2010中国（上海）国际门业博览会暨门窗产品展览会
Door Expo 2010
2010/10/26-28
上海Shanghai 3770

中国南宁国际建筑装饰博览会
China Nanning Intl building decoration fair
2010/10/29-31
广西南宁Guangxi-Nanning 5600

2010年第七届中国成都建筑科技、装饰材料（冬季）博览会
2010/11/07-12
四川成都Sichuan-Chengdu 6895

2010第八届中国（上海）国际保温材料与节能技术展览会
2010 Eighth China (Shanghai) Intl rmal insulation materials and energy-saving Technology Expo
2010/11/30-02
上海Shanghai 3950

2010中国（上海）国际建材及室内装饰展览会
2010 Shanghai Intl Construction Material and Indoor Decoration Exhibition
2010/8/17-20
上海Shanghai 3170

# 28. 交通 轨道 航运 公路 Transportation

2010中国国际轨道交通展览会/ 2010 中国国际隧道与地下工程技术展览会
Metro China 2010

Tunnel China 2010
2010/05/19-21
上海Shanghai 2320

2010第三届中国西部交通建设博览会
Western China Transportation Expo
2010/04/13-15
四川成都Sichuan-Chengdu 6800

世界客车博览亚洲展览会
Busworld Asia
2010/05/06-08
上海Shanghai 2190

2010第五届中国(青岛)房车及休旅车展览会
5th Qingdao Recreational Vehicle Show
2010/05/20-24
山东青岛Shandong-Qingdao 6670

2010北京国际物流、卡车、起重运输机械展览会
China Beijing Intl Logistics Expo 2010
2010/08/10-12
北京Beijing 1145

2010上海国际智能交通论坛暨技术和应用展览会/2010上海国际停车设备和智能系统展览会
Intl ITS Conference & Expo Shanghai 2010/ INTERPARKING SHANGHAI 2010
2010/09/01-03
上海Shanghai 3270

## 29. 教育 教学设备 Education & Teaching Instrument

2010第三届西部教育技术装备及高职教育仪器展览会/第五届中国西部国际科技仪器及实验室装备展
2010 Chengdu Intl Educational Technology and Equipment Exhibition
2010/03/05-07
四川成都Sichuan-Chengdu 6750

第十五届中国国际教育巡回展
15th China Intl Education Exhibition Tour
2010/03/13-14
北京Beijing 100

2010年中国（四川）教育博览会
2010/03/22-28
四川成都Sichuan-Chengdu 6895

第59届中国教学仪器设备展示会
59th China National Exhibition of Education Instruments
2010/04/26-30
浙江义乌Zhejiang-Yiwu 6750

第二届中国郑州教育服务大会
2th China Zhengzhou Education Service Fair
2010/05 -
河南郑州Henan-Zhengzhou 5830

希望2009四川首届青少年文化暨四川国际青少年博览会
2010/05/27-30
四川成都Sichuan-Chengdu 6895

2010第五届上海国际幼儿教育展
2010 5th Shanghai Intl KIDS Education EXPO
2010/05/30-01
上海Shanghai 2440

出国留学展
2010/06/17-22
四川成都Sichuan-Chengdu 6895

北京国际教育展
Education Expo 2010
2010/06/18-20
北京Beijing 1145

高校咨询
2010/06/25-27
四川成都Sichuan-Chengdu 6895

中国（北京）玩具动漫教育文化博览会
China toys and animation educational expo
2010/07/29-08/01
北京Beijing 765

2010中国国际教育展
China Education Expo 2010
2010/10/16-17
北京Beijing 940

## 30. 金属加工 冶金 铸造锻造技术设备 Metalworking, Metallurgy & Foundry

第十届中国西部国际金属工业展
10th West China Intl Metal Exhibition
2010/03/11-13
重庆Chongqing 1150

第六届上海国际钢管工业展览会
SHANGHAI TUBE EXPO
2010/05/11-13
上海Shanghai 2210

第十二届中国国际冶金工业展览会
12th China Intl Metallurgical Industry Expo
2010/05/11-14
北京Beijing 470

2010中国国际铸件博览会
2010 CASTING CHINA
2010/05/11-14
北京Beijing 460

第十届中国国际铸造、锻压及工业炉展览会
2010 METAL CHINA
2010/05/11-14
北京Beijing 450

SCCE 2010第五届上海国际硬质合金及生产技术和应用展览会
5th Shanghai Intl Cemented Carbides Exhibition
2010/05/17-19
上海Shanghai 2280

第七届中国国际压铸会议暨展览会
7th China Intl Diecasting Congress & Exhibition
2010/06/16-18
上海Shanghai 2710

2010第十届中国东北国际冶金及金属工业展览会；同期举办：第九届中国东北电气、自动化、仪器仪表展览会/ 中国东北国际铸造、锻压、焊接、热处理、工业炉技术与设备展览会，2010第九届中国东北节能技术与设备展览会/ 中国东北国际耐火材料展览会，2010东北国际冶金工业暨不锈钢技术与制品展览会/ 东北国际冶金工业暨铝型材及技术设备展览会，2010中国东北国际模具制造技术设备展览会/ 中国东北国际煤矿安全生产及相关物资装备展览会
2009 Norast China Metal Expo
2010/06/16-18
辽宁沈阳Liaoning-Shenyang 6570

第十一届广州国际金属暨冶金工业展览会
11th China (Guangzhou) intl Metal & Metallurgy Exhibition
2010/06/23-26
广东广州Guangdong-Guangzhou 4880

第八届深圳国际磁性材料及粉末冶金工业展览会
8th China(Shenzhen) Intl Magnetic Materials and Powder Metallurgy Industry Exhibition
2010/06/24-26
广东深圳Guangdong-Shenzhen 5300

第六届中国国际金属加工技术设备展览会
6th China Intl Metals Working Technologyo & Equipment Exhibition
2010/08/18-21
天津Tianjin 4130

2010中国特殊钢工业展览会
China Special Steel Industry Exhibition 2010
2010/09/21-23
上海Shanghai 3560

第四届中国国际管材展览会
4th All-China Intl Tube & Pipe Trade Fair
2010/09/21-24
上海Shanghai 3550

2010华南（东莞）金属新材料、新技术、新设备及制品展览会
South China Expo (Dongguan) for New Metal Materials, New Technologies, New equipments and Products
2010/09/27-29
广东东莞Guangdong-Dongguan 5439

2010第七届中国(北京)国际冶金工业博览会
China (Beijing) Intl Metallurgy Industry Exhibition, 2010
2010/11/10-12
北京Beijing 1010

第十二届东莞国际模具及金属加工展/ 第十二届东莞国际橡塑胶及包装展
12th China Dongguan Intl Mould & Metalworking Exhibition/ 12th China Dongguan Intl Plastics, Packaging & Rubber Exhibition
2010/11/17-20
广东东莞Guangdong-Dongguan 4543

# 31. 酒店业 Hotel & Restaurant

上海国际酒店用品博览会
Hotelex
2010/03/29-01
上海Shanghai 1640

2010中国国际酒店博览会
2010 China Intl Hotel Fair
2010/05/10-12
北京Beijing 410

中国国际酒店博览会
Hhotel China 2010
2010/05/10-13
北京Beijing 440

2010年第六届中国成都酒店设备用品及旅游工艺品博览会
2010/06/11-16
四川成都Sichuan-Chengdu 6895

北京国际酒店用品博览会
Hotelex Beijing
2010/08/31-02
北京Beijing 810

# 32. 机械 制造 工业装备自动化 Machinery, Machine Tools and Technology & Automation

中国广州国际工业自动化技术及装备展览会
SPS-Industrial Automation Fair Guangzhou
2010/03/08-11
广东广州Guangdong-Guangzhou 4590

中国广州国际工业自动化技术及装备展览会
SPS-Industrial Automation Fair Guangzhou - Fuyang
2010/03/08-11
广东广州Guangdong-Guangzhou 4660

12届中原国际工业控制自动化及仪器仪表展
Central China Automation and Instrument Exhibition
2010/03/18-20
河南郑州Henan-Zhengzhou 5770

2010中国中部(郑州)国际装备制造业博览会
Central China (Zhengzhou) Intl Equipment Manufacturing Exposition(2010)
2010/03/18-20
河南郑州Henan-Zhengzhou 5790

第十一届中国国际机械工业展览会
11TH CHINA INTL MACHINERY INDUSTRY EXHIBITION
2010/03/18-21
浙江宁波Zhejiang-Ningbo 6960

2010第11届中国东北国际机床、工模具技术展览会
Norast 11th Intl Machine Tool and Tools & Moulds Technique Exhibition China 2010
2010/03/18-21
辽宁沈阳Liaoning-Shenyang 6390

2010年第四届广西机械工业博览会
fourth Guangxi mechanical industry exposition, 2010
2010/03/26-28
广西南宁Guangxi-Nanning 5520

2010第11届深圳国际机械、模具及制品、塑胶工业展览会
China Shenzhen Intl Machinery Manufacturing Industry Exhibition （SIMM2010）
2010/03/28-31
广东深圳Guangdong-Shenzhen 5140

2010第11届深圳国际机械、模具及制品、塑胶工业展览会
China Shenzhen Intl Machinery Manufacturing Industry Exhibition （SIMM2010）
2010/03/28-31
广东深圳Guangdong-Shenzhen 5130

2010年第三届中国东北国际流体机械展览会
3rd China (Norast) Fluid Machinery Exhibition
2010/04/01-03
辽宁沈阳Liaoning-Shenyang 6520

2010第十二届中国东北国际动力传动与控制技术展览会
2010 12th China Norast Intl Power Transmission and Control Technique Exhibition
2010/04/01-03
辽宁沈阳Liaoning-Shenyang 6490

2010中国（成都）国防科技工业及装备博览会暨第15届成都国际机床展
Chengdu China Natl Defense Science & Technology Industry and Equipment Manufacturing Expo/ 15th Chengdu Intl Machine Exhibition
2010/04/02-04
四川成都Sichuan-Chengdu 6790

第十四届对台进出口商品交易会
14th China Xiamen Machinery and Electronics Exhibition (CXMEE)
2010/04/08-11
福建厦门Fujian-Xiamen 4340

2010中国数控机床展览会（CCMT2010）
China CNC Machine Tool Fair 2010 (CCMT2010)
2010/04/12-16
江苏南京Jiangsu-Nanjing 6110

2010中国中部（合肥）国际装备制造业博览会
Cental China Intl Equipment Manufacturing Exposition
2010/05/07-09
安徽合肥Anhui-Hefei 4180

汉诺威工业装备展
2010/05/07-14
四川成都Sichuan-Chengdu 6895

2010大连国际工业博览会
2010 Dalian Intl industry fair
2010/05/12-14
辽宁大连Liaoning-Dalian 6250

2010国际现代工厂/ 过程自动化技术与装备展览会
2010FA/PA
2010/05/12-15
北京Beijing 1145

2010北京动力传动与控制技术展览会
DMBC 2010
2010/05/12-15
北京Beijing 1145

2010中国中部（长沙）国际装备制造业博览会
Changsha Intl Equipment Manufacturing Exhibition
2010/05/18-20
湖南长沙Hunan-Changsha 6010

2010中国（杭州）国际工业博览会
CHINA(HANGZHOU)INTL INDUSTRY EXPO
2010/05/20-22
浙江杭州Zhejiang-Hangzhou 6950

第十一届新疆国际农业机械博览会暨农业生产资料交易洽谈会
11th Xinjing Intl Machinery Exhibition
2010/05/20-22
新疆乌鲁木齐Xinjiang-Urumqi 6900

第六届中国（天津）国际工业控制自动化及仪器仪表展览会
Sixth China (Tianjin)Intl Industrial Control Automation &InstrumentExhibition
2010/05/26-28
天津Tianjin 4090

第六届中国（天津）国际动力传动与控制技术展览会、第六届中国天津液压、气动、密封件及空压机展览会
6th China (Tianjin) Intl power Transmission and Control TechnologyExhibition
2010/05/26-28
天津Tianjin 4070

2010第六届中国（天津）国际机床展览会
6th China (Tianjin) Intl Machine Tool Exhibition
2010/05/26-28
天津Tianjin 4080

第十五届北京埃森焊接与切割展览会
15th Beijing Essen Welding & Cutting Fair
2010/05/27-30
北京Beijing 540

2010第十届北京国际机械装备、模具、塑料橡胶、动力传动自动化仪器仪表展览会
China Intl Machinery Equipment Mould, Rubber and Plastic Industry & Power Transmission automation instrument and meter exhibition
2010/06/08-10
北京Beijing 1145

2010年中国国际铝工业展览会
ALUMINIUM CHINA 2010

2010/06/09-11
上海Shanghai 2650

第十届中国国际机床工具展览会
The 10th China Intl Machine Tool & Tools Exhibition
2010/06/11-18
北京Beijing 660

中国国际动力传动与自动化控制展览会
PTAC CHINA 2010
2010/06/23-25
北京Beijing 715

第十五届华南国际机械及模具展/ 第十五届华南国际塑胶展
15th South China Intl Machinery & Mould Exhibition/ 15th South China Intl Plastics Exhibition
2010/06/30-02
广东广州Guangdong-Guangzhou 4890

2010年第12上海国际机床展（东博展）
12th Shanghai Intl Machine Tool Fair - Eastpo 2010
2010/07/15-18
上海Shanghai 3040

三联工业装备展
2010/08/01-03
四川成都Sichuan-Chengdu 6895

中国北京国际工程项目、机械设备及建筑材料博览会
2010 China （Beijing) Intl Engineering Projects, Mechanical Equipment and Building Materials Exposition
2010/08/04-06
北京Beijing 1145

第四届上海国际工业装配与传输技术展览会
4th Shanghai Intl Assembly & Handling Technology Exhibition
2010/08/11-14
上海Shanghai 3130

华南国际工业组装技术与装备展览会
Automotive Electronics South China
2010/08/31-02
广东深圳Guangdong-Shenzhen 5410

第九届中国国际装备制造业博览会
9th China Intl Equipment Manufacturing Exposition
2010/09/01-05
辽宁沈阳Liaoning-Shenyang 6595

立嘉工业展
2010/09/07-09
四川成都Sichuan-Chengdu 6895

第十一届中国国际机电产品博览会
11th China Intl Machinery & Electronic Products Exposition
2010/09/23-26
湖北武汉Hubei-Wuhan 5960

第八届国际粉体工业/散装技术展览会暨会议
8th Intl Powder/Bulk Conference & Exhibition
2010/09/27-29
上海Shanghai 3575

2010洛阳机电产品博览会
Luoyang Machinery and Electronic Products Expo
2010/10 -
河南洛阳Henan-Luoyang 5680

2010第四届中国（芜湖）装备制造业博览会
4th China (Wuhu) Equipment Manufacturing Exposition
2010/10 -
安徽芜湖Hubei-Wuhu 4220

亚洲国际动力传动与控制技术展览会/亚洲国际物流技术与运输系统展览会
PTC ASIA
Power Transmission and Control
2010/10/25-28
上海Shanghai 3760

第12届中国国际工业博览会
China Intl Industry Fair 2010
2010/11/02-06
上海Shanghai 3860

第十二届中国国际机床展览会（CIMT2011）
12th China Intl Machine Tool Show (CIMT2011)
2011/04/11-16
北京Beijing 1130

## 33. 空调 制冷 供暖 通风 Air-conditioning, Heating, Refrigeration & Ventilation

第七届广州国际车用空调及冷藏链技术展览会
Guangzhou Intl automotive Air-conditioning& cold China exhibition
2010/03/04-06
广东广州Guangdong-Guangzhou 4580

第十届中国国际供热、通风及空调产品与技术博览会
10th China Intl Heating, Ventilation & Air-conditioning Expo
2010/03/16-18
北京Beijing 112

第13届中国东北国际供热供暖、空调、新能源设备展览会
13th China (Norast) Intl Equipments of Heating, Air-Condition & New Energy Sources Exhibition
2010/03/25-27
辽宁沈阳Liaoning-Shenyang 6470

第二十一届国际制冷、空调、供暖、通风及食品冷冻加工展览会
21st Intl Exhibition for Refrigeration, Air-conditioning, Heating and Ventilation, Frozen Food Processing, Packaging and Storage
2010/04/07-09
北京Beijing 290

2010年中国国际燃气、供热技术与设备展览会
GAS&HEATING CHINA 2010
2010/05/17-21
北京Beijing 500

## 34. 矿业 Mining

2010中国（上海）国际地球物理勘探技术展览会
2010 China (Shanghai) Intl Geophysical Exploration Technology Exhibition
2010/04/08-10
上海Shanghai 1840

2010第六届北京国际煤炭装备及矿山技术设备展览会
6th China Intl Coal Equipment and Mine Technical Equipment Exhibition 2010
2010/06/03-05
北京Beijing 1145

煤碳展
2010/09/01-03
四川成都Sichuan-Chengdu 6895

## 35. 零售业 Retail

2010上海国际物联网大会
Internet of Things Conference Shanghai 2010
2010/06 -
上海Shanghai 2450

2010年（第五届）中国零售商大会暨展会
2010 China Retailers Convention & Exhibition
2010/06/18-21
四川成都Sichuan-Chengdu 6830

2010第七届中国国际自动售货系统及商用自助服务产品展/ 2010第二届上海国际数字标牌及触摸查询技术展览会/ 2010上海互动多媒体信息技术及虚拟仿真产品展览会暨大屏幕投影显示、数字会议系统产品展览会
7th China Intl Vending & Kiosk show/ Shanghai Intl Digital Signage & Touch Inquiry Technology Show 2010/
2010/06/25-27
上海Shanghai 2780

2010上海国际零售业展览会
2010 Shanghai Intl Retail Exhibition
2010/07/07-10
上海Shanghai 2920

中国药店展览会
China Drug Store Show
2010/08/12-14
上海Shanghai 3255

阿里巴巴网货大会
2010/12/14-19
四川成都Sichuan-Chengdu 6895

中国国际加油加气站高新技术及设备暨便利店业务博览会
Gas station
2011 -
北京Beijing 1145

# 36. 礼品 Gifts

2010北京国际创意礼品与工艺品展览会
Beijing Intl Gift and Graft Show
2010/03/06-09
北京Beijing 70

第七届中国国际文具礼品博览会暨世纪文具网国际采购会
7th China Intl Stationery & Gifts Exposition & Stationery Trade Com Purchasing Fair
2010/03/20-22
浙江宁波Zhejiang-Ningbo 6970

第二十一届中国国际礼品、赠品及家庭用品展览会
21 st China Intl Gifts,Premium & Houseware Exhibition
2010/04/04-07
北京Beijing 270

第十八届中国（深圳）国际礼品、工艺品、钟表及家庭用品展览会
17th China (Shenzhen) Intl Gifts, Handicrafts, Watches & Houseware Fair
2010/04/25-28
广东深圳Guangdong-Shenzhen 5180

成都家居、休闲用品及礼品展览会
Chengdu Houseware, Leisure Goods & Gifts Fair
2010/06/18-20
四川成都Sichuan-Chengdu 6810

第二十二届中国国际礼品、赠品及家庭用品展览会
22nd China Intl Gifts, Premium & Houseware Exhibition
2010/08/15-18
北京Beijing 770

第十八届中国（深圳）国际玩具及礼品展览会
18th China (Shenzhen) Intl Toys &Gifts Fair
2010/10/21-24
广东深圳Guangdong-Shenzhen 5460

2010北京国际礼品、赠品及家庭用品（年底）采购订货会
China Intl Gifts, Premium & Houseware Exhibition
2010/11/27-29
北京Beijing 1080

# 37. 铝业 Aluminum Industry

2010年中国国际铝工业展览会
ALUMINIUM CHINA 2010
2010/06/09-11
上海Shanghai 2650

# 38. 旅游 Tourism

2010中国出境旅游交易会
China Outbound Travel & Tourism Market
2010/04/27-30
北京Beijing 390

上海世界旅游资源博览会
World Travel Fair
2010/05/27-29
上海Shanghai 2430

2010年第六届中国成都酒店设备用品及旅游工艺品博览会
2010/06/11-16
四川成都Sichuan-Chengdu 6895

中国国际旅游商品博览会
China Intl Tourism Commodities Fair
2010/06/17-20
浙江义乌Zhejiang-Yiwu 6760

2010北京国际旅游博览会暨北方旅游交易会
BEIJING INTL TOURISM EXPO 2010
2010/06/25-27
北京Beijing 720

中国（北京）国际商务及会奖旅游展览会
China Incentive, Business Travel & Meetings Exhibition
2010/09 -
北京Beijing 830

旅游展
2010/09/01-08
四川成都Sichuan-Chengdu 6895

中国国际旅游交易会
China Intl Travel Mart
2010/11/18-21
上海Shanghai 3920

# 39. 美容美发 化妆品 水疗 Beauty, Cosmetics, Hairdressing & Spa

第32届广州国际美容美发化妆用品进出口博览会
GUANGZHOU INTL BEAUTY & COSMETICIMPORT-EXPORT- SPRING 2010
2010/03/09-11
广东广州Guangdong-Guangzhou 4670

2010第十六届中国北京国际美容美发化妆用品博览会(春季)
16th Chinese Intl Beauty, Hairdressing & Cosmetics Expo in Beijing 2010
2010/04/10-12
北京Beijing 340

第十六届中国国际美容化妆洗涤用品博览会
China Beauty Expo
2010/05/19-21
上海Shanghai 2360

中国国际美发美容博览会
China Intl Hair & Beauty Expo
2010/07/05-07
北京Beijing 750

2010北京国际美容化妆品及医学养生健康产业博览会
2010 Beijing Intl Beauty, Hairdressing, Cosmetics & Health Products Expo
2010/10/26-28
北京Beijing 1145

# 40. 模具 Mold

2010第11届中国东北国际机床、工模具技术展览会
North 11th Intl Machine Tool and Tools & Moulds Technique Exhibition China 2010
2010/03/18-21
辽宁沈阳Liaoning-Shenyang 6390

2010第11届深圳国际机械、模具及制品、塑胶工业展览会
China Shenzhen Intl Machinery Manufacturing Industry Exhibition （SIMM2010）
2010/03/28-31
广东深圳Guangdong-Shenzhen 5130

2010第六届上海国际模型展览会
7th Shanghai Intl Model Exhibition 2010 （SIMS 2010）
2010/04/03-05
上海Shanghai 1810

第22届广州国际玩具及模型展览会
22nd Guangzhou (China) Intl Toy & Hobby Fair
2010/04/08-10
广东广州Guangdong-Guangzhou 4810

第十三届中国国际模具技术和设备展览会
DIE & MOULD CHINA 2010 (DMC 2010)
2010/05/11-15
上海Shanghai 2230

第六届中国(天津)国际模具技术与设备展览会
6th China (Tianjin) Intl Die & Mould Technology Exhibitionexhibition
2010/05/26-28
天津Tianjin 4100

2010第十届中国东北国际冶金及金属工业展览会
同期举办：东北国际模具制造技术设备展览会
2009 North China Metal Expo
2010/06/16-18
辽宁沈阳Liaoning-Shenyang 6570

第十五届华南国际机械及模具展
第十五届华南国际塑胶展
15th South China Intl Machinery & Mould Exhibition
15th South China Intl Plastics Exhibition
2010/06/30-02
广东广州Guangdong-Guangzhou 4890

第九届中国国际玩具、模型及婴儿用品展
9th Intl Trade Fair for Toys, Hobby & Baby Articles
2010/10/12-14
上海Shanghai 3650

第十二届东莞国际模具及金属加工展
第十二届东莞国际橡塑胶及包装展
12th China Dongguan Intl Mould & Metalworking Exhibition
12th China Dongguan Intl Plastics, Packaging & Rubber

Exhibition
2010/11/17-20
广东东莞Guangdong-Dongguan 4543

# 41. 能源 新能源 节能 New Energy & Energy-Saving

2010中国国际新能源暨节能环保产业展览会
2nd China Intl New Energy & Energy Conservation and Environmental Protection Exhibition
2010/03/17-19
北京Beijing 1145

2010中国可持续建筑国际大会
China Sustainable Building Forum 2010
2010/03/23-25
上海Shanghai 1600

2010中国（沈阳）国际建设科技博览会暨第八届东北建筑节能、新型墙体材料及设备展览会
8th (Shenyang) Intl Energy-saving & New Wall Material and Equipment Exhibition
2010/03/25-27
辽宁沈阳Liaoning-Shenyang 6440

第13届中国东北国际供热供暖、空调、新能源设备展览会
13th China (North) Intl Equipments of Heating, Air-Condition & New Energy Sources Exhibition
2010/03/25-27
辽宁沈阳Liaoning-Shenyang 6470

中国东北第13届国际电力电工及能源技术设备展览会
13th North China Intl Electric Power, Electrician and Energy Tech & Equipment Exhibition 2010
2010/04/01-03
辽宁沈阳Liaoning-Shenyang 6510

2010重庆国际生态环保与节能减排技术展览会
Chongqing Eco, Energy Saving Exhibition
2010/04/08-11
重庆Chongqing 1160

第二届太阳能产品西部（成都）展示交易会
2010/04/12-16
四川成都Sichuan-Chengdu 6895

第四届中国国际新光源&新能源照明展览会暨论坛
Green Lighting China Expo and Forum 2010
2010/04/20-22
上海Shanghai 2035

中国（上海）国际风能展览会暨研讨会/ 第8届中国国际动力设备及发电机组展览会
4th China Intl Wind Energy Exhibition and Conference
2010/04/27-29
上海Shanghai 2070

国际太阳能及光伏会议暨展览会
11th China PV Power Expo
2010/05/05-07
上海Shanghai 2160

第四届中国（西安）国际绿色建筑与建筑节能博览会
4th China Intl green building and energy-
2010/05/19-21
陕西西安Shaanxi-Xi'an 6605

2010第六届北京国际煤炭装备及矿山技术设备展览会
6th China Intl Coal Equipment and Mine Technical Equipment Exhibition 2010
2010/06/03-05
北京Beijing 1145

中国国际海上风电和风电产业链大会暨展览会
China Intl Offshore Wind Energy & Wind Energy Industry Chain Conference and Exhibition
2010/06/08-10
上海Shanghai 2600

2010北京国际电子工业节能技术、产品展览会
China Television Shopping Exposition 2010
2010/06/10-12
北京Beijing 1145

中国国际清洁能源博览会
Clean Energy Expo China
2010/06/23-25
北京Beijing 700

亚洲风能大会暨国际风能设备展览会
Wind Power Asia - Asian Wind Energy Exhibition & Conference
2010/06/23-25
北京Beijing 690

2010第六届北京国际电动车清洁能源汽车暨休闲运动车展览会
6th Beijing Intl Pure Electric Vehicle, Hybrid Power & Clean Energy Vehicle, and Accessories Exhibition
2010/07/16-18
北京Beijing 1145

第四届中国（青岛）国际建筑节能和可再生能源应用博览会
4th China Qingdao Intl Building Energy Saving & Renewable Energy Utilization Fair
2010/07/17-19
山东青岛Shandong-Qingdao 6700

北京国际风能、太阳能核电工业暨电力设备技术展览会
2010 Beijing Intl Wind, Solar, Nuclear Power Industry and Power Electrical Equipment and Technology Exhibition
2010/09/19-21
北京Beijing 1145

2010成都新能源国际论坛暨新能源博览会
2010/09/28-30
四川成都Sichuan-Chengdu 6895

2010北京国际风能大会暨展览会
China Windpower Beijing 2010
2010/10/14-16
北京Beijing 930

第十三届国际电力设备及技术展览会
2010国际节能、电力环保及脱硫脱硝装备展览会
第六届国际电机工程及电工装备展览会
EP China 2010
2010/10/19-21
北京Beijing 1145

2010第三届上海国际可再生能源大会暨展览会
3rd Intl Congress & Exhibition On Reproducible Energy
2010/10/21-23
上海Shanghai 3730

2010第11届中国太阳能光伏会议暨展览
2010 11th China Solar PV Conference and Exhibition
2010/11/18-20
江苏南京Jiangsu-Nanjing 6180

2010第八届中国（上海）国际保温材料与节能技术展览会
2010 8th China (Shanghai) Intl Insulation Materials and Energy-saving Technology Expo
2010/11/30-12/02
上海Shanghai 3950

# 42. 农业 林业 畜牧业 渔业 Agriculture, Animal Husbandry, Fishery & Forestry

第二十二届河南家禽交易会
22th Henan Poultry Trade Fair
-
河南郑州Henan-Zhengzhou 5690

2010北京年货博览会
Beijing happy Spring Festival
2010/01/22-02/07
北京Beijing 1145

农业展览
Xiamen Agriculture Show
2010/02/05-08
福建厦门Fujian-Xiamen 4300

第二届全国杂粮产业大会
2nd National Cereals Industry Convention
2010/03/12-13
天津Tianjin 4020

第四届全国鸭鹅产业大会
4th National Ducks and Geese Convention
2010/03/17-18
天津Tianjin 4030

2010第五届中国东北畜牧及饲料工业展览会；同期举办：第五届东北农业生产资料交易会
5th North-East China Livestock and Feed Exhibition
2010/03/21-23
辽宁沈阳Liaoning-Shenyang 6420

第五届全国粳稻米大会
5th National Rice Conference

2010/04/08-09
吉林长春Jilin-Changchun 6230

第十一届新疆国际农业机械博览会暨农业生产资料交易洽谈会
11th Xinjing Intl Machinery Exhibition
2010/05/20-22
新疆乌鲁木齐Xinjiang-Urumqi 6900

中国南宁国际农业科技博览会
China Nanning Intl agriculture fair
2010/07/23-25
广西南宁Guangxi-Nanning 5570

第五届成都农资信息交流
2010/08/27-29
四川成都Sichuan-Chengdu 6895

2010中国国际集约化畜牧展览会
VIV China 2010
2010/09/21-23
北京Beijing 1145

2010中国国际农产品交易会
2010 China Int'l Agriculture Products Trade Fair
2010/10 -
河南郑州Henan-Zhengzhou 5900

2010第九届中国武汉国际农业机械展览会
9th Wuhan Agricultural Machinery Exhibition
2010/11 -
湖北武汉Hubei-Wuhan 5980

中国国际渔业博览会
CHINA FISHERIES & SEAFOOD EXPO
2010/11/01-04
辽宁大连Liaoning-Dalian 6310

中国义乌（国际）森林产品博览会
China Yiwu ( Intl ) Forest Product Fair
2010/11/01-04
浙江义乌Zhejiang-Yiwu 6780

中国杨凌农业高新科技成果博览会
China Yangling agricultural Hi-Tech Fair
2010/11/01-05
陕西杨凌Shaanxi-Yangling 6610

# 43. 汽车 摩托车 电动车 Automobiles & Motorcycles

上海通用雪佛兰新赛欧发布会
2010/01/01-12
四川成都Sichuan-Chengdu 6895

奇瑞年会
2010/01/22-23
四川成都Sichuan-Chengdu 6895

第六届中国（广州）国际汽车改装服务业展览会
6th China Intl Automotive Aftermarket Industry and Tuning Trade Fair (AAITF)
2010/03/03-05
广东广州Guangdong-Guangzhou 4570

第七届广州国际车用空调及冷藏链技术展览会
Guangzhou Intl automotive Air-conditioning& cold China exhibition
2010/03/04-06
广东广州Guangdong-Guangzhou 4580

第十届中国国际汽车用品展览会
10th China Intl Auto Accessories Commercial Expo 2010
2010/03/12-14
北京Beijing 90

第五届哈尔滨春季汽车展览会
5th Harbin Intl Automobile Exhibition - Spring
2010/03/23-29
黑龙江哈尔滨Heilongjiang-Harbin 5630

第七届中国国际橡胶及轮胎工业展览会
7th China Intl Rubber and Tire Fair
2010/04/08-10
山东青岛Shandong-Qingdao 6660

2010第十二届东北沈阳国际汽车维修技术及设备、汽车零配件、汽车用品展览会
12th Vehicle Maintenance and Parts Show
2010/04/14-17
辽宁沈阳Liaoning-Shenyang 6550

2010沈阳第十三届国际家用轿车及商用、专用汽车展览会
13th Shenyang Auto Show
2010/04/14-18
辽宁沈阳Liaoning-Shenyang 6560

2010北京国际汽车展览会
Auto China 2010
2010/04/24-02
北京Beijing 388

2010年常州第二届汽车展
2nd Changzhou Auto Show
2010/05/01-03
江苏常州Jiangsu-Changzhou 6040

2010第五届中国(青岛)房车及休旅车展览会
5th Qingdao Recreational Vehicle Show
2010/05/20-24
山东青岛Shandong-Qingdao 6670

2010第七届中国国际轮胎资源循环利用展览会
7th China Intl Tire Resource Cyclic Utilization Expo
2010/05/26-28
天津Tianjin 4060

2010(第十二届)重庆国际汽车工业展览会
China Chongqing Intl Auto Industry Fair
2010/06/10-14
重庆Chongqing 1190

海峡西岸汽车博览会
West Taiwan Strait Auto Expo 2010
2010/06/17-21
福建厦门Fujian-Xiamen 4380

第四届中国常州电动车展览会
4th Changzhou Electric Vehicle Exhibition
2010/06/18-20
江苏常州Jiangsu-Changzhou 6060

2010中国上海国际汽车零部件展览会
Auto Components Shanghai 2010
2010/06/21-23
上海Shanghai 2720

2010第七届汽车用品交易会暨第六届汽车羊剪绒产品订货会
2010 7th Auto Products Trade Fair& 6th Auto-Use Wool Products Fair
2010/07 -
河南郑州Henan-Zhengzhou 5850

2010第六届北京国际电动车清洁能源汽车暨休闲运动车展览会
6th Beijing Intl Pure Electric Vehicle, Hybrid Power & Clean Energy Vehicle, and Accessories Exhibition
2010/07/16-18
北京Beijing 1145

第13届哈尔滨国际汽车工业展览会
13th Harbin Intl Automobile Exhibition
2010/08/02-09
黑龙江哈尔滨Heilongjiang-Harbin 5670

2010北京国际物流、卡车、起重运输机械展览会
China Beijing Intl Logistics Expo 2010
2010/08/10-12
北京Beijing 1145

2010上海国际汽车制造技术与装备及材料展览会
Shanghai Intl Automotive Manufacturing Technology & Material Show 2010
2010/08/11-14
上海Shanghai 3120

第四届上海国际家用车务车展览会
shanghai Intl exhibition on family & commercial auto 2010
2010/08/12-15
上海Shanghai 3150

第八届中国汽车用品采购交易会
8th China Intl Auto Supplies Sourcing Fair
2010/08/18-20
上海Shanghai 3180

2010（第十五届）大连国际汽车展览会
15th Dalian Intl Automotive Exhibition
2010/08/18-22
辽宁大连Liaoning-Dalian 6290

华南国际汽车电子展览会
Automotive Electronics South China
2010/08/31-09/02
广东深圳Guangdong-Shenzhen 5400

第十一届中国（湖北-武汉）国际汽车工业展览会
11th China(Hubei/Wuhan) Intl Auto Industry Exhibition
2010/09/09-13
湖北武汉Hubei-Wuhan 5950

第十三届成都国际汽车展览会汽车用品展
2010/09/17-19
四川成都Sichuan-Chengdu 6865

成都国际汽车展览会
Chengdu Motor Show

2010/09/19-25
四川成都Sichuan-Chengdu 6868

2010第九届南京国际汽车展览会
9th Nanjing Intl Auto Exposition
2010/09/29-04
江苏南京Jiangsu-Nanjing 6170

2010第九届南京国际汽车展览会
2010 Nanjing Auto Exposition
2010/09/29-04
江苏南京Jiangsu-Nanjing 6160

厦门日报房车大联展
Xiamen Housing and Automotive Exhibition
2010/10 -
福建厦门Fujian-Xiamen 4410

2010中国（济南）国际卡车暨零部件博览会
Truckworld2010
2010/10/15-17
山东济南Shandong-Jinan 6645

第九届中国国际摩托车博览会
9th China Intl Motorcycle Trade Exhibition
2010/10/21-24
重庆Chongqing 1220

2010中国国际汽车制造及生产设备博览会
CIAMPFE2010
2010/10/25-27
北京Beijing 1145

2010中国（郑州）国际汽车博览会
2010 Zhengzhou Intl Automobile Expo
2010/11 -
河南郑州Henan-Zhengzhou 5920

汽体展
2010/11/10-12
四川成都Sichuan-Chengdu 6895

中国国际橡胶技术展览会/亚洲埃森轮胎展
REIFEN CHINA
2010/11/25-27
上海Shanghai 3940

上海国际汽车零配件、维修检测诊断设备及服务用品展览会
automechanika Shanghai
2010/12/08-11
上海Shanghai 3960

中国国际加油加气站高新技术及设备暨便利店业务博览会
Gas station
2011/ -
北京Beijing 1145

## 44. 清洁 Cleaning

中国国际洗涤设备展览会
Laundry China 2010
2010/03/29-01
上海Shanghai 1680

中国清洁博览会
11th China Clean
2010/03/29-31
上海Shanghai 1790

第十六届中国国际美容化妆洗涤用品博览会
China Beauty Expo
2010/05/19-21
上海Shanghai 2360

中国国际清洁能源博览会
Clean Energy Expo China
2010/06/23-25
北京Beijing 700

中国清洁博览会(北京)
China Clean Expo-Beijing
2010/08/31-02
北京Beijing 820

## 45. 奢侈品 Luxury Life

2010第3届中国(深圳)国际奢侈品展览会暨深圳企业家生活方式展览会
TOP LUXURY SHOW
2010/07/08-10
广东深圳Guangdong-Shenzhen 5350

北京国际顶级私人物品展
TOP ESSENCE BEIJING
2010/11/05-07
北京Beijing 980

## 46. 设计 Design

第八届上海国际园林景观设计及城市建设展览会
8th Shanghai Int\'l Landscape Design & Urban Construction Expo
2010/03/23-25
上海Shanghai 1550

家居设计展览会
Expo Deco
2010/03/29-04/01
上海Shanghai 1750

中国国际建筑及室内设计节
Home Fashion & Design Shanghai
2010/03/29-04/01
上海Shanghai 1700

创意展
2010/06/18-23
四川成都Sichuan-Chengdu 6895

2010中国宁波国际工业设计博览会
2010 World Industrial Design Fair Ningbo China
2010/09 -
宁波Zhejiang-Ningbo 6700

2010第五届上海设计双年展
5th Shanghai Design Biennial
2010/09/16-18
上海Shanghai 3500

2010 "100%设计" 上海展
100% Design Shanghai
2010/10/21-23
上海Shanghai 3720

第八届中国（无锡）国际工业设计博览会
8th China (Wuxi) Intl Industrial Design Expo
2010/11/06-08
江苏无锡Jiangsu-Wuxi 6190

## 47. 摄影 影像 Photography & Image

第十七届中国上海国际婚纱摄影器材展览会暨国际儿童摄影、主题摄影展览会(春季)
17th China (Shanghai) Intl Wedding Photographic Equipment Exhibition & Intl Children's Photography, me Photography Exhibition (Spring)
2010/01/20-23
上海Shanghai 1340

中国国际婚纱及摄影器材博览会
China Wedding and Photo Equipment Expo
2010/03/21-24
北京Beijing 120

第十三届中国国际照相机械影响器材与技术博览会
13th China Intl Photograph & Electrical Imaging Machinery
2010/06/10-13
北京Beijing 650

第十二届中国（上海）国际摄影器材和数码影像展览会
PHOTO & IMAGING SHANGHAI 2010
2010/07/01-04
上海Shanghai 2810

第十八届中国上海国际婚纱摄影器材展览会暨国际儿童摄影、主题摄影展览会(秋季)
18th China (Shanghai) Intl Wedding Photographic Equipment Exhibition & Intl Children's Photography, me Photography Exhibition (Autumn)
2010/07/01-04
上海Shanghai 2820

## 48. 食品 饮料 茶 酒及生产 Food, Beverage, Tea, Spirit & Processing

中国中部食品与饮料加工及包装展览会
2010/ -
河南Henan- 5700

北京国际名酒文化节暨世界名酒产业博览会
Winefest Beijing
2010/01/20-24
北京Beijing 30

广东（厚街）茶业博览会
Guangdong (Houjie) Tea Expo
2010/01/22-25
广东东莞Guangdong-Dongguan 4456

第十四届中国国际食品添加剂和配料展览会暨第二十届全国食品添加剂生产应用展示会
Food Ingredients China 2010
2010/03/23-25
上海Shanghai 1520

中国国际咖啡与茶用品展览会
Coffee & Tea China 2010
2010/03/29-01
上海Shanghai 1670

中国国际葡萄酒及烈酒展览会
Wine China Exhibition
2010/04 -
北京Beijing 385

第二十一届国际制冷、空调、供暖、通风及食品冷冻加工展览会
21st Intl Exhibition for Refrigeration, Air-conditioning, Heating and Ventilation, Frozen Food Processing, Packaging and Storage
2010/04/07-09
北京Beijing 290

第八届中国北京国际食品加工与包装机械展览会
8th China Beijing Intl Food Processing & Packaging Machinery Exhibition
2010/04/10-12
北京Beijing 330

2010中国国际冰淇淋加工技术设备及冷链展览会
China Intl Ice Cream Industry Exhibition
2010/04/21-23
上海Shanghai 2050

2010第六届中国郑州糖酒食品交易会/ 2010第六届中国粮油调味品（郑州）交易会
2010 6th China City and Countryside Planning/ 2010 6th China Zhengzhou Candy & Spirit Fair
2010/05 -
河南郑州Henan-Zhengzhou 5820

2010北京国际咖啡博览会
2010 China Intl Coffee Industry Exhibition
2010/05/10-12
北京Beijing 430

2010第13届中国国际焙烤展览会
13th China Intl Trade Fair For Bakery & Confectionery
2010/05/12-15
上海Shanghai 2240

第十一届中国国际食品和饮料展览会
SIAL China 2010
2010/05/19-21
上海Shanghai 2350

2010年第十四届中国国际烘焙展览会
2010 14th CHINA BAKERY EXHIBITION
2010/05/20-22
广东广州Guangdong-Guangzhou 4840

2010第二届中国（山东）国际食品博览会
2010 2nd China( Shandong) food fair
2010/05/21-23
山东济南Shandong-Jinan 6620

2010中国（上海）国际茶业博览会
2010 China (Shanghai) Intl Tea Exhibition
2010/05/21-24
上海Shanghai 2380

2010中国国际有机食品博览会
BioFach China 2010
2010/05/27-29
上海Shanghai 2420

第五届中国（郑州）国际酒店、餐饮、泳池沐浴SPA设备及用品博览会/ 第五届中国（郑州）国际家纺、布艺及工艺品、礼品家居装饰博览会
5th China (Zhengzhou) Intl Hotel, F&B, Swimming pool and SPA Equipment and Product Expo/ 5th China (Zhengzhou) Household Textile, Cloth Art, Handicraft and Decoration Article Expo
2010/06 -
河南郑州Henan-Zhengzhou 5840

2010年中国国际葡萄酒博览会
2010 Topwine China
2010/06/01-03
北京Beijing 580

亚洲食品配料、天然原料、 健康原料展览会
Fi Asia - China/ Hi China/ Ni China
Food Ingredients Asia China 2010
Health Ingredient China 2010
Natural Ingredients China 2010
2010/06/02-04
上海Shanghai 2550

第二届成都端午食品博览会
2010/06/06-16
四川成都Sichuan-Chengdu 6895

第八届中国（厦门）食品交易博览会
8th China (Xiamen) Food Fair
2010/06/25-27
福建厦门Fujian-Xiamen 4390

第八届中国国际肉类工业展览会
Eighth China Intl Meat Industry Exhibition
2010/06/29-01
北京Beijing 730

2010年中国国际酒业博览会
China Intl Alcoholic Drinks Expo 2010
2010/07/09-11
北京Beijing 1145

首届食品博览会
2010/08/27-29
四川成都Sichuan-Chengdu 6895

第三届中国（重庆）茶叶博览会暨海峡两岸文化交流会
3rd China (Chongqing) Tea Expo
2010/09 -
重庆Chongqing 1200

中国国际啤酒饮料制造技术及设备展览会
China Brew 2010
2010/09/07-10
北京Beijing 1145

第十届中国四川月饼节
2010/09/09-21
四川成都Sichuan-Chengdu 6895

第十一届国际果蔬、食品博览会
11th Intl Fruit/Vegetable/Food Exposition
2010/09/23-26
山东烟台Shagndong-Yantai 6730

第六届中国国际有机食品和绿色食品博览会
ORGANIC CHINA EXPO BEIJING 2010
2010/09/24-27
北京Beijing 900

美食节
2010/09/27-08
四川成都Sichuan-Chengdu 6895

第十二届中国上海国际食品加工及包装机械展览会
Intl FoodTec China/Interfood Shanghai 2010
2010/10/19-21
上海Shanghai 3690

2010中国糖果文化节暨第七届中国国际甜食及休闲食品展览会
China Confectionery Culture Festival 2010, Sweets & Snacks China 2010
2010/10/28-30
上海Shanghai 3780

2010中意国际葡萄酒展
VINITALY CHINA 2010
2010/11 -
上海Shanghai 3800

2010第二届中国（西安）糖酒食品交易会/ 第二届中国（西安）国际纺织服装博览会
2010/11/04-10
陕西西安Shaanxi-Xi'an 00

2010中国烘焙展览会（西部）
China Bakery Exhibition 2010 (West)
2010/11/11-13
四川成都Sichuan-Chengdu 6890

首届四川名优食品博览会
2010/11/25-30
四川成都Sichuan-Chengdu 6895

## 49. 实验室设备 Laboratory Equipment

2010第三届西部教育技术装备及高职教育仪器展览会/第五届中国西部国际科技仪器及实验室装备展
2010 Chengdu Intl Educational Technology and Equipment Exhibition
2010/03/05-07
四川成都Sichuan-Chengdu 6750

第八届中国国际科学仪器及实验室装备展览会
8th China Intl Scientific Instrument and Laboratory Equipment Exhibition
2010/04/08-10
北京Beijing 310

第60届中国实验室技术及装备交易会
60th China Laboratory Technology and Equipment Exhibition
2010/06/22-24
上海Shanghai 2740

## 50. 石油 石化 天然气 燃气 Petroleum, Gas,Petrochemical

中国国际石油石化技术装备展览会及中国国际输配电防爆工业展览会
CIPPE 2010
2010/03/22-24
北京Beijing 1145

2010年中国国际燃气、供热技术与设备展览会
GAS&HEATING CHINA 2010
2010/05/17-21
北京Beijing 500

2010中国西部（成都）国际化工、石油天然气及化工技术装备展览会
2010/06/02-07
四川成都Sichuan-Chengdu 6895

中国（上海）国际石油石化技术装备展览会/中国（上海）国际海洋石油天然气展览会
China (Shanghai) Intl Petroleum & Petrochemical Technology and Equipment Exhibition
2010/09/01-03
上海Shanghai 3310

## 51. 水 水处理 Water Treatment

中国中部国际环境保护与水处理展览会
Central China Intl Environment Protection and Water Treatment Exhibition
2010 -
河南郑州Henan-Zhengzhou 5710

第11届中国（广州）国际给排水、水处理技术设备展览会
中国（广州）国际泵、阀门、管道展览会
11th China (Guangzhou) Waste water & Water Treatment, Pump, Vale & Pipe China
2010/03/09-11
广东广州Guangdong-Guangzhou 4700

第11届中国东北国际给排水、水处理技术设备及泵、阀、管道展览会
11th Norast China Intl, Water Supply & Drainage, Water Disposal Technique & Equipment, and Pump & Value and Pipeline Exhibition
2010/03/25-27
辽宁沈阳Liaoning-Shenyang 6460

第六届成都给排水处理及流体机械展暨环保、固废物及资源综合利用博览会
2010/03/31-05
四川成都Sichuan-Chengdu 6895

2010中国国际水处理化学品及水溶性高分子展览会
China Intl Water Treatment Chemicals Exhibition
2010/04/08-10
北京Beijing 325

2010中国西部（成都）给排水处理技术装备博览会暨流体机械+泵阀门+管道展
2010/05/18-22
四川成都Sichuan-Chengdu 6895

第十三届膜与水处理技术暨装备展览会
water and membrane China 2010
2010/10/19-21
北京Beijing 1145

2010中国国际水处理化学品、水溶高分子、造纸化学品、工业表面活性剂技术及应用展览会
2010 Intl Exhibition on Water-treatment chemicals & Water-soluble Polymer Products & Papermaking Chemicals & Industrial Surfactants, Technology and Application
2010/11/03-04
上海Shanghai 1145

## 52. 塑料 橡胶 Plastics & Rubbers

2010第11届中国东北国际塑胶机械及包装工业展览会
11th Norast China Intl Plastics Machinery & Packaging Exhibition 2010
2010/03/18-21
辽宁沈阳Liaoning-Shenyang 6370

2010第11届深圳国际机械、模具及制品、塑胶工业展览会
China Shenzhen Intl Machinery Manufacturing Industry Exhibition （SIMM2010）
2010/03/28-31
广东深圳Guangdong-Shenzhen 5130

第七届中国国际橡胶及轮胎工业展览会
7th China Intl Rubber and Tire Fair
2010/04/08-10
山东青岛Shandong-Qingdao 6660

中国国际橡塑展
Chinaplas 2010
2010/04/19-22
上海Shanghai 2020

2010第七届中国国际轮胎资源循环利用展览会
7th China Intl Tire Resource Cyclic Utilization Expo
2010/05/26-28
天津Tianjin 4060

2010第十届北京国际机械装备、模具、塑料橡胶、动力传动自动化仪器仪表展览会
China Intl Machinery Equipment Mould, Rubber and Plastic Industry & Power Transmission automation instrument and meter exhibition
2010/06/08-10
北京Beijing 1145

第十五届华南国际机械及模具展/ 第十五届华南国际塑胶展
15th South China Intl Machinery & Mould Exhibition/ 15th South China Intl Plastics Exhibition
2010/06/30-02
广东广州Guangdong-Guangzhou 4890

中国国际塑料橡胶注射成型工业展览会
China Intl Exhibition on Plastics and Rubber Injection Moulding Industry (CIM 2010)
2010/09/15-17
天津Tianjin 4140

第十二届中国塑料博览会
12th China Plastics Expo
2010/11/06-09
浙江余姚Zhejiang-Yuyao 6800

第十二届东莞国际橡塑胶及包装展
12th China Dongguan Intl Mould & Metalworking Exhibition/ 12th China Dongguan Intl Plastics, Packaging & Rubber Exhibition
2010/11/17-20
广东东莞Guangdong-Dongguan 4543

中国国际橡胶技术展览会/亚洲埃森轮胎展
REIFEN CHINA
2010/11/25-27
上海Shanghai 3940

## 53. 陶瓷 玻璃 Ceramic and Glass

中国广州国际陶瓷展览会
China Intl Ceramics Exhibititon (Guangzhou)
2010/03/18-21
广东广州Guangdong-Guangzhou 4710

中国国际建筑陶瓷及卫浴科技精品展览会
11th Ceramics, Tile & Sanitary Ware China
2010/03/29-04/01
上海Shanghai 1690

中国国际建筑陶瓷色釉料及原辅材料展览会
Building Ceramics Glaze & Pigment China 2010
2010/03/29-04/01
上海Shanghai 1630

第21届中国国际玻璃工业技术展览会
China Glass 2010
2010/06/04-07
北京Beijing 1145

第七届中国(上海)国际玻璃工业新技术展览会
China (ShangHai) Int'l Glass Industry New Tech. Expo, 2010
2010/10/09-11
上海Shanghai 3620

# 54. 特许经营 连锁加盟 Franchising

2010中国特许展
China Franchise Expo
2010/04/16-18
北京Beijing 360

2010国际特许加盟（上海）展览会
Franchise (Shanghai) Expo
2010/09/08-12
上海Shanghai 3410

# 55. 体育 休闲 Sports & Leisure

中国国际钓鱼用品贸易展览会
CHINA FISH 2010
2010/02/23-25
北京Beijing 50

第二十届中国国际钓鱼用品贸易展览会
20th China Intl Fishing Tackle Trade Exhibition
2010/02/23-25
北京Beijing 40

亚洲国际品牌体育用品及运动时尚博览会
ispo china
2010/03/04-06
北京Beijing 60

中国广州户外及休闲展览会
China Intl Outdoor & Leisure Fair
2010/03/18-21
广东广州Guangdong-Guangzhou 4750

中国国际康体健身、休闲娱乐与运动器材展览会
Fitness, Sports & Leisure China
2010/03/29-01
上海Shanghai 1660

第三届东北国际渔具、户外用品博览会
3rd Fishing and Outdoor Sports Fair
2010/04/09-11
东北沈阳Liaoning-Shenyang 6540

中国高尔夫球博览会
China golf show
2010/04/16-18
北京Beijing 370

第二届中国（西安）国际户外运动博览会/ 第二届中国（西安）国际健身运动用品展览会
China (Xi' an) Intl outdoor sports expo/ China (Xi'an) Intl Trade Show for Fitness Sport & Leisure Fair
2010/04/28-01
陕西西安Shaanxi-Xi'an

第二届中国（西安）国际健身机运动用品展览会
China (xi' an) Intl trade show for fitness sport & leisure fair
2010/04/28-01
陕西西安Shaanxi-Xi'an

2010第五届北京国际游泳沐浴SPA展览会
Beijing Intl Swimming Pools, Bath, SPA Expo 2010
2010/05/07-10
北京Beijing 1145

2010（第26届）中国国际体育用品博览会
China Intl Sporting Goods Show 2010
2010/05/20-23
北京Beijing 520

2010第五届中国(青岛)房车及休旅车展览会
5th Qingdao Recreational Vehicle Show
2010/05/20-24
山东青岛Shandong-Qingdao 6670

2010第六届北京国际电动车清洁能源汽车暨休闲运动车展览会
6th Beijing Intl Pure Electric Vehicle, Hybrid Power & Clean Energy Vehicle, and Accessories Exhibition
2010/07/16-18
北京Beijing 1145

2010年健身大会
Fitness China 2010
2010/08/05-07
北京Beijing 1145

中国（上海）国际马博会
China (Shanghai) Intl Horse Fair
2010/10 -
上海Shanghai 3600

2010第四届中国国际马业马术展览会
4th China Intl Equestrian & Horse Industry Fair
2010/10/26-28
北京Beijing 950

路博2010泛北部湾新生活方式展览会
Broad2010 Guangxi Fan-Beibu Gulf New Lifestyle Exhibition
2010/12/18-20
广西南宁Guangxi-Nanning 5610

# 56. 投资 金融 Investment & Finance

2010年金融展
China Intl Financial Exhibition
2010/06/17-20
北京Beijing 680

广东外商投资企业产品（内销）博览会
Guangdong Foreign-invested Enterprises Commodities Fair
2010/06/18-21
广东东莞Guangdong-Dongguan 5436

河南省投资贸易洽谈会
Henan Investment and Trade Fair
2010/08 -
河南郑州Henan-Zhengzhou 5860

第十四届中国国际投资贸易洽谈会
14th China Intl Fair for Investment & Trade
2010/09/08-11
福建厦门Fujian-Xiamen 4400

第七届中国-东盟博览会
中国-东盟商务与投资分会
7th China ASEAN Expo
2010/10/20-24
广西南宁Guangxi-Nanning 5590

2010北京国际钱币博览会
Beijing Intl Coins Exposition 2010
2010/10/28-31
北京Beijing 970

中国对外投资合作洽谈会
China Overseas Investment Fair
2010/11/10-11
北京Beijing 990

# 57. 图书 Books

2010北京图书订货会
Beijing Book Fair 2010 commodities Fair
2010/01/10-11
北京Beijing 1145

2010年第二十届全国图书交易博览会
2010/04/22-26
四川成都Sichuan-Chengdu 6895

北京国际图书博览会
BIBF 2010
2010/08/29-02
北京Beijing 1145

# 58. 玩具 儿童用品 Toys & Children's Products

环球资源流行服饰配件采购交易会
及环球资源婴儿及儿童采购交易会
环球资源及赠品采购交易会
China Sourcing Fair：
Fashion Accessories
Baby & Children' s Products
Gifts & Premiums
2010/01/13-15
上海Shanghai 1320

中国（上海）第十五届国际玩具展暨上海玩具第46届博览会
Toy China 2010 (Spring)
2010/03/05-07
上海Shanghai 1360

2010第三届东北孕婴童产品展览会
3rd Baby and Children Products Show
2010/03/11-14
辽宁沈阳Liaoning-Shenyang 6340

2010年广州国际婴幼儿用品展
Guangzhou Intl Baby Product Fair 2010
2010/04/08-10
广东广州Guangdong-Guangzhou 4800

第22届广州国际玩具及模型展览会
22nd Guangzhou (China) Intl Toy & Hobby Fair
2010/04/08-10
广东广州Guangdong-Guangzhou 4810

第十一届京正北京孕婴童用品展览会
Mor & baby China 2010
2010/04/10-12
北京Beijing 1145
玩具展
2010/04/28-06
四川成都Sichuan-Chengdu 6895

第12届北京国际玩具及幼教用品展览会
12thBeijing Intl Toys & Preschool Tools Exhibition
2010/05/15-17
北京Beijing 480

2010第五届中国（济南）儿童产业国际博览会
5th 2010 China (Jinan) Intl Children Industry Fair
2010/05/29-31
山东济南Shandong-Jinan 6630

北京国际儿童及婴幼儿食品博览会
Beijing Intl Exhibition of Infant Food
2010/07/10-12
北京Beijing 1145

上海儿童、婴儿、孕妇产品博览会
2010 Shanghai Intl Children-Baby-Maternity Products Expo
2010/07/21-23
上海Shanghai 3050

中国（北京）国际妇女儿童产业博览会
China children and women industry expo
2010/07/29-08/01
北京Beijing 766

中国（北京）玩具动漫教育文化博览会
China toys and animation educational expo
2010/07/29-08/01
北京Beijing 765

2010年北京国际儿童婴儿孕妇产品博览会
Children-Baby-Maternity Products Expo
2010/09/11-12
北京Beijing 870

第九届中国国际玩具、模型及婴儿用品展
9th Intl Trade Fair for Toys, Hobby & Baby Articles
2010/10/12-14
上海Shanghai 3650

第十八届中国（深圳）国际玩具及礼品展览会
18th China (Shenzhen) Intl Toys & Gifts Fair
2010/10/21-24
广东深圳Guangdong-Shenzhen 5460

# 59. 文化产业 Culture Industry

中国（深圳）国际文化产业博览交易会
China （Shenzhen） Intl Cultural Industries Fair
2010/05/14-17
广东深圳Guangdong-Shenzhen 5200

第104届中国文化用品商品交易会暨中国国际制笔文具博览会
104th China Stationery Commodity Fair
2010/06/10-12
上海Shanghai 2680

创意展
2010/06/18-23
四川成都Sichuan-Chengdu 6895

第一届（2010）上海国际美术材料展览会
Shanghai Intl Art Materials Exhibition
2010/09/09-11
上海Shanghai 3420

第五届中国厦门国际佛事用品展览会
5th China Xiamen Intl Buddhist Items & Crafts Fair
2010/11/05-08
福建厦门Fujian-Xiamen 4430

第五届中国北京国际文化创意产业博览会
FOURTH CHINA BEIJING INTL HIGH-TECH EXPO
2010/11/18-21
北京Beijing 1040

# 60. 文具 办公用品 Stationery & Office Supplies

第七届中国国际文具礼品博览会暨世纪文具网国际采购会
7th China Intl Stationery & Gifts Exposition& StationeryTrade. Com Purchasing Fair
2010/03/20-22
浙江宁波Zhejiang-Ningbo 6970

中国义乌文化产品交易博览会
China Yiwu Stationery & Arts Trade Fair
2010/04/20-23
浙江义乌Zhejiang-Yiwu 6720

第104届中国文化用品商品交易会暨中国国际制笔文具博览会
104th China Stationery Commodity Fair
2010/06/10-12
上海Shanghai 2680

中国国际文具及办公用品展览会
Paperworld China
2010/09/15-17
上海Shanghai 3450

ReChina 2010 第七届亚洲打印耗材展览会
ReChina Asia Expo 2010
2010/09/27-29
上海Shanghai 3570

# 61. 五金工具 Hardware & Tools

中国国际五金博览会
China Intl Hardware Fair
2010/03/10-12
上海Shanghai 1390

中国国际门窗、幕墙、五金与遮阳　品展览会
Doors, Windows, Structures & Sunshades China
2010/03/29-04/01
上海Shanghai 1720

第十三届中国东北国际五金工具展览会
13th China (Norast) Intl Hardware & Tool Exhibition
2010/04/08-10
辽宁沈阳Liaoning-Shenyang 6530

中国国际五金电器博览会
China Intl Hardware & Electrical Appliances Trade Fair
2010/04/20-23
浙江义乌Zhejiang-Yiwu 6740

中国（北京）国际五金机电工业博览会暨电池电子工业展览会
China Intl Hardware Industry Expo, Beijing
2010/08/05-07
北京Beijing 1145

2010 中国国际五金展－科隆国际五金展-;强力推动
China Intl Hardware Show
-Powered by PRACTICAL WORLD
2010/09/28-30
上海Shanghai 3580

# 62. 物流 仓储 运输 Logistics

中国中部国际物流、物料运输与储藏展览会
Central China Logistics Exhibition
2010/03/18-20
河南郑州Henan-Zhengzhou 5780

第十一届中国东北国际物流技术及运输系统展览会
Norast 11th Intl physical Distributibon & Transpor System Exhibition China 2010
2010/03/18-21
辽宁沈阳Liaoning-Shenyang 6380

2010第十届中国(青岛)国际物流展览会
10th China Intl Material Handling and Logistics Expo
2010/03/25-27
山东青岛Shandong-Qingdao 6650

中国国际物流、交通运输及远程信息处理博览会
transport logistic China
2010/06/08-10
上海Shanghai 2630

GLE2010广西泛北部湾港口、物流及仓储设备展览会
GLE 2010 Guangxi Fan-Beibu Gulf Equipment Of Port & Logistics & Storage Exhibition
2010/07/02-04
广西南宁Guangxi-Nanning 5530

第四届上海国际工业装配与传输技术展览会
4th Shanghai Intl Assembly & Handling Technology Exhibition
2010/08/11-14
上海Shanghai 3130

亚洲国际物流技术与运输系统展览会
CeMAT ASIA 2010
2010/10/25-28
上海Shanghai 3750

亚洲国际动力传动与控制技术展览会/亚洲国际物流技术与运输系统展览会
PTC ASIA
Power Transmission and Control
2010/10/25-28
上海Shanghai 3760

## 63. 线、缆 Cable

2010四川线材线缆及相关设备展
2010/06/04-09
四川成都Sichuan-Chengdu 6895

2010深圳国际线圈工业、绝缘材料展览会/ 2010深圳国际漆包线展览会
2010Shenzhen Internationa Coils Industry&Insulating Materials Exhibition/ 2010Shenzhen Intl Enamelled Wire Exhibition
2010/06/24-26
广东深圳Guangdong-Shenzhen 5330

中国国际线缆及线材展览会
4th All China-Intl Wire & Cable Industry Trade Fair
2010/09/21-24
上海Shanghai 3540

## 64. 消费电子 家用电器 Consumer Electronics & Appliances

中国广州国际厨房家具和电器展览会
China Kitchen Furniture and Appliance Fair (CKFA)
2010/03 -
广东广州Guangdong-Guangzhou 4550

2010中国国际消费电子博览会
2010 China Intl Consumer Electronics Show (SINOCES)
2010/07/08-11
山东青岛Shandong-Qingdao 6680

中国（广州）国际厨房设备及配件展
China Kitchen Furniture and Appliance Fair
2010/07/08-11
广东广州Guangdong-Guangzhou 4990

2010广东国际家电配件采购博览会
2010 Guangdong Intl Appliance Parts Procurement Fair
2010/07/15-17
广东广州Guangdong-Guangzhou 5030

2010中国顺德国际家用电器博览会
China Shunde Intl Exposition for Household Electrical Appliances 2010
2010/10/18-21
广东顺德Guangdong-Shunde 5510

## 65. 消费品 家居用品 Consumer Goods

2010快乐新年北京购物节
2010Beijing happy Shopping Festival
2009/12/26-03
北京Beijing 1145

2010北京年货博览会
2010 Beijing happy Spring Festival
2010/01/22-07
北京Beijing 1145

2010新春年货购物节
2010/01/26-11
四川成都Sichuan-Chengdu 6895

第7届元宵商品交易会
2010/02/20-01
四川成都Sichuan-Chengdu 6895

中国广州国际家居饰品/用品展览会
Homedecor & Housewares China 2010
2010/03/18-21
广东广州Guangdong-Guangzhou 4720

第25届深圳国际家具/家居饰品/家具配料展览会
25th Shenzhen Intl furniture exhibition
2010/03/19-22
广东深圳Guangdong-Shenzhen 5120

家居设计展览会
Expo Deco
2010/03/29-01
上海Shanghai 1750

第二十一届中国国际礼品、赠品及家庭用品展览会
21st China Intl Gifts, Premium & Houseware Exhibition
2010/04/04-07
北京Beijing 270

义乌消费品出口交易会
Yiwu Sourcing Fair: Consumer Goods
2010/04/20-23
浙江义乌Zhejiang-Yiwu 6730

第十八届中国（深圳）国际礼品、工艺品、钟表及家庭用品展览会
17th China (Shenzhen) Intl Gifts, Handicrafts, Watches & Houseware Fair
2010/04/25-28
广东深圳Guangdong-Shenzhen 5180

第九届中国国际日用消费品博览会
9th China Intl Consumer Goods Fair
2010/06/08-11
浙江宁波Zhejiang-Ningbo 6990

成都家居、休闲用品及礼品展览会
Chengdu Houseware, Leisure Goods & Gifts Fair
2010/06/18-20
四川成都Sichuan-Chengdu 6810

第104届中国日用百货商品交易会
104thchina Daily-use Articles Trade Fair & China Modern Home Expo
2010/07/22-24
上海Shanghai 3060

夏日国际香港购物嘉年华
Intl-Hong Kong Shopping Carnival
2010/08/05-09
北京Beijing 1145

第十届中国（上海）国际墙纸、地毯、布艺展览会暨中国国际家居软装饰博览会
China Wallpaper
2010/08/02-04
上海Shanghai 3110

第二十二届中国国际礼品、赠品及家庭用品展览会
22nd China Intl Gifts, Premium & Houseware Exhibition
2010/08/15-18
北京Beijing 770

中国国际家居饰品布艺及灯饰展览会
Finishing Fabrics & Lightings China 2010
2010/09/07-10
上海Shanghai 3370

国际家居装饰艺术展
Intl Home Décor & Design
2010/10/21-23
上海Shanghai 3830

第十八届中国（深圳）国际玩具及礼品展览会
18th China (Shenzhen) Intl Toys &Gifts Fair
2010/10/21-24
广东深圳Guangdong-Shenzhen 5460

2010北京国际礼品、赠品及家庭用品（年底）采购订货会
China Intl Gifts, Premium & Houseware Exhibition
2010/11/27-29
北京Beijing 1080

路博2010泛北部湾新生活方式展览会
Broad2010 Guangxi Fan-Beibu Gulf New Lifestyle Exhibition
2010/12/18-20
广西南宁Guangxi-Nanning 5610

2010第九届东莞嘉年华时尚生活用品购物节
9th Dongguan Shopping Festival
2010/12/21-02
广东东莞Guangdong-Dongguan 4548

## 66. 鞋 皮革 Shoes & Leather

第十一届中国(东莞)国际鞋机鞋材工业技术展
11th China (Dongguan) Intl Footwear Machinery &

Material Industry Fair
2010/03/29-01
广东东莞Guangdong-Dongguan 4470

第十二届中国(晋江)国际鞋业博览会
12TH JINJIANG FOOTWEAR (INT\'L) EXPOSITION,CHINA
2010/04/19-22
福建晋江Fujian-Jinjiang 4240

中国东莞国际鞋展·鞋机展·手袋展
China Shoes·China Shoetec & China Bags
2010/05/04-06
广东东莞Guangdong-Dongguan 4505

广州国际鞋类、皮革及工业设备展览会
Intl Shoes & Lear Exhibition (Machinery & Raw Material)
2010/06/01-03
广东广州Guangdong-Guangzhou 4850

中国国际鞋类展暨中国国际箱包、裘革服装及服饰展
China Intl Footwear Fair
Moda Shanghai
2010/09/01-03
上海Shanghai 3300

中国国际皮革展
All China Lear Exhibitions
2010/09/01-03
上海Shanghai 3290

2010中国东莞国际鞋展/ 鞋机展
Dongguan Shoes/ China Shoetes/ China Bags
2010/10/28-30
广东东莞Guangdong-Dongguan 4540

鞋类、加工
2010/11/12-17
四川成都Sichuan-Chengdu 6895

第三十七届中国国际裘皮革皮制品交易会
37th China Fur & Lea r Products Fair
2011/01/11-14
北京Beijing 1120

## 67. 信息技术 通信技术 Information Technology & Communication Technology

第十届西北（兰州）广告印刷LED及办公设备展览会
Lanzhou AD, Printing, LED, Office Equipment Exhibition
2010/03/19-21
甘肃兰州Gansu-Lanzhou 4455

第十八届中国国际广播电视信息网路展览会
CCBN 2010
2010/03/23-25
北京Beijing 1145

2010中国（上海）国际测绘仪器及GPS/GIS/RS技术展览会
China（Shanghai）Intl Survey and Mapping Equipment & Technology exhibition
2010/04/08-10
上海Shanghai 1860

第六届中国（深圳）文化产业博览交易会数字影视*动漫游戏展
China （Shenzhen） Intl Cultural Industries Fair “DTV/COM & ANI EXHIBITION"
2010/05/14-17
广东深圳Guangdong-Shenzhen 5210

第十三届中国国际智能卡博览会
13th Intl Fair of Smart Cards, China 2010(SCC2010)
2010/05/26-28
北京Beijing 530

2010上海国际物联网大会
Internet of Things Conference Shanghai 2010
2010/06 -
上海Shanghai 2450

2010第十四届中国国际软件博览会
INTL SOFT CHINA 2010
2010/06/02-04
北京Beijing 600

中国国际物流、交通运输及远程信息处理博览会
transport logistic China
2010/06/08-10
上海Shanghai 2630

2010第七届中国国际自动售货系统及商用自助服务产品展/ 2010第二届上海国际数字标牌及触摸查询技术展览会/ 2010上海互动多媒体信息技术及虚拟仿真产品展览会暨大屏幕投影显示、数字会议系统产品展览会
7th China Intl Vending & Kiosk Show/ Shanghai Intl Digital Signage & Touch Inquiry Technology Show 2010/
2010/06/25-27
上海Shanghai 2780

2010上海国际数字营销展览会
Shanghai Intl Digital Media Exhibition 2010
2010/07/07-10
上海Shanghai 2870

第六届中国（南京）国际软件产品博览会
6th China (Nanjing) Intl Software Product Expo
2010/09/03-05
江苏南京Jiangsu-Nanjing 6150

2010中国国际嵌入式大会暨展览会
Embedded China 2010
2010/09/07-09
上海Shanghai 3340

ReChina 2010
第七届亚洲打印耗材展览会
ReChina Asia Expo 2010
2010/09/27-29
上海Shanghai 3570

2010年中国国际信息通信展览会
P&T/EXPO COMM CHINA 2010
2010/10/11-15
北京Beijing 920

第十七届国际自动识别技术展览会
16th Intl Exhibition of Automatic Identification Technology
2010/11/10-12
北京Beijing 1000

## 68. 印刷 Printing

2010东莞数字喷印及广告技术展览会
Dongguan Digital Printing Exhibition
2010/03/02-06
广东东莞Guangdong-Dongguan 4458

四川印刷器材展览会
2010/03/04-07
四川成都Sichuan-Chengdu 6895

2010安徽印刷包装工业展览会
Anhui Printing & Packaging Industry Exhibition
2010/03/06-08
安徽合肥Anhui-Hefei 4170

第十七届华南国际印刷工业展览会/ 2010中国国际标签印刷技术展览会
17th South China Intl Exhibition on Printing Industry, China Intl Exhibition on Label Printing Technology
2010/03/09-11
广东广州Guangdong-Guangzhou 4680

第十届西北（兰州）广告印刷LED及办公设备展览会
Lanzhou AD, Printing, LED, Office Equipment Exhibition
2010/03/19-21
甘肃兰州Gansu-Lanzhou 4455

2010第十四届武汉广告展览会
第二届武汉印刷/包装/纸业展览会
2010 Wuhan Ad Exhibition
2010/03/30-04/01
湖北武汉Hubei-Wuhan 5930

第27届中国国际丝网印刷及数字技术展览会/2010年中国国际服装服饰及面料印花技术展览会
27th China Screen Print Expo/ 2010 China Textile Print Expo
2010/04/27-29
上海Shanghai 2060

第十届东莞国际印刷造纸胶粘带及广告展览会
10th Dongguan Intl Printing and Packaging and paper advertising, adhesive tape, protective film exhibition
2010/05/27-29
广东东莞Guangdong-Dongguan 5435

2010上海国际数码及快速印刷设备展览会
Shanghai Intl Digital & Express Printing Exhibition 2010
2010/07/07-10
上海Shanghai 2970

2010上海国际标签展览会
Label Shanghai 2010
2010/07/07-10
上海Shanghai 2960

第五届中国（北方）印刷及设备器材展览会
Print North 2010
2010/07/23-30
北京Beijing 1145

2010中国国际标签技术展览会
China Intl Exhibition for Label Technology
2010/12/15-17
上海Shanghai 3990

## 69. 仪器仪表 Instrument

2010第三届西部教育技术装备及高职教育仪器展览会/第五届中国西部国际科技仪器及实验室装备展
2010 Chengdu Intl Educational Technology and Equipment Exhibition
2010/03/05-07
四川成都Sichuan-Chengdu 6750

第12届中原国际工业控制自动化及仪器仪表展
Central China Automation and Instrument Exhibition
2010/03/18-20
河南郑州Henan-Zhengzhou 5770

2010第十三届中国东北仪器仪表及工业自动化展览会
13th Norast China Intl Instrument & Automation Exhibition 2010
2010/04/01-03
辽宁沈阳Liaoning-Shenyang 6500

2010中国（上海）国际测绘仪器及GPS/GIS/RS技术展览会
2010China (shanghai) Intl Survey and Mapping Equipment & Technology exhibition
2010/04/08-10
上海Shanghai 1860

第八届中国国际科学仪器及实验室装备展览会
8th China Intl Scientific Instrument and Laboratory Equipment Exhibition
2010/04/08-10
北京Beijing 310

自动化仪器仪表
2010/04/12-17
四川成都Sichuan-Chengdu 6895

第59届中国教学仪器设备展示会
59th China National Exhibition of Education Instruments
2010/04/26-30
浙江义乌Zhejiang-Yiwu 6750

2010年华南（东莞）环境与可靠性实验技术论坛暨仪器展
South China Intl Certification Technology Forum & Instrument Equipment Fair
2010/05/14-16
广东东莞Guangdong-Dongguan 4510

第六届中国（天津）国际工业控制自动化及仪器仪表展览会
6th China (Tianjin) Intl Industrial Control Automation & InstrumentExhibition
2010/05/26-28
天津Tianjin 4090

中国国际生物技术和仪器设备博览会
BIOTECH CHINA 2010
2010/06/02-04
上海Shanghai 2530

2010第十届北京国际机械装备、模具、塑料橡胶、动力传动自动化仪器仪表展览会
China Intl Machinery Equipment Mould, Rubber and Plastic Industry & Power Transmission automation instrument and meter exhibition
2010/06/08-10
北京Beijing 1145

第60届中国实验室技术及装备交易会
60th China Laboratory Technology and Equipment Exhibition
2010/06/22-24
上海Shanghai 2740

第二十一届多国仪器仪表学术会议暨展览会
21st Intl Conference and Fair for Measurement Instrumentation and Automation
2010/09/06-09
北京Beijing 860

2010北京国际在线分析测试技术及设备展览会
2010 China Intl On-line Analytical Testing Technology and Equipment Exhibition
2010/10/19-21
北京Beijing 1145

## 70. 艺术 Arts

2010中艺博国际画廊博览会
China Intl Gallery Exposition
2010/04/21-25
北京Beijing 380

艺术北京2010当代艺术博览会
Art Beijing 2010 Contemporary Art Fair
2010/04/29-02
北京Beijing 400

第九届中国国际古典家具展览会
2010上海国际古董及艺术品展览会
Antique Furniture China 2010
Antiques & Arts Shanghai
2010/05/20-23
上海Shanghai 2375

2010第二届中国仿古工艺品及技术展览会
China Archaistic Craft & Technology Exhibition Expo
2010/06/26-28
上海Shanghai 2790

2010北京国际艺术博览会
13th Beijing Intl Art Exposition
2010/08/19-23
北京Beijing 790

2010第四届中国（北京）国际红木古典家具、现代家居及室内装饰艺术展览会
CIRCFE 2010
2010/08/28-30
北京Beijing 1145

第一届（2010）上海国际美术材料展览会
Shanghai Intl Art Materials Exhibition
2010/09/09-11
上海Shanghai 3420

国际家居装饰艺术展
Intl Home Décor & Design
2010/10/21-23
上海Shanghai 3830

## 71. 医药 医疗设备 生物保健 Medical Equipment, Pharmaceuticals & Health Care

2010第十六届沈阳药交会
16th Shenyang Medicine Fair
2010/01/16-16
辽宁沈阳Liaoning-Shenyang 6320

第37届东北药品保健品交易会
37th North-East China Medicine and Health Products Fair
2010/03/01-02
东北沈阳Liaoning-Shenyang 6330

2010福建（第二十一届）国际医疗仪器与设备展览会
China Tianjin Intl Medical Instruments and Equipment Exhibition
2010/03/03-05
福建福州Fujian-Fuzhou 4230

中国中西部（合肥）医疗器械展览会暨第11届安徽医疗器械（2010年春季）展览会
Hefei Medical Devices Exhibition
2010/03/05-07
安徽合肥Anhui-Hefei 4160

2010中国中西部（成都）医疗器械展览会暨第10届中国西部医疗器械及口腔设备展览会
Chengdu Medical Device Exhibition
2010/03/07-09
四川成都Sichuan-Chengdu 6760

中国国际化妆品、个人及家庭护理用品原料展览会
Personal Care and Home Ingredients
2010/03/10-12
上海Shanghai 1370

中国中西部（郑州）医疗器械展览会暨第18届中原国际医疗器械(2010年春季)展览会
2010 China Central (Zhengzhou) Medical Equipment

Show
2010/03/10-12
河南郑州Henan-Zhengzhou 5750

2010第十二届中国东北口腔设备及材料展览会暨东北国际口腔学术交流会
12th China Norast Intl Dental Equipment & Affiliated Facilities Exhibition 2010 / Norast Intl Symposium On Oral Health
2010/03/11-14
辽宁沈阳Liaoning-Shenyang 6350

第七届中国国际成人保健及生殖健康展览会
7th China Intl Adult Toys & Reproductive Health Exhibition
2010/03/12-14
上海Shanghai 1450

2010中国中西部（长沙）医疗器械展览会暨第16届湖南医疗器械技术与设备(2010年春季)展览会
Changsha Medical Devices Exhibition
2010/03/17-
湖南长沙Hunan-Changsha 5990

2010第二十一届（春季）沈阳国际医疗器械设备展览会
2010 21th Shenyang Intl Medical Equipment Fair
2010/03/23-25
辽宁沈阳Liaoning-Shenyang 6430

2010中国中西部（昆明）医疗器械展览会
Kunming Medical Devices Exhibition
2010/03/24-27
云南昆明Yunnan-Kunming 6920

第二十二届医疗仪器设备展览会
22nd Intl Medical Instruments and Equipment Exhibition
2010/03/26-28
北京Beijing 150

第二十二届国际医疗仪器设备展览会
22nd Intl Medical Instruments and Equipment Exhibition
2010/03/26-28
北京Beijing 160

第23届国际FOM 2010学术年会
23rd Focus On Microscopy 2010 Conference
2010/03/28-31
上海Shanghai 1620

2010第二十二届中国长春国际医疗器械卫生产业博览会
2010 22th Intl Medical Equipment Industry Hygiene Industrial Expo Chang chun-china Chang chun-china
2010/03/30-01
吉林长春Jilin-Changchun 6220

湖北武汉国际先进医疗仪器设备展览会
hubei wuhan Intl madical equipment & instrument exhibition
2010/03/30-01
湖北武汉Hubei-Wuhan 5940

第十届中国国际眼科和视光技术及设备展览会
10th Intl congress of Ophthalmology and Optometry China (COOC 2010)
2010/04/09-11
江西南昌Jiangxi-Nanchang 6195

2010年中国国际医药生物产业展览会
2010 China Beijing Intl Pharmacy Biology Industry Exhibition
2010/04/09-11
北京Beijing 1145

第九届中国西部国际口腔设备及材料展
2010/04/09-14
四川成都Sichuan-Chengdu 6895

第二届中国（北京）国际优生优育计生用品（成人用品）展览会
2nd Beijing Intl Adult-goods Exhibition
2010/04/10-12
北京Beijing 1145

第10届中国国际医疗器械设计与制造技术展览会（春季）
10th ICMD
-Intl Component Manufacturing & Design Show (Spring)
2010/04/18-21
广东深圳Guangdong-Shenzhen 5170

第63届中国国际医疗器械春季博览会
63rd CMEF (China Int'l Medical Equipment Fair 2010 - Spring )
2010/04/18-21
广东深圳Guangdong-Shenzhen 5160

第63届全国药品交易会（春季）
63rd PHARMCHINA (China National Pharmaceuticals Fair)
2010/04/24-26
福建厦门Fujian-Xiamen 4350

1第10届中国（北京）国际健康产业产品博览会
10th China(Beijing) Intl Healthcare Industry Exhibition
2010/05/07-09
北京Beijing 1145

中国中西部（太原）医疗器械展览会暨第11届山西医疗器械(2010年春季)展览会
Taiyuan Medical Device Exhibition
2010/05/13-15
山西太原Shanxi-Taiyuan 6740

2010中国（上海）国际残疾人和老年人康复护理技术及辅助器具展览会
5th China Intl Exhibition of Rehabilitation, Nursing & Health care for Elderly and Disabled People
2010/05/17-19
上海Shanghai 2300

2010中国（天津）国际医疗仪器与设备展览会
China Tianjin Intl Medical Instruments and Equipment Exhibition
2010/05/18-20
天津Tianjin 4040

第64届中国国际医药原料药、中间体、包装、设备交易会（春季）
64th API China(active pharmaceutical ingredient)
2010/05/18-20
黑龙江哈尔滨Heilongjiang-Harbin 5640

世界制药工业中国展（医药、包装材料、制药设备展区）
INTERPHEX CHINA
2010/05/18-20
黑龙江哈尔滨Heilongjiang-Harbin 5650

中国国际生物技术和仪器设备博览会
BIOTECH CHINA 2010
2010/06/02-04
上海Shanghai 2530

中国国际生物技术和仪器设备博览会
BIOTECH CHINA 2010
2010/06/02-04
上海Shanghai 2480

第12届上海国际生物技术与医药研讨会（BIO-FORUM2010）
12th Shanghai Intl Forum on Biotechnology & Pharmaceutical Industry
2010/06/02-04
上海Shanghai 2490

世界 药原料中国展
CPhi China
2010/06/02-04
上海Shanghai 2560

第60届中国实验室技术及装备交易会
60th China Laboratory Technology and Equipment Exhibition
2010/06/22-24
上海Shanghai 2740

第11届全国医疗器械区域博览会
11th CMEF Regional
2010/07 -
天津Tianjin 4125

第45届全国新特药品交易会
45th New Drugs China
2010/07/09-11
北京Beijing 755

中国中西部（合肥）医疗器械展览会暨第12届安徽医疗器械（2010年秋季）展览会
Hefei Medical Devices Exhibition (2010 autumn)
2010/08 -
安徽合肥Anhui-Hefei 4200

2010 大连国际医疗器械展览会
2010 Dalian Intl Exhibition for Medical Instrument
2010/08/10-12
辽宁大连Liaoning-Dalian 6270

中国药店展览会
China Drug Store Show
2010/08/12-14
上海Shanghai 3255

中国医用仪器设备展览会暨技术交流会
China-hospeo
2010/08/19-21
北京Beijing 780

中国国际保健博览会
Health Expo 2010

2010/09 -
北京Beijing 865

2010中国中西部（南宁）医疗器械展览会
China (Xining) Medical Devices Exhibition
2010/09 -
广西南宁Guangxi-Nanning 5580

2010中国中西部（长沙）医疗器械展览会暨第17届湖南医疗器械技术与设备(2010年秋季)展览会
Changsha Medical Devices Exhibition
2010/09 -
湖南长沙Hunan-Changsha 6030

中国中西部（郑州）医疗器械展览会暨第19届中原国际医疗器械(2010年秋季)展览会
2010 China Central (Zhengzhou) Medical Equipment Show
2010/09 -
河南郑州Henan-Zhengzhou 5870

2010国际健康生活方式博览会
2010 Intl Healthy Lifestyle Expo
2010/09/01-03
北京Beijing 850

2010第十一届（成都）全国医疗器械及口腔设备展览会
2010/09/02-08
四川成都Sichuan-Chengdu 6895

第10 届中国国际保健博览会暨保健节
10th China Intl Healthcare Expo & 10th China Intl Healthcare Festival
2010/09/09-11
北京Beijing 865

2010第三届中国国际植物提取物展览会及研讨会
Shanghai Intl Nature Extract Exhibition & Conference
2010/09/21-22
上海Shanghai 3530

2010中国国际教育展
China Education Expo 2010
2010/10/16-17
北京Beijing 940

2010北京国际美容化妆品及医学养生健康产业博览会
Beijing Intl Beauty, Hairdressing, Cosmetics & Health Products Expo
2010/10/26-28
北京Beijing 1145

第十五届中国国际医药（工业）展览会暨技术交流会暨中国医药工业国际论坛
15th China Intl Pharmaceutical Industry Exhibition — China Intl Pharmaceutical Industry Forum
2010/10/26-29
北京Beijing 960

第64届全国药品交易会（秋季）
64th PHARMCHINA
(China National Pharmaceuticals Fair )
2010/11 -
四川成都Sichuan-Chengdu 6370

2010中医药国际科技博览会
Traditional Chinese Medicine Exposition 2010
2010/11 -
四川成都Sichuan-Chengdu 6880

中国国际口腔器材展览会/ 首届全球华人口腔医学大会暨中国国际口腔医学大会
CDEI – China Dental Exhibition Intl/ GCCD – Global Congress of Chinese Dentists
2010/12/01-04
福建厦门Fujian-Xiamen 4453

上海国际健康大会
Intl Congress & Exhibition on Nutrition Fitness and Health (NFH)
2010/12/09-11
上海Shanghai 3970

## 72. 乐器 Music Instrument

第十九届中国国际专业音响、灯光、乐器及技术展览会
19th China Intl Exhibition on Pro Audio, Light, Music & Technology
2010/05/20-23
北京Beijing 510

中国(上海)国际乐器展览会
Music China
2010/10/12-15
上海Shanghai 3670

## 73. 展览展示 Show Business

第11届中国国际展览和会议展示会
11th China Intl Trade Show for Exhibition and Conference Industry
2010/01/14-15
陕西西安Shaanxi-Xi'an 6600

2010上海国际展览展示、POP及商用设施展览会
Shanghai Intl Displaying, POP and Commercial Facility Exhibition 2010
2010/07/07-10
上海Shanghai 2910

## 74. 招聘 人力资源 Job Fairs

上海市高校毕业生就业招聘会
Shanghai Job Fair for College Graduates
2010/01/09-
上海Shanghai 1310

招聘会
2010/03/06-07
四川成都Sichuan-Chengdu 6895

人才展
2010/03/27-28
四川成都Sichuan-Chengdu 6895

人才展
2010/05/29-30
四川成都Sichuan-Chengdu 6895

人才展
2010/08/28-29
四川成都Sichuan-Chengdu 6895

人才展
2010/12/04-05
四川成都Sichuan-Chengdu 6895

## 75. 纸业 Paper

第十届东莞国际印刷造纸胶粘带及广告展览会
10th Dongguan Intl Printing and Packaging and Paper Advertising, Adhesive Tape, Protective Film Exhibition
2010/05/27-29
广东东莞Guangdong-Dongguan 5435

第18届上海国际印刷包装纸业展览会
2010上海国际印刷包装产品交易会
Shanghai Intl Print Exhibition 2010
2010/07/07-10
上海Shanghai 2890

第十八届中国国际纸浆造纸暨纸制品展览会及会议
China Paper Shanghai 2010 – 18th Intl Exhibition and Conference Reaching All of China's Paper-Related Industries
2010/09/15-17
上海Shanghai 3460

2010中国国际水处理化学品、水溶高分子、造纸化学品、工业表面活性剂技术及应用展览会
2010 Intl Exhibition on Water-treatment Chemicals & Water-soluble Polymer Products & Papermaking Chemicals & Industrial Surfactants, Technology and Application
2010/11/03-04
上海Shanghai 1145

亚洲纸业世界展览会
Tissue World Asia
2010/11/17-19
上海Shanghai 3910

## 76. 钟表 眼镜 Watches, Clocks & Optics

第十八届中国（深圳）国际礼品、工艺品、钟表及家庭用品展览会
17th China (Shenzhen) Intl Gifts, Handicrafts, Watches & Houseware Fair
2010/04/25-28
广东深圳Guangdong-Shenzhen 5180

第21届中国（深圳）国际钟表展览会
21st China Watch Fair
2010/07/01-04
广东深圳Guangdong-Shengzhen 5340

中国国际眼镜业展览会
China Intl Optics Fair 2010
2010/09/14-16
北京Beijing 1145

# 77. 珠宝 Jewelry

中国(深圳)国际黄金珠宝玉石展览会
China Intl Gold, Jewelry & Gem Fair
2010/03/09-12
广东深圳Guangdong-Shenzhen 5110

2010第三届天津国际珠宝首饰展览会
2010 Tianjin 3rd Intl Jewelry Fair
2010/05/06-09
天津Tianjin 4035

中国(广州)国际黄金珠宝玉石展览会
China Intl Gold, Jewelry & Gem Fair
2010/06/17-20
广东广州Guangdong-Guangzhou 4870

中国昆明珠宝玉石展览会
China Jewellery Fair 2010
2010/07/10-14
云南昆明Yunnan-Kunming 6940

第十一届北京国际珠宝展览会
11th Beijing Intl Jewellery Fair
2010/07/16-19
北京Beijing 760

2010北京国际珠宝展览会
11th Beijing Intl Jewelry Fair
2010/07/16-19
北京Beijing 760

2010深圳国际珠宝展
2010 Shenzhen Intl Jewellery Fair
2010/09/15-19
广东深圳Guangdong-Shenzhen 5440

# 78. 自行车 电动自行车 Bikes

2010中国自行车展览会/ 2010中国国际电动车及零配件展览会
China Intl Bicycle & Motor Fair (CHINA CYCLE 2010)/ China E-BIKE 2010
2010/04/27-30
上海Shanghai 2110

第四届中国常州电动车展览会
4th Changzhou Electric Vehicle Exhibition
2010/06/18-20
江苏常州Jiangsu-Changzhou 6060

# 79. 其他 Others

北京活力澳门推广周
Business and Trade Fair Beijing
2010/01/08-10
北京Beijing 10

2010北京旅居人士服务展览会
2010 Expat Show
2010/03/26-28
北京Beijing 170

2010中国国际福祉博览会
China Intl Wellbeing Expo 2010
2010/09/19-21
北京Beijing 1145

第五届中国厦门国际佛事用品展览会
5th China Xiamen Intl Buddhist Items & Crafts Fair
2010/11/05-08
福建厦门Fujian-Xiamen 4430

# 国内展览会议

# 日期索引

# Exhibitions and Conference in Chronological Order

## 2010

第二十二届河南家禽交易会
22th Henan Poultry Trade Fair
河南郑州 Henan-Zhengzhou 5690

中国中部食品与饮料加工及包装展览会
Central China Food & Beverage Processing and Packaging Exhibition
河南郑州 Henan-Jinan 5700

中国中部国际环境保护与水处理展览会
Central China Intl Environment Protection and Water Treatment Exhibition
河南郑州 Henan-Jinan 5710

## January 2010 一月

2010/01/01-12
上海通用雪佛兰新赛欧发布会
四川成都 Sichuan-Chengdu 6895

2010/01/05-05
四川省卫生巡诊车交接仪式
四川成都 Sichuan-Chengdu 6895

2010/01/06-17
2010名品衣装（厦门）博览会
Brand Name Apparel (Xiamen) Show
福建厦门 Fujian-Xiamen 4270

2010/01/08-10
北京活力澳门推广周
Business and Trade Fair Beijing
北京 Beijing 10

2010/01/09-
上海市高校毕业生就业招聘会
Shanghai Job Fair for College Graduates
上海 Shanghai 1310

2010/01/09-13
2010第四届西南（成都）农资推广暨畜牧业展览会
四川成都 Sichuan-Chengdu 6895

2010/01/10-11
2010订货会
Beijing Book Fair 2010 commodities Fair
北京 Beijing 1145

2010/01/13-15
环球资源流行服饰配件采购交易会及环球资源婴儿及儿童采购交易会，环球资源及赠品采购交易会
China Sourcing Fair：Fashion Accessories
Baby & Children' s Products
Gifts & Premiums
上海 Shanghai 1320

2010/01/13-19
北京2010年TOP100名牌服饰折扣购物展
Top 100 Brand Name Apparel Sale
北京 Beijing 20

2010/01/14-15
第11届中国国际展览和会议展示会
11th China Intl Trade Show for Exhibition and Conference Industry
陕西西安 Shaanxi-Xi'an 6600

2010/01/14-20
2010成都品牌家具春季直销周
四川成都 Sichuan-Chengdu 6895

2010/01/15-17
居民家庭和沿街商铺实用技防产品展示会
Safety and Security Exhibition
南京江苏 Nanjing-Jiangsu 6100

2010/01/16-16
2010第十六届沈阳药交会
16th Shenyang Medicine Fair
辽宁沈阳 Liaoning-Shenyang 6320

2010/01/19-20
一汽丰田晚宴
四川成都 Sichuan-Chengdu 6895

2010/01/19-29
新品服装暨名优产品年货会
New Apparel and Brand Name Products Shopping Fair
福建厦门 Fujian-Xiamen 4280

2010/01/20-23
第十七届中国上海国际婚纱摄影器材展览会暨国际儿童摄影、主题摄影展览会(春季)
17th China (Shanghai) Intl Wedding Photographic Equipment Exhibition & Intl Children' s Photography, Theme Photography Exhibition (Spring)
上海 Shanghai 1340

2010/01/20-24
北京国际名酒文化节暨世界名酒产业博览会
Winefest Beijing
北京 Beijing 30

2010/01/22-07
2010北京年货博览会
2010 Beijing happy Spring Festival
北京 Beijing 1145

2010/01/22-23
奇瑞年会
四川成都 Sichuan-Chengdu 6895

2010/01/22-25
广东（厚街）茶业博览会
Guangdong (Houjie) Tea Expo
广东东莞 Guangdong-Dongguan 4456

2010/01/26-11
2010新春年货购物节
四川成都 Sichuan-Chengdu 6895

2010/01/30-09
北方服装节厦门博览会
Fashion Festival
福建厦门 Fujian-Xiamen 4290

## February 2010 二月

2010/02/05-08
农业展览
Xiamen Agriculture Show
福建厦门 Fujian-Xiamen 4300

2010/02/20-01
第7届元宵商品交易会
四川成都 Sichuan-Chengdu 6895

2010/02/23-25
第二十届中国国际钓鱼用品贸易展览会
20th China Intl Fishing Tackle Trade Exhibition
北京 Beijing 40

2010/02/23-25
中国国际钓鱼用品贸易展览会
CHINA FISH 2010
北京 Beijing 50

## March 2010 三月

2010/03/-
中国广州国际厨房家具和电器展览会
China Kitchen Furniture and Appliance Fair (CKFA)
广东广州 Guangdong-Guangzhou 4550

2010/03/-
2010年（春季）中国郑州第十六届中原广告展暨2010年中国中部LED霓虹灯展
2010(Spring)China Zhengzhou 16th Central China Advertisement Show and 2010 China Central LED Neon-lights Show
河南郑州 Henan-Zhengzhou 5795

2010/03/01-02
第37届东北药品保健品交易会
37th North-East China Medicine and Health Products Fair
东北沈阳 Dongbei-Shenyang 6330

2010/03/01-05
中国华东进出口商品交易会
East China Fair
上海 Shanghai 1350

2010/03/02-05
2010广东国际广告展
SIGN CHINA 2010
广东广州 Guangdong-Guangzhou 4560

2010/03/02-06
2010东莞数字喷印及广告技术展览会
Dongguan Digital Printing Exhibition
广东东莞 Guangdong-Dongguan 4458

2010/03/03-05
第六届中国（广州）国际汽车改装服务业展览会
6th China Intl Automotive Aftermarket Industry and Tuning Trade Fair (AAITF)
广东广州 Guangdong-Guangzhou 4570

2010/03/03-05
2010福建（第二十一届）国际医疗仪器与设备展览会

China Tianjin Intl Medical Instruments and Equipment Exhibition
福州福建 Fuzhou-Fujian 4230

2010/03/03-07
2010/03/04-06
第七届广州国际车用空调及冷藏链技术展览会
Guangzhou Intl automotive Air-conditioning& cold China exhibition
广东广州 Guangdong-Guangzhou 4580

2010/03/04-06
亚洲国际品牌体育用品及运动时尚博览会
ispo china
北京 Beijing 60

2010/03/04-07
四川印刷器材展览会
四川成都 Sichuan-Chengdu 6895

2010/03/05-07
中国中西部（合肥）医疗器械展览会暨第11届安徽医疗器械（2010年春季）展览会
Hefei Medical Devices Exhibition
安徽合肥 Anhui-Hefei 4160

2010/03/05-07
中国（上海）第十五届国际玩具展暨上海玩具第46届博览会
Toy China 2010 (Spring)
上海 Shanghai 1360

2010/03/05-07
2010第三届西部教育技术装备及高职教育仪器展览会/2010第五届中国西部国际科技仪器及实验室装备展
2010 Chengdu Intl Educational Technology and Equipment Exhibition
四川成都 Sichuan-Chengdu 6750

2010/03/06-07
招聘会
四川成都 Sichuan-Chengdu 6895

2010/03/06-08
2010安徽视觉广告技术及标识制作展览会
Anhui Ad Technology and Label Exhibition
河南郑州 Henan-Jinan 4175

2010/03/06-08
2010安徽印刷包装工业展览会
Anhui Printing & Packaging Industry Exhibition 河南郑州 Henan-Jinan 4170

2010/03/06-09
2010北京国际创意礼品与工艺品展览会
Beijing Intl Gift and Graft Show
北京 Beijing 70

2010/03/06-09
第十届中国厦门国际石材展览会
10th China Xiamen Intl Stone Fair
福建厦门 Fujian-Xiamen 4310

2010/03/06-09
中国厦门国际厨柜展
China (Xiamen) Cabinets Show
福建厦门 Fujian-Xiamen 4330

2010/03/07-09
2010中国中西部（成都）医疗器械展览会暨第10届中国西部医疗器械及口腔设备展览会
Chengdu Medical Device Exhibition
四川成都 Sichuan-Changzhou 6760

2010/03/08-10
2010长春第十三届广告博览会
2010 Changchun 13th session of advertisement exposition
吉林长春 Jilin-Changchun 6210

2010/03/08-11
中国广州国际工业自动化技术及装备展览会
SPS-Industrial Automation Fair Guangzhou
广东广州 Guangdong-Guangzhou 4590

2010/03/08-11
中国广州国际工业自动化技术及装备展览会
SPS-Industrial Automation Fair Guangzhou - Fuyang
广东广州 Guangdong-Guangzhou 4660

2010/03/09-11
第十七届华南国际印刷工业展览会/ 2010中国国际标签印刷技术展览会
17th South China Intl Exhibition on Printing Industry, China Intl Exhibition on Label Printing Technology
广东广州 Guangdong-Guangzhou 4680

2010/03/09-11
第11届中国（广州）国际给排水、水处理技术设备展览会、中国（广州）国际泵、阀门、管道展览会
11th China (Guangzhou)_Water Wasterwater & Water Treatment 、Pump,Vale&Pipe China
广东广州 Guangdong-Guangzhou 4700

2010/03/09-11
第32届广州国际美容美发化妆用品进出口博览会
GUANGZHOU INTL BEAUTY & COSMETICIMPORT-EXPORT- SPRING 2010
广东广州 Guangdong- Guangzhou 4670

2010/03/09-12
中国(深圳)国际黄金珠宝玉石展览会
China International Gold, Jewelry & Gem Fair 广东深圳 Guangdong-Shenzhen 5110

2010/03/10-12
中国国际化妆品、个人及家庭护理用品原料展览会
Personal Care and Home Ingredients
上海 Shanghai 1370

2010/03/10-12
第十六届上海国际服装纺织品贸易博览会
Shanghai Intl Clothing & Textile Expo
上海 Shanghai 1400

2010/03/10-12
中国国际五金博览会
China Intl Hardware Fair
上海 Shanghai 1390

2010/03/10-12
中国中西部（郑州）医疗器械展览会暨第18届中原国际医疗器械(2010年春季)展览会
2010 China Central (Zhengzhou) Medical Equipment Show
河南郑州 Henan-Jinan 5750

2010/03/10-13
第十三届国际木工机械及家具生产设备展览会暨第十三届国际家具配件、材料及木制品展览会
Wood Work Fair 2010
北京 Beijing 1145

2010/03/11-13
第十届中国西部国际金属工业展
10th West China International Metal Exhibition
重庆 Chongqing 1150

2010/03/11-14
2010第十二届中国东北口腔设备及材料展览会暨东北国际口腔学术交流会
12th China Northeast Intl Dental Equipment & Affiliated Facilities Exhibition 2010 / Northeast Intl Symposium On Oral Health
辽宁沈阳 Liaoning-Shenyang 6350

2010/03/11-14
2010第三届东北孕婴童产品展览会
3rd Baby and Children Products Show
辽宁沈阳 Liaoning-Shenyang 6340

2010/03/12-13
第二届全国杂粮产业大会
2nd National Cereals Industry Convention
天津 Tianjin 4020

2010/03/12-14
第十届中国国际汽车用品展览会
10th China Intl Auto Accessories Commercial Expo 2010
北京 Beijing 90

2010/03/12-14
第七届中国国际成人保健及生殖健康展览会
7th China Intl Adult Toys & Reproductive Health Exhibition
上海 Shanghai 1450

2010/03/12-14
2010上海宠物大会暨第三届上海宠物医疗学术研讨会
Pet Fair Shanghai 2010
上海 Shanghai 1460

2010/03/12-20
春季品牌服装博览会
四川成都 Sichuan-Chengdu 6895

2010/03/13-14
第十五届中国国际教育巡回展
14th China International Education Exhibition Tour
北京 Beijing 100

2010/03/15-18
中国国际采暖、供热暨空调、通风产品与技术展览会
CIEC
北京 Beijing 1145

2010/03/15-18
第十七届中国（北京）国际建筑装饰及材料博览会
17th China Intl Building Decorations and Building Materials Exposition
北京 Beijing 110

2010/03/15-18
中国国际建筑装饰博览会
China Intl Building Decoration and Building Materials Exposition
北京 Beijing 1145

2010/03/16-18
慕尼黑上海电子展
electronica & Productronica China
上海 Shanghai 1480

2010/03/16-18
第十届中国国际供热、通风及空调产品与技术博览会
10th China Intl Heating, Ventilation & Air-conditioning Expo
北京 Beijing 112

2010/03/16-18
慕尼黑上海激光、光电展
LASER World of PHOTONICS CHINA
上海 Shanghai 1470

2010/03/16-20
国际名家具（东莞）展览会
Intl Famous Furniture Fair(Dongguan)
广东东莞 Guangdong-Dongguan 4460

2010/03/17-
2010中国中西部（长沙）医疗器械展览会暨第16届湖南医疗器械技术与设备(2010年春季)展览会
Changsha Medical Devices Exhibition
湖南长沙 Hunan-Changsha 5990

2010/03/17-18
第四届全国鸭鹅产业大会
4th National Ducks and Geese Convention
天津 Tianjin 4030

2010/03/17-19
2010中国（上海）国际突发事件灾难预防及救援装备技术展览会暨中国（上海）国际紧急医疗救援装备技术展览会
China Rescue Expo 2010
上海 Shanghai 1500

2010/03/17-19
2010中国国际新能源暨节能环保产业展览会
2nd China Intl New Energy & Energy Conservation and Environmental Protection Exhibition 2010
北京 Beijing 1145

2010/03/18-20
中国中部国际物流、物料运输与储藏展览会
Central China Logistics Exhibition
河南郑州 Henan-Jinan 5780

2010/03/18-20
第12届中原国际工业控制自动化及仪器仪表展
Central China Automation and Instrument Exhibition
河南郑州 Henan-Zhengzhou 5770

2010/03/18-20
2010中国中部(郑州)国际装备制造业博览会
Central China (Zhengzhou) Intl Equipment Manufacturing Exposition(2010)
河南郑州 Henan-Zhengzhou 5790

2010/03/18-21
中国广州户外及休闲展览会
China Intl Outdoor & Leisure Fair
广东广州 Guangdong-Guangzhou 4750

2010/03/18-21
第十一届中国国际机械工业展览会
11TH CHINA INTL MACHINERY INDUSTRY EXHIBITION
浙江宁波 Zhejiang-Ningbo 6960

2010/03/18-21
上海之春房产展示交易会
Shanghai Spring Real Estate Market
上海 Shanghai 1510

2010/03/18-21
2010第11届中国东北国际机床、工模具技术展览会
Northeast 11th Intl Machine Tool and Tools & Moulds Technique Exhibition China 2010
辽宁沈阳 Liaoning-Shenyang 6390

2010/03/18-21
2010第11届中国东北国际塑胶机械及包装工业展览会
11th Northeast China Intl Plastics Machinery & Packaging Exhibition 2010
辽宁沈阳 Liaoning-Shenyang 6370

2010/03/18-21
第十一届中国东北国际物流技术及运输系统展览会
Northeast 11th Intl physical Distributibon & Transpor System Exhibition China 2010
辽宁沈阳 Liaoning-Shenyang 6380

2010/03/18-21
东北第14届国际焊接、切割、激光技术设备展览会
14th China (Northeast) Intl Welding, Cutting, & Laser Technology and Equipment Exhibition
辽宁沈阳 Liaoning-Shenyang 6360

2010/03/18-21
中国（广州）国际家用纺织品及辅料博览会
China (Guangzhou) Intl Trade Fair for Home Textiles
广东广州 Guangdong-Guangzhou 4730

2010/03/18-21
中国广州国际家具博览会(民用家具展)
China Intl Furniture Fair (Guangzhou)-Home Furniture
广东广州 Guangdong-Guangzhou 4760

2010/03/18-21
中国广州国际家居饰品/用品展览会
Homedecor & Housewares China 2010
广东广州 Guangdong-Guangzhou 4720

2010/03/18-21
中国广州国际陶瓷展览会
China Intl Ceramics Exhibititon (Guangzhou)
广东广州 Guangdong-Guangzhou 4710

2010/3/19-21
中国（国际）婚博会
Wedding Expo
北京 Beijing 115

2010/03/19-21
第十届西北（兰州）广告印刷LED及办公设备展览会
Lanzhou AD, Printing, LED, Office Equipment Exhibition
甘肃兰州 Gansu-Lanzhou 4455

2010/03/19-22
第25届深圳国际家具/家居饰品/家具配料展览会
25th Shenzhen Intl furniture exhibition
广东深圳 Guangdong-Shenzhen 5120

2010/03/19-22
2010辽宁第十四届国际广告四新技术暨印刷/数码技术设备展示会
Shenyang AD and Digital Exhibition
辽宁沈阳 Liaoning-Shenyang 6400

2010/03/20-22
第七届中国国际文具礼品博览会暨世纪文具网国际采购会
7th China Intl Stationery & Gifts Exposition& StationeryTrade. Com Purchasing Fair
宁波 Zhejiang-Ningbo 6970

2010/03/21-23
2010第五届中国东北畜牧及饲料工业展览会；同期举办：第五届东北农业生产资料交易会
5th North-East China Livestock and Feed Exhibition
辽宁沈阳 Liaoning-Shenyang 6420

2010/03/22-24
中国国际石油石化技术装备展览会及中国国际输配电防爆工业展览会
CIPPE 2010
北京 Beijing 1145

2010/03/22-24
2010中国国际婚纱及摄影器材博览会
China Wedding and Photo Equipment Expo
北京 Beijing 120

2010/03/22-28
2010年中国（四川）教育博览会
四川成都 Sichuan-Chengdu 6895

2010/03/23-25
第八届上海国际园林景观设计及城市建设展览会
8th Shanghai Int\'l Landscape Design & Urban Construction Expo
上海 Shanghai 1550

2010/03/23-25
第十四届中国国际食品添加剂和配料展览会暨第二十届全国食品添加剂生产应用展示会
Food Ingredients China 2010
上海 Shanghai 1520

2010/03/23-25
第十八届中国国际广播电视信息网路展览会
CCBN 2010
北京 Beijing 1145

2010/03/23-25
2010第二十一届（春季）沈阳国际医疗器械设备展览会
2010 21th Shenyang Intl Medical Equipment Fair
辽宁沈阳 Liaoning-Shenyang 6430

2010/03/23-25
2010中国可持续建筑国际大会
China Sustainable Building Forum 2010
上海 Shanghai 1600

2010/03/23-25
第12届中国国际地面材料及铺装技术展览会
DOMOTEX asia
CHINAFLOOR 2010
上海 Shanghai 1590

2010/03/23-29
第五届哈尔滨春季汽车展览会
5th Harbin Intl Automobile Exhibition - Spring
黑龙江哈尔滨 Heilongjiang-Harbin 5630

2010/03/24-27
2010中国中西部（昆明）医疗器械展览会
Kunming Medical Devices Exhibition
云南 Yunnan 6920

2010/03/25-27
2010中国（沈阳）国际建设科技博览会暨第八届东北建筑节能、新型墙体材料及设备展览会
2010 8th (Shenyang) Intl Energy-saving & New Wall Muterial and Equipment Exhibition
辽宁沈阳 Liaoning-Shenyang 6440

2010/03/25-27
2010第十届中国(青岛)国际物流展览会
The10th China Intl Material Handling and Logistics Expo
山东青岛 Shandong-Qingdao 6650

2010/03/25-27
第13届中国东北国际供热供暖、空调、新能源设备展览会
13th China (Northeast) Intl Equipments of Heating, Air-Condition & New Energy Sources Exhibition
辽宁沈阳 Liaoning-Shenyang 6470

2010/03/25-27
第十二届中国东北国际门窗、幕墙、玻璃与加工设备展览会
12th Northeast China Intl Door & Window, Curtain, Wall, Glass and Fabric Exhibition
辽宁沈阳 Liaoning-Shenyang 6480

2010/03/25-27
第11届中国东北国际给排水、水处理技术设备及泵、阀、管道展览会
11th Northeast China Intl, Water Supply & Drainage, Water Disposal Technique & Equipment, and Pump & Value and Pipeline Exhibition
辽宁沈阳 Liaoning-Shenyang 6460

2010/03/25-27
第十六届东北沈阳国际建筑装饰博览会
16th Northeast Intl Building Decoration Exhibition
辽宁沈阳 Liaoning-Shenyang 6450

2010/03/26-28
第二十二届医疗仪器设备展览会
22nd Intl Medical Instruments and Equipment Exhibition
北京 Beijing 150

2010/03/26-28
2010第三届华展云南广告四新展览会
Yunnan AD Exhibition
云南昆明 Yunnan-Kunming 6930

2010/03/26-28
第二十二届国际医疗仪器设备展览会
22nd Intl Medical Instruments and Equipment Exhibition
北京 Beijing 160

2010/03/26-28
2010年第四届广西机械工业博览会
fourth Guangxi mechanical industry exposition, 2010
广西南宁 Guangxi-Nanning 5520

2010/03/26-28
2010北京旅居人士服务展览会
Yunnan AD Exhibition
北京 Beijing 170

2010/03/27-28
人才展
四川成都 Sichuan-Chengdu 6895

2010/03/27-29
2010第十一届中国(上海)广告四新展览会
11th China (Shanghai) Advertising Four New Exhibition
上海 Shanghai 1610

2010/03/27-30
中国广州国际家具博览会（办公环境展）
China Intl Furniture Fair (Guangzhou)-Office Show
广东广州 Guangdong-Guangzhou 4790

2010/03/27-30
中国广州国际木工机械、家具配料展览会
Interzum Guangzhou
广东广州 Guangdong-Guangzhou 4770

2010/03/28-31
第23届国际FOM 2010学术年会
23rd Focus On Microscopy 2010 Conference
上海 Shanghai 1620

2010/03/28-31
第十八届中国国际服装服饰博览会
18th China Intl Clothing & Accessories Fair (CHIC2010)
北京 Beijing 180

2010/03/28-31
2010第11届深圳国际机械、模具及制品、塑胶工业展览会
China Shenzhen Intl Machinery Manufacturing Industry Exhibition （SIMM2010）
广东深圳 Guangdong-Shenzhen 5130

2010/03/28-31
中国国际服装服饰博览会
China Intl Clothing & Accessories Fair
北京 Beijing 200

2010/03/28-31
中国国际服装服饰博览会
CHIC 2010
北京 Beijing 200

2010/03/28-31
2010第11届深圳国际机械、模具及制品、塑胶工业展览会
China Shenzhen Intl Machinery Manufacturing Industry Exhibition （SIMM2010）
广东深圳 Guangdong-Shenzhen 5140

2010/03/29-01
中国国际咖啡与茶用品展览会
Coffee & Tea China 2010
上海 Shanghai 1670

2010/03/29-01
中国国际门窗、幕墙、五金与遮阳　品展览会
Doors, Windows, Structures & Sunshades China
上海 Shanghai 1720

2010/03/29-01
中国国际建筑陶瓷及卫浴科技精品展览会
11th Ceramics, Tile & Sanitary Ware China
上海 Shanghai 1690

2010/03/29-01
中国国际康体健身、休　娱乐与运动器材展览会
Fitness, Sports & Leisure China
上海 Shanghai 1660

2010/03/29-01
上海国际酒店用品博览会
Hotelex
上海 Shanghai 1640

2010/03/29-01
中国国际建筑及室内设计节
Home Fashion & Design Shanghai
上海 Shanghai 1700

2010/03/29-01
中国国际洗涤设备展览会
Laundry China 2010
上海 Shanghai 1680

2010/03/29-01
第十八届中国国际建筑装饰展览会
18 TH EXPO BUILD CHINA 2010
上海 Shanghai 1650

2010/03/29-01
家居设计展览会
Expo Deco
上海 Shanghai 1750

2010/03/29-01
第十一届中国(东莞)国际鞋机鞋材工业技术展
11th China (Dongguan) Int' l Footwear Machinery & Material Industry Fair
广东东莞 Guangdong-dongguan 4470

2010/03/29-01
第十一届中国(东莞)国际纺织制衣工业技术展
11th China (Dongguan) Int' l Textile & Clothing Industry Fair
广东东莞 Guangdong-dongguan 4480

2010/03/29-01
中国国际建筑陶瓷色釉料及原辅材料展览会
Building Ceramics Glaze & Pigment China 2010
上海 Shanghai 1630

2010/03/29-01
中国国际木　品及原材料展览会
Sustainable Building Woodwork Expo
上海 Shanghai 1740

2010/03/29-31
第五届国际胶粘带、保护膜及光学膜（上海）展览会/ 国际模切材料及加工设备（上海）展览会
5th Intl Adhesive tape Protective Films & Optical Film (Shanghai) Expo/ Intl Diecyt Materials and Fabrication Plants (Shanghai) Expo
上海 Shanghai 1770

2010/03/29-31
中国清洁博览会
11th China Clean
上海 Shanghai 1790

2010/03/30-01
2010第十四届武汉广告展览会/ 第二届武汉印刷/包装/纸业展览会
2010 Wuhan Ad Exhibition
湖北武汉 Hubei-Wuhan 5930

2010/03/30-01
湖北武汉国际先进医疗仪器设备展览会
hubei wuhan Intl madical equipment & instrument exhibition
湖北武汉 Hubei-Wuhan 5940

2010/03/30-01
2010第二十二届中国长春国际医疗器械卫生产业博览会
201022th Intl Medical Equipment Industry Hygiene Industrial Expo Chang chun-china Chang chun-china
辽宁沈阳 Liaoning-Shenyang 6220

2010/03/30-01
中国国际纺织面料及辅料（春夏）博览会
China Intl Trade Fair for Apparel Fabrics and Accessories
北京 Beijing 220

2010/03/31-02
中国国际纺织纱线（春夏）展览会
China Intl Trade Fair for Fibres and Yarns
北京 Beijing 240

2010/03/31-02
2010北京国际喷涂聚脲技术、屋顶（木屋）绿化及沥青展览会
Polyurea Technology, Green Roof and Asphalt Show
北京 Beijing 250

2010/03/31-05
第六届成都给排水处理及流体机械展暨环保、固废物及资源综合利用博览会
四川成都 Sichuan-Chengdu 6895

2010/03/31-05
第十届成都照明+建筑电气博览会暨LED展览会
四川成都 Sichuan-Chengdu 6895

## April 2010 四月

2010/04/-
2010第八届中国（郑州）社会公共安全产品博览会
2010 8th China Zhengzhou Public Security Product Expo
河南郑州 Henan-Zhengzhou 5800

2010/04/-
2010中部住宅及科技产业博览会
2010 China Central Real Estate and Tech Industry Expo
河南郑州 Henan-Zhengzhou 5810

2010/04/01-03
2010第十三届中国东北仪器仪表及工业自动化展览会
13th Northeast China Intl Instrument & Automation Exhibition 2010
辽宁沈阳 Liaoning-Shenyang 6500

2010/04/01-03
2010年第三届中国东北国际流体机械展览会
3rd China (Northeast) Fluid Machinery Exhibition 2010
辽宁沈阳 Liaoning-Shenyang 6520

2010/04/01-03
中国东北第13届国际电力电工及能源技术设备展览会
13th Northeast China Intl Electric Power, Electrician and Energy Tech & Equipment Exhibition 2010
辽宁沈阳 Liaoning-Shenyang 6510

2010/04/01-03
中国（上海）国际袜业采购交易会
China (Shanghai) Intl Hosiery Purchasing Expo
上海 Shanghai 1800

2010/04/01-03
2010第十二届中国东北国际动力传动与控制技术展览会
2010 12th China Northeast Intl Power Transmission and Control Technique Exhibition
辽宁沈阳 Liaoning-Shenyang 6490

2010/04/02-04
2010中国（成都）国防科技工业及装备博览会暨第15届成都国际机床展
Chengdu China Natl Defense Science & Technology Industry and Equipment Manufacturing Expo/ 15th Chengdu Intl Machine Exhibition
四川成都 Sichuan-Chengdu 6790

2010/04/03-05
2010深圳国际婚博会暨深圳婚庆文化节
Shenzhen Intl Wedding Exhibition &Wedding Cultural Festival 2010
广东深圳 Guangdong-Shenzhen 5140

2010/04/03-05
2010第六届上海国际模型展览会

7th Shanghai International Model Exhibition 2010 (SIMS 2010)
上海 Shanghai 1810

2010/04/04-07
第二十一届中国国际礼品、赠品及家庭用品展览会
21 st China Intl Gifts,Premium & Houseware Exhibition
北京 Beijing 270

2010/04/04-07
第二十一届中国国际礼品、赠品及家庭用品展览会
China Intl Gifts, Premium & Houseware Exhibition
北京 Beijing 270

2010/04/06-09
第17届中国国际石材产品及石材技术装备展览会
STONETECH 2010
17th China Intl Stone Processing Machinery, Equipment and Products Exhibition
上海 Shanghai 1830

2010/04/07-09
第二十一届国际制冷、空调、供暖、通风及食品冷冻加工展览会
21st Intl Exhibition for Refrigeration, Air-conditioning, Heating and Ventilation, Frozen Food Processing, Packaging and Storage
北京 Beijing 290

2010/04/07-09
励华国际瓦楞展2010中国展
SinoCorrugated
广东东莞 Guangdong-Dongguan 4490

2010/04/07-09
第二十一届国际制冷、空调、供暖、通风及食品冷冻加工展览会
21st Intl Exhibition for Refrigeration, Air-conditioning, Heating and Ventilation, Frozen Food Processing, Packaging and Storage
北京 Beijing 300

2010/04/07-09
2010励华国际彩盒展
广东东莞 Guangdong-Dongguan 4500

2010/04/08-09
第五届全国粳稻米大会
5th National Rice Conference
吉林长春 Jilin-Changchun 6230

2010/04/08-10
第八届中国国际科学仪器及实验室装备展览会
8th China Intl Scientific Instrument and Laboratory Equipment Exhibition
北京 Beijing 310

2010/04/08-10
2010中国国际水处理化学品及水溶性高分子展览会
China Intl Water Treatment Chemicals Exhibition
北京 Beijing 325

2010/04/08-10
2010年广州国际婴幼儿用品展
Guangzhou Intl Baby Product Fair 2010
广东广州 Guangdong-Guangzhou 4800

2010/04/08-10
第七届中国国际橡胶及轮胎工业展览会
7th China Intl Rubber and Tire Fair
山东青岛 Shandong-Qingdao 6660

2010/04/08-10
2010中国（上海）国际测绘仪器及GPS/GIS/RS技术展览会
2010China (shanghai) Intl Survey and Mapping Equipment & Technology exhibition
上海 Shanghai 1860

2010/04/08-10
第十三届中国东北国际五金工具展览会
13th China (Northeast) Intl Hardware & Tool Exhibition
辽宁沈阳 Liaoning-Shenyang 6530

2010/04/08-10
第二届中国（上海）国际电源产业展览会
2nd China (ShangHai) Intl Power Supply Industry Fair
上海 Shanghai 1880

2010/04/08-10
2010中国（上海）国际地球物理勘探技术展览会
2010 China (Shanghai) Intl Geophysical Exploration Technology Exhibition
上海 Shanghai 1840

2010/04/08-10
二届中国（上海）国际铅酸蓄电池展览会
2nd China (ShangHai) Intl Lead Battery Industry Fair
上海 Shanghai 1890

2010/04/08-10
2010中国（上海）国际超级电容器产业展览会
2nd China (ShangHai) Intl Lead Battery Industry Fair
上海 Shanghai 1850

2010/04/08-10
第22届广州国际玩具及模型展览会
22nd Guangzhou (China) Intl Toy & Hobby Fair
广东广州 Guangdong-Guangzhou 4810

2010/04/08-10
第二届中国（上海）国际电池产品及技术展览会
2nd China (ShangHai) Intl Battery Industry Fair
上海 Shanghai 1870

2010/04/08-11
2010重庆国际生态环保与节能减排技术展览会
Chongqing Eco, Energy Saving Exhibition
重庆 Chongqing 1160

2010/04/08-11
2010年中国北京春季房地产展示交易会
Springtime Real Estate Trade Fair Beijing China
北京 Beijing 320

2010/04/08-11
中国(上海)国际游艇展
China (Shanghai) International Boat Show 2010
上海 Shanghai 1900

2010/04/08-11
第十四届对台出口商品交易会
14th China Xiamen Machinery and Electronics Exhibition (CXMEE)
福建厦门 Fujian-Xiamen 4340

2010/04/09-11
第十届中国国际眼科和视光技术及设备展览会
10th Intl congress of Ophthalmology and Optometry China_(COOC 2010)
江西南昌 Jiangxi-Nanchang 6195

2010/04/09-11
2010年中国国际医药生物产业展览会
2010 China Beijing Intl Pharmacy Biology Industry Exhibition
北京 Beijing 1145

2010/04/09-11
第三届东北国际渔具、户外用品博览会
3rd Fishing and Outdoor Sports Fair
东北沈阳 Dongbei-Shenyang 6540

2010/04/09-11
2010年春季（第75届）中国电子展
75th China Electronics Fair (CEF Shenzhen)
广东深圳 Guangdong-Shenzhen 5150

2010/04/09-11
德纳广告展
四川成都 Sichuan-Chengdu 6895

2010/04/09-12
第八届中国国际家居博览会
7th China Intl Housing and Furnishing Exposition
浙江宁波 Zhejiang-Ningbo 6980

2010/04/09-12
第十五届中国国际建筑装饰材料展览会
The15th China Int\'l Construction & Decoration Materials Exhibition
辽宁大连 Liaoning-Dalian 6240

2010/04/09-14
全国门窗展
四川成都 Sichuan-Chengdu 6895

2010/04/09-14
2010年城市建设科技博览会
四川成都 Sichuan-Chengdu 6895

2010/04/09-14
第九届中国西部国际口腔设备及材料展
四川成都 Sichuan-Chengdu 6895

2010/04/10-12
中国（北京）第十一届国际照明电器博览会
Beijing Intl Illumination Exhibition
北京 Beijing 1145

2010/04/10-12
2010第十六届中国北京国际美容美发化妆用品博览会(春季)
16th Chinese Intl Beauty, Hairdressing & Cosmetics Expo in Beijing 2010
北京 Beijing 340

2010/04/10-12
2010年北京国际美容美发美体化妆及洗涤用品博览会
Chinese Intl Beauty, Hairdressing & Cosmetics and cleaning products Expo 2010
北京 Beijing 1145

2010/04/10-12
第二届中国（北京）国际优生优育计生用品（成人用品）展览会
2nd Beijing Intl Adult-goods Exhibition
北京 Beijing 1145

2010/04/10-12
第十一届京正北京孕婴童用品展览会
Mother& baby China 2010
北京 Beijing 1145

2010/04/10-12
2010北京国际烘焙、食品加工与包装设备展览会
Beijing baking, drink, starch, food processing and package equipment exhibition 2010
北京 Beijing 1145

2010/04/10-12
第八届中国北京国际食品加工与包装机械展览会
8th China Beijing Intl Food Processing & Packaging Machinery Exhibition
北京 Beijing 330

2010/04/10-15
第十届成都国际社会公共安全产品与技术展览会
四川成都 Sichuan-Chengdu 6895

2010/04/11-13
2010中国内衣面料辅料博览会
Underwear fabric accessories in 2010 Expo in China
上海 Shanghai 1950

2010/04/11-13
2010中国家用纺织品面料及家居布艺博览会
2010 China's home textile fabric and home sewing expo
上海 Shanghai 1960

2010/04/12-14
第92届中国针棉织品交易会
China Intl Trade Fair Mode Underwear and Home

Textiles
上海 Shanghai 1920

2010/04/12-16
2010中国数控机床展览会（CCMT2010）
China CNC Machine Tool Fair 2010 (CCMT2010)
江苏南京 Jiangsu-Nanjing 6110

2010/04/12-16
第二届太阳能产品西部（成都）展示交易会
四川成都 Sichuan-Chengdu 6895

2010/04/12-17
自动化仪器仪表
四川成都 Sichuan-Chengdu 6895

2010/04/13-15
2010第三届中国西部交通建设博览会
Western China Transportation Expo
四川成都 Sichuan-Changzhou 6800

2010/04/13-16
动保展
四川成都 Sichuan-Chengdu 6895

2010/04/14-16
第十届中国国际染料工业暨有机颜料、纺织化学品展览会
CHINA INTERDYE 2010 (10th China Intl Dye Industry, Pigments and Textile Chemicals Exhibition)
上海 Shanghai 2000

2010/04/14-17
2010第十二届东北沈阳国际汽车维修技术及设备、汽车零配件、汽车用品展览会
12th Vehicle Maintenance and Parts Show
辽宁沈阳 Liaoning-Shenyang 6550

2010/04/14-18
2010沈阳第十三届国际家用轿车及商用、专用汽车展览会
13th Shenyang Auto Show
辽宁沈阳 Liaoning-Shenyang 6560

2010/04/15-18
CIDE—2010第九届中国国际门业展览会
9th China Intl Door Industry Exhibition
北京 Beijing 350

2010/04/15 – 19
第107届中国进出口商品交易会（第一期）
107th China Import and Export Fair Phase 1
广东广州 Guangdong-Guangzhou 4815

2010/04/16-18
2010中国特许展
China Franchise Expo
北京 Beijing 360

2010/04/16-18
中国高尔夫球博览会
China golf show
北京 Beijing 370

2010/04/18-21
第10届中国国际医疗器械设计与制造技术展览会（春季）
10th ICMD
广东深圳 Guangdong-Shenzhen 5170

2010/04/18-21
第十三届海峡两岸纺织服装博览会暨2010年休闲服装博览会
thirteenth Strait Textile & Clothing Fairs（STCF）
广东石狮 Guangdong-Shishi 4250

2010/04/18-21
第63届中国国际医疗器械春季博览会
63rd CMEF (China Int'l Medical Equipment Fair 2010 - Spring )
广东深圳 Guangdong-Shenzhen 5160

2010/04/19-22
中国国际橡塑展
Chinaplas 2010
24th International Exhibition on Plastic and Rubber Industries
上海 Shanghai 2020

2010/04/19-22
第十二届中国(晋江)国际鞋业博览会
12TH JINJIANG FOOTWEAR (INT\'L) EXPOSITION,CHINA
晋江 Fujian-Jinjiang 4240

2010/04/20-22
第二十届中国国际电子生产设备暨微电子工业展/ 中国国际电子制造技术展览会
NEPCON/ EMT China 2010
上海 Shanghai 2030

2010/04/20-22
第四届中国国际新光源&新能源照明展览会暨论坛
Green Lighting China Expo and Forum 2010
上海 Shanghai 2035

2010/04/20-22
2010中国国际工业转包展览会
China Industrial Subcontracting & Outsourcing Fair 2010
重庆 Chongqing 1170

2010/04/20-23
中国义乌文化产品交易博览会
China Yiwu Stationery & Arts Trade Fair
浙江义乌 Zhejiang-Yiwu 7020

2010/04/20-23
中国国际五金电器博览会
China Intl Hardware & Electrical Appliances Trade Fair
浙江义乌 Zhejiang-Yiwu 7040

2010/04/20-23
义乌消费品出口交易会
Yiwu Sourcing Fair: Consumer Goods
浙江义乌 Zhejiang-Yiwu 7030

2010/04/21-23
2010中国国际冰淇淋加工技术设备及冷链展览会
China Intl Ice Cream Industry Exhibition
上海 Shanghai 2050

2010/04/21-23
第十届中国国际电力电工设备暨电厂脱硫脱硝展览会
China Epower 2010
上海 Shanghai 2040

2010/04/21-25
2010中艺博国际画廊博览会
China International Gallery Exposition
北京 Beijing 380

2010/04/22-24
湖南公共安全产品与技术博览会
Hunan Safety and Security Expo
湖南长沙 Hunan-Changsha 6000

2010/04/22-26
2010年第二十届全国图书交易博览会
四川成都 Sichuan-Chengdu 6895

2010/04/23-04/25
中国国际葡萄酒及烈酒展览会
Wine China Exhibition
北京 Beijing 385

2010/04/23 – 27
第107届中国进出口商品交易会（第二期）
107th China Import and Export Fair Phase 2
广东广州 Guangdong-Guangzhou 4816

2010/04/24-26
第63届全国药品交易会（春季）
63rd PHARMCHINA (China National Pharmaceuticals Fair )
福建厦门 Fujian-Xiamen 4350

2010/04/24-05/02
2010北京国际汽车展览会
Auto China 2010
2010 Beijing International Automotive Exhibition
北京 Beijing 388

2010/04/25-28
第十八届中国（深圳）国际礼品、工艺品、钟表及家庭用品展览会
17th China (Shenzhen) Intl Gifts, Handicrafts, Watches & Houseware Fair
广东深圳 Guangdong-Shenzhen 5180

2010/04/26-30
第59届中国教学仪器设备展示会
59th China National Exhibition of Education Instruments
浙江义乌 Zhejiang-Yiwu 7050

2010/04/27-29
2010第九届南京社会公共安全防范产品展览会
Nanjing public security defensive proocts exhibition
南京江苏 Nanjing-Jiangsu 6120

2010/04/27-29
第27届中国国际丝网印刷及数字技术展览会/2010年中国国际服装服饰及面料印花技术展览会
27th China Screen Print Expo/ 2010 China Textile Print Expo
上海 Shanghai 2060

2010/04/27-29
中国（上海）国际风能展览会暨研讨会/ 第8届中国国际动力设备及发电机组展览会
4th China Intl Wind Energy Exhibition and Conference
上海 Shanghai 2070

2010/04/27-29
2010南京智能建筑产品博览会
Nanjing building intelligence exhibition 2010
南京江苏 Nanjing-Jiangsu 6130

2010/04/27-30
2010中国自行车展览会
2010中国国际电动车及零配件展览会
China Intl Bicycle & Motor Fair
(CHINA CYCLE 2010)
China E-BIKE 2010
上海 Shanghai 2110

2010/04/27-30
2010中国出境旅游交易会
China Outbound Travel & Tourism Market
北京 Beijing 390

2010/04/28-01
第二届中国（西安）国际户外运动博览会
第二届中国（西安）国际健身运动用品展览会
China (Xi' an) Intl outdoor sports expo/ China (Xi'an) Intl Trade Show for Fitness Sport & Leisure Fair
陕西西安 Shaanxi-Xi'an 6603

2010/04/28-06
玩具展
四川成都 Sichuan-Chengdu 6895

2010/04/28-16
春夏服装博览会
四川成都 Sichuan-Chengdu 6895

2010/04/29-02
艺术北京2010当代艺术博览会
Art Beijing 2010 Contemporary Art Fair
北京 Beijing 400

## May 2010 五月

2010/05/-
2010第六届中国郑州糖酒食品交易会/ 2010第六届中国粮油调味品（郑州）交易会

2010 6th China City and Countryside Planning/ 2010 6th China Zhengzhou Candy & Spirit Fair
河南郑州 Henan-Zhengzhou 5820

2010/05/-
第二届中国郑州教育服务大会
2th China Zhengzhou Education Service Fair
河南郑州 Henan-Zhengzhou 5830

2010/05/01-03
2010年常州第二届汽车展
2nd Changzhou Auto Show
江苏常州 Jiangsu-Changzhou 6040

2010/05/01-04
上海房地产春季展示会
Holiday Real Estate Market
上海 Shanghai 2120

2010/05/01 – 05
第107届中国进出口商品交易会（第三期）
107th China Import and Export Fair Phase 3
广东广州 Guangdong-Guangzhou 4817

2010/05/01-06
春季房地产交易会
四川成都 Sichuan-Chengdu 6895

2010/05/04-06
中国东莞国际鞋展•鞋机展•手袋展
China Shoes•China Shoetec & China Bags
广东东莞 Guangdong-Dongguan 4505

2010/05/05-07
国际太阳能及光伏会议暨展览会
11th China PV Power Expo
上海 Shanghai 2160

2010/05/05-07
中国国际环保、废弃物及资源利用展览会和中国国际给排水水处理展览会
IFAT CHINA+EPTEE+CWS
上海 Shanghai 2130

2010/05/06-08
世界客车博览亚洲展览会
Busworld Asia
上海 Shanghai 2190

2010/05/06-08
2010第四届中国（上海）国际室内供暖、通风及净化产品展览会
4th Shanghai Intl Indoor Heating, Ventilation and Purification Products Expo
上海 Shanghai 2170

2010/05/06-09
2010第三届天津国际珠宝首饰展览会
2010 Tianjin 3rd Intl Jewelry Fair
天津 Tianjin 4035

2010/05/07-09
2010中国中部（合肥）国际装备制造业博览会
Cental China Intl Equipment Manufacturing Exposition
安徽合肥 Anhui-Hefei 4180

2010/05/07-09
1第10届中国（北京）国际健康产业产品博览会
10th China(Beijing) Intl Healthcare Industry Exhibition
北京 Beijing 1145

2010/05/07-09
2010第六届北京国际LED展览会
6th Beijing Intl LED exposition
北京 Beijing 1145

2010/05/07-10
2010第五届北京国际游泳沐浴SPA展览会
Beijing Intl Swimming Pools, Bath, SPA Expo 2010
北京 Beijing 1145

2010/05/07-14
汉诺威工业装备展
四川成都 Sichuan-Chengdu 6895

2010/05/08-13
电力展
四川成都 Sichuan-Chengdu 6895

2010/05/10-12
2010北京国际咖啡博览会
2010 China International Coffee Industry Exhibition
北京 Beijing 430

2010/05/10-13
中国国际酒店博览会
Hhotel China 2010
北京 Beijing 440

2010/05/11-13
第六届上海国际钢管工业展览会
SHANGHAI TUBE EXPO
上海 Shanghai 2210

2010/05/11-14
2010中国国际铸件博览会
2010 CASTING CHINA
北京 Beijing 460

2010/05/11-14
第十二届中国国际冶金工业展览会
12th China Intl Metallurgical Industry Expo
北京 Beijing 470

2010/05/11-14
2010中国国际铸件博览会/ 第八届中国国际耐火材料及工业陶瓷展览会
Casting china Intl 2010/ 8th china Intl refractories and industrial ceramics exhibition
北京 Beijing 460

2010/05/11-14
第十届中国国际铸造、锻压及工业炉展览会
2010 METAL CHINA
北京 Beijing 450

2010/05/11-15
第十三届中国国际模具技术和设备展览会
DIE & MOULD CHINA 2010 (DMC 2010)
上海 Shanghai 2230

2010/05/11-15
第十二届中国国际冶金工业展览会/ 第十届中国国际铸造、锻压及工业炉展览会/ 2010中国国际铸件展览会
Metallurgy China 2010/ 2010 Metal China/ 2010 Casting China
北京 Beijing 470

2010/05/12-14
2010大连国际工业博览会
2010 Dalian Intl industry fair
辽宁大连 Liaoning-Dalian 6250

2010/05/12-15
2010国际现代工厂/ 过程自动化技术与装备展览会
2010FA/PA
北京 Beijing 1145

2010/05/12-15
2010第13届中国国际焙烤展览会
13th China Intl Trade Fair For Bakery & Confectionery
上海 Shanghai 2240

2010/05/13-15
第十一届中国重庆国际工业装备博览会
11th Chongqing Intl Industry Equipment Fair 重庆 Chongqing 1180

2010/05/13-15
中国中西部（太原）医疗器械展览会暨第11届山西医疗器械(2010年春季)展览会
Yiwu Sourcing Fair: Consumer Goods
山西太原 Shanxi-Taiyuan 6740

2010/05/13-15
第十届上海社会公共安全产品国际博览会
10th Shanghai Intl Exhibition On Public Safety And Security
上海 Shanghai 2260

2010/05/13-24
李宁订货会
四川成都 Sichuan-Chengdu 6895

2010/05/14-16
第十九届华南（东莞）国际电子制造采购博览会
South China Electronic Fair
广东东莞 Guangdong-Dongguan 4530

2010/05/14-16
2010年华南（东莞）环境与可靠性实验技术论坛暨仪器展
South China Intl Certification Technology Forum & Instrument Equipment Fair
广东东莞 Guangdong-Dongguan 4510

2010/05/14-16
第四届亚洲（东莞）国际激光加工技术论坛暨应用展
Laser Bocessing Technology Forum and Equipment Application Fair
广东东莞 Guangdong-Dongguan 4520

2010/05/14-17
第六届中国（深圳）文化产业博览交易会数字影视-动漫游戏展
China （Shenzhen） Intl Cultural Industries Fair "DTV/COM & ANI EXHIBITION"
广东深圳 Guangdong-Shenzhen 5210

2010/05/14-17
中国（深圳）国际文化产业博览交易会
China （Shenzhen） Intl Cultural Industries Fair
广东深圳 Guangdong-Shenzhen 5200

2010/05/15-17
第12届北京国际玩具及幼教用品展览会
12thBeijing Intl Toys & Preschool Tools Exhibition
上海 Shanghai 480

2010/05/17-19
2010中国（上海）国际残疾人和老年人康复护理技术及辅助器具展览会
5th China Intl Exhibition of Rehabilitation, Nursing & Health care for Elderly and Disabled People
上海 Shanghai 2300

2010/05/17-19
SCCE 2010第五届上海国际硬质合金及生产技术和应用展览会
5th Shanghai Intl Cemented Carbides Exhibition
上海 Shanghai 2280

2010/05/17-19
第98届中国鞋业/皮具商品博览会暨"名品进名店"对接展会
98th Chinese Shoes & Leather Commodity and "Well-Known Brands & Famous Shops" Exposition
Into Shoppes at Famous Butt Show
上海 Shanghai 2270

2010/05/17-21
2010年中国国际燃气、供热技术与设备展览会
GAS&HEATING CHINA 2010
北京 Beijing 500

2010/05/18-20
2010中国中部（长沙）国际装备制造业博览会
Changsha International Equipment Manufacturing Exhibition
湖南长沙 Hunan-Changsha 6010

2010/05/18-20
世界制药工业中国展（医药、包装材料、制药设备展区）
INTERPHEX CHINA
黑龙江哈尔滨 Heilongjiang-Harbin 5650

2010/05/18-20
2010中国（天津）国际医疗仪器与设备展览会
China Tianjin Intl Medical Instruments and Equipment Exhibition
天津 Tianjin 4040

2010/05/18-20
第64届中国国际医药原料药、中间体、包装、设备交易会（春季）
64th API China(active pharmaceutical ingredient )
黑龙江哈尔滨 Heilongjiang-Harbin 5640

2010/05/18-22
2010年常州房地产交易会
2010 Changzhou Real Estate Fair
江苏常州 Jiangsu-Changzhou 6050

2010/05/18-22
2010中国西部（成都）给排水处理技术装备博览会暨流体机械+泵阀门+管道展
四川成都 Sichuan-Chengdu 6895

2010/05/18-23
动漫展
四川成都 Sichuan-Chengdu 6895

2010/05/19-21
2010第七届上海纺织服装采购交易会
2010 (7th) Shanghai Textile & Apparel Trade Fair
上海 Shanghai 2370

2010/05/19-21
第十一届中国国际食品和饮料展览会
SIAL China 2010
上海 Shanghai 2350

2010/05/19-21
第四届中国（西安）国际绿色建筑与建筑节能博览会
4th China Intl green building and energy
陕西西安 Shaanxi-Xian 6605

2010/05/19-21
2010中国国际轨道交通展览会/ 2010 中国国际隧道与地下工程技术展览会
Metro China 2010
Tunnel China 2010
上海 Shanghai 2320

2010/05/19-21
第十六届中国国际美容化妆洗涤用品博览会
China Beauty Expo
上海 Shanghai 2360

2010/05/19-23
2010中国西部（成都）国际电玩展览会
四川成都 Sichuan-Chengdu 6895

2010/05/20-22
第十一届新疆国际农业机械博览会暨农业生产资料交易洽谈会
11 th xinjing Intl Machinery Exhibition
新疆乌鲁木齐 Xinjiang-Urmuqi 6900

2010/05/20-22
2010中国（杭州）国际工业博览会
CHINA(HANGZHOU)INTL INDUSTRY EXPO 2010
浙江杭州 Zhejiang-Hangzhou 6950

2010/05/20-22
2010年第十四届中国国际烘焙展览会
2010 14th CHINA BAKERY EXHIBITION
广东广州 Guangdong-Guangzhou 4840

2010/05/20-23
2010（第26届）中国国际体育用品博览会
China Intl Sporting Goods Show 2010
北京 Beijing 520

2010/05/20-23
第十九届中国国际专业音响、灯光、乐器及技术展览会
19th China Intl Exhibition on Pro Audio, Light, Music & Technology
北京 Beijing 510

2010/05/20-23
第九届中国国际古典家具展览会 & 2010上海国际古董及艺术品展览会
Antique Furniture China 2010 & Antiques & Arts Shanghai 2010
上海 Shanghai 2375

2010/05/20-23
中国国际舞台灯光音响展
PALM EXPO 2010
北京 Beijing 1145

2010/05/20-24
2010第五届中国(青岛)房车及休旅车展览会
5th Qingdao Recreational Vehicle Show
山东青岛 Shandong-Qingdao 6670

2010/05/21-23
2010第二届中国（山东）国际食品博览会
2010 2nd China( Shandong) food fair
山东济南 Shandong-Jinan 6620

2010/05/21-24
2010中国（上海）国际茶业博览会
2010 China (Shanghai) Intl Tea Exhibition
上海 Shanghai 2380

2010/05/23-25
2010深圳光电显示周
CHINA OPTOELECTRONICS&DISPLAY EXPO
广东深圳 Guangdong-Shenzhen 5220

2010/05/26-28
第7届中国（天津）国际涂装、电镀及表面处理展览会
7th china(tianjin) Intl coating,electroplating and surface finishing exhibition
天津 Tianjin 4120

2010/05/26-28
2010第七届中国（天津）国际涂料展览会
7TH CHINA (TIANJIN) INTL COATINGS EXHIBITION
天津 Tianjin 4050

2010/05/26-28
第六届中国（天津）国际动力传动与控制技术展览会、第六届中国天津液压、气动、密封件及空压机展览会
6th China (Tianjin) Intl power Transmission and Control TechnologyExhibition
天津 Tianjin 4070

2010/05/26-28
第八届中国国际聚氨酯展览会
PU China 2010
深圳 Guangdong-Shenzhen 5230

2010/05/26-28
第六届中国(天津)国际模具技术与设备展览会
6th China (Tianjin) Intl Die & Mould Technology Exhibitionexhibition
天津 Tianjin 4100

2010/05/26-28
第六届中国（天津）国际工业控制自动化及仪器仪表展览会
Sixth China (Tianjin)Intl Industrial Control Automation &InstrumentExhibition
天津 Tianjin 4090

2010/05/26-28
第十三届中国国际智能卡博览会
13th Intl Fair of Smart Cards, China 2010(SCC2010)
北京 Beijing 530

2010/05/26-28
2010第六届中国（天津）国际机床展览会
6th China (Tianjin) Intl Machine Tool Exhibition
天津 Tianjin 4080

2010/05/26-28
2010第七届中国国际轮胎资源循环利用展览会
7th China International Tire Resource Cyclic Utilization Expo
天津 Tianjin 4060

2010/05/26-29
第15届中国国际建筑贸易博览会
Intl Building & Construction Trade Fair 2010
上海 Shanghai 2410

2010/05/26-29
第15届中国国际厨房、卫浴设施展览会
Kitchen & Bath China 2010
上海 Shanghai 2400

2010/05/27-29
2010中国国际有机食品博览会
BioFach China 2010
上海 Shanghai 2420

2010/05/27-29
第十届东莞国际印刷造纸胶粘带及广告展览会
10th Dongguan Intl Printing and Packaging and paper advertising, adhesive tape, protective film exhibition
广东东莞 Guangdong-Dongguan 5435

2010/05/27-29
上海世界旅游资源博览会
World Travel Fair
上海 Shanghai 2430

2010/05/27-30
第十五届北京埃森焊接与切割展览会
15th Beijing Essen Welding & Cutting Fair
北京 Beijing 540

2010/05/27-30
希望2009四川首届青少年文化暨四川国际青少年博览会
四川成都 Sichuan-Chengdu 6895

2010/05/27-30
北京埃森焊接与切割展览会
Beijing Essen Welding & Cutting Fair
北京 Beijing 540

2010/05/27-31
第十三届中国北京国际科技产业博览会
13th China Beijing Intl High-Tech Expo
北京 Beijing 550

2010/05/28-30
第七届厦门人居环境展示会
7th Xiamen Living Environment Show
福建厦门 Fujian-Xiamen 4360

2010/05/28-30
2010成都绿色健康、保健产业展览会/ 第三届西部成都成人保健品计生及生殖健康用品展
四川成都 Sichuan-Chengdu 6895

2010/05/29-30
人才展
四川成都 Sichuan-Chengdu 6895

2010/05/29-31
2010第三届大连市出口企业产品展销会
Dalian Export Enterprise Products Fair
辽宁大连 Liaoning-Dalian 6260

2010/05/29-31
2010第五届中国（济南）儿童产业国际博览会
5th 2010 China (Jinan) Intl Children Industry Fair
山东济南 Shandong-Jinan 6630

2010/05/30-01
2010第五届上海国际幼儿教育展

2010 5th Shanghai Intl KIDS Education EXPO
上海 Shanghai 2440

## June 2010 六月

2010/06/-
第五届中国（郑州）国际酒店、餐饮、泳池沐浴SPA设备及用品博览会/ 第五届中国（郑州）国际家纺、布艺及工艺品、礼品家居装饰博览会
5th China (Zhengzhou) Intl Hotel, F&B, Swimming pool and SPA Equipment and Product Expo/ 5th China (Zhengzhou) Household Textile, Cloth Art, Handicraft and Decoration Article Expo
河南郑州 Henan-Zhengzhou 5840

2010/06/-
中国国际动力传动与自动化控制展览会
PTAC CHINA 2010
北京 Beijing 570

2010/06/-
2010上海国际物联网大会
Internet of Things Conference Shanghai 2010
上海 Shanghai 2450

2010/06/01-03
广州国际鞋类、皮革及工业设备展览会
20th Inl Exhibition Shoes & Leather Industry
Incoporate with:
Guangzhou Intl Leather Exhibition
Intl Tanning Technology & Machinery Exhibition (Machinery & Raw Material)
广东广州 Guangdong-Guangzhou 4850

2010/06/01-03
2010年中国国际葡萄酒博览会
2010 Topwine China
北京 Beijing 580

2010/06/02-04
2010中国国际包装博览会
Beijing Intl Packaging Fair 2010
北京 Beijing 1145

2010/06/02-04
2010第十四届中国国际软件博览会
INTL SOFT CHINA 2010
北京 Beijing 600

2010/06/02-04
中国国际生物技术和仪器设备博览会
BIOTECH CHINA 2010
上海 Shanghai 2480

2010/06/02-04
亚洲食品配料、天然原料、健康原料展览会
Fi Asia - China/ Hi China/ Ni China
Food Ingredients Asia China 2010
Health Ingredient China 2010
Natural Ingredients China 2010
上海 Shanghai 2550

2010/06/02-04
环球资源消费类电子产品采购交易会
China Sourcing Fair-Electronics
上海 Shanghai 2520

2010/06/02-04
第12届上海国际生物技术与医药研讨会（BIO-FORUM2010）
12th Shanghai Intl Forum on Biotechnology & Pharmaceutical Industry
上海 Shanghai 2490

2010/06/02-04
世界制药原料中国展
CPhi China
上海 Shanghai 2560

2010/06/02-04
中国(上海)国际家具展览会暨上海国际家居饰品展示会
上海 Shanghai 2470

2010/06/02-04
中国国际生物技术和仪器设备博览会
BIOTECH CHINA 2010
上海 Shanghai 2530

2010/06/02-07
2010中国西部（成都）国际化工、石油天然气及化工技术装备展览会
四川成都 Sichuan-Chengdu 6895

2010/06/03-05
第四届中国国际新型墙体材料技术装备及产品展览会
4th CHINA INTL BUILDING MATERIAL TECHNOLOGY & EQUIPMENT EXPO
北京 Beijing 650

2010/06/03-05
第四届中国国际墙体材料及保温技术展览会
4th CHINA INTL WALL MATERIAL & INSULATION TECHNOLOGY EXHIBITION
北京 Beijing 630

2010/06/03-05
第三届中国国际建筑材料技术及设备展览会暨第四届中国国际新型墙体材料技术装备及产品展览会
WALLEXPO CHINA 2010
北京 Beijing 610

2010/06/03-05
2010第六届中国（北京）国际动力传动及控制技术暨液压气动密封件展览会
China Intl Power Transmission and Automatic Control 2010
北京 Beijing 1145

2010/06/03-05
中国国际散装水泥暨预拌混凝土与预拌砂浆技术装备及产品展览会
2010 CHINA INTL BULK CEMENT TECHNOLOGY & EQUIPMENT EXPO
北京 Beijing 640

2010/06/03-05
第三届粉煤灰、脱硫石膏综合利用技术装备及产品展览会
3rd FINE COAL ASH & DESULFURIZED GYPSUM COMPREHENSIVE UTILIZATION TECHNOLOGY & EQUIPMENT EXPO
北京 Beijing 620

2010/06/03-05
2010第六届北京国际煤炭装备及矿山技术设备展览会
6th China Intl Coal Equipment and Mine Technical Equipment Exhibition 2010
北京 Beijing 1145

2010/06/03-05
第三届中国国际建筑材料技术装备展览会
3rd CHINA INTL BUILDING MATERIAL TECHNOLOGY EXPO
北京 Beijing 610

2010/06/04-07
第21届中国国际玻璃工业技术展览会
China Glass 2010
北京 Beijing 1145

2010/06/04-09
2010四川线材线缆及相关设备展
四川成都 Sichuan-Chengdu 6895

2010/06/04-09
工程机械
四川成都 Sichuan-Chengdu 6895

2010/06/06-07
第三届中国国际服务外包合作大会
China Intl Service Outsourcing Cooperation Conference 2010
江苏南京 Jiangsu-Nanjing 6140

2010/06/06-10
第三届南亚国家商品展
3rd South Asian Countries Commodity Fair
云南昆明 Yunnan-Kunming 6933

2010/06/06-10
第十八届中国昆明进出口商品交易会
18th China Import & Export Fair, Kunming
云南昆明 Yunnan-Kungming 6935

2010/06/06-16
第二届成都端午食品博览会
四川成都 Sichuan-Chengdu 6895

2010/06/07-09
2010年第六届中国成都建筑科技装饰材料博览会暨建筑电气展览会
四川成都 Sichuan-Chengdu 6895

2010/06/08-10
2010第九届中国（上海）国际纺织品面辅料博览会
2010 9TH CHINA（SHANGHAI）INTL TEXTILES, FABRICS & ACCESSORIES EXHIBITION2010 9TH CHINA（SHANGHAI）INTL TEXTILES, FABRICS & ACCESSORIES EXHIBITION
上海 Shanghai 2620

2010/06/08-10
2010第十届北京国际机械装备、模具、塑料橡胶、动力传动自动化仪器仪表展览会
China Intl Machinery Equipment Mould, Rubber and Plastic Industry & Power Transmission automation instrument and meter exhibition
北京 Beijing 1145

2010/06/08-10
中国国际海上风电和风电产业链大会暨展览会
China Int' l Offshore Wind Energy & Wind Energy Industry Chain Conference and Exhibition
上海 Shanghai 2600

2010/06/08-10
中国国际物流、交通运输及远程信息处理博览会
transport logistic China
上海 Shanghai 2630

2010/06/08-10
上海国际非开挖技术展览会暨研讨会
2010 No-Dig Shanghai
上海 Shanghai 2610

2010/06/08-11
第九届中国国际日用消费品博览会
9th China Intl Consumer Goods Fair
浙江宁波 Zhejiang-Ningbo 6990

2010/06/09-11
2010年中国国际铝工业展览会
ALUMINIUM CHINA 2010
上海 Shanghai 2650

2010/06/09-11
第八届中国（广州）国际环保展
8th Intl Enviro Guangzhou
广东广州 Guangdong-Guangzhou 4860

2010/06/09-13
中国国际照相机械影像器材与技术博览会
China Intl Photograph & Electrical Imaging Machinery and Technology Fair 2010
北京 Beijing 650

2010/06/10-12
2010北京国际电子工业节能技术、产品展览会
China Television Shopping Exposition 2010
北京 Beijing 1145

2010/06/10-12
第104届中国文化用品商品交易会暨中国国际制笔文具博览会
104th China Stationery Commodity Fair
上海 Shanghai 2680

2010/06/10-13
第十三届中国国际照相机械影响器材与技术博览会
13th China Intl Photograph & Electrical Imaging Machinery
北京 Beijing 650

2010/06/10-14
2010(第十二届)重庆国际汽车工业展览会
China Chongqing Intl Auto Industry Fair
重庆 Chongqing 1190

2010/06/11-13
建材展览会
Building Material Show
福建厦门 Fujian-Xiamen 4370

2010/06/11-16
2010年第六届中国成都酒店设备用品及旅游工艺品博览会
四川成都 Sichuan-Chengdu 6895

2010/06/14-18
第十届中国国际机床工具展览会
10th China Intl Machine Tool & Tools Exhibition
北京 Beijing 660

2010/06/15-19
第二十一届中国哈尔滨国际经济贸易洽谈会
21th China Harbin Intl Economiv and Trade Fair
黑龙江哈尔滨市 Heilongjiang-Harbin 5660

2010/06/16-18
2010第十届中国东北国际冶金及金属工业展览会；同期举办：2010第九届中国东北电气、自动化、仪器仪表展览会，2010中国东北国际铸造、锻压、焊接、热处理、工业炉技术与设备展览会，2010第九届中国东北节能技术与设备展览会，2010中国东北国际耐火材料展览会，2010东北国际冶金工业暨不锈钢技术与制品展览会，2010东北国际冶金工业暨铝型材及技术设备展览会，2010中国东北国际模具制造技术设备展览会，2010中国东北国际煤矿安全生产及相关物资装备展览会
2009 Northeast China Metal Expo
辽宁沈阳 Liaoning-Shenyang 6570

2010/06/16-18
第七届中国国际压铸会议暨展览会
7th China Intl Diecasting Congress & Exhibition
上海 Shanghai 2710

2010/06/17-20
中国(广州)国际黄金珠宝玉石展览会
China International Gold, Jewelry & Gem Fair 广东广州 Guangdong- 4870

2010/06/17-20
中国国际旅游商品博览会
China Intl Tourism Commodities Fair
浙江义乌 Zhejiang-Yiwu 7060

2010/06/17-20
2010年金融展
China Intl Financial Exhibition
北京 Beijing 680

2010/06/17-21
海峡西岸汽车博览会
West Taiwan Strait Auto Expo 2010
福建厦门 Fujian-Xiamen 4380

2010/06/17-22
出国留学展
四川成都 Sichuan-Chengdu 6895

2010/06/18-20
第四届中国常州电动车展览会
4th Changzhou Electric Vehicle Exhibition
江苏常州 Jiangsu-Changzhou 6060

2010/06/18-20
成都家居、休闲用品及礼品展览会
Chengdu Houseware, Leisure Goods & Gifts Fair
四川成都 Sichuan-Chengdu 6810

2010/06/18-20
北京国际教育展
Education Expo 2010
北京 Beijing 1145

2010/06/18-21
广东外商投资企业产品（内销）博览会
Guangdong Foreign-invested Enterprises Commodities Fair
广东东莞 Guangdong-Dongguan 5436

2010/06/18-21
2010年（第五届）中国零售商大会暨展会
2010 China Retailers Convention & Exhibition
四川成都 Sichuan-Chengdu 6830

2010/06/18-23
创意展
四川成都 Sichuan-Chengdu 6895

2010/06/21-23
2010中国上海国际汽车零部件展览会
Auto Components Shanghai 2010
上海 Shanghai 2720

2010/06/22-24
第60届中国实验室技术及装备交易会
60th China Laboratory Technology and Equipment Exhibition
上海 Shanghai 2740

2010/06/22-24
中国（成都）国际电子生产设备及技术展览会
NEPCON West China 2010
四川成都 Sichuan-Chengdu 6840

2010/06/22-24
微电子展
四川成都 Sichuan-Chengdu 6895

2010/06/23-25
中国国际清洁能源博览会
Clean Energy Expo China
北京 Beijing 700

2010/06/23-25
亚洲风能大会暨国际风能设备展览会
Wind Power Asia - Asian Wind Energy Exhibition & Conference
北京 beijing 690

2010/06/23-25
2010北京国际动力传动及控制技术与液态气动密封件展览会
China Intl Power Transmission and Automatic Control 2010
北京 Beijing 1145

2010/06/23-25
2010第十一多人行广告、标识、LED展
2010 11th DAX Advertising, Sign Board & LED Exhibition
广东深圳 Guangdong-Shenzhen 5250

2010/06/23-25
2010第十八届多人行电子展、光电展
2010 18th DEX Electronic Exhibition & Photonics Exhibition
广东深圳 Guangdong-Shenzhen 5240

2010/06/23-26
第十一届广州国际金属暨冶金工业展览会
11th China (Guangzhou) intl Metal & Metallurgy Exhibition
广东广州 Guangdong-Guangzhou 4880

2010/06/24-25
第六届亚洲不动产投资峰会
Asia Property Investment Showcase & Conference
上海 Shanghai 2770

2010/06/24-26
第九届中国国际电池技术交流会/展览会
9th China Intl Battery Fair
广东深圳 Guangdong-Shenzhen 5280

2010/06/24-26
第八届深圳国际小电机及电机工业展览会
8th China(Shenzhen) Intl Small Motor and Electric Machinery Exhibition
广东深圳 Guangdong-Shenzhen 5290

2010/06/24-26
2010深圳国际线圈工业、绝缘材料展览会/ 2010深圳国际漆包线展览会
2010Shenzhen Internationa Coils Industry&Insulating Materials Exhibition/ 2010Shenzhen Intl Enamelled Wire Exhibition
广东深圳 Guangdong-Shenzhen 5330

2010/06/24-26
第八届深圳国际磁性材料及粉末冶金工业展览会
8th China(Shenzhen) Intl Magnetic Materials and Powder Metallurgy Industry Exhibition
广东深圳 Guangdong-Shenzhen 5300

2010/06/24-27
2010年中国北京夏季房地产展示交易会
Summer Real Estate Trade Fair Beijing China
北京 Beijing 710

2010/06/25-27
2010第七届中国国际自动售货系统及商用自助服务产品展/ 2010第二届上海国际数字标牌及触摸查询技术展览会/ 2010上海互动多媒体信息技术及虚拟仿真产品展览会暨大屏幕投影显示、数字会议系统产品展览会
7th China Intl Vending & Kiosk show/ Shanghai Intl Digital Signage & Touch Inquiry Technology Show 2010/
上海 Shanghai 2780

2010/06/25-27
第八届中国（厦门）食品交易博览会
8th China (Xiamen) Food Fair
福建厦门 Fujian-Xiamen 4390

2010/06/25-27
2010北京国际旅游博览会暨北方旅游交易会
BEIJING INTL TOURISM EXPO 2010
北京 Beijing 720

2010/06/25-27
高校咨询
四川成都 Sichuan-Chengdu 6895

2010/06/26-11
成都夏季丝绸服装展
四川成都 Sichuan-Chengdu 6895

2010/06/26-28
2010第二届中国仿古工艺品及技术展览会
China Archaistic Craft & Technology Exhibition Expo
上海 Shanghai 2790

2010/06/29-01
第八届中国国际肉类工业展览会
Eighth China Intl Meat Industry Exhibition
北京 Beijing 730

2010/06/30-02
第十五届华南国际机械及模具展/ 第十五届华南国际塑胶展
15th South China Intl Machinery & Mould Exhibition/

15th South China Intl Plastics Exhibition
广东广州 Guangdong-Guangzhou 4890

## July 2010 七月

2010/07/-
第11届全国医疗器械区域博览会
11th CMEF Regional
天津 Tianjin 4125

2010/07/-
2010第七届汽车用品交易会暨第六届汽车羊剪绒产品订货会
2010 7th Auto Products Trade Fair& 6th Auto-Use Wool Products Fair
河南郑州 Henan-Zhengzhou 5850

2010/07/01-04
第十二届中国（上海）国际摄影器材和数码影像展览会
PHOTO & IMAGING SHANGHAI 2010
上海 Shanghai 2810

2010/07/01-04
中国（北京）国际家具及木工机械展览会
2010 China Beijing Intl Furniture Woodworking machinery & Wood Products Exhibition
北京 Beijing 1145

2010/07/01-04
第21届中国（深圳）国际钟表展览会
21st China Watch Fair
广东深圳 Guangdong-Shengzhen 5340

2010/07/01-04
第十八届中国上海国际婚纱摄影器材展览会暨国际儿童摄影、主题摄影展览会(秋季)
18th China (Shanghai) Intl Wedding Photographic Equipment Exhibition & Intl Children's Photography, Theme Photography Exhibition (Autumn)
上海 Shanghai 2820

2010/07/02-04
GICE 2010第二届广西泛北部湾工程机械展览会
GICE 2010 Guangxi Fan-Beibu Gulf Construction Machinery Exhibition
广西南宁 Guangxi-Nanning 5540

2010/07/02-04
GLE2010广西泛北部湾港口、物流及仓储设备展览会
GLE 2010 Guangxi Fan-Beibu Gulf Equipment Of Port & Logistics & Storage Exhibition
广西南宁 Guangxi-Nanning 5530

2010/07/02-06
第十一届成都国际家具工业展
11th International Furniture Fair Chengdu
四川成都 Sichuan-Chengdu 6850

2010/07/02-11
2010年北京欧美超级家具展览会
European and American Furniture Show
北京 Beijing 740

2010/07/03-06
2010/07/05-07
中国国际美发美容博览会
China Intl Hair & Beauty Expo
北京 Beijing 750

2010/07/07-10
2010上海国际数字营销展览会
Shanghai Int'l Digital Media Exhibition 2010
上海 Shanghai 2870

2010/07/07-10
2010上海国际照明展
SHANGHAI INT'L LIGHTING EXPO 2010
上海 Shanghai 2840

2010/07/07-10
2010上海国际户外广告发光体技术及城市景观照明设备展览会
Shanghai Int'l Outdoor AD Illuminating & City Lighting Technology & Equipment Exhibition 2010
上海 Shanghai 2940

2010/07/07-10
2010上海国际数码及快速印刷设备展览会
Shanghai Int'l Digital & Express Printing Exhibition 2010
上海 Shanghai 2970

2010/07/07-10
2010上海国际标签展览会
Label Shanghai 2010
上海 Shanghai 2960

2010/07/07-10
2010上海国际零售业展览会
2010 Shanghai Intl Retail Exhibition
上海 Shanghai 2920

2010/07/07-10
2010上海国际展览展示、POP及商用设施展览会
Shanghai Intl Displaying, POP and Commercial Facility Exhibition 2010
上海 Shanghai 2910

2010/07/07-10
第十八届上海国际印刷包装纸业展览会/2010上海国际印刷包装产品交易会
Shanghai Intl Print Exhibition 2010
上海 Shanghai 2890

2010/07/07-10
2010上海国际照明技术设备展览会
Shanghai Int'l Lighting Technology & Equipment Exhibition 2010
上海 Shanghai 2930

2010/07/08-10
第十届中国（深圳）国际品牌服装服饰交易会
10th China (Shenzhen) Intl Brand Clothing &Accessories Fair
广东深圳 Guangdong-Shenzhen 5360

2010/07/08-10
2010第3届中国(深圳)国际奢侈品展览会暨深圳企业家生活方式展览会
TOP LUXURY SHOW
广东深圳 Guangdong-Shenzhen 5350

2010/07/08-10
深圳国际纺织面料及辅料博览会
Shenzhen Intl Trade Fair for Apparel Fabrics and Accessories
广东深圳 Guangdong-Shenzhen 5370

2010/07/08-11
中国（广州）国际厨房设备及配件展
China Kitchen Furniture and Appliance Fair
广东广州 Guangdong-Guangzhou 4990

2010/07/08-11
中国（广州）国际建筑装饰博览会
12th China(Guangzhou) Intl Building Decoration Fair
广东广州 Guangdong-Guangzhou 5020

2010/07/08-11
2010中国国际消费电子博览会
2010 China Intl Consumer Electronics Show (SINOCES)
山东青岛 Shandong-Qingdao 6680

2010/07/08-11
中国（广州）国际地面铺装材料展
China(Guangzhou) Int'l Floor Covering Fair
广东广州 Guangdong-Guangzhou 5010

2010/07/08-11
中国（广州）国际卫浴及建筑陶瓷展
China(Guangzhou) Int'l Exhibition for Sanitary Ware and Building Ceramics
广东广州 Guangdong-Guangzhou 5000

2010/07/09-11
第45届全国新特药品交易会
45th New Drugs China
北京 Beijing 755

2010/07/09-11
2010年中国国际酒业博览会
China Intl Alcoholic Drinks Expo 2010
北京 Beijing 1145

2010/07/10-12
北京国际儿童及婴幼儿食品博览会
Beijing Intl Exhibition of Infant Food
北京 Beijing 1145

2010/07/10-14
中国昆明珠宝玉石展览会
China Jewellery Fair 2010
云南昆明 Yunnan-Kunming 6940

2010/07/15-17
2010广东国际家电配件采购博览会
2010 Guangdong Intl Appliance Parts Procurement Fair
广东广州 Guangdong-Guangzhou 5030

2010/07/15-18
2010年第12上海国际机床展（东博展）
12th Shanghai Intl Machine Tool Fair - Eastpo 2010
上海 Shanghai 3040

2010/07/16-18
2010第六届北京国际电动车清洁能源汽车暨休闲运动车展览会
6th Beijing Intl Pure Electric Vehicle, Hybrid Power & Clean Energy Vehicle, and Accessories Exhibition
北京 Beijing 1145

2010/07/16-19
第四届中国（青岛）国际石材工业及机械设备展览会
4th China Qingdao Intl Stone Industry & Machinery Exhibition
山东青岛 Shandong-Qingdao 6690

2010/07/16-19
第十一届北京国际珠宝展览会
11th Beijing Intl Jewellery Fair
北京 Beijing 760

2010/07/17-18
建材团购（派达）
四川成都 Sichuan-Chengdu 6895

2010/07/17-19
第四届中国（青岛）国际建筑节能和可再生能源应用博览会
4th China Qingdao Intl Building Energy Saving & Renewable Energy Utilization Fair
山东青岛 Shandong-Qingdao 6700

2010/07/17-19
第六届中国（青岛）国际建筑材料及装饰材料博览会
6th China Qingdao Intl Construction & Decoration Materials Exposition
山东青岛 Shandong-Qingdao 6710

2010/07/21-23
上海儿童、婴儿、孕妇产品博览会
2010 Shanghai International Children-Baby-Maternity Products Expo
上海 Shanghai 3050

2010/07/22-24
第104届中国日用百货商品交易会
104thchina Daily-use Articles Trade Fair & China Modern Home Expo
上海 Shanghai 3060

2010/07/23-25
中国南宁国际农业科技博览会
China Nanning Intl agriculture fair
广西南宁 Guangxi-Nanning 5570

2010/07/23-30
第五届中国（北方）印刷及设备器材展览会
Print North 2010
北京 Beijing 1145

2010/07/29-01
中国（北京）玩具动漫教育文化博览会
China toys and animation educational expo
北京 Beijing 765

2010/07/29-01
中国国际数码互动娱乐产品及技术应用展览会
China Joy
7th China Digital Entertainment Expo & Conference
上海 Shanghai 3090

2010/07/29-01
中国（北京）国际妇女儿童产业博览会
China children and women industry expo
北京 Beijing 766

## August 2010 八月

2010/08/-
河南省投资贸易洽谈会
Henan Investment and Trade Council
河南郑州 Henan-Zhengzhou 5860

2010/08/-
中国中西部（合肥）医疗器械展览会暨第12届安徽医疗器械（2010年秋季）展览会
Hefei Medical Devices Exhibition (2010 autumn)
安徽合肥 Anhui-Hefei 4200

2010/08/01-03
三联工业装备展
四川成都 Sichuan-Chengdu 6895

2010/08/02-04
第十届中国（上海）国际墙纸、地毯、布艺展览会暨中国国际家居软装饰博览会
China Wallpaper
上海 Shanghai 3110

2010/08/02-09
第13届哈尔滨国际汽车工业展览会
13th Harbin Intl Automobile Exhibition
黑龙江哈尔滨 Heilongjiang-Harbin 5670

2010/08/04-06
中国北京国际工程项目、机械设备及建筑材料博览会
2010 China (Beijing) Intl Engineering Projects, Mechanical Equipment and Building Materials Exposition
北京 Beijing 1145

2010/08/05-07
中国（北京）国际五金机电工业博览会暨电池电子工业展览会
China Intl Hardware Industry Expo, Beijing
北京 Beijing 1145

2010/08/05-07
2010年健身大会
Fitness China 2010
北京 Beijing 1145

2010/08/05-09
夏日国际香港购物嘉年华
Intl-Hong Kong Shopping Carnival
北京 Beijing 1145

2010/08/10-12
2010 大连国际医疗器械展览会
2010 Dalian Intl Exhibition for Medical Instrument
辽宁大连 Liaoning-Dalian 6270

2010/08/10-12
中国（北京）国际管业展览会
China Beijing Intl Steel Tube Industry Expo, 2010
北京 Beijing 1145

2010/08/10-12
2010北京国际物流、卡车、起重运输机械展览会
China Beijing Intl Logistics Expo 2010
北京 Beijing 1145

2010/08/11-14
第四届上海国际工业装配与传输技术展览会
4th Shanghai Intl Assembly & Handling Technology Exhibition
上海 Shanghai 3130

2010/08/11-14
2010上海国际汽车制造技术与装备及材料展览会
Shanghai Intl Automotive Manufacturing Technology & Material Show 2010
上海 Shanghai 3120

2010/08/12-14
2010大连国际广告技术与设备展览会
Dalian Ad Exhibition
辽宁大连 Liaoning-Dalian 6280

2010/08/12-14
中国药店展览会
China Drug Store Show
上海 Shanghai 3255

2010/08/12-15
第四届上海国际家用车务车展览会
shanghai Intl exhibition on family&commercial auto 2010
上海 Shanghai 3150

2010/08/12-16
第二届动漫节
2nd Shenzhen Animation Festival
广东深圳 Guangdong-Shenzhen 5380

2010/08/15-18
第二十二届中国国际礼品、赠品及家庭用品展览会
22nd China Intl Gifts, Premium & Houseware Exhibition
北京 Beijing 770

2010/08/17-20
第六届中国（上海）国际建筑节能及新型建材展览会
6th Shanghai Intl Energy-saving & Advanced Building Materials Exhibition
上海 Shanghai 3160

2010/8/17-20
2010中国（上海）国际建材及室内装饰展览会
2010 Shanghai Intl Construction Material and Indoor Decoration Exhibition
上海 Shanghai 3170

2010/08/18-20
第八届中国汽车用品采购交易会
8th China Intl Auto Supplies Sourcing Fair
上海 Shanghai 3180

2010/08/18-20
第四届中国(上海)国际船舶工业博览会 暨第十五届全国海事科学技术研讨会
4th Intl Shipbuilding Industry Expo Of China 15th National Marine Science and Technology Seminar
上海 Shanghai 3190

2010/08/18-21
第六届中国国际金属加工技术设备展览会
6th China Intl Metals Working Technologyo & Equipment Exhibition
天津 Tianjin 4130

2010/08/18-22
建材装饰展装协
四川成都 Sichuan-Chengdu 6895

2010/08/18-22
2010（第十五届）大连国际汽车展览会
15th Dalian Intl Automotive Exhibition
辽宁大连 Liaoning-Dalian 6290

2010/08/19-21
中国医用仪器设备展览会暨技术交流会
China-hospeo
北京 Beijing 780

2010/08/19-21
2010第四届中国东北（沈阳）政府采购展览会
Northeast China (Shenyang) International Exhibition for Government Purchase
辽宁沈阳 Liaoning-Shenyang 6580

2010/08/19-23
2010北京国际艺术博览会
13th Beijing Intl Art Exposition
北京 Beijing 790

2010/08/21-24
中国国际家具及木工机械（济南）博览会
9th Jinan Intl Furniture Fair
山东济南 Shandong-Jinan 6640

2010/08/23-26
第十九届北京国际广播电影电视设备展览会
Beijing Intl Radio, TV & Film Equipment Exhibition 2010
北京 BeiJing 800

2010/08/24-26
中国国际针织博览会
China Intl Knitting Trade Fair
上海 Shanghai 3210

2010/08/24-26
第十六届中国国际家用纺织品及辅料博览会
16th China Intl Trade Fair for Home Textiles and Accessories
上海 Shanghai 3200

2010/08/26-29
2010第四届上海进口商品博览会
4th Shanghai Imports Expo 2010
上海 Shanghai 3250

2010/08/27-29
第五届成都农资信息交流
四川成都 Sichuan-Chengdu 6895

2010/08/27-29
首届食品博览会
四川成都 Sichuan-Chengdu 6895

2010/08/28-29
人才展
四川成都 Sichuan-Chengdu 6895

2010/08/28-30
2010第四届中国（北京）国际红木古典家具、现代家居及室内装饰艺术展览会
CIRCFE 2010
北京 Beijing 1145

2010/08/29-02
北京国际图书博览会
BIBF 2010
北京 Beijing 1145

2010/08/31-02
华南国际工业组装技术与装备展览会
Automotive Electronics South China
广东深圳 Guangdong-Shenzhen 5410

2010/08/31-02
华南国际汽车电子展览会
广东深圳 Guangdong-Shenzhen 5400

2010/08/31-02
中国清洁博览会(北京)
China Clean Expo-Beijing
北京 Beijing 820

2010/08/31-02
第十五届华南国际电子生产设备暨微电子工业展/ 华南国际电子制造技术展览会
NEPCON/ EMT South China 2010
广东深圳 Guangdong-Shenzhen 5390

2010/08/31-02
北京国际酒店用品博览会
Hotelex Beijing
北京 Beijing 810

## September 2010 九月

2010/09/-
2010中国宁波国际工业设计博览会
2010 World Industrial Design Fair Ningbo China
浙江宁波 Zhejiang-Ningbo 7000

2010/09/-
中国国际产业用纺织品及非织造布展览会
Intl Trade Fair For Technical Textiles and Nonwovens
上海 Shanghai 3260

2010/09/-
中国中西部（郑州）医疗器械展览会暨第19届中原国际医疗器械(2010年秋季)展览会
2010 China Central (Zhengzhou) Medical Equipment Show
河南郑州 Henan-Jinan 5870

2010/09/-
第三届中国（重庆）茶叶博览会暨海峡两岸文化交流会
3rd China (Chongqing) Tea Expo
重庆 Chongqing 1200

2010/09/-
中国国际保健博览会
Health Expo 2010
北京 Beijing 865

2010/09/-
第四届中国东北亚（沈阳）进口商品博览会
4th China Northeast Asia (Shenyang) Import Fair
辽宁沈阳 Liaoning-Shenyang 6590

2010/09/-
2010中国中西部（长沙）医疗器械展览会暨第17届湖南医疗器械技术与设备(2010年秋季)展览会
Changsha Medical Devices Exhibition
湖南长沙 Hunan-Changsha 6030

2010/09/-
第二届中国绿化博览会
2nd China Green Expo
河南郑州 Henan-Zhengzhou 5890

2010/09/-
2010中国中西部（南宁）医疗器械展览会
China (Xining) Medical Devices Exhibition
广西南宁 Guangxi-Nanning 5580

2010/09/-
中国（北京）国际商务及会奖旅游展览会
China Incentive, Business Travel & Meetings Exhibition
北京 Beijing 830

2010/09/01-03
中国国际皮革展
All China Leather Exhibitions
上海 Shanghai 3290

2010/09/01-03
2010上海国际智能交通论坛暨技术和应用展览会/ 2010上海国际停车设备和智能系统展览会
Intl ITS Conference & Expo Shanghai 2010/ INTERPARKING SHANGHAI 2010
上海 Shanghai 3270

2010/09/01-03
中国（上海）国际石油石化技术装备展览会/中国（上海）国际海洋石油天然气展览会
China (Shanghai) Intl Petroleum & Petrochemical Technology and Equipment Exhibition
上海 Shanghai 3310

2010/09/01-03
煤碳展
四川成都 Sichuan-Chengdu 6895

2010/09/01-03
中国国际鞋类展暨中国国际箱包、裘革服装及服饰展
China International Footwear Fair
Moda Shanghai
上海 Shanghai 3300

2010/09/01-03
第五届中国国际安全生产及职业健康展览会
5th China Intl Occupational Safety & Health Exhibition (COS+H 2010)
北京 Beijing 855

2010/09/01-03
2010国际健康生活方式博览会
2010 International Healthy Lifestyle Expo
北京 Beijing 850

2010/09/01-05
第二十四届国际名家具（东莞）展览会
24th Intl Famous Furniture Fair (Dongguan)
广东东莞 Guangdong-Dongguan 5437

2010/09/01-05
中国乌鲁木齐对外经济贸易洽谈会
China Urumqi Foreign Economic Relations & Trade Fair
新疆乌鲁木齐 Xinjiang-Urumqi 6910

2010/09/01-06
2010成都新能源国际论坛暨新能源博览会
四川成都 Sichuan-Chengdu 6895

2010/09/01-08
旅游展
四川成都 Sichuan-Chengdu 6895

2010/09/02-05
第十三届亚洲宠物展览会
Pet Fair Asia 2010
上海 Shanghai 3330

2010/09/02-07
第二届服装及缝制设备展览会
四川成都 Sichuan-Chengdu 6895

2010/09/02-07
纺织工业及面辅料展览会
四川成都 Sichuan-Chengdu 6895

2010/09/02-08
2010第十一届（成都）全国医疗器械及口腔设备展览会
四川成都 Sichuan-Chengdu 6895

2010/09/03-05
第六届中国（南京）国际软件产品博览会
6th China (Nanjing) Intl Software Product Expo
江苏南京 Jiangsu-Nanjing 6150

2010/09/06-09
第十二届中国国际光电博览会（CIOE2010）
12th China Intl Optoelectronic Expo（CIOE2010）
广东深圳 Guangdong-Shenzhen 5420

2010/09/06-09
第二十一届多国仪器仪表学术会议暨展览会
21st Intl Conference and Fair for Measurement Instrumentation and Automation
北京 Beijing 860

2010/09/07-09
2010中国国际嵌入式大会暨展览会
Embedded China 2010
上海 Shanghai 3340

2010/09/07-09
立嘉工业展
四川成都 Sichuan-Chengdu 6895

2010/09/07-09
2010中国（西部）电子展
Chengdu – China Electronics Fair
四川成都 Sichuan-Chengdu 6860

2010/09/07-10
中国国际家居饰品布艺及灯饰展览会
Finishing Fabrics & Lightings China 2010
上海 Shanghai 3370

2010/09/07-10
中国国际办公家具展览会
Office Furniture China 2010
上海 Shanghai 3360

2010/09/07-10
中国国际家具展览会
Furniture China 2010
上海 Shanghai 3350

2010/09/07-10
中国国际家具生产设备及原辅材料展览会
Furniture Manufacturing & Supply China 2010 上海 Shanghai 3400

2010/09/07-10
中国国际啤酒饮料制造技术及设备展览会
China Brew 2010
北京 Beijing 1145

2010/09/07-10
中国国际橱柜展览会
Kitchen & Cabinet China 2010
上海 Shanghai 3380

2010/09/08-11
第十四届中国国际投资贸易洽谈会
14th China International Fair for Investment & Trade
福建厦门 Fujian-Xiamen 4400

2010/09/08-12
2010国际特许加盟（上海）展览会
Franchise (Shanghai) Expo
上海 Shanghai 3410

2010/09/09-11
第一届（2010）上海国际美术材料展览会
Shanghai Intl Art Materials Exhibition
上海 Shanghai 3420

2010/09/09-11
第10届中国国际保健博览会暨保健节
10th China Intl Healthcare Expo & 10th China Intl Healthcare Festival
北京 Beijing 865

2010/09/09-13
第十一届中国（湖北-武汉）国际汽车工业展览会
11th China(Hubei/Wuhan) Intl Auto Industry Exhibition
湖北武汉 Hubei-Wuhan 5950

2010/09/09-21
第十届中国四川月饼节
四川成都 Sichuan-Chengdu 6895

2010/09/11-12
2010年北京国际儿童婴儿孕妇产品博览会
Children-Baby-Maternity Products Expo
北京 Beijing 870

2010/09/13-15
第十届中国重庆城市建设及建筑科技博览会
UCBE & LFAD Chongqing 2010
Urban Construction & Building Exhibition
重庆 Chongqing 1210

2010/09/14-16
中国国际眼镜业展览会
China Intl Optics Fair 2010
北京 Beijing 1145

2010/09/14-16
2010年秋季北京国际广告标识展、中国国际数码与喷墨印刷技术展览会
China Sign Expo 2010
北京 Beijing 1145

2010/09/14-16
2010中国国际机场技术、设备和服务展览会
Inter Airport China 2010
北京 Beijing 1145

2010/09/15-17
2010（第十届）中国国际化工展览会
ICIF China 2010
上海 Shanghai 3430

2010/09/15-17
中国国际塑料橡胶注射成型工业展览会
China Intl Exhibition on Plastics and Rubber Injection Moulding Industry (CIM 2010)
天津 Tianjin 4140

2010/09/15-17
中国国际文具及办公用品展览会
Paperworld China
China Intl Stationery & Office Supplies Exhibition
上海 Shanghai 3450

2010/09/15-17
上海聚氨酯展览会/阻燃展/复合材料展
2010 China International Exhibition on Polyurethane
上海 Shanghai 3440

2010/09/15-17
第十八届中国国际纸浆造纸暨纸制品展览会及会议
China Paper Shanghai 2010 – 18th Intl Exhibition and Conference Reaching All of China' s Paper-Related Industries
上海 Shanghai 3460

2010/09/15-19
2010深圳国际珠宝展
2010 Shenzhen Intl Jewellery Fair
广东深圳 Guangdong-Shenzhen 5440

2010/09/16-17
第十五届国际集成电路研讨会暨展览会
15th Intl IC-China Conference & Exhibition
广东东莞 Guangdong-Dongguan 5438

2010/09/16-18
2010第五届上海设计双年展
5th Shanghai Design Biennial
上海 Shanghai 3500

2010/09/16-18
2010年中国（上海）国际跨国采购大会
2010 Intl Sourcing Fair (Shanghai, China.)
上海 Shanghai 3510

2010/09/16-19
2010年中国北京秋季房地产展示交易会
Autumn Real Estate Trade Fair Beijing China
北京 Beijing 880

2010/09/17-19
第十三届成都国际汽车展览会汽车用品展
Chengdu Motor Show 2010
四川成都 Sichuan-Chengdu 6865

2010/09/17-19
中国国际高端物业展
China Intl Luxury Property Show
上海 Shanghai 3520

2010/09/19-21
2010第五届中国国际军民两用技术展览会
5th Military and Civil Technology Exhibition
北京 Beijing 890

2010/09/19-21
2010第五届北京国际居民两用技术展览会
2010 China Intl Military and Civil Mutually Used Technology Exhibition
北京 Beijing 1145

2010/09/19-21
2010中国国际福祉博览会
China Intl Wellbeing Expo 2010
北京 Beijing 1145

2010/09/19-21
北京国际风能、太阳能核电工业暨电力设备技术展览会
2010 Beijing Intl Wind, Solar, Nuclear Power Industry and Power Electrical Equipment and Technology Exhibition
北京 Beijing 1145

2010/09/19-25
成都国际汽车展览会
Chengdu Motor Show
四川成都 Sichuan-Chengdu 6868

2010/09/20-23
2010年常州科技经贸洽谈会
Changzhou Technological and Economic Fair
江苏常州 Jiangsu-Changzhou 6080

2010/09/21-22
2010第三届中国国际植物提取物展览会及研讨会
Shanghai Intl Nature Extract Exhibition & Conference
上海 Shanghai 3530

2010/09/21-23
2010中国国际集约化畜牧展览会
VIV China 2010
北京 Beijing 1145

2010/09/21-23
2010中国特殊钢工业展览会
China Special Steel Industry Exhibition 2010
上海 Shanghai 3560

2010/09/21-24
中国国际线缆及线材展览会
4th All China-Intl Wire & Cable Industry Trade Fair
上海 Shanghai 3540

2010/09/21-24
第四届中国国际管材展览会
4th All-China Intl Tube & Pipe Trade Fair
上海 Shanghai 3550

2010/09/21-24
2010广州宠物水族用品展
2010 Guangzhou Pet &Auqarium Show
广东广州 Guangdong-Guangzhou 5050

2010/09/23-26
第十一届国际果蔬、食品博览会
11th Intl Fruit/Vegetable/Food Exposition
山东烟台 Shagndong-Yantai 6730

2010/09/23-26
第十一届中国国际机电产品博览会
11th China Intl Machinery & Electronic Products Exposition
湖北武汉 Hubei-Wuhan 5960

2010/09/24-27
第六届中国国际有机食品和绿色食品博览会
ORGANIC CHINA EXPO BEIJING 2010
北京 Beijing 900

2010/09/27-08
美食节
四川成都 Sichuan-Chengdu 6895

2010/09/27-29
2010华南（东莞）金属新材料、新技术、新设备及制品展览会
South China Expo (Dongguan) for New Metal Materials, New Technologies, New equipments and Products
广东东莞 Guangdong-Dongguan 5439

2010/09/27-29
第八届国际粉体工业/散装技术展览会暨会议
8th Intl Powder/Bulk Conference & Exhibition
上海 Shanghai 3575

2010/09/27-29
ReChina 2010 第七届亚洲打印耗材展览会
ReChina Asia Expo 2010
上海 Shanghai 3570

2010/09/28-30
2010 中国国际五金展－«科隆国际五金展»强力推动
China Intl Hardware Show —Powered by PRACTICAL WORLD
上海 shanghai 3580

2010/09/28-30
2010成都新能源国际论坛暨新能源博览会
四川成都 Sichuan-Chengdu 6895

2010/09/29-04
2010第九届南京国际汽车展览会
2010 Nanjing Auto Exposition
江苏南京 Jiangsu-Nanjing 6160

2010/09/29-04
2010第九届南京国际汽车展览会
9th Nanjing Intl Auto Exposition
江苏南京 Jiangsu-Nanjing 6170

## October 2010 十月

2010/10/-
2010第四届中国（芜湖）装备制造业博览会
4th China (Wuhu) Equipment Manufacturing Exposition
安徽合肥 Anhui-Hefei 4220

2010/10/-
厦门日报房车大联展
Xiamen Housing and Automotive Exhibition
福建厦门 Fujian-Xiamen 4410

2010/10/-
2010洛阳机电产品博览会
Luoyang Machinery and Electronic Products Expo
河南郑州 Henan-Jinan 5680

2010/10/-
2010中国国际农产品交易会
2010 China Int'l Agriculture Products Trade Fair
河南郑州 Henan-Zhengzhou 5900

2010/10/-
2010郑州全国商品交易会
2010 Zhengzhou National Commodity Fair
河南郑州 Henan-Zhengzhou 5910

2010/10/-
中国（上海）国际马博会
China (Shanghai) Intl Horse Fair
上海 Shanghai 3600

2010/10/01-06
秋季房交会
四川成都 Sichuan-Chengdu 6895

2010/10/01-24
成都秋季服装展销会
四川成都 Sichuan-Chengdu 6895

2010/10/03-06
上海房地产秋季展示会
Holiday Real Estate Market
上海 Shanghai 3610

2010/10/09-11
第七届中国(上海)国际玻璃工业新技术展览会
China (ShangHai) Int'l Glass Industry New Tech. Expo
上海 Shanghai 3620

2010/10/10-25
中国国际西部博览会
四川成都 Sichuan-Chengdu 6895

2010/10/11-13
北京国际减灾应急技术设备博览会
Beijing Intl Disaster Reduction Expo
北京 Beijing 910

2010/10/11-15
2010年中国国际信息通信展览会
P&T/EXPO COMM CHINA 2010
北京 Beijing 920

2010/10/12-14
第九届中国国际玩具、模型及婴儿用品展
9th Intl Trade Fair for Toys, Hobby & Baby Articles
上海 Shanghai 3650

2010/10/12-15
上海国际专业灯光音响展览会
prolight + Sound Shanghai
上海 Shanghai 3660

2010/10/12-15
中国(上海)国际乐器展览会
Music China
上海 Shanghai 3670

2010/10/13-15
PPI彩盒印刷包装展
China Folding Carton
3rd PPI Folding Carton, Printing & Packing Industry Exhibition and Forum
天津 Tianjin 4150

2010/10/14-16
2010上海司法警用及安全防范技术产品博览会
Shanghai Security Products Expo
上海 Shanghai 3680

2010/10/14-16
2010北京国际风能大会暨展览会
China Windpower Beijing 2010
北京 Beijing 930

2010/10/15-17
2010中国（济南）国际卡车暨零部件博览会
Truckworld2010
山东济南 Shandong-Jinan 6645

2010/10/15 – 30
第108届中国进出口商品交易会
108th China Import and Export Fair
广东广州 Guangdong-Guangzhou 5055

2010/10/16-17
2010中国国际教育展
China Education Expo 2010
北京 Beijing 940

2010/10/18-21
2010中国顺德国际家用电器博览会
China Shunde Intl Exposition for Household Electrical Appliances 2010
广东顺德 Guangdong-Shunde 5510

2010/10/19-21
第十二届中国上海国际食品加工及包装机械展览会
Intl FoodTec China/Interfood Shanghai 2010
上海 Shanghai 3690

2010/10/19-21
第十三届膜与水处理技术暨装备展览会
water and membrane China 2010
北京 Beijing 1145

2010/10/19-21
第十三届国际电力设备及技术展览会/ 2010国际节能、电力环保及脱硫脱硝装备展览会/ 第六届国际电机工程及电工装备展览会
EP China 2010
北京 Beijing 1145

2010/10/19-21
2010北京国际在线分析测试技术及设备展览会
2010 China Intl On-line Analytical Testing Technology and Equipment Exhibition
北京 Beijing 1145

2010/10/19-22
中国国际纺织面料及辅料（秋冬）博览会
China Intl Trade Fair for Apparel Fabrics and Accessories
上海 Shanghai 3710

2010/10/20-24
第七届中国-东盟博览会/ 中国-东盟商务与投资分会
7th China ASEAN Expo
广西南宁 Guangxi-Nanning 5590

2010/10/21-23
2010第三届上海国际可再生能源大会暨展览会
3rd Intl Congress & Exhibition On Reproducible Energy
上海 Shanghai 3730

2010/10/21-23
国际家居装饰艺术展
International Home Décor & Design
上海 Shanghai 3830

2010/10/21-23
2010“100%设计”上海展
100% Design Shanghai
上海 Shanghai 3720

2010/10/21-24
第九届中国国际摩托车博览会
9th China Intl Motorcycle Trade Exhibition
重庆 Chongqing 1220

2010/10/21-24
第十八届中国（深圳）国际玩具及礼品展览会
18th China (Shenzhen) Intl Toys &Gifts Fair
广东深圳 Guangdong-Shenzhen 5460

2010/10/21-25
中国义乌国际小商品博览会
China Yiwu Intl Commodities Fair
浙江义乌 Zhejiang-Yiwu 7070

2010/10/25-27
2010中国国际汽车制造及生产设备博览会
CIAMPFE2010
北京 Beijing 1145

2010/10/25-28
亚洲国际动力传动与控制技术展览会/亚洲国际物流技术与运输系统展览会
PTC ASIA
Power Transmission and Control
上海 Shanghai 3760

2010/10/25-28
亚洲国际物流技术与运输系统展览会
CeMAT ASIA 2010
上海 Shanghai 3750

2010/10/26-28
2010北京国际美容化妆品及医学养生健康产业博览会
2010 Beijing Intl Beauty, Hairdressing, Cosmetics & Health Products Expo
北京 Beijing 1145

2010/10/26-28
2010第四届中国国际马业马术展览会
4th China International Equestrian & Horse Industry Fair
北京 Beijing 950

2010/10/26-28
2010中国（上海）国际门业博览会暨门窗产品展览会
Door Expo 2010
China Shanghai Intl Door Industry Expo
上海 Shanghai 3770

2010/10/26-29
第十五届中国国际医药（工业）展览会暨技术交流会暨中国医药工业国际论坛
15th China Intl Pharmaceutical Industry Exhibition ---China Intl Pharmaceutical Industry Forum
北京 Beijing 960

2010/10/27-29
2010北京国际广告技术设备展及LED展览会
China Exhibition of Advertisement & Sign 2010, Beijing
北京 Beijing 1145

2010/10/27-29
中国国际光电产业博览会暨中国国际激光，电子及光显产业展览会/中国国际机器视觉展览会暨机器视觉技术及工业应用研讨会
Optoelectronics Industry Exposition (Beijing) & Intl Lasers, Optoelectronics and Photonics Exhibition
北京 Beijing 1145

2010/10/28-02
2010年中国（常州）国际动漫艺术周
China (Changzhou) Animation Festival
江苏常州 Jiangsu-Changzhou 6090

2010/10/28-30
2010中国糖果文化节暨第七届中国国际甜食及休闲食品展览会
China Confectionery Culture Festival 2010, Sweets & Snacks China 2010
上海 Shanghai 3780

2010/10/28-30
2010中国东莞国际鞋展/ 鞋机展
Dongguan Shoes/ China Shoetes/ China Bags
广东东莞 Guangdong-Dongguan 4540

2010/10/28-31
2010北京国际钱币博览会
Beijing Intl Coins Exposition 2010
北京 Beijing 970

2010/10/29-31
中国南宁国际建筑装饰博览会
China Nanning Intl building decoration fair
广西南宁 Guangxi-Nanning 5600

2010/10/30-02
第十四届中国国际宠物水族用品展览会
CIPS 2010
北京 Beijing 1145

## November 2010 十一月

2010/11/-
第十五届中国宁波国际住宅产品博览会
15th china ningbo Intl exhibition on rlousing industry products
浙江宁波 Zhejiang-Ningbo 7010

2010/11/-
2010中意国际葡萄酒展
VINITALY CHINA 2010
上海 Shanghai 3800

2010/11/-
2010第九届中国武汉国际农业机械展览会
9th Wuhan Agricultural Machinery Exhibition 湖北武汉 Hubei-Wuhan 5980

2010/11/-
第64届全国药品交易会（秋季）
64th PHARMCHINA
(China National Pharmaceuticals Fair)
四川成都 Sichuan-Chengdu 6870

2010/11/-
2010中医药国际科技博览会
Traditional Chinese Medicine Exposition 2010
四川成都 Sichuan-Chengdu 6880

2010/11/-
2010中国（郑州）国际汽车博览会
2010 Zhengzhou Intl Automobile Expo
河南郑州 Henan-Zhengzhou 5920

2010/11/01-04
中国国际渔业博览会
CHINA FISHERIES & SEAFOOD EXPO
辽宁大连 Liaoning-Dalian 6310

2010/11/01-04
中国义乌（国际）森林产品博览会
China Yiwu ( Intl ) Forest Product Fair
浙江义乌 Zhejiang-Yiwu 7080

2010/11/01-05
中国杨凌农业高新科技成果博览会
China Yangling agricultural Hi-Tech Fair
陕西杨凌 Shaanxi-Yangling 6610

2010/11/02-04
第五届微波及天线技术交流展览会
5th Intl conference& exhibition on microwave and antenna
上海 Shanghai 3810

2010/11/02-04
第九届国际电磁兼容与安规认证暨微波展览会
9th Intl conference& exhibition on elcctromagnetic compatibility
上海 Shanghai 3820

2010/11/02-05
2010年中国国际社会公共安全产品博览会
10th China Intl Exhibition on Public Safety and Security
北京 Beijing 1145

2010/11/02-06
第12届中国国际工业博览会
China International Industry Fair 2010
上海 Shanghai 3860

2010/11/03-04
2010中国国际水处理化学品、水溶高分子、造纸化学品、工业表面活性剂技术及应用展览会
2010 Intl Exhibition on Water-treatment chemicals & Water-soluble Polymer Products & Papermaking Chemicals & Industrial Surfactants, Technology and Application
上海 Shanghai 3825

2010/11/04-07
第四届中国（深圳）国际游艇及设备展览会
SIBEX - China (Shenzhen) Intl Boat Show
广东深圳 Guangdong-Shenzhen 5480

2010/11/04-10
2010第二届中国（西安）糖酒食品交易会/ 第二届中国（西安）国际纺织服装博览会
2nd Xi'an Sugar and Spirits Fair
2nd Xi'an Textile and Apparel Expo
陕西西安 Shaanxi-Xi'an 6608

2010/11/05-07
北京国际顶级私人物品展
TOP ESSENCE BEIJING
北京 Beijing 980

2010/11/05-08
第五届中国厦门国际佛事用品展览会
5th China Xiamen Intl Buddhist Items & Crafts Fair
福建厦门 Fujian-Xiamen 4430

2010/11/06-08
第八届中国（无锡）国际工业设计博览会
8th China (Wuxi) Intl Industrial Design Expo
江苏无锡 Jiangsu-Wuxi 6190

2010/11/06-09
第十二届中国塑料博览会
12th China Plastics Expo
浙江余姚 Zhejiang-Yuyao 7100

2010/11/06-17
沿海地区服装展
Coastal Area Apparel Show
福建厦门 Fujian-Xiamen 4440

2010/11/07-12
2010年第七届中国成都建筑科技、装饰材料（冬季）博览会
四川成都 Sichuan-Chengdu 6895

2010/11/07-14
香港博览会
四川成都 Sichuan-Chengdu 6895

2010/11/08-10
第三届中国国际造船工业装备和船舶设计建造技术展
China Intl Exhibition on Shipbuilding Equipment, Ship Design & Manufacturing Tech 2010
上海 Shanghai 3850

2010/11/08-10
第二届中国国际海洋工程技术和装备展
China Intl Exhibition on Ocean EngineeringTechnology & Equipment 2010
上海 Shanghai 3840

2010/11/09-11
第10届中国国际染料工业及纺织化学品、印花技术展览会
10th China Intl Exhibition for Dye Industry & Textile Chemical、Printing Industrial Technology
广东广州 Guangdong-Guangzhou 5060

2010/11/09-11
第10届中国（广州）国际制衣技术设备展览会
10th China (Guangzhou) Intl Exhibition for Clothing Technology and Equipment
广东广州 Guangdong-Guangzhou 5080

2010/11/09-11
第10届中国（广州）国际纺织机械展览会
10th China (Guangzhou) Intl Exhibition For Textile Machinery
广东广州 Guangdong-Guangzhou 5090

2010/11/09-11
第10届中国（广州）国际纺织面料辅料及纱线展览会
10th China（Guangzhou）Intl Exhibition For Apparel Fabric & Accessories
广东广州 Guangdong-Guangzhou 5070

2010/11/10-11
中国对外投资合作洽谈会
China Overseas Investment Fair
北京 Beijing 990

2010/11/10-12
第75届中国电子展暨2010亚洲电子展
China Electronics Fair
上海 Shanghai 3870

2010/11/10-12
汽体展
四川成都 Sichuan-Chengdu 6895

2010/11/10-12
第十七届国际自动识别技术展览会
16th Intl Exhibition of Automatic Identification Technology
北京 Beijing 1000

2010/11/10-12
2010第七届中国(北京)国际冶金工业博览会
China (Beijing) Intl Metallurgy Industry Exhibition, 2010
北京 Beijing 1010

2010/11/10-12
中国（北京）国际金属及管业展
China Beijing Intl Metal & Steel Tube Industry Expo, 2010
北京 Beijing 1145

2010/11/11-13
2010中国烘焙展览会（西部）
China Bakery Exhibition 2010 (West)
四川成都 Sichuan-Chengdu 6890

2010/11/11-15
2010中国国际珠宝展览会
China Intl Jewelry Fair 2010
北京 Beijing 1020

2010/11/12-17
鞋类、加工
四川成都 Sichuan-Chengdu 6895

2010/11/16-21
中国国际航空航天博览会
China Intl Aviation & Aerospace Exhibition
广东珠海 Guangdong-Zhuhai 5515

2010/11/16-21
第十二届中国国际高新技术成果交易会信息技术与产品展
China Hi-Tech Fair/ComNet2010
广东深圳 Guangdong-Shenzhen 5490

2010/11/16-21
第十二届中国国际高新技术成果交易会电子展
China Hi-Tech Fair/Elec
广东深圳 Guangdong-Shenzhen 5500

2010/11/17-19
2010年中国国际过滤工业展览会
Filtration 2010, China
上海 Shanghai 3900

2010/11/17-19
亚洲纸业世界展览会
Tissue World Asia
上海 Shanghai 3910

2010/11/17-20
第十二届东莞国际模具及金属加工展/ 第十二届东莞国际橡塑胶及包装展
12th China Dongguan Intl Mould & Metalworking Exhibition/ 12th China Dongguan Intl Plastics, Packaging & Rubber Exhibition
广东东莞 Guangdong-dongguan 4543

2010/11/18-20
2010第11届中国太阳能光伏会议暨展览
2010 11th China Solar PV Conference and Exhibition
江苏南京 Jiangsu-Nanjing 6180

2010/11/18-20
第十一届中国（义乌）国际袜子、针织及染整机械展览会/ 第四届中国（义乌）国际针织纱线展览会
10th Yiwu Intl Exhibition on Hosiery, Knitting, Dyeing

& Finishing Machinery/ 3rd China (Yiwu) Intl Exhibition on Knitting Yarns
浙江义乌 Zhejiang-Yiwu 7090

2010/11/18-21
中国北京国际文化创意产业博览会
China Beijing Intl Cultural & Creative Industry Expo 2010
北京 Beijing 1040

2010/11/18-21
中国国际旅游交易会
China International Travel Mart
上海 Shanghai 3920

2010/11/19-02
大连服装展
Dalian Clothing Show
福建厦门 Fujian-Xiamen 4450

2010/11/22-24
2010中国国际润滑油、脂及调和技术设备展览会
2010 China Intl lubricating oil, Grease and Refining Technology Exhibition
上海 Shanghai 3930

2010/11/23-26
中国国际工程机械、建筑机械、工程车辆及设备博览会
2010 China Intl lubricating oil, Grease and Refining Technology Exhibition
上海 Shanghai 3930

2010/11/25-27
中国国际橡胶技术展览会/亚洲埃森轮胎展
REIFEN CHINA
4th Asian Essen Tire Show
上海 Shanghai 3940

2010/11/25-28
2010年中国北京冬季房地产展示交易会
Winter Real Estate Trade Fair Beijing China
北京 Beijing 1070

2010/11/25-30
首届四川名优食品博览会
四川成都 Sichuan-Chengdu 6895

2010/11/27-29
2010北京国际礼品、赠品及家庭用品（年底）采购订货会
China International Gifts, Premium & Houseware Exhibition
北京 Beijing 1080

2010/11/30-02
2010第八届中国（上海）国际保温材料与节能技术展览会
2010 Eighth China (Shanghai) Intl thermal insulation materials and energy-saving Technology Expo
上海 Shanghai 3950

## December 2010 十二月

2010/12/01-03
第十三届中国国际胶粘剂及密封剂展览会暨第五届中国国际胶粘剂与标签展览会
China Adhesive 2010
上海 Shanghai 3955

2010/12/01-04
中国国际口腔器材展览会/ 首届全球华人口腔医学大会暨中国国际口腔医学大会
CDEI – China Dental Exhibition Intl/ GCCD – Global Congress of Chinese Dentists
福建厦门 Fujian-Xiamen 4453

2010/12/04-05
人才展
四川成都 Sichuan-Chengdu 6895

2010/12/04-07
全国库存商品及闲置物资博览交易会
China Store Goods and Idle Products Trade Fair
山东青岛 Shandong-Qingdao 6720

2010/12/08-11
上海国际汽车零配件、维修检测诊断设备及服务用品展览会
automechanika Shanghai
Shanghai Intl Trade Fair for Automotive Parts, Equipment and Service Supplies
上海 Shanghai 3960

2010/12/09-11
上海国际健康大会
Intl Congress & Exhibition on Nutrition Fitness and Health (NFH)
上海 Shanghai 3970

2010/12/11-19
成都冬季服装博览会
四川成都 Sichuan-Chengdu 6895

2010/12/14-19
阿里巴巴网货大会
四川成都 Sichuan-Chengdu 6895

2010/12/15-17
2010中国国际标签技术展览会
China Intl Exhibition for Label Technology
上海 Shanghai 3990

2010/12/18-20
路博2010泛北部湾新生活方式展览会
Broad2010 Guangxi Fan-Beibu Gulf New Lifestyle Exhibition
广西南宁 Guangxi-Nanning 5610

2010/12/21-02
2010第九届东莞嘉年华时尚生活用品购物节
9th Dongguan Shopping Festival
广东东莞 Guangdong-Dongguan 4548

2011-
中国国际加油加气站高新技术及设备暨便利店业务博览会
Gas station
北京 Beijing 1100

2011/01/11-14
第三十七届中国国际裘皮革皮制品交易会
37th China Fur & Leather Products Fair
北京 Beijing 1120

2011/04/11-16
第十二届中国国际机床展览会（CIMT2011）
12th China Intl Machine Tool Show (CIMT2011)
北京 Beijing 1130

2011/11/18-21
第五届中国北京国际文化创意产业博览会
Fourth China BeiJing Intl High-Tech Expo
北京 Beijing 140

# 中国香港展览会议

## Exhibitions and Fairs Overseas

| 日期 Date | 展览会议 Event | 地点 Venue | 主办 Organizer |
| --- | --- | --- | --- |
| 2010.1.3-8 | IEEE International NanoElectronics Conference 2010 | 香港城市大学<br>City University of Hong Kong | 香港城市大学<br>City University of Hong Kong<br>☎ 852-3442 5481<br>🖷 852-3442 0264<br>✉ apkyfu@city.edu.hk<br>www.cityu.edu.hk/ieeeinec |
| 2010.1.8-10 | 推进慢性疾病护理国际研讨会<br>International Conference on Promoting Chronic Care | 香港理工大学<br>The Hong Kong Polytechnic University | International Conference Consultants Ltd<br>☎ 852-2559 9973<br>🖷 852-2547 9528<br>✉ cmai@icc.com.hk<br>www.Chronic-Care2010.org |
| 2010.1.11-13 | 香港贸发局香港国际专利授权展<br>HKTDC Hong Kong International Licensing Show | 香港会议展览中心<br>Hong Kong Convention & Exhibition Centre | 香港贸易发展局<br>Hong Kong Trade Development Council<br>☎ 852-1830 668<br>🖷 852-2824 0249<br>✉ hktdc@hktdc.org<br>www.hktdc.com/hktradefairs<br>详细介绍见☆1<br>Detail See ☆1 |
| 2010.1.11-14 | 香港贸发局香港婴儿用品展<br>HKTDC Hong Kong Baby Products Fair | 香港会议展览中心<br>Hong Kong Convention & Exhibition Centre | 香港贸易发展局<br>Hong Kong Trade Development Council<br>☎ 852-1830 668<br>🖷 852-2824 0249<br>✉ exhibitions@hktdc.org<br>www.hktdc.com/hktradefairs<br>详细介绍见☆3<br>Detail See ☆3 |
| 2010.1.11-14 | 香港国际文具展<br>Hong Kong International Stationery Fair | 香港会议展览中心<br>Hong Kong Convention & Exhibition Centre | 香港贸易发展局<br>Hong Kong Trade Development Council<br>☎ 852-1830 668<br>🖷 852-2824 0249<br>✉ exhibitions@hktdc.org<br>www.hktdc.com/hktradefairs<br>详细介绍见☆4<br>Detail See ☆4 |
| 2010.1.11-14 | 香港贸发局香港玩具展<br>HKTDC Hong Kong Toys & Games Fair | 香港会议展览中心<br>Hong Kong Convention & Exhibition Centre | 香港贸易发展局<br>Hong Kong Trade Development Council<br>☎ 852-1830 668<br>🖷 852-2824 0249<br>✉ exhibitions@hktdc.org<br>www.hktdc.com/hktradefairs<br>详细介绍见☆2<br>Detail See ☆2 |

# 2010MIECF

Macao International Environmental Co-operation Forum & Exhibition

2010年澳门国际环保合作发展论坛及展览

主办单位/Host
中华人民共和国
澳门特别行政区政府
Government of the Macao Special Administrative Region of the People's Republic of China

# THE GREEN GATEWAY

# 綠色通道

8 -10 April 2010 • Macao

2010年4月8日至10日 • 澳门

关于登记或索取更多资讯，请联络 • For registration or more information, contact:

2010MIECF官方承办单位 • 2010MIECF Host Co-ordinator
澳门特别行政区政府 • Macao Special Administrative Region

澳门贸易投资促进局 • Macao Trade and Investment Promotion Institute
电话/Tel : (853) 8798 9675 传真/Fax: (853) 2872 7123
电邮/Email : miecf2010@ipim.gov.mo

环境保护局 • Environmental Protection Bureau
电话/Tel: (853) 2872 5134 传真/Fax : (853) 2872 5129
电邮/Email: info@dspa.gov.mo

2010MIECF项目经理 • 2010MIECF Event Manager
慕尼黑国际博览亚洲(香港)有限公司 • MMI Asia (Hong Kong) Limited

澳門/Macao: 电话/Tel: (853) 8798 9675 传真/Fax : (853) 2872 7123
电邮/Email: miecf2010@ipim.gov.mo

香港/Hong Kong: 电话/Tel: (852) 2511 0738 传真/Fax: (852) 2511 5099
电邮/Email : info@macaomiecf.com

新加坡/Singapore : 电话/Tel: (65) 6236 0988 传真/Fax : (65) 6236 1966
电邮/Email: info@macaomiecf.com

www.macaomiecf.com

| 日期<br>Date | 展览会议<br>Event | 地点<br>Venue | 主办<br>Organizer |
|---|---|---|---|
| 2010.1.18-21 | 香港贸发局香港国际时尚荟萃<br>HKTDC Education & Careers Expo | 香港会议展览中心<br>Hong Kong Convention & Exhibition Centre | 香港贸易发展局<br>Hong Kong Trade Development Council<br>☎ 852-1830 668<br>🖷 852-2824 0249<br>✉ exhibitions@hktdc.org<br>www.hktdc.com/hktradefairs<br>详细介绍见☆6<br>Detail See ☆6 |
| 2010.1.18-21 | 香港贸发局香港时装节秋冬系列<br>HKTDC Hong Kong Fashion Week for Fall/Winter | 香港会议展览中心<br>Hong Kong Convention & Exhibition Centre | 香港贸易发展局<br>Hong Kong Trade Development Council<br>☎ 852-1830 668<br>🖷 852-2824 0249<br>✉ exhibitions@hktdc.org<br>www.hktdc.com/hktradefairs<br>详细介绍见☆5<br>Detail See ☆5 |
| 2010.1.23-24 | 香港药剂学术年会2010<br>Hong Kong Pharmacy Conference 2010 | 香港会议展览中心<br>Hong Kong Convention and Exhibition Centre | ☎ 852-9633 4533<br>✉ hkpharmacyconference@gmail.com<br>www.pharmacyconference.org |
| 2010.1.24-28 | 23rd IEEE International Conference on Micro Electro Mechanical Systems (MEMS 2010) | 香港会议展览中心<br>Hong Kong Convention and Exhibition Centre | 香港科技大学<br>The Hong Kong University of Science & Technology<br>☎ 852-2358 7057<br>🖷 852-2358 1485<br>✉ eemwong@ust.hk<br>www.ncsu.edu/IEEE-RAS |
| 2010.1.25-27 | LINC Asia-Pacific 2010 | 亚洲国际博览馆<br>AsiaWorld-Expo | CongO Congress Organisation and more GmbH<br>☎ +498 912 954 40<br>✉ toniejaeger@aol.com<br>www.lincasiapacific.cn |
| 2010.1.28-30 | 1st International Congress on Abdominal Obesity: Bridging the Gap Between Cardiology and Diabetology | 香港会议展览中心<br>Hong Kong Convention and Exhibition Centre | Kenas International<br>☎ +41 229080488<br>🖷 +41 229069140<br>✉ abob@kenes.com<br>www.kenes.com/abob |
| 2010.1.30-31 | 英国教育展<br>Education UK Exhibition 2010 | 香港会议展览中心<br>Hong Kong Convention and Exhibition Centre | The British Council<br>☎ 852-2913 5100<br>🖷 852-2913 5102<br>✉ enquiries@britishcouncil.org.hk<br>www.britishcouncil.org/hongkong |
| 2010.2.3-10 | 世界气象组织航空气象学委员会第十四届会议<br>The 14th Session of the Commission for Aeronautical Meteorology of the World Meteorological Organization | 香港会议展览中心<br>Hong Kong Convention and Exhibition Centre | 太古旅游<br>Hong Kong Observatory<br>☎ 852-3151 8900<br>🖷 852-2590 0099<br>wmo.homeip.net |

| 日期<br>Date | 展览会议<br>Event | 地点<br>Venue | 主办<br>Organizer |
|---|---|---|---|
| 2010.2.4-7 | 香港贸发局教育及职业博览<br>HKTDC Education & Careers Expo | 香港会议展览中心<br>Hong Kong Convention & Exhibition Centre | 香港贸易发展局<br>Hong Kong Trade Development Council<br>☎ 852-1830 668<br>🖷 852-2824 0249<br>✉ exhibitions@hktdc.org<br>www.hktdc.com/hktradefairs<br>详细介绍见☆7<br>Detail See ☆7 |
| 2010.2.5-7 | 第五届香港宠物节<br>第五届国际宠物及水族用品博览<br>The 5th Hong Kong Pet Show | 香港会议展览中心<br>Hong Kong Convention and Exhibition Centre | 展汇香港投资有限公司<br>World Hong Kong Investment Limited<br>☎ 852-2756 2888<br>🖷 852-2360 2222<br>✉ marketing@petshow.com.hk<br>www.petshow.com.hk |
| 2010.2.19-21 | 第58届情人节婚纱、婚宴及结婚服务博览<br>58th Valentine's Wedding Service & Banquet Expo 2010 | 香港会议展览中心<br>Hong Kong Convention and Exhibition Centre | 香港亚洲展览集团有限公司<br>Hongkong-Asia Exhibition (Holdings) Ltd<br>☎ 852-2591 9823<br>🖷 852-2573 3311<br>✉ E-mail: hkexhi@hka.com.hk<br>www.iweddingclub.com |
| 2010.2.25-28 | 2010香港国际毛皮时装展览会<br>2010 Hong Kong International Fur & Fashion Fair | 香港会议展览中心<br>Hong Kong Convention and Exhibition Centre | 香港毛皮业协会<br>Hong Kong Fur Federation<br>☎ 852-2367 4646<br>🖷 852-2739 0799<br>✉ fur@hkff.org<br>www.hkff.org/en/events/fair.do |
| 2010.2.26-28 | International Congress of Cardiology 2010 | 香港会议展览中心<br>Hong Kong Convention and Exhibition Centre | 香港中文大学<br>Division of Cardiology, Department of Medicine and Therapeutis, The Chinese University of Hong Kong<br>☎ 852-2632-3194<br>🖷 852-2144-5343<br>✉ cardiology@cuhk.edu.hk<br>www.icc-hongkong.com |
| 2010.2.26-28 | 2010春季BB购物节暨儿童成长教育展<br>2010 Baby Show in Spring & Child Growth Education Expo | 香港会议展览中心<br>Hong Kong Convention and Exhibition Centre | 荷花集团<br>Eugene International Limited<br>☎ 852-2811 4522<br>🖷 852-2565 0258<br>✉ marketing@eugenegroup.com.hk<br>www.eugenegroup.com.hk |
| 2010.3 - | 香港音乐汇展<br>Hong Kong Music Fair | 香港会议展览中心<br>Hong Kong Convention & Exhibition Centre | 香港贸易发展局<br>Hong Kong Trade Development Council<br>☎ 852-1830 668<br>🖷 852-2824 0249<br>✉ hktdc@hktdc.org<br>www.hktdc.com/hktradefairs<br>详细介绍见☆10<br>Detail See ☆10 |

| 日期<br>Date | 展览会议<br>Event | 地点<br>Venue | 主办<br>Organizer |
|---|---|---|---|
| 2010.3.3-6 | 三月亚洲时尚首饰及配饰展<br>Asia Fashion Jewelry Accessories Fair-March | 亚洲国际博览馆<br>AsiaWorld-Expo | 亚洲博闻有限公司<br>UMB Asia Ltd<br>☎ 852-2585 6179, 2516 2158<br>🖷 852-3749 7542<br>✉ salesafj@cmpasia.com<br>www.asiafja.com |
| 2010.3.5-9 | 香港贸发局香港国际珠宝展<br>HKTDC Hong Kong International Jewellery Show | 香港会议展览中心<br>Hong Kong Convention & Exhibition Centre | 香港贸易发展局<br>Hong Kong Trade Development Council<br>☎ 852-1830 668<br>🖷 852-2824 0249<br>✉ exhibitions@hktdc.org<br>www.hktdc.com/hktradefairs<br>详细介绍见☆8<br>Detail See ☆8 |
| 2010.3.11-12 | 第二届学术图书馆馆员国际学术会议-风雨唱咏 继往开来<br>Academic Librarian 2:<br>Singing in the Rain -<br>Conference Towards Future Possibilities | 香港理工大学<br>The Hong Kong Polytechnic University | 香港理工大学<br>The Hong Kong Polytechnic University<br>☎ 852-2766 6855<br>🖷 852-2765 8274<br>✉ steve.oconnor@polyu.edu.hk<br>www.lib.polyu.edu.hk/ALSR2010 |
| 2010.3.16-18 | 亚洲智能卡暨身份识别技术工业展<br>Cartes in Asia | 亚洲国际博览馆<br>AsiaWorld-Expo | 法国高美爱博展览集团<br>☎ 010-6588 5968, 6588 5969<br>🖷 010-6588 5970<br>✉ jackiezhang@promosalons-china.com<br>www.cartes-asia.com |
| 2010.3.16-18 | China Maritime 2010 | 香港会议展览中心<br>Hong Kong Convention and Exhibition Centre | Baird Publications Pty Ltd<br>☎ +61-3 9645 0411<br>🖷 +61-3 9645 0475 |
| 2010.3.17-19 | 香港国际春季成衣及时装材料展<br>Interstoff Asia Essential - Spring 2010 | 香港会议展览中心<br>Hong Kong Convention and Exhibition Centre | 法兰克福展览(香港)有限公司<br>Messe Frankfurt (HK) Ltd<br>☎ 852-2238 9932<br>🖷 852-2598 8771<br>✉ olivia.ho@hongkong.messefrankfurt.com<br>www.messefrankfurt.com.hk |
| 2010.3.19-21 | 香港婚纱暨结婚博览<br>Hong Kong Wedding Expo 2010 | 香港会议展览中心<br>Hong Kong Convention and Exhibition Centre | 隽杰国际展览有限公司<br>Audace International Fairs Limited<br>☎ 852-2367 8385<br>🖷 852-2367 8488<br>✉ info@expo.com.hk<br>www.expo.com.hk |
| 2010.3.19-21 | 香港婚宴博览2010<br>Hong Kong Wedding Banquet Expo 2010 | 香港会议展览中心<br>Hong Kong Convention and Exhibition Centre | 隽杰国际展览有限公司<br>Audace International Fairs Limited<br>☎ 852-2367 8385<br>🖷 852-2367 8488<br>✉ info@expo.com.hk<br>www.expo.com.hk |

| 日期<br>Date | 展览会议<br>Event | 地点<br>Venue | 主办<br>Organizer |
|---|---|---|---|
| 2010.3.22-25 | 香港贸发局香港国际影视展<br>HKTDC Hong Kong International Film & TV Market<br>(FILMART) | 香港会议展览中心<br>Hong Kong Convention & Exhibition Centre | 香港贸易发展局<br>Hong Kong Trade Development Council<br>☎ 852-1830 668<br>🖷 852-2824 0249<br>✉ hktdc@hktdc.org<br>www.hktdc.com/hktradefairs<br>详细介绍见☆9<br>Detail See ☆9 |
| 2010.3.28-30 | International Symposium on Spine and Paravertebral Sonography for Anaesthesia and Pain Medicine 2010 | 威尔斯亲王医院<br>Prince of Wales Hospital | 香港中文大学<br>The Chinese University of Hong Kong<br>☎ 852-2632 1311<br>🖷 852-2637 8010<br>✉ issps2010@gmail.com<br>www.usgraweb.hk/issps2010 |
| 2010.3.29-31 | 亚太区皮革展-原料及制造技术展<br>APLF-Materials, Manufacturing and Techonology | 香港会议展览中心<br>Hong Kong Convention & Exhibition Centre | 亚太区皮革展有限公司<br>APLF Ltd<br>☎ 852-2827 6211<br>🖷 852-3749 7310<br>✉ sales@aplf.com<br>www.aplf.com |
| 2010.3.29-31 | 时尚汇集（三月展）<br>Fashion Access | 香港会议展览中心<br>Hong Kong Convention and Exhibition Centre | 亚太区皮革展有限公司<br>Asia Pacific Leather Fair Ltd<br>☎ 852-2827 6211<br>🖷 852-3749 7346<br>✉ sales@aplf.com<br>www.fashionaccess.aplf.com |
| 2010.3.29-31 | 国际服装业高峰论坛<br>Prime Source Forum Hong Kong | 香港会议展览中心<br>Hong Kong Convention and Exhibition Centre | 亚太区皮革展有限公司<br>Asia Pacific Leather Fair Ltd<br>☎ 852-2827 6211<br>🖷 852-3749 7831<br>✉ info@primesourceforum.com<br>www.primesourceforum.com |
| 2010.3.30-31 | 香港国际时尚内衣展<br>Hong Kong Mode Lingerie | 香港会议展览中心<br>Hong Kong Convention and Exhibition Centre | EUROVET ASIA LTD<br>☎ 852-2815 0667<br>🖷 852-2815 0691<br>✉ hongkong@la-federation.com<br>www.eurovet.fr |
| 2010.4.2-4 | 第五届香港国际宠物用品展暨水族博览<br>5th Hong Kong International Pet Accessory & Aqua Expo | 香港国际展贸中心<br>Hong Kong Intl Trade & Exhibition Centre (Kowloon Bay) | 讯通展览公司<br>Paper Communication Exhibition Services<br>☎ 852-2763 9011<br>🖷 852-2341 0379<br>✉ info@paper-com.com.hk<br>www.paper-com.com.hk |
| 2010.4.7-10 | New Frontiers: CAADRIA2010 | 香港中文大学<br>The Chinese University of Hong Kong | 香港中文大学<br>The Chinese University of Hong Kong<br>☎ 852-2609 6593<br>🖷 852-2603 5267<br>✉ i@caadria2010.org<br>www.caadria2010.org |

| 日期<br>Date | 展览会议<br>Event | 地点<br>Venue | 主办<br>Organizer |
|---|---|---|---|
| 2010.4.12-15 | 环球资源安防产品采购交易会<br>China Souring Fair-Security Products | 亚洲国际博览馆<br>AsiaWorld-Expo | 环球资源<br>Global Sources Exhibitions<br>☎ 852-2814 5605<br>🖷 852-2580 7988<br>✉ Efu@globalsources.com<br>www.chinasourcingfair.com |
| 2010.4.12-15 | 环球资电子产品及零件采购交易会<br>China Souring Fair-Electronics & Components | 亚洲国际博览馆<br>AsiaWorld-Expo | 环球资源<br>Global Sources Exhibitions<br>☎ 852-8199 7308<br>🖷 852-8199 7628<br>✉ visit@chinasourcingfair.com<br>www.chinasourcingfair.com |
| 2010.4.13-16 | 香港贸发局香港国际春季灯饰展<br>HKTDC Hong Kong International Lighting Fair (Spring Edition) | 香港会议展览中心<br>Hong Kong Convention & Exhibition Centre | 香港贸易发展局<br>Hong Kong Trade Development Council<br>☎ 852-1830 668<br>🖷 852-2824 0249<br>✉ exhibitions@hktdc.org<br>www.hktdc.com/hktradefairs<br>详细介绍见☆13<br>Detail See ☆13 |
| 2010.4.13-16 | 香港贸发局香港春季电子产品展<br>HKTDC Hong Kong Electronics Fair (Spring Edition) | 香港会议展览中心<br>Hong Kong Convention & Exhibition Centre | 香港贸易发展局<br>Hong Kong Trade Development Council<br>☎ 852-1830 668<br>🖷 852-2824 0249<br>✉ exhibitions@hktdc.org<br>www.hktdc.com/hktradefairs<br>详细介绍见☆11<br>Detail See ☆11 |
| 2010.4.13-16 | 香港贸发局国际资讯科技博览<br>HKTDC International ICT Expo | 香港会议展览中心<br>Hong Kong Convention & Exhibition Centre | 香港贸易发展局<br>Hong Kong Trade Development Council<br>☎ 852-1830 668<br>🖷 852-2824 0249<br>✉ exhibitions@hktdc.org<br>www.hktdc.com/hktradefairs<br>详细介绍见☆12<br>Detail See ☆12 |
| 2010.4.20-23 | 香港贸发局香港国际家用纺织品展<br>HKTDC Hong Kong International Home Textiles Fair | 香港会议展览中心<br>Hong Kong Convention & Exhibition Centre | 香港贸易发展局<br>Hong Kong Trade Development Council<br>☎ 852-1830 668<br>🖷 852-2824 0249<br>✉ exhibitions@hktdc.org<br>www.hktdc.com/hktradefairs<br>详细介绍见☆15<br>Detail See ☆15 |
| 2010.4.20-23 | 香港贸发局香港家庭用品展<br>HKTDC Hong Kong Houseware Fair | 香港会议展览中心<br>Hong Kong Convention & Exhibition Centre | 香港贸易发展局<br>Hong Kong Trade Development Council<br>☎ 852-1830 668<br>🖷 852-2824 0249<br>✉ exhibitions@hktdc.org<br>www.hktdc.com/hktradefairs<br>详细介绍见☆14<br>Detail See ☆14 |

| 日期<br>Date | 展览会议<br>Event | 地点<br>Venue | 主办<br>Organizer |
|---|---|---|---|
| 2010.4.20-23 | 环球资源印度家居用品采购交易会<br>The Chinese University of Hong Kong | 亚洲国际博览馆<br>AsiaWorld-Expo | 环球资源<br>Global Sources Exhibitions<br>☎ 852-2814 5605<br>🖷 852-2580 7988<br>✉ visit@chinasourcingfair.com<br>http://tradeshow.globalsources.com |
| 2010.4.20-23 | 环球资礼品及赠品采购交易会<br>China Souring Fair-Gifts & Premiums | 亚洲国际博览馆<br>AsiaWorld-Expo | 环球资源<br>Global Sources Exhibitions<br>☎ 852-8199 7308<br>🖷 852-8199 7628<br>✉ visit@chinasourcingfair.com<br>www.chinasourcingfair.com |
| 2010.4.20-23 | 环球资源流行服饰配件采购交易会<br>China Souring Fair-Fashion Accessories | 亚洲国际博览馆<br>AsiaWorld-Expo | 环球资源<br>Global Sources Exhibitions<br>☎ 852-2814 5605<br>🖷 852-2580 7988<br>✉ Efu@globalsources.com<br>www.chinasourcingfair.com |
| 2010.4.20-23 | 环球资源家居用品采购交易会<br>China Souring Fair-Home Products | 亚洲国际博览馆<br>AsiaWorld-Expo | 环球资源<br>Global Sources Exhibitions<br>☎ 852-2814 5605<br>🖷 852-2580 7988<br>✉ Efu@globalsources.com<br>www.chinasourcingfair.com |
| 2010.4.20-23 | 环球资源内衣及泳衣采购交易会<br>China Souring Fair-Underwear & Swimwear | 亚洲国际博览馆<br>AsiaWorld-Expo | 环球资源<br>Global Sources Exhibitions<br>☎ 852-2814 5605<br>🖷 852-2580 7988<br>✉ Efu@globalsources.com<br>www.chinasourcingfair.com |
| 2010.4.20-23 | 环球资源婴儿及儿童产品采购交易会<br>China Souring Fair-Baby & Children's Products | 亚洲国际博览馆<br>AsiaWorld-Expo | 环球资源<br>Global Sources Exhibitions<br>☎ 852-2814 5605<br>🖷 852-2580 7988<br>✉ Efu@globalsources.com<br>www.chinasourcingfair.com |
| 2010.4.27-30 | 香港贸发局香港礼品及赠品展<br>HKTDC Hong Kong Gifts & Premium Fair | 香港会议展览中心<br>Hong Kong Convention & Exhibition Centre | 香港贸易发展局<br>Hong Kong Trade Development Council<br>☎ 852-1830 668<br>🖷 852-2824 0249<br>✉ exhibitions@hktdc.org<br>www.hktdc.com/hktradefairs<br>详细介绍见☆16<br>Detail See ☆16 |
| 2010.4.27-30 | 香港国际印刷及包装展<br>Hong Kong International Printing & Packaging Fair | 亚洲国际博览馆<br>AsiaWorld-Expo | 香港贸易发展局<br>Hong Kong Trade Development Council<br>☎ 852-1830 668<br>🖷 852-2824 0249<br>✉ exhibitions@hktdc.org<br>www.hktdc.com/hktradefairs<br>详细介绍见☆17<br>Detail See ☆17 |

| 日期<br>Date | 展览会议<br>Event | 地点<br>Venue | 主办<br>Organizer |
|---|---|---|---|
| 2010.5.12-16 | 香港国际艺术展2010<br>Art HK 10 - Hong Kong International Art Fair | 香港会议展览中心<br>Hong Kong Convention and Exhibition Centre | Asian Art Fairs Ltd<br>☎ 852-2918 8793<br>🖷 852-2918 8793<br>✉ info@hongkongartfair.com<br>www.hongkongartfair.com |
| 2010.5.13-15 | 思源博览2010<br>Asia Senior Fair 2010 | 香港会议展览中心<br>Hong Kong Convention and Exhibition Centre | 纵延展业<br>Vertical Expo Services Co Ltd<br>☎ 852-2528 0062<br>🖷 852-2528 0072<br>✉ asf@verticalexpo.com<br>www.verticalexpo.com |
| 2010.5.13-15 | 2010 亚洲殡仪博览<br>The Chinese University of Hong Kong | 香港会议展览中心<br>Hong Kong Convention and Exhibition Centre | 纵延展业<br>Vertical Expo Services Co Ltd<br>☎ 852-2528 0062<br>🖷 852-2528 0072<br>✉ afe@verticalexpo.com<br>www.asiafuneralexpo.com |
| 2010.5.14-17 | 亚洲瑜伽研讨会<br>Evolution Asia Yoga Conference | 香港会议展览中心<br>Hong Kong Convention and Exhibition Centre | Asia Yoga Conference Ltd<br>☎ 852-3691 3981<br>🖷 852-3520 4999<br>✉ info@asiayogaconference.com<br>www.asiayogaconference.com |
| 2010.5.15-17 | 第9届育儿天地博览<br>The 9th Parents' Journal Baby, Children & Family Expo | 香港会议展览中心<br>Hong Kong Convention and Exhibition Centre | 百家宝集团<br>Peegaboo Group<br>☎ 852-3741 1720<br>🖷 852-3741 1725<br>✉ info@peegaboo.com<br>www.peegaboo.com |
| 2010.5.20-22 | USANA亚太年会2010<br>USANA Asia Pacific Convention 2010 | 香港会议展览中心<br>Hong Kong Convention and Exhibition Centre | USANA Health Sciences<br>☎ 852-2162 1818<br>🖷 852-2162 1828 |
| 2010.5.21-23 | 2010第五届亚洲国际艺术古董展<br>5th Asia International Arts & Antiques Fair 2010 | 亚洲国际博览馆<br>AsiaWorld-Expo | 讯通展览公司(香港)<br>Paper Communication Exhibition Services<br>☎ 852-2950 1999<br>🖷 852-2341 0379<br>✉ shirley@paper-com.com.hk<br>www.aiaa.com.hk |
| 2010.5.25-27 | 国际葡萄酒及烈酒商贸展<br>Vinexpo Asia-Pacific 2010 | 香港会议展览中心<br>Hong Kong Convention and Exhibition Centre | Vinexpo Overseas<br>☎ +33 5 56 56 00 22<br>🖷 +33 5 56 56 00 00<br>✉ info@vinexpo.com<br>http://blog.vinexpo.com |
| 2010.5.27-30 | 香港国际艺术展10<br>ART HK 10 | 香港会议展览中心<br>Hong Kong Convention and Exhibition Centre | Asian Art Fairs Ltd<br>☎ 852-2918 8793<br>🖷 852-2918 8794<br>✉ enquiries@hongkongartfair.com<br>www.hongkongartfair.com |

| 日期<br>Date | 展览会议<br>Event | 地点<br>Venue | 主办<br>Organizer |
|---|---|---|---|
| 2010.5.28-30 | 拥抱健康生活博览2010<br>Health Expo 2010 | 香港会议展览中心<br>Hong Kong Convention and Exhibition Centre | Metro Finance<br>☎ 852-3698 8848<br>🖷 852-2123 9868<br>✉ lettym@metroradio.com.hk |
| 2010.5.30-6.1 | 16th International Sustainable Development Research Conference 2010 | 香港会议展览中心<br>Hong Kong Convention and Exhibition Centre | Kadoorie Institute, The University of Hong Kong<br>☎ 852-2219 4768<br>🖷 852-2857 2521<br>✉ sdconf10@hku.hk<br>www.kadinst.hku.hk |
| 2010.6.2-4 | 第十二届长者及伤残人士交通输服务国际大会<br>12th International Conference on Mobility and Transport for Elderly and Disabled Persons (TRANSED 2010) | 香港会议展览中心<br>Hong Kong Convention and Exhibition Centre | 香港复康会<br>The Hong Kong Society for Rehabilitation<br>☎ 852-2817 6277<br>🖷 852-2855 1947<br>✉ secretariat@transevd2010.hk<br>www.transed2010.hk |
| 2010.6.2-4 | 2010第三届亚洲(香港)国际建材装饰及照明展<br>第十四届亚洲国际电气电子工程及节能科技展览会<br>Asian Elenex 2010<br>Asian Building Technologies 2010<br>Asian Building Interiors 2010<br>Asian Securitex | 香港会议展览中心<br>Hong Kong Convention and Exhibition Centre | 香港展览服务有限公司<br>Hong Kong Exhibition Services Ltd<br>☎ 852-2804 1500<br>🖷 852-2528 3103<br>✉ exhibit@hkesallworld.com<br>www.asianelenex.com |
| 2010.6.5-6 | SMART Investment and International Property Expo 2010 | 香港会议展览中心<br>Hong Kong Convention and Exhibition Centre | Corporate Consumer Communications Ltd<br>☎ 852-2576 8008<br>🖷 852-2945 6424<br>✉ mwong@4-ltd.com<br>http://hk.wrs.yahoo.com |
| 2010.6.10-13 | 第五届商务及会奖旅游展<br>The 5th M.I.C.E. Business & Incentive Travel Expo | 香港会议展览中心<br>Hong Kong Convention and Exhibition Centre | 汇众展览服务有限公司<br>TKS Exhibition Services Ltd<br>☎ 852-3155 0600<br>🖷 852-3520 1500<br>✉ maggie.chiu@tkshk.com<br>www.itehkmice.com |
| 2010.6.10-13 | 第二十四届香港国际旅游展<br>ITE 2010 - The 24th International Travel Expo Hong Kong | 香港会议展览中心<br>Hong Kong Convention and Exhibition Centre | 汇众展览服务有限公司<br>TKS Exhibition Services Ltd<br>☎ 852-3155 0600<br>🖷 852-3520 1500<br>✉ maggie.chiu@tkshk.com<br>www.itehk.com |
| 2010.6.10-14 | 2010国际联合会议社会工作及社会发展的愿景与蓝图<br>The 2010 Joint World Conference on Social Work and Social Development: The Agenda | 香港会议展览中心<br>Hong Kong Convention and Exhibition Centre | The Hong Kong Council of Social Service<br>☎ 852-2864 2997<br>🖷 852-2528 4230<br>✉ info@swsd2010.org<br>www.swsd2010.org |

| 日期<br>Date | 展览会议<br>Event | 地点<br>Venue | 主办<br>Organizer |
|---|---|---|---|
| 2010.6.16-19 | Congress of the Int'l Liver Transplantation Soc - ILTS | 香港会议展览中心<br>Hong Kong Convention and Exhibition Centre | International Liver Transplantation Society |
| 2010.6.18-20 | 第一届香港国际牙科展暨研讨会<br>1st Hong Kong International Dental Expo And Symposium | 香港会议展览中心<br>Hong Kong Convention and Exhibition Centre | CMPMedica Pacific Ltd<br>☎ 852-2116 4340<br>🖷 852-2559 6910<br>✉ info@hkideas.org<br>www.hkideas.org |
| 2010.6.22-24 | 亚洲零售博览会<br>Retail Asia Expo 2010 | 香港会议展览中心<br>Hong Kong Convention and Exhibition Centre | Asia Business Events Ltd<br>☎ 852-3105 3970<br>🖷 852-3105 3974<br>✉ stuart@retailasiaexpo.com<br>www.retailasiaexpo.com |
| 2010.6.24-27 | 六月香港珠宝首饰展览会<br>Hong Kong Jewellery & Gems Fair | 香港会议展览中心<br>Hong Kong Convention and Exhibition Centre | 亚洲博闻有限公司<br>UMB Asia Ltd<br>☎ 852-2516 1677, 2516 2158<br>🖷 852-3749 7542<br>✉ salesjwf@cmpasia.com<br>www.jewellerynetasia.com |
| 2010.6.24-27 | 六月亚洲时尚首饰及配饰展<br>Asia' s Fashion Jewellery & Accessories Fair – June | 亚洲国际博览馆<br>AsiaWorld-Expo | 亚洲博闻有限公司<br>UMB Asia Ltd<br>☎ 852-2585 6179, 2516 2158<br>🖷 852-3749 7542<br>✉ salesafj@cmpasia.com<br>www.asiafja.com |
| 2010.7.5-8 | 香港贸发局香港时装节春夏系列<br>HKTDC Hong Kong Fashion Week for Spring/Summer | 香港会议展览中心<br>Hong Kong Convention & Exhibition Centre | 香港贸易发展局<br>Hong Kong Trade Development Council<br>☎ 852-1830 668<br>🖷 852-2824 0249<br>✉ exhibitions@hktdc.org<br>www.hktdc.com/hktradefairs<br>详细介绍见☆19<br>Detail See ☆19 |
| 2010.7.5-8 | 香港贸发局香港夏季礼品、家庭用品及玩具展<br>HKTDC Summer Sourcing Show for Gifts, Houseware & Toys | 香港会议展览中心<br>Hong Kong Convention & Exhibition Centre | 香港贸易发展局<br>Hong Kong Trade Development Council<br>☎ 852-1830 668<br>🖷 852-2824 0249<br>✉ exhibitions@hktdc.org<br>www.hktdc.com/hktradefairs<br>详细介绍见☆18<br>Detail See ☆18 |
| 2010.7.10-11 | 第8届香港国际教育展<br>The 8th Hong Kong International Education Expo | 香港会议展览中心<br>Hong Kong Convention and Exhibition Centre | 立新国际展览有限公司<br>Neway International Trade Faris Limited<br>☎ 852-2561 5566<br>🖷 852-2811 9156<br>✉ info@newayfairs.com<br>www.newayfairs.com |

| 日期<br>Date | 展览会议<br>Event | 地点<br>Venue | 主办<br>Organizer |
|---|---|---|---|
| 2010.7.11-15 | Congress of the Asia Pacific League of Associations for Rheumatology | 香港会议展览中心<br>Hong Kong Convention and Exhibition Centre | 香港风湿病学学会<br>HK Society of Rheumatology<br>☎ 852-2882 3108<br>🖷 852-2882 6931<br>✉ takhinc@alumni.cuhk.edu.hk<br>www.ilar.org/regionalleagues/aplar.htm |
| 2010.7.16-18 | 香港婚纱、婚宴暨结婚贺礼博览会2010<br>Hong Kong Wedding, Banquet & Wedding Gifts Expo 2010 | 香港会议展览中心<br>Hong Kong Convention and Exhibition Centre | 隽杰国际展览有限公司<br>Audace International Fairs Limited<br>☎ 852-2367 8385<br>🖷 852-2367 8488<br>✉ info@expo.com.hk<br>www.expo.com.hk |
| 2010.7.16-18 | International Liver Transplant Society 16th Annual International Congress | 香港会议展览中心<br>Hong Kong Convention and Exhibition Centre | International Liver Transplantation Society (ILTS)<br>☎ +1-856 4390500 转ext.4428<br>🖷 +1-856 4390525<br>✉ sfagan@ahint.com<br>www.ilts.org |
| 2010.7.18-21 | The 7th Conference of the International Test Commission | 香港中文大学<br>The Chinese University of Hong Kong | International Test Commission<br>www.itc2010hk.com |
| 2010.7.21-27 | 香港贸发局香港书展<br>HKTDC Hong Kong Book Fair | 香港会议展览中心<br>Hong Kong Convention & Exhibition Centre | 香港贸易发展局<br>Hong Kong Trade Development Council<br>☎ 852-1830 668<br>🖷 852-2824 0249<br>✉ exhibitions@hktdc.org<br>www.hktdc.com/hktradefairs<br>详细介绍见☆20<br>Detail See ☆20 |
| 2010.7.30-8.1 | 第五届香港国际宠物用品展<br>6th Hong Kong International Pet & Accessory Expo | 亚洲国际博览馆<br>AsiaWorld-Expo | 讯通展览公司<br>Paper Communication Exhibition Services<br>☎ 852-2763 9011<br>🖷 852-2341 0379<br>✉ petexpo@paper-com.com.hk<br>www.petexpo.hk |
| 2010.7.30-8.1 | 2010香港国际水族博览及香港屋企展<br>Hong Kong International Aqua & Family Expo 2010 | 亚洲国际博览馆<br>AsiaWorld-Expo | 讯通展览公司<br>Paper Communication Exhibition Services<br>☎ 852-2763 9011<br>🖷 852-2341 0379<br>✉ petexpo@paper-com.com.hk<br>www.petexpo.hk |
| 2010.7.31-8.1 | 第九届香港国际教育展<br>The 9th Hong Kong International Education Expo | 香港会议展览中心<br>Hong Kong Convention and Exhibition Centre | 立新国际展览有限公司<br>Neway International Trade Faris Limited<br>☎ 852-2561 5566<br>🖷 852-2811 9156<br>✉ info@newayfairs.com<br>www.newayfairs.com |

| 日期 Date | 展览会议 Event | 地点 Venue | 主办 Organizer |
|---|---|---|---|
| 2010.8.6-8 | 2010香港高级视听展<br>2010 Hong Kong High-End Audio-Visual Show | 香港会议展览中心<br>Hong Kong Convention and Exhibition Centre | Audio Technique<br>☎ 852-28811252<br>🖷 852-28903999<br>✉ mag@audiotechnique.com |
| 2010.8.12-14 | 香港国际茶展<br>Hong Kong International Tea Fair<br>香港国际茶展<br>Hong Kong International Tea Fair | 香港会议展览中心<br>Hong Kong Convention & Exhibition Centre | 香港贸易发展局<br>Hong Kong Trade Development Council<br>☎ 852-1830 668<br>🖷 852-2824 0249<br>✉ exhibitions@hktdc.org<br>www.hktdc.com/hktradefairs<br>详细介绍见☆21<br>Detail See ☆21 |
| 2010.8.12-16 | 香港贸发局美食博览<br>HKTDC Food Expo | 香港会议展览中心<br>Hong Kong Convention & Exhibition Centre | 香港贸易发展局<br>Hong Kong Trade Development Council<br>☎ 852-1830 668<br>🖷 852-2824 0249<br>✉ exhibitions@hktdc.org<br>www.hktdc.com/hktradefairs<br>详细介绍见☆22<br>Detail See ☆22 |
| 2010.8.12-16 | 国际现代化中医药及健康产品展览会暨会议<br>International Conference & Exhibition of the Modernization of Chinese Medicine & Health | 香港会议展览中心<br>Hong Kong Convention & Exhibition Centre | 香港贸易发展局<br>Hong Kong Trade Development Council<br>☎ 852-1830 668<br>🖷 852-2824 0249<br>✉ exhibitions@hktdc.org<br>www.hktdc.com/hktradefairs<br>详细介绍见☆23<br>Detail See ☆23 |
| 2010.8.20-23 | 香港电脑通讯节2010<br>Hong Kong Computer & Communications Festival 2010 | 香港会议展览中心<br>Hong Kong Convention and Exhibition Centre | The Chamber of HK Computer Industry<br>☎ 852-2785 8867<br>🖷 852-3526 0898<br>✉ enquiry@chkci.org.hk<br>www.chkci.org.hk |
| 2010.8.26-28 | 亚洲天然产品博览<br>Natural Products Expo Asia 201 | 香港会议展览中心<br>Hong Kong Convention and Exhibition Centre | Penton Media Asia Limited<br>☎ 852-2975 9051<br>🖷 852-2857 6144<br>✉ info@penton.com<br>www.naturalproductsasia.com |
| 2010.8.27-29 | 第60届婚纱、婚宴及结婚服务博览<br>60th Fall/Winter Wedding Service & Banquet Expo | 香港会议展览中心<br>Hong Kong Convention and Exhibition Centre | 香港亚洲展览（集团）有限公司<br>Hongkong-Asia Exhibition (Holdings) Ltd<br>☎ 852-2591 9823<br>🖷 852-2573 3311<br>✉ hkexhi@hka.com.hk<br>www.iweddingclub.com |
| 2010.9.3-7 | The Options for the Control of Influenza VII Conference 2010 | 香港会议展览中心<br>Hong Kong Convention and Exhibition Centre | 香港大学<br>Options for the Control of Influneza VII<br>☎ 852-2819 9828<br>🖷 852-2819 9827<br>✉ gjsmith@hku.hk<br>www.controlinfluenza.com |

| 日期<br>Date | 展览会议<br>Event | 地点<br>Venue | 主办<br>Organizer |
|---|---|---|---|
| 2010.9.6-10 | 香港贸发局香港钟表展<br>HKTDC Hong Kong Watch & Clock Fair | 香港会议展览中心<br>Hong Kong Convention & Exhibition Centre | 香港贸易发展局<br>Hong Kong Trade Development Council<br>☎ 852-1830 668<br>🖷 852-2824 0249<br>✉ exhibitions@hktdc.org<br>www.hktdc.com/hktradefairs<br>详细介绍见☆24<br>Detail See ☆24 |
| 2010.9.7-9 | 亚洲海鲜展<br>Asian Seafood Expo | 香港会议展览中心<br>Hong Kong Convention and Exhibition Centre | Diversified Events Hong Kong<br>☎ 852-3105 3975<br>🖷 852-3105 3974<br>✉ xiao@restaurantandbarhk.com<br>http://seafoodsource.com |
| 2010.9.7-9 | 国际佳肴、餐饮、酒廊设备展览会<br>Restaurant & Bar 2010 | 香港会议展览中心<br>Hong Kong Convention and Exhibition Centre | Asia Business Events Ltd<br>☎ 852-3105 3970<br>🖷 852-3105 3974<br>✉ stuart@restaurantandbarhk.com<br>www.restaurantandbarhk.com/en/index.html |
| 2010.9.8-10 | 2010年亚洲国际水果蔬菜展<br>Asia Fruit Logistica / Asiafruit Congress 2010 | 香港会议展览中心<br>Hong Kong Convention and Exhibition Centre | Gloabl Produce Event GmbH<br>☎ 6636700608<br>🖷 50 30 30387060<br>✉ Baramirattanachai@messe-berlin.de<br>www.mintel.webbler.co.uk |
| 2010.9.20-23 | 九月亚洲时尚首饰及配饰展<br>Asia' s Fashion Jewellery & Accessories Fair – September | 亚洲国际博览馆<br>AsiaWorld-Expo | 亚洲博闻有限公司<br>UMB Asia Ltd<br>☎ 852-2585 6179, 2516 2158<br>🖷 852-3749 7542<br>✉ salesafj@cmpasia.com<br>www.asiafja.com |
| 2010.9.20-23 | 九月香港珠宝首饰展览会<br>September Hong Kong Jewellery & Gems Fair | 亚洲国际博览馆<br>AsiaWorld-Expo | 亚洲博闻有限公司<br>UMB Asia Ltd<br>☎ 852-2516 1677, 25162158<br>🖷 852-3749 7542<br>✉ salesjwf@cmpasia.com<br>www.jewellerynetasia.com |
| 2010.9.20-23 | 九月香港珠宝首饰展览会<br>September Hong Kong Jewellery & Gems Fair | 香港会议展览中心<br>Hong Kong Convention and Exhibition Centre | 亚洲博闻有限公司<br>UMB Asia Ltd<br>☎ 852-2516 1677, 25162158<br>🖷 852-3749 7542<br>✉ salesjwf@cmpasia.com<br>www.jewellerynetasia.com |
| 2010.9.26-29 | 中外货代物流企业洽谈会 | 亚洲国际博览馆<br>AsiaWorld-Expo | Intuitive Logistic Resources Co. Ltd.<br>☎ 662 726 9060<br>🖷 662 726 9070<br>✉ douglas@intuitivelogisticresources.com<br>www.worldcargoconnections.com |

| 日期<br>Date | 展览会议<br>Event | 地点<br>Venue | 主办<br>Organizer |
|---|---|---|---|
| 2010.9.26-29 | IEEE International Conference on Image Processing (ICIP) 2010 | 香港会议展览中心<br>Hong Kong Convention and Exhibition Centre | IEEE Hong Kong Chapter of Signal Processing<br>☎ 852-2766 6213<br>🖷 852-2362 8439<br>✉ enylchan@polyu.edu.hk<br>www.signalprocessingsociety.org |
| 2010.9.26-30 | 15th Conference of International Society for Respiratory Protection (ISRP) | 香港朗廷酒店<br>Smartworx Studios | ☎ +61 299774073<br>✉ dana@isrp.com<br>www.isrp.com/hongkong |
| 2010.9.28-30 | 时尚汇集秋季展<br>Fashion Access | 香港会议展览中心<br>Hong Kong Convention and Exhibition Centre | 亚太区皮革展有限公司<br>Asia Pacific Leather Fair Ltd<br>☎ 852-2827 6211<br>🖷 852-3749 7346<br>✉ sales@aplf.com<br>www.fashionaccess.aplf.com |
| 2010.10 - | 香港国际建筑装饰材料及五金展<br>Hong Kong International Building and Decoration Materials & Hardware Fair | 亚洲国际博览馆<br>AsiaWorld-Expo | 香港贸易发展局<br>Hong Kong Trade Development Council<br>☎ 852-1830 668<br>🖷 852-2824 0249<br>✉ exhibitions@hktdc.org<br>www.hktdc.com/hktradefairs<br>详细介绍见☆29<br>Detail See ☆29 |
| 2010.10 - | 亚洲运动用品展<br>Sports Source Asia | 亚洲国际博览馆<br>AsiaWorld-Expo | 香港贸易发展局<br>Hong Kong Trade Development Council<br>☎ 852-1830 668<br>🖷 852-2824 0249<br>✉ exhibitions@hktdc.org<br>www.hktdc.com/hktradefairs<br>详细介绍见☆28<br>Detail See ☆28 |
| 2010.10.6-8 | 香港国际成衣及时装材料展 2010<br>Interstoff Asia Essential - Autumn 2010 | 香港会议展览中心<br>Hong Kong Convention and Exhibition Centre | 法兰克福展览(香港)有限公司<br>Messe Frankfurt (HK) Ltd<br>☎ 852-2238 9917<br>🖷 852-2598 8771<br>✉ cindy.chee@hongkong.messefrankfurt.com |
| 2010.10.12-15 | 环球资源电子产品及零件采购交易会<br>China Sourcing Fair - Security Products (Fall 2010) | 亚洲国际博览馆<br>AsiaWorld-Expo | 环球资源<br>Global Sources Exhibitions<br>☎ 852-2814 5605<br>🖷 852-2580 7988<br>✉ Efu@globalsources.com<br>www.chinasourcingfair.com |
| 2010.10.12-15 | 环球资源安防产品采购交易会<br>China Sourcing Fair - Security Products (Fall 2010) | 亚洲国际博览馆<br>AsiaWorld-Expo | 环球资源<br>Global Sources Exhibitions<br>☎ 852-2814 5605<br>🖷 852-2580 7988<br>✉ Efu@globalsources.com |

| 日期<br>Date | 展览会议<br>Event | 地点<br>Venue | 主办<br>Organizer |
|---|---|---|---|
| 2010.10.13-16 | 国际电子组件及生产技术展<br>electronicAsia | 香港会议展览中心<br>Hong Kong Convention & Exhibition Centre | 香港贸易发展局<br>Hong Kong Trade Development Council<br>☎ 852-1830 668<br>🖷 852-2824 0249<br>✉ exhibitions@hktdc.org<br>www.hktdc.com/hktradefairs<br>详细介绍见☆26<br>Detail See ☆26 |
| 2010.10.13-16 | 香港贸发局香港秋季电子产品展<br>HKTDC Hong Kong Electronics Fair (Autumn Edition) | 香港会议展览中心<br>Hong Kong Convention & Exhibition Centre | 香港贸易发展局<br>Hong Kong Trade Development Council<br>☎ 852-1830 668<br>🖷 852-2824 0249<br>✉ exhibitions@hktdc.org<br>www.hktdc.com/hktradefairs<br>详细介绍见☆25<br>Detail See ☆25 |
| 2010.10.20-23 | 环球资源婴儿及儿童产品采购交易会<br>China Sourcing Fair - Baby & Children's Products (Fall 2010) | 亚洲国际博览馆<br>AsiaWorld-Expo | 环球资源<br>Global Sources Exhibitions<br>☎ 852-2814 5605<br>🖷 852-2580 7988<br>✉ efu@globalsources.com<br>www.chinasourcingfair.com |
| 2010.10.20-23 | 环球资源印度家居用品采购交易会<br>India Sourcing Fair - Home Products (Fall 2010) | 亚洲国际博览馆<br>AsiaWorld-Expo | 环球资源<br>Global Sources Exhibitions<br>☎ 852-2814 5605<br>🖷 852-2580 7988<br>✉ visit@chinasourcingfair.com<br>www.india-sourcingfair.com |
| 2010.10.20-23 | 环球资源流行服饰配件采购交易会<br>China Sourcing Fair - Fashion Accessories (Fall 2010) | 亚洲国际博览馆<br>AsiaWorld-Expo | 环球资源<br>Global Sources Exhibitions<br>☎ 852-2814 5605<br>🖷 852-2580 7988<br>✉ Efu@globalsources.com<br>www.chinasourcingfair.com |
| 2010.10.20-23 | 环球资源内衣及泳衣采购交易会<br>China Sourcing Fair - Underwear & Swimwear (Fall 2010) | 亚洲国际博览馆<br>AsiaWorld-Expo | 环球资源<br>Global Sources Exhibitions<br>☎ 852-2814 5605<br>🖷 852-2580 7988<br>✉ visit@chinasourcingfair.com<br>www.chinasourcingfair.com |
| 2010.10.20-23 | 环球资源礼品及赠品采购交易会<br>China Sourcing Fair - Gifts & Premiums (Fall 2010) | 亚洲国际博览馆<br>AsiaWorld-Expo | 环球资源<br>Global Sources Exhibitions<br>☎ 852-2814 5605<br>🖷 852-2580 7988<br>✉ efu@globalsources.com<br>www.chinasoucringfair.com |
| 2010.10.20-23 | 环球资源家居用品交易会<br>China Sourcing Fair - Home Products (Fall 2010) | 亚洲国际博览馆<br>AsiaWorld-Expo | 环球资源<br>Global Sources Exhibitions<br>☎ 852-2814 5605<br>🖷 852-2580 7988<br>✉ efu@globalsources.com<br>www.chinasoucringfair.com |

| 日期<br>Date | 展览会议<br>Event | 地点<br>Venue | 主办<br>Organizer |
|---|---|---|---|
| 2010.10.20-23 | 亚洲展览盛世第一部分<br>Mega Show Part 1 | 香港会议展览中心<br>Hong Kong Convention and Exhibition Centre | Group Idea International Limited<br>☎ 852-2311 8216<br>🖷 852-2311 6629<br>✉ cs@kenfair.com |
| 2010.10.27-30 | 香港国际照明科技展 2010<br>LED + Light Tech Show-HK 2010 | 亚洲国际博览馆<br>AsiaWorld-Expo | 捷霖国际企业有限公司<br>D&A International Corp<br>☎ 886 2 2649 4888<br>🖷 886 2 2649 4999<br>✉ da.ico@msa.hinet.net / da@data-asia.com<br>www.ledlightfair.com |
| 2010.10.27-30 | 香港贸发局香港国际秋季灯饰展<br>HKTDC Hong Kong International Lighting Fair (Autumn Edition) | 香港会议展览中心<br>Hong Kong Convention & Exhibition Centre | 香港贸易发展局<br>Hong Kong Trade Development Council<br>☎ 852-1830 668<br>🖷 852-2824 0249<br>✉ exhibitions@hktdc.org<br>www.hktdc.com/hktradefairs<br>详细介绍见☆27<br>Detail See ☆27 |
| 2010.10.28-30 | 亚洲展览盛世第二部分:礼品、装璜摆设及家居用品<br>Mega Show Part 2 - Gifts, Decor & Home | 香港会议展览中心<br>Hong Kong Convention and Exhibition Centre | Group Idea International Limited<br>☎ 852-2311 8216<br>🖷 852-2311 6629<br>✉ cs@kenfair.com<br>www.kenfair.com |
| 2010.11 - | 香港贸发局香港国际医疗器材及用品展<br>HKTDC Hong Kong International Medical Devices and Supplies Fair | 香港会议展览中心<br>Hong Kong Convention & Exhibition Centre | 香港贸易发展局<br>Hong Kong Trade Development Council<br>☎ 852-1830 668<br>🖷 852-2824 0249<br>✉ exhibitions@hktdc.org<br>www.hktdc.com/hktradefairs<br>详细介绍见☆31<br>Detail See ☆31 |
| 2010.11.3-5 | 香港贸发局香港眼镜展<br>HKTDC Hong Kong Optical Fair | 香港会议展览中心<br>Hong Kong Convention & Exhibition Centre | 香港贸易发展局<br>Hong Kong Trade Development Council<br>☎ 852-1830 668<br>🖷 852-2824 0249<br>✉ exhibitions@hktdc.org<br>www.hktdc.com/hktradefairs<br>详细介绍见☆33<br>Detail See ☆33 |
| 2010.11.3-6 | 国际环保博览<br>Eco Expo Asia – International Trade Fair on Environmental Protection | 亚洲国际博览馆<br>AsiaWorld-Expo | 香港贸易发展局<br>Hong Kong Trade Development Council<br>☎ 852-1830 668<br>🖷 852-2824 0249<br>✉ exhibitions@hktdc.org<br>www.hktdc.com/hktradefairs<br>详细介绍见☆30<br>Detail See ☆30 |

| 日期<br>Date | 展览会议<br>Event | 地点<br>Venue | 主办<br>Organizer |
|---|---|---|---|
| 2010.11.4-6 | 香港贸发局香港国际美酒展<br>HKTDC Hong Kong International Wine & Spirits Fair | 香港会议展览中心<br>Hong Kong Convention & Exhibition Centre | 香港贸易发展局<br>Hong Kong Trade Development Council<br>☎ 852-1830 668<br>🖷 852-2824 0249<br>✉ exhibitions@hktdc.org<br>www.hktdc.com/hktradefairs<br>详细介绍见☆32<br>Detail See ☆32 |
| 2010.11.5-7 | 全球市长论坛<br>Global Mayars Forum | 亚洲国际博览馆<br>AsiaWorld-Expo | 国际市长交流中心<br>International Mayors Communication Centre<br>☎ 0755-8610 0515<br>🖷 0755-8610 0235<br>✉ jinlan@hk-imcc.com<br>✉ inquiry@hk-imcc.com<br>www.hk-imcc.com |
| 2010.11.5-7 | 香港婚纱及婚宴博览2010<br>Hong Kong Wedding Banquet Expo 2010 | 香港会议展览中心<br>Hong Kong Convention and Exhibition Centre | 隽杰国际展览有限公司<br>Audace International Fairs Limited<br>☎ 852-2367 8385<br>🖷 852-2367 8488<br>✉ info@expo.com.hk<br>www.expo.com.hk |
| 2010.11.10-12 | 亚洲香港"国际地产投资交易会"<br>MIPIM Asia: The World's Property Market in Asia Pacific | 香港会议展览中心<br>Hong Kong Convention & Exhibition Centre | 励展博览集团国际销售部<br>☎ 86-10-5933 9288<br>🖷 86-10-5933 9233<br>✉ ronald.wu@reedexpo.com.cn<br>www.reedexport.cn<br>详细介绍见☆34<br>Detail See ☆34 |
| 2010.11.10-12 | 亚太区美容展<br>Cosmoprof Asia | 香港会议展览中心<br>Hong Kong Convention and Exhibition Centre | 亚太区美容展有限公司<br>Cosmoprof Asia Ltd<br>☎ 852-2827 6211<br>🖷 852-3749 7345<br>✉ cosmasia@cmpasia.com<br>www.cosmoprof-asia.com |
| 2010.11.15-17 | 第6届公共交通国际联会亚太区大会暨国际公交财务融资会议<br>6th UITP Asia-Pacific Congress and UITP International Conference on Public Transport Financing | 亚洲国际博览馆<br>AsiaWorld-Expo | 公共交通国际联会<br>International Association of Public Transport<br>☎ 852- 2993 3254<br>www.uitp.org/events/2010/hongkong/en |
| 2010.11.16-18 | Railway Interiors Expo 2010 | 亚洲国际博览馆<br>AsiaWorld-Expo | UKIP Media & Events Ltd<br>☎ +44 (0) 1306 743744<br>✉ m.blackhurst@ukintpress.com<br>www.ukipme.com<br>www.railwayinteriors-expo.com |
| 2010.11.17-19 | 中国国际视听集成设备与技术展2010<br>InfoComm Asia 2010 | 香港会议展览中心<br>Hong Kong Convention and Exhibition Centre | InfoCommAsia Pte Ltd<br>☎ +65 6281 8607<br>🖷 +65 6725 8362<br>✉ rtan@infocommasia.org<br>www.infocomm-asia.com |

| 日期<br>Date | 展览会议<br>Event | 地点<br>Venue | 主办<br>Organizer |
|---|---|---|---|
| 2010.12.2-4 | 香港贸发局创新科技及设计博览<br>HKTDC Inno Design Tech Expo | 香港会议展览中心<br>Hong Kong Convention & Exhibition Centre | 香港贸易发展局<br>Hong Kong Trade Development Council<br>☎ 852-1830 668<br>🖷 852-2824 0249<br>✉ hktdc@hktdc.org<br>www.hktdc.com/hktradefairs<br>详细介绍见☆36<br>Detail See ☆36 |
| 2010.12.2-4 | 香港贸发局国际中小企博览<br>HKTDC World SME Expo | 香港会议展览中心<br>Hong Kong Convention & Exhibition Centre | 香港贸易发展局<br>Hong Kong Trade Development Council<br>☎ 852-1830 668<br>🖷 852-2824 0249<br>✉ exhibitions@hktdc.org<br>www.hktdc.com/hktradefairs<br>详细介绍见☆35<br>Detail See ☆35 |
| 2010.12.5-7 | Society of Construction Law International Construction Law Conference 2010: Local Problems – Global Perspectives | 香港会议展览中心<br>Hong Kong Convention and Exhibition Centre | Society of Construction Law Hong Kong<br>☎ 852-2525 2381<br>🖷 852-2524 2171<br>✉ admin@scl.hk |
| 2010.12.5-8 | 第七届引导教育会议"东西汇聚：发展与适应"<br>7th World Congress on Conductive Education "East meets West: Adaptation & Development" | 香港会议展览中心<br>Hong Kong Convention and Exhibition Centre | 香港耀能协会<br>SAHK<br>☎ 852-2527 8978<br>🖷 852-2866 3727<br>✉ ho@sahk1963.org.hk<br>www.ce-congress2010.org |
| 2010.12.10-12 | 第61届圣诞婚纱、婚宴及结婚服务博览<br>61st Christmas Wedding Service & Banquet Expo 2010 | 香港会议展览中心<br>Hong Kong Convention and Exhibition Centre | 香港亚洲展览（集团）有限公司<br>Hongkong-Asia Exhibition (Holdings) Ltd<br>☎ 852-2591 9823<br>🖷 852-2573 3311<br>✉ hkexhi@hka.com.hk<br>www.iweddingclub.com |
| 2011.1.31-2.2 | Overseas CBMC Korea Convention 2011 | 香港会议展览中心<br>Hong Kong Convention and Exhibition Centre | CBMC Korea (China)<br>☎ 852-6384 5555<br>🖷 852-2886 5002<br>✉ cmre001@gmail.com<br>cbmc.or.kr |
| 2011.2.25-28 | 2011 Hong Kong International Fur & Fashion Fair | 香港会议展览中心<br>Hong Kong Convention and Exhibition Centre | 香港毛皮业协会<br>Hong Kong Fur Federation<br>☎ 852-2367 4646<br>🖷 852-2367 4646<br>✉ fur@hkff.org |
| 2011.3 - | 国际管线管理及安全会议<br>The Second International Conference on Utility Management and Safety (ICUMAS) | （排版说明，此处地点空白） | Hong Kong Institute of Utility Specialists<br>☎ 852-2690 3899<br>🖷 852-2618 4500<br>✉ sicichong@uti.hk<br>www.hkius.org.hk |

| 日期<br>Date | 展览会议<br>Event | 地点<br>Venue | 主办<br>Organizer |
|---|---|---|---|
| 2011.5.11-14 | HOFEX 2011 - The 14th Asian International Exhibition of Food & Drink, Hotel, Restaurant & Foodservice Equipment, Supplies & Services | 香港会议展览中心<br>Hong Kong Convention and Exhibition Centre | 香港展览服务有限公司<br>☎ 852-2804 1500<br>🖷 852-2528 3103<br>✉ exhibit@hkesallworld.com<br>www.hofex.com |
| 2011.5.14-17 | Combined Scientific Meeting 2011 | 香港会议展览中心<br>Hong Kong Convention and Exhibition Centre | International Conference Consultants Ltd.<br>☎ 852-2559 9973<br>🖷 852-2547 9528<br>✉ cmai@icc.com.hk<br>www.csm2011.com |
| 2011.5.23-27 | 14th Asian Regional Conference on Soil Mechanics and Geotechnical Engineering | 香港理工大学<br>The Hong Kong Polytechnic University | 香港理工大学<br>The Hong Kong Polytechnic University<br>☎ 852-2766 6065<br>🖷 852-2334 6389<br>✉ cejhyin@polyu.edu.hk<br>www.cse.polyu.edu.hk |
| 2011.7.3-9 | 15th International Symposium on Toxicity Assessment | 香港城市大学<br>City University of Hong Kong | ☎ 852-2788 9710<br>🖷 852-2788 7406<br>✉ bhdwtau@cityu.edu.hk<br>123.203.212.73 |
| 2011.7.8-11 | 3rd Asia Pacific Region Conference of International Union Against Tuberculosis and Lung Disease | 香港会议展览中心<br>Hong Kong Convention and Exhibition Centre | 香港防痨心脏及胸病协会<br>Hong Kong Tuberculosis, Chest & Heart Diseases Association<br>☎ 852-2572 3466<br>🖷 852-2834 0711<br>✉ antitb@ha.org.hk<br>www.antitb.org.hk |
| 2011.7.10-14 | 国际电机工程会议 2011<br>International Conference on Electrical Engineering 2011 | | 香港工程师学会<br>The Hong Kong Institution of Engineers<br>☎ 852-2859 4446<br>🖷 852-2203 4133<br>✉ conf3@hkie.org.hk<br>www.icee-hk.org |
| 2011.7.25-29 | The School Nurses International 16th Biennial Conference 2011 | 香港理工大学<br>The Hong Kong Polytechnic University | 香港理工大学<br>The Hong Kong Polytechnic University<br>☎ 852-2766 4147<br>传真hspamela@inet.polyu.edu.hk |
| 2011.8.16-21 | The 17th International Congress of Phonetic Sciences | 香港会议展览中心<br>Hong Kong Convention and Exhibition Centre | 香港城市大学<br>City University of Hong Kong<br>☎ 852-2788 7594<br>🖷 852-2788 8706 |

☆1 ☎ 852-1830 668
🖷 852- 2824 0249
✉ hktdc@hktdc.org
www.hktdc.com/hktradefairs

HKTDC
Hong Kong International Licensing Show
香港國際專利授權展

## 香港贸发局香港国际专利授权展

日期： 2010/01/11-13
地点： 香港会议展览中心，香港
内容： 专利授权之品牌或设计、卡通人物、动漫及数码娱乐、艺术设计、专上学府品牌、知名企业品牌、娱乐名人、生活时尚及服饰、运动品牌、设计及市场推广服务、法律及专业顾问服务
上届规模 2008： 展出面积3,627平方米，参展商132家
主办： 香港贸易发展局
地址： 香港湾仔港湾道一号会展广场办公大楼38字楼

## HKTDC Hong Kong International Licensing Show

Date: 2010/01/11-13
Venue: Hong Kong Convention & Exhibition Centre, Hong Kong
Profile: Properties and brands for licensing, animation & digital entertainment, art & design, characters, collegiate, corporate brands, entertainment, fashion & lifestyle, sports, design & marketing services, legal & professional services
Statistics 2008: Gross Area 3,627sqm, Exhibitors 132
Organizer: Hong Kong Trade Development Council
Address: 38/F, Office Tower, Convention Plaza, 1 Harbour Road, Wan Chai, Hong Kong

☆2 ☎ 852-1830 668
🖷 852-2824 0249
✉ exhibitions@hktdc.org
www.hktdc.com/hktradefairs

HKTDC
**Hong Kong Toys & Games Fair**
**香港玩具展**

## 香港贸发局香港玩具展

日期： 2010/01/11-14
地点： 香港会议展览中心，香港
内容： 糖果玩具、益智玩具及游戏、电子及遥控玩具、嗜好玩具、魔术用具、户外及运动用品、纸品及玩具包装、派对用品、玩具零件及配件、软身玩具及洋娃娃、模型、机械玩具及动作玩偶、电子游戏
上届规模2009： 展出面积55,580平方米，参展商2,021家
主办： 香港贸易发展局
地址： 香港湾仔博览道1号香港会议展览中心博览商场13号展览事务部

## HKTDC Hong Kong Toys & Games Fair

Date: 2010/01/11-14
Venue: Hong Kong Convention & Exhibition Centre, Hong Kong
Profile: Candy toys, educational toys & games, electronic & remote control toys, hobby goods, magic items, outdoor & sporting items, paper products & toy packaging, party items, toy parts & accessories, soft toys & dolls, vehicles, mechanical toys & action figures, video games
Statistics 2009: Gross Area 55,580sqm, Exhibitors 2,021
Organizer: Hong Kong Trade Development Council
Address: Exhibitions Department, Unit 13, Expo Galleria, Hong Kong Convention and Exhibition Centre, 1 Expo Drive, Wan Chai, Hong Kong

☆3 ☎ 852-1830 668
🖷 852-28240249
✉ exhibitions@hktdc.org
www.hktdc.com/hktradefairs

HKTDC
Hong Kong Baby Products Fair
香港嬰兒用品展

## 香港贸发局香港婴儿用品展

日期： 2010/01/11-14
地点： 香港会议展览中心，香港
内容： 婴儿服及鞋、婴儿手推车、婴儿椅及相关产品、护肤及沐浴产品、育婴产品、寝具及家具、婴儿玩具及游戏用品、婴儿礼品及纪念品、孕妇用品
附注： 2010年首次举办
主办： 香港贸易发展局
地址： 香港湾仔博览道1号香港会议展览中心博览商场13号展览事务部

## HKTDC Hong Kong Baby Products Fair

Date: 2010/01/11-14
Venue: Hong Kong Convention & Exhibition Centre, Hong Kong
Profile: Baby wear and footwear, strollers and gear, skincare and bath products, feeding and nursery products, bedding and furniture, baby toys and activities, gift sets, maternity products
Remarks: Fair launches in 2010
Organizer: Hong Kong Trade Development Council
Address: Exhibitions Department, Unit 13, Expo Galleria, Hong Kong Convention and Exhibition Centre, 1 Expo Drive, Wan Chai, Hong Kong

☆4 ☎ 852-1830 668
🖷 852-2824 0249
✉ exhibitions@hktdc.org
www.hktdc.com/hktradefairs

香港国际文具展
日期：　2010/01/11-14
地点：　香港会议展览中心，香港
内容：　美术用品、儿童文具及学校用品、电脑周边设备及配件、办公室设备用消耗品、礼品文具、办公室设备、纸品及印刷品、书写设备
上届规模 2009：　展出面积5,075平方米，参展商223家
主办：　香港贸易发展局
地址：　香港湾仔博览道1号香港会议展览中心博览商场13号展览事务部

Hong Kong International Stationery
FairDate:　2010/01/11-14
Venue:　Hong Kong Convention & Exhibition Centre, Hong
KongProfile:　Artist supplies, children stationery & school supplies, computer peripherals & related accessories, consumables for office equipment, gift stationery, office equipment, paper & printing products, writing equipment
Statistics 2009:　Gross Area 5,075sqm, Exhibitors 223
Organizer:　Hong Kong Trade Development Council
Address:　Exhibitions Department, Unit 13, Expo Galleria, Hong Kong Convention and Exhibition Centre, 1 Expo Drive, Wan Chai, Hong Kong

☆5 ☎ 852-1830 668
🖷 852-2824 0249
✉ exhibitions@hktdc.org
www.hktdc.com/hktradefairs

HKTDC
**Hong Kong Fashion Week for Fall/Winter**
香港時裝節秋冬系列

香港贸发局香港时装节秋冬系列
日期：　2010/01/18-21
地点：　香港会议展览中心，香港
内容：　秋冬时装系列、服装配件、饰品及布料
上届规模 2009：　展出面积42,306平方米，参展商1,421家
主办：　香港贸易发展局
地址：　香港湾仔博览道1号香港会议展览中心博览商场13号展览事务部

HKTDC Hong Kong Fashion Week for Fall/Winter
Date:　2010/01/18-21
Venue:　Hong Kong Convention & Exhibition Centre, Hong Kong
Profile:　Fall/Winter fashion collections, garment accessories
Statistics 2009:　Gross Area 42,306sqm, Exhibitors 1,421
Organizer:　Hong Kong Trade Development Council
Address:　Exhibitions Department, Unit 13, Expo Galleria, Hong Kong Convention and Exhibition Centre, 1 Expo Drive, Wan Chai, Hong Kong

☆6 ☎ 852-1830 668
🖷 852-2824 0249
✉ exhibitions@hktdc.org
www.hktdc.com/hktradefairs

HKTDC
**World Boutique, Hong Kong**
香港國際時尚薈萃

香港贸发局香港国际时尚荟萃
日期：　2010/01/18-21
地点：　香港会议展览中心，香港
内容：　品牌时装及设计师系列、时装饰品、家居时尚用品及赠品
上届规模 2009：　展出面积 9,417平方米，参展商274家
主办：　香港贸易发展局
地址：　香港湾仔博览道1号香港会议展览中心博览商场13号展览事务部

HKTDC World Boutique, Hong Kong
Date:　2010/01/18-21
Venue:　Hong Kong Convention & Exhibition Centre, Hong Kong
Profile:　Fashion designers' collection, branded fashion products, home fashion & lifestyle products, small gifts
Statistics 2009:　Gross Area 9,417sqm, Exhibitors 274
Organizer:　Hong Kong Trade Development Council
Address:　Exhibitions Department, Unit 13, Expo Galleria, Hong Kong Convention and Exhibition Centre, 1 Expo Drive, Wan Chai, Hong Kong

☆7 ☎ 852-1830 6687
🖷 852-2824 0249
✉ exhibitions@hktdc.org
www.hktdc.com/hktradefairs

HKTDC
**Education & Careers Expo**
**教育及職業博覽**

香港贸发局教育及职业博览
日期： 2010/02/04-07
地点： 香港会议展览中心，香港
内容： 大专院校及理工、大学、专科及进修学校、职业训练机构、语文学校、外地教育机构、政府部门、半政府机构、专业学会、私人机构、出版商及书店、教学／学习辅助器材
上届规模 2009： 展出面积8,505平方米，参展商514家
主办： 香港贸易发展局
地址： 香港湾仔博览道1号香港会议展览中心博览商场13号展览事务部

HKTDC Education & Careers Expo
Date: 2010/02/04-07
Venue: Hong Kong Convention & Exhibition Centre, Hong Kong
Profile: Colleges & polytechnics, universities, school for continue education, vocational training, language schools, outside Hong Kong educational institutions, government departments, semi-government organizations, professional associations, private enterprises, book publishers/book stores, learning aids/educational equipment
Statistics 2009: Gross Area 8,505sqm, Exhibitors 514
Organizer: Hong Kong Trade Development Council
Address: Exhibitions Department, Unit 13, Expo Galleria, Hong Kong Convention and Exhibition Centre, 1 Expo Drive, Wan Chai, Hong Kong

☆8 ☎ 852-1830 6687
🖷 852-2824 0249
✉ exhibitions@hktdc.org
www.hktdc.com/hktradefairs

HKTDC
**Hong Kong International Jewellery Show**
**香港國際珠寶展**

香港贸发局香港国际珠宝展
日期： 2010/03/05-09
地点： 香港会议展览中心，香港
内容： 珠宝首饰、银首饰、制成首饰、古董首饰、翡翠首饰、钻石、贵重宝石、南洋珠及大溪地珍珠、淡水珠及养珠、半宝石、珠宝配件、宝石陈列及包装用品、工具及仪器、珠宝刊物及服务、贸易商会、品牌表及时钟、成表及时钟
上届规模 2009： 展出面积70,617平方米，参展商2,360家
主办： 香港贸易发展局
地址： 香港湾仔博览道1号香港会议展览中心博览商场13号展览事务部

HKTDC Hong Kong International Jewellery Show
Date: 2010/03/05-09
Venue: Hong Kong Convention & Exhibition Centre, Hong Kong
Profile: Fine jewellery, silver jewellery, finished jewellery, antique jewellery, jade jewellery, diamonds, precious stones, south sea pearls & tahiti pearls, fresh water & cultured pearls, semi-precious stones, jewellery accessories, jewellery display & packaging material, jewellery tools & equipment, trade publications & services, trade associations, brand name watches & clocks, complete watches & clocks
Statistics 2009: Gross Area 70,617sqm, Exhibitors 2,360
Organizer: Hong Kong Trade Development Council
Address: Exhibitions Department, Unit 13, Expo Galleria, Hong Kong Convention and Exhibition Centre, 1 Expo Drive, Wan Chai, Hong Kong

☆9 ☎ 852-1830 6687
🖷 852-2824 0249
✉ hktdc@hktdc.org
www.hktdc.com/hktradefairs

HKTDC
**Hong Kong International Film & TV Market (FILMART)**
**香港國際影視展**

香港贸发局香港国际影视展
日期： 2010/03/22-25
地点： 香港会议展览中心，香港
内容： 电影、电视节目、动画、数码娱乐、有关产品及服务
上届规模 2009： 展出面积12,636平方米，参展商505家
主办： 香港贸易发展局
地址： 香港湾仔港湾道1号会展广场办公大楼38楼

HKTDC Hong Kong International Film & TV Market (FILMART)
Date: 2010/03/22-25
Venue: Hong Kong Convention & Exhibition Centre, Hong Kong
Profile: Movies, TV programmes, animation, digital entertainment, related products & services.
Statistics 2009: Gross Area 12,636sqm, Exhibitors 505
Organizer: Hong Kong Trade Development Council
Address: 38/F, Office Tower, Convention Plaza, 1 Harbour Road, Wan Chai, Hong Kong

☆10 ☎ 852-1830 668
🖷 852-2824 0249
✉ hktdc@hktdc.org
www.hktdc.com/hktradefairs

香港音乐汇展
日期： 2010/03
地点： 香港会议展览中心，香港
内容： 唱片公司及代理商、音乐出版社、流动电话服务公司、便携音乐播放仪器制造及营运商、互联网音乐供应商、支持电子商贸科技公司、音乐数码娱乐制作公司、演唱会制作公司、卡拉OK营运商及卡拉OK系统供应商、唱片、版权协会及商会、或相关之新媒体产品及机构、传媒
上届规模 2009： 展出面积2,000平方米，参展商70家
主办： 香港贸易发展局
地址： 香港湾仔港湾道1号会展广场办公大楼38楼

Hong Kong Music Fair
Date: 2010/03
Venue: Hong Kong Convention & Exhibition Centre, Hong Kong
Profile: Record companies & labels, music publishers, mobile phone makers and service providers, portable music device manufacturers & vendors, internet music service providers, technology companies in support of music e-commerce, digital music entertainment & production company, artist management & concert promoters, karaoke operators & system providers, industry associations, media
Statistics 2009: Gross Area 2,000sqm, Exhibitors 70
Organizer: Hong Kong Trade Development Council
Address: 38/F, Office Tower, Convention Plaza, 1 Harbour Road, Wan Chai, Hong Kong

☆11 ☎ 852-1830 6687
🖷 852-2824 0249
✉ exhibitions@hktdc.org
www.hktdc.com/hktradefairs

HKTDC
**Hong Kong Electronics Fair (Spring Edition)**
香港春季電子產品展

香港贸发局香港春季电子产品展
日期： 2010/04/13-16
地点： 香港会议展览中心，香港
内容： 视听产品、数码影像产品、电子配件、电子游戏产品、电子制造服务、电子组件及生产技术、电子保健产品、家用电器、汽车电子及导航系统、办公室自动化及设备、个人电子产品、保安产品、检测和认证服务、电子产品保护／储存设备、电讯产品、商贸服务
上届规模 2009： 展出面积51,761平方米，参展商2,121家
主办： 香港贸易发展局
地址： 香港湾仔博览道1号香港会议展览中心博览商场13号展览事务部

HKTDC Hong Kong Electronics Fair (Spring Edition)
Date: 2010/04/13-16
Venue: Hong Kong Convention & Exhibition Centre, Hong Kong
Profile: Audio & visual, digital imaging, electronic accessories, electronic gaming, electronic manufacturing services (EMS), electronic parts, components and production technology, healthcare electronics, home appliances, in-vehicle electronics & navigation systems, office automation & equipment, personal electronics, securityproducts, testing and certification, protective & storage solutions for electronics, telecommunication products, trade services
Statistics 2009: Gross Area 51,761sqm, Exhibitors 2,121
Organizer: Hong Kong Trade Development Council
Address: Exhibitions Department, Unit 13, Expo Galleria, Hong Kong Convention and Exhibition Centre, 1 Expo Drive, Wan Chai, Hong Kong

☆12 ☎ 852-1830 6687
🖷 852-2824 0249
✉ exhibitions@hktdc.org
www.hktdc.com/hktradefairs

HKTDC
**International ICT Expo**
國際資訊科技博覽

香港贸发局国际资讯科技博览
日期： 2010/04/13-16
地点： 香港会议展览中心，香港
内容： 电讯、网络及无线科技、企业解决方案、电脑及周边设备、数码娱乐及多媒体、电子物流及零售科技、本土创意科技、资讯科技外包服务、商贸服务

上届规模 2009：展出面积9,115平方米，参展商568家
主办：香港贸易发展局
地址：香港湾仔博览道1号香港会议展览中心博览商场13号展览事务部

HKTDC International ICT Expo
Date: 2010/04/13-16
Venue: Hong Kong Convention & Exhibition Centre, Hong Kong
Profile: Telecom, networking & wireless technology, enterprise solutions, computer & peripherals, digitainment & multimedia, e-logistics & retail technologies, home-grown innovations, IT outsourcing, trade services
Statistics 2009: Gross Area 9,115sqm, Exhibitors 568
Organizer: Hong Kong Trade Development Council
Address: Exhibitions Department, Unit 13, Expo Galleria, Hong Kong Convention and Exhibition Centre, 1 Expo Drive, Wan Chai, Hong Kong

☆13 ☎ 852-1830 668
852-2824 0249
exhibitions@hktdc.org
www.hktdc.com/hktradefairs

HKTDC

**Hong Kong International Lighting Fair (Spring Edition)**
**香港國際春季燈飾展**

香港贸发局香港国际春季灯饰展
日期：2010/04/13-16
地点：香港会议展览中心，香港
内容：水晶灯饰、环保照明、节庆照明、LED照明、户外照明、灯饰配件及零件、枱灯
上届规模 2009：展出面积5,336平方米，参展商235家
主办：香港贸易发展局
地址：香港湾仔博览道1号香港会议展览中心博览商场13号展览事务部

HKTDC Hong Kong International Lighting Fair (Spring Edition)
Date: 2010/04/13-16
Venue: Hong Kong Convention & Exhibition Centre, Hong Kong
Profile: Crystal lighting, green lighting, holiday lighting, LED lighting, outdoor lighting, lighting accessories & components, table lamps
Statistics 2009: Gross Area 5,336sqm, Exhibitors 235
Organizer: Hong Kong Trade Development Council
Address: Exhibitions Department, Unit 13, Expo Galleria, Hong Kong Convention and Exhibition Centre, 1 Expo Drive, Wan Chai, Hong Kong

☆14 ☎ 852-1830 6687
852-2824 0249
exhibitions@hktdc.org
www.hktdc.com/hktradefairs

HKTDC

**Hong Kong Houseware Fair**
**香港家庭用品展**

香港贸发局香港家庭用品展
日期：2010/04/20-23
地点：香港会议展览中心，香港
内容：人造花饰、酒吧用具、浴室用具、美容及健身用品、蜡烛及香熏饰品、清洁用品、家具、园艺及户外用品、手工艺品、五金用具及自行装配产品、保健及个人护理产品、家居装饰品、厨具及厨房小器具、油画及艺术作品、宠物用品、长者用品、小型家庭电器、餐具、商贸服务
上届规模 2009：展出面积59,776平方米，参展商2,207家
主办：香港贸易发展局
地址：香港湾仔博览道1号香港会议展览中心博览商场13号展览事务部

HKTDC Hong Kong Houseware Fair
Date: 2010/04/20-23
Venue: Hong Kong Convention & Exhibition Centre, Hong Kong
Profile: Artificial flowers, bar accessories, bathroom accessories, beauty & fitness, candles & scent sensation, cleaning & supplies, furniture, gardening & outdoor accessories, handicrafts, hardware & DIY products, health & personal care items, home decorations, kitchenware and gadgets, paintings & objets d' Art, pet supplies, silver generation products, small electrical appliances, tableware, trade services
Statistics 2009: Gross Area 59,776sqm, Exhibitors 2,207
Organizer: Hong Kong Trade Development Council
Address: Exhibitions Department, Unit 13, Expo Galleria, Hong Kong Convention and Exhibition Centre, 1 Expo Drive, Wan Chai, Hong Kong

☆15 ☎ 852-1830 6687
🖷 852-2824 0249
✉ exhibitions@hktdc.org
www.hktdc.com/hktradefairs

HKTDC
**Hong Kong International Home Textiles Fair**
**香港國際家用紡織品展**

### 香港贸发局香港国际家用纺织品展

日期：　2010/04/20-23
地点：　香港会议展览中心，香港
内容：　浴室纺织品、寝室纺织品、地毯及铺地制品、家居饰品、餐桌及厨房纺织品、铺墙制品、婴儿纺织品、家用纺织相关产品、设计及贸易服务
附注：　2010年首次举办
主办：　香港贸易发展局
地址：　香港湾仔博览道1号香港会议展览中心博览商场13号展览事务部

### HKTDC Hong Kong International Home Textiles Fair

Date: 2010/04/20-23
Venue: Hong Kong Convention & Exhibition Centre, Hong Kong
Profile: Bathroom textiles, bedroom textiles, carpet & floor coverings, interior & décor textiles, table & kitchen textiles, wall coverings, baby textiles, home textile-related products & design, trade services
Remarks: Fair launches in 2010
Organizer: Hong Kong Trade Development Council
Address: Exhibitions Department, Unit 13, Expo Galleria, Hong Kong Convention and Exhibition Centre, 1 Expo Drive, Wan Chai, Hong Kong

☆16 ☎ 852-1830 6687
🖷 852-2824 0249
✉ exhibitions@hktdc.org
www.hktdc.com/hktradefairs

HKTDC
**Hong Kong Gifts & Premium Fair**
**香港禮品及贈品展**

### 香港贸发局香港礼品及赠品展

日期：　2010/04/27-30
地点：　香港会议展览中心，香港
内容：　宣传赠品、公司礼品、时尚首饰及饰品、小型摆设及装饰品、综合礼品、户外及旅游用品、包装产品、派对及节庆用品、画框及相架、文具及纸品、科技礼品、玩具及体育用品、钟表、新婚贺礼及用品、商贸服务
上届规模 2009：　展出面积79,060平方米，参展商3,983家
主办：　香港贸易发展局
地址：　香港湾仔博览道1号香港会议展览中心博览商场13号展览事务部

### HKTDC Hong Kong Gifts & Premium Fair

Date: 2010/04/27-30
Venue: Hong Kong Convention & Exhibition Centre, Hong Kong
Profile: Advertising premiums, corporate gifts, fashion jewellery & accessories, figurines & decorations, general gift items, outdoor & travel goods, packaging, party & festive items, pictures & photo frames, stationery & paper, tech gifts, toys & sporting goods, watches & clocks, wedding favours, trade services
Statistics 2009: Gross Area 79,060sqm, Exhibitors 3,983
Organizer: Hong Kong Trade Development Council
Address: Exhibitions Department, Unit 13, Expo Galleria, Hong Kong Convention and Exhibition Centre, 1 Expo Drive, Wan Chai, Hong Kong

☆17 ☎ 852-1830 6687
🖷 852-2824 0249
✉ exhibitions@hktdc.org
www.hktdc.com/hktradefairs

### 香港国际印刷及包装展

日期：　2010/04/27-30
地点：　香港亚洲国际博览馆，香港
内容：　印刷服务、包装服务、印刷耗材、包装材料及配件、印刷及包装机械及设备、美容用品包装、食品包装、药品包装、书刊印刷、印前处理、图像及设计服务、整饰及纸品加工服务、多谋体印刷科技及服务、电脑喷画及广告牌印刷服、设备及配件、机器设备维修及保养服务、咨询及培训服务
上届规模 2009：　展出面积11,360平方米，参展商240家
主办：　香港贸易发展局
地址：　香港湾仔博览道1号香港会议展览中心博览商场13号展览事务部

### Hong Kong International Printing & Packaging Fair

Date: 2010/04/27-30
Venue: AsiaWorld-Expo, Hong Kong
Profile: Printing services, packaging services, printing consumables, packaging materials & accessories, printing & packaging equipment & systems, cosmetic packaging, food

packaging, medicine packaging, book printing, pre-press services, graphic arts and design services, finishing & converting services, multimedia technologies and services, inkjet printing & signage production services, equipment & accessories, equipment repair and maintenance services, consultancy and training services

Statistics 2009: Gross Area 11,360sqm, Exhibitors 240
Organizer: Hong Kong Trade Development Council
Address: Exhibitions Department, Unit 13, Expo Galleria, Hong Kong Convention and Exhibition Centre, 1 Expo Drive, Wan Chai, Hong Kong

☆18 ☎ 852-1830 6687
🖷 852-2824 0249
✉ exhibitions@hktdc.org
www.hktdc.com/hktradefairs

HKTDC
**Summer Sourcing Show for Gifts, Houseware & Toys**
**香港夏季禮品、家庭用品及玩具展**

### 香港贸发局香港夏季礼品、家庭用品及玩具展
日期: 2010/07/05-08
地点: 香港会议展览中心，香港
内容: 礼品及赠品、家庭用品、家居装饰品、玩具及游戏、节日及派对装饰品、设计服务
上届规模 2009: 展出面积8,941平方米，参展商444家
主办: 香港贸易发展局
地址: 香港湾仔博览道1号香港会议展览中心博览商场13号展览事务部

### HKTDC Summer Sourcing Show for Gifts, Houseware & Toys
Date: 2010/07/05-08
Venue: Hong Kong Convention & Exhibition Centre, Hong Kong
Profile: Gifts and premium, household products, home decorations, toys and games, festive and party items, design services
Statistics 2009: Gross Area 8,941sqm, Exhibitors 444
Organizer: Hong Kong Trade Development Council
Address: Exhibitions Department, Unit 13, Expo Galleria, Hong Kong Convention and Exhibition Centre, 1 Expo Drive, Wan Chai, Hong Kong

☆19 ☎ 852-1830 6687
🖷 852-2824 0249
✉ exhibitions@hktdc.org
www.hktdc.com/hktradefairs

HKTDC
**Hong Kong Fashion Week for Spring/Summer**
**香港時裝節春夏系列**

### 香港贸发局香港时装节春夏系列
日期: 2010/07/05-08
地点: 香港会议展览中心，香港内容: 春夏时装系列、服装配件、饰品及布料
上届规模 2009: 展出面积31,394平方米，参展商1,164家
主办: 香港贸易发展局
地址: 香港湾仔博览道1号香港会议展览中心博览商场13号展览事务部

### HKTDC Hong Kong Fashion Week for Spring/Summer
Date: 2010/07/05-08
Venue: Hong Kong Convention & Exhibition Centre, Hong Kong
Profile: Spring/Summer fashion collections, garment accessories
Statistics 2009: Gross Area 31,394sqm, Exhibitors 1,164
Organizer: Hong Kong Trade Development Council
Address: Exhibitions Department, Unit 13, Expo Galleria, Hong Kong Convention and Exhibition Centre, 1 Expo Drive, Wan Chai, Hong Kong

☆20 ☎ 852-1830 6687
🖷 852-2824 0249
✉ exhibitions@hktdc.org
www.hktdc.com/hktradefairs

HKTDC
**Hong Kong Book Fair**
**香港書展**

### 香港贸发局香港书展
日期: 2010/07/21-27
地点: 香港会议展览中心，香港
内容: 各类书籍及刊物、儿童及青少年图书、宗教书籍、多媒体产品、各类文具及印刷品
上届规模 2009: 展出面积44,595平方米，参展商504家
主办: 香港贸易发展局
地址: 香港湾仔博览道1号香港会议展览中心博览商场13号展览事务部

### HKTDC Hong Kong Book Fair
Date: 2010/07/21-27
Venue: Hong Kong Convention & Exhibition Centre, Hong Kong
Profile: Books and publications, children's and teen's books, religious books, multimedia, stationery and printing products
Statistics 2009: Gross Area 44,595sqm, Exhibitors 504
Organizer: Hong Kong Trade Development Council
Address: Exhibitions Department, Unit 13, Expo Galleria, Hong Kong Convention and Exhibition Centre, 1 Expo Drive, Wan Chai, Hong Kong

☆21 ☎ 852-1830 6687
🖷 852-2824 0249
✉ exhibitions@hktdc.org
www.hktdc.com/hktradefairs

香港国际茶展
日期： 2010/08/12-14
地点： 香港会议展览中心，香港
内容： 各地名茶、加工茶、茶饮料、茶食品、各种茶相关加工产品、茶叶包装、茶叶机械与检测、茶具、茶业机构、茶叶技术、茶艺术品、茶业媒体
上届规模 2009： 展出面积6,604平方米，参展商259家
主办： 香港贸易发展局
地址： 香港湾仔博览道1号香港会议展览中心博览商场13号展览事务部

Hong Kong International Tea Fair
Date: 2010/08/12-14
Venue: Hong Kong Convention & Exhibition Centre, Hong Kong
Profile: Tea, processed tea and tea product, tea packaging, tea processing equipment and testing service, tea ware, tea bar/organization, tea technology, tea art, tea media
Statistics 2009: Gross Area 6,604sqm, Exhibitors 259
Organizer: Hong Kong Trade Development Council
Address: Exhibitions Department, Unit 13, Expo Galleria, Hong Kong Convention and Exhibition Centre, 1 Expo Drive, Wan Chai, Hong Kong

☆22 ☎ 852-1830 6687
🖷 852-2824 0249
✉ exhibitions@hktdc.org
www.hktdc.com/hktradefairs

HKTDC
Food Expo
美食博覽

香港贸发局美食博览
日期： 2010/08/12-16
地点： 香港会议展览中心，香港
内容： 食品及饮品、食品包装、标签、物流及服务、食品处理产品、食品科技、机械及服务
上届规模 2009： 展出面积25,820平方米，参展商607家
主办： 香港贸易发展局
地址： 香港湾仔博览道1号香港会议展览中心博览商场13号展览事务部

HKTDC Food Expo
Date: 2010/08/12-16
Venue: Hong Kong Convention & Exhibition Centre, Hong Kong
Profile: Food and beverage, food packaging, food processing products, machinery & related services
Statistics 2009: Gross Area 25,820sqm, Exhibitors 607
Organizer: Hong Kong Trade Development Council
Address: Exhibitions Department, Unit 13, Expo Galleria, Hong Kong Convention and Exhibition Centre, 1 Expo Drive, Wan Chai, Hong Kong

☆23 ☎ 852-1830 6687
🖷 852-2824 0249
✉ exhibitions@hktdc.org
www.hktdc.com/hktradefairs

HKTDC
International Conference & Exhibition of the Modernization of Chinese Medicine & Health Products
國際現代化中醫藥及健康產品展覽會暨會議

国际现代化中医药及健康产品展览会暨会议
日期： 2010/08/12-16
地点： 香港会议展览中心，香港
内容： 中药、保健食品、健康护理及疗法、原料、设备及相关服务、科研及开发、商会
上届规模 2009： 展出面积3,784平方米，参展商125家
主办： 香港贸易发展局
地址： 香港湾仔博览道1号香港会议展览中心博览商场13号展览事务部

International Conference & Exhibition of the Modernization of Chinese Medicine & Health Products
Date: 2010/08/12-16
Venue: Hong Kong Convention & Exhibition Centre, Hong Kong
Profile: Chinese medicine, health supplement, health care & therapy, raw material, equipment & related services, research & development, trade association
Statistics 2009: Gross Area 3,784sqm, Exhibitors 125
Organizer: Hong Kong Trade Development Council
Address: Exhibitions Department, Unit 13, Expo Galleria, Hong Kong Convention and Exhibition Centre, 1 Expo Drive, Wan Chai, Hong Kong

☆24 ☎ 852-1830 6687
🖷 852-2824 0249
✉ exhibitions@hktdc.org
www.hktdc.com/hktradefairs

HKTDC

## Hong Kong Watch & Clock Fair
## 香港鐘表展

香港贸发局香港钟表展
日期： 2010/09
地点： 香港会议展览中心，香港
内容： 表及钟、配件／零件／设备、机械、包装用品、商贸服务及刊物
上届规模 2009： 展出面积34,418平方米，参展商708家
主办： 香港贸易发展局
地址： 香港湾仔博览道1号香港会议展览中心博览商场13号展览事务部

HKTDC Hong Kong Watch & Clock Fair
Date: 2010/09
Venue: Hong Kong Convention & Exhibition Centre, Hong Kong
Profile: Complete watches & clocks, parts & components, equipment, machinery, packaging, trade services
Statistics 2009: Gross Area 34,418sqm, Exhibitors 708
Organizer: Hong Kong Trade Development Council
Address: Exhibitions Department, Unit 13, Expo Galleria, Hong Kong Convention and Exhibition Centre, 1 Expo Drive, Wan Chai, Hong Kong

☆25 ☎ 852-1830 6687
🖷 852-2824 0249
✉ exhibitions@hktdc.org
www.hktdc.com/hktradefairs

HKTDC

## Hong Kong Electronics Fair (Autumn Edition)
## 香港秋季電子產品展

香港贸发局香港秋季电子产品展
日期： 2010/10/13-16
地点： 香港会议展览中心，香港
内容： 视听产品、电脑及周边产品、数码影像产品、电子配件、电子游戏产品、家用电器、电子保健产品、汽车电子及导航系统、办公室自动化及设备、个人电子产品、保安产品、电讯产品、商贸服务
上届规模 2009： 展出面积77,391平方米，参展商2,852家
主办： 香港贸易发展局
地址： 香港湾仔博览道1号香港会议展览中心博览商场13号展览事务部

HKTDC Hong Kong Electronics Fair (Autumn Edition)
Date: 2010/10/13-16
Venue: Hong Kong Convention & Exhibition Centre, Hong Kong
Profile: Audio visual products, computer & peripherals, digital imaging, electronic accessories, electronic gaming, home appliances, healthcare electronics, in-vehicle electronics and navigation systems, office automation, personal electronics, security products, telecommunications products, trade services
Statistics 2009: Gross Area 77,391sqm, Exhibitors 2,852
Organizer: Hong Kong Trade Development Council
Address: Exhibitions Department, Unit 13, Expo Galleria, Hong Kong Convention and Exhibition Centre, 1 Expo Drive, Wan Chai, Hong Kong

☆26 ☎ 852-1830 6687
🖷 852-2824 0249
✉ exhibitions@hktdc.org
www.hktdc.com/hktradefairs

国际电子组件及生产技术展
日期： 2010/10/13-16
地点： 香港会议展览中心，香港
内容： 电子科技、元器件、组件、显示技术、太阳能光伏电子技术
上届规模 2009： 展出面积12,007平方米，参展商570家
主办： 香港贸易发展局
地址： 香港湾仔博览道1号香港会议展览中心博览商场13号展览事务部

electronicAsia
Date: 2010/10/13-16
Venue: Hong Kong Convention & Exhibition Centre, Hong Kong
Profile: Electronic components, assemblies, electronics production, display technologies, photovoltaic technology
Statistics 2009: Gross Area 12,007sqm, Exhibitors 570
Organizer: Hong Kong Trade Development Council
Address: Exhibitions Department, Unit 13, Expo Galleria, Hong Kong Convention and Exhibition Centre, 1 Expo Drive, Wan Chai, Hong Kong

☆27 ☎ 852-1830 6687
🖷 852-2824 0249
✉ exhibitions@hktdc.org
www.hktdc.com/hktradefairs

HKTDC
**Hong Kong International Lighting Fair (Autumn Edition)**
香港國際秋季燈飾展

### 香港贸发局香港国际秋季灯饰展

日期： 2010/10
地点： 香港会议展览中心，香港
内容： LED照明、环保照明、家居照明、商业照明、户外照明、灯饰配件及零件、灯饰管理、设计及技术
上届规模 2008： 展出面积47,056平方米，参展商1,572家
主办： 香港贸易发展局
地址： 香港湾仔博览道1号香港会议展览中心博览商场13号展览事务部

### HKTDC Hong Kong International Lighting Fair (Autumn Edition)

Date: 2010/10
Venue: Hong Kong Convention & Exhibition Centre, Hong Kong
Profile: LED lighting, green lighting, household lighting, commercial lighting, outdoor lighting, lighting accessories, parts & components, lighting management, design & technology
Statistics 2008: Gross Area 47,056sqm, Exhibitors 1,572
Organizer: Hong Kong Trade Development Council
Address: Exhibitions Department, Unit 13, Expo Galleria, Hong Kong Convention and Exhibition Centre, 1 Expo Drive, Wan Chai, Hong Kong

☆28 ☎ 852-1830 6687
🖷 852-2824 0249
✉ exhibitions@hktdc.org
www.hktdc.com/hktradefairs

### 亚洲运动用品展

日期： 2010/10
地点： 香港亚洲国际博览馆，香港
内容： 球类运动装备、自行车运动用品、运动服装布料／物料、健身及健美器材、高尔夫球用品、室内运动、户外运动及休闲用品、球拍运动、滚轴及滑板用品、体育防护配件、运动鞋、运动用品店装置及设备、运动服装及配件、田径运动、水上运动、冰上运动
上届规模 2009： 展出面积5,832平方米，参展商216家
主办： 香港贸易发展局
地址： 香港湾仔博览道1号香港会议展览中心博览商场13号展览事务部

### Sports Source Asia

Date: 2010/10
Venue: AsiaWorld-Expo, Hong Kong
Profile: Ball game equipment, cycling, fabrics & materials for sportswear, fitness & gymnastic training equipment, golf equipment & supplies, indoor sports, outdoor sports, racket sports, skating & skateboarding supplies, sports safety & protection gear, sports shoes, sports shop fittings & equipment, sportswear & accessories, track & field sports, water sports, winter sports
Statistics 2009: Gross Area 5,832sqm, Exhibitors 216
Organizer: Hong Kong Trade Development Council
Address: Exhibitions Department, Unit 13, Expo Galleria, Hong Kong Convention and Exhibition Centre, 1 Expo Drive, Wan Chai, Hong Kong

☆29 ☎ 852-1830 6687
🖷 852-2824 0249
✉ exhibitions@hktdc.org
www.hktdc.com/hktradefairs

### 香港国际建筑装饰材料及五金展

日期： 2010/10
地点： 香港亚洲国际博览馆，香港
内容： 卫浴／厨房、建筑装饰五金、室内装饰材料、门及窗、天花及幕墙、涂料、化学建材、陶瓷及石材、建筑科技及家具
上届规模 2009： 展出面积5,542平方米，参展商208家
主办： 香港贸易发展局
地址： 香港湾仔博览道1号香港会议展览中心博览商场13号展览事务部

### Hong Kong International Building and Decoration Materials & Hardware Fair

Date: 2010/10
Venue: AsiaWorld-Expo, Hong Kong
Profile: Bathroom & kitchen, building & decorative hardware, indoor decorative materials, door & window, ceiling & curtain wall, coating & chemicals, ceramics, stone & marble, building technology, furniture
Statistics 2009: Gross Area 5,542sqm, Exhibitors 208
Organizer: Hong Kong Trade Development Council
Address: Exhibitions Department, Unit 13, Expo Galleria, Hong Kong Convention and Exhibition Centre, 1 Expo Drive, Wan Chai, Hong Kong

☆30 ☎ 852-1830 6687
℡ 852-2824 0249
✉ exhibitions@hktdc.org
www.hktdc.com/hktradefairs

国际环保博览

日期：2010/11
地点：香港亚洲国际博览馆，香港
内容：空气质素、管理、监测及实验室技术、环保产品、能源效益及能源、环保工程方案、服务及研究、水质及废物及循环再造
上届规模 2008：展出面积4,297平方米，参展商123家
主办：香港贸易发展局
地址：香港湾仔博览道1号香港会议展览中心博览商场13号展览事务部

Eco Expo Asia – International Trade Fair on Environmental Protection

Date: 2010/11
Venue: AsiaWorld-Expo, Hong Kong
Profile: Air quality , control, measuring & laboratory technology, eco-friendly product, energy efficiency & energy, environmental project solution, services & research, water quality and waste & recycling
Statistics 2008: Gross Area 4,297sqm, Exhibitors 123
Organizer: Hong Kong Trade Development Council
Address: Exhibitions Department, Unit 13, Expo Galleria, Hong Kong Convention and Exhibition Centre, 1 Expo Drive, Wan Chai, Hong Kong

☆31 ☎ 852-1830 6687
℡ 852-2824 0249
✉ exhibitions@hktdc.org
www.hktdc.com/hktradefairs

HKTDC
Hong Kong International Medical Devices and Supplies Fair
香港國際醫療器材及用品展

香港贸发局香港国际医疗器材及用品展

日期：2010/11
地点：香港会议展览中心，香港
内容：意外及急救设备、建筑科技及医院家具、中医设备、通讯、系统及资讯科技、牙科设备及用品、诊断工具及仪器、电子医疗设备／医疗科技、化验室设备、医疗设备部件及物料、医疗用品及消耗用品、物理治疗／整形外科／复健技术及设备、医疗纺织品
上届规模 2009：展出面积4,101平方米，参展商153家
主办：香港贸易发展局
地址：香港湾仔博览道1号香港会议展览中心博览商场13号展览事务部

HKTDC Hong Kong International Medical Devices and Supplies Fair

Date: 2010/11
Venue: Hong Kong Convention & Exhibition Centre, Hong Kong
Profile: Accident and emergency equipment, building technology and hospital furniture, chinese medical devices, communication, systems and information technology, dental equipment and supplies, diagnostics, electromedical equipment/medical technology, laboratory equipment, medical components and materials, medical supplies and disposables, physiotherapy / orthopaedic / rehabilitation technology, textiles
Statistics 2009: Gross Area 4,101sqm, Exhibitors 153
Organizer: Hong Kong Trade Development Council
Address: Exhibitions Department, Unit 13, Expo Galleria, Hong Kong Convention and Exhibition Centre, 1 Expo Drive, Wan Chai, Hong Kong

☆32 ☎ 852-1830 6687
℡ 852-2824 0249
✉ exhibitions@hktdc.org
www.hktdc.com/hktradefairs

HKTDC
Hong Kong International Wine & Spirits Fair
香港國際美酒展

香港贸发局香港国际美酒展

日期：2010/11
地点：香港会议展览中心，香港
内容：含酒精饮品、美酒之友、酒类生产及物流、酒类产品及器具、酒类相关服务
上届规模 2009：展出面积13,090平方米，参展商525家
主办：香港贸易发展局
地址：香港湾仔博览道1号香港会议展览中心博览商场13号展览事务部

HKTDC Hong Kong International Wine & Spirits Fair

Date: 2010/11
Venue：Hong Kong Convention & Exhibition Centre, Hong Kong
Profile: Liquor & beverage products, friends of wine, wine production & logistics, wine accessories & equipmentm, other related services
Statistics 2009: Gross Area 13,090sqm, Exhibitors 525
Organizer: Hong Kong Trade Development Council
Address: Exhibitions Department, Unit 13, Expo Galleria, Hong Kong Convention and Exhibition Centre, 1 Expo Drive, Wan Chai, Hong Kong

☆33 ☎ 852-1830 6687
🖷 852-2824 0249
✉ exhibitions@hktdc.org
www.hktdc.com/hktradefairs

HKTDC
**Hong Kong Optical Fair**
**香港眼鏡展**

### 香港贸发局香港眼镜展

日期： 2010/11
地点： 香港会议展览中心，香港
内容： 隐形眼镜、镜框及镜架、镜片、眼镜配件、护目镜、运动眼镜、太阳眼镜、视光仪器、眼镜盒及眼镜袋、相关之机械及技术、相关之化学原料、相关之包装物料、相关之服务及专业刊物、零售及店铺设计、陈列设备及技术
上届规模 2008： 展出面积24,911平方米，参展商523家
主办： 香港贸易发展局
地址： 香港湾仔博览道1号香港会议展览中心博览商场13号展览事务部

### HKTDC Hong Kong Optical Fair

Date: 2010/11
Venue: Hong Kong Convention & Exhibition Centre, Hong Kong
Profile: Contact lenses, frames & mountings, lenses, parts & accessories, safety eyewear, sportswear, sunglasses, optometric instruments, spectacle cases & holders, related equipment & technology, related chemical & materials, related packaging materials, retail & shop design, equipment & technology
Statistics 2008: Gross Area 24,911sqm, Exhibitors 523
Organizer: Hong Kong Trade Development Council
Address: Exhibitions Department, Unit 13, Expo Galleria, Hong Kong Convention and Exhibition Centre, 1 Expo Drive, Wan Chai, Hong Kong

☆34 ☎ 010-5933 9288
🖷 010-5933 9233
✉ ronald.wu@reedexpo.com.cn
www.reedexport.cn

mipimasia

### 亚洲香港“国际地产投资交易会”

日期： 2010/11
地点： 香港会展中心
内容： 三天的展会是亚太地区房地产业内人士向国际投资者推介房地产项目、建立高层联系、创建伙伴关系以及探索新市场的最佳机会。 展会运用各种方式鼓励参会者建立联系和交流。除展出外，展会还将组织会谈，以便最优秀的国际房地产专家分享知识。
周期： 每年一届
市场范围： 国际性
性质： 面向贸易观众
参展联络： 励展博览集团国际销售部
地址： 北京朝阳区新源里南路1-3号平安国际金融中心A座15层01-03，05（100027）
联系人： 吴祥

MIPIM Asia: The World's Property Market in Asia Pacific
Date: 2010/11
Venue: Hong Kong Convention & Exhibition Centre, Hong Kong
Frequency: Annual
Market Area: International
Nature: Trade only

☆35 ☎ 852-1830 6687
🖷 852-2824 0249
✉ hktdc@hktdc.org
www.hktdc.com/hktradefairs

HKTDC
**World SME Expo**
**國際中小企博覽**

### 香港贸发局国际中小企博览

日期： 2010/12
地点： 香港会议展览中心，香港
内容： 一站式国际商贸平台，提供中小企业支持服务及环球商机
上届规模 2008： 展出面积12,402平方米，参展商287家
主办： 香港贸易发展局
地址： 香港湾仔港湾道一号会展广场办公大楼38字楼

### HKTDC World SME Expo

Date: 2010/12
Venue: Hong Kong Convention & Exhibition Centre, Hong Kong
Profile: A one-stop international marketplace for SMEs, providing business solutions and market opportunities
Statistics 2008: Gross Area 12,402sqm, Exhibitors 287
Organizer: Hong Kong Trade Development Council
Address: 38/F, Office Tower, Convention Plaza, 1 Harbour Road, Wan Chai, Hong Kong

☆36 ☎ 852-1830 6687
🖷 852-2824 0249
✉ hktdc@hktdc.org
www.hktdc.com/hktradefairs

HKTDC
**Inno Design Tech Expo**
**創新科技及設計博覽**

### 香港贸发局创新科技及设计博览

| | |
|---|---|
| 日期： | 2010/12 |
| 地点： | 香港会议展览中心，香港 |
| 内容： | 第五届「创新科技及设计博览」，是创意及科技业界发掘生意契机、物色合适商贸伙伴的理想平台。 |
| 上届规模 2008： | 展出面积4,670平方米，参展商327家 |
| 主办： | 香港贸易发展局 |
| 地址： | 香港湾仔港湾道一号会展广场办公大楼38字楼 |

### HKTDC Inno Design Tech Expo

| | |
|---|---|
| Date: | 2010/12 |
| Venue: | Hong Kong Convention & Exhibition Centre, Hong Kong |
| Profile: | The fifth HKTDC Inno Design Tech Expo (IDT Expo) provides a unique platform for creative and technology professionals to exchange ideas and explore business opportunities. |
| Statistics 2008: | Gross Area 4,670sqm, Exhibitors 327 |
| Organizer: | Hong Kong Trade Development Council |
| Address: | 38/F, Office Tower, Convention Plaza, 1 Harbour Road, Wan Chai, Hong Kong |

☆37 ☎ 86-10-5933 9288
🖷 86-10-5933 9233
✉ www.reedexport.cn
www.asianaerospace.com

### 亚洲航天航空设备与技术展

| | |
|---|---|
| 日期： | 2011/09 - |
| 地点： | 亚洲国际展览馆, 香港 |
| 内容： | 该展会一直在全球商业航空展中占据首要的地位，为亚太区各大航空买家开展业务交易、建立业务联系、获取丰富的业内资讯提供了绝佳的机遇。在中国民用航空总局（CAAC）的支持下，亚洲航天航空设备与技术展将邀请中国航空领域的高层官员前来参展，届时将为广大展商和观众提供领先技术与最佳商业实践知识交流的平台。 产品及服务 飞机（固定翼与旋转翼）、飞机保养、飞机维修与检修系统、机场基础设施/服务、飞机零部件、航空电子、雷达系统、商务航空、化学品、油漆、涂料、通讯设备/服务、引擎、空中交通管制设备、陆地交通工具与配 |
| 周期： | 两年一届 |
| 市场范围： | 国际性 |
| 展览性质： | 仅向贸易观众开放 |
| 上届规模 '07： | 展商总数527家, 贸易观众11,527人 |
| 主办： | 励展博览集团 |

### Asian Aerospace

| | |
|---|---|
| Date: | 2011/09 - |
| Venue: | AsiaWorld-Expo, Hong Kong |
| Frequency: | Biennial |
| Market Area: | International |
| Nature: Trade only | |
| Statistics '07: | Exhibitors 527, Visitors 11,527 |
| Organizer: | Reed Exhibitions |

# 中国澳门展览会议

# Exhibitions in Macao China

☎ +65 6780 4669
✉ David.lim@reedexpo.com.sg
www.asianaerospace.com

## 亚洲商务航空展览会

日期：2010/06/08-10
地点：澳门商用航空中心
周期：每年一届
主办：励展博览集团

## Asian Business Aviation (ABA)

Venue: Macau Business Aviation Center
Profile: The business aviation exhibition will be a gathering of manufacturers of business jets and helicopters unveiling the latest innovations for the business, general aviation industry. The products, services and technologies showcased in the exhibition will aim at meeting the growing demand generated by China and the rest of Asia.
Frequency: Annual
Organizer: Reed Exhibitions

2010/04/8 -10
www.macaomiecf.com

## 2010年澳门国际环保合作发展论坛及展览（第三届）

周期：每年一届
市场范围：国际性
官方承办：澳门特别行政区政府；澳门贸易投资促进局；澳门环境保护局
澳门贸易投资促进局
☎ 853-8798 9675 　 853-2872 7123 　 ✉ miecf2010@ipim.gov.mo
澳门环境保护局
☎ 853-2872 5134 　 853-2872 5129 　 ✉ info@dspa.gov.mo
项目经理：慕尼黑国际博览亚洲（香港）有限公司
☎ 853-8798 9675 　 853-2872 7123 　 ✉ miecf2010@ipim.gov.mo
香港：☎ 852-2511 0738 　 852-2511 5099 　 ✉ info@macaomiecf.com
新加坡：☎ 65-6236 0988 　 65-6263 1966

## Macao International Environmental Co-operation Forum & Exhibition (3rd edition)

Venue：Macao
Frequency: Annual
Market Area: International
Host Co-ordinator: Macao Special Administrative Region; Macao Trade Investment Promotion Institute; Environmental Protection Bureau
Macao Trade and Investment Promotion Institute:
☎ 853-8798 9675 　 853-2872 7123 　 ✉ miecf2010@ipim.gov.mo
Environment Protection Bureau
☎ 853-2872 5134 　 853-2872 5129 　 ✉ info@dspa.gov.mo
Event Manager: MMI Asia (Hong Kong) Limited
Macao：☎ 853-8798 9675 　 853-2872 7123 　 ✉ miecf2010@ipim.gov.mo
Hong Kong：☎ 852-2511 0738 　 852-2511 5099 　 ✉ info@macaomiecf.com
Singapore：☎ 65-6236 0988 　 65-6263 1966

2010/05/13 – 14
☎ 021-6289 5385
🖷 021-6247 2950
✉ info@remacau.com
www.remacauexpo.com.cn

## 2010 澳门国际打印耗材展览会

| | |
|---|---|
| 地点： | 澳门威尼斯人度假村酒店金光会展中心 |
| 内容： | 墨盒、硒鼓、墨水、碳粉、色带等各种打印耗材；兼容、再生、循环使用等打印机和复印机耗材；相纸、喷绘纸、热敏纸等各种特殊打印用纸；打印耗材的制造、翻新、罐装、测试等设备和工具；喷绘机、打印机、复印机等打印输出设备和零部件；打印设备与打印耗材的技术、信息等服务类产品 |
| 首届举办 | |
| 周期： | 每年一届 |
| 市场范围： | 国际性 |
| 性质： | 面向贸易观众 |
| 入场券价格： | 50元人民币 |
| 参展费用： | 1600元/$m^2$ |
| 预计规模： | 总面积5000$m^2$, 参展商120家，贸易观众3,000人 |
| 主办： | ReChina Expo Inc.USA, Recharger Magazine (USA)；上海广会会展有限公司 |
| 地址： | 上海市镇宁路200号欣安大厦东峰18A(200040) |
| 联系人： | 陈文瑾 小姐 |

## ReMacau Expo 2010

| | |
|---|---|
| Venue: | The Venetian Macao-Resort-Hotel |
| Profile： | Ink cartridges, Toner cartridges, Ink, Toner, Ribbons, and other printer consumables; Compatible, Remanufactured and renewable consumables of printers and copiers; Photo paper, Inkjet paper, Thermal transfer paper and other special printing papers; Manufacturing, Remanufacturing, Refilling, Testing equipment & tools for printer consumables; Wide-format Inkjet printers, printers, copiers and other printing-out equipment and components; Technologies, information and other services for printing equipment and con |
| First Session | |
| Frequency： | Annual |
| Market Area: | International |
| Nature: | Trade only |
| Cost to Attend： | RMB 50:- |
| Participation Fee: | RMB1600/$m^2$; USD265/$m^2$ |
| Expectation： | Exhibition Area 5,000$m^2$, Exhibitors 120, Visitors 3,000 |
| Organizer: | ReChina Expo Inc.USA; Recharger Magazine(USA); Shanghai GrandView Expo Co.,Ltd. |
| Address: | 18A East Wing Xin'An Building 200 ZhenNing Rd, Shanghai 200040, China |
| Contact: | Ms. Cheyenne Chen |

2010/06/08 – 10
☎ 010-5933 9288
🖷 010-5933 9233
✉ liang.wang@reedexpo.com.cn
www.g2easia.com

global gaming expo
G2E ASIA

## 亚洲全球博彩业博览会

| | |
|---|---|
| 地点： | 澳门威尼斯人度假村 Cotai Strip会展中心 |
| 内容： | 亚洲全球博彩业博览会是亚洲博彩市场的首要行业展会兼研讨会。展会集中展现亚洲博彩行业的迅猛发展、最新产品及最新潮流，吸引优质买家，且创造亚太地区博彩业最好的互联氛围。作为全球博彩业博览会（G2E）系列展会的一部分，亚洲全球博彩业博览会是来自博彩行业且专为博彩行业主办的展会，展会每年都与时俱进，满足行业需求并迎合最新行业潮流。 |
| 周期： | 每年一届 |
| 市场范围： | 国际性 |
| 性质： | 面向贸易观众 |
| 参展费用： | 光地展位360美元/$m^2$, 标准展位410美元/$m^2$ |
| 主办： | 励展香港公司；励展博览集团国际销售部 |
| 地址： | 北京市朝阳区新源里南路1-3号平安国际金融中心A座15层01-03,05(100027) |
| 联系人： | 王亮 |
| 展会赞助商： | 博彩器械厂商协会；澳大拉西亚博彩机械厂商协会；澳大利亚赌场协会 |
| 白金赞助商： | 高盛集团 |

| | |
|---|---|
| G2E Asia： | Global Gaming Expo Asia |
| Venue： | The Venetian Macao and Cotai Strip CotaiExpo |
| Frequency： | Annual |
| Market Area： | International |
| Nature： | Trade Only |
| Participation Fee： | Raw Space USD 360/$m^2$, Standard Booth USD 410/$m^2$ |
| Organizer： | Reed Exhibitions |

2010/11/03 – 05
2011/11 -
☎ 010-6590 7766转ext 715
🖷 010-6590 6139
✉ j.xu@koelnmesse.cn
www.wineandgourmetasia.cn

### 亚洲美食佳酿暨酒店及餐饮设备展

地点： 威尼斯人会议展览中心
内容： 亚洲美食佳酿暨酒店及餐饮设备展是亚洲地区唯一致力于国际精制食品与高级葡萄酒，酒店与餐饮设备及供应与服务行业的专业展览会。同期举办丰富活动，是美食主义者的盛会。
主要展品范围： 酒店设备与服务、葡萄酒和烈酒、食品和饮料
周期： 每年一届
市场范围： 国际性
展览性质： 面向贸易观众
主办： 科隆国际展览有限公司
地址： 北京市东三环北路8号亮马河大厦2座1018室（100004）
联系人： 徐畅

### Wine & Gourmet Asia

Venue: The Venetian Macao and Cotai Strip CotaiExpo
Market Area: International
Nature: Trade Only
Organizer: Koelnmesse GmbH
Address: Unit 1018, Landmark Tower II, No 8 Dongsanhuan North Road, Beijing 100004, China

# 台湾展览信息

# Exhibitions in Taiwan

☎ 010-6859 4964
🖷 010-6859 4964

## 台湾海峡两岸塑料橡胶工业展览会

日期： 2010/03/05 – 09
地点： 台北
周期： 每年一届
性质： 面向贸易观众
参展联络： 中国机械汽车展览联合会

☎ 010-8460 0551
🖷 010-8460 0394
✉ zhaolingna@ciec.com.cn
www.jingmu.com.cn

## 台北国际汽车零配件展览会

日期： 2010/04-
地点： 台北
内容： 汽车零配件
周期： 每年一届
市场范围： 国际性
性质： 面向公众/贸易观众
参展联络： 京慕国际展览有限公司（Jing Mu International Exhibition Co., Ltd.）
地址： 北京市朝阳区北三环东路6号中国国际展览中心服务楼3层（6 East Beisanhuan Rd., Beijing 100028，China）
联系人： 张辉，刘舰

☎ 010-8460 0551
🖷 010-8460 0394
✉ zhaolingna@ciec.com.cn
www.jingmu.com.cn

## 台北国际体育用品展览会
Taispo

日期： 2010/4/29 – 2010/5/2
地点： 台北
内容： 各类运动用球具、健身器材、溜冰器具、露营用具、运动服饰、运动器具、户外用品
周期： 每年一届
市场范围： 国际性
性质： 面向公众/贸易观众
参展联络： 京慕国际展览有限公司（Jing Mu International Exhibition Co., Ltd.）
地址： 北京市朝阳区北三环东路6号中国国际展览中心服务楼3层（6 East Beisanhuan Rd., Beijing100028, China）
联系人： 张翠元；滕昊

☎ 010-8460 0551
🖷 010-8460 0394
✉ zhaolingna@ciec.com.cn
www.jingmu.com.cn

## 台湾国际太阳能光电论坛暨展览会

日期： 2010/10 –
地点： 台北
内容： 太阳能光伏产品及技术、太阳能电池、光热产品
周期： 每年一届
市场范围： 国际性
参展联络： 京慕国际展览有限公司
地址： 北京市朝阳区北三环东路6号中国国际展览中心服务楼3层
联系人： 张晚霞，俞亮

☎ 010-6642 6288
🖷 010-6642 6556
www.ptexpo.com.cn

## 2010年海峡两岸宽频通讯展

日期： 2010/10/11 – 14
地点： 台北世界贸易中心南港展览馆Taipei World Trade Center Nangang Exhibition Hall
内容： 通讯运营与服务、内容提供、通讯设备、通讯零组件、应用服务、检测验证、FTTx、WiMAX、媒体等。
周期： 每年一届
始办年份： 2008
参展费用： 光地展位1600元/$m^2$，每家参展企业报名费人民币3000元
主办： 中国邮电器材集团公司；台湾区电机电子工业同业公会（PTAC, TEEMA）
地址： 北京西城区复兴门内大街156号北京招商国际金融中心A座10层A1008室（）
联系人： 张宝林

# 海外展览会议

# Exhibitions and Fairs Overseas

www.reedexport.cn
多样资源一手掌握
轻松玩转海外市场
建筑
音乐
五金
礼品
安防
图书
机械
能源
眼镜
石油
印刷
工程
制造
施工
海事
航天
国防
励展博览集团是全球首屈一指的展览及会议主办机构。每年举办的大型展览和会议超过 470 个，足迹遍及世界 37 个国家和地区。展览会涵盖 44 个行业。作为国际展览业的佼佼者，励展举办的展会每年都能成功汇聚七百万采购商和超过十万供货商，并促成上百亿美元的交易。

# 阿尔及利亚
# Algeria

### 阿尔及利亚汽配展
### EQUIP'AUTO Algérie

**日期**：2010/04/19 - 22
**地点**：阿尔及利亚阿尔及尔SAFEX展览中心
**内容**：轻型车、工业用车及售后网络所需设备和配件，汽车维修设备和相关服务，石油产品，润滑油和保养品，车身所需设备和产品，轮胎和轮辋，汽车服务场所所需设备，产品和配件，个人保护设备
**始办年份**：2006
**周期**：每年一届
**市场范围**：国际性
**上届规模**‘07：展览面积70,000m$^2$，参展商157家，参观人数4,680人
**主办**：法国高美爱博展览集团
**地址**：北京市朝阳区朝外大街20号联合大厦710室（100020）
**联系人**：张静
☎ 010-6588 5968, 6588 5969
🖷 010-6588 5970
✉ jackiezhang@promosalons-china.com

### EQUIP'AUTO Algérie

Date: 2010/04/19 - 22
Venue: SAFEX, Algiers, Algeria
Established Year: 2006
Frequency: Annual
Market Area: International
Statistics '07: Exhibition Area 70,000m$^2$, Exhibitors 157, Visitors 4,680
Organizer: COMEXPOSIUM
Address: 710# Union Plaza NO.20 ChaoWaiDaJie Beijing 100020, CHINA
☎ 010-6588 5968, 6588 5969
🖷 010-6588 5970
Contact: Jackie ZHANG
✉ jackiezhang@promosalons-china.com

### 国际农业机械展览会

**日期**：2010/05 -
**地点**：阿尔及利亚阿尔及尔
**周期**：每年一届
**市场范围**：国际性
**参展联络**：中国机械汽车展览联合会
☎ 010-6859 4964
🖷 010-6859 4964

### 阿尔及利亚环保及水处理设备展
### SIEE – Pollutec 2010: 6th International Exhibition of Equipment & Services for Water

SIEE - Pollutec

**日期**：2010/05 -
**地点**：阿尔及利亚阿尔及尔Safex-Pins Maritimes
**内容**：阿尔及利亚环保及水处理设备展是其境内业界唯一的专业展览，它汇聚300多家展出公司展示来自世界各地的不同水处理装备，服务，和技术解决方案，同时将有6,000多名有业务意向的观众在4天的时间里寻觅绝佳商机。SIEE – Pollutec每年一届，致力于提供广泛技术方案，解决各国所遇到的各种水处理问题，并且辅以高质量的会议日程，覆盖所有重要主题，这对于在阿尔及利亚的水处理行业专业人士是必不可少的。
**周期**：每年一届
**市场范围**：国际性
**赞助单位**：阿尔及利亚水资源部
**主办**：励展法国公司
**参展联络**：励展博览集团国际销售部
**地址**：北京市朝阳区新源里南路1-3号平安国际金融中心A座15层01-03，05（100027）
**联系人**：王亮
☎ 010-5933 9288
🖷 010-5933 9233
✉ liang.wang@reedexpo.com.cn
www.reedexport.cn

### 国际工程机械及施工设备展览会

**日期**：2010/11 -
**地点**：阿尔及利亚阿尔及尔
**周期**：每年一届
**市场范围**：国际性
**参展联络**：中国机械汽车展览联合会
☎ 010-6859 4964
🖷 010-6859 4964

### 第8届阿尔及利亚国际建筑工程展览会
### (SITP)

**日期**：2010/11 -
**地点**：阿尔及利亚阿尔及尔
**内容**：建筑工程
**市场范围**：国际性
**参展联络**：北京中仕达兴业展览有限公司
**地址**：北京市海淀区蓝靛厂东路2号金源时代商务中心2号楼A座11B（100097）
**联系人**：贾倩，赵仕忱，牟向东，张露
☎ 010-5129 8900
🖷 010-8886 2939
✉ mail@chinstar.cn
www.chinstar.cn

### 阿尔及利亚环保及水处理设备展
### SIEE – Pollutec 2011: 6th International Exhibition of Equipment & Services for Water

SIEE - Pollutec

**日期**：2011/05 -
**地点**：阿尔及利亚阿尔及尔
**内容**：阿尔及利亚环保及水处理设备展是其境内业界唯一的专业展览，它汇聚300多家展出公司展示来自世界各地的不同水处理装备，服务，和技术解决方案，同时将有6,000多名有业务意向的观众在4天的时间里寻觅绝佳商机。SIEE – Pollutec每年一届，致力于提供广泛技术方案，解决各国所遇到的各种水处理问题，并且辅以高质量的会议日程，覆盖所有重要主题，这对于在阿尔及利亚的水处理行业专业人士是必不可少的。
**周期**：每年一届
**市场范围**：国际性
**赞助**：阿尔及利亚水资源部
**主办**：励展法国公司
**参展联络**：励展博览集团国际销售部
**地址**：北京市朝阳区新源里南路1-3号平安国际金融中心A座15层01-03，05（100027）
**联系人**：王亮
☎ 010-5933 9288
🖷 010-5933 9233
✉ liang.wang@reedexpo.com.cn
www.reedexport.cn

# 安哥拉
# Angola

### 中国工业产品展览会

**日期**：2010 -
**地点**：安哥拉罗安达
**周期**：每年一届
**市场范围**：国际性
**参展联络**：中国机械汽车展览联合会
☎ 010-6859 4964
🖷 010-6859 4964

### 国际贸易博览会

**日期**：2010/07/14 - 19
**地点**：安哥拉罗安达
**周期**：每年一届
**市场范围**：国际性
**参展联络**：中国机械汽车展览联合会
☎ 010-6859 4964
🖷 010-6859 4964

### 第7届安哥拉国际建筑建材博览会

**日期**：2010/10 -
**地点**：安哥拉卢安达
**内容**：建筑建材
**市场范围**：国际性
**参展联络**：北京中仕达兴业展览有限公司
**地址**：北京市海淀区蓝靛厂东路2号金源时代商务中心2号楼A座11B（100097）
**联系人**：贾倩，赵仕忱，牟向东，张露
☎ 010-5129 8900
🖷 010-8886 2939
✉ mail@chinstar.cn
www.chinstar.cn

### 国际工程机械及建筑材料展览会

**日期**：2010/10 -
**地点**：安哥拉罗安达
**周期**：每年一届
**市场范围**：国际性
**参展联络**：中国机械汽车展览联合会
☎ 010-6859 4964
🖷 010-6859 4964

# 阿根廷
# Argentina

### 南美国际建筑工业展览会
### BATIMAT EXPOVIVIENDA: International Event for the Construction & Building Industry

BATIMAT EXPOVIVIENDA
Exposición Internacional de la Construcción y la Vivienda

**日期**：2010/06/01 - 05
**地点**：阿根廷布宜诺斯艾利斯
**内容**：表面装饰材料（包括油漆涂料、墙纸、地毯、地板、墙体、铸模、灯光等）；器具设备（厨房及卫浴器具设备、取暖及制冷设备、下水设备、保安防盗系统、木器、塑料器具等）；肆造服务及产品（建造工程公司、升降电梯及电动扶梯、作业保安系统、电话通讯系统及其他技术设备、机械、工具等）；机械（重型机械设备、推土机、起重机、挖掘机及相关工程运输机械）。
观众来源 建筑师、设计师、工程师、独立专业人士、顾问、咨询师、总裁、总监、首席执行管、合伙人、副总裁、工程安装部门经理、总经理、项目负责人、政府智能部门、企业单位负责人、 企业主、专业职称人士
**周期**：每年一届
**市场范围**：国际性
**参展联络**：励展博览集团国际销售部
**地址**：北京市朝阳区新源里南路1-3号平安国际金融中心A座15层01-03，05（100027）
**联系人**：吴祥
☎ 010-5933 9288
🖷 010-5933 9233
✉ ronald.wu@reedexpo.com.cn
www.reedexport.cn

### 国际物流展览会

日期：2010/08/10 - 31
地点：阿根廷布宜诺斯艾利斯
周期：每年一届
市场范围：国际性
参展联络：中国机械汽车展览联合会
☎ 010-6859 4964
🖷 010-6859 4964

### 阿根廷国际食品及饮料展

Alimentaria Mercosur: International Food & Beverage Exhibition

Alimentaria Mercosur

日期：2010/09 -
地点：阿根廷布宜诺斯艾利斯
内容：阿根廷国际食品及饮料展是南美食品、饮料和设备最大型且具有代表性的展会 产品和服务 食品饮料和设备的生产商、制造商、分销商及进出口公司。
观众来源：阿根廷、巴西和南美的买家、分销商（包括超市、批发、进口商和出口商…）餐厅和食品公司
周期：每年一届
市场范围：国际性
参展费用：欢迎垂询展位费用（单位：比索Peso）
赞助商：COPAL; FUNDACION EXPORTAR; CAS; FASA; SECRETARIA DE AGRICULTURA GANADERIA Y PESCA
主办：励展阿根廷公司
参展联络：励展博览集团国际销售部
地址：北京市朝阳区新源里南路1-3号平安国际金融中心A座15层01-03，05（100027）
联系人：杜一鸣
☎ 010-5933 9288
🖷 010-5933 9233
✉ martin.du@reedexpo.com.cn
www.reedexport.cn

### 国际电信联盟2010年美洲电信展

ITU TELECOM AMERICAS 2010

日期：2010/09/21 - 24
地点：阿根廷布宜诺斯艾利斯
周期：5年一届
市场范围：国际性
主办：国际电信联盟
承办：中国邮电器材集团公司国际展览部
地址：北京西城区复兴门内大街156号北京招商国际金融中心A座10层A1008室
联系人：张宝林
☎ 010-6642 6288
🖷 010-6642 6556
www.ptexpo.com.cn

### ITU TELECOM AMERICAS 2010

Date: 2010/09/21 - 24
Venue: Buenos Aires, Argentina
Frequency: Every 5 Years
Market Area: International
Organizer: International Telecommunication Union
☎ 86-10-6642 6288
🖷 86-10-6642 6556
www.ptexpo.com.cn

### 国际工程机械与建筑机械展览会

日期：2010/10 -
地点：阿根廷布宜诺斯艾利斯
周期：每年一届
市场范围：国际性
参展联络：中国机械汽车展览联合会
☎ 010-6859 4964
🖷 010-6859 4964

### 2010年南美洲（阿根廷）国际汽车零部件及售后服务展览会

Automechanika Argentina

日期：2010/11/03 - 06
4567
地点：阿根廷布宜诺斯艾利斯
周期：每年一届
市场范围：国际性
主办：法兰克福展览公司
承办：中国汽车工业国际合作总公司
地址：北京市海淀区中关村丹棱街3号A座5层（100080）
联系人：何萌
☎ 010-8260 6880
🖷 010-8260 6883
✉ exhibition@cnaico.com.cn

### 南美国际建筑工业展览会

BATIMAT EXPOVIVIENDA: International Event for the Construction & Building Industry

BATIMAT EXPOVIVIENDA
Exposición Internacional de la Construcción y la Vivienda

日期：2011/06 -
地点：阿根廷布宜诺斯艾利斯
内容：表面装饰材料（包括油漆涂料、墙纸、地毯、地板、墙体、铸模、灯光等）；器具设备（厨房及卫浴器具设备、取暖及制冷设备、下水设备、保安防盗系统、木器、塑料器具等）；建造服务及产品（建造工程公司、升降电梯及电动扶梯、作业保安系统、电话通讯系统及其他技术设备、机械、工具等）；机械（重型机械设备、推土机、起重机、挖掘机及相关工程运输机械）。
观众来源：建筑师、设计师、工程师、独立专业人士、顾问、咨询师、总裁、总监、首席执行管、合伙人、副总裁、工程安装部门经理、总经理、项目负责人、政府智能部门、企业单位负责人、 企业主、专业职称人士
周期：每年一届
市场范围：国际性
主办：参展联络：励展博览集团国际销售部
地址：北京市朝阳区新源里南路1-3号平安国际金融中心A座15层01-03，05（100027）
联系人：吴祥
☎ 010-5933 9288
🖷 010-5933 9233
✉ ronald.wu@reedexpo.com.cn
www.reedexport.cn

## 澳大利亚 Australia

### 悉尼国际SPA及美容展览会

Sydney International Spa & Beauty Expo

sydney international spa & beauty expo

日期：2010 -
地点：澳大利亚悉尼达令港 悉尼会展中心
内容：悉尼国际SPA及美容展览会是澳大利亚SPA及美容行业最大、最悠久的专业展会，方便行业人士从最广大的供应商中采购产品，并学习如何将业务领向成功。
产品及服务：最新技术、疗法、沙龙服务及设备。数百位展商将带来全球最好的美容品牌。从传统面部美容、蜜蜡脱毛及全身美容，到非外科面部整容、健康项目及全自由体验。
周期：每年一届
市场范围：国际性
参展费用：标准展位534澳大利亚元/m²
主办：励展澳大利亚公司
参展联络：励展博览集团国际销售部
地址：北京市朝阳区新源里南路1-3号平安国际金融中心A座15层01-03，05（100027）
联系人：吴祥
☎ 010-5933 9288
🖷 010-5933 9233
✉ ronald.wu@reedexpo.com.cn
www.reedexport.cn

### 第10届澳大利亚悉尼国际家具展

AIFF 2010

日期：2010/02/03 - 05
地点：澳大利亚悉尼
内容：适合软体沙发、套房、原木家具和户外家具等
周期：每年一届
市场范围：国际性
参展联络：大连上选会展服务有限公司
地址：大连市西岗区鞍山路13号兴业广场大厦B座508室（116011）
☎ 0411-8378 8326, 8378 8396, 8378 9165, 8378 8821
🖷 0411-8378 8830, 8378 8823
✉ cicyhuang@vip.sina.com
MSN：cicyhuang@msn.com
www.sun-show.com

### 2010年西澳大利亚国际电力能源行业展示会及高层战略商务论谈

Power & Electricity West Australia

日期：2010/03/02 - 04
地点：澳大利亚柏斯Parmelia Hilton
内容：Focusing on Power Generation, T&D and Environment, Electric Power Equipment and Technology。电力、电网建设：电站设备、电网建设、电力装置、高压开关、传输、配电网络、变压器、电流互感器、电压互感器、电力电容器、高压开柜、监控器、电机工程、电力供应和附件、电线电缆、绝缘材料、测量设备等；输变电设备：电网系统、变压器、仪表互感器、电力变频器、电缆线材、电力电容避雷器，接地电阻，电抗器，电炉和加热设备，电焊机，绝缘器及其它；配电装置和控制设备；清洁能源等设备制造；发电机设备；各类发电设备，风力发电设备，太阳能技术及设备，清洁可再生能源，原子核反应堆，蒸汽锅炉，蒸汽透平以及其它能源发电系统。核能、可再生能源
周期：每年一届
市场范围：国际性
主办：特兰展览
参展联络：北京中杰城设国际展览有限公司
地址：北京市海淀区三里河路9号建设部机关门诊楼5层（100835）
联系人：李娜
☎ 010-8838 5291
🖷 010-5885 7468, 5893 4708
✉ info@btfi.cn
www.top-fairs.com.cn
www.btfi.cn

### 澳大利亚劳保展

SAFETY IN ACTION

日期：2010/04/20 - 22
地点：澳大利亚墨尔本
内容：个人防护设备（手套、工装、安全鞋、反光材料等）工作环境下安全的传送装置、噪音防护方面的软硬件设备、防火设备、放射防护、触电保护、安全组织和服务等
周期：每年一届
市场范围：国际性
参展联络：京慕国际展览有限公司
地址：北京市朝阳区北三环东路6号中国国际展览中心服务楼3层
联系人：薛磊，国曦
☎ 010-8460 0551

☎ 010-8460 0394
✉ zhaolingna@ciec.com.cn
www.jingmu.com.cn

## 澳大利亚机械制造周

National Manufacturing Week

**日期：** 2010/05 -
**地点：** 澳大利亚黄金海岸南岸墨尔本国际会展中心
**内容：** 是大洋洲规模最大、水平最高、涉及范围最广的工业技术展示与交易场所，分别在悉尼和墨尔本两个城市轮回展出。08年的展览会在悉尼举办，参展的人员数为3823人，是全澳洲业内人士争相关注的盛会。澳大利亚国际机械制造周展览会围绕10大主题：澳大利亚国际工程展、焊接热处理展、气动液压技术、物料搬运、计算机控制、安保展、流程与控制展及机床工具展等。中国组团参展是有史以来规模最多参展公司最多的一次，展出面积在海外参展团中独树一帜共有550m²，中国参展展品主要有机床、剪板机、电机、柴油机、机械零配件、五金工具、电动工具、轴承、搬运车、摩托车、割草机、小五金等。其次是德国200m²，瑞士和新西兰各100m²，还有捷克、印度等小规模参展团体；观众分别来自美国、英国、德国、秘鲁、新加坡、阿联酋、印度、意大利日本、马来西亚、挪威、丹麦、香港、中国等众多国家.澳大利亚国际机械制造周展览会的展品范围极其广泛，几乎涵盖了工业制造流程的各个方面。
**周期：** 每年一届
**市场范围：** 国际性
**上届规模** ’08：展览面积12,000m²，参展商400家，参观人数12,000人
**参展联络：** 励展博览集团国际销售部
**地址：** 北京朝阳区新源里南路1-3号平安国际金融中心A座15层01-03，05（100027）
**联系人：** 宫卫
☎ 010-5933 9288
☎ 010-5933 9233
✉ david.gong@reedexpo.com.cn
www.reedexport.cn
www.nmw.reedexhibitions.com.au

## 2010年澳大利亚全球商品采购交易会

201 The Global Sourcing & Merchandising Expo

**日期：** 2010/05/05 - 07
**地点：** 澳大利亚墨尔本展览中心
**内容：** 服装纺织区：日常服装、婚礼服装、布料、鞋类、手提包、时尚配件、皮革制品、孕妇服装、运动装；男士用品区：日常用品、随身小器具及漫画书、五金工具类；家居园艺区：家具、手工艺品、家庭及厨房用具、家庭防护、灯具、户外及休闲产品、季节性装饰品、家居储藏；企业商品区：小礼品、促销礼品、IT系统、办公家具、办公用品、包装及纸质用品、印刷出版物、安全装置、通信、制服；休闲用品区：汽车相关、化妆品、消费电子及电脑产品、眼镜、礼品、珠宝手表、奢侈品、个人护理用品、运动器具；自主品牌区：服饰、化妆品、食品、健康产品、家居服装、护肤品、软件；0-12岁区：婴儿用品、儿童服装、玩具等。
**周期：** 每年一届
**主办：** International Conferences & Exhibitions LLC（IC&E）
**参展联络：** 杭州思诺博会展服务有限公司
**地址：** 杭州市体育场路229号浙江粮油大厦1202室（310003）
☎ 0571-8577 8500
☎ 0571-8577 9709
✉ expo@sinobal.com
www.sinobal.com

## 2010年澳大利亚国际机械制造周展览会

National Manufacturing Week

**日期：** 2010/05/11 - 14
数据库会展编号3651
**地点：** 澳大利亚悉尼奥林匹克公园展馆
**内容：** 澳大利亚国际机械制造周展览会（National Manufacturing Week）是大洋州规模最大、水平最高、涉及范围最广的工业技术展示与交易场所，每年一届，分别在悉尼和墨尔本两个城市轮回展出。该展为澳大利亚最大的机械工业展会，展览范围较广，基本揽括了机械工业方面的各种产品。其中以机床、工程机械、五金工具为主。分为十个主题，其中主要有：澳大利亚国际工程展、焊接热处理展、气动液压技术、物料搬运、计算机控制、安保产品、流程与控制展、机床工具、金属加工、电力设备、电子器件等。在展会调查中显示，关于矿业、能源以及其他资源的工业制造及服务展示特别得到参观商的重视。
**周期：** 每年一届
**市场范围：** 国际性
**上届规模** ‘09：展览面积10,000m²，参展商441家，参观人数10,174人
**参展联络：**
**地址：** 广州市海珠区新港中路350号C1204（510310）
**联系人：** 周文槟
☎ 020-3405 2086, 13710318991
☎ 020-3405 0629
✉ tai1234567@21cn.com
MSN：gdwenbin@hotmail.com
QQ：406372636

## 2010 年澳大利亚国际机械制造周展览

AIEE

(Australia's International Engineering Exhibition) with National Manufacturing Week
**日期：** 2010/05/11 - 14
**地点：** 澳大利亚悉尼奥林匹克公园展馆
**内容：** 该展会所设主题：共10个主题：电力展（ELECTRIX）；电子工业展（Electronics Industry Exhibition -AusTronics）；澳大利亚的国际工程设备展（Australia's International Engineering Exhibitions）；物流，物料搬运配展（Logistics, Materials Handling & Distribution Exhibition LMHD）；航空技术（AIR Technology）；自动化及机器人展（Automation & Robotics Exhibition）；计算计软件技术、服务系统（CIMtech Exhibition）；健康及安全（Health and Safety Exhibition）；仪器仪表，控制及自动化展览会（Instrumentation, Control and Automation Exhibition ICEX-IICA）；大焊接、热处理展（Welding, heat-treating, joining Exhibition-WeldTech）
**始办年份：** 1969
**周期：** 两年一届
**市场范围：** 国际性
**主办：** 国际电工委员会电气工程分会
**参展联络：** 北京中杰城设国际展览有限公司
**地址：** 北京市海淀区三里河路9号建设部机关门诊楼5层（100835）
**联系人：** 李娜
☎ 010-8838 5291
☎ 010-5885 7468, 5893 4708
✉ info@btfi.cn
www.top-fairs.com.cn
www.btfi.cn

## 2010年澳大利亚国际工程机械展

**日期：** 2010/05/21 - 23
**地点：** 澳大利亚悉尼
**内容：** 通风设备、操作设备、建筑维修、化学制品、切割机、清洁装置、商业用车、压土机、混凝土机械、工程顾问、施工设备、起重机、刀具切割机、排水装置、钻孔装置、挖掘机、电子控制系统、发动机、发动装置、腐蚀调控系统、开凿机、打洞机、过滤器、打磨处理、燃料管理系统、全球定位器械调节装置、高压水泵、灌溉装置、草根供应和培养、原料处理、公园和街道设备、铺路砖块、管道维护、运动场设备、预制塑胶产品、出版、抽水机、管道、电子管装置、再循环产品、公路维修设备、公路安全设备、下水道系统和维修、支柱、标记、软件、喷淋系统、街道清洁装备、测量装备、调控设计装备和工具、挖沟设备、卡车及配件、轮胎及配件、防毒服装、安全服装、垃圾处理系统、废水处理系统、水控制系统、焊接设备和服务、木材切割机、除草机
**周期：** 每年一届
**市场范围：** 国际性
**主办：** 澳大利亚公共建设工程协会
**参展联络：** 北京麦田通会国际展览有限公司
**联系人：** 吴珊
☎ 010-5165 9302转8005, 8633 1235, 13426437438
☎ 010-5165 9302
✉ xiaoxiangzhishui@yahoo.com.cn
MSN：xiaoxiangzhishui@hotmail.com

## 澳大利亚昆士兰采矿机械展

Queensland Mining & Engineering Exhibition (QME)

**日期：** 2010/07/27 - 29
**地点：** 澳大利亚
**内容：** 关于展会 QME是在煤矿开采区的核心地区举办的最大的区域性展会，主要展出采矿、矿物加工、发电、糖类加工及金属熔炼业的产品及服务。QME2006 是第二次与QCME(Queensland Construction & Machinery Exhibition)合办的展会。
**周期：** 两年一届
**市场范围：** 国际性
**参展费用：** 欢迎垂询参展费（单位：澳大利亚元）
**主办：** 澳大利亚励展博览集团
**参展联络：** 励展博览集团国际销售部
**地址：** 北京朝阳区新源里南路1-3号平安国际金融中心A座15层01-03，05（100027）
**联系人：** 王亮
☎ 010-5933 9288
☎ 010-5933 9233
✉ liang.wang@reedexpo.com.cn
www.reedexport.cn

## 澳大利亚机械制造周

National Manufacturing Week

**日期：** 2011/05 -
插入logo，数据库会展编号3554
**地点：** 澳大利亚 黄金海岸，南岸，墨尔本国际会展中心
**内容：** 大洋州规模最大、水平最高、涉及范围最广的工业技术展示与交易场所。08年的展览会在悉尼举办，参展的人员数为3823人，是全澳洲业内人士争相关注的盛会。澳大利亚国际机械制造周展览会围绕10大主题：澳大利亚国际工程展、焊接热处理展、气动液压技术、物料搬运、计算机控制、安保展、流程与控制展及机床工具展等。

中国组团参展是有史以来规模最多参展公司最多的一次，展出面积在海外参展团中独树一帜共有550m²，中国参展展品主要有机床、剪板机、电机、柴油机、机械零配件、五金工具、电动工具、轴承、搬运车、摩托车、割草机、小五金等。其次是德国200m²，瑞士和新西兰各100m²，还有捷克、印度等小规模参展团体。

观众分别来自美国、英国、德国、秘鲁、新加

坡、阿联酋、印度、意大利日本、马来西亚、挪威、丹麦、香港、中国等众多国家。

展品范围极其广泛，几乎涵盖了工业制造流程的各个方面。

**周期：** 每年一届（分别在悉尼和墨尔本两个城市轮回展出）

**市场范围：** 国际性

**上届规模** ’08：展览面积12,000m$^2$，参展商400家，参观人数12,000人

**参展联络：** 励展博览集团国际销售部

**地址：** 北京朝阳区新源里南路1-3号平安国际金融中心A座15层01-03，05（100027）

**联系人：** 宫卫

☎ 010-5933 9288

🖷 010-5933 9233

✉ david.gong@reedexpo.com.cn

www.reedexport.cn

www.nmw.reedexhibitions.com.au

## 2011年澳大利亚全球商品采购交易会

2011 The Global Sourcing & Merchandising Expo

**日期：** 2011/05 -

**地点：** 澳大利亚墨尔本展览中心

**内容：** 服装纺织区：日常服装、婚礼服装、布料、鞋类、手提包、时尚配件、皮革制品、孕妇服装、运动装；男士用品区：日常用品、随身小器具及漫画书、五金工具类；家居园艺区：家具、手工艺品、家庭及厨房用具、家庭防护、灯具、户外及休闲产品、季节性装饰品、家居储藏；企业商品区：小礼品、促销礼品、IT系统、办公家具、办公用品、包装及纸质用品、印刷出版物、安全装置、通信、制服；休闲用品区：汽车相关、化妆品、消费电子及电脑产品、眼镜、礼品、珠宝手表、奢侈品、个人护理用品、运动器具；自主品牌区：服饰、化妆品、食品、健康产品、家居服装、护肤品、软件；0-12岁区：婴儿用品、儿童服装、玩具等。

**周期：** 每年一届

**市场范围：** 国际性

**主办：** International Conferences & Exhibitions LLC (IC&E)

**参展联络：** 杭州思诺博会展服务有限公司

**地址：** 杭州市体育场路229号浙江粮油大厦1202室（310003）

☎ 0571-8577 8500

🖷 0571-8577 9709

✉ expo@sinobal.com

www.sinobal.com

## 悉尼亚太国际矿业展

AIMEX:

Asia Pacific's International Mining Exhibition

**日期：** 2011/09/06 - 09

**日期：** 2014 -

插入logo，数据库会展编号3361

**地点：** 澳大利亚悉尼奥林匹克公园悉尼展览场

**内容：** 面向世界采矿以及相关工程行业最大的产品及服务展会之一。

**产品及服务：** 采矿设备、供应及服务、计算机-软件及硬件、传送装置及相关操作设备、电子设备、消防设备、安全设备、地下采矿、运输、环境保护及尘埃控制、露天采矿、矿物开采、矿物加工及选煤、粉碎、碾压及筛选设备、发电、传送、布缆、能源系统、进程控制、水泵及阀门。**市场范围：** 国际性

**赞助：** 澳大利亚采矿设备及服务委员会(MESCA)；建筑及采矿设备工业集团(CMEIG)；澳大拉西亚采矿及冶金学院(AUSIMM)；澳大利亚采矿设备技术及服务(AUSTMINE)；澳大利亚贸易委员会(AUSTRADE)

**参展联络：** 励展博览集团国际销售部

**地址：** 北京朝阳区新源里南路1-3号平安国际金融中心A座15层01-03，05（100027）

**联系人：** 王亮

☎ 010-5933 9288

🖷 010-5933 9233

✉ liang.wang@reedexpo.com.cn

www.reedexport.cn

## 澳大利亚昆士兰采矿机械展

Queensland Mining & Engineering Exhibition (QME)

**日期：** 2012/07 -

**地点：** 澳大利亚

**内容：** QME是在煤矿开采区的核心地区举办的最大的区域性展会，主要展出采矿、矿物加工、发电、糖类加工及金属熔炼业的产品及服务。QME 2006是第二次与QCME(Queensland Construction & Machinery Exhibition)合办的展会。

**周期：** 两年一届

**市场范围：** 国际性

**参展费用：** 欢迎垂询参展费用（单位：澳大利亚元AU$）

**主办：** 澳大利亚励展博览集团

**参展联络：** 励展博览集团国际销售部

**地址：** 北京朝阳区新源里南路1-3号平安国际金融中心A座15层01-03，05（100027）

**联系人：** 王亮

☎ 010-5933 9288

🖷 010-5933 9233

✉ liang.wang@reedexpo.com.cn

www.reedexport.cn

# 奥地利 Austria

## 维也纳国际汽车展

Vienna Auto Show

**日期：** 2010/01/14 - 17

**地点：** 奥地利维也纳Messe Wien（维也纳展览中心）

**内容：** 由奥地利汽车进口商支持的汽车展。**产品及服务：** 新汽车产品、轮胎及各类汽车配件。

**周期：** 两年一届

**市场范围：** 国际性

**主办：** 励展奥地利公司

**参展联络：** 励展博览集团海外展览部

**地址：** 北京朝阳区新源里南路1-3号平安国际金融中心A座15层01-03，05（100027）

**联系人：** 杜一鸣

☎ 010-5933 9288

🖷 010-5933 9233

✉ martin.du@reedexpo.com.cn

www.reedexport.cn

## 奥地利国际汽车生产设备及加油站设备、化学品及环境技术展

Auto Zum:

International Trade Fair for the Car & Vehicle Industry

AutoZum Salzburg

**日期：** 2011/01 -

**日期：** 2013/01 -

**地点：** 奥地利萨尔斯堡贸易展览中心

**内容：** AutoZum 是奥地利最大的汽车零部件及加油站设备、汽车化学产品及环保产品国际专业展览会，至今已成功举办了28届。该展是在奥地利地区汽车行业人士汇聚的的唯一场所，同时它也无可置疑成为奥地利主要的国际贸易展览会。作为衡量下一个财政年度的标准，该展被称为是在多瑙河和阿尔卑斯山区域的市场指南针。展览会具有明确的主题，高质量的专业讲座、专业的观众，这些都为参展提供了必要的增值服务。作为专业贸易展览会，AutoZum是接触新客户、增进现有客户关系，扩大贸易的最好机会。也是为专业观众展示革新产品的最好场所。展览会组办单位通过各种渠道包括多个步骤的直接邮寄、媒体、广告等方式推广专业客商到展会参观洽谈，以及与相关协会和管理部门包括来自捷克、匈牙利、斯洛文尼亚、斯洛伐克等紧密合作，使Autozum成为阿尔卑斯山及莱茵河区域在汽车零部件及汽车售后服务领域最重要的展览会。

展会主要数据：参观客商24,873名客商，主要来自汽车、加油站及美容和维修行业的雇主、经理、执行人员和雇员。据统计，有90%的参观客商对AutoZum表示满意，89%的客商来自行业的代表，87%的客商认为参加此展的好处多于其他种交流方式，71%的客商把此展作为本年度参加的贸易展览会计划，83%的客商表示继续参加AutoZum展览会

**周期：** 两年一届

**市场范围：** 国际性

**参展联络：** 励展博览集团国际销售部

**地址：** 北京朝阳区新源里南路1-3号平安国际金融中心A座15层01-03，05（100027）

**联系人：** 杜一鸣

☎ 010-8515 1376

🖷 010-5933 9233

✉ martin.du@reedexpo.com.cn

www.reedexport.cn

## 奥地利国际食品技术及制造展览会

L-TEC: The Trade Fair for Food Technology & Manufacturing

**日期：** 2011/03 -

**地点：** 奥地利萨尔茨堡

**内容：** 奥地利国际食品技术及制造展览会是奥地利独一无二的食品行业综合展会。展会的展示重点为面包糕点、肉类、奶类、包装及商店设备。产品及服务 食品技术和生产所需的产品及服务。

**周期：** 三年一届

**市场范围：** 国际性

**主办：** 励展奥地利公司

**参展联络：** 励展博览集团国际销售部

**地址：** 北京朝阳区新源里南路1-3号平安国际金融中心A座15层01-03，05（100027）

**联系人：** 杜一鸣

☎ 010-5933 9288

☎ 010-5933 9233
✉ martin.du@reedexpo.com.cn
www.reedexport.cn

### 奥地利国际木材加工、处理、装配、木匠用品展

BWS: International Trade Fair for Woodworking

日期：2011/04 -
2013/04 -
地点：奥地利萨尔茨堡展览中心
内容：BWS是国际顶级的木工机械和金属制品的展览会，和"奥地利五金展"同是木工业和五金业内全国性和国际性供应商和购买商必须参加的盛会。吸引着来自整个欧洲的供货商和采购商。观众主要是欧洲的木工、工匠、门窗制造厂、木制产品加工厂、家具制造商、木工贸易、油漆贸易公司、伐木厂、五金商、建筑公司、钥匙锁具贸易公司、安全科技企业、金属处理加工公司、建筑师。
产品和服务：木工五金配件、防护衣及工作安全用品、铰链和配件、工具、锁具及锁具技术、安全设备、金属加工、紧固及固定技术、环境技术、木具加工及成套设备、木工材料&加工材料、木工和细木供应，表面磨光、加工聚合材料机器和工具、木工和细木机械/工具、锯木技术、锯木机械及工具、门窗设备、结构设备、森林伐木设备，机械，工具
始办年份：1974
周期：两年一届
市场范围：国际性
主办：励展博览集团国际销售部
地址：北京朝阳区新源里南路1-3号平安国际金融中心A座15层01-03、05（100027）
联系人：杜一鸣
☎ 010-5933 9288
☎ 010-5933 9233
✉ martin.du@reedexpo.com.cn
www.reedexport.cn

## 阿塞拜疆 Azerbaijan

### 第七届阿塞拜疆国际汽车及零配件展览会

Auto Show Azerbaijan 2010

日期：2010/04/01 - 04
地点：阿塞拜疆巴库
周期：每年一届
市场范围：国际性
主办：法兰克福展览公司
参展联络：中国汽车工业国际合作总公司
地址：北京市海淀区中关村丹棱街3号A座5层（100080）
联系人：何萌
☎ 010-8260 6880
☎ 010-8260 6883
✉ exhibition@cnaico.com.cn

### 国际运输及物流展览会

日期：2010/06/01 - 04
地点：阿塞拜疆巴库
周期：每年一届
市场范围：国际性
参展联络：中国机械汽车展览联合会
☎ 010-6859 4964
☎ 010-6859 4964

## 巴林 Bahrain

### 中东国际地球物理科学展览会暨研讨会

日期：2010/03/08 - 10
地点：巴林
内容：勘探、测井、数据采集分析、成像、定位
主办：北京邦企展览有限公司
地址：北京市朝阳区惠新东街11号紫光发展大厦B1-501（100029）
联系人：雷邵军，赖玉宝
☎ 010-6482 3808
☎ 010-6482 3670
✉ bbes@china.com

### 中东精练及石化展览会

日期：2010/05/24 - 26
地点：巴林
内容：石油炼化、化工、管道闸门
主办：北京邦企展览有限公司
地址：北京市朝阳区惠新东街11号紫光发展大厦B1-501（100029）
联系人：雷邵军，赖玉宝
☎ 010-6482 3808
☎ 010-6482 3670
✉ bbes@china.com

## 比利时 Belgium

### EUROPEAN SEAFOOD EXPO

Date：2010/04/27 - 29
Venue: PARC DEC EXPOSITIONS
Frequency: Annual
Market Area: International
Organizer: DIVERSIFIED BUSINESS COMMUNICATIONS
☎ 86-10-5919 4405
☎ 86-10-6591 8986
✉ joy@agri.gov.cn

## 孟加拉 Bengal

### 孟加拉国际电力能源及照明展览会

EL-POWER&LIGHTING BANGLADESH

日期：2010/01/07 - 10
地点：孟加拉达卡中孟友谊会展中心
内容：电力和热能生产设备：发电设备及系统，独立的能源来源，锅炉及锅炉辅助设备，蒸汽涡轮机，电力产品，联合循环和燃气涡轮机组，热、电转换设备，各种发电机。转换和存储电能设备与产品：蓄电池，电力变压器，充电设备及产品。输配电设备与产品：传输和分配电能，电源开关，高、低电压程控系统及设备，绝缘和非绝缘产品，变电站设备及产品，低压配电设备和程控系统，输电线路，继电保护装置及系统。可再生能源、电力设备及技术：天然气发电工程，生物能学，风力发电工程，氢气发电工程，地热电站工程，小水电工程，太阳能电力工程等可再生电力能源。节能产品，工业电力工程及技术，电动机，电力驱动设备，电气控制设备，燃料电池材料，泵类和压缩机，照明设备，管道和管道配件，工业通风系统，水处理技术和系统，测量，控制和诊断仪器，诊断设备
周期：每年一届
市场范围：国际性
参展联络：北京中杰城设国际展览有限公司

地址：北京市海淀区三里河路9号建设部机关门诊楼5层（100835）
联系人：李娜
☎ 010-8838 5291
☎ 010-5885 7468, 5893 4708
✉ info@btfi.cn
www.top-fairs.com.cn, www.btfi.cn

### 国际印刷、包装及塑胶展览会

日期：2010/01/25 - 28
地点：孟加拉达卡
周期：每年一届
市场范围：国际性
参展联络：中国机械汽车展览联合会
☎ 010-6859 4964
☎ 010-6859 4964

### 国际汽车展览会

日期：2010/03/18 - 20
地点：孟加拉达卡
周期：每年一届
市场范围：国际性
参展联络：中国机械汽车展览联合会
☎ 010-6859 4964
☎ 010-6859 4964

## 博茨瓦纳 Botswana

### 国际交易会

日期：2010/11/04 - 07
地点：博茨瓦纳哈博罗内
周期：每年一届
市场范围：国际性
参展联络：中国机械汽车展览联合会
☎ 010-6859 4964
☎ 010-6859 4964

## 巴西 Brazil

### 巴西国际影像贸易展览会

PHOTOIMAGE BRAZIL: International Image Trade Fair

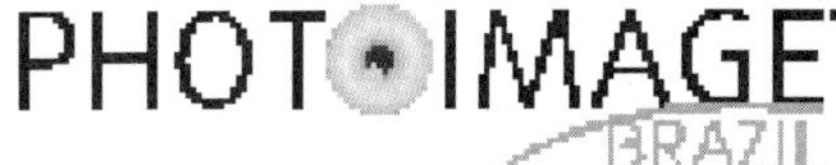


日期：2010 -
地点：巴西圣保罗 Imigrantes会展中心
内容：作为南美地区规模最大、最具影响力的影像类专业博览会,将呈献传统和数码摄影业及相关产业的最新创新。展会将吸引摄影器材及配件的主要厂商、代表及进口商。展会期间举办的业内大会和研讨会，使整个展会充满卓越的商业机会，长期以来一直是国际知名影像类企业向南美乃至整个美洲市场展示自身最新技术及产品的最佳平台。在活动期间，访客可以找到来自世界各地的与摄影和图像有关的大型公司，比如Kodak, FujiFilm, Noritsu, Samsung, Apple, HP, Pentax, Canon, Olympus, Kingston 和Roland。巴西影像展最具影响力的参展公司除Roland 和Elgin之外，还有Panasonic, Sony, Sharp (通过巴西发行商, Optec)等。近年来，随着中国影像产业的不断壮大，在完成欧洲以及美国等地区的市场拓展后，巴西 — 将成为您打开南美市场的最佳通道。
周期：每年一届
市场范围：国际性

**赞助：** ABIMFI-SEAFESP
**主办：** 励展博览集团巴西Alcantara Machado公司
**参展联络：** 励展博览集团国际销售部
**地址：** 北京朝阳区新源里南路1-3号平安国际金融中心A座15层01-03，05（100027）
**联系人：** 宫卫
☎ 010-5933 9288
🖷 010-5933 9233
✉ david.gong@reedexpo.com.cn
www.reedexport.cn

## 巴西圣保罗国际牙科展

## CIOSP

**日期：** 2010/01 -
**地点：** 巴西圣保罗
**内容：** 牙科医疗器械与设备；牙科医疗材料、工具；颌面外科专用器械、材料；牙体牙髓专用器械、材料；牙周病科专用器械、材料；正畸专用器械、材料
**周期：** 每年一届
**市场范围：** 国际性
**参展联络：** 京慕国际展览有限公司
**地址：** 北京市朝阳区北三环东路6号中国国际展览中心服务楼3层
**联系人：** 安红彦；孙铁兵
☎ 010-8460 0551
🖷 010-8460 0394
✉ zhaolingna@ciec.com.cn
www.jingmu.com.cn

## 巴西国际鞋业、皮革制品及附件展览会

## COUROMODA

**日期：** 2010/01/18 - 21
**地点：** 巴西圣保罗
**内容：** 鞋材、制鞋设备、箱包、皮革服饰以及与其相关的皮革制品等
**市场范围：** 国际性
**参展联络：** 京慕国际展览有限公司
**地址：** 北京市朝阳区北三环东路6号中国国际展览中心服务楼3层
**联系人：** 李嘉羊，古莹
☎ 010-8460 0551
🖷 010-8460 0394
✉ zhaolingna@ciec.com.cn
www.jingmu.com.cn

## 巴西国际五金及工具展览会

## Tools & Hardware Fair

**日期：** 2010/03 -
**地点：** 巴西圣保罗
**内容：** 建筑装饰五金、日用五金、电动机手动工具、建筑设备、固定装置及电子产品；户外用品周
**期：** 每年一届
**市场范围：** 国际性
**参展联络：** 京慕国际展览有限公司
**地址：** 北京市朝阳区北三环东路6号中国国际展览中心服务楼3层
**联系人：** 国曦，王爽
☎ 010-8460 0551
🖷 010-8460 0394
✉ zhaolingna@ciec.com.cn
www.jingmu.com.cn

## 国际印刷及包装展览会

**日期：** 2010/03/08 - 12
4457
**地点：** 巴西圣保罗
**周期：** 每年一届
**市场范围：** 国际性
**参展联络：** 中国机械汽车展览联合会
☎ 010-6859 4964
🖷 010-6859 4964

## 巴西国际机床工具展览会

## TECHMEI 2010

**日期：** 2010/03/15 - 18
**地点：** 巴西圣保罗
**周期：** 两年一届
**市场范围：** 国际性
**主办：** 中国国际贸易促进委员会机械行业分会
**地址：** 北京市西城区三里河路46号（100823）
**联系人：** 周海明，叶海青，聂飞
☎ 010-6859 5495, 6859 5247, 6851 3586, 6859 4938
🖷 010-6859 5057
✉ info@ccpitmsc.org jix@ccpit.org
www.chinamachin.org.cn
www.ccpitmsc.org

## 2010年巴西国际工业机械和设备展览会

## 2010 Brazil International Industrial Machinery and Equipment Exhibition

**日期：** 2010/03/15 - 18
**地点：** 巴西北方展览中心（红馆和绿馆）
**内容：** 机床和外设计量设备、机器人和工业机器人、切削工具、钢板和管成型机、压力机、工业工程院/ CAD / CAM软件、控制系统和工业自动化、塑料机械改造、Technical书籍和杂志、银行和金融机构
**周期：** 两年一届
**市场范围：** 国际性
**参展费用：** （3x3m）人民币28,000元
**上届规模** '08：展览面积30,000m²，参展商200家（来自114个国家），参观人数50,000人（其中专业和贸易观众20,000人）
**主办：** AP3
**地址：** 广东省深圳市福田区新洲大厦15层深圳创明展览设计有限公司（518048）
**联系人：** 雷明，朱利萍
☎ 0755-2393 8881, 2393 8025
🖷 0755-2393 8426
✉ cmffok@163.com
MSN：lm83573425@21cn.com

## 2010 Brazil International Industrial Machinery and Equipment Exhibition

**Date：** 2010/03/15 - 18
**Venue:** EXPO CENTER NORTE, Brazil
**Profile:** Machine tools and peripherals, Metrology equipments, Robots and industrial manipulators, Cutting tools Steel sheets and tube shaping machines, Presses Industrial CAE / CAD / CAM software, Control systems and industrial automation, Plastic transformation machinery, Technical books and magazines, Banks and financial institutions
**Frequency:** Biannual
**Market Area:** International
**Participated Fee:** （3x3m）RMB 28,000
**Statistics '08:** Exhibition Area 30,000m², Exhibitors 200（came from 114 countries）, Visitors 50,000 （trade visitors 20, 000）
**Organizer:** AP3
**Address:** 15/Fl Xinzhou Building, Futian District, Shenzhen, Guangdong
**Contact:** Rei Ming, Julius Ping
☎ 86-755-2393 8881, 2393 8025
🖷 86-755-2393 8426
✉ cmffok@163.com
MSN: lm83573425@21cn.com

## 巴西国际建材展

## Feicon Batimat - International Construction Industry Trade Fair

FEICON BATIMAT

**日期：** 2010/04/06 - 10
**地点：** 巴西圣保罗
**内容：** FEICON BATIMAT是在建筑业开展业务的最佳平台。它的成功是基于高质量的观众、其传播战略以及参展商的声望。它是建筑业内唯一的综合展会，在国内已经举办了20年，在国际上则已有40年历史。圣保罗的"国际建筑周"集合了拉美建筑业最优秀的项目。这是一个了解世界上最重要、最富盛名的品牌之创新和投资的绝佳机会。
**产品及服务：** 空调、休闲区（花园家具、凉篷、运动场及配件）。挂锁、锁及配件、金属屋顶及墙壁、门窗外框、石膏、比重计、水泵和水箱、放水、隔热/隔音、百叶帘和遮阳篷、游泳池、工业地坪、技术出版物、PVC、瓷砖、木质及橡胶地板及地毯、服务、安全系统和产品、木地板、木板、复合木地板、镶板、壁板、油漆、清漆及油漆附件、玻璃。
**周期：** 每年一届
**市场范围：** 国际性
**赞助：** ANAMACO；ABIMAQ；AREMASP；ABRAFATI；SIAMFESP；SINCOMAVI；ABIROCHAS
**参展联络：** 励展博览集团国际销售部
**地址：** 北京朝阳区新源里南路1-3号平安国际金融中心A座15层01-03，05（100027）
**联系人：** 宫卫
☎ 010-5933 9288
🖷 010-5933 9233
✉ david.gong@reedexpo.com.cn
www.reedexport.cn

## 巴西国际安防产品博览会

## ISC BRASIL – International Security & Conference Expo

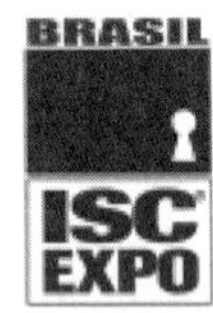


**日期：** 2010/04/14 - 16
**地点：** 巴西圣保罗Transamerica 展览中心
**内容：** 2008年巴西国际安保产品展览会（ISC BRASIL）是美国国际安保展览会继美国西部拉斯维加斯展和东部纽约展之后在南美地区召开的又一届盛会。2006年首届展会获得圆满成功，近3500位来自南美的主要采购商到会与展商进行接洽。目前国际知名公司如BOSCH、GE、HDL、SONY、HID等许多公司以及巴西当地知名公司均已订购2009年展位。随着全球安保产品工业的发展，巴西市场十分旺盛，估计目前超过9.2亿美元、年增长10%。参加巴西安保产品展览会具有如下优势：增加与当地客商扩大贸易的机会，与当地主要批发商建立联系，建立新的全球贸易伙伴，与来自全球主要的安保专业人士建立网络联系，了解来自该地区及全球安保产品的信息，与最终买家建立联系，结识来自巴西及南美地区的产品组装厂商，推广产品的使用和服务功能
**始办年份：** 2006
**周期：** 每年一届
**市场范围：** 国际性
**参展费用：** 净地展位220美元/m²，标准展位300美元/m²
**主办：** 励展博览集团美国公司和巴西公司；巴西Alcantara Machado Trade Fair展览公司
**协办：** 美国安保协会（SIA）；拉美安保协会（ALAS）；巴西电子电器工业协会（ABINEE）
**支持：** 巴西展览协会
**参展联络：** 励展博览集团国际销售部
**地址：** 北京朝阳区新源里南路1-3号平安国际金融中心A座15层01-03，05（100027）
**联系人：** 宫卫
☎ 010-5933 9288
🖷 010-5933 9233
✉ david.gong@reedexpo.com.cn
www.reedexport.cn

## 2010年巴西国际重型及商务汽车零配件展

## AUTOMEC Pesados & Comercias 2010

**日期：** 2010/04/27 – 05/01
**地点：** 巴西圣保罗安年比展览中心
**内容：** 该展如今已经进展成为南半球最重要的重型车辆、商用车及其零配件的展览盛事。
**周期：** 每年一届
**市场范围：** 国际性

**上届规模** ‘08：展览面积30,000m²，参展商437家（来自20个国家），贸易观众20,000人
**主办**：法兰克福展览公司
**参展联络**：中国汽车工业国际合作总公司
**地址**：北京市海淀区中关村丹棱街3号A座5层（100080）
**联系人**：何萌
☎ 010-8260 6880
🖷 010-8260 6883
✉ exhibition@cnaico.com.cn

## 巴西国际圣诞节日装饰品及玩具博览会

### Toys, Parties & Christmas Fair South America

**日期**：2010/05 -
**地点**：巴西圣保罗巴西
**内容**：圣诞用品、圣诞及派对装饰品、人造花果、焰火、宗教装饰品、蜡烛、烛台、薰香制品、装饰品包装、玩具、贺卡及文具、工艺品
**市场范围**：国际性
**参展联络**：京慕国际展览有限公司
**地址**：北京市朝阳区北三环东路6号中国国际展览中心服务楼3层
**联系人**：古莹
☎ 010-8460 0551
🖷 010-8460 0394
✉ zhaolingna@ciec.com.cn
www.jingmu.com.cn

## 国际机械及工业装备贸易展览会

### International Machinery and Industrial Supplies Trade Fair 2010

**日期**：2010/05/11 - 15
**地点**：巴西圣保罗
**周期**：两年一届
**市场范围**：国际性
**参展联络**：中国机械汽车展览联合会
☎ 010-6859 4964
🖷 010-6859 4964
**参展联络**：中国贸促会机械行业分会
**地址**：北京市西城区三里河路46号（100823）
**联系人**：吴琼
☎ 010-6859 4909
🖷 010-6859 4995
✉ info@ccpitmsc.org
✉ jix@ccpit.org
www.chinamachin.org.cn
www.ccpitmsc.org

## 巴西国际铝工业展

### The ALUMINIUM International Pavilion

**日期**：2010/05/18 - 20

EXPOALUMÍNIO 2010
Exposição Internacional do Alumínio
International Aluminum Exhibition

**地点**：巴西圣保罗Imigrantes展览中心
**内容**：由于铝材的特殊性质，可塑性极高，可以制成各种产品，为各种行业提供各种商务解决方案，是一种取之不尽，开发性极强的原材料。无论是在巴西国内还是海外，经过业内人士不断研究和采用先进的技术，使得铝的使用价值得以提高。参加巴西国际铝工业展ExpoAlumínio2010将带给您更多惊喜。展会为您提供绝佳良机推广您的公司，建立商务往来，推荐最新产品、设备、服务和科技创新等。展会将汇集来自铝业的公司、专家及消费者，涉及行业包括包装、建筑、机械、设备和消费品。
**周期**：每年一届
**市场范围**：国际性
**主办**：励展巴西公司Alcantara Machado
**参展联络**：励展博览集团国际销售部
**地址**：北京朝阳区新源里南路1-3号平安国际金融中心A座15层01-03，05（100027）
**联系人**：宫卫
☎ 010-5933 9288
🖷 010-5933 9233
✉ david.gong@reedexpo.com.cn
www.reedexport.cn

## 巴西安防展

### EXPO SEC

**日期**：2010/05/25 - 27
**地点**：圣保罗巴西
**内容**：中央监控、闭路、门禁系统、安全锁、身份识别、数据安全、无线通讯、保险箱及个人防护设备（手套、工装、安全鞋、反光材料）等
**周期**：每年一届
**市场范围**：国际性
**参展联络**：京慕国际展览有限公司
**地址**：北京市朝阳区北三环东路6号中国国际展览中心服务楼3层
**联系人**：薛磊，国曦
☎ 010-8460 0551
🖷 010-8460 0394
✉ zhaolingna@ciec.com.cn
www.jingmu.com.cn

## 巴西纺织服装展

**日期**：2010/06 -
**地点**：巴西圣保罗
**内容**：男女服装、童装、内衣泳装、劳保服装、服装饰品、各种服装附件、各种面料、家用纺织品、皮革制品、箱包手袋
**市场范围**：国际性
**参展联络**：京慕国际展览有限公司
**地址**：北京市朝阳区北三环东路6号中国国际展览中心服务楼3层
**联系人**：由慧；柳川
☎ 010-8460 0551
🖷 010-8460 0394
✉ zhaolingna@ciec.com.cn
www.jingmu.com.cn

## 巴西国际医疗展

### Hospitalar

**日期**：2010/06 -
**地点**：巴西圣保罗
**内容**：医院设备、医疗技术、实验室设备、医用耗材、整形及康复用品、成品药等
**周期**：每年一届
**市场范围**：国际性
**参展联络**：京慕国际展览有限公司
**地址**：北京市朝阳区北三环东路6号中国国际展览中心服务楼3层
**联系人**：魏亦山
☎ 010-8460 0551
🖷 010-8460 0394
✉ zhaolingna@ciec.com.cn
www.jingmu.com.cn

## 国际食品及饮料包装机械展览会

第26届巴西国际食品、饮料工业加工技术和包装工业博览会
Flspal Tecnologia 2010
**日期**：2010/06/08 - 11
**地点**：巴西圣保罗
**周期**：每年一届
**市场范围**：国际性
**参展联络**：中国机械汽车展览联合会
☎ 010-6859 4964
🖷 010-6859 4964
**参展联络**：中国贸促会机械行业分会
**地址**：北京市西城区三里河路46号（100823）
**联系人**：吕静，于奇琳，张垚
☎ 010-6859 4909, 6859 5498, 6859 4192
🖷 010-6859 5485
✉ info@ccpitmsc.org
✉ jix@ccpit.org
www.chinamachin.org.cn
www.ccpitmsc.org

## 第五届巴西库里提巴国际汽车配件展览会

**日期**：2010/06/09 - 12
**地点**：巴西巴拉那州库里蒂巴市展览馆
**内容**：各类机动车零部件、工具、轮胎、汽车配件、发动机、汽车电子、改装车、检修设备、涂料、清洁用品、汽油、润滑剂、添加剂、汽车服务及售后服务用品等等。
此展是巴西第二大的汽配专业展览，该展览的目的是为了推动行业发展，制造新的商机，寻求合作伙伴，交流最新技术信息。库里提巴距圣保罗300公里，是巴西第6大城市，也是巴西最发达的南部城市之一，集中了巴西机械制造业，汽车工业和建筑工业的城市，也是巴西产品通往南锥体其他国家的集散地。参展单位包括产品进口商,经销商、产品制造商、采购商、技术研发中心
**始办年份**：2000
**周期**：两年一届
**市场范围**：国际性
**上届规模** ‘08：展览面积30,000m²，参观人数37,620人,参展商类别：零售商 32%，汽车修理维护中心19%，制造商 14%，进口商 21%，技术研发中心9%，汽车销售商 4%，其他 1% 3、成果：交流合作42%，采购 33%，新品展示 12%，其他 2%
**主办**：DIRETRIZ
**参展联络**：中国贸促会建设行业分会/北京中杰城设国际展览有限公司
**地址**：北京市海淀区三里河路9号建设部（100835）
**联系人**：全静
☎ 010-8838 4563
🖷 010-5885 7468
✉ quanjing68@126.com
MSN：quanjing_hotmail.com
QQ：602693071

## 拉美国际环保及卫生展览会

### AmbientalExpo: Latin America Sanitation & Environmental Solutions Fair

Ambientalexpo

**日期**：2010/06/22 - 24
**地点**：巴西圣保罗
**内容**：拉美国际环保及卫生展览会（Ambiental Expo）将成为新供应商、买家和其它专业人士在圣保罗会面的理想平台。圣保罗市也是整个南美最重要的城市之一。展览将展示最新产品、系统和解决方案，用于水、土壤、空气、滤渣、能源，及嘈音等领域，预计将有来自公共机构和私人公司的近5000名高端访客来此与90多个展出公司洽谈业务。
**周期**：每年一届
**市场范围**：国际性
**主办**：励展巴西公司
**参展联络**：励展博览集团国际销售部
**地址**：北京朝阳区新源里南路1-3号平安国际金融中心A座15层01-03，05（100027）
**联系人**：王亮
☎ 010-5933 9288
🖷 010-5933 9233
✉ liang.wang@reedexpo.com.cn
www.reedexport.cn

## 拉丁美洲印刷展览会

### EXPOPRINT 2010

**日期**：2010/06/23 - 29
**地点**：巴西圣保罗
**周期**：四年一届
**市场范围**：国际性
**参展联络**：中国贸促会机械行业分会
**地址**：北京市西城区三里河路46号（100823）
**联系人**：孙晓光，江彦明，陈媛蓉
☎ 010-6859 5406, 6859 4927, 6859 4826
🖷 010-6859 4948
✉ info@ccpitmsc.org
✉ jix@ccpit.org
www.chinamachin.org.cn
www.ccpitmsc.org

## 2010年第13届巴西国际电力、能源及电子展

**日期**：2010/06/29 – 07/01
**地点**：巴西圣保罗北方展览中心
**内容**：电力产品部分：高、低压电器及成套设备，变压器，发电机，电动机，电流互感器，电压互感

器，电力电容器，输配电设备，发电设备，电网自动化技术及设备，电力测量和自动控制系统，电线电缆，光缆，绝缘材料，测量仪器仪表，电力照明工程及设备，灯具，光源，建筑电气，能源工业相关产品，系统及自动化过程控制系统、能源安全设备、节能技术及设备、可再生能源开发与利用、太阳能加热设备和系统；电子产品部分：电力元器件，电子元器件及组件，高低压电源及开关设备，电源电池，低压线缆，连接线，线束，机电元件及连接技术，天线技术等。
**周期**：每年一届
**市场范围**：国际性
**主办**：ARANDA公司
**参展联络**：中国贸促会建设行业分会/北京中杰城设国际展览有限公司
**地址**：北京市海淀区三里河路9号建设部机关门诊楼5层（100835）
**联系人**：李娜
☎ 010-8838 5291
🖷 010-5885 7468, 5893 4708
✉ info@btfi.cn
www.top-fairs.com.cn
www.btfi.cn

## 巴西圣保罗国际家具展
MOVINTER 2010
**日期**：2010/07/27 - 30
**地点**：巴西圣保罗
**周期**：每年一届
**市场范围**：国际性
**参展联络**：大连上选会展服务有限公司
**地址**：大连市西岗区鞍山路13号兴业广场大厦B座508室（116011）
☎ 0411-8378 8326, 8378 8396, 8378 9165, 8378 8821
🖷 0411-8378 8830, 8378 8823
✉ cicyhuang@vip.sina.com
MSN：cicyhuang@msn.com
www.sun-show.com

## 巴西国际家庭用品及礼品博览会
House & Gift Fair South America
**日期**：2010/08 -
**地点**：巴西圣保罗巴西
**市场范围**：国际性
**参展联络**：京慕国际展览有限公司
**地址**：北京市朝阳区北三环东路6号中国国际展览中心服务楼3层
**联系人**：孟琳；古莹
☎ 010-8460 0551
🖷 010-8460 0394
✉ zhaolingna@ciec.com.cn
www.jingmu.com.cn

## 巴西圣保罗国际体育用品展
SPORTS BUSINESS SHOW
**日期**：2010/08 -
**地点**：巴西圣保罗
**内容**：体育用品及场馆设施
**周期**：每年一届
**市场范围**：国际性
**参展联络**：京慕国际展览有限公司
**地址**：北京市朝阳区北三环东路6号中国国际展览中心服务楼3层
**联系人**：林航，刘靖
☎ 010-8460 0551
🖷 010-8460 0394
✉ zhaolingna@ciec.com.cn
www.jingmu.com.cn

## 巴西圣保罗国际家庭用品及礼品博览会
**日期**：2010/08/14 - 17
**地点**：巴西圣保罗EXPO CENTER NORTE
**内容**：南美国际家庭用品及礼品博览会已成为南美最大的消费品及礼品类博览会，巴西本土的家庭用品和礼品类的大企业均斥资参与该展。该展2008年的展出面积达到了4.6万m$^2$，有来自24个国家的900多家公司参展，四天的展出时间共吸引了48346名来自巴西及其他南美洲国家的采购商光顾此展（其中402名来自巴西以外）。2009年该展将增加In light(装饰灯)和Supri Shop（超市用品）两个展区，预计展出总规模将达到5.6万平方米。消费品市场是南美现今增长速度最快的市场之一，而巴西圣保罗南美国际家庭用品及礼品博览会将是中国企业进入该市场的最佳途径之一。随着现在每年出席人数的稳定增长，越来越多的专业高层人士的到场参观，该展会已经成为一个最富活力的展览贸易交易平台。

展品范围：家居用品（餐桌用品、厨房用具、清洁用品、收纳用具）、家用电器（小家电、便携式电子设备、音像制品）、家庭装饰（室内照明、人造花、花园风景、装饰配件、油画及相框、装饰蜡烛、工艺礼品）、室内家具（餐厅、起居室、厨房、办公室、浴室、游泳池、花园等）、家用纺织品（卧室、浴室、餐厅用纺织品，毛巾，地毯，家居面料）、精选礼品（礼品、文具、公文包、旅游用品）、灯（装饰灯、圣诞灯）、超市用品
**始办年份**：1981
**周期**：每年一届
**市场范围**：国际性
**上届规模** '09：展览面积50,000m$^2$，参展商900多家，参观人数48,346人
**主办**：格拉费特展览及推广公司
**地址**：广州市海珠区新港中路350号C1204（510310）
**联系人**：周文槟
☎ 020-3405 2086 13710318991
🖷 020-3405 0629
✉ abzhanlan@21cn.com
MSN：gdwenbin@hotmail.com
QQ：406372636

## 巴西圣保罗户外探险及生态旅游博览会
Adventure Sports Fair
**日期**：2010/09 -
**地点**：巴西圣保罗
**内容**：户外装备、运动服装、露营用品及背包、自行车运动用品、登山及攀岩用品、水上运动用品
**周期**：每年一届
**市场范围**：国际性
**参展联络**：京慕国际展览有限公司
**地址**：北京市朝阳区北三环东路6号中国国际展览中心服务楼3层
**联系人**：林航，刘靖
☎ 010-8460 0551
🖷 010-8460 0394
✉ zhaolingna@ciec.com.cn
www.jingmu.com.cn

## 圣保罗酒店用品及餐饮设备博览会
Equipotel
**日期**：2010/09 -
**地点**：巴西圣保罗巴西
**内容**：家用纺织品及床上用品，制服，餐具，厨具，清洁卫生产品及设备，厨房及餐馆设备，浴室及浴室设备等
**市场范围**：国际性
**参展联络**：京慕国际展览有限公司
**地址**：北京市朝阳区北三环东路6号中国国际展览中心服务楼3层
**联系人**：王海琼；滕昊
☎ 010-8460 0551
🖷 010-8460 0394
✉ zhaolingna@ciec.com.cn
www.jingmu.com.cn

## 巴西国际美容展览会
Cosmetica:
International Beauty Trade Fair

**日期**：2010/09 -
**地点**：巴西圣保罗
**内容**：巴西国际美容展览会是化妆品和个人护理领域独一无二的展会。展商包括行业中最知名的公司。展会为期4天，将展出当前市场中的技术发展及创新产品。其主要目的是保持高质量的观众、买家。
**周期**：每年一届
**市场范围**：国际性
**主办**：巴西Reed Exhibitions Alcantara Machado
**参展联络**：励展博览集团国际销售部
**地址**：北京市朝阳区新源里南路1-3号平安国际金融中心A座15层01-03，05（100027）
**联系人**：吴祥
☎ 010-5933 9288
🖷 010-5933 9233
✉ ronald.wu@reedexpo.com.cn
www.reedexport.cn

## 巴西国际乐器音响展
EXPOMUSIC
**日期**：2010/09 -
**地点**：巴西圣保罗
**内容**：小型乐器、大型乐器、电子乐器；乐器配件与乐器用家具、刊物、专业音效及录音设备、舞台灯光、配件、多媒体
**周期**：每年一届
**市场范围**：国际性
**参展联络**：京慕国际展览有限公司
**地址**：北京市朝阳区北三环东路6号中国国际展览中心服务楼3层
**联系人**：王英瑶；王芳
☎ 010-8460 0551
🖷 010-8460 0394
✉ zhaolingna@ciec.com.cn
www.jingmu.com.cn

## 国际石油与天然气展览会
**日期**：2010/09/13 - 16
**地点**：巴西里约热内卢
**周期**：每年一届
**市场范围**：国际性
**参展联络**：中国机械汽车展览联合会
☎ 010-6859 4964
🖷 010-6859 4964

## 圣保罗户外花园家具展
**日期**：2010/09/23 - 26
**地点**：巴西圣保罗
**周期**：每年一届
**市场范围**：国际性
**参展联络**：大连上选会展服务有限公司
**地址**：大连市西岗区鞍山路13号兴业广场大厦B座508室（116011）
☎ 0411-8378 8326, 8378 8396, 8378 9165, 8378 8821
🖷 0411-8378 8830, 8378 8823
✉ cicyhuang@vip.sina.com
MSN：cicyhuang@msn.com
www.sun-show.com

## 第六届巴西国际摩托车及配件展览会
Motorcycle Show Brazil
**日期**：2010/10/20 - 24
**地点**：巴西圣保罗
**周期**：每年一届
**市场范围**：国际性
**主办**：法兰克福展览公司
**参展联络**：中国汽车工业国际合作总公司
**地址**：北京市海淀区中关村丹棱街3号A座5层（100080）
**联系人**：何萌
☎ 010-8260 6880
🖷 010-8260 6883
✉ exhibition@cnaico.com.cn

## 巴西国际健身器材博览会
Fitness Brasil
**日期**：2010/10 -

**地点：**巴西圣保罗
**内容：**健身器材，运动服装，背包，体操用品，瑜伽垫，划船、滑雪器械、运动保健等
**周期：**每年一届
**市场范围：**国际性
**参展联络：**京慕国际展览有限公司
**地址：**北京市朝阳区北三环东路6号中国国际展览中心服务楼3层
**联系人：**刘靖，林航
☎ 010-8460 0551
🖷 010-8460 0394
✉ zhaolingna@ciec.com.cn
www.jingmu.com.cn

### 国际工业配件展览会

**日期：**2010/10/26 - 29
**地点：**巴西南卡希亚斯
**周期：**每年一届
**市场范围：**国际性
**参展联络：**中国机械汽车展览联合会
☎ 010-6859 4964
🖷 010-6859 4964

## 巴西石油化工设备展

Química & Petroquímica:
International Trade Fair of Machinery & Equipment for the Chemical & Petrochemical Industry

**日期：**2011 -

**地点：**巴西圣保罗Pavilh & atilde
**内容：**现在石油化工业的发展，在巴西甚至是在世界范围内都十分迅猛。除了世界人口自然增长这个原因之外，另一个原因是由于环境保护和关注意识越来越强，这促使人们去利用可持续资源来改善生活质量。根据相关部门统计：工业的装机容量为87%，年收入已达1,030亿美元，平均增长8%，预期2012年吸引投资200亿美元。
本展会将是南美首个专门以石油化工、制药、化妆品、食品饮料、纤维素及纸张、农产品贸易等为内容的展会，在展会中，参展商都是机械、设备、零件及服务的供应商。
**周期：**两年一届
**市场范围：**国际性
**主办：**励展巴西公司Alcantara Machado
**参展联络：**励展博览集团国际销售部；
**地址：**北京朝阳区新源里南路1-3号平安国际金融中心A座15层01-03，05（100027）
**联系人：**宫卫
☎ 010-5933 9288
🖷 010-5933 9233
✉ david.gong@reedexpo.com.cn
www.reedexport.cn

## 巴西国际制冷、空调、通风、供暖和空气处理贸易展

Febrava:
International Refrigeration, Air-conditioning, Ventilation, Heating and Air Treatment Trade Fair

**日期：**2011 -
**地点：**巴西圣保罗 Imigrantes会展中心
**内容：**巴西国际制冷、空调、通风、供暖和空气处理贸易展是美洲第二大制冷、空调、通风、供暖和空气处理行业展会。展会吸引来自巴西和国际的业内最重要公司，是发布推动行业发展的解决方案和创新技术的理想场所。
**周期：**两年一届
**市场范围：**国际性
**参展费用：**净地260美元/m²，标准展位340美元/m²
**赞助：**ABRAVA；SINDRATAR；ABIMAQ
**主办：**励展巴西Reed Exhibitions Alcantara Machado BRAZIL
**参展联络：**励展博览集团国际销售部
**地址：**北京朝阳区新源里南路1-3号平安国际金融中心A座15层01-03，05（100027）
**联系人：**宫卫
☎ 010-5933 9288
🖷 010-5933 9233
✉ david.gong@reedexpo.com.cn
www.reedexport.cn

## 巴西国际建材展

Feicon Batimat -
International Construction Industry Trade Fair

**日期：**2011 -
**地点：**巴西圣保罗
**内容：**FEICON BATIMAT是在建筑业开展业务的最佳平台。它的成功是基于高质量的观众、其传播战略以及参展商的声望。它是建筑业内唯一的综合展会，在国内已经举办了20年，在国际上则已有40年历史。圣保罗的"国际建筑周"集合了拉美建筑业最优秀的项目。这是一个了解世界上最重要、最富盛名的品牌之创新和投资的绝佳机会。
**产品及服务：**空调、休闲区（花园家具、凉篷、运动场及配件）。挂锁、锁及配件、金属屋顶及墙壁、门窗外框、石膏、比重计、水泵和水箱、放水、隔热/隔音、百叶帘和遮阳篷、游泳池、工业地坪、技术出版物、PVC、瓷砖、木质及橡胶地板及地毯、服务、安全系统和产品、木地板、木板、复合木地板、镶板、壁板、油漆、清漆及油漆附件、玻璃。
**周期：**每年一届
**市场范围：**国际性
**赞助：**ANAMACO；ABIMAQ；AREMASP；ABRAFATI；SIAMFESP；SINCOMAVI；ABIROCHAS
**参展联络：**励展博览集团国际销售部
**地址：**北京朝阳区新源里南路1-3号平安国际金融中心A座15层01-03，05（100027）
**联系人：**宫卫
☎ 010-5933 9288
🖷 010-5933 9233
✉ david.gong@reedexpo.com.cn
www.reedexport.cn

## 巴西国际安防产品博览会

ISC BRASIL –
International Security & Conference Expo

**日期：**2011 -
**地点：**巴西圣保罗Transamerica 展览中心
**内容：**ISC BRASIL是美国国际安保展览会继美国西部拉斯维加斯展和东部纽约展之后在南美地区召开的又一届盛会。该展由得到的巴西展览协会等单位的大力支持。2006年首届展会获得圆满成功，近3500位来自南美的主要采购商到会与展商进行接洽。目前国际知名公司如BOSCH、GE、HDL、SONY、HID等许多公司以及巴西当地知名公司均已订购2009年展位。随着全球安保产品工业的发展，巴西市场十分旺盛，估计目前超过9.2亿美元、年增长10%。
参加巴西安保产品展览会具有如下优势：增加与当地客商扩大贸易的机会，与当地主要批发商建立联系，建立新的全球贸易伙伴，与来自全球主要的安保专业人士建立网络联系，了解来自该地区及全球安保产品的信息，与最终买家建立联系，结识来自巴西及南美地区的产品组装厂商，推广产品的使用和服务功能
**始办年份：**2006
**周期：**每年一届
**市场范围：**国际性
**参展费用：**净地220美元/m²,标准展位300美元/m²
**协办：**美国安保协会（SIA）；拉美安保协会（ALAS）；巴西电子电器工业协会（ABINEE）
**主办：**励展博览集团美国公司；励展巴西公司；巴西Alcantara Machado Trade Fair展览公司
**参展联络：**励展博览集团国际销售部
**地址：**北京朝阳区新源里南路1-3号平安国际金融中心A座15层01-03，05（100027）
**联系人：**宫卫
☎ 010-5933 9288
🖷 010-5933 9233
✉ david.gong@reedexpo.com.cn
www.reedexport.cn

## 拉美国际环保及卫生展览会

AmbientalExpo:
Latin America Sanitation & Environmental Solutions Fair

**日期：**2011 -
**地点：**巴西圣保罗
**内容：**拉美国际环保及卫生展览会（Ambiental Expo）将成为新供应商、买家和其它专业人士在圣保罗会面的理想平台。圣保罗市也是整个南美最重要的城市之一。展览将展示最新产品、系统和解决方案，用于水、土壤、空气、滤渣、能源，及嘈音等领域，预计将有来自公共机构和私人公司的近5000名高端访客来此与90多个展出公司洽谈业务。
**周期：**每年一届
**市场范围：**国际性
**主办：**励展巴西公司
**参展联络：**励展博览集团国际销售部
**地址：**北京朝阳区新源里南路1-3号平安国际金融中心A座15层01-03，05（100027）
**联系人：**王亮
☎ 010-5933 9288
🖷 010-5933 9233
✉ liang.wang@reedexpo.com.cn
www.reedexport.cn

## 巴西纺织机械展

ITMEX Americas:
International Textile Machinery Trade Fair

**日期：**2011/03 -
**地点：**巴西圣保罗
**内容：**巴西纺织机械展（ITMEX Americas）再次展出创新型高技术非织造品，机械装备、必需件及零件、卫生用品（尿布、卫生巾、湿纸巾），非织造品转换器，转换用机械及装备，转换必需材料及零件。同时举办的展会还有 Fenatec, Feimaco, Expolav and Ponto Final。
**产品及服务：**非织造品、高技术纺织品、其它技术纺织品、机械和设备，生产必需品和零件、一次性卫生用品（尿布、卫生巾、湿纸巾）、非织造品转换器、转换机械及设备、转换器必需品及零件。
**周期：**两年一届
**市场范围：**国际性

**参展费用：**净地260美元/m²，标准展位340美元/m²
**上届规模** ‘09：展览面积52,000m²，参展商602家（国外展商283家），参观人数23,609人
**主办：**励展巴西公司
**参展联络：**励展博览集团国际销售部
**地址：**北京朝阳区新源里南路1-3号平安国际金融中心A座15层01-03，05（100027）
**联系人：**宫卫
☎ 010-5933 9288
🖷 010-5933 9233
✉ david.gong@reedexpo.com.cn
www.reedexport.cn

## 巴西国际电子展

FIEE Elétrica:
International Electrical, Energy & Automation Industry Trade Fair

**日期：**2011/04 -
**地点：**巴西圣保罗
**内容：**在过去的42年中，作为巴西最重要的电力工业展，FIEE Elétrica一直给予能源生产，传输和分销领域广泛支持，提供商业机遇，发布前沿科技，与本展同期举行的electronicAmerica——一个集组件、组件生产设备、激光技术和光电业的国际贸易展会。

产品及服务:能源生产，传送和分配装备—GTD必需元件-供电组件-电力安装材料-电力工具和自动控制-公用设施组件-电力工程，安装和维修-银行服务，实体公司，贸易发布及服务。
**周期：**两年一届
**市场范围：**国际性
**参展费用：**净地260美元/m²，标准展位340美元/m²
**上届规模** ‘09：展览面积60,000m²，参展商394家（国外展商267家），参观人数50,535人
**主办：**励展巴西公司
**参展联络：**励展博览集团国际销售部
**地址：**北京朝阳区新源里南路1-3号平安国际金融中心A座15层01-03，05（100027）
**联系人：**宫卫
☎ 010-5933 9288
🖷 010-5933 9233
MSN：david.gong@reedexpo.com.cn
www.reedexport.cn

## 巴西机械工具展

Feimafe:
International Machine Tools and Integrated Manufacturing Systems Trade Fair

FEIMAFE

**日期：**2011/05 -
**地点：**巴西圣保罗
**内容：**由于机床市场的快速增长，巴西机械工具展（FEIMAFE）占领了拉丁美洲地区，被认为是该地区最大最重要的展会，展会的发展也非常成功。2007年，展商人数达到1,383名，其中有724名来自巴西，另外659名来自海外。展会场地面积为78,000平方公尺，观众人数达到65,614人。届时，国际质量控制贸易展览会（QUALIDADE）也将同期举办。

产品及服务:机床、自动化、质量控制整合生产技术、辅助设备,配件和零部件、工具、服务
**周期：**两年一届
**市场范围：**国际性
**参展费用：**净地展位260美元/m²，标准展位340美元
**上届规模** ‘09：展览面积78,000m²，参展商1,383家（国外展商659家），参观人数65,614人
**主办：**励展巴西公司
**参展联络：**励展博览集团国际销售部
**地址：**北京朝阳区新源里南路1-3号平安国际金融中心A座15层01-03，05（100027）
**联系人：**宫卫
☎ 010-5933 9288
🖷 010-5933 9233
电邮：david.gong@reedexpo.com.cn
www.reedexport.cn

## 巴西国际汽车配件展

Automec：
International Autoparts, Equipment and Services Trade Fair

**日期：**2011/05/05 - 09
**地点：**巴西圣保罗
**内容：**拉美地区最大的汽车配件展——巴西国际汽车配件展即将迎来第9个年头，目前该展会以其规模已跻身全球五大汽车配件展之一。Automec 展现的高科技配件、附件、机器和装备，曾为整个汽车业创造了独一无二的商业良机。
**市场范围：**国际性
**参展费用：**净地260美元/m²，标准展位340美元/m²
**赞助：**SINDIPE；ABRIVE；ANDAP；SICAP；SINCOPE；SINDIREPA
**主办：**励展巴西公司
**参展联络：**励展博览集团国际销售部
**地址：**北京朝阳区新源里南路1-3号平安国际金融中心A座15层01-03，05（100027）
**联系人：**宫卫
☎ 010-5933 9288
🖷 010-5933 9233
✉ david.gong@reedexpo.com.cn
www.reedexport.cn

## 巴西国际海洋石油及天然气工业设备展

Brazil Offshore:
International Offshore Oil and Gas Industry Trade Show and Conference

**日期：**2011/06/14 - 17
**日期：**2013 -
**地点：**巴西里约州马珈耶Macaé, Roberto Marinho展览中心
**内容：**作为世界第三大海洋石油工业产品贸易展会，巴西国际海洋石油天然气工业设备展是众多成功业内贸易展会之一，在参展公司和观众的数量和质量上有突飞猛进的增长。展会举办地点在Macaé，也是Petrobras UNBC的基地。Campos Watershed目前是世界最大的海洋实验室，巨大的投资焦点在于探索新发现并将海洋石油的前沿推向超深水域，而巴西在这一领域正处于世界领先水平。同期举办的展会：- 国际海洋石油与天然气工业会议/IBP-巴西石油及生物燃料研究所/SPE-汽油工程师组织 - 商务谈判/ONIP-国家汽油工业组织/ SEBRAE-RJ
**周期：**两年一届
**市场范围：**国际性
**赞助：**IBP; ONIP; SPE; FIRJAN; Macaé市政厅; 里约州政府; Upstream; Offshore Engineer; Brasil Energia, Click Macaé.
**主办：**励展巴西公司
**参展联络：**励展博览集团国际销售部
**地址：**北京朝阳区新源里南路1-3号平安国际金融中心A座15层01-03，05（100027）
**联系人：**宫卫
☎ 010-5933 9288
🖷 010-5933 9233
✉ david.gong@reedexpo.com.cn
www.reedexport.cn

### 第27届巴西国际家具工业贸易展览会

**日期：**2011/08 -
**地点：**巴西
**周期：**两年一届
**市场范围：**国际性
**参展联络：**大连上选会展服务有限公司
**地址：**大连市西岗区鞍山路13号兴业广场大厦B座508室（116011）
☎ 0411-8378 8326, 8378 8396, 8378 9165, 8378 8821
🖷 0411-8378 8830, 8378 8823
✉ cicyhuang@vip.sina.com
MSN：cicyhuang@msn.com
www.sun-show.com

## 巴西纺织机械展

ITMEX Americas:
International Textile Machinery Trade Fair

**日期：**2013 -
**地点：**巴西圣保罗
**内容：**巴西纺织机械展（ITMEX Americas）再次展出创新型高技术非织造品，机械装备、必需件及零件、卫生用品（尿布、卫生巾、湿纸巾），非织造品转换器，转换用机械及装备，转换必需材料及零件。同时举办的展会还有 Fenatec, Feimaco, Expolav and Ponto Final
**产品及服务：**非织造品、高技术纺织品、其它技术纺织品、机械和设备，生产必需品和零件、一次性卫生用品（尿布、卫生巾、湿纸巾）、非织造品转换器、转换机械及设备、转换器必需品及零件。
**周期：**两年一届
**市场范围：**国际性
**参展费用：**净地260美元/m²，标准展位340美元/m²
**主办：**励展巴西公司
**参展联络：**励展博览集团国际销售部
**地址：**北京朝阳区新源里南路1-3号平安国际金融中心A座15层01-03，05（100027）
**联系人：**宫卫
☎ 010-5933 9288
🖷 010-5933 9233
✉ david.gong@reedexpo.com.cn
www.reedexport.cn

# 加拿大
# Canada

### 国际卡车展览会

**日期：**2010/04 -
**地点：**加拿大多伦多
**周期：**每年一届
**市场范围：**国际性
**参展联络：**中国机械汽车展览联合会
☎ 010-6859 4964
🖷 010-6859 4964

### 2010年加拿大蒙特利尔国际食品饮料展览会

2010 SIAL Montreal

**日期：**2010/04/21 - 23
**地点：**加拿大蒙特利尔展览中心
**内容：**食品添加剂、佐料、熟食、奶制品、蛋制

品、猪肉制品和腌制品、新鲜肉类和肠类、新鲜家禽和野味、海产品、新鲜水果蔬菜、水果干和脱水蔬菜、甜食、饼干、面包、罐头食品、冷冻食品、生物制品、宠物食品、食品杂货、冰淇淋、含酒精饮料、一般饮料等各类食品饮料。
始办年份：2001
周期：每年一届
市场范围：国际性
上届规模 '09：参展商520家，参观人数12043人
主办：SIAL Montréal
参展联络：杭州思诺博会展服务有限公司
地址：杭州市体育场路229号浙江粮油大厦1202室（310003）
☎ 0571-8577 8500
🖷 0571-8577 9709
✉ expo@sinobal.com
www.sinobal.com

### 2010年27届加拿大国际矿山设备展暨加拿大国际矿业年会

CIM

日期：2010/05/09 - 12
地点：加拿大多伦多Metro Toronto Convention Centre
内容：该展分矿山机械及科技应用、矿山贸易租赁、及矿山协会年会等主题，是加拿大最大的专业矿山展。同时召开第三届加拿大国际岩石年会。大展期间将有来自世界38个国际的近600家展商参与。展品涵盖范围广泛。同时该展也得到加拿大及国际展商的认可，相信中国企业高质量的产品会在CIM上找到合适商机 CIM加拿大采矿冶金石油协会，成立于1898年，是加拿大矿业资源、金属加工、石油开采的专业协会组织。该协会有超过12000的国家级会员，每年的该展，都会邀请会员参加，形成专业技术交流和贸易服务为主的专业活动。保证了展会的专业性，促进了展商和采购商的有效交流。
周期：每年一届
市场范围：国际性
主办：北京麦田通会国际展览有限公司
联系人：吴珊
☎ 010-5165 9302转8005, 8633 1235, 13426437438
🖷 010-5165 9302
✉ xiaoxiangzhishui@yahoo.com.cn
MSN：xiaoxiangzhishui@hotmail.com

### 全球石油展览会

日期：2010/06/08 - 10
地点：加拿大卡尔加里
周期：每年一届
市场范围：国际性
参展联络：中国机械汽车展览联合会
☎ 010-6859 4964
🖷 010-6859 4964

### 国际管道展览会

日期：2010/09/28 - 30
4438
地点：加拿大卡尔加里
周期：每年一届
市场范围：国际性
参展联络：中国机械汽车展览联合会
☎ 010-6859 4964
🖷 010-6859 4964

### 国际印刷展览会

日期：2010/11/20 - 22
地点：加拿大多伦多
周期：每年一届
市场范围：国际性
参展联络：中国机械汽车展览联合会
☎ 010-6859 4964
🖷 010-6859 4964

### 2011年加拿大蒙特利尔国际食品饮料展览会

2011 SIAL Montreal

日期：2011/04 -
地点：加拿大蒙特利尔展览中心
内容：食品添加剂、佐料、熟食、奶制品、蛋制品、猪肉制品和腌制品、新鲜肉类和肠类、新鲜家禽和野味、海产品、新鲜水果蔬菜、水果干和脱水蔬菜、甜食、饼干、面包、罐头食品、冷冻食品、生物制品、宠物食品、食品杂货、冰淇淋、含酒精饮料、一般饮料等各类食品饮料。
始办年份：2001
周期：每年一届
市场范围：国际性
主办：SIAL Montréal
参展联络：杭州思诺博会展服务有限公司
地址：杭州市体育场路229号浙江粮油大厦1202室（310003）
☎ 0571-8577 8500
🖷 0571-8577 9709
✉ expo@sinobal.com
www.sinobal.com

## 智利 Chile

### 2010第十届智利国际矿业及工程机械展览会

EXPOMIN 2010

日期：2010/04/12 - 16
地点：智利圣地亚哥雷斯克会展中心
内容：该展是拉美地区最重要、且最大的矿业展览会，2008年该展览会有来自美国、德国、澳大利亚、比利时、加拿大、西班牙、芬兰、英国、南非、巴西公司参展，展会成交12亿美元。智利矿展是全世界向拉丁美洲采矿业提供机械、设备、技术、服务以及供给品的专业展览会。参观者包括矿业领域的专业人士。同时，展会还将举办各种专业与技术领域的国际座谈会。智利矿展将为企业和个人提供重要的商业机会。
周期：两年一届
市场范围：国际性
上届规模 '08：展览面积30,000m$^2$，参展商1,020家（来自36个国家），专业和贸易观众43,000人）
主办：圣地亚哥国际展览公司
参展联络：北京麦田通会国际展览有限公司
联系人：吴珊
☎ 010-5165 9302转ext 8005, 8633 1235, 13426437438
🖷 010-5165 9302
✉ xiaoxiangzhishui@yahoo.com.cn
MSN：xiaoxiangzhishui@hotmail.com

### 智利国际建筑建材展览会

日期：2010/05/12 - 15
地点：智利圣地亚哥
内容：建筑建材
市场范围：国际性
参展联络：北京中仕达兴业展览有限公司
地址：北京市海淀区蓝靛厂东路2号金源时代商务中心2号楼A座11B（100097）
联系人：贾倩，赵仕忱，牟向东，张露
☎ 010-5129 8900
🖷 010-8886 2939
✉ mail@chinstar.cn
www.chinstar.cn

### 智利国际工程机械及混凝土展览会

日期：2010/05/12 - 15
地点：智利圣地亚哥
内容：工程机械及混凝土
市场范围：国际性
参展联络：北京中仕达兴业展览有限公司
地址：北京市海淀区蓝靛厂东路2号金源时代商务中心2号楼A座11B（100097）
联系人：贾倩，赵仕忱，牟向东，张露
☎ 010-5129 8900
🖷 010-8886 2939
✉ mail@chinstar.cn
www.chinstar.cn

## 古巴 Cuba

### 国际博览会

日期：2010/11 -
地点：古巴哈瓦那
周期：每年一届
市场范围：国际性
参展联络：中国机械汽车展览联合会
☎ 010-6859 4964
🖷 010-6859 4964

## 捷克 Czech

### 捷克布拉格国际体育用品和时装贸易博览会

Sport Prague & Sport Fashion

日期：2010/02 -
地点：捷克布拉格
内容：运动服饰、运动器材、各类体育用品
周期：每年一届
市场范围：国际性
参展联络：京慕国际展览有限公司
地址：北京市朝阳区北三环东路6号中国国际展览中心服务楼3层
联系人：李雪寒
☎ 010-8460 0551
🖷 010-8460 0394
✉ zhaolingna@ciec.com.cn
www.jingmu.com.cn

### 捷克国际电子电力展览会

Amper

日期：2010/03/31 - 03
地点：捷克布拉格布拉格
内容：电子组件和模块，发电和配电设备，电气设备组件，导体和电缆，测量装置等
周期：每年一届
市场范围：国际性
参展联络：京慕国际展览有限公司
地址：北京市朝阳区北三环东路6号中国国际展览中心服务楼3层
联系人：薛亮；孙铁兵
☎ 010-8460 0551
🖷 010-8460 0394
✉ zhaolingna@ciec.com.cn
www.jingmu.com.cn

### 捷克国际汽车及零配件博览会

International Fair of Utility Vehicles, Parts and Garage Equipment

日期：2010/06/05 - 10
地点：捷克
内容：整车类：卡车货车、巴士、拖车；汽车零部件；汽车制造、操作和修理；汽车配件；燃油、润滑油和加油站；公路交通服务；相关机构和组织；汽车相关外围产品及设备包括车用装饰品等；汽车相关维修设备/工具、手工具
市场范围：国际性
主办：开国咨询（上海）有限公司-捷克布尔诺商展中心中国代表处
地址：上海市浦东新区福山路450号7楼A座（200122）
联系人：朱小姐
☎ 021-5109 5546转8006
🖷 021-6875 2877
✉ cindy@kaigo.com.cn
www.kaigo.com.cn

### 2010捷克国际劳保展
### 捷克国际工业展览会

**日期：** 2010/09/13 - 17
**地点：** 捷克布鲁诺商展中心
**内容：** 个人安全：个人防护设备，防护工作服，企业时装/形象/识别服装，防护服及工作服面料，安全设备及工作场所安全设施，安全组织/商业媒体/刊物；工作场所安全设施：防火、安全产品及系统，爆炸及毒物防护，辐射防护，电力安全，空气污染控制，减噪/消音装置/震动防护设备，工作环境保护，环境保护及废料处理，测量和控制技术，安全设备及系统，机械安全装置，安全站立区域，相关设备及配件，设备、装置的维护、服务及维修，交通及车辆安全，质量保证，物品防护，装置及配件，媒体、职业安全培训，职业安全服务及咨询等
**市场范围：** 国际性
**主办：** 开国咨询（上海）有限公司
**地址：** 中国上海市浦东新区福山路450号7楼A座（200122）
**联系人：** 朱小姐
☎ 021-5109 5546转8006
🖷 021-6875 2877
✉ cindy@kaigo.com.cn
www.kaigo.com.cn

### 2010捷克国际工业展
### 2010捷克国际机床工具展览会

**日期：** 2010/09/13 - 17
**地点：** 捷克布鲁诺商展中心
**内容：** 采矿，冶金，铸造，陶瓷 和玻璃工程 驱动器，液压系统和气动 工具，冷却技术和空调技术 塑料，橡胶機械 金属加工和成型机，工具， 表面处理，热处理， 焊接机 电力工程和重型电气工程 电子，自动化和测量技术 研究，服务机构
**周期：** 每年一届
**市场范围：** 国际性
**主办：** 开国咨询（上海）有限公司
**地址：** 中国上海市浦东新区福山路450号7楼A座（200122）
**联系人：** 朱小姐
☎ 021-5109 5546转ext 8006
🖷 021-6875 2877
✉ cindy@kaigo.com.cn
www.kaigo.com.cn

### 捷克国际消费类电子展览会
DIGITEX

**日期：** 2010/10 -
**地点：** 捷克布尔诺
**内容：** 影音系统、数码设备、家用电器等
**周期：** 每年一届
**市场范围：** 国际性
**参展联络：** 京慕国际展览有限公司
**地址：** 北京市朝阳区北三环东路6号中国国际展览中心服务楼3层
**联系人：** 宋秋爽，刘舰
☎ 010-8460 0551
🖷 010-8460 0394
✉ zhaolingna@ciec.com.cn
www.jingmu.com.cn

## 埃及
## Egypt

### 国际博览会

**日期：** 2010/03/17 - 28
**地点：** 埃及开罗
**周期：** 每年一届
**市场范围：** 国际性
**参展联络：** 中国机械汽车展览联合会
☎ 010-6859 4964
🖷 010-6859 4964

### 开罗办公自动化和办公服务展

**日期：** 2010/04/10 - 13
**地点：** 埃及开罗
**周期：** 每年一届
**市场范围：** 国际性
**参展联络：** 大连上选会展服务有限公司
**地址：** 大连市西岗区鞍山路13号兴业广场大厦B座508室（116011）
☎ 0411-8378 8326, 8378 8396, 8378 9165, 8378 8821
🖷 0411-8378 8830, 8378 8823
✉ cicyhuang@vip.sina.com
MSN：cicyhuang@msn.com
www.sun-show.com

### 泛阿拉伯/非洲塑料橡胶材料展览会

**日期：** 2010/05/13 - 16
**地点：** 埃及开罗
**周期：** 每年一届
**市场范围：** 国际性
**参展联络：** 中国机械汽车展览联合会
☎ 010-6859 4964
🖷 010-6859 4964

### 埃及建材及石材展览会
E.S.E & Inter Build

**日期：** 2010/06 -
**地点：** 埃及开罗
**内容：** 建筑机械、管道设备、陶瓷、石材、修饰材料、卫浴设施、厨具、各类石材
**周期：** 每年一届
**市场范围：** 国际性
**参展联络：** 京慕国际展览有限公司
**地址：** 北京市朝阳区北三环东路6号中国国际展览中心服务楼3层
**联系人：** 薛涵，王芳
☎ 010-8460 0551
🖷 010-8460 0394
✉ zhaolingna@ciec.com.cn
www.jingmu.com.cn

### 第15届北非汽车、摩托车及零配件展览会
Automech

**日期：** 2010/06 -
**地点：** 埃及开罗
**内容：** 汽车、摩托车、汽摩配件、组件及零部件、汽车设备、保养产品、车轮轮胎、音箱系统和设备、车内娱乐系统、汽车加工业产品、加油站设备、电池电源、空调制冷系统、汽摩装饰产品、电子机械系统、发动机、各种工具、涂料、安全系统。
**周期：** 每年一届
**市场范围：** 国际性
**主办：** 法兰克福展览公司
**参展联络：** 中国汽车工业国际合作总公司
**地址：** 北京市海淀区中关村丹棱街3号A座5层（100080）
**联系人：** 何萌
☎ 010-8260 6880
🖷 010-8260 6883
✉ exhibition@cnaico.com.cn

### 第30届埃及国际酒店食品及相关设备展

**日期：** 2010/10/24 - 27
**地点：** 埃及开罗国际会议中心
**内容：** 该展会已有二十九年的历史，由埃及最著名的EGM ( Egyptian Group for Marketing ) 展览公司与埃及国家对外经济贸易部、青年部以及国家电视台传媒运营商联合举办，受到了埃及各届人士的热烈欢迎。同时得到了当地政府部门的大力支持。此展不仅是埃及最大的酒店食品展，也是开罗市民的盛会。酒店设备：厨具餐具、保鲜设备、冷冻冷藏设备、康体健身娱乐设施、音响视听器材、酒店智能管理系统；酒店家具：桌面用品、客房大堂用品、纺织布艺酒店制服、卧室配置、房间内部设计、室内通风设备；清洁设备：洗涤设备；咖啡茶餐饮供应设备；食品饮料：茶、咖啡及相关设备用具。饮料、酒、农产品、方便食品、速冻食品健康食品、保健食品、罐头食品、肉类品、禽制品、乳制品、调味品、粮油制品、干鲜果蔬、烘烤食品、休闲食品
**市场范围：** 国际性
**上届规模：** 展览面积20,000m², 专业贸易观众40,000人
**主办：** 中国国际广告公司国际展览部
**地址：** 北京市西直门内南小街国英1号楼423室
**联系人：** 郭小姐，黄小姐
☎ 010-5856 1270转103/104
🖷 010-5856 1136
✉ yolanda@bcpit.com, bcpit@china.com

### 国际机床工具展览会

**日期：** 2010/11 -
**地点：** 埃及开罗
**周期：** 每年一届
**市场范围：** 国际性
**参展联络：** 中国机械汽车展览联合会
☎ 010-6859 4964
🖷 010-6859 4964

## 法国
## France

### 法国国际视觉广告技术及标识制作展
Viscom Paris:
The International Event for Visual Communication

**日期：** 2010 -
**地点：** 法国巴黎Paris Porte de Versailles
**内容：** 法国国际视觉广告技术及标识制作展(Viscom Paris)为您带来视觉行业的创新性的产品、潮流和技术，展会汇集了制图行业专家，将所有的最新概念和技术一一呈现，其中涉及数码打印，丝网印刷。展会针对数码打印和视觉效果，以及丝网印刷和标牌制作的新动态，进行深度挖掘和比较开发。展会范围涉及面广泛，几乎涵盖业内所有竞争力强的技术和极具创新性的产品。
**周期：** 每年一届
**市场范围：** 国际性
**参展费用：** 欢迎垂询参展费用
**赞助：** 法国标牌协会（SYNAFEL）；法国数字标牌协会（APCAD）
**主办：** 励展法国公司
**参展联络：** 励展博览集团国际销售部
**地址：** 北京朝阳区新源里南路1-3号平安国际金融中心A座15层01-03、05（100027）
**联系人：** 王亮
☎ 010-5933 9288
🖷 010-5933 9233
✉ liang.wang@reedexpo.com.cn
www.reedexport.cn

### 巴黎国际服装、珠宝、银饰及配件展览会
Eclat de Mode / Bijorhca Paris: The Fashion side of Jewelry. Bi-annual International Trade Show

日期：2010/01 -
地点：法国巴黎凡尔赛门展览中心
内容：巴黎专为世界时尚珠宝业举办的唯一国际展会。集中展示秋／冬时装珠宝、银质珠宝、高级女士时装及时尚附件等产品。Eclat de Mode 是时尚世界的旗帜性展会，每年两届在巴黎举办（一月及九月）。展商包括来自全球30多个国家的设计师、厂商、批发商、进口商。
产品及服务：设计师珠宝及服装珠宝、银质及镀金珠宝、时尚手表、品牌及高级定制珠宝、春夏时尚配件。
周期：每年一届
市场范围：国际性
主办：励展法国公司
参展联络：励展博览集团国际销售部
地址：北京市朝阳区新源里南路1-3号平安国际金融中心A座15层01-03，05（100027）
联系人：吴祥
☎ 010-5933 9288
🖷 010-5933 9233
✉ ronald.wu@reedexpo.com.cn
www.reedexport.cn

### 巴黎国际成衣展

Pret a Porter Paris

日期：2010/01/23 - 26
地点：法国巴黎凡尔赛门展览馆
内容：是欧洲最大、历史最悠久的服装及相关产品的综合类展会。展会主要定位在以服装，服饰为主的产品展示上，汇集了来自世界各地的知名服装品牌，连场的时装发布展示着最新时尚潮流。世界各大著名零售店和大型百货公司每年都会来此展会制定计划、洽谈订货。巴黎国际成衣展与著名的国际时尚流行趋势新品发布会（WHO' S NEXT ）及巴黎国际内衣泳装展（MODE CITY）同期同馆，每一届均能吸引大量专业客商到会。在2009年9月的展会上，参展商和参观者的人数又有所增加。总展出面积为65,000m²，共有1,550个品牌参展，有450个新品牌参展。其中有45%来自于法国以外的其他国家。展出产品多达1,800种服装系列，7,800套服装，42,236名买家参观采购。观众来自60多个国家，40.2%为国际买家，其中以意大利、西班牙、英国、日本、希腊、荷兰、土耳其、德国、瑞士、比利时和美国的买家居多。“巴黎国际内衣展M O D E C I T Y”为提升展会档次自09年起不再设置SOUCING加工区，而改为接受品牌企业参展，报名企业应符合展会新标准。
周期：每年两届
市场范围：国际性
入场券价格：45
主办：法国女装协会
参展联络：德国欧野有限公司
地址：北京朝阳区广渠东路3号申奥商务楼203B（100022）
联系人：李艳艳
☎ 010-8721 5659
✉ evitagroup_exhibition@hotmail.com
QQ：190687477
www.pretparis.com

### 世界音乐博览会

MIDEM:
The World's Music Market

日期：2010/01/23 - 27
地点：法国戛纳
内容MIDEM国际音乐博览会（暨为期2天的MidemNet数码与移动音乐论坛）始创于1967年，每年在法国戛纳举办一届，每届为期5天，观众包括来自93个国家、覆盖各种音乐类别和所有产业细分市场的10,000多名音乐界专业人士。MIDEM致力于为国际音乐产业提供交易、联络、交流、发现新音乐风格与人才、吸取资讯的贸易展会平台。在展览同时，该展会通过每日会议、圆桌论坛、音乐会与在线音乐产业数据库等多种形式为业界提供更多增值服务。此外，MIDEM还设立了MIDEM Classique & Jazz (www.midem.com/classique)、MIDEM Electronic & Urban Village等专门展区。
始办年份：1967
周期：每年一届
市场范围：国际性
参展费用：净地展位3,800欧元起
主办：励展法国公司
参展联络：励展博览集团国际销售部
地址：北京市朝阳区新源里南路1-3号平安国际金融中心A座15层01-03，05（100027）
联系人：吴祥
☎ 010-5933 9288
🖷 010-5933 9233
✉ ronald.wu@reedexpo.com.cn
www.reedexport.cn

### 法国卫浴展

Ideo Bain: The Bathroom Exhibition

日期：2010/02/09 - 14
地点：法国巴黎
内容：浴室设备、厨房设备、供暖设备、泵类产品：管道阀门
周期：两年一届
市场范围：国际性
参展联络：京慕国际展览有限公司
地址：北京市朝阳区北三环东路6号中国国际展览中心服务楼3层
联系人：薛涵，王芳
☎ 010-8460 0551
🖷 010-8460 0394
✉ zhaolingna@ciec.com.cn
www.jingmu.com.cn

### 巴黎国际供暖、制冷、空调、新能源及家用电气展览会

Interclima+elec Home&building

日期：2010/02/09 - 12
地点：法国巴黎Paris Expo - Porte de Versailles
内容：由国际知名展览机构--励展博览法国公司主办的Interclima每两年一届，2010年将是第19届，是目前世界上供暖、制冷、空调及智能建筑领域规模最大、影响力最强的专业展会之一。2008年的Interclima展会，无论是在展出面积还是观众人数上，均又创历史新高。展出净面积超过7万平方米，展商增加了22.5%。平均每个展商在展出期间建立的有效联系为650个。2008年的Interclima接待观众人数达102620人次，比2006年增加20.5%。其中，来自法国以外的观众有7700多名，占总数的7.53%；贸易商与制造商占35%强，安装商占39%强。Interclima展的潜力却非常巨大。因为德国、意大利的相关市场已经进入成熟期，而法国却还处于发展期。也正因如此，所以法国政府对建筑住宅用冷凝锅炉、制冷、供暖设备提供高达40%的补贴，对某些太阳能采暖设施及加热泵的补贴更高达50%。另外，法国工业部长亲临参观上届展会也说明了法国政府对新能源技术的高度重视。
周期：两年一届
市场范围：国际性
参展费用：净地展位240欧元/m²，标准展位（9m²）325-517欧元/m²（价格不含增值税19%）
主办：励展博览法国公司
参展联络：励展博览集团国际销售部
地址：北京朝阳区新源里南路1-3号平安国际金融中心A座15层01-03，05（100027）
联系人：杜一鸣
☎ 010-5933 9288
🖷 010-5933 9233
✉ martin.du@reedexpo.com.cn
www.reedexport.cn

### 国际重卡及专用车辆展览会

日期：2010/03/02 - 06
地点：法国里昂
周期：每年一届
市场范围：国际性
参展联络：中国机械汽车展览联合会
☎ 010-6859 4964
🖷 010-6849 4964

### 世界面点展

EUROPAIN

日期：2010/03/06 - 10
地点：法国巴黎北维勒班展览中心
内容：面点、甜食、西餐配料、巧克力、冰淇淋、外卖食品业、餐饮酒店业、生产设备
始办年份：1967
周期：两年一届
市场范围：国际性
上届规模 ‘08：展览面积80,000m²，参展商670家（来自20个国家），参观人数78,537人
主办：法国国际专业展促进会
地址：北京市朝阳区朝外大街20号联合大厦710室（100020）
联系人：张静
☎ 010-6588 5968, 6588 5969
🖷 010-6588 5970
✉ jackiezhang@promosalons-china.com

### 巴黎国际特许经营展览会

Franchise Expo Paris:
International Franchise Show

日期：2010/03/14 - 17
地点：法国巴黎
内容：授予特许经营者，服务供应商及机构
周期：每年一届
市场范围：国际性
主办：法国励展展览公司
参展联络：励展博览集团国际销售部
地址：北京朝阳区新源里南路1-3号平安国际金融中心A座15层01-03，05（100027）
联系人：王亮
☎ 010-5933 9288
🖷 010-5933 9233
✉ liang.wang@reedexpo.com.cn
www.reedexport.cn

### 法国国际地产投资交易会

MIPIM

日期：2010/03/16 - 19
地点：法国戛纳影节宫
内容：MIPIM是世界上唯一聚集全球房地产界最具影响力的人物的交易会。它创造独一无二的、绝佳的联络、展示以及商业机会。房地产顾问、开发商、地区官员、投资者以及公司最终用户可在展会上搜集新楼信息、开展新交易以及创建新的伙伴关系。产品及服务 为投资者，公司最终用户、当地及地区官员、开发商、经纪商、资产管理者以及服务供应商提供商业机会。另有内容丰富的研讨会活动以及各种社交联络活动，令参会者深刻理解房地产业并获取国际房地产业的最新资讯动态。
周期：每年一届

**市场范围**：国际性
**参展联络**：励展博览集团国际销售部
**地址**：北京市朝阳区新源里南路1-3号平安国际金融中心A座15层01-03，05（100027）
**联系人**：吴祥
☎ 010-5933 9288
🖷 010-5933 9233
✉ ronald.wu@reedexpo.com.cn
www.reedexport.cn

## 里昂国际博览会

### Foire Internationale de Lyon

**日期**：2010/03/19 - 29
**地点**：法国里昂欧洲国际展览中心
**内容**：手工艺，世界民族之林，表演/小家电/家里的修补用品，居住，厨房/浴室/大家电，室内家具，土地，葡萄酒和美味，运动和休闲，室外布置（阳台-露台-花园），车辆和户外休闲，游泳池，水疗和康体，女性专区，服务，多媒体新科技
**周期**：每年一届
**市场范围**：国际性
**上届规模** '09：展览面积1,000,000m$^2$，参展商1,100家
**主办**：法国智奥展览集团
**地址**：北京市朝阳区朝外大街20号联合大厦710室（100020）
**联系人**：张静
☎ 010-6588 5968, 6588 5969
🖷 010-6588 5970
✉ jackiezhang@promosalons-china.com

### Foire Internationale de Lyon

Date：2010/03/19 - 29
Venue: France
Frequency: Annual
Market Area: International
Statistics '09: Exhibition Area 1,000,000m$^2$, Exhibitors 1,100
Organizer: G.L. events
Address: 710# Union Plaza NO.20 ChaoWaiDaJie Beijing 100020, China
☎ 010-6588 5968, 6588 5969
🖷 010-6588 5970
Contact: Zhang Jing
✉ jackiezhang@promosalons-china.com

## 欧洲国际运输及物流周

### SITL Europe: International Event for Transport & Logistics

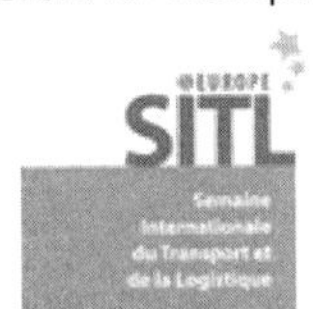


**日期**：2010/03/23 - 26
**地点**：法国巴黎北维勒班特展馆
**内容**：向业界展示营销供应链管理中的整套服务及产品，是运输与物流业界必不可少的重要B2B商业平台。观众及参展商通过参加商务会议获得新知，并交流市场的最新动态，以获得提升企业经营及策略规划等竞争优势。
**周期**：两年一届
**市场范围**：国际性
**主办**：励展法国公司
**参展联络**：励展博览集团国际销售部
**地址**：北京朝阳区新源里南路1-3号平安国际金融中心A座15层01-03，05（100027）
**联系人**：王亮
☎ 010-5933 9288
🖷 010-5933 9233
✉ liang.wang@reedexpo.com.cn
www.reedexport.cn

## 2010年法国里昂照明展

### LumiVille and InLight Expo

**日期**：2010/06/01 - 03
**地点**：法国里昂国际展览中心
**内容**：室外照明灯具、室内照明灯具及光源、高新技术产品、电器附件、产品服务、相关能源系统等
**周期**：每年一届
**市场范围**：国际性
**参展联络**：中国轻工业展览中心
**地址**：北京市东城区东四六条64号（100007）
**联系人**：应艳梅
☎ 010-6401 6504
🖷 010-6401 6504
✉ cy888@vip.163.com
MSN：lengfeier@msn.com
QQ：71229011
www.cliexpo.org

## 中国纺织品服装贸易展览会（巴黎）

### China Textile and Apparel Trade Show (Paris)

**日期**：2010/09 -
**地点**：法国
**内容**：各类服装,家用纺织品,服装面料,服饰等
**始办年份**：2006
**周期**：每年一届
**市场范围**：国际性
**入场券价格**：名片换取
**参展费用**：标准展位（3x3m）5,300欧元
**上届规模** '09：参展商80家，专业贸易观众6,000人
**主办**：中国纺织工业协会
**承办**：中国贸促会纺织行业分会；中国服装协会；法兰克福展览（法国）有限公司
**地址**：中国北京东长安街12号450室（100742）
**联系人**：王彤
☎ 010-8522 9482
🖷 010-8522 9544
✉ wangtong@ccpittex.com
www.eurofair.com.cn

### China Textile and Apparel Trade Show (Paris)

Date：2010/09 -
Venue: Parc d' expositions Paris Le Bourget, France
Profile: All kinds of Wear, Hometextiles, Apparel fabrics & Accessories
Established Year: 2006
Frequency: Annual
Market Area: International
Participated Fee: Standard Booth （3x3m） EUR 5,300
Statistics '09: Exhibitors 80, Trade Visitors 6,000
Sponsor: China National Textile & Apparel Council
Organizer: The Sub-Council of Textile Industry CCPIT; China National Garment Association; Messe Frankfurt (France) Ltd
Address: Room 450, No.12 Chang An Street, Beijing, China
Contact: Wang Tong
☎ 86-10-8522 9482
🖷 86-10-8522 9544
✉ wangtong@ccpittex.com
www.eurofair.com.cn

## 法国巴黎Maison & Objet 2010

**日期**：2010/09/03 - 07
**地点**：法国巴黎
**周期**：每年一届
**市场范围**：国际性
**参展联络**：大连上选会展服务有限公司
**地址**：大连市西岗区鞍山路13号兴业广场大厦B座508室（116011）
☎ 0411-8378 8326, 8378 8396, 8378 9165, 8378 8821
🖷 0411-8378 8830, 8378 8823
✉ cicyhuang@vip.sina.com
MSN：cicyhuang@msn.com
www.sun-show.com

## 2010年法国巴黎国际美容展览会

### 2010 Beyond Beauty Paris

**日期**：2010/09/12 - 15
**地点**：法国巴黎凡尔赛门展览中心
**内容**：COSMEETING展区：香水、化妆品、美容护理、护肤产品、天然化妆品、家用香料、美容配件(美甲工具、镊子、化妆镜、海绵产品、化妆刷、头梳等美容工具及美容礼品、饰品、化妆包、包装盒)；CREATIVE展区：包装，设备，私有标牌、定单生产，咨询与设计，促销产品，广告材料，陈列与展示；EUROPEAN SPA展区 ：专业的皮肤护理产品（脸部、身体、抗衰老、香氛等），专业附件产品（服饰、装饰、护理附件），专业设备仪器（SPA美容仪器、日光浴设备、浴疗设备、桑拿蒸汽房设备）。
**周期**：每年一届
**上届规模** '08：参展商600家，参观人数18,300人
**主办**：ITEC(法国)公司
**参展联络**：杭州思诺博会展服务有限公司
**地址**：杭州市体育场路229号浙江粮油大厦1202室（310003）
☎ 0571-8577 8500
🖷 0571-8577 9709
✉ expo@sinobal.com
www.sinobal.com

## 巴黎国际眼镜展

### SILMO PARIS

**日期**：2010/09/23 - 26
**地点**：法国巴黎凡尔赛门展览中心
**内容**：眼镜片，眼镜架，太阳镜，隐形眼镜，运动眼镜，时尚眼镜，与眼镜销售相关的各种附件产品，配镜师专用仪器工具和设备，眼镜店设备和装置，生产制造设备和配件
**始办年份**：1967
**周期**：每年一届
**市场范围**：国际性
**上届规模** '09：展览面积95,000m$^2$，参展商1,000家（国外展商770家，来自99个国家），参观人数42,700人
**主办**：法国高美爱博展览集团
**地址**：北京市朝阳区朝外大街20号联合大厦710室（100020）
**联系人**：张静
☎ 010-6588 5968, 6588 5969
🖷 010-6588 5970
✉ jackiezhang@promosalons-china.com

## 法国巴黎国际门窗展

**日期**：2010/10 -
**地点**：法国巴黎
**内容**：门、窗系列
**周期**：每年一届
**市场范围**：国际性
**参展联络**：京慕国际展览有限公司
**地址**：北京市朝阳区北三环东路6号中国国际展览中心服务楼3层
**联系人**：许艳，孙铁兵
☎ 010-8460 0551
🖷 010-8460 0394
✉ zhaolingna@ciec.com.cn
www.jingmu.com.cn

## 巴黎国际两轮车展

### MONDIAL DU DEUX ROUES

**日期**：2010/10 -
**地点**：法国巴黎凡尔赛门展览中心
**内容**：自行车展会：所有类型整车（赛车，越野自行车，城市自行车，电动自行车，越野自行车...），零件（车架，脚踏板，车叉，传动装置，轮圈...）摩托车展会：摩托车，小轮摩托车，轻骑摩托车，四轮摩托车，三轮摩托车，装备和摩托车手服装（头盔，靴子，手套...）
**周期**：每年一届
**市场范围**：国际性
**上届规模** '07：展览面积80,000m$^2$，参展商1,200家，参观人数400,000人
**主办**：法国汽车摩托车及自行车促进公司
**地址**：北京市朝阳区朝外大街20号联合大厦710室（100020）
**联系人**：张静
☎ 010-6588 5968, 6588 5969
🖷 010-6588 5970
✉ jackiezhang@promosalons-china.com

### MONDIAL DU DEUX ROUES

Date：2010/10 -
Venue: Paris, France
Frequency: Annual
Market Area: International
Statistics '07: Exhibition Area 80,000m$^2$, Exhibitors 1,200
Organizer: AMC PROMOTION
Address: 710# Union Plaza, NO.20 ChaoWaiDaJie, Beijing 100020, CHINA
☎ 010-6588 5968, 6588 5969
🖷 010-6588 5970
Contact: Jackie ZHANG
✉ jackiezhang@promosalons-china.com

### 巴黎国际服装批发商博览会
### INTERSELECTION

**日期**：2010/10 -
**地点**：法国巴黎
**内容**：各类女装、男装、童装及相关服饰配件、服装面料、家纺产品
**市场范围**：国际性
**参展联络**：京慕国际展览有限公司
**地址**：北京市朝阳区北三环东路6号中国国际展览中心服务楼3层
**联系人**：由慧
☎ 010-8460 0551
🖷 010-8460 0394
✉ zhaolingna@ciec.com.cn
www.jingmu.com.cn

### 巴黎国际服装及纺织品定牌贸易展
### FATEX

**日期**：2010/10 -
**地点**：法国巴黎
**内容**：各类女装、男装、童装及相关服饰配件、服装面料、家纺产品
**市场范围**：国际性
**参展联络**：京慕国际展览有限公司
**地址**：北京市朝阳区北三环东路6号中国国际展览中心服务楼3层
**联系人**：由慧
☎ 010-8460 0551
🖷 010-8460 0394
✉ zhaolingna@ciec.com.cn
www.jingmu.com.cn

## 法国国际现代艺术展览会

### FIAC:
### International Modern & Contemporary Art Fair

**日期**：2010/10 -
**地点**：法国巴黎Grand Palais展览馆及Cour Carree du Louvre展览馆
**内容**：FIAC是法国及外国现代和当代艺术的年度展，包括油画、摄影、雕塑和装置艺术。有220多个法国及国际画廊、经销商参加展会。
**产品及服务**：现代和当代艺术交易市场，展示油画、雕塑、素描、印刷品、纸上作品、摄影、录像及装置艺术。
**周期**：每年一届
**市场范围**：国际性
**主办**：励展法国公司；
**参展联络**：励展博览集团国际销售部
**地址**：北京市朝阳区新源里南路1-3号平安国际金融中心A座15层01-03，05（100027）
**联系人**：吴祥
☎ 010-5933 9288
🖷 010-5933 9233
✉ ronald.wu@reedexpo.com.cn
www.reedexport.cn

### 巴黎世界汽车展
### MONDIAL DE L'AUTOMOBILE

**日期**：2010/10/02 - 17
**地点**：法国巴黎凡尔赛门展览中心
**内容**：乘用车，小型车，运动车辆，四轮驱动摩托车，沙滩车，车身，汽车设计，汽车工程，调谐，用途车及商用车，商用车车身，房车，汽车配套零部件、配件和原材料，服务，媒体，官方和专业组织，汽车制造商的零售店等
**始办年份**：1898
**周期**：两年一届
**市场范围**：国际性
**上届规模** '08：展览面积220,000m$^2$，参展商500家（国外展商33家），参观人数1431883人
**主办**：法国汽车摩托车及自行车促进公司(AMC PROMOTION)
**地址**：北京市朝阳区朝外大街20号联合大厦710室（100020）
**联系人**：张静
☎ 010-6588 5968, 6588 5969
🖷 010-6588 5970
✉ jackiezhang@promosalons-china.com

### 国际食品加工机械设备展览会

**日期**：2010/10/17 - 21
4352
**地点**：法国巴黎
**周期**：每年一届
**市场范围**：国际性
**参展联络**：中国机械汽车展览联合会
☎ 010-6859 4964
🖷 010-6859 4964

### 巴黎国际食品展
### SIAL

**日期**：2010/10/17 - 21
**地点**：法国巴黎北郊维勒班展览中心
**内容**：酒精饮料；罐头制品，饼干和精细烘烤食品；腊肉；奶制品和蛋类；冷冻制品；减肥食品，健康食品，儿童食品；精细食品；原辅料和添加剂；新鲜制品；水果和蔬菜；食品杂货业；肉类；本国展区和世界各地区的展区；非酒精饮料；营养罐头制品，饼干和精细烘烤食品；有机食品；家禽和野味；腌货；法国各个地区；海鲜产品；葡萄酒和烈性酒
**周期**：两年一届
**市场范围**：国际性
**上届规模** '08：展览面积200,000m$^2$，参展商5,302家（国外展商4,082家，来自99个国家），参观人数140,423人
**主办**：法国高美爱博展览集团
**地址**：北京市朝阳区朝外大街20号联合大厦710室（100020）
**联系人**：卢晓成
☎ 010-6588 5968, 6588 5969
🖷 010-6588 5970
✉ louislu@promosalons-china.com

### SIAL

Date：2010/10/17 - 21
Venue: Pairs, France
Frequency: Biennial
Market Area: International
Statistics '08: Exhibition Area 200,000m$^2$, Exhibitors 5,302 (foreigners 4,082, came from 99 countries)
Organizer: COMEXPOSIUM
Address: 710# Union Plaza NO.20 ChaoWaiDaJie Beijing 100020, China
☎ 010-6588 5968, 6588 5969
🖷 010-6588 5970
Contact: Louis LU
✉ louislu@promosalons-china.com

## 法国国际安防展/消防设备展

### Expoprotection/Feu:
### The Exhibition for Risk Management

**日期**：2010/11/02 - 04
**地点**：法国巴黎维勒班特国际展览中心
**内容**：法国国际安防展/消防设备展将在巴黎盛大开幕，该展会是安防及消防业界的盛会。届时，安防、消防等领域展品都将在此全面展示，包括工作服、行业风险及自然风险等。
**周期**：两年一届
**市场范围**：国际性
**主办**：励展法国公司
**参展联络**：励展博览集团国际销售部
**地址**：北京朝阳区新源里南路1-3号平安国际金融中心A座15层01-03，05（100027）
**联系人**：宫卫
☎ 010-5933 9288
🖷 010-5933 9233
✉ david.gong@reedexpo.com.cn
www.reedexport.cn

### 2010年第40届法国巴黎国际工业配件展览会

**日期**：2010/11/02 - 05
**地点**：法国巴黎诺德-维勒班展览中心
**内容**：金属加工：铸锻件、铸造原辅材料及铸造技术、汽车配件、工业标准件、紧固件、泵、阀门、电机、索具、轴承、铸造及锻造机械、半成品、金属热处理、表面处理、工螺纹切割、机加工、专业机械加工、冲压切断/成型、工程、研发、质量控制、工业维修保养；模具、工具、塑料、橡胶、及合成材料；电子电器、微电子技术、集成电路、开关、连接器、二极管/三极管、显示器、光电子激光器件、继电器、传感器、电阻器、电位器、变频器等电子元器件
**周期**：每年一届
**市场范围**：国际性
**主办**：北方国际展览有限公司
**地址**：北京市宣武区菜园街1号中环假日酒店写字楼1102-1103室（100053）
**联系人**：穆超
☎ 010-8355 9740
🖷 010-8355 7940
✉ woody.m@northexpo.com.cn
MSN：mr_angel_boy@hotmail.com
QQ：26327995
www.northexpo.com.cn

## 法国国际酒店及餐饮设备展

### Equip' Hotel:
### The World Class Event for the Restaurant, Hotel, Cafes & Catering Industries

EQUIP'HOTEL
PARIS

**日期**：2010/11/14 - 18
**地点**：法国凡尔赛门巴黎展览馆
**内容**：餐馆、酒店、咖啡馆与餐饮业的世界级展会。
**展品范围**：浴室、健身与健美、饮料、建筑装配与翻新、咖啡制作与酒吧、家具与装饰、酒店连锁、厨房设备与材料、洗衣与卫生、服务、点心与简餐、餐具与桌布、技术。
**周期**：两年一届
**市场范围**：国际性
**参展费用**：净地展位249欧元/m$^2$，标准展位354欧元/m$^2$
**赞助**：法国金属制造商协会
**主办**：励展法国公司
**参展联络**：励展博览集团海外展览部
**地址**：北京朝阳区新源里南路1-3号平安国际金融中心A座15层01-03，05（100027）
**联系人**：杜一鸣
☎ 010-5933 9288
🖷 010-5933 9233
✉ martin.du@reedexpo.com.cn
www.reedexport.cn

## 法国国际建筑门窗展：汇聚国际领先的门窗、防护和遮阳设备

International Windows, Doors, Shutters & Solar Protection Exhibition

**日期**：2010/11/16 - 19
**地点**：法国凡尔赛门展览中心
**内容**：作为建筑行业中创新领域的一大亮点，Equip'Baie在业内具有极高地位，展会致力于提高建筑物的能源利用率、安全保障和舒适度。EQUIP' BAIE是致力于建材和建筑的国际型展会，展览范围包括木工类、门窗类、玻璃类和遮阳产品。每一届展会均成为业内专家、开发商、承包人、分销商和产品制造商汇集的地方。与此同时，Equip'Baie也为制造商和机械设备供应商交流提供了一个绝佳的平台。由于强大的合约促进力，EQUIP' BAIE被业内高度赞誉，展会致力于在一个友好的环境下，将业内专家汇集一堂，把握时机尽情和同行们探讨热点话题。METAL EXPO是一个致力于建筑行业内的金属产品应用的展会，同时也是EQUIP' BAIE展会的联合主办方。
**周期**：两年一届
**市场范围**：国际性
**参展费用**：净地展位205欧元/m²，标准展位286欧元/m²
**主办**：法国励展博览集团
**参展联络**：励展博览集团国际销售部
**地址**：北京朝阳区新源里南路1-3号平安国际金融中心A座15层01-03，05（100027）
**联系人**：王颖
☎ 010-5933 9288
🖷 010-5933 9233
✉ winnie.wang@reedexpo.com.cn
www.reedexport.cn

## 法国国际工业配件展

MIDEST

**日期**：2010/11/17 - 20
**地点**：法国巴黎维勒班特展览中心
**内容**：法国最大的国际金属、塑料、电器电力加工转包技术及服务展，为业内人士提供从产量导向型转包到涉及最新技术的产品完全工业化的最佳方案。
**产品及服务**：金属加工、塑料/橡胶/合成物加工机械、加工、装配、模具、显微技术、电器、电力、工业服务、工业维护
**周期**：每年一届
**市场范围**：国际性
**参展费用**：净地展位208欧元/m²
**主办**：Reed Expositions France
**参展联络**：励展博览集团国际销售部
**地址**：北京市东长安街1号东方广场东1办公楼1204室（100738）
**联系人**：宫卫先生
☎ 010-5933 9288
🖷 010-5933 9233
✉ david.gong@reedexpo.com.cn
www.reedexport.cn

## 国际包装博览会与食品包装展览会

EMBALLAGE & IPA 2010

**日期**：2010/11/22 - 25
**地点**：法国巴黎
**周期**：两年一届
**市场范围**：国际性
**参展联络**：中国机械汽车展览联合会
☎ 010-6859 4964
🖷 010-6859 4964
**参展联络**：中国贸促会机械行业分会
**地址**：北京市西城区三里河路46号（100823）
**联系人**：吕静，于奇琳，张垚
☎ 010-6859 4909, 6859 5498, 6859 4192
🖷 010-6859 5485
✉ info@ccpitmsc.org
✉ jix@ccpit.org
www.chinamachin.org.cn
www.ccpitmsc.org

## 法国里昂国际环保工业展览会

Pollutec- Lyon

**日期**：2010/12 -
**地点**：法国里昂会议展览中心EUREXPO
**内容**：在为期4天的展会中，将有超过4万名来自业内和当地政府的决策者和专家参加Pillutec Horizons展会，了解并交流相关信息，讨论关于当今及未来在环境和经济方面面临的挑战，发现防污治污技术的新进展，并积极贯彻由1400名"环境和可持续发展"业内人士和专家提出的应对未来的解决方案。
**产品及服务**：与以下领域相关的技术与服务：污染治理，资源优化，能源与气候变化，风险防范与管理，可持续发展，城镇规划与环境，资金流与网络管理，运输与后勤，储藏，分析、测量、追踪，规划、审计、咨询及研究与工程、培训，防范与保护，展团、机构、研究、教育
**周期**：每年一届（在巴黎和里昂轮换举办）
**市场范围**：国际性
**赞助单位**：法国环境能源署（ADEME）
**参展联络**：励展博览集团国际销售部
**地址**：北京朝阳区新源里南路1-3号平安国际金融中心A座15层01-03，05（100027）
**联系人**：王亮
☎ 010-5933 9288
🖷 010-5933 9233
✉ liang.wang@reedexpo.com.cn
www.reedexport.cn

## 法国国际工业自动化展

SCS

**日期**：2010/12 -
**地点**：法国
**内容**：自动化：工业自动化设备和系统，自动化零部件，传感器，工业自动化信息技术及软件，有线和无线通讯技术；电气能源，传动装置，线性导向装置，驱动装置，测试，检测
**周期**：每年一届
**市场范围**：国际性
**上届规模**　'07：展览面积20,000m²，参展商600家（国外展商121家），参观人数25,000人
**主办**：法国智奥展览集团
**地址**：北京市朝阳区朝外大街20号联合大厦710室（100020）
**联系人**：张静
☎ 010-6588 5968, 6588 5969
🖷 010-6588 5970
✉ jackiezhang@promosalons-china.com

## 2011年巴黎国际殡葬展：殡葬行业供应商与经销商的展会

Funéraire Paris 2011: The Exhibition for Funeral Suppliers & Distributors

**日期**：2011 -
**地点**：法国巴黎 Paris Le Bourget
**内容**：在2009年巴黎国际殡葬展（FUNERAIRE PARIS 2009）上，您将会看到欧洲及世界范围内殡葬业产品以及与之相配套的服务，包括：纪念碑，墓碑，棺材，骨灰瓮，殡葬服务，殡葬防腐产品，殡仪运输，大理石，专业媒体与组织。
**周期**：两年一届
**市场范围**：国际性
**参展费用**：净地展位203欧元/m²，标准展位：269欧元/m²
**主办**：励展法国公司
**参展联络**：励展博览集团国际销售部
**地址**：北京朝阳区新源里南路1-3号平安国际金融中心A座15层01-03，05（100027）
**联系人**：王颖
☎ 010-, 5933 9288
🖷 010-5933 9233
✉ winnie.wang@reedexpo.com.cn
www.reedexport.cn

## 世界音乐博览会

MIDEM:
The World's Music Market

**日期**：2011/01 -
**地点**：法国戛纳
**内容**：MIDEM国际音乐博览会（暨为期2天的MidemNet数码与移动音乐论坛）每年在法国戛纳举办一届，每届为期5天，观众包括来自93个国家、覆盖各种音乐类别和所有产业细分市场的10,000多名音乐界专业人士。MIDEM致力于为国际音乐产业提供交易、联络、交流、发现新音乐风格与人才、吸取资讯的贸易展会平台。在展览同时，该展会通过每日会议、圆桌论坛、音乐会与在线音乐产业数据库等多种形式为业界提供更多增值服务。此外，MIDEM还设立了MIDEM Classique & Jazz（www.midem.com/classique）、MIDEM Electronic & Urban Village等专门展区。
**始办年份**：1967
**周期**：每年一届
**市场范围**：国际性
**参展费用**：净地展位3,800欧元/m²
**主办**：励展法国公司
**参展联络**：励展博览集团国际销售部
**地址**：北京市朝阳区新源里南路1-3号平安国际金融中心A座15层01-03，05（100027）
**联系人**：吴祥
☎ 010-5933 9288
🖷 010-5933 9233
✉ ronald.wu@reedexpo.com.cn
www.reedexport.cn

## 法国国际农牧业设备及技术展览会

SIMA

**日期**：2011/02/20 - 24
**地点**：法国巴黎北维勒班展览中心
**内容**：多功能设备，专业设备。巴黎国际农牧业展览会（SIMAGENA）：畜牧饲养者和育种者的国际商务会晤，再生能源
**周期**：两年一届
**市场范围**：国际性
**上届规模**　'09：展览面积122,446m²，参展商1,323家（国外展商529家），参观人数208,550人
**主办**：法国爱博西玛公司
**地址**：北京市朝阳区朝外大街20号联合大厦710室（100020）
**联系人**：卢晓成
☎ 010-6588 5968, 6588 5969
🖷 010-6588 5970
✉ louislu@promosalons-china.com

## 巴黎国际实时运输及物流展

SITL Real Time:
International Show for Logistics Solutions

日期：2011/03 -
2013/03 -
地点：法国巴黎凡尔赛门展览馆
内容：SITL Real Time为运输及物流业展览会，旨在向业界展示营销供应链管理中的整套服务及产品，是运输与物流业界必不可少的重要B2B商业平台。观众及参展商通过参加商务会议获得新知，并交流市场的最新动态，以获得提升企业经营及策略规划等竞争优势。
产品及服务 运输与联合运输服务—海外服务—物流服务-运输、物流设备及服务-运输、物流技术与信息服务-物流基础设施-物流地产-其他相关服务
周期：两年一届
市场范围：国际性
主办：励展法国公司；
参展联络：励展博览集团国际销售部
地址：北京朝阳区新源里南路1-3号平安国际金融中心A座15层01-03，05（100027）
联系人：王亮
☎ 010-5933 9288
🖷 010-5933 9233
✉ liang.wang@reedexpo.com.cn
www.reedexport.cn
www.sitl.eu

## 法国国际地产投资交易会

MIPIM

日期：2011/03 -
地点：法国戛纳影节宫
内容：MIPIM是世界上唯一聚集全球房地产界最具影响力的人物的交易会。它创造独一无二的、绝佳的联络、展示以及商业机会。房地产顾问、开发商、地区官员、投资者以及公司最终用户可在展会上搜集新楼信息、开展新交易以及创建新的伙伴关系。
产品及服务：为投资者，公司最终用户、当地及地区官员、开发商、经纪商、资产管理者以及服务供应商提供商业机会。另有内容丰富的研讨会活动以及各种社交联络活动，令参会者深刻理解房地产业并获取国际房地产业的最新资讯动态。
周期：每年一届
市场范围：国际性
参展联络：励展博览集团国际销售部
地址：北京市朝阳区新源里南路1-3号平安国际金融中心A座15层01-03，05（100027）
联系人：吴祥
☎ 010-5933 9288
🖷 010-5933 9233
✉ ronald.wu@reedexpo.com.cn
www.reedexport.cn

## 巴黎国际特许经营展览会

Franchise Expo Paris:
International Franchise Show

日期：2011/03 -
地点：法国巴黎
内容：展品范围有授予特许经营者，服务供应商及机构
周期：每年一届
市场范围：国际性
主办：法国励展展览公司
参展联络：励展博览集团国际销售部
地址：北京朝阳区新源里南路1-3号平安国际金融中心A座15层01-03，05（100027）
联系人：王亮
☎ 010-5933 9288
🖷 010-5933 9233
✉ liang.wang@reedexpo.com.cn
www.reedexport.cn

## 巴黎国际汽车工业展

EQUIP'AUTO

日期：2011/10 -
地点：法国巴黎北维勒班展览中心
内容：汽车工程、转包加工项目；汽车零部件和配饰、售后网络；物流；个人防护产品；石化产品、润滑油、护理产品；渠道管理系统、信息技术；维修、护养；车身、油漆；汽车服务；专业人士服务、业务分化；其它相关展示
始办年份：1975
周期：两年一届
市场范围：国际性
上届规模 '07：展览面积160,000m²，参展商2,022家（国外展商1,617家），参观人数106,407人
主办：法国高美爱博展览集团
地址：北京市朝阳区朝外大街20号联合大厦710室（100020）
联系人：卢晓成
☎ 010-6588 5968, 6588 5969
🖷 010-6588 5970
✉ louislu@promosalons-china.com

EQUIP'AUTO

Date：2011/10 -
Venue: Paris, France
Established Year: 1975
Frequency: Biennial
Market Area: International
Statistics '07: Exhibition Area 160,000m², Exhibitors 2,022（foreigners 1,617），Visitors 106,407
Organizer: COMEXPOSIUM
Address: 710# Union Plaza, NO.20 ChaoWaiDaJie, Beijing 100020, China
☎ 86-10-6588 5968, 6588 5969
🖷 86-10-6588 5970
Contact: Louis LU
✉ louislu@promosalons-china.com

## 法国国际葡萄酒及果蔬技术展

SITEVI

日期：2011/11 -
地点：法国蒙彼利埃展览中心
内容：葡萄、果蔬种植设备，葡萄收获，葡萄酒酿制、葡萄酒工艺，包装，水果与蔬菜，灌溉，农用物资和服务类
始办年份：1977
周期：两年一届
市场范围：国际性
上届规模 '09：展览面积35,190m²，参展商720家（国外展商174家），参观人数44,592人
主办：法国爱博西玛公司
地址：北京市朝阳区朝外大街20号联合大厦710室（100020）
联系人：卢晓成
☎ 010-6588 5968, 6588 5969
🖷 010-6588 5970
✉ louislu@promosalons-china.com

SITEVI

Date：2011/11 -
Venue: France
Established Year: 1977
Frequency: Biennial
Market Area: International
Statistics '09: Exhibition Area 35,190m², Exhibitors 720（foreigners 174），Visitors 44,592
Organizer: EXPOSIMA
Address: 710# Union Plaza NO.20 ChaoWaiDaJie Beijing 100020, CHINA
☎ 86-10-6588 5968, 6588 5969
🖷 86-10-6588 5970
Contact: Louis LU
✉ louislu@promosalons-china.com

## 巴黎国际建材及设备展

BATIMAT: International Building Exhibition

BATIMAT®

日期：2011/11 -
地点：法国巴黎
内容：主体工程区：屋架、结构构件、屋顶、防水材料、保温隔热材料、主体结构材料和构配件、水处理系统、排水系统；门窗及五金区：门窗、木门窗、金属门窗、塑料门窗、复合材料门窗、门窗闭锁开启系统、遮阳帘（蓬）及其自动开启设备、门窗密封材料、门窗小五金、门锁、玻璃制品、铁艺制品；装饰装修区：各种隔段材料、橱柜、墙地面装饰材料、瓷砖、大理石、花岗石、其它石材、石板、木质板材、木地板、油漆涂料、壁炉及烟道、厨房装饰、照明、装饰材料、游泳池装修及其设备、露天家具及设施、户外运动及娱乐设施；建筑施工设备区：木材加工设备、金属加工设备、塑料加工设备、施工机具、工具、工地安全和防护设备及用品、建筑工地所使用的各种专用车辆 智能化楼宇区 有线和无线网络和安装系统、舒适度、安全、门禁、照明和多媒体功能的管理和控制、智能屋顶、整合系统、各种电梯、中央真空除尘系统、整合安装和设备管理系统 IT区 管理系统、CAD、计算机外围设备、因特网方案；服务类区：专业和技术组织、贸易媒体、各类服务型企业
周期：两年一届
市场范围：国际性
参展联络：励展博览集团国际销售部
地址：北京市朝阳区新源里南路1-3号平安国际金融中心A座15层01-03，05（100027）
联系人：吴祥
☎ 010-5933 9288
🖷 010-5933 9233
✉ ronald.wu@reedexpo.com.cn
www.reedexport.cn

## 国际环保工业展

POLLUTEC

日期：2011/12 -
地点：法国巴黎凡尔赛门展览中心
内容：自来水技术，城市污水处理，工业废水处理，垃圾处理，废物再生利用技术，能源及环境，地面去污，气体污染治理，防治噪声，分析及监测设备，洁净工业技术，景观保护，清洁工业，生态工业区，污染预防，太阳能、风能及小水电站，隔热保温及热能的回收利用，地热，热力网。巴黎展侧重工业环保，里昂展既有工业环保，又有城市环保
周期：每年一届
市场范围：国际性
上届规模 '09：展览面积25,800m²，参展商1,451家，参观人数35,890人
主办：励展博览集团-法国励展公司
地址：北京市朝阳区信源里南路1-3号平安国际金融中心A座01-03, 05（100020）
联系人：张静
☎ 010-5933 9288
🖷 010-5933 9233
✉ jackiezhang@promosalons-china.com

## 法国国际工业自动化展

SCS

日期：2011/12 -
地点：法国巴黎北维勒班展览中心
内容：自动化：工业自动化设备和系统，自动化零

部件，传感器，工业自动化信息技术及软件，有线和无线通讯技术；电气能源：BT器材和工业检测设备，BT电气零部件，控制装置和分配系统，能源的持续、质量和转换，功率电子元件，数据的测试、分析和采集，电气能源的制造，电气能源的经营和供给；传动装置：液压泵、零部件和传动装置，气动压缩机、零部件和传动装置，机械零部件和传动装置，轴承和限位器，H.P.V.操作和连接

**周期：**每年一届

**市场范围：**国际性

**上届规模** '07：展览面积20,000m²，参展商600家（国外展商121家），参观人数25,000人

**主办：**法国智奥展览集团

**地址：**北京市朝阳区朝外大街20号联合大厦710室（100020）

**联系人：**张静

☎ 010-6588 5968, 6588 5969

🖷 010-6588 5970

✉ jackiezhang@promosalons-china.com

## 巴黎国际供暖、制冷、空调、新能源及家用电气展览会

Interclima+elec Home & building

interclima
+elec
home&building

**日期：**2012/02 -

**地点：**法国巴黎Paris Expo - Porte de Versailles

**内容：**由国际知名展览机构——励展博览法国公司主办的Interclima，2010年将是第19届，是目前世界上供暖、制冷、空调及智能建筑领域规模最大、影响力最强的专业展会之一。2008年的Interclima展会，无论是在展出面积还是观众人数上，均又创历史新高。展商比2004年增加了22.5%。平均每个展商在展出期间建立的有效联系为650个。2008年的Interclima接待观众人数比2006年增加20.5%。其中，来自法国以外的观众有7700多名，占总数的7.53%；贸易商与制造商占35%强，安装商占39%强。Interclima展的潜力却非常巨大。因为德国、意大利的相关市场已经进入成熟期，而法国却还处于发展期。也正因如此，所以法国政府对建筑住宅用冷凝锅炉、制冷、供暖设备提供高达40%的补贴，对某些太阳能采暖设施及加热泵的补贴更高达50%。另外，法国工业部长亲临参观上届展会也说明了法国政府对新能源技术的高度重视。

**周期：**两年一届

**市场范围：**国际性

**参展费用：**净地展位240欧元/m²，标准展位（9m²）325～517欧元/m²（不含增值税19%）

**上届规模** '08：展览面积70,000m²，参观人数102,620人

**主办：**励展博览法国公司

**参展联络：**励展博览集团国际销售部

**地址：**北京朝阳区新源里南路1-3号平安国际金融中心A座15层01-03，05（100027）

**联系人：**杜一鸣

☎ 010-5933 9288

🖷 010-5933 9233

✉ martin.du@reedexpo.com.cn

www.reedexport.cn

## 欧洲国际运输及物流周

SITL Europe:
International Event for Transport & Logistics

**日期：**2012/03 -

**地点：**法国巴黎北维勒班特展馆

**内容：**欧洲国际运输及物流周（SITL Europe）向业界展示营销供应链管理中的整套服务及产品，是运输与物流业界必不可少的重要B2B商业平台。观众及参展商通过参加商务会议获得新知，并交流市场的最新动态，以获得提升企业经营及策略规划等竞争优势。

**周期：**两年一届

**市场范围：**国际性

**主办：**励展法国公司

**参展联络：**励展博览集团国际销售部

**地址：**北京朝阳区新源里南路1-3号平安国际金融中心A座15层01-03，05（100027）

**联系人：**王亮

☎ 010-5933 9288

🖷 010-5933 9233

✉ liang.wang@reedexpo.com.cn

www.reedexport.cn

## 法国国际酒店及餐饮设备展

Equip' Hotel:
The World Class Event for the Restaurant, Hotel, Cafes & Catering Industries

EQUIP'HOTEL
PARIS

**日期：**2012/11 -

**地点：**法国凡尔赛门巴黎展览馆

**内容：**餐馆、酒店、咖啡馆与餐饮业的世界级展会。

**展品范围：**浴室——健身与健美、饮料、建筑装配与翻新、咖啡制作与酒吧、家具与装饰、酒店连锁、厨房设备与材料、洗衣与卫生、服务、点心与简餐、餐具与桌布、技术。

**周期：**两年一届

**市场范围：**国际性

**参展费用：**净地249欧元/m²，标准展位354欧元/m²

**赞助：**法国金属制造商协会

**主办：**励展法国公司

**参展联络：**励展博览集团海外展览部

**地址：**北京朝阳区新源里南路1-3号平安国际金融中心A座15层01-03，05（100027）

**联系人：**杜一鸣

☎ 010-5933 9288

🖷 010-5933 9233

✉ martin.du@reedexpo.com.cn

www.reedexport.cn

## 法国国际安防展/消防设备展

Expoprotection/Feu: The Exhibition for Risk Management

**日期：**2012/11 -

**地点：**法国巴黎维勒班特国际展览中心

**内容：**两年一届法国国际安防展/消防设备展将在巴黎盛大开幕，该展会是安防及消防业界的盛会。届时，安防、消防等领域展品都将在此全面展示，包括工作服、行业风险及自然风险等。

**周期：**两年一届

**市场范围：**国际性

**主办：**励展法国公司

**参展联络：**励展博览集团国际销售部

**地址：**北京朝阳区新源里南路1-3号平安国际金融中心A座15层01-03，05（100027）

**联系人：**宫卫

☎ 010-5933 9288

🖷 010-5933 9233

✉ david.gong@reedexpo.com.cn

www.reedexport.cn

## 法国国际建筑门窗展：汇聚国际领先的门窗、防护和遮阳设备

International Windows, Doors, Shutters & Solar Protection Exhibition

**日期：**2012/11 -

**地点：**法国凡尔赛门展览中心

**内容：**作为建筑行业中创新领域的一大亮点，Equip'Baie在业内具有极高地位，展会致力于提高建筑物的能源利用率、安全保障和舒适度。EQUIP' BAIE是致力于建材和建筑的国际型展会，展览范围包括木工类、门窗类、玻璃类和遮阳产品。每一届展会均成为业内专家、开发商、承包人、分销商和产品制造商汇集的地方。与此同时，Equip'Baie也为制造商和机械设备供应商交流提供了一个绝佳的平台。由于强大的合约促进力，EQUIP' BAIE被业内高度赞誉，展会致力于在一个友好的环境下，将业内专家汇集一堂，把握时机尽情和同行们探讨热点话题。METAL EXPO是一个致力于建筑行业内的金属产品应用的展会，同时也是EQUIP' BAIE展会的联合主办方。

**周期：**两年一届

**市场范围：**国际性

**参展费用：**净地205欧元/m²，标准展位286欧元/m²

**主办：**法国励展博览集团

**参展联络：**励展博览集团国际销售部

**地址：**北京朝阳区新源里南路1-3号平安国际金融中心A座15层01-03，05（100027）

**联系人：**王颖

☎ 010-5933 9288

🖷 010-5933 9233

✉ winnie.wang@reedexpo.com.cn

www.reedexport.cn

# 德国
# Germany

## 柏林国际水利技术、污水处理展览会暨学术会议

Wasser Berlin

**日期：**2010 -

**地点：**德国柏林

**内容：**通讯技术、工业设备、信息技术、测量体系、分析技术、泵站技术、驱动技术、液态气体技术、调节和控制技术、交流技术、服务、污水处理技术、污水、游泳池装置、地下工程、建筑体系、水体保护、供水技术、水处理设备、水处理技术

**周期：**三年一届

**市场范围：**国际性

**参展联络：**德国工商会（香港）南中国办事处/柏林国际展览有限公司香港及中国代表处

**地址：**广州市天河北路大都会广场2915室

**联系人：**孟昕

☎ 020-8755 8204, 8755 2353

🖷 020-8755 1889

✉ meng.sophie@gz.china.ahk.de

www.messe-berlin.de

## 国际会展及媒体技术展览会

Showtech

**日期：**2010/ -

**地点：**德国柏林

**内容：**声像技术、视听技术、通讯技术、灯光装潢、舞台搭建、舞台技术、图像技术、安全技术、服务、音响技术、演播室设备、各类活动的举办技术、建筑展、培训

**周期：**两年一届

**市场范围：**国际性

**参展联络**：德国工商会（香港）南中国办事处/柏林国际展览有限公司香港及中国代表处
**地址**：广州市天河北路大都会广场2915室
**联系人**：孟昕
☎ 020-8755 8204, 8755 2353
🖷 020-8755 1889
✉ meng.sophie@gz.china.ahk.de
www.messe-berlin.de

## 柏林国际建筑物清洁、管理及服务展览会暨学术会议

### CMS - Cleaning Management Service

**日期**：2010 -
**地点**：德国柏林
**内容**：清洁设备、清洁技术、商品清洁、洗涤剂、设备管理、楼层清洁、保养、监控、维修、服务
**周期**：两年一届
**市场范围**：国际性
**参展联络**：德国工商会（香港）南中国办事处/柏林国际展览有限公司香港及中国代表处
**地址**：广州市天河北路大都会广场2915室
**联系人**：孟昕
☎ 020-8755 8204, 8755 2353
🖷 020-8755 1889
✉ meng.sophie@gz.china.ahk.de
www.messe-berlin.de

## 埃森国际建材展

### DEUBAU

**日期**：2010/01 -
**地点**：德国埃森
**内容**：建材，门窗及其五金，玻璃幕墙，屋顶材料，铝材，卫浴，瓷砖，玻璃纤维，地板
首届
**周期**：两年一届
**市场范围**：国际性
**参展联络**：京慕国际展览有限公司
**地址**：北京市朝阳区北三环东路6号中国国际展览中心服务楼3层
**联系人**：安红彦；孙铁兵
☎ 010-8460 0551
🖷 010-8460 0394
✉ zhaolingna@ciec.com.cn
www.jingmu.com.cn

## 法兰克福家纺展

### Heimtextil

**日期**：2010/01/13 - 16
**地点**：德国法兰克福
**内容**：地布、窗饰布、家具面料及皮革、卧室纺织品、浴室纺织品、厨房用纺织品、面料后整理等
**市场范围**：国际性
**参展联络**：京慕国际展览有限公司
**地址**：北京市朝阳区北三环东路6号中国国际展览中心服务楼3层
**联系人**：由慧；柳川
☎ 010-8460 0551
🖷 010-8460 0394
✉ zhaolingna@ciec.com.cn
www.jingmu.com.cn

## 柏林绿色周−食品工业、农业及园艺博览会

### Internationale Grune Woche Berlin

**日期**：2010/01/15 - 24
**地点**：德国柏林
**内容**：农业机械、农业、啤酒、饮料、烹饪用具、鱼类、粮食、园艺用品、园艺物料、园艺设备、家庭用品、畜产品、肉制品、香肠、汽酒、烈酒、酒
**周期**：每年一届
**市场范围**：国际性
**参展费用**：118～148欧元/$m^2$
**参展联络**：德国工商会（香港）南中国办事处/柏林国际展览有限公司香港及中国代表处
**地址**：广州市天河北路大都会广场2915室
**联系人**：孟昕
☎ 020-8755 8204, 8755 2353
🖷 020-8755 1889
✉ meng.sophie@gz.china.ahk.de
www.messe-berlin.de

# 国际工程机械与建筑机械展览会

## 慕尼黑国际眼镜及光学镜片博览会

### OPTI

**日期**：2010/01/15 - 17
**地点**：德国慕尼黑
**内容**：眼镜及隐形眼镜相关、太阳镜、潮流镜架、光学设备仪器工具、店面设备、助听器、视力矫正仪器、三脚架、工场设备等
**周期**：每年一届
**市场范围**：国际性
**参展联络**：京慕国际展览有限公司
**地址**：北京市朝阳区北三环东路6号中国国际展览中心服务楼3层
**联系人**：张璋
☎ 010-8460 0551
🖷 010-8460 0394
✉ zhaolingna@ciec.com.cn
www.jingmu.com.cn

# 科隆国际家具展

### imm cologne

**日期**：2010/01/19 - 24
**地点**：德国科隆国际展览中心
**内容**：科隆国际家具展（imm cologne）始于1949年，是当今世界最负盛名的家具展览会。每年一月份在德国科隆国际展览中心举行。展品无以伦比的广度和深度是科隆国际家具展作为全球第一品牌的独特性。在这里，全球的观众将领略到来自世界范围的包罗万象的设计一流的家具以及经典家居用品世界，其间，丰富多彩的配套活动也为科隆国际家具展增色不少
**始办年份**：1949
**周期**：每年一届
**市场范围**：国际性
**入场券价格**：710元人民币
**参展费用**：统一特装560欧元/$m^2$，自行特装155欧元/$m^2$
**主办**：德国科隆展览国际有限公司
**地址**：北京市朝阳区东三环北路8号亮马河大厦二座1018室（100004）
**联系人**：郑志强
☎ 010-6590 7766转 717
🖷 010-6590 6139
✉ info@koelnmesse.cn
www.imm-cologne.cn

# imm cologne

**Date**：2010/01/19 - 24
**Venue**: Koelnmesse Trade Fair Center, Germany
**Profile**: imm cologne is the international leading trade fair for the furnishing sector. Each year, imm cologne is the first event to present the latest home trends for Europe and overseas. The unparalleled breadth and depth of the exhibits is the trademark and claim to top quality of imm cologne. Here, international trade visitors discover furniture and home style ideas from all over the world.
**Established Year**: 1949
**Frequency**: Annual
**Market Area**: International
**Cost to Attend**: 710 RMB
**Organizer**: Koelnmesse GmbH
**Address**: Unit 1018 Landmark Tower II, No. 8 Dongsanhuan N. Road, Beijing 100004
**Contact**: KEN ZHENG
☎ 86-10-6590 7766 ext 717
🖷 86-10-6590 6139
✉ info@koelnmesse.cn
www.imm-cologne.cn

## 欧洲国际压铸展览会

### EUROGUSS 2010

**日期**：2010/01/19 - 21
**地点**：德国纽伦堡
**周期**：两年一届
**市场范围**：国际性
**主办**：中国贸促会机械行业分会
**地址**：北京市西城区三里河路46号（100823）
**联系人**：严静，陈媛蓉
☎ 010-6859 4938, 6859 5296, 6851 2883
🖷 010-6859 5057
✉ info@ccpitmsc.org
✉ jix@ccpit.org
www.chinamachin.org.cn
www.ccpitmsc.org

## 柏林国际服装服饰博览会

### Premium Berlin

**日期**：2010/01/20 - 22
**地点**：德国柏林
**内容**：2009年7月的第14届Premium，31.672位专业买家到访，创造了今年服装服饰展会业买家访问率的最高值。买家来自62% 德语区国家,21%意大利,7%英伦三国,5%荷卢比三国,4%北欧四国,1%欧洲外买家（日本、中国、俄罗斯、美国）。来自世界各地的近700家展商，超过900个系列的展品，包括服装、鞋包、服饰等，1200多家专业媒体，31,672位专业买家。展会组织方一直以来对于每一位参展商所设立的高标准参展要求，使得来自中国的品牌企业一直还没有机会能够在该展会中展示自己的设计，现在，德国欧野有限公司与Premium主办方达成协议，为中国的原创品牌铺平道路，真正以品牌企业的形象亮相于Premium这个欧洲高端品牌展会，与欧洲高端品牌企业同台竞技。
**周期**：每年两届
**市场范围**：国际性
**主办**：德国Premium博览中心
**参展联络**：德国欧野有限公司
**地址**：北京朝阳区广渠东路3号申奥商务楼203B（100022）
**联系人**：李艳艳
☎ 010-8721 5659
✉ evitagroup_exhibition@hotmail.com
www.premiumexhibitions.com

## 法兰克福国际圣诞礼品博览会

### ChristmasWorld

**日期**：2010/01/29 - 02
**地点**：德国法兰克福德国
**内容**：圣诞用品、节日装饰品等
**市场范围**：国际性
**参展联络**：京慕国际展览有限公司
**地址**：北京市朝阳区北三环东路6号中国国际展览中心服务楼3层
**联系人**：古莹，孟琳
☎ 010-84600551
🖷 010-84600394
✉ zhaolingna@ciec.com.cn
www.jingmu.com.cn

## 法兰克福国际美容美发及流行饰品博览会

### BeautyWorld

**日期**：2010/01/30 - 02
**地点**：德国法兰克福
**内容**：香水、化妆品、珠宝及饰品、卫生用品、护牙用品、假发、护发用品、美甲用品、化妆沐浴用品等
**市场范围**：国际性
**参展联络**：京慕国际展览有限公司
**地址**：北京市朝阳区北三环东路6号中国国际展览中

心服务楼3层
联系人：孟琳，古莹
☎ 010-8460 0551
🖷 010-8460 0394
✉ zhaolingna@ciec.com.cn
www.jingmu.com.cn

### 法兰克福国际文具及办公用品博览会
### PaperWorld

**日期**：2010/01/30 - 02
**地点**：德国法兰克福
**内容**：文具、办公用品等
**市场范围**：国际性
**参展联络**：京慕国际展览有限公司
**地址**：北京市朝阳区北三环东路6号中国国际展览中心服务楼3层
**联系人**：孟琳，古莹
☎ 010-8460 0551
🖷 010-8460 0394
✉ zhaolingna@ciec.com.cn
www.jingmu.com.cn

### 科隆国际糖果及休闲食品展
### ISM-international Sweets and Biscuits Fair

**日期**：2010/01/31 - 03
**地点**：德国科隆国际博览中心
**内容**：ISM——全球市场成功的标志 在德国科隆举办的科隆国际糖果及休闲食品展（ISM）是全球最大、最重要的甜食和休闲食品的展览会。每年，来自全球贸易界的专业人士汇聚在这里，相互介绍、发掘和探讨国际最新流行趋势、最新的产品，寻找最近最好的商机。
**始办年份**：1972
**周期**：每年一届
**市场范围**：国际性
**入场券价格**：人民币600元
**参展费用**：标准展位420欧元/m²（12m²起），净地150欧元/m²(36m²起)
**上届规模**‘09：展览面积110, 000m², 参展商1, 593家（国外展商1, 274家），专业贸易观众32, 500人
**主办**：科隆展览国际有限公司
**地址**：北京东三环北路8号亮马河大厦2座1018室（100004）
**联系人**：徐畅，王迎
☎ 010-6590 7766 转 715
🖷 010-6590 6139
✉ j.xu@koelnmesse.cn
www.ism-cologne.cn

### ISM- international Sweets and Biscuits Fair

**Date**：2010/01/31 - 03
**Venue**: Cologne Exhibition Center, Germany
**Profile**: ISM is the largest and most important sweets and biscuits fair in the world. Every year the international sector meets to introduce, discover and discuss the latest trends, the newest products and the most up-to-dates perspectives.
**Established Year**: 1972
**Frequency**: Annual
**Market Area**: International
**Cost to Attend**: RMB 600:-
**Participated Fee**: Standard Booth EUR 420/m²(min 12m²), Raw Space EUR 150/m²(min 36m²)
**Statistics** ‘09: Exhibition Area 110, 000m², Exhibitors 1, 593（foreigners 1, 274）, Trade Visitors 32,500
**Organizer**: Koelnmesse
**Address**: Unit 1018, Landmark Tower Ⅱ, No. 8 Dongsanhuan North Rd, Beijing 100004, China
**Contact**: Joyce Xu, Elan Wang*
☎ 010-6590 7766 ext 715
🖷 86-10-6590 6139
✉ j.xu@koelnmesse.cn
www.ism-cologne.cn

### 杜塞尔多夫国际服装博览会（春季）
### CPD

**日期**：2010/02 -
**地点**：德国杜塞尔多夫
**内容**：各种女装、男装、针织服装、裘皮服装、晚装、婚装、服饰、浴装、内衣、帽子、围巾等
**周期**：每年两届
**市场范围**：国际性
**参展联络**：京慕国际展览有限公司
**地址**：北京市朝阳区北三环东路6号中国国际展览中心服务楼3层
**联系人**：由慧；柳川
☎ 010-8460 0551
🖷 010-8460 0394
✉ zhaolingna@ciec.com.cn
www.jingmu.com.cn

### 国际果蔬展览会
### Fruit Logistica

**日期**：2010/02/03 - 05
4093
**地点**：德国柏林
**内容**：生态产品、水果、商品展示、坚果、服务、仓储技术、计算机软件、包装技术、运输、蔬菜、干果
**周期**：每年一届
**市场范围**：国际性
**参展费用**：180欧元/m²
**参展联络**：德国工商会（香港）南中国办事处/柏林国际展览有限公司香港及中国代表处
**地址**：广州市天河北路大都会广场2915室
**联系人**：孟昕
☎ 020-8755 8204, 8755 2353
🖷 020-8755 1889
✉ meng.sophie@gz.china.ahk.de
www.messe-berlin.de

### 纽伦堡春季国际玩具博览会
### International Toy Fair Nürnberg

**日期**：2010/02/04 - 09
**地点**：德国纽伦堡纽伦堡
**内容**：儿童玩具、婴儿玩具、电动玩具、户外运动玩具、木制玩具、圣诞饰品等
**市场范围**：国际性
**参展联络**：京慕国际展览有限公司
**地址**：北京市朝阳区北三环东路6号中国国际展览中心服务楼3层
**联系人**：付颖，古莹
☎ 010-8460 0551
🖷 010-8460 0394
✉ zhaolingna@ciec.com.cn
www.jingmu.com.cn

### 春季马术用品展
### spoga horse(spring)

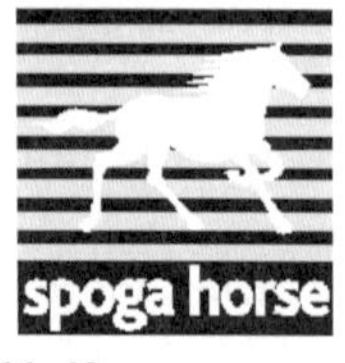


**日期**：2010/02/06 - 08
**地点**：德国科隆国际展览中心展馆
**内容**：马术用品、相关服务
**始办年份**：2008
**周期**：每年两届
**市场范围**：国际性
**参展费用**：标准展位381 欧元/m²（9m²起），净地136欧元/m²（36m²起）
**上届规模**‘08：展览面积28,500m², 参展商379家，参观人数38,600人
**主办**：科隆展览中国有限公司
**地址**：北京市东三环北路8号亮马河大厦2座1018室（100004）
**联系人**：张昱，贾宁
☎ 010-6590 7766转738
🖷 010-6590 6139
✉ j.zhang@koelnmesse.cn

### 慕尼黑冬季国际体育用品及运动时装展
### ispo winter

**日期**：2010/02/07 - 10
**地点**：德国慕尼黑
**内容**：冬季体育世界、球拍及室内运动、板类运动、体育服装、户外运动、运动鞋团队世界、健身运动、休闲服饰等
**周期**：每年一届
**市场范围**：国际性
**参展联络**：京慕国际展览有限公司
**地址**：北京市朝阳区北三环东路6号中国国际展览中心服务楼3层
**联系人**：林航，刘靖
☎ 010-8460 0551
🖷 010-8460 0394
✉ zhaolingna@ciec.com.cn
www.jingmu.com.cn

### 法兰克福国际消费品博览会（春季）
### AMBIENTE / DECORATE LIFE

**日期**：2010/02/12 - 16
**地点**：德国法兰克福德国
**内容**：礼品、家庭用品、钟表、美术陶瓷、日用陶瓷、餐具、文具、手工艺品、箱包和皮革制品等
**市场范围**：国际性
**参展联络**：京慕国际展览有限公司
**地址**：北京市朝阳区北三环东路6号中国国际展览中心服务楼3层
**联系人**：张翠元，滕昊
☎ 010-8460 0551
🖷 010-8460 0394
✉ zhaolingna@ciec.com.cn
www.jingmu.com.cn

### 柏林国际建筑技术展览会
### Bautec

**日期**：2010/02/16 - 20
**地点**：德国柏林
**内容**：气象设备，建筑设备，建筑用品，餐馆建筑，建筑系统，建筑化学，城市规划，木土工程，通讯技术，门，大门，热技术，内部建筑，市政大厦，公共卫生技术，脚手架，服务，表面承载技术，窗户，屋顶工程，房屋立面系统，防火，房屋技术，木结构建筑物，护壁板
**周期**：两年一届
**市场范围**：国际性
**参展联络**：德国工商会（香港）南中国办事处/柏林国际展览有限公司香港及中国代表处
**地址**：广州市天河北路大都会广场2915室
**联系人**：孟昕
☎ 020-8755 8204, 8755 2353
🖷 020-8755 1889
✉ meng.sophie@gz.china.ahk.de
www.messe-berlin.de

### 欧洲国际钟表、珠宝首饰、银器及加工设备展
### inhorgenta Europe

**日期**：2010/02/19 - 22
**地点**：德国慕尼黑
**内容**：钟表、手表、珠宝、宝石、珍珠、银器、首饰盒、包袋、店面设施、珠宝加工生产设备等
**市场范围**：国际性
**参展联络**：京慕国际展览有限公司
**地址**：北京市朝阳区北三环东路6号中国国际展览中心服务楼3层
**联系人**：张璋

☎ 010-8460 0551
🖷 010-8460 0394
✉ zhaolingna@ciec.com.cn
www.jingmu.com.cn

## 科隆国际五金博览会

INTERNATIONAL HARDWARE FAIR COLOGNE

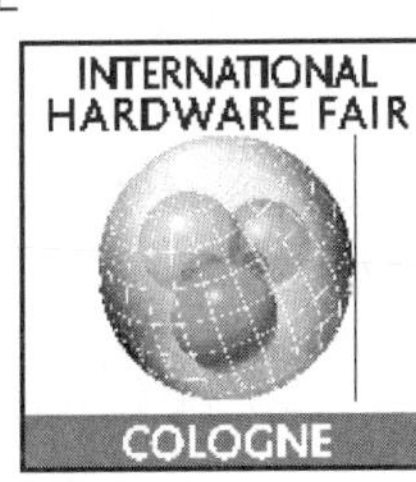


**日期：**2010/02/28 – 03/03
**地点：**德国科隆国际展览中心
**内容：**科隆国际五金博览会是国际五金行业规模最大最有影响力的盛会，代表着国际化的发展和顶级品质。全球没有任何其他展会能在一次展会上涵盖如此全面和齐备的展品范围，科隆国际五金博览会现在及将来都是全球这一行业内最具竞争力和主导博览会。

科隆国际五金博览会在2010 年采用新的LOGO和名称后，在五金领域将更加专业化。博览会包括三大展品系列—工具；锁具及安全系统；紧固件和家居改进，来自全球相关领域的零售商、供应商及采购商都聚集在此。随着中国产品的国际竞争力的增强以及参展取得的卓越的效果，中国企业参加科隆国际五金博览会的规模和数量也在最近数年内有着突飞猛进的增长。在2008 年的展览上，共有超过900 家来自中国大陆的企业向欧美的采购商展示了自己最新的产品和服务，展出面积超过了9,000 m$^2$。
**周期：**两年一届
**市场范围：**国际性
**参展费用：**标准展位540欧元/m$^2$(含净地租金、展位装修、公共能源费、德国展览业协会费用及AUMA费、基本会刊登录费用、观众推广费用)，359欧元/家(垃圾清运费、展位电费、其它杂费及19 %增值税)
**主办：**德国科隆展览国际有限公司
**地址：**北京市朝阳区东三环北路8号亮马河大厦二座1018室（100004）
**联系人：**郑志强
☎ 010-6590 7766转 717
🖷 010-6590 6139
✉ k.zheng@koelnmesse.cn
www.koelnmesse.cn

## INTERNATIONAL HARDWARE FAIR COLOGNE

Date：2010/02/28 - 03
Venue: Koelnmesse Trade Fair Center, Germany
Profile: The world' s leading trade fair for the hardware sector regarding: Internationality of exhibitors and visitors Comprehensive survey of the hardware industry "One-Stop-Shopping".
Frequency: Biennial
Market Area: International
Participated Fee: Standard Booth EUR 540/m$^2$
Organizer: Koelnmesse GmbH
Address: Unit 1018 Landmark Tower II, No. 8 Dongsanhuan N. Road, Beijing 100004
Contact: KEN ZHENG
☎ 86-10-6590 7766 ext 717
🖷 86-10-6590 6139
✉ k.zheng@koelnmesse.cn
www.koelnmesse.cn

### 杜塞尔多夫国际鞋业及皮革制品博览会（春季）

Global Shoes & Accessories

**日期：**2010/03 -
**地点：**德国杜塞尔多夫
**内容：**男女鞋、童鞋、功夫鞋、劳保鞋、雪地靴、工作鞋、制鞋机械及鞋类饰物等
**周期：**每年两届
**市场范围：**国际性
**参展联络：**京慕国际展览有限公司
**地址：**北京市朝阳区北三环东路6号中国国际展览中心服务楼3层
**联系人：**李嘉羊，古莹
☎ 010-8460 0551
🖷 010-8460 0394
✉ zhaolingna@ciec.com.cn
www.jingmu.com.cn

### 柏林国际旅游展览会

ITB Berlin

**日期：**2010/03/10 - 14
**地点：**德国柏林
**内容：**会议中心、旅游设备、信息技术、国际旅游业协会、市政工程、服务、旅游、旅行社讯息、旅行、旅行团
**周期：**每年一届
**市场范围：**国际性
**参展联络：**德国工商会（香港）南中国办事处/柏林国际展览有限公司香港及中国代表处
**地址：**广州市天河北路大都会广场2915室
**联系人：**孟昕
☎ 020-8755 8204, 8755 2353
🖷 020-8755 1889
✉ meng.sophie@gz.china.ahk.de
www.messe-berlin.de

## 科隆教育与培训展览会

Didacta

**日期：**2010/03/16 - 20
**地点：**德国科隆国际博览中心
**市场范围：**国际性
**主办：**科隆展览国际有限公司
**地址：**科隆展览中国有限公司 北京东三环北路8号亮马河大厦2座1018室（100004）
**联系人：**徐畅，王迎
☎ 010-6590 7766 转715
🖷 010-6590 6139
✉ j.xu@koelnmesse.cn

### 国际仪器分析，生化技术，诊断和实验技术贸易博览会暨国际研讨会

Analytica

**日期：**2010/03/23 - 26
3935
**地点：**德国慕尼黑
**内容：**分析仪器设备、工业质量控制、材料测试及鉴定、实验室技术和仪器、化学制品和试剂. 药剂和诊断、生物化学、生物技术和生命科学等
**周期：**两年一届
**市场范围：**国际性
**参展联络：**京慕国际展览有限公司
**地址：**北京市朝阳区北三环东路6号中国国际展览中心服务楼3层
**联系人：**韩芳，俞亮
☎ 010-8460 0551
🖷 010-8460 0394
✉ zhaolingna@ciec.com.cn
www.jingmu.com.cn

### 2010德国纽伦堡门窗幕墙博览会

12th International Trade Fair Windows Doors and Facade

**日期：**2010/03/24 - 27
**地点：**德国纽伦堡国际会展中心
**内容：**设计及型材系统、用于幕墙、窗/窗门、大门、房门、暖房或封闭式凉台半成品、材料、加工辅料、涂料、密封材料、木材与木材加工材料、粘合剂、清洁剂、磨料、闭锁系统、建筑元件、加工元件、遮阳与通风技术、玻璃、玻璃制品、门窗五金件、门、紧固技术、安全技术、组织技术、机器、设备、工具、用于玻璃加工、木材加工、塑料加工、金属加工、表面与应用技术、环境技术、操作技术、工厂装备、服务、协会及联合会、研究与发展、专业信息。
**周期：**两年一届
**市场范围：**国际性
**参展联络：**福建省国际贸易展览公司；福建省新天国际会展有限公司
**地址：**福建省福州市鼓楼区五四北路283号天骅大厦20层2088单元
**联系人：**范心锦，卢建光
☎ 0591-2808 6523, 8773 5017
✉ barryfan@valuedshow.com
MSN：barryvanfan@hotmail.com
QQ：30249576
www.valuedshow.com

### 法兰克福国际乐器展
### 法兰克福国际舞台灯光及音响展

Musikmesse,
ProLight + Sound

**日期：**2010/03/24 - 27
**地点：**德国法兰克福
**内容：**小型乐器、大型乐器、电子乐器；乐器配件与乐器用家具、刊物、专业音效及录音设备、舞台灯光、配件、多媒体
**周期：**每年一届
**市场范围：**国际性
**参展联络：**京慕国际展览有限公司
**地址：**北京市朝阳区北三环东路6号中国国际展览中心服务楼3层
**联系人：**王英瑶；王芳
☎ 010-8460 0551
🖷 010-8460 0394
✉ zhaolingna@ciec.com.cn
www.jingmu.com.cn

### 国际室内照明器材展览会

**日期：**2010/04/11 - 16
**地点：**德国法兰克福
**周期：**每年一届
**市场范围：**国际性
**参展联络：**中国机械汽车展览联合会
☎ 010-6859 4964
🖷 010-6849 4964

### 德国国际管材、线缆及线材展览会

Tube & Wire 2010

**日期：**2010/04/12 - 16
**地点：**德国杜塞尔多夫
**周期：**两年一届
**市场范围：**国际性
**主办：**中国贸促会机械行业分会
**地址：**北京市西城区三里河路46号（100823）
**联系人：**严静，陈媛蓉
☎ 010-6859 4938, 6859 5296, 6851 2883
🖷 010-6859 5057
✉ info@ccpitmsc.org
✉ jix@ccpit.org
www.chinamachin.org.cn
www.ccpitmsc.org

## 欧洲化妆品原料展

in-cosmetics:
The Leading Global Platform for Personal Care Ingredients

**日期：**2010/04/13 - 15

**地点：**德国新慕尼黑博览中心
**内容：**in-cosmetics是世界领先的化妆品、化妆用具及个人护理业原料及配料国际展会。每年春季在欧洲轮回举办。展会吸引全世界最好的供应商、研发人士，以及生产和营销专业人士。是一个最富启发

性的新配料、新技术、新方案及前沿产品的平台；同时也是一次全面的教育机会，可以学到化妆品业内的科技突破、潮流以及相关规定。
**周期：**每年一届
**市场范围：**国际性
**参展费用：**净地355欧元/m²起，标准展位434欧元/ m²起
**参展联络：**励展博览集团国际销售部
**地址：**北京市朝阳区新源里南路1-3号平安国际金融中心A座15层01-03，05（100027）
**联系人：**杜一鸣
☎ 010-5933 9288
🖷 010-5933 9233
✉ martin.du@reedexpo.com.cn
www.reedexport.cn

### 2010年德国汉诺威工业博览会
### HANNOVER MESSE 2010

**日期：**2010/04/19 - 23
**地点：**德国汉诺威展览中心
**内容：**汉诺威工业博览会（HANNOVER MESSE）始创于1947年8月，经过半个多世纪的不断发展与完善，已成为当今规模最大的国际工业盛会，被认为是联系全世界技术领域和商业领域的重要国际活动。近年来也有越来越多的亚洲、美洲及非洲不远万里从前来洽谈，使博览会成为一个真正的全球性的盛会，并被认为全世界技术领域和商业领域的重要国际活动。来自中国、美国、加拿大、俄罗斯、英国、法国、意大利、瑞士、日本、韩国、印度、巴基斯坦、土耳其、马来西亚、台湾等国和地区厂商参展，专业观众的比例达到96%。中国展商成为一大生力军，共有441家企业（中国大陆426家，中国香港15家）积极参展，展商数量仅次位居海外参展首位的意大利。2010年汉诺威工业博览会"移动技术"将首次以专题展形式亮相，全面聚焦包括混合动力和电力驱动系统的移动技术、移动能源、储存装备和可替代燃料。2010汉诺威工业博览会合作伙伴国为意大利。
**始办年份：**1960
**周期：**每年一届
**市场范围：**国际性
**上届规模** '09：展览面积225,000m²，参展商6,400家（来自60个国家），参观人数200,000人
**主办：**上海达欧展览服务有限公司
**地址：**上海市春申路3758弄凯利大楼1号206（201100）
**联系人：**朱志强
☎ 021-3412 3509
🖷 021-3412 3496
✉ dail_zhuzhiqiang@yahoo.com.cn
MSN：lyn_zhuzhiqiang@hotmail.com
QQ：417438558

### 慕尼黑工程机械展
### 德国国际工程机械、建材机械、矿山机械、工程车辆博览会
### BAUMA

**日期：**2010/04/19 - 25
**地点：**德国慕尼黑
**内容：**土木工程机械、起重机械、部件与零配件、道路机械、挖掘机械、混凝土机械、脚手架等
**周期：**三年一届
**市场范围：**国际性
**参展联络：**京慕国际展览有限公司
**地址：**北京市朝阳区北三环东路6号中国国际展览中心服务楼3层
**联系人：**马赛，俞亮
☎ 010-8460 0551
🖷 010-8460 0394
✉ zhaolingna@ciec.com.cn
www.jingmu.com.cn
**参展联络：**中国贸促会机械行业分会
**地址：**北京市西城区三里河路46号（100823）
**联系人：**张同丽
☎ 010-6859 4805
✉ info@ccpitmsc.org
✉ jix@ccpit.org
www.chinamachin.org.cn
www.ccpitmsc.org

### 科隆国际艺术展
### ART COLOGNE 2009

**日期：**2010/04/21 - 25
**地点：**德国科隆国际展览中心
**内容：**科隆艺术展是一个以传播和销售被国际认可的现代及当 代艺术作品展览会。科隆艺术展是世界上最重要的艺术 展览会之一。 主要展品范围：油画作品 绘图作品 雕塑作品 行为艺术 摄影作品 展会观众
**始办年份：**1967
**周期：**每年一届
**市场范围：**国际性
**入场券价格：**日票 20欧元，两日票30欧元，团体票（10人以上）14欧元
**上届规模：**展览面积43,700m²，参展商253家
**主办：**科隆展览国际有限公司
**地址：**科隆展览中国有限公司 北京东三环北路8号亮马河大厦2座1018室（100004）
**联系人：**游千仪
☎ 010-6590 7766
🖷 010-6590 6139
✉ m.yu@koelnmesse.cn
www.artcologne.cn

### 世界健美、健身及休闲博览会
### FIBO - The Leading International Trade Show for Fitness & Wellness

**日期：**2010/04/22 - 25
**地点：**德国埃森展览中心
**内容：**一听到FIBO，健身中心经营者、健身教练、体育医生、理疗师、宾馆经营者、桑拿浴经营者、投资者及多功能健康中心经营者会立刻想到每年春季在埃森举办的世界最专业的健美与健身展会。每年的FIBO都是一个独一无二的思想和创新的市场，涵盖健身器材、服务、营养、健康、美容、服饰、娱乐、运动等领域。 产品及服务 健身及训练器材、咨询、健康宣传、医疗健身、运动营养、健美及美容器材、桑拿浴、日光浴床、化妆品、健身房器材、电脑软硬件、协会、音乐、运动及健身服饰。
**周期：**每年一届
**市场范围：**国际性
**参展费用：**净地展位136～156欧元/m²
**参展联络：**励展博览集团国际销售部
**地址：**北京朝阳区新源里南路1-3号平安国际金融中心A座15层01-03，05（100027）
**联系人：**王亮
☎ 010-5933 9288
🖷 010-5933 9233
✉ liang.wang@reedexpo.com.cn
www.reedexport.cn

### 国际咖啡展览会
### coffeena: International Coffee Fair

**日期：**2010/06 -
**地点：**德国科隆国际博览中心
**市场范围：**国际性
**主办：**科隆展览国际有限公司
**地址：**科隆展览中国有限公司 北京东三环北路8号亮马河大厦2座1018室（100004）
**联系人：**徐畅，王迎
☎ 010-6590 7766 转 715
🖷 010-6590 6139
✉ j.xu@koelnmesse.cn

### 国际太阳能光伏展览会

**日期：**2010/06 -
**地点：**德国慕尼黑
**周期：**每年一届
**市场范围：**国际性
**参展联络：**中国机械汽车展览联合会
☎ 010-6859 4964
🖷 010-6859 4964

### 2010年德国埃森国际轮胎展览会（德国雷芬展）

**日期：**2010/06/01 - 04
**地点：**德国埃森展览中心
**内容：**各种轮胎；轮胎配件；汽车修理厂、轮胎服务和轮胎翻新企业的设备；用于轮胎翻新和硫化的设备、机器和工具；用于修理的材料；轮胎回收处理；运营机构、仓库、办公室及销售点设施/销售辅助；用于轮胎贸易和修理厂的IT方案；用于轮胎专业厂的服务；其他相关产品及服务。
**始办年份：**1960
**周期：**两年一届
**市场范围：**国际性
**上届规模** '08：展览面积50,138m²，参展商580家，参观人数17,355人
**主办：**德国埃森展览公司
**参展联络：**杭州思诺博会展服务有限公司
**地址：**杭州市体育场路229号浙江粮油大厦1202室（310003）
☎ 0571-8577 8500
🖷 0571-8577 9709
✉ expo@sinobal.com
www.sinobal.com

### 慕尼黑国际机器人和自动化技术贸易博览会
### AUTMATICA

**日期：**2010/06/08 - 11
**地点：**德国慕尼黑
**内容：**装配和控制技术、机器人技术、工业制图、定位系统、驱动技术、传感技术、控制技术、劳动安全技术、供给技术、软件、服务项目和服务人员、科研与工艺
**周期：**两年一届
**市场范围：**国际性
**参展联络：**京慕国际展览有限公司
**地址：**北京市朝阳区北三环东路6号中国国际展览中心服务楼3层
**联系人：**马赛
☎ 010-8460 0551
🖷 010-8460 0394
✉ zhaolingna@ciec.com.cn
www.jingmu.com.cn

### 柏林-勃兰登堡国际航空航天展览会
### ILA - Berlin Air Show

**日期：**2010/06/08 - 13
**地点：**德国柏林
**内容：**新型材料；航空设备；航空航天研究；航天研究；航天技术；飞机；飞机发动机；飞机维护；机场设备；组件；防御技术；电子设备；电子系统；直升机；电源装置；太空技术
**周期：**两年一届
**市场范围：**国际性
**参展联络：**德国工商会（香港）南中国办事处/柏林国际展览有限公司香港及中国代表处
**地址：**广州市天河北路大都会广场2915室
**联系人：**孟昕
☎ 020-8755 8204, 8755 2353
🖷 020-8755 1889
✉ meng.sophie@gz.china.ahk.de
www.messe-berlin.de

### 慕尼黑国际太阳能技术展
### Intersolar

**日期：**2010/06/09 - 11

地点：德国慕尼黑
内容：太阳能供水系统及产品，太阳能集热采暖设备，太阳能建筑应用，太阳能其它应用产品
周期：每年一届
参展联络：京慕国际展览有限公司
地址：北京市朝阳区北三环东路6号中国国际展览中心服务楼3层
联系人：张晚霞，俞亮
☎ 010-8460 0551
🖷 010-8460 0394
✉ zhaolingna@ciec.com.cn
www.jingmu.com.cn

### 德国国际光学展览会
### Optatec

日期：2010/06/15 - 18
地点：德国法兰克福
内容：光学零部件，原材料和系统，光学机械零部件/装置，光电子零部件/装置，纤维光学，纤维电缆及零部件，灯光指引，纤维电缆制造设备/测试设备，灯光源/雷射
周期：两年一届
市场范围：国际性
参展联络：京慕国际展览有限公司
地址：北京市朝阳区北三环东路6号中国国际展览中心服务楼3层
联系人：韩芳，俞亮
☎ 010-8460 0551
🖷 010-8460 0394
✉ zhaolingna@ciec.com.cn
www.jingmu.com.cn

### 德国慕尼黑国际自行车博览会
### BIKE EXPO

日期：2010/07 -
地点：德国慕尼黑
内容：自行车整车、电动自行车、自行车零配件、自行车户外运动、自行车服装/配饰、相关活动
周期：每年一届
市场范围：国际性
参展联络：京慕国际展览有限公司
地址：北京市朝阳区北三环东路6号中国国际展览中心服务楼3层
联系人：林航，刘靖
☎ 010-8460 0551
🖷 010-8460 0394
✉ zhaolingna@ciec.com.cn
www.jingmu.com.cn

### 杜塞尔多夫国际服装博览会（秋季）
### CPD

日期：2010/07 -
地点：德国杜塞尔多夫
内容：各种女装、男装、针织服装、裘皮服装、晚装、婚装、服饰、浴装、内衣、帽子、围巾等
周期：每年两届
市场范围：国际性
参展联络：京慕国际展览有限公司
地址：北京市朝阳区北三环东路6号中国国际展览中心服务楼3层
联系人：由慧；柳川
☎ 010-8460 0551
🖷 010-8460 0394
✉ zhaolingna@ciec.com.cn
www.jingmu.com.cn

### 2010年德国法兰克福国际时尚消费品展览会
### AMBIENTE/ DECORATE LIFE

日期：2010/07/02 - 06
地点：德国法兰克福展览中心
内容：礼品区和餐具厨具区,中国企业主要集中此馆；家居用品、花园用品区：礼品及节庆，游戏、玩具、玩偶、包袋及皮制礼品、手工艺品、民族工艺品、文具、各类柳藤编制篮及工艺品、室内香薰物品、蜡烛和附件、风水及阴阳摆设、商店橱窗展示品、珠宝、节庆装饰品、丝绸和干花；家居用品及花园用品：家具和小件摆设、家用品及附件、家饰、家纺、墙上挂饰、灯具、挂钟及台钟、户外和园艺品附件、花盆；餐具及厨具：玻璃、水晶玻璃、瓷器、陶器、刃具及附件、茶道及附件、银制或镀银器皿、金属器皿、餐桌饰品、餐桌花卉饰品、厨房用品、烹饪及烘焙炊具、烹饪用电器设备、酒吧及饮酒用具、厨房及桌上用布艺纺织品、清洁用品及器皿、厨房家具及各类厨房附件、家用器皿、购物篮及包袋、小电器、塑料产品
周期：每年一届
市场范围：国际性
上届规模：展览面积78,200m²，参展商2,091家，参观人数50,000人
参展联络：中国轻工业展览中心
地址：北京市东城区东四六条64号（100007）
联系人：应艳梅
☎ 010-6401 6504
🖷 010-6401 6504
✉ cy888@vip.163.com
MSN：lengfeier@msn.com
QQ：71229011
www.cliexpo.org

### 2010年德国菲德里斯哈芬户外休闲运动博览会
### 2010 European Outdoor Trade Fair

日期：2010/07/15 - 18
地点：德国菲德烈斯哈芬市展览中心
内容：各类休闲用具：户外家具、花园设备、休闲桌椅；露营器材类：睡袋、帐篷、吊床、配件等；背包类：旅行袋、旅行帆布背包、越野帆布背包、登山包、攀岩包及配件等；各类运动健身器械：水上运动用具、充气艇、橡皮艇、马具用品、望远镜、球类用品等；运动休闲服装：夹克、登山服、羽绒服、自行车服、滑雪服、越野服、休闲运动鞋、帽子等。
始办年份：1994
周期：每年一届
市场范围：国际性
上届规模 '08：参展商787家（来自40个国家），参观人数18,900人
主办：德国菲德烈斯哈芬展览公司
参展联络：杭州思诺博会展服务有限公司
地址：杭州市体育场路229号浙江粮油大厦1202室（310003）
☎ 0571-8577 8500
🖷 0571-8577 9709
✉ expo@sinobal.com
www.sinobal.com

### 柏林电子消费品展
### IFA

日期：2010/08 -
地点：德国柏林
内容：家用电器、娱乐电子、音响设备、各式电子材料和设备等；电脑、远程通讯、卫星接收设备周期：每年一届
市场范围：国际性
参展联络：京慕国际展览有限公司
地址：北京市朝阳区北三环东路6号中国国际展览中心服务楼3层
联系人：宋秋爽，刘舰
☎ 010-8460 0551
🖷 010-8460 0394
✉ zhaolingna@ciec.com.cn
www.jingmu.com.cn

**科隆国际游戏展**

### gamescom

日期：2010/08/18 - 22
地点：德国科隆国际博览中心
内容：科隆国际游戏展(gamescom)由创办于2002年的原莱比锡游戏展(Games Convention)发展而来，09年起正式移师科隆，是欧洲最专业的综合性互动式游戏软件、信息软件和硬件设备展览，也是德国唯一一个集中了游戏软件、硬件、娱乐设备、信息软件和设备的大型国际展会。科隆国际游戏展由科隆国际展览公司与联邦互动娱乐软件协会(BIU)联合举办。科隆国际展览中心完备的基础设施和优越的地理位置、科隆国际展览公司遍布全球的营销及服务网络、以及具备多年举办大型国际展会的丰富经验，将为gamescom提供一个良好的发展空间。
始办年份：2002
周期：每年一届
市场范围：国际性
主办：科隆国际展览公司；联邦互动娱乐软件协会(BIU)
地址：北京东三环北路8号亮马河大厦2座1018室（100004）
联系人：陈瑞
☎ 010-6590 7766转750
🖷 010-6590 6139
✉ r.chen@koelnmesse.cn

**gamescom**

Date：2010/08/18 - 22
Venue: Cologne Exhibition Center, Germany
Established Year: 2002
Frequency: Annual
Market Area: International
Organizer: KOELNMESSE
Address: Unit 1018 Landmark Tower Ⅱ, No. 8 Dongsanhuan North Rd., Beijing 100004, China
☎ 86-10-6590 7766 ext 750
🖷 86-10-6590 6139
Contact: Ryan Chen
✉ r.chen@koelnmesse.cn

### 德国国际安装及操纵技术展览会
### MOTEX 2010

日期：2010/09/ -
地点：德国斯图加特
周期：每年一届
市场范围：国际性
参展联络：中国贸促会机械行业分会
地址：北京市西城区三里河路46号（100823）
联系人：李华龙，曹姗姗，李静
☎ 010-6859 5039, 6859 5043, 6859 5067
🖷 010-6857 2287
✉ info@ccpitmsc.org
✉ jix@ccpit.org
www.chinamachin.org.cn
www.ccpitmsc.org

### 德国国际金属加工设备及技术展览会
### AMB 2010

日期：2010/09/ -
地点：德国斯图加特
周期：两年一届
市场范围：国际性
参展联络：中国贸促会机械行业分会
地址：北京市西城区三里河路46号（100823）
联系人：王建飞
☎ 010-6859 4952
🖷 010-6859 4995
✉ info@ccpitmsc.org
✉ jix@ccpit.org
www.chinamachin.org.cn
www.ccpitmsc.org

### 国际园艺展览会

日期：2010/09 -
地点：德国科隆
周期：每年一届
市场范围：国际性
参展联络：中国机械汽车展览联合会
☎ 010-6859 4964
🖷 010-6859 4964

### 德国国际汽车修理、加油设备及零部件博览会
### Automechanika 2010

日期：2010/09 -
地点：德国法兰克福
周期：两年一届
市场范围：国际性
参展联络：中国贸促会机械行业分会
地址：北京市西城区三里河路46号（100823）
联系人：邹京玲
☎ 010-6859 4952, 6859 4804, 6859 5055
℻ 010-6859 4917
✉ info@ccpitmsc.org
✉ jix@ccpit.org
www.chinamachin.org.cn
www.ccpitmsc.org

### 杜塞尔多夫国际鞋业及皮革制品博览会（秋季）

### Global Shoes & Accessories

日期：2010/09 -
地点：德国杜塞尔多夫
内容：男女鞋、童鞋、功夫鞋、劳保鞋、雪地靴、工作鞋、制鞋机械及鞋类饰物等
周期：每年两届
市场范围：国际性
参展联络：京慕国际展览有限公司
地址：北京市朝阳区北三环东路6号中国国际展览中心服务楼3层
联系人：李嘉羊，古莹
☎ 010-8460 0551
℻ 010-8460 0394
✉ zhaolingna@ciec.com.cn
www.jingmu.com.cn

### 欧洲光伏太阳能展览会

### European Photovoltaic Solar Energy Conference and Exhibition

日期：2010/09 -
地点：德国汉堡
内容：太阳能光伏产品及技术，太阳能电池，光热产品
周期：每年一届
市场范围：国际性
参展联络：京慕国际展览有限公司
地址：北京市朝阳区北三环东路6号中国国际展览中心服务楼3层
联系人：薛亮
☎ 010-8460 0551
℻ 010-8460 0394
✉ zhaolingna@ciec.com.cn
www.jingmu.com.cn

### 国际电子消费品展览会

### IFA

日期：2010/09 -
地点：德国柏林
内容：声像技术、嵌入式厨具、电缆技术、计算机软件、计算机技术、家电、数据保护技术、数据传输、电子家电、信息技术、多媒体技术、网络技术、在线服务、电信、电视技术
周期：每年一届
市场范围：国际性
参展联络：德国工商会（香港）南中国办事处/柏林国际展览有限公司香港及中国代表处
地址：广州市天河北路大都会广场2915室
联系人：孟昕
☎ 020-8755 8204, 8755 2353
℻ 020-8755 1889
✉ meng.sophie@gz.china.ahk.de
www.messe-berlin.de

### 德国法兰克福国际汽车零部件及售后服务展览会

日期：2010/09 -
地点：德国法兰克福
内容：汽车配件
周期：每年一届
市场范围：国际性
参展联络：京慕国际展览有限公司
地址：北京市朝阳区北三环东路6号中国国际展览中心服务楼3层
联系人：张辉，刘舰
☎ 010-8460 0551
℻ 010-8460 0394
✉ zhaolingna@ciec.com.cn
www.jingmu.com.cn

### 科隆国际体育、露营用品及花园家具展

### Spoga

日期：2010/09 -
地点：德国科隆
内容：露营用品、花园家具工具及用品、休闲体育用品、烧烤用品等
周期：每年一届
市场范围：国际性
参展联络：京慕国际展览有限公司
地址：北京市朝阳区北三环东路6号中国国际展览中心服务楼3层
联系人：张翠元，滕昊
☎ 010-8460 0551
℻ 010-8460 0394
✉ zhaolingna@ciec.com.cn
www.jingmu.com.cn

### 秋季马术用品展

### spoga horse (Autumn)

日期：2010/09/05 - 07
地点：德国科隆国际展览中心展馆
内容：马术用品、相关服务
始办年份：2008
周期：每年两届
市场范围：国际性
参展费用：标准展位381欧元/m²(最小9m²),净地136欧元/m²（最小36 m²）
上届规模‘08：展览面积28,500m²，参展商379家，参观人数38,600人
主办：科隆展览中国有限公司
地址：北京市东三环北路8号亮马河大厦2座1018室（100004）
联系人：张昱，贾宁
☎ 010-6590 7766转738
℻ 010-6590 6139
✉ j.zhang@koelnmesse.cn

### spoga horse (Autumn)

Date：2010/09/05 - 07
Venue: Germany
Established Year: 2008
Frequency: Biannual
Market Area: International
Participated Fee: Standard Booth EUR 381/m²(min 9m²), Raw Space EUR 136/m²（min 36m²）
Statistics '08: Exhibition Area 28,500m², Exhibitors 379，Visitors 38,600
Organizer: Koelnmesse Co Ltd
Address: Unit 1018 Landmark Tower II, No 8 Dongsanhuan N Rd., Beijing, China
☎ 010-6590 7766 ext738
℻ 86-10-6590 6139
Contact: Joesy Zhang, Maggie Jia
✉ j.zhang@koelnmesse.cn

### 国际体育用品、露营设备及园林生活博览会/国际园艺博览会

### spoga/gafa

日期：2010/09/05 - 07
地点：德国科隆国际展览中心
内容：户外生活（户外家具）；户外运动（烧烤设备，露营休闲用品，体育及比赛用品）；户内和户外休闲（植物和植物护理，花卉栽培和装饰，水处理和室外照明，花园规划和维护，其它设备和花园布置，宠物用品）；马术用品及服务
周期：每年一届
上届规模：展览面积265,600m²，参展商2,236家（来自57个国家），参观人数38,433人
主办：科隆展览中国有限公司
地址：北京市东三环北路8号亮马河大厦2座1018室（100004）
联系人：张昱，贾宁
☎ 010-6590 7766转738
℻ 010-6590 6139
✉ j.zhang@koelnmesse.cn
www.spogagafa.cn

### spoga/gafa

Date：2010/09/05 - 07
Venue: Germany
Frequency: Annual
Statistics '09: Exhibition Area 265,600m², Exhibitors 2,236（came from 57 countries），Visitors 38,433
Organizer: Koelnmesse Co Ltd
Address: Unit 1018 Landmark Tower II, No 8 Dongsanhuan N Rd., Beijing, China
☎ 86-10-6590 7766 ext 738
℻ 86-10-6590 6139
Contact: Joesy Zhang, Maggie Jia
✉ j.zhang@koelnmesse.cn
www.spogagafa.cn

### 德国汉堡国际海事展览会

### Europort Maritime 2010

日期：2010/09/07 - 10
地点：德国汉堡
周期：两年一届
市场范围：国际性
参展联络：中国贸促会机械行业分会
地址：北京市西城区三里河路46号（100823）
联系人：郭霞
☎ 010-6859 4985, 6859 5056
℻ 010-6853 3354
✉ info@ccpitmsc.org
✉ jix@ccpit.org
www.chinamachin.org.cn
www.ccpitmsc.org

### 慕尼黑国际环博会

### IFAT

日期：2010/09/13 - 17
地点：德国慕尼黑
内容：水及污水处理、包装回收再利用、空气净化与污染防治
周期：两年一届
市场范围：国际性
参展联络：京慕国际展览有限公司
地址：北京市朝阳区北三环东路6号中国国际展览中心服务楼3层
联系人：马赛，俞亮
☎ 010-8460 0551
℻ 010-8460 0394
✉ zhaolingna@ciec.com.cn
www.jingmu.com.cn

### 2010年法兰克福国际汽车零配件及售后服务展

### Automechanika - International Trade Fair for the Automobile Aftermarket And Original Equipment Market

日期：2010/09/14 - 19
地点：德国法兰克福德国法兰克福展览中心
内容：汽车行业的国际盛会，其在世界汽车工业展览会具有领先地位。2010 年的Automechanika 还将会启用新近落成的11 号馆，这将会为整个展会带来新的亮点。
展品范围：部件及系统：汽车驱动、底盘、车身、电气设备及电子系统的部件及组件 汽车内部、外部、驱动、驾驶动力及电子操控的系统及模块；附

件及改装：汽车附件、特殊设备、改装系统、性能系统、精装饰；维修及保养：汽车服务和维修设备、车身维修及涂漆、维修站建造及管理；IT 及管理：IT 产品、车辆交易所、保险、金融、租赁管理、破损管理、车辆检测服务、经销商管理系统、代理权的计划与设计、代理权市场；加油站和洗车房：加油站设备、汽车保养及清洗
**始办年份**：2000
**周期**：两年一届
**市场范围**：国际性
**上届规模** ‘09：展览面积285,800m$^2$(国外展商面积200,000m$^2$)，参展商4,471家（国外展商140家，来自145个国家），参观人数161,000人（其中专业和贸易观众100,000人）
**主办**：德国法兰克福展览公司
**参展联络**：北京中杰城设国际展览有限公司
**地址**：北京市海淀区三里河路9号建设部（100835）
**联系人**：全静
☎ 010-8838 4563
🖷 010-5885 7468
✉ quanjing68@126.com
MSN：quanjing_2008@hotmail.com
QQ：602693071
**参展联络**：中国汽车工业国际合作总公司
**地址**：北京市海淀区中关村丹棱街3号A座5层（100080）
**联系人**：何萌
☎ 010-8260 6880
🖷 010-8260 6883
✉ exhibition@cnaico.com.cn

## 2010德国埃森国际铝工业展览会

### 第八届世界铝工业博览会暨学术会议

### ALUMINIUM 2010

**日期**：2010/09/14 - 16
**地点**：德国埃森展览中心
**内容**：ALUMINIUM 2010是铝工业和其相关应用配套设备展览的首选之地。本展览覆盖整个价值链从提炼到成品应用于汽车制造和运输、建筑、机械电机工程、包装设计以及铝加工及精炼技术等主要领域。
**产品及服务**：来自40多个国家约900个展商将展示近千种创新产品，以及深层技术开发和最新趋势。德国国际铝工业展览会（ALUMINIUM）是铝工业及相关配套应用设备最重要的展示平台。铝生产商、加工商、精炼商以及科技和附加产品供应商，以及各种配套应用产品供应商将于九月汇聚德国埃森。
**周期**：两年一届
**市场范围**：国际性
**参展费用**：净地展位185欧元/m$^2$
**主办**：励展德国公司
**参展联络**：励展博览集团国际销售部
**地址**：北京朝阳区新源里南路1-3号平安国际金融中心A座15层01-03，05（100027）
**联系人**：王颖
☎ 86-010-5933 9288
🖷 010-5933 9233
✉ winnie.wang@reedexpo.com.cn
www.reedexport.cn

## 数码营销博览会

### dmexco

**日期**：2010/09/15 - 16
**地点**：德国科隆国际博览中心
**市场范围**：国际性
**主办**：科隆展览国际有限公司
**地址**：北京东三环北路8号亮马河大厦2座1018室100004（100004）
**联系人**：陈瑞
☎ 010-6590 7766转750
🖷 010-6590 6139
✉ r.chen@koelnmesse.cn

### dmexco

**Date**：2010/09/15 - 16
**Venue**: Cologne Exhibition Center, Germany
**Market Area**: International
**Organizer**: KOELNMESSE
**Address**: Unit 1018, Landmark Tower Ⅱ, No. 8 Dongsanhuan North Rd., Beijing 100004, China
☎ 86-10-6590 7766 ext 750
🖷 86-10-6590 6139
**Contact**: Ryan Chen
✉ r.chen@koelnmesse.cn

## 科隆国际少儿用品展

### Kind + Jugend

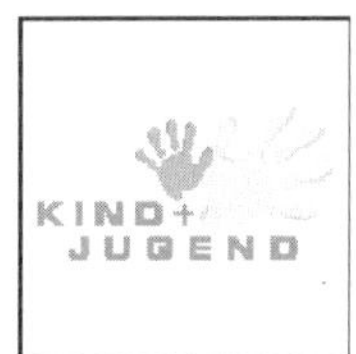


**日期**：2010/09/16 - 19
插入logo，数据库会展编号4592
**地点**：德国科隆国际展览中心
**内容**：儿车及附件，安全座椅及设备，家具及附件，纺织品，婴儿、儿童、青年时装及孕妇装，玩具，育婴用品，电器，出版物，团体，其它。
**始办年份**：1960
**周期**：每年一届
**市场范围**：国际性
**参展费用**：展位费340欧元/m$^2$(min 9m$^2$)
**上届规模** ‘09：展览面积80,000m$^2$，参展商781家（国外展商612家，来自41个国家），专业贸易观众18,000人
**主办**：科隆国际展览有限公司
**地址**：北京市亮马河大厦2座1018室（100004）
**联系人**：齐志宇
☎ 010-6590 7766 转727
🖷 010-6590 6139
✉ k.qi@koelnmesse.cn
www.kindundjugend.cn

## Kind + Jugend

**Date**：2010/09/16 - 19
**Venue**: Cologne exhibition center, Germany
**Profile**: Prams, car/bicycle seats, children's furniture, hygiene articles, electric appliances, textiles, baby cosmetics, toys and games for babies and toddlers, fashion for babies and toddlers, maternity wear, shop equipment, publications, organizations
**Established Year**: 1960
**Frequency**: Annual
**Market Area**: International
**Participated Fee**: EUR 340/m$^2$(min 9m$^2$)
**Statistics** ‘09: Exhibition Area 80,000m$^2$, Exhibitors 781 (foreigners 612, came from 41 countries), Trade Visitors 18,000
**Organizer**: Koelnmesse
**Address**: Unit 1018, Landmark Tower 2, No.8 Dongsanhuan North Rd., Beijing, China
☎ 010-6590 7766 转727
🖷 86-10-6590 6139
**Contact**: Kevin Qi
✉ k.qi@koelnmesse.cn
www.kindundjugend.cn

### 交通、车辆、组件－革新产品展览会

### InnoTrans

**日期**：2010/09/21 - 24
**地点**：德国柏林
**内容**：通讯技术；数据安装处理；高速公路规划；后勤；客运服务；铁路交通技术；铁路通信工具；隧道建设
**周期**：两年一届
**市场范围**：国际性
**参展联络**：德国工商会（香港）南中国办事处/柏林国际展览有限公司香港及中国代表处
**地址**：广州市天河北路大都会广场2915室
**联系人**：孟昕
☎ 020-8755 8204, 8755 2353
🖷 020-8755 1889
✉ meng.sophie@gz.china.ahk.de
www.messe-berlin.de

### InnoTrans

**Date**：2010/09/21 - 24
**Venue**: Berlin, Germany
**Frequency**: Biennial
**Market Area**: International
**Organizer**: Messe Berlin GmbH
☎ 86-20-8755 8204, 8755 2353
🖷 86-20-8755 1889
**Contact**: Meng Xin
✉ meng.sophie@gz.china.ahk.de
www.messe-berlin.de

## 世界影像博览会

### Photokina

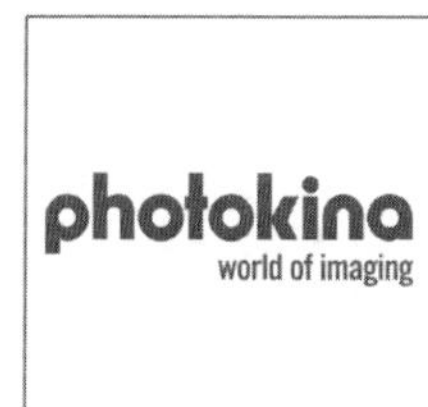


**日期**：2010/09/21 - 26
**地点**：德国科隆国际博览中心
**内容**：两年一届的世界影像博览会（photokina）是照相与成 像工业领域领先的展览会，是世界上唯一的为大众消 费者和专业人士提供所有成像介质、成像技术与成像市场综合性展示的展览会。因此，世界影像博览会（photokina）在成像领域具有独特的竞争优势，使其成为所有影像用户提供综合性解决方案的展示平台。世界影像博览会（photokina）不仅为照相与成像产业 部门提供新的销售动力，而且是集中展示面向未来的 各种技术和产品的趋势论坛。
**周期**：两年一届
**市场范围**：国际性
**上届规模** ‘08：参展商1,523家（国外展商161家），参观人数169, 000人（专业贸易观众109,850人）
**主办**：科隆国际展览有限公司
**地址**：北京市亮马河大厦2座1018室（100004）
**联系人**：徐畅，王迎
☎ 010-6590 7766 转715
🖷 010-6590 6139
✉ j.xu@koelnmesse.cn
www.photokina.cn
**主办**：北方国际展览有限公司
**地址**：北京市宣武区莱园街1号，中环假日酒店写字楼1102-1103室（100053）
**联系人**：潘容
☎ 010-8355 7740
🖷 010-6354 7597
✉ gracepan@northexpo.com.cn

## Photokina

**Date**：2010/09/21 - 26
**Venue**: Cologne Exhibition Center, Germany
**Frequency**: Biennial

Market Area: International
Statistics '08: Exhibitors 1,523 (foreigners 161), Visitors 169, 000
Organizer: Koelnmesse
Address: Unit 1018, Landmark Tower 2, No.8 Dongsanhuan North Rd., Beijing, China
☎ 86-10-6590 7766 ext 715
☏ 86-10-6590 6139
Contact: Joyce Xu, Elan Wang
✉ j.xu@koelnmesse.cn
www.photokina.cn

### 德国柏林国际铁路、机车、车辆展览会

日期：2010/09/21 - 24
地点：德国柏林
内容：铁路技术、机车技术、铁路设施、车厢装饰
周期：每年一届
市场范围：国际性
参展联络：京慕国际展览有限公司
地址：北京市朝阳区北三环东路6号中国国际展览中心服务楼3层
联系人：张辉；刘舰
☎ 010-8460 0551
☏ 010-8460 0394
✉ zhaolingna@ciec.com.cn
www.jingmu.com.cn

## 数码管理解决方案展览会

### DMS EXPO

日期：2010/09/21 - 23
地点：德国科隆国际博览中心
市场范围：国际性
主办：科隆展览国际有限公司
地址：北京东三环北路8号亮马河大厦2座1018室(100004)
联系人：陈瑞
☎ 010-6590 7766转750
☏ 010-6590 6139
✉ r.chen@koelnmesse.cn

## DMS EXPO

Date：2010/09/21 - 23
Venue: Cologne Exhibition Center, Germany
Market Area: International
Organizer: KOELNMESSE
Address: Unit 1018 Landmark Tower Ⅱ, No. 8 Dongsanhuan North Rd., Beijing 100004, China
☎ 86-10-6590 7766 ext 750
☏ 86-10-6590 6139
Contact: Ryan Chen
✉ r.chen@koelnmesse.cn

### 2010年德国汉诺威商用车及配件博览会

### IAA 2010

日期：2010/09/23 - 30
地点：德国汉诺威
周期：每年一届
市场范围：国际性
主办：法兰克福展览公司
参展联络：中国汽车工业国际合作总公司
地址：北京市海淀区中关村丹棱街3号A座5层(100080)
联系人：何萌
☎ 010-8260 6880
☏ 010-8260 6883
✉ exhibition@cnaico.com.cn

### 慕尼黑国际高尔夫运动用品博览会

### Golf Europe

日期：2010/09/26 - 28
地点：德国慕尼黑
内容：高尔夫用具、服装、配件、商店装备、发球练习场及室内果岭、室内高尔夫、专业书刊等
周期：每年一届
市场范围：国际性
参展联络：京慕国际展览有限公司
地址：北京市朝阳区北三环东路6号中国国际展览中心服务楼3层
联系人：张璋
☎ 010-8460 0551
☏ 010-8460 0394
✉ zhaolingna@ciec.com.cn
www.jingmu.com.cn

### 2010年杜塞尔多夫国际玻璃技术博览会

### 12th International Trade Fair For Glass Production- Processing- Products

日期：2010/09/28 - 01
地点：德国杜塞尔多夫展览中心
内容：玻璃制造、生产技术；玻璃深加工和精加工；工具，配件和维修部件；工艺玻璃及玻璃控制技术，加工机械；建筑行业和外墙用玻璃、幕墙；太阳能，透明隔热；电脑显示器玻璃激光技术。
周期：两年一届
市场范围：国际性
参展联络：福建省国际贸易展览公司；福建省新天国际会展有限公司
地址：福建省福州市鼓楼区五四北路283号天骅大厦20层2088单元
联系人：范心锦，卢建光
☎ 0591-2808 6523, 8773 5017
✉ barryfan@valuedshow.com
MSN：barryvanfan@hotmail.com
QQ：30249576
www.valuedshow.com

## 欧洲复合材料展

### COMPOSITES EUROPE

日期：2010/10 -
地点：德国斯图加特新展览中心
内容：涵盖整个复合材料产业的新兴国际性展会。研讨会由行业协会以及合作媒体举办。
产品及服务：复合材料的原料、中间产品、半成品和成品、技术和设备，以及服务。媒体，国内展区、演讲区、产品演示区。
周期：每年一届
市场范围：国际性
参展费用：净地展位172欧元/m²
主办：励展德国公司
参展联络：励展博览集团国际销售部
地址：北京市朝阳区新源里南路1-3号平安国际金融中心A座15层01-03，05（100027）
联系人：王颖
☎ 010-5933 9288
☏ 010-5933 9233
✉ winnie.wang@reedexpo.com.cn
www.reedexport.cn

### 柏林国际现代艺术展

### Art Forum Berlin

日期：2010/10 -
地点：德国柏林
内容：美术、图像、摄影、雕塑、影像艺术、画
周期：每年一届
市场范围：国际性
参展费用：190欧元/m²
参展联络：德国工商会（香港）南中国办事处/柏林国际展览有限公司香港及中国代表处
地址：广州市天河北路大都会广场2915室
联系人：孟昕
☎ 020-8755 8204, 8755 2353
☏ 020-8755 1889
✉ meng.sophie@gz.china.ahk.de
www.messe-berlin.de

### Art Forum Berlin

Date：2010/10 -
Venue: Berlin, Germany
Frequency: Annual
Market Area: International
Participated Fee: EUR 190/m²
Organizer: Messe Berlin GmbH
☎ 86-20-8755 8204, 8755 2353
☏ 86-20-8755 1889
Contact: Meng Xin
✉ meng.sophie@gz.china.ahk.de
www.messe-berlin.de

### 慕尼黑国际信息技术、通讯和新媒体展

### SYSTEMS

日期：2010/10 -
地点：德国慕尼黑
内容：基础应用软件、计算机和系统外围设备、电脑硬件和系统、电子商务、电信和网络、移动电信设备、网络安全、网络基础设施等
周期：每年一届
市场范围：国际性
参展联络：京慕国际展览有限公司
地址：北京市朝阳区北三环东路6号中国国际展览中心服务楼3层
联系人：韩芳，俞亮
☎ 010-8460 0551
☏ 010-8460 0394
✉ zhaolingna@ciec.com.cn
www.jingmu.com.cn

### 慕尼黑国际商业地产展

### EXPO REAL

日期：2010/10 -
地点：德国慕尼黑
内容：商铺、大型购物中心、经济开发区、主题公园、办公用房和工业用房等非直接住宅地产、房地产投资及金融机构、规划及建筑设计公司
周期：每年一届
市场范围：国际性
参展联络：京慕国际展览有限公司
地址：北京市朝阳区北三环东路6号中国国际展览中心服务楼3层
联系人：许艳
☎ 010-8460 0551
☏ 010-8460 0394
✉ zhaolingna@ciec.com.cn
www.jingmu.com.cn

## 德国国际视觉广告技术与标识制作展

### Viscom Frankfurt 2010: International Trade Fair for Visual Communication

日期：2010/10 -
地点：德国法兰克福展览中心
内容：德国国际视觉广告技术与标识制作展涵盖视觉传播领域的各个方面。该展之前名为PRO SIGN，一直以创新的产品、高质量的展会服务而闻名。
周期：两年一届
市场范围：国际性

**参展费用：** 净地展位145～202欧元/ m²，标准展位235～322欧元/m²
**主办：** 励展德国公司
**参展联络：** 励展博览集团国际销售部
**地址：** 北京市朝阳区新源里南路1-3号平安国际金融中心A座15层01-03，05（100027）
**联系人：** 王亮
☎ 010-5933 9288
🖷 010-5933 9233
✉ liang.wang@reedexpo.com.cn
www.reedexport.cn

## 德国埃森国际工业安全用品展览会

## Security Essen

**日期：** 2010/10/05 - 08
**地点：** 德国埃森
**内容：** 中央监控设备、门禁系统、机械安全系统、建筑防火、防盗及火灾报警系统、专用安全车辆、个人防护用具、专用服装、犯罪预警设备、监控巡逻设备等
**周期：** 两年一届
**市场范围：** 国际性
**参展联络：** 京慕国际展览有限公司
**地址：** 北京市朝阳区北三环东路6号中国国际展览中心服务楼3层
**联系人：** 王爽，薛磊
☎ 010-8460 0551
🖷 010-8460 0394
✉ zhaolingna@ciec.com.cn
www.jingmu.com.cn

## 科隆国际摩托车、滑板车及自行车展览会

## INTERMOT Cologne

**日期：** 2010/10/06 - 10
**地点：** 德国科隆国际展览中心
**内容：** 动力车 拖车和边车 摩托车零件及配件 发动机及组件 电动设备 摩托服及用具 摩托生产工具、车间和商店设备 原材料、半成品、及包装材料 润滑油及防护用品 摩托车旅游及相关户外用品
**始办年份：** 1988
**周期：** 两年一届
**市场范围：** 国际性
**入场券价格：** 370元人民币
**参展费用：** 标准展位460 欧元/m²（9m²起）含净地租金、展位装修、公共能源费、德国展览业协会费用（AUMA 费）、基本会刊登录费用、垃圾清 运费、展位电费、其它杂费及19%增值税；净地（36m²起）一面开口136.50欧元/m²，两面开口141.50 欧元/m²，三面开口144.50欧元/m²，四面开口146.50欧元/m²；室外场地75欧元/m²不包括标准展位提及的其他费用及19%增值税
**上届规模** '08：展览面积120,000m²，参展商1,068家（国外展商696家，来自36个国家），参观人数200,000人（专业贸易观众193,000人）
**主办：** 科展览有中国限公司
**地址：** 北京市亮马河大厦2座1018室（100004）
**联系人：** 齐志宇
☎ 010-6590 7766转727
🖷 010-6590 6139
✉ k.qi@koelnmesse.cn
www.ids-cologne.cn

## INTERMOT Cologne

**Date：** 2010/10/06 - 10
**Venue:** Cologne Exhibition Center, Germany
**Profile:** Motorized vehicles, Trailers and sidecars, Components and accessories for motorcycles, Engines and components, Electrical equipment, Clothing, Motorcyclists' gear, Machines and tools, Workshop and shop equipment, Raw materials, Semi-finished products, Packaging materials, Lubricants, Gear-box/transmission oil, Care products, Tourism, Contact groups
**Established Year:** 1988
**Frequency:** Biennial
**Market Area:** International
**Cost to Attend:** RMB 370
**Participated Fee:** Standard Booth EUR 460/m² (min 9m²) ; Raw Space (min 36m²) : EUR 136.50/m², Corner Unit EUR 141.50/m², Peninsula Unit EUR 144.50/m², Island Unit EUR 146.50/m²; Outdoor EUR 75/m²
**Statistics '08:** Exhibition Area 120,000m², Exhibitors 1,068 (foreigners 696, came from 36 countries) , Visitors 200,000 (trade visitors 193,000)
**Organizer:** Koelnmesse Co Ltd
**Address:** Unit 1018, Landmark Tower 2, No.8 Dongsanhuan North Rd., Beijing, China
☎ 86-10-6590 7766 ext 727
🖷 86-10-6590 6139
**Contact:** Kevin Qi
✉ k.qi@koelnmesse.cn
www.ids-cologne.cn

## 国际制冷、空调与通风展览会

**日期：** 2010/10/13 - 15
**地点：** 德国纽伦堡
**周期：** 每年一届
**市场范围：** 国际性
**参展联络：** 中国机械汽车展览联合会
☎ 010-6859 4964
🖷 010-6859 4964

## 科隆国际糖果原料和机械展览会

## ProSweets Cologne 2010

**日期：** 2010/10/18 - 21
**地点：** 德国科隆国际博览中心
**内容：** 甜食生产原材料，甜食包装材料，甜食包装机械，甜食工业机器与设备，甜食生产中冷藏与空调技术，甜食生产中的食品安全、质量管理，甜食生产中的自动化、数据处理、开环和闭环控制技术，甜食生产用加工设备和辅助装置，服务提供商、组织机构、出版社，垃圾处理、废物循环利用
**始办年份：** 2006
**周期：** 每年一届
**市场范围：** 国际性
**参展费用：** 标准展位（9m²起）：一面开口450欧元/m²，两面开口460欧元/m²，三面开口470欧元/m²，岛形展位470欧元/m²；净地（36m²起）：一面开口175欧元/m²，两面开口185欧元/m²，三面开口195欧元/m²，岛形展位195欧元/m²
**上届规模** '09：展览面积17,000m²，参展商307家（国外展商158家），专业贸易观众14,700人
**主办：** 科隆国际展览有限公司
**地址：** 北京市东三环北路8号亮马河大厦2座1018室（100004）
**联系人：** 张昱，贾宁
☎ 010-6590 7766转738
🖷 010-6590 6139
✉ j.zhang@koelnmesse.cn
www.prosweets.cn

## ProSweets Cologne 2010

**Date：** 2010/10/18 - 21
**Venue:** Cologne Exhibition Center, Germany
**Profile:** Raw materials and ingredients for confectionery production; Confectionery packaging; Packaging machines for confectionery; Machines and systems for the confectionery industry; Refrigeration and air conditioning technology for confectionery production; Food safety and quality management in confectionery production (incl. operating hygiene); Automation, data processing, control technology for confectionery production; Operating equipment and auxiliary devices for confectionery production; Service providers, organizations, publishers; Waste disposal / Recycling
**Established Year:** 2006
**Frequency:** Annual
**Market Area:** International
**Participated Fee:** Standard Booth (min 9m²): EUR 450/m², Corner Unit EUR 460/m², Peninsula Unit EUR 470/m², Island Unit EUR 470/m²; Raw Space (min 36m²) : EUR 175/m², Corner Unit EUR 185/m², Peninsula Unit EUR 195/m², Island Unit EUR 195/m²
**Statistics '09:** Exhibition Area 17,000m², Exhibitors 307 (foreigners 158) , Trade Visitors 14,700)
**Organizer:** Koelnmesse GmbH
**Address:** Unit 1018, Landmark Tower II, No.8 Dongsanhuan North Rd., Beijing 100004, China
☎ 86-10-6590 7766 ext 738
🖷 86-10-6590 6139
**Contact:** Joesy Zhang, Maggie Jia
✉ j.zhang@koelnmesse.cn
www.prosweets.cn

## 2010第21届国际金属板材加工技术展览会

## 21st European International Sheet Metal Processing Technology Exhibition

**日期：** 2010/10/26 - 30
**地点：** 德国汉诺威展览中心
**内容：** 金属板材、半成品和成品（铁/非铁）、金属冲压模具、精冲模具、压铸模具、多工位级进模具等，搬运技术、分离技术、成型技术、柔性金属板加工技术、机械零件、管材/型材加工、接合与紧固技术、用于金属板材/盘的表面技术（与流程相关）、用于金属板材/盘加工的机床技术、流程控制与品质保证、资料处理（硬件和软件）、厂房与仓库设备、安全工作/环境保护、服务、资讯和交流
**始办年份：** 2004
**周期：** 每年一届
**市场范围：** 国际性
**参展费用：** 标准展位326欧元/m²（12m²起），中高档装修、双面开口加收5%，另加增值税19%
**上届规模** '08：展览面积130,000m²，参展商1,409家（来自40个国家），参观人数64,300人
**主办：** 国际金属板材协会
**地址：** 广东省深圳市福田区新洲大厦15层深圳创明展览设计有限公司（518048）
**联系人：** 雷明，朱利萍
☎ 0755-2393 8881, 2393 8025
🖷 0755-2393 8426
✉ cmffok@163.com
MSN：lm83573425@21cn.com
**参展联络：** 中国贸促会机械行业分会
**地址：** 北京市西城区三里河路46号（100823）
**联系人：** 江彦明，袁丽娜
☎ 010-6859 4927, 6851 5863
🖷 010-6859 4948
✉ info@ccpitmsc.org
✉ jix@ccpit.org
www.chinamachin.org.cn
www.ccpitmsc.org

## 21st European International Sheet Metal Processing Technology Exhibition

**Date：** 2010/10/26 - 30
**Venue:** Hannover Exhibition Center, Germany
**Profile:** Die-casting molds, multi-position progressive die technology, separation technology such as handling sheet metal forming technology, processing technology of flexible mechanical parts pipe/profile bonding and fastening technology for processing of sheet metal/plate surface technology (and process related). For sheet metal/plate processing, machine tool technology in process control and quality assurance data processing (hardware and software) plant and warehouse equipment safety, environmental services, information and communication
**Established Year:** 2004
**Frequency:** Annual
**Market Area:** International

Participated Fee: Standard Booth EUR 326/m$^2$ (min 12m$^2$), Corner Unit add 5%
Statistics '08: Exhibition Area 130,000m$^2$, Exhibitors 1,409（came from 40 countries）, Visitors 64,300
Organizer: The International Association of Sheet Metal
Address: 15/Fl Xinzhou Building, Futian District, Shenzhen, Guangdong
☎ 86-755-2393 8881, 2393 8025
℻ 86-755-2393 8426
Contact: Rei Ming, Julius Ping
✉ cmffok@163.com
MSN: lm83573425@21cn.com

## 科隆办公展

### Orgatec 2010

日期：2010/10/26 - 30
地点：德国科隆
周期：两年一届
市场范围：国际性
参展联络：大连上选会展服务有限公司
地址：大连市西岗区鞍山路13号兴业广场大厦B座508室（116011）
☎ 0411-8378 8326, 8378 8396, 8378 9165, 8378 8821
℻ 0411-8378 8830, 8378 8823
✉ cicyhuang@vip.sina.com
MSN：cicyhuang@msn.com
www.sun-show.com

### Orgatec 2010

Date：2010/10/26 - 30
Venue: Germany
Frequency: Biennial
Market Area: International
Contact: Dalian Sun Show Convention & Exhibition Service Co Ltd
☎ 86-411-8378 8326, 8378 8396, 8378 9165
℻ 86-411-8378 8830, 8378 8823
✉ cicyhuang@vip.sina.com
MSN: cicyhuang@msn.com
www.sun-show.com

## 国际塑料及橡胶展览会

日期：2010/10/27 - 03
地点：德国杜塞尔多夫
周期：每年一届
市场范围：国际性
参展联络：中国机械汽车展览联合会
☎ 010-6859 4964
℻ 010-6859 4964

## 杜塞尔多夫医疗设备展

### Medica

日期：2010/11 -
地点：德国杜塞尔多夫
内容：实验室设备、急救服务、手术室设备、医院技术设施及设备；诊断及治疗设备；生化及检验设备
周期：每年一届
市场范围：国际性
参展联络：京慕国际展览有限公司
地址：北京市朝阳区北三环东路6号中国国际展览中心服务楼3层
联系人：魏亦山，孙铁兵
☎ 010-8460 0551
℻ 010-8460 0394
✉ zhaolingna@ciec.com.cn
www.jingmu.com.cn

### Medica

Date：2010/11 -
Venue: Dusseldorf, Germany
Frequency: Annual
Market Area: International
Organizer: Jing Mu International Exhibition Co Ltd
Address: 6 East Beisanhuan Rd., Beijing 100028, China
☎ 86-10-8460 0551
℻ 86-10-8460 0394
✉ zhaolingna@ciec.com.cn
www.jingmu.com.cn

## 德国国际电子自动化系统及元件展览会

### SPS/IPC/DRIVES Electric Automation Systems and Components 2010

日期：2010/11 -
地点：德国纽伦堡
周期：每年一届
市场范围：国际性
参展联络：中国贸促会机械行业分会
地址：北京市西城区三里河路46号（100823）
联系人：李华龙，曹姗姗，李静
☎ 010-6859 5039, 6859 5043, 6859 5067
℻ 010-6857 2287
✉ info@ccpitmsc.org
✉ jix@ccpit.org
www.chinamachin.org.cn
www.ccpitmsc.org

## 慕尼黑国际电子元器件博览会

### electronica

日期：2010/11/09 - 12
地点：德国慕尼黑
内容：显示设备、电源、变压器、电池、封装工艺、伺服系统及驱动元素、电子设计、检验检测、组件和辅助系统、半导体、嵌入系统、传感器和微系统、线缆、开关等
周期：每年一届
市场范围：国际性
参展联络：京慕国际展览有限公司
地址：北京市朝阳区北三环东路6号中国国际展览中心服务楼3层
联系人：韩芳；俞亮
☎ 010-8460 0551
℻ 010-8460 0394
✉ zhaolingna@ciec.com.cn
www.jingmu.com.cn

### electronica

Date：2010/11/09 - 12
Venue: Munich, Germany
Frequency: Annual
Market Area: International
Organizer: Jing Mu International Exhibition Co Ltd
Address: 6 East Beisanhuan Rd., Beijing 100028, China
☎ 86-10-8460 0551
℻ 86-10-8460 0394
✉ zhaolingna@ciec.com.cn
www.jingmu.com.cn

## 国际饮料设备展览会

日期：2010/11/12 - 14
地点：德国纽伦堡
周期：每年一届
市场范围：国际性
参展联络：中国机械汽车展览联合会
☎ 010-6859 4964
℻ 010-6859 4964

## 科隆国际优秀艺术及古董展

### Cologne Fine Art And Antiques

日期：2010/11/17 - 21
地点：德国科隆国际展览中心
内容：艺术品及古董 非欧洲艺术、部落艺术、人类学艺术、古代宗教绘画和 19世纪艺术、家具、古董、摄影作品、挂毯、地毯、武器装备、军事纪念品、音乐设备、钟表、珠宝、袖珍模型、图示、新近艺术、装饰艺术风格(Art Deco)、包豪斯风格、现代设计艺术、书籍和艺术杂志 现代艺术 现代古典艺术、战后艺术、当代艺术、艺术版画、摄影作品、录像、原生艺术（Art Brut）、书籍和艺术杂志 古董书籍 书籍、手稿、地图、图像及印刷品
始办年份：2006
周期：每年一届
市场范围：国际性
入场券价格：日票20欧元(需现场购买)，二日票30欧元，10人以上团体票12欧元/人，夜间票(下午5点后入场)14欧元，预展日票50欧元
参展费用：参展审核费250欧元
上届规模：展览面积35, 000m$^2$，参展商172家，专业贸易观众30, 000人
主办：科隆展览国际有限公司
地址：科隆展览中国有限公司北京东三环北路8号亮马河大厦2座1018室（100004）
联系人：游千仪
☎ 010-6590 7766
℻ 010-6590 6139
✉ m.yu@koelnmesse.cn

### Cologne Fine Art And Antiques

Date：2010/11/17 - 21
Venue: Cologne Exhibition Center, Germany
Established Year: 2006
Frequency: Annual
Market Area: International
Cost to Attend: EUR 20:-
Statistics '09: Exhibition Area 35,000m$^2$, Exhibitors 172, Trade Visitors 30,000
Organizer: KOELNMESSE
Address: Unit 1018 Landmark Tower Ⅱ, No. 8 Dongsanhuan North Rd., Beijing 100004, China
☎ 86-10-6590 7766
℻ 86-10-6590 6139
Contact: Monika
✉ m.yu@koelnmesse.cn

## 欧洲模具及机床技术展览会

### Euro Mold and Turntec 2010

日期：2010/12 -
地点：德国法兰克福
周期：每年一届
市场范围：国际性
参展联络：中国贸促会机械行业分会
地址：北京市西城区三里河路46号（100823）
联系人：孙晓光，吴琼，纪冬冬
☎ 010-68595431, 6858 0868, 6859 4909，6859 4826
℻ 010-6859 5485
✉ info@ccpitmsc.org
✉ jix@ccpit.org
www.chinamachin.org.cn
www.ccpitmsc.org

## 世界健美、健身及休闲博览会

### FIBO - The Leading International Trade Show for Fitness & Wellness

日期：2011 -
地点：德国埃森展览中心
内容：一听到FIBO，健身中心经营者、健身教练、体育医生、理疗师、宾馆经营者、桑拿浴经营者、投资者及多功能健康中心经营者会立刻想到每年春季在埃森举办的世界最专业的健美与健身展会。每年的FIBO都是一个独一无二的思想和创新的市场，涵盖健身器材、服务、营养、健康、美容、服饰、娱乐、运动等领域。 产品及服务 健身及训练器材、咨询、健康宣传、医疗健身、运动营养、健美及美容器材、桑拿浴、日光浴床、化妆品、健身房器材、电脑软硬件、协会、音乐、运动及健身服饰。
周期：每年一届
市场范围：国际性
参展费用：净地展位136～156欧元/ m$^2$
参展联络：励展博览集团国际销售部

地址：北京朝阳区新源里南路1-3号平安国际金融中心A座15层01-03，05（100027）
联系人：王亮
☎ 010-5933 9288
🖷 010-5933 9233
✉ liang.wang@reedexpo.com.cn
www.reedexport.cn

## 2011年德国科隆国际糖果及休闲食品展览会（ISM）

2011 ISM

日期：2011/01 -
地点：德国科隆国际展览中心
内容：可可、巧克力和巧克力制品，饼干，休闲食品，糖制品，冰淇淋和糖浆
周期：每年一届
市场范围：国际性
上届规模 '09：展览面积110,000m$^2$，参展商1,593家（国外展商1,274家，来自56个国家），参观人数35,200人
主办：德国科隆国际展览有限公司
参展联络：杭州思诺博会展服务有限公司
地址：杭州市体育场路229号浙江粮油大厦1202室（310003）
☎ 0571-8577 8500
🖷 0571-8577 9709
✉ expo@sinobal.com
www.sinobal.com

## 科隆国际家具展

imm cologne

日期：2011/01/18 - 23
地点：德国科隆国际展览中心
内容：科隆国际家具展（imm cologne）始于1949年，是当今世界最负盛名的家具展览会。每年一月份在德国科隆国际展览中心举行。展品无以伦比的广度和深度是科隆国际家具展作为全球第一品牌的独特性。在这里，全球的观众将领略到来自世界范围的包罗万象的设计一流的家具以及经典家居用品世界，其间，丰富多彩的配套活动也为科隆国际家具展增色不少
周期：每年一届
市场范围：国际性
参展费用：统一特装560欧元/m$^2$，自行特装155欧元/m$^2$
主办：德国科隆展览国际有限公司
地址：北京市朝阳区东三环北路8号亮马河大厦二座1018室（100004）
联系人：郑志强
☎ 010-6590 7766转 717
🖷 010-6590 6139
✉ info@koelnmesse.cn
www.imm-cologne.cn

## imm cologne

Date：2011/01/18 - 23
Venue: Koelnmesse Trade Fair Center, Germany
Profile: imm cologne is the international leading trade fair for the furnishing sector. Each year, imm cologne is the first event to present the latest home trends for Europe and overseas. The unparalleled breadth and depth of the exhibits is the trademark and claim to top quality of imm cologne. Here, international trade visitors discover furniture and home style ideas from all over the world.
Frequency: Annual
Market Area: International
Participated Fee: EUR 155～560/m$^2$
Organizer: Koelnmesse GmbH
Address: Unit 1018 Landmark Tower II, No. 8 Dongsanhuan N. Road, Beijing 100004, China
☎ 86-10-6590 7766 ext 717
🖷 86-10-6590 6139
Contact: KEN ZHENG
✉ info@koelnmesse.cn
www.imm-cologne.cn

## 2011年德国柏林国际水果蔬菜博览会

2011 Fruit Logistica

日期：2011/02 -
地点：德国柏林展览中心
内容：水果、蔬菜、干果、坚果、香料、调料、有机食品、冷冻水果、冷冻蔬菜、生物产品、包装技术、运输、储藏技术、软件、服务等。
周期：每年一届
市场范围：国际性
主办：Messe Berlin GmbH
参展联络：杭州思诺博会展服务有限公司
地址：杭州市体育场路229号浙江粮油大厦1202室（310003）
☎ 0571-8577 8500
🖷 0571-8577 9709
✉ expo@sinobal.com
www.sinobal.com

## 科隆国际糖果原料和机械展览会

ProSweets Cologne 2011

日期：2011/02 -
地点：德国科隆国际博览中心
内容：甜食生产原材料 甜食包装材料 甜食包装机械 甜食工业机器与设备 甜食生产中冷藏与空调技术 甜食生产中的食品安全、质量管理 甜食生产中的自动化、数据处理、开环和闭环控制技术 甜食生产用加工设备和辅助装置 服务提供商、组织机构、出版社 垃圾处理、废物循环利用
始办年份：2006
周期：每年一届
市场范围：国际性
参展费用：标准展位（9m$^2$起）：一面开口450欧元/m$^2$，两面开口460欧元/m$^2$，三面开口470欧元/m$^2$，岛形展位470欧元/m$^2$；净地（36m$^2$起）：一面开口175欧元/m$^2$，两面开口185欧元/m$^2$，三面开口195欧元/m$^2$，岛形展位195欧元/m$^2$
主办：科隆国际展览有限公司
地址：北京市东三环北路8号亮马河大厦2座1018室（100004）
联系人：张昱，贾宁
☎ 010-6590 7766转738
🖷 010-6590 6139
✉ j.zhang@koelnmesse.cn
www.prosweets.cn

## ProSweets Cologne 2010

Date：2011/02 -
Venue: Cologne Exhibition Center, Germany
Profile: Raw materials and ingredients for confectionery production; Confectionery packaging; Packaging machines for confectionery; Machines and systems for the confectionery industry; Refrigeration and air conditioning technology for confectionery production; Food safety and quality management in confectionery production (incl. operating hygiene); Automation, data processing, control technology for confectionery production; Operating equipment and auxiliary devices for confectionery production; Service providers, organizations, publishers; Waste disposal / Recycling
Established Year: 2006
Frequency: Annual
Market Area: International
Participated Fee: Standard Booth (min 9m$^2$)：EUR 450/m$^2$, Corner Unit EUR 460/m$^2$, Peninsula Unit EUR 470/m$^2$, Island Unit EUR 470/m$^2$; Raw Space (min 36m$^2$)：EUR 175/m$^2$, Corner Unit EUR 185/m$^2$, Peninsula Unit EUR 195/m$^2$, Island Unit EUR 195/m$^2$
Organizer: Koelnmesse GmbH
Address: Unit 1018, Landmark Tower II, No.8 Dongsanhuan North Rd., Beijing 100004, China
☎ 86-10-6590 7766 ext738
🖷 86-10-6590 6139
Contact: Joesy Zhang, Maggie Jia
✉ j.zhang@koelnmesse.cn
www.prosweets.cn

## 科隆国际糖果及休闲食品展

ISM -
international Sweets and Biscuits Fair

日期：2011/02 -
地点：德国科隆国际博览中心
内容：ISM——全球市场成功的标志，在德国科隆举办的科隆国际糖果及休闲食品展（ISM）是全球最大、最重要的甜食和休闲食品的展览会。每年，来自全球贸易界的专业人士汇聚在这里，相互介绍、发掘和探讨国际最新流行趋势、最新的产品，寻找最近最好的商机。
始办年份：1972
周期：每年一届
市场范围：国际性
入场券价格：人民币600元
参展费用：标准展位（12m$^2$起）420欧元/m$^2$，净地（36m$^2$起）150欧元/m$^2$
上届规模 '09：展览面积110, 000m$^2$，参展商1,593家（国外展商1,274家），专业贸易观众32, 500人
主办：科隆展览国际有限公司
地址：科隆展览中国有限公司 北京东三环北路8号亮马河大厦2座1018室（100004）
联系人：徐畅，王迎
☎ 010-6590 7766转715
🖷 010-6590 6139
✉ j.xu@koelnmesse.cn
www.ism-cologne.cn

## ISM -

International Sweets and Biscuits Fair

Date：2011/02 -
Venue: Cologne Exhibition Center, Germany
Profile: ISM is the largest and most important sweets and biscuits fair in the world. Every year the international sector meets to introduce, discover and discuss the latest trends, the newest products and the most up-to-dates perspectives.
Established Year: 1972
Frequency: Annual
Market Area: International
Cost to Attend: RMB 600
Participated Fee: Standard Booth EUR 420/m$^2$（min 12m$^2$）, Raw Space EUR 150/m$^2$ (min 36m$^2$)
Statistics '09: Exhibition Area 110,000m$^2$, Exhibitors 1,593（foreigners 1,274）, Trade Visitors 32,500）
Organizer: Koelnmesse
Address: Unit 1018, Landmark Tower Ⅱ, No. 8 Dongsanhuan North Rd,, Beijing 100004, China
☎ 86-10-6590 7766 ext 715
🖷 86-10-6590 6139
Contact: Joyce Xu, Elan Wang
✉ j.xu@koelnmesse.cn
www.ism-cologne.cn

## 春季马术用品展

spoga horse(spring)

**日期**：2011/02/05 - 07
**地点**：德国科隆国际展览中心
**内容**：马术用品、相关服务
**始办年份**：2008
**周期**：每年两届
**市场范围**：国际性
**参展费用**：标准展位381欧元/m²(9m²起)，净地136欧元/m²（36m²起）
**上届规模**‘08：展览面积28,500m²，参展商379家，参观人数38,600人
**主办**：科隆展览中国有限公司
**地址**：北京市东三环北路8号亮马河大厦2座1018室（100004）
**联系人**：张昱，贾宁
☎ 010-6590 7766转738
🖷 010-6590 6139
✉ j.zhang@koelnmesse.cn

## spoga horse(spring)

Date：2011/02/05 - 07
Venue: Germany
Established Year: 2008
Frequency: Biannual
Market Area: International
Participated Fee: Standard Booth EUR 381/m² (min 9m²), Raw Space EUR 136/m²（min 36m²）
Statistics ‘08: Exhibition Area 28,500m², Exhibitors 379，Visitors 38,600
Organizer: Koelnmesse Co Ltd
Address: Unit 1018 Landmark Tower II, No 8 Dongsanhuan N Rd., Beijing, China
Contact: Joesy Zhang, Maggie Jia
☎ 86-10-6590 7766 ext 738
🖷 86-10-6590 6139
✉ j.zhang@koelnmesse.cn

## 欧洲化妆品原料展

in-cosmetics:
The Leading Global Platform for Personal Care Ingredients

**日期**：2011/04 -
**地点**：德国新慕尼黑博览中心
**内容**：in-cosmetics是世界领先的化妆品、化妆用具及个人护理业原料及配料国际展会。每年春季在欧洲轮回举办。展会吸引全世界最好的供应商、研发人士，以及生产和营销专业人士。是一个最富启发性的新配料、新技术、新方案及前沿产品的平台；同时也是一次全面的教育机会，可以学到化妆品业内的科技突破、潮流以及相关规定。
**周期**：每年一届
**市场范围**：国际性
**参展费用**：净地展位355欧元/m²起，标准展位434欧元/m²起
**参展联络**：励展博览集团国际销售部
**地址**：北京市朝阳区新源里南路1-3号平安国际金融中心A座15层01-03，05（100027）
**联系人**：杜一鸣
☎ 010-5933 9288
🖷 010-5933 9233
✉ martin.du@reedexpo.com.cn
www.reedexport.cn

## 科隆亚太采购交易会

——五金、家居、家电、园艺产品

Asia Pacific Sourcing

**日期**：2011/04/03 - 05
**地点**：德国科隆国际展览中心
**内容**：从2005年起，一个旨在创造新的环太平洋地区与欧洲、北美洲之间的进出口贸易的平台——科隆亚太采购交易会—五金、家居、家电、园艺产品每单数年在科隆国际博览中心举办。APS取得了令人振奋的成功，几乎所有的参展商和观众都表示展会效果完全超出了他们的期望，获得巨大的收获。APS已经成为亚太地区的制造商向欧洲和北美地区的客户展示自己最新的产品和技术的重要平台。
**始办年份**：2005
**周期**：两年一届
**市场范围**：国际性
**参展费用**：490欧元/m²，165欧元/m²
**上届规模**‘09：展览面积32,000m²，参展商406家，专业贸易观众5, 300人
**主办**：科隆展览国际有限公司
**地址**：科隆展览中国有限公司 北京东三环北路8号亮马河大厦2座1018室（100004）
**联系人**：郑志强
☎ 010-6590 7766 转717
🖷 010-6590 6139
✉ k.zheng@koelnmesse.cn
www.asiapacificsourcing.cn

## Asia Pacific Sourcing

Date：2011/04/03 - 05
Venue: Koelnmesse Trade Fair Center, Germany
Profile: The event is a separate platform presenting Asian products from the house, garden and leisure sector. The aim is to link product ranges from Asian growth markets with the growing demand in Europe and North America, all in a concentrated format in Cologne. This trade fair is scheduled to be held every two years, serving as a multi-lateral hub for the import and export business. Asia-Pacific Sourcing is the ordering and communication platform for products, innovations and trends for the house, garden and leisure segment.
Established Year: 2005
Frequency: Biennial
Market Area: International
Participated Fee: EUR 165～490/m²
Statistics ‘09: Exhibition Area 32,000m², Exhibitors 406，Trade Visitors 5,300
Organizer: KOELNMESSE
Address: Unit 1018 Landmark Tower Ⅱ, No. 8 Dongsanhuan North Rd., Beijing 100004, China
Contact: KEN ZHENG
☎ 86-10-6590 7766 ext 717
🖷 86-10-6590 6139
✉ k.zheng@koelnmesse.cn
www.asiapacificsourcing.cn

## 科隆国际艺术展

ART COLOGNE 2011

**日期**：2011/04/13 - 17
**地点**：德国科隆国际展览中心
**内容**：油画作品、绘图作品、雕塑作品、行为艺术、摄影作品
**始办年份**：1967
**周期**：每年一届
**市场范围**：国际性
**入场券价格**：日票20欧元，两日票30欧元，团体票（10人以上）14欧元
**上届规模**：展览面积43,000m²，参展商253家
**主办**：科隆展览国际有限公司
**地址**：科隆展览中国有限公司 北京东三环北路8号亮马河大厦2座1018室（100004）
**联系人**：游千仪
☎ 010-6590 7766
🖷 010-6590 6139
✉ m.yu@koelnmesse.cn

## ART COLOGNE 2011

Date：2011/04/13 - 17
Venue: Cologne Exhibition Center, Germany
Established Year: 1967
Frequency: Annual
Market Area: International
Cost to Attend: EUR 20:-, Two days EUR 30:-, Group Rate (min 10 people) EUR 14:-
Statistics‘09': Exhibition Area 43,000m², Exhibitors 253
Organizer: KOELNMESSE
Address: Unit 1018 Landmark Tower Ⅱ, No. 8 Dongsanhuan North Rd., Beijing 100004, China
Contact: Monika
☎ 86-10-6590 7766
🖷 86-10-6590 6139
✉ m.yu@koelnmesse.cn

## 科隆国际牙科展

International Dental Show 2011

**日期**：2011/04/22 - 26
**地点**：德国科隆国际展览中心
**内容**：牙科临床实践；牙科技工室；感染控制与维护；服务、信息、交流和机构
**周期**：两年一届
**市场范围**：国际性
**入场券价格**：260元人民币
**参展费用**：标准展位（9 m²起）545欧元/m²含净地租金、展位装修、公共能源费，其它费用：基本会刊登录费349.00 欧元/参展商（净价），垃圾清运10 欧元/m²，电费15 欧元/m²，其中会刊登录费为净价需要加收19%增值税；净地（36m²起）238欧元/m²，其它费用：公共能源费6欧元/m²，会刊登录费349欧元/参展商，暂缴杂费25欧元/m²（300m²以上展位另计）及19%增值税
**上届规模**‘09：展览面积138,000m²，参展商1,820家（来自57个国家），参观人数106,000人
**主办**：科隆展览有中国限公司
**地址**：北京市亮马河大厦2座1018室（100004）
**联系人**：齐志宇
☎ 010-6590 7766转727
🖷 010-6590 6139
✉ k.qi@koelnmesse.cn
www.ids-cologne.cn

## International Dental Show 2011

Date：2011/04/22 - 26
Venue: Cologne exhibition centre, Germany
Profile: Dental practice, Dental laboratory, Infection control and maintenance, Services, information, communication and organization
Frequency: Biennial
Market Area: International
Cost to Attend: RMB 260:-
Participated Fee: Standard Booth (min 9m²) EUR 545/m², Raw Space (min 36m²) EUR 238/m²
Statistics ‘09: Exhibition Area 138,000m², Exhibitors 1,820 (came from 57 countries)，Visitors 106,000
Organizer: Koelnmesse Co Ltd
Address: Unit 1018, Landmark Tower 2, No.8 Dongsanhuan North Rd., Beijing, China
Contact: Kevin Qi
☎ 86-10-6590 7766 ext 727

86-10-6590 6139
k.qi@koelnmesse.cn
www.ids-cologne.cn

## 科隆国际家具生产、木工及室内装饰展

interzum cologne

**日期：** 2011/05/25 - 28
**地点：** 德国科隆国际展览中心
**内容：** 科隆国际家具生产、木工及室内装饰展（interzum）始于1959年，是针对家具生产及其原辅料方面的一个全球性盛会，是目前世界上木工机械、家具生产设备及家具原材料、配件领域规模最大、影响力最大的专业展览会之一，每两年举办一届（逢单年举办），其展品范围之广位居所有同类展会之首。
**周期：** 两年一届
**市场范围：** 国际性
**参展费用：** 490欧元/$m^2$，165欧元/$m^2$
**主办：** 德国科隆展览国际有限公司
**地址：** 北京市朝阳区东三环北路8号亮马河大厦二座1018室（100004）
**联系人：** 贾宁
010-6590 7766转729
010-6590 6139
m.jia@koelnmesse
www.interzum.cn

## interzum cologne

**Date：** 2011/05/25 - 28
**Venue:** Koelnmesse Trade Fair Center, Germany
**Profile:** interzum is the leading global event for the furniture and interior construction industries' supplying sections. This is where the trends and visions that will create future living spaces using modern materials, outstanding design, and exclusive innovations come to life.
**Frequency:** Biennial
**Market Area:** International
**Participated Fee:** EUR 165～490/$m^2$
**Organizer:** Koelnmesse GmbH
**Address:** Unit 1018 Landmark Tower II, No. 8 Dongsanhuan N. Road, Beijing 100004, China
**Contact:** Maggie Jia
86-10-6590 7766 ext 729
86-10-6590 6139
m.jia@koelnmesse
www.interzum.cn

## 国际废物处理博览会

ENTECO

**日期：** 2011/06/06 - 09
**地点：** 德国科隆国际博览中心
**内容：** 废物管理和再循环、水处理和废水治理、焚化和可再利用能源、市政及环境服务、环保技术和物流管理、空气质量和污染控制、职业安全和噪音保护、环保调查和组织机构
**始办年份：** 1976
**周期：** 两年一届
**市场范围：** 国际性
**参展费用：** 360欧元/$m^2$（12$m^2$起）；净地：（36$m^2$起）一面开口129欧元/$m^2$，两面开口135欧元/$m^2$，三面开口139欧元/$m^2$，岛形展位139欧元/$m^2$，室外场地70欧元/$m^2$
**上届规模** '09：展览面积72,000$m^2$，参展商784家（来自235个国家），专业贸易观众36,000人
**主办：** 科隆展览国际有限公司
**地址：** 北京东三环北路8号亮马河大厦2座1018室（100004）
**联系人：** 陈瑞
010-6590 7766转750
010-6590 6139
r.chen@koelnmesse.cn

## ENTECO

**Date：** 2011/06/06 - 09
**Venue:** Cologne Exhibition Center, Germany
**Profile:** Waste Management & Recycling, Health and Safety At Work & Noises Protection, Research & Organization, Local Authority & Environmental Service, Air Quality Control & Emissions Protection, Technology & Logistics, Incineration & Renewable Energy, Water & Liquid Waste
**Established Year:** 1976
**Frequency:** Biennial
**Market Area:** International
**Participated Fee:** EUR 360/$m^2$（min 12$m^2$）; Raw Space（min 36$m^2$）EUR 129/$m^2$, Corner Unit EUR 135/$m^2$, Peninsula Unit EUR 139/$m^2$, Island Unit EUR 139/$m^2$; Outdoor EUR 70/$m^2$
**Statistics** '09: Exhibition Area 72,000$m^2$, Exhibitors 784（came from 235 countries）, Trade Visitors 36,000
**Organizer:** KOELNMESSE
**Address:** Unit 1018 Landmark Tower Ⅱ, No. 8 Dongsanhuan North Rd., Beijing 100004, China
010-6590 7766 ext 750
86-10-6590 6139
**Contact:** Ryan Chen
r.chen@koelnmesse.cn

## 柏林国际会展技术及媒体技术展览会

SHOWTECH – International Trade Show & Conference for Event Technology & Services

**日期：** 2011/06/07 - 09
**地点：** 德国柏林展览中心
**内容：** 国际会展技术及媒体技术展览会是针对舞台表演及展会活动行业的著名欧洲展览会，是向业内技术决策人、制造商、展会活动经理人、主办者及经销商展示灯光、音响科技领域最新创新、解决方案及行业潮流的高水平业务交流平台。由展会赞助机构德国影剧院技术协会（DTHG）于展会同期主办的专业会议将邀请顶级业内专家介绍最新的国际影剧院技术及管理经验。
**周期：** 两年一届
**市场范围：** 国际性
**赞助：** 德国影剧院技术协会（DTHG）——剧院、影院、电视、演出及展会活动专业协会
**参展联络：** 励展博览集团国际销售部
**地址：** 北京朝阳区新源里南路1-3号平安国际金融中心A座15层01-03，05（100027）
**联系人：** 杜一鸣
010-5933 9288
010-5933 9233
martin.du@reedexpo.com.cn
www.reedexport.cn

## 科隆国际游戏展

gamescom

**日期：** 2011/08 -
**地点：** 德国科隆国际博览中心
**内容：** 科隆国际游戏展(gamescom)由创办于2002年的原莱比锡游戏展(Games Convention)发展而来，09年起正式移师科隆，是欧洲最专业的综合性互动式游戏软件、信息软件和硬件设备展览，也是德国唯一一个集中了游戏软件、硬件、娱乐设备、信息软件和设备的大型国际展会。 科隆国际游戏展由科隆国际展览公司与联邦互动娱乐软件协会(BIU)联合举办。科隆国际展览中心完备的基础设施和优越的地理位置、科隆国际展览公司遍布全球的营销及服务网络、以及具备多年举办大型国际展会的丰富经验，将为gamescom提供一个良好的发展空间。
**始办年份：** 2002
**周期：** 每年一届
**市场范围：** 国际性
**主办：** 科隆展览国际有限公司
**地址：** 北京东三环北路8号亮马河大厦2座1018室（100004）
**联系人：** 陈瑞
010-6590 7766转750
010-6590 6139
r.chen@koelnmesse.cn

## gamescom

**Date：** 2011/08 -
**Venue:** Cologne Exhibition Center, Germany
**Established Year:** 2002
**Frequency:** Annual
**Market Area:** International
**Organizer:** KOELNMESSE
**Address:** Unit 1018 Landmark Tower Ⅱ, No. 8 Dongsanhuan North Rd., Beijing 100004, China
**Contact:** Ryan Chen
86-10-6590 7766 ext 750
86-10-6590 6139
r.chen@koelnmesse.cn

## 数码营销博览会

dmexco

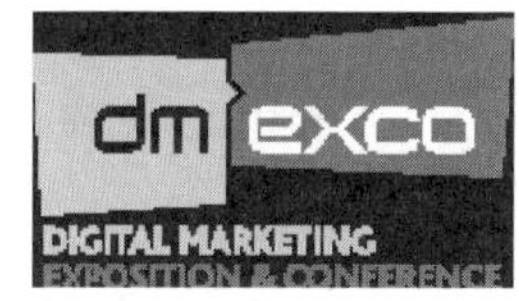


**日期：** 2011/09 -
**地点：** 德国科隆国际博览中心
**市场范围：** 国际性
**主办：** 科隆展览国际有限公司
**地址：** 北京东三环北路8号亮马河大厦2座1018室（100004）
**联系人：** 陈瑞
010-6590 7766转750
010-6590 6139
r.chen@koelnmesse.cn

## dmexco

**Date：** 2011/09 -
**Venue:** Cologne Exhibition Center, Germany
**Market Area:** International
**Organizer:** KOELNMESSE
**Address:** Unit 1018 Landmark Tower Ⅱ, No. 8 Dongsanhuan North Rd., Beijing 100004, China
**Contact:** Ryan Chen
86-10-6590 7766ext 750
86-10-6590 6139
r.chen@koelnmesse.cn

## 数码管理解决方案展览会

DMS EXPO

**日期：** 2011/09 -
**地点：** 德国科隆国际博览中心
**市场范围：** 国际性
**主办：** 科隆展览国际有限公司

地址：北京东三环北路8号亮马河大厦2座1018室（100004）
联系人：陈瑞
☎ 010-6590 7766转 750
🖷 010-6590 6139
✉ r.chen@koelnmesse.cn

## DMS EXPO

Date：2011/09 -
Venue: Cologne Exhibition Center, Germany
Market Area: International
Organizer: KOELNMESSE
Address: Unit 1018 Landmark Tower Ⅱ, No. 8 Dongsanhuan North Rd., Beijing 100004, China
☎ 86-10-6590 7766ext 750
🖷 86-10-6590 6139
Contact: Ryan Chen
✉ r.chen@koelnmesse.cn

## 国际体育用品、露营设备及园林生活博览会/国际园艺博览会

spoga/gafa

日期：2011/09/04 - 06
地点：德国科隆国际展览中心
内容：户外生活（户外家具），户外运动（烧烤设备、露营休闲用品、体育及比赛用品），户内和户外休闲（植物和植物护理、花卉栽培和装饰、水处理和室外照明、花园规划和维护、其它设备和花园布置、宠物用品），马术用品及服务
周期：每年一届
主办：科隆展览中国有限公司
地址：北京市东三环北路8号亮马河大厦2座1018室（100004）
联系人：张昱，贾宁
☎ 010-6590 7766转738
🖷 010-6590 6139
✉ j.zhang@koelnmesse.cn
www.spogagafa.cn

## spoga/gafa

Date：2011/09/04 - 06
Venue: Cologne Exhibition Center, Germany
Frequency: Annual
Organizer: Koelnmesse Co Ltd
Address: Unit 1018 Landmark Tower II, No 8 Dongsanhuan N Rd., Beijing, China
Contact: Joesy Zhang, Maggie Jia
☎ 86-10-6590 7766 ext 738
🖷 86-10-6590 6139
✉ j.zhang@koelnmesse.cn
www.spogagafa.cn

## 秋季马术用品展

spoga horse (Autumn)

日期：2011/09/04 - 06
地点：德国科隆国际展览中心展馆
内容：马术用品、相关服务
始办年份：2008
周期：每年两届
市场范围：国际性
参展费用：标准展位381欧元/$m^2$(9$m^2$起)，净地136欧元/$m^2$（36$m^2$起）
上届规模‘08：展览面积28,500$m^2$，参展商379家，参观人数38,600人
主办：科隆展览中国有限公司
地址：北京市东三环北路8号亮马河大厦2座1018室（100004）
联系人：张昱，贾宁
☎ 010-6590 7766转738
🖷 010-6590 6139
✉ j.zhang@koelnmesse.cn

## spoga horse (Autumn)

Date：2011/09/04 - 06
Venue: Cologne Exhibition Center, Germany
Established Year: 2008
Frequency: Biannual
Market Area: International
Participated Fee: Standard Booth EUR 381/$m^2$ (min 9m2), Raw Space EUR 136/$m^2$（min 36$m^2$）
Statistics ‘08: Exhibition Area 28,500$m^2$, Exhibitors 379, Visitors 38,600
Organizer: Koelnmesse Co Ltd
Address: Unit 1018 Landmark Tower II, No 8 Dongsanhuan N Rd., Beijing, China
☎ 86-10-6590 7766 ext 738
🖷 86-10-6590 6139
Contact: Joesy Zhang, Maggie Jia
✉ j.zhang@koelnmesse.cn

## 科隆国际少儿用品展

Kind + Jugend

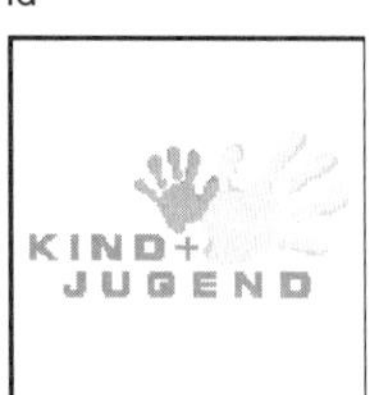


日期：2011/09/15 - 18
地点：德国科隆国际展览中心
内容：儿车及附件，安全座椅及设备，家具及附件，纺织品，婴儿、儿童、青年时装及孕妇装，玩具，育婴用品，电器，出版物，团体
始办年份：1960
周期：每年一届
市场范围：国际性
参展费用：340欧元/$m^2$(9$m^2$起)
上届规模‘09：展览面积80,000$m^2$，参展商781家（国外展商612家，来自41个国家），专业贸易观众18,000人
主办：科隆国际展览有限公司
地址：北京市亮马河大厦2座1018室（100004）
联系人：齐志宇
☎ 010-6590 7766 转 727
🖷 010-6590 6139
✉ k.qi@koelnmesse.cn
www.kindundjugend.cn

## Kind + Jugend

Date：2011/09/15 - 18
Venue: Cologne Exhibition Center, Germany
Profile: Prams, car/bicycle seats, children’s furniture, hygiene articles, electric appliances, textiles, baby cosmetics, toys and games for babies and toddlers, fashion for babies and toddlers, maternity wear, shop equipment, publications, organizations
Established Year: 1960
Frequency: Annual
Market Area: International
Participated Fee: EUR 340/$m^2$ (min 9$m^2$)
Statistics ‘09: Exhibition Area 80,000$m^2$, Exhibitors 781（foreigners 612, came from 41 countries）, Trade Visitors 18,000
Organizer: Koelnmesse
Address: Unit 1018, Landmark Tower 2, No.8 Dongsanhuan North Rd., Beijing, China
Contact: Kevin Qi
☎ 86-10-6590 7766 ext 727
🖷 86-10-6590 6139
✉ k.qi@koelnmesse.cn
www.kindundjugend.cn

## 世界食品博览会

Anuga

日期：2011/10/08 - 12
地点：德国科隆国际博览中心
内容：全世界的食品展数不胜数，但只有Anuga才是食品和饮料行业规模最大、地位最重要的展览会，也是唯一一个为您的未来精心规划的展览会。
展品范围：基本食品和精细食品，冷冻食品，肉制品，冷藏食品，奶制品，面包、焙烤食品和热饮，饮料，有机食品，餐饮技术，零售技术。
其他：非处方药OTC论坛、健康及功能性食品论坛、协会、组织、贸易媒体、服务提供商和信息技术
周期：两年一届
市场范围：国际性
参展费用：440欧元/$m^2$（12$m^2$起）含净地租金、展位装修、公共能源费、AUMA费
上届规模‘09：展览面积287,000$m^2$，参展商6,522家（国外展商5,307家），专业贸易观众153,500人
主办：科隆展览国际有限公司
地址：科隆展览中国有限公司 北京东三环北路8号亮马河大厦2座1018室（100004）
联系人：徐畅，王迎
☎ 010-6590 7766 转 715
🖷 010-6590 6139
✉ j.xu@koelnmesse.cn
www.anuga.cn

## Anuga

Date：2011/10/08 - 12
Venue: Cologne Exhibition Center, Germany
Profile: Trade Fair for the International Food Industry Leading fair for industry, trade and catering trade in the food and beverage sector Manufacturers, importers and wholesalers of food and drinks; of catering technology; of retail technology/shop fittings. Suppliers of services for the catering sector and the food retail trade, Trade agencies, Suppliers of specialties, Suppliers of fresh convenience products
Frequency: Biennial
Market Area: International
Participated Fee: EUR 440/$m^2$（min 12$m^2$）
Statistics ‘09: Exhibition Area 287,000$m^2$, Exhibitors 6,522（foreigners 5,307）, Trade Visitors 153,500
Organizer: KOELNMESSE
Address: Unit 1018 Landmark Tower Ⅱ, No. 8 Dongsanhuan North Rd., Beijing 100004, China
Contact: Joyce Xu, Elan Wang
☎ 86-10-6590 7766 ext 715
🖷 86-10-6590 6139
✉ j.xu@koelnmesse.cn
www.anuga.cn

## 国际休闲、体育设施及泳池设备展

FSB

日期：2011/10/26 - 28
地点：德国科隆国际博览中心
内容：运动设施，公共泳池设施，公共桑拿设施，运动场的规划设计、建设及其配套设施，城市规划/景观建筑，服务及专业媒体
始办年份：1969
周期：两年一届

市场范围：国际性
参展费用：标准展台410 欧元/$m^2$（$12m^2$起）费用包括：含净地租金、展位装修、公共能源费、AUMA费及19%增值税，不包含基本会刊登录费、垃圾清运及电费。净地147 欧元/$m^2$（$36m^2$起） 费用包括：公共能源费、AUMA费、会刊登录费用、垃圾清运费、展位电费、暂缴杂费及19%增值税。企业需要自行安排展位装修
上届规模 ‘09：展览面积36,000$m^2$，参展商271家（国外展商106家，来自46个国家），参观人数24,000人
主办：科隆展览国际有限公司
地址：北京东三环北路8号亮马河大厦2座1018室（100004）
联系人：陈瑞
☎ 010-6590 7766转 750
🖷 010-6590 6139
✉ r.chen@koelnmesse.cn

## FSB

Date：2011/10/26 - 28
Venue: Cologne Exhibition Center, Germany
Established Year: 1969
Frequency: Biennial
Market Area: International
Participated Fee: Standard Booth EUR 410/$m^2$（min $12m^2$），Raw Space EUR 147/$m^2$ (min 36 $m^2$)
Statistics '09: Exhibition Area 36,000$m^2$, Exhibitors 271（foreigners 106, came from 46 countries），Visitors 24,000
Organizer: KOELNMESSE
Address: Unit 1018 Landmark Tower Ⅱ, No. 8 Dongsanhuan North Rd., Beijing 100004, China
☎ 86-10-6590 7766ext 750
🖷 86-10-6590 6139
Contact: Ryan Chen
✉ r.chen@koelnmesse.cn

## 国际桑拿及泳池设备展

FSB

日期：2011/10/26 - 29
地点：德国科隆国际博览中心
内容：游泳池、桑拿房的设计、建设及其维护；游泳池、桑拿房相关设施、设备、器材、用品；游泳休闲设备、疗养设备；游泳池、桑拿房卫生设备、各类处理设备；服务、专业媒体及其它
周期：两年一届
市场范围：国际性
上届规模 ‘09：展览面积36,000$m^2$，参展商106家（国外展商46家），专业贸易观众24,000人
主办：科隆展览国际有限公司
地址：科隆展览中国有限公司 北京东三环北路8号亮马河大厦2座1018室（100004）
联系人：张昱，贾宁
☎ 010-6590 7766 转 738
🖷 010-6590 6139
✉ j.zhang@koelnmesse.cn

## 国际博物馆及展示技术展览会

EXPONATEC

日期：2011/11/15 - 18
地点：德国科隆国际展览中心
内容：国际博物馆及展示技术展览会是全球最大的博物行业的展会。
主要展品范围：楼宇新建、重建与规划；人事服务供应商；公共关系；观众研究与定位；展览设计；建筑与展览技术；媒体；入口出口区域；博物馆商店；博物馆餐饮；安全与运输；行政后勤；修复与保存；分解；材料测试；继续教育；研究机构
始办年份：2004
周期：两年一届
市场范围：国际性
主办：科隆展览国际有限公司
地址：北京东三环北路8号亮马河大厦2座1018室（100004）
联系人：陈瑞
☎ 010-6590 7766转 750
🖷 010-6590 6139
✉ r.chen@koelnmesse.cn

## EXPONATEC

Date：2011/11/15 - 18
Venue: Cologne Exhibition Center, Germany
Established Year: 2004
Frequency: Biennial
Market Area: International
Organizer: KOELNMESSE
Address: Unit 1018 Landmark Tower Ⅱ, No. 8 Dongsanhuan North Rd., Beijing 100004, China
Contact: Ryan Chen
☎ 86-10-6590 7766 ext 750
🖷 86-10-6590 6139
✉ r.chen@koelnmesse.cn

## 科隆国际优秀艺术及古董展

Cologne Fine Art And Antiques

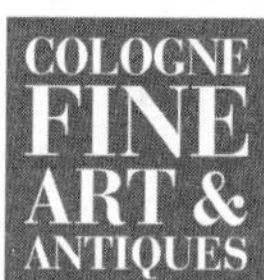


日期：2011/11/16 - 20
地点：德国科隆国际展览中心
内容：艺术品及古董 非欧洲艺术、部落艺术、人类学艺术、古代宗教绘画和 19世纪艺术、家具、古董、摄影作品、挂毯、地毯、武 器装备、军事纪念品、音乐设备、钟表、珠宝、袖珍模 型、图示、新近艺术、装饰艺术风格(Art Deco)、包豪 斯风格、现代设计艺术、书籍和艺术杂志 现代艺术 现代古典艺术、战后艺术、当代艺术、艺术版画、摄影 作品、录像、原生艺术（Art Brut）、书籍和艺术杂志 古董书籍 书籍、手稿、地图、图像及印刷品
始办年份：2006
周期：每年一届
市场范围：国际性
入场券价格：日票20欧元需现场购买，两日票30欧元，团体票12欧元/人（10人以上），夜间票(下午5点后入场)14欧元，预展日票50欧元
参展费用：参展审核费250 欧元
上届规模：展览面积35,000$m^2$，参展商172家，专业贸易观众30,000人
主办：科隆展览国际有限公司
地址：科隆展览中国有限公司 北京东三环北路8号亮马河大厦2座1018室（100004）
联系人：游千仪
☎ 010-6590 7766
🖷 010-6590 6139
✉ m.yu@koelnmesse.cn

## Cologne Fine Art And Antiques

Date：2011/11/16 - 20
Venue: Cologne Exhibition Center, Germany
Established Year: 2006
Frequency: Annual
Market Area: International
Cost to Attend: EUR 20:-
Statistics: Exhibition Area 35,000$m^2$, Exhibitors 172, Trade Visitors 30,000
Organizer: KOELNMESSE
Address: Unit 1018 Landmark Tower Ⅱ, No. 8 Dongsanhuan North Rd., Beijing 100004, China
Contact: Monika
☎ 86-10-6590 7766
🖷 86-10-6590 6139
✉ m.yu@koelnmesse.cn

## 德国国际视觉广告技术与标识制作展

Viscom Frankfurt 2012: International Trade Fair for Visual Communication

日期：2012 -
地点：德国法兰克福展览中心
内容：德国国际视觉广告技术与标识制作展涵盖视觉传播领域的各个方面。该展之前名为PRO SIGN，一直以创新的产品、高质量的展会服务而闻名。
周期：两年一届
市场范围：国际性
参展费用：净地展位145～200欧元/$m^2$，标准展位235～322欧元/$m^2$
主办：励展德国公司
参展联络：励展博览集团国际销售部
地址：北京市朝阳区新源里南路1-3号平安国际金融中心A座15层01-03，05（100027）
联系人：王亮
☎ 010-5933 9288
🖷 010-5933 9233
✉ liang.wang@reedexpo.com.cn
www.reedexport.cn

## 2012德国埃森国际铝工业展览会；第八届世界铝工业博览会暨学术会议

ALUMINIUM 2012

日期：2012/09 -
地点：德国埃森展览中心
内容：ALUMINIUM 2010是铝工业和其相关应用配套设备展览的首选之地。本展览覆盖整个价值链从提炼到成品应用于汽车制造和运输、建筑、机械电机工程、包装设计以及铝加工及精炼技术等主要领域。 产品及服务 来自40多个国家约900个展商将展示近千种创新产品，以及深层技术开发和最新趋势。德国国际铝工业展览会（ALUMINIUM）是铝工业及相关配套应用设备最重要的展示平台。铝生产商、加工商、精炼商以及科技和附加产品供应商，以及各种配套应用产品供应商将于九月汇聚德国埃森。
周期：两年一届
市场范围：国际性
参展费用：净地展位185欧元/$m^2$
主办：励展德国公司
参展联络：励展博览集团国际销售部
地址：北京朝阳区新源里南路1-3号平安国际金融中心A座15层01-03，05（100027）
联系人：王颖
☎ 010-5933 9288
🖷 010-5933 9233
✉ winnie.wang@reedexpo.com.cn
www.reedexport.cn

## 柏林国际会展技术及媒体技术展览会

SHOWTECH – International Trade Show & Conference for Event Technology & Services

## SHOWTECH

日期：2013/06 -
地点：德国柏林展览中心
内容：国际会展技术及媒体技术展览会是针对舞台表演及展会活动行业的著名欧洲展览会，是向业内技术决策人、制造商、展会活动经理人、主办者及经销商展示灯光、音响科技领域最新创新、解决方案及行业潮流的高水平业务交流平台。由展会赞助机构德国影剧院技术协会（DTHG）于展会同期主办的专业会议将邀请顶级业内专家介绍最新的国际影剧院技术及管理经验。
周期：两年一届
市场范围：国际性
赞助：德国影剧院技术协会（DTHG）——剧院、影院、电视、演出及展会活动专业协会
参展联络：励展博览集团国际销售部
地址：北京朝阳区新源里南路1-3号平安国际金融中心A座15层01-03，05（100027）
联系人：杜一鸣
☎ 010-5933 9288
🖷 010-5933 9233
✉ martin.du@reedexpo.com.cn
www.reedexport.cn

# 希腊
# Greece

## 国际海事展览会

日期：2010/06/08 - 11
地点：希腊比雷埃夫斯
周期：每年一届
市场范围：国际性
参展联络：中国机械汽车展览联合会
☎ 010-6859 4964
🖷 010-6859 4964

# 洪都拉斯
# Honduras

## 中国贸易展览会

日期：2010/09 -
地点：洪都拉斯圣佩德罗苏拉
周期：每年一届
市场范围：国际性
参展联络：中国机械汽车展览联合会
☎ 010-6859 4964
🖷 010-6859 4964

# 匈牙利
# Hungary

## 第29届匈牙利国际建材展览会

日期：2010/04/14 - 18
地点：匈牙利布达佩斯
内容：建材
市场范围：国际性
参展联络：北京中仕达兴业展览有限公司
地址：北京市海淀区蓝靛厂东路2号金源时代商务中心2号楼A座11B（100097）
联系人：贾倩，赵仕忱，牟向东，张露
☎ 010-5129 8900
🖷 010-8886 2939

✉ mail@chinstar.cn
www.chinstar.cn

# 印度
# India

## 2010年印度国际汽车摩托车零配件展览会
## The 10th Auto Expo India 2010

日期：2010/01/05 - 11
地点：印度新德里
周期：每年一届
市场范围：国际性
主办：法兰克福展览公司
参展联络：中国汽车工业国际合作总公司
地址：北京市海淀区中关村丹棱街3号A座5层（100080）
联系人：何萌
☎ 010-8260 6880
🖷 010-8260 6883
✉ exhibition@cnaico.com.cn

## 第10届国际包装印刷展览会

日期：2010/01/19 - 22
地点：印度新德里
周期：每年一届
市场范围：国际性
参展联络：中国机械汽车展览联合会
☎ 010-6859 4964
🖷 010-6859 4964

## 国际机床工具展览会

日期：2010/01/21 - 26
地点：印度班加罗尔
周期：每年一届
市场范围：国际性
参展联络：中国机械汽车展览联合会
☎ 010-6859 4964
🖷 010-6859 4964

## 印度国际宝石及珠宝展览会

日期：2010/01/23 – 25
地点：印度钦奈贸易中心
性质：仅对贸易观众
主办：博闻印度公司
联络：博闻（广州）展览有限公司
☎ 020-8666 0158. 8666 3338 转 1151
🖷 020-8667 7120
Email: info@cmpchina.com
www.jewelleryfair.in

## Gem and Jewelry India International Exhibition 2010

Date：2010/01/23 – 25
Venue: Chennai Trade Center, Chennai, India
Nature: Trade Only
Organizer: UBM India Pvt. Ltd
☎ 011-2376 5551
✉ info@ubmindia.com
Contact: UBM China Ltd – Guangzhou
☎ 86-20-8666 0158. 8666 3338 ext. 1151
🖷 86-20-8667 7120
✉ info@cmpchina.com
www.jewelleryfair.in

## 国际铸造展览会

日期：2010/02/05 - 07
地点：印度艾哈迈德巴德
周期：每年一届
市场范围：国际性
参展联络：中国机械汽车展览联合会
☎ 010-6859 4964
🖷 010-6859 4964

## 印度焊接展览会

日期：2010/02/10 - 12
地点：印度孟买
周期：每年一届
市场范围：国际性
参展联络：中国机械汽车展览联合会
☎ 010-6859 4964
🖷 010-6859 4964

## ACREX India

日期：2010/02/17 –20
地点：印度孟买展览中心
主办：博闻印度公司
联络：博闻（广州）展览有限公司
☎ 020-8666 0158. 8666 3338 转 1151
🖷 020-8667 7120
✉ info@cmpchina.com
www.ubmasia.com

## ACREX India

Date：2010/02/17 –20
Venue: Mumbai, India
Organizer: UBM India Pvt. Ltd
Contact: UBM China Ltd – Guangzhou
☎ 86-20-8666 0158. 8666 3338 ext. 1151
🖷 86-20-8667 7120
✉ info@cmpchina.com
www.ubmasia.com

## 印度旅游贸易展览会

日期：2010/02/18 –20
地点：印度孟买展览中心
主办：博闻印度公司
联络：博闻（广州）展览有限公司
☎ 020-8666 0158. 8666 3338 转 1151
🖷 020-8667 7120
✉ info@cmpchina.com
www.ubmasia.com

## India Travel Trade Expo

Date: 2010/02/18 – 20
Venue: Bombay Exhibition Center, India
Contact: UBM China Ltd – Guangzhou
☎ 86-20-8666 0158. 8666 3338 ext. 1151
🖷 86-20-8667 7120
Email: info@cmpchina.com
www.ubmasia.com

## 2010年印度国际铝展
## Aluminium India 2010

日期：2010/02/25 - 27
地点：印度孟买展览中心
内容：蓬勃发展中的印度铝业市场预计将在未来数年内持续增长。随着印度厂商生产能力的不断扩展、新企业的加入以及当前市场对高品质产品需求的不断增长，印度铝业正在越来越多地采用新科技与新设备以求提升生产质量。为满足印度铝业对国际铝业新技术及新产品的迫切需求，Alcastek（印度国际铝制造技术会议暨贸易展）和励展博览集团将联合举办"印度国际铝展（ALUMINIUM INDIA）"，届时将吸引3,000多名行业决策者、厂商代表、用户及技术研发人员与会观展。而Alcastek印度国际铝制造技术会议也将于同期继续举行，期间将邀请世界级专家共同探讨国际铝业的最新进展、打造高标准的技术交流平台。2010年印度国际铝展（Aluminium India 2010）将在印度铝制造业及汽车制造业的中心举办，是进入印度铝业市场的独特贸易展会平台。
周期：两年一届
市场范围：国际性
参展费用：净地250美元/ $m^2$，标准展位325美元/ $m^2$

参展联络：励展博览集团国际销售部
地址：北京市朝阳区新源里南路1-3号平安国际金融中心A座15层01-03，05（100027）
联系人：王颖
☎ 010-5933 9288
🖷 010-5933 9233
✉ winnie.wang@reedexpo.com.cn
www.reedexport.cn

## 印度国际医疗展

### Medical Fair India

日期：2010/03 -
地点：印度孟买
内容：医疗设备及仪器、医用消耗品、医疗科技、医疗保健品、医院办公设备、医院病房、医用电子仪器、超声仪器等
周期：每年一届
市场范围：国际性
参展联络：京慕国际展览有限公司
地址：北京市朝阳区北三环东路6号中国国际展览中心服务楼3层
联系人：魏亦山
☎ 010-8460 0551
🖷 010-8460 0394
✉ zhaolingna@ciec.com.cn
www.jingmu.com.cn

## 国际石油和天然气展览会

日期：2010/03/03 - 06
地点：印度孟买
周期：每年一届
市场范围：国际性
参展联络：中国机械汽车展览联合会
☎ 010-6859 4964
🖷 010-6859 4964

## 第六届印度国际木工机械家具配件及工具专业展

日期：2010/03/04 - 08
地点：印度
主办：北京邦企展览服务有限公司
地址：北京市朝阳区惠新东街11号紫光发展大厦B1-501（100029）
联系人：雷绍军先生，赖玉宝小姐
☎ 010-6482 3808
🖷 010-6482 3670
✉ bbes@china.com

## 2010印度机械工业和电子家电家居展览会

### 2010 Indian machinery industry and electrical appliances at home show

日期：2010/03/10 - 13
地点：印度孟买展览中心
内容：机床及金属加工设备、配件，印刷机械设备、材料及配件，塑料、包装机械设备、材料及配件，纺织机械设备、材料及配件，纺织机械设备、材料及配件，建筑机械，工程机械设备、材料及配件；搬用机械及设备，轴承及专用设备、机械零配件及相关配套和其他
始办年份：2009
周期：每年一届
市场范围：国际性
参展费用：（3x3m）人民币22,000元
参展联络：深圳市创明展览设计有限公司
地址：广东省深圳市福田区新洲大厦15层（518048）
联系人：雷明，朱利萍
☎ 0755-2393 8881, 2393 8025
🖷 0755-2393 8426
✉ cmffok@163.com
MSN：lm83573425@21cn.com
地址：广州市海珠区新港中路350号C1204（510310）
联系人：周文槟
☎ 020-3405 2086 13710318991
🖷 020-3405 0629
✉ abzhanlan@21cn.com
MSN：gdwenbin@hotmail.com
QQ：406372636

### 2010 Indian machinery industry and electrical appliances at home show

Date：2010/03/10 - 13
Venue: Exhibition Center, Mumbai, India
Profile: Machine tools and metal processing equipment, spare parts, printing machinery and equipment, materials and accessories, plastic, packaging machinery and equipment, materials and accessories, textile machinery and equipment, materials and accessories, textile machinery and equipment, materials and parts, construction machinery, engineering machinery and equipment, materials, and accessories; borrowed machinery and equipment, bearings and special equipment, machinery spare parts and related ancillary and other
Established Year: 2009
Frequency: Annual
Market Area: International
Participated Fee: （3x3m）RMB 22,000
Address: 15/Fl Xinzhou Building, Futian District, Shenzhen, Guangdong
☎ 0755-2393 8881, 2393 8025
🖷 0755-2393 8426
Contact: Rei Ming, Julius Ping
✉ cmffok@163.com
MSN: lm83573425@21cn.com

## 2010 第二届印度国际消费电子、家电及家居用品展

### 2010 The 2nd India International Electronics Fair

日期：2010/03/10 - 13
4361
地点：印度孟买展览中心
内容：消费类电子：视盘机(VCD,DVD,EVD),功放,音响,家庭影院等娱乐产品,数码相机,数码摄像机等影像视频产品,显示器,掌上电脑,电子辞典,电脑等信息技术产品,汽车电子,导航系统,汽车音响. 家电:家用制冷器具,家用空调,家用清洁器具,厨卫电器,居室空气调节电器,个人护理电器,卫生保健电器,水处理电器等. 家居产品:家居装饰品,厨卫用品,家用五金产品和工具,餐具和餐桌用品,灯饰,钟表,园艺用品等.
始办年份：2009
周期：每年一届
市场范围：国际性
参展费用：标准展位费（3x3m$^2$）人民币22,000元，净地（18m$^2$起）人民币2,200元/m$^2$
上届规模 '09：展览面积1,000m$^2$(国外展商面积40m$^2$)，参展商100家（国外展商60家，来自10个国家），参观人数10,000人（专业贸易观众2,000人）
主办：中华人民共和国商务部
承办：商务部外贸发展事务局
地址：广东省深圳市福田区新洲大厦15层深圳市创明展览设计有限公司（518038）
联系人：雷明，朱利萍
☎ 0755-2393 8881, 2193 8025
🖷 0755-2393 7426
✉ cmffok@163.com
MSN：leiming1188@hotmail.com

### 2nd India International Electronics Fair

Date：2010/03/10 - 13
Venue: Bombay Exhibition Center, India
Profile: Consumer Electronics: video player (VCD, DVD, EVD), power amplifier, audio, home theater and other entertainment products, digital cameras, digital video camcorders and other video products, monitors, handheld computers, electronic dictionaries, computers and other information technology products, automotive electronics, navigation systems, car audio. Appliances: Household refrigerating appliances, household air-conditioning, household cleaning appliances, kitchen appliances, room air-conditioning appliances, personal care appliances, health appliances, water treatment appliances. Household Products
Established Year: 2009
Frequency: Annual
Market Area: International
Participated Fee: Standard Booth RMB 22,000 (3x3m), Raw Space (min 18m$^2$) RMB 2,200/m$^2$
Statistics '09: Exhibition Area 1,000m$^2$(foreigners 40m$^2$), Exhibitors 100（foreigners 60, came from 10 countries），Visitors 10,000（trade visitors 2,000）
Organizer: The People's Republic of China Ministry of Commerce
Sponsor: Foreign Trade Development Bureau Ministry of Commerce
Address: 15/Fl Xinzhou Building, Futian District, Shenzhen, Guangdong
☎ 86-755-2393 8881, 2193 8025
🖷 86-755-2393 7426
Contact: Rei Ming, Julius Ping
✉ cmffok@163.com
MSN: leiming1188@hotmail.com

## 印度国际模具及机床展览会

### 7TH DIEMOULD INDIA 201

日期：2010/03/18 - 21
地点：印度班加罗尔
周期：两年一届
市场范围：国际性
参展联络：中国贸促会机械行业分会
地址：北京市西城区三里河路46号（100823）
联系人：孙晓光，吴琼，纪冬冬
☎ 010-68595431，6858 0868，6859 4909，6859 4826
🖷 010-6859 5485
✉ info@ccpitmsc.org
✉ jix@ccpit.org
www.chinamachin.org.cn
www.ccpitmsc.org

## 2010年（第18届）印度国际信息通讯博览会

### 18th Convergence India 2010 International Exhibition and conference

日期：2010/03/23 - 25
地点：印度新德里
周期：每年一届
市场范围：国际性
主办：印度通讯与信息技术部
参展联络：中国邮电器材集团公司国际展览部
地址：北京西城区复兴门内大街156号北京招商国际金融中心A座10层A1008室
联系人：张宝林
☎ 010-6642 6288
🖷 010-6642 6556
www.ptexpo.com.cn

## 印度及中亚国际电力展览会

### POWER-GEN India & Central Asia 2010

日期：2010/04/21 - 23
地点：印度新德里
周期：每年一届
市场范围：国际性
参展联络：中国贸促会机械行业分会
地址：北京市西城区三里河路46号（100823）
联系人：刘博
☎ 010-6859 4807, 6859 4804, 6859 5499
🖷 010-6859 4917
✉ info@ccpitmsc.org
✉ jix@ccpit.org
www.chinamachin.org.cn
www.ccpitmsc.org

## 印度国际机械展览会

### India International Machinery and Equipment Exhibition 2010

日期：2010/05/ -
地点：印度孟买
周期：每年一届
市场范围：国际性
参展联络：中国贸促会机械行业分会
地址：北京市西城区三里河路46号（100823）

联系人：王昊燕
☎ 010-6859 4802
🖷 010-6859 4995
✉ info@ccpitmsc.org
✉ jix@ccpit.org
www.chinamachin.org.cn
www.ccpitmsc.org

## 印度鞋履配饰、原料及技术国际商贸展

日期：2010/05/07 – 09
地点：印度新德里
主办：亚太区皮革展有限公司（亚洲博闻有限公司及SIC集团合办）
☎ 852-2827 6211
🖷 852-2827 7831
✉ sales@aplf.com
www.aplf.com

## fMM&T

Foodware, Materials, Manufacturing and Technology
Date：2010/05/07 – 09
Venue: India Expo Mart, Greater Noida, New Delhi
Organizer: APLF Limited
☎ 852-2827 6211
🖷 852-2827 7831
✉ sales@aplf.com
www.aplf.com

## 海德拉巴珠宝珍珠玉石展览会

日期：2010/06/18 – 20
地点：印度海德拉巴
内容：成品首饰、珠宝首饰、钻石、宝石、珍珠及银饰
主办：亚洲博闻有限公司
联络：博闻（广州）展览有限公司
☎ 020-8666 0158. 8666 3338 转 1151
🖷 020-8667 7120
www.ubmasia.com

## Hyderabad Jewelry, Pearl & Gem Fair

Date: 2010/06/18 – 20
Venue: Hitex Exhibition Center, India
Organizer: USB Asia
Contact: UBM China Ltd – Guangzhou
☎ 86-20-8666 0158. 8666 3338 ext. 1151
🖷 86-20-8667 7120
✉ info@cmpchina.com
www.ubmasia.com

## 嵌入式系统会议（印度）

日期：2010/07/21 – 23
地点：印度班加洛Nimhans Convention Center
主办：亚洲博闻有限公司
联络：博闻（广州）展览有限公司
☎ 020-8666 0158. 8666 3338 转 1151
🖷 020-8667 7120
www.ubmasia.com

## 亚洲国际机床展览会

## AMTEX 2010

日期：2010/07/23 - 26
地点：印度新德里
周期：每年一届
市场范围：国际性
参展联络：中国贸促会机械行业分会
地址：北京市西城区三里河路46号（100823）
联系人：周海明，叶海青，聂飞
☎ 010-6859 5495, 6859 5247, 6851 3586, 6859 4938
🖷 010-6859 5057
✉ info@ccpitmsc.org
✉ jix@ccpit.org
www.chinamachin.org.cn
www.ccpitmsc.org

## 印度国际自动化设备暨机器人展览会

## AUTOMATION 2010

日期：2010/09 -
地点：印度孟买
周期：两年一届
市场范围：国际性
参展联络：中国贸促会机械行业分会
地址：北京市西城区三里河路46号（100823）
联系人：王建飞
☎ 010-6859 4952
🖷 010-6859 4995
✉ info@ccpitmsc.org
✉ jix@ccpit.org
www.chinamachin.org.cn
www.ccpitmsc.org

## 班加罗尔国际电子元器件展

## ELECTRONIC INDIA

日期：2010/09 -
地点：印度班加罗尔班加罗尔
内容：各种电子元件，半导体，线缆，电源，传感器，继电器，开关，连接器，显示器，电机， PCB等
周期：每年一届
市场范围：国际性
参展联络：京慕国际展览有限公司
地址：北京市朝阳区北三环东路6号中国国际展览中心服务楼3层
联系人：韩芳；俞亮
☎ 010-8460 0551
🖷 010-8460 0394
✉ zhaolingna@ciec.com.cn
www.jingmu.com.cn

## 南亚地球物理学研讨会

日期：2010/9/17 - 19
地点：印度新德里
内容：勘探、测井、数据采集分析、成像、定位
主办：北京邦企展览有限公司
地址：北京市朝阳区惠新东街11号紫光发展大厦B1-501（100029）
联系人：雷邵军、赖玉宝
☎ 010-6482 3808
🖷 010-6482 3670
✉ bbes@china.com

## Interop India

日期：2010/09/28 – 30
地点：印度孟买展览中心
主办：亚洲博闻有限公司
联络：博闻（广州）展览有限公司
☎ 020-8666 0158. 8666 3338 转 1151
🖷 020-8667 7120
✉ info@cmpchina.com
www.ubmasia.com

## 国际食品加工技术和包装展览会

日期：2010/09/30 – 10/03
地点：印度孟买
周期：每年一届
市场范围：国际性
参展联络：中国机械汽车展览联合会
☎ 010-6859 4964
🖷 010-6859 4964

## 孟买国际家具展览会

## INDEX MUBAI 2010

日期：2010/10/08 - 12
地点：印度孟买
周期：每年一届
市场范围：国际性
参展联络：大连上选会展服务有限公司
地址：大连市西岗区鞍山路13号兴业广场大厦B座508室（116011）
☎ 0411-8378 8326, 8378 8396, 8378 9165, 8378 8821
🖷 0411-8378 8830, 8378 8823
✉ cicyhuang@vip.sina.com
MSN：cicyhuang@msn.com
www.sun-show.com

## INDEX MUBAI 2010

Date：2010/10/08 - 12
Venue: India
Frequency: Annual
Market Area: International
Organizer: Dalian Sun Show Convention & Exhibition Service Co Ltd
☎ 86-411-8378 8326, 8378 8396, 8378 9165
🖷 86-411-8378 8830, 8378 8823
✉ cicyhuang@vip.sina.com
MSN: cicyhuang@msn.com
www.sun-show.com

## 印度食品配料展

日期：2010/10/22 – 23
地点：印度孟买展览中心
主办：亚洲博闻有限公司
联络：博闻（广州）展览有限公司
☎ 020-8666 0158. 8666 3338 转 1151
🖷 020-8667 7120
✉ info@cmpchina.com
www.ubmasia.com

## Food Ingredients India 2010

Date：2010/10/22 – 23
Venue: Mumbai, India
Organizer: UBM India Pvt Ltd
☎ 91-22-6612 2600
UMB Asia Ltd
☎ 852-2516 1634
🖷 852-2802 9934
www.ubmasia.com

## 2010年印度国际包装塑料展览会

日期：2010/11 -
地点：印度
主办：北京邦企展览服务有限公司
地址：北京市朝阳区惠新东街11号紫光发展大厦B1-501（100029）
联系人：雷绍军先生，赖玉宝小姐
☎ 010-6482 3808
🖷 010-6482 3670
✉ bbes@china.com

## 第7届工程机械展览会

日期：2010/11 -
地点：印度班加罗尔
周期：每年一届
市场范围：国际性
参展联络：中国机械汽车展览联合会
☎ 010-6859 4964
🖷 010-6859 4964

## 国际工程及工业自动化展览会

日期：2010/12 -
地点：印度孟买
周期：每年一届
市场范围：国际性
参展联络：中国机械汽车展览联合会
☎ 010-6859 4964

## 印度国际安全与消防技术设备展览会
## 内部安全展览会
## 印度防火展

日期：2010/11/23 – 25
地点：印度孟买展览中心
主办：亚洲博闻有限公司；博闻印度公司
☎ 852-2827 6211
🖷 852-2827 7831
www.ubmasia.com

## 国际五金工具展览会

日期：2010/12 -
地点：印度金奈
周期：每年一届
市场范围：国际性
参展联络：中国机械汽车展览联合会

☎ 010-6859 4964
🖷 010-6859 4964

### 印度工程机械展
### COMMEX

**日期：** 2010/12 -
**地点：** 印度海得拉巴
**内容：** 工程机械、矿山机械、建筑机械及其配件
**周期：** 每年一届
**市场范围：** 国际性
**参展联络：** 京慕国际展览有限公司
**地址：** 北京市朝阳区北三环东路6号中国国际展览中心服务楼3层
**联系人：** 宋秋爽，刘舰
☎ 010-8460 0551
🖷 010-8460 0394
✉ zhaolingna@ciec.com.cn
www.jingmu.com.cn

### 国际工业装备展览会
### Industrial Automation India 2010

**日期：** 2010/12 -
**地点：** 印度孟买
**周期：** 每年一届
**市场范围：** 国际性
**参展联络：** 中国贸促会机械行业分会
**地址：** 北京市西城区三里河路46号（100823）
**联系人：** 王建飞
☎ 010-6859 4952
🖷 010-6859 4995
✉ info@ccpitmsc.org
✉ jix@ccpit.org
www.chinamachin.org.cn
www.ccpitmsc.org

### 世界制药机械、包装设备与材料印度展
### 国际合同定制服务印度展
### 世界制药机械、包装设备与材料印度展

**日期：** 2010/12/01 - 03
**地点：** 印度孟买展览中心
**主办：** 亚洲博闻有限公司；博闻印度公司
☎ 852-2827 6211
🖷 852-2827 7831
www.ubmasia.com

### P-MEC India 2010
### ICSE India 2010
### CPhI India 2010

**Date:** 2010/12/01 - 03
**Venue:** Bombay Exhibition Center, Mumbai, India
**Organizer:** UMB Asia Ltd
☎ 852-2827 6211
🖷 852-2827 7831
www.ubmasia.com

### 印度石油技术展
### —2011年第9届国际石油与天然气展览会
### PETROTECH-2011 9th International Oil & Gas Conference and Exhibition

**日期：** 2011/01 -
**地点：** 印度新德里Pragati Maidan展览中心
**内容：** 印度石油技术展系列之国际石油与天然气展览会是全球烃工业的一次盛会。博览会围绕石油经济、安全、可持续发展、环境、新兴技术、加工技术等问题进行研讨及经验交流，并展望烃工业的未来发展方向。作为展示印度烃工业的平台，国际石油与天然气展览会每年吸引来自世界各地极具实力的代表团、技术使用及提供商、科学家、工程师、技术（专家）官员、政府官员、主张环保的企业家等齐聚于此。经过多年的稳固发展，第8 届印度国际石油与天然气展览会已成为全球烃工业之不容错过的盛会。
**产品及服务：** 所有烃类产业价值链
**周期：** 两年一届
**市场范围：** 国际性
**参展费用：** 净地展位550美元/m²，标准展位650美元/m²
**主办：** 励展印度公司
**参展联络：** 励展博览集团国际销售部
**地址：** 北京朝阳区新源里南路1-3号平安国际金融中心A座15层01-03，05（100027）
**联系人：** 宫卫
☎ 010-5933 9288
🖷 010-5933 9233
✉ david.gong@reedexpo.com.cn
www.reedexport.cn
www.petrotech2009.org

### 2012年印度国际铝展
### Aluminium India 2012

**日期：** 2012 -
**地点：** 印度孟买展览中心
**内容：** 蓬勃发展中的印度铝业市场预计将在未来数年内持续增长。随着印度厂商生产能力的不断扩展、新企业的加入以及当前市场对高品质产品需求的不断增长，印度铝业正在越来越多地采用新科技与新设备以求提升生产质量。为满足印度铝业对国际铝业新技术及新产品的迫切需求，Alcastek（印度国际铝制造技术会议暨贸易展）和励展博览集团将联合举办"印度国际铝展（ALUMINIUM INDIA）"，届时将吸引3,000多名行业决策者、厂商代表、用户及技术研发人员与会观展。而Alcastek印度国际铝制造技术会议也将于同期继续举行，期间将邀请世界级专家共同探讨国际铝业的最新进展、打造高标准的技术交流平台。2010年印度国际铝展（Aluminium India 2010）将在印度铝制造业及汽车制造业的中心举办，是进入印度铝业市场的独特贸易展会平台。
**周期：** 两年一届
**市场范围：** 国际性
**参展费用：** 净地展位250美元/m²，标准展位325美元/m²
**主办：** 励展博览集团
**参展联络：** 励展博览集团国际销售部
**地址：** 北京市朝阳区新源里南路1-3号平安国际金融中心A座15层01-03，05（100027）
**联系人：** 王颖
☎ 010-5933 9288
🖷 010-5933 9233
✉ winnie.wang@reedexpo.com.cn
www.reedexport.cn

## 印度尼西亚
## Indonesia

### 2010印度尼西亚国际包装技术展览会

**日期：** 2010/05/05 - 08
**地点：** 印度尼西亚亚雅加达国际展览中心
**内容：** 包装机械及加工设备，包装材料、容器及辅助设备，包装设计及创新，协助手动包装的设备和工具，包装设计及创新，包装类纸箱，包装译码和条形码设备，化妆品行业包装设备，环保技术-再生利用类包装，设备、产品、材料，食品、饮料类包装，医药行业包装设备，综合吸塑类包装设备，标签设备，包装业相关的仓储技术
**市场范围：** 国际性
**参展联络：** 正博会议展览（上海）有限公司
**地址：** 上海市浦东新区福山路450号7楼A座（200122）
**联系人：** 朱小姐
☎ 021-5109 5546转8006
🖷 021-6875 2877
✉ cindy@kaigo.com.cn
www.kaigo.com.cn

### 2010印度尼西亚国际汽车、摩托车及零配件展
### INDOAUTOMOTIVE 2010

**日期：** 2010/05/05 - 08
**地点：** 印度尼西亚雅加达会议展览中心
**内容：** 汽车、摩托车整车；各类汽摩零部件、配件；汽车导航系统；汽车制造、操作管理系统；汽车相关维修设备/工具、手工具；汽车相关外围产品及设备包括车用装饰品等；相关机构、组织、杂志
**市场范围：** 国际性
**主办：** PT. Wahana Kemalaniaga Makmur
**参展联络：** 正博会议展览（上海）有限公司
**地址：** 上海市浦东新区福山路450号7楼A座（200122）
**联系人：** 朱小姐
☎ 021-5109 5546转8006
🖷 021-6875 2877
✉ cindy@kaigo.com.cn
www.kaigo.com.cn

### Indo Signtech
### Indo-Powertools
### 8th International Printing, Plastic, Packaging & Food Processing Machinery Fair

（印刷、塑料、包装及食品机械展）
**日期：** 2010/05/13 - 16
**地点：** 印度尼西亚
**周期：** 每年一届
**市场范围：** 国际性
**主办：** 讯通展览公司
**地址：** 香港九龙观塘成业街11号华成工商中心5字楼15室
☎ 852-2763 9011
🖷 852-2341 0379
✉ info@paper-com.com.hk
www.paper-com.com.hk

Indo Signtech
Indo-Powertools
8th International Printing, Plastic, Packaging & Food Processing Machinery Fair / **Date：** 2010/05/13 - 16
**Venue:** Jakarta International Expo, Indonesia
**Frequency:** Annual
**Market Area:** International
**Organizer:** Paper Communication Exhibition Services
**Address:** Rm. 15, 5/F., Wah Shing Centre, 11 Shing Yip St., Kwun Tong, Kowloon, Hong Kong.
☎ 852-2763 9011
🖷 852-2341 0379
✉ info@paper-com.com.hk
www.paper-com.com.hk

### 中国机械和电子产品展览会

**日期：** 2010/05/26 -
**地点：** 印尼雅加达
**周期：** 每年一届
**市场范围：** 国际性
**参展联络：** 中国机械汽车展览联合会
☎ 010-6859 4964
🖷 010-6859 4964
**参展联络：** 中国贸促会机械行业分会
**地址：** 北京市西城区三里河路46号（100823）
**联系人：** 丁苏卫
☎ 010-6859 4989
🖷 010-6859 4995
✉ info@ccpitmsc.org
✉ jix@ccpit.org
www.chinamachin.org.cn
www.ccpitmsc.org

### 印度尼西亚中国工程机械、矿山机械展览会

日期：2010/05/26 - 29
地点：印度尼西亚雅加达
周期：每年一届
市场范围：国际性
参展联络：中国贸促会机械行业分会
地址：北京市西城区三里河路46号（100823）
联系人：杨 明
☎ 010-6859 4937
✉ info@ccpitmsc.org
✉ jix@ccpit.org
www.chinamachin.org.cn
www.ccpitmsc.org

### 国际汽车展览会

日期：2010/07 -
地点：印尼雅加达
周期：每年一届
市场范围：国际性
参展联络：中国机械汽车展览联合会
☎ 010-6859 4964
🖷 010-6859 4964

### 亚洲食品配料展

日期：2010/09/29 – 10/01
地点：印尼雅加达国际博览馆
主办：亚洲博闻有限公司
☎ 852-2827 6211
🖷 852-2827 7831
www.ubmasia.com
联络：上海博华国际展览有限公司
☎ 021-6437 1178
🖷 021-6437 0982

### 国际医疗器械、医院用品、实验室设备及医药展览会

日期：2010/10/19 - 22
地点：印尼雅加达
周期：每年一届
市场范围：国际性
参展联络：中国机械汽车展览联合会
☎ 010-6859 4964
🖷 010-6859 4964

### 印尼国际汽车制造机械及零部件展览会

International Automobile, Auto Parts & ACCESSORIES Exhibition 2010

日期：2010/12 -
地点：印度尼西亚雅加达
周期：每年一届
市场范围：国际性
参展联络：中国贸促会机械行业分会
地址：北京市西城区三里河路46号（100823）
联系人：范卓英
☎ 010-6859 4952, 6859 4804, 6859 5055
🖷 010-6859 4917
✉ info@ccpitmsc.org
✉ jix@ccpit.org
www.chinamachin.org.cn
www.ccpitmsc.org

### 印尼国际机床及金属工具展览会

日期：2010/12/03 - 06
地点：印尼雅加达
内容：数控机床、精密工程机械、金属加工及零件制造、机械检测
周期：每年一届
主办：北京邦企展览有限公司
地址：北京市朝阳区惠新东街11号紫光发展大厦B1-501（100029）
联系人：雷邵军，赖玉宝
☎ 010-6482 3808
🖷 010-6482 3670
✉ bbes@china.com

## 伊朗 Iran

### 国际石油及天然气设备展览会

日期：2010/05 -
地点：伊朗德黑兰
周期：每年一届
市场范围：国际性
参展联络：中国机械汽车展览联合会
☎ 010-6859 4964
🖷 010-6859 4964

### 伊朗国际工程机械、建材机械及矿山机械展览会

Iran Conmin 2010

日期：2010/06 -
地点：伊朗德黑兰
周期：两年一届
市场范围：国际性
参展联络：中国贸促会机械行业分会
地址：北京市西城区三里河路46号（100823）
联系人：康薇
☎ 010-6859 4982
✉ info@ccpitmsc.org
✉ jix@ccpit.org
www.chinamachin.org.cn
www.ccpitmsc.org

### 第10届伊朗国际建筑建材展

日期：2010/07 -
地点：伊朗德黑兰
内容：建筑建材
市场范围：国际性
参展联络：北京中仕达兴业展览有限公司
地址：北京市海淀区蓝靛厂东路2号金源时代商务中心2号楼A座11B（100097）
联系人：贾倩，赵仕忱，牟向东，张露
☎ 010-5129 8900
🖷 010-8886 2939
✉ mail@chinstar.cn
www.chinstar.cn

### 第9届伊朗国际建材石材及工程机械矿业展

日期：2010/07/05 - 08
地点：伊朗德黑兰
内容：建材石材及工程机械矿业
市场范围：国际性
参展联络：北京中仕达兴业展览有限公司
地址：北京市海淀区蓝靛厂东路2号金源时代商务中心2号楼A座11B（100097）
联系人：贾倩，赵仕忱，牟向东，张露
☎ 010-5129 8900
🖷 010-8886 2939
✉ mail@chinstar.cn
www.chinstar.cn

### 中国工业展览会

日期：2010/10 -
地点：伊朗德黑兰
周期：每年一届
市场范围：国际性
参展联络：中国机械汽车展览联合会
☎ 010-6859 4964
🖷 010-6859 4964

### 国际供暖、制冷、空调与通风展览会

日期：2010/10 -
地点：伊朗德黑兰
周期：每年一届
市场范围：国际性
参展联络：中国机械汽车展览联合会
☎ 010-6859 4964
🖷 010-6859 4964

### 国际工业博览会

日期：2010/10/06 - 09
地点：伊朗德黑兰
周期：每年一届
市场范围：国际性
参展联络：中国机械汽车展览联合会
☎ 010-6859 4964
🖷 010-6859 4964

### 伊朗国际汽车零配件展览会

日期：2010/11 -
地点：伊朗德黑兰
周期：每年一届
市场范围：国际性
主办：法兰克福展览公司
参展联络：中国汽车工业国际合作总公司
地址：北京市海淀区中关村丹棱街3号A座5层（100080）
联系人：何萌
☎ 010-8260 6880
🖷 010-8260 6883
✉ exhibition@cnaico.com.cn

### 国际橡胶机械展览会

日期：2010/11 -
地点：伊朗德黑兰
周期：每年一届
市场范围：国际性
参展联络：中国机械汽车展览联合会
☎ 010-6859 4964
🖷 010-6859 4964

## 伊拉克 Iraq

### 第五届伊拉克重建国际工业展览会

IRAQ INTERNATIONAL FAIR 2010

日期：2010/11/ -
地点：伊拉克巴格达
周期：每年一届
参展联络：中国贸促会机械行业分会
地址：北京市西城区三里河路46号（100823）
联系人：罗红
☎ 010-6851 2883
🖷 010-6859 4995
✉ info@ccpitmsc.org
✉ jix@ccpit.org
www.chinamachin.org.cn
www.ccpitmsc.org

## 意大利 Italy

### 米兰马契夫国际博览会（春季）

Macef Spring / Autumn

日期：2010/01/16 - 19
地点：意大利米兰意大利
内容：水晶、玻璃制品、流行首饰及配饰、厨房用品、家庭用品、家居装饰品、装饰画、节庆装饰品
周期：每年两届
市场范围：国际性
参展联络：京慕国际展览有限公司
地址：北京市朝阳区北三环东路6号中国国际展览中心服务楼3层
联系人：王海琼；滕昊
☎ 010-84600551
🖷 010-84600394
✉ zhaolingna@ciec.com.cn
www.jingmu.com.cn

## 2010年法兰克福（罗马）国际汽车配件及售后服务展览会

### Automechanika Roma

**日期：**2010/02/11 - 14
**地点：**意大利罗马
**内容：**汽车配件及零部件、汽车修理保养产品设备、车轮、车内娱乐及音箱系统和设备、汽车加工产品、加油站设备、电池电源、空调制冷、汽车装饰、电子机械系统、发动机、工具、涂料、安全系统等。
**周期：**两年一届
**市场范围：**国际性
**主办：**法兰克福展览公司
**参展联络：**中国汽车工业国际合作总公司
**地址：**北京市海淀区中关村丹棱街3号A座5层（100080）
**联系人：**何萌
☎ 010-8260 6880
🖷 010-8260 6883
✉ exhibition@cnaico.com.cn

## 博罗尼亚门窗及室内装修建材展

### Saie Spring

**日期：**2010/03/18 - 21
**地点：**意大利博罗尼亚
**内容：**室内建材、门窗、环保建材、太阳能源再生系统等
**周期：**每年一届
**市场范围：**国际性
**参展联络：**京慕国际展览有限公司
**地址：**北京市朝阳区北三环东路6号中国国际展览中心服务楼3层
**联系人：**许艳；孙铁兵
☎ 010-8460 0551
🖷 010-8460 0394
✉ zhaolingna@ciec.com.cn
www.jingmu.com.cn

## 米兰国际卫浴展

### EXPOBAGNO

**日期：**2010/03/23 - 27
**地点：**意大利米兰国际展览中心Rho新展馆
**内容：**国际知名的、新兴的国际卫浴展，主要展出注重精致、现代、舒适和设计的高端产品。EXPOBAGNO展品的设计和风格满足市场需求，引领时尚潮流。首届展会在新米兰展览中心举办。
**产品及服务：**陶瓷洁具、浴缸、淋浴房及附件、健身设备、按摩浴缸、装饰淋浴隔间、卫浴家具、迷你水疗、贴面材料、瓷砖、大理石、桑拿浴房、龙头及配件、配件、浴室附件以及烘干毛巾架等。
**周期：**两年一届
**市场范围：**国际性
**参展联络：**励展博览集团国际销售部
**地址：**北京朝阳区新源里南路1-3号平安国际金融中心A座15层01-03，05（100027）
**联系人：**宫卫
☎ 010-5933 9288
🖷 010-5933 9233
✉ david.gong@reedexpo.com.cn
www.reedexport.cn

## 意大利米兰供暖、空调、制冷、再生能源及太阳能展

### Mostra Convegno Expocomfort: Production & Distribution line for the HVAC & Plumbing Sector

**日期：**2010/03/23 - 27
**地点：**意大利米兰国际展览中心Rho新展馆
**内容：**MCE（Mostra Convegno Expocomfort）是在民用和工业用供暖、再生能源、空调、制冷、通风、水处理、相关服务及零部件领域首屈一指、最具影响力的国际专业展会。始创于1960年，从1982年起每两年一届在意大利米兰市举行。作为意大利第一个致力于工业的展览，40多年的发展历程证明了MCE是这个领域的领跑者。该展会由米兰国际展览公司（Fiera Milano Exhibitions）和意大利励展展览公司共同组建的合资公司（Fiera Milano International SPA）主办，受到了意大利政府的高度重视，并得到了意大利贸易部、环境和领土保护部、教育研究部的大力支持和赞助。产品及服务 多年来，MCE始终保持着丰富及鲜明的主题，供暖（暖气设备、零部件、工具-器具）；能源（光电 - 太阳能 - 热电、生物能源 - 共生能源、绝缘）；制冷（空调设备、通风装置、商业和工业制冷）；供水（饮水卫生技术、水处理）等四个主要内容历久弥新
**始办年份：**1960
**周期：**两年一届
**市场范围：**国际性
**参展费用：**净地展位：189欧元/m²
**主办：**意大利励展展览公司；米兰国际展览公司
**参展联络：**励展博览集团国际销售部
**地址：**北京朝阳区新源里南路1-3号平安国际金融中心A座15层01-03，05（100027）
**联系人：**宫卫
☎ 010-5933 9288
🖷 010-5933 9233
✉ david.gong@reedexpo.com.cn
www.reedexport.cn

## 国际铸造展览会

**日期：**2010/04 -
**地点：**意大利布雷西亚
**周期：**每年一届
**市场范围：**国际性
**参展联络：**中国机械汽车展览联合会
☎ 010-6859 4964
🖷 010-6849 4964

## 意大利米兰展

### SALONEUFFICIO 2010

**日期：**2010/04/14 - 19
**地点：**意大利米兰
**周期：**每年一届
**市场范围：**国际性
**参展联络：**大连上选会展服务有限公司
**地址：**大连市西岗区鞍山路13号兴业广场大厦B座508室（116011）
☎ 0411-8378 8326, 8378 8396, 8378 9165, 8378 8821
🖷 0411-8378 8830, 8378 8823
✉ cicyhuang@vip.sina.com
MSN：cicyhuang@msn.com
www.sun-show.com

### SALONEUFFICIO 2010

**Date：**2010/04/14 - 19
**Venue:** Italy
**Frequency:** Annual
**Market Area:** International
**Organizer:** Dalian Sun Show Convention & Exhibition Service Co Ltd
☎ 0411-8378 8326, 8378 8396, 8378 9165
🖷 0411-8378 8830, 8378 8823
✉ cicyhuang@vip.sina.com
MSN: cicyhuang@msn.com
www.sun-show.com

## 国际流体传动与控制展览会

FLUIDTRANS 2010

**日期：**2010/05/04 - 07
**地点：**意大利米兰
**周期：**两年一届
**市场范围：**国际性
**参展联络：**中国机械汽车展览联合会
☎ 010-6859 4964
🖷 010-6849 4964
**参展联络：**中国贸促会机械行业分会
**地址：**北京市西城区三里河路46号（100823）
**联系人：**李华龙，曹姗姗，李静
☎ 010-6859 5039, 6859 5043, 6859 5067
🖷 010-6857 2287
✉ info@ccpitmsc.org
✉ jix@ccpit.org
www.chinamachin.org.cn
www.ccpitmsc.org

## 意大利国际木工机械及技术展览会

### XYLEXPO 2010

**日期：**2010/05/04 - 08
**地点：**意大利米兰
**周期：**两年一届
**市场范围：**国际性
**参展联络：**中国贸促会机械行业分会
**地址：**北京市西城区三里河路46号（100823）
**联系人：**严立群
☎ 010-6859 4807, 6859 4804, 6859 5499
🖷 010-6859 4917
✉ info@ccpitmsc.org
✉ jix@ccpit.org
www.chinamachin.org.cn
www.ccpitmsc.org

## 米兰马契夫国际博览会（秋季）

### Macef Spring / Autumn

**日期：**2010/09 -
**地点：**意大利米兰
**内容：**水晶、玻璃制品、流行首饰及配饰、厨房用品、家庭用品、家居装饰品、装饰画、节庆装饰品等
**周期：**每年两届
**市场范围：**国际性
**参展联络：**京慕国际展览有限公司
**地址：**北京市朝阳区北三环东路6号中国国际展览中心服务楼3层
**联系人：**王海琼；滕昊
☎ 010-8460 0551
🖷 010-8460 0394
✉ zhaolingna@ciec.com.cn
www.jingmu.com.cn

## 博罗尼亚国际建筑业博览会

### Saie

**日期：**2010/10 -
**地点：**意大利博洛尼亚
**内容：**建筑机械、建材加工设备、建筑材料的生产设备和机械及设备、电动工具、紧固件；水处理系统等
**周期：**每年一届
**市场范围：**国际性
**参展联络：**京慕国际展览有限公司
**地址：**北京市朝阳区北三环东路6号中国国际展览中心服务楼3层
**联系人：**安红彦，孙铁兵
☎ 010-8460 0551
🖷 010-8460 0394
✉ zhaolingna@ciec.com.cn
www.jingmu.com.cn

## 欧洲户外休闲与沙滩用品贸易展

### The SUN

**日期：**2010/10 -
**地点：**意大利里米尼
**内容：**运动休闲服饰及鞋类、背包、野营用品、登山及攀岩用品、渔具、自行车运动用品、滑板车、水上运动等
**周期：**每年一届

市场范围：国际性
参展联络：京慕国际展览有限公司
地址：北京市朝阳区北三环东路6号中国国际展览中心服务楼3层
联系人：薛亮，孙铁兵
☎ 010-8460 0551
℻ 010-8460 0394
✉ zhaolingna@ciec.com.cn
www.jingmu.com.cn

## 意大利国际牙科器具及材料展

### International Expodental

日期：2010/10/15 - 17
地点：意大利罗马
内容：牙科医疗器械与设备；牙科医疗材料、工具；颌面外科专用器械、材料；牙体牙髓专用器械、材料；牙周病科专用器械、材料；正畸专用器械、材料
周期：每年一届
市场范围：国际性
参展联络：京慕国际展览有限公司
地址：北京市朝阳区北三环东路6号中国国际展览中心服务楼3层
联系人：安红彦，孙铁兵
☎ 010-8460 0551
℻ 010-8460 0394
✉ zhaolingna@ciec.com.cn
www.jingmu.com.cn

## 意大利里米尼国际户外、设计及装饰材料博览会

### The SUN

日期：2010/10/28 - 31
地点：意大利里米尼
内容：运动休闲服饰及鞋类、背包、野营用品、帐篷、休闲桌椅、登山及攀岩用品、渔具用品、自行车运动用品、滑板车、滑板、水上运动用品、户外休闲用品与配件等
周期：每年一届
市场范围：国际性
参展联络：京慕国际展览有限公司
地址：北京市朝阳区北三环东路6号中国国际展览中心服务楼3层
联系人：薛亮，孙铁兵
☎ 010-8460 0551
℻ 010-8460 0394
✉ zhaolingna@ciec.com.cn
www.jingmu.com.cn

### The SUN

Date：2010/10/28 - 31
Venue: Rimini, Italy
Frequency: Annual
Market Area: International
Organizer: Jing Mu International Exhibition Co Ltd
Address: 6 East Beisanhuan Rd., Beijing 100028, China
☎ 86-10-8460 0551
℻ 86-10-8460 0394
✉ zhaolingna@ciec.com.cn
www.jingmu.com.cn

## 米兰摩托车贸易博览会

### EICMA MOTO

日期：2010/11 -
地点：意大利米兰
内容：摩托车、两轮车及配件、附件、头盔、摩托服及用具等
周期：每年一届
市场范围：国际性
参展联络：京慕国际展览有限公司
地址：北京市朝阳区北三环东路6号中国国际展览中心服务楼3层
联系人：张辉，刘舰
☎ 010-8460 0551
℻ 010-8460 0394
✉ zhaolingna@ciec.com.cn
www.jingmu.com.cn

### EICMA MOTO

Date：2010/11 -
Venue: Milan, Italy
Frequency: Annual
Market Area: International
Organizer: Jing Mu International Exhibition Co Ltd
Address: 6 East Beisanhuan Rd., Beijing 100028, China
☎ 86-10-8460 0551
℻ 86-10-8460 0394
✉ zhaolingna@ciec.com.cn
www.jingmu.com.cn

## 国际能源回收与可持续发展贸易博览会

### ECOMONDO

日期：2010/11 -
地点：意大利里米尼
内容：废弃物再生循环，可再生能源，民用工业与农业中水的再利用，空气质量监控
周期：每年一届
市场范围：国际性
参展联络：京慕国际展览有限公司
地址：北京市朝阳区北三环东路6号中国国际展览中心服务楼3层
联系人：薛亮，孙铁兵
☎ 010-8460 0551
℻ 010-8460 0394
✉ zhaolingna@ciec.com.cn
www.jingmu.com.cn

### ECOMONDO

Date：2010/11 -
Venue: Rimini, Italy
Frequency: Annual
Market Area: International
Organizer: Jing Mu International Exhibition Co Ltd
Address: 6 East Beisanhuan Rd., Beijing 100028, China
☎ 86-10-8460 0551
℻ 86-10-8460 0394
✉ zhaolingna@ciec.com.cn
www.jingmu.com.cn

## 意大利国际视觉传播展

### Viscom Visual Communication Italy: The International Trade Fair on Visual Communication & Events Services

日期：2010/11 -
地点：意大利米兰展览中心
内容：意大利国际视觉传播展是欧洲最大的视觉传播业展会。
产品及服务：标志及标志制作、数码印刷及成像、大幅面数码印刷、POP广告、移动印刷、雕铣、营销物品及服装、活动服务以及传播
周期：每年一届
市场范围：国际性
参展费用：净地展位253欧元/m²，标准展位315欧元/m²
参展联络：励展博览集团国际销售部
地址：北京市朝阳区新源里南路1-3号平安国际金融中心A座15层01-03，05（100027）
联系人：王亮
☎ 010-5933 9288
℻ 010-5933 9233
✉ liang.wang@reedexpo.com.cn
www.reedexport.cn

## 2010年第68届意大利米兰国际摩托车及自行车展览会

### 2010 EICMA Show

日期：2010/11/10 - 15
地点：意大利米兰新国际展览中心
内容：摩托车、电动摩托车、动力车、助动车、踏板车、零配件、轮胎及胎圈、发动机及组件、电动设备、生产设备、工具设备、摩托服及用具、防护用品、原材料、半成品、润滑油和包装材料、摩托车旅游及相关户外用品等。
周期：每年一届
市场范围：国际性
上届规模 '08：展览面积300,000m²，参展商1,560家，参观人数500,000人
主办：意大利国际展览集团
参展联络：杭州思诺博会展服务有限公司
地址：杭州市体育场路229号浙江粮油大厦1202室（310003）
☎ 0571-8577 8500
℻ 0571-8577 9709
✉ expo@sinobal.com
www.sinobal.com

## 国际农业机械展览会

日期：2010/11/12 - 16
地点：意大利博洛尼亚
周期：每年一届
市场范围：国际性
参展联络：中国机械汽车展览联合会
☎ 010-6859 4964
℻ 010-6859 4964

## 意大利安全及防护用品展览会

### SICUREZZA

日期：2010/11/16 - 19
地点：意大利米兰
内容：商业安全防护类，CCTV及监视系统、门禁系统、报警系统、犯罪预警设备、监控巡逻设备
周期：每年一届
市场范围：国际性
参展联络：京慕国际展览有限公司
地址：北京市朝阳区北三环东路6号中国国际展览中心服务楼3层
联系人：国曦，薛磊
☎ 010-8460 0551
℻ 010-8460 0394
✉ zhaolingna@ciec.com.cn
www.jingmu.com.cn

## 意大利劳保用品展览会

### SICURTECH Expo

日期：2010/11/16 - 19
地点：意大利米兰
内容：个人防护设备（手套、工装、安全鞋、反光材料等）工作环境下安全的传送装置、噪音防护方面的软硬件设备、防火设备、放射防护、触电保护、安全组织和服务等
周期：每年一届
市场范围：国际性
参展联络：京慕国际展览有限公司
地址：北京市朝阳区北三环东路6号中国国际展览中心服务楼3层
联系人：国曦，薛磊
☎ 010-8460 0551
℻ 010-8460 0394
✉ zhaolingna@ciec.com.cn
www.jingmu.com.cn

### SICURTECH Expo

Date：2010/11/16 - 19
Venue: Milan, Italy
Frequency: Annual
Market Area: International
Organizer: Jing Mu International Exhibition Co Ltd
Address: 6 East Beisanhuan Rd., Beijing 100028, China
☎ 86-10-8460 0551
℻ 86-10-8460 0394

✉ zhaolingna@ciec.com.cn
www.jingmu.com.cn

### 意大利米兰供暖、空调、制冷、再生能源及太阳能展

Mostra Convegno Expocomfort: Production & Distribution Line for the HVAC & Plumbing Sector

www.mcexpocomfort.it

**日期：** 2012/03 -
**地点：** 意大利米兰国际展览中心Rho新展馆
**内容：** MCE（Mostra Convegno Expocomfort）是在民用和工业用供暖、再生能源、空调、制冷、通风、水处理、相关服务及零部件领域首屈一指、最具影响力的国际专业展会。始创于1960年，从1982年起每两年一届在意大利米兰市举行。作为意大利第一个致力于工业的展览，40多年的发展历程证明了MCE是这个领域的领跑者。该展会由米兰国际展览公司（Fiera Milano Exhibitions）和意大利励展展览公司共同组建的合资公司（Fiera Milano International SPA）主办，受到了意大利政府的高度重视，并得到了意大利贸易部、环境和领土保护部、教育研究部的大力支持和赞助。
**产品及服务：** 多年来，MCE始终保持着丰富及鲜明的主题，供暖（暖气设备、零部件、工具、器具）；能源（光电、太阳能、热电、生物能源、共生能源、绝缘）；制冷(空调设备、通风装置、商业和工业制冷)；供水(饮水卫生技术、水处理）等四个主要内容历久弥新
**始办年份：** 1960
**周期：** 两年一届
**市场范围：** 国际性
**参展费用：** 净地展位189欧元/$m^2$
**主办：** 意大利励展展览公司；米兰国际展览公司
**参展联络：** 励展博览集团国际销售部
**地址：** 北京朝阳区新源里南路1-3号平安国际金融中心A座15层01-03、05（100027）
**联系人：** 宫卫
☎ 010-5933 9288
🖷 010-5933 9233
✉ david.gong@reedexpo.com.cn
www.reedexport.cn

### 米兰国际卫浴展

EXPOBAGNO

**日期：** 2012/03 -
**地点：** 意大利米兰国际展览中心Rho新展馆
**内容：** 国际知名的、新兴的国际卫浴展，主要展出注重精致、现代、舒适和设计的高端产品。EXPOBAGNO展品的设计和风格满足市场需求，引领时尚潮流。首届展会在新米兰展览中心举办。
**产品及服务：** 陶瓷洁具、浴缸、淋浴房及附件、健身设备、按摩浴缸、装饰淋浴隔间、卫浴家具、迷你水疗、贴面材料、瓷砖、大理石、桑拿浴房、龙头及配件、配件、浴室附件以及烘干毛巾架等。
**周期：** 两年一届
**市场范围：** 国际性
**参展联络：** 励展博览集团国际销售部
**地址：** 北京朝阳区新源里南路1-3号平安国际金融中心A座15层01-03、05（100027）
**联系人：** 宫卫
☎ 010-5933 9288
🖷 010-5933 9233
✉ david.gong@reedexpo.com.cn
www.reedexport.cn

# 日本
# Japan

### 日本汽车电子展

Intl Automotive Electronics Technology Expo (CAR-ELE JAPAN)

**Int'l Automotive Electronics Technology Expo** CAR-ELE JAPAN

**日期：** 2010/01/20 - 22
**地点：** 日本东京国际展示场
**内容：** 日本汽车电子展(CAR-ELE JAPAN)是日本首个国际展会，展品范围涵盖所有汽车电子技术。
**周期：** 每年一届
**市场范围：** 国际性
**赞助：** INCOM CO LTD；AUTOMOTIVE ELECTRONICS GICHO PUBLISHING & ADVERTISING CO LTD；KOGYOCHOSAKAI PUBLISHING CO LTD；COSMO BRAINS CORP；SANGYO TIMES INC；ELECTRONIC JOURNAL INC；THE NIKKAN KOGYO SHIMBUN LTD；JAPAN INDUSTRIAL PUBLISH
**主办：** 励展日本公司
**参展联络：** 励展博览集团国际销售部
**地址：** 北京朝阳区新源里南路1-3号平安国际金融中心A座15层01-03、05（100027）
**联系人：** 杜一鸣
☎ 010-5933 9288
🖷 010-5933 9233
✉ martin.du@reedexpo.com.cn
www.reedexport.cn

### 2010日本东京春季国际礼品博览会

**日期：** 2010/02/02 - 05
**地点：** 日本东京
**内容：** 东京国际礼品博览会是日本最大、最负盛名的礼品及装饰品博览会。每年分春秋两季举行。本届是第69届博览会，来自全球的2,450多家参展商将在86,410$m^2$的展览面积上展示最新潮流的精品。届时，将吸引世界各地逾200,000买家将与会洽谈。深受中西双重文化的熏陶和影响的日本人十分重视各种中西方的节日。每逢节日他们都会精心挑选礼物相互馈赠。因此日本的消费市场（金额高达1200亿美元）是全球最大的市场之一，为各国的出口企业都展开了诱人的前景。该展会为国内企业开拓日本市场提供了一条最便捷有效的途径。
　　展品范围：工艺品、节日用品、饰品、家居时尚精品、人造花、个性化小礼品、玻璃制品、家居用品、户外用品、室内装饰品、办公文具及纸制品、包装饰品、箱包及皮革制品、编织品、毛绒玩具、机动玩具、美容用品、浴室和床上用品、青少年用品、珠宝及时尚饰品、体育及休闲用品、宠物用品、IT产品等。
**始办年份：** 1976
**周期：** 每年两届
**市场范围：** 国际性
**联络：** 广州市海珠区新港中路350号C1204（510310）
**联系人：** 周文槟
☎ 020-3405 2086 13710318991
🖷 020-3405 0629
✉ dbzh88@163.com
MSN：gdwenbin@hotmail.com
QQ：406372636

### 综合医疗展及会议
### 医疗护理食品博览会

**日期：** 2010/02/09 –10
**地点：** 日本东京有明国际展览中心
**主办：** 博闻日本公司
**联络：** 博闻（广州）展览有限公司
☎ 020-8666 0158. 8666 3338 转 1151
🖷 020-8667 7120
✉ info@cmpchina.com

### Integrated Medicine Exhibition & Conference

Date：2010/02/09 – 10
Venue: Tokyo Big Sight, Japan
Organizer: UBM
Contact: UBM China Ltd – Guangzhou
☎ 86-20-8666 0158. 8666 3338 ext. 1151
🖷 86-20-8667 7120
Email: info@cmpchina.com

### 国际供暖、通风、空调与制冷展览会

**日期：** 2010/02/16 - 19
**地点：** 日本东京
**周期：** 每年一届
**市场范围：** 国际性
**参展联络：** 中国机械汽车展览联合会
☎ 010-6859 4964
🖷 010-6859 4964

### 网上及流动直销方案展

**日期：** 2010/02/25 – 26
**地点：** 日本东京阳光城市展览中心
**主办：** 博闻日本有限公司
**联络：** 博闻（广州）展览有限公司
☎ 020-8666 0158. 8666 3338 转 1151
🖷 020-8667 7120
✉ info@cmpchina.com
www.ubmasia.com

### Net & Mobile Direct Marketing Solution Fair

Date: 2010/02/25 – 26
Venue: Tokyo, Japan
Organizer: UMB Business Media Co Ltd
Contact: UBM China Ltd – Guangzhou
☎ 86-20-8666 0158. 8666 3338 ext. 1151
🖷 86-20-8667 7120
✉ info@cmpchina.com
www.ubmasia.com

### 东京健康博览会

**日期：** 2010/03/17 – 19
**地点：** 东京阳光城市展览中心
**主办：** 博闻日本有限公司
**联络：** 博闻（广州）展览有限公司
☎ 020-8666 0158. 8666 3338 转 1151
🖷 020-8667 7120
✉ info@cmpchina.com
www.ubmasia.com

### Tokyo Health Industry Show

Date: 2010/03/17 – 19
Venue: Tokyo, Japan
Organizer: UMB Business Media Co Ltd
Contact: UBM China Ltd – Guangzhou
☎ 86-20-8666 0158. 8666 3338 ext. 1151
🖷 86-20-8667 7120
Email: info@cmpchina.com
www.ubmasia.com

### 中国日本纺织成衣博览会（春季）

CFF

**日期：** 2010/03 -
**地点：** 日本大阪
**内容：** 纺织品、成衣、辅料、新技术、新材料
**周期：** 每年两届
**市场范围：** 国际性
**参展联络：** 京慕国际展览有限公司
**地址：** 北京市朝阳区北三环东路6号中国国际展览中心服务楼3层
**联系人：** 由慧；柳川
☎ 010-8460 0551
🖷 010-8460 0394

✉ zhaolingna@ciec.com.cn
www.jingmu.com.cn

## 2010 日本国际食品与饮料展览会
## 2010 Foodex Japan

日期：2010/03/02 - 05
地点：日本千叶幕张展览中心
内容：食品：农产品（新鲜、冷冻、干货）、农产加工品、谷物、畜产品（冷冻、干货）、肉加工品、乳制品、水产品（新鲜、冷冻、干货）、水产加工品、已加工食品、蒸煮袋食品、副食品、西式副食品、调料、香辣佐料、各种面类、西式糕点、甜食。饮料：含酒精饮料（日本酒、烧酒、啤酒、葡萄酒等）饮料、矿泉水、咖啡、红茶、绿茶、以及其它茶类。
始办年份：1976
周期：每年一届
市场范围：国际性
上届规模 '09：展览面积27,911m²，参展商2,393家（来自59个国家），参观人数80,000人
主办：Japan Management Association
参展联络：杭州思诺博会展服务有限公司
地址：杭州市体育场路229号浙江粮油大厦1202室（310003）
☎ 0571-8577 8500
🖷 0571-8577 9709
✉ expo@sinobal.com
www.sinobal.com

## 东京国际光伏发电展览会
## PV EXPO 2010: International Photovoltaic Power Generation Expo

Int'l Photovoltaic Power Generation Expo
PV EXPO

日期：2010/03/03 - 05
地点：日本东京Tokyo Big Sight
内容：2010年东京国际光伏发电展览会是亚洲最大的B to B展会，它汇集了与光伏制造业、太阳能电池、组件和光伏系统有关的各种材料、设备和技术。预期世界范围内的参展商数量为400家、贸易相关观众30,000人次。作为亚洲光伏发电产业综合性最强的展会，2010年东京国际光伏发电展览会将起重要作用。
周期：每年一届
市场范围：国际性
参展费用：欢迎垂询
主办：日本励展博览有限公司
参展联络：励展博览集团国际销售部
地址：北京朝阳区新源里南路1-3号平安国际金融中心A座15层01-03，05（100027）
联系人：杜一鸣
☎ 010-5933 9288
🖷 010-5933 9233
✉ martin.du@reedexpo.com.cn
www.reedexport.cn

## 2010年日本国际汽车售后市场展览会
## IAAE 2010

日期：2010/03/18 - 20
地点：日本东京
周期：每年一届
市场范围：国际性
主办：法兰克福展览公司
参展联络：中国汽车工业国际合作总公司
地址：北京市海淀区中关村丹棱街3号A座5层（100080）
联系人：何萌
☎ 010-8260 6880
🖷 010-8260 6883
✉ exhibition@cnaico.com.cn

## 日本美食佳酿暨酒店及餐饮设备展
## Wine & Gourmet Japan 2010

日期：2010/04/07 - 09
地点：日本东京国际展览中心
内容：罐头食品、乳制品、精制烘焙食品、精制特色食品、食品配料、新鲜食品、冷冻、冷藏食品、精制巧克力、鲜美食品、肉禽制品、海鲜、非酒精饮料（茶和咖啡）、休闲食品、糖果、甜食 葡萄酒、烈酒、啤酒、食品招待和餐饮服务相关设备
始办年份：2009
周期：每年一届
市场范围：国际性
入场券价格：3000日元，预登记者免费
参展费用：高级标准展位355欧元/m²，净地215欧元/m²（18m²起）
上届规模 '09：专业贸易观众60,867人
主办：科隆国际展览有限公司
地址：北京市东三环北路8号亮马河大厦2座1018室（100004）
联系人：徐畅，王迎
☎ 010-6590 7766转 715
🖷 010-6590 6139
✉ j.xu@koelnmesse.cn
www.wineandgourmetjapan.com

## Wine & Gourmet Japan 2009

Date：2010/04/07 - 09
Venue: Tokyo Big Sight, Japan
Established Year: 2009
Frequency: Annual
Market Area: International
Cost to Attend: JP￥3,000
Participated Fee: Standard Booth EUR 355/m², Raw Space EUR 215/m² (min 18m²)
Statistics '09: Trade Visitors 60,867
Organizer: Koelnmesse
Address: Unit 1018, Landmark Tower II, No 8 Dongsanhuan North Rd. Beijing, China
☎ 86-10-6590 7766 ext 715
🖷 86-10-6590 6139
Contact: Joyce Xu, Elan Wang
✉ j.xu@koelnmesse.cn
www.wineandgourmetjapan.com

## 电子电机零配件及材料博览会

日期：2010/04/14 - 16
地点：日本千叶
周期：每年一届
市场范围：国际性
参展联络：中国机械汽车展览联合会
☎ 010-6859 4964
🖷 010-6859 4964

## 第21届日本国际模具暨金属加工展览会
## 21th INTERMOLD 2010

日期：2010/04/14 - 17
地点：日本大阪
周期：两年一届
市场范围：国际性
参展联络：中国贸促会机械行业分会
地址：北京市西城区三里河路46号（100823）
联系人：孙晓光，吴琼，纪冬冬
☎ 010-68595431, 6858 0868, 6859 4909，6859 4826
🖷 010-6859 5485
✉ info@ccpitmsc.org
✉ jix@ccpit.org
www.chinamachin.org.cn
www.ccpitmsc.org

## FPD制造设备及技术国际展览会
## FINETECH JAPAN

FINETECH JAPAN

日期：2010/04/14 - 16
地点：日本东京Big Sight展览中心
内容：世界最大的平面显示器制造业配件、原料、设备及生产技术展，包括液晶显示器（LCD）、等离子显示器（PDP）、有机电激发光显示器（Organic EL）、表面传导电子发射显示器（SED）、场发射显示器（FED）、电子纸显示器（Electronic Paper）等。
周期：每年一届
市场范围：国际性
参展联络：励展博览集团国际销售部
地址：北京朝阳区新源里南路1-3号平安国际金融中心A座15层01-03，05（100027）
联系人：杜一鸣
☎ 010-5933 9288
🖷 010-5933 9233
✉ martin.du@reedexpo.com.cn
www.reedexport.cn

## 焊接展览会

日期：2010/04/21 - 24
地点：日本东京
周期：每年一届
市场范围：国际性
参展联络：中国机械汽车展览联合会
☎ 010-6859 4964
🖷 010-6859 4964

## 世界制药机械、包装设备及材料日本展

日期：2010/04/21 – 23
地点：日本东京有明国际展览中心
内容：制药机械及辅助设备，医药包装机械设备及辅助材料，药品检测及分析仪器设备等
周期：每年一届
主办：博闻日本有限公司
联络：博闻（广州）展览有限公司
☎ 020-8666 0158. 8666 3338 转 1151
🖷 020-8667 7120
✉ info@cmpchina.com
www.ubmasia.com

## P-MEC Japan

Date: 2010/04/21 – 23
Venue: Tokyo Big Sight Exhibition Center
Profile: Analytical Equipment Batching Systems, Equipment Filling equipment Filtration, Separation, Purification Packaging Equipment & Supplies
Frequency：Annual
Organizer: UMB Business Media Co Ltd
Contact: UBM China Ltd – Guangzhou
☎ 86-20-8666 0158. 8666 3338 ext. 1151
🖷 86-20-8667 7120
✉ info@cmpchina.com
www.ubmasia.com

## 国际合同定制服务日本展

日期：2010/04/21 – 23
地点：日本东京有明国际展览中心
主办：博闻日本有限公司
联络：博闻（广州）展览有限公司
☎ 020-8666 0158. 8666 3338 转 1151
🖷 020-8667 7120
✉ info@cmpchina.com
www.ubmasia.com

## ICSE Japan

Date: 2010/04/21 – 23
Venue: Tokyo Big Sight Exhibition Center
Organizer: UMB Business Media Co Ltd
Contact: UBM China Ltd – Guangzhou
☎ 86-20-8666 0158. 8666 3338 ext. 1151
🖷 86-20-8667 7120
✉ info@cmpchina.com
www.ubmasia.com

## 日本国际海事展示会及会议

时间：2010/04/21 – 23
地点：日本东京有明国际展览中心
主办：博闻日本有限公司
联络：博闻（广州）展览有限公司

☎ 020-8666 0158. 8666 3338 转 1151
🖷 020-8667 7120
✉ info@cmpchina.com
www.ubmasia.com

### Sea Japan

Date: 2010/04/21 – 23
Venue: Tokyo Big Sight Exhibition Center
Organizer: UMB Business Media Co Ltd
Contact: UBM China Ltd – Guangzhou
☎ 86-20-8666 0158. 8666 3338 ext. 1151
🖷 86-20-8667 7120
✉ info@cmpchina.com
www.ubmasia.com

### 日本软件开发展览会

SODEC:
Software Development Expo

**日期：**2010/05/12 - 14
**地点：**日本东京国际展览中心
**内容：**东京软件开发展是亚洲嵌入式软件系统领域规模最大的展览会。2008年，该展会吸引了来自全球1,551家领先企业前来参展，这一数据使得东京软件开发展成为该行业的专业展示平台。众多海外企业已透过该平台顺利进入日本市场。凭借展会所取得的瞩目成绩，东京软件开发展每年都在不断地发展壮大，它将为软件行业参展商及观展群众搭建互相联络的高效平台。
**周期：**每年一届
**市场范围：**国际性
**主办：**励展日本公司
**参展联络：**励展博览集团国际销售部
**地址：**北京朝阳区新源里南路1-3号平安国际金融中心A座15层01-03，05（100027）
**联系人：**杜一鸣
☎ 010-5933 9288
🖷 010-5933 9233
✉ martin.du@reedexpo.com.cn
www.reedexport.cn

### 客户服务中心/客户关系管理展览会及会议大阪展

Call Centre/ CRM Demo & Conference Osaka 2010

**日期：**2010/05/26 – 27
**地点：**日本大阪MyDome Osaka
**主办：**亚洲博闻有限公司；博闻日本有限公司
☎ 852-2827 6211
🖷 852-2827 7831
www.ubmasia.com

### 日本（东京）国际食品机械展览会

FOOMA

**日期：**2010/06 -
**地点：**日本东京
**内容：**专用食品机械、加工设备、辅助机械、包装机械等
**周期：**每年一届
**市场范围：**国际性
**参展联络：**京慕国际展览有限公司
**地址：**北京市朝阳区北三环东路6号中国国际展览中心服务楼3层
**联系人：**薛亮，孙铁兵
☎ 010-8460 0551
🖷 010-8460 0394
✉ zhaolingna@ciec.com.cn
www.jingmu.com.cn

### 东京机械零部件及材料技术展

M-Tech: Mechanical Components & Materials Technology Expo

**日期：**2010/06/23 - 25
**地点：**日本东京Big Sight展览中心
**内容：**日本最大的机械零部件、材料及加工装配技术行业贸易展会，是日本机械加工行业的门户平台。
**产品及服务：**轴承、齿轮、离合器、传动带/链条、线性传动、减震、轴封、电机、传感器、其它传动相关的机械零部件、紧固件及紧固技术、螺栓、螺母、垫圈、铆钉、粘结剂与粘合剂、种紧固件及相关产品/技术、工程塑料、塑料、聚合物、金属/有色金属、合金、陶瓷、橡胶、人造橡胶、硅零件、塑料零件/技术、金属零件/技术、橡胶零件/技术、其他材质零件/技术、机械加工技术如冲压、轧制、锻造（压模、脱腊、精密铸造及其他铸造工艺）、成形（射出、转送、吹塑及其他成形工艺）、挤出成形（薄膜、型材、片材及其他挤出成形工艺）、机械、轧制、锻造、成型、表面加工、净化材料、润滑剂、去毛刺技术、表面处理技术、出版物、其他机械零部件。
**周期：**每年一届
**市场范围：**国际性
**参展联络：**励展博览集团国际销售部
**地址：**北京朝阳区新源里南路1-3号平安国际金融中心A座15层01-03，05（100027）
**联系人：**宫卫
☎ 010-5933 9288
🖷 010-5933 9233
✉ david.gong@reedexpo.com.cn
www.reedexport.cn

### 日本东京国际玩具博览会

Tokyo Toy Show

**日期：**2010/07 -
**地点：**日本东京
**内容：**玩具、儿童用品、车船飞机模型、电池、游戏类产品和设备等
**市场范围：**国际性
**参展联络：**京慕国际展览有限公司
**地址：**北京市朝阳区北三环东路6号中国国际展览中心服务楼3层
**联系人：**付颖，古莹
☎ 010-8460 0551
🖷 010-8460 0394
✉ zhaolingna@ciec.com.cn
www.jingmu.com.cn

### 东京国际礼品展览会

International Variety-Gift Expo Tokyo (GIFTEX)

GIFTEX
INTERNATIONAL VARIETY-GIFT EXPO TOKYO

**日期：**2010/07/07 - 09
插入logo，数据库会展编号3450
**地点：**日本东京Big Sight展览中心
**内容：**日本全新的礼品博览会，展品琳琅满目。与亚洲最大的文具行业展会及日本最大的书展同期举行，定会吸引重要买家参观。
**周期：**每年一届
**市场范围：**国际性
**主办：**励展日本公司
**参展联络：**励展博览集团国际销售部
**地址：**北京朝阳区新源里南路1-3号平安国际金融中心A座15层01-03，05（100027）
**联系人：**杜一鸣
☎ 010-5933 9288
🖷 010-5933 9233
✉ martin.du@reedexpo.com.cn
www.reedexport.cn

### 东京国际办公家具展览会

International Office Furniture Expo

OFFICE FURNITURE JAPAN International Office Furniture Expo

**日期：**2010/07/07 - 09
**地点：**日本东京国际展览中心
**内容：**近年来，办公室家具一直吸引着各行各业人士的目光，这是因为办公家具是提高工作效率、优化办公环境、激励员工工作等的一个重要工具。2009年是首次在日本举办的专为办公家具产品举办的展会。快来加入到东京国际办公家具展览会行列中吧，紧跟销售量上升的趋势，扩展贵公司在日本的市场！
**周期：**每年一届
**市场范围：**国际性
**主办：**励展日本公司
**参展联络：**励展博览集团国际销售部
**地址：**北京朝阳区新源里南路1-3号平安国际金融中心A座15层01-03，05（100027）
**联系人：**申健
☎ 010-8518 2644, 5933 9288
🖷 010-5933 9233
✉ jerry.shen@reedexpo.com.cn
www.reedexport.cn

### 东京国际办公机械及设备展览会

OFMEX:
International Office Machines & Equipment Expo Tokyo

**日期：**2010/07/07 - 09
**地点：**日本东京Big Sight展览中心
**内容：**亚洲最佳的办公机械及设备行业展会。
**产品及服务：**复印机、打印机、传真机、电视会议系统、剪裁机、压膜机、装订机、写字板、投影仪、OHP（高架投影仪）、屏幕、工时记录器、磁带复写器、电子文具、空气清新剂、电子打卡机、收银机、计算器、音响系统、电子产品、前台系统、邮寄机、碳粉盒、商业电脑软件、扫描器、办公安全系统。
**周期：**每年一届
**市场范围：**国际性
**赞助：**日本办公机械经销商协会
**主办：**励展日本公司
**参展联络：**励展博览集团国际销售部
**地址：**北京市朝阳区新源里南路1-3号平安国际金融中心A座15层01-03，05（100027）
**联系人：**申健
☎ 010-8518 2644, 5933 9288
🖷 010-5933 9233
✉ jerry.shen@reedexpo.com.cn
www.reedexport.cn

### 日本书展

TIBF: Tokyo International Book Fair

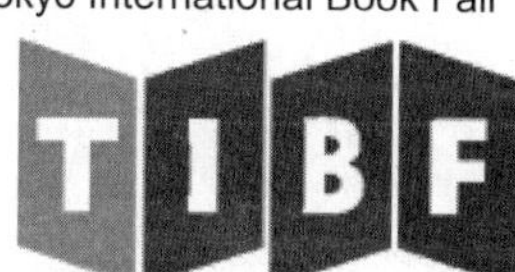


**日期：**2010/07/08 - 11
**地点：**日本东京Tokyo Big Sight
**内容：**日本最大的国际图书展会，由日本书展执委会主办，日本书展执委会由主要的几家出版协会和励展日本公司组成。TIBF是版权谈判、合作出版项目、直接出口方面的理想平台。
**周期：**每年一届
**市场范围：**国际性
**参展费用：**欢迎垂询参展费用

赞助：日本书展执委会
主办：励展日本公司
参展联络：励展博览集团国际销售部
地址：北京朝阳区新源里南路1-3号平安国际金融中心A座15层01-03，05（100027）
☎ 010-5933 9288
🖷 010-5933 9233
✉ david.gong@reedexpo.com.cn
www.reedexport.cn

### 日本国际五金及DIY展览会

### Japan DIY Show 2010

日期：2010/08 -
地点：日本东京
周期：每年一届
市场范围：国际性
参展联络：中国贸促会机械行业分会
地址：北京市西城区三里河路46号（100823）
联系人：江彦明，袁丽娜
☎ 010-6859 4927, 6851 5863
🖷 010-6859 4948
✉ info@ccpitmsc.org
✉ jix@ccpit.org
www.chinamachin.org.cn
www.ccpitmsc.org

### 东京国际礼品博览会（秋季）

### TIGS

日期：2010/09 -
地点：日本
内容：礼品、日用品、家庭用品、装饰品、厨房用品、纺织品、时尚饰品、手表、钟表等
市场范围：国际性
参展联络：京慕国际展览有限公司
地址：北京市朝阳区北三环东路6号中国国际展览中心服务楼3层
联系人：孟琳
☎ 010-84600551
🖷 010-84600394
✉ zhaolingna@ciec.com.cn
www.jingmu.com.cn

### 中国日本纺织成衣博览会（秋季）

### CFF

日期：2010/09 -
地点：日本东京
内容：纺织品、成衣、辅料、新技术、新材料
周期：每年两届
市场范围：国际性
参展联络：京慕国际展览有限公司
地址：北京市朝阳区北三环东路6号中国国际展览中心服务楼3层
联系人：由慧；柳川
☎ 010-8460 0551
🖷 010-8460 0394
✉ zhaolingna@ciec.com.cn
www.jingmu.com.cn

### 日本光电博览会

### INTEROPTO

日期：2010/09 -
地点：日本千叶
内容：光学设备、光学仪器、光学装置、光学元件、光显示、红外技术、光电印刷、光学制造技术、感应器件、激光及光电子、光通讯、光学成像、生产工程设计等
周期：每年一届
市场范围：国际性
参展联络：京慕国际展览有限公司
地址：北京市朝阳区北三环东路6号中国国际展览中心服务楼3层
联系人：宋秋爽；刘舰
☎ 010-8460 0551
🖷 010-8460 0394
✉ zhaolingna@ciec.com.cn
www.jingmu.com.cn

### 日本珠宝展

### Japan Jewelry Fair

日期：2010/09/01 – 03
地点：日本东京有明国际展览中心
主办：亚洲博闻有限公司；博闻日本有限公司
☎ 852-2827 6211
🖷 852-2827 7831
www.ubmasia.com
www.jewellerynetasia.com

### 纤体与美容展

### Diet & Beauty

日期：2010/09/13 – 15
地点：日本东京有明国际展览中心
主办：亚洲博闻有限公司；博闻日本有限公司
☎ 852-2827 6211
🖷 852-2827 7831
www.ubmasia.com
www.dirtandbeauty.jp

### 第四届日本东京国际花园及景观博览会

### Gardex 2010

GARDEX

日期：2010/10 -
地点：日本千叶幕张国际展览中心
内容：日本东京国际花园及景观博览会（Gardex）是目前是日本最大的国际花园贸易展，着眼于各种花园、景观及温室等产品。上一届展会取得了巨大的成功，从全世界各地云集与此的各花园工业公司，都已通过Gardex展会的契机拓展了业务。据展会主办方统计，2008年Gardex展会有超过300家参展企业参展，以及32000多专业观众到会洽谈，希望共同创造出更多的现场销售业绩。同期同馆举行“日本东京国际花卉展IFEX ”，IFEX展由日本植物行业协会和日本励展公司主办的亚洲最大及最重要的花卉园艺贸易展之一。花卉及园艺业的出口商，种植者和制造商云集与此，展出了切花，植物，种子，包装及配件，花盆，花瓶，园艺机械，以及各种形式的花卉相关产品，将有行业专业买家，如零售商，批发商，进口商及从日本各地和亚洲种植商前来参观。日本东京国际花卉展已成为了解日本市场，以及其他国际市场的贸易中心和通往日本市场的大门。因两会同期举行，将吸引更多的展商参展，更多的专业买家参观洽谈，是企业进军日本及亚洲市场不可多得的机会！
周期：每年一届
市场范围：面向贸易观众
主办：日本植物行业协会；日本励展公司
参展联络：励展博览集团国际销售部
地址：北京市朝阳区新源里南路1-3号平安国际金融中心A座15层01-03，05（100027）
联系人：吴祥
☎ 010-8518 9064，5933 9288
🖷 010-5933 9233
✉ ronald.wu@reedexpo.com.cn
www.reedexport.cn

### 国际包装展览会

### TOKYO PACK 2010

日期：2010/10/05 - 08
地点：日本东京
周期：两年一届
市场范围：国际性
参展联络：中国机械汽车展览联合会
☎ 010-6859 4964
🖷 010-6859 4964
参展联络：中国贸促会机械行业分会
地址：北京市西城区三里河路46号（100823）
联系人：吕静，于奇琳，张垚
☎ 010-6859 4909, 6859 5498, 6859 4192
🖷 010-6859 5485
✉ info@ccpitmsc.org
✉ jix@ccpit.org
www.chinamachin.org.cn
www.ccpitmsc.org

### 日本健康食品原料展

### 日本食品安全及品质控制展

### Health Ingredients Japan

日期：2010/10/13 – 15
地点：日本东京有明国际展览中心
主办：亚洲博闻有限公司；博闻日本有限公司
☎ 852-2827 6211
🖷 852-2827 7831
www.ubmasia.com
www.hijapan.info
联络：上海博华国际展览有限公司
☎ 021-6437 1178
🖷 021-6437 0982

### 日本国际机床展览会

### JIMTOF 2010

日期：2010/10/28 - 02
地点：日本东京
周期：两年一届
市场范围：国际性
参展联络：中国贸促会机械行业分会
地址：北京市西城区三里河路46号（100823）
联系人：周海明，叶海青，聂飞
☎ 010-6859 5495, 6859 5247, 6851 3586, 6859 4938
🖷 010-6859 5057
✉ info@ccpitmsc.org
✉ jix@ccpit.org
www.chinamachin.org.cn
www.ccpitmsc.org

### 日本大型连锁零售企业贴标（OEM）采购展

### PRIVATE LABEL SUPPLIERS SHOW

日期：2010/11 -
地点：日本东京
内容：食品、饮料、美容美发、保健等消费品类
周期：每年一届
市场范围：国际性
参展联络：京慕国际展览有限公司
地址：北京市朝阳区北三环东路6号中国国际展览中心服务楼3层
联系人：李嘉羊，古莹
☎ 010-8460 0551
🖷 010-8460 0394
✉ zhaolingna@ciec.com.cn
www.jingmu.com.cn

### PRIVATE LABEL SUPPLIERS SHOW

Date：2010/11 -
Venue: Tokyo, Japan
Frequency: Annual
Market Area: International
Organizer: Jing Mu International Exhibition Co Ltd
Address: 6 East Beisanhuan Rd., Beijing 100028, China
☎ 86-10-8460 0551
🖷 86-10-8460 0394
✉ zhaolingna@ciec.com.cn
www.jingmu.com.cn

### 客户服务中心/客户关系管理展览会及会议

日期：2010/11/10 – 12
地点：日本东京阳光城市展览中心
主办：亚洲博闻有限公司；博闻日本有限公司
☎ 852-2827 6211
🖷 852-2827 7831
www.ubmasia.com

### Call Center/ CRM Demo & Conference 2010

Date: 2010/11/10 – 12
Venue: Tokyo, Japan
Organizer: UMB Asia Ltd
☎ 852-2827 6211
🖷 852-2827 7831
www.ubmasia.com

### 东京国际家具展览会
IFFT / ILL 2010

**日期：**2010/11/24 - 26
**地点：**日本东京
**内容：**该展已申请好国家中小企业补贴，一个展位补贴人民币15000元。针对日本市场
**周期：**每年一届
**市场范围：**国际性
**参展联络：**大连上选会展服务有限公司
**地址：**大连市西岗区鞍山路13号兴业广场大厦B座508室（116011）
☎ 0411-8378 8326, 8378 8396, 8378 9165, 8378 8821
🖷 0411-8378 8830, 8378 8823
✉ cicyhuang@vip.sina.com
MSN：cicyhuang@msn.com
www.sun-show.com

## 日本汽车电子展
(CAR-ELE JAPAN)
Intl Automotive Electronics Technology Expo

Int'l Automotive Electronics Technology Expo CAR-ELE JAPAN

**日期：**2011/01 -
**地点：**日本东京国际展示场
**内容：**日本汽车电子展(CAR-ELE JAPAN)是日本首个国际展会，展品范围涵盖所有汽车电子技术。
**周期：**每年一届
**市场范围：**国际性
**赞助：**INCOM CO LTD；AUTOMOTIVE ELECTRONICS GICHO PUBLISHING & ADVERTISING CO LTD；KOGYOCHOSAKAI PUBLISHING CO LTD；COSMO BRAINS CORP；SANGYO TIMES INC；ELECTRONIC JOURNAL INC；THE NIKKAN KOGYO SHIMBUN LTD；JAPAN INDUSTRIAL PUBLISH
**主办：**励展日本公司
**参展联络：**励展博览集团国际销售部
**地址：**北京朝阳区新源里南路1-3号平安国际金融中心A座15层01-03，05（100027）
**联系人：**杜一鸣
☎ 010-5933 9288
🖷 010-5933 9233
✉ martin.du@reedexpo.com.cn
www.reedexport.cn

### 2011年日本国际食品及饮料展览会
2011 Foodex Japan

**日期：**2011/03 -
**地点：**日本千叶幕张国际会展中心
**内容：**食品：农产品（新鲜、冷冻、干货）、农产加工品、谷物、畜产品（冷冻、干货）、速冻蔬菜、罐头、肉加工品、乳制品、水产品（新鲜、冷冻、干货）、水产加工品、已加工食品、蒸煮袋食品、副食品、西式副食品、调料、香辣佐料、各种面类、西式糕点、甜食。饮料：含酒精饮料（日本酒、烧酒、啤酒、葡萄酒等）饮料、矿泉水、咖啡、红茶、日本茶、以及其它茶类。
**始办年份：**1976
**周期：**每年一届
**市场范围：**国际性
**主办：**Japan Management Association
**参展联络：**杭州思诺博会展服务有限公司
**地址：**杭州市体育场路229号浙江粮油大厦1202室（310003）
☎ 0571-8577 8500
🖷 0571-8577 9709
✉ expo@sinobal.com
www.sinobal.com

## 东京国际光伏发电展览会
PV EXPO 2011:
International Photovoltaic Power Generation Expo

Int'l Photovoltaic Power Generation Expo PV EXPO

**日期：**2011/03 -
**地点：**日本东京Tokyo Big Sight
**内容：**2011年东京国际光伏发电展览会是亚洲最大的B to B展会，它汇集了与光伏制造业、太阳能电池、组件和光伏系统有关的各种材料、设备和技术。预期世界范围内的参展商数量为400家，贸易相关观众30000人次。作为亚洲光伏发电产业综合性最强的展会，2011年东京国际光伏发电展览会将起重要作用。
**周期：**每年一届
**市场范围：**国际性
**参展费用：**欢迎垂询参展费用
**主办：**日本励展博览有限公司
**参展联络：**励展博览集团国际销售部
**地址：**北京朝阳区新源里南路1-3号平安国际金融中心A座15层01-03，05（100027）
**联系人：**杜一鸣
☎ 010-5933 9288
🖷 010-5933 9233
✉ martin.du@reedexpo.com.cn
www.reedexport.cn

## 日本美食佳酿暨酒店及餐饮设备展
Wine & Gourmet Japan 2011

**日期：**2011/04 -
**地点：**日本东京国际展览中心
**内容：**罐头食品、乳制品、精制烘焙食品、精制特色食品、食品配料、新鲜食品、冷冻、冷藏食品、精制巧克力、鲜美食品、肉禽制品、海鲜、非酒精饮料（茶和咖啡）、休闲食品、糖果、甜食 葡萄酒、烈酒、啤酒、食品招待和餐饮服务相关设备
**始办年份：**2009
**周期：**每年一届
**市场范围：**国际性
**入场券价格：**3,000日元，预登记者免费
**参展费用：**高级标摊355欧元/m²，净地215欧元/m²（18m²起）
**上届规模** '09：专业贸易观众60,867人
**主办：**科隆国际展览有限公司
**地址：**北京市东三环北路8号亮马河大厦2座1018室（100004）
**联系人：**徐畅，王迎
☎ 010-6590 7766转 715
🖷 010-6590 6139
✉ j.xu@koelnmesse.cn
www.wineandgourmetjapan.com

### Wine & Gourmet Japan 2011
Date：2011/04 -
Venue: Tokyo Big Sight, Japan
Established Year: 2009
Frequency: Annual
Market Area: International
Cost to Attend: JP￥3,000
Participated Fee: Standard Booth EUR 355/m², Raw Space EUR 215/m²（min 18m²）
Statistics '09: Trade Visitors 60,867
Organizer: Koelnmesse
Address: Unit 1018, Landmark Tower II, No 8 Dongsanhuan North Rd. Beijing, China
☎ 86-10-6590 7766 ext 715
🖷 86-10-6590 6139
Contact: Joyce Xu, Elan Wang
✉ j.xu@koelnmesse.cn
www.wineandgourmetjapan.com

## FPD制造设备及技术国际展览会
FINETECH JAPAN

FINETECH JAPAN

**日期：**2011/04 -
**地点：**日本东京Big Sight展览中心
**内容：**世界最大的平面显示器制造业配件、原料、设备及生产技术展，包括液晶显示器（LCD）、等离子显示器（PDP）、有机电激发光显示器（Organic EL）、表面传导电子发射显示器（SED）、场发射显示器（FED）、电子纸显示器（Electronic Paper）等。
**周期：**每年一届
**市场范围：**国际性
**参展联络：**励展博览集团国际销售部
**地址：**北京朝阳区新源里南路1-3号平安国际金融中心A座15层01-03，05（100027）
**联系人：**杜一鸣
☎ 010-5933 9288
🖷 010-5933 9233
✉ martin.du@reedexpo.com.cn
www.reedexport.cn

## 日本软件开发展览会
SODEC:
Software Development Expo

**日期：**2011/05 -
**地点：**日本东京国际展览中心
**内容：**东京软件开发展是亚洲嵌入式软件系统领域规模最大的展览会。众多海外企业已透过该平台顺利进入日本市场。凭借展会所取得的瞩目成绩，东京软件开发展每年都在不断地发展壮大，它将为软件行业参展商及观展群众搭建互相联络的高效平台。
**周期：**每年一届
**市场范围：**国际性
**主办：**励展日本公司
**参展联络：**励展博览集团国际销售部
**地址：**北京朝阳区新源里南路1-3号平安国际金融中心A座15层01-03，05（100027）
**联系人：**杜一鸣
☎ 010-5933 9288
🖷 010-5933 9233
✉ martin.du@reedexpo.com.cn
www.reedexport.cn

## 东京机械零部件及材料技术展
M-Tech:
Mechanical Components & Materials Technology Expo

**日期：**2011/06 -

**内容：**日本最大的机械零部件、材料及加工装配技术行业贸易展会，是日本机械加工行业的门户平台。
**产品及服务：**轴承、齿轮、离合器、传动带/链条、线性传动、减震、轴封、电机、传感器、其它传动相关的机械零部件、紧固件及紧固技术、螺栓、螺母、垫圈、铆钉、粘结剂与粘合剂、种紧固件及相关产品/技术、工程塑料、塑料、聚合物、金属/有色金属、合金、陶瓷、橡胶、人造橡胶、硅零件、塑料零件/技术、金属零件/技术、橡胶零件/技术、其他材质零件/技术、机械加工技术如冲压、轧制、锻造（压模、脱腊、精密铸造及其他铸造工艺）、成形（射出、转送、吹塑及其他成形工艺）、挤出成形（薄膜、型材、片材及其他挤出成形工艺）、机械、轧制、锻造、成型、表面加工、净化材料、润滑剂、去毛刺技术、表面处理技术、出版物、其他机械零部件。
**周期：**每年一届
**市场范围：**国际性
**主办：**励展博览集团国际销售部
**地址：**北京朝阳区新源里南路1-3号平安国际金融中心A座15层01-03，05（100027）
**联系人：**宫卫

☎ 010-5933 9288
🖷 010-5933 9233
✉ david.gong@reedexpo.com.cn
www.reedexport.cn

### 东京国际办公家具展览会

International Office Furniture Expo

OFFICE FURNITURE JAPAN International Office Furniture Expo

**日期：** 2011/07 -
**地点：** 日本东京国际展览中心
**内容：** 近年来，办公室家具一直吸引着各行各业人士的目光，这是因为办公家具是提高工作效率、优化办公环境、激励员工工作等的一个重要工具。2009年首次在日本举办的专为办公家具产品举办的展会。快来加入到东京国际办公家具展览会行列中吧，紧跟销售量上升的趋势，扩展贵公司在日本的市场！
**周期：** 每年一届
**市场范围：** 国际性
**主办：** 励展日本公司
**参展联络：** 励展博览集团国际销售部
**地址：** 北京朝阳区新源里南路1-3号平安国际金融中心A座15层01-03，05（100027）
**联系人：** 申健
☎ 010-8518 2644, 5933 9288
🖷 010-5933 9233
✉ jerry.shen@reedexpo.com.cn
www.reedexport.cn

### 日本书展

TIBF:
Tokyo International Book Fair

**日期：** 2011/07 -
**地点：** 日本东京Tokyo Big Sight
**内容：** 日本最大的国际图书展会，由日本书展执委会主办，日本书展执委会由主要的几家出版协会和励展日本公司组成。TIBF是版权谈判、合作出版项目、直接出口方面的理想平台。
**周期：** 每年一届
**市场范围：** 国际性
**参展费用：** 欢迎垂询参展费用
**协办：** 日本书展执委会
**主办：** 励展日本公司
**参展联络：** 励展博览集团国际销售部
**地址：** 北京朝阳区新源里南路1-3号平安国际金融中心A座15层01-03，05（100027）
☎ 010-5933 9288
🖷 010-5933 9233
✉ david.gong@reedexpo.com.cn
www.reedexport.cn

### 东京国际礼品展览会

International Variety
- Gift Expo Tokyo (GIFTEX)

GIFTEX INTERNATIONAL VARIETY-GIFT EXPO TOKYO

**日期：** 2011/07 -
**地点：** 日本东京Big Sight展览中心
**内容：** 日本全新的礼品博览会，展品琳琅满目。与亚洲最大的文具行业展会及日本最大的书展同期举行，定会吸引重要买家参观。
**周期：** 每年一届
**市场范围：** 国际性
**主办：** 励展日本公司
**参展联络：** 励展博览集团国际销售部
**地址：** 北京朝阳区新源里南路1-3号平安国际金融中心A座15层01-03，05（100027）
**联系人：** 杜一鸣
☎ 010-5933 9288
🖷 010-5933 9233
✉ martin.du@reedexpo.com.cn
www.reedexport.cn

### 东京国际办公机械及设备展览会

OFMEX: International Office Machines & Equipment Expo Tokyo

**日期：** 2011/07 -
**地点：** 日本东京Big Sight展览中心
**内容：** 亚洲最佳的办公机械及设备行业展会。
**产品及服务：** 复印机、打印机、传真机、电视会议系统、剪裁机、压膜机、装订机、写字板、投影仪、OHP（高架投影仪）、屏幕、工时记录器、磁带复写器、电子文具、空气清新剂、电子打卡机、收银机、计算器、音响系统、电子产品、前台系统、邮寄机、碳粉盒、商业电脑软件、扫描器、办公安全系统。
**周期：** 每年一届
**市场范围：** 国际性
**赞助：** 日本办公机械经销商协会
**主办：** 励展日本公司
**参展联络：** 励展博览集团国际销售部
**地址：** 北京市朝阳区新源里南路1-3号平安国际金融中心A座15层01-03，05（100027）
**联系人：** 申健
☎ 010-8518 2644, 5933 9288
🖷 010-5933 9233
✉ jerry.shen@reedexpo.com.cn
www.reedexport.cn

## 约旦
## Jordan

### 第3届约旦国际建筑建材暨工程机械展

**日期：** 2010/09/27 - 30
**地点：** 约旦安曼
**内容：** 建筑建材暨工程机械
**市场范围：** 国际性
**参展联络：** 北京中仕达兴业展览有限公司
**地址：** 北京市海淀区蓝靛厂东路2号金源时代商务中心2号楼A座11B（100097）
**联系人：** 贾倩，赵仕忱，牟向东，张露
☎ 010-5129 8900
🖷 010-8886 2939
✉ mail@chinstar.cn
www.chinstar.cn

## 哈萨克斯坦
## Kazakhstan

### 国际工程机械及矿业机械展览会

**日期：** 2010/09 -
**地点：** 哈萨克斯坦阿拉木图
**周期：** 每年一届
**市场范围：** 国际性
**参展联络：** 中国机械汽车展览联合会
☎ 010-6859 4964
🖷 010-6859 4964

## 肯尼亚
## Kenya

### 东非肯尼亚建筑机械及材料展览会

**日期：** 2010/05/18 - 22
**地点：** 肯尼亚内罗毕
**内容：** 建筑设备、建筑机械、建筑材料、卫浴等
**周期：** 每年一届
**市场范围：** 国际性
**参展联络：** 京慕国际展览有限公司
**地址：** 北京市朝阳区北三环东路6号中国国际展览中心服务楼3层
**联系人：** 宋秋爽，刘舰
☎ 010-8460 0551
🖷 010-8460 0394
✉ zhaolingna@ciec.com.cn
www.jingmu.com.cn

### 国际贸易展览会

**日期：** 2010/09/28 - 04
**地点：** 肯尼亚内罗毕
**周期：** 每年一届
**市场范围：** 国际性
**参展联络：** 中国机械汽车展览联合会
☎ 010-6859 4964
🖷 010-6859 4964

## 黎巴嫩
## Lebanon

### 2010年第15届黎巴嫩工程建材展会

The 15th International Trade Exhibition for Construction, Building Materials,

**日期：** 2010/06/01 - 04
**地点：** 黎巴嫩贝鲁特国际展会中心
**内容：** 各种重建的基础设施产品、服务、系统包括：石油设备、建筑、制冷、电力、通讯设备、新能源、供水设施、公路、桥梁建设、学校重建、医疗保健、医院及设备、医药、安全设施及服务和环境工具、农业和食品生产设备和机械
市场介绍：黎巴嫩重建展（PROJECT LEBANON）是中东地区规模最大、效果最好的专业览会，该会由原来的黎巴嫩的建材展演变而来，已经成功举办了十四届，是中东地区最具影响力的建材展。为了使机遇最大化并扩大客户的商业领域，IFP的举办此次展会的初衷是为了给跨国际的和地区的客户提供一个独一无二的机会来参加一个同时服务于约旦，伊拉克，叙利亚，黎巴嫩和巴勒斯坦这五个国家市场的展会。
**周期：** 每年一届
**主办：** IFP集团
**联系人：** 杨亚男
☎ 010-8763 5663
🖷 010-8763 5688
✉ ifp5633@ifpchina.com
MSN：laurayangyanan@hotmail.com
www.ifpchina.com

## 利比亚
## Libya

### 第7届利比亚国际建筑建材展

**日期：** 2010/05/16 - 20
**地点：** 利比亚的黎波里
**内容：** 国际建筑建材
**市场范围：** 国际性
**参展联络：** 北京中仕达兴业展览有限公司

**地址**：北京市海淀区蓝靛厂东路2号金源时代商务中心2号楼A座11B（100097）
**联系人**：贾倩，赵仕忱，牟向东，张露
☎ 010-5129 8900
🖷 010-8886 2939
✉ mail@chinstar.cn
www.chinstar.cn

# 科特迪瓦
# Lvory Coast

### 亚洲商品展览会

**日期**：2010/11/19 - 21
**地点**：科特迪瓦阿比让
**周期**：每年一届
**市场范围**：国际性
**参展联络**：中国机械汽车展览联合会
☎ 010-6859 4964
🖷 010-6859 4964

### 电力展览会

**日期**：2010/06 -
**地点**：德国圣彼得堡
**周期**：每年一届
**市场范围**：国际性
**参展联络**：中国机械汽车展览联合会
☎ 010-6859 4964
🖷 010-6859 4964

# 马来西亚
# Malaysia

### 亚太地区海洋石油及天然气展览会

**日期**：2010/03/16 - 18
**地点**：马来西亚吉隆坡
**周期**：每年一届
**市场范围**：国际性
**参展联络**：中国机械汽车展览联合会
☎ 010-6859 4964
🖷 010-6859 4964

### 第十二届马来西亚国防展

**日期**：2010/04/19 - 22
**地点**：马来西亚
**主办**：北京邦企展览服务有限公司
**地址**：北京市朝阳区惠新东街11号紫光发展大厦B1-501（100029）
**联系人**：雷绍军先生，赖玉宝小姐
☎ 010-6482 3808
🖷 010-6482 3670
✉ bbes@china.com

### 马来西亚国际精密工程机床金属工业设备展

**日期**：2010/05/07 - 09
**地点**：马来西亚吉隆坡
**内容**：数控机床、精密工程机械、金属加工及零配件制造
**主办**：北京邦企展览有限公司
**地址**：北京市朝阳区惠新东街11号紫光发展大厦B1-501（100029）
**联系人**：雷邵军，赖玉宝
☎ 010-6482 3808
🖷 010-6482 3670
✉ bbes@china.com

### 亚洲海洋、深水技术展览会

**日期**：2010/06/11 - 13
**地点**：马来西亚吉隆坡
**内容**：海洋工程、深水技术
**主办**：北京邦企展览有限公司
**地址**：北京市朝阳区惠新东街11号紫光发展大厦B1-501（100029）
**联系人**：雷邵军，赖玉宝
☎ 010-6482 3808
🖷 010-6482 3670
✉ bbes@china.com

### 马来西亚槟城电子/微电子展览会

Nepcon/Microelectronics Penang

**日期**：2010/06/15 - 17
**地点**：马来西亚槟城国际体育场
**内容**：在槟城举办的每年一届的马来西亚电子产品业展会。展示先进的电子配件、组装、生产及测试设备、微电子产品、PCB/SMT、半导体技术。
**展品范围**：印刷电路板及半导体行业的设备、原料、系统及服务、包装、生产、设计、测试、组装、转包 承包生产、模具和表面处理技术、电子零配件。
**周期**：每年一届
**市场范围**：国际性
**参展费用**：净地展位RM$ 960/m², 标准展位RM$1,060/ m²
**参展联络**：励展博览集团国际销售部
**地址**：北京朝阳区新源里南路1-3号平安国际金融中心A座15层01-03，05（100027）
**联系人**：杜一鸣
☎ 010-5933 9288
🖷 010-5933 9233
✉ martin.du@reedexpo.com.cn
www.reedexport.cn

### 国际制冷、通风及空调展览

**日期**：2010/06/17 - 20
4209
**地点**：马来西亚吉隆坡
**周期**：每年一届
**市场范围**：国际性
**参展联络**：中国机械汽车展览联合会
☎ 010-6859 4964
🖷 010-6859 4964

### 马来西亚国际橡塑胶机械暨模具工业技术展
### 第21届马来西亚国际广告与设备展
### 第21届马来西亚国际食品加工与包装设备展

21st Malaysia International Rubber Plastic Mould and Die Exhibition
21st Malaysia International Sign & Technology Fair
21st Malaysia International Food Processing & Packaging Exhibition

**日期**：2010/07/15 - 18
**地点**：马来西亚
**周期**：每年一届
**市场范围**：国际性
**主办**：讯通展览公司
**地址**：香港九龙观塘成业街11号华成工商中心5字楼15室
☎ 852-2763 9011
🖷 852-2341 0379
✉ info@paper-com.com.hk
www.paper-com.com.hk

### 21st Malaysia International Rubber Plastic Mould and Die Exhibition
### 21st Malaysia International Sign & Technology Fair
### 21st Malaysia International Food Processing & Packaging Exhibition

**Date**: 2010/07/15 - 18
**Venue**: Putra World Trade Centre, Malaysia
**Frequency**: Annual
**Market Area**: International
**Organizer**: Paper Communication Exhibition Services
**Address**: Rm. 15, 5/F., Wah Shing Centre, 11 Shing Yip St., Kwun Tong, Kowloon, Hong Kong.
☎ 852-2763 9011
🖷 852-2341 0379
✉ info@paper-com.com.hk
www.paper-com.com.hk

# 墨西哥
# Mexico

### 第16届墨西哥国际家具工业展

**日期**：2010/01/20 - 23
**地点**：墨西哥
**周期**：每年一届
**市场范围**：国际性
**参展联络**：大连上选会展服务有限公司
**地址**：大连市西岗区鞍山路13号兴业广场大厦B座508室（116011）
☎ 0411-8378 8326, 8378 8396, 8378 9165, 8378 8821
🖷 0411-8378 8830, 8378 8823
✉ cicyhuang@vip.sina.com
MSN：cicyhuang@msn.com
www.sun-show.com

### 2010年墨西哥国际通信技术设备展览会

Expo Comm Mexico 2010

**日期**：2010/02/23 - 25
**地点**：墨西哥Centro Banamex会展中心，墨西哥城
**内容**：该展已成功举办过18届，是拉美最大的专业通信设备与技术展览会。2009展会仍吸引了来自墨西哥、巴西、美国、加拿大、中国、西班牙、法国、乌拉圭、台湾地区等近200家企业参展，可见墨西哥通信市场的巨大潜力。展地规模近万平凡米，参展的著名公司有Microsoft、IBM、Motorola、LG、Nokia、Notel、Siemens等。专业观众超过万人次，97%的参展商对观众质量表示满意。
**展品范围**：信息通信交换、传输技术与设备；通信终端设备及配套产品；信息通信服务；电信增值业务；下一代网络、网络电视、网络游戏、互动娱乐产品及服务；数据通信与网络技术及相关产品；通信电源、仪器仪表、通信机房用品；计算机硬件设备与软件产品；通信电子元器件；通信终端配件；其它信息通信配套产品等。数字设备及系统：数码影像、办公自动化；计算机（个人电脑、笔记本、PDA）；计算机配件及部件，数码娱乐，消费电子产品。
**周期**：每年一届
**市场范围**：国际性
**上届规模**　'09：展览面积10,000m², 专业贸易观众10,000人
**主办**：美国克劳斯国际展览会议公司
**地址**：广州市海珠区新港中路350号C1204（510310）
**联系人**：周文槟
☎ 020-3405 2086 13710318991
🖷 020-3405 0629
✉ dbzh88@@1cn.com
MSN：gdwenbin@hotmail.com
QQ：406372636

### 第十六届墨西哥国际塑料橡胶工业展览会

PLASTIMAGEN 2010

**日期**：2010/03/23 - 26
**地点**：墨西哥墨西哥城展览中心
**内容**：塑料工业和橡胶工业的机械与设备类：预加工机械设备、二次加工设备、回收利用设备、挤出机、注塑机、成型机、成型机零部件、熔接技术设备、辅助设备、车间设备及仪器；材料类：颜料、着色剂、塑料添加剂和辅助剂，塑料合成材料，丙乙酸树脂、含氟聚合物、热固塑料、改良剂、铝箔材料，医疗材料及渔具材料等；FRP原材料，FRP相关设备装置（成型装置，循环利用，成型件等）；塑料及橡胶的成品和半成品：薄片、棍、杆、泡沫塑料等半成品，用于航空宇宙、卫生保健、通讯、营业设

备、家具等方面的成品；供应商服务机构及塑料橡胶的行业组织；工艺设计、制造服务、质量担保等
**始办年份：**2008
**周期：**两年一届
**市场范围：**国际性
**参展费用：** （3x3m）24,600元人民币
**上届规模** ‘08：参展商来自42个国家，参观人数60,000人（专业贸易观众40,000人）
**主办：**国际塑胶橡胶工业协会
**承办：**商务部外贸发展事务局
**参展联络：**深圳市创明展览设计有限公司
**地 址：**广东省深圳市福田区新洲大厦15层（518038）
**联系人：**雷明，朱利萍
☎ 0755-2393 8881, 21938025
℻ 0755-2393 7426
✉ cmffok@163.com
MSN：leiming1188@hotmail.com

### PLASTIMAGEN 2010

Date：2010/03/23 - 26
**Venue:** Centro Banamex, Mexico
**Profile:** Plastics and rubber industry machinery and equipment categories: pre-processing machinery and equipment, secondary processing equipment, recycling equipment, extrusion machines, injection molding machine, molding machine, molding machine parts, welding technology and equipment, auxiliary equipment, Workshop equipment and apparatus; Materials: paint, coloring agents, plastic additives and auxiliary agents, plastic composite materials, C-acetic acid resins, fluorine-containing polymers, thermosetting plastics, improvers, foil materials, medical materials and fishing gear materials, etc.; FRP raw materials, FRP-related equipment unit (forming equipment, recycling, molding parts, etc.); plastic and rubber finished products and semi-finished products
**Established Year:** 2008
**Frequency:** Biennial
**Market Area:** International
**Participated Fee:** RMB 24,600 （3x3m）
**Statistics '08:** Exhibitors came from 42 countries, Visitors 60,000 （trade visitors 40, 000）
**Organizer:** International Plastics and Rubber Industries Association
**Sponsor:** Foreign Trade Development Bureau Ministry of Commerce
**Address:** 15/Fl Xinzhou Building, Futian District, Shenzhen, Guangdong
☎ 86-755-2393 8881, 2193 8025
℻ 86-755-2393 7426
**Contact:** Rei Ming, Julius Ping
✉ cmffok@163.com
**MSN:** leiming1188@hotmail.com

### 墨西哥国际制药工业展览会

### Expofarma INTERPHEX Mexico

**日期：**2010/04/21 - 23
**地点：**墨西哥墨西哥城 世界贸易中心
**内容：**EXPOFARMA——墨西哥医药界最负盛名的展会，与INTERPHEX——全球制药业的权威展会将联合打造业内全新的盛会——EXPOFARMA INTERPHEX，创造无限商机。
**产品及服务：**加工设备、工程设备、分析设备、器材及控制、代码解决方案、承包制造、设备维护、自动化加工、卫生调节设备、质量保证、质量控制（QA&QC）、技术认证
**周期：**每年一届
**市场范围：**国际性
**主办：**励展美洲公司（美国）
**参展联络：**励展博览集团国际销售部
**地址：**北京市朝阳区新源里南路1-3号平安国际金融中心A座15层01-03，05（100027）
**联系人：**申健
☎ 010-8518 2644, 5933 9288
℻ 010-5933 9233
✉ jerry.shen@reedexpo.com.cn
www.reedexport.cn

### 墨西哥国际包装机械展览会

### EXPO PACK Mexico 2010

**日期：**2010/06 -
**地点：**墨西哥墨西哥城
**周期：**每年一届
**市场范围：**国际性
**参展联络：**中国贸促会机械行业分会
**地址：**北京市西城区三里河路46号（100823）
**联系人：**吕静，于奇琳，张垚
☎ 010-6859 4909, 6859 5498, 6859 4192
℻ 010-6859 5485
✉ info@ccpitmsc.org
✉ jix@ccpit.org
www.chinamachin.org.cn
www.ccpitmsc.org

### 2010年第十三届墨西哥电力电工设备及技术展

### Expo Electrica International 2010

**日期：**2010/06/02 - 04
4487
**地点：**墨西哥
**周期：**每年一届
**市场范围：**国际性
**参展联络：**北京中杰城设国际展览有限公司
**地址：**北京市海淀区三里河路9号建设部机关门诊楼5层（100835）
**联系人：**李娜
☎ 010-8838 5291
℻ 010-5885 7468, 5893 4708
✉ info@btfi.cn
www.top-fairs.com.cn
www.btfi.cn

### 墨西哥国际食品及饮料展

### Alimentaria Mexico: International Food & Beverage Exhibition

MÉXICO Alimentaria

**日期：**2010/06/01 - 03
**地点：**墨西哥墨西哥城
**内容：**Alimentaria México每年汇聚大量食品、饮料业者以及墨西哥与国际领先的最新产品，已成为墨西哥食品饮料销售商、零售商、酒店、餐饮业、食品业及款待业专业人士的重要贸易展会平台。Alimentaria México的观众专业程度相当高：80%拥有采购决策权、53%有意寻找新供应商，而且其中大部分为零售商。Alimentaria México共吸引来自28个国家的410家参展公司、近11,500位观众，展品超过5,000，是墨西哥领先的食品与饮料贸易展会。

展商来源：食品饮料类-包括以下种类食品饮料的生产商或经销商：肉制品、禽类产品、海产品、农产品、奶制品、冰冻食品、罐装食品、甜味品、面包及糖果类、无酒精饮料、酒类。食品设备类-包括以下种类设备的制造商及经销商：食品饮料制作、储存及售卖设备，餐馆饭店、咖啡 酒吧及其他相关附加服务专用设备件
**周期：**每年一届
**市场范围：**国际性
**参展费用：**净地展位315美元/m²，标准展位 3,195美元起(+VAT增值税)
**参展联络：**励展博览集团国际销售部
**地址：**北京朝阳区新源里南路1-3号平安国际金融中心A座15层01-03，05（100027）
**联系人：**杜一鸣
☎ 010-8515 1376
℻ 010-5933 9233
✉ martin.du@reedexpo.com.cn
www.reedexport.cn
www.alimentaria-mexico.com

### 国际摩托车展览会

**日期：**2010/07 -
**地点：**墨西哥墨西哥城
**周期：**每年一届
**市场范围：**国际性
**参展联络：**中国机械汽车展览联合会
☎ 010-6859 4964
℻ 010-6859 4964

### 2010年中美洲国际汽车零部件、原料加工及售后服务贸易展览会

### PAACE Automechanika Mexico

**日期：**2010/07/14 - 16
**地点：**墨西哥墨西哥城
**内容：**汽车原件和零配件、汽车电子、电器零件、照明系统、汽车音响和娱乐设备、汽车配件、附件及汽车改装服务、汽车商贸、陈列室、车间和维修站装备及物流处理、汽车维修、检测工具和设备、汽车美容、护理产品、服务及设备、汽车烤漆房、涂料、光漆、打磨产品、服务及设备，汽车环保、循环再造、废物处理等等。
**周期：**每年一届
**市场范围：**国际性
**主办：**法兰克福展览公司
**参展联络：**中国汽车工业国际合作总公司
**地 址：**北京市海淀区中关村丹棱街3号A座5层（100080）
**联系人：**何萌
☎ 010-8260 6880
℻ 010-8260 6883
✉ exhibition@cnaico.com.cn

### 墨西哥五金展

**日期：**2010/09 -
**地点：**墨西哥瓜达拉哈拉
**内容：**建筑装饰五金、日用五金、电动机手动工具、建筑设备、固定装置及电子产品；户外用品
**周期：**每年一届
**市场范围：**国际性
**参展联络：**京慕国际展览有限公司
**地址：**北京市朝阳区北三环东路6号中国国际展览中心服务楼3层
**联系人：**王爽，薛磊
☎ 010-8460 0551
℻ 010-8460 0394
✉ zhaolingna@ciec.com.cn
www.jingmu.com.cn

### 墨西哥建筑与制造业展

EXPO CIHAC
**日期：**2010/10 -
**地点：**墨西哥墨西哥城
**内容：**建筑材料、建设机械和电动手用工具；厨房和浴室橱柜家俱；太阳能产品；防水系统、空调和家用电器
**周期：**每年一届
**市场范围：**国际性
**参展联络：**京慕国际展览有限公司
**地址：**北京市朝阳区北三环东路6号中国国际展览中心服务楼3层
**联系人：**安红彦，孙铁兵
☎ 010-8460 0551
℻ 010-8460 0394
✉ zhaolingna@ciec.com.cn
www.jingmu.com.cn

### 国际供暖、制冷与空调展览会

**日期：**2010/10/26 - 28
**地点：**墨西哥墨西哥城
**周期：**每年一届
**市场范围：**国际性
**参展联络：**中国机械汽车展览联合会
☎ 010-6859 4964
℻ 010-6859 4964

### 国际交通运输工具展览会

**日期：**2010/11 -
**地点：**墨西哥瓜达拉哈拉

周期：每年一届
市场范围：国际性
参展联络：中国机械汽车展览联合会
☎ 010-6859 4964
🖷 010-6859 4964

### 国际石油及天然气展览会

日期：2010/11/17 - 19
地点：墨西哥比亚埃尔莫萨
周期：每年一届
市场范围：国际性
参展联络：中国机械汽车展览联合会
☎ 010-6859 4964
🖷 010-6859 4964

### 墨西哥国际制药工业展览会

Expofarma INTERPHEX Mexico

日期：2011/04 -
地点：墨西哥墨西哥城 世界贸易中心
内容：EXPOFARMA——墨西哥医药界最负盛名的展会，与INTERPHEX——全球制药业的权威展会将联合打造业内全新的盛会——EXPOFARMA INTERPHEX，创造无限商机。
产品及服务：加工设备、工程设备、分析设备、器材及控制、代码解决方案、承包制造、设备维护自动化加工、卫生调节设备、质量保证、质量控制（QA&QC）、技术认证
周期：每年一届
市场范围：国际性
主办：励展美洲公司（美国）
参展联络：励展博览集团国际销售部
地址：北京市朝阳区新源里南路1-3号平安国际金融中心A座15层01-03，05（100027）
联系人：申健
☎ 010-8518 2644, 5933 9288
🖷 010-5933 9233
✉ jerry.shen@reedexpo.com.cn
www.reedexport.cn

### 墨西哥国际食品及饮料展

Alimentaria Mexico:
International Food & Beverage Exhibition

日期：2011/06 -
地点：墨西哥墨西哥城
内容：Alimentaria México每年汇聚大量食品、饮料业者以及墨西哥与国际领先的最新产品，已成为墨西哥食品饮料销售商、零售商、酒店、餐饮业、食品业及款待业专业人士的重要贸易展会平台。Alimentaria México的观众专业程度相当高：80%拥有采购决策权、53%有意寻找新供应商，而且其中大部分为零售商。Alimentaria México共吸引来自28个国家的410家参展公司、近11,500位观众，展品超过5,000，是墨西哥领先的食品与饮料贸易展会。
展商来源：食品饮料类-包括以下种类食品饮料的生产商或经销商：肉制品、禽类产品、海产品、农产品、奶制品、冰冻食品、罐装食品、甜味品、面包及糖果类、无酒精饮料、酒类。食品设备类-包括以下种类设备的制造商及经销商：食品饮料制作、储存及售卖设备，餐馆饭店、咖啡 酒吧及其他相关附加服务专用设备件
周期：每年一届
市场范围：国际性
参展费用：净地展位315美元/m$^2$，标准展位 3,195美元/m$^2$起(+VAT增值税)
参展联络：励展博览集团国际销售部
地址：北京朝阳区新源里南路1-3号平安国际金融中心A座15层01-03，05（100027）
联系人：杜一鸣
☎ 010-8515 1376
🖷 010-5933 9233
✉ martin.du@reedexpo.com.cn
www.reedexport.cn
www.alimentaria-mexico.com

## 摩洛哥
## Morocco

### 2010年摩洛哥工程机械展
### BTP 2010

日期：2010/05/26 - 30
地点：摩洛哥卡萨布兰卡展览中心
内容：随着北非地区工业的发展，对工程机械类产品的需求量越来越大，特别是经济位居北非第三位的摩洛哥。自2005年来，摩洛哥政府为鼓励外国企业投资，制定了不少优惠政策和鼓励措施，因此，中国工程机械产品对北非的出口有进一步扩大的可能。摩洛哥工业市场资源单一，经济结构单一，仅有采油业和石化业，其他工业极为薄弱。现在摩洛哥政府也看到了这一点，正在大力发展石化工业以外的其他工业，以减少对国外的依赖。目前中国在摩洛哥市场所占的比例还很小，去年在摩洛哥地区的出口额约为70亿至80亿美元，而摩洛哥工程机械行业的进口额每年约为额500亿美元，可见还有很大的出口潜力。
周期：每年一届
市场范围：国际性
主办：FNBTP摩洛哥联合展览公司
参展联络：北京麦田通会国际展览有限公司
联系人：吴珊
☎ 010-5165 9302转8005, 8633 1235, 13426437438
🖷 010-5165 9302
✉ xiaoxiangzhishui@yahoo.com.cn
MSN：xiaoxiangzhishui@hotmail.com

### 国际塑料与橡胶工业展览会

日期：2010/06 -
地点：摩洛哥卡萨布兰卡
周期：每年一届
市场范围：国际性
参展联络：中国机械汽车展览联合会
☎ 010-6859 4964
🖷 010-6859 4964

### 2010年摩洛哥卡萨布兰卡中国商品展

日期：2010/07 -
地点：摩洛哥卡萨布兰卡
内容：纺织品及服装鞋帽；轻工产品；食品；机电产品；汽车、摩托车及零配件；建筑材料等。
首届
市场范围：国际性
预计规模：展出面积3,000m$^2$，参展厂商150人，参观人数6,000人
主办：中企国际展览广告有限公司
地址：北京东土城路8号林达大厦B座3L（100013）
联系人：顾洪涛，杨光
☎ 010-6446 6671
🖷 010-8838 2248
✉ eaciecco@mx.cei.gov.cn
MSN：ceieac407@hotmail.com

## 新西兰
## New Zealand

### 2010年第12届新西兰国际电力能源行业展示会及高层战略论谈
### 12th Power & Electricity World New Zealand

日期：2010/02/15 - 18
地点：新西兰
内容：Focusing on Power Generation, T&D and Environment, Electric Power Equipment and Technology。电力、电网建设：电站设备、电网建设、电力装置、高压开关、传输、配电网络、变压器、电流互感器、电压互感器、电力电容器、高压开柜、监控器、电机工程、电力供应和附件、电线电缆、绝缘材料、测量设备等；输变电设备：电网系统、变压器，仪表互感器，电力变频器，电缆线材、电力电容避雷器，接地电阻，电抗器，电炉和加热设备，电焊机，绝缘器及其它；配电装置和控制设备，开关装置，高压开关，高压断路器，低压断路器；清洁能源等设备制造；发电机设备：直流发电机，交流发电机，发电机，电动机，电动工具及其它电机和发电机；各类发电设备，风力发电设备，太阳能技术及设备，清洁可再生能源
周期：每年一届
市场范围：国际性
主办：特兰展览
参展联络：北京中杰城设国际展览有限公司
地址：北京市海淀区三里河路9号建设部机关门诊楼5层（100835）
联系人：李娜
☎ 010-8838 5291
🖷 010-5885 7468, 5893 4708
✉ info@btfi.cn
www.top-fairs.com.cn
www.btfi.cn

## 尼日利亚
## Nigeria

### 第7届尼日利亚拉各斯国际汽车展览会
### Lagos Motor Fair

日期：2010/10 -
地点：尼日利亚拉各斯
周期：每年一届
市场范围：国际性
主办：法兰克福展览公司
参展联络：中国汽车工业国际合作总公司
地址：北京市海淀区中关村丹棱街3号A座5层（100080）
联系人：何萌
☎ 010-8260 6880
🖷 010-8260 6883
✉ exhibition@cnaico.com.cn

## 朝鲜
## North Korea

### 国际商品博览会

日期：2010/05 -
地点：朝鲜平壤
周期：每年一届
市场范围：国际性
参展联络：中国机械汽车展览联合会
☎ 010-6859 4964
🖷 010-6859 4964

## 挪威
## Norway

### 北海国际石油及天然气展览会

日期：2010/08/26 - 29

**地点**：挪威斯达旺格
**周期**：每年一届
**市场范围**：国际性
**参展联络**：中国机械汽车展览联合会
☎ 010-6859 4964
🖷 010-6859 4964

# 阿曼 Oman

## 第7届阿曼国际建筑建材展

**日期**：2010/03/15 - 17
**地点**：阿曼马斯喀特
**内容**：建筑建材展
**周期**：每年一届
**市场范围**：国际性
**参展联络**：北京中仕达兴业展览有限公司
**地址**：北京市海淀区蓝靛厂东路2号金源时代商务中心2号楼A座11B（100097）
**联系人**：贾倩，赵仕忱，牟向东，张露
☎ 010-5129 8900
🖷 010-8886 2939
✉ mail@chinstar.cn
www.chinstar.cn

# 巴基斯坦 Pakistan

## 国际包装、塑料及印刷机械展览会

**日期**：2010/05/07 - 09
**地点**：巴基斯坦卡拉奇
**周期**：每年一届
**市场范围**：国际性
**参展联络**：中国机械汽车展览联合会
☎ 010-6859 4964
🖷 010-6859 4964

## 第8届巴基斯坦国际石油、天然气及电力能源展览会

POGEE 2010

**日期**：2010/05/19 - 22
**地点**：巴基斯坦卡拉奇展览中心
**内容**：电力产品及设备：电站设备、电厂设备、发电机、高压输电设备、配电网络设备、变压器、监控管理设备、便携式发电机、电机产品、应急供电设备及其配件、开关装置、电力保护装置、测试器材、各类照明灯具、空调和通风设备等电力相关产品及设备；石油天然气能源设备及技术：油井、钻探、焊接设备、油罐设备、起重、吊装、升降、保温、制冷、通风、遥控监测、维修保养设备；加油机、透平机、涡轮机、汽轮机、叶轮机等机械；阀门、泵、压缩机、风机、空分设备、真空设备、锅炉、压力容器，冷却机器、法兰、管道、软管及其连接装置、工业防爆产品等；仪器仪表：稳定器、记录器、过滤器、温度感应器、测量计量仪器、过滤网、筛网等； 技术服务：勘测、勘探、提炼、分离、液化、焊接、压力传递检测、质量检测、流量流速控制等技术；计算机数据管理；油库工程、工程顾问；安全、报警、险情控制、操作进程控制、管道线路保护、消防报警设备、安全及劳保用品、实验及模拟等系统；石油、天然气产品；钻井平台、钢铁架构；绝缘材料；指示器材。
**周期**：每年一届
**市场范围**：国际性
**主办**：Pegasus Consultancy(pvt)Ltd
**参展联络**：北京中杰城设国际展览有限公司
**地址**：北京市海淀区三里河路9号建设部机关门诊楼5层（100835）
**联系人**：李娜
☎ 010-8838 5291
🖷 010-5885 7468, 5893 4708
✉ info@btfi.cn
www.top-fairs.com.cn
www.btfi.cn

## 第6届巴基斯坦国际建筑建材展

**日期**：2010/07/27 - 29
**地点**：巴基斯坦卡拉奇
**内容**：建筑建材
**市场范围**：国际性
**参展联络**：北京中仕达兴业展览有限公司
**地址**：北京市海淀区蓝靛厂东路2号金源时代商务中心2号楼A座11B（100097）
**联系人**：贾倩，赵仕忱，牟向东，张露
☎ 010-5129 8900
🖷 010-8886 2939
✉ mail@chinstar.cn
www.chinstar.cn

## 巴基斯坦国际汽车、摩托车及配件展览会

6th International Automobile, Auto Parts & Accessories Exhibition 2010

**日期**：2010/11 -
**地点**：巴基斯坦卡拉奇
**周期**：每年一届
**市场范围**：国际性
**参展联络**：中国贸促会机械行业分会
**地址**：北京市西城区三里河路46号（100823）
**联系人**：范卓英
☎ 010-6859 4952, 6859 4804, 6859 5055
🖷 010-6859 4917
✉ info@ccpitmsc.org
✉ jix@ccpit.org
www.chinamachin.org.cn
www.ccpitmsc.org

# 巴拿马 Panama

## 巴拿马第28届国际博览会

Expocomer 2010

**日期**：2010/03/03 - 06
**地点**：巴拿马
**内容**：国内数百家外向型企业和专业外贸公司参展，宣传了中国企业形象和中国产品，促进了中国与巴拿马和中南美洲国家的贸易合作关系。这些参展单位在博览会上均收到良好的效果，仅2009年，中国展团总成交1.27亿美元，主要商品是家具、纺织服装、鞋帽、五金工具、轻工制品、玩具、家用电器、装饰品、汽摩配件、文具用品以及灯具等。
**展出内容**：机械、电子、仪器、化工、五矿、五金工具、食品、服装、轻工产品、照明设备、灯具、建材、消费品、纺织品、家用电器、石油化工、加工机械、农用机械、电子通讯、轻工家电、汽车配件、五矿建材、农机具、文具玩具、体育用品、汽车、摩托车、农产品、畜牧产品等。
**始办年份**：1982
**周期**：两年一届
**市场范围**：国际性
**主办**：巴拿马农工商协会
**地址**：广州市海珠区新港中路350号C1204（510310）
**联系人**：周文槟
☎ 020-3405 2086 13710318991
🖷 020-3405 0629
✉ wbtd88@163.com
MSN：gdwenbin@hotmail.com
QQ：406372636

# 秘鲁 Peru

## 秘鲁国际天然气、液化气展览会

**日期**：2010/08/19 - 21
**地点**：秘鲁利马
**内容**：天然气勘探、钻采、运输、加气站、天然气汽车
**主办**：北京邦企展览有限公司
**地址**：北京市朝阳区惠新东街11号紫光发展大厦B1-501（100029）
**联系人**：雷邵军，赖玉宝
☎ 010-6482 3808
🖷 010-6482 3670
✉ bbes@china.com

## 第30届南美秘鲁国际矿业机械设备展

**日期**：2011/09 -
**地点**：秘鲁阿雷基帕
**内容**：矿业机械设备
**市场范围**：国际性
**参展联络**：北京中仕达兴业展览有限公司
**地址**：北京市海淀区蓝靛厂东路2号金源时代商务中心2号楼A座11B（100097）
**联系人**：贾倩，赵仕忱，牟向东，张露
☎ 010-5129 8900
🖷 010-8886 2939
✉ mail@chinstar.cn
www.chinstar.cn

# 菲律宾 Philippines

## 中国机械电子产品贸易展览会

**日期**：2010/06 -
**地点**：菲律宾马尼拉
**周期**：每年一届
**市场范围**：国际性
**参展联络**：中国机械汽车展览联合会
☎ 010-6859 4964
🖷 010-6859 4964

## 第20届菲律宾国际建筑建材展

**日期**：2010/11 -
**地点**：菲律宾马尼拉
**内容**：建筑建材展
**市场范围**：国际性
**参展联络**：北京中仕达兴业展览有限公司
**地址**：北京市海淀区蓝靛厂东路2号金源时代商务中心2号楼A座11B（100097）
**联系人**：贾倩，赵仕忱，牟向东，张露
☎ 010-5129 8900
🖷 010-8886 2939
✉ mail@chinstar.cn
www.chinstar.cn

# 波兰 Poland

## 第19届波兰国际建筑建材展

**日期**：2010/01/19 - 22
**地点**：波兰波兹南
**内容**：建筑建材
**周期**：每年一届
**市场范围**：国际性
**参展联络**：北京中仕达兴业展览有限公司
**地址**：北京市海淀区蓝靛厂东路2号金源时代商务中

心2号楼A座11B（100097）
**联系人：**贾倩，赵仕忱，牟向东，张露
☎ 010-5129 8900
🖷 010-8886 2939
✉ mail@chinstar.cn
www.chinstar.cn

### 国际供热、壁炉、空调及制冷博览会

**日期：**2010/04/26 - 29
**地点：**波兰波兹南
**周期：**每年一届
**市场范围：**国际性
**参展联络：**中国机械汽车展览联合会
☎ 010-6859 4964
🖷 010-6849 4964

### 波兰国际工程机械展览会

**日期：**2010/05 -
**地点：**波兰科尔采
**内容：**工程机械、矿山机械等
**周期：**每年一届
**市场范围：**国际性
**参展联络：**京慕国际展览有限公司
**地址：**北京市朝阳区北三环东路6号中国国际展览中心服务楼3层
**联系人：**宋秋爽，刘舰
☎ 010-8460 0551
🖷 010-8460 0394
✉ zhaolingna@ciec.com.cn
www.jingmu.com.cn

### 波兰国际塑料加工工业展
PLASTPOL

**日期：**2010/05 -
**地点：**波兰科尔采
**内容：**塑料加工技术、设备及机械；塑料包装设备
**周期：**每年一届
**市场范围：**国际性
**参展联络：**京慕国际展览有限公司
**地址：**北京市朝阳区北三环东路6号中国国际展览中心服务楼3层
**联系人：**薛亮，孙铁兵
☎ 010-8460 0551
🖷 010-8460 0394
✉ zhaolingna@ciec.com.cn
www.jingmu.com.cn

### 波兰国际建筑设备和特殊交通车辆展览会
International Construction Equipment and Special Vehicles Fair

**日期：**2010/05 -
**地点：**波兰凯尔采
**内容：**土方工作机械;混凝土搅拌设备和运输设备，起重和接入机械，工程车辆，工程机械配件；气动、液压设备
**周期：**每年一届
**市场范围：**国际性
**参展联络：**京慕国际展览有限公司
**地址：**北京市朝阳区北三环东路6号中国国际展览中心服务楼3层
**联系人：**薛亮，孙铁兵
☎ 010-8460 0551
🖷 010-8460 0394
✉ zhaolingna@ciec.com.cn
www.jingmu.com.cn

### 国际机械与创新技术展览会

**日期：**2010/06/08 - 11
**地点：**波兰波兹南
**周期：**每年一届
**市场范围：**国际性
**参展联络：**中国机械汽车展览联合会
☎ 010-6859 4964
🖷 010-6859 4964

### 国际工业展览会

**日期：**2010/06/08 - 11
**地点：**波兰波兹南
**周期：**每年一届
**市场范围：**国际性
**参展联络：**中国机械汽车展览联合会
☎ 010-6859 4964
🖷 010-6859 4964

### 波兰国际机床工具展览会
MACH-TOOL 2010

**日期：**2010/06/15 - 18
**地点：**波兰波兹南
**周期：**每年一届
**市场范围：**国际性
**参展联络：**中国贸促会机械行业分会
**地址：**北京市西城区三里河路46号（100823）
**联系人：**周海明，叶海青，聂飞
☎ 010-6859 5495, 6859 5247, 6851 3586, 6859 4938
🖷 010-6859 5057
✉ info@ccpitmsc.org
✉ jix@ccpit.org
www.chinamachin.org.cn
www.ccpitmsc.org

## 葡萄牙
## Portugal

### 里斯本国际食品展
Alimentaria Lisboa:
International Food & Beverage Exhibition

Alimentaria Lisboa

**日期：**2011/04 -
2013/04 -
**地点：**葡萄牙里斯本国际展览馆
**内容：**里斯本国际食品展在2009年庆祝了第10届盛会，并再次证明了自己在葡萄牙食品饮料业的领先参照点地位。是每奇数年一次在伊比利亚半岛上举办的食品饮料领域最重要的商业展会。在葡萄牙配销公司协会（APED）以及每个葡萄牙零售渠道的支持下，展会凝聚了食品市场最大最全面的视野，展会期间还为观众和展商提供丰富多彩的活动。
**周期：**两年一届
**市场范围：**国际性
**参展费用：**净地96.5～121.8欧元
**参展联络：**励展博览集团国际销售部
**地址：**北京朝阳区新源里南路1-3号平安国际金融中心A座15层01-03，05（100027）
**联系人：**杜一鸣
☎ 010-5933 9288
🖷 010-5933 9233
✉ martin.du@reedexpo.com.cn
www.reedexport.cn

## 波多黎各
## Puerto Rico

### 波多黎各国际制药工业展览会：生物科技及制药商展览会
INTERPHEX Puerto Rico:
Exhibition & Conference for Pharmaceutical & Biotechnology Manufacturers

Conference & Exhibition INTERPHEX PUERTO RICO

**日期：**2010/03/04 - 05
2011/02 -
**地点：**波多黎各圣胡安波多黎各会议中心
**内容：**波多黎各国际制药工业展览会(INTERPHEX Puerto Rico)已经成为加勒比地区最主要的专业性展会，包括：药品的审批，生产，包装，以及生物制药。展览会将展出超过350种设备，技术，另外还有为期两天的教学项目和丰富的网上活动。展会由下列五个不同的展区组成：监管、生产技术、设备/工程、生物技术和包装。届时，波多黎各国际制药工业展览会将与波多黎各供应链及物流展（Supply Chain & Logistics Puerto Rico）和波多黎各医疗仪器展（MEDICAL DEVICE Puerto Rico）同期举办。
**周期：**每年一届
**市场范围：**国际性
**参展费用：**欢迎垂询参展费用（按美元计算）
**主办：**励展美国公司
**参展联络：**励展博览集团国际销售部
**地址：**北京朝阳区新源里南路1-3号平安国际金融中心A座15层01-03，05（100027）
**联系人：**申健
☎ 010-8518 2644, 5933 9288
🖷 010-5933 9233
✉ jerry.shen@reedexpo.com.cn
www.reedexport.cn

## 卡塔尔
## Qatar

### 2010年第9届中东国际电力、能源、水力展
Power-Gen Middle East

**日期：**2010/11/01 - 03
**地点：**卡塔尔卡塔尔国际展览中心
**内容：**电力、水力产品及设备：电站设备、电网建设、电力装置、高低压开关、传输、配电网络、变压器、电流互感器、电压互感器、电力电容器、高压电柜、监控器及系统、电机工程、电力、水供应和附件、电线电缆、绝缘材料、测量设备等；输变电设备：电网系统、变压器，仪表互感器，电力变频器，电缆线材、电力电容避雷器，接地电阻，电抗器，电炉和加热设备，电焊机，绝缘器及其它；配电装置和控制设备，开关装置，高、低压开关，高、低压断路器；清洁能源等设备制造；发电机设备：直流发电机，交流发电机，发电机，电动机，电动工具及其它电机和发电机；各类发电设备，风力发电设备，水力发电设备及建设，太阳能技术及设备等；能源产品，清洁可再生能源，原子核反应堆。技术监测及维护系统。
**始办年份：**2001
**周期：**每年一届
**市场范围：**国际性
**主办：**美国派尼韦尔公司
**参展联络：**北京中杰城设国际展览有限公司
**地址：**北京市海淀区三里河路9号建设部机关门诊楼5层（100835）
**联系人：**李娜
☎ 010-8838 5291
🖷 010-5885 7468, 5893 4708
✉ info@btfi.cn
www.top-fairs.com.cn
www.btfi.cn

## 罗马尼亚
## Romania

### 罗马尼亚国际门窗玻璃博览会
CONSTRUCT EXPO

**日期：**2010/05 -
**地点：**罗马尼亚布加勒斯特布加勒斯特
**内容：**门、窗系列

**周期**：每年一届
**市场范围**：国际性
**参展联络**：京慕国际展览有限公司
**地址**：北京市朝阳区北三环东路6号中国国际展览中心服务楼3层
**联系人**：许艳；孙铁兵
☎ 010-8460 0551
🖷 010-8460 0394
✉ zhaolingna@ciec.com.cn
www.jingmu.com.cn

# 俄罗斯
# Russia

## 俄罗斯国际家居用品博览会
## Consumexpo

**日期**：2010/01/18 - 22
**地点**：俄罗斯莫斯科俄罗斯
**内容**：日用品、家具、室内装饰品；礼品、圣诞节用品；鞋、服装、流行首饰、服饰佩饰等
**市场范围**：国际性
**参展联络**：京慕国际展览有限公司
**地址**：北京市朝阳区北三环东路6号中国国际展览中心服务楼3层
**联系人**：王海琼；滕昊
☎ 010-84600551
🖷 010-84600394
✉ zhaolingna@ciec.com.cn
www.jingmu.com.cn

## 莫斯科安保展
## （俄罗斯国际安防技术论坛）
## Security & Safety Technologies Moscow (SST Moscow)

**日期**：2010/02/02 - 05
**地点**：俄罗斯莫斯科Crocus Expo会展中心
**内容**：SST-莫斯科安保展（俄罗斯国际安防技术论坛）是俄罗斯、独联体及东欧地区领先的安防行业展会，其参展商包括来自25个国家的近500家公司，同时举办40多场会议，观众包括买家、终端用户与系统安装商。SST是全世界安防公司展示新产品与解决方案的最佳平台。俄罗斯安防与安全产业与市场发展非常迅速。

**展品范围**：SST紧密联系俄罗斯与全球安防业市场，集中展示业内各领域的相关产品：闭路电视、门禁、生物识别、火灾报警、IT与特殊通讯系统、反恐、搜索器材、安防服务、工业安防、工作安全等
**周期**：每年一届
**市场范围**：国际性
**参展费用**：净地221欧元/m²，标准展位272欧元/m²
**主办**：励展俄罗斯公司
**参展联络**：励展博览集团国际销售部
**地址**：北京朝阳区新源里南路1-3号平安国际金融中心A座15层01-03，05（100027）
**联系人**：宫卫
☎ 010-5933 9288
🖷 010-5933 9233
✉ david.gong@reedexpo.com.cn
www.reedexport.cn

## 第14届莫斯科国际供暖、卫浴、通风及空调和环保展览会
## aqua-therm Moscow: 14th International Exhibition for Heating, Ventilation, Air-Conditioning, Water Supply, Sanitary Equipment, Environmental Technology & Pools

**日期**：2010/02/02 - 05
**地点**：俄罗斯莫斯科Crocus Expo会展中心
**内容**：此展由励展博览集团（Reed Exhibitions）和领先的国际展会主办机构ITE Moscow共同主办，至今为止，aqua-therm Moscow已成功举办过13届，2010年2月，第14届展会即将以全新的面貌展现在大家的面前。在行业专家的鼎力支持下，主办单位广泛调查了解俄罗斯地区的行业消费者的购买意愿，并通过采取一系列有针对性的宣传策略，致力于为参展商提供最大价值的服务，定能为展商吸引更多顶级买家。本届展会将带来的一大亮点：除往届皆有的供暖产品展区，本届展会专为服务于泳池和Spa市场的展商设立了一个全新展区：World of Water & Spa。Aqua-therm将在位于莫斯科的Crocus Expo会展中心拉开帷幕。这也是莫斯科现代化程度最高、设备最好的展览中心，与莫斯科机场毗邻，位于商业区和市中心周边，交通便利。
**周期**：每年一届
**市场范围**：国际性
**参展费用**：净地295欧元/m²，标准展位320欧元/m²
**主办**：励展俄罗斯公司；俄罗斯联邦
**参展联络**：励展博览集团国际销售部
**地址**：北京朝阳区新源里南路1-3号平安国际金融中心A座15层01-03，05（100027）
**联系人**：宫卫
☎ 010-85185787, 5933 9288
🖷 010-5933 9233
✉ david.gong@reedexpo.com.cn
www.reedexport.cn

## 第8届俄罗斯国际建筑钢结构及金属材料设备展

**日期**：2010/02/16 - 19
**地点**：俄罗斯莫斯科
**内容**：建筑钢结构及金属材料
**周期**：每年一届
**市场范围**：国际性
**参展联络**：北京中仕达兴业展览有限公司
**地址**：北京市海淀区蓝靛厂东路2号金源时代商务中心2号楼A座11B（100097）
**联系人**：贾倩，赵仕忱，牟向东，张露
☎ 010-5129 8900
🖷 010-8886 2939
✉ mail@chinstar.cn
www.chinstar.cn

## 第4届俄罗斯国际水泥、混凝土技术及装备展

**日期**：2010/02/16 - 19
**地点**：俄罗斯莫斯科
**内容**：水泥、混凝土技术及装备
**周期**：每年一届
**市场范围**：国际性
**参展联络**：北京中仕达兴业展览有限公司
**地址**：北京市海淀区蓝靛厂东路2号金源时代商务中心2号楼A座11B（100097）
**联系人**：贾倩，赵仕忱，牟向东，张露
☎ 010-5129 8900
🖷 010-8886 2939
✉ mail@chinstar.cn
www.chinstar.cn

## 国际园艺展览会

**日期**：2010/03 -
**地点**：俄罗斯莫斯科
**周期**：每年一届
**市场范围**：国际性
**参展联络**：中国机械汽车展览联合会
☎ 010-6859 4964
🖷 010-6849 4964

## 俄联邦轻工纺织及设备博览会（春季）
## Trade Fair For Textile & Light Industry Goods & Equipments

**日期**：2010/03 -
**地点**：俄罗斯莫斯科
**内容**：纺织面料、服装、家用针纺织品、地毯、鞋帽、室内装饰品、皮革制品、各种纺织原料、设备
**周期**：每年两届
**市场范围**：国际性
**参展联络**：京慕国际展览有限公司
**地址**：北京市朝阳区北三环东路6号中国国际展览中心服务楼3层
**联系人**：崔文佳，柳川
☎ 010-8460 0551
🖷 010-8460 0394
✉ zhaolingna@ciec.com.cn
www.jingmu.com.cn

## 俄罗斯圣彼得堡国际体育用品展
## SPORT-CNOPT

**日期**：2010/03 -
**地点**：俄罗斯圣彼得堡
**内容**：冬季体育世界、球拍及室内运动、板类运动、体育服装、户外运动、运动鞋团队世界、健身运动、休闲服饰等
**周期**：每年一届
**市场范围**：国际性
**参展联络**：京慕国际展览有限公司
**地址**：北京市朝阳区北三环东路6号中国国际展览中心服务楼3层
**联系人**：林航，刘靖
☎ 010-8460 0551
🖷 010-8460 0394
✉ zhaolingna@ciec.com.cn
www.jingmu.com.cn

## 俄罗斯圣彼得堡国际两轮车展
## Velo-Expo

**日期**：2010/03 -
**地点**：俄罗斯圣彼得堡
**内容**：自行车整车、电动车整车、摩托车整车、两轮车零配件、两轮车服装等
**周期**：每年一届
**市场范围**：国际性
**参展联络**：京慕国际展览有限公司
**地址**：北京市朝阳区北三环东路6号中国国际展览中心服务楼3层
**联系人**：林航，刘靖
☎ 010-8460 0551
🖷 010-8460 0394
✉ zhaolingna@ciec.com.cn
www.jingmu.com.cn

## 法兰克福国际汽车配件展览会

**日期**：2010/03/03 - 05
**地点**：俄罗斯莫斯科
**周期**：每年一届
**市场范围**：国际性
**参展联络**：中国机械汽车展览联合会
☎ 010-6859 4964
🖷 010-6849 4964

## 国际汽车配件、售后服务及设备展览会

**日期**：2010/03/10 - 12
**地点**：俄罗斯莫斯科
**周期**：每年一届
**市场范围**：国际性
**参展联络**：中国机械汽车展览联合会
☎ 010-6859 4964
🖷 010-6849 4964

## 2010年第9届俄罗斯国际专业线缆、线材及紧固件和安装设备展览会
## CABEX 2010

**日期**：2010/03/16 - 19
**地点**：俄罗斯索科尔尼基展览中心

**内容：**线缆（高中低压电力电缆，油田，矿业，安防专用）、特种线缆、线材制品（民用，工业用，电力用，通信用）、电缆（线）绝缘材料、紧固件、安装及专业工具；电线电缆、光纤光缆专用机械、线材制造及精加工机械、原材料及辅助加工材料；测控技术、检测工程及实验设备；电线电缆附件、线缆接插件、连接器连接系统、布线系统、电线电缆保护设备及用品；相关领域其他产品。
**始办年份：**2002
**周期：**每年一届
**市场范围：**国际性
**上届规模** '09：展览面积4,500m$^2$，参观人数6,768人（专业贸易观众5,872人）
**主办：**北方国际展览有限公司
**地址：**北京市宣武区菜园街1号中环假日酒店写字楼1102-1103室（100053）
**联系人：**穆超
☎ 010-8355 9740
🖷 010-8355 7940
✉ woody.m@northexpo.com.cn
MSN：mr_angel_boy@hotmail.com
QQ：26327995
www.northexpo.com.cn

### 莫斯科国际玩具、母婴用品博览会
### MITGE-Toy & Game Mother & Baby

**日期：**2010/03/16 - 19
**地点：**俄罗斯莫斯科
**内容：**玩具、礼品、各类婴幼儿用品、孕妇服装及用品；婴儿车及辅件、家具及辅件、青少年用品等
**市场范围：**国际性
**参展联络：**京慕国际展览有限公司
**地址：**北京市朝阳区北三环东路6号中国国际展览中心服务楼3层
**联系人：**付颖；古莹
☎ 010-8460 0551
🖷 010-8460 0394
✉ zhaolingna@ciec.com.cn
www.jingmu.com.cn

### 2010年俄罗斯国际电力展览会
### Russia Power 2010

**日期：**2010/03/24 - 26
**地点：**俄罗斯
**内容：**电力设备：电站设备、电力装置、高压开关、传输、配电网络、变压器、电流互感器、电压互感器、电力电容器、高压开柜、监控器、电机工程、电力供应和附件、电线电缆、绝缘材料、测量设备等；输变电设备：变压器，仪表互感器，电力变频器，电缆线材、电力电容避雷器，接地电阻，电抗器，电炉和加热设备，电焊机，绝缘器及其它；配电装置和控制设备，开关装置，高压开关，高压断路器，低压断路器；清洁能源等设备制造；发电机设备：直流发电机，交流发电机，发电机，电动机，电动工具及其它电机和发电机；各类发电设备，风力发电设备，太阳能技术及设备，清洁可再生能源，原子核反应堆，蒸汽锅炉，蒸汽透平以及其它能源发电系统。
**周期：**每年一届
**市场范围：**国际性
**主办：**美国派尼韦尔公司
**参展联络：**北京中杰城设国际展览有限公司
**地址：**北京市海淀区三里河路9号建设部机关门诊楼5层（100835）
**联系人：**李娜
☎ 010-8838 5291
🖷 010-5885 7468, 5893 4708
✉ info@btfi.cn
www.top-fairs.com.cn
www.btfi.cn

### 国际商用车展览会

**日期：**2010/04 -
**地点：**俄罗斯莫斯科
**周期：**每年一届
**市场范围：**国际性
**参展联络：**中国机械汽车展览联合会
☎ 010-6859 4964
🖷 010-6849 4964

### 2010年莫斯科国际建筑建材展
### MOSBUILD

**日期：**2010/04/06 - 09
**地点：**俄罗斯莫斯科红宝石展览中心、奥林匹克展览中心
**内容：**Expocenter 展馆-建筑材料：建筑材料、建筑工具及设备、智能建筑系统、五金、五金工具及配件、各类板材、管道及附件、建筑安全设备、屋顶材料、混凝土等；卫浴类：浴室五金及配件、水龙头、水疗按摩器设备、卫生洁具、沐浴洁具、淋浴房、厨房及浴室设备等；瓷砖及石材类：各类瓷砖、陶瓷、陶瓷工具、大理石、花岗岩、马赛克、石材工具等；暖通制冷类：空调、空气过滤系统、温度自动调节系统、锅炉、能源供电系统、加热器及系统、热交换器、绝缘材料、抽水机、散热器、制冷设备、排污、过滤器等。水加热设备等；Crocus 展馆-地面区：各类地毯、木地板、地砖、门垫、浴室垫、工业地板材、地板镶铺技术设备、密封剂、胶水、粘合剂；门锁类,窗及玻璃类,内部装饰材料,园林园景等。
**始办年份：**1995
**周期：**每年一届
**市场范围：**国际性
**上届规模** '09：展览面积160,000m$^2$，参展商2,483家（来自45个国家），参观人数98,393人
**主办：**北京领汇国际展览有限公司
**地址：**北京市朝阳区农展馆南路13号瑞辰国际中心719（100125）
**联系人：**张爽
☎ 010-5129 5359转8810
🖷 010-5129 5379转8810
✉ bangni5858@163.com
MSN：expo8810@worldfairs.cn
QQ：574000135
www.worldfairs.cn

### 第七届俄罗斯国际摩托车及零配件展览会
### International Specialized Exhibition of Motorcycles, Scooters and Service

**日期：**2010/04/08 - 11
**地点：**俄罗斯莫斯科
**周期：**每年一届
**市场范围：**国际性
**主办：**法兰克福展览公司
**参展联络：**中国汽车工业国际合作总公司
**地址：**北京市海淀区中关村丹棱街3号A座5层（100080）
**联系人：**何萌
☎ 010-8260 6880
🖷 010-8260 6883
✉ exhibition@cnaico.com.cn

### 2010年俄罗斯国际矿业展览会

**日期：**2010/04/14 - 16
**地点：**俄罗斯莫斯科CROCUS展馆
**内容：**该展至今已经成功举办了十二届。俄罗斯矿产开发与加工领域的重要人士出席每届盛会。2009年有来自世界各地的包括小松、SANDVIK、ATLAS COPCO、CETCO等国际知名公司。此外，展场还特设挪威展区、加拿大展区和德国展区。并于2009年首次设立中国展区。参展观众人数达到10000人次。2008年的展会上，90%以上的参展商对观众质量和数量表示满意。40%的参展商现场预订了2010年展位。
展品：矿产勘探技术、矿藏加工、矿产开采、回收与再利用、矿产工业安全技术、地表矿产、矿产品深加工、原材料加工与处理、矿产运输与物流技术。具体展品有：采矿机械设备；铲运机，运输车；露天坑口技术；辅助机械和设备；开矿工程工具与设备，硬金属工具，研磨剂，金刚刀具；工艺设备；采矿工程通风；钻探技术和爆破材料；地块应力与变形状况的探测装置；自然生态系统控制装置与设备；工程与测量装置；防爆电气。
**始办年份：**1995
**周期：**每年一届
**市场范围：**国际性
**上届规模** '09：参展商250家（来自30个国家）
**主办：**北京麦田通会国际展览有限公司
**联系人：**吴珊
☎ 010-5165 9302转8005, 8633 1235, 13426437438
🖷 010-5165 9302
✉ xiaoxiangzhishui@yahoo.com.cn
MSN：xiaoxiangzhishui@hotmail.com

### 俄罗斯电子元器件展
### Expo Electronica

**日期：**2010/04/20 - 22
**地点：**俄罗斯莫斯科
**内容：**各种电子元件，半导体，线缆，电源，传感器，继电器，开关，连接器，显示器，电机，PCB等
**周期：**每年一届
**市场范围：**国际性
**参展联络：**京慕国际展览有限公司
**地址：**北京市朝阳区北三环东路6号中国国际展览中心服务楼3层
**联系人：**韩芳；俞亮
☎ 010-8460 0551
🖷 010-8460 0394
✉ zhaolingna@ciec.com.cn
www.jingmu.com.cn

### 供热、制冷、通风、水处理及卫生洁具展览会

**日期：**2010/04/20 - 23
**地点：**俄罗斯莫斯科
**周期：**每年一届
**市场范围：**国际性
**参展联络：**中国机械汽车展览联合会
☎ 010-6859 4964
🖷 010-6849 4964

### 国际物流技术与运输系统展览会

**日期：**2010/04/27 - 30
**地点：**俄罗斯莫斯科
**周期：**每年一届
**市场范围：**国际性
**参展联络：**中国机械汽车展览联合会

### 2010年俄罗斯莫斯科国际交通与物流展览会
### Trans Russia 2010

**日期：**2010/04/27 - 30
**地点：**俄罗斯莫斯科
**周期：**每年一届
**市场范围：**国际性
**主办：**法兰克福展览公司
**参展联络：**中国汽车工业国际合作总公司
**地址：**北京市海淀区中关村丹棱街3号A座5层（100080）
**联系人：**何萌
☎ 010-8260 6880
🖷 010-8260 6883
✉ exhibition@cnaico.com.cn

### 国际工业配件展览会

**日期：**2010/05 -
**地点：**俄罗斯莫斯科
**周期：**每年一届
**市场范围：**国际性
**参展联络：**中国机械汽车展览联合会
☎ 010-6859 4964
🖷 010-6849 4964

### 俄罗斯国际管材及线材展览会
### Tube & Wire Russia 2010

**日期：**2010/05 -
**地点：**俄罗斯莫斯科
**周期：**每年一届
**市场范围：**国际性
**参展联络：**中国贸促会机械行业分会
**地址：**北京市西城区三里河路46号（100823）
**联系人：**严静，陈媛蓉
☎ 010-6859 4938, 6859 5296, 6851 2883
🖷 010-6859 5057
✉ info@ccpitmsc.org
✉ jix@ccpit.org
www.chinamachin.org.cn
www.ccpitmsc.org

### 国际包装工业展览会

**日期**：2010/05 -
**地点**：俄罗斯莫斯科
**周期**：每年一届
**市场范围**：国际性
**参展联络**：中国机械汽车展览联合会
☎ 010-6859 4964
📠 010-6849 4964

### 俄罗斯国际机床工具展览会
### METALLOOBRABOTKA 2010

**日期**：2010/05 -
**地点**：俄罗斯莫斯科
**周期**：每年一届
**市场范围**：国际性
**参展联络**：中国贸促会机械行业分会
**地址**：北京市西城区三里河路46号（100823）
**联系人**：周海明，叶海青，聂飞
☎ 010-6859 5495, 6859 5247, 6851 3586, 6859 4938
📠 010-6859 5057
✉ info@ccpitmsc.org
✉ jix@ccpit.org
www.chinamachin.org.cn
www.ccpitmsc.org

### 2010年俄罗斯国家电信展
### SVIAZ/ EXPO COMM MOSCOW 2010

**日期**：2010/05/11 - 14
**地点**：俄罗斯莫斯科
**周期**：每年一届
**市场范围**：国际性
**主办**：中国邮电器材集团公司国际展览部
**地址**：北京西城区复兴门内大街156号北京招商国际金融中心A座10层A1008室
**联系人**：张宝林
☎ 010-6642 6288
📠 010-6642 6556
www.ptexpo.com.cn

### 西伯利亚贝加尔建设周展览会
### BAIKAL WEEK OF CONSTRUCTION TECHNOLOGIES

**日期**：2010/05/12 - 15
**地点**：俄罗斯伊尔库茨克
**内容**：新建筑技术、设备、原材料、服务等
**周期**：每年一届
**市场范围**：国际性
**参展联络**：京慕国际展览有限公司
**地址**：北京市朝阳区北三环东路6号中国国际展览中心服务楼3层
**联系人**：薛涵
☎ 010-8460 0551
📠 010-8460 0394
✉ zhaolingna@ciec.com.cn
www.jingmu.com.cn

## 莫斯科国际家具生产、木工及室内装饰展 俄罗斯春季家具展

### interzum moscow 2010
### EEM
### EuroExpoFurniture 2010

**日期**：2010/05/12 - 15
**地点**：俄罗斯莫斯科Crokus 博览中心
**内容**：莫斯科国际家具生产、木工及室内装饰展（interzum Moscow/Interkomplekt）和俄罗斯春季家具展(EEM/EuroExpoFurniture 2010) 同期于莫斯科Crocus 博览中心（Crocus Expo Exhibition Center）举行，后者是俄罗斯最重要的春季家具展。作为interzum 的系列展会，莫斯科国际家具生产、木工及室内装饰展在展示一系列国际领先的家具生产材料和辅助配件的同时，也让您对俄罗斯及东欧的家具市场及潮流走向拥有更深入的了解。
**周期**：两年一届
**市场范围**：国际性
**参展费用**：净地（24m²起）260欧元/m²，标准展位（9m²起）380欧元/m²
**上届规模** ‘08：展览面积20,174m²，专业贸易观众63,700人
**主办**：德国科隆展览国际有限公司；MVK JSC
**承办**：德国科隆展览国际有限公司
**地址**：科隆展览中国有限公司 北京东三环北路8号亮马河大厦2座1018室（100004）
**联系人**：贾宁
☎ 010-6590 7766 转 729
📠 010-6590 6139
✉ m.jia@koelnmesse
www.interzum-moscow.cn

## interzum moscow 2010
### EEM
### EuroExpoFurniture 2010

**Venue**: Crokus Expo Exhibition Center,
**Profile**: interzum moscow/ Interkomplekt provide a comprehensive overview into the broad country specific spectrum of the sector, held at the new Crokus Expo Exhibition Centre in Moscow. The fair presents an impressive range of materials and components for furniture production as well as an inside view of the Russian furniture market and Russian trends.
**Frequency**: Biennial
**Market Area**: International
**Participated Fee**: Raw Space EUR 260/m² (min 24m²), Standard Booth EUR 380/m² (min 9m²)
**Statistics '08**: Exhibition Area 20,174m², Trade Visitors 63,700
**Organizer**: Koelnmesse GmbH; MVK JSC
**Address**: Unit 1018, Landmark Tower Ⅱ, No. 8 Dongsanhuan North Rd,, Beijing 100004, China
**Contact**: Maggie Jia
☎ 86-10-6590 7766 ext 729
📠 86-10-6590 6139
✉ m.jia@koelnmesse
www.interzum-moscow.cn

### 国际焊接展览会

**日期**：2010/05/19 - 21
**地点**：俄罗斯圣彼得堡
**周期**：每年一届
**市场范围**：国际性
**参展联络**：中国机械汽车展览联合会
☎ 010-6859 4964
📠 010-6849 4964

### 国际机床展览会

**日期**：2010/05/24 - 28
**地点**：俄罗斯莫斯科
**周期**：每年一届
**市场范围**：国际性
**参展联络**：中国机械汽车展览联合会
☎ 010-6859 4964
📠 010-6849 4964

### 莫斯科国际工程机械展
### CTT

**日期**：2010/06 -
**地点**：俄罗斯莫斯科
**内容**：工程机械、矿山机械、建筑机械及其配件
**周期**：每年一届
**市场范围**：国际性
**参展联络**：京慕国际展览有限公司
**地址**：北京市朝阳区北三环东路6号中国国际展览中心服务楼3层
**联系人**：马赛，俞亮
☎ 010-8460 0551
📠 010-8460 0394
✉ zhaolingna@ciec.com.cn
www.jingmu.com.cn

### 第5届俄罗斯国际模具制造与技术展览会
### 5th Rosmould 2010

**日期**：2010/06 -
**地点**：俄罗斯莫斯科
**周期**：每年一届
**市场范围**：国际性
**参展联络**：中国贸促会机械行业分会
**地址**：北京市西城区三里河路46号（100823）
**联系人**：孙晓光，吴琼，纪冬冬
☎ 010-68595431, 6858 0868, 6859 4909, 6859 4826
📠 010-6859 5485
✉ info@ccpitmsc.org
✉ jix@ccpit.org
www.chinamachin.org.cn
www.ccpitmsc.org

### 俄罗斯国际包装工业展览会
### Rospack 2010

**日期**：2010/06 -
**地点**：俄罗斯莫斯科
**周期**：每年一届
**市场范围**：国际性
**参展联络**：中国贸促会机械行业分会
**地址**：北京市西城区三里河路46号（100823）
**联系人**：吕静，于奇琳，张垚
☎ 010-6859 4909, 6859 5498, 6859 4192
📠 010-6859 5485
✉ info@ccpitmsc.org
✉ jix@ccpit.org
www.chinamachin.org.cn
www.ccpitmsc.org

### 国际塑料及设备展览会

**日期**：2010/06/02 - 04
**地点**：俄罗斯莫斯科
**周期**：每年一届
**市场范围**：国际性
**参展联络**：中国机械汽车展览联合会
☎ 010-6859 4964
📠 010-6849 4964

### 第十七届俄罗斯国际采矿技术及煤矿设备展
### UGOL ROSSII & MINING 2010

**日期**：2010/06/04 - 07
**地点**：俄罗斯新库兹涅茨克市展览中心
**内容**：新库兹涅茨克位于库兹涅茨克煤田（简称库兹巴斯），该地区是俄罗斯规模最大的产煤区，面积2.67万平方公里，煤炭的工业储量居全国第一位。从二十世纪三十年代初开始，乌拉尔一库兹巴斯煤炭一冶金基地建立，新库兹涅茨克迅速发展。钢铁、电力、焦化、机械制造及有色冶金业均十分发达，成为俄罗斯乌拉尔以东最大的重工业基地。该展和当地库兹巴斯展览公司联合主办，受到了当地政府和协会的大力支持。
**周期**：每年一届
**市场范围**：国际性
**上届规模**：参展商552家（来自19个国家），参观人数21,000人
**主办**：德国杜塞尔多夫展览公司；库兹巴斯展览公司
**参展联络**：北京麦田通会国际展览有限公司
**联系人**：吴珊
☎ 010-5165 9302转 8010, 13426437438
📠 010-5165 9302转 8013

### 国际电力电子展览会

**日期**：2010/06/07 - 10
**地点**：俄罗斯莫斯科
**周期**：每年一届
**市场范围**：国际性
**参展联络**：中国机械汽车展览联合会
☎ 010-6859 4964
📠 010-6849 4964

### 2010年莫斯科国际汽车零部件展览会
### MIMS Automechanika Moscow 2010

**日期**：2010/08/25 - 29
**地点**：俄罗斯莫斯科
**周期**：每年一届
**市场范围**：国际性
**主办**：法兰克福展览公司

**参展联络**：中国汽车工业国际合作总公司
**地址**：北京市海淀区中关村丹棱街3号A座5层（100080）
**联系人**：何萌
☎ 010-8260 6880
🖷 010-8260 6883
✉ exhibition@cnaico.com.cn

### 第14届俄罗斯国际汽车及配件博览会
### Moscow International Motor Show

**日期**：2010/08/26 - 31
**地点**：俄罗斯莫斯科
**内容**：各类整车、机动车、自行车、各类汽车配件及附件、汽车用电子设备及安装设备、轮胎等;汽车发动机、底盘、车身及电器系统的各种零部件；汽车随车工具及检测、测试设备；汽车维修装备和机器厂房设备；汽车涂料及其设备；汽车装饰件及用品。
该展是俄罗斯及独联体国家最大的汽车配件展览会，也是该地区经国际汽车工业协会认证的唯一车展。展览品已含盖了汽车工业的所有产品，主要有汽车零部件、车用电器及维护产品等。2009 MIM参展商国家团组有中国、中国台湾、韩国、泰国、日本、美国、意大利、德国、西班牙、土耳其、新加坡、马来西亚、巴西等。中国展商2008年达到了几年来的参展高峰，展出面积高达2600多$m^2$，参展企业超过200余家。
**始办年份**：1991
**周期**：每年一届
**市场范围**：国际性
**上届规模** '09：展览面积2,600$m^2$，(来自48个国家)
**主办**：英国ITE
**参展联络**：北京中杰城设国际展览有限公司
**地址**：北京市海淀区三里河路9号建设部（100835）
**联系人**：全静
☎ 010-8838 4563
🖷 010-5885 7463
✉ quanjing68@126.com
MSN：quanjing_2008@hotmail.com
QQ：602693071

### 圣彼得堡国际建筑建材展览会
### Balticbuild

**日期**：2010/09 -
**地点**：俄罗斯圣彼得堡
**内容**：建筑材料、玻璃，建筑技术、建筑机械、建筑工具、五金、结构设计、卫浴设施、地砖、石材、涂料油漆保温隔热材料、屋面结构、墙体材料、防水材料、门、窗等
**周期**：每年一届
**市场范围**：国际性
**参展联络**：京慕国际展览有限公司
**地址**：北京市朝阳区北三环东路6号中国国际展览中心服务楼3层
**联系人**：薛涵，王芳
☎ 010-8460 0551
🖷 010-8460 0394
✉ zhaolingna@ciec.com.cn
www.jingmu.com.cn

### 俄罗斯国际五金工具展览会
### Intertool Moscow: 13th International Exhibition for Tools, Metal-Working & Manufacturing Industries

**日期**：2010/09 -
**地点**：俄罗斯莫斯科Crocus展览中心
**内容**：俄罗斯国际五金工具展览会于1998年创立，是俄罗斯工具行业最大、最顶级的国际展会，且被认为是最重要的交流和信息平台。展会吸引来自21个国家的530个展商以及15,000名观众。
**周期**：每年一届
**市场范围**：国际性
**参展费用**：净地295欧元/$m^2$，标准展位325欧元/$m^2$
**主办**：励展俄罗斯公司
**参展联络**：励展博览集团国际销售部
**地址**：北京市朝阳区新源里南路1-3号平安国际金融中心A座15层01-03，05（100027）
**联系人**：吴祥
☎ 010-5933 9288
🖷 010-5933 9233
✉ ronald.wu@reedexpo.com.cn
www.reedexport.cn

### 俄罗斯国际家用及室内纺织品展览会
### Heimtextil Russia

**日期**：2010/09 -
**地点**：俄罗斯莫斯科
**内容**：地布、窗饰布；家具面料及皮革；卧房纺织品；浴室纺织品；厨房用纺织品；面料后整理等**市场范围**：国际性
**参展联络**：京慕国际展览有限公司
**地址**：北京市朝阳区北三环东路6号中国国际展览中心服务楼3层
**联系人**：由慧；柳川
☎ 010-8460 0551
🖷 010-8460 0394
✉ zhaolingna@ciec.com.cn
www.jingmu.com.cn

### 俄联邦轻工纺织及设备博览会（秋季）
### Trade Fair For Textile & Light Industry Goods & Equipments

**日期**：2010/09 -
**地点**：俄罗斯莫斯科
**内容**：纺织面料、服装、家用针纺织品、地毯、鞋帽、室内装饰品、皮革制品、各种纺织原料、设备
**周期**：每年两届
**市场范围**：国际性
**参展联络**：京慕国际展览有限公司
**地址**：北京市朝阳区北三环东路6号中国国际展览中心服务楼3层
**联系人**：崔文佳；柳川
☎ 010-8460 0551
🖷 010-8460 0394
✉ zhaolingna@ciec.com.cn
www.jingmu.com.cn

### 莫斯科国际乐器展
### MUSIC MOSCOW

**日期**：2010/09 -
**地点**：俄罗斯莫斯科
**内容**：小型乐器、大型乐器、电子乐器；乐器配件与乐器用家具、刊物、专业音效及录音设备、舞台灯光、配件、多媒体
**周期**：每年一届
**市场范围**：国际性
**参展联络**：京慕国际展览有限公司
**地址**：北京市朝阳区北三环东路6号中国国际展览中心服务楼3层
**联系人**：王英瑶；王芳
☎ 010-8460 0551
🖷 010-8460 0394
✉ zhaolingna@ciec.com.cn
www.jingmu.com.cn

### 莫斯科国际健身及康体器材贸易展会
### MIOFF

**日期**：2010/09 -
**地点**：俄罗斯莫斯科
**内容**：健身器材，运动服装，背包，体操用品，瑜伽垫，划船、滑雪器械、运动保健等
**周期**：每年一届
**市场范围**：国际性
**参展联络**：京慕国际展览有限公司
**地址**：北京市朝阳区北三环东路6号中国国际展览中心服务楼3层
**联系人**：张璋
☎ 010-8460 0551
🖷 010-8460 0394
✉ zhaolingna@ciec.com.cn
www.jingmu.com.cn

### 西伯利亚森林利用和木材加工展览会
### Siberian Wood Industry

**日期**：2010/09/14 - 17
**地点**：俄罗斯伊尔库茨克
**内容**：木材加工设备，工具、机械、森林管理等
**周期**：每年一届
**市场范围**：国际性
**参展联络**：京慕国际展览有限公司
**地址**：北京市朝阳区北三环东路6号中国国际展览中心服务楼3层
**联系人**：薛涵
☎ 010-8460 0551
🖷 010-8460 0394
✉ zhaolingna@ciec.com.cn
www.jingmu.com.cn

### 2010莫斯科食品展
### World food moscow 2010

**日期**：2010/09/14 - 17
**地点**：俄罗斯莫斯科
**内容**：食品、饮料、酒类、食品原料、罐头食品、肉制品、乳制品、水果、蔬菜、海产品、咖啡、茶、糖果、饼干点心、婴儿食品、食品加工、包装技术及设备、保健食品、餐饮服务及相关技术等。
**始办年份**：1992
**周期**：每年一届
**市场范围**：国际性
**上届规模** '09：展览面积36,000$m^2$(国外展商面积20,000$m^2$)，参展商1,096家（国外展商55家，来自646个国家），专业贸易观众53,988人
**参展联络**：中企国际展览广告有限公司
**地址**：北京东土城路8号林达大厦B座3L（100013）
**联系人**：顾洪涛，杨光
☎ 010-6446 6671
🖷 010-8838 2248
✉ eaciecco@mx.cei.gov.cn
MSN：ceieac407@hotmail.com

### 俄罗斯国际计算机信息系统安全展览会
### Infosecurity Russia

**日期**：2010/10 -
**地点**：俄罗斯莫斯科
**内容**：莫斯科Infosecurity展会是俄罗斯、独联体及东欧等国在信息安全领域的绝佳展示及研讨平台。每年吸引众多专家及企业管理人来此获取信息安全技术，并寻求更好的方案以对抗信息方面的威胁。Infosecurity展馆占地4,000多平方米，吸引了70多家参展商及4,000多位信息安全专家参会。此次展会包含众多免费的会议项目，其中包括70多场圆桌会议、行业专区及研讨专题会等，围绕该行业诸多受关注的话题展开讨论。
**产品及服务**：Infosecurity是世界领先的IT业安全展会品牌，已分别在英国、加拿大、荷兰、比利时、法国、斯堪的纳维亚地区、意大利、印度及美国成功举办。
展览主题包括：访问令牌、反病毒、生物测定、证书管理机构、内容监控/过滤、数据存储、灾难恢复/业务延续、加密技术、防火墙、入侵探测系统、IT取证、虚拟专用网（VPN）、LAN/ WAN安全、管理安全服务、公开密钥体系（PKI）、物理安全措施程序、无线网络安全、渗透测试、风险评估、安全网络服务、政策发展、培训。
**周期**：每年一届
**市场范围**：国际性
**参展费用**：净地展位340欧元/$m^2$，报名费330欧元。展位升级附加费：两侧开放（拐角）10%，三侧开放（半岛状）15%，全开放（岛状）20%（如展商只在净地展位基础上搭建双层展台将收取50%附加费）

**赞助**：微软白金赞助，Tsifrovii Technologii大会赞助
**主办**：励展俄罗斯公司
**参展联络**：励展博览集团国际销售部
**地址**：北京市朝阳区新源里南路1-3号平安国际金融中心A座15层01-03，05（100027）
**联系人**：杜一鸣
☎ 010-5933 9288
🖷 010-5933 9233
✉ martin.du@reedexpo.com.cn
www.reedexport.cn

## 俄罗斯国际化妆品、美容博览会

InterCHARM:
The Largest Perfumery & Cosmetics Exhibition in Russia, Eastern & Central Europe

**日期**：2010/10 -
**地点**：俄罗斯莫斯科Crocus展览中心
**内容**：该展会是国际展会联盟UFI认证展会，是俄罗斯、独联体、东欧及中欧地区的领先美容行业展会。第14届InterCHARM净展览面积达19,500m$^2$（总展览面积：45,000m$^2$），参展商总数达876家 - 其中三分之一为国际参展商（包括来自保加利亚、巴西、中国、法国、德国、意大利、韩国、波兰、西班牙、台湾等地的国家展团与联合参展团），所占展览面积较上届增长8%。InterCHARM致力于通过丰富的展览及活动安排聚集行业决策者、满足观众及参展商需求、展示市场机会，是美容市场专业人士进行会面交流、寻求区域与国际合作伙伴、讨论重要话题、发现新产品的领先贸易展会平台。
**周期**：每年一届
**市场范围**：国际性
**参展费用**：净地295欧元/m$^2$,标准展位390欧元/m$^2$
**赞助**：俄罗斯联邦商业与工业部；俄罗斯香水与化妆品协会；莫斯科市政府
**主办**：励展俄罗斯公司
**参展联络**：励展博览集团国际销售部
**地址**：北京市朝阳区新源里南路1-3号平安国际金融中心A座15层01-03，05（100027）
**联系人**：吴祥
☎ 010-5933 9288
🖷 010-5933 9233
✉ ronald.wu@reedexpo.com.cn
www.reedexport.cn

## 新西伯利亚家具展

SIBFURNITURE 2010

**日期**：2010/10/05 - 08
**地点**：俄罗斯西伯利亚
**周期**：每年一届
**市场范围**：国际性
**参展联络**：大连上选会展服务有限公司
**地址**：大连市西岗区鞍山路13号兴业广场大厦B座508室（116011）
☎ 0411-8378 8326, 8378 8396, 8378 9165, 8378 8821
🖷 0411-8378 8830, 8378 8823
✉ cicyhuang@vip.sina.com
MSN：cicyhuang@msn.com
www.sun-show.com

## 2010俄罗斯金秋农业展览会

Golden Autumn 2010

**日期**：2010/10/08 - 11
**地点**：俄罗斯莫斯科
**内容**：各类食品饮料、食品加工、包装技术及设备；农业机械和设备：用于农作物种植、畜牧养殖等机械设备以及相关零部件及服务；灌溉和排水系统；饲料和饲料机械；农业化学产品；林业用品；各种牲畜，家禽及畜牧饲料工业；动物医学、兽医药相关产品；植物育种及相关技术等
**始办年份**：1998
**周期**：每年一届
**市场范围**：国际性
**上届规模**　'09：展览面积50,000m$^2$(国外展商面积35,000m$^2$)，参展商1,000家（国外展商350家，来自23个国家），专业贸易观众35,000人
**主办**：俄罗斯联邦农业部；莫斯科市政府；俄罗斯农业科学院；俄罗斯联邦农业联盟；全俄展览中心
**参展联络**：中企国际展览广告有限公司
**地址**：北京东土城路8号林达大厦B座3L（100013）
**联系人**：顾洪涛，杨光
☎ 010-6446 6671
🖷 010-8838 2248
✉ eaciecco@mx.cei.gov.cn
MSN：ceieac407@hotmail.com

## 俄罗斯石油和天然气技术展览会

SPE Russian Oil & Gas Technical Conference & Exhibition

**日期**：2010/10/26 - 28
　　　2012/10 -
**地点**：俄罗斯莫斯科All-Russian会展中心
**内容**：该展览会和研讨会是石油和天然气勘探及生产业的一次国际盛会。展会由石油工程师协会与励展公司共同举办。这个以研讨会为主的盛会将主要关注适合世界级工业发展的技术应用方面。
　　**展品范围**：钻井、井完成、地质和地球物理、油藏监测、测井与油井地层评价、设施工程、生产运作、渗流机制与原油回收方法、油藏工程、天然气技术、项目管理、出射和外围技术、健康/安全与环境。
**周期**：两年一届
**市场范围**：国际性
**参展费用**：净地235英磅/m$^2$，标准展位275英磅/m$^2$
**赞助**：Rosneft；Lukoil；TNK-BP Shell；Chevron；Halliburton；Schlumberger；OMV；Weatherford
**主办**：励展英国公司
**参展联络**：励展博览集团国际销售部
**地址**：北京朝阳区新源里南路1-3号平安国际金融中心A座15层01-03，05（100027）
**联系人**：宫卫
☎ 010-5933 9288
🖷 010-5933 9233
✉ david.gong@reedexpo.com.cn
www.reedexport.cn

## 俄罗斯国际冶金展览会

Metallurgy 2010

**日期**：2010/11 -
**地点**：俄罗斯莫斯科
**周期**：每年一届
**市场范围**：国际性
**参展联络**：中国贸促会机械行业分会
**地址**：北京市西城区三里河路46号（100823）
**联系人**：严静，陈媛蓉
☎ 010-6859 4938, 6859 5296, 6851 2883
🖷 010-6859 5057
✉ info@ccpitmsc.org
✉ jix@ccpit.org
www.chinamachin.org.cn
www.ccpitmsc.org

## 俄罗斯国际五金工具展览会

**日期**：2010/11 -
**地点**：俄罗斯莫斯科
**周期**：每年一届
**市场范围**：国际性
**参展联络**：中国贸促会机械行业分会
**地址**：北京市西城区三里河路46号（100823）
**联系人**：江彦明，袁丽娜
☎ 010-6859 4927, 6851 5863
🖷 010-6859 4948
✉ info@ccpitmsc.org
✉ jix@ccpit.org
www.chinamachin.org.cn
www.ccpitmsc.org

## 俄罗斯国际家具、配件及室内装潢展

MEBEL 2010

**日期**：2010/11 -
**地点**：俄罗斯
**周期**：每年一届
**市场范围**：国际性
**参展联络**：大连上选会展服务有限公司
**地址**：大连市西岗区鞍山路13号兴业广场大厦B座508室（116011）
☎ 0411-8378 8326, 8378 8396, 8378 9165, 8378 8821
🖷 0411-8378 8830, 8378 8823
✉ cicyhuang@vip.sina.com
MSN：cicyhuang@msn.com
www.sun-show.com

## 国际照明展览会

**日期**：2010/11 -
**地点**：俄罗斯莫斯科
**周期**：每年一届
**市场范围**：国际性
**参展联络**：中国机械汽车展览联合会
☎ 010-6859 4964
🖷 010-6859 4964

## 俄罗斯国际纸浆造纸、林业、生活用纸及纸包装展览会

PAP-FOR Russia:
International Exhibition and Conference for Russia's Pulp & Paper, Forestry, Tissue & Converting & Packaging Industries

**日期**：2010/11/08 - 11
　　　2012 -
**地点**：俄罗斯圣彼得堡
**内容**：俄罗斯及独联体地区规模最大、历史最悠久的纸浆造纸、林业、生活用纸及纸包装行业国际贸易博览会。 产品及服务 纸浆、纸板、纸转化产品、造纸系统和产品（储木场、纸浆制造、漂白、浆料准备、纸机、涂层、表面处理、化学材料、计算机、建造、数据处理、能源、工程、环保、仪器、维护、过程控制、质量控制、安全、测试）、纸转化系统和产品（印压、复卷设备、涂层设备、卷纸机、干燥设备、卷筒与卷轴、印刷、检查与扫描设备等）
**周期**：两年一届
**市场范围**：国际性
**参展费用**：净地430欧元/m$^2$，标准展位711欧元/m$^2$
**赞助**：俄罗斯联邦工业与电力工程部工业司；RAO Bumprom；西北部林业联盟；VNIIB - 俄罗斯纸浆造纸产业研究所；圣彼得堡植物聚合物科技大学；Pulp.Paper.Board 杂志；列宁格勒地区自然资源与环保委员会；芬兰纸业工程师协会
**主办**：励展俄罗斯公司
**参展联络**：励展博览集团国际销售部
**地址**：北京朝阳区新源里南路1-3号平安国际金融中心A座15层01-03，05（100027）
**联系人**：杜一鸣
☎ 010-5933 9288
🖷 010-5933 9233
✉ martin.du@reedexpo.com.cn
www.reedexport.cn

## 第15届莫斯科国际供暖、卫浴、通风及空调和环保展览会

aqua-therm Moscow:
15th International Exhibition for Heating, Ventilation, Air-Conditioning, Water Supply, Sanitary Equipment, Environmental Technology & Pools

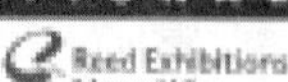

**日期**：2011/02 -
**地点**：俄罗斯莫斯科Crocus Expo会展中心
**内容**：由励展博览集团（Reed Exhibitions）和领先的国际展会主办机构ITE Moscow共同主办，至今为止，aqua-therm Moscow已成功举办过13届。在行业专家的鼎力支持下，主办单位广泛调查了解俄罗斯地区的行业消费者的购买意愿，并通过采取一系列有针对性的宣传策略，致力于为参展商提供最大价值的服务，定能为展商吸引更多顶级买家。本届展会将带来的一大亮点：除往届皆有的供暖产品展区，本届展会专为服务于泳池和Spa市场的展商设立了一个全新展区：World of Water & Spa。Aqua-therm将在位于莫斯科的Crocus Expo会展中心拉开帷幕。这也是莫斯科现代化程度最高、设备最好的展览中心，与莫斯科机场毗邻，位于商业区和市中心周边，交通便利。
**周期**：每年一届
**市场范围**：国际性
**参展费用**：净地295欧元/m²，标准展位320欧元/m²
**主办**：励展俄罗斯公司；俄罗斯联邦
**参展联络**：励展博览集团国际销售部
**地址**：北京朝阳区新源里南路1-3号平安国际金融中心A座15层01-03，05（100027）
**联系人**：宫卫
☎ 010-85185787, 5933 9288
🖷 010-5933 9233
✉ david.gong@reedexpo.com.cn
www.reedexport.cn

### 莫斯科安保展
### （俄罗斯国际安防技术论坛）
### Security & Safety Technologies Moscow (SST Moscow)

**日期**：2011/02 -
**地点**：俄罗斯莫斯科Crocus Expo会展中心
**内容**：SST-莫斯科安保展（俄罗斯国际安防技术论坛）是俄罗斯、独联体及东欧地区领先的安防行业展会，其参展商包括来自25个国家的近500家公司，同时举办40多场会议，观众包括买家、终端用户与系统安装商。SST是全世界安防公司展示新产品与解决方案的最佳平台。俄罗斯安防与安全产业与市场发展非常迅速。

展品范围：SST紧密联系俄罗斯与全球安防业市场，集中展示业内各领域的相关产品：闭路电视、门禁、生物识别、火灾报警、IT与特殊通讯系统、反恐、搜索器材、安防服务、工业安防、工作安全等
**周期**：每年一届
**市场范围**：国际性
**参展费用**：净地221欧元/m²，标准展位272欧元/m²
**主办**：励展俄罗斯公司
**参展联络**：励展博览集团国际销售部
**地址**：北京朝阳区新源里南路1-3号平安国际金融中心A座15层01-03，05（100027）
**联系人**：宫卫
☎ 010-5933 9288
🖷 010-5933 9233
✉ david.gong@reedexpo.com.cn
www.reedexport.cn

## 萨尔瓦多
## SALVADOR

### 中国贸易展览会

**日期**：2010/09 -
**地点**：萨尔瓦多圣萨尔瓦多
**周期**：每年一届
**市场范围**：国际性
**参展联络**：中国机械汽车展览联合会
☎ 010-6859 4964
🖷 010-6859 4964

## 沙特阿拉伯
## Saudi Arabia

### 国际石油、天然气及石化设备展览会

**日期**：2010/01/17 - 20
**地点**：沙特利雅得
**周期**：每年一届
**市场范围**：国际性
**参展联络**：中国机械汽车展览联合会
☎ 010-6859 4964
🖷 010-6859 4964

### 2010沙特医疗及医疗机械展

**日期**：2010/04/12 - 15
**地点**：沙特利雅得国际展览中心
**内容**：诊断设备、治疗设备、放疗设备、理疗设备、内外科手术设备、保健产品及设备、辅助设备（消毒灭菌设备、制冷设备、中央吸引供氧设备、空调设备、血库设备、医用化验及分析仪器设备、水处理设备、医用摄录像设备、分析仪器光电恒温设备等）、辅助材料（医用卫生材料、医用橡胶制品、医用搪瓷制品、玻璃仪器、不锈钢器皿等）、急救设备、制药机械和设备等
**周期**：每年一届
**市场范围**：国际性
**主办**：IFP集团
**联系人**：杨亚男
☎ 010-8763 5663
🖷 010-8763 5688
✉ ifp5633@ifpchina.com
MSN：laurayangyanan@hotmail.com
www.ifpchina.com

### 2010年第九届沙特（利雅得）国际电子通讯展

**日期**：2010/04/25 - 29
**地点**：沙特利雅得国际展览中心
**内容**：固定电话、移动电话及其配件：各种固定电话机、手机、手机耳机、免提设备、摄像头、红外、蓝牙设备、数据线、手机电池、按键、显示屏、充电器、SIM卡座、手机壳等。传输、交换设备：光纤放大器、光接收机、发射机、调制解调器、光纤收发器、网桥、分配器、交换机、网卡、无线网卡、路由器、集线器、转换器、切换器、中继器等。通信线缆、布线产品、天线：电脑接口线、光缆、网络线、通讯电缆，线卡、线扣、线槽、穿线管、跳线架、水晶头，通信天线、手机天线、卫星天线等其它：显示器、数码产品、对讲机、传真机、寻呼机、电信系统和设备、IT和软件、造卫星、无线电广播设备、远程信息处理。
**周期**：每年一届
**市场范围**：国际性
**预计规模**：展览总面积15,000m²
**主办**：IFP集团
**联系人**：杨亚男
☎ 010-8763 5663
🖷 010-8763 5688
✉ ifp5633@ifpchina.com
MSN：laurayangyanan@hotmail.com
www.ifpchina.com

### 2010沙特电力、能源、照明、水处理展

**日期**：2010/05/24 - 27
**地点**：沙特利雅得国际展览中心
**内容**：电站设备、电力装置、高压开关、低压电器、传输、配电网络、变压器、电流互感器、电压互感器、电力电容器、高压开关柜、监控器、电机工程、电力供应和附件、电线电缆、绝缘材料、测量设备
**周期**：每年一届
**市场范围**：国际性
**主办**：IFP集团
**联系人**：杨亚男
☎ 010-8763 5663
🖷 010-8763 5688
✉ ifp5633@ifpchina.com
MSN：laurayangyanan@hotmail.com
www.ifpchina.com

### 第22届沙特国际建筑及石材贸易博览会

**日期**：2010/10/03 - 06
**地点**：沙特利雅得
**内容**：建筑及石材贸易博览会
**市场范围**：国际性
**参展联络**：北京中仕达兴业展览有限公司
**地址**：北京市海淀区蓝靛厂东路2号金源时代商务中心2号楼A座11B（100097）
**联系人**：贾倩，赵仕忱，牟向东，张露
☎ 010-5129 8900
🖷 010-8886 2939
✉ mail@chinstar.cn
www.chinstar.cn

### 2010沙特建材—PMV
### （重工机械展）
### The International Exhibition for Construction Equipment Plant, Machinery and Vehicles

**日期**：2010/10/18 - 21
**地点**：沙特利雅得展览中心
**内容**：建筑车辆：自卸车，牵引车，混合机、开凿机、推土机、卡车、拖车、叉车、升降车半挂牵引车、运输特殊部件的卡车、路面清扫车、沥青铺路设备、车体部件、运土设备、各类零配件；建筑机械：隧道工程专用机械、隧道掘进机、开凿机、挖掘装载机、升降机、铲运机、推土机、零部件、堆垛机钻孔设备及系统、焊接设备和配附件、电缆敷设机械、管道和电缆探测器、压缩机、压路机、平板式振捣器、夯、土壤固化剂、垃圾压实机、道路施工、养护及修复专用机械、铁路铺设机械、墙体切割机；起重和传送装置：吊车、起重机、传送平台、工作平台、高空作业平台、升降机、滑轮铰链、电动吊车、电动葫芦、真空搬运系统、压土机、压缩机、泵、爆破施工机械、重机械及设备、钻孔机、起卸机、挖掘机及支柱、水压机械
**始办年份**：2009
**周期**：每年一届
**市场范围**：国际性
**主办**：IFP集团
**联系人**：杨亚男
☎ 010-8763 5663
🖷 010-8763 5688
✉ ifp5633@ifpchina.com
MSN：laurayangyanan@hotmail.com
www.ifpchina.com

### 2010年沙特利雅得中国商品展

**日期**：2010/12/05 - 08
**地点**：沙特阿拉伯利雅得展览中心
**内容**：纺织品及服装鞋帽；轻工产品；食品；机电产品；汽车、摩托车及零配件；建筑材料等。
首届
**市场范围**：国际性
**预计规模**：展出面积3,000m²，参展厂商150家，参观人数6,000人
**主办**：中企国际展览广告有限公司
**地址**：北京东土城路8号林达大厦B座3L（100013）
**联系人**：顾洪涛，杨光
☎ 010-6446 6671
🖷 010-8838 2248
✉ eaciecco@mx.cei.gov.cn
MSN：ceieac407@hotmail.com

## 新加坡
## Singapore

### 新加坡国际家具展
### IFFS 2010

**日期**：2010/03/09 - 12
**地点**：新加坡新加坡

内容：针对欧美市场的家具展，中国每年有近百个厂家参加的最热门展览，且为参展成本最低。
周期：每年一届
市场范围：国际性
参展联络：大连上选会展服务有限公司
地址：大连市西岗区鞍山路13号兴业广场大厦B座508室（116011）
☎ 0411-8378 8326, 8378 8396, 8378 9165, 8378 8821
传真 0411-8378 8830, 8378 8823
✉ cicyhuang@vip.sina.com
MSN：cicyhuang@msn.com
www.sun-show.com

## 亚太海事展

Asia Pacific Maritime

日期：2010/03/24 - 26
2012/03 -
地点：新加坡博览中心
内容：亚太海事展是亚太地区海事行业一站式的交易会，展示海事工程及港口科技领域的最新产品和技术。APM被誉为新加坡最重要的国际海事展，它集展会、研讨会和小组讨论为一体，提供完整的行业体验；同时，它的一系列联络活动将亚太地区的高级买家与国际海事供应商联系起来。APM为您节省时间，使您在最快的时间内找到可以让您的公司领先于海事市场的产品。APM也为您提供开拓国际市场和扩展全球业务的机会。

展商来源：造船、船只维修和改造、海事设备、推进力系统（主推进力和辅助推进力）、船只运行设备、海事技术、电子/电力工程、港口技术、货物传输系统、货代、货代设备、配件及存储、海事服务、海事安全、导航与通讯技术。
周期：两年一届
市场范围：国际性
参展费用：净地630新加坡元/m²，标准展位760～800新加坡元/m²
主办：励展新加坡公司（亚太总部）
参展联络：励展博览集团国际销售部
地址：北京朝阳区新源里南路1-3号平安国际金融中心A座15层01-03，05（100027）
联系人：宫卫
☎ 010-85185787, 5933 9288
传真 010-5933 9233
✉ david.gong@reedexpo.com.cn
www.reedexport.cn

### 新加坡牙科展览会

IDEM

日期：2010/04 -
地点：新加坡
内容：牙科实验室用设备和仪器
周期：每年一届
市场范围：国际性
参展联络：京慕国际展览有限公司
地址：北京市朝阳区北三环东路6号中国国际展览中心服务楼3层
联系人：安红彦，孙铁兵
☎ 010-8460 0551
传真 010-8460 0394
✉ zhaolingna@ciec.com.cn
www.jingmu.com.cn

### 第十七届新加坡食品酒店站

日期：2010/04/20 - 23
地点：新加坡
主办：北京邦企展览服务有限公司
地址：北京市朝阳区惠新东街11号紫光发展大厦B1-501（100029）
联系人：雷绍军先生，赖玉宝小姐
☎ 010-6482 3808
传真 010-6482 3670
✉ bbes@china.com

### 新加坡国际水族及配件展

Aquarama

日期：2010/05 -
地点：新加坡新加坡
内容：海洋淡水鱼类、水族植物、鱼食、水上家具与照明、喷泉、庭院植物、庭院诗品、土壤灌溉、宠物用品等
周期：两年一届
市场范围：国际性
参展联络：京慕国际展览有限公司
地址：北京市朝阳区北三环东路6号中国国际展览中心服务楼3层
联系人：滕昊，李萌
☎ 010-8460 0551
传真 010-8460 0394
✉ zhaolingna@ciec.com.cn
www.jingmu.com.cn

## 2010年亚洲建筑及室内装饰展览会

BEX asia 2010

日期：2010/05 -
地点：新加坡SUNTEC会展中心
内容：该展会将成为东南亚建筑与建造业的潮流风向标，为业界全面展示国际最新、最先进的产品、材料、应用、技术、科技、服务与设备，同时也是业界专业人士聚会、交流、开展合作、洽谈业务的理想平台。
周期：每年一届
市场范围：国际性
参展费用：净地展位595新加坡元/m²，标准展位715新加坡元/m²*
支持：新加坡建筑协会（SIA）；建筑及施工委员会（BCA） 新加坡会展局（SECB）新加坡旅游局分支机构；新加坡相关行业组织：空调及制冷协会（ARA）；天然石材协会；新加坡建筑材料供应商协会（SBMSA）；新加坡电气行业协会（SETA）；新加坡电气工程承包商及持照电工协会（SECA）；新加坡家具工业委员会；新加坡玻璃协会（SGA）；新加坡电梯工程承包商及制造商协会（SLECMA）；新加坡水管业协会（SPS）
主办：新加坡励展私人有限公司
参展联络：励展博览集团国际销售部
地址：北京市朝阳区新源里南路1-3号平安国际金融中心A座15层01-03，05（100027）
联系人：王颖
☎ 010-5933 9288
传真 010-5933 9233
✉ winnie.wang@reedexpo.com.cn
www.reedexport.cn

## 亚洲制药工业展览会

Interphex Asia:
Asia's Dedicated Sourcing Platform for Pharmaceutical Manufacturing

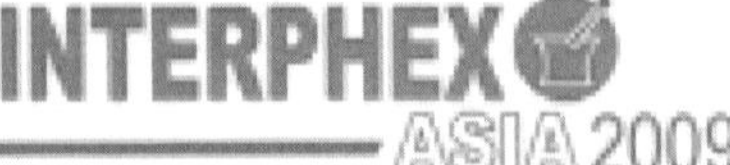


日期：2010/06 -
2011 -
地点：新加坡新达城展览中心
内容：亚洲制药工业展览会(INTERPHEX Asia)致力于全面展示亚洲制药行业的机械设备与材料新品，展会汇集了许多来自亚太地区的药品生产专家和国际供应商。新加坡作为活动主办地，在地理位置上，处在像印度尼西亚，马来群岛，菲律宾和泰国这样的发展中市场的中心，加之展会中举办的同期会议ISPE Singapore Conference，意味着您将会在展会中与该地区制药生产链上的资深人士不期而遇，与其交换意见并共同探讨亚洲地区的行业发展。
周期：每年一届
市场范围：国际性
参展费用：净地485美元/m²，标准展位585美元/m²
主办：励展新加坡公司
参展联络：励展博览集团国际销售部
地址：北京朝阳区新源里南路1-3号平安国际金融中心A座15层01-03，05（100027）
联系人：申健
☎ 010-8518 2644, 5933 9288
传真 010-5933 9233
✉ jerry.shen@reedexpo.com.cn
www.reedexport.cn

### 国际汽车配件展览会

日期：2010/06 -
地点：新加坡新加坡城
周期：每年一届
市场范围：国际性
参展联络：中国机械汽车展览联合会
☎ 010-6859 4964
传真 010-6859 4964

### 第十五届国际数字多媒体与广播科技展览会及研讨会

日期：2010/06/15 - 18
地点：新加坡
主办：北京邦企展览服务有限公司
地址：北京市朝阳区惠新东街11号紫光发展大厦B1-501（100029）
联系人：雷绍军先生，赖玉宝小姐
☎ 010-6482 3808
传真 010-6482 3670
✉ bbes@china.com

### 第21届国际通讯与资讯科技展览及研讨会

日期：2010/06/15 - 18
地点：新加坡
主办：北京邦企展览服务有限公司
地址：北京市朝阳区惠新东街11号紫光发展大厦B1-501（100029）
联系人：雷绍军先生，赖玉宝小姐
☎ 010-6482 3808
传真 010-6482 3670
✉ bbes@china.com

## 新加坡电子展

Global TRONINCS

日期：2010/09/15 - 17
2012/09 -
地点：新加坡Suntec展览馆
内容：新加坡环球电子展是东南亚及亚太地区最具影响力、规模最大、专业水平很高的电子专业展，由世界上最大的展览公司之一励展国际博览集团组织。参展商有来自世界各国的千余家企业，观众数万人，其中近半数来自亚太各国。共有中国、德国、意大利、英国、日本、韩国、马来西亚、新加坡、香港、台湾等十个国家和地区馆，来自美国、比利时、瑞士、芬兰、法国、匈牙利、澳大利亚、新西兰、爱尔兰、墨西哥、斯里兰卡等国家的展商参加。参展商普遍反映此次展会观众质量较高，效果明显。欢迎各有关企业报名参展。由于展位有限，请尽快申请！
产品及服务：应用集成电路、光电半导体器件、功率半导体器件、半导体传感器及固体传感器、各类阻容元件、真空电子器件、光导纤维、封装材料、PCB组件及原材料、电子保护装置、接插件、各种连

接器、开关、按键及键盘、无源微波器件、各种显示器件、磁盘驱动器、光盘驱动器及配件、磁性材料、网卡、电机、计算机外部设备及材料、电子工模具、各种电子测量仪器、电子整机配套组件、防静电器材、各种电源等。
**周期：**两年一届
**市场范围：**国际性
**参展费用：**净地展位675新加坡元/m²，标准展位775新加坡元/m²
**参展联络：**励展博览集团国际销售部
**地址：**北京朝阳区新源里南路1-3号平安国际金融中心A座15层01-03，05（100027）
**联系人：**杜一鸣
☎ 010-5933 9288
🖷 010-5933 9233
✉ martin.du@reedexpo.com.cn
www.reedexport.cn

### 亚洲电视论坛

Asia Television Forum (ATF)

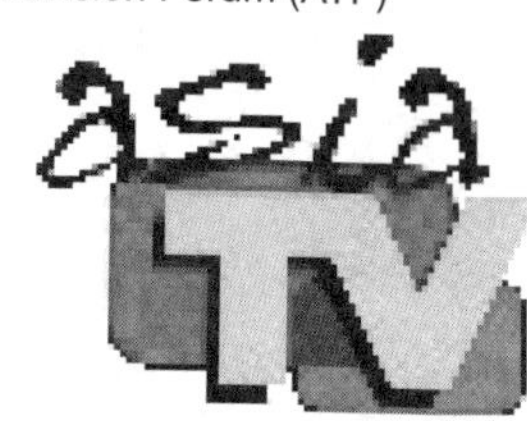

**日期：**2010/12 -
**地点：**新加坡Suntec展览中心
**内容：**亚洲电视论坛是亚洲最好的电视节目集市，聚集了国际电视节目销售商和亚洲的电视节目采购商及合伙人。ATF与亚洲影片交流与研讨会同场举办，造就了亚太地区最全面的一站式电影电视采购平台。每年都有来自超过22个亚洲国家的电影电视节目采购商参加。
**产品及服务：**17个类别的地面、有线及卫星电视节目：动画、儿童节目、喜剧、时事、纪实剧、记录片、电视剧、教育片、长片电影、轻娱乐节目、古典音乐和芭蕾、连续片、连续剧、系列片、短节目、情景喜剧、体育以及音乐录影带。
**周期：**每年一届
**市场范围：**国际性
**参展联络：**励展博览集团国际销售部
**地址：**北京朝阳区新源里南路1-3号平安国际金融中心A座15层01-03，05（100027）
**联系人：**杜一鸣
☎ 010-8515 1376
🖷 010-85151 304
✉ martin.du@reedexpo.com.cn
www.reedexport.cn
www.asiatvforum.com

### 东南亚石油及天然气科技展览会暨研讨会

**日期：**2010/12/03 - 06
**地点：**新加坡
**内容：**石油、天然气、勘探、钻采、管道阀门
**主办：**北京邦企展览有限公司
**地址：**北京市朝阳区惠新东街11号紫光发展大厦B1-501（100029）
**联系人：**雷邵军，赖玉宝
☎ 010-6482 3808
🖷 010-6482 3670
✉ bbes@china.com

### 新加坡国际缝制设备展览会

International Apparel Machinery Trade Show (JIAM 2011)

**日期：**2011/05 -
**地点：**新加坡展览中心
**内容：**世界三大缝制设备展会之一的JIAM首次于2008年5月在新加坡举行。本届展会为期4天，其主题为“将技术从JIAM推向世界之门”，将展出来自世界领先厂商和供应商的最新、最先进机械及设备，并展示为服装、服饰产业提供解决方案的高度创新、尖端的技术。JIAM展会在亚洲出口商和世界服装市场间起着关键的桥梁作用。
**始办年份：**2008
**市场范围：**国际性
**参展费用：**净地展位315,000日元（9m²）
**主办：**励展新加坡公司（亚太总部）
**参展联络：**励展博览集团国际销售部
**地址：**北京朝阳区新源里南路1-3号平安国际金融中心A座15层01-03，05（100027）
**联系人：**杜一鸣
☎ 010-5933 9288
🖷 010-5933 9233
✉ martin.du@reedexpo.com.cn
www.reedexport.cn

## 斯洛伐克 Slovakia

### 第31届斯洛伐克国际建筑工程展

**日期：**2010/03/23 - 27
**地点：**斯洛伐克布拉迪斯拉发
**内容：**国际建筑工程
**周期：**每年一届
**市场范围：**国际性
**参展联络：**北京中仕达兴业展览有限公司
**地址：**北京市海淀区蓝靛厂东路2号金源时代商务中心2号楼A座11B（100097）
**联系人：**贾倩，赵仕忱，牟向东，张露
☎ 010-5129 8900
🖷 010-8886 2939
✉ mail@chinstar.cn
www.chinstar.cn

## 南非 South Africa

### 第4届非洲石油、天然气和石油化工展览会

**日期：**2010/03/16 - 18
**地点：**南非开普敦
**周期：**每年一届
**市场范围：**国际性
**参展联络：**中国机械汽车展览联合会
☎ 010-6859 4964
🖷 010-6859 4964

### 中国贸易博览会

**日期：**2010/07 -
**地点：**南非米德兰德
**周期：**每年一届
**市场范围：**国际性
**参展联络：**中国机械汽车展览联合会
☎ 010-6859 4964
🖷 010-6859 4964

### 南非建材展

Interbuild

**日期：**2010/07 -
**地点：**南非约翰内斯堡
**内容：**建筑材料、玻璃，建筑技术、建筑机械、建筑工具、五金、结构设计、卫浴设施、地砖、石材、涂料油漆保温隔热材料、屋面结构、墙体材料、防水材料、门、窗等
**周期：**每年一届
**市场范围：**国际性
**参展联络：**京慕国际展览有限公司
**地址：**北京市朝阳区北三环东路6号中国国际展览中心服务楼3层
**联系人：**薛涵，王芳
☎ 010-8460 0551
🖷 010-8460 0394
✉ zhaolingna@ciec.com.cn
www.jingmu.com.cn

### 国际五金工具展览会

**日期：**2010/08 -
**地点：**南非约翰内斯堡
**周期：**每年一届
**市场范围：**国际性
**参展联络：**中国机械汽车展览联合会
☎ 010-6859 4964
🖷 010-6859 4964

### 南非约翰内斯堡家具家居及室内装饰展

Decorex 2010

**日期：**2010/08/05 - 09
**地点：**南非约翰内斯堡
**周期：**每年一届
**市场范围：**国际性
**参展联络：**大连上选会展服务有限公司
**地址：**大连市西岗区鞍山路13号兴业广场大厦B座508室（116011）
☎ 0411-8378 8326, 8378 8396, 8378 9165, 8378 8821
🖷 0411-8378 8830, 8378 8823
✉ cicyhuang@vip.sina.com
MSN：cicyhuang@msn.com
www.sun-show.com

### 国际采矿设备、电机工程、石油机械、一般工业及材料处理展览会

**日期：**2010/10/04 - 08
**地点：**南非约翰内斯堡
**周期：**每年一届
**市场范围：**国际性
**参展联络：**中国机械汽车展览联合会
☎ 010-6859 4964
🖷 010-6859 4964

### 2010年南非国际建筑建材博览会

**日期：**2010/9/8 - 11
**地点：**南非约翰内斯堡展览中心
**内容：**建筑材料：陶瓷、天然石材、人造石材、塑料异型材、铝型材、修饰材料、涂料、油漆、镶边瓷砖、墙纸及墙板镶嵌等、门窗材料（木、铝合金、塑料、塑钢等）顶棚和房顶材料；灯具灯饰、室内装饰材料、玻璃及金属型材、新型建材；建筑五金工具、涂料、管件阀门、消防安全器材；门窗、厨房设施、厨房设备；卫浴洁具、瓷砖、建筑石材；保温材料及设备、环保设备及用品；建筑器材、建筑机械设备等。
**始办年份：**1968
**周期：**两年一届
**上届规模** ‘08：展览面积25,000m²，参展商650家，参观人数18,000人
**主办：**北京领汇国际展览有限公司
**地址：**北京市朝阳区农展馆南路13号瑞辰国际中心718-719（100125）
**联系人：**张爽
☎ 010-5129 5359-8810
🖷 010-5129 5379-8810
✉ bangni5858@163.com
MSN：expo8810@worldfairs.cn
QQ：574000135
www.worldfairs.cn

### 南非国际贸易展览会

SAITEX 2010

**日期：**2010/10 -
**地点：**南非约翰内斯堡
**周期：**每年一届

市场范围：国际性
参展联络：中国贸促会机械行业分会
地址：北京市西城区三里河路46号（100823）
联系人：严立群
☎ 010-6859 4807
🖷 010-6859 4917
✉ info@ccpitmsc.org
✉ jix@ccpit.org
www.chinamachin.org.cn
www.ccpitmsc.org

### 南非国际矿山与电力博览会

### Electra Mining Africa 2010

日期：2010/10/04 - 08
地点：南非约翰内斯堡
周期：两年一届
市场范围：国际性
参展联络：中国贸促会机械行业分会
地址：北京市西城区三里河路46号（100823）
联系人：赵小轶
☎ 010-6859 5176
✉ info@ccpitmsc.org
✉ jix@ccpit.org
www.chinamachin.org.cn
www.ccpitmsc.org

## 韩国 South Korea

### 2010韩国大邱国际纤维展

### Preview in Daegu 2010

日期：2010/03/10 - 12
地点：韩国大邱展览会议中心
内容：各类家用纺织品：铺地材料、墙布、窗帘、床上及浴用亚麻制品、桌布、装饰布。各类天然原料、面料：丝、棉、麻、毛、羊绒及混纺面料。各种制衣用纱线、面料：针织布、梭织布、坯布、化纤、印染布。各种服装辅料、辅件：拉链、扣子、衬、垫、饰物。各类工业用纺织品原料、面料：纤维、线、无纺布、涂层织物、压层织物、合成织物。各种相关出版物：书籍、图案、软件等。
始办年份：2001
周期：每年一届
市场范围：国际性
性质：面向公众
入场券价格：免费
参展费用：标准展位2,000美元，净地展位1,800美元
主办：韩国纤维产业联合会；大韩贸易投资振兴公社（KOTRA）；大邱广域市
联系人：慕晗
☎ 021-5108 8771转126
🖷 021-6219 6015
✉ kotra@yahoo.cn
MSN：m_muhan@hotmail.com
www.previewin.com

### Preview in Daegu 2010

Date：2010/03/10 - 12
Venue: EXCO
Profile: Preview In DAEGU(PID), the Spring/Summer international textile fair, represents the excellence of Korean textile manufacturers in terms of innovative technology in high-tech & functional fabrics, and invites trend-seekers in order to cope with rapid & unpredictable contemporary trends in daily basis.
Established Year: 2001
Frequency: Annual
Market Area: International
Nature: Open to public
Cost to Attend: Free
Participated Fee: Standard Booth USD 2,000, Raw Space USD 1,800
Contact: MU Han
☎ 86-21-5108 8771 ext 126
🖷 86-21-6219 6015
✉ kotra@yahoo.cn
MSN: m_muhan@hotmail.com
www.previewin.com

### 2010韩国国际太阳能、风能、地能展览会

### SWEET 2010

日期：2010/03/17 - 19
地点：韩国光州金大中会展中心
内容：太阳能、太阳光、风能、地热、生物能、燃料电池及第二代电池、海洋能、氢气、煤气化、煤液化、环保•资源再利用、节能•高效能源
市场范围：国际性
性质：面向公众
参展费用：标准展位2,000美元，净地展位1,700美元
主办：大韩贸易投资振兴公社（KOTRA）；韩国光州广域市政府；全罗南道政府；金大中会展中心；韩国能源经济新闻
地址：上海市长宁区兴义路8号万都中心3110室（200336）
联系人：慕晗
☎ 021-5108 8771转126
🖷 021-6219 6015
✉ kotra@yahoo.cn
MSN：m_muhan@hotmail.com
www.previewin.com

### SWEET 2010

Date：2010/03/17 - 19
Venue: Kimdaejung Convention Center
Profile: Photovoltaics; Solar Thermal; Wind Power; Hydrogen; Fuel Cell; Geothermal; Biomass; Marine Energy; Integrated Gasification Combined Cycle; Hydropower; Waste Energy; Environmental Protection & Resource-recycling; High Energy-efficient & Energy Saving;
Market Area: International
Nature: Open to public
Participated Fee: Standard Booth USD 2,000, Raw Space USD 1,700
Contact: MU Han
Address: No. 8 Xingyi Road, Room 3110 Maxdo Centre, Changning District, Shanghai
☎ 86-21-5108 8771 ext 126
🖷 86-21-6219 6015
✉ kotra@yahoo.cn
MSN: m_muhan@hotmail.com
www.previewin.com

## 韩国电子展

### Nepcon Korea: SMT/PCB & NEPCON KOREA

日期：2010/03/31 - 02
地点：韩国首尔Coex会展中心
内容：韩国领先的电子元件和配套产品生产展会。
产品和服务：SMT相关设备和材料，PCB生产设备和材料，电子零件生产设备和材料，IT终端产品的自动化生产设备和材料，电子元件和测试检测设备，控制设备和材料，微电子技术和包装技术
周期：每年一届
市场范围：国际性
参展费用：净地展位400美元，标准展位450美元
主办：励展日本公司
参展联络：励展博览集团国际销售部
地址：北京市朝阳区新源里南路1-3号平安国际金融中心A座15层01-03，05（100027）
联系人：杜一鸣
☎ 010-5933 9288
🖷 010-5933 9233
✉ martin.du@reedexpo.com.cn
www.reedexport.cn

### 第14届韩国国际机床展览会

### The 14th Republic of Korea (Seoul) International Machine Tool Exhibition

日期：2010/04/13 - 18
地点：韩国国际展览厅
内容：属切削机床，金属成型机床，工业机器人领域，制造单元/系统及自动化设备领域，工具、检验和测量设备领域，机床零部件、辅助设备、数控系统领域，其他
始办年份：1984
周期：两年一届
市场范围：国际性
参展费用：净地280美元/m²
主办：韩国产业资源部
参展联络：机床工业协会
地址：广东省深圳市福田区新洲大厦15层（518048）
联系人：雷明，朱利萍
☎ 0755-2393 8881, 2393 8025
🖷 0755-2393 8426
✉ cmffok@163.com
MSN：lm83573425@21cn.com
参展联络：中国贸促会机械行业分会
地址：北京市西城区三里河路46号（100823）
联系人：周海明，叶海青，聂飞
☎ 010-6859 5495, 6859 5247, 6851 3586, 6859 4938
🖷 010-6859 5057
✉ info@ccpitmsc.org jix@ccpit.org
www.chinamachin.org.cn
www.ccpitmsc.org

### The 14th Republic of Korea (Seoul) International Machine Tool Exhibition

Date：2010/04/13 - 18
Venue: KINTEX, Seoul
Profile: Metal cutting machine tools, metal forming machine tools, industrial robotics, manufacturing units/systems and automation equipment, tools, testing and measuring equipment, machine tools Zero Parts, Auxiliary Equipment. CNC systems, the other
Established Year: 1984
Frequency: Biennial
Market Area: International
Participated Fee: Raw Space USD 280/m²
Organizer: South Korea's Ministry of Industry and Energy
Contact: Machine Tool Industry Association
Address: 15/Fl Xinzhou Building, Futian District, Shenzhen, Guangdong
☎ 0755-2393 8881, 2393 8025
🖷 0755-2393 8426
Contact: Rei Ming, Julius Ping
✉ cmffok@163.com
MSN: lm83573425@21cn.com

### 2010年第28届韩国首尔国际食品展

### International Food Industry Exhibition Seoul 2010 (IFIES)

日期：2010/05/12 - 15
地点：韩国首尔国际展览中心
内容：糖果，面包，乳制品，小吃，休闲/方便食品；健康/保健食品，调料品/香料，食品添加剂及原材料；饮料、酒精饮料（葡萄酒，啤酒，白酒，各国特色酒，软饮料，果汁，健康饮料）咖啡；蔬菜，水果，禽，谷，水产品等，冷冻与方便食物，熟食品；茶及咖啡/茶的消费用品等；食品加工器材，面包糖果加工器材及加工附件，饮料/酿酒加工机，冷饮/制冷机械设备，及其食品家电等。饭馆，酒店，超级市场的装备与机器入厨房器具&器材，烹饪用具，酒吧/咖啡馆的服务设备，食品服务设备，食品储存设备，食品预备装置。
始办年份：1982
周期：每年一届

市场范围：国际性
性质：面向公众
参展费用：净地展位280美元/m²(18m²起)，标准展位3,015美元/9m²
主办：大韩贸易投资振兴公社（KOTRA）；韩国食品工业协会（KFIA）
地址：上海市长宁区兴义路8号万都中心3110室（200336）
联系人：慕晗
☎ 021-5108 8771转126
🖷 021-6219 6015
✉ kotra@yahoo.cn
MSN：m_muhan@hotmail.com
www.previewin.com

## International Food Industry Exhibition Seoul 2010 (IFIES)

Date：2010/05/12 - 15
Venue: KINTEX
Established Year: 1982
Frequency: Annual
Market Area: International
Nature: Open to public
Participated Fee: Raw Space USD 280/m² (min 18m²) , Standard Booth USD 3,015/9m²
Organizer: KOTRA; KIFA; Allworld; KEM
Address: No. 8 Xingyi Road, Room 3110 Maxdo Centre, Changning District, Shanghai
Contact: MU Han
☎ 86-21-51088771 ext 126
🖷 86-21-6219 6015
✉ kotra@yahoo.cn
MSN: m_muhan@hotmail.com
www.previewin.com

## 2010韩国国际游艇展

## Korea International Boat Show 2010

日期：2010/06/09 - 13
地点：韩国京畿道华城市田谷港
内容：舰艇及豪华游艇：动力艇及帆船、豪华及超豪华游艇、橡皮艇、充气艇、游览船。复合材料及设备:动力装置、推进系统、配套设备、硬件、便携式设备、通讯导航设备、发动机/驱动器、救生装置。水上运动:独木舟和皮筏、潜水、帆船运动、帆板、水橇设备、潜水装置、航行及帆船驾驶课程，便携式健康运动设备。码头、休闲活动及服务:码头开发商、港口和船坞设备、码头设备、船艇设计公司。与海洋有关的政府机关、教育部门及团体
始办年份：2008
周期：每年一届
市场范围：国际性
性质：面向公众
主办：韩国文化经济部；韩国文化体育旅游部；京畿道政府；华城市政府；大韩贸易投资振兴公社
地址：上海市长宁区兴义路8号万都中心3110室（200336）
联系人：慕晗
☎ 021-5108 8771转126
🖷 021-6219 6015
✉ kotra@yahoo.cn
MSN：m_muhan@hotmail.com
www.previewin.com

## Korea International Boat Show 2010

Date：2010/06/09 - 13
Venue: Jeongok Marina, Hwaseong City, Gyeonggi
Established Year: 2008
Frequency: Annual
Market Area: International
Nature: Open to public
Contact: MU Han
Address: No. 8 Xingyi Road, Room 3110 Maxdo Centre, Changning District, Shanghai
☎ 86-21-5108 8771ext 126
🖷 86-21-6219 6015
✉ kotra@yahoo.cn
MSN: m_muhan@hotmail.com
www.previewin.com

## 2010年韩国汽车零配件展览会

## KOAA Show 2010

日期：2010/09 -
地点：韩国高阳
内容：各种汽车、商务用车、摩托机车、大篷车的相关零部件；发动机部分，身体部分，刹车部分，掌舵部分，悬挂部分，电部分，驾驶和输送部分等等；汽车有关货物整理，协调工具，电气产品，汽车仪器；AV/GPS和各种各样的汽车附件 AV 确定，CD 变换器，GPS 传感器，mp3/CDP，航行，扩音器/低音扬声器，小汽车电视，汽车音响，调谐设备/ 放大器，各类汽车美容；其它高科技项目，新开发的汽车和有关的技术等
周期：每年一届
市场范围：国际性
主办：法兰克福展览公司
参展联络：中国汽车工业国际合作总公司
地址：北京市海淀区中关村丹棱街3号A座5层（100080）
联系人：何萌
☎ 010-8260 6880
🖷 010-8260 6883
✉ exhibition@cnaico.com.cn

## 国际印刷机械设备展览会

日期：2010/09/08 - 11
地点：韩国高阳
周期：每年一届
市场范围：国际性
参展联络：中国机械汽车展览联合会
☎ 010-6859 4964
🖷 010-6859 4964

## 2010 光州国际文化创意产业展

## Gwangju ACE Fair 2010

日期：2010/09/09 - 12
地点：韩国光州金大中国际会展中心
内容：电影电视类展馆、游戏卡通人物类展馆、CGI动画类展馆、文化教育类展馆、光州之梦展馆、新传媒类展馆、海外文化展馆
周期：每年一届
市场范围：国际性
性质：面向公众
入场券价格：免费
主办：光州光域市；金大中国际会展中心；KOTRA；光州情报文化产业振兴院；湖南有线电视振兴协会；光州设计中心
地址：上海市长宁区兴义路8号万都中心3110室（200336）
联系人：慕晗
☎ 021-5108 8771转126
🖷 021-6219 6015
✉ kotra@yahoo.cn
MSN：m_muhan@hotmail.com
www.previewin.com

## Gwangju ACE Fair 2010

Date：2010/09/09 - 12
Venue: Kimdaejung Convention Center
Frequency: Annual
Market Area: International
Nature: Open to public
Cost to Attend: Free
Organizer: Gwangju Metropolitan City; Kimdaejung Convention Center; Gwangju Information & Culture Industry Promotion Agency(GITCT); Korea Trade Investment Promotion Agency(KOTRA); Honam Cable Television Association; Gwangju Design Center
Address: No. 8 Xingyi Road, Room 3110 Maxdo Centre, Changning District, Shanghai
Contact: MU Han
☎ 86-21-5108 8771 ext 126
🖷 86-21-6219 6015
✉ kotra@yahoo.cn
MSN: m_muhan@hotmail.com
www.previewin.com

## 2010韩国新可再生能源展

## Renewable Energy Korea 2010

日期：2010/10/21 - 24
地点：韩国首尔COEX
内容：太阳能、风能、地热、生物能、燃料电池及第二代电池、海洋能、氢气、煤气化、煤液化、环保、资源再利用、节能、高效能源。
首届
周期：每年一届
市场范围：国际性
性质：面向公众
入场券价格：免费
参展费用：净地展位1,300美元/9m²，标准展位1,650美元/9m²
主办：KOTRA(大韩贸易投资振兴公社)；MKE（韩国知识经济部）；韩国能源管理公团
地址：上海市长宁区兴义路8号万都中心3110室（200336）
联系人：慕晗
☎ 021-5108 8771转126
🖷 021-6219 6015
✉ kotra@yahoo.cn
MSN：m_muhan@hotmail.com
www.previewin.com

## Renewable Energy Korea 2010

Date：2010/10/21 - 24
Venue: COEX
First Session
Frequency: Annual
Market Area: International
Nature: Open to public
Cost to Attend: Free
Participated Fee: Raw Space USD 1,300 美元/9m², Standard Booth USD 1,650/9m²
Contact: MU Han
Address: No. 8 Xingyi Road, Room 3110 Maxdo Centre, Changning District, Shanghai
☎ 86-21-5108 8771 ext 126
🖷 86-21-6219 6015
✉ kotra@yahoo.cn
MSN: m_muhan@hotmail.com
www.previewin.com

## 韩国电子展

## Nepcon Korea：SMT/PCB & NEPCON KOREA

日期：2011 -
地点：韩国首尔Coex会展中心
内容：韩国领先的电子元件和配套产品生产展会。
产品和服务：SMT相关设备和材料，PCB生产设备和材料，电子零件生产设备和材料，IT终端产品的自动化生产设备和材料，电子元件和测试检测设备，控制设备和材料，微电子技术和包装技术
周期：每年一届
市场范围：国际性
参展费用：净地400美元/m²，标准展位450美元/m²
主办：励展日本公司
参展联络：励展博览集团国际销售部
地址：北京市朝阳区新源里南路1-3号平安国际金融中心A座15层01-03，05（100027）
联系人：杜一鸣
☎ 010-5933 9288
🖷 010-5933 9233
✉ martin.du@reedexpo.com.cn
www.reedexport.cn

## 韩国海事展

## KORMARINE

日期：2011/10 -
地点：韩国釜山会展中心

内容：关于展会 韩国海事及造船业最主要的展会活动。 产品及服务 船只设计、建造和装备、起重机械、火警与安全系统、烟气探测、防火设备、电子设备、船只及港口导航/通讯系统、引擎、海上防卫系统、分级与出版物。
周期：两年一届
市场范围：国际性
主办：励展日本公司
参展联络：励展博览集团国际销售部
地址：北京朝阳区新源里南路1-3号平安国际金融中心A座15层01-03，05（100027）
联系人：宫卫
☎ 010-5933 9288
🖷 010-5933 9233
✉ david.gong@reedexpo.com.cn
www.reedexport.cn

# 西班牙
# Spain

## 国际农业机械展览会

日期：2010/02 -
地点：西班牙萨拉戈萨
周期：每年一届
市场范围：国际性
参展联络：中国机械汽车展览联合会
☎ 010-6859 4964
🖷 010-6859 4964

## 西班牙瓦伦西亚卫浴展
## CEVISAMA

日期：2010/02/09 - 12
地点：西班牙瓦伦西亚
内容：卫浴、陶瓷、机械及配件
周期：每年一届
市场范围：国际性
参展联络：京慕国际展览有限公司
地址：北京市朝阳区北三环东路6号中国国际展览中心服务楼3层
联系人：薛涵，王芳
☎ 010-8460 0551
🖷 010-8460 0394
✉ zhaolingna@ciec.com.cn
www.jingmu.com.cn

## 2010年世界移动通信大会
## Mobile World Congress 2010

日期：2010/02/15 - 18
地点：西班牙巴塞罗那展览中心
内容：移动电话及配套设备、GPS、移动电话应用软件、蓝牙设备及相关应用、无线区域网络、天线、电力设备、无线电、PDA及配套产品、微波通信设备、IP电信及网络产品与服务、电线电缆和电子商务应用等。
周期：每年一届
市场范围：国际性
参展费用：净地865英镑/m²(36m²起）（不含税），标准展位（9m²起）935英镑/m²（不含税），参展保险费370英镑/家，参展注册费人民币3000元/家
主办：GSM协会
承办：中国邮电器材集团公司国际展览部
地址：北京西城区复兴门内大街156号北京招商国际金融中心A座10层A1008室
联系人：张宝林
☎ 010-6642 6288
🖷 010-6642 6556
www.ptexpo.com.cn

## 国际水务与环境展览会

日期：2010/03/02 - 05
地点：西班牙萨拉戈萨
周期：每年一届
市场范围：国际性
参展联络：中国机械汽车展览联合会
☎ 010-6859 4964
🖷 010-6849 4964

## 西班牙巴塞罗那国际餐馆用品博览会
## Restaurama

日期：2010/03/10 - 14
地点：西班牙巴塞罗那
内容：厨具、餐馆酒吧家具、花园家具、灯具、室内外装饰品、清洁用品、餐厨用纺织品和制服服装、烹饪设备、电器设备、一次性耗用品
周期：两年一届
市场范围：国际性
参展联络：京慕国际展览有限公司
地址：北京市朝阳区北三环东路6号中国国际展览中心服务楼3层
联系人：王海琼，滕昊
☎ 010-8460 0551
🖷 010-8460 0394
✉ zhaolingna@ciec.com.cn
www.jingmu.com.cn

## 西班牙巴塞罗那食品展

日期：2010/03/22 - 26
地点：西班牙巴塞罗那
内容：肉制品、乳制品、海产品、果菜、餐饮、酒类、饮料、罐头食品、糖果、饼干、冷冻食品、调料、粮油食品等
周期：两年一届
市场范围：国际性
参展联络：京慕国际展览有限公司
地址：北京市朝阳区北三环东路6号中国国际展览中心服务楼3层
联系人：崔文佳
☎ 010-8460 0551
🖷 010-8460 0394
✉ zhaolingna@ciec.com.cn
www.jingmu.com.cn

## 2010年西班牙国际食品饮料展览会
## Alimentaria 2010: International Food & Beverage Exhibition

Alimentaria 2010

日期：2010/03/22 - 26
地点：西班牙巴塞罗那Fira Barcelona展览中心
内容：西班牙国际食品饮料展览会是西班牙最重要的食品饮料展，也是世界范围内重要的展会之一。展会的分区、革新、创造与活力氛围，及其专业精神和国际影响力都是该展会成功的重要因素。展会吸引了5,000家领先的食品饮料制造商和经销商和158,000位来自五大洲的专业采购，它为食品与饮料工业再次提供一个国际经济舞台。
周期：两年一届
市场范围：国际性
参展费用：欢迎垂询。以欧元为单位
主办：励展博览集团国际销售部，西班牙Alimentaria Exhibitions S. A.
地址：北京朝阳区新源里南路1-3号平安国际金融中心A座15层01-03，05（100027）
联系人：杜一鸣
☎ 010-5933 9288
🖷 010-5933 9233
MSN：martin.du@reedexpo.com.cn
www.reedexport.cn

## 国际物流与物料操作展览会

日期：2010/05 -
地点：西班牙巴塞罗那
周期：每年一届
市场范围：国际性
参展联络：中国机械汽车展览联合会
☎ 010-6859 4964
🖷 010-6849 4964

## 2010年西班牙马德里门窗幕墙博览会
## 12th International Window, Curtain Walls and Structural Glass Trade Show

日期：2010/05/04 - 07
地点：西班牙马德里国际展览中心
内容：钢质窗、铝质窗、木质窗、PVC窗、其他材料、天花板和天窗、幕墙、结构玻璃、玻璃；机械类：铝、木材、PVC、玻璃；工具和配件；自动化产品；粘合剂;覆盖物；门：室内门、室外门、工业用门、车库门；太阳能保护：百叶窗、遮阳篷；有机硅，铰链，紧固件，合页；太阳能应用系统；软件等周边服务。
周期：两年一届
市场范围：国际性
参展联络：福建省国际贸易展览公司；福建省新天国际会展有限公司
地址：福建省福州市鼓楼区五四北路283号天骅大厦20层2088单元
联系人：范心锦，卢建光
☎ 0591-2808 6523, 8773 5017
✉ barryfan@valuedshow.com
MSN：barryvanfan@hotmail.com
QQ：30249576
www.valuedshow.com

## 第26届西班牙国际机床展览会
## The 26th International Machine Tool Exhibition Spain

日期：2010/05/31 - 05
地点：西班牙毕尔堡国际展览中心
内容：机械设备：金属切削，切削与量度、成型；.机械工具：焊接，氧气切割，热处理设备，表面处理工具设备，研磨工具产品，机械控制设备，加工系统，调节，平衡和固定系统；其他设备及零部件：机械设备零配件，液压，气压，电子自动系统设备，控制与驱动系统，润滑与冷却，材料，废物处理系统，安全生产系统。自动化生产：自动化操作系统，自动化存储技术和集合系统，工作站，机器人及软件；测量与质量控制：测量工具，测试机械，图像数据流程与质量控制。
周期：两年一届
市场范围：国际性
参展费用：标准展位3,150欧元/9㎡
主办：毕尔堡展览中心（BEC）；西班牙机床制造商协会（AFM）
承办：欧洲机床合作委员会
地 址：广东省深圳市福田区新洲大厦15层（518048）
联系人：雷明，朱利萍
☎ 0755-2393 8881, 2393 8025
🖷 0755-2393 8426
✉ cmffok@163.com
MSN：lm83573425@21cn.com

## The 26th International Machine Tool Exhibition Spain

Date：2010/05/31 - 05
Venue: Spain Bilbao International Exhibition Center,
Profile: Machinery & Equipment: metal cutting, cutting and measuring, molding; Machine tools: welding, oxygen cutting, heat treatment equipment, surface equipment, processing tools, grinding tools, machinery control equipment, processing systems, regulation, balanced and fixed systems; Other equipment and parts: machinery and equipment spare parts, hydraulic, pneumatic, electronic automatic system equipment, control and drive systems, lubrication and cooling, materials, waste treatment systems, safety production systems; Automated production
Frequency: Biennial
Market Area: International
Participated Fee: Standard Booth EUR 3,150/9㎡
Organizer: BEC；AFM Sponsor: CECIMO
Address: 15/Fl Xinzhou Building, Futian District, Shenzhen, Guangdong

☎ 86-755-2393 8881, 2393 8025
🖷 86-755-2393 8426
Contact: Rei Ming, Julius Ping
✉ cmffok@163.com
MSN: lm83573425@21cn.com

### 第47届瓦伦西亚国际家具展

**日期：**2010/09/28 - 02
**地点：**西班牙瓦伦西亚
**周期：**每年一届
**市场范围：**国际性
**参展联络：**大连上选会展服务有限公司
**地址：**大连市西岗区鞍山路13号兴业广场大厦B座508室（116011）
☎ 0411-8378 8326, 8378 8396, 8378 9165, 8378 8821
🖷 0411-8378 8830, 8378 8823
✉ cicyhuang@vip.sina.com
MSN：cicyhuang@msn.com
www.sun-show.com

### 西班牙瓦伦西亚Ideas & Pasion

**日期：**2010/09/28 - 02
**地点：**西班牙瓦伦西亚
**周期：**每年一届
**市场范围：**国际性
**参展联络：**大连上选会展服务有限公司
**地址：**大连市西岗区鞍山路13号兴业广场大厦B座508室（116011）
☎ 0411-8378 8326, 8378 8396, 8378 9165, 8378 8821
🖷 0411-8378 8830, 8378 8823
✉ cicyhuang@vip.sina.com
MSN：cicyhuang@msn.com
www.sun-show.com

### 西班牙标识视觉传播及图像设计行业展

Viscom-Sign Espana

**日期：**2010/10 -
**地点：**西班牙马德里IFEMA展览中心
**内容：**标识视觉传播及图像设计行业展（Viscom）精益求精，展品更佳、规模更大、国际化程度更高，正在成为欧洲视觉传播行业的领导型展会，为您展览最新的数码印刷、户外广告、卖场视觉传播产品、服务以及平面设计领域的最新潮流趋势。
**展品范围：**采用新材料和新幅面尺寸的高品质数码印刷技术，使用各类材料和尺寸的创新广告解决方案，专业图像管理服务、图形处理输出设备、专用软件与工具。
**周期：**每年一届
**市场范围：**国际性
**参展费用：**净地展位177欧元/m$^2$
**主办：**励展西班牙公司
**参展联络：**励展博览集团国际销售部
**地址：**北京市朝阳区新源里南路1-3号平安国际金融中心A座15层01-03，05（100027）
**联系人：**王亮
☎ 010-5933 9288
🖷 010-5933 9233
✉ liang.wang@reedexpo.com.cn
www.reedexport.cn

### 第15届西班牙国际电力及电子产品博览会（MATELEC 2010）

International Exhibition of Electrical and Electronic Equipment

**日期：**2010/10/26 - 29
**地点：**西班牙马德里IFEMA展览中心
**内容：**电子，电源、电力，电工产品及设备、电机工程、电气设备、空调及装置、气象设备、电讯设备、测量系统、调控设备、照明技术及设备及电子类产品等。
**周期：**两年一届
**市场范围：**国际性
**参展联络：**北京中杰城设国际展览有限公司
**地址：**北京市海淀区三里河路9号建设部机关门诊楼5层（100835）
**联系人：**李娜
☎ 010-8838 5291
🖷 010-5885 7468, 5893 4708
✉ info@btfi.cn
www.top-fairs.com.cn, www.btfi.cn

### 2010年第十五届西班牙巴塞罗那国际餐厅、酒店及相关用品展

Hostelco 2010

**日期：**2010/11/05 - 09
**地点：**西班牙巴塞罗那
**内容：**酒店餐饮领域设备，机械；烹饪用具，餐具；电脑管理，控制，及安全系统；纺织用品；家具及家具用品；酒店餐饮业的食品及饮料；洗衣店，干洗，及清洁卫生设备和用品；自动贩卖机。国际餐厅，酒店及相关用品展2008由西班牙FIRA DE BARCELONA-FELAC协会主办，已成为欧洲餐厅、酒店用品领域的专业展览之一。今年是第十四届，展出面积超过7万平方米，1000多家主要企业参展，接待专业客商98，000人，海外观众增加了9%。在上届展会上，35%的观众是公司所有者，11%的观众是总经理，6%的观众是销售经理；这一系列数据表明很大一部分观众都是决策者。观众表现出来的忠实性惊人的。该展会在德国、奥地利、瑞士、法国、英国、意大利、葡萄牙、荷兰、比利时和卢森堡、巴西都设有销售代表处。这对于中国企业开发欧洲市场及北美市场是一个极好的门户。
**始办年份：**1981
**周期：**两年一届
**市场范围：**国际性
**主办：**北方国际展览有限公司
**地址：**北京市宣武区菜园街1号中环假日酒店写字楼1102-1103室（100053）
**联系人：**穆超
☎ 010-8355 9740
🖷 010-8355 7940
✉ woody.m@northexpo.com.cn
MSN：mr_angel_boy@hotmail.com
QQ：26327995
www.northexpo.com.cn

### 西班牙毕尔巴鄂国际五金工具展

Ferroforma

**日期：**2011/03 -
**地点：**西班牙毕尔巴鄂展览中心
**内容：**锁具、安防设备及配件；工具；电动工具和木工机械；建筑五金和建材；工业供应品 劳保用品；紧固件；商店、仓储设备与配件；家居用品；装潢五金；电气产品，照明；管件；家居改进和DIY产品；园艺工具和产品
**始办年份：**1974
**周期：**两年一届
**市场范围：**国际性
**入场券价格：**17欧元
**参展费用：**标准展位310欧元/m$^2$，净地180欧元/m$^2$
**主办：**科隆展览国际有限公司
**地址：**北京东三环北路8号亮马河大厦2座1018室（100004）
**联系人：**陈瑞
☎ 010-6590 7766转 750
🖷 010-6590 6139
✉ r.chen@koelnmesse.cn

### Ferroforma

Date：2011/03 -
Venue: BILBAO EXHIBITION CENTRE, Spain
Established Year: 1974
Frequency: Biennial
Market Area: International
Cost to Attend: EUR 17
Participated Fee: Standard Booth EUR 310/m$^2$, Raw Space EUR 180/m$^2$
Organizer: KOELNMESSE
Address: Unit 1018 Landmark Tower Ⅱ, No. 8 Dongsanhuan North Rd., Beijing 100004, China
☎ 86-10-6590 7766 ext 750
🖷 86-10-6590 6139
Contact: Ryan Chen
✉ r.chen@koelnmesse.cn

### 2012年西班牙国际食品饮料展览会

Alimentaria 2012:
International Food & Beverage Exhibition

**日期：**2012/03 -
**地点：**西班牙Fira Barcelona展览中心
**内容：**西班牙国际食品饮料展览会是西班牙最重要的食品饮料展，也是世界范围内重要的展会之一。展会的分区、革新、创造与活力氛围，及其专业精神和国际影响力都是该展会成功的重要因素。展会吸引了5,000家领先的食品饮料制造商和经销商和158,000位来自五大洲的专业采购，它为食品与饮料工业再次提供一个国际经济舞台。
**周期：**两年一届
**市场范围：**国际性
**主办：**励展博览集团国际销售部；西班牙Alimentaria Exhibitions S. A.
**地址：**北京朝阳区新源里南路1-3号平安国际金融中心A座15层01-03，05（100027）
**联系人：**杜一鸣
☎ 010-5933 9288
🖷 010-5933 9233
MSN：martin.du@reedexpo.com.cn
www.reedexport.cn

### 巴塞罗那国际食品、饮料设备及技术展

Bta. Barcelona tecnologías de la alimentación:
Bta. Barcelona Food Technology Exhibition

Bta.
Barcelona tecnologías
de la alimentación

**日期：**2012/05 -
2015 -
**地点：**西班牙巴塞罗那
**内容：**国际食品及饮料加工机械、技术及配料行业展会。一个展览，三个行业子展会，涵盖食品加工行业的所有技术。作为一个重要的国际商贸平台，巴塞罗那国际食品、饮料设备及技术展览会通过其三个子展会——Tecnoalimentaria、Tecnocárnica及Ingretecno——为食品和饮料业的各个领域提供机械及中间食品（调料、添加剂、功能性配料）的技术方案。2009年，BTA将成为欧洲食品饮料业最重要的三大行业展会之一，成为一个真正的行业国际基准。BTA与HISPACK，瞄准同样观众群的两大展会将联合同期举办，为顾客带来更高价值，同时为食品和饮料界人士提供满足他们生产需求的所有选择：加工机械、中间食品、容器及包装。从配料到包装，面积8万5千m$^2$的展会将吸引3500个展商和6万观众。
产品及服务：食品和饮料业各领域的机械和技术、中间产品（调料、添加剂、功能性配料等）后勤，冷藏、清洁、安全、销售的技术应用。
**周期：**三年一届
**市场范围：**国际性
**参展费用：**净地每135～145欧元/m$^2$+增值税
**赞助：**AMEC；ICEX；IRTA；AECOC协作
**主办：**西班牙Alimentaria展览公司
**参展联络：**励展博览集团国际销售部
**地址：**北京朝阳区新源里南路1-3号平安国际金融中心A座15层01-03，05（100027）
**联系人：**杜一鸣
☎ 010-5933 9288

📠 010-5933 9233
MSN：martin.du@reedexpo.com.cn
www.reedexport.cn

# 苏丹
# Sudan

### 国际建筑机械、工程机械及建筑材料展览会

**日期**：2010/10/21 - 25
**地点**：苏丹喀士穆
**周期**：每年一届
**市场范围**：国际性
**参展联络**：中国机械汽车展览联合会
☎ 010-6859 4964
📠 010-6859 4964

# 叙利亚
# Syria

### 2010年叙利亚国际电力、石油，天然气展览会
### Oil &Gas Exhibition

**日期**：2010/04/05 - 08
**地点**：叙利亚大马士革
**内容**：国际知名石油公司及电力能源公司及电力相关产品；机械设备：油井、钻探、焊接、油罐设备、起重、吊装、升降、保温、制冷、通风、遥控监测、维修、保养等设备；发电机、加油机、透平机、涡轮机、汽轮机、叶轮机等机械；阀门、泵、压缩机、风机、空分设备、真空设备、千斤顶、锅炉、熔炉，压力容器，冷却机器、法兰、管道、软管及其连接装置、工业防爆产品、工业供电，电动传送装置及其装配,及各种配套设备及化工机械；仪器仪表；技术服务；计算机数据管理；油库工程、电气工程、工程顾问；安全、报警；其它：一切石油、石化、天然气产品；钻井平台。
**始办年份**：1998
**周期**：两年一届
**市场范围**：国际性
**参展联络**：北京中杰城设国际展览有限公司
**地址**：北京市海淀区三里河路9号建设部机关门诊楼5层（100835）
**联系人**：李娜
☎ 010-8838 5291
📠 010-5885 7468，5893 4708
✉ info@btfi.cn
www.top-fairs.com.cn
www.btfi.cn

### 国际石油及天然气设备展览会

**日期**：2010/04/05 - 08
**地点**：叙利亚大马士革
**周期**：每年一届
**市场范围**：国际性
**参展联络**：中国机械汽车展览联合会
☎ 010-6859 4964
📠 010-6859 4964

### 第16届叙利亚国际建筑建材展

**日期**：2010/05/12 - 16
**地点**：叙利亚大马士革
**内容**：建筑建材
**市场范围**：国际性
**参展联络**：北京中仕达兴业展览有限公司
**地址**：北京市海淀区蓝靛厂东路2号金源时代商务中心2号楼A座11B（100097）
**联系人**：贾倩，赵仕忱，牟向东，张露
☎ 010-5129 8900
📠 010-8886 2939
✉ mail@chinstar.cn
www.chinstar.cn

### 国际机械工业展览会

**日期**：2010/05/27 - 31
**地点**：叙利亚大马士革
**周期**：每年一届
**市场范围**：国际性
**参展联络**：中国机械汽车展览联合会
☎ 010-6859 4964
📠 010-6859 4964

### 国际汽车零部件展览会

**日期**：2010/07/01 - 07
**地点**：叙利亚大马士革
**周期**：每年一届
**市场范围**：国际性
**参展联络**：中国机械汽车展览联合会
☎ 010-6859 4964
📠 010-6859 4964

# 坦桑尼亚
# Tanzania

### 国际贸易博览会

**日期**：2010/06/28 - 08
**地点**：坦桑尼亚达累斯萨拉姆
**周期**：每年一届
**市场范围**：国际性
**参展联络**：中国机械汽车展览联合会
☎ 010-6859 4964
📠 010-6859 4964

# 泰国
# Thailand

### 泰国国际化妆品原料展

### in-cosmetics Asia - The leading Exhibition & Conference for Personal Care Ingredients in Asia

**日期**：2010 -
**地点**：泰国曼谷国际贸易展览中心
**内容**：亚洲国际化妆品原料展是亚洲首个国际性化妆品研发、配方、科技、销售及营销展会。展会官方名称为PCIA，在亚洲巡回展出。展会涵盖广泛的科技及商业内容，专为配方商和供应商而设计。
**产品及服务**：磨砂、抗衰老、抗菌、抗脂、去屑、香薰、植物药材、体内/体外临床、润肤剂、乳化剂、去死皮、填料、配方、芳香剂、湿润剂、杂志、生产、营销、微生物学、包装、颜料/色素、防腐剂、肥皂/合成洗涤剂、溶剂、遮光剂、表面活性剂、鞣剂、稠化剂、维他命。观众来源 研发经理、科学家、配方师、药剂师、销售与营销专家以及来自成品厂商、为成品采购新原料及配料的买家。
**周期**：每年一届
**市场范围**：国际性
**参展费用**：净地309英镑/m$^2$，标准展位334英镑/m$^2$
**主办**：励展英国公司
**参展联络**：励展博览集团国际销售部
**地址**：北京朝阳区新源里南路1-3号平安国际金融中心A座15层01-03，05（100027）
**联系人**：杜一鸣
☎ 010-5933 9288
📠 010-5933 9233
✉ martin.du@reedexpo.com.cn
www.reedexport.cn

### 亚洲纸业展览会

**日期**：2010/04/21 – 23
**地点**：皇后国际会议中心，泰国曼谷
**内容**：包括新生产技术展、纸品及办公用品展，及高层管理论坛。
**主办**：亚洲博闻有限公司
**联络**：博闻（广州）展览有限公司
☎ 020-8666 0158. 8666 3338 转 1151
📠 020-8667 7120
✉ info@cmpchina.com
www.ubmasia.com
www.asianpapershow.com

### Asian Paper

**Date**: 2010/04/21 – 23
**Venue**: Queen Sirikit National Convention & Exhibition Center, Bangkok
**Profile**: New production technology, paper products and office supplies, new applied technology conference; senior management symposium
**Frequency**: Annual
**Organizer**: UBM Asia
**Contact**: UBM China Ltd – Guangzhou
☎ 86-20-8666 0158. 8666 3338 ext. 1151
📠 86-20-8667 7120
✉ info@cmpchina.com
www.ubmasia.com
www.asianpapershow.com

### 泰国国际工业转包展
### 国际机械展
### 国际工业工具、测量、分析及监控科技展

### Subson Thailand
### Automotive Engineering Asia
### Sheet Metal Asia

**日期**：2010/05/13 – 16
**地点**：泰国曼谷国际贸易展览中心
**主办**：亚洲博闻有限公司
☎ 852-2827 6211
📠 852-2827 7831
www.ubmasia.com

### 国际环保技术展
### 亚洲水泵及阀门展
### 亚洲再生能源展

### Entech Pollutec Asia
### Pumps & Valves Asia
### Renewable Energy Asia

**日期**：2010/06/02 – 05
**地点**：泰国曼谷国际贸易展览中心
**主办**：亚洲博闻有限公司
☎ 852-2827 6211
📠 852-2827 7831
www.ubmasia.com

### 亚洲世界食品博览会

### Thaifex–World of Food Asia

**日期**：2010/05/12 - 16
**地点**：泰国曼谷IMPACT展览中心
**内容**：Thaifex 亚洲世界食品博览会在泰国成功举办，由科隆国际展览有限公司和泰国出口推广部及泰国商会共同筹备，回顾2009年泰国的亚洲世界食品博览会，展会展示了所有食品领域相关的五大块内容，吸引了来自33个国家的共1,011家展商参展，展览总面积为42,250m$^2$。
**产品**：食品和饮料、食品技术、餐饮、招待、零售和连锁
**始办年份**：2004
**周期**：每年一届
**市场范围**：国际性
**入场券价格**：免费

**参展费用：** 标准展位270美元/m²，净地200美元/m²
**上届规模** '08：展览面积42,250m²，参展商1,011家，专业贸易观众21,833人
**主办：** 科隆国际展览有限公司
**地址：** 北京市东三环北路8号亮马河大厦2座1018室（100004）
**联系人：** 徐畅，王迎
☎ 010-6590 7766转 715
🖷 010-6590 6139
✉ j.xu@koelnmesse.cn
www.world-of-food.cn

### Thaifex – World of Food Asia

Date：2010/05/12 - 16
Venue: IMPACT, Bangkok, Thailand
Established Year: 2004
Frequency: Annual
Market Area: International
Cost to Attend: Free
Participated Fee: Standard Booth USD 270/m², Raw Space USD 200/m²
Statistics '08: Exhibition Area 42,250m², Exhibitors 1,011, Trade visitors 21,833
Organizer: Koelnmesse
Address: Unit 1018, Landmark Tower II, No 8 Dongsanhuan North Rd., Beijing, China
☎ 86-10-6590 7766 ext 715
🖷 86-10-6590 6139
Contact: Joyce Xu, Elan Wang
✉ j.xu@koelnmesse.cn
www.world-of-food.cn

### 国际自动化生产和装配展览会
### ASSEMBLY TECH 2010

**日期：** 2010/06 -
**地点：** 泰国曼谷
**周期：** 每年一届
**市场范围：** 国际性
**参展联络：** 中国机械汽车展览联合会
☎ 010-6859 4964
🖷 010-6859 4964

## 泰国国际塑料及橡胶机械展

### InterPlas Thailand 2010

**日期：** 2010/06/24 - 27
**地点：** 泰国曼谷国际贸易展览中心
**内容：** 泰国国际塑料和橡胶技术贸易展会及研讨会。同期举办：泰国国际模具展、泰国国际汽车制造展、泰国国际装配技术展、泰国国际电子产品制造贸易展及会议。
**周期：** 每年一届
**市场范围：** 国际性
**参展联络：** 励展博览集团国际销售部
**地址：** 北京市朝阳区新源里南路1-3号平安国际金融中心A座15层01-03，05（100027）
**联系人：** 王亮
☎ 010-5933 9288
🖷 010-5933 9233
✉ liang.wang@reedexpo.com.cn
www.reedexport.cn

## 泰国国际装配技术展

### Assembly Technology 2010: The International Automated Manufacturing & Assembly Technology Exhibition

**日期：** 2010/06/24 - 27
**地点：** 泰国曼谷国际贸易展览中心
**内容：** 2010年第11届泰国国际装配技术展（Assembly Technology 2010）是泰国唯一的由行业组织的自动化及装配技术展，Assembly Technology 2010是汽车配件和电子配件制造技术类领域4个国际展会其中之一。同期展会：泰国国际塑料及橡胶机械展（InterPlas Thailand）；泰国国际塑料和橡胶技术贸易展会及研讨会；泰国国际模具展（InterMold Thailand），东南亚唯一针对模具生产的机械技术行业展会；泰国国际汽车生产制造展览会（Automotive Manufacturing），东南亚唯一针对汽车配件制造技术的展会。同期举办的还有：国际工厂自动化技术与设备展览会（Factory Automation）；国际工厂自动化，电子与电力传输以及物料输送技术展会及研讨会 Fluid Power；国际液压，压缩技术展会及研讨会
**周期：** 每年一届
**市场范围：** 国际性
**主办：** 励展博览集团国际销售部；励展泰国公司 Tradex
**地址：** 北京市朝阳区新源里南路1-3号平安国际金融中心A座15层01-03，05（100027）
**联系人：** 王亮
☎ 010-5933 9288
🖷 010-5933 9233
✉ liang.wang@reedexpo.com.cn
www.reedexport.cn

## 泰国国际模具展

### InterMold Thailand 2010

**日期：** 2010/06/24 - 27
**地点：** 泰国曼谷国际贸易展览中心
**内容：** 东南亚唯一针对模具生产的机械技术行业展会。
**周期：** 每年一届
**市场范围：** 国际性
**参展联络：** 励展博览集团国际销售部
**地址：** 北京朝阳区新源里南路1-3号平安国际金融中心A座15层01-03，05（100027）
**联系人：** 王亮
☎ 010-5933 9288
🖷 010-5933 9233
✉ liang.wang@reedexpo.com.cn
www.reedexport.cn

## 泰国汽车电子展

### Automotive Electronics 2010: ASEAN's Only Machinery Expo for Automotive Electronics Parts and Components Manufacturing / Co-located with Automotive Manufacturing 2010

AUTOMOTIVE ELECTRONICS

**日期：** 2010/06/24 - 27
**地点：** 泰国曼谷国际会展中心
**内容：** 东南亚地区唯一的汽车电子零部件展会。Automotive Electronics展会同期举办国际装配展（ASSEMBLY）、国际模具展（INTERMOLD）、国际橡胶展（INTERPLAS）、国际汽车展（AUTOMOTIVE）四个主题展会。经过多年精心培育与专业化、国际化运作，目前此展会已成为东南亚规模大、国际性强、影响力大、专业化程度高的知名 展会。 东盟是东南亚地区10个国家联盟的总称，拥有大约4亿人口。自1995年以来,中国与东盟的双边贸易额年增长速度均超过15%。现在东盟已经 成为中国第5大贸易伙伴。泰国是我国的近邻，由于东盟十国间将实现零关税，故泰国处于东盟国家的经济核心地位，也是今后我国产品进入东盟市场的"桥头堡" 和重要的转口基地。中国与泰国将率先建立自由贸易区，基于泰国良好的投资环境和区位优势，随着两国汽车工业、电子信息行业的迅猛发展，两国贸易必将迎来更 为广阔的前景。泰国是东盟成员之一，人口6400万，是东南亚最大的汽车市场，有"东方底特律"之称。汽车巨头均云集于此，投入巨额资金， 建立生产线，设立合资厂，使泰国的汽车工业飞速发展。飞速发展的泰国汽车工业，给汽车零配件生产企业及经销商带来了巨大商机，给汽车电子产品的研发与生产 带来勃勃生机。
**周期：** 每年一届
**市场范围：** 国际性
**参展费用：** 净地展位2,280美元/m²，标准展位365美元/m²
**参展联络：** 励展博览集团国际销售部
**地址：** 北京市朝阳区新源里南路1-3号平安国际金融中心A座15层01-03，05（100027）
**联系人：** 杜一鸣
☎ 010-5933 9288
🖷 010-5933 9233
✉ martin.du@reedexpo.com.cn
www.reedexport.cn

## 泰国国际汽车生产制造展览会

### Automotive Manufacturing 2010 - ASEAN's Only Machinery Expo for Automotive Parts Manufacturing

AUTOMOTIVE MANUFACTURING

**日期：** 2010/06/24 - 27
**地点：** 泰国曼谷国际贸易展览中心
**内容：** 东盟唯一的汽车零部件制造展会，它是在汽车零部件和电子零件制造技术行业中四个国际性展会其中之一。泰国国际装配技术展（Assembly Technology），致力于展示自动化和组装的前沿技术泰国国际塑料及橡胶机械展（InterPlas Thailand），致力于展示塑料和橡胶前沿生产技术。泰国国际模具展（InterMold Thailand 2010），东南亚唯一针对模具生产的机械技术行业展会。
**周期：** 每年一届
**市场范围：** 国际性
**主办：** 励展泰国公司
**参展联络：** 励展博览集团国际销售部
**地址：** 北京朝阳区新源里南路1-3号平安国际金融中心A座15层01-03，05（100027）
**联系人：** 杜一鸣
☎ 010-5933 9288
🖷 010-5933 9233
✉ martin.du@reedexpo.com.cn
www.reedexport.cn

## 泰国国际服装及纺织品用机械、设备、材料及附件展

### GFT 2010: Thailand's 16th International Presentation of Machinery, Tools & Equipment for Garment & Textile Industries

**日期：** 2010/07/01 - 04
**地点：** 泰国曼谷国际贸易展览中心
**内容：** 泰国国际服装及纺织品用机械、设备、材料及附件展
**周期：** 每年一届
**市场范围：** 面向贸易观众
**主办：** 励展泰国公司
**参展联络：** 励展博览集团国际销售部
**地址：** 北京市朝阳区新源里南路1-3号平安国际金融中心A座15层01-03，05（100027）
**联系人：** 王亮
☎ 010-5933 9288
🖷 010-5933 9233
✉ liang.wang@reedexpo.com.cn
www.reedexport.cn

### 泰国曼谷国际医院及医疗设备展览会

Medical Fair Thailand

**日期：** 2010/09 -
**地点：** 泰国曼谷
**内容：** 医疗设备、外科手术设备；实验室设备和配置；急诊及运输设施；医学技术；整形外科和康复技术；各类处方药和非处方药；营养和医用厨房设备；看护和监控系统
**周期：** 每年一届
**市场范围：** 国际性
**参展联络：** 京慕国际展览有限公司
**地址：** 北京市朝阳区北三环东路6号中国国际展览中心服务楼3层
**联系人：** 魏亦山，孙铁兵
☎ 010-8460 0551
🖷 010-8460 0394
✉ zhaolingna@ciec.com.cn
www.jingmu.com.cn

### 第十八届泰国国际食品、酒店展览会

**日期：** 2010/09 -
**地点：** 泰国
**主办：** 北京邦企展览服务有限公司
**地址：** 北京市朝阳区惠新东街11号紫光发展大厦B1-501（100029）
**联系人：** 雷绍军先生，赖玉宝小姐
☎ 010-6482 3808
🖷 010-6482 3670
✉ bbes@china.com

### 东南亚国际管材、线材展览会

**日期：** 2010/10 -
4240
**地点：** 泰国曼谷
**周期：** 每年一届
**市场范围：** 国际性
**参展联络：** 中国机械汽车展览联合会
☎ 010-6859 4964
🖷 010-6859 4964

### 泰国国际机床及金属加工机械贸易展

METALEX 2009:
ASEAN's Largest International Machine Tool & Metalworking Technology Trade Exhibition & Conference

METALEX

**日期：** 2010/11/24 - 27
**地点：** 泰国曼谷国际贸易展览中心
**内容：** 亚洲最大的国际机床及金属加工机械贸易展会。
**产品及服务：** 组装技术、弹性制造系统、制造系统、软件、控制测量、测试设备及工具、工具与模具、机床、机械加工中心、电火花机床、各式模具、铸造工具、钣金加工、焊接技术、电线/弹簧/紧固件，管工技术、电线技术
**周期：** 每年一届
**市场范围：** 国际性
**主办：** 励展泰国公司
**参展联络：** 励展博览集团国际销售部
**地址：** 北京市朝阳区新源里南路1-3号平安国际金融中心A座15层01-03，05（100027）
**联系人：** 王亮
☎ 010-5933 9288
🖷 010-5933 9233
✉ liang.wang@reedexpo.com.cn
www.reedexport.cn

### 泰国安防展

Intersec Thailand

**日期：** 2010/12/02 - 04
**地点：** 泰国曼谷
**内容：** 安全防范类，警用装备类，个人安保类：防护服装、工装鞋和工作服等
**周期：** 每年一届
**市场范围：** 国际性
**参展联络：** 京慕国际展览有限公司
**地址：** 北京市朝阳区北三环东路6号中国国际展览中心服务楼3层
**联系人：** 国曦，薛磊
☎ 010-8460 0551
🖷 010-8460 0394
✉ zhaolingna@ciec.com.cn
www.jingmu.com.cn

### 亚洲世界食品博览会

Thaifex – World of Food Asia

**日期：** 2011/05 -
**地点：** 泰国曼谷IMPACT展览中心
**内容：** Thaifex 亚洲世界食品博览会，在泰国成功举办-由科隆国际展览有限公司和泰国出口推广部及泰国商会共同筹备。展会展示了所有食品领域相关的五大块**内容：** 食品和饮料、食品技术、餐饮、招待、零售和连锁
**始办年份：** 2004
**周期：** 每年一届
**市场范围：** 国际性
**入场券价格：** 免费
**参展费用：** 标准展位270美元/m²，净地200美元/m²
**主办：** 科隆国际展览有限公司
**地址：** 北京市东三环北路8号亮马河大厦2座1018室（100004）
**联系人：** 徐畅，王迎
☎ 010-6590 7766转 715
🖷 010-6590 6139
✉ j.xu@koelnmesse.cn
www.world-of-food.cn

### 泰国国际模具展

InterMold Thailand 2010

**日期：** 2011/06 -
**地点：** 泰国曼谷国际贸易展览中心
**内容：** 东南亚唯一针对模具生产的机械技术行业展会。
**周期：** 每年一届
**市场范围：** 国际性
**参展联络：** 励展博览集团国际销售部
**地址：** 北京朝阳区新源里南路1-3号平安国际金融中心A座15层01-03，05（100027）
**联系人：** 王亮
☎ 010-5933 9288
🖷 010-5933 9233
✉ liang.wang@reedexpo.com.cn
www.reedexport.cn

### 泰国国际装配技术展

Assembly Technology 2011:
The International Automated Manufacturing & Assembly Technology Exhibition

**日期：** 2011/06 -
**地点：** 泰国曼谷国际贸易展览中心
**内容：** 泰国唯一的由行业组织的自动化及装配技术展，是汽车配件和电子配件制造技术类领域4个国际性展会其中之一。同期展会：泰国国际塑料及橡胶机械展（InterPlas Thailand）；泰国国际塑料和橡胶技术贸易展会及研讨会 泰国国际模具展（InterMold Thailand）：东南亚唯一针对模具生产的机械技术行业展会 泰国国际汽车生产制造展览会（Automotive Manufacturing）：东南亚唯一针对汽车配件制造技术的展会 同期举办的还有：国际工厂自动化技术与设备展览会（Factory Automation）；国际工厂自动化，电子与电力传输以及物料输送技术展会及研讨会 Fluid Power；国际液压，压缩技术展会及研讨会
**周期：** 每年一届
**市场范围：** 国际性
**主办：** 励展博览集团国际销售部；励展泰国公司 Tradex
**地址：** 北京市朝阳区新源里南路1-3号平安国际金融中心A座15层01-03，05（100027）
**联系人：** 王亮
☎ 010-5933 9288
🖷 010-5933 9233
✉ liang.wang@reedexpo.com.cn
www.reedexport.cn

### 泰国汽车电子展

Automotive Electronics 2011:
ASEAN's Only Machinery Expo for Automotive Electronics Parts and Components Manufacturing / Co-located with Automotive Manufacturing 2011

AUTOMOTIVE
ELECTRONICS

**日期：** 2011/06 -
**地点：** 泰国曼谷国际会展中心
**内容：** 东南亚地区唯一的汽车电子零部件展会。Automotive Electronics展会同期举办国际装配展（ASSEMBLY）、国际模具展（INTERMOLD）、国际橡胶展（INTERPLAS）、国际汽车展（AUTOMOTIVE）四个主题展会。经过多年精心培育与专业化、国际化运作，目前此展会已成为东南亚规模大、国际性强、影响力大、专业化程度高的知名 展会。 东盟是东南亚地区10个国家联盟的总称，拥有大约4亿人口。自1995年以来,中国与东盟的双边贸易额年增长速度均超过15%。现在东盟已经成为中国第5大贸易伙伴。泰国是我国的近邻，由于东盟十国间将实现零关税，故泰国处于东盟国家的经济核心地位，也是今后我国产品进入东盟市场的“桥头堡” 和重要的转口基地。中国与泰国将率先建立自由贸易区，基于泰国良好的投资环境和区位优势，随着两国汽车工业、电子信息行业的迅猛发展，两国贸易必将迎来更 为广阔的前景。泰国是东盟成员之一，人口6400万，是东南亚最大的汽车市场，有“东方底特律”之称。汽车巨头均云集于此，投入巨额资金， 建立生产线，设立合资厂，使泰国的汽车工业飞速发展。飞速发展的泰国汽车工业，给汽车零配件生产企业及经销商带来了巨大商机，给汽车电子产品的研发与生产带来勃勃生机。
**周期：** 每年一届
**市场范围：** 国际性
**参展费用：** 净地280美元/m²，标准展位365美元/m²
**参展联络：** 励展博览集团国际销售部
**地址：** 北京市朝阳区新源里南路1-3号平安国际金融中心A座15层01-03，05（100027）
**联系人：** 杜一鸣
☎ 010-5933 9288
🖷 010-5933 9233
✉ martin.du@reedexpo.com.cn
www.reedexport.cn

### 泰国国际塑料及橡胶机械展

InterPlas Thailand 2011

**日期：** 2011/06 -
插入logo，数据库会展编号3501
**地点：** 泰国曼谷国际贸易展览中心
**内容：** 同期举办泰国国际模具展、泰国国际汽车制造展、泰国国际装配技术展、泰国国际电子产品制造贸易展及会议。
**周期：** 每年一届
**市场范围：** 国际性
**参展联络：** 励展博览集团国际销售部
**地址：** 北京市朝阳区新源里南路1-3号平安国际金融中心A座15层01-03，05（100027）
**联系人：** 王亮

☎ 010-5933 9288
🖷 010-5933 9233
✉ liang.wang@reedexpo.com.cn
www.reedexport.cn

## 泰国国际汽车生产制造展览会

Automotive Manufacturing 2011 - ASEAN's Only Machinery Expo for Automotive Parts Manufacturing

AUTOMOTIVE MANUFACTURING

**日期：** 2011/06 -
**地点：** 泰国曼谷国际贸易展览中心
**内容：** 是东盟唯一的汽车零部件制造展会，它是在汽车零部件和电子零件制造技术行业中四个国际性展会其中之一。 泰国国际装配技术展（Assembly Technology），致力于展示自动化和组装的前沿技术 泰国国际塑料及橡胶机械展（InterPlas Thailand），致力于展示塑料和橡胶前沿生产技术 泰国国际模具展（InterMold Thailand），东南亚唯一针对模具生产的机械技术行业展会。
**周期：** 每年一届
**市场范围：** 国际性
**主办：** 励展泰国公司
**参展联络：** 励展博览集团国际销售部
**地址：** 北京朝阳区新源里南路1-3号平安国际金融中心A座15层01-03，05（100027）
**联系人：** 杜一鸣
☎ 010-5933 9288
🖷 010-5933 9233
✉ martin.du@reedexpo.com.cn
www.reedexport.cn

## 2011年泰国电子展：国际电子产品制造贸易展及会议

NEPCON Thailand 2011: The International Electronics Manufacturing Technology Trade Exhibition and Conference

**日期：** 2011/06/23 - 26
2013/06 -
**地点：** 泰国曼谷国际贸易展览中心
**内容：** 2011年第11届泰国电子展（NEPCON Thailand 2011）是国际电子元器件及生产设备展览会(NEPCON)系列展会之一，曾在亚洲8个国家举办。同地举办的展会：泰国国际塑料及橡胶机械展（InterPlas Thailand）：泰国国际塑料和橡胶技术贸易展会及研讨会。泰国国际模具展（InterMold Thailand）：东南亚唯一针对模具生产的机械技术行业展会 泰国国际汽车生产制造展览会（Automotive Manufacturing）：东南亚唯一针对汽车配件制造展会 泰国国际装配技术展（Assembly Technology）：国际自动化制造和装配技术展会
**周期：** 两年一届
**市场范围：** 国际性
**主办：** 励展泰国公司
**参展联络：** 励展博览集团国际销售部
**地址：** 北京市朝阳区新源里南路1-3号平安国际金融中心A座15层01-03，05（100027）
**联系人：** 杜一鸣
☎ 010-5933 9288
🖷 010-5933 9233
✉ martin.du@reedexpo.com.cn
www.reedexport.cn

## 泰国国际服装及纺织品用机械、设备、材料及附件展

GFT 2012: Thailand's 17th International Presentation of Machinery, Tools & Equipment for Garment & Textile Industries

**日期：** 2012 -
**地点：** 泰国曼谷国际贸易展览中心
**内容：** 泰国国际服装及纺织品用机械、设备、材料及附件展
**周期：** 两年一届
**市场范围：** 面向贸易观众
**主办：** 励展泰国公司
**参展联络：** 励展博览集团国际销售部
**地址：** 北京市朝阳区新源里南路1-3号平安国际金融中心A座15层01-03，05（100027）
**联系人：** 王亮
☎ 010-5933 9288
🖷 010-5933 9233
✉ liang.wang@reedexpo.com.cn
www.reedexport.cn

## 泰国国际木工机械、家具制造机械、零件及相关技术展

Furnitech Woodtech 2012

**日期：** 2012 -
**地点：** 泰国曼谷国际会展中心
**内容：** 泰国国际木工机械、家具制造机械、零件及相关技术展会及研讨会
**周期：** 三年一届
**市场范围：** 国际性
**参展费用：** 净地270美元/m²，标准展位340美元/m²
**赞助：** 泰国家具工业协会（合办方）
**主办：** 励展泰国公司
**参展联络：** 励展博览集团国际销售部
**地址：** 北京市朝阳区新源里南路1-3号平安国际金融中心A座15层01-03，05（100027）
**联系人：** 王亮
☎ 010-5933 9288
🖷 010-5933 9233
✉ liang.wang@reedexpo.com.cn
www.reedexport.cn

# 土耳其 Turkey

## 第4届土耳其国际矿业展览会

**日期：** 2010 -
**地点：** 土耳其伊斯坦布尔
**内容：** 国际矿业
**周期：** 每年一届
**市场范围：** 国际性
**参展联络：** 北京中仕达兴业展览有限公司
**地址：** 北京市海淀区蓝靛厂东路2号金源时代商务中心2号楼A座11B（100097）
**联系人：** 贾倩，赵仕忱，牟向东，张露
☎ 010-5129 8900
🖷 010-8886 2939
✉ mail@chinstar.cn
www.chinstar.cn

# 土耳其 Turkey

## 2010年土耳其伊斯坦布尔国际家具展

IMOB 2010

**日期：** 2010/02/02 - 06
**地点：** 土耳其伊斯坦布尔
**周期：** 每年一届
**市场范围：** 国际性
**参展联络：** 大连上选会展服务有限公司
**地址：** 大连市西岗区鞍山路13号兴业广场大厦B座508室（116011）
☎ 0411-8378 8326, 8378 8396, 8378 9165, 8378 8821
🖷 0411-8378 8830, 8378 8823
✉ cicyhuang@vip.sina.com
MSN：cicyhuang@msn.com
www.sun-show.com

## 国际管材展览会

**日期：** 2010/03/04 - 07
**地点：** 土耳其伊斯坦布尔
**周期：** 每年一届
**市场范围：** 国际性
**参展联络：** 中国机械汽车展览联合会
☎ 010-6859 4964
🖷 010-6859 4964

## 国际照明、电子及电力展览会

**日期：** 2010/03/11 - 14
**地点：** 土耳其伊斯坦布尔
**周期：** 每年一届
**市场范围：** 国际性
**参展联络：** 中国机械汽车展览联合会
☎ 010-6859 4964
🖷 010-6859 4964

## 第十一届伊斯坦布尔国际门窗博览会

Istanbul Window: 11th International Window, Glass Technology, Accessory, Related Industry and Auxiliary Products Fair

**日期：** 2010/03/11 - 14
**地点：** 土耳其伊斯坦布尔
**内容：** 塑钢门窗、铝合金门窗、不锈钢门窗、彩板门窗、木质门窗等其他不同材质门窗，五金配件、相关辅料、挤出设备、组装设备；各种玻璃幕墙、幕墙相关产品、设备等；门窗幕墙设计软件、玻璃优化下料系统等软件；各种建筑玻璃、钢化玻璃、艺术玻璃、装饰玻璃、特种玻璃等。
**周期：** 每年一届
**市场范围：** 国际性
**参展联络：** 福建省国际贸易展览公司；福建省新天国际会展有限公司
**地址：** 福建省福州市鼓楼区五四北路283号天骅大厦20层2088单元
**联系人：** 范心锦；卢建光
☎ 0591-2808 6523, 8773 5017
✉ barryfan@valuedshow.com
MSN：barryvanfan@hotmail.com
QQ：30249576
www.valuedshow.com

## 第18届土耳其国际建筑工程机械展览会

ANKOMAK 2010

**日期：** 2010/03/31 - 04
**地点：** 土耳其伊斯坦布尔
**周期：** 两年一届
**市场范围：** 国际性
**主办：** 中国贸促会机械行业分会
**地址：** 北京市西城区三里河路46号（100823）
**联系人：** 张立昂
☎ 010-6859 5012
✉ info@ccpitmsc.org
✉ jix@ccpit.org
www.chinamachin.org.cn
www.ccpitmsc.org

## 2010年伊斯坦布尔家电展没

International Exhibition and Conference for Household Appliances

**日期：** 2010/04/22 - 25

地点：土耳其伊斯坦布尔世界贸易中心
内容：2010年伊斯坦布尔家电展是一个国际性的贸易展会，并在大小家电及配件的最新发展及技术创新上给出一次扩展性的研究。
首届
周期：每年两届
市场范围：国际性
主办：科隆展览国际有限公司
地址：北京东三环北路8号亮马河大厦2座1018室（100004）
联系人：陈瑞
☎ 010-6590 7766转 750
🖷 010-6590 6139
✉ r.chen@koelnmesse.cn

### International Exhibition and Conference for Household Appliances

Date：2010/04/22 - 25
Venue: World Trade Centre Istanbul, Turkey
Profile: Domotechnica Istanbul is an international trade fair and gives an expanded survey of the latest developments and innovations of major household appliances, small household appliances and components.
First Session
Frequency: Biannual
Market Area: International
Organizer: KOELNMESSE
Address: Unit 1018 Landmark Tower Ⅱ, No. 8 Dongsanhuan North Rd., Beijing 100004, China
☎ 86-10-6590 7766 ext 750
🖷 86-10-6590 6139
Contact: Ryan Chen
✉ r.chen@koelnmesse.cn

### 国际供暖、制冷、空调及卫浴展览会

日期：2010/05/05 - 08
地点：土耳其伊斯坦布尔
周期：每年一届
市场范围：国际性
参展联络：中国机械汽车展览联合会
☎ 010-6859 4964
🖷 010-6859 4964

### 2010年土耳其国际建筑建材展览会

日期：2010/05/05 - 09
地点：土耳其伊斯坦布尔国际展览中心
内容：TURKEYBUILD是土耳其及其周边地区最大规模的综合建筑建材展。它由土耳其著名展览公司Yapi-Endustri Merkezi主办，并因其专业性强、规模大的特点在国际上赢得了一定的知名度，展会每年在伊斯坦布尔、安卡拉及伊兹米尔三地分别举办。其中，展会在伊斯坦布尔自1978年开始举办，迄今已举办31届。
始办年份：1985
周期：每年一届
市场范围：国际性
参展联络：北京领汇国际展览有限公司
地址：北京市朝阳区农展馆南路13号瑞辰国际中心719（100125）
联系人：段宇
☎ 010-5129 5359-8801
🖷 010-5129 5379-8801
✉ lewayfair@126.com
MSN：expo8801@worldfairs.cn

### 国际印刷技术与纸工业展览会

日期：2010/05/29 - 06
地点：土耳其伊斯坦布尔
周期：每年一届
市场范围：国际性
参展联络：中国机械汽车展览联合会
☎ 010-6859 4964
🖷 010-6859 4964

### 国际建筑及工程机械展览会

日期：2010/06/09 - 13
地点：土耳其伊斯坦布尔
周期：每年一届
市场范围：国际性
参展联络：中国机械汽车展览联合会
☎ 010-6859 4964
🖷 010-6859 4964

### 土耳其国际建筑业博览会
### BAUCON YAPEX

日期：2010/10 -
地点：土耳其安塔利亚
内容：建筑材料、新型建筑材料、门窗、卫浴和陶瓷等
周期：每年一届
市场范围：国际性
参展联络：京慕国际展览有限公司
地址：北京市朝阳区北三环东路6号中国国际展览中心服务楼3层
联系人：安红彦，孙铁兵
☎ 010-8460 0551
🖷 010-8460 0394
✉ zhaolingna@ciec.com.cn
www.jingmu.com.cn

### 国际汽车工业及配件展览会

日期：2010/10 -
地点：土耳其伊斯坦布尔
周期：每年一届
市场范围：国际性
参展联络：中国机械汽车展览联合会
☎ 010-6859 4964
🖷 010-6859 4964

### 国际灯具展览会

日期：2010/10 -
地点：土耳其伊斯坦布尔
周期：每年一届
市场范围：国际性
参展联络：中国机械汽车展览联合会
☎ 010-6859 4964
🖷 010-6859 4964

### 土耳其国际金属加工技术（机床）展览会
### TATEF 2010

日期：2010/10/12 - 17
地点：土耳其伊斯坦布尔
周期：两年一届
市场范围：国际性
主办：中国贸促会机械行业分会
地址：北京市西城区三里河路46号（100823）
联系人：周海明，叶海青，聂飞
☎ 010-6859 5495, 6859 5247, 6851 3586, 6859 4938
🖷 010-6859 5057
✉ info@ccpitmsc.org
✉ jix@ccpit.org
www.chinamachin.org.cn
www.ccpitmsc.org

### 土耳其国际塑料工业展览会
### Plas Eurasia Istanbul

日期：2010/11 -
地点：土耳其伊斯坦布尔
内容：塑料机械及设备，橡胶机械及设备，橡塑加工质量检测仪器及设备，橡塑加工用化工原料、助剂及辅助材料，工用模具及配件，橡塑制品
周期：每年一届
市场范围：国际性
参展联络：京慕国际展览有限公司
地址：北京市朝阳区北三环东路6号中国国际展览中心服务楼3层
联系人：薛亮，孙铁兵
☎ 010-8460 0551
🖷 010-8460 0394
✉ zhaolingna@ciec.com.cn
www.jingmu.com.cn

# 乌克兰
# Ukraine

### 2010年乌克兰国际玻璃及门窗专业展览会

日期：2010/02/23 - 26
地点：乌克兰基辅基辅国际展览中心
内容：此展是由一个世界巡回专业品牌展，将在哈撒克斯坦，乌克兰，莫斯科等东欧及中亚城市巡回展出。展出面积预计一万平方米，2010年2月在乌克兰举办的此展是乌克兰地区最专业最具规模的的玻璃及门窗展。
周期：每年一届
市场范围：国际性
参展联络：福建省国际贸易展览公司；福建省新天国际会展有限公司
地址：福建省福州市鼓楼区五四北路283号天骅大厦20层2088单元
联系人：范心锦，卢建光
☎ 0591-2808 6523, 8773 5017
✉ barryfan@valuedshow.com
MSN：barryvanfan@hotmail.com
QQ：30249576
www.valuedshow.com

### 乌克兰国际五金工具展
### INTERTOOL KIEV

日期：2010/03 -
地点：乌克兰基辅
内容：五金工具、模具制造，塑料，橡胶，质量控制材料，工程工具，机床，动力手工具，精密工具
周期：每年一届
市场范围：国际性
参展联络：京慕国际展览有限公司
地址：北京市朝阳区北三环东路6号中国国际展览中心服务楼3层
联系人：薛亮，孙铁兵
☎ 010-8460 0551
🖷 010-8460 0394
✉ zhaolingna@ciec.com.cn
www.jingmu.com.cn

### 乌克兰国际空调、暖通及工业制冷贸易博览会
### Cool Clima Kiev

日期：2010/03 -
地点：乌克兰基辅
内容：空调及相关设备配件，通风系统；各类相关耗材、工具，各式采暖器、壁挂炉；电机、锅炉；制冷等
周期：每年一届
市场范围：国际性
参展联络：京慕国际展览有限公司
地址：北京市朝阳区北三环东路6号中国国际展览中心服务楼3层
联系人：薛亮，孙铁兵
☎ 010-8460 0551
🖷 010-8460 0394
✉ zhaolingna@ciec.com.cn
www.jingmu.com.cn

### 国际摩托车展览会

日期：2010/03/11 - 14
地点：乌克兰基普
周期：每年一届
市场范围：国际性
参展联络：中国机械汽车展览联合会
☎ 010-6859 4964
🖷 010-6849 4964

### 第8届乌克兰国际建材展

日期：2010/03/23 - 27
地点：乌克兰基辅
内容：建材
周期：每年一届
市场范围：国际性
参展联络：北京中仕达兴业展览有限公司

地址：北京市海淀区蓝靛厂东路2号金源时代商务中心2号楼A座11B（100097）
联系人：贾倩，赵仕忱，牟向东，张露
☎ 010-5129 8900
🖷 010-8886 2939
✉ mail@chinstar.cn
www.chinstar.cn

### 2010年第14届乌克兰国际电力及电子展览会
Elcom Ukraine

日期：2010/04/13 - 16
地点：乌克兰基辅Kiev Expo Plaza
内容：发电机组、控制开关和相关设备等；电厂环保技术及设备；电力控制系统及检测设备；发电设备、电站设备、高低压电器、变电设备；输配电设备、工程安装配套产品、施工工具；自动化技术及设备，配件、组件；电表、电能计量产品。
周期：每年一届
市场范围：国际性
主办：Fairtrade组委会
参展联络：中国贸促会建设行业分会/北京中杰城设国际展览有限公司
地址：北京市海淀区三里河路9号建设部机关门诊楼5层（100835）
联系人：李娜
☎ 010-8838 5291
🖷 010-5885 7468, 5893 4708
✉ info@btfi.cn
www.top-fairs.com.cn
www.btfi.cn

### 国际供暖、卫浴与空调展览会

日期：2010/05/12 - 15
地点：乌克兰基普
周期：每年一届
市场范围：国际性
参展联络：中国机械汽车展览联合会
☎ 010-6859 4964
🖷 010-6849 4964

### 国际商用车展览会

日期：2010/09 -
地点：乌克兰基普
周期：每年一届
市场范围：国际性
参展联络：中国机械汽车展览联合会
☎ 010-6859 4964
🖷 010-6859 4964

### 第19届乌克兰国际建筑建材展

日期：2010/09 -
地点：乌克兰基辅
内容：建筑建材展
市场范围：国际性
参展联络：北京中仕达兴业展览有限公司
地址：北京市海淀区蓝靛厂东路2号金源时代商务中心2号楼A座11B（100097）
联系人：贾倩，赵仕忱，牟向东，张露
☎ 010-5129 8900
🖷 010-8886 2939
✉ mail@chinstar.cn
www.chinstar.cn

## 阿联酋
## United Arab Emirates

### 第5届沙迦金属加工展览会

日期：2010/01/11 - 14
地点：阿联酋沙迦
周期：每年一届
市场范围：国际性
参展联络：中国机械汽车展览联合会
☎ 010-6859 4964
🖷 010-6859 4964

### 2010年中东（迪拜）国际秋季商品交易会
2010 Dubai Autumn Fair

日期：2010/01/17 - 19
地点：阿联酋迪拜世界贸易中心
内容：生活用品类、粮油食品类、美容包材类、服装纺织类、五金机电类、皮革鞋帽类、塑料制品类、钟表文具类、礼品玩具类、电子通讯类、石油开采类、五矿化工类、建筑材料类、室内装饰类、汽摩配件类、家电制冷类、医疗保健类、体育用品类等。
始办年份：1986
周期：每年一届
市场范围：国际性
上届规模 '08：展览面积15,750m²，参展商793家（来自25个国家），参观人数15,000人
主办：Al Fajer展览公司
参展联络：杭州思诺博会展服务有限公司
地址：杭州市体育场路229号浙江粮油大厦1202室（310003）
☎ 0571-8577 8500
🖷 0571-8577 9709
✉ expo@sinobal.com
www.sinobal.com

### 2010年中东（迪拜）国际商业安全及消防器材博览会
2010 Intersec Middle East

日期：2010/01/17 - 19
地点：阿联酋迪拜国际会展中心
内容：商业安全类：门禁设备、警报器、iDVR、闭路电视、监视器、可视出入监控设备、身份识别设备、锁、保险柜、保安服务设备、安防用传感器、声控设备、无线遥控安防用设备；警用装备类：警用交通工具、警用装甲车、警用通讯器材、侦察和排除炸弹设备、警用制服、法庭用设备、生物测定设备、交通控制设备、雷达设备、营救设备、辐射检测和处理设备、武器模拟器、警用路障、毒品侦测设备、X射线检测设备、监控和反监控设备；消防监控类：灭火设备、救火车、水上火灾营救设备、防火设备、火警警报器、紧急警报设备；工业安全类：个人防护设备、安防用品（绳索/挂钩等）、梯子/脚手架、特种容器、急救设备（医）、高危工作防护设备、建筑/露天工作安全防护设备、无菌环境/专业消毒设备、空气污染处理设备、废物循环处理设备。
周期：每年一届
市场范围：国际性
上届规模 '09：展览面积38,200m²，参展商710家，专业贸易观众17,206人
主办：德国法兰克福（迪拜）展览公司
参展联络：杭州思诺博会展服务有限公司
地址：杭州市体育场路229号浙江粮油大厦1202室（310003）
☎ 0571-8577 8500
🖷 0571-8577 9709
✉ expo@sinobal.com
www.sinobal.com

### 2010年迪拜国际消费品、礼品贸易博览会（IATF）

日期：2010/01/17 - 19
地点：阿联酋迪拜世界贸易中心展馆
内容：由世界著名的展览公司 Al fajer 主办。该展经过20多年的努力，赢得中东贸易发展"晴雨表"的美誉，是中东历史最悠久、最有影响力的年度盛会。中东迪拜作为中东地区第二大自由港口，近年来，迪拜的转口贸易得到空前的发展，转口国家有伊朗、印度、沙特、科威特、土耳其、伊拉克、英国等200多个国家，贸易覆盖人口达到13亿。
展品内容：家居、餐厨用品、塑料制品、陶瓷、礼品、赠品、玩具、玻璃制品、家用电器、办公用品、日用消费品、流行饰品、珠宝首饰、五金工具、建筑材料、建筑机械、医疗保健、体育用品、轻工工艺、纺织品、机电产品、皮革制品、游戏、工艺品及手工艺品、烟具、系列的产品等轻工产品。
周期：每年两届
市场范围：国际性
上届规模 '08：参展商793家（来自24个国家）
主办：Al fajer
地址：广州市海珠区新港中路350号C1204（510310）
联系人：周文槟
☎ 020-3405 2086 13710318991
🖷 020-3405 0629
✉ dbzh88@163.com
MSN：gdwenbin@hotmail.com
QQ：406372636

### 阿布扎比环保展
ENVIRONMENT 2010

日期：2010/01/18 - 21
地点：阿联酋阿联酋阿布扎比国家展览中心
内容：ENVIRONMENT 2009是本地区最重要的展览及会议，关注环保设备、技术和服务部门的综合解决方案。ENVIRONMENT 2009获阿联酋总统Sheikh Khalifa Bin Zayed Al Nahyan阁下的大力支持，本届展会将是自2001年首次举办以来的第五届展会。POLLUTEC的主办方、世界最大的环境贸易展会主办机构励展博览集团将依靠其全面的资源拓展ENVIRONMENT展会在未来的规模和展出效率。
始办年份：1991
周期：每年一届
市场范围：国际性
参展费用：净地展位AED 1,100/m²，标准展位AED 1,300/m²
主办：励展法国公司
参展联络：励展博览集团国际销售部
地址：北京市朝阳区新源里南路1-3号平安国际金融中心A座15层01-03，05（100027）
联系人：杜一鸣
☎ 010-5933 9288
🖷 010-5933 9233
✉ martin.du@reedexpo.com.cn
www.reedexport.cn

### 阿布扎比世界未来能源展览会
WORLD FUTURE ENERGY SUMMIT: Leading Conference and Exhibition focusing on Future Energy

日期：2010/01/18 - 21
地点：阿联酋阿布扎比新国家展览中心
内容：由Turret中东公司与阿布扎比政府联合主办，阿布扎比皇储默罕默德、扎耶德、阿勒纳哈扬和MASDAR生态城对本展会表示大力支持。展会提供了一个良好的平台，为前来参加的领导以及各界人士提供机会共同讨论热点问题，比如可以持续发展，以及替代能源解决方案和技术等。参加展会的政界人士，商业专家和高级顾问超过11,000人次，分别来自72个国家。励展博览集团从Turrent中东公司收购了阿布扎比世界未来能源展览会，使其成为"能源和环境展会"的一员。WFES是一个世界级的展会，关注问题包括可持续发展，可替代能源解决方案和技术，并且致力于建立高质量会议以及国际展会，形成强大的行业关系网。
周期：每年一届
市场范围：国际性
参展费用：净地480美元/m²，标准展位530美元/m²
主办：励展中东公司；阿拉伯联合酋长国
参展联络：励展博览集团国际销售部
地址：北京朝阳区新源里南路1-3号平安国际金融中心A座15层01-03，05（100027）
联系人：杜一鸣
☎ 010-5933 9288
🖷 010-5933 9233
✉ martin.du@reedexpo.com.cn
www.reedexport.cn

### 阿拉伯国际医疗设备展览会

ARAB HEALTH

**日期：** 2010/01/25 - 28
**地点：** 阿联酋迪拜
**内容：** 医疗设备等
**周期：** 每年一届
**市场范围：** 国际性
**参展联络：** 京慕国际展览有限公司
**地址：** 北京市朝阳区北三环东路6号中国国际展览中心服务楼3层
**联系人：** 魏亦山
☎ 010-8460 0551
🖷 010-8460 0394
✉ zhaolingna@ciec.com.cn
www.jingmu.com.cn

### 2010年中东（阿布扎比）国际美容美发博览会

2010 Beauty Vision

**日期：** 2010/02/02 - 04
**地点：** 阿联酋阿布扎比国家展览中心
**内容：** 零售：化妆品，香水，美容工具，天然化妆品，护甲、美甲产品，护肤品，美容卫生用品，防晒品，脱毛产品，牙齿美容，时装首饰；医药：实验室，高级抗老化产品，服务，西药房，药店，营养治疗，美容保养品，保健食品；美发：护发产品，发型装置，美发辅助工具，染发剂，烫发产品，美发沙龙辅助工具，沙龙设计/装置/摆设；原材料：成份，包装，包装材料，标签，装配，原材料，市场推广中介，设计师，咨询师，展示；SPA水疗：自然健康产品，水疗仪器，有机美容，美体仪器，咨询及管理
**周期：** 每年一届
**市场范围：** 国际性
**主办：** Channels Exhibitions
**参展联络：** 杭州思诺博会展服务有限公司
**地址：** 杭州市体育场路229号浙江粮油大厦1202室（310003）
☎ 0571-8577 8500
🖷 0571-8577 9709
✉ expo@sinobal.com
www.sinobal.com

### 迪拜办公家具展

The Office Exhibition

**日期：** 2010/02/09 - 11
**地点：** 阿联酋迪拜
**周期：** 每年一届
**市场范围：** 国际性
**参展联络：** 大连上选会展服务有限公司
**地址：** 大连市西岗区鞍山路13号兴业广场大厦B座508室（116011）
☎ 0411-8378 8326, 8378 8396, 8378 9165, 8378 8821
🖷 0411-8378 8830, 8378 8823
✉ cicyhuang@vip.sina.com
MSN：cicyhuang@msn.com
www.sun-show.com

### 中东国际工业自动化、动力传动及物流技术展

**日期：** 2010/02/09 - 11
**地点：** 阿联酋迪拜
**周期：** 每年一届
**市场范围：** 国际性
**参展联络：** 中国机械汽车展览联合会
☎ 010-6859 4964
🖷 010-6859 4964

### 中东迪拜国际两轮车展

GULF BIKE EXPO

**日期：** 2010/03 -
**地点：** 阿联酋迪拜
**内容：** 自行车整车、电动车整车、摩托车整车、两轮车零配件、两轮车服装等
**周期：** 每年一届
**市场范围：** 国际性
**参展联络：** 京慕国际展览有限公司
**地址：** 北京市朝阳区北三环东路6号中国国际展览中心服务楼3层
**联系人：** 林航，刘靖
☎ 010-8460 0551
🖷 010-8460 0394
✉ zhaolingna@ciec.com.cn
www.jingmu.com.cn

### 中东国际玩具博览会

The Middle East's Toy Fair

**日期：** 2010/03 -
**地点：** 阿联酋迪拜迪拜
**内容：** 玩具、童车、儿童服饰、儿童家具、电动游戏、游戏机、户外游戏设备
**市场范围：** 国际性
**参展联络：** 京慕国际展览有限公司
**地址：** 北京市朝阳区北三环东路6号中国国际展览中心服务楼3层
**联系人：** 付颖；古莹
☎ 010-8460 0551
🖷 010-8460 0394
✉ zhaolingna@ciec.com.cn
www.jingmu.com.cn

### 中东迪拜国际牙防展览会

AEEDC

**日期：** 2010/03 -
**地点：** 阿联酋迪拜
**内容：** 牙科医疗器械与设备；牙科医疗材料、工具；颌面外科专用器械、材料；牙体牙髓专用器械、材料；牙周病科专用器械、材料；正畸专用器械、材料
**周期：** 每年一届
**市场范围：** 国际性
**参展联络：** 京慕国际展览有限公司
**地址：** 北京市朝阳区北三环东路6号中国国际展览中心服务楼3层
**联系人：** 安红彦，孙铁兵
☎ 010-8460 0551
🖷 010-8460 0394
✉ zhaolingna@ciec.com.cn
www.jingmu.com.cn

### 阿布扎比国际反恐安全展览会

ISNR (Abu Dhabi) International Security & National Resilience

**日期：** 2010/03/01 - 03
**地点：** 阿联酋阿布扎比国家展览中心
**内容：** 国际反恐安全展览会（ISNR）是独特而及时的一次盛事，展示有效保护国土与对抗国际恐怖主义所需的尖端器械。ISNR是唯一涵盖整个国土安全领域的展会。四天的研讨会及展览将为主要行业商家提供讨论以下相关最新技术方案的独特平台：情报侦察与威胁防范；国界安防及运输安防；反恐；重要基础设施防卫；危机管理；应急准备及救援。
**展品范围：** 展会是体验国际安保业最新技术的绝好机会。最新安保方法与政策；重要安保课程；最新安保方案与战略
**周期：** 两年一届
**市场范围：** 国际性
**参展费用：** 净地355美元/m²，标准展位400美元/m²
**主办：** 励展中东公司
**参展联络：** 励展博览集团国际销售部
**地址：** 北京朝阳区新源里南路1-3号平安国际金融中心A座15层01-03，05（100027）
**联系人：** 宫卫
☎ 010-5933 9288
🖷 010-5933 9233
✉ david.gong@reedexpo.com.cn
www.reedexport.cn

### 2010中东门窗及幕墙博览会

6th International Trade Fair for Doors, Windows & Roofing

**日期：** 2010/03/08 - 10
**地点：** 阿联酋沙迦国际展览中心
**内容：** 门：木门、玻璃门、UPVC门、自动门、机械自动门、电子自动门、滑行门系统、门锁系统、门把手等配件、工业用门、门控系统、室内门、室外门、组合门、折叠门、防火门；窗：UPVC窗、木质窗、玻璃窗、圆型窗、拱型窗、多边型窗、滑动窗、折叠窗、铝型材；附件：密封剂、粘合剂、配件、垫圈、铰链带、紧固件、门窗锁系统、建筑五金；屋顶：屋顶系统、工程建筑外墙面砖、钢结构屋顶、露天防水系统、绝缘材料、可拉伸膜、铝型材、沥青、混凝土、墙面、玻璃制品、工业屋面解决方案、金属与钢结构系统、PVC材料、聚碳酸酯材料；墙体
**周期：** 每年一届
**市场范围：** 国际性
**参展联络：** 福建省国际贸易展览公司；福建省新天国际会展有限公司
**地址：** 福建省福州市鼓楼区五四北路283号天骅大厦20层2088单元
**联系人：** 范心锦；卢建光
☎ 0591-2808 6523, 8773 5017
✉ barryfan@valuedshow.com
MSN：barryvanfan@hotmail.com
QQ：30249576
www.valuedshow.com

### 2010年中东（迪拜）国际商用车展览会

2010 Commercial Vehicles Middle East

**日期：** 2010/03/09 - 11
**地点：** 阿联酋迪拜阿国际会展中心
**内容：** 重型商用车：货车、客车；轻型商用车：面包车、小型客车、小卡车、拖车；工程机械车：搅拌车、挖掘车、推土机、起重机；专用车：牵引车、冷藏车、救护车、警用车、消防车、餐车、市政车；警用车；商用车附件：平板挂车、货柜、倾卸装置、铝质厢式车身、挂车、多轴拖车；商用车零件、部件、配件及设备；商用车服务：商用车保险、融资/租赁、数据处理、通讯/刊物、司机培训、导航产品/服务、燃料工艺；综合/其他
首届
**周期：** 每年一届
**市场范围：** 国际性
**主办：** SMG展览公司
**地址：** 杭州市体育场路229号浙江粮油大厦1202室（310003）
☎ 0571-8577 8500
🖷 0571-8577 9709
✉ expo@sinobal.com
www.sinobal.com

### 2011年中东（迪拜）国际木材及木工机械展

2011 Dubai Wood Show

**日期：** 2010/04 -
**地点：** 阿联酋迪拜机场展览中心
**内容：** 木材制品类：木制家具及配件，修整配件，木制门窗，木材，原木，硬木，软木，胶合板，薄板，装饰硬纸板，各类面板，木线条，木地板，木制工艺品，装饰木材和木制装饰物，橱柜，磨料产品，表面加工及处理设备，气钉，钉枪，个人保护相关设备，建筑用木工技术；木工机械类：木材加工器械，成型板，玻璃珠，壁板/嵌板/覆层设备，木材处理设备，木材五金工具及配件，刀片/小刀，镗床，磨边机/合角机，切割工具，榫眼机，切削和成型机，成圆机，砂光/磨光机，行业服务（运输和后勤）
**周期：** 每年一届
**市场范围：** 国际性
**上届规模** ‘09：展览面积16,000m²，参展商300家（来自30个国家），参观人数3,000人
**主办：** SMG展览公司
**参展联络：** 杭州思诺博会展服务有限公司
**地址：** 杭州市体育场路229号浙江粮油大厦1202室

(310003)
☎ 0571-8577 8500
🖷 0571-8577 9709
✉ expo@sinobal.com
www.sinobal.com

## 中东迪拜国际服装、纺织、鞋类、皮革及时尚配饰博览会

### Motexha

**日期：**2010/04 -
**地点：**阿联酋迪拜迪拜
**内容：**男女服装、童装、内衣泳装、劳保服装、服装饰品、各种服装配件、各种面料、家用纺织品、皮革制品、箱包手袋
**市场范围：**国际性
**参展联络：**京慕国际展览有限公司
**地址：**北京市朝阳区北三环东路6号中国国际展览中心服务楼3层
**联系人：**由慧；柳川
☎ 010-8460 0551
🖷 010-8460 0394
✉ zhaolingna@ciec.com.cn
www.jingmu.com.cn

## 世界城市可持续发展论坛

### Global City Abu Dhabi

**日期：**2010/04 -
**地点：**阿联酋阿布扎比酋长国宫殿酒店
**内容：**世界城市可持续发展论坛是全球各界领导人交流可持续发展最佳方案，并探讨可持续发展战略的唯一国际性论坛。市长、城市规划师、决策者及各界领导人齐聚阿布扎比参加这一盛会。亚洲、欧洲、中东及北美洲等地区的代表城市将互相分享并探讨可持续发展经验及专业技术。通过本届论坛，主办方希望令世界看到阿布扎比正崛起为一个新的国际城市，吸引着全球众多城市聚集于此，参加讨论城市发展及规划等可持续发展问题。
**周期：**每年一届
**市场范围：**国际性
**主办：**励展中东公司（阿联酋）
**参展联络：**励展博览集团国际销售部
**地址：**北京市朝阳区新源里南路1-3号平安国际金融中心A座15层01-03，05（100027）
**联系人：**吴祥
☎ 010-5933 9288
🖷 010-5933 9233
✉ ronald.wu@reedexpo.com.cn
www.reedexport.cn

## 2010年中东（迪拜）国际服装、纺织、鞋类及皮革制品博览会

### 2010 Motexha

**日期：**2010/04/06 - 08
**地点：**阿联酋迪拜国际会展中心
**内容：**服装及面料类：男女服装、运动休闲服装、童装、劳保服装、纺织工艺、服装饰品（领带、围巾、胸针等）、各种面料、棉麻织品、针织品、纺织制品、纺织机械、家用纺织品、床上用品、裘皮制品； 辅料及配件：拉链、纽扣、衬布等、及辅料；各类鞋：男女皮鞋、拖鞋、时装鞋、童鞋、休闲鞋；皮革产品：皮革制品、书包、背包、拉杆包、手提包、钱包
**始办年份：**1978
**周期：**每年一届
**市场范围：**国际性
**上届规模** '09：展览面积2,325m², 参展商220家（来自23个国家），参观人数3,643人
**主办：**IIR展览公司
**参展联络：**杭州思诺博会展服务有限公司
**地址：**杭州市体育场路229号浙江粮油大厦1202室（310003）
☎ 0571-8577 8500
🖷 0571-8577 9709
✉ expo@sinobal.com
www.sinobal.com

## 中东（迪拜）木材及木工机械展览会

### Dubai Wood Show

**日期：**2010/04/13 - 15
**地点：**阿联酋迪拜机场展览中心
**内容：**中东地区唯一的木材及木材机械的专业展会。展品包括材制品类：木制家具及配件，修整配件，木制门窗，木材，原木，硬木，软木，胶合板，薄板，装饰硬纸板，各类面板，木线条，木地板，木制工艺品，装饰木材和木制装饰物，橱柜，磨料产品，表面加工及处理设备，气钉，钉枪，个人保护相关设备，建筑用木工技术。木工机械类：木材加工器械，成型板，玻璃珠，壁板/嵌板/覆层设备，木材处理设备，刀片/小刀，镗床，磨边机/合角机，切割工具，榫眼机，切削和成型机，成圆机，砂光/磨光机，旋切机器，胶合机器，小木板设备，碾压设备，化纸浆设备，制木专用设备，行业服务。
**周期：**每年一届
**市场范围：**国际性
**上届规模** '09：展览面积16,000m², 参展商200家（国外展商30家）
**主办：**SMG展览公司
**参展联络：**杭州思诺博会展服务有限公司
**地址：**杭州市体育场路229号粮油大厦1205（310003）
**联系人：**吴雷
☎ 0571-8577 8500
🖷 0571-8577 9709
✉ expo@sinobal.com
www.sinobal.com

## 2010年中东迪拜国际乐器、舞台灯光及舞台音响技术展览会

### 2010 PALME Middle East

**日期：**2010/04/18 - 20
**地点：**阿联酋迪拜国际会展中心
**内容：**小型乐器：弦乐器、铜乐器、口风琴、敲击乐器、木管乐器 大型乐器：钢琴、键盘乐器、教堂管风琴、古典键盘乐器；电子乐器：键盘、合成乐器、数字钢琴、电子鼓、电吉他/贝斯；专业音效及录音设备：舞台工程技术、舞台灯光、激光技术、专业音响、载声设备、功放、卡拉OK系统、麦克风与配件、公共广播系统、录音与重制设备、混音桌与箱架、配件、家具
**周期：**每年一届
**市场范围：**国际性
**上届规模** '09：展览面积5,369m², 参展商162家，参观人数6,048人
**主办：**英国IIR展览公司
**参展联络：**杭州思诺博会展服务有限公司
**地址：**杭州市体育场路229号浙江粮油大厦1202室（310003）
☎ 0571-8577 8500
🖷 0571-8577 9709
✉ expo@sinobal.com
www.sinobal.com

## 迪拜机场设备展览会

### Airport Show Dubai 2009

**日期：**2010/04/25 - 27
**地点：**阿联酋迪拜航空会展中心
**内容：**迪拜机场设备展览会始创于2001年，是中东地区专注于机场建设、发展及运营的重要展会。展示新建及现有机场建造及供应的方方面面，如行李操作、雷达系统、机场内部设施及建筑供应。2008年，为促使迪拜机场设备展会的不断壮大，将2007年成功举办的会议项目发展成为独立并相互关联的展示区域：中东航空安全展示、中东地勤服务安全展示及中东交通控制展示。2009年，主办方计划增加新的会议项目及垂直展示体系。将维护、修理及操作纳入这一体系将具有非常重要的战略意义，在加燃料、服务、特许权经营方面也具有同等意义。此外，我们与各地政府建立的良好关系，进一步挖掘该地区就业及培训等方面的潜力。
**产品及服务：**机场设计与建造—规划、设计与建筑、建造、建筑材料。机场供应—行李运输、客运、内部机场终端 机场运营—维护、管理及服务、航行服务；技术—信息技术/软件、灯光、乘客信息、技术装置及体系 地面支持设备—飞行操作、行李推车、（托车、货物装载机、ULD），客梯、多用途车、饮食装备；安全—准入及周界控制、CCTV及监控体系、X-光及探测体系、安全培训及咨询 航空管理及控制体系—ATC塔/移动控制塔、通讯及数据处理系统、控制台及围护结构、着陆体系及航空急救
**始办年份：**2001
**周期：**每年一届
**市场范围：**国际性
**参展联络：**励展博览集团国际销售部
**地址：**北京朝阳区新源里南路1-3号平安国际金融中心A座15层01-03，05（100027）
**联系人：**宫卫
☎ 010-5933 9288
🖷 010-5933 9233
✉ david.gong@reedexpo.com.cn
www.reedexport.cn

## 2010年中东（阿布扎比）国际食品及饮料展

### 2010 Middle East Food

**日期：**2010/04/26 - 28
**地点：**阿联酋阿布扎比阿联酋阿布扎比国家展览中心
**内容：**食品及饮料：特色食品、精美食品、冷冻食品、肉类、伊斯兰食品、乳制品、未加工食品、罐头食品/加工食品、海产品、饮料及咖啡等；食品原料：抗氧化剂、生理活性成份、膨松剂、添加剂、补给品、食用油及食用脂肪、草药/香料及原料、乳酸菌、营养物、防腐剂、蛋白质、维他命及矿物等；甜食巧克力及糕点：甜食、巧克力及巧克力产品、可可、烘培产品、冰淇淋、糖果、饼干、浓缩食品； 有机健康食品：功能性食品、高级包装天然食品、绿色食品、有机肉类、有机乳制品、饮料及饮用水、能量食品、减肥食品等；食品处理、包装及机械；餐饮技术及设备
**周期：**每年一届
**市场范围：**国际性
**主办：**Channels Exhibition
**参展联络：**杭州思诺博会展服务有限公司
**地址：**杭州市体育场路229号浙江粮油大厦1202室（310003）
☎ 0571-8577 8500
🖷 0571-8577 9709
✉ expo@sinobal.com
www.sinobal.com

## 中东国际五金工具博览会

### The Middle East's Leading Trade Show for Hardware & Tools

**日期：**2010/05 -
**地点：**阿联酋迪拜
**内容：**建筑装饰五金、日用五金、电动机手动工具、园艺工具、锁类、防盗及报警产品、照明器材
**周期：**每年一届
**市场范围：**国际性
**参展联络：**京慕国际展览有限公司
**地址：**北京市朝阳区北三环东路6号中国国际展览中心服务楼3层
**联系人：**国曦，薛磊
☎ 010-8460 0551
🖷 010-8460 0394
✉ zhaolingna@ciec.com.cn
www.jingmu.com.cn

## 中东国际厨房、卫浴洁具博览会

### ISH Kitchen & Bathroom Gulf

**日期：**2010/05 -

**地点**：阿联酋迪拜
**内容**：卫生洁具、浴室设备、水处理系统等相关设备；供暖设备、热能循环和利用、通风装置等
**周期**：每年一届
**市场范围**：国际性
**参展联络**：京慕国际展览有限公司
**地址**：北京市朝阳区北三环东路6号中国国际展览中心服务楼3层
**联系人**：罗晓龙，王芳
☎ 010-8460 0551
🖷 010-8460 0394
✉ zhaolingna@ciec.com.cn
www.jingmu.com.cn

### 中东国际家用电器博览会
### Hometech Middle East

**日期**：2010/05 -
**地点**：阿联酋迪拜迪拜
**内容**：家用电器、消费电子产品
**周期**：每年一届
**市场范围**：国际性
**参展联络**：京慕国际展览有限公司
**地址**：北京市朝阳区北三环东路6号中国国际展览中心服务楼3层
**联系人**：宋秋爽，刘舰
☎ 010-8460 0551
🖷 010-8460 0394
✉ zhaolingna@ciec.com.cn
www.jingmu.com.cn

### 2010年中东（迪拜）国际地面铺装展览会
### 2010 DOMOTEX Middle East

**日期**：2010/05/10 - 12
**地点**：阿联酋迪拜国际会展中心
**内容**：地板：实木地板、强化复合木地板、实木复合地板、竹地板、集成材地板、软木地板、人造板材；地毯；地砖：釉面砖、通体砖、大理石、花岗岩、毛石、各种复合地材；塑料地面材料：地板砖、地板革、PVC板材、工程用或特种用塑料地铺；地面材料配件、耗材及铺盖技术：衬垫、模具、安装工具、清洁设备、粘合剂、装饰用品；加工制造机械设备；设计及印制。
**周期**：每年一届
**市场范围**：国际性
**上届规模**　‘09：展览面积12,000m$^2$，参展商215家（来自27个国家），参观人数51,496人
**主办**：德国博览会集团公司
**参展联络**：杭州思诺博会展服务有限公司
**地址**：杭州市体育场路229号浙江粮油大厦1202室（310003）
☎ 0571-8577 8500
🖷 0571-8577 9709
✉ expo@sinobal.com
www.sinobal.com

### 2010年中东（阿布扎比）国际通讯展（Mecom 2010）

**日期**：2010/05/17 - 19
**地点**：阿联酋阿布扎比国家展览中心
**内容**：观众来自海湾联合会成员国（GCC）：阿联酋、沙特阿拉伯、科威特、阿曼、卡塔尔和巴林。加上伊拉克、伊朗和也门的参观者，及其他中东国家如埃及、利比亚、突尼斯、叙利亚、黎巴嫩、约旦的参观者和非洲国家、黑海周边国家和中亚前俄罗斯、印度次大陆。
展出范围：信息通信交换、传输技术与设备；通信终端设备及配套产品；信息通信服务；电信增值业务；移动通信系统和移动通信终端产品；数据通信与网络技术及相关产品；下一代网络、网络电视、网络游戏、互动娱乐产品及服务；通信电源、仪器仪表、通信机房用品；通信电子元器件；通信终端配件；通信线缆；存储、显示技术；数码娱乐、消费电子产品。
**周期**：每年一届
**市场范围**：国际性
**联络**：广州市海珠区新港中路350号C1204（510310）
**联系人**：周文槟
☎ 020-3405 2086 13710318991
🖷 020-3405 0629
✉ cntai88@sina.com
MSN：gdwenbin@hotmail.com
QQ：406372636

### 中东（迪拜）国际园艺及户外休闲用品展览会

**日期**：2010/05/17 - 19
**地点**：阿联酋迪拜
**内容**：花园家具及家居用品、露营及休闲用品、烧烤设备、花园机械和设备、花园手工具和附件、其它设备和花园布置、植物和植物护理、水处理和室外照明
**周期**：每年一届
**市场范围**：国际性
**参展联络**：京慕国际展览有限公司
**地址**：北京市朝阳区北三环东路6号中国国际展览中心服务楼3层
**联系人**：滕昊，张翠元
☎ 010-8460 0551
🖷 010-8460 0394
✉ zhaolingna@ciec.com.cn
www.jingmu.com.cn

### 2010中东国际五金工具展览会
### 2010 Hardware & Tools Middle East

**日期**：2010/05/17 - 19
**地点**：阿联酋迪拜国际会展中心
**内容**：五金：建筑五金、家具装饰五金、轴承、锁类、密封件、紧固件、铆钉、螺丝、水龙头、管件阀门；工具：气动工具、电动工具、手工工具、木工工具、钳子、刀具、量具、焊接设备、钻头、玻璃切割工具、喷枪；建材：门窗、油漆涂料、黏合剂、地板、铝合金、塑钢、木工、铁器、防盗及报警产品、安防器材；机械：木工机械、金属加工机械、焊接机械等设备及配件
**始办年份**：1998
**周期**：每年一届
**市场范围**：国际性
**上届规模**　‘09：展览面积14,000m$^2$，参展商389家（来自20个国家），参观人数18,000人（专业贸易观众6,000人）
**主办**：法兰克福展览公司
**参展联络**：杭州思诺博会展服务有限公司
**地址**：杭州市体育场路229号浙江粮油大厦1202室（310003）
☎ 0571-8577 8500
🖷 0571-8577 9709
✉ expo@sinobal.com
www.sinobal.com

### 2010年中东（迪拜）国际花卉园艺及户外休闲用品展览会
### 2010 Garden & Landscaping Middle East

**日期**：2010/05/17 - 19
**地点**：阿联酋迪拜阿联酋迪拜世贸中心
**内容**：花园机械，工具，花园建筑，家具，花园装饰，池塘装饰品；化学肥料，植物种子，灭虫产品，胶皮软管，灌溉系统；灯具照明设备，罐，锅，栅栏，烧烤架，烧烤用品
**周期**：每年一届
**市场范围**：国际性
**上届规模**　‘09：参展商来自40个国家，参观人数5,162人
**主办**：法兰克福展览公司
**参展联络**：杭州思诺博会展服务有限公司
**地址**：杭州市体育场路229号浙江粮油大厦1202室（310003）
☎ 0571-8577 8500
🖷 0571-8577 9709
✉ expo@sinobal.com
www.sinobal.com

### 国际五金工具 / 商业照明展览会

**日期**：2010/05/17 - 19
**地点**：阿联酋迪拜
**周期**：每年一届
**市场范围**：国际性
**参展联络**：中国机械汽车展览联合会
☎ 010-6859 4964
🖷 010-6859 4964

### 2010年中东国际眼镜眼科用品展览会
### 2010 Vision-X Dubai

**日期**：2010/05/18 - 20
**地点**：阿联酋迪拜国际会展中心
**内容**：各种光学眼镜、太阳镜、运动用和防护类眼镜产品、眼用消费品和护眼产品、眼镜镜片、框架、配件、人造眼、观景镜头和透镜用织物、镜片镜头切割设备、眼镜器械和设备、眼科外科设备、诊断设备和器械、折光仪器和设备，视轴矫正设备、眼镜展示架。
**周期**：每年一届
**市场范围**：国际性
**上届规模**　‘09：展览面积6,489m$^2$，参展商142家（来自23个国家），参观人数3,297人
**主办**：迪拜世贸中心组委会
**参展联络**：杭州思诺博会展服务有限公司
**地址**：杭州市体育场路229号浙江粮油大厦1202室（310003）
☎ 0571-8577 8500
🖷 0571-8577 9709
✉ expo@sinobal.com
www.sinobal.com

### 2010中东阿布扎比国际工程机械展

**日期**：2010/05/24 - 26
**地点**：阿联酋阿布扎比
**内容**：工程机械
**市场范围**：国际性
**参展联络**：北京中仕达兴业展览有限公司
**地址**：北京市海淀区蓝靛厂东路2号金源时代商务中心2号楼A座11B（100097）
**联系人**：贾倩，赵仕忱，牟向东，张露
☎ 010-5129 8900
🖷 010-8886 2939
✉ mail@chinstar.cn
www.chinstar.cn

### 国际汽车配件博览会

**日期**：2010/05/25 - 27
**地点**：阿联酋迪拜
**周期**：每年一届
**市场范围**：国际性
**参展联络**：中国机械汽车展览联合会
☎ 010-6859 4964
🖷 010-6859 4964

### 2010年中东（迪拜）国际汽车配件及售后服务展览会
### Automechanika Middle East

**日期**：2010/05/25 - 27
**地点**：阿联酋迪拜
**内容**：汽车配件及零部件、汽车修理保养产品设备、车轮、车内娱乐及音箱系统和设备、汽车加工产品、加油站设备、电池电源、空调制冷、汽车装饰、电子机械系统、发动机、工具、涂料、安全系统等。**周期**：每年一届
**市场范围**：国际性
**主办**：法兰克福展览公司
**参展联络**：中国汽车工业国际合作总公司
**地址**：北京市海淀区中关村丹棱街3号A座5层（100080）
**联系人**：何萌
☎ 010-8260 6880
🖷 010-8260 6883
✉ exhibition@cnaico.com.cn

### 2010年中东（迪拜）国际美容美发用品展览会
### 2010 Beautyworld Middle East

**日期**：2010/06/01 - 03
**地点**：阿联酋迪拜国际会展中心
**内容**：化妆品、护肤品、香水香熏、护发产品、防晒产品；疗养沙龙设备用具、美发沙龙配件设备、美容沙龙用具及设备、美容治疗仪、皮肤护理设

备、水治疗设备、植发设备、健身房设备、健身器材、超声波按摩器；美体用品、指甲护理及修脸产品、理发工具、口腔护理用品、假发、发饰等有关产品；美容产品包装、原材料、礼品，蜡烛、美容服务、杂志。
**始办年份**：1995
**周期**：每年一届
**市场范围**：国际性
**上届规模** '08：展览面积10,121m$^2$，参展商950家（来自55个国家）
**主办**：德国法兰克福（迪拜）展览公司
**参展联络**：杭州思诺博会展服务有限公司
**地址**：杭州市体育场路229号浙江粮油大厦1202室（310003）
☎ 0571-8577 8500
📠 0571-8577 9709
✉ expo@sinobal.com
www.sinobal.com

### 中东厨房卫浴设备展览会

**日期**：2010/09 -
**地点**：阿联酋迪拜
**周期**：每年一届
**市场范围**：国际性
**参展联络**：中国机械汽车展览联合会
☎ 010-6859 4964
📠 010-6859 4964

### 中东游泳池设备及SPA展览会

Middle East Pool & Spa Exhibition

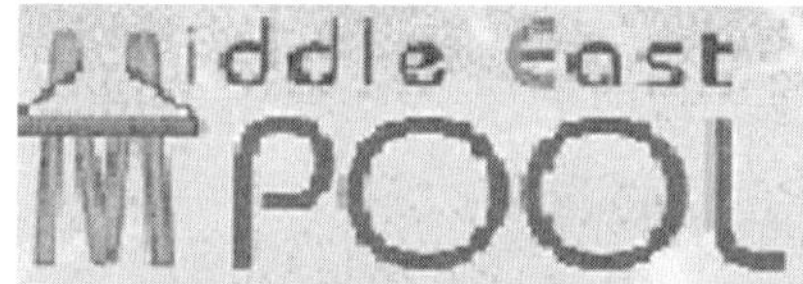


**日期**：2010/09/26 - 28
**地点**：阿联酋迪拜国际会展中心
**内容**：中东游泳池设备及SPA展览会（ME Pool）是中东地区唯一专门针对游泳池及SPA行业的展览会。展会在充满机遇的中东未来商业中心迪拜举行。中东地区最近的建筑热潮促使数以千计的世界级游泳池及娱乐中心拔地而起。ME Pool聚焦最新最现代的舒适技术，为游泳池业开创了新的天地。展会地点位于东西方贸易中心、世界上最富有地区之一的迪拜。ME Pool为全世界的厂商、经销商和投资者提供了一个独一无二的交流与信息平台。
**周期**：两年一届
**市场范围**：国际性
**参展费用**：净地315美元/m$^2$，标准展位360美元/m$^2$
**主办**：阿联酋励展中东公司
**参展联络**：励展博览集团国际销售部
**地址**：北京市朝阳区新源里南路1-3号平安国际金融中心A座15层01-03，05（100027）
**联系人**：申健
☎ 010-8518 2644, 5933 9288
📠 010-5933 9233
✉ jerry.shen@reedexpo.com.cn
www.reedexport.cn

### 中东国际城市、建筑及商用照明展览会

Light Middle East

**日期**：2010/09/27 - 29
**地点**：阿联酋迪拜迪拜
**内容**：照明用品
**周期**：每年一届
**市场范围**：国际性
**参展联络**：京慕国际展览有限公司
**地址**：北京市朝阳区北三环东路6号中国国际展览中心服务楼3层
**联系人**：宋秋爽，刘舰
☎ 010-8460 0551
📠 010-8460 0394
✉ zhaolingna@ciec.com.cn
www.jingmu.com.cn

### 中东（沙迦）国际工程机械展

CONMEX

**日期**：2010/10 -
**地点**：阿联酋沙迦
**内容**：工程机械、矿山机械、建筑机械及其配件
**周期**：每年一届
**市场范围**：国际性
**参展联络**：京慕国际展览有限公司
**地址**：北京市朝阳区北三环东路6号中国国际展览中心服务楼3层
**联系人**：马赛，俞亮
☎ 010-8460 0551
📠 010-8460 0394
✉ zhaolingna@ciec.com.cn
www.jingmu.com.cn

### 中东国际石油、天然气展览会

**日期**：2010/10 -
**地点**：阿联酋迪拜
**周期**：每年一届
**市场范围**：国际性
**参展联络**：中国机械汽车展览联合会
☎ 010-6859 4964
📠 010-6859 4964

### 2010年中东（阿布扎比）国际电力及水能展

2010 Power Generation & Water Middle East

**日期**：2010/10/17 - 19
**地点**：阿联酋阿布扎比国家展览中心
**内容**：电力-电站设备，变电设备和电力传输设备，高、低压电气开电力控制系统，检测设备，电缆电线材料，发电机组，开关设备和相关设备；水能-水利设备和技术，蓄水罐，输水管，真空管，排灌设备，水泵和发动机，纯水净化设备，水污染监控分析设备和各种水处理技术，各类阀门；环保节能安全设备和技术。
**始办年份**：2008
**周期**：每年一届
**市场范围**：国际性
**主办**：英国IIR展览公司
**参展联络**：杭州思诺博会展服务有限公司
**地址**：杭州市体育场路229号浙江粮油大厦1202室（310003）
☎ 0571-8577 8500
📠 0571-8577 9709
✉ expo@sinobal.com
www.sinobal.com

### 中东国际建筑机械、车辆和设备展

PMV

**日期**：2010/11 -
**地点**：阿联酋迪拜
**内容**：工程机械/工程车辆，建材机械，建筑机械，生产设备，技术与服务，测量与控制系统等
**周期**：每年一届
**市场范围**：国际性
**参展联络**：京慕国际展览有限公司
**地址**：北京市朝阳区北三环东路6号中国国际展览中心服务楼3层
**联系人**：宋秋爽，刘舰
☎ 010-8460 0551
📠 010-8460 0394
✉ zhaolingna@ciec.com.cn
www.jingmu.com.cn

### 国际机床和金属加工技术展览会

**日期**：2010/11 -
**地点**：阿联酋迪拜
**周期**：每年一届
**市场范围**：国际性
**参展联络**：中国机械汽车展览联合会
☎ 010-6859 4964
📠 010-6859 4964

### 迪拜国际体育用品博览会

Sportex Dubai

**日期**：2010/11 -
**地点**：阿联酋迪拜
**内容**：运动服装、鞋、帽、健身器材及附件、户外运动及休闲用品、运动器材、旅游休闲产品、运动、体健等
**周期**：每年一届
**市场范围**：国际性
**参展联络**：京慕国际展览有限公司
**地址**：北京市朝阳区北三环东路6号中国国际展览中心服务楼3层
**联系人**：林航，刘靖
☎ 010-8460 0551
📠 010-8460 0394
✉ zhaolingna@ciec.com.cn
www.jingmu.com.cn

### 国际石油、天然气及石化设备展览会

**日期**：2010/11/01 - 04
**地点**：阿联酋阿布扎比
**周期**：每年一届
**市场范围**：国际性
**参展联络**：中国机械汽车展览联合会
☎ 010-6859 4964
📠 010-6859 4964

### 2010年中东（迪拜）国际甜食及休闲食品展

2010 Sweets Middle East

**日期**：2010/11/01 - 01
**地点**：阿联酋迪拜国际会展中心
**内容**：可可、巧克力和巧克力制品，饼干、零食，糖制品，休闲食品，焙烤制品，冰淇淋和生意粉，面包类食品，胶质糖，小点心等。
**始办年份**：2007
**周期**：每年一届
**市场范围**：国际性
**上届规模** '08：参展商160家（来自32个国家），参观人数4,545人
**主办**：德国科隆展览公司
**参展联络**：杭州思诺博会展服务有限公司
**地址**：杭州市体育场路229号浙江粮油大厦1202室（310003）
☎ 0571-8577 8500
📠 0571-8577 9709
✉ expo@sinobal.com
www.sinobal.com

### 2010年中东迪拜国际家具和室内装饰博览会

2010 INDEX

**日期**：2010/11/08 - 11
**地点**：阿联酋迪拜国际会展中心
**内容**：家具展区：酒店/餐馆家具、休闲家具、办公家具、公寓家具、零售家具、室外/园艺家具、居室家具、厨房家具、餐厅家具；家居配件：厨房用具、装饰花瓶、陶器、玻璃制品、家庭用品、镜子、雕刻装饰、窗帘窗饰；地面展区：手工制地毯、机器制地毯、纺织铺地、木板铺地、纤维/纱线/织物；家纺展区：纺织品、亚麻织物、窗帘，家居装饰。
**周期**：每年一届
**市场范围**：国际性
**上届规模** '07：展览面积35,700m$^2$，参展商1,690家（国外展商1,491家，来自56个国家），参观人数12,014人
**主办**：DMG展览公司
**参展联络**：杭州思诺博会展服务有限公司
**地址**：杭州市体育场路229号浙江粮油大厦1202室（310003）
☎ 0571-8577 8500
📠 0571-8577 9709
✉ expo@sinobal.com
www.sinobal.com

### 第20届中东迪拜国际家具展

INDEX 2010

**日期**：2010/11/08 - 11
**地点**：阿联酋迪拜
**周期**：每年一届
**市场范围**：国际性

参展联络：大连上选会展服务有限公司
地址：大连市西岗区鞍山路13号兴业广场大厦B座508室（116011）
☎ 0411-8378 8326, 8378 8396, 8378 9165, 8378 8821
🖷 0411-8378 8830, 8378 8823
✉ cicyhuang@vip.sina.com
MSN：cicyhuang@msn.com
www.sun-show.com

### 2010年中东（迪拜）五大行业—国际建筑机械、车辆及设备展览会

### 2010 BIG 5 PMV

日期：2010/11/21 - 24
地点：阿联酋迪拜国际会展中心
内容：建筑车辆：自卸车，牵引车，半挂牵引车，运输特殊部件的卡车，路面清扫车，车体部件，各类零配件；建筑机械：隧道工程专用机械，隧道掘进机，开凿机，挖掘装载机，升降机，铲运机，推土机，零部件，堆垛机钻孔设备及系统，电缆敷设机械，管道和电缆探测器，压缩机，压路机，平板式振捣器，夯，土壤固化剂，垃圾压实机，道路施工、养护及修复专用机械，铁路铺设机械，墙体切割机；起重和传送装置：吊车，起重机，传送平台，工作平台，高空作业平台，升降机，滑轮铰链，电动吊车、电动葫芦，真空搬运系统，叉车，升降车。
始办年份：2007
周期：每年一届
市场范围：国际性
上届规模　'08：展览面积40,000m²，参展商412家（来自299个国家），专业贸易观众6,464人
主办：DMG展览公司和SMG展览公司
参展联络：杭州思诺博会展服务有限公司
地址：杭州市体育场路229号浙江粮油大厦1202室（310003）
☎ 0571-8577 8500
🖷 0571-8577 9709
✉ expo@sinobal.com
www.sinobal.com

### 中东迪拜国际饮料技术及机械设备展

日期：2010/12 -
3921
地点：阿联酋迪拜
内容：生产包装机械、净化技术及设备、清洗设备、饮料罐装设备及生产线、输送设备、生产无酒精饮料的设备、混合搅拌设备等
周期：每年一届
市场范围：国际性
参展联络：京慕国际展览有限公司
地址：北京市朝阳区北三环东路6号中国国际展览中心服务楼3层
联系人：许艳，孙铁兵
☎ 010-8460 0551
🖷 010-8460 0394
✉ zhaolingna@ciec.com.cn
www.jingmu.com.cn

### 阿布扎比国际汽车展览会

### Abu Dhabi International Motor Show

日期：2010/12/15 - 19
插入logo，数据库会展编号3358
地点：阿联酋阿布扎比国家展览中心
内容：中东地区最大且最全面的汽车展览会，承蒙阿拉伯联合酋长国内政部部长赛义夫-扎耶德-阿勒纳哈扬的大力支持。来自励展中东公司的展会项目总监Ara Fernezian介绍到："展会举办得非常成功，得到了大家的积极响应，观众人数达到50,000名，展商也对展会的结果表示满意。"展会由励展中东公司举办，展览场地包括室内和户外，面积达38,000m²。80家展商在展会上展示了50个品牌的豪华车、高性能车、个性特制车、箱式轿车、概念混合动力汽车、运动车、越野车、家庭房车及运动型多用途汽车(SUVs)、摩托车和沙滩车以及商务车型，比如卡车，厢型车和迷你车、豪华客车、豪华轿车、拖车和宿营房车。同时，展会还为您带来汽车配件和自动设备等。展会拥有400个最新车型，来自30个不同的车辆生产商，其中19辆车型是中东首发。其他品牌車还包括Ultimate Aero和Shelby的超级车和概念车，并且Ferrari还带来了他们的F1轿车。
产品及服务：汽车类：豪华轿车，高性能名车，个性特制车，高级轿车，概念混合动力汽车，运动车，四驱越野车，家庭房车及运动型多用途汽车(SUVs)，摩托车，沙滩车(quad bikes) 商务用车：敞蓬小型载货卡车，货车及中巴车，豪华长途客车，豪华轿车，拖车及宿营房车 其他相关汽车服务：车库及修理公司，保险公司，汽车金融公司，汽车维修公司，维护设备，汽车媒体
周期：两年一届
市场范围：国际性
参展费用：净地展位840迪拉姆/m²，标准展位1,010迪拉姆/m²
主办：励展博览集团国际销售部；励展中东公司（阿联酋）
地址：北京市朝阳区新源里南路1-3号平安国际金融中心A座15层01-03，05（100027）
联系人：杜一鸣
☎ 010-5933 9288
🖷 010-5933 9233
✉ martin.du@reedexpo.com.cn
www.reedexport.cn

### 迪拜机场设备展览会

### Airport Show Dubai 2009

日期：2011 -
地点：阿联酋迪拜航空会展中心
内容：中东地区专注于机场建设、发展及运营的重要展会。展示新建及现有机场建造及供应的方方面面，如行李操作、雷达系统、机场内部设施及建筑供应。为促使迪拜机场设备展会的不断壮大，将会议项目发展成为独立并相互关联的展示区域：中东航空安全展示、中东地勤服务安全展示及中东交通控制展示。2009年，主办方计划增加新的会议项目及垂直展示体系。将维护、修理及操作纳入这一体系将具有非常重要的战略意义，在加燃料、服务、特许权经营方面也具有同等意义。
产品及服务：机场设计与建造：规划、设计与建筑、建造、建筑材料。机场供应一行李运输、客运、内部机场终端 机场运营—维护、管理及服务、航行服务；技术：信息技术/软件、灯光、乘客信息、技术装置及体系 地面支持设备：飞行操作、行李推车（托车、货物装载机、ULD），客梯、多用途车、饮食装备 安全—准入及周界控制、CCTV及监控体系、X-光及探测体系、安全培训及咨询 航空管理及控制体系—ATC塔/移动控制塔、通讯及数据处理系统、控制台及围护结构、着陆体系及航空急救
始办年份：2001
周期：每年一届
市场范围：国际性
参展联络：励展博览集团国际销售部
地址：北京朝阳区新源里南路1-3号平安国际金融中心A座15层01-03，05（100027）
联系人：宫卫
☎ 010-5933 9288
🖷 010-5933 9233
✉ david.gong@reedexpo.com.cn
www.reedexport.cn

### 2011年中东（迪拜）国际秋季商品交易会

### 2011 IATF

日期：2011/01 -
地点：阿联酋迪拜世界贸易中心
内容：生活用品、粮油食品、美容包材、服装纺织、五金机电、皮革鞋帽、塑料制品、钟表文具、礼品玩具、电子通讯、石油开采、五矿化工、建筑材料、室内装饰、汽摩配件、家电制冷、医疗保健、体育用品。
周期：每年一届
市场范围：国际性
上届规模　'08：展览面积15,750m²，参展商800家（来自25个国家），参观人数15,000人
主办：Al Fajer展览公司
参展联络：杭州思诺博会展服务有限公司
地址：杭州市体育场路229号浙江粮油大厦1202室（310003）
☎ 0571-8577 8500
🖷 0571-8577 9709
✉ expo@sinobal.com
www.sinobal.com

### 2011年中东（迪拜）国际商业安全及消防器材博览会

### 2011 Intersec Middle East

日期：2011/01 -
地点：阿联酋迪拜国际会展中心
内容：商业安全类,警用装备类,消防监控类,工业安全类,高危工作防护设备、建筑/露天工作安全防护设备、无菌环境/专业消毒设备、空气污染处理设备、废物循环处理设备。
周期：每年一届
市场范围：国际性
上届规模　'09：参展商710家（来自50个国家），参观人数17,200人
主办：德国法兰克福（迪拜）展览公司
参展联络：杭州思诺博会展服务有限公司
地址：杭州市体育场路229号浙江粮油大厦1202室（310003）
☎ 0571-8577 8500
🖷 0571-8577 9709
✉ expo@sinobal.com
www.sinobal.com

### 阿布扎比环保展

### ENVIRONMENT 2011

日期：2011/01 -
地点：阿联酋阿布扎比国家展览中心
内容：ENVIRONMENT是本地区最重要的展览及会议，关注环保设备、技术和服务部门的综合解决方案。ENVIRONMENT获阿联酋总统Sheikh Khalifa Bin Zayed Al Nahyan阁下的大力支持。POLLUTEC的主办方、世界最大的环境贸易展会主办机构励展博览集团将依靠其全面的资源拓展ENVIRONMENT展会在未来的规模和展出效率。
周期：每年一届
市场范围：国际性
参展费用：净地展位AED 1,100/m²，标准展位AED 1,300/m²
主办：励展法国公司
参展联络：励展博览集团国际销售部
地址：北京市朝阳区新源里南路1-3号平安国际金融中心A座15层01-03，05（100027）
联系人：杜一鸣
☎ 010-5933 9288
🖷 010-5933 9233
✉ martin.du@reedexpo.com.cn
www.reedexport.cn

### 2011年中东（阿布扎比）国际美容美发博览会

### 2011 Beauty Vision

日期：2011/02 -
地点：阿联酋阿布扎比国家展览中心
内容：零售：化妆品，香水，美容工具，天然化妆品，护甲、美甲产品，护肤品，美容卫生用品，防晒品，脱毛产品，牙齿美容，时装首饰等；医药：实验室，高级抗老化产品，服务，西药房，药店，营养治疗，美容保养品，保健食品；美发护发；原材料；SPA水疗
周期：每年一届
市场范围：国际性
主办：Channels Exhibitions
参展联络：杭州思诺博会展服务有限公司
地址：杭州市体育场路229号浙江粮油大厦1202室（310003）
☎ 0571-8577 8500

☎ 0571-8577 9709
✉ expo@sinobal.com
www.sinobal.com

## 2011年中东（迪拜）海湾食品展览会
## 2011 Gulfood

**日期**：2011/02 -
**地点**：阿联酋迪拜国际会展中心
**内容**：食品及饮料：食品添加剂，罐装食品，食品加工技术，酒精饮品，无酒精饮料，海洋食品，烘焙食品，糖食及糖果加工技术，冷冻食品，冷藏食品，奶制品，咖啡及茶，肉食产品，家禽食品，清真食品，保健食品，特质食品及精细食品，快餐及小吃，方便食品；酒店设备：公共饮食业产品，厨房设备，冷藏设施，酒店设备，酒店供给产品及服务，餐饮服务及产品，餐具及配件，酒店家具，商店装饰品，商店展示台；机械设备及技术
**始办年份**：1987
**周期**：每年一届
**市场范围**：国际性
**上届规模**　‘09：展览面积20,494m$^2$，参展商3000家（来自70个国家），参观人数40,000人
**主办**：阿联酋迪拜世界贸易中心
**参展联络**：杭州思诺博会展服务有限公司
**地址**：杭州市体育场路229号浙江粮油大厦1202室（310003）
☎ 0571-8577 8500
☎ 0571-8577 9709
✉ expo@sinobal.com
www.sinobal.com

## 2011年中东（迪拜）国际商用车展览会
## 2011 Commercial Vehicles Middle East

**日期**：2011/3 -
**地点**：阿联酋迪拜国际会展中心
**内容**：重型商用车、轻型商用车、工程机械车、专用车、商用车附件、商用车服务、综合/其他
**周期**：每年一届
**市场范围**：国际性
**主办**：SMG展览公司
**参展联络**：杭州思诺博会展服务有限公司
**地址**：杭州市体育场路229号浙江粮油大厦1202室（310003）
☎ 0571-8577 8500
☎ 0571-8577 9709
✉ expo@sinobal.com
www.sinobal.com

## 2011 年法兰克福中东（迪拜）国际玩具及文具用品展览会
## 2011 Toy Fair Middle East

**日期**：2011/03 -
**地点**：阿联酋迪拜国际会展中心
**内容**：玩具：自行车，童车，滑板车，电动玩具，填充玩具，木制玩具，益智玩具，模型玩具，动漫产品，玩具乐器，气球，洋娃娃，户外游戏设备，游戏机，糖果和软饮料；文具及学校用品、礼品；婴幼儿用品：婴儿家具，婴儿玩具，婴儿被褥，婴儿护肤品，婴儿衣服。
**周期**：每年一届
**市场范围**：国际性
**上届规模**　‘09：参展商101家（来自30个国家），参观人数3,234人
**主办**：德国法兰克福（迪拜）展览公司
**参展联络**：杭州思诺博会展服务有限公司
**地址**：杭州市体育场路229号浙江粮油大厦1202室（310003）
☎ 0571-8577 8500
☎ 0571-8577 9709
✉ expo@sinobal.com
www.sinobal.com

## 2011年中东（迪拜）国际服装、纺织、鞋类及皮革制品博览会
## 2011 Motexha

**日期**：2011/04 -
**地点**：阿联酋迪拜国际会展中心
**内容**：服装及面料类：男女服装、运动休闲服装、童装、劳保服装、纺织工艺、服装饰品（领带、围巾、胸针等）、各种面料、棉麻织品、针织品、纺织制品、纺织机械、家用纺织品、床上用品、裘皮制品；辅料及配件：拉链、纽扣、衬布等、及辅料；各类鞋；皮革产品
**始办年份**：1978
**周期**：每年一届
**市场范围**：国际性
**上届规模**　‘08：展览面积2,748m$^2$，参展商200家（来自24个国家），参观人数3,300人
**主办**：IIR展览公司
**参展联络**：杭州思诺博会展服务有限公司
**地址**：杭州市体育场路229号浙江粮油大厦1202室（310003）
☎ 0571-8577 8500
☎ 0571-8577 9709
✉ expo@sinobal.com
www.sinobal.com

## 2011年中东迪拜国际乐器、舞台灯光及舞台音响技术展览会
## 2011 PALME Middle East

**日期**：2011/04 -
**地点**：阿联酋迪拜国际会展中心
**内容**：小型乐器: 弦乐器、铜乐器、口风琴、敲击乐器、木管乐器 大型乐器: 钢琴、键盘乐器、教堂管风琴、古典键盘乐器 电子乐器: 键盘、合成乐器、数字钢琴、电子鼓、电吉他/贝斯；专业音效及录音设备: 舞台工程技术、舞台灯光、激光技术、专业音响、载声设备、功放、卡拉OK系统、麦克风与配件、公共广播系统；音乐出版品
**周期**：每年一届
**市场范围**：国际性
**上届规模**　‘09：展览面积5,369m$^2$，参展商162家，参观人数5,369人
**主办**：英国IIR展览公司
**参展联络**：杭州思诺博会展服务有限公司
**地址**：杭州市体育场路229号浙江粮油大厦1202室（310003）
☎ 0571-8577 8500
☎ 0571-8577 9709
✉ expo@sinobal.com
www.sinobal.com

## 2011年中东（阿布扎比）国际食品及饮料展
## 2011 Middle East Food

**日期**：2011/04 -
**地点**：阿联酋阿布扎比国家展览中心
**内容**：食品及饮料,食品原料,甜食巧克力及糕点,有机健康食品,食品处理、包装及机械，餐饮技术及设备。
**周期**：每年一届
**市场范围**：国际性
**主办**：Channels Exhibitions
**参展联络**：杭州思诺博会展服务有限公司
**地址**：杭州市体育场路229号浙江粮油大厦1202室（310003）
☎ 0571-8577 8500
☎ 0571-8577 9709
✉ expo@sinobal.com
www.sinobal.com

## 2011年迪拜中东国际铝工业展览会
## ALUMINIUM Dubai 2011

**日期**：2011/04/12 - 14
2013/ -
**地点**：阿联酋迪拜国际会议展览中心
**内容**：2011年迪拜铝业展将利用展会品牌ALUMINIUM促进各国公司的发展。此外，人们期待在本地区各重要组织（如EMAL、Dubal和有关政府单位，如：迪拜出口发展公司（DEDC））的支持下，能促使更多海湾合作理事会国家（GCC）、北美和中东其他国家的铝业单位前来参展。2011年迪拜铝业展与2009年展会相似，本届展会将引入可以促进本地区铝业发展的新产品、新设备、新技术与新投资。其中包括许多主流技术，例如：铝材挤压成型技术、铸造与热处理技术，冶炼技术，厂房工程和建筑类技术等。另外还有应用于建筑、交通、机电工程、工厂设备、包装容器生产、设计专用工具等方面的产品。此外，除了吸引了本地区已有的和新兴的铝业企业外，2011年迪拜铝业展还吸引了世界各地杰出的铝业公司前来参展。
**周期**：两年一届
**市场范围**：国际性
**主办**：励展中东公司
**参展联络**：励展博览集团国际销售部
**地址**：北京朝阳区新源里南路1-3号平安国际金融中心A座15层01-03，05（100027）
**联系人**：王颖
☎ 0105933 9288
☎ 010-5933 9233
MSN：winnie.wang@reedexpo.com.cn
www.reedexport.cn

## 2011年中东（迪拜）国际地面铺装展览会
## 2011 DOMOTEX Middle East

**日期**：2011/05 -
**地点**：阿联酋迪拜国际会展中心
**内容**：地板、地毯、地砖、塑料地面材料、地面材料配件、耗材及铺盖技术、地面装饰材料及地毯的加工制造机械设备、地面材料的图案设计及印制。
**周期**：每年一届
**上届规模**　‘09：展览面积12,000m$^2$，参展商280家（来自26个国家），参观人数6,000人
**主办**：德国博览会集团公司
**参展联络**：杭州思诺博会展服务有限公司
**地址**：杭州市体育场路229号浙江粮油大厦1202室（310003）
**联系人**：展览部
☎ 0571-8577 8500
☎ 0571-8577 9709
✉ expo@sinobal.com
www.sinobal.com

## 2011 年中东国际眼镜眼科用品展览会
## 2011 Vision-X Dubai

**日期**：2011/05 -
**地点**：阿联酋迪拜国际会展中心
**内容**：各种光学眼镜、太阳镜、运动用和防护类眼镜产品、眼用消费品和护眼产品、眼镜镜片、框架、配件、人造眼、观景镜头和透镜用织物、镜片镜头切割设备、眼镜器械和设备、眼科外科设备、诊断设备和器械、折光仪器和设备, 视轴矫正设备、眼镜展示架。
**周期**：每年一届
**市场范围**：国际性
**上届规模**　‘09：展览面积6,489m$^2$，参展商142家（来自23个国家），参观人数3,297人
**主办**：迪拜世贸中心组委会
**参展联络**：杭州思诺博会展服务有限公司
**地址**：杭州市体育场路229号浙江粮油大厦1202室（310003）
☎ 0571-8577 8500
☎ 0571-8577 9709
✉ expo@sinobal.com
www.sinobal.com

## 2011 年中东（迪拜）国际汽车零配件及售后服务展览会
## 2011 Automechanika Middle East

**日期**：2011/05 -
**地点**：阿联酋迪拜国际会展中心
**内容**：汽车部件和装置、汽车配件和改装车、汽车维修和保养、汽车服务站和清洗站。
**周期**：每年一届
**市场范围**：国际性

**上届规模** ‘09：展览面积30,000m²，参展商958家，参观人数15,275人
**主办：**德国法兰克福（迪拜）展览公司
**参展联络：**杭州思诺博会展服务有限公司
**地址：**杭州市体育场路229号浙江粮油大厦1202室（310003）
☎ 0571-8577 8500
🖷 0571-8577 9709
✉ expo@sinobal.com
www.sinobal.com

### 2011年中东（迪拜）国际美容美发用品展览会
### 2011 Beautyworld Middle East

**日期：**2011/06 -
**地点：**阿联酋迪拜国际会展中心
**内容：**化妆品、护肤品，疗养沙龙设备用具、美发沙龙配件设备，美体用品、指甲护理及修脸产品、理发工具，美容产品包装、原材料、礼品
**始办年份：**1994
**周期：**每年一届
**市场范围：**国际性
**主办：**德国法兰克福（迪拜）展览公司
**参展联络：**杭州思诺博会展服务有限公司
**地址：**杭州市体育场路229号浙江粮油大厦1202室（310003）
☎ 0571-8577 8500
🖷 0571-8577 9709
✉ expo@sinobal.com
www.sinobal.com

## 阿布扎比国际反恐安全展览会
### ISNR (Abu Dhabi) International Security & National Resilience

**日期：**2012/03 -
**地点：**阿联酋阿布扎比国家展览中心
**内容：**是独特而及时的一次盛事，展示有效保护国土与对抗国际恐怖主义所需的尖端器械。ISNR是唯一涵盖整个国土安全领域的展会。四天的研讨会及展览将为主要行业商家提供讨论以下相关最新技术方案的独特平台：情报侦察与威胁防范；国界安防及运输安防；反恐；重要基础设施防卫；危机管理；应急准备及救援。
　　展品范围：展会是体验国际安保业最新技术的绝好机会。最新安保方法与政策；重要安保课程；最新安保方案与战略
**周期：**两年一届
**市场范围：**国际性
**参展费用：**净地展位355美元/m²，标准展位400美元/m²
**主办：**励展中东公司
**参展联络：**励展博览集团国际销售部
**地址：**北京朝阳区新源里南路1-3号平安国际金融中心A座15层01-03，05（100027）
**联系人：**宫卫
☎ 010-5933 9288
🖷 010-5933 9233
✉ david.gong@reedexpo.com.cn
www.reedexport.cn

## 阿布扎比国际汽车展览会
### Abu Dhabi International Motor Show

**日期：**2012/12 -
**地点：**阿联酋阿布扎比国家展览中心
**内容：**中东地区最大且最全面的汽车展览会。
**产品及服务：**汽车类：豪华轿车，高性能名车，个性特制车，高级轿车，概念混合动力汽车，运动车，四驱越野车，家庭房车及运动型多用途汽车(SUVs)，摩托车，沙滩车(quad bikes)商务用车：敞篷小型载货卡车，货车及中巴车，豪华长途客车，豪华轿车，拖车及宿营房车 其他相关汽车服务：车库及修理公司，保险公司，汽车金融公司，汽车维修公司，维护设备，汽车媒体
**周期：**两年一届
**市场范围：**国际性
**参展费用：**净地展位840迪拉姆/m²，标准展位1,010迪拉姆/m²
**主办：**励展博览集团国际销售部；励展中东公司（阿联酋）
**地址：**北京市朝阳区新源里南路1-3号平安国际金融中心A座15层01-03，05（100027）
**联系人：**杜一鸣
☎ 010-5933 9288
🖷 010-5933 9233
✉ martin.du@reedexpo.com.cn
www.reedexport.cn

# 英国
# United Kingdom

### 伯明翰春季国际博览会
### Spring Fair Birmingham

**日期：**2010/02/07 - 11
**地点：**英国伯明翰英国
**内容：**礼品、家庭用品、流行饰品、文具、装饰用品、灯饰、家居用品等
**参展联络：**京慕国际展览有限公司
**地址：**北京市朝阳区北三环东路6号中国国际展览中心服务楼3层
**联系人：**李萌；滕昊
☎ 010-8460 0551
🖷 010-8460 0394
✉ zhaolingna@ciec.com.cn
www.jingmu.com.cn

## 英国酒店设备展
### Hotelympia

**日期：**2010/02/28 - 04
**地点：**英国伦敦ExCeL展览馆
**内容：**英国酒店设备展（Hotelympia）展览范围广泛，包括最新产品和创新科技，为您提供一个与众不同的参展环境和浓郁的展会氛围。 参加Hotelympia 2010，您可以挖掘更多业内最新理念和解决方案以及重要商业信息，扩展人际网，与来自业内的朋友和同事们，感受展会现场的热烈气氛和烹饪比赛带来的乐趣。 英国酒店设备展分为6个部分，包括食品和饮料、餐饮设备、餐桌、装饰设计、浴室和Spa、建筑设计和设备管理。同时展会将与Hostec-Europe同期举办，期间还会举办酒店职业日活动等。
**周期：**两年一届
**市场范围：**国际性
**主办：**励展博览集团国际销售部；英国Fresh RM
**地址：**北京市朝阳区新源里南路1-3号平安国际金融中心A座15层01-03，05（100027）
**联系人：**杜一鸣
☎ 010-5933 9288
🖷 010-5933 9233
✉ martin.du@reedexpo.com.cn
www.reedexport.cn

### 国际节能环保和未来建筑展览会

**日期：**2010/03/02 - 04
**地点：**英国伦敦
**周期：**每年一届
**市场范围：**国际性
**参展联络：**中国机械汽车展览联合会
☎ 010-6859 4964
🖷 010-6859 4964

### 伯明翰国际厨卫展
### KBB

**日期：**2010/03/21 - 24
**地点：**英国伯明翰
**内容：**浴室设备：浴室配件、照明、镜子、浴室五金挂件等，厨房设备：厨房下水道装置等
**周期：**每年一届
**市场范围：**国际性
**参展联络：**京慕国际展览有限公司
**地址：**北京市朝阳区北三环东路6号中国国际展览中心服务楼3层
**联系人：**罗晓龙，王芳
☎ 010-8460 0551
🖷 010-8460 0394
✉ zhaolingna@ciec.com.cn
www.jingmu.com.cn

## 伦敦书展
### The London Book Fair

**日期：**2010/04/19 - 21
**地点：**英国伦敦Earls Court展览中心
**内容：**伦敦书展是出版商进行书籍版权交易、书品贸易及产品服务交流的平台，每年吸引世界各地的业界人士齐聚于此；同时，研讨会及其他活动项目将贯穿整个展会。伦敦书展是全球性的大聚会，已发展成为国际性的出版业中心。它不仅是行业人士进行商务往来、与客户及行业间进行交流、招揽新业务、学习新技术的绝佳平台，来此观展更是一次愉快的经历。
**周期：**每年一届
**市场范围：**国际性
**参展费用：**净地254英磅/m²，标准展位301英磅/m²
**主办：**励展英国公司
**参展联络：**励展博览集团国际销售部
**地址：**北京朝阳区新源里南路1-3号平安国际金融中心A座15层01-03，05（100027）
**联系人：**宫卫
☎ 010-5933 9288
🖷 010-5933 9233
✉ david.gong@reedexpo.com.cn
www.reedexport.cn

## 欧洲国际计算机信息系统安全展览会
### Infosecurity Europe

**日期：**2010/04/27 - 29
**地点：**英国伦敦Earls Court展览中心
**内容：**是欧洲涵盖面最广的信息安全专业会展。展会在展出各种创新产品和服务的同时为参会者就当今的战略及技术问题提供无与伦比的教育机会。展会丰富的知识及信息给观众提供如何、何种、为何以及何时定购产品的答案。
**产品及服务：**信息安全产品及服务，包括应用安全、反垃圾邮件、杀毒、生物测定、业务延续/灾难恢复、证书管理机构、内容监控、加密/PKI、防火墙、身份管理、IT取证、互联网安全、入侵防卫/探测、立法和标准/BS7799、托管安全服务、网络安全服务、漏洞修补管理、穿透测试/弱点评估、物理安全、远程访问、安全存储、安全策略制订、安全令牌、安全培训/普及/教育、安全网络服务、smart卡、统一威胁管理、VPN与无线/手提安全。
**周期：**每年一届
**市场范围：**国际性
**参展费用：**净地455英镑/m²，标准展位500英镑/m²
**参展联络：**励展博览集团国际销售部
**地址：**北京市朝阳区新源里南路1-3号平安国际金融中心A座15层01-03，05（100027）
**联系人：**杜一鸣

☎ 010-5933 9288
🖷 010-5933 9233
✉ martin.du@reedexpo.com.cn
www.reedexport.cn

### 英国包装展览会
TOTAL PROCESESSING & PACKAGING

日期：2010/05 -
地点：英国伯明翰
周期：三年一届
市场范围：国际性
参展联络：中国贸促会机械行业分会
地址：北京市西城区三里河路46号（100823）
联系人：吕静，于奇琳，张垚
☎ 010-6859 4909, 6859 5498, 6859 4192
🖷 010-6859 5485
✉ info@ccpitmsc.org
✉ jix@ccpit.org
www.chinamachin.org.cn
www.ccpitmsc.org

### 英国国际安防展
IFSEC

日期：2010/05/10 - 13
地点：英国伯明翰
内容：商业安全防护类，CCTV及监视系统、门禁系统、报警系统、犯罪预警设备、监控巡逻设备
周期：每年一届
市场范围：国际性
参展联络：京慕国际展览有限公司
地址：北京市朝阳区北三环东路6号中国国际展览中心服务楼3层
联系人：薛磊，国曦
☎ 010-8460 0551
🖷 010-8460 0394
✉ zhaolingna@ciec.com.cn
www.jingmu.com.cn

### 英国国际职业安全与健康科技大展
SAFETY&HELTH EXPO

日期：2010/05/11 - 13
地点：英国伯明翰
内容：个人防护设备（手套、工装、安全鞋、反光材料等）工作环境下安全的传送装置、噪音防护方面的软硬件设备、防火设备、放射防护、触电保护、安全组织和服务等
周期：每年一届
市场范围：国际性
参展联络：京慕国际展览有限公司
地址：北京市朝阳区北三环东路6号中国国际展览中心服务楼3层
联系人：薛磊，国曦
☎ 010-8460 0551
🖷 010-8460 0394
✉ zhaolingna@ciec.com.cn
www.jingmu.com.cn

### 国际印刷展览会
IPEX 2010

日期：2010/05/18 - 25
地点：英国伯明翰
周期：四年一届
市场范围：国际性
参展联络：中国贸促会机械行业分会
地址：北京市西城区三里河路46号（100823）
联系人：孙晓光，江彦明，陈媛蓉
☎ 010-6859 5406, 6859 4927, 6859 4826
🖷 010-6859 4948
✉ info@ccpitmsc.org
✉ jix@ccpit.org
www.chinamachin.org.cn
www.ccpitmsc.org
参展联络：中国机械汽车展览联合会
☎ 010-6859 4964
🖷 010-6849 4964

### 英国国际包装新技术展览会
Total Processing & Packaging

日期：2010/05/25 - 27
地点：英国伯明翰国家展览中心
内容：涵盖加工和包装行业各领域，提供完整的生产线方案、行业内情及创新信息。
产品及服务 包装原料和容器、加工设备、包装机械、包装设计、其他相关产品及服务。
周期：三年一届
市场范围：国际性
赞助：与英国加工与包装机械协会（PPMA）
协办：英国材料、矿石和冶金协会
参展联络：励展博览集团国际销售部
地址：北京朝阳区新源里南路1-3号平安国际金融中心A座15层01-03，05（100027）
联系人：杜一鸣
☎ 010-5933 9288
🖷 010-5933 9233
✉ martin.du@reedexpo.com.cn
www.reedexport.cn

### 国际工业配件展览会

日期：2010/06 -
地点：英国伯明翰
周期：每年一届
市场范围：国际性
参展联络：中国机械汽车展览联合会
☎ 010-6859 4964
🖷 010-6859 4964

### 英国制造技术博览会
MACH 2010

日期：2010/06/07 - 11
地点：英国伯明翰
周期：两年一届
市场范围：国际性
参展联络：中国贸促会机械行业分会
地址：北京市西城区三里河路46号（100823）
联系人：罗红
☎ 010-6851 2883
🖷 010-6859 4995
✉ info@ccpitmsc.org
✉ jix@ccpit.org
www.chinamachin.org.cn
www.ccpitmsc.org

### 国际动力传动与工业零部件展览会

日期：2010/06/08 - 10
地点：英国伯明翰
周期：每年一届
市场范围：国际性
参展联络：中国机械汽车展览联合会
☎ 010-6859 4964
🖷 010-6849 4964

### 英国国际舞台灯光音响技术展
THE PLASA SHOW

日期：2010/09 -
地点：英国伦敦
内容：专业音效及录音设备、舞台灯光、录音与重制设备、混音桌与箱架、配件、多媒体
周期：每年一届
市场范围：国际性
参展联络：京慕国际展览有限公司
地址：北京市朝阳区北三环东路6号中国国际展览中心服务楼3层
联系人：王英瑶；王芳
☎ 010-8460 0551
🖷 010-8460 0394
✉ zhaolingna@ciec.com.cn
www.jingmu.com.cn

### 伦敦国际珠宝展
International Jewelry London

日期：2010/09 -
地点：英国伦敦Earls Court展览馆
内容：珠宝，手饰，宝石，钻石，手表，钟表，银饰，礼品，英式手饰，包装，陈列品
周期：每年一届
市场范围：国际性
参展联络：励展博览集团国际销售部
地址：北京市朝阳区新源里南路1-3号平安国际金融中心A座15层01-03，05（100027）
联系人：吴祥
☎ 010-5933 9288
🖷 010-5933 9233
✉ ronald.wu@reedexpo.com.cn
www.reedexport.cn

### 伯明翰国际建材展
Interbuild

日期：2010/10 -
地点：英国伯明翰
内容：建筑材料；建筑五金；门窗类；卫浴设备及地面材料；其他材料
周期：每年一届
市场范围：国际性
参展联络：京慕国际展览有限公司
地址：北京市朝阳区北三环东路6号中国国际展览中心服务楼3层
联系人：安红彦，孙铁兵
☎ 010-8460 0551
🖷 010-8460 0394
✉ zhaolingna@ciec.com.cn
www.jingmu.com.cn

### 英国酒店用品展
Hospitality

日期：2011/01/24 - 26
2013/01
地点：英国伯明翰国家展览中心
内容：英国酒店用品展（Hospitality）将于2011年举办，机会难得，不容错过，展会将为酒店行业人士提供面对面的交流机会，扩展关系网，建立商务友谊。
周期：两年一届
市场范围：国际性
参展费用：净地252欧元/m$^2$，标准展位307欧元/m$^2$
主办：励展博览集团国际销售部；英国Fresh RM
地址：北京朝阳区新源里南路1-3号平安国际金融中心A座15层01-03，05（100027）
联系人：杜一鸣
☎ 010-5933 9288
🖷 010-5933 9233
✉ martin.du@reedexpo.com.cn
www.reedexport.cn

## 英国食品、饮料包装机械、设备展览会

Pro2Pac:
Processing & Packaging Solutions Event, Exclusively for the Food & Drink Industry

**日期**：2011/03/13 - 16
2013/03 -
**地点**：英国伦敦ExCeL会展中心
**内容**：英国食品、饮料包装机械、设备展览会(Pro2Pac)是唯一一个专为食品和饮料行业提供包装机械、设备的展会，Pro2Pac将与英国最大的食品饮料展IFE——英国国际食品和饮料展同期举办，两个展会将带领大家全方位地透视食品和饮料行业。
**周期**：两年一届
**市场范围**：国际性
**参展费用**：净地230英镑/m$^2$，标准展位274英镑/m$^2$
**主办**：励展英国公司
**参展联络**：励展博览集团国际销售部
**地址**：北京市朝阳区新源里南路1-3号平安国际金融中心A座15层01-03，05（100027）
**联系人**：杜一鸣
☎ 010-5933 9288
🖷 010-5933 9233
✉ martin.du@reedexpo.com.cn
www.reedexport.cn

## 伦敦书展

The London Book Fair

**日期**：2011/04 -
**地点**：英国伦敦Earls Court展览中心
**内容**：伦敦书展是出版商进行书籍版权交易、书品贸易及产品服务交流的平台，每年吸引世界各地的业界人士齐聚于此；同时，研讨会及其他活动项目将贯穿整个展会。伦敦书展是全球性的大聚会，已发展成为国际性的出版业中心。它不仅是行业人士进行商务往来、与客户及行业间进行交流、招揽新业务、学习新技术的绝佳平台，来此观展更是一次愉快的经历。
**周期**：每年一届
**市场范围**：国际性
**参展费用**：净地254英磅/m$^2$，标准展位301英磅/m$^2$
**主办**：励展英国公司
**参展联络**：励展博览集团国际销售部
**地址**：北京朝阳区新源里南路1-3号平安国际金融中心A座15层01-03，05（100027）
**联系人**：宫卫
☎ 010-5933 9288
🖷 010-5933 9233
✉ david.gong@reedexpo.com.cn
www.reedexport.cn

## 欧洲国际计算机信息系统安全展览会

Infosecurity Europe

**日期**：2011/04 -
**地点**：英国伦敦Earls Court展览中心
**内容**：欧洲涵盖面最广的信息安全专业会展。展会在展出各种创新产品和服务的同时为参会者就当今的战略及技术问题提供无与伦比的教育机会。展会丰富的知识及信息给观众提供如何、何种、为何以及何时定购产品的答案。
**产品及服务**：信息安全产品及服务，包括应用安全、反垃圾邮件、杀毒、生物测定、业务延续、灾难恢复、证书管理机构、内容监控、加密、PKI、防火墙、身份管理、IT取证、互联网安全、入侵防卫、探测、立法和标准、BS7799、托管安全服务、网络安全服务、漏洞修补管理、穿透测试、弱点评估、物理安全、远程访问、安全存储、安全策略制订、安全令牌、安全培训、普及/教育、安全网络服务、smart卡、统一威胁管理、VPN与无线、手提安全。
**周期**：每年一届
**市场范围**：国际性
**参展费用**：净地455英镑/m$^2$，标准展位500英镑/m$^2$
**参展联络**：励展博览集团国际销售部
**地址**：北京朝阳区新源里南路1-3号平安国际金融中心A座15层01-03，05（100027）
**联系人**：杜一鸣
☎ 010-5933 9288
🖷 010-5933 9233
✉ martin.du@reedexpo.com.cn
www.reedexport.cn

## 2011 英国石油工业技术展

Offshore Europe 2011:
Oil & Gas Exhibition & Conference

**日期**：2011/09 -
**地点**：英国阿伯丁会展中心
**内容**：作为东半球最重要的石油勘探及生产工业展会，英国石油工业技术展一直不断发展，全面真实地反映着世界石油工业不断发展的技术要求。
**产品及服务**：涉及石油勘探与生产各个环节的上游油田技术、服务。
**周期**：两年一届
**市场范围**：国际性
**参展费用**：净地展位191～320英磅/m$^2$，标准展位370英磅/m$^2$
**参展联络**：励展博览集团国际销售部
**地址**：北京朝阳区新源里南路1-3号平安国际金融中心A座15层01-03，05（100027）
**联系人**：宫卫
☎ 010-5933 9288
🖷 010-5933 9233
✉ david.gong@reedexpo.com.cn
www.reedexport.cn
www.offshore-europe.co.uk

## 英国全套生产线，暨加工及包装机械展

PPMA Show:
UK's annual showcase for Processing & Packaging Machinery

**日期**：2011/09 -
**地点**：英国伯明翰国家展览中心
**内容**：PPMA展会是英国一年一度的加工和包装机械展会。在即将举办的第20届展会上，参展商将获得一个绝佳的机会，向慕名而来的英国买家现场展示自己的机器和技术。PPMA的参展商将从这一英国唯一的、业内专家云集的展会上获益良多。
**周期**：每年一届
**市场范围**：国际性
**赞助**：PPMA Ltd（加工与包装机械协会）
**主办**：励展英国公司
**参展联络**：励展博览集团国际销售部
**地址**：北京朝阳区新源里南路1-3号平安国际金融中心A座15层01-03，05（100027）
**联系人**：杜一鸣
☎ 010-5933 9288
🖷 010-5933 9233
✉ martin.du@reedexpo.com.cn
www.reedexport.cn

## 英国国际食品和饮料展

IFE:
International Food & Drink Event

**日期**：2011/3/13 - 16
2013/3 -
**地点**：英国伦敦ExCel 会展中心
**内容**：汇集了全球范围内食品和饮料行业创新产品。本地和国际观众不仅可以率先体验来自1,500家厂商带来的最新产品，还可以了解行业最新动态及未来发展趋势，接触到食品及饮料行业各个层次的客户资源及深入的合作机遇。
**周期**：两年一届
**市场范围**：国际性
**参展费用**：净地展位261英镑，标准展位313英镑
**主办**：励展博览集团国际销售部；英国Fresh RM
**地址**：北京市朝阳区新源里南路1-3号平安国际金融中心A座15层01-03，05（100027）
**联系人**：杜一鸣
☎ 010-5933 9288
🖷 010-5933 9233
✉ martin.du@reedexpo.com.cn
www.reedexport.cn

## 英国酒店设备展

Hotelympia

**日期**：2012/02 -
**地点**：英国伦敦ExCeL展览馆
**内容**：展览范围广泛，包括最新产品和创新科技，为您提供一个与众不同的参展环境和浓郁的展会氛围。参加Hotelympia 2012，您可以挖掘更多业内最新理念和解决方案以及重要商业信息，扩展人际网，与来自业内的朋友和同事们，感受展会现场的热烈气氛和烹饪比赛带来的乐趣。英国酒店设备展分为6个部分，包括食品和饮料、餐饮设备、餐桌、装饰设计、浴室和Spa、建筑设计和设备管理。同时展会将与Hostec-Europe同期举办，期间还会举办酒店职业日活动等。
**周期**：两年一届
**市场范围**：国际性
**主办**：励展博览集团国际销售部；英国Fresh RM
**地址**：北京市朝阳区新源里南路1-3号平安国际金融中心A座15层01-03，05（100027）
**联系人**：杜一鸣
☎ 010-5933 9288
🖷 010-5933 9233
✉ martin.du@reedexpo.com.cn
www.reedexport.cn

## 英国国际包装新技术展览会

Total Processing & Packaging

**日期：** 2013-
**地点：** 英国伯明翰国家展览中心
**内容：** 涵盖加工和包装行业各领域，提供完整的生产线方案、行业内情及创新信息。
**产品及服务：** 包装原料和容器、加工设备、包装机械、包装设计、其他相关产品及服务。
**周期：** 三年一届
**市场范围：** 国际性
**协办：** 英国加工与包装机械协会（PPMA）；英国材料、矿石和冶金协会
**参展联络：** 励展博览集团国际销售部
**地址：** 北京朝阳区新源里南路1-3号平安国际金融中心A座15层01-03，05（100027）
**联系人：** 杜一鸣
☎ 010-5933 9288
🖷 010-5933 9233
✉ martin.du@reedexpo.com.cn
www.reedexport.cn

# 美国
# USA

## 美国职业高尔夫球协会高尔夫用品秋季展

PGA Fall Expo

**日期：** 2010 -
**地点：** 美国内华达州拉斯维加斯曼德勒海湾会议中心
**内容：** 全美最佳的高尔夫服饰、装备、配件秋季购买预定盛会。展会召集350余个高尔夫及相关行业展商展示他们的产品，为数以千计的职业高尔夫球协会球员以及高尔夫零售商提供预览春季最热门的高尔夫装备、配件以及服饰的机会。对高尔夫零售商来说是全美最好的秋季交易盛会。
**产品及服务：** 高尔夫装备、高尔夫产品及服务、高尔夫及度假服饰、旅行、助学用品、球场标志及固定装置、草皮与球场维护、高尔夫推车以及俱乐部管理
**周期：** 每年一届
**市场范围：** 国际性
**参展费用：** 净地展位17美元/平方英尺
**赞助：** 美国职业高尔夫球协会
**参展联络：** 励展博览集团国际销售部
**地址：** 北京市朝阳区新源里南路1-3号平安国际金融中心A座15层01-03，05（100027）
**联系人：** 申健
☎ 010-8518 2644，5933 9288
🖷 010-5933 9233
✉ jerry.shen@reedexpo.com.cn
www.reedexport.cn

## 美国国际消费类电子产品博览会

CES

**日期：** 2010/01/07 - 10
**地点：** 美国拉斯维加斯
**内容：** 数字视听产品、家庭娱乐产品、车载视听设备、多媒体音箱、电子礼品等
**周期：** 每年一届
**市场范围：** 国际性
**参展联络：** 京慕国际展览有限公司
**地址：** 北京市朝阳区北三环东路6号中国国际展览中心服务楼3层
**联系人：** 宋秋爽；刘舰
☎ 010-8460 0551
🖷 010-8460 0394
✉ zhaolingna@ciec.com.cn
www.jingmu.com.cn

## 2010年美国AG CONNECT农机展

AG CONNECT 2010

**日期：** 2010/01/13 - 15
**地点：** 美国奥兰多橘郡国际会展中心
**内容：** 新产品/新技术，除动物外所有农业相关的设备，工具，配件，种子，服务等
首届
**周期：** 每年一届
**市场范围：** 国际性
**主办：** 美国设备制造商协会
**地址：** 北京东城区建国门北大街8号华润大厦501室（100005）
**联系人：** 孙红宇
☎ 010-8519 1566
🖷 010-8519 1567
✉ hsun@cm-1.com
www.agconnect.com

## AG CONNECT 2010

**Date：** 2010/01/13 - 15
**Venue:** Orlando Orange County Convention Center,
**Profile:** New innovations/technologies, All sectors except live animals Equipment, Implements, Components, Inputs, Services
First Session
**Frequency:** Annual
**Market Area:** International
**Organizer:** Association of Equipment Manufacturers (AEM)
**Address:** China Resources Building, Suite 501, No.8 Jianguomenbei Avenue, Beijing, China
☎ 86-10-8519 1566
🖷 86-10-8519 1567
**Contact:** Helen Sun
✉ hsun@cm-1.com
www.agconnect.com

## 2010年拉斯维加斯建材展

International Builders' Show

**日期：** 2010/01/19 - 22
**地点：** 美国拉斯维加斯会展中心
**内容：** 是世界规模的建筑行业盛会，由拥有20多万家会员单位的美国最大建筑协会—全美房屋建造协会(National Association of Home Builders) 主办。自1944年首次举办以来，IBS逐步成为建筑行业进军北美市场的重要贸易平台。展会将给参展商和参观者提供一个非常有吸引力的打开国际市场的通道，是建筑业企业展示新产品、确认新代理、发布新信息最佳窗口
**周期：** 每年一届
**市场范围：** 国际性
**上届规模** '09：展览面积150,000m²(国外展商面积148,000m²)，参展商1,258家（来自108个国家），专业贸易观众100,000人
**主办：** 北京领汇国际展览有限公司
**地址：** 北京市朝阳区农展馆南路13号瑞辰国际中心719（100125）
**联系人：** 段宇
☎ 010-5129 5359-8801
🖷 010-5129 5379-8801
✉ lewayfair@126.com
MSN：expo8801@worldfairs.cn
www.worldfairs.cn

## International Builders' Show

**Date：** 2010/01/19 - 22
**Venue:** Las Vegas Convention Center, USA
**Profile:** The International Builders' Show is THE premier industry event. As the largest building industry tradeshow in the country, this is the place to recharge your business! Get inspired with the more than 175 education sessions and network with the best in the industry!
**Frequency:** Annual
**Market Area:** International
**Statistics '09:** Exhibition Area 150,000m²(foreigners 148,000m²), Exhibitors 1,258 (came from 108 countries), Trade Visitors 100,000
**Contact:** Beijing Leway Intl Fairs Co Ltd
☎ 86-10-5129 5359 ext 8801
🖷 86-10-5129 5379 ext 8801
✉ lewayfair@126.com
MSN: expo8801@worldfairs.cn
www.worldfairs.cn/

## 盐湖城冬季/夏季户外运动用品博览会（冬季）

Outdoor Retailer Winter / Summer Market

**日期：** 2010/01/21 - 24
**地点：** 美国盐湖城
**内容：** 户外装备、运动服装、露营用品及背包、自行车运动用品、登山及攀岩用品、水上运动用品
**周期：** 每年两届
**市场范围：** 国际性
**参展联络：** 京慕国际展览有限公司
**地址：** 北京市朝阳区北三环东路6号中国国际展览中心服务楼3层
**联系人：** 李雪寒
☎ 010-8460 0551
🖷 010-8460 0394
✉ zhaolingna@ciec.com.cn
www.jingmu.com.cn

## 美国国际空调、制冷和供热展览会

AHR 2010

**日期：** 2010/01/25 - 27
**地点：** 美国奥兰多
**周期：** 每年一届
**市场范围：** 国际性
**参展联络：** 中国贸促会机械行业分会
**地址：** 北京市西城区三里河路46号（100823）
**联系人：** 丁苏卫
☎ 010-6859 4989
🖷 010-6859 4917
✉ info@ccpitmsc.org
✉ jix@ccpit.org
www.chinamachin.org.cn
www.ccpitmsc.org

## 美国西部光电博览会

Photonics West

**日期：** 2010/01/26 - 28
**地点：** 美国圣何塞
**内容：** 光学元件、光显示、红外技术、光电印刷、光学制造技术、光学测试测量技术、激光及光电子
**周期：** 每年一届
**市场范围：** 国际性
**参展联络：** 京慕国际展览有限公司
**地址：** 北京市朝阳区北三环东路6号中国国际展览中心服务楼3层
**联系人：** 宋秋爽；刘舰
☎ 010-8460 0551
🖷 010-8460 0394
✉ zhaolingna@ciec.com.cn
www.jingmu.com.cn

## 美国职业高尔夫球协会高尔夫用品展

PGA Merchandise Show

**日期：** 2010/01/28 - 30
**地点：** 美国佛罗里达州奥兰多橙郡会议中心
**内容：** 由美国职业高尔夫协会创办，已成为世界顶

级高尔夫专业展览盛会，在国际高尔夫球市场中起着引领潮流的作用。在上届展会中，博览会纪录的总参观人数达到了45,019人，相较前一年增长3%。其中包括PGA的专业人士，主要分销商、零售商、高尔夫俱乐部经理、私人培训学校决策人、高尔夫相关媒体等等。在专业观众方面，博览会每年均保持着14%的人数上的增长。其主办宗旨即是构筑与会参展公司与专业观众的桥梁。国际高尔夫产业的知名品牌将悉数参展，已经报名参展的有Callaway Golf, TaylorMade Golf, the Titleist Performance Institute, Srixon, Nike Golf, Adidas, Cutter & Buck, MacGregor, Ahead, Ashworth, Tehama, Gear For Sports, Bridgstone, the Greg Norman Collection等。作为专业的高尔夫贸易展览，展会同时还举办高尔夫展示日和专家讲座与商务会议，不仅为展商提供良好的贸易洽谈环境，还为买家和观众提供学习和提高高尔夫球技的机会

**始办年份**：1954
**周期**：每年一届
**市场范围**：国际性
**参展费用**：净地展位32美元/每平方英尺
**参展联络**：励展博览集团国际销售部
**地址**：北京市朝阳区新源里南路1-3号平安国际金融中心A座15层01-03，05（100027）
**联系人**：申健
☎ 010-8518 2644, 5933 9288
🖷 010-5933 9233
✉ jerry.shen@reedexpo.com.cn
www.reedexport.cn

## 拉斯维加斯国际鞋业博览会（春季）

## WSA

**日期**：2010/02 -
**地点**：美国拉斯维加斯
**内容**：各种鞋类、鞋架、手提袋以及鞋的辅料等
**周期**：每年两届
**市场范围**：国际性
**参展联络**：京慕国际展览有限公司
**地址**：北京市朝阳区北三环东路6号中国国际展览中心服务楼3层
**联系人**：李嘉羊，古莹
☎ 010-8460 0551
🖷 010-8460 0394
✉ zhaolingna@ciec.com.cn
www.jingmu.com.cn

## 拉斯维加斯国际服装服饰博览会（春季）

## MAGIC

**日期**：2010/02 -
**地点**：美国拉斯维加斯
**内容**：各种男装、女装、休闲服装、童装、皮装、服饰、浴装、内衣、帽子、围巾；各种面料、辅料等
**周期**：每年两届
**市场范围**：国际性
**参展联络**：京慕国际展览有限公司
**地址**：北京市朝阳区北三环东路6号中国国际展览中心服务楼3层
**联系人**：崔文佳；柳川
☎ 010-8460 0551
🖷 010-8460 0394
✉ zhaolingna@ciec.com.cn
www.jingmu.com.cn

## 2010年春季美国拉斯维加斯国际家具展

**日期**：2010/02/01 - 05
**地点**：美国拉斯维加斯
**周期**：每年一届
**市场范围**：国际性
**参展联络**：大连上选会展服务有限公司
**地址**：大连市西岗区鞍山路13号兴业广场大厦B座508室（116011）
☎ 0411-8378 8326, 8378 8396, 8378 9165, 8378 8821
🖷 0411-8378 8830, 8378 8823
✉ cicyhuang@vip.sina.com
MSN：cicyhuang@msn.com
www.sun-show.com

## 美国圣地亚哥极限运动及运动时尚博览会

## ASR Trade Expo

**日期**：2010/02/03 - 04
**地点**：美国圣地亚哥
**内容**：冲浪运动用品、滑冰运动用品、雪类运动用品、游泳用品、板类运动用品、运动鞋服、时尚服装
**周期**：每年一届
**市场范围**：国际性
**参展联络**：京慕国际展览有限公司
**地址**：北京市朝阳区北三环东路6号中国国际展览中心服务楼3层
**联系人**：李雪寒
☎ 010-8460 0551
🖷 010-8460 0394
✉ zhaolingna@ciec.com.cn
www.jingmu.com.cn

## 国际摩托车展览会

**日期**：2010/02/12 - 15
**地点**：美国印第安纳波利斯
**周期**：每年一届
**市场范围**：国际性
**参展联络**：中国机械汽车展览联合会
☎ 010-6859 4964
🖷 010-6859 4964

## 纽约国际玩具博览会

## American International Toy Fair

**日期**：2010/02/14 - 17
**地点**：美国纽约
**内容**：各种玩具、圣诞饰品、节日用品等
**市场范围**：国际性
**参展联络**：京慕国际展览有限公司
**地址**：北京市朝阳区北三环东路6号中国国际展览中心服务楼3层
**联系人**：付颖；古莹
☎ 010-8460 0551
🖷 010-8460 0394
✉ zhaolingna@ciec.com.cn
www.jingmu.com.cn

## 美国拉斯维加斯春季国际服装服饰博览会

**日期**：2010/02/15 - 18
**地点**：美国拉斯维加斯会展中心
**内容**：休闲装、职业装、西装、流行时装 、青春时装 、纺织服装、针织服饰、街头装、前卫服装、牛仔装、工作服、特制服装、民族服装、皮革服装、裘皮时装、婚纱礼服、运动装、泳装、内衣、睡衣、披肩、围巾、帽子、袜子、领带、服装辅料、纺织面料、相关缝纫设备、纺织媒体、电脑设计软件及时装书籍等

展会概况：该展目前是世界上最大的综合男装、女装、童装、前卫时装及服装面料为一体的专业服装类综合展会，也是美洲服装业界公认的美洲服装市场的"风向标"，是美洲服装市场最为重要的市场信息发布中心及交易场所。据展会的统计数字显示，"每年的MAGIC SHOW均吸引来自世界各地的3500多家参展企业带来约5500个品牌的21000类产品，集中了几乎世界上所有知名的成衣品牌，包括美国最著名的服装贸易商和生产商。

该展览主要特点：规模大，影响力强，专业观众数量多，是世界上规模及影响最大的服装博览会，在服装界具有权威地位。

**周期**：每年两届
**市场范围**：国际性
**主办**：拉斯维加斯会展中心
**参展联络**：上海达欧展览服务有限公司
**联系人**：杭小姐
☎ 021-3412 3215
🖷 021-3412 3496
✉ joyce1231@126.com
MSN：dail_joyce@hotmail.com
QQ：496953608
www.dail.com.cn

## 沥青大世界

## World of Asphalt 2010

**日期**：2010/02/15 - 18
**地点**：美国俄亥俄州辛辛那提
**内容**：沥青相关的设备和材料等
**周期**：每年一届
**市场范围**：国际性
**主办**：美国设备制造商协会
**地址**：北京东城区建国门北大街8号华润大厦501室（100005）
**联系人**：孙红宇
☎ 010-8519 1566
🖷 010-8519 1567
✉ hsun@cm-1.com
www.agconnect.com

## World of Asphalt 2010

**Date**：2010/02/15 - 18
**Venue**: Cincinnati, OH, USA
**Frequency**: Annual
**Market Area**: International
**Organizer**: Association of Equipment Manufacturers (AEM)
**Address**: China Resources Building, Suite 501, No.8 Jianguomenbei Avenue, Beijing, China
☎ 86-10-8519 1566
🖷 86-10-8519 1567
**Contact**: Helen Sun
✉ hsun@cm-1.com
www.agconnect.com

## 2010年48届美国篱笆与护栏展

## fencetech 2010

**日期**：2010/02/17 - 19
**地点**：美国奥兰多橘子郡展览中心
**内容**：世界上唯一的护栏行业的专业展，展会由美国国家护栏和篱笆协会发起，该协会是世界上最大的护栏厂家的协会，在北美地区拥有2,400个成员单位。该展会分为" fencetech" 与" decktech" 两个主题。展览期间，除各顶级护栏生产企业展示最新的产品和技术以外，还有一系列的教育和培训，并研讨相关的前沿技术和动态。

展品范围：各类用途护栏，护栏原料类，护栏构建、加工机械类别，木塑制品

**始办年份**：1962(轮流在奥兰多、拉斯维加斯和芝加哥举办)
**周期**：每年一届
**市场范围**：国际性
**上届规模**　'09：展览面积10,000m²(国外展商面积9,000m²)，参展商200家（国外展商190家，来自15个国家），参观人数30,000人（专业和贸易观众5,000人）
**主办**：北京领汇国际展览有限公司
**地址**：北京市朝阳区农展馆南路13号瑞辰国际中心719室（100125）
**联系人**：梁建伟
☎ 010-5129 5359-8501
🖷 010-5129 5379-8501
✉ liangjw512@yahoo.com.cn
MSN：expo8501@worldfairs.cn
QQ：59827042
www.lewayfairs.com
www.worldfairs.cn

## fencetech 2010

**Date**：2010/02/17 - 19
**Venue**: Orange Country Convention Center, Orlando, USA
**Profile**: FENCETECH is the American Fence Association' s annual convention and trade show and is the industry' s premier marketplace. FENCETECH brings together the industry' s leading manufacturers, distributors, contractors and specifiers to showcase the latest in the fence industry to thousands of AFA members and other fence, deck and railing professionals. main product： wire mesh fence\ Vinyl Fence\ concrete fence\ iron fence\ aluminum fence\ railing\\deck\ decking\ accessories
**Established Year**: 1962

Frequency: Annual
Market Area: International
Statistics '09: Exhibition Area 10,000m²(foreigners 9,000m²), Exhibitors 200 (foreigners 190, came from 15 countries), Trade Visitors 5,000
Organizer: Beijing Leway International Fairs Co Ltd
Address: Room 719,Ruichen International Centre, No.13 Nongzhanguan South Road,Chaoyang District, Beijing, China
☎ 86-10-5129 5359 ext 8501
🖷 86-10-5129 5379 ext 8501
Contact: Anthony
✉ liangjw512@yahoo.com.cn
MSN: expo8501@worldfairs.cn
QQ: 59827042
www.lewayfairs.com
www.worldfairs.cn

## 国际印刷艺术展览会

日期：2010/02/25 - 27
地点：美国迈阿密
周期：每年一届
市场范围：国际性
参展联络：中国机械汽车展览联合会
☎ 010-6859 4964
🖷 010-6859 4964

## 美国国际水处理展览会

日期：2010/03 -
地点：美国芝加哥
内容：工业水处理，家用水处理
周期：每年一届
市场范围：国际性
参展联络：京慕国际展览有限公司
地址：北京市朝阳区北三环东路6号中国国际展览中心服务楼3层
联系人：安宏彦，孙铁兵
☎ 010-8460 0551
🖷 010-8460 0394
✉ zhaolingna@ciec.com.cn
www.jingmu.com.cn

## 2010美国芝加哥国际家庭用品博览会

International Home & Housewares Show

日期：2010/03/14 - 16
地点：美国芝加哥迈考密展览中心
内容：国际展区（World Pavilion）的设立大大扩大了中国参展商的规模。展品内容:家庭日用品、小家电、金属器皿、餐具、家庭五金工具、家庭装饰品、厨房用品、塑料制品、陶瓷及瓷器；健康保健和个人保健产品、清洁用具、浴室和个人护理用品、室内用品、铁器和户外用品、家具、灯饰、儿童用品、宠物用具及圣诞工艺品等。
周期：每年一届
市场范围：国际性
上届规模 '09：参展商2,000家（来自35个国家），参观人数21,000人
主办：美国全国家庭用品制造商协会
地址：广州市海珠区新港中路350号C1204（510310）
联系人：周文槟
☎ 020-3405 2086 13710318991
🖷 020-3405 0629
✉ dbzh88@163.com
MSN：gdwenbin@hotmail.com
QQ：406372636

## 美国东部国际光学展

International Vision Expo East

日期：2010/03/18 - 21
地点：美国纽约Jacob K Javits会议中心
内容：美国东部领先的眼科保健盛会，聚集所有眼科保健专业人员。
周期：每年一届
市场范围：国际性
参展费用：净地展位31.75～35.50美元/平方公尺
参展联络：励展博览集团国际销售部
地址：北京朝阳区新源里南路1-3号平安国际金融中心A座15层01-03，05（100027）
联系人：杜一鸣
☎ 010-5933 9288
🖷 010-5933 9233
✉ martin.du@reedexpo.com.cn
www.reedexport.cn

## 美国纸业世界展览会

Tissue World Americas 2010
日期：2010/03/24 – 26
地点：美国迈阿密海滩会议中心
主办：博闻公司
☎ 65-6592 0890
🖷 65-6438 6090
www.tissueworld.com
联络：亚洲博闻有限公司
☎ 852-2827 6211
🖷 852-2827 7831
www.ubmasia.com

## 美国西部国际安防产品博览会

ISC West:
International Security Conference West

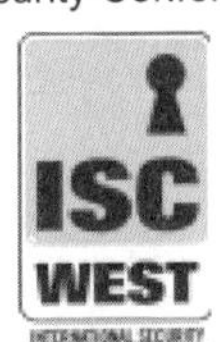


日期：2010/03/24 - 26
地点：美国拉斯维加斯会展中心 & 金沙会展中心
内容：该展由世界著名的励展公司主办、美国安保协会（SIA）协办、并经加州警报协会（CAA）及美国防盗防火协会授权（NBFAA），每年分别在美国西部拉斯维加斯和东部纽约举办，2009年西部拉斯维加斯展将是第42届。展览会由于增加了许多新的项目和产品，世界级的行业培训、大量的展期和展会网络联络机会，使该展继续成为为安保产品制造商，经销商、安装商、综合商以及最终使用客户参加的主要的行业盛会。相关人员均是来自这些行业的高级经理或贸易的决策者。展会的国际展团包括中国、韩国、台湾省。

展品集中在CCTV、接入控制和生物测定学。参展商包括世界知名公司，包括BOSCH、CANNON、GE、PANASONIC、SAMSUNG、SONY等。9%客商来自美国以外。
周期：每年两届
市场范围：国际性
参展费用：净地展位44.50美元/平方英尺
参展联络：励展博览集团国际销售部
地址：北京市朝阳区新源里南路1-3号平安国际金融中心A座15层01-03，05（100027）
联系人：宫卫
☎ 010-5933 9288
🖷 010-5933 9233
✉ david.gong@reedexpo.com.cn
www.reedexport.cn

## 美国中西部卡车展览会

日期：2010/03/25 - 27
地点：美国路易斯维尔
周期：每年一届
市场范围：国际性
参展联络：中国机械汽车展览联合会
☎ 010-6859 4964
🖷 010-6859 4964

## 美国洛杉矶国际纺织品展览会（春季）

Globaltex

日期：2010/04 -
地点：美国洛杉矶洛杉矶
内容：各类服装、面料、纺织品
周期：每年两届
市场范围：国际性
参展联络：京慕国际展览有限公司
地址：北京市朝阳区北三环东路6号中国国际展览中心服务楼3层
联系人：崔文佳；柳川
☎ 010-8460 0551
🖷 010-8460 0394
✉ zhaolingna@ciec.com.cn
www.jingmu.com.cn

## 2010年汽车工程学会世界大会及汽车零配件展览会-SAE底特律汽配展

2010 SAE

日期：2010/04/12 - 15
地点：美国底特律Cobo会议展览中心
内容：汽车相关行业产品、工程工具和服务。如各类汽车零配件、发动机、安全带、制动器零件、底盘、离合器、面板、设备、配套、仪表、冷却系统、蓄电池、环保废物处理、传动及变速器、提升设备、服务设备、调试设备、专用工具、修理设备、汽车电器、重型车辆及附件等。
始办年份：1974
周期：每年一届
市场范围：地区性全国性国际性
主办：SAE
地址：上海市春申路3758弄凯利大厦1号206室（201100）
联系人：徐小姐
☎ 021-34123495-806
🖷 021-34123496
✉ dail_xuhongzhuan@yahoo.com.cn
MSN：xhzhuan@hotmail.com
QQ：305693255
www.dail.com.cn

## 芝加哥国际厨房浴室设备博览会

K/BIS

日期：2010/04/16 - 18
地点：美国芝加哥
内容：浴室设备：浴室配件、照明、镜子、浴室五金挂件等，厨房设备：厨房下水道装置等
周期：每年一届
市场范围：国际性
参展联络：京慕国际展览有限公司
地址：北京市朝阳区北三环东路6号中国国际展览中心服务楼3层
联系人：薛涵，王芳
☎ 010-8460 0551
🖷 010-8460 0394
✉ zhaolingna@ciec.com.cn
www.jingmu.com.cn

## 美国国际制药工业展览会

INTERPHEX
incorporating PharmaManufacturing, PharmaSourcing & Services, PharmaIT and PharmaFacilities

INTERPHEX

日期：2010/04/20 - 22
地点：美国纽约 Jacob K Javits会展中心
内容：世界领先的制药行业论坛。
产品及服务：加工设备及供应品、包装设备及材料、实验设备及供应品、研发产品及服务、污染控制、清洁室供应品及服务、进程自动化及控制、原材料、信息技术、外包及承包服务、设施产品及服务、药品交付技术、合成产品等等。
周期：每年一届
市场范围：国际性
赞助：ISPE（国际药物工程协会）；Pharmaceutical Processing（药品加工杂志）
主办：励展美洲公司
参展联络：励展博览集团国际销售部

地址：北京市朝阳区新源里南路1-3号平安国际金融中心A座15层01-03，05（100027）
联系人：申健
☎ 010-8518 2644, 5933 9288
🖷 010-5933 9233
✉ jerry.shen@reedexpo.com.cn
www.reedexport.cn

### 2010年美国国际输配电设备和技术展（IEEE 2010）

### IEEE, PES-Transmission & Distribution Conference and exposition

日期：2010/04/20 - 22
地点：美国
内容：输配电设备、电网自动化技术及设备、电能计量产品、发电设备、电力施工工具、低压电器和建筑电气、电厂环保产品。
周期：每年一届
市场范围：国际性
主办：国际电工委员会电气工程分会
参展联络：北京中杰城设国际展览有限公司
地址：北京市海淀区三里河路9号建设部机关门诊楼5层（100835）
联系人：李娜
☎ 010-8838 5291
🖷 010-5885 7468, 5893 4708
✉ info@btfi.cn
www.top-fairs.com.cn, www.btfi.cn

### 国际物料搬运及物流展览会

日期：2010/04/26 - 29
地点：美国克里夫兰
周期：每年一届
市场范围：国际性
参展联络：中国机械汽车展览联合会
☎ 010-6859 4964
🖷 010-6859 4964

### 美国休斯顿国际石油展览会

### Offshore Technology Conference

日期：2010/05/03 - 06
地点：美国休斯顿
内容：与石油、石化、天然气等产品相关的机械设备、仪表仪器、工业安全及防护用品、技术服务等
周期：每年一届
市场范围：国际性
参展联络：京慕国际展览有限公司
地址：北京市朝阳区北三环东路6号中国国际展览中心服务楼3层
联系人：由慧
☎ 010-8460 0551
🖷 010-8460 0394
✉ zhaolingna@ciec.com.cn
www.jingmu.com.cn

### 美国国际小家电及家居用品展览会

### Homewares Show

where housewares is always at home
Homewares SHOW

日期：2010/05/04 - 06
地点：美国拉斯维加斯会议中心
内容：针对家用器具产品类零售商需求的日渐强大。
展商来源：小家电、家庭存储与收纳、家庭环境与照明、家用小器具、水处理、清洁用品、小器具、地板、窗户及家装、宠物产品
周期：每年一届
市场范围：国际性
参展联络：励展博览集团国际销售部
地址：北京市朝阳区新源里南路1-3号平安国际金融中心A座15层01-03，05（100027）
联系人：吴祥
☎ 010-5933 9288
🖷 010-5933 9233
✉ ronald.wu@reedexpo.com.cn
www.reedexport.cn

### 美国国际五金工具及花园用品展览会

### National Hardware Show

日期：2010/05/04 - 06
地点：美国拉斯维加斯会议中心
内容：作为与家居用品市场联系的纽带，国际五金制品展览会专注于“户外生活”的流行趋势，提供关于居家维修、重塑、重建、保养及装饰的一切展示，其中包括一个完整的展中展-园艺世界。展商与观众可共同参与内容丰富的各个行业会议，业内专业人士将在会上发表关于时尚潮流及当前家居/家居装饰零售商的市场机遇等方面的演讲。
周期：每年一届
市场范围：国际性
参展费用：净地展位20.95美元/平方英尺
赞助：Paint and Decorating Retailers Association; U.S. Commercial Service; China International Hardware Show; Lawn & Garden Retailer; Spoga+gafa, Spoga; Hardlines; HomeWorldBusiness.com
主办：励展美国公司
参展联络：励展博览集团国际销售部
地址：北京市朝阳区新源里南路1-3号平安国际金融中心A座15层01-03，05（100027）
联系人：吴祥
☎ 010-5933 9288
🖷 010-5933 9233
✉ ronald.wu@reedexpo.com.cn
www.reedexport.cn

### 2010年美国芝加哥国际酒店用品及餐饮展会

### The NRA Show 2010

日期：2010/05/22 - 25
地点：美国芝加哥国际会展中心
内容：酒店设备、浴室设备、厨房设备、清洁用品、娱乐健身设备、家具、装饰、餐饮、教育培训及专业服务。The NRA Show是全球规模最大的酒店用品及餐饮展。该展是由1919年成立的餐馆协会发起、主办和管理的。美国餐馆协会在美国餐馆行业占有主导地位，销售额达到476亿美元，为1,220万劳动力提供就业机会,成为美国经济、就业和社会服务的基石。全美50个洲的餐馆协会、7,100多家酒店都隶属于它的会员，该展的特点是全美酒店大连锁集团的采购，很多美国的酒店是世界连锁集团，有很强的购买力。该展每年吸引全球各地100多个国家75,000多名行业专业人士参加，到会的国际媒体超过300多位，该展会得到了美国农业部的海外事业服务处及美国商务部的国际买方企划处赞助，并云集了当今世界酒店业领先者，以及业内商用最具创意的尖端、时尚的产品与设备。
周期：每年一届
市场范围：国际性
主办：北方国际展览有限公司
地址：北京市宣武区菜园街1号中环假日酒店写字楼1102-1103室（100053）
联系人：穆超
☎ 010-8355 9740
🖷 010-8355 7940
✉ woody.m@northexpo.com.cn
MSN：mr_angel_boy@hotmail.com
QQ：26327995
www.northexpo.com.cn

### 2010美国波士顿国际环保建材展

日期：2010/05/24 - 26
地点：美国波士顿
内容：环保建材
周期：每年一届
市场范围：国际性
参展联络：北京中仕达兴业展览有限公司
地址：北京市海淀区蓝靛厂东路2号金源时代商务中心2号楼A座11B（100097）
联系人：贾倩，赵仕忱，牟向东，张露
☎ 010-5129 8900
🖷 010-8886 2939
✉ mail@chinstar.cn
www.chinstar.cn

### 美国书展－原美国书商协会大会及贸易展

### BookExpo America

日期：2010/05/25 - 27
地点：美国纽约 Jacob K Javits会展中心
内容：美洲书展集合了世界最多的英文书籍与行业及作者的特别活动，为展商及观众创造无可比拟的学习、联络、采购以及建立商业关系的机会。
产品及服务：大众商业出版物、非图书出版物、儿童/教育出版物、音像出版物、艺术出版物、宗教出版物、库存图书、精神/灵感出版物、旅游出版物、地图及地球仪、专业/技术/科学出版物、小出版社、国际/外语书籍、大学出版社、礼品/附带产品等等。
周期：每年一届
市场范围：国际性
参展费用：净地展位33美元/平方英尺，标准展位42美元/平方英尺
参展联络：励展博览集团国际销售部
地址：北京朝阳区新源里南路1-3号平安国际金融中心A座15层01-03，05（100027）
联系人：宫卫
☎ 010-5933 9288
🖷 010-5933 9233
✉ david.gong@reedexpo.com.cn
www.reedexport.cn

### 中国纺织品服装贸易展览会(纽约)

### China Textile and Apparel Trade Show (New York)

日期：2010/06 -
地点：美国纽约贾维茨会议中心
内容：各类纺织品、服装、服饰及家用纺织品
始办年份：2000
周期：每年一届
市场范围：国际性
入场券价格：名片换取
参展费用：标准展位（3x3m）人民币32,000元
上届规模 ‘09：参展商100家，专业贸易观众3,000人
主办：中国纺织工业协会
承办：中国贸促会纺织行业分会
地址：中国北京东长安街12号450室（100742）
联系人：张涛，王静
☎ 010-8522 9550，8522 9017
🖷 010-8522 9544
✉ zhangg@ccpittex.com,
✉ joycewang@ccpittex.com
www.usfair.com.cn

### China Textile and Apparel Trade Show (New York)

Date：2010/06 -
Venue: Javits Convention Center, New York
Profile: All kinds of textiles, Wear, Accessories, Hometextiles
Established Year: 2000
Frequency: Annual
Market Area: International
Participated Fee: Standard Booth （3x3m）RMB 32,000

Statistics '09: Exhibitors 100，Trade Visitors 3,000
Sponsor: China National Textile & Apparel Council
Organizer: The Sub-Council of Textile Industry, CCPIT
Address: Room 450, No.12 Chang An Street, Beijing, China
Contact: Zhang Tao, Wang Jing
☎ 86-10-8522 9550，8522 9017
🖷 86-10-8522 9544
✉ zhangg@ccpittex.com
✉ joycewang@ccpittex.com
www.usfair.com.cn

### 美国智能交通展览会
### ITS America's 2010 Exposition

**日期：** 2010/06/01 - 03
**地点：** 美国马里兰
**周期：** 每年一届
**市场范围：** 国际性
**参展联络：** 中国贸促会机械行业分会
**地址：** 北京市西城区三里河路46号（100823）
**联系人：** 范卓英
☎ 010-6859 4807, 6859 4804, 6859 5499
🖷 010-6859 4917
✉ info@ccpitmsc.org
✉ jix@ccpit.org
www.chinamachin.org.cn
www.ccpitmsc.org

### 美国芝加哥办公家具展
### NEOCON 2010

**日期：** 2010/06/14 - 16
**地点：** 美国芝加哥
**周期：** 每年一届
**市场范围：** 国际性
**参展联络：** 大连上选会展服务有限公司
**地址：** 大连市西岗区鞍山路13号兴业广场大厦B座508室（116011）
☎ 0411-8378 8326, 8378 8396, 8378 9165, 8378 8821
🖷 0411-8378 8830, 8378 8823
✉ cicyhuang@vip.sina.com
MSN：cicyhuang@msn.com
www.sun-show.com

### 国际传动及电机展览会

**日期：** 2010/06/27 - 29
**地点：** 美国奥兰多
**周期：** 每年一届
**市场范围：** 国际性
**参展联络：** 中国机械汽车展览联合会
☎ 010-6859 4964
🖷 010-6859 4964

### 北美国际太阳能技术展
### intersolar North America

**日期：** 2010/07 -
**地点：** 美国旧金山
**内容：** 太阳能供水系统及产品，太阳能集热采暖设备，太阳能建筑应用，太阳能其它应用产品
**周期：** 每年一届
**市场范围：** 国际性
**参展联络：** 京慕国际展览有限公司
**地址：** 北京市朝阳区北三环东路6号中国国际展览中心服务楼3层
**联系人：** 张晚霞，俞亮
☎ 010-8460 0551
🖷 010-8460 0394
✉ zhaolingna@ciec.com.cn
www.jingmu.com.cn

### 拉斯维加斯国际鞋业博览会（秋季）
### WSA

**日期：** 2010/07 -
**地点：** 美国拉斯维加斯
**内容：** 各种鞋类、鞋架、手提袋以及鞋的辅料等
**周期：** 每年两届
**市场范围：** 国际性
**参展联络：** 京慕国际展览有限公司
**地址：** 北京市朝阳区北三环东路6号中国国际展览中心服务楼3层
**联系人：** 李嘉羊；古莹
☎ 010-8460 0551
🖷 010-8460 0394
✉ zhaolingna@ciec.com.cn
www.jingmu.com.cn

### 盐湖城冬季/夏季户外运动用品博览会（夏季）
### Outdoor Retailer Winter/ Summer Market

**日期：** 2010/07 -
**地点：** 美国盐湖城
**内容：** 户外装备、运动服装、露营用品及背包、自行车运动用品、登山及攀岩用品、水上运动用品
**周期：** 每年两届
**市场范围：** 国际性
**参展联络：** 京慕国际展览有限公司
**地址：** 北京市朝阳区北三环东路6号中国国际展览中心服务楼3层
**联系人：** 李雪寒
☎ 010-8460 0551
🖷 010-8460 0394
✉ zhaolingna@ciec.com.cn
www.jingmu.com.cn

### 美国AACC临床化学年会暨国际临床实验室设备展
### Clinical Lab Expo and the American Association of Clinical Chemistry's (AACC) Annual Meeting

**日期：** 2010/07 -
**地点：** 美国芝加哥
**内容：** 电解质、毒理学与治疗性药物监控、免疫测定法、自动化与机器人学、内分泌、癌症及血糖检验、DNA分析、酶学、分子诊断学、血液学与止血法、心脏病检验
**周期：** 每年一届
**市场范围：** 国际性
**参展联络：** 京慕国际展览有限公司
**地址：** 北京市朝阳区北三环东路6号中国国际展览中心服务楼3层
**联系人：** 魏亦山，孙铁兵
☎ 010-8460 0551
🖷 010-8460 0394
✉ zhaolingna@ciec.com.cn
www.jingmu.com.cn

### 北美国际太阳能科技展览会

**日期：** 2010/07/14 - 16
**地点：** 美国旧金山
**周期：** 每年一届
**市场范围：** 国际性
**参展联络：** 中国机械汽车展览联合会
☎ 010-6859 4964
🖷 010-6859 4964

### 拉斯维加斯国际服装服饰博览会（秋季）
### MAGIC

**日期：** 2010/08 -
**地点：** 美国拉斯维加斯
**内容：** 各种男装、女装、休闲服装、童装、皮装、服饰、浴装、内衣、帽子、围巾；各种面料、辅料
**周期：** 每年两届
**市场范围：** 国际性
**参展联络：** 京慕国际展览有限公司
**地址：** 北京市朝阳区北三环东路6号中国国际展览中心服务楼3层
**联系人：** 崔文佳，柳川
☎ 010-8460 0551
🖷 010-8460 0394
✉ zhaolingna@ciec.com.cn
www.jingmu.com.cn

### 美国亚洲商品采购大会
### ASD/AMD SOURCE DIRECT

**日期：** 2010/08 -
**地点：** 美国拉斯维加斯
**市场范围：** 国际性
**参展联络：** 京慕国际展览有限公司
**地址：** 北京市朝阳区北三环东路6号中国国际展览中心服务楼3层
**联系人：** 李嘉羊；古莹
☎ 010-8460 0551
🖷 010-8460 0394
✉ zhaolingna@ciec.com.cn
www.jingmu.com.cn

### 丹佛健康与健身博览会
### Denver Health + Fitness Business & Expo

**日期：** 2010/08 -
**地点：** 美国丹佛
**内容：** 健身器材，运动服装，背包，体操用品，瑜伽垫，划船、滑雪器械、运动保健等
**周期：** 每年一届
**市场范围：** 国际性
**参展联络：** 京慕国际展览有限公司
**地址：** 北京市朝阳区北三环东路6号中国国际展览中心服务楼3层
**联系人：** 张璋
☎ 010-8460 0551
🖷 010-8460 0394
✉ zhaolingna@ciec.com.cn
www.jingmu.com.cn

### 美国国际医疗设备展览会
### FIME

**日期：** 2010/08 -
**地点：** 美国迈阿密
**内容：** 治疗仪器及配件、检测分析诊断仪及配件、医用家具、实验室用品、医用耗材、残疾人辅助用品、护理康复仪器、监护仪器、牙科设备医用包装、家庭护理
**周期：** 每年一届
**市场范围：** 国际性
**参展联络：** 京慕国际展览有限公司
**地址：** 北京市朝阳区北三环东路6号中国国际展览中心服务楼3层
**联系人：** 魏亦山，孙铁兵
☎ 010-8460 0551
🖷 010-8460 0394
✉ zhaolingna@ciec.com.cn
www.jingmu.com.cn

### 美国国际物流技术展览会
### MATTECH 2010

**日期：** 2010/08/05 - 06
**地点：** 美国迈阿密
**周期：** 每年一届
**市场范围：** 国际性
**参展联络：** 中国贸促会机械行业分会
**地址：** 北京市西城区三里河路46号（100823）
**联系人：** 郭霞
☎ 010-6859 4985, 6859 5056
🖷 010-6853 3354
✉ info@ccpitmsc.org
✉ jix@ccpit.org
www.chinamachin.org.cn
www.ccpitmsc.org

### 亚特兰大国际木工机械展览会
### IWF

**日期：** 2010/08/25 - 28
**地点：** 美国亚特兰大
**内容：** 木工机械、五金配件、锁具等
**周期：** 每年一届
**市场范围：** 国际性
**参展联络：** 京慕国际展览有限公司
**地址：** 北京市朝阳区北三环东路6号中国国际展览中心服务楼3层

联系人：王爽，薛磊
☎ 010-8460 0551
🖷 010-8460 0394
✉ zhaolingna@ciec.com.cn
www.jingmu.com.cn

## 美国ABC国际婴童用品展览会

ABC Kids Expo

日期：2010/09 -
地点：美国拉斯维加斯
内容：婴幼儿服装及用品、儿童服装、孕妇装、婴幼儿用品、青少年家具、玩具、婴儿推车、儿童汽车座椅等
市场范围：国际性
参展联络：京慕国际展览有限公司
地址：北京市朝阳区北三环东路6号中国国际展览中心服务楼3层
联系人：付颖；古莹
☎ 010-8460 0551
🖷 010-8460 0394
✉ zhaolingna@ciec.com.cn
www.jingmu.com.cn

## 美国国际桥梁、隧道与公路展览会

Annual meeting & Exhibition 2010

日期：2010/09 -
地点：美国芝加哥
周期：每年一届
市场范围：国际性
参展联络：中国贸促会机械行业分会
地址：北京市西城区三里河路46号（100823）
联系人：范卓英
☎ 010-6859 4807, 6859 4804, 6859 5499
🖷 010-6859 4917
✉ info@ccpitmsc.org
✉ jix@ccpit.org
www.chinamachin.org.cn
www.ccpitmsc.org

## 美国芝加哥国际机械制造周展览会

NMW

日期：2010/09 -
地点：美国芝加哥
内容：工程设计、工业自动化、工厂工程之维护/修理及运营、机械零部件/工业转包/代加工
周期：每年一届
市场范围：国际性
参展联络：京慕国际展览有限公司
地址：北京市朝阳区北三环东路6号中国国际展览中心服务楼3层
联系人：薛亮，孙铁兵
☎ 010-8460 0551
🖷 010-8460 0394
✉ zhaolingna@ciec.com.cn
www.jingmu.com.cn

## 美国圣地亚哥极限运动及运动时尚博览会

ASR Trade Expo

日期：2010/09 -
地点：美国圣地亚哥
内容：冲浪运动用品、滑冰运动用品、雪类运动用品、游泳用品、板类运动用品、运动鞋服、时尚服装
周期：每年一届
市场范围：国际性
参展联络：京慕国际展览有限公司
地址：北京市朝阳区北三环东路6号中国国际展览中心服务楼3层
联系人：李雪寒
☎ 010-8460 0551
🖷 010-8460 0394
✉ zhaolingna@ciec.com.cn
www.jingmu.com.cn

## 美国国际自行车及零部件展览会

Interbike

日期：2010/09 -
地点：美国拉斯维加斯
内容：各类自行车及零配件、三轮车，婴儿车，滑板车，电动自行车；服饰、背包；健身器材，运动营养品和安全产品等
周期：每年一届
市场范围：国际性
参展联络：京慕国际展览有限公司
地址：北京市朝阳区北三环东路6号中国国际展览中心服务楼3层
联系人：薛亮，孙铁兵
☎ 010-8460 0551
🖷 010-8460 0394
✉ zhaolingna@ciec.com.cn
www.jingmu.com.cn

## 美国国际制造技术（机床）展览会

IMTS 2010

日期：2010/09/13 - 18
地点：美国芝加哥
周期：两年一届
市场范围：国际性
参展联络：中国贸促会机械行业分会
地址：北京市西城区三里河路46号（100823）
联系人：周海明，叶海青，聂飞
☎ 010-6859 5495, 6859 5247, 6851 3586, 6859 4938
🖷 010-6859 5057
✉ info@ccpitmsc.org
✉ jix@ccpit.org
www.chinamachin.org.cn www.ccpitmsc.org

## 第八届美国国际玻璃门窗展览会

8th The Glass Build, Window & Door Expo

日期：2010/09/14 - 16
地点：美国拉斯维加斯国际会议展览中心
内容：塑钢门窗、铝合金门窗、不锈钢门窗、彩板门窗、木质门窗等其他不同材质门窗，五金配件、相关辅料、挤出设备、组装设备；各种玻璃幕墙、幕墙相关产品、设备等；门窗幕墙设计软件、玻璃优化下料系统等软件；各种建筑玻璃、钢化玻璃、艺术玻璃、装饰玻璃、特种玻璃等。
周期：每年一届
市场范围：国际性
参展联络：福建省国际贸易展览公司；福建省新天国际会展有限公司
地址：福建省福州市鼓楼区五四北路283号天骅大厦20层2088单元
联系人：范心锦；卢建光
☎ 0591-2808 6523, 8773 5017
✉ barryfan@valuedshow.com
MSN：barryvanfan@hotmail.com
QQ：30249576
www.valuedshow.com

## 芝加哥休闲户外家具及用品展

Casual Outdoor Expo

日期：2010/09/21 - 24
地点：美国芝加哥
周期：每年一届
市场范围：国际性
参展联络：大连上选会展服务有限公司
地址：大连市西岗区鞍山路13号兴业广场大厦B座508室（116011）
☎ 0411-8378 8326, 8378 8396, 8378 9165, 8378 8821
🖷 0411-8378 8830, 8378 8823
✉ cicyhuang@vip.sina.com
MSN：cicyhuang@msn.com
www.sun-show.com

## 美国潜水设备行销协会展

DEMA Show

日期：2010/10 -
地点：美国拉斯维加斯
内容：各式潜水装备，水下灯具、车辆、通讯设备，潜水服、眼镜，潜水培训及救援设备等
周期：每年一届
市场范围：国际性
参展联络：京慕国际展览有限公司
地址：北京市朝阳区北三环东路6号中国国际展览中心服务楼3层
联系人：薛亮，孙铁兵
☎ 010-8460 0551
🖷 010-8460 0394
✉ zhaolingna@ciec.com.cn
www.jingmu.com.cn

## 美国国际康复展

Medtrade

日期：2010/10 -
地点：美国亚特兰大
内容：家居保健产品、呼吸产品、医疗/外科设备、日用援助品、伤口/皮肤护理、矫正/义肢、运动药物/复健、管理咨询、零售销售规划、消耗
周期：每年一届
市场范围：国际性
参展联络：京慕国际展览有限公司
地址：北京市朝阳区北三环东路6号中国国际展览中心服务楼3层
联系人：魏亦山，孙铁兵
☎ 010-8460 0551
🖷 010-8460 0394
✉ zhaolingna@ciec.com.cn
www.jingmu.com.cn

## 美国东部国际安防产品博览会

ISC East:
International Security Conference East

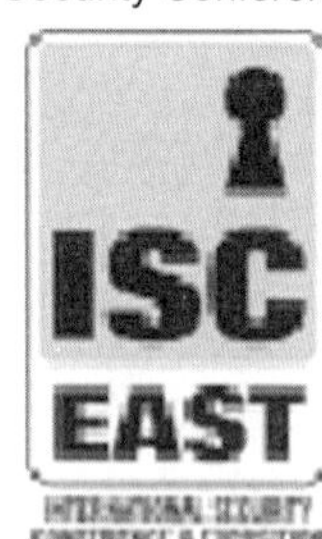


日期：2010/10 -
地点：美国纽约Jacob K Javits会展中心
内容：该展每年秋季在美国东部举办，与春季在拉斯维加斯举办的美国西部国际安保展(ISC West)为姊妹展。2004年起该展从华盛顿移至经济发达的纽约举办。在移至纽约后，该展取得了极大的成功，人气也更加兴旺。共有400多家参展商参展，9,000名专业客商到会参观洽谈，其中100多家是世界知名的公司或人士，分别来自美国50个洲和70多个国家和地区，展会面积超过7万平方英尺。展览会吸引世界知名品牌公司参展，包括：ADI, Fire Lite Alarms Inc., HID Corp, Honeywell, Panasonic, Pelco, NAPCO, Silent Knight and Vicon等。ISC是世界安保、防盗、防火、防护产品行业的重要活动。世界各国安全、防护、保险等领域人士均与会交流、学习和贸易促进。
产品及服务：防盗类电子产品：闭路电视、监视器、门路控制、家庭保险设备、摄像设备、报警装置和系统、电子防盗装置、门用控制装置；防盗类五金：安保五金、各种锁类产品、保险柜、工具箱、门用五金件、电子锁、安装工具、门铃 信息网络安全：通讯控制、计算机安全管理、IT保护等产品 无线、通讯产品：安保产品电池和动力设备、无线报警设备、探测器、传感器、超声器、无线通讯装置、电话系统、收录机、声控装置；防护产品：温度报警装置、车量安全检测室外庭院护拦、梯子、仪表及测量装置、电线电缆等一切与生活相关的安全、安保、保险有关的产品、劳保用品、交通警示和反光保护用品等；家庭自动化产品；消防产品：灭火器、火灾报警、火灾控制等产品
周期：每年一届
市场范围：国际性
参展费用：36.50美元/平方英尺
协办：美国安保协会
主办：励展博览集团美国公司
参展联络：励展博览集团国际销售部
地址：北京朝阳区新源里南路1-3号平安国际金融中心A座15层01-03，05（100027）

联系人：宫卫
☎ 010-5933 9288
🖷 010-5933 9233
✉ david.gong@reedexpo.com.cn
www.reedexport.cn

### 国际园艺机械展览会

日期：2010/10 -
地点：美国路易斯维尔
周期：每年一届
市场范围：国际性
参展联络：中国机械汽车展览联合会
☎ 010-6859 4964
🖷 010-6859 4964

### 美国牙科协会第150届年会
ADA

日期：2010/10 -
地点：美国夏威夷
内容：牙科医疗器械与设备；牙科医疗材料、工具；颌面外科专用器械、材料；牙体牙髓专用器械、材料；牙周病科专用器械、材料；正畸专用器械、材料
周期：每年一届
市场范围：国际性
参展联络：京慕国际展览有限公司
地址：北京市朝阳区北三环东路6号中国国际展览中心服务楼3层
联系人：安红彦，孙铁兵
☎ 010-8460 0551
🖷 010-8460 0394
✉ zhaolingna@ciec.com.cn
www.jingmu.com.cn

### 美国洛杉矶国际纺织品展览会（秋季）
Globaltex

日期：2010/10 -
地点：美国洛杉矶洛杉矶
内容：各类服装、面料、纺织品
周期：每年两届
市场范围：国际性
参展联络：京慕国际展览有限公司
地址：北京市朝阳区北三环东路6号中国国际展览中心服务楼3层
联系人：崔文佳；柳川
☎ 010-8460 0551
🖷 010-8460 0394
✉ zhaolingna@ciec.com.cn
www.jingmu.com.cn

### 美国劳保用品展览会
Congress & Expo

日期：2010/10/04 - 06
地点：美国圣地亚哥
内容：个人防护设备（手套、工装、安全鞋、反光材料等）工作环境下安全的传送装置、噪音防护方面的软硬件设备、防火设备、放射防护、触电保护、安全组织和服务等
周期：每年一届
市场范围：国际性
参展联络：京慕国际展览有限公司
地址：北京市朝阳区北三环东路6号中国国际展览中心服务楼3层
联系人：薛磊，国曦
☎ 010-8460 0551
🖷 010-8460 0394
✉ zhaolingna@ciec.com.cn
www.jingmu.com.cn

### 美国西部国际光学展
International Vision Expo West

日期：2010/10/07 - 09
地点：美国拉斯维加斯金沙会展中心
内容：美国西部领先的眼科保健盛会，聚集所有眼科保健专业人员。
产品及服务：眼科保健业的眼镜和眼科护理产品及服务。
周期：每年一届
市场范围：国际性
参展费用：净地展位29.75～35美元/平方英尺
赞助：美国视力协会（VCA）
参展联络：励展博览集团国际销售部
地址：北京朝阳区新源里南路1-3号平安国际金融中心A座15层01-03，05（100027）
联系人：杜一鸣
☎ 010-5933 9288
🖷 010-5933 9233
✉ martin.du@reedexpo.com.cn
www.reedexport.cn

### 纽约国际动漫博览会
New York Comic Con

日期：2010/10/08 - 10
地点：美国纽约Jacob K Javits中心
内容：像Publishers Weekly and Variety这样的顶级行业出版商、数以千计的追求时尚与新潮大众文化的其他行业人士，以及公众都会参加纽约国际动漫博览会。如果您想寻找最具活力、进行最大的交易以及决定将来突破的地方，纽约国际动漫博览会都是唯一的选择。它不仅仅是一个漫画书籍展，它也是东部海岸独一无二的展会，带您进入美国最大的大众文化、媒体和版权交易城市。
周期：每年一届
市场范围：国际性
参展费用：净地展位18美元/平方英尺
主办：励展美国公司
参展联络：励展博览集团国际销售部
地址：北京朝阳区新源里南路1-3号平安国际金融中心A座15层01-03，05（100027）
联系人：杜一鸣
☎ 010-5933 9288
🖷 010-5933 9233
✉ martin.du@reedexpo.com.cn
www.reedexport.cn

### 国际太阳能展览会

日期：2010/10/12 - 14
地点：美国拉斯维加斯
周期：每年一届
市场范围：国际性
参展联络：中国机械汽车展览联合会
☎ 010-6859 4964
🖷 010-6859 4964

### 帕米亚盆地国际石油及天然气展览会

日期：2010/10/18 - 21
地点：美国敖德萨
周期：每年一届
市场范围：国际性
参展联络：中国机械汽车展览联合会
☎ 010-6859 4964
🖷 010-6859 4964

### 纸加工与包装展览会

日期：2010/10/31 – 11/03
地点：美国芝加哥
周期：每年一届
市场范围：国际性
参展联络：中国机械汽车展览联合会
☎ 010-6859 4964
🖷 010-6859 4964

### 全球博彩业博览会
Global Gaming Expo (G2E)

日期：2010/11 -
地点：美国拉斯维加斯会议中心
内容：全球博彩业博览会（G2E）是世界博彩业的盛事，每年11月在拉斯维加斯举办。届时，国内外博彩业管理人、采购商及行业专家将齐聚一堂，提供最有深度的先进产品、观念、信息，并建立众多联络。在博览会现场（拉斯维加斯）您可以亲自参与其中并体会诸多乐趣。如果您已经经营或正打算涉足博采业，全球博彩业博览会将不容错过。该博览会参展商达750多家，设140多个研讨项目及其他特别活动。
周期：每年一届
市场范围：国际性
赞助：博彩设备制造协会（AGEM）；澳洲博彩器材制造商协会（AGMMA）；Asociacion Latinoamericana de Juegos de Azar (ALAJA)；美国博彩业协会(ACA)；博彩标准协会(GSA)；北美负责任赌博中心(NCRG)
主办：励展博览集团国际销售部；美国博彩业协会（AGA）
地址：北京市朝阳区新源里南路1-3号平安国际金融中心A座15层01-03，05（100027）
联系人：王亮
☎ 010-5933 9288
🖷 010-5933 9233
✉ liang.wang@reedexpo.com.cn
www.reedexport.cn

### 纽约国际餐饮及酒店用品博览会
The Intl Hotel/Motel & Restaurant Show

日期：2010/11 -
地点：美国纽约美国
内容：家用纺织品及床上用品，制服，餐具，厨具，清洁卫生产品及设备，厨房及餐馆设备，浴室及浴室设备等
市场范围：国际性
参展联络：京慕国际展览有限公司
地址：北京市朝阳区北三环东路6号中国国际展览中心服务楼3层
联系人：王海琼；滕昊
☎ 010-8460 0551
🖷 010-8460 0394
✉ zhaolingna@ciec.com.cn
www.jingmu.com.cn

### 美国国际包装机械博览会
Pack Expo International 2010

日期：2010/11 -
地点：美国芝加哥
周期：每年一届
市场范围：国际性
参展联络：中国贸促会机械行业分会
地址：北京市西城区三里河路46号（100823）
联系人：吕静，于奇琳，张垚
☎ 010-6859 4909, 6859 5498, 6859 4192
🖷 010-6859 5485
✉ info@ccpitmsc.org
✉ jix@ccpit.org
www.chinamachin.org.cn
www.ccpitmsc.org

### 2010年拉斯维加斯改装车零配件展览会
SEMA Show

日期：2010/11/02 - 05
地点：美国拉斯维加斯

内容：一般汽车、卡车、厢型车、越野休旅车等的各类改装产品。汽车电子产品。国产及进口小跑车的外形升级，引擎修复，电子产品，及汽车悬吊系统等产品。越野车专用悬吊系统，车灯，内胎，油压起重机等及其他产品。引擎改装车，古典式汽车及古董车的复制品及再制品。各式轮胎，轮圈，轮胎配件，轮胎相关工具及设备。
周期：每年一届
市场范围：国际性
主办：法兰克福展览公司
参展联络：中国汽车工业国际合作总公司
地址：北京市海淀区中关村丹棱街3号A座5层（100080）
联系人：何萌
☎ 010-8260 6880
🖷 010-8260 6883
✉ exhibition@cnaico.com.cn

### 国际制造技术与焊接展览会

日期：2010/11/02 - 04
地点：美国亚特兰大
周期：每年一届
市场范围：国际性
参展联络：中国机械汽车展览联合会
☎ 010-6859 4964
🖷 010-6859 4964

### 2010年拉斯维加斯国际汽车零部件及售后市场展览会

### AAPEX Show

日期：2010/11/02 - 04
地点：美国拉斯维加斯
内容：汽车发动机、底盘、车身及电器系统的各种零部件；汽车方面的计算机辅助设计；汽车随车工具及检测、测试设备；汽车维修装备和机器厂房设备；汽车涂料及其设备；汽车音响、汽车轮胎及轮毂；汽车装饰件及用品等。
周期：每年一届
市场范围：国际性
参展联络：中国汽车工业国际合作总公司
地址：北京市海淀区中关村丹棱街3号A座5层（100080）
联系人：何萌
☎ 010-8260 6880
🖷 010-8260 6883
✉ exhibition@cnaico.com.cn

### 美国国际电力展览会

### POWER-GEN 2010

日期：2010/12 -
地点：美国奥兰多
周期：每年一届
市场范围：国际性
参展联络：中国贸促会机械行业分会
地址：北京市西城区三里河路46号（100823）
联系人：范卓英
☎ 010-6859 4807, 6859 4804, 6859 5499
🖷 010-6859 4917
✉ info@ccpitmsc.org
✉ jix@ccpit.org
www.chinamachin.org.cn
www.ccpitmsc.org

## 美国书展
## －原美国书商协会大会及贸易展

### BookExpo America

日期：2011 -
地点：美国纽约 Jacob K Javits会展中心
内容：美洲书展集合了世界最多的英文书籍与行业及作者的特别活动，为展商及观众创造无可比拟的学习、联络、采购以及建立商业关系的机会。产品及服务 大众商业出版物、非图书出版物、儿童/教育出版物、音像出版物、艺术出版物、宗教出版物、库存图书、精神/灵感出版物、旅游出版物、地图及地球仪、专业/技术/科学出版物、小出版社、国际/外语书籍、大学出版社、礼品/附带产品等等。
周期：每年一届
市场范围：国际性
参展费用：净地展位33美元/平方英尺，标准展位42美元/平方英尺
参展联络：励展博览集团国际销售部
地址：北京朝阳区新源里南路1-3号平安国际金融中心A座15层01-03，05（100027）
联系人：宫卫
☎ 010-5933 9288
🖷 010-5933 9233
✉ david.gong@reedexpo.com.cn
www.reedexport.cn

## 美国职业高尔夫球协会高尔夫用品展

### PGA Merchandise Show

日期：2011/01 -
地点：美国佛罗里达州奥兰多橙郡会议中心
内容：该展览会由美国职业高尔夫协会创办于1954年，已成为世界顶级高尔夫专业展览盛会，在国际高尔夫球市场中起着引领潮流的作用。其中包括PGA的专业人士，主要分销商、零售商、高尔夫俱乐部经理、私人培训学校决策人、高尔夫相关媒体等。其主办宗旨即是构筑与会参展公司与专业观众的桥梁。作为专业的高尔夫贸易展览，展会同时还举办高尔夫展示日和专家讲座与商务会议，不仅为展商提供良好的贸易洽谈环境，还为买家和观众提供学习和提高高尔夫球技的机会
周期：每年一届
市场范围：国际性
参展费用：净地展位32美元/平方英尺
参展联络：励展博览集团国际销售部
地址：北京市朝阳区新源里南路1-3号平安国际金融中心A座15层01-03，05（100027）
联系人：申健
☎ 010-8518 2644, 5933 9288
🖷 010-5933 9233
✉ jerry.shen@reedexpo.com.cn
www.reedexport.cn

## 美国东部国际光学展

### International Vision Expo East

日期：2011/03 -
地点：美国纽约Jacob K Javits会议中心
内容：美国东部领先的眼科保健盛会，聚集所有眼科保健专业人员。
周期：每年一届
市场范围：国际性
参展费用：净地展位31.75～35.50美元/平方英尺
参展联络：励展博览集团国际销售部
地址：北京朝阳区新源里南路1-3号平安国际金融中心A座15层01-03，05（100027）
联系人：杜一鸣
☎ 010-5933 9288
🖷 010-5933 9233
✉ martin.du@reedexpo.com.cn
www.reedexport.cn

### 美国工程机械博览会

### CONEXPO CON/AGG 2011

日期：2011/03/22 - 26
地点：美国拉斯维加斯国际会展中心
内容：工程车辆，工程机械，起重运输设备，施工设备、工具及特殊系统，施工工地砂浆、混凝土处置设备，模板及脚手架，建筑工地设施 建材机械
周期：三年一届
市场范围：国际性
主办：美国设备制造商协会
地址：北京东城区建国门北大街8号华润大厦501室（100005）
联系人：孙红宇
☎ 010-8519 1566
🖷 010-8519 1567
✉ hsun@cm-1.com
www.agconnect.com

### CONEXPO CON/AGG 2011

Date：2011/03/22 - 26
Venue: Las Vegas Convention Center, USA
Profile: Construction vehicles, Construction machines, Lifting appliances and conveyors, Construction equipment, tools and special systems, Handling and processing concrete and mortar at construction sites, Formwork and scaffoldings, Site installations
Frequency: Every 3 years
Market Area: International
Organizer: Association of Equipment Manufacturers (AEM)
Address: China Resources Building, Suite 501, No. 8 Jianguomenbei Avenue, Beijing, China
☎ 86-10-8519 1566
🖷 86-10-8519 1567
Contact: Helen Sun
✉ hsun@cm-1.com
www.agconnect.com

### 美国液压、气动、零部件展

### IFPE

日期：2011/03/22 - 26
地点：美国拉斯维加斯会展中心
内容：液压、气动、零部件等
周期：三年一届
市场范围：国际性
主办：美国设备制造商协会
地址：北京东城区建国门北大街8号华润大厦501室（100005）
联系人：孙红宇
☎ 010-8519 1566
🖷 010-8519 1567
✉ hsun@cm-1.com
www.agconnect.com

### IFPE

Date：2011/03/22 - 26
Venue: Las Vegas Convention Center, USA
Profile: Off-Highway Vehicles (includes Construction, Mining, Forestry, Agriculture, Lawn & Garden, and Airport Support vehicles) Fluid Power/Power Transmission Products, Electrical Machinery, Instruments/Controls Distribution Material Handling (includes overhead/straddle cranes, industrial trucks, tractors and stackers) Manufacturing/Production Automation/Machine Tools (includes chemical, petroleum, metal, plastics, and rubber processing) Automotive/Commercial Vehicles (includes Class 8 trucks, vocational trucks, and trucks for other applications) Engineering Services Defense/Aerospace Amusement/Entertainment Technology Other Products/ Services
Frequency: Every 3 years
Market Area: International
Organizer: Association of Equipment Manufacturers (AEM)
Address: China Resources Building, Suite 501, No.8 Jianguomenbei Avenue, Beijing
☎ 86-10-8519 1566
🖷 86-10-8519 1567
Contact: Helen Sun
✉ hsun@cm-1.com
www.agconnect.com

### 美国西部国际安防产品博览会

ISC West:
International Security Conference West

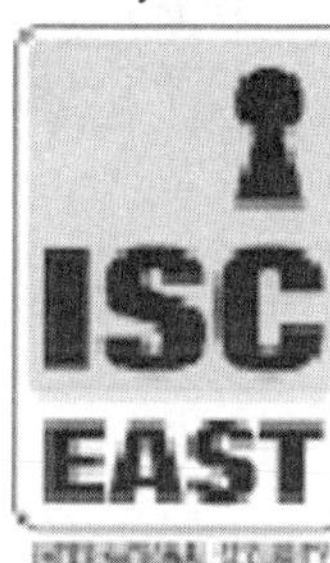


日期：2011/04 -
地点：美国拉斯维加斯会展中心 & 金沙会展中心
内容：该展由世界著名的励展公司主办、美国安保协会（SIA）协办、并经加州警报协会（CAA）及美国防盗防火协会授权（NBFAA），展览会增加了许多新的项目和产品，世界级的行业培训、大量的展期和展会网络联络机会，使该展继续成为为安保产品制造商，经销商、安装商、综合商以及最终使用客户参加的主要的行业盛会。相关人员均是来自这些行业的高级经理或贸易的决策者。展会的国际展团包括中国、韩国、台湾省等，主要展出展品集中在CCTV、接入控制和生物测定学。参展商包括世界知名公司。
周期：每年一届(分别在拉斯维加斯和纽约举办)
市场范围：国际性
参展费用：净地展位44.50美元/平方英尺
参展联络：励展博览集团国际销售部
地址：北京朝阳区新源里南路1-3号平安国际金融中心A座15层01-03，05（100027）
联系人：宫卫
☎ 010-5933 9288
🖷 010-5933 9233
✉ david.gong@reedexpo.com.cn
www.reedexport.cn

### 美国国际五金工具及花园用品展览会

National Hardware Show

日期：2011/05 -
地点：美国拉斯维加斯会议中心
内容：作为与家居用品市场联系的纽带，国际五金制品展览会专注于“户外生活”的流行趋势，提供关于居家维修、重塑、重建、保养及装饰的一切展示，其中包括一个完整的展中展-园艺世界。展商与观众可共同参与内容丰富的各个行业会议，业内专业人士将在会上发表关于时尚潮流及当前家居/家居装饰零售商的市场机遇等方面的演讲。
周期：每年一届
市场范围：国际性
参展费用：净地展位20.95美元/平方英尺
赞助：Paint and Decorating Retailers Association; U.S. Commercial Service; China International Hardware Show; Lawn & Garden Retailer; Spoga+gafa, Spoga; Hardlines; HomeWorldBusiness.com
主办：励展美国公司
参展联络：励展博览集团国际销售部
地址：北京市朝阳区新源里南路1-3号平安国际金融中心A座15层01-03，05（100027）
联系人：吴祥
☎ 010-5933 9288
🖷 010-5933 9233
✉ ronald.wu@reedexpo.com.cn
www.reedexport.cn

### 美国国际小家电及家居用品展览会

Homewares Show

日期：2011/05 -
地点：美国拉斯维加斯会议中心
内容：针对家用器具产品类零售商需求的日渐强大，美国国际小家电及家居用品展将于09年继续举办。
展商来源：小家电、家庭存储与收纳、家庭环境与照明、家用小器具、水处理、清洁用品、小器具、地板、窗户及家装、宠物产品
周期：每年一届
市场范围：国际性
参展联络：励展博览集团国际销售部
地址：北京市朝阳区新源里南路1-3号平安国际金融中心A座15层01-03，05（100027）
联系人：吴祥
☎ 010-5933 9288
🖷 010-5933 9233
✉ ronald.wu@reedexpo.com.cn
www.reedexport.cn

### 纽约国际动漫博览会

New York Comic Con



日期：2011/10 -
地点：美国纽约Jacob K Javits中心
内容：像Publishers Weekly and Variety这样的顶级行业出版商、数以千计的追求时尚与新潮大众文化的其他行业人士，以及公众都会参加纽约国际动漫博览会。如果您想寻找最具活力、进行最大的交易以及决定将来突破的地方，纽约国际动漫博览会都是唯一的选择。它不仅仅是一个漫画书籍展，它也是东部海岸独一无二的展会，带您进入美国最大的大众文化、媒体和版权交易城市。
周期：每年一届
市场范围：国际性
参展费用：净地展位18美元/平方英尺
主办：励展美国公司
参展联络：励展博览集团国际销售部
地址：北京朝阳区新源里南路1-3号平安国际金融中心A座15层01-03，05（100027）
联系人：杜一鸣
☎ 010-5933 9288
🖷 010-5933 9233
✉ martin.du@reedexpo.com.cn
www.reedexport.cn

## 乌兹别克斯坦 Uzbekistan

### 第三届中国工业产品展览会

日期：2010/09/16 - 19
地点：乌兹别克斯坦塔什干
周期：每年一届
市场范围：国际性
参展联络：中国机械汽车展览联合会
☎ 010-6859 4964
🖷 010-6859 4964

## 委内瑞拉 Venezuela

### 拉丁美洲石油展览会

日期：2010/06 -
地点：委内瑞拉马拉开波
周期：每年一届
市场范围：国际性
参展联络：中国机械汽车展览联合会
☎ 010-6859 4964
🖷 010-6859 4964

### 2010年中国工业产品展

China Industry Expo
日期：2010/06/18 - 21
地点：委内瑞拉加拉加斯
周期：每年一届
市场范围：国际性
参展联络：中国汽车工业国际合作总公司
地址：北京市海淀区中关村丹棱街3号A座5层（100080）
联系人：何萌
☎ 010-8260 6880
🖷 010-8260 6883
✉ exhibition@cnaico.com.cn

## 越南 Vietnam

### （VietShip 2010）

### 第5届越南国际造船技术及海事展览会

The 5th Vietnam Intl Exhibition on Shipbuilding & Marine Technology

日期：2010/03/17 - 19
地点：越南河内国家会议中心
内容：造船、航海、运输技术；船艇舾装及相关配套材料与用品；商用、专用船舶及特种船舶；船舶制造及维修设备和设施；船舶部件、舱体、材料及半成品；发动机、推进装置；泵、压缩机、配件和辅机；电子技术和电子设备；补给系统和废水处理系统；救生、救捞设备及安全消防器材；船坞和浮码头；船舶检验与管理体系；游艇及各类休闲船艇；水纹气象预报设备；高速艇、工作船艇及各类专业用途船艇；各种船用防水，防火漆；船艇动力、操纵、推进系统及仪器设备；二手船艇交易及船艇维护保养技术与装备
始办年份：2000
周期：两年一届
市场范围：国际性
参展费用：标准展位1,900元/个，净地1900元/$m^2$
上届规模 ‘08：展览面积10,000$m^2$(国外展商面积7,000$m^2$)，参展商600家（国外展商300家，来自30个国家），参观人数15,000人（其中专业和贸易观众8,000人）
主办：越南社会主义共和国政府；越南工业贸易部
承办：越南船舶工业总公司
地址：广西南宁市新民路3号永嘉大厦C座1208室南宁越中会展商务有限公司（530012）
联系人：凌峰，覃学海
☎ 0771-261 5157，263 0881转1007，263 4998
🖷 0771-263 0917
✉ exhibition@china-vn.com
MSN：exhibition-cv@163.com
QQ：980303370
www.china-vn.com

## 第5届越南（河内）国际建筑建材装饰博览会

Vietbuild 2010

**日期：** 2010/04/01 - 04
**地点：** 越南河内越南国际展览中心
**内容：** 建筑装饰材料展区、建筑装饰五金展区、厨房卫浴展区、电梯门窗及门控五金展区、照明及灯饰展区、楼宇智能自动化展区、建筑涂料/化学建材展区。
**始办年份：** 2005
**周期：** 每年一届
**市场范围：** 国际性
**上届规模** '09：展览面积19,800m²(国外展商面积3,420m²)，参展商500家（国外展商380家，来自20个国家），参观人数100,000人（其中专业和贸易观众12,000人）
**主办：** 越南国家建设部
**承办：** 越南国家建设部信息中心
**地址：** 广西南宁市新民路3号永嘉大厦C座1208室南宁越中会展商务有限公司（530012）
**联系人：** 凌峰，覃学海
☎ 0771-261 5157, 263 0881转1007, 263 4998
🖷 0771-263 0917
✉ exhibition@china-vn.com
MSN：exhibition-cv@163.com
QQ：980303370
www.china-vn.com

## 第20届越南（河内）国际贸易博览会

The 20th Vietnam International Trade Fair In Ha Noi City

**日期：** 2010/04/14 – 17
**地点：** 越南河内国际会展中心
**内容：** 投资洽谈、酒店用品、消费电子及家电产品、体育及休闲用品、玩具及钟表眼镜、文具及办公用品、珠宝首饰、建筑建材、室内外装饰品。
**预计规模：** 展出面积17,000m²，参展商580家，参观人数48,000人
**主办：** 越南国家工业贸易部
**地址：** 广西南宁市新民路3号永嘉大厦C座1208室南宁越中会展商务有限公司（530012）
**联系人：** 凌峰，覃学海
☎ 0771-261 5157, 263 0881转1007, 263 4998
🖷 0771-263 0917
✉ exhibition@china-vn.com
MSN：exhibition-cv@163.com
QQ：980303370
www.china-vn.com

## 越南国际金属加工设备及技术展览会

Metaltech - Vietnam

**日期：** 2010/05/11 - 14
**地点：** 越南胡志明市西贡会议展览中心
**内容：** 金属加工设备
**始办年份：** 1993
**周期：** 每年一届
**市场范围：** 国际性
**参展费用：** 标准展位2,700美元/9m²
**上届规模：** 参展商140家（来自11个国家），参观人数12,000人
**主办：** 显辉国际展览有限公司
**地址：** 香港上环禧利街27号富辉商业中心2403室
**联系人：** 张小姐
☎ (852) 2851 8603
🖷 (852) 2851 8637
✉ topreput@top-repute.com
www.topreputе.com.hk

## Metaltech – Vietnam

**Date:** 2010/05/11 - 14
**Venue:** Saigon Exhibition & Convention Centre (SECC), Ho Chi Minh City, Vietnam,
**Profile:** Metal working machinery material & technology, machine tools
**Established Year:** 1993
**Frequency:** Annual
**Market Area:** International
**Participated Fee:** Standard Booth USD 2,700/booth (9m²)
**Statistics '09:** Exhibitors 140 (came from 11 countries), Visitors 12,000
**Organizer:** Top Repute Co Ltd
**Address:** Rm. 2403, Fu Fai Commercial Centre, 27 Hillier Street, Sheung Wan, Hong Kong
☎ 852-2851 8603
🖷 852-2851 8637
**Contact:** Ms. Cheung
✉ topreput@top-repute.com
www.topreputе.com.hk

## 越南国际塑胶机械及技术展览会

Vietnam Plastic Fair

VIETNAM PLASTICS FAIR

**日期：** 2010/05/11 - 14
**地点：** 越南胡志明市西贡会议展览中心
**内容：** 塑胶机械、物料及技术
**始办年份：** 1993
**周期：** 每年一届
**市场范围：** 国际性
**参展费用：** 标准展位2,700 美元/9m²
**上届规模** '09：参展商140家（来自11个国家），参观人数12,000人
**主办：** 中国对外贸易中心（集团）；显辉国际展览有限公司
**地址：** 香港上环禧利街27号富辉商业中心2403室
**联系人：** 张小姐
☎ 852-2851 8603
🖷 852-2851 8637
✉ topreput@top-repute.com
www.shoesleather-guangzhou.com/index.html

## Vietnam Plastic Fair

**Date:** 2010/05/11 - 14
**Venue:** Saigon Exhibition & Convention Centre (SECC), Ho Chi Minh City, Vietnam
**Profile:** Plastic machinery, product and raw material
**Established Year:** 1993
**Frequency:** Annual
**Market Area:** International
**Participated Fee:** Standard Booth USD 2,700/booth (9m²)
**Statistics '09:** Exhibitors 140 (came from 11 countries), Visitors 12,000
**Organizer:** China Foreign Trade Center (Group); Top Repute Co Ltd
**Address:** Rm 2403, Fu Fai Commercial Centre, 27 Hillier Street, Sheung Wan, Hong Kong
☎ 852-2851 8603
🖷 852-2851 8637
**Contact:** Ms. Cheung
✉ topreput@top-repute.com
www.shoesleather-guangzhou.com/index.html

## 越南国际食品包装机械及技术展览会

Foodpack - Vietnam

**日期：** 2010/05/11 - 14
**地点：** 越南胡志明市西贡会议展览中心
**内容：** 各类食品包装机械、原料及技术
**始办年份：** 1993
**周期：** 每年一届
**市场范围：** 国际性
**参展费用：** 标准展位2,700美元/9m²
**主办：** 显辉国际展览有限公司
**地址：** 香港上环禧利街27号富辉商业中心2403室
**联系人：** 张小姐
☎ 852-2851 8603
🖷 852-2851 8637
✉ topreput@top-repute.com
www.topreputе.com.hk

## Foodpack – Vietnam

**Date:** 2010/05/11 - 14
**Venue:** Saigon Exhibition & Convention Centre (SECC), Ho Chi Minh City, Vietnam,
**Profile:** Food packaging machinery, material & technology
**Established Year:** 1993
**Frequency:** Annual
**Market Area:** International
**Participated Fee:** Standard Booth USD 2,700/booth (9m²)
**Organizer:** Top Repute Co Ltd
**Address:** Rm. 2403, Fu Fai Commercial Centre, 27 Hillier Street, Sheung Wan, Hong Kong
☎ 852-2851 8603
🖷 852-2851 8637
**Contact:** Ms. Cheung
✉ topreput@top-repute.com
www.topreputе.com.hk

## 越南国际印刷、包装机械设备及技术展览会

Print & Pack – Vietnam

PRINT & PACK

**日期：** 2010/05/11 - 14
**地点：** 越南胡志明市西贡会议展览中心
**内容：** 印刷包装机械
**始办年份：** 1993
**周期：** 每年一届
**市场范围：** 国际性
**参展费用：** 标准展位2,700美元/9m²
**上届规模** '09：参展商140家（来自11个国家），参观人数12,000人
**主办：** 显辉国际展览有限公司
**地址：** 香港上环禧利街27号富辉商业中心2403室
**联系人：** 张小姐
☎ 852-2851 8603
🖷 852-2851 8637
✉ topreput@top-repute.com
www.topreputе.com.hk

## Print & Pack – Vietnam

**Date:** 2010/05/11 - 14
**Venue:** Saigon Exhibition & Convention Centre (SECC), Ho Chi Minh City, Vietnam
**Profile:** Printing and packaging technology, machinery & equipment
**Established Year:** 1993
**Frequency:** Annual
**Market Area:** International
**Participated Fee:** Standard Booth USD 2,700/booth

(9m²)
Statistics '09: Exhibitors 140 (came from 11 countries), Visitors 12,000
Organizer: Top Repute Co Ltd
Address: Rm. 2403, Fu Fai Commercial Centre, 27 Hillier Street, Sheung Wan, Hong Kong
☎ 852-2851 8603
℡ 852-2851 8637
Contact: Ms. Cheung
✉ topreput@top-repute.com
www.toprepute.com.hk

### 国际医药制药、医疗器械展览会暨中国医药制药、医疗器械展览会

日期：2010/05/12 - 15
地点：越南河内
周期：每年一届
市场范围：国际性
参展联络：中国机械汽车展览联合会
☎ 010-6859 4964
℡ 010-6859 4964

### 越南国际模具展

InterMold Vietnam 2010:
Vietnam's Only Machinery and Technology Trade Exhibition & Conference for Mould & Die Manufacturing

日期：2010/05/20 - 22
地点：越南河内国际展览中心
内容：2010年第三届越南国际模具展（InterMold Vietnam 2010）是越南唯一针对模具生产的机械及技术行业展会，该展会是越南工业配件制造技术领域四个国际性制造展会其中之一。同期展会：第三届国际塑料及橡胶机械技术展会及研讨会 Automation Vietnam 2010；第三届越南国际工业自动化、电力传输及材料处理技术展览及研讨会 Automotive Manufacturing Vietnam 2010；越南唯一针对汽车零部件制造的机械行业展会（第三届），该展会也将与越南电子展（NEPCON Vietnam 2010）同期举办。
周期：每年一届
市场范围：国际性
主办：励展博览集团国际销售部；励展泰国公司
地址：北京市朝阳区新源里南路1-3号平安国际金融中心A座15层01-03，05（100027）
联系人：王亮
☎ 010-5933 9288
℡ 010-5933 9233
✉ liang.wang@reedexpo.com.cn
www.reedexport.cn

### 2010年第五届越南国际环保技术展览会

Vietnam International Exhibition Fair Environment Technology 2010

日期：2010/05/27 – 30
地点：越南河内国际会展中心
内容：环境处理技术与设备、固体废弃物处理技术、资源综合利用、新能源和节能、水和污水处理设备、环境控制及生态环境、生态服务等。
预计规模：展览面积26,000m²，标准展位200家，参展商130家，参观人数22,000人
主办：越南工业贸易部；越南自然环境保护协会
地址：广西南宁市新民路3号永嘉大厦C座1208室南宁越中会展商务有限公司（530012）
联系人：凌峰，覃学海
☎ 0771-261 5157, 263 0881转1007, 263 4998
℡ 0771-263 0917
✉ exhibition@china-vn.com
MSN：exhibition-cv@163.com
QQ：980303370
www.china-vn.com

### 第5届越南国际汽车摩托车及零配件展览会

The 5th Vietnam International Automobile Motorcycle Parts & Accessories Exhibition

同期举办：
2010越南国际汽车用品展览会
2010越南国际交通及配套产业展
日期：2010/06/09 - 12
地点：越南河内讲武国际会展中心
内容：汽车制造技术装备、汽车用品、汽车维护保养设备及用品、智能交通系统及设施、汽车停车技术设备、汽车加油站设备；汽车摩托车零部件展区 各种汽车摩托车发动机、弹簧、消声器、转向、刹车片、滤清器、电制品、引擎零部件、汽车摩托车底盘、车体零部件、传感器、活塞销、柴油机、点火线圈、点火器、缸体、连接件、凸轮轴、斩壳、离合器、制动器、减振器、万向节、油泵、压缩机、汽车空调、零配件、轮毂、轴承、传动、电子、电器、仪表、轮胎、玻璃、线束、车灯、粘结剂、蓄电池、安全、防盗、保护装置、汽车模具及相关产品；汽车零部件及与新产品、新技术、专利成果等。
始办年份：2005
周期：每年一届
市场范围：国际性
上届规模 '09：展览面积12,000m²(国外展商面积8,500m²)，参展商150家（国外展商100家，来自18个国家），参观人数70,000人（其中专业和贸易观众5,000人）
主办：越南工业政策研究院
承办：越南汽车工程师协会
地址：广西南宁市新民路3号永嘉大厦C座1208室南宁越中会展商务有限公司（530012）
联系人：凌峰，覃学海
☎ 0771-261 5157, 263 0881转1007, 263 4998
℡ 0771-263 0917
✉ exhibition@china-vn.com
MSN：exhibition-cv@163.com
QQ：980303370
www.china-vn.com

### 中国（越南）建筑机械及建材展览会

日期：2010/06/15 - 18
地点：越南河内友谊文化宫
内容：铝、钢门窗，木门窗，复合门窗，建筑幕墙，门窗，五金件，结构胶，玻璃等相关配套产品，检测设备，建筑材料，建筑技术，建筑及建材机械，建筑工程用车，建材成品，材料及加工设备，二手建材设备等。五金用品，电动工具，交电产品，化工原料。
首届
周期：每年一届
市场范围：国际性
参展费用：标准展位15,000元/展位，净地1,450元/m²
主办：中国建筑金属结构协会；越南工贸部广告博览中心；越南建设部；越南社会主义共和工贸部
承办：深圳亚太会议展览有限公司；越南贸易广告博览公司
地址：深圳市福田区南园路70号上田大厦5D（518031）
联系人：贾海其
☎ 0755-8301 8681, 8301 8682
℡ 0755-8301 8685
✉ vivian@asiancapital,net
QQ：4032342722

### 中国商品（越南）交易会

Chinese Commodities (Vietnam) Fair

日期：2010/06/15 - 18
地点：越南河内友谊文化宫
内容：五金用品、电动工具、交电产品、化工原料、纺织品原材料、服装、皮革、鞋帽产品和原材料、纺织类加工机械、皮革种植产品、农副产品、农业设备器具、农用运输设备、食品加工原材料、乳制品、调味品、糖酒类、建材、建械、普通汽车、重型卡车、摩托车、电脑、家具、手工艺品、文具、学具等。
始办年份：2005
周期：每年一届
市场范围：国际性
参展费用：标准展位15,000元人民币/9m²，净地1,450元人民币/m²
主办：中国商业联合会；越南社会注意共和国工贸部
承办：中国商业联合会展览部；深圳亚太会议展览有限公司；越南工贸部广告博览公司
地址：深圳市福田区南园路70号上田大厦5D（518031）
联系人：贾海其
☎ 0577-8301 8681, 8301 8682
℡ 0577-8301 8685
✉ vivian@asiancnpital,net
QQ：403234272

### 越南国际精密工程机械金属工业设备展

日期：2010/07/07 - 09
地点：越南胡志明市
参展联络：北京邦企展览有限公司
地址：北京市朝阳区惠新东街11号紫光发展大厦B1-501（100029）
联系人：雷邵军，赖玉宝
☎ 010-6482 3808
℡ 010-6482 3670
✉ bbes@china.com

### 国际制冷空调与建材展览会

日期：2010/08 -
地点：越南胡志明市
周期：每年一届
市场范围：国际性
参展联络：中国机械汽车展览联合会
☎ 010-6859 4964
℡ 010-6859 4964

### 第十届越南国际药品及医疗设备展览会

VIETNAM MEDI-PHARM EXPO 2010
2010 10th Vietnam International Medical Pharmaceutical,
Medical Equipment Exhibition

日期：2010/08/18 - 21
地点：越南胡志明新平国际展览中心 TBECC
内容：药品类展区：制药产品—中药，西药，补养药品，健康药品；生产药品的原料—化工原料，草药等；制药及包装机械展区；药品制作的化妆品。医院装备及用品展区：诊断和治病的设备，家庭医疗设备，救护车及其设备，眼科装设备，眼科及眼睛，在近临床诊断的设备；保健品展区；骨科及口腔展区；医疗康复护理用品用具展区；医药器械及实验室用品展区。
始办年份：2000
周期：两年一届
市场范围：国际性
入场券价格：免费
参展费用：标准展位14,800元人民币/9m²，净地1,380元人民币/m²
上届规模 '09：展出面积5,610m²，标准展位292个，参展商216家，参观人数20,140人
主办：越南卫生部；越南工贸部

地址：广西南宁市新民路3号永嘉大厦C座1208室南宁越中会展商务有限公司（530012）
联系人：凌峰，覃学海
☎ 0771-261 5157, 263 0881转1007, 263 4998
🖷 0771-263 0917
✉ exhibition@china-vn.com
MSN：exhibition-cv@163.com
QQ：980303370
www.china-vn.com

## 越南国际工程机械、建材机械、工程车辆及设备展览会

Con-Building Vietnam 2010

日期：2010/09 -
地点：越南胡志明
周期：每年一届
市场范围：国际性
参展联络：中国贸促会机械行业分会
地址：北京市西城区三里河路46号（100823）
联系人：张同丽
☎ 010-6859 4805
✉ info@ccpitmsc.org
✉ jix@ccpit.org
www.chinamachin.org.cn
www.ccpitmsc.org

## 越南国际精密工程机床金属工业设备展

日期：2010/09 -
地点：越南河内
内容：数控机床、精密工程机械、金属加工及零配件制造、机械检
主办：北京邦企展览有限公司
地址：北京市朝阳区惠新东街11号紫光发展大厦B1-501（100029）
联系人：雷邵军，赖玉宝
☎ 010-6482 3808
🖷 010-6482 3670
✉ bbes@china.com

## 越南国际汽车及零配件展览会

日期：2010/09 -
地点：越南胡志明市
内容：汽车及零配件展览会
周期：每年一届
市场范围：国际性
参展联络：京慕国际展览有限公司
地址：北京市朝阳区北三环东路6号中国国际展览中心服务楼3层
联系人：张辉，刘舰
☎ 010-8460 0551
🖷 010-8460 0394
✉ zhaolingna@ciec.com.cn
www.jingmu.com.cn

## 越南国际鞋类、皮革及工业设备展览会

International Shoes & Leather Exhibition – Vietnam

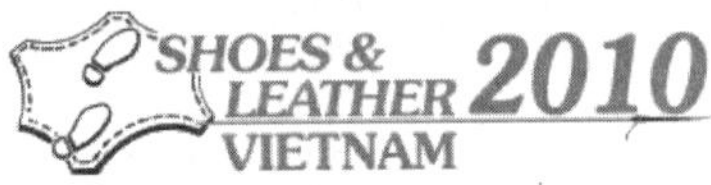


日期：2010/09/08 - 10
地点：越南
内容：鞋类机械、制革机、皮具机、皮革、原皮料、鞋材、化工、配件/辅料、成品
周期：每年一届
市场范围：国际性
上届规模 '09：参展商110家，参观人数6,300人
主办：显辉国际展览有限公司
地址：香港上环禧利街27号富辉商业中心2403室
联系人：郭小姐
☎ 852-2851 8603
🖷 852-2851 8637
✉ topreput@top-repute.com
www.toprepute.com.hk

## International Shoes & Leather Exhibition - Vietnam

Date：2010/09/08 - 10
Venue: Vietnam
Profile: Tanning machinery, shoes machinery, raw materials, leather, chemicals, accessories, finished products, etc.
Frequency: Annual
Market Area: International
Statistics '09: Exhibitors 110，Visitors观众
Organizer: Top Repute Co Ltd
Address: Rm. 2403, Fu Fai Commercial Centre, 27 Hillier Street, Sheung Wan, Hong Kong
Contact: Ms. Kwok
☎ 852-2851 8603
🖷 852-2851 8637
✉ topreput@top-repute.com
www.toprepute.com.hk

## 越南国际建筑展览会

"VICB 2010" -
Vietnam International Construction & Building Exhibition 2010

日期：2010/09/08 - 10
地点：越南西贡会议展览中心
内容：建筑/楼宇工程机械、设备、工具、建材及技术
周期：每年一届
市场范围：国际性
参展费用：标准展位2,430美元/9m²
主办：显辉国际展览有限公司
地址：香港上环禧利街27号富辉商业中心2403室
联系人：林先生
☎ 852-2851 8603
🖷 852-2851 8637
✉ topreput@hkabc.net
✉ dennis@top-repute.com
www.toprepute.com.hk
www.construction-vietnam.com

## "VICB 2010" -

Vietnam International Construction & Building Exhibition 2010
Date：2010/09/08 - 10
Venue: Saigon Exhibition & Convention Center (SECC), Vietnam
Profile: Machinery, Equipment, Material & technology for construction and building industries
Frequency: Annual
Market Area: International
Participated Fee: Standard Booth USD 2,430/9m²
Organizer: Top Repute Co Ltd
Address: Rm. 2403, Fu Fai Commercial Centre, 27 Hillier Street, Sheung Wan, Hong Kong
☎ 852-2851 8603
🖷 852-2851 8637
Contact: Mr. Dennis Lam
✉ topreput@hkabc.net
✉ dennis@top-repute.com
www.toprepute.com.hk
www.construction-vietnam.com

## RAHV 2010

越南国际制冷、空调、供暖、通风系统展览会

日期：2010/09/08 - 10
地点：越南西贡会议展览中心（SECC）
内容：制冷、空调、供暖、通风、冷冻设备及技术
周期：每年一届
市场范围：国际性
参展费用：标准展位2,430美元/9m²
主办：显辉国际展览有限公司
地址：香港上环禧利街27号富辉商业中心2403室
联系人：林先生
☎ 852-2851 8603
🖷 852-2851 8637
✉ topreput@hkabc.net,
✉ dennis@top-repute.com
www.toprepute.com.hk
www.construction-vietnam.com

## International Exhibition on Refrigeration, Air-conditioning, Heating & Ventilation System

Date：2010/09/08 - 10
Venue: Saigon Exhibition & Convention Center (SECC), Vietnam
Profile: Machinery, equipment & technology for refrigeration, air-conditioning, heating & ventilation
Frequency: Annual
Market Area: International
Participated Fee: Standard Booth USD 2,430/9m²
Organizer: Top Repute Co Ltd
Address: Rm. 2403, Fu Fai Commercial Centre, 27 Hillier Street, Sheung Wan, Hong Kong
☎ 852-2851 8603
🖷 852-2851 8637
Contact: Mr. Dennis Lam
✉ topreput@hkabc.net
✉ dennis@top-repute.com
www.toprepute.com.hk
www.construction-vietnam.com

## 第14届越南国际食品及饮料展览会

第14届越南国际食品及饮料加工、包装工艺设备展览会

The 14th International Exhibition on Food & Beverage -
The 14th International Exhibition on Food Processing / Packing Technology & Equipment

日期：2010/09/08 - 11
插入logo，数据库会展编号4117
地点：越南胡志明新平国际展览中心
内容：食品医疗、食品加工包装机械、食品添加剂及原料、冰激凌加工技术设备。食品：糖果各种；包装食品；加工食品；黄油、牛奶产；方便食品；调未；草木品、草木制品；蔬菜各种；食用油、粮油；唐产品；肉、禽及肉制品；海产品：海鲜产品；鱼、虾、螃蟹、墨鱼等冷藏水产品。鱼路、火锅、海产春卷等加工水海产品。饮料产品：茶叶、咖啡；名种酒类（烈酒、开胃酒、葡萄酒、香槟酒、药酒）；名种啤酒；无酒精等饮料；汽水及无汽水饮料；矿泉水；纯净水、保健饮料、果汁。保健食品及药品：燕水；名种糖尿病人用的产品；人参及名种人参产品；功能性食品、营养品及维生素产品；凉草木；有机食品、滋补品等。食品原料：调味料、甜味素、味精、酶制剂、保鲜剂等；食品加工包装机械：食品工艺机械；包装设备；水产品加工、包装及保鲜设备；食品冷链储运及保鲜设备；糖果糕点加工机械；饮料加工机械（酒、啤酒、饮料、矿泉水）；食品清洗设备等 提供酒店用品及设备：设备 & 供应商用通用设备；冷冻冷藏设备；食具及配件；运输及分配；配制设备 贸易权转让：国内外食品、饮料、酒店产品的贸易权转让
始办年份：1996
周期：两年一届
市场范围：国际性

**参展费用**：标准展位16,000元人民币/9m$^2$，净地1,500元人民币/m$^2$
**上届规模**　'09：展览面积3,760m$^2$，参展商150家，标准展位260家，参观人数15,000人
**主办**：越南科学工艺部；越南工贸部；越南农业及农村发展部；越南卫生部；越南质量衡量标准总局
**承办**：越南贸易广告博览公司
**地址**：广西南宁市新民路3号永嘉大厦C座1208室南宁越中会展商务有限公司（530012）
**联系人**：凌峰，覃学海
☎ 0771-261 5157, 263 0881转1007, 263 4998
🖷 0771-263 0917
✉ exhibition@china-vn.com
MSN：exhibition-cv@163.com
QQ：980303370
www.china-vn.com

## 越南国际安防、技防、消防设备和技术展览会

SECURITY & FIRE VIETNAM 2010 – Vietnam International Security System, Fire Protection Equipment and Technology Exhibition 2010

**日期**：2010/09/08 - 10
**地点**：越南西贡会议展览中心（SECC）
**内容**：安防、技防、消防产品、设备和技术
**市场范围**：国际性
**参展费用**：标准展位2,430美元/9m$^2$
**主办**：显辉国际展览有限公司
**地址**：香港上环禧利街27号富辉商业中心2403室
**联系人**：林先生
☎ 852-2851 8603
🖷 852-2851 8637
✉ topreput@hkabc.net
✉ dennis@top-repute.com
www.toprepute.com.hk
www.construction-vietnam.com

## SECURITY & FIRE VIETNAM 2010

– Vietnam International Security System, Fire Protection Equipment and Technology Exhibition 2010

**Date**：2010/09/08 - 10
**Venue**: Saigon Exhibition & Convention Center (SECC), Vietnam
**Profile**: Machinery, equipment & technology for refrigeration, air-conditioning、heating & ventilation
**Market Area**: International
**Participated Fee**: Standard Booth USD 2,430/9m$^2$
**Organizer**: Top Repute Co Ltd
**Address**: Rm. 2403, Fu Fai Commercial Centre, 27 Hillier Street, Sheung Wan, Hong Kong
**Contact**: Mr. Dennis Lam
☎ 852-2851 8603
🖷 852-2851 8637
✉ topreput@hkabc.net
✉ dennis@top-repute.com
www.toprepute.com.hk
www.construction-vietnam.com

## 越南国际鞋类、皮革制成品展览会

International Footwear & Leather Products Exhibition – Vietnam

**日期**：2010/09/11 - 14
**地点**：越南西贡会议展览中心
**内容**：所有鞋类、皮包和箱包、皮革衣服和产品、时尚皮制饰物配件、知名品牌产品
**周期**：每年一届
**市场范围**：国际性
**主办**：显辉国际展览有限公司
**地址**：香港上环禧利街27号富辉商业中心2403室
**联系人**：刘小姐、黄先生
☎ 852-2851 8603
🖷 852-2851 8637
✉ topreput@top-repute.com
www.toprepute.com.hk

## International Footwear & Leather Products Exhibition – Vietnam

**Date**：2010/09/11 - 14
**Venue**: Saigon Exhibition & Convention Center, Vietnam,
**Profile**: All kinds of footwear, Bags & Suitcases, Leather Garments & Leather Product, Fashion Accessories, Brand Name Products
**Frequency**: Annual
**Market Area**: International
**Organizer**: Top Repute Co Ltd
**Address**: Rm. 2403, Fu Fai Commercial Centre, 27 Hillier Street, Sheung Wan, Hong Kong
**Contact**: Ms. Lau, Mr. Wong
☎ 852-2851 8603
🖷 852-2851 8637
✉ topreput@top-repute.com
www.toprepute.com.hk

## 第13届越南（胡志明）国际建筑建材装饰博览会

Vietbuild 2010

**日期**：2010/09/16 - 20
**地点**：越南胡志明富寿体育展览中心
**内容**：建筑装饰材料展区、建筑装饰五金展区、厨房卫浴展区、电梯门窗及门控五金展区、照明及灯饰展区、楼宇智能自动化展区、建筑涂料/化学建材展区。
**始办年份**：1998
**周期**：每年一届
**市场范围**：国际性
**上届规模**　'09：展览面积30,000m$^2$，标准展位2,600个，参展商800家（国外展商372家，来自20个国家），参观人数200,000人（其中专业和贸易观众12,000人）
**主办**：越南国家建设部
**承办**：越南国家建设部信息中心
**地址**：广西南宁市新民路3号永嘉大厦C座1208室南宁越中会展商务有限公司（530012）
**联系人**：凌峰,覃学海
☎ 0771-261 5157, 263 0881转ext 1007, 263 4998
🖷 0771-2630917
✉ exhibition@china-vn.com
MSN：exhibition-cv@163.com
QQ：980303370
www.china-vn.com

## 第十届越南国际橡塑胶工业展

(Vietnam Plas 2010)

## 第十届越南国际包装工业展　第十届越南国际印刷工业展

The 10th Vietnam Intl Plastics, Rubber Industry Exhibition/ The 10th Vietnam Intl Packaging & Printing Industry Exhibition The 10th Vietnam Intl Print & Label Industry Exhibition
**日期**：2010/09/22 - 25
**地点**：越南胡志明国际展览中心
**周期**：每年一届
**主办**：讯通展览公司
**地址**：香港九龙观塘成业街11号华成工商中心5字楼15室
☎ 852-2763 9011
🖷 852-2341 0379
✉ info@paper-com.com.hk
www.paper-com.com.hk

## The 10th Vietnam Intl Plastics, Rubber Industry Exhibition/ The 10th Vietnam Intl Packaging & Printing Industry Exhibition/ The 10th Vietnam Intl Print & Label Industry Exhibition

**Date**：2010/09/22 - 25
**Venue**: SECC-Saigon Exhibition & Convention Center, Vietnam
**Frequency**: Annual
**Organizer**: Paper Communication Exhibition Services
**Address**: Rm. 15, 5/F., Wah Shing Centre, 11 Shing Yip St., Kwun Tong, Kowloon, Hong Kong
☎ 852-2763 9011
🖷 852-2341 0379
✉ info@paper-com.com.hk
www.paper-com.com.hk

## 国际医药及医疗器械展览会

**日期**：2010/09/22 - 25
**地点**：越南胡志明市
**周期**：每年一届
**市场范围**：国际性
**参展联络**：中国机械汽车展览联合会
☎ 010-6859 4964
🖷 010-6859 4964

## 越南国际汽车－摩托车及零配件展览会

SAIGON AUTOTECH

**日期**：2010/10 -
**地点**：越南胡志明
**内容**：整车及零部件等
**周期**：每年一届
**市场范围**：国际性
**参展联络**：京慕国际展览有限公司
**地址**：北京市朝阳区北三环东路6号中国国际展览中心服务楼3层
**联系人**：张辉，刘舰
☎ 010-8460 0551
🖷 010-8460 0394
✉ zhaolingna@ciec.com.cn
www.jingmu.com.cn

## 越南国际机床及金属加工机械贸易展

METALEX Vietnam 2010: Vietnam's Premier International Machine Tool Metalworking Technology Trade Exhibition and Conference – 4th Edition

**日期**：2010/10/07 - 09
**地点**：越南胡志明市国际展览会议中心
**内容**：该展隶属于METALEX--东南亚地区最大的机床及金属加工机械专业性展览会。METALEX Vietnam 2010 将展出越南买家所需的各种尖端技术，如机床、加工中心、金属板材加工、焊接技术、工厂自动化、模具、控制测量、工具及加工。
**市场范围**：国际性
**参展费用**：净地展位（36m$^2$起）335美元/m$^2$，标准展位（3×3m）420美元/m$^2$，注册费：每公司200美元
**主办**：励展泰国公司

参展联络：励展博览集团国际销售部
地址：北京市朝阳区新源里南路1-3号平安国际金融中心A座15层01-03，05（100027）
联系人：王亮
☎ 010-5933 9288
🖷 010-5933 9233
✉ liang.wang@reedexpo.com.cn
www.reedexport.cn

## 第19届越南国际工业产品展览会

19th Vietnam International Industrial Fair

日期：2010/10/19 – 23
地点：越南讲武会展中心
内容：工业自动化技术、工业仪器仪表、工业制冷设备与技术、金属加工技术设备、机床及五金工具、工业模具技术
预计规模：展出面积12,000m²，标准展位850个，参展商500家，参观人数15,000人
主办：越南工业贸易部；越南交通运输部
主办：越南国家建设部
承办：越南国家建设部信息中心
地址：广西南宁市新民路3号永嘉大厦C座1208室南宁越中会展商务有限公司（530012）
联系人：凌峰，覃学海
☎ 0771-261 5157, 263 0881转ext 1007, 263 4998
🖷 0771-2630917
✉ exhibition@china-vn.com
MSN：exhibition-cv@163.com
QQ：980303370
www.china-vn.com

## 第八届越南汽车摩托车工业博览会

Vietnam Auto Expo

日期：2010/11 -
地点：越南胡志明市
周期：每年一届
市场范围：国际性
参展联络：中国汽车工业国际合作总公司
地址：北京市海淀区中关村丹棱街3号A座5层（100080）
联系人：何萌
☎ 010-8260 6880
🖷 010-8260 6883
✉ exhibition@cnaico.com.cn

## 2010越南国际农业博览会

Vietnam International Agriculture Fair 2010

Agro viet 2010

日期：2010/11/12 – 15
地点：越南农业展览馆，越南河内
内容：农业生产；种子、农药、化肥；农业机械及农产品加工；饲料及畜牧养殖技术；茶叶种植加工技术；农业高新科技、产品等。
预计规模：展出面积10,000m²，标准展位450个，参展商246家，观众人数17,000人
主办：越南农业与农村发展部
地址：广西南宁市新民路3号永嘉大厦C座1208室南宁越中会展商务有限公司（530012）
联系人：凌峰，覃学海
☎ 0771-261 5157, 263 0881转ext 1007, 263 4998
🖷 0771-2630917
✉ exhibition@china-vn.com
MSN：exhibition-cv@163.com
QQ：980303370
www.china-vn.com

## 第八届越南（胡志明）国际贸易博览会

The 8th Vietnam International Trade Fair in Ho Chi Minh City

日期：2010/12/01 - 04
地点：越南西贡国际会展中心SECC
内容：投资洽谈、酒店用品、消费电子及家电、体育及休闲用品、玩具及钟表眼镜、文具及办公用品、珠宝首饰、建筑建材、室内外装饰品。
预计规模：展出面积9,000m²，标准展位600个，参展商370家，参观人数25,000人
主办：越南国际工业贸易部
地址：广西南宁市新民路3号永嘉大厦C座1208室南宁越中会展商务有限公司（530012）
联系人：凌峰，覃学海
☎ 0771-261 5157, 263 0881转ext 1007, 263 4998
🖷 0771-2630917
✉ exhibition@china-vn.com
MSN：exhibition-cv@163.com
QQ：980303370
www.china-vn.com

## 越南国际工程机械、建材机械、工程车辆、建筑材料、技术及服务博览会

Con-Build Vietnam

日期：2010/12/01 - 04
地点：越南胡志明
内容：施工机械/施工车辆，建筑材料和机械，建材材料、技术与服务，矿业与林业，运输和公路建设
周期：每年一届
市场范围：国际性
参展联络：京慕国际展览有限公司
地址：北京市朝阳区北三环东路6号中国国际展览中心服务楼3层
联系人：安红彦，孙铁兵
☎ 010-8460 0551
🖷 010-8460 0394
✉ zhaolingna@ciec.com.cn
www.jingmu.com.cn

## 国际贸易博览会

日期：2010/12/08 - 11
地点：越南胡志明市
周期：每年一届
市场范围：国际性
参展联络：中国机械汽车展览联合会
☎ 010-6859 4964
🖷 010-6859 4964

## 越南国际模具展

InterMold Vietnam 2011:

Vietnam's Only Machinery and Technology Trade Exhibition & Conference for Mould & Die Manufacturing

日期：2011/05 -
地点：越南河内国际展览中心
内容：是越南唯一针对模具生产的机械及技术行业展会，该展会是越南工业配件制造技术领域四个国际性制造展会其中之一。同期展会：越南国际塑料及橡胶机械展（InterPlas Vietnam）、国际塑料及橡胶机械技术展会及研讨会 Automation Vietnam、第三届越南国际工业自动化、电力传输及材料处理技术展览及研讨会 Automotive Manufacturing Vietnam越南唯一针对汽车零部件制造的机械行业展会，该展会也将与越南电子展（NEPCON Vietnam）同期举办。
周期：每年一届
市场范围：国际性
主办：励展博览集团国际销售部；励展泰国公司
地址：北京市朝阳区新源里南路1-3号平安国际金融中心A座15层01-03，05（100027）
联系人：王亮
☎ 010-5933 9288
🖷 010-5933 9233
✉ liang.wang@reedexpo.com.cn
www.reedexport.cn

## 越南国际塑料及橡胶机械展

InterPlas Vietnam:
Vietnam's International Plastic and Rubber Technology Trade Exhibition and Conference

日期：2011/05 -
地点：越南越南河内国际展览中心
内容：该展会是越南工业配件制造技术领域四个国际性制造展会其中之一。同期展会：Automation Vietnam、越南国际工业自动化、电力传输及材料处理技术展览及研讨会 Automotive Manufacturing Vietnam——越南唯一针对汽车零部件制造的机械行业展会、越南国际模具展（InterMold Vietnam）——越南唯一针对模具生产的机械及技术行业展会。该展会也将与越南电子展（NEPCON Vietnam）同期举办。
周期：每年一届
市场范围：国际性
主办：励展泰国公司
参展联络：励展博览集团国际销售部
地址：北京市朝阳区新源里南路1-3号平安国际金融中心A座15层01-03，05（100027）
联系人：王亮
☎ 010-5933 9288
🖷 010-5933 9233
✉ liang.wang@reedexpo.com.cn
www.reedexport.cn

## 越南电子展

NEPCON Vietnam 2011:
The International Electronics Manufacturing Technology Trade Exhibition and Conference – Vietnam Edition

日期：2011/05 -
地点：越南河内国际展览中心
内容：越南国际电子生产技术行业展会与研讨会。产品及服务包括表面贴装技术设备及服务、测试及测量设备及服务、电子产品生产服务、电子元器件及移动电话元器件、平板显示模块及应用、汽车部件及元器件生产技术、精密部件及金属部件相关产品、汽车检测与维护仪器及设备相关电子产品、汽车产业相关软件及电子设计、车载电子组件、车载通讯及导航系统、安全与保安系统相关电子设备及设计、发动机控制系统、汽车电器及车载电子系统。
周期：每年一届
市场范围：国际性
主办：励展泰国公司
参展联络：励展博览集团国际销售部
地址：北京市朝阳区新源里南路1-3号平安国际金融中心A座15层01-03，05（100027）
联系人：杜一鸣
☎ 010-5933 9288
🖷 010-5933 9233
✉ martin.du@reedexpo.com.cn
www.reedexport.cn

## 越南国际自动化展览会

Automation - Vietnam

日期：2011/05/11 - 14
地点：越南胡志明市西貢会议展览中心
内容：各类自动化机械
始办年份：1993
周期：每年一届
市场范围：国际性
参展费用：标准展位2,700美元/9m$^2$
主办：显辉国际展览有限公司
地址：香港上环禧利街27号富辉商业中心2403室
联系人：张小姐
☎ 852-2851 8603
🖷 852-2851 8637
✉ topreput@top-repute.com
www.toprepute.com.hk

## Automation – Vietnam

Date：2011/05/11 - 14
Venue: Saigon Exhibition & Convention Centre (SECC), Ho Chi Minh City, Vietnam
Profile: Industrial automation machinery
Established Year: 1993
Frequency: Annual
Market Area: International
Participated Fee: Standard Booth USD 2,700/booth (9m$^2$)
Organizer: Top Repute Co Ltd
Address: Rm. 2403, Fu Fai Commercial Centre, 27 Hillier Street, Sheung Wan, Hong Kong
Contact: Ms. Cheung
☎ 852-2851 8603
🖷 852-2851 8637
✉ topreput@top-repute.com
www.toprepute.com.hk

# 海外展览会议行业分类

# Exhibitions Overseas Listed by Industry Category

## 安全
## Safety and Security

中东（迪拜）国际商业安全及消防器材博览会
2010 Intersec Middle East
2010/01/17-2010/01/19
阿联酋迪拜 United Arab Emirates-Dubai

莫斯科安保展（俄罗斯国际安防技术论坛）
Security & Safety Technologies Moscow (SST Moscow)
2010/02/02-2010/02/05
俄罗斯莫斯科 Russia-Moscow

阿布扎比国际反恐安全展览会
ISNR (Abu Dhabi) Intl Security & National Resilience
2010/03/01-2010/03/03
阿联酋阿布扎比 United Arab Emirates-Abu Dhabi

美国西部国际安防产品博览会
ISC West : Intl Security Conference West
2010/03/24-2010/03/26
美国拉斯维加斯 USA-Las Vegas

巴西国际安防产品博览会
ISC BRASIL － Intl Security & Conference Expo
2010/04/14-2010/04/16
巴西圣保罗 Brazil-Sao Paulo

澳大利亚劳保展
SAFETY IN ACTION
2010/04/20-2010/04/22
澳大利亚墨尔本 Australia-Melbourne

英国国际安防展
IFSEC
2010/05/10-2010/05/13
英国伯明翰 United Kingdom-Birmingham

英国国际职业安全与健康科技大展
SAFETY&HELTH EXPO
2010/05/11-2010/05/13
英国伯明翰 United Kingdom-Birmingham

巴西安防展
EXPO SEC
2010/05/25-2010/05/27
巴西圣保罗 Brazil-Sao Paulo

越南国际安防、技防、消防设备和技术展览会
SECURITY & FIRE VIETNAM 2010 -
Vietnam Intl Security System, Fire Protection Equipment and Technology Exhibition 2010
2010/09/08-2010/09/10
越南胡志明市 Vietnam-Ho Chi Minh City

2010捷克国际劳保展
捷克国际工业展览会
2010/09/13-2010/09/17
捷克布鲁诺 Czech-Brno

俄罗斯国际计算机信息系统安全展览会
Infosecurity Russia
2010/10 -
俄罗斯莫斯科 Russia-Moscow

美国东部国际安防产品博览会
ISC East:
Intl Security Conference East
2010/10 -
美国纽约 USA-New York

俄罗斯国际计算机信息系统安全展览会
Infosecurity Russia
2010/10 -
俄罗斯莫斯科 Russia-Moscow

美国劳保用品展览会
Congress & Expo
2010/10/04-2010/10/06
美国圣地亚哥 USA-Santiago

德国埃森国际工业安全用品展览会
Security Essen
2010/10/05-2010/10/08
德国埃森 Germany-Essen

法国国际安防展
消防设备展
Expoprotection
Feu: The Exhibition for Risk Management
2010/11/02-2010/11/04
法国巴黎 France-Paris

意大利劳保用品展览会
SICURTECH Expo
2010/11/16-2010/11/19
意大利米兰 Italy-Milan

意大利安全及防护用品展览会
SICUREZZA
2010/11/16-2010/11/19
意大利米兰 Italy-Milan

泰国安防展
Intersec Thailand
2010/12/02-2010/12/04
泰国曼谷 Thailand-Bangkok

巴西国际安防产品博览会
ISC BRASIL －
Intl Security & Conference Expo
2011 -
巴西圣保罗 Brazil-Sao Paulo

中东（迪拜）国际商业安全及消防器材博览会
2011 Intersec Middle East
2011/01 -
阿联酋迪拜 United Arab Emirates-Dubai

莫斯科安保展（俄罗斯国际安防技术论坛）
Security & Safety Technologies Moscow (SST Moscow)
2011/02 -
俄罗斯莫斯科 Russia-Moscow

美国西部国际安防产品博览会
ISC West:
Intl Security Conference West
2011/04 -
美国拉斯维加斯 USA-Las Vegas

欧洲国际计算机信息系统安全展览会
Infosecurity Europe
2011/04 -
英国伦敦 United Kingdom-Lon Don

阿布扎比国际反恐安全展览会
ISNR (Abu Dhabi)
Intl Security & National Resilience
2012/03 -
阿联酋阿布扎比
United Arab Emirates-Abu Dhabi

法国国际安防展
消防设备展
Expoprotection
Feu: The Exhibition for Risk Management
2012/11 -
法国巴黎 France-Paris

## 包装
## Packaging

第10届国际包装印刷展览会
2010/01/19-2010/01/22
印度新德里 India-New Delhi

国际印刷、包装及塑胶展览会
2010/01/25-2010/01/28
孟加拉达卡 Bengal

国际印刷及包装展览会
2010/03/08-2010/03/12
巴西圣保罗 Brazil-Sao Paulo

英国包装展览会
TOTAL PROCESESSING & PACKAGING 2010
2010/05 -
英国伯明翰 United Kingdom-Birmingham

国际包装工业展览会
2010/05 -
俄罗斯莫斯科 Russia-Moscow

2010印度尼西亚国际包装技术展览会
2010/05/05-2010/05/08
印度尼西亚 Indonesia

国际包装、塑料及印刷机械展览会
2010/05/07-2010/05/09
巴基斯坦卡拉奇 Pakistan-Karachi

越南国际印刷、包装机械设备及技术展览会
Print & Pack － Vietnam
2010/05/11-2010/05/14
越南胡志明市 Vietnam-Ho Chi Minh City

越南国际食品包装机械及技术展览会
Foodpack / Vietnam
2010/05/11-2010/05/14
越南胡志明市 Vietnam-Ho Chi Minh City

英国国际包装新技术展览会
Total Processing & Packaging
2010/05/25-2010/05/27
英国伯明翰
United Kingdom-Birmingham

第26届巴西国际食品、饮料工业加工技术和包装工业博览会
Flspal Tecnologia 2010
2010/06 -
巴西圣保罗 Brazil-Sao Paulo

墨西哥国际包装机械展览会
EXPO PACK Mexico 2010
2010/06 -
墨西哥墨西哥城
Mexico-Mexico City

俄罗斯国际包装工业展览会
Rospack 2010
2010/06 -
俄罗斯莫斯科 Russia-Moscow

国际食品及饮料包装机械展览会
2010/06/08-2010/06/11
巴西圣保罗 Brazil-Sao Paulo

国际包装展览会
2010/10/05-2010/10/08
日本东京 Japan-Tokyo

纸加工与包装展览会
2010/10/31-2010/11/03
美国芝加哥 USA-Chicago

美国国际包装机械博览会
Pack Expo Intl 2010
2010/11 -
美国芝加哥 America-Chicago

印度国际包装塑料展览会
2010/11 -
印度 India

俄罗斯国际纸浆造纸、林业、生活用纸及纸包装展
PAP/FOR Russia:
Intl Exhibition and Conference for Russia's
Pulp & Paper, Forestry, Tissue & Converting & Packaging Industries
2010/11/08-2010/11/11
俄罗斯圣彼得堡 Russia-St.Petersburg

国际包装博览会与食品包装展览会
2010/11/22-2010/11/25
法国巴黎 France-Paris

英国全套生产线，暨加工及包装机械展
PPMA Show:
UK's annual showcase for Processing & Packaging Machinery
2011/09 -
英国伯明翰
United Kingdom-Birmingham

俄罗斯国际纸浆造纸、林业、生活用纸及纸包装展
PAP/FOR Russia:
Intl Exhibition and Conference for Russia's Pulp & Paper, Forestry, Tissue & Converting & Packaging Industries
2012 -
俄罗斯圣彼得堡 Russia-St.Petersburg

英国国际包装新技术展览会
Total Processing & Packaging
2013 -
英国伯明翰 United Kingdom-Birmingham

## 材料
## Materials

国际管材线材展览会
2010/04/12-2010/04/16
德国杜塞尔多夫 Germany-Dusseldorf

电子电机零配件及材料博览会
2010/04/14-2010/04/16
日本东京 Japan-Tokyo

俄罗斯国际管材及线材展览会
Tube & Wire Russia 2010
2010/05 -
俄罗斯莫斯科 Russia-Moscow

东京机械零部件及材料技术展
M/Tech:
Mechanical Components & Materials Technology Expo
2010/06/23-2010/06/25
日本东京 Japan-Tokyo

中美洲国际汽车零部件、原材料加工及服务贸易展览会
2010/07/14-2010/07/16
墨西哥墨西哥城 Mexico-Mexico City

东南亚国际管材、线材展览会
2010/10 -
泰国曼谷 Thailand-Bangkok

欧洲复合材料展
COMPOSITES EUROPE
2010/10 -
德国斯图加特 Germany-Stuttgart

东京机械零部件及材料技术展
M/Tech: Mechanical Components & Materials Technology Expo
2011/06 -
日本东京 Japan-Tokyo

## 宠物
## Pets

新加坡国际水族及配件展
Aquarama
2010/05 -
新加坡 Singapore

## 船艇、海事
## Boata, Ship Building and Marine

第5届越南国际造船技术及海事展览会
（VietShip 2010）
5th Vietnam Intl Exhibition on Shipbuilding & Marine Technology
2010/03/17-2010/03/19
越南 Vietnam

亚太海事展
Asia Pacific Maritime
2010/03/24-2010/03/26
新加坡 Singapore

国际海事展览会
2010/06/08-2010/06/11
希腊比雷埃夫斯 Greece

2010韩国国际游艇展
Korea Intl Boat Show 2010
2010/06/09-2010/06/13
韩国 Korea

德国汉堡国际海事展览会
Europort Maritime 2010
2010/09/07-2010/09/10
德国汉堡 Germany-

韩国海事展
KORMARINE
2011/10 -
韩国釜山 Korea-Busan

亚太海事展
Asia Pacific Maritime
2012/03 -
新加坡 Singapore

## 灯光照明、灯饰
## Lighting

孟加拉国际电力能源及照明展览会
EL/POWER&LIGHTING BANGLADESH
2010/01/07-2010/01/10
孟加拉达卡 Bengal

阿纳海姆国际乐器、舞台灯光及音响展
THE NAMM SHOW
2009/01/14-2009/01/17
美国阿纳海姆 USA-Anaheim

国际室内照明器材展览会
2010/04/11-2010/04/16
德国法兰克福 Germany-Frankfort

中东迪拜国际舞台灯光、音响及乐器展
PALME
2010/04/18-2010/04/20
阿联酋迪拜 United Arab Emirates-Dubai

国际五金工具/ 商业照明展览会
2010/05/17-2010/05/19
阿联酋迪拜
United Arab Emirates-Dubai

2010沙特电力、能源、照明、水处理展
2010/05/24-2010/05/27
沙特阿拉伯利雅得 Saudi Arabia-Riyadh

法国里昂照明展
LumiVille and InLight Expo
2010/06/01-2010/06/03
法国里昂 France-Lyon

中东国际城市、建筑及商用照明展览会
Light Middle East
2010/09/27-2010/09/29
阿联酋迪拜
United Arab Emirates-Dubai

国际灯具展览会
2010/10 -
土耳其伊斯坦布尔 Turkey-Istanbul

国际制冷、照明、能源与建筑材料展览会
2010/10/26-2010/10/29
利比亚的黎波里 Libya

国际电子及照明展览会
2010/10/26-2010/10/29
西班牙马德里 Spain-Madrid

国际照明展览会
2010/11 -
俄罗斯莫斯科 Russia-Moscow

## 电力、电工
## Electric Power, Electrical Engineering

第12届新西兰国际电力能源行业展示会及高层战略论谈
12th Power &Electricity World New Zealand
2010/02/15-2010/02/18
新西兰 New Zealand

西澳大利亚国际电力能源行业展示会及高层战略商务论谈
Power & Electricity West Australia
2010/03/02–2010/03/04
澳大利亚柏斯Australia-

第9届俄罗斯国际专业线缆、线材及紧固件和安装设备展览会
CABEX 2010
2010/03/16–2010/03/19
俄罗斯索科尔尼基 Russia

俄罗斯国际电力展览会
Russia Power 2010
2010/03/24–2010/03/26
俄罗斯 Russia

捷克国际电子电力展览会
Amper
2010/03/31–2010/04/03
捷克布拉格 Czech–Prague

杜塞尔多夫国际管材、线缆及紧固件展览会
2010/04/12–2010/04/16
德国杜塞尔多夫 Germany–Dusseldorf

第14届乌克兰国际电力及电子展览会
Elcom Ukraine
2010/04/13–2010/04/16
乌克兰基辅 Ukraine–Kiev

美国国际输配电设备和技术展
（IEEE 2010）
IEEE, PES/Transmission & Distribution Conference and Exposition
2010/04/20–2010/04/22
美国 USA

印度及中亚国际电力展览会
POWER/GEN India & Central Asia 2010
2010/04/21–2010/04/23
印度新德里 India–New Delhi

第8届巴基斯坦国际石油、天然气及电力能源展览会
POGEE 2010
2010/05/19–2010/05/22
巴基斯坦卡拉奇 Pakistan– Karachi

2010沙特电力、能源、照明、水处理展
2010/05/24–2010/05/27
沙特阿拉伯利雅得 Saudi Arabia– Riyadh

国际电子电力水利展览会
2010/06 –
墨西哥墨西哥城 Mexico–Mexico City

电力展览会
2010/06 –
德国圣彼得堡 Germany–St.Petersburg

第十三届墨西哥电力电工设备及技术展览会
Expo Electrica Intl 2010
2010/06/02–2010/06/04
墨西哥 Moxico

俄罗斯国际电力电子展览会
2010/06/07–2010/06/10
俄罗斯莫斯科 Russia–Moscow

国际电力电子展览会
2010/06/07–2010/06/10
俄罗斯莫斯科 Russia–Moscow

德国国际光学展览会
Optatec
2010/06/15–2010/06/18
德国法兰克福 Germany–Frankfurt

中东（阿布扎比）国际电力及水能展览会
Power Generation & Water Middle East
2010/10/17–2010/10/19
阿联酋阿布扎比
United Arab Emirates– Abu Dhabi

第9届中东国际电力、能源、水力展览会
Power/Gen Middle East
2010/11/01–2010/11/03
卡塔尔 Qatar

美国国际电力展览会
POWER/GEN 2010
2010/12 –
美国奥兰多 USA–Orlando

美国东部国际光学展
Intl Vision Expo East
2010/03/18–2010/03/21
美国纽约 USA–New York

# 电子
# Electronics

韩国电子展
Nepcon Korea:
SMT/PCB & NEPCON KOREA
2010/03/31–2010/04/02
韩国首尔 South Korea–Soul

捷克国际电子电力展览会
Amper
2010/03/31–2010/04/03
捷克布拉格 Czech–Prague

第14届乌克兰国际电力及电子展览会
Elcom Ukraine
2010/04/13–2010/04/16
乌克兰基辅 Ukraine– Kiev

电子电机零配件及材料博览会
2010/04/14–2010/04/16
日本千叶 Japan

俄罗斯电子元器件展
Expo Electronica
2010/04/20–2010/04/22
俄罗斯莫斯科 Russia–Moscow

第九届沙特（利雅得）国际电子通讯展
2010/04/25–2010/04/29
沙特阿拉伯利雅得 Saudi Arabia– Riyadh

美国国际小家电及家居用品展览会
Homewares Show
2010/05/04–2010/05/06
美国拉斯维加斯 USA–Las Vegas

马来西亚槟城电子/微电子展览会
Nepcon/Microelectronics Penang
2010/06/15–2010/06/17
马来西亚槟城 Malaysia–PISA

泰国汽车电子展
Automotive Electronics 2010:
ASEAN's Only Machinery Expo for Automotive Electronics Parts and Components Manufacturing / Co–located with Automotive Manufacturing 2010
2010/06/24–2010/06/27
泰国曼谷 Thailand–Bangkok

第13届巴西国际电力、能源及电子展览会
2010/06/29–2010/07/01
巴西圣保罗 Brazil–Sao Paulo

班加罗尔国际电子元器件展
ELECTRONIC INDIA
2010/09 –
印度班加罗尔 India–BangaloreBangalore

新加坡电子展
Global TRONINCS
2010/09/15–2010/09/17
新加坡 Singapore

美国西部国际光学展
Intl Vision Expo West
2010/10/07–2010/10/09
美国拉斯维加斯 USA–Las Vegas

第15届西班牙国际电力及电子产品博览会
（MATELEC 2010）
Intl Exhibition of Electrical and Electronic Equipment
2010/10/26–2010/10/29
西班牙马德里 Spain–Madrid

德国国际电子自动化系统及元件展览会
SPS/IPC/DRIVES Electric Automation Systems and Components 2010
2010/11 –
德国纽伦堡 Germany–Nuremberg

慕尼黑国际电子元器件博览会
electronica
2010/11/09–2010/11/12
德国慕尼黑 Germany–Munich

韩国电子展
Nepcon Korea : SMT/PCB & NEPCON KOREA
2011 –
韩国首尔 Korea– Seoul

日本汽车电子展
Intl Automotive Electronics Technology Expo
(CAR/ELE JAPAN)
2011/01 –
日本东京 Japan–Tokyo

美国东部国际光学展
Intl Vision Expo East
2011/03 –
美国纽约 USA–New York

巴西国际电子展
FIEE El é trica:
Intl Electrical, Energy & Automation Industry Trade Fair
2011/04 –
巴西圣保罗 Brazil–Sao Paulo

越南电子展
NEPCON Vietnam 2010:
The Intl Electronics Manufacturing Technology Trade Exhibition and Conference – Vietnam Edition
2011/05 –
越南河内 Vietnam–Hanoi

美国国际小家电及家居用品展览会
Homewares Show
2011/05 –
美国拉斯维加斯 USA–Las Vegas

泰国汽车电子展
Automotive Electronics 2011:
ASEAN's Only Machinery Expo for Automotive Electronics Parts and Components Manufacturing / Co–located with Automotive Manufacturing 2011
2011/06 –
泰国曼谷 Thailand–Bangkok

2011年泰国电子展：
国际电子产品制造贸易展及会议
NEPCON Thailand 2011:
Intl Electronics Manufacturing Technology Trade Exhibition and Conference
2011/06/23–2011/06/26
泰国曼谷 Thailand–Bangkok

新加坡电子展
Global TRONINCS
2012/09 –
新加坡 Singapore

2013年泰国电子展：
国际电子产品制造贸易展及会议
NEPCON Thailand 2013:
Intl Electronics Manufacturing Technology Trade Exhibition and Conference
2013/06 -
泰国曼谷 Thailand-Bangkok

## 动漫、游戏
## Comics and Games

科隆国际游戏展
gamescom
2010/08/18-2010/08/22
德国科隆 Germany-Cologne

纽约国际动漫博览会
New York Comic Con
2010/10/08-2010/10/10
美国纽约 USA-New York

科隆国际游戏展
gamescom
2011/08 -
德国科隆 Germany-Cologne

纽约国际动漫博览会
New York Comic Con
2011/10 -
美国纽约 USA-New York

## 防务、警用设备
## Defense and Police Equipment

中东（迪拜）国际商业安全及消防器材博览会
2010 Intersec Middle East
2010/01/17-2010/01/19
阿联酋迪拜 United Arab Emirates-Dubai

莫斯科安保展（俄罗斯国际安防技术论坛）
Security & Safety Technologies Moscow
(SST Moscow)
2010/02/02-2010/02/05
俄罗斯莫斯科 Russia-Moscow

阿布扎比国际反恐安全展览会
ISNR (Abu Dhabi) Intl Security & National Resilience
2010/03/01-2010/03/03
阿联酋阿布扎比 United Arab Emirates-Abu Dhabi

第十二届马来西亚国防展
2010/04/19-2010/04/22
马来西亚 Malaysia

阿布扎比国际反恐安全展览会
ISNR (Abu Dhabi) Intl Security & National Resilience
2012/03 -
阿联酋阿布扎比 United Arab Emirates-Abu Dhabi

莫斯科安保展（俄罗斯国际安防技术论坛）
Security & Safety Technologies Moscow (SST Moscow)
2011/02 -
俄罗斯莫斯科 Russia-Moscow

## 房地产
## Real Estate

法国国际地产投资交易会
MIPIM
2010/03/16-2010/03/19
法国 France

慕尼黑国际商业地产展
EXPO REAL
2010/10 -
德国慕尼黑 Germany-Munich

法国国际地产投资交易会
MIPIM
2011/03 -
法国 France

## 纺织、服装、服饰及相关机械
## Clothing and Textiles

法兰克福家纺展
Heimtextil
2010/01/13-2010/01/16
德国法兰克福 Germany-Frankfurt

柏林国际服装服饰博览会
Premium Berlin
2010/01/20-2010/01/22
德国Germany

巴黎国际成衣展
Pret a Porter Paris
2010/01/23-2010/01/26
法国巴黎 France-Paris

杜塞尔多夫国际服装博览会（春季）
CPD
2010/02 -
德国杜塞尔多夫 Germany-Dusseldorf

拉斯维加斯国际服装服饰博览会（春季）
MAGIC
2010/02 -
美国拉斯维加斯 USA-Las Vegas

美国拉斯维加斯春季国际服装服饰博览会
2010/02/15-2010/02/18
美国拉斯维加斯 USA-Las Vegas

俄联邦轻工纺织及设备博览会（春季）
Trade Fair For Textile & Light Industry Goods & Equipments
2010/03 -
俄罗斯莫斯科 Russia-Moscow

中国日本纺织成衣博览会（春季）
CFF
2010/03 -
日本大阪 Japan-Osaka

2010韩国大邱国际纤维展
Preview in Daegu 2010
2010/03/10-2010/03/12
韩国大邱 Korea

中东迪拜国际服装、纺织、鞋类、皮革及时尚配饰博览会
Motexha
2010/04 -
阿联酋迪拜 United Arab Emirates-Dubai

美国洛杉矶国际纺织品展览会（春季）
Globaltex
2010/04 -
美国洛杉矶 USA-Los Angeles

中东（迪拜）国际服装、纺织、鞋类及皮革制品博览会
2010 Motexha
2010/04/06-2010/04/08
阿联酋迪拜 United Arab Emirates-Dubai

中国纺织品服装贸易展览会(纽约)
China Textile and Apparel Trade Show (New York)
2010/06 -
美国纽约 America- New York

巴西纺织服装展
2010/06 -
巴西圣保罗 Brazil-Sao Paulo

杜塞尔多夫国际服装博览会（秋季）
CPD
2010/07 -
德国杜塞尔多夫 Germany-Dusseldorf

泰国国际服装及纺织品用机械、设备、材料及附件展
GFT 2010:
Thailand's 16th Intl Presentation of Machinery, Tools & Equipment for Garment & Textile Industries
2010/07/01-2010/07/04
泰国曼谷 Thailand-Bangkok

拉斯维加斯国际服装服饰博览会（秋季）
MAGIC
2010/08 -
美国拉斯维加斯 USA-Las Vegas

中国纺织品服装贸易展览会(巴黎)
China Textile and Apparel Trade Show (Paris)
2010/09 -
法国 France

俄联邦轻工纺织及设备博览会（秋季）
Trade Fair For Textile & Light Industry Goods & Equipments
2010/09 -
俄罗斯莫斯科 Russia-Moscow

中国日本纺织成衣博览会（秋季）
CFF
2010/09 -
日本东京 Japan-Tokyo

俄罗斯国际家用及室内纺织品展览会
Heimtextil Russia
2010/09 -
俄罗斯莫斯科 Russia-Moscow

巴黎国际服装及纺织品定牌贸易展
FATEX
2010/10 -
法国巴黎 France-Paris

巴黎国际服装批发商博览会
INTERSELECTION
2010/10 -
法国巴黎 France-Paris

美国洛杉矶国际纺织品展览会（秋季）
Globaltex
2010/10 -
美国洛杉矶 USA-Los Angeles

巴西纺织机械展
ITMEX Americas:
Intl Textile Machinery Trade Fair
2011/03 -
巴西圣保罗 Brazil-Sao Paulo

2011年中东（迪拜）国际服装、纺织、鞋类及皮革制品博览会
2011 Motexha
2011/04 -
阿联酋迪拜 United Arab Emirates-Dubai

新加坡国际缝制设备展览会
Intl Apparel Machinery Trade Show (JIAM 2011)
2011/05 -
新加坡 Singapore

泰国国际服装及纺织品用机械、设备、材料及附件展
GFT 2012:
Thailand's 17th Intl Presentation of Machinery, Tools &

Equipment for Garment & Textile Industries
2012 –
泰国曼谷 Thailand–Bangkok

巴西纺织机械展
ITMEX Americas:
Intl Textile Machinery Trade Fair
2013 –
巴西圣保罗 Brazil–Sao Paulo

## 工程机械
## Construction Machinery

第31届斯洛伐克国际建筑工程展
2010/03/23–2010/03/27
斯洛伐克布拉迪斯拉发
Slovakia–Bratislava

第4届土耳其国际矿业展览会
2010 –
土耳其伊斯坦布尔 Turkey–Istanbul

第18届土耳其国际建筑工程机械展览会
ANKOMAK 2010
2010/03/31–2010/04/04
土耳其伊斯坦布尔 Turkey–Istanbul

第十届智利国际矿业及工程机械展览会
EXPOMIN 2010
2010/04/12–2010/04/16
智利圣地亚哥 Chile–Santiago

第11届智利国际矿业展览会
2010/04/12–2010/04/16
智利圣地亚哥 Chile–Santiago

俄罗斯国际矿业展览会
2010/04/14–2010/04/16
俄罗斯 Russia

慕尼黑工程机械展
BAUMA
2010/04/19–2010/04/25
德国慕尼黑 Germany–Munich

波兰国际工程机械展览会
2010/05 –
波兰Poland

波兰国际建筑设备和特殊交通车辆展览会
Intl Construction Equipment and Special Vehicles Fair
2010/05 –
波兰凯Poland

27届加拿大国际矿山设备展暨加拿大国际矿业年会
CIM
2010/05/09–2010/05/12
加拿大多伦多 Canada–Toronto

巴西国际机械及工业设备贸易博览会
2010/05/11–2010/05/15
巴西圣保罗 Brazil–Sao Paulo

智利国际工程机械及混凝土展览会
2010/05/12–2010/05/15
智利圣地亚哥 Chile–Santiago

澳大利亚国际工程机械展
2010/05/21–2010/05/23
澳大利亚悉尼 Australia–Sydney

2010中东阿布扎比国际工程机械展
2010/05/24–2010/05/26
阿联酋阿布扎比 United Arab Emirates–Abu Dhabi

印度尼西亚中国工程机械、矿山机械展览会
2010/05/26–2010/05/29
印度尼西亚雅加达 Indonesia–Jakarta

摩洛哥工程机械展
BTP 2010
2010/05/26–2010/05/30
摩洛哥卡萨布兰卡 Morocco–Casablanca

伊朗国际工程机械、建材机械及矿山机械展览会
Iran Conmin 2010
2010/06 –
伊朗德黑兰 Iran–Tehran

第十七届俄罗斯国际采矿技术及煤矿设备展览会
UGOL ROSSII & MINING 2010
2010/06/04–2010/06/07
俄罗斯Russia

越南国际工程机械、建材机械、工程车辆及设备展览会
Con/Building Vietnam 2010
2010/09 –
越南胡志明 Vietnam–Ho Chi Minh City

第3届约旦国际建筑建材暨工程机械展
2010/09/27–2010/09/30
约旦安曼 Jordan–Rabbah

中东(沙迦)国际工程机械展
CONMEX
2010/10 –
阿联酋沙迦 United Arab Emirates

南非国际矿山与电力博览会
Electra Mining Africa 2010
2010/10/04–2010/10/08
南非约翰内斯堡 South Africa–Johannesburg

国际采矿设备、电机工程、石油机械、一般工业及材料处理展览会
2010/10/04–2010/10/08
南非约翰内斯堡 South Africa–Johannesburg

沙特建材—PMV(重工机械展)
The Intl Exhibition for Construction Equipment Plant, Machinery and Vehicles
2010/10/18–2010/10/21
沙特阿拉伯利雅得 Saudi Arabia–Riyadh

印度工程机械展
COMMEX
2010/12 –
印度海得拉巴 India–Hyder ā b ā d

越南国际工程机械、建材机械、工程车辆、建筑材料、技术及服务博览会
Con/Build Vietnam
2010/12/01–2010/12/04
越南胡志明市 Vietnam–Ho Chi Minh City

美国工程机械博览会
CONEXPO CON/AGG 2011
2011/03/22–2011/03/26
美国拉斯维加斯 USA–Las Vegas

第30届南美秘鲁国际矿业机械设备展
2011/09 –
秘鲁阿雷基帕 Peru–Arequipa

悉尼亚太国际矿业展
AIMEX:
Asia Pacific's Intl Mining Exhibition
2011/09/06–2011/09/09
澳大利亚悉尼 Australia–Sydney

悉尼亚太国际矿业展
AIMEX: Asia Pacific's Intl Mining Exhibition
2014–
澳大利亚悉尼 Australia–Sydney

## 管道
## Pipline

国际管材展览会
2010/03/04–2010/03/07
土耳其伊斯坦布尔 Turkey–Istanbul

德国国际管材、线缆及线材展览会
Tube & Wire 2010
2010/04/12–2010/04/16
德国杜塞尔多夫 Germany–Dusseldorf

俄罗斯国际管材及线材展览会
Tube & Wire Russia 2010
2010/05 –
俄罗斯莫斯科 Russia–Moscow

国际管道展览会
2010/09/28–2010/09/30
加拿大卡尔加里 Canada–Calgary

## 光电
## Opto-Electronic

美国西部光电博览会
Photonics West
2010/01/26–2010/01/28
美国圣何塞 USA–San Jose

东京国际光伏发电展览会
PV EXPO 2010:
Intl Photovoltaic Power Generation Expo
2010/03/03–2010/03/05
日本东京 Japan–Tokyo

美国东部国际光学展
Intl Vision Expo East
2010/03/18–2010/03/21
美国纽约 USA–New York

中东国际眼镜眼科用品展览会
2010 Vision/X Dubai
2010/05/18–2010/05/20
阿联酋迪拜 United Arab Emirates–Dubai

德国国际光学展览会
Optatec
2010/06/15–2010/06/18
德国法兰克福 Germany–Frankfurt

日本光电博览会
INTEROPTO
2010/09 –
日本千叶 Japan

美国西部国际光学展
Intl Vision Expo West
2010/10/07–2010/10/09
美国拉斯维加斯 USA–Las Vegas

东京国际光伏发电展览会
PV EXPO 2010:
Intl Photovoltaic Power Generation Expo
2011/03 –
日本东京 Japan–Tokyo

美国东部国际光学展
Intl Vision Expo East
2011/03 –
美国纽约 USA–Las Vegas

## 广播、电影、电视设备
## Broadcasting, Film and Television

中东迪拜国际乐器、舞台灯光及舞台音响技术展
2010 PALME Middle East
2010/04/18–2010/04/20
阿联酋迪拜
United Arab Emirates–Dubai

第十五届国际数字多媒体与广播科技展览会及研讨会
2010/06/15–2010/06/18
新加坡 Singapore

亚洲电视论坛
Asia Television Forum (ATF)
2010/12 –
新加坡 Singapore

2011年中东迪拜国际乐器、舞台灯光及舞台音响技术展览会
2011 PALME Middle East
2011/04 –
阿联酋迪拜 United Arab Emirates–Dubai

柏林国际会展技术及媒体技术展览会
SHOWTECH –
Intl Trade Show & Conference for Event Technology & Services
2011/06/07–2011/06/09
德国柏林 Germany–Berlin

柏林国际会展技术及媒体技术展览会
SHOWTECH –
Intl Trade Show & Conference for Event Technology & Services
2013/06 –
德国柏林Germany–Berlin

## 广告
## Advertising

法国国际视觉广告技术及标识制作展
Viscom Paris:
The Intl Event for Visual Communication
2010 –
法国巴黎 France–Paris

## 焊接
## Welding

印度焊接展览会
2010/02/10–2010/02/12
印度孟买 India–Bombay

焊接展览会
2010/04/21–2010/04/24
日本东京 Japan–Tokyo

国际焊接展览会
2010/05/19–2010/05/21
俄罗斯圣彼得堡 Russia–St.Petersburg

国际制造技术与焊接展览会
2010/11/02–2010/11/04
美国亚特兰大 USA–Atlanta

## 化工
## Chemical Industry

巴西石油化工设备展
Quí mica & Petroquí mica:
Intl Trade Fair of Machinery & Equipment for the Chemical & Petrochemical Industry
2011 –
巴西圣保罗 Brazil–Sao Paulo

## 航空
## Aviation

迪拜机场设备展览会
Airport Show Dubai 2009
2010/04/25–2010/04/27
阿联酋迪拜 United Arab Emirates–Dubai

柏林/勃兰登堡国际航空航天展览会
ILA / Berlin Air Show
2010/06/08–2010/06/13
德国柏林 Germany–Berlin

迪拜机场设备展览会
Airport Show Dubai 2009
2011 –
阿联酋迪拜United Arab Emirates–Dubai

## 环境保护
## Environment Protection

柏林国际水利技术、污水处理展览会暨学术会议
Wasser Berlin
2010 –
德国柏林 Germany–Berlin

阿布扎比环保展
ENVIRONMENT 2010
2010/01/18–2010/01/21
阿联酋阿布扎比
United Arab Emirates–Abu Dhabi

国际节能环保和未来建筑展览会
2010/03/02–2010/03/04
英国伦敦 United Kingdom–London

国际水务与环境展览会
2010/03/02–2010/03/05
西班牙 Spain

2010美国波士顿国际环保建材展
2010/05/24–2010/05/26
美国波士顿 USA–Boston

2010年第五届越南国际环保技术展览会
Vietnam International Exhibition Fair Environmental Technology 2010
2010/05/27–2010/05/30
越南河内 Vietnam

国际环保技术展 亚洲水泵及阀门展 亚洲再生能源展
Entech Pollutec Asia Pumps & Valves Asia Renewable Energy Asia
2010/06/02–2010/06/05
泰国 Thailand

拉美国际环保及卫生展览会
AmbientalExpo:
Latin America Sanitation & Environmental Solutions Fair
2010/06/22–2010/06/24
巴西圣保罗 Brasil–Sao Paulo

慕尼黑国际环博会
IFAT
2010/09/13–2010/09/17
德国慕尼黑 Germany–Munich

法国里昂国际环保工业展览会
Pollutec/ Lyon
2010/12 –
法国里昂 France– Lyon

拉美国际环保及卫生展览会
AmbientalExpo:
Latin America Sanitation & Environmental Solutions Fair
2011 –
巴西圣保罗 Brazil–Sao Paulo

奥地利国际汽车生产设备及加油站设备、化学品及环境技术展
Auto Zum:
Intl Trade Fair for the Car & Vehicle Industry
2011/01 –
奥地利萨尔斯堡 Austria–Salzburg

阿布扎比环保展
ENVIRONMENT 2011
2011/01 –
阿联酋阿布扎比 United Arab Emirates–Abu Dhabi

国际废物处理博览会
ENTECO
2011/06/06–2011/06/09
德国科隆 Germany–Cologne

国际环保工业展
POLLUTEC
2011/12 –
法国巴黎 France–Paris

奥地利国际汽车生产设备及加油站设备、化学品及环境技术展
Auto Zum:
Intl Trade Fair for the Car & Vehicle Industry
2013/01 –
奥地利萨尔斯堡 Austria–Salzburg

## 机械、制造、工业装备、自动化
## Machinery, Machine Tools and Technology & Automation

中国工业产品展览会
2010 –
安哥拉 Angola

国际农业机械展览会
2010/02 –
西班牙 Spain–

中东国际工业自动化、动力传动及物流技术展览会
2010/02/09–2010/02/11
阿联酋迪拜 United Arab Emirates–Dubai

巴西国际工业机械和设备展览会
2010 Brazil Intl Industrial Machinery and Equipment Exhibition
2010/03/15–2010/03/18
巴西 Brazil

印度国际模具及机床展览会
7TH DIEMOULD INDIA 201
2010/03/18–2010/03/21
印度 India

第14届韩国国际机床展览会
The 14th Republic of Korea (Seoul) Intl Machine Tool Exhibition
2010/04/13–2010/04/18
韩国 Korea

FPD制造设备及技术国际展览会
FINETECH JAPAN
2010/04/14-2010/04/16
日本东京 Japan-Tokyo

第21届日本国际模具暨金属加工展览会
21th INTERMOLD 2010
2010/04/14-2010/04/17
日本大阪 Japan-Osaka

德国汉诺威工业博览会
HANNOVER MESSE 2010
2010/04/19-2010/04/23
德国汉诺威 Germany-Hannover

焊接展览会
2010/04/21-2010/04/24
日本东京 Japan-Tokyo

巴西国际机械展览会
Intl Machinery and Industrial Supplies Trade Fair 2010
2010/05 -
巴西圣保罗 Brazil-Sao Paulo

伊拉克重建国际工业展览会
2010/05 -
土耳其 Turkey

印度国际机械展览会
India Intl Machinery and Equipment Exhibition 2010
2010/05 -
印度孟买 India-Mumbai

国际工业配件展览会
2010/05 -
俄罗斯莫斯科 Russia-Moscow

俄罗斯国际机床工具展览会
METALLOOBRABOTKA 2010
2010/05 -
俄罗斯莫斯科 Russia-Moscow

澳大利亚机械制造周
National Manufacturing Week
2010/05 -
澳大利亚墨尔本 Australia-Melbourne

国际农业机械展览会
2010/05 -
阿尔及利亚阿尔及尔 Algeria-Algiers

国际流体传动与控制展览会
2010/05/04-2010/05/07
意大利米兰 Italy-Milan

2010 年澳大利亚国际机械制造周展览
AIEE
(Australia's Intl Engineering Exhibition)
with Natl Manufacturing Week
2010/05/11-2010/05/14
澳大利亚悉尼 Australia-Sydney

巴西国际机械及工业设备贸易博览会
2010/05/11-2010/05/15
巴西圣保罗 Brazil-Sao Paulo

泰国国际工业转包展 国际机械展/国际工业工具、测量、分析及监控科技展
Subson Thailand Automotive Engineering Asia Sheet Metal Asia
2010/05/13-2010/05/16
泰国 Thailand

越南国际模具展
InterMold Vietnam 2010:
Vietnam's Only Machinery and Technology Trade Exhibition & Conference for Mould & Die Manufacturing
2010/05/20-2010/05/22
越南河内 Vietnam-Hanoi

国际机床展览会
2010/05/24-2010/05/28
俄罗斯莫斯科 Russia-Moscow

中国机械和电子产品展览会
2010/05-
印尼雅加达 Indonesia-Jakarta

国际机械工业展览会
2010/05/27-2010/05/31
叙利亚大马士革 Syria-Damascus

第26届西班牙国际机床展览会
The 26th Intl Machine Tool Exhibition Spain
2010/05/31-2010/06/05
西班牙 Spain

第5届俄罗斯国际模具制造与技术展览会
5th Rosmould 2010
2010/06 -
俄罗斯莫斯科 Russia-Moscow

莫斯科国际工程机械展
CTT
2010/06 -
俄罗斯莫斯科 Russia-Moscow

国际工业配件展览会
2010/06 -
英国伯明翰 United Kingdom-Birmingham

日本(东京) 国际食品机械展览会
FOOMA
2010/06 -
日本东京 Japan-Tokyo

中国机械电子产品贸易展览会
2010/06 -
菲律宾马尼拉 Philippines-Manila

东京国际机械零部件、材料及技术展览会
M/Tech
2010/06 -
日本东京 Japan-Tokyo

国际自动化生产和装配展览会
2010/06 -
泰国曼谷 Thailand-Bangkok

英国制造技术博览会
MACH 2010
2010/06/07-2010/06/11
英国伯明翰 United Kingdom-Birmingham

国际动力传动与工业零部件展览会
2010/06/08-2010/06/10
英国伯明翰 United Kingdom-Birmingham

国际机械与创新技术展览会
2010/06/08-2010/06/11
波兰波兹南 Poland-Poznan

国际工业展业会
2010/06/08-2010/06/11
波兰波兹南 Poland-Poznan

波兰国际机床工具展览会
MACH/TOOL 2010
2010/06/15-2010/06/18
波兰波兹南 Poland-Poznan

东京机械零部件及材料技术展
M/Tech:
Mechanical Components & Materials Technology Expo
2010/06/23-2010/06/25
日本东京 Japan-Tokyo

泰国国际模具展
InterMold Thailand 2010
2010/06/24-2010/06/27
泰国曼谷 Thailand-Bangkok

泰国国际装配技术展
Assembly Technology 2010:
The Intl Automated Manufacturing & Assembly Technology Exhibition
2010/06/24-2010/06/27
泰国曼谷 Thailand-Bangkok

国际传动及电机展览会
2010/06/27-2010/06/29
美国奥兰多 USA-Orlando

第9届伊朗国际建材石材及工程机械矿业展
2010/07/05-2010/07/08
伊朗德黑兰 Iran-Tehran

亚洲国际机床展览会
AMTEX 2010
2010/07/23-2010/07/26
印度新德里 India-New Delhi

美国芝加哥国际机械制造周展览会
NMW
2010/09 -
美国芝加哥 USA-Chicago

国际工程机械及矿业机械展览会
2010/09 -
哈萨克斯坦 Kazakhstan

印度国际自动化设备暨机器人展览会
AUTOMATION 2010
2010/09 -
印度孟买 India-Mumbai

德国国际安装及操纵技术展览会
MOTEX 2010
2010/09 -
德国斯图加特 Germany-Stuttgart

国际印刷机械设备展览会
2010/09/08-2010/09/11
韩国 Korea

国际工业博览会
2010/09/13-2010/09/17
捷克布鲁诺 Czech-Brno

2010捷克国际劳保展/捷克国际工业展览会
2010/09/13-2010/09/17
捷克布鲁诺 Czech-Brno

2010捷克国际工业展
2010捷克国际机床工具展览会
2010/09/13-2010/09/17
捷克布鲁诺 Czech-Brno

美国国际制造技术（机床）展览会
IMTS 2010
2010/09/13-2010/09/18
美国芝加哥 USA-Chicago

美国芝加哥国际机床制造技术展览会
（IMTS 2010）
2010/09/13-2010/09/18
美国芝加哥 USA-Chicago

国际工业博览会
2010/10/06-2010/10/09
伊朗德黑兰 Iran-Teheran

越南国际机床及金属加工机械贸易展
METALEX Vietnam 2010:
Vietnam's Premier Intl Machine Tool Metalworking Technology Trade Exhibition and Conference - 4rd Edition
2010/10/07-2010/10/09
越南胡志明市 Vietnam-Ho Chi Minh City

第19届国际工业产品展览会
19th Vietnam Intl Industrial Fair
2010/10/19-2010/10/23
越南Vietnam

土耳其国际金属加工技术(机床)展览会
TATEF 2010
2010/10/12-2010/10/17
土耳其伊斯坦布尔 Turkey-Istanbul

国际工业配件展览会
2010/10/26-2010/10/29
巴西南卡希亚斯 Brazil-Caxias do Sul

日本国际机床展览会
JIMTOF 2010
2010/10/28-2010/11/02
日本东京 Japan-Tokyo

第五届伊拉克重建国际工业展览会
IRAQ INTL FAIR 2010
2010/11 -
伊拉克 Iraq

国际橡胶机械展览会
2010/11 -
伊朗德黑兰 Iran-Teheran

国际机床和金属加工技术展览会
2010/11 -
阿联酋迪拜
United Arab Emirates-Dubai

国际机床工具展览会
2010/11 -
埃及开罗 Egypt-Cairo

国际制造技术与焊接展览会
2010/11/02-2010/11/04
美国亚特兰大 USA-Atlanta

第40届法国巴黎国际工业配件展览会
2010/11/02-2010/11/05
法国巴黎 France-Paris

国际农业机械展览会
2010/11/12-2010/11/16
意大利博洛尼亚 Italy- Bologna

法国国际工业配件展
MIDEST
2010/11/17-2010/11/20
法国巴黎 France-Paris

泰国国际机床及金属加工机械贸易展
METALEX:
ASEAN's Largest Intl Machine Tool & Metalworking Technology Trade Exhibition & Conference
2010/11/24-2010/11/27
泰国曼谷 Thailand-Bangkok

国际工业装备展览会
Industrial Automation India 2010
2010/12 -
印度孟买 India- Bombay

欧洲模具及机床技术展览会
Euro Mold and Turntec 2010
2010/12 -
德国法兰克福 Germany-Frankfurt

国际工程及工业自动化展览会
2010/12 -
印尼孟买 Indonesia-Bombay

法国国际工业自动化展
SCS
2010/12 -
法国 France

印尼国际机床及金属加工技术展览会
2010/12 -
印尼雅加达 Indonesia-Jakarta

印尼国际机床及金属工具展览会
2010/12/03-2010/12/06
印尼雅加达 Indonesia-Jakarta

美国液压、气动、零部件展
IFPE
2011/03/22-2011/03/26
美国拉斯维加斯 USA-Las Vegas

FPD制造设备及技术国际展览会
FINETECH JAPAN
2011/04 -
日本东京 Japan-Tokyo

新加坡国际缝制设备展览会
Intl Apparel Machinery Trade Show
(JIAM 2011)
2011/05 -
新加坡 Singapore

越南国际模具展
InterMold Vietnam 2011:
Vietnam's Only Machinery and Technology Trade Exhibition & Conference for Mould & Die Manufacturing
2011/05 -
越南河内 Vietnam-Hanoi

澳大利亚机械制造周
National Manufacturing Week
2011/05 -
澳大利亚墨尔本 Australia-Melbourne

巴西机械工具展
Feimafe:
Intl Machine Tools and Integrated Manufacturing Systems Trade Fair
2011/05 -
巴西圣保罗 Brazil-Sao Paulo

越南国际自动化展览会
Automation / Vietnam
2011/05/11-2011/05/14
越南胡志明市 Vietnam-Ho Chi Minh City

东京机械零部件及材料技术展
M/Tech:
Mechanical Components & Materials Technology Expo
2011/06 -
日本东京 Japan-Tokyo

泰国国际模具展
InterMold Thailand 2010
2011/06 -
泰国曼谷 Thailand-Bangkok

泰国国际装配技术展
Assembly Technology 2011:
Intl Automated Manufacturing & Assembly Technology Exhibition
2011/06 -
泰国曼谷 Thailand-Bangkok

英国全套生产线暨加工及包装机械展
PPMA Show:
UK's annual showcase for Processing & Packaging Machinery
2011/09 -
英国伯明翰
United Kingdom-Birmingham

法国国际工业自动化展
SCS
2011/12 -
法国巴黎France-Paris

## 家具、木工机械
## Furniture, Woodworking

科隆国际家具展
imm cologne
2010/01/19-2010/01/24
德国科隆 Germany-Cologne

第16届墨西哥国际家具工业展
2010/01/20-2010/01/23
墨西哥 Mexico

春季美国拉斯维加斯国际家具展
2010/02/01-2010/02/05
美国拉斯维加斯 USA-Las Vegas

土耳其伊斯坦布尔国际家具展
IMOB 2010
2010/02/02-2010/02/06
土耳其伊斯坦布尔 Turkey-Istanbul

第10届澳大利亚悉尼国际家具展
AIFF 2010
2010/02/03-2010/02/05
澳大利亚悉尼 Australia-Sydney

第六届印度国际木工机械家具配件及工具专业展
2010/03/04-2010/03/08
印度 India

新加坡国际家具展
IFFS 2010
2010/03/09-2010/03/12
新加坡 Singapore

2011年中东（迪拜）国际木材及木工机械展览会
2011 Dubai Wood Show
2010/04 -
阿联酋迪拜 United Arab Emirates-Dubai

中东（迪拜）木材及木工机械展览会
Dubai Wood Show
2010/04/13-2010/04/15
阿联酋迪拜 United Arab Emirates-Dubai

意大利国际木工机械及技术展览会
XYLEXPO 2010
2010/05/04-2010/05/08
意大利米兰 Italy-Milan

莫斯科国际家具生产、木工及室内装饰展/俄罗斯春季家具展
interzum moscow 2010
EEM/EuroExpoFurniture 2010
2010/05/12-2010/05/15
俄罗斯莫斯科 Russia-Moscow

东京国际办公家具展览会
Intl Office Furniture Expo
2010/07/07-2010/07/09
日本东京 Japan-Tokyo

巴西圣保罗国际家具展
MOVINTER 2010
2010/07/27-2010/07/30
巴西圣保罗 Brazil-Sao Paulo

国际五金、DIY及家具展览会
2010/08 -
日本东京 Japan-Tokyo

南非约翰内斯堡家具家居及室内装饰展
Decorex 2010
2010/08/05-2010/08/09
南非约翰内斯堡
South Africa-Johannesburg

亚特兰大国际木工机械展览会
IWF
2010/08/25-2010/08/28
美国亚特兰大 USA-Atlanta

法国巴黎Maison & Objet 2010
2010/09/03-2010/09/07
法国巴黎 France-Paris

西伯利亚森林利用和木材加工展览会
Siberian wood industry
2010/09/14-2010/09/17
俄罗斯伊尔库茨克 Russia-Irkutsk

芝加哥休闲户外家具及用品展
Casual Outdoor Expo
2010/09/21-2010/09/24
美国芝加哥 USA-Chicago

圣保罗户外花园家具展
2010/09/23-2010/09/26
巴西圣保罗 Brazil-Sao Paulo

第47届瓦伦西亚国际家具展
2010/09/28-2010/10/02
西班牙瓦伦西亚 Spain-

新西伯利亚家具展
SIBFURNITURE 2010
2010/10/05-2010/10/08
俄罗斯 Russia

孟买国际家具展览会
INDEX MUBAI 2010
2010/10/08-2010/10/12
印度孟买 India-Mumbai

俄罗斯国际家具、配件及室内装潢展
MEBEL 2010
2010/11 -
俄罗斯 Russia

第20届中东迪拜国际家具展
INDEX 2010
2010/11/08-2010/11/11
阿联酋迪拜 United Arab Emirates-Dubai

中东迪拜国际家具和室内装饰博览会
2010 INDEX
2010/11/08-2010/11/11
阿联酋迪拜 United Arab Emirates-Dubai

东京国际家具展览会
IFFT / ILL 2010
2010/11/24-2010/11/26
日本东京 Japan-Tokyo

科隆国际家具展
imm cologne
2011/01/18-2011/01/23
德国科隆 Germany-Cologne

奥地利国际木材加工、处理、装配、木匠用品展
BWS: Intl Trade Fair for Woodworking
2011/04 -
奥地利萨尔茨堡 Austria-Salzburg

科隆国际家具生产、木工及室内装饰展
interzum cologne
2011/05/25-2011/05/28
德国科隆 Germany-Cologne

东京国际办公家具展览会
Intl Office Furniture Expo
2011/07 -
日本东京 Japan-Tokyo

第27届巴西国际家具工业贸易展览会
2011/08 -
巴西 Brazil

泰国国际木工机械、家具制造机械、零件及相关技术展
Furnitech Woodtech 2012
2012 -
泰国曼谷 Thailand-Bangkok

奥地利国际木材加工、处理、装配、木匠用品展
BWS: Intl Trade Fair for Woodworking
2013/04 -
奥地利萨尔茨堡 Austria-Salzburg

阿根廷国际建材五金及厨具、卫浴设备展
阿根廷布宜诺斯艾利斯 Argentina-Buenos Aires

# 建筑、建材、装饰及相关机械
# Building, Construction, Decoration and Materials

埃森国际建材展
DEUBAU
2010/01 -
德国埃森 Germany-Essen

拉斯维加斯建材展
Intl Builders' Show
2010/01/19-2010/01/22
美国拉斯维加斯 USA-Las Vegas

第19届波兰国际建筑建材展
2010/01/19-2010/01/22
波兰波兹南 Poland-Poznan

西班牙瓦伦西亚卫浴展
CEVISAMA
2010/02/09-2010/02/12
西班牙瓦伦西亚 Spain-Valencia cf

法国卫浴展
Ideo Bain: The Bathroom Exhibition
2010/02/09-2010/02/14
法国巴黎 France-Paris

第4届俄罗斯国际水泥、混凝土技术及装备展览会
2010/02/16-2010/02/19
俄罗斯莫斯科 Russia-Moscow

第8届俄罗斯国际建筑钢结构及金属材料设备展
2010/02/16-2010/02/19
俄罗斯莫斯科 Russia-Moscow

柏林国际建筑技术展览会
Bautec
2010/02/16-2010/02/20
德国柏林 Germany-Berlin

48届美国篱笆与护栏展
fencetech 2010
2010/02/17-2010/02/19
美国奥兰多 USA-Orlando

乌克兰国际玻璃及门窗专业展览会
2010/02/23-2010/02/26
乌克兰基辅 Ukraine-Kiev

国际节能环保和未来建筑展览会
2010/03/02-2010/03/04
英国伦敦 United Kingdom-London

2010中东门窗及幕墙博览会
6th Intl Trade Fair for Doors, Windows & Roofing
2010/03/08-2010/03/10
阿联酋沙迦 United Arab Emirates

第十一届伊斯坦布尔国际门窗博览会
11th Intl Window, Glass Technology, Accessory, Related Industry and Auxiliary Products Fair
2010/03/11-2010/03/14
土耳其 Turkey

土耳其门窗、玻璃技术及配件展
Istanbul Window
2010/03/11-2010/03/14
土耳其伊斯坦布尔 Turkey-Istanbul

第7届阿曼国际建筑建材展
2010/03/15-2010/03/17
阿曼马斯喀特 Oman-Muscat

博罗尼亚门窗及室内装修建材展
Saie Spring
2010/03/18-2010/03/21
意大利博洛尼亚 Italy-Bologna

伯明翰国际厨卫展
KBB
2010/03/21-2010/03/24
英国伯明翰 United Kingdom-Birmingham

第8届乌克兰国际建材展
2010/03/23-2010/03/27
乌克兰基辅 Ukraine-Kiev

米兰国际卫浴展
EXPOBAGNO
2010/03/23-2010/03/27
意大利米兰 Italy-Milan

2010德国纽伦堡门窗幕墙博览会
12th Intl Trade Fair Windows Doors and Facade
2010/03/24-2010/03/27
德国纽伦堡 Germany-Nuremberg

第5届越南（河内）国际建筑建材装饰博览会
Vietbuild 2010
2010/04/01-2010/04/04
越南 Vietnam

莫斯科国际建筑建材展
MOSBUILD
2010/04/06-2010/04/09
俄罗斯莫斯科 Russia-Moscow

巴西国际建材展
Feicon Batimat
Intl Construction Industry Trade Fair
2010/04/06-2010/04/10
巴西圣保罗 Brazil-Sao Paulo

第29届匈牙利国际建材展览会
2010/04/14-2010/04/18
匈牙利布达佩斯 Hungary-Budapest

芝加哥国际厨房浴室设备博览会
K/BIS
2010/04/16-2010/04/18
美国芝加哥 USA-Chicago

中东国际厨房、卫浴洁具博览会
ISH Kitchen & Bathroom Gulf
2010/05 -
阿联酋迪拜 United Arab Emirates-Dubai

罗马尼亚国际门窗玻璃博览会
CONSTRUCT EXPO
2010/05 -
罗马尼亚布加勒斯特
Romania-Bucharest

亚洲建筑及室内装饰展览会
BEX asia 2010
2010/05 -
新加坡 Singapore

西班牙马德里门窗幕墙博览会
12th Intl Window, Curtain Walls and Structural Glass Trade Show
2010/05/04-2010/05/07
西班牙马德里 Spain-Madrid

土耳其国际建筑建材展览会
2010/05/05-2010/05/09
土耳其伊斯坦布尔 Turkey-Istanbul

中东（迪拜）国际地面铺装展览会
2010 DOMOTEX Middle East
2010/05/10-2010/05/12
阿联酋迪拜 United Arab Emirates-Dubai

西伯利亚贝加尔建设周展览会
BAIKAL WEEK OF CONSTRUCTION TECHNOLOGIES
2010/05/12-2010/05/15
俄罗斯伊尔库茨克 Russia-Irkutsk

智利国际建筑建材展览会
2010/05/12-2010/05/15
智利圣地亚哥 Chile-Santiago

第16届叙利亚国际建筑建材展
2010/05/12-2010/05/16
叙利亚大马士革 Syria-Damascus

第7届利比亚国际建筑建材展
2010/05/16-2010/05/20
利比亚的黎波里 Libya-Tripoli

东非肯尼亚建筑机械及材料展览会
2010/05/18-2010/05/22
肯尼亚内罗毕 Kenya-

2010美国波士顿国际环保建材展
2010/05/24-2010/05/26
美国波士顿 USA-Boston

埃及建材及石材展览会
E.S.E & Inter Build
2010/06 -
埃及开罗 Egypt-Cairo

第15届黎巴嫩工程建材展会
15th Intl Trade Exhibition for Construction, Building Materials,
2010/06/01-2010/06/04
黎巴嫩 Lebanon

南美国际建筑工业展览会
BATIMAT EXPOVIVIENDA:
Intl Event for the Construction & Building Industry
2010/06/01-2010/06/05
阿根廷布宜诺斯艾利斯
Argentina-Buenos Aires

第5届越南国际汽车摩托车及零配件展览会
2010/06/09-2010/06/12
越南河内 Vietnam-Hanoi

国际建筑及工程机械展览会
2010/06/09-2010/06/13
土耳其伊斯坦布尔 Turkey-Istanbul

中国（越南）建筑机械及建材展览会
2010/06/15-2010/06/18
越南河内 Vietnam-Hanoi

南非建材展
Interbuild
2010/07 -
南非约翰内斯堡 South Africa-Johannesburg

第10届伊朗国际建筑建材展
2010/07 -
伊朗德黑兰 Iran-Tehran

第9届伊朗国际建材石材及工程机械矿业展
2010/07/05-2010/07/08
伊朗德黑兰 Iran-Tehran

第6届巴基斯坦国际建筑建材展
2010/07/27-2010/07/29
巴基斯坦卡拉奇 Pakistan-Karachi

国际制冷空调与建材展览会
2010/08 -
越南胡志明市 Vietnam-Ho Chi Minh City

第19届乌克兰国际建筑建材展
2010/09 -
乌克兰基辅 Ukraine-Kiev

圣彼得堡国际建筑建材展览会
Balticbuild
2010/09 -
俄罗斯圣彼得堡 Russia-St.Petersburg

越南国际建筑展览会
VICB 2010
Vietnam Intl Construction & Building Exhibition 2010
2010/09/08-2010/09/10
越南 Vietnam

第八届美国国际玻璃门窗展览会
8th The Glass Build, Window & Door Expo
2010/09/14-2010/09/16
美国拉斯维加斯 USA-Las Vegas

第13届越南（胡志明）国际建筑建材装饰博览会
Vietbuild 2010
2010/09/16-2010/09/20
越南胡志明市 Vietnam-Ho Chi Minh City

中东游泳池设备及SPA展览会
Middle East Pool & Spa Exhibition
2010/09/26-2010/09/28
阿联酋迪拜 United Arab Emirates-Dubai

第3届约旦国际建筑建材暨工程机械展
2010/09/27-2010/09/30
约旦安曼 Jordan-Rabbah

第7届安哥拉国际建筑建材博览会
2010/10 -
安哥拉卢安达 Angola-Rwanda

墨西哥建筑与制造业展
EXPO CIHAC
2010/10 -
墨西哥墨西哥城 Mexico-Mexico City

国际汽车工业及配件展览会
2010/10 -
土耳其伊斯坦布尔 Turkey-Istanbul

中国工业展览会
2010/10 -
伊朗德黑兰 Iran-Teheran

法国巴黎国际门窗展
2010/10 -
法国巴黎 France-Paris

土耳其国际建筑业博览会
BAUCON YAPEX
2010/10 -
土耳其 Turkey

伯明翰国际建材展
Interbuild
2010/10 -
英国伯明翰
United Kingdom-Birmingham

国际工程机械及建筑材料展览会
2010/10 -
安哥拉卢安达 Angola-Rwanda

博罗尼亚国际建筑业博览会
Saie
2010/10 -
意大利博洛尼亚 Italy-Bologna

国际工程机械与建筑机械展览会
2010/10 -
阿根廷布宜诺斯艾利斯
Argentina-Buenos Aires

第四届日本东京国际花园及景观博览会
Gardex 2010
2010/10 -
日本千叶 Japan-Makuhari Messe

第22届沙特国际建筑及石材贸易博览会
2010/10/03-2010/10/06
沙特阿拉伯利雅得
Saudi Arabia-Riyadh

国际建筑机械、工程机械及建筑材料展览会
2010/10/21-2010/10/25
苏丹喀土穆 Sudan-

第7届工程机械展览会
2010/11 -
印度班加罗尔 India-Bangalore

第20届菲律宾国际建筑建材展
2010/11 -
菲律宾马尼拉 Philippines-Manila

第8届阿尔及利亚国际建筑工程展览会
（SITP）
2010/11 -
阿尔及利亚阿尔及尔 Algeria-Algiers

国际工程机械及施工设备展览会
2010/11 -
阿尔及利亚阿尔及尔 Algeria-Algiers

法国国际建筑门窗展：汇聚国际领先的门窗、防护和遮阳设备
Intl Windows, Doors, Shutters & Solar Protection Exhibition
2010/11/16-2010/11/19
法国巴黎 France-Paris

南非国际建筑建材博览会
2010/9/8-2010/9/11
南非约翰内斯堡 South Africa-Johannesburg

巴西国际建材展
Feicon Batimat
Intl Construction Industry Trade Fair
2011 -
巴西圣保罗 Brazil-Sao Paulo

2011年中东（迪拜）国际地面铺装展览会
2011 DOMOTEX Middle East
2011/05 -
阿联酋迪拜 United Arab Emirates-Dubai

南美国际建筑工业展览会
BATIMAT EXPOVIVIENDA:
Intl Event for the Construction & Building Industry
2011/06 -
阿根廷布宜诺斯艾利斯 Argentina-Buenos Aires

巴黎国际建材及设备展
BATIMAT: Intl Building Exhibition
2011/11 -
法国巴黎 France-Paris

米兰国际卫浴展
EXPOBAGNO
2012/03 -
意大利米兰 Italy-Milan

法国国际建筑门窗展：汇聚国际领先的门窗、防护和遮阳设备
Intl Windows, Doors, Shutters & Solar Protection Exhibition
2012/11 -
法国巴黎 France-Paris

## 交通、运输、物流、铁路
## Transportation, Logistics

沥青大世界
World of Asphalt 2010
2010/02/15-2010/02/18
美国辛辛那提 USA-Cincinnati

欧洲国际运输及物流周
SITL Europe:
Intl Event for Transport & Logistics
2010/03/23-2010/03/26
法国巴黎 France-Paris

国际物料搬运及物流展览会
2010/04/26-2010/04/29
美国克里夫兰 USA-Cleveland

国际物流技术与运输系统展览会
2010/04/27-2010/04/30
俄罗斯莫斯科 Russia-Moscow

俄罗斯莫斯科国际交通与物流展览会
Trans Russia 2010
2010/04/27-2010/04/30
俄罗斯莫斯科 Russia-Moscow

国际建筑机械与施工车辆展览会、国际公路建设展览会及国际基础设备展览会
2010/05/11-2010/05/14
波兰 Poland

美国智能交通展览会
ITS America's 2010 Exposition
2010/06/01-2010/06/03
美国 USA

国际运输及物流展览会
2010/06/01-2010/06/04
阿塞拜疆 Azerbaijan

美国国际物流技术展览会
MATTECH 2010
2010/08/05-2010/08/06
美国迈阿密 USA-Miami

美国国际桥梁、隧道与公路展览会
Annual meeting & Exhibition 2010
2010/09 -
美国芝加哥 USA-Chicago

德国柏林国际铁路、机车、车辆展览会
2010/09/21-2010/09/24
德国柏林 Germany-Berlin

国际交通运输工具展览会
2010/11 -
墨西哥瓜达拉哈拉 Mexico-Guadalajara

巴黎国际实时运输及物流展
SITL Real Time:
Intl Show for Logistics Solutions
2011/03 -
法国巴黎 France-Paris

欧洲国际运输及物流周
SITL Europe:
Intl Event for Transport & Logistics
2012/03 -
法国巴黎 France-Paris

巴黎国际实时运输及物流展
SITL Real Time: Intl Show for Logistics Solutions
2013/03 -
法国巴黎 France-Paris

## 教育
## Education

科隆教育与培训展览会
Didacta
2010/03/16-2010/03/20
德国科隆 Germany-Cologne

## 金属加工、冶金、铸造锻造
## Metalworking, Metallurgy and Foundry

第5届沙迦金属加工展览会
2010/01/11-2010/01/14
阿联酋沙迦 United Arab Emirates

欧洲国际压铸展览会
EUROGUSS 2010
2010/01/19-2010/01/21
德国纽伦堡 Germany-Nuremberg

国际铸造展览会
2010/02/05-2010/02/07
印度艾哈迈德巴德 India

第8届俄罗斯国际建筑钢结构及金属材料设备展
2010/02/16-2010/02/19
俄罗斯莫斯科 Russia-Moscow

国际铸造展览会
2010/04 -
意大利布雷西亚 Italy

第21届日本国际模具暨金属加工展览会
21th INTERMOLD 2010
2010/04/14-2010/04/17
日本大阪 Japan-Osaka

马来西亚国际精密工程机床金属工业设备展
2010/05/07-2010/05/09
马来西亚吉隆坡 Malaysia-Kuala Lumpur

越南国际金属加工设备及技术展览会
Metaltech / Vietnam
2010/05/11-2010/05/14
越南胡志明市 Vietnam-Ho Chi Minh City

第5届俄罗斯国际模具制造与技术展览会
5th Rosmould 2010
2010/06 -
俄罗斯莫斯科 Russia-Moscow

越南国际精密工程机械金属工业设备展
2010/07/07-2010/07/09
越南胡志明市 Vietnam-Ho Chi Minh City

德国国际金属加工设备及技术展览会
AMB 2010
2010/09 -
德国斯图加特 Germany-Stuttgart

越南国际精密工程机床金属工业设备展
2010/09 -
越南河内 Vietnam-Hanoi

美国芝加哥国际机床制造技术展览会
（IMTS 2010）
2010/09/13-2010/09/18
美国芝加哥 USA-Chicago

2010国际金属板材加工技术展览会
21st European Intl Sheet Metal Processing Technology Exhibition
2010/10/26-2010/10/30
德国汉诺威 Germany-Hannover

国际机床及金属加工机械展览会
2010/11 -
泰国曼谷 Thailand-Bangkok

俄罗斯国际冶金展览会
Metallurgy 2010
2010/11 -
俄罗斯莫斯科 Russia-Moscow

泰国国际机床及金属加工机械贸易展
METALEX:
ASEAN's Largest Intl Machine Tool & Metalworking Technology Trade Exhibition & Conference
2010/11/24-2010/11/27
泰国曼谷 Thailand-Bangkok

印尼国际机床及金属工具展览会
2010/12/03-2010/12/06
印尼雅加达 Indonesia-Jakarta

## 酒店业
## Hotel and Restaurant

英国酒店设备展
Hotelympia
2010/02/28-2010/03/04
英国伦敦 United Kingdom-London

西班牙巴塞罗那国际餐馆用品博览会
Restaurama
2010/03/10-2010/03/14
西班牙 Spain

日本美食佳酿暨酒店及餐饮设备展
Wine & Gourmet Japan 2009
2010/04/07-2010/04/09
日本东京 Japan-Tokyo

第十七届新加坡食品酒店站
2010/04/20-2010/04/23
新加坡 Singapore

芝加哥国际餐饮、酒店用品博览会
NRA Restaurant Hotel - Motel Show
2010/05/16-2010/05/19
美国 USA

美国芝加哥国际酒店用品及餐饮展会
The NRA Show 2010
2010/05/22-2010/05/25
美国芝加哥 USA-Chicago

第十八届泰国国际食品、酒店展览会
2010/09 -
泰国 Thailand

圣保罗酒店用品及餐饮设备博览会
Equipotel
2010/09 -
巴西 Brazil

第30届埃及国际酒店食品及相关设备展
2010/10/24-2010/10/27
埃及开罗 Egypt-Cairo

纽约国际餐饮及酒店用品博览会
The Intl Hotel/motel & Restaurant Show
2010/11 -
美国 USA

第十五届西班牙巴塞罗那国际餐厅、酒店及相关用品展
Hostelco 2010
2010/11/05-2010/11/09
西班牙巴塞罗那 Spain

法国国际酒店及餐饮设备展
Equip' Hotel:
The World Class Event for the Restaurant, Hotel, Cafes & Catering Industries
2010/11/14-2010/11/18
法国巴黎 France-Pairs

法国巴黎国际餐饮、酒店设备展览会
Equip Hotel
2010/11/15-2010/11/19
法国巴黎 France-Pairs

英国酒店用品展
Hospitality
2011/01/24-2011/01/26
英国伯明翰 United Kingdom-Birmingham

日本美食佳酿暨酒店及餐饮设备展
Wine & Gourmet Japan 2009
2011/04 -
日本东京 Japan-Tokyo

英国酒店设备展
Hotelympia
2012/02 -
英国伦敦 United Kingdom-London

法国国际酒店及餐饮设备展
Equip' Hotel:
The World Class Event for the Restaurant, Hotel, Cafes & Catering Industries
2012/11 -
法国巴黎 France-Paris

英国酒店用品展
Hospitality
2013/01 -
英国伯明翰 United Kingdom-Birmingham

## 空调、制冷、供暖 Air-conditioning, Heating, Refrigeration, Ventilation

美国国际空调、制冷和供热展览会
AHR 2010
2010/01/25-2010/01/27
美国奥兰多 USA-Orlando

第14届莫斯科国际供暖、卫浴、通风及空调和环保展览会
aqua/therm Moscow:
14th Intl Exhibition for Heating, Ventilation, Air/Conditioning, Water Supply, Sanitary Equipment, Environmental Technology & Pools
2010/02/02-2010/02/05
俄罗斯莫斯科 Russia-Moscow

巴黎国际供暖、制冷、空调、新能源及家用电气展
Interclima+elec Home&building
2010/02/09-2010/02/12
法国巴黎 France-Paris

国际供暖、通风、空调与制冷展览会
2010/02/16-2010/02/19
日本东京 Japan-Tokyo

乌克兰国际空调、暖通及工业制冷贸易博览会
Cool Clima Kiev
2010/03 -
乌克兰基辅 Ukraine-Kiev

意大利米兰供暖、空调、制冷、再生能源及太阳能展
Mostra Convegno Expocomfort : Production & Distribution line for the HVAC & Plumbing Sector
2010/03/23-2010/03/27
意大利米兰 Italy-Milan

米兰国际供暖、空调、制冷及卫生洁具博览会
MCE
2010/03/23-2010/03/27
意大利米兰 Italy-Milan

供热、制冷、通风、水处理及卫生洁具展览会
2010/04/20-2010/04/23
俄罗斯莫斯科 Russia-Moscow

国际供热、壁炉、空调及制冷博览会
2010/04/26-2010/04/29
波兰波兹南 Poland-Poznan Poznan

国际供暖、制冷、空调及卫浴展览会
2010/05/05-2010/05/08
土耳其伊斯坦布尔 Turkey-Istanbul

国际供暖、卫浴与空调展览会
2010/05/12-2010/05/15
乌克兰基普 Ukraine- Kiev

国际制冷、通风及空调展览
2010/06/17-2010/06/20
马来西亚吉隆坡 Malaysia-Kuala Lumpur

国际制冷空调与建材展览会
2010/08 -
越南胡志明市 Vietnam-Ho Chi Minh City

RAHV 2010
越南国际制冷、空调、供暖、通风系统展览会
2010/09/08-2010/09/10
越南西贡 Vietnam

国际供暖、制冷、空调与通风展览会
2010/10 -
伊朗德黑兰 Iran-Teheran

国际制冷、空调与通风展览会
2010/10/13-2010/10/15
德国纽伦堡 Germany-Nuremberg

国际供暖、制冷与空调展览会
2010/10/26-2010/10/28
墨西哥墨西哥城 Mexico-Mexico City

巴西国际制冷、空调、通风、供暖和空气处理贸易展
Febrava:
Intl Refrigeration, Air/conditioning, Ventilation, Heating and Air Treatment Trade Fair
2011 -
巴西圣保罗 Brazil-Sao Paulo

第15届莫斯科国际供暖、卫浴、通风及空调和环保展览会
aqua/therm Moscow:
15th Intl Exhibition for Heating, Ventilation, Air/Conditioning, Water Supply, Sanitary Equipment, Environmental Technology & Pools
2011/02 -
俄罗斯莫斯科 Russia-Moscow

巴黎国际供暖、制冷、空调、新能源及家用电气展
Interclima+elec Home&building
2012/02 -
法国巴黎 France-Paris

意大利米兰供暖、空调、制冷、再生能源及太阳能展
Mostra Convegno Expocomfort:
Production & Distribution line for the HVAC & Plumbing Sector
2012/03 -
意大利米兰 Italy-Milan

## 矿业 Mining

第4届土耳其国际矿业展览会
2010-
土耳其伊斯坦布尔 Turkey-Istanbul

2010第十届智利国际矿业及工程机械展览会
EXPOMIN 2010
2010/04/12-2010/04/16
智利圣地亚哥 Chile-Santiago

俄罗斯国际矿业展览会
2010/04/14-2010/04/16
俄罗斯 Russia

27届加拿大国际矿山设备展暨加拿大国际矿业年会
CIM
2010/05/09-2010/05/12
加拿大多伦多 Canada-Toronto

伊朗国际工程机械、建材机械及矿山机械展览会
Iran Conmin 2010
2010/06 -
伊朗德黑兰 Iran-Tehran

第十七届俄罗斯国际采矿技术及煤矿设备展览会
UGOL ROSSII & MINING 2010
2010/06/04-2010/06/07
俄罗斯新库兹涅茨克市 Russia

澳大利亚昆士兰采矿机械展
Queensland Mining & Engineering Exhibition (QME)
2010/07/27-2010/07/29
澳大利亚 Australia

南非国际矿山与电力博览会
Electra Mining Africa 2010
2010/10/04-2010/10/08
南非约翰内斯堡 South Africa-Johannesburg

第30届南美秘鲁国际矿业机械设备展
2011/09 -
秘鲁阿雷基帕 Peru-Arequipa

悉尼亚太国际矿业展
AIMEX:
Asia Pacific's Intl Mining Exhibition
2011/09/06-2011/09/09
澳大利亚悉尼 Australia-Sydney

澳大利亚昆士兰采矿机械展
Queensland Mining & Engineering Exhibition (QME)
2012/07 -
澳大利亚 Australia

悉尼亚太国际矿业展
AIMEX: Asia Pacific' s Intl Mining Exhibition
2014 -
澳大利亚悉尼 Australia-Sydney

## 乐器 Music Instrument

法兰克福国际乐器展；法兰克福国际舞台灯光及音响展
Musikmesse, ProLight + Sound
2010/03/24-2010/03/27
德国法兰克福 Germany-Frankfurt

中东迪拜国际乐器、舞台灯光及舞台音响技术展览会
2010 PALME Middle East
2010/04/18-2010/04/20
阿联酋迪拜 United Arab Emirates-Dubai

巴西国际乐器音响展
EXPOMUSIC
2010/09 -
巴西圣保罗 Brazil-Sao Paulo

莫斯科国际乐器展
MUSIC MOSCOW
2010/09 -
俄罗斯莫斯科 Russia-Moscow

英国国际舞台灯光音响技术展
THE PLASA SHOW
2010/09 -
英国伦敦 United Kingdom-London

2011年中东迪拜国际乐器、舞台灯光及舞台音响技术展览会
2011 PALME Middle East
2011/04 -
阿联酋迪拜 United Arab Emirates-Dubai

## 礼品 Gifts

迪拜国际消费品、礼品贸易博览会（IATF）
2010/01/17-2010/01/19
阿联酋迪拜 United Arab Emirates-Dubai

法兰克福国际圣诞礼品博览会
ChristmasWorld
2010/01/29-2010/02/02
德国 Germany

2010日本东京春季国际礼品博览会
2010/02/02-2010/02/05
日本东京 Japan-Tokyo

伯明翰春季国际博览会
Spring Fair Birmingham
2010/02/07-2010/02/11
英国伯明翰 United Kingdom-Birmingham

巴西国际圣诞节日装饰品及玩具博览会
Toys, Parties & Christmas Fair South America
2010/05 -
巴西 Brazil

东京国际礼品展览会
Intl Variety/Gift Expo Tokyo (GIFTEX)
2010/07/07-2010/07/09
日本东京 Japan-Tokyo

巴西国际家庭用品及礼品博览会
House & Gift Fair South America
2010/08 -
巴西 Brazil

巴西圣保罗国际家庭用品及礼品博览会
2010/08/14-2010/08/17
巴西圣保罗 Brazil-Sao Paulo

东京国际礼品博览会（秋季）
TIGS
2010/09 -
日本东京 Japan-Tokyo

东京国际礼品展览会
Intl Variety/Gift Expo Tokyo
(GIFTEX)
2011/07 -
日本东京 Japan-Tokyo

## 零售业 Retail

巴黎国际特许经营展览会
Franchise Expo Paris:
Intl Franchise Show
2010/03/14-2010/03/17
法国巴黎 France-Paris

客户服务中心/客户关系管理展览会及会议大阪展
Call Centre/ CRM Demo & Conference Osaka 2010
2010/05/26-2010/05/27
日本 Japan-Tokyo

数码营销博览会
dmexco
2010/09/15-2010/09/16
德国科隆 Germany-Cologne

日本大型连锁零售企业贴标（OEM）采购展
PRIVATE LABEL SUPPLIERS SHOW
2010/11 -
日本东京 Japan-Tokyo

巴黎国际特许经营展览会
Franchise Expo Paris:
Intl Franchise Show
2011/03 -
法国巴黎 France-Paris

数码营销博览会
dmexco
2011/09 -
德国科隆 Germany-Cologne

## 旅游 Tourism

柏林国际旅游展览会
ITB Berlin
2010/03/10-2010/03/14
德国柏林 Germany-Berlin

德国菲德里斯哈芬户外休闲运动博览会
2010 European Outdoor Trade Fair
2010/07/15-2010/07/18
德国菲德烈斯哈芬 Germany

巴西圣保罗户外探险及生态旅游博览会
Adventure Sports Fair
2010/09 -
巴西圣保罗 Brazil-Sao Paulo

## 铝业 Aluminums Industry

印度国际铝展
Aluminium India 2010
2010/02/25-2010/02/27
印度孟买 India-Mumbai

巴西国际铝工业展
The ALUMINIUM Intl Pavilion
2010/05/18-2010/05/20
巴西圣保罗 Brazil-Sao Paulo

德国埃森国际铝工业展览会
第八届世界铝工业博览会暨学术会议
ALUMINIUM 2010
2010/09/14-2010/09/16
德国埃森 Germany-Essen

2011年迪拜中东国际铝工业展览会
ALUMINIUM Dubai 2011
2011/04/12-2011/04/14
阿联酋迪拜
United Arab Emirates-Dubai

2012年印度国际铝展
Aluminium India 2012
2012 -
印度孟买 India-Mumbai

2012德国埃森国际铝工业展览会
第八届世界铝工业博览会暨学术会议
ALUMINIUM 2012
2012/09 -
德国埃森 Germany-Essen

2013年迪拜中东国际铝工业展览会
ALUMINIUM Dubai 2013
2013 -
阿联酋迪拜国
United Arab Emirates-Dubai

## 媒体 Media

国际会展及媒体技术展览会
Showtech
2010 -
德国柏林 Germany-Berlin

法国国际视觉广告技术及标识制作展
Viscom Paris:
The Intl Event for Visual Communication
2010 -
法国巴黎 France-Paris

德国国际视觉广告技术与标识制作展
Viscom Frankfurt 2010:
Intl Trade Fair for Visual Communication
2010/10 -
德国法兰克福 Germany- Frankfurt

西班牙标识视觉传播及图像设计行业展
Viscom/Sign Espana
2010/10 -
西班牙马德里 Spain-Madrid

意大利国际视觉传播展
Viscom Visual Communication Italy:
The Intl Trade Fair on Visual Communication & Events Services
2010/11 -
意大利米兰 Italy-Milano

德国国际视觉广告技术与标识制作展
Viscom Frankfurt 2012:
Intl Trade Fair for Visual Communication
2012 -
德国法兰克福 Germany-Frankfurt

## 美容美发、化妆品 Beauty, Cosmetics and Hairdressing

泰国国际化妆品原料展
in/cosmetics Asia
The leading Exhibition & Conference for Personal Care Ingredients in Asia
2010 -
泰国曼谷 Thailand-Bangkok

悉尼国际SPA及美容展览会
Sydney Intl Spa & Beauty Expo
2010 -
澳大利亚悉尼 Australia-Sydney

法兰克福国际美容美发及流行饰品博览会
BeautyWorld
2010/01/30-2010/02/02
德国 Germany

中东（阿布扎比）国际美容美发博览会
2010 Beauty Vision
2010/02/02-2010/02/04
阿联酋阿布扎比 United Arab Emirates-Abu Dhabi

欧洲化妆品原料展
in/cosmetics:
The Leading Global Platform for Personal Care Ingredients
2010/04/13-2010/04/15
德国慕尼黑 Germany-Munich

中东（迪拜）国际美容美发用品展览会
2010 Beautyworld Middle East

2010/06/01-2010/06/03
阿联酋迪拜 United Arab Emirates-Dubai

巴西国际美容展览会
Cosmetica:
Intl Beauty Trade Fair
2010/09 -
巴西圣保罗 Brazil-Sao Paulo

法国巴黎国际美容展览会
Beyond Beauty Paris
2010/09/12-2010/09/15
法国巴黎 France-Paris

俄罗斯国际化妆品、美容博览会
InterCHARM:
The Largest Perfumery & Cosmetics Exhibition in Russia, Eastern & Central Europe
2010/10 -
俄罗斯莫斯科 Russia-Moscow

中东（阿布扎比）国际美容美发博览会
2011 Beauty Vision
2011/02 -
阿联酋阿布扎比
United Arab Emirates-Abu Dhabi

欧洲化妆品原料展
in/cosmetics:
The Leading Global Platform for Personal Care Ingredients
2011/04 -
德国慕尼黑 Germany-Munich

中东（迪拜）国际美容美发用品展览会
2011 Beautyworld Middle East
2011/06 -
阿联酋迪拜 United Arab Emirates-Dubai

## 能源、节能
## Energy and Energy-Saving

第12届新西兰国际电力能源行业展示会及高层战略论谈
12th Power &Electricity World New Zealand
2010/02/15-2010/02/18
新西兰 New Zealand

西澳大利亚国际电力能源行业展示会及高层战略商务论谈
Power &Electricity West Australia
2010/03/02-2010/03/04
澳大利亚柏斯 Australia-

国际石油、天然气与能源展览会
2010/05 -
巴基斯坦卡拉奇 Pakistan-Karachi

第13届巴西国际电力、能源及电子展览会
2010/06/29-2010/07/01
巴西圣保罗 Brazil-Sao Paulo

中东（阿布扎比）国际电力及水能展览会
2010 Power Generation & Water Middle East
2010/10/17-2010/10/19
阿联酋阿布扎比
United Arab Emirates-Abu Dhabi

第9届中东国际电力、能源、水力展览会
Power/Gen Middle East
2010/11/01-2010/11/03
卡塔尔 Qatar

## 农业、林业、畜牧业、渔业、花卉
## Agriculture, Fishery, Floriculture, Forestry

国际农业机械展览会
2010/01/12-2010/01/15
美国奥兰多 USA-Orlando

美国AG CONNECT农机展
AG CONNECT 2010
2010/01/13-2010/01/15
美国奥兰多 USA-Orlando

国际果蔬展览会
Fruit Logistica
2010/02/03-2010/02/05
德国柏林 Germany-Berlin

欧洲国际水产品展览会
EUROPEAN SEAFOOD EXPO
2010/04/27-2010/04/29
比利时 Belgium

国际农业机械展览会
2010/05 - 2010/05/
阿尔及利亚阿尔及尔
Algeria-Algiers

2010俄罗斯金秋农业展览会
Golden Autumn 2010
2010/10/08-2010/10/11
俄罗斯莫斯科 Russia-Moscow

2010 越南国际农业博览会
Vietnam Intl Agriculture Fair
2010/11/12-2010/11/15
越南河内 Vietnam

法国国际农牧业设备及技术展览会
SIMA
2011/02/20-2011/02/24
法国巴黎 France-Paris

## 汽车、摩托车
## Automobiles, Motorcycles

印度国际汽车摩托车零配件展览会
The 10th Auto Expo India 2010
2010/01/05-2010/01/11
印度新德里 India-New Delhi

维也纳国际汽车展
Vienna Auto Show
2010/01/14-2010/01/17
奥地利维也纳 Austria-Vienna

日本汽车电子展
Intl Automotive Electronics Technology Expo
(CAR/ELE JAPAN)
2010/01/20-2010/01/22
日本东京 Japan-Tokyo

法兰克福（罗马）国际汽车配件及售后服务展览会
Automechanika Roma
2010/02/11-2010/02/14
意大利罗马 Italy- Roma

国际摩托车展览会
2010/02/12-2010/02/15
美国印第安纳波利斯 USA-Indianapolis

俄罗斯圣彼得堡国际两轮车展
Velo/Expo
2010/03 -
俄罗斯圣彼得堡 Russia-St.Petersburg

中东迪拜国际两轮车展
GULF BIKE EXPO
2010/03 -
阿联酋迪拜 United Arab Emirates-Dubai

国际重卡及专用车辆展览会
2010/03/02-2010/03/06
法国里昂 France-Lyon

法兰克福国际汽车配件展览会
2010/03/03-2010/03/05
俄罗斯莫斯科 Russia-Moscow

中东（迪拜）国际商用车展览会
2010 Commercial Vehicles Middle East
2010/03/09-2010/03/11
阿联酋迪拜 United Arab Emirates-Dubai

国际汽车配件、售后服务及设备展览会
2010/03/10-2010/03/12
俄罗斯莫斯科 Russia-Moscow

国际汽车售后市场展览会
2010/03/11-2010/03/13
日本东京 Japan-Tokyo

国际摩托车展览会
2010/03/11-2010/03/14
乌克兰基普 Ukraine-Kiev

日本国际汽车售后市场展览会
IAAE 2010
2010/03/18-2010/03/20
日本东京 Japan-Tokyo

国际汽车展览会
2010/03/18-2010/03/20
孟加拉 Bengal

美国中部卡车展览会
MID/AMERICA TRUCKING SHOW
2010/03/25-2010/03/27
美国路易斯维尔 USA-Louisville

国际商用车展览会
2010/04 -
俄罗斯莫斯科 Russia-Moscow

国际卡车展览会
2010/04 -
加拿大多伦多 Canada-Toronto

第七届阿塞拜疆国际汽车及零配件展览会
Auto Show Azerbaijan 2010
2010/04/01-2010/04/04
阿塞拜疆巴库 Azerbaijan

第七届俄罗斯国际摩托车及零配件展览会
Intl Specialized Exhibition of Motorcycles, Scooters and Service
2010/04/08-2010/04/11
俄罗斯莫斯科 Russia-Moscow

汽车工程学会世界大会及汽车零配件展览会/SAE底特律汽配展
2010 SAE
2010/04/12-2010/04/15
美国底特律 USA-

阿尔及利亚汽配展
EQUIP' AUTO Algérie
2010/04/19-2010/04/22
阿尔及利亚 Algeria

巴西国际重型及商务汽车零配件展
AUTOMEC Pesados & Comercias 2010
2010/04/27-2010/05/01
巴西圣保罗 Brazil-Sao Paulo

波兰国际建筑设备和特殊交通车辆展览会
Intl Construction Equipment and Special Vehicles Fair
2010/05 –
波兰Poland

2010印度尼西亚国际汽车、摩托车及零配件展
INDOAUTOMOTIVE 2010
2010/05/05–2010/05/08
印度尼西亚 Indonesia

中东（迪拜）国际汽车配件及售后服务展览会
Automechanika Middle East
2010/05/25–2010/05/27
阿联酋迪拜 United Arab Emirates–Dubai

国际汽车配件展览会
2010/06 –
新加坡 Singapore

第15届北非汽车、摩托车及零配件展览会
Automech
2010/06 –
埃及开罗 Egypt–Cairo

德国埃森国际轮胎展览会
（德国雷芬展）
2010/06/01–2010/06/04
德国埃森 Germany–Essen

捷克国际汽车及零配件博览会
Intl Fair of Utility Vehicles, Parts and Garage Equipment
2010/06/05–2010/06/10
捷克 Czech

第5届越南国际汽车摩托车零配件展览会
2010越南国际汽车用品展览会
2010越南国际交通及配套产业展
5th Vietnam Intl Automobile Motorcycle Parts & Accessories Exhibition
2010/06/09–2010/06/12
越南 Vietnam

第五届巴西库里提巴国际汽车配件展览会
2010/06/09–2010/06/12
巴西 Brazil

泰国国际汽车生产制造展览会
Automotive Manufacturing 2010
ASEAN's Only Machinery Expo for Automotive Parts Manufacturing
2010/06/24–2010/06/27
泰国曼谷 Thailand–Bangkok

泰国汽车电子展
Automotive Electronics 2010:
ASEAN's Only Machinery Expo for Automotive Electronics Parts and Components Manufacturing / Co-located with Automotive Manufacturing 2010
2010/06/24–2010/06/27
泰国曼谷 Thailand–Bangkok

国际汽车展览会
2010/07 –
印尼雅加达 Indonesia–Jakarta

国际摩托车展览会
2010/07 –
墨西哥墨西哥城 Mexico–Mexico City

国际汽车零部件展览会
2010/07/01–2010/07/07
叙利亚大马士革 Syria–Damascus

中美洲国际汽车零部件、原料加工及售后服务贸易展览会
PAACE Automechanika Mexico
2010/07/14–2010/07/16
墨西哥墨西哥城 Mexico– Mexico City

第14届俄罗斯国际汽车及配件博览会
Moscow Intl Motor Show (UFI)
2010/08/26–2010/08/31
俄罗斯莫斯科 Russia–Moscow

德国国际汽车修理、加油设备及零部件博览会
Automechanika 2010
2010/09 –
德国法兰克福 Germany–Frankfurt

法国巴黎国际两轮车展
PARIS INTL TWO WHEEL SHOW
2010/09 –
法国巴黎 France–Paris

越南国际汽车及零配件展览会
2010/09 –
越南胡志明市 Vietnam–Ho Chi Minh City

韩国汽车零配件展览会
KOAA Show 2010
2010/09 –
韩国高阳 Korea–

国际商用车展览会
2010/09 –
乌克兰基普 Ukraine–Kiev

2010 年法兰克福国际汽车零配件及售后服务展
Automechanika:
Intl Trade Fair for the Automobile Aftermarket And Original Equipment Market
2010/09/14–2010/09/19
德国法兰克福 Germany– Frankfurt

交通、车辆、组件/革新产品展览会
InnoTrans
2010/09/21–2010/09/24
德国柏林 Germany–Berlin

德国汉诺威商用车及配件博览会
IAA 2010
2010/09/23–2010/09/30
德国汉诺威 Germany–Hannover

巴黎国际两轮车展
MONDIAL DU DEUX ROUES
2010/10 –
法国巴黎 France–Paris

第7届尼日利亚拉各斯国际汽车展览会
Lagos Motor Fair
2010/10 –
尼日利亚拉各斯 Nigeria–Lagos

越南国际汽车/摩托车及零配件展览会
SAIGON AUTOTECH
2010/10 –
越南胡志明市 Vietnam–Ho Chi Minh City

第六届巴西国际摩托车及配件展览会
Motorcycle Show Brazil
2010/10 –
巴西圣保罗 Brazil–Sao Paulo

巴黎世界汽车展
MONDIAL DE L' AUTOMOBILE
2010/10/02–2010/10/17
法国巴黎 France–Paris

科隆国际摩托车、滑板车及自行车展览会
INTERMOT Cologne
2010/10/06–2010/10/10
德国科隆 Germany–Cologne

米兰两轮车展览会
2010/11 –
意大利米兰 Italy–Milan

巴基斯坦国际汽车、摩托车及配件展览会
6th Intl Automobile, Auto Parts & Accessories Exhibition 2010
2010/11 –
巴基斯坦卡拉奇 Pakistan– Karachi

伊朗国际汽车零配件展览会
2010/11 –
伊朗德黑兰 Iran–Tehran

第八届越南汽车摩托车工业博览会
Vietnam Auto Expo
2010/11 –
越南胡志明市 Vietnam–Ho Chi Minh City

米兰摩托车贸易博览会
EICMA MOTO
2010/11 –
意大利米兰 Italy–Milan

美国拉斯维加斯国际汽车零配件及售后服务展览会
AAPEX SHOW /SEMA SHOW 2010
2010/11/02–2010/11/04
美国拉斯维加斯 USA–Las Vegas

美国拉斯维加斯国际汽车零配件及售后市场展览会
2010 AAPEX
2010/11/02–2010/11/04
美国拉斯维加斯 USA–Las Vegas

拉斯维加斯改装车零配件展览会
SEMA Show
2010/11/02–2010/11/05
美国拉斯维加斯 USA–Las Vegas

南美洲（阿根廷）国际汽车零部件及售后服务展览会
Automechanika Argentina
2010/11/03–2010/11/06
阿根廷布宜诺斯艾利斯 Argentina–Buenos Aires

第68届意大利米兰国际摩托车及自行车展览会EICMA
2010 EICMA
2010/11/10–2010/11/15
意大利米兰 Italy–Milan

印尼国际汽车制造机械及零部件展览会
Intl Automobile,Auto Parts & ACCESSORIES Exhibition 2010
2010/12 –
印尼雅加达 Indonesia–Jakarta

阿布扎比国际汽车展览会
Abu Dhabi Intl Motor Show
2010/12/15–2010/12/19
阿联酋阿布扎比
United Arab Emirates–Abu Dhabi

日本汽车电子展
Intl Automotive Electronics Technology Expo (CAR/ELE JAPAN)
2011/01 –
日本东京 Japan–Tokyo

奥地利国际汽车生产设备及加油站设备、化学品及环境技术展
Auto Zum:
Intl Trade Fair for the Car & Vehicle Industry
2011/01 –
奥地利萨尔斯堡 Austria–Salzburg

中东（迪拜）国际汽车零配件及售后服务展览会
2011 Automechanika Middle East
2011/05 –
阿联酋迪拜
United Arab Emirates–Dubai

巴西国际汽车配件展
Automec:
Intl Autoparts, Equipment and Services Trade Fair
2011/05/05–2011/05/09
巴西圣保罗 Brazil–Sao Paulo

泰国汽车电子展
Automotive Electronics 2011:
ASEAN's Only Machinery Expo for Automotive Electronics Parts and Components Manufacturing
Co-located with Automotive Manufacturing 2011
2011/06 -
泰国曼谷 Thailand-Bangkok

泰国国际汽车生产制造展览会
Automotive Manufacturing 2011
ASEAN's Only Machinery Expo for Automotive Parts Manufacturing
2011/06 -
泰国曼谷 Thailand-Bangkok

巴黎国际汽车工业展
EQUIP' AUTO
2011/10 -
法国巴黎 France-Paris

2011年中东（迪拜）国际商用车展览会
2011 Commercial Vehicles Middle East
2011/3 -
阿联酋迪拜 United Arab Emirates-Dubai

阿布扎比国际汽车展览会
Abu Dhabi Intl Motor Show
2012/12 -
阿联酋阿布扎比国家展览中心
United Arab Emirates- Abu Dhabi

奥地利国际汽车生产设备及加油站设备、化学品及环境技术展
Auto Zum:
Intl Trade Fair for the Car & Vehicle Industry
2013/01 -
奥地利萨尔斯堡 Austria-Salzburg

## 清洁
## Cleaning

柏林国际建筑物清洁、管理及服务展览会暨学术会议
CMS / Cleaning Management Service
2010 -
德国柏林 Germany-Berlin

## 摄影、摄像
## Photography and Image

世界影像博览会
Photokina
2010/09/21-2010/09/26
德国科隆 Germany-Cologne

西班牙标识视觉传播及图像设计行业展
Viscom/Sign Espana
2010/10 -
西班牙马德里 Spain-Madrid

西班牙标识视觉传播及图像设计行业展
Viscom/Sign Espana
2009/10/22-2009/10/24
西班牙马德里 Spain-Madrid

国际会展及媒体技术展览会
Showtech
2010 -
德国柏林 Germany-Berlin

巴西国际影像贸易展览会
PHOTOIMAGE BRAZIL:
Intl Image Trade Fair
2010 -
巴西圣保罗 Brazil-Sao Paulo

## 石油、燃气
## Petroleum and Gas

国际石油、天然气及石化设备展览会
2010/01/17-2010/01/20
沙特阿拉伯利雅得 Saudi Arabia-Riyadh

国际石油和天然气展览会
2010/03/03-2010/03/06
印度孟买 India-Bombay

第4届非洲石油、天然气和石油化工展览会
2010/03/16-2010/03/18
南非开普敦 South Africa

叙利亚国际电力、石油，天然气展览会
Oil & Gas Exhibition
2010/04/05-2010/04/08
叙利亚 Syria

国际石油及天然气设备展览会
2010/04/05-2010/04/08
叙利亚大马士革 Syria-Damascus

国际石油及天然气设备展览会
2010/05 -
伊朗德黑兰 Iran-Teheran

美国休斯顿国际石油展览会
Offshore Technology Conference
2010/05/03-2010/05/06
美国休斯顿 USA-Houston

第8届巴基斯坦国际石油、天然气及电力能源展览会
POGEE 2010
2010/05/19-2010/05/22
巴基斯坦卡拉奇 Pakistan-Karachi

中东精练及石化展览会
2010/05/24-2010/05/26
巴林 Bahrain

拉丁美洲石油展览会
2010/06 -
委内瑞拉马拉开波 Venezuela-Maracaibo

全球石油展览会
2010/06/08-2010/06/10
加拿大卡尔加里 Canada-Calgary

秘鲁国际天然气、液化气展览会
2010/08/19-2010/08/21
秘鲁利马 Peru

北海国际石油及天然气展览会
2010/08/26-2010/08/29
挪威斯达旺格 Norway

国际石油与天然气展览会
2010/09/13-2010/09/16
巴西里约热内卢 Brazil-Rio de Janeiro

中东国际石油、天然气展览会
2010/10 -
阿联酋迪拜 United Arab Emirates-Dubai

帕米亚盆地国际石油及天然气展览会
2010/10/18-2010/10/21
美国敖德萨 USA-Odessa

俄罗斯石油和天然气技术展览会
SPE Russian Oil & Gas Technical Conference & Exhibition
2010/10/26-2010/10/28
俄罗斯莫斯科 Russia-Moscow

国际石油、天然气及石化设备展览会
2010/11/01-2010/11/04
阿联酋阿布扎比
United Arab Emirates-Abu Dhabi

国际石油及天然气展览会
2010/11/17-2010/11/19
墨西哥比亚埃尔莫萨 Mexico

东南亚石油及天然气科技展览会暨研讨会
2010/12/03-2010/12/06
新加坡 Singapore

巴西石油化工设备展
Química & Petroquímica:
Intl Trade Fair of Machinery & Equipment for the Chemical & Petrochemical Industry
2011 -
巴西圣保罗 Brazil-Sao Paulo

印度石油技术展—2011年第9届国际石油与天然气展览会
PETROTECH/2011
9th Intl Oil & Gas Conference and Exhibition
2011/01 -
印度新德里 India-New Delhi

巴西国际海洋石油及天然气工业设备展览会
Brazil Offshore:
Intl Offshore Oil and Gas Industry Trade Show and Conference
2011/06/14-2011/06/17
巴西里约热内卢 Brazil-Rio de Janeiro

2011 英国石油工业技术展
Offshore Europe 2011:
Oil & Gas Exhibition & Conference
2011/09 -
英国阿伯丁 United Kingdom

俄罗斯石油和天然气技术展览会
SPE Russian Oil & Gas Technical Conference & Exhibition
2012/10 -
俄罗斯莫斯科 Russia-Moscow

巴西国际海洋石油及天然气工业设备展览会
Brazil Offshore:
Intl Offshore Oil and Gas Industry Trade Show and Conference
2013 -
巴西里约热内卢 Brazil-Rio de Janeiro

## 食品、茶、酒、饮料及相关机械
## Food, Beverage

柏林绿色周/食品工业、农业及园艺博览会
Intle Grune Woche Berlin
2010/01/15-2010/01/24
德国柏林 Germany-Berlin

科隆国际糖果及休闲食品展
ISM/ Intl Sweets and Biscuits Fair
2010/01/31-2010/02/03
德国科隆 Germany-Cologne

国际果蔬展览会
Fruit Logistica
2010/02/03-2010/02/05
德国柏林 Germany-Berlin

2010 日本国际食品与饮料展览会
2010 Foodex Japan
2010/03/02-2010/03/05
日本千叶 Japan-

世界面点展
EUROPAIN
2010/03/06-2010/03/10
法国巴黎 France-Paris

西班牙国际食品饮料展览会
Alimentaria2010:
Intl Food & Beverage Exhibition
2010/03/22-2010/03/26
西班牙 Spain

日本美食佳酿暨酒店及餐饮设备展
Wine & Gourmet Japan 2009
2010/04/07-2010/04/09
日本东京 Japan-Tokyo

第十七届新加坡食品酒店站
2010/04/20-2010/04/23
新加坡 Singapore

加拿大蒙特利尔国际食品饮料展览会
2010 SIAL Montreal
2010/04/21-2010/04/23
加拿大蒙特利尔 Canada-Montreal

中东（阿布扎比）国际食品及饮料展览会
2010 Middle East Food
2010/04/26-2010/04/28
阿联酋阿布扎比
United Arab Emirates-Abu Dhabi

欧洲国际水产品展览会
EUROPEAN SEAFOOD EXPO
2010/04/27-2010/04/29
比利时 Belgium

第二十八届韩国首尔国际酒店食品展
2010/05 -
韩国 Korea

第28届韩国首尔国际食品展
Intl Food Industry Exhibition Seoul 2010 (IFIES)
2010/05/12-2010/05/15
韩国首尔 Korea-Seoul

亚洲世界食品博览会
Thaifex - World of Food Asia
2010/05/12-2010/05/16
泰国曼谷 Thailand-Bangkok

美国芝加哥国际酒店用品及餐饮展会
The NRA Show 2010
2010/05/22-2010/05/25
美国芝加哥 USA-Chicago

日本(东京）国际食品机械展览会
FOOMA
2010/06 -
日本东京 Japan-Tokyo

第26届巴西国际食品、饮料工业加工技术和包装工业博览会
Flspal Tecnologia 2010
2010/06 -
巴西圣保罗 Brazil-Sao Paulo

国际咖啡展览会
coffeena Intl Coffee Fair
2010/06 -
德国科隆 Germany-Cologne

国际包装机械及食品饮料加工机械设备展览会
2010/06 -
墨西哥墨西哥城 Mexico-Mexico City

墨西哥国际食品及饮料展
Alimentaria Mexico:
Intl Food & Beverage Exhibition
2010/06/01-2010/06/03
墨西哥墨西哥城 Mexico-Mexico City

国际食品及饮料包装机械展览会
2010/06/08-2010/06/11
巴西圣保罗 Brazil-Sao Paulo

第十八届泰国国际食品、酒店展览会
2010/09 -
泰国 Thailand

圣保罗酒店用品及餐饮设备博览会
Equipotel
2010/09 -
巴西 Brazil

阿根廷国际食品及饮料展
Alimentaria Mercosur:
Intl Food & Beverage Exhibition
2010/09 -
阿根廷布宜诺斯艾利斯
Argentina-Buenos Aires

第14届越南国际食品及饮料展
第14届越南国际食品及饮料加工，包装工艺设备展
14th Intl Exhibition on Food & Beverage
The 14th Intl Exhibitionon Food Processing / Packing Technology & Equipment
2010/09/08-2010/09/11
越南新平 Vietnam

2010莫斯科食品展
World food moscow 2010
2010/09/14-2010/09/17
俄罗斯莫斯科 Russia-Moscow

第十四届越南国际食品饮料工业博览会
14th Vietnam Intl Industrial Fair- Food and Beverage
2010/09/08-2010/09/11
越南胡志明市 Vietnam

亚洲食品配料展
2010/09/29-2010/10/01
印度 India

国际食品加工技术和包装展览会
2010/09/30-2010/10/03
印度孟买 India-Bombay

国际食品加工机械设备展览会
2010/10/17-2010/10/21
法国巴黎 France-Paris

巴黎国际食品展
SIAL
2010/10/17-2010/10/21
法国巴黎 France-Paris

科隆国际糖果原料和机械展览会
ProSweets Cologne 2010
2010/10/18-2010/10/21
德国科隆 Germany-Cologne

第30届埃及国际酒店食品及相关设备展
2010/10/24-2010/10/27
埃及开罗 Egypt-Cairo

日本大型连锁零售企业贴标（OEM）采购展
PRIVATE LABEL SUPPLIERS SHOW
2010/11 -
日本东京 Japan-Tokyo

纽约国际餐饮及酒店用品博览会
The Intl Hotel/motel & Restaurant Show
2010/11 -
美国纽约 USA-New York

中东（迪拜）国际甜食及休闲食品展览会
2010 Sweets Middle East
2010/11/01-2010/11/01
阿联酋迪拜 United Arab Emirates-Dubai

国际饮料设备展览会
2010/11/12-2010/11/14
德国纽伦堡 Germany-Nuremberg

中东迪拜国际饮料技术及机械设备展
2010/12 -
阿联酋迪拜 United Arab Emirates-Dubai

德国科隆国际糖果及休闲食品展览会
2011 ISM
2011/01 -
德国科隆 Germany-Cologne

科隆国际糖果原料和机械展览会
ProSweets Cologne 2010
2011/02 -
德国科隆 Germany-Cologne

2011年中东（迪拜）海湾食品展览会
2011 Gulfood
2011/02 -
阿联酋迪拜 United Arab Emirates-Dubai

2011年德国柏林国际水果蔬菜博览会
2011 Fruit Logistica
2011/02 -
德国柏林 Germany-Berlin

奥地利国际食品技术及制造展览会
L/TEC:
The Trade Fair for Food Technology & Manufacturing
2011/03 -
奥地利萨尔茨堡
Austria-Messezentrum Salzburg

日本国际食品及饮料展览会
2011 Foodex Japan
2011/03 -
日本千叶 Japan

英国食品、饮料包装机械、设备展览会
Pro2Pac:
Processing & Packaging Solutions Event, Exclusively for the Food & Drink Industry
2011/03/13-2011/03/16
英国伦敦 United Kingdom-London

日本美食佳酿暨酒店及餐饮设备展
Wine & Gourmet Japan 2009
2011/04 -
日本东京 Japan-Tokyo

2011年加拿大蒙特利尔国际食品饮料展览会
2011 SIAL Montreal
2011/04 -
加拿大蒙特利尔 Canada-Montreal

里斯本国际食品展
Alimentaria Lisboa:
Intl Food & Beverage Exhibition
2011/04 -
葡萄牙里斯本 Portugal

中东（阿布扎比）国际食品及饮料展览会
2011 Middle East Food
2011/04 -
阿联酋阿布扎比
United Arab Emirates-Abu Dhabi

亚洲世界食品博览会
Thaifex - World of Food Asia
2011/05 -
泰国曼谷 Thailand-Bangkok

墨西哥国际食品及饮料展
Alimentaria Mexico:
Intl Food & Beverage Exhibition
2011/06 -
墨西哥墨西哥城 Mexico-Mexico City

世界食品博览会
Anuga
2011/10/08-2011/10/12
德国科隆 Germany-Cologne

法国国际葡萄酒及果蔬技术展
SITEVI
2011/11 –
法国蒙彼利埃 France

英国国际食品和饮料展
IFE:
Intl Food & Drink Event
2011/3/13–2011/3/16
英国伦敦 United Kingdom–London

2012年西班牙国际食品饮料展览会
Alimentaria2012:
Intl Food & Beverage Exhibition
2012/03 –
西班牙 Spain

巴塞罗那国际食品、饮料设备及技术展览会
Bta. Barcelona tecnolog í as de la alimentaci ó n:
Bta. Barcelona Food Technology Exhibition
2012/05 –
西班牙巴塞罗那 Spain–Barcelona

英国食品、饮料包装机械、设备展览会
Pro2Pac:
Processing & Packaging Solutions Event, Exclusively for the Food & Drink Industry
2013/03 –
英国伦敦 United Kingdom–London

里斯本国际食品展
Alimentaria Lisboa:
Intl Food & Beverage Exhibition
2013/04 –
葡萄牙里斯本 Portugal

英国国际食品和饮料展
IFE: Intl Food & Drink Event
2013/03–
英国伦敦 United Kingdom–London

巴塞罗那国际食品、饮料设备及技术展览会
Bta. Barcelona tecnolog í as de la alimentaci ó n:
Bta. Barcelona Food Technology Exhibition
2015 –
西班牙巴塞罗那 Spain–Barcelona

## 水
## Water

柏林国际水利技术、污水处理展览会暨学术会议
Wasser Berlin
2010 –
德国柏林 Germany–Berlin

美国国际水处理展览会
2010/03 –
美国芝加哥 USA–Chicago

国际水务与环境展览会
2010/03/02–2010/03/05
西班牙萨拉戈萨 Spain

国际供暖、制冷、空调、卫浴与水处理设备展览会
2010/03/23–2010/03/27
意大利米兰 Italy–Milan

供热、制冷、通风、水处理及卫生洁具展览会
2010/04/20–2010/04/23
俄罗斯莫斯科 Russia–Moscow

亚洲海洋、深水技术展览会
2010/06/11–2010/06/13
马来西亚吉隆坡 Malaysia–Kuala Lumpur

阿尔及利亚环保及水处理设备展
SIEE – Pollutec 2011:
6th Intl Exhibition of Equipment & Services for Water
2011/05 –
阿尔及利亚阿尔及尔 Algeria

## 塑料、橡胶
## Plastics and Rubbers

第十六届墨西哥国际塑料橡胶工业展览会
PLASTIMAGEN 2010
2010/03/23–2010/03/26
墨西哥墨西哥城 Mexico–Mexico City

第五届越南国际包装机械展览会暨研讨会
第五届越南国际塑料机械&橡胶加工材料展览会
2010/03/17–2010/03/20
越南 Vietnam

波兰国际塑料加工工业展
PLASTPOL
2010/05 –
波兰Poland

国际包装、塑料及印刷机械展览会
2010/05/07–2010/05/09
巴基斯坦卡拉奇 Pakistan–Karachi

越南国际塑胶机械及技术展览会
Vietnam Plastic Fair
2010/05/11–2010/05/14
越南胡志明市 Vietnam–Ho Chi Minh City

泛阿拉伯/非洲塑料橡胶材料展览会
2010/05/13–2010/05/16
埃及开罗 Egypt–Cairo

国际塑料与橡胶工业展览会
2010/06 –
摩洛哥卡萨布兰卡 Morocco–Casablanca

国际塑料及设备展览会
2010/06/02–2010/06/04
俄罗斯莫斯科 Russia–Moscow

泰国国际塑料及橡胶机械展
InterPlas Thailand 2010
2010/06/24–2010/06/27
泰国曼谷 Thailand–Bangkok

第21届马来西亚国际橡塑胶机械暨模具工业技术展
第21届马来西亚国际广告与设备展
第21届马来西亚国际食品加工与包装设备展
21st Malaysia Intl Rubber Plastic Mould and Die Exhibition/ 21st Malaysia Intl Sign & Technology Fair/ 21st Malaysia Intl Food Processing & Packaging Exhibition
2010/07/15–2010/07/18
马来西亚 Malaysia

第十届越南国际橡塑胶工业展
(Vietnam Plas 2010)
第十届越南国际包装工业展
第十届越南国际印刷工业展
The 10th Vietnam Intl Plastics, Rubber Industry Exhibition/ The 10th Vietnam Intl Packaging & Printing Industry Exhibition / The 10th Vietnam Intl Print & Label Industry Exhibition
2010/09/22–2010/09/25
越南胡志明市 Vietnam–Ho Chi Minh City

国际塑料及橡胶展览会
2010/10/27–2010/11/03
德国杜塞尔多夫 Germany–Dusseldorf

杜塞尔多夫国际塑料及橡胶展(K展)
2010/10/27–2010/11/03
德国杜塞尔多夫 Germany–Dusseldorf

国际橡胶机械展览会
2010/11 –
伊朗德黑兰 Iran–Teheran

印度国际包装塑料展览会
2010/11 –
印度 India

土耳其国际塑料工业展览会
Plas Eurasia Istanbul
2010/11 –
土耳其伊斯坦布尔 Turkey–Istanbul

越南国际塑料及橡胶机械展
InterPlas Vietnam:
Vietnam's Intl Plastic and Rubber Technology Trade Exhibition and Conference
2011/05 –
越南河内 Vietnam–Hanoi

泰国国际塑料及橡胶机械展
InterPlas Thailand 2011
2011/06 –
泰国曼谷 Thailand–Bangkok

## 陶瓷、玻璃
## Ceramics and Glass

西班牙瓦伦西亚卫浴展
CEVISAMA
2010/02/09–2010/02/12
西班牙瓦伦西亚 Spain–Valencia cf

法国卫浴展
Ideo Bain:
The Bathroom Exhibition
2010/02/09–2010/02/14
法国巴黎 France–Paris

乌克兰国际玻璃及门窗专业展览会
2010/02/23–2010/02/26
乌克兰基辅 Ukraine–Kiev

伯明翰国际厨卫展
KBB
2010/03/21–2010/03/24
英国伯明翰
United Kingdom–Birmingham

米兰国际卫浴展
EXPOBAGNO
2010/03/23–2010/03/27
意大利米兰 Italy–Milan

米兰国际供暖、空调、制冷及卫生洁具博览会
MCE
2010/03/23–2010/03/27
意大利米兰 Italy–Milan

芝加哥国际厨房浴室设备博览会
K/BIS
2010/04/16–2010/04/18
美国芝加哥 USA–Chicago

第八届美国国际玻璃门窗展览会
8th The Glass Build, Window & Door Expo
2010/09/14–2010/09/16
美国拉斯维加斯 USA–Las Vegas

中东国际厨房、卫浴洁具博览会
ISH Kitchen & Bathroom Gulf
2010/05 –
阿联酋迪拜 United Arab Emirates–Dubai

罗马尼亚国际门窗玻璃博览会
CONSTRUCT EXPO
2010/05 –
罗马尼亚布加勒斯特
Romania–Bucharest

西班牙马德里国际门窗、幕墙及玻璃博览会
2010/05/04–2010/05/07

西班牙马德里 Spain-Madrid

杜塞尔多夫国际玻璃技术博览会
12th Intl Trade Fair For Glass Production/ Processing/ Products
2010/09/28-2010/10/01
德国杜塞尔多夫 Germany-Dusseldorf

美国国际玻璃及门窗展览会
2010/09/30-2010/10/02
美国亚特兰大 USA-Atlanta

杜塞尔多夫国际塑料及橡胶展(K展)
2010/10/27-2010/11/03
德国德国杜塞尔多夫 Germany-Dusseldorf

米兰国际卫浴展
EXPOBAGNO
2012/03 -
意大利米兰 Italy-Milan

## 特许经营 Franchinsing

巴黎国际特许经营展览会
Franchise Expo Paris: Intl Franchise Show
2010/03/14-2010/03/17
法国巴黎 France-Paris

巴黎国际特许经营展览会
Franchise Expo Paris: Intl Franchise Show
2011/03 -
法国巴黎 France-Paris

## 体育、休闲 Sports and Leisure

美国职业高尔夫球协会高尔夫用品秋季展
PGA Fall Expo
2010 -
美国拉斯维加斯 USA-Las Vegas

盐湖城冬季/夏季户外运动用品博览会（冬季）
Outdoor Retailer Winter / Summer Market
2010/01/21-2010/01/24
美国盐湖城 USA-Salt Lake City

美国职业高尔夫球协会高尔夫用品展
PGA Merchandise Show
2010/01/28-2010/01/30
美国佛罗里达州 USA

捷克布拉格国际体育用品和时装贸易博览会
Sport Prague & Sport Fashion
2010/02 -
捷克布拉格 Czech-Prague

美国圣地亚哥极限运动及运动时尚博览会
ASR Trade Expo
2010/02/03-2010/02/04
美国圣地亚哥 USA-Santiago

春季马术用品展
spoga horse(spring)
2010/02/06-2010/02/08
德国科隆 Germany-Cologne

慕尼黑冬季国际体育用品及运动时装展
ispo winter
2010/02/07-2010/02/10
德国慕尼黑 Germany-Munich

俄罗斯圣彼得堡国际体育用品展
SPORT/CNOPT
2010/03 -
俄罗斯圣彼得堡 Russia-St.Petersburg

世界健美、健身及休闲博览会
FIBO
The Leading Intl Trade Show for Fitness & Wellness
2010/04/22-2010/04/25
德国埃森 Germany-Essen

中东（迪拜）国际园艺及户外休闲用品展览会
2010/05/17-2010/05/19
阿联酋迪拜 United Arab Emirates-Dubai

盐湖城冬季/夏季户外运动用品博览会（夏季）
Outdoor Retailer Winter / Summer Market
2010/07 -
美国盐湖城 USA-Salt Lake City

德国菲德里斯哈芬户外休闲运动博览会
2010 European Outdoor Trade Fair
2010/07/15-2010/07/18
德国菲德烈斯哈芬 Germany-

丹佛健康与健身博览会
Denver Health + Fitness Business & Expo
2010/08 -
美国丹佛 USA-Denver

巴西圣保罗国际体育用品展
SPORTS BUSINESS SHOW
2010/08 -
巴西圣保罗 Brazil-Sao Paulo

ASR美国圣地亚哥极限运动及运动时尚博览会
ASR Trade Expo
2010/09 -
美国圣地亚哥 USA-Santiago

巴西圣保罗户外探险及生态旅游博览会
Adventure Sports Fair
2010/09 -
巴西圣保罗 Brazil-Sao Paulo

科隆国际体育、露营用品及花园家具展
Spoga
2010/09 -
德国科隆 Germany-Cologne

莫斯科国际健身及康体器材贸易展会
MIOFF
2010/09 -
俄罗斯莫斯科 Russia-Moscow

秋季马术用品展
spoga horse (Autumn)
2010/09/05-2010/09/07
德国科隆 Germany-Cologne

国际体育用品、露营设备及园林生活博览会/国际园艺博览会
spoga/gafa
2010/09/05-2010/09/07
德国科隆 Germany-Cologne

中东游泳池设备及SPA展览会
Middle East Pool & Spa Exhibition
2010/09/26-2010/09/28
阿联酋迪拜 United Arab Emirates-Dubai

慕尼黑国际高尔夫运动用品博览会
Golf Europe
2010/09/26-2010/09/28
德国慕尼黑 Germany-Munich

美国潜水设备行销协会展
DEMA Show
2010/10 -
美国拉斯维加斯 USA-Las Vegas

巴西国际健身器材博览会
Fitness Brasil
2010/10 -
巴西圣保罗 Brazil-Sao Paulo

科隆国际摩托车、滑板车及自行车展览会
INTERMOT Cologne
2010/10/06-2010/10/10
德国科隆 Germany-Cologne

欧洲户外休闲与沙滩用品贸易展
The SUN
2010/10 -
意大利里米尼 Italy-Rimini

意大利里米尼国际户外、设计及装饰材料博览会
The SUN
2010/10/28-2010/10/31
意大利里米尼 Italy-Rimini

迪拜国际体育用品博览会
Sportex Dubai
2010/11 -
阿联酋迪拜 United Arab Emirates-Dubai

世界健美、健身及休闲博览会
FIBO
The Leading Intl Trade Show for Fitness & Wellness
2011 -
德国埃森 Germany-Essen

美国职业高尔夫球协会高尔夫用品展
PGA Merchandise Show
2011/01 -
美国佛罗里达州 USA-

春季马术用品展
spoga horse(spring)
2011/02/05-2011/02/07
德国科隆国 Germany-Cologne

春季马术用品展
spoga horse(spring)
2011/02/05-2011/02/07
德国科隆 Germany-Cologne

秋季马术用品展
spoga horse (Autumn)
2011/09/04-2011/09/06
德国科隆 Germany-Cologne

国际体育用品、露营设备及园林生活博览会
国际园艺博览会
spoga/gafa
2011/09/04-2011/09/06
德国科隆 Germany-Cologne

国际休闲、体育设施及泳池设备展
FSB
2011/10/26-2011/10/28
德国科隆 Germany-Cologne

国际桑拿及泳池设备展
2011/10/26-2011/10/29
德国科隆 Germany-Cologne

## 图书 Books

伦敦书展
The London Book Fair
2010/04/19-2010/04/21
英国伦敦 United Kingdom-London

美国书展 / 原美国书商协会大会及贸易展
BookExpo America
2010/05/25-2010/05/27
美国纽约 USA-New York

日本书展
TIBF:
Tokyo Intl Book Fair
2010/07/08-2010/07/11
日本东京 Japan-Tokyo

纽约国际动漫博览会
New York Comic Con
2010/10/08-2010/10/10
美国纽约 USA-New York

美国书展
(原美国书商协会大会及贸易展)
BookExpo America
2011 -
美国纽约 USA-New York

伦敦书展
The London Book Fair
2011/04 -
英国伦敦 United Kingdom-London

日本书展
TIBF : Tokyo Intl Book Fair
2011/07 -
日本东京 Japan-Tokyo

纽约国际动漫博览会
New York Comic Con
2011/10 - 2011/10/
美国纽约 USA-New York

## 玩具、儿童用品
## Toys

纽伦堡春季国际玩具博览会
Intl Toy Fair N ü rnberg
2010/02/04-2010/02/09
德国纽伦堡 Germany-Nuernberg

纽约国际玩具博览会
American Intl Toy Fair
2010/02/14-2010/02/17
美国纽约 USA-New York

中东国际玩具博览会
The Middle East's Toy Fair
2010/03 -
阿联酋迪拜
United Arab Emirates-Dubai

莫斯科国际玩具、母婴用品博览会
MITGE/Toy & Game Mother & Baby
2010/03/16-2010/03/19
俄罗斯莫斯科 Russia-Moscow

巴西国际圣诞节日装饰品及玩具博览会
Toys, Parties & Christmas Fair South America
2010/05 - 2010/05/
巴西 Brazil

美国ABC国际婴童用品展览会
ABC Kids Expo
2010/09 -
美国拉斯维加斯 USA-Las Vegas

科隆国际婴幼儿及少年儿童用品展
Kind+Jugend
2010/09 -
德国科隆 Germany-Cologne

科隆国际少儿用品展
Kind + Jugend
2010/09/16-2010/09/19
德国科隆 Germany-Cologne

法兰克福中东（迪拜）国际玩具及文具用品展览会
2011 Toy Fair Middle East
2011/03 -
阿联酋迪拜 United Arab Emirates-Dubai

科隆国际少儿用品展
Kind + Jugend
2011/09/15-2011/09/18
德国科隆 Germany-Cologne

## 文化产业
## Cultural Industry

2010 光州国际文化创意产业展
Gwangju ACE Fair 2010
2010/09/09-2010/09/12
韩国 Korea

## 文具、办公用品
## Stationery and Office Supplies

迪拜办公家具展
The Office Exhibition
2010/02/09-2010/02/11
阿联酋迪拜 United Arab Emirates-Dubai

开罗办公自动化和办公服务展
2010/04/10-2010/04/13
埃及开罗 Egypt- Cairo

美国芝加哥办公家具展
NEOCON 2010
2010/06/14-2010/06/16
美国芝加哥 USA- Las Vegas

东京国际办公机械及设备展览会
OFMEX : Intl Office Machines & Equipment Expo Tokyo
2010/07/07-2010/07/09
日本东京 Japan-Tokyo

科隆办公展
Orgatec 2010
2010/10/26-2010/10/30
德国科隆 Germany-Cologne

法兰克福中东（迪拜）国际玩具及文具用品展览会
2011 Toy Fair Middle East
2011/03 -
阿联酋迪拜 United Arab Emirates-Dubai

东京国际办公机械及设备展览会
OFMEX:
Intl Office Machines & Equipment Expo Tokyo
2011/07 -
日本东京 Japan-Tokyo

## 五金、工具
## Hardware and Tools

国际机床工具展览会
2010/01/21-2010/01/26
印度班加罗尔 India-Bangalore

科隆国际五金博览会
INTL HARDWARE FAIR COLOGNE
2010/02/28-2010/03/03
德国科隆 Germany-Cologne

乌克兰国际五金工具展
INTERTOOL KIEV
2010/03 -
乌克兰基辅 Ukraine-Kiev

巴西国际五金及工具展览会
Tools & Hardware Fair
2010/03 -
巴西圣保罗 Brazil-Sao Paulo

圣保罗国际建材及五金展览会
FEICON BATIMAT
2010/04/06-2010/04/10
巴西圣保罗 Brazil-Sao Paulo

中东国际五金工具博览会
The Middle East's Leading Trade Show for Hardware & Tools
2010/05 -
阿联酋迪拜
United Arab Emirates-Dubai

国际五金工具展览会
2010/05/04-2010/05/06
美国拉斯维加斯 USA-Las Vegas

美国国际五金工具及花园用品展览会
National Hardware Show
2010/05/04-2010/05/06
美国拉斯维加斯 USA-Las Vegas

国际五金工具 / 商业照明展览会
2010/05/17-2010/05/19
阿联酋迪拜
United Arab Emirates-Dubai

2010中东国际五金工具展览会
2010 Hardware & Tools Middle East
2010/05/17-2010/05/19
阿联酋迪拜
United Arab Emirates-Dubai

国际五金工具展览会
2010/08 -
南非约翰内斯堡
South Africa-Johannesburg

日本国际五金及DIY展览会
Japan DIY Show 2010
2010/08 -
日本东京 Japan-Tokyo

国际五金工具展览会
2010/09 -
俄罗斯莫斯科 Russia-Moscow

墨西哥五金展
2010/09 -
墨西哥瓜达拉哈拉
Mexico-Guadalajara

俄罗斯国际五金工具展览会
Intertool Moscow:
13th Intl Exhibition for Tools, Metal/Working & Manufacturing Industries
2010/09 -
俄罗斯莫斯科 Russia-Moscow

俄罗斯国际五金工具展览会
2010/11 -
俄罗斯莫斯科 Russia-Moscow

国际五金工具展览会
2010/12 -
印度金奈 India-

科隆亚太采购交易会——
五金、家居、家电、园艺产品
Asia Pacific Sourcing
2011/04/03-2011/04/05
德国科隆 Germany-Cologne

美国国际五金工具及花园用品展览会
National Hardware Show
2011/05 -
美国拉斯维加斯 USA-Las Vegas

## 物流、仓储
## Logistics

中东国际工业自动化、动力传动及物流技术展览会
2010/02/09-2010/02/11
阿联酋迪拜
United Arab Emirates-Dubai

国际物流与物料操作展览会
2010/05 -
西班牙巴塞罗那
Spain-Barcelona

国际物流展览会
2010/08/10-2010/08/31
阿根廷布宜诺斯艾利斯
Argentina-Buenos Aires

## 消费电子、家用电器
## Consumer Electronics

美国国际消费类电子产品博览会
CES
2010/01/07-2010/01/10
美国拉斯维加斯 USA-Las Vegas

第二届印度国际消费电子、家电及家居用品展
The 2nd India Intl Electronics Fair
2010/03/10-2010/03/13
印度孟买 India-Mumbai

伊斯坦布尔家电展
Intl Exhibition and Conference for Household Appliances
2010/04/22-2010/04/25
土耳其伊斯坦布尔 Turkey-Istanbul

中东国际家用电器博览会
Hometech Middle East
2010/05 -
阿联酋迪拜
United Arab Emirates-Dubai

美国国际小家电及家居用品展览会
Homewares Show
2010/05/04-2010/05/06
美国拉斯维加斯 USA-Las Vegas

科隆亚太采购交易会
——五金、家居、家电、园艺产品
Asia Pacific Sourcing
2011/04/03-2011/04/05
德国科隆 Germany-Cologne

美国国际小家电及家居用品展览会
Homewares Show
2011/05 -
美国拉斯维加斯 USA-Las Vegas

## 消费品、家居
## Consumer Goods

迪拜国际消费品、礼品贸易博览会（IATF）
2010/01/17-2010/01/19
阿联酋迪拜 United Arab Emirates-Dubai

俄罗斯国际家居用品博览会
Consumexpo
2010/01/18-2010/01/22
俄罗斯 Russia

法兰克福国际消费品博览会（春季）
AMBIENTE / DECORATE LIFE
2010/02/12-2010/02/16
德国 Germany

2010美国芝加哥国际家庭用品博览会
Intl Home & Housewares Show
2010/03/14-2010/03/16
美国芝加哥 USA-Chicago

国际商品博览会
2010/05 -
朝鲜平壤 North Korea-Pyongyang

美国国际五金工具及花园用品展览会
National Hardware Show
2010/05/04-2010/05/06
美国拉斯维加斯 USA-Las Vegas

德国法兰克福国际时尚消费品展览会
2010/07/02-2010/07/06
德国法兰克福 Germany- Frankfurt

巴西国际家庭用品及礼品博览会
House & Gift Fair South America
2010/08 - 2010/08/
巴西 Brazil

柏林电子消费品展
IFA
2010/08 -
德国柏林 Germany-Berlin

巴西圣保罗国际家庭用品及礼品博览会
2010/08/14-2010/08/17
巴西圣保罗 Brazil-Sao Paulo

国际电子消费品展览会
IFA
2010/09 -
德国柏林 Germany-Berlin

中东厨房卫浴设备展览会
2010/09 -
阿联酋迪拜 United Arab Emirates-Dubai

捷克国际消费类电子展览会
DIGITEX
2010/10 -
捷克布鲁诺 Czech-Brno

中东迪拜国际家具和室内装饰博览会
2010 INDEX
2010/11/08-2010/11/11
阿联酋迪拜
United Arab Emirates-Dubai

西班牙毕尔巴鄂国际五金工具展
Ferroforma
2011/03 -
西班牙毕尔巴鄂 Spain

美国国际五金工具及花园用品展览会
National Hardware Show
2011/05 -
美国拉斯维加斯 USA-Las Vegas

## 鞋、皮革
## Leather, Shoes

巴西国际鞋业、皮革制品及附件展览会
COUROMODA
2010/01/18-2010/01/21
巴西圣保罗 Brazil-Sao Paulo

拉斯维加斯国际鞋业博览会（春季）
WSA
2010/02 -
美国拉斯维加斯 USA-Las Vegas

杜塞尔多夫国际鞋业及皮革制品博览会（春季）
Global Shoes & Accessories
2010/03 -
德国杜塞尔多夫
Germany-Dusseldorf

拉斯维加斯国际鞋业博览会（秋季）
WSA
2010/07 -
美国拉斯维加斯 USA-Las Vegas

杜塞尔多夫国际鞋业及皮革制品博览会（秋季）
Global Shoes & Accessories
2010/09 -
德国杜塞尔多夫 Germany-Dusseldorf

越南国际鞋类、皮革制成品展览会
Intl Footwear & Leather Products Exhibition - Vietnam
2010/09/11-2010/09/14
越南西贡 Vietnam-

越南国际鞋类、皮革及工业设备展览会
Intl Shoes & Leather Exhibition - Vietnam
2011/09/08-2011/09/10
越南 Vietnam

## 新能源、节能
## New Energy

孟加拉国际电力能源及照明展览会
EL/POWER&LIGHTING BANGLADESH
2010/01/07-2010/01/10
孟加拉 Bengal

阿布扎比世界未来能源展览会
WORLD FUTURE ENERGY SUMMIT:
Leading Conference and Exhibition focusing on Future Energy
2010/01/18-2010/01/21
阿联酋阿布扎比
United Arab Emirates-Abu Dhabi

东京国际光伏发电展览会
PV EXPO 2010:
Intl Photovoltaic Power Generation Expo
2010/03/03-2010/03/05
日本东京Japan-Tokyo

中东国际地球物理科学展览会暨研讨会
2010/03/08-2010/03/10
巴林 Bahrain

2010韩国国际太阳能、风能、地能展览会
SWEET 2010
2010/03/17-2010/03/19
韩国 Korea

意大利米兰供暖、空调、制冷、再生能源及太阳能展
Mostra Convegno Expocomfort:
Production & Distribution line for the HVAC & Plumbing Sector
2010/03/23-2010/03/27
意大利米兰 Italy-Milan

国际太阳能光伏展览会
2010/06 -
德国慕尼黑 Germany-Munich

慕尼黑国际太阳能技术展
Intersolar
2010/06/09-2010/06/11
德国慕尼黑 Germany-Munich

北美国际太阳能技术展
intersolar North America
2010/07 -
美国旧金山 USA-San Francisco

北美国际太阳能科技展览会
2010/07/14-2010/07/16
美国旧金山 USA-San Francisco

欧洲光伏太阳能展览会
European Photovoltaic Solar Energy Conference and Exhibition
2010/09 -
德国汉堡 Germany-Hamburg

国际太阳能展览会
2010/10/12-2010/10/14
美国拉斯维加斯 USA-Las Vegas

2010韩国新可再生能源展
Renewable Energy Korea 2010
2010/10/21-2010/10/24
韩国首尔 Korea-Seoul

国际能源回收与可持续发展贸易博览会
ECOMONDO
2010/11 -
意大利里米尼 Italy-Rimini

南亚地球物理科学研讨会
2010/9/17-2010/9/19
印度新德里 India-New Delhi

东京国际光伏发电展览会
PV EXPO 2010:
Intl Photovoltaic Power Generation Expo
2011/03 -
日本东京 Japan-Tokyo

意大利米兰供暖、空调、制冷、再生能源及太阳能展
Mostra Convegno Expocomfort:
Production & Distribution line for the HVAC & Plumbing Sector
2012/03 -
意大利米兰 Italy-Milan

## 信息技术、通信技术
## Information Technology and Telecommunication Technology

世界移动通信大会
Mobile World Congress 2010
2010/02/15-2010/02/18
西班牙巴塞罗那 Spain- Barcelona

墨西哥国际通信技术设备展览会
Expo Comm Mexico 2010
2010/02/23-2010/02/25
墨西哥墨西哥城 Mexico- Mexico City

第18届印度国际信息通讯博览会
18th Convergence India 2010 Intl Exhibition and conference
2010/03/23-2010/03/25
印度新德里 India-New Delhi

欧洲国际计算机信息系统安全展览会
Infosecurity Europe
2010/04/27-2010/04/29
英国伦敦 United Kingdom-London

俄罗斯国家电信展
SVIAZ/ EXPO COMM MOSCOW 2010
2010/05/11-2010/05/14
俄罗斯莫斯科 Russia-Moscow

日本软件开发展览会
SODEC : Software Development Expo
2010/05/12-2010/05/14
日本东京 Japan-Tokyo

中东（阿布扎比）国际通讯展（Mecom 2010）
2010/05/17-2010/05/19
阿联酋阿布扎比 United Arab Emirates-Abu Dhabi

客户服务中心/客户关系管理展览会及会议大阪展
Call Centre/ CRM Demo & Conference Osaka 2010
2010/05/26-2010/05/27
日本 Japan

慕尼黑国际机器人和自动化技术贸易博览会
AUTMATICA
2010/06/08-2010/06/11
德国慕尼黑 Germany-Munich

第21届国际通讯与资讯科技展览及研讨会
2010/06/15-2010/06/18
新加坡 Singapore

数码营销博览会
dmexco
2010/09/15-2010/09/16
德国科隆 Germany-Cologne

数码管理解决方案展览会
DMS EXPO
2010/09/21-2010/09/23
德国科隆 Germany-Cologne

国际电信联盟美洲电信展
ITU TELECOM AMERICAS 2010
2010/09/21-2010/09/24
阿根廷布宜诺斯艾利斯
Argentina-Buenos Aires

俄罗斯国际计算机信息系统安全展览会
Infosecurity Russia
2010/10 -
俄罗斯莫斯科 Russia-Moscow

慕尼黑国际信息技术、通讯和新媒体展
SYSTEMS
2010/10 -
德国慕尼黑 Germany-Munich

欧洲国际计算机信息系统安全展览会
Infosecurity Europe
2011/04 -
英国伦敦 United Kingdom-London

日本软件开发展览会
SODEC : Software Development Expo
2011/05 -
日本东京 Japan-Tokyo

数码营销博览会
dmexco
2011/09 -
德国科隆 Germany-Cologne

数码管理解决方案展览会
DMS EXPO
2011/09 -
德国科隆 Germany-Cologne

## 医药、医疗设备、保健、生物
## Medicao Equipment, Pharmaceuticals and Health Care

巴西圣保罗国际牙科展
CIOSP
2010/01 -
巴西圣保罗 Brazil-Sao Paulo

阿拉伯国际医疗设备展览会
ARAB HEALTH
2010/01/25-2010/01/28
阿联酋迪拜 United Arab Emirates-Dubai

中东迪拜国际牙防展览会
AEEDC
2010/03 -
阿联酋迪拜 United Arab Emirates-Dubai

印度国际医疗展
Medical Fair India
2010/03 -
印度孟买 India-Mumbai

日本健康博览会
2010/03 -
日本东京 Japan-Tokyo

波多黎各国际制药工业展览会
生物科技及制药商展览会
INTERPHEX Puerto Rico:
Exhibition & Conference for Pharmaceutical & Biotechnology Manufacturers
2010/03/04-2010/03/05
波多黎各 Puerto Rico

国际仪器分析,生化技术,诊断和实验技术贸易博览会暨国际研讨会
Analytica
2010/03/23-2010/03/26
德国慕尼黑 Germany-Munich

新加坡牙科展览会
IDEM
2010/04 -
新加坡 Singapore

2010沙特医疗及医疗机械展
2010/04/12-2010/04/15
沙特阿拉伯利雅得 Saudi Arabia-Riyadh

美国国际制药工业展览会
INTERPHEX incorporating
PharmaManufacturing,
PharmaSourcing & Services,
PharmaIT and
PharmaFacilities
2010/04/20-2010/04/22
美国纽约 USA-New York

墨西哥国际制药工业展览会
Expofarma INTERPHEX Mexico
2010/04/21-2010/04/23
墨西哥墨西哥城 Mexico-Mexico City

国际医药制药、医疗器械展览会暨
中国医药制药、医疗器械展览会
2010/05/12-2010/05/15
越南河内 Vietnam-Hanoi

中东国际眼镜眼科用品展览会
2010 Vision/X Dubai
2010/05/18-2010/05/20
阿联酋迪拜 United Arab Emirates-Dubai

巴西国际医疗展
Hospitalar
2010/06 -
巴西圣保罗 Brazil-Sao Paulo

亚洲制药工业展览会
Interphex Asia:
Asia's Dedicated Sourcing Platform for Pharmaceutical Manufacturing
2010/06 -
新加坡 Singapore

美国AACC临床化学年会暨国际临床实验室设备展
Clinical Lab Expo and the American Association of Clinical Chemistry's (AACC) Annual Meeting
2010/07 -
美国芝加哥 USA-Chicago

美国国际医疗设备展览会
FIME
2010/08 -
美国迈阿密 USA-Miami

第十届越南国际药品及医疗设备展览会
越南第十届越南国际医药制药、医疗器材展览会

VIETNAM MEDI/PHARM EXPO 2010
10th Vietnam Intl Medical Pharmaceuticals, Medical Equipment Exhibition
2010/08/18-2010/08/21
越南胡志明市Vietnam

泰国曼谷国际医院及医疗设备展览会
Medical Fair Thailand
2010/09 -
泰国曼谷 Thailand-Bangkok

国际医药及医疗器械展览会
2010/09/22-2010/09/25
越南胡志明市 Vietnam-Ho Chi Minh City

美国国际康复展
Medtrade
2010/10 -
美国亚特兰大 USA-Atlanta Botanical

美国牙科协会第150届年会
ADA
2010/10 -
美国 USA

意大利国际牙科器具及材料展
Intl Expodental
2010/10/15-2010/10/17
意大利罗马 Italy-Rome

国际医疗器械、医院用品、实验室设备及医药展览会
2010/10/19-2010/10/22
印尼雅加达 Indonesia-Jakarta

杜塞尔多夫医疗设备展
Medica
2010/11 -
德国杜塞尔多夫 Germany-Dusseldorf

亚洲制药工业展览会
Interphex Asia:
Asia's Dedicated Sourcing Platform for Pharmaceutical Manufacturing
2011 -
新加坡 Singapore

波多黎各国际制药工业展览会：生物科技及制药商展览会
INTERPHEX Puerto Rico:
Exhibition & Conference for Pharmaceutical & Biotechnology Manufacturers
2011/02 -
波多黎各 Puerto Rico

墨西哥国际制药工业展览会
Expofarma INTERPHEX Mexico
2011/04 -
墨西哥墨西哥城 Mexico-Mexico City

科隆国际牙科展
Intl Dental Show 2011
2011/04/22-2011/04/26
德国科隆 Germany-Cologne

## 仪器仪表 Instrument

杜塞尔多夫国际管材、线缆及紧固件展览会
2010/04/12-2010/04/16
德国杜塞尔多夫 Germany-Dusseldorf

马来西亚国际精密工程机床金属工业设备展
2010/05/07-2010/05/09
马来西亚吉隆坡
Malaysia-Kuala Lumpur

越南国际精密工程机械金属工业设备展
2010/07/07-2010/07/09
越南胡志明市
Vietnam-Ho Chi Minh City

越南国际精密工程机床金属工业设备展
2010/09 -
越南河内 Vietnam-Hanoi

## 艺术 Arts

国际印刷艺术展览会
2010/02/25-2010/02/27
美国迈阿密 USA-Miami

科隆国际艺术展
ART COLOGNE 2009
2010/04/21-2010/04/25
德国科隆 Germany-Cologne

柏林国际现代艺术展
Art Forum Berlin
2010/10 -
德国柏林 Germany-Berlin

法国国际现代艺术展览会
FIAC:
Intl Modern & Contemporary Art Fair
2010/10 -
法国巴黎 France-Paris

科隆国际优秀艺术及古董展
Cologne Fine Art And Antiques
2010/11/17-2010/11/21
德国科隆 Germany-Cologne

科隆国际艺术展
ART COLOGNE 2009
2011/04/13-2011/04/17
德国科隆 Germany-Cologne

科隆国际优秀艺术及古董展
Cologne Fine Art And Antiques
2011/11/16-2011/11/20
德国科隆 Germany-Cologne

## 音乐 Music

世界音乐博览会
MIDEM:
The World's Music Market
2010/01/23-2010/01/27
法国戛纳 France-

世界音乐博览会
MIDEM:
The World's Music Market
2011/01 -
法国戛纳 France

## 印刷 Printing

第10届国际包装印刷展览会
2010/01/19-2010/01/22
印度新德里 India-New Delhi

国际印刷、包装及塑胶展览会
2010/01/25-2010/01/28
孟加拉达卡 Bengal-

国际印刷艺术展览会
2010/02/25-2010/02/27
美国迈阿密 USA-Miami

国际印刷及包装展览会
2010/03/08-2010/03/12
巴西圣保罗 Brazil-Sao Paulo

越南国际印刷、包装机械设备及技术展览会
Print & Pack - Vietnam
2010/05/11-2010/05/14
越南胡志明市 Vietnam-Ho Chi Minh City

8th Intl Printing, Plastic, Packaging & Food Processing Machinery Fair / Indo Signtech / Indo/Powertools
2010/05/13-2010/05/16
印度尼西亚 Indonesia

英国国际印刷展览会
IPEX 2010
2010/05/18-2010/05/25
英国伯明翰 UK-Birmingham

国际印刷技术与纸工业展览会
2010/05/29-2010/06/06
土耳其伊斯坦布尔 Turkey-Istanbul

拉丁美洲印刷展览会
EXPOPRINT 2010
2010/06/23-2010/06/29
巴西圣保罗 Brazil-Sao Paulo

国际印刷展览会
2010/11/20-2010/11/22
加拿大多伦多 Canada-toronto

## 园艺、花卉 Gardening

柏林绿色周/食品工业、农业及园艺博览会
Intle Grune Woche Berlin
2010/01/15-2010/01/24
德国柏林 Germany-Berlin

国际园艺展览会
2010/03 -
俄罗斯莫斯科 Russia-Moscow

中东（迪拜）国际花卉园艺及户外休闲用品展览会
2010 Garden & Landscaping Middle East
2010/05/17-2010/05/19
阿联酋迪拜 United Arab Emirates-Dubai

中东（迪拜）国际园艺及户外休闲用品展览会
2010/05/17-2010/05/19
阿联酋迪拜 United Arab Emirates-Dubai

国际园艺展览会
2010/09 -
德国科隆 Germany-Cologne

国际体育用品、露营设备及园林生活博览会/国际园艺博览会
spoga/gafa
2010/09/05-2010/09/07
德国科隆 Germany-Cologne

国际园艺机械展览会
2010/10 -
美国路易斯维尔 USA-Louisville

国际体育用品、露营设备及园林生活博览会/国际园艺博览会
spoga/gafa
2011/09/04-2011/09/06
德国科隆 Germany-Cologne

## 展览展示
## Exhibition and Display

国际博物馆及展示技术展览会
EXPONATEC
2011/11/15-2011/11/18
德国科隆 Germany-Cologne

## 纸业
## Paper

美国纸业世界展览会
Tissue World Americas 2010
2010/03/24-2010/03/26
美国 USA

国际印刷技术与纸工业展览会
2010/05/29-2010/06/06
土耳其伊斯坦布尔 Turkey-Istanbul

纸加工与包装展览会
2010/10/31-2010/11/03
美国芝加哥 USA-Chicago

俄罗斯国际纸浆造纸、林业、生活用纸及纸包装展览会
PAP/FOR Russia: Intl Exhibition and Conference for Russia's Pulp & Paper, Forestry, Tissue & Converting & Packaging Industries
2010/11/08-2010/11/11
俄罗斯圣彼得堡 Russia- St.Petersburg

俄罗斯国际纸浆造纸、林业、生活用纸及纸包装展览会
PAP/FOR Russia: Intl Exhibition and Conference for Russia's Pulp & Paper, Forestry, Tissue & Converting & Packaging Industries
2012 -
俄罗斯圣彼得堡 Russia-St.Petersburg

## 钟表、眼镜
## Watche, Clocks and Optics

慕尼黑国际眼镜及光学镜片博览会
OPTI
2010/01/15-2010/01/17
德国慕尼黑 Germany-Munich

巴黎国际眼镜展
SILMO PARIS
2010/09/23-2010/09/26
法国巴黎 France-Paris

2011 年中东国际眼镜眼科用品展览会
2011 Vision/X Dubai
2011/05 -
阿联酋迪拜 United Arab Emirates-Dubai

## 珠宝
## Jewelry

巴黎国际服装、珠宝、银饰及配件展览会
Eclat de Mode / Bijorhca Paris: The Fashion side of Jewellery. Bi/annual Intl Trade Show
2010/01 -
法国巴黎 France-Paris

欧洲国际钟表、珠宝首饰、银器及加工设备展
inhorgenta Europe
2010/02/19-2010/02/22
德国 Germany

伦敦国际珠宝展
Intl Jewellery London
2010/09 -
英国伦敦 United Kingdom- London

日本珠宝展
Japan Jewellery Fair
2010/09/01-2010/09/03
日本 Japan

## 自行车
## Bikes

德国慕尼黑国际自行车博览会
BIKE EXPO
2010/07 -
德国慕尼黑 Germany-Munich

美国国际自行车及零部件展览会
Interbike
2010/09 -
美国拉斯维加斯 USA-Las Vegas

巴黎国际两轮车展
MONDIAL DU DEUX ROUES
2010/10 -
法国巴黎 France-Paris

意大利米兰国际两轮车展
EICMA
2010/11 -
意大利米兰 Italy-Milan

第68届意大利米兰国际摩托车及自行车展览会
2010 EICMA 2010 EICMA 2010 Eicma Show
2010/11/10-2010/11/15
意大利米兰 Italy-Milan

## 综合博览会
## General Fair

米兰马契夫国际博览会（春季）
Macef Spring / Autumn
2010/01/16-2010/01/19
意大利米兰 Italy-Milan

中东（迪拜）国际秋季商品交易会
2010 Dubai Autumn Fair
2010/01/17-2010/01/19
阿联酋迪拜 United Arab Emirates-Dubai

巴拿马第28届国际博览会
Expocomer 2010
2010/03/03-2010/03/06
巴拿马 Panama

国际博览会
2010/03/17-2010/03/28
埃及开罗 Egypt-Cairo

里昂国际博览会
Foire Intle de Lyon
2010/03/19-2010/03/29
法国里昂 France-Lyon

第20届越南（河内）国际贸易博览会
20th Vietnam Intl Trade Fair In Ha Nor City
2010/04/14-17
越南河内 Vietnam-Ha Noi City

意大利米兰展
SALONEUFFICIO 2010
2010/04/14-2010/04/19
意大利米兰 Italy-Milan

澳大利亚全球商品采购交易会
201 The Global Sourcing & Merchandising Expo
2010/05/05-2010/05/07
澳大利亚墨尔本 Australia-Melbourne

委内瑞拉中国工业产品展览会
2010/06 -
委内瑞拉 Venezuela

中国商品（越南）交易会
Chinese Commodities (Vietnam) Fair
2010/06/15-2010/06/18
越南河内 Vietnam-Hanoi

中国工业产品展
China Industry Expo
2010/06/18-2010/06/21
委内瑞拉加拉加斯 Venezuela-

国际贸易博览会
2010/06/28-2010/07/08
坦桑尼亚达累斯萨拉姆 Tanzania-

中国贸易博览会
2010/07 -
南非米德兰德 South Africa

摩洛哥卡萨布兰卡中国商品展
2010/07 -
摩洛哥卡萨布兰卡 Morocco-Casablanca

国际贸易博览会
2010/07/14-2010/07/19
安哥拉罗安达 Angola

美国亚洲商品采购大会
ASD/AMD SOURCE DIRECT
2010/08 -
美国 USA

米兰马契夫国际博览会（秋季）
Macef Spring / Autumn
2010/09 -
意大利 Italy

中国贸易展览会
2010/09 -
洪都拉斯圣佩德罗苏拉 Honduras

中国贸易展览会
2010/09 -
萨尔瓦多圣萨尔瓦多
SALVADOR-SAN SALVADOR

第三届中国工业产品展览会
2010/09/16-2010/09/19
乌兹别克斯坦塔什干
Uzbekistan-Tashkent

西班牙瓦伦西亚Ideas & Pasion
2010/09/28-2010/10/02
西班牙瓦伦西亚 Spain

国际贸易展览会
2010/09/28-2010/10/04
肯尼亚内罗毕 Kenya

南非国际贸易展览会
SAITEX 2010
2010/10 -
南非约翰内斯堡
South Africa-Johannesburg

国际博览会
2010/11 -
古巴哈瓦那 Cuba

国际交易会
2010/11/04-2010/11/07
博茨瓦纳哈博罗内
Botswana

亚洲商品展览会
2010/11/19-2010/11/21
科特迪瓦阿比让 Cote/d/Ivoire

中东（迪拜）五大行业—
国际建筑机械、车辆及设备展览会
2010 BIG 5 PMV
2010/11/21-2010/11/24
阿联酋迪拜 United Arab Emirates-Dubai

第八届越南（胡志明）国际贸易博览会
8th VIETNAM INTL TRADE FAIR IN HO CHI MINH CITY
2010/12/01-2010/12/04
越南胡志明市Vietname

沙特利雅得中国商品展
2010/12/05-2010/12/08
沙特阿拉伯利雅得 Saudi Arabia-Riyadh

国际贸易博览会
2010/12/08-2010/12/11
越南胡志明市 Vietnam-Ho Chi Minh City

年中东（迪拜）国际秋季商品交易会
IATF
2011/01 -
阿联酋迪拜 United Arab Emirates-Dubai

年澳大利亚全球商品采购交易会
The Global Sourcing & Merchandising Expo
2011/05 -
澳大利亚墨尔本 Australia-Melbourne

## 其他
## Others

世界城市可持续发展论坛
Global City Abu Dhabi
2010/04 -
阿联酋阿布扎比 United Arab Emirates-Abu Dhabi

全球博彩业博览会
Global Gaming Expo (G2E)
2010/11 -
美国拉斯维加斯 USA-Las Vegas

2011年巴黎国际殡葬展：
殡葬行业供应商与经销商的展会
Fun é raire Paris 2011:
The Exhibition for Funeral Suppliers & Distributors
2011 -
法国巴黎 France-Paris

# 行业先锋

## 展览会议组织与管理

### 科隆国际展览有限公司

科隆国际展览有限公司 Koelnmesse GmbH 成立于1922年，是世界上最大的展览公司之一。其每年以不同周期定期主办的60多个国际专业博览会和展览会是世界上25个行业的主导博览会。在这些领域，全球90%以上的出口型产品在此展出。科隆展览的核心主题包括：食品行业；居室、园林与休闲；健康与设施；通讯、媒体与时装；家具、室内装饰与纺织品；艺术与文化；技术与环境；IT与数字娱乐。

国内联系方式：
科隆展览中国有限公司
地址：北京市东三环北路8号亮马河大厦2座1018室
邮编：100004
电话：010-6590 7878/7766
传真：010-6590 6139
电邮：info@koelnmesse.cn
网址：www.Koelnmesse.cn

科隆展览中国有限公司　上海办事处
地址：中国上海市淮海中路283号香港广场南楼1202室
邮编：200021
电话：021-6390 6161
传真：021-6390 6858
电邮：info2@koelnmesse.cn

科隆展览中国有限公司　广州办事处
地址：广州市天河区天河北路183号大都会广场3311室
邮编：510620
电话：020-8755 2468
传真：020-8755 2970
电邮：info3@koelnmesse.cn

### 中国国际贸易中心股份有限公司

中国国际贸易中心股份有限公司展览部是中国国际贸易中心股份有限公司下从事展览组织、管理的专业部门。拥有一支业务娴熟、人员精干的专业队伍，下设展览业务部、市场开发部、现场管理部等，可提供包括展览策划、立项报批、宣传招展、搭建展台、现场管理、展厅设施维护、出租场地设备的全套展览专业服务。凭借丰富的实践经验、外语技能、完善健全的管理制度、同国内外展览业同行的广泛联系以及来自外经贸部等中央国家部委的支持协助，国贸中心展览部参与组织、主办、协办了大量重要展览会，并赢得了国内外同行和展商的普遍好评。

地址：北京建国门外大街一号中国国际贸易中心展览部
邮编：100004
电话：010-6505 2288转80448
传真：010-6505-3260
电邮：cwtced@public3.bta.net.cn
网址：www.cwtc.com.cn

### 亚洲博闻公司

亚洲博闻是亚洲地区首要的专业商贸展会主办商之一。集团并透过旗下专业刊物及相关网站，致力为企业提供高质素商业市场信息。集团的总公司——联合企业媒体(United Business Media，简称UBM)是世界知名的跨国公司，专门从事企业对企业媒体及市场资讯的服务。

亚洲博闻总部设于香港，在亚洲及美国13个主要城市共有员工600名。其业务遍布12个市场领域，共有逾100个媒体产品，包括在12个国家和地区举办的约80个贸易展会、20份专业刊物及相关市场网站。

亚洲博闻的展会享负盛名，吸引逾30,000多家参展商及来自150个国家的1,270,000名专业观众。其专业刊物为5,800多名广告客户将信息推广至135,000名业内人士。

亚洲博闻有限公司－香港总办事处：
香港湾仔港湾道26号华润大厦17楼
电话：852-2827 6211
传真：852-2827 7831
电邮：info@cmpasia.com
网址：www.cmpasia.com

上海博华国际展览有限公司
上海襄阳南路218号现代大厦十楼　（邮编：200031）
电话：021-6437 1178
传真：021-6437 0982
电子邮箱：info@cmpsinoexpo.com
网址：www.cmpsinoexpo.com

博闻(广州)展览有限公司
中国广州市流花路中国大酒店商业大厦1151-1153室
邮编：510015
电话：020-8666 0158/8666 3388转ext 1151
传真：020-8667 7120
电子邮箱：info@cmpchina.com
网址：www.cmpchina.com

### 越中会展商务有限公司

**VN-CN Convention Exhibition & Business Co Ltd**

是一家专业从事策划和运作中国－越南两国之间双向展览会议、商务考察、市场调研、投资咨询、贸易配对、学术交流、商旅等多项服务融为一体的专业商务机构。

本公司与越南各层次政府及商务机构、会展公司、行业协会、企业界有着广泛人脉关系和紧密合作，所开展的商务活动一直得到越南贸易促进局、越南外商投资局、越南工商会、越南驻华大使馆商务处、越南驻南宁总领事馆等官方的大力支持。

由本公司和越南工业贸易部贸易广告博览公司牵头成立的“中越会展联盟”将致力于打造成为中越会展业务开拓先锋，

致力于整合中越优势资源联手合作组织承揽中国参展参会商前往越南参加各类展会和合作组织承揽越南参展参会商来华参加各类展会。凭借着联盟的超前合作理念和专业操作平台，现已吸纳了多家中国和越南会展业界有识人士和实体参与联盟合作，目的是将合作操作的项目效果最大化及维护展商、会商利益最大化。

同时，本公司在组织越南商家来华参展参会采购和来华开展各类商务活动等领域也颇有成就，每年均组织和接待近2000名越南商家来华进行各类商务活动。我们曾为广交会、昆交会、、西博会、义乌小商品博览会、中国国际广告节、中国渔博会等国内20多个知名展览会成功邀请越南展商或采购商前来参会，并一直延续着合作关系。另，我司连续多年成为中国－东盟博览会越南参会客商组织接待和越南采购商招商协办机构。

（越南－中国）越中会展商务有限公司
VN-CN Convention Exhibition & Busiess Co Ltd
广西南宁市新民路3号永嘉大厦12楼
电话：0771-261 5157, 263 4998
传真：0771-263 0917
电邮：exhibition@china-vn.com

越南工业贸易部贸易广告博览股份公司（中国南宁办事处）
Vietnam National Trade Fair And Advertising Company
广西南宁市新民路3号永嘉大厦12楼
电话：0771-261 7885, 263 1887
传真：0771-263 1887
电子邮箱：vinexad.xttm@gmail.com

## 显辉国际展览有限公司

显辉国际展览有限公司成立于1989年，是一家发展迅速、专业从事在中国及东南亚地区筹办各类形专业展览会和会议服务的公司。

自成立以来，本公司便专注于发展展览业务，致力筹办不同的工业展览会，展览题材范围主要包括 ：鞋类、皮革及工业设备；医疗设备及技术；动漫画展；金属加工、塑料、印刷、食品包装的工业机械设备和技术；制冷、空调、供暖、通风及食品冷冻技术；建筑工程及建材设备；酒店、餐饮设备及服务；食品博览会；国际展销会和博览会等。

凭著已累积了20年的展览服务业经验，对亚洲各国和地区的市场动态充分了解、加上高效益的管理与营运，以及广阔的人脉网络，时至今天，我们每年所举办的国际大型展览会都已成为区内的触目盛事，部分的展览会更成为业内翘楚，亦是参展商及供应商推广业务的有效平台。 其中，在广州举办的“国际鞋类、皮革及工业设备展览会”已被誉为国内同类专业展中规模最大及最成功的国际展；还有在越南举办的工业机械展，包括“国际塑胶机械及技术展”；“国际金属加工设备及技术展”；“国际印刷、包装机械设备及技术展”；“国际食品包装机械设备及技术展”均在行内享有相当的美誉和地位。

为配合业务的迅速发展及日益频繁的商业活动需求，我们除了以香港作为总部外，亦早于公司成立之初在上海，广州，越南开设分公司，并在世界各国（包括中国大陆，台湾地区，日本，韩国，新加坡，巴基斯坦，澳大利亚，意大利，西班牙，德国等国家）建立代理服务网络，提供快捷和尽善尽美的服务。

显辉公司力求至臻，凭借广阔的人脉网络极富经验的管理层 ，具专业、富动力的员工团队，我们挚诚为世界各地的客户提供最全面的信息，最完善的服务。

地址：香港上环禧利街27号富辉商业中心2403室
电话：00852-2851 8603
传真：00852-2851 8637
电邮：topreput@hkabc.ne
网址：www.toprepute.com.hk

世界一流的展览及会议活动主办机构—英国励展博览集团早于上世纪80年代就进入中国办展览，现已发展为中国最活跃的国际展览及会议主办机构之一，拥有五家在华成员公司，包括励展中国公司、国药励展展览有限责任公司、励展华博展览（深圳）有限公司、北京励展华群展览有限公司和上海励华国际展览有限公司。励展大中华区现共有员工约450人。未来，励展还将通过持续增长现有展会、开发新项目和建立战略合作合资伙伴关系，为中国相关行业提供更多高品质的展览会，编奏面对面的力量。

励展博览集团在华举办的展览及会议在行业上涵盖了航天与航空，电子制造与组装，机床、金属加工及工业材料，包装，医药医疗及保健，礼品与家居，生活方式、旅游、博彩及地产7个在中国快速增长的专业领域。

2009年，励展各成员公司在华共举办逾40场市场领先展会，将来自海内外的逾2万名供应商和近70万名买家汇聚在一起进行面对面的业务交流和洽谈。

在不断促进相关产业及地区繁荣的同时，励展博览集团还积极履行企业公民责任，通过以下行动促进了中国会展业的可持续发展和回馈社会：

支持并在励展的展会里践行知识产权保护；

拥护展会数据审计及透明化，确保励展展会公布的数据真实有效；

关注环保，带动展会参与者及合作伙伴共同打造绿色展会；

通过“励展中国大学”持续培训中国本地员工；

实施“励展中国奖学金”，推进中国会展教育和人才培养；

捐资扶贫帮困；

举办“励展大中华区高峰会”，与行业领先企业携手推进中国展览业的提升与发展。

欲了解更多励展博览集团大中华区业务，请访问：
www.reedexpo.com.cn

# 澳门贸易投资促进局
# 为您提供全方位的商业服务

作为澳门特别行政区促进贸易和投资的机构，我们的使命是：促进本地对外贸易及引进外资，推动澳门与世界各地之间经贸关系的发展，加强相互了解，发展友好合作。

具体来讲，我们提供以下服务：

对投资者的“一站式”服务

对于在澳门的投资计划，我们向投资者提供有专人跟进的“一站式”服务：接受咨询、评估项目、专责公证办理成立公司手续、指引投资程序及所需牌照／准照申請、寻找合作伙伴、跟进有关行政手续及其它协助以便落实投资项目。为了使此项服务更加便捷完善，本局内设“专责公证员”，并且也设立了由九个政府部门主管组成的“投资委员会”。

离岸服务

本局负责非金融离岸业务的审批、技术协助和监管工作，并通过推广活动促进非金融离岸业务在澳之发展。允许在澳门经营的离岸机构分为“离岸商业服务机构”和“离岸辅助服务机构”。政府向离岸商业活动提供多项税务优惠。离岸机构只需向本局缴付一次性的设立费，及每半年一次的运作费。

经贸推广活动

本局每年主办、协办及参与在澳门及全球各地举行的经贸会展和贸易投资合作活动，主要包括：澳门国际贸易投资展览会(MIF)、中国内地及葡语国家的大型经贸洽谈会，以及各地区的投资环境推介会等。同时，本局每年亦曾组织经贸代表团出外考察访问，并接待外地代表到访，促进澳门与海内外企业家的交流与合作。此外，本局对澳门企业参加世界各地的展览会提供多方面支持，包括资助部分的参展及宣传品印刷经费，提供全球多项展览会信息等。

澳门商务促进中心

“中心”的设立是为了让外來投资者在低成本及短时间内了解澳门的营商环境和办理有关行政手续，减低在澳经商的启动成本，并为本地的企业和商会提供一个直接与外地企业和商会交流与合作的服务平台。“中心”向企业提供：

设施设备－包括现代化办公室、洽谈室、产品展示区、电脑设备、无线宽频互联网。另设有收费多功能会议厅、影印及传真等商务设备。

商贸服务—包括“贸促局咨询服务专柜”、“内地商务咨询服务”、秘书服务，以及提供有关本地企业、驻“中心”商会、政府部门行政手续及本地统计资料。另外，尚有与商会合作举办商贸推介及交流活动等。

企业之间及企业与办事处互相交流的平台—“中心”有多间外地商会、团体、机构、组织代表处(统称：办事处)进驻，如“渝澳经济合作促进会澳门秘书处”、“世界华商组织联盟”、“葡中工商协会”、“国际葡语市场企业家商会”、“中国国际贸易促进委员会驻港澳代表处”、“澳门德国商会”、“澳洲商务署澳门办事处”、“欧洲咨询中心”、“澳门葡萄牙商务中心”、“澳门英国商会”及“日资商业服务中心(澳门)有限公司”。企业可向驻“中心”的办事处直接咨询。“中心”为企业及各驻场办事处提供了交流与合作的机会。

中小企服务中心

为加強本澳中小企业之综合竞争力，把握澳门经济发展所带来之商机，并按照澳门政府支持中小企业发展的政策，于澳门贸易投资促进局属下之“澳门商务促进中心”將推出一系列协助本地中小企业之服务，并设立“中小企服务中心”，目的是协助本地中小企开拓海外和本地市场，并结合海外及本地市场需求，促进企业交流合作，引导中小企把握澳门服务业及会展业所带来之商机。

咨询服务

为了推广澳门的经贸环境，向海内外商界提供最新的商贸讯息，本局定期出版“贸易投资快讯”和“澳门经济之窗”，也經常发行“投资者指南”及有关宣传性刊物及光碟。本局的网页是我们向公众提供资讯的。

主要途径：

除了关于澳门和本局的一般资料及主要刊物内容，还有本澳制造商和出口商的资料库以及免费的主商易站等一系列丰富及不断更新的资料，为用户提供在世界各地寻找贸易投资伙伴的机会。

资讯中心

资讯中心也是我们对外提供信息咨询服务的重要窗口之一。公众可以阅读、直接向服务人员或通过电脑查寻资料，并可借阅一些特定刊物。

资讯中心主要有以下的参考资料：

外国及本澳经贸方面的基本情况
本澳经贸政策与规例
本澳及海内外统计数据
本澳及海内外厂商名录

申请居留

在本澳作出有利于澳门特别行政区的重大投资计划或重大投资的权利人、或获本地雇主聘用的、其所具备的学历、专业资格及经验被视为特别有利于本澳的管理人员或具备特别资格的技术人员，均可透过本局的投资居留暨法律处申请本澳的临时居留许可。

地址：澳门友谊大马路918号世界贸易中心一至四楼
电话：853-28 710300
传真：853-28 590309, 710304
电邮：ipim@ipim.gov.mo
网址：www.ipim.gov.mo
24小时电话查询热线 853-28 881212

## 香港贸易发展局

香港贸易发展局成立于1966年，是专责推广香港特别行政区对外贸易的法定机构，服务对象包括以香港为基地的贸易商、制造商及服务业者。我们在世界各地设有40多个办事处，其中11个在中国内地，致力推广香港作为全球企业与中国内地及亚洲经商的平台。

香港贸发局通过不同的服务，包括：贸易展览会、网上的贸易平台及产品杂志，把全世界数以百万计的买家及供应商联系起来。

香港贸发局每年在香港举办超过30个国际性贸易展览会，其中有八国外是亚洲同类型展览中规模最大的。

香港贸发局的网站 - www.hktdc.com，广受全球商家欢迎，载有来自香港、中国内地及海外90万名注册买家及超过12万名供应商的资料。用户可以于网站搜寻超过7,000个产品类别，寻找所需的产品或服务，简单快捷。

香港贸发局出版15本产品杂志及行业专刊，读者超过500万，遍及全球。我们每年出版150份贸易研究报告、针对个别行业的快讯及商业通讯，提供有关香港、中国内地及海外市场的最新情报。

同时，香港贸发局为中小企业提供商贸配对服务，我们的资料库载有全球120万家企业的资料，能为企业物色理想的合作伙伴。

香港贸发局每年举办超过160项研讨会、大型会议、工作坊及论坛，协助港商拓展新市场。此外，我们每年在世界各地举办约600项贸易推广活动，把香港的产品、服务及讯息传达给约10万名来自主要市场的商家，并在香港接待约600个访港贸易代表团。

香港贸发局和欧盟、法国、日本、韩国、英国和美国先后成立了六个双边贸易委员会，以加强香港和这些国家及地区的经贸联系。同时，香港贸发局亦担任“环球香港商业协会联盟”秘书处，通过遍及全球的香港商业协会与世界各地建立连系。

有关香港贸发局的其它资料，请浏览 www.hktdc.com

地址 ： 香港湾仔港湾道1号会展广场办公大楼38楼
电话 ： (852) 1830 668
传真 ： (852) 2824 0249
电邮 ： hktdc@tdc.org.hk

## 上海里扬展览服务有限公司

2002年1月成立的里扬集团，下属公司分别有：（上海里扬展览服务有限公司、里扬展览（香港）有限公司、上海尼奥建筑装潢有限公司、韩国成都设计（株）。我们紧紧把握时代脉搏，凭借对现代展览、展示形式和内涵的深刻理解，逐渐发展成为具实力和影响力的综合型专业展览公司，是上海市会展行业协会、北京展览馆协会、上海展览展示工程协会、上海韩国商会的会员单位，同时也是韩国釜山国际展览馆上海办事处。公司的主要业务包括：主办、承办、合作举办大型国际展览会；组织出国展览；策划大型商务活动；展台搭建以及品牌产品专柜设计。

目前，公司每年自主举办“上海国际幼儿教育展”、中韩技术转移暨投资洽谈会、产业机器人高峰论坛，专业代理海外28个知名展览会，涉及的行业有建材、电子、教育、食品、IT、化妆品等，并参与400多场展会的特装设计和制作，与SAMSUNG、INTEL、MICROSOFT、GOODYEAR、HYUNDAI、HITACHI、SIEMENS、中国电信等众多国际知名企业建立了良好的合作关系，并吸引了一批韩国和中国优秀的展览技术人才。

地址：上海市天山路600弄同达创业大厦2506室
邮编：201801
电话：021-6113 9515，6113 9516
传真：021-6113 9511
电邮：simon@neon-expo.com

## 中国对外贸易广州展览公司

中国对外贸易广州展览公司是中国对外贸易中心（中华人民共和国商务部直属机构，承办著名的“中国第一展”-- 中国进出口商品交易会）的直属企业，是目前中国最具实力和影响力的专业展览公司之一。公司以主办、承办、合作举办各类大型国际博览会和组织出国展览为主业，每年举办各类大型国际专业博览会10多个并组团参加世界各地20多个国家和地区的80多个著名国际专业展览会，展览规模和出展面积在全国同行业中名列前茅。

公司秉承“诚信可靠、优质服务、专业办展”的宗旨，赢得业内广泛好评。公司荣获了国内外多项殊荣，包括：西班牙贸易领导者俱乐部颁发的“第29届国际贸易品牌奖”和给公司总经理的“全球质量管理奖章”、商务部综合贸易经济合作研究院授予的 “诚信综合等级AAA单位”，税务部门核定的“纳税‘A’级企业”和广东省工商行政管理局连续5年授予的“重合同守信用企业”等。

地址：中国广州市流花路117号
邮编：510014
电话：020-8667 2120， 2608 1605， 2608 1608
传真：020-8666 3416
北京办事处 电话：010-6559 9082
上海办事处 电话：021-6360 5188
网址：www.fairwindow.com

## 法国爱博西雅展览（北京）有限公司

爱博集团（EXPOSIUM）是世界最著名的展览公司之一，具有五十年主办展会的经验和专长，得到国际展览界的公认。

爱博集团目前举办115个展览会，其中11个展览会在法国以外的国家举办。爱博集团办展的领域包括：农牧业、工业设备、建筑、印刷、电子、电信、信息、信息技术、食品、食品加工、包装、销售、城市规划与生活环境、旅游等。

爱博集团积极推行国际发展战略，以自己的强势市场为依托，围绕农业，食品工业，公共工程以及物流运输等行业开发市场，并以有潜力的亚洲和拉美地区的新兴国家作为开拓重点。

2004年，爱博集团在北京建立了自己的展览公司（北京爱博西雅展览有限公司），在上海设有代表处。其任务是为在法国举办的展会组织各种宣传促进活动，同时和中国的行业机构或展览公司发展合作关系，积极在华开拓新的展览会业务。

SIAL法国国际食品和饮料展览会创建于1964年，每两年一届，迄今已有40多年的历史，现已成为世界第一品牌的食品专业展会。自2000年SIAL展移植中国以来，SIAL CHINA中国国际食品和饮料展览会已成功举办了七届。SIAL CHINA展会秉承其母展－SIAL巴黎国际食品展国际性、专业性、贸易性的特点，以客户服务作为展会组织工作的中心，规模不断扩大，现已发展成为中国国际食品第一大展，是国内外食品厂商开拓中国大陆市场、亚洲市场和海外市场的不二选择，是您不容错过的贸易和合作交流平台。

法国爱博西雅展览（北京）有限公司
北京市朝外大街22号泛利大厦1605室
邮编：100020
电话：010-6588 6235，8879
传真：010-6588 6233
电邮：info@sialchina.cn
网址：www.sialchina.cn

## 上海国际展览公司

上海市国际展览有限公司成立于1984年是全国首家国营企业专业从事国际来展的展览公司，现由上海世博（集团）有限公司与上海市国际贸易促进委员会共同投资；公司成立以来，已成功举办各类展览会近500个，展览面积近500万平方米；公司现为国际博览联盟（UFI）正式会员，举办的"中国国际模具技术和设备展览会"、"上海国际汽车工业展览会"和"中国国际染料工业暨有机颜料、纺织化学品展会"是国际博览联盟认证的展览会；在2005年会展行业协会首次试评的上海首批8个优质展览会中，本公司举办的5个展览会榜上有名；公司下属的一些投资和合资公司，提供从展览运输、展馆管理、展览搭建、广告业务、展品留购和会议会务等全方位的会展服务产业链。

地址：上海市延安中路841号东方海外大厦8楼
邮编：200040
电话：021-6279 2828
传真：021-6545 5124
网址：www.siec-ccpit.com
电邮：info@siec-ccpit.com

## 义乌中国小商品城展览有限公司

义乌中国小商品城展览有限公司（以下简称义乌商展）是浙江中国小商品城集团股份有限公司（沪证代码600415）旗下控股企业，注册资金800万元，拥有50多人年轻化、高学历的专业团队，专门从事国内外展览组织业务，是UFI、IAEE的会员企业。

公司最早创办于1998年，为义乌地区首家展览企业，是历届中国义乌国际小商品博览会的唯一展务执行机构，公司承办的义博会已跻身为广交会、华交会之后的中国第三大出口商品展，成为唯一经国务院批准的日用消费品类国际大型展会。

公司成立多年以来，先后承办过浙江省旅交会、浙江省农博会、全国百货会、全国化洗会、中国会展财富论坛等国家级、省级会展项目，并自主培育及合作开发了多个品牌展览项目，包括中国义乌文化产品交易博览会、中国国际五金电器博览会、义乌消费品出口交易会、义乌国际针织及服装机械展、中国水晶及玻璃制品博览会，中国义乌国际森林产品博览会，还组织展商参加法兰克福、拉斯维加斯、伯明翰、马契夫、迪拜等境外知名展会，并取得部分境外知名展览会的出国组展权。

在中国经济新一轮发展的重要时期，我们将继续以"搭建会展平台，促进贸易机会"为宗旨，努力做好工业经济和商业经济的产业纽带。我们愿意在各界朋友的大力支持下，密切同行合作，提升企业服务，打造精英团队，逐步向国际一流的现代展览服务企业迈进。

地址：浙江省义乌市宾王路301号梅湖会展中心三楼
电话：0086-0579-85415888
传真：0086-0579-85415777

## 北京广角视野展览有限公司

作为中国展览馆协会会员单位，是主要从事国际会展策划与组织、展览工程服务等的专业化公司。公司已通过ISO9001:2000国际质量管理体系认证，是目前中国最为专业的展览公司之一。

公司成立于2004年，拥有业内资深的策划师、一流的设计师和业内知名策划顾问，以及专业的施工团队和加工工厂。业务涉及国际展会（大型活动）的策划与组织、展览工程服务、展览展示设计与制作，展厅和博物馆的设计与承建等。

公司总部位于北京，已开通4007060747服务热线，公司服务网络覆盖上海、广州、香港等八座中国大中城市，并在美国、德国等六个国家和地区设有业务网。公司自成立以来，一直致力于构建一个兼具国际视野；气氛浓厚；融会优秀企业文化的卓越建设团队。无论您在哪里，我们都能随时随地为您提供最佳的服务。

地址：北京市朝阳区曙光西里甲6号时间国际H座8层
邮编：100028
电话：010-5128 1558转ext 802
传真：010-5128 1558转ext 817
电邮：wideview@bjwav.cn

## 宁波雅卓展览服务有限公司
地址：宁波百丈东路650号贵都商务楼7楼
邮编：315040
电话：0574-2771 6625
传真：0574-8784 9306
电邮：younage@younage
网址：www.chinamaching.cn

## 晋江市展务有限公司
地址：福建省晋江市青阳外经贸大厦3楼
邮编：362200
电话：0595-8560 0609，8530 3030
传真：0595-8567 4572
电邮：jif@cn-jif.com
网址：www.cn-jif.com

## 中国演艺设备技术协会
地址：北京市东城区安定门东大街28号雍和大厦东楼C座10层
邮编：100007
电话：010-8402 9994,6403 3098转ext201/203
传真：010-8401 0152
电邮：chen@palmexpo.com
网址：www.palmexpo.com

## 中国哈尔滨国际经济贸易洽谈会
地址：哈尔滨市南岗区美顺街35号
邮编：150090
电话：0451-8234 0100
传真：0451-8234 0226
电邮：chn@ichtf.com
网址：www.ichtf.com

## 广东玩具文化经济发展研究会
地址：广州市淘金北路正平南街1号2楼
邮编：510095
电话：020-8358 7012，8358 7037
传真：020-8358 7016
电邮：expo@ctoy.cn
网址：www.chinatoyfair.com

## 中国贸促会轻工行业分会
地址：北京阜外大街乙22号
邮编：100833
电话：010-6839 6330
传真：010-6839 6422
电邮：ccpitsli@public3.bta.net.cn
网址：www.fi-c.com

## 中国食品添加剂和配料协会
地址：北京朝外大街甲6号万通中心3座1402
邮编：100020
电话：010-5979 5833
传真：010-5907 1335
电邮：cfaa1990@yahoo.com.cn
网址：www.fi-c.com

## 中国铸造协会
地址：北京市海淀区紫竹院路甲32号
邮编：100048
电话：010-8851 4541
传真：010-8851 4541
电邮：wangkunyi@foundry.com.cn
网址：www.foundry.com.cn

## 中国昆明进出口商品交易会办公室
地址：云南省昆明市北京路175号
邮编：650011
电话：0871-316 4305
传真：0871-316 4304
电邮：kmfair@kmfair.org
网址：www.kmsacc.com

## 中国化学与物理电源行业协会
地址：天津市南开区凌庄子道18号
邮编：300381
电话：022-2395 9049，2395 9268
传真：022-2338 0938
电邮：CIAPS@public.tpt.tj.cn
网址：www.cibf.org.cn

## 乌鲁木齐对外经济贸易洽谈会
地址：新疆乌鲁木齐市新华南路1292号乌洽会办公室
邮编：830049
电话：0991-285 0497，287 9890
传真：0991-287 9890
电邮：urumqifairoffice@163.com
网址：www.urumqifair.com

## 中国机床总公司/北京国机展览中心
地址：北京市朝阳区新源南路1-3号平安国际金融中心A座15层01-03,05
电话：010-5933 9075，5933 9078
传真：010-5933 9099
电邮：Jenny.chen@reedces.com.cn
网址：www.cimes.net.cn

## 中国邮电器材集团公司
地址：西城区复兴门内大街156号北京招商国际金融中心A座10层A1008室
电话：010-6642 6288
传真：010-6642 6556
网址：www.ptexpo.com.cn

## 中国机械工程学会及其焊接分会
地址：北京市海淀区莲花小区2-5-1607
邮编：100036
电话：010-6397 2404，6398 2928
传真：010-6398 0554
电邮：Whj@cmes.org
网址：essen.cmes.org

# 行业先锋

## 展览设计与施工搭建

### 奥克坦姆集团大中华区
### -奥克坦姆系统科技（苏州）有限公司

奥克坦姆系统科技（苏州）有限公司（www.octanorm.cn）是全球展览展示系统的行业领导者德国OCTANORM集团（www.octanorm.de）在苏州新加坡工业园区投资成立的全资子公司。以先进的理念创造出高效环保并且美观的铝制产品系统，除了广泛应用于展览展示行业外，还在室内装饰，陈列以及洁净室领域得到了极大的推广。提供一流的产品和服务是我们的一贯宗旨。奥克坦姆产品是真正的绿色产品，而且安装和拆除及其快捷，可以重复投入使用，运输和储存也极为方便。

“OSPI”（奥克坦姆国际服务伙伴www.ospi-network.com），是一个在OCTANORM倡导下成立的展览行业权威组织。“构筑世界会展”是奥克坦姆国际服务伙伴的宏伟目标。“本地设计，异地搭建”是其基本理念和原则。奥克坦姆国际服务伙伴使世界变得更小，借助于这个组织可以使我们的客户克服语言障碍，同时免去繁琐的海关手续。此外，OSPI还开发了专业的绘图软件，比如OCTACAD和OCTADesign等，为国际间的高效合作提供了诸多便利。

随着中国会展经济日新月异的发展，奥克坦姆在华业务日益扩大，先后设立了上海和北京分公司，且更宽广的发展网络正在不断展开。持续创新的技术，世界一流的产品，以系统实现美。奥克坦姆将在全球尤其是中国继续提供最高品质的服务。

地址：江苏省苏州工业园区星龙街428号苏春工业坊3A
邮编：215126
电话：0512-6283 3338
传真：0512-6283 3330
电邮：info@octanorm.cn

### 上海里扬展览服务有限公司

2002年1月成立的里扬集团，下属公司分别有：（上海里扬展览服务有限公司、里扬展览（香港）有限公司、上海尼奥建筑装潢有限公司、韩国成都设计（株））。我们紧紧把握时代脉搏，凭借对现代展览、展示形式和内涵的深刻理解，逐渐发展成为具实力和影响力的综合型专业展览公司，是上海市会展行业协会、北京展览馆协会、上海展览展示工程协会、上海韩国商会的会员单位，同时也是韩国釜山国际展览馆上海办事处。公司的主要业务包括：主办、承办、合作举办大型国际展览会；组织出国展览；策划大型商务活动；展台搭建以及品牌产品专柜设计。

目前，公司每年自主举办“上海国际幼儿教育展”、中韩技术转移暨投资洽谈会、产业机器人高峰论坛，专业代理海外28个知名展览会，涉及的行业有建材、电子、教育、食品、IT、化妆品等，并参与400多场展会的特装设计和制作，与SAMSUNG、INTEL、MICROSOFT、GOODYEAR、HYUNDAI、HITACHI、SIEMENS、中国电信等众多国际知名企业建立了良好的合作关系，并吸引了一批韩国和中国优秀的展览技术人才。

地址：上海市天山路600弄同达创业大厦2506室
邮编：201801
电话：021-6113 9515，6113 9516
传真：021-6113 9511
电邮：simon@neon-expo.com

### 上海新思维传播策划有限公司

上海新思维传播策划有限公司是一家从事与展会相关的综合性展览服务公司：其业务范围包括：展览展示设计制作、商业空间设计制作、会议活动策划布置、室内设计与活动硬件设施的提供；公司业务还包括：企业形象策划、创意与制作、户外媒体发布、电视广告、拍摄、期刊采编，提供影视策划与营销以及商业公关服务等等。

我司在上海浦东新区拥有面积近10000平方米的制作工厂，一支近200人的具有多年展览经验、技艺精湛的制作队伍；公司吸收及培养了一批经验丰富，具有专业素质、实战经验的专业人才；公司也有完善的硬件设施如1000多套用于标准展位的铝合金展架、烤漆房、多台意大利进口三维雕刻机、高精度写真机等。

我司成立于1995年，是上海最早从事展览行业的公司之一。在展览会上成功地完成了意大利馆、韩国馆、新加坡馆、非洲馆等国家馆的展台设计与制作；历年来我们都为全国电子展、玩具展、服装纺织展等知名展览会的主场搭建商，并获得客户的肯定和好评；特殊展台方面，我们已与众多的知名公司成功合作过，如日本马自达、通用、吉利、绿地、农工商、招商地产，顾家工艺、卡森、中国移动等等。

目前我司荣幸的被指定为2010年上海世博会的指定供应商之一，我们将以专业、完善的服务为目标，永远站在高质量不断创新的前列！

地址：上海浦东合庆镇龙江路180号
电话：021-6891 1200
传真：021-6891 1211
电邮：xiaozi1980@126.com

### 北京广角视野展览有限公司

北京广角视野展览有限公司成立于2004年，隶属于广角视野传播机构，是一家专业致力于会展组织策划、展览工程服务专业化公司，公司已通过ISO9000国际质量体系认证，中国展览协会会员单位，国家展览工程企业二级资质，河南展览协会理事单位。是目前中国展览行业发展最具潜力的展览公司。

公司以会展组织、策划、设计、创意、为专长，长期为政府展示工程项目服务，曾多次受国家部委的重任与委托，承接过各类政府展览大中型展示厅、展区的策划、设计制作工作，并屡获殊荣。

广角视野公司以“实现自身价值、凝聚团队力量、推动行业发展、传播人类梦想”为奋斗使命；秉承“服务创造价值”的经营理念，为客户提供最佳的会展组织解决方案，并力求将展览工程的商业价值与艺术形式实现完美结合。

地址：北京市朝阳区曙光西里甲6号时间国际H座8层
邮编：100028
电话：010-5128 1558转ext 802
传真：010-5128 1558转ext 817
电邮：wideview@bjwav.cn

# 行业先锋

## 展览会议中心

### 中国国际展览中心集团公司

中国国际展览中心集团公司（简称“中展集团”）是中国国际贸易促进委员会直属企业，中国展览馆协会理事长单位、国际展览业协会（UFI）成员和国际展览与项目协会（IAEE）成员。中展集团的业务范围涵盖场馆经营管理、国内外组展以及各种展览配套服务。

中国国际展览中心位于北京市朝阳区北三环东路6号，占地面积13.6万平方米，室内展馆面积6万多平方米。每年举办各类展会100多个，展出面积超过100万平方米。

2008年初开业运营的中国国际展览中心（新馆）位于北京顺义天竺空港城商务区，紧邻首都国际机场，第一期工程建筑面积24万平方米、室内展馆面积10万平方米。中国国际展览中心（新馆）是目前北京市规模最大、设施先进、功能完备的展览场馆。

电话：010-8460 0000
网址：www.ciec-expo.com

### 中国国际贸易中心

中国国际贸易中心展览大厅是中国最大的中外合资商务服务企业——中国国际贸易中心股份有限公司的一个组成部分，于1989年建成并开始投入使用，截止2001年底的十二年间，已经累计举办了各类展览会460多个，成为目前北京知名度最高、展项密度最大、国际展览最多的展览设施之一。

展览大厅地处国贸中心东翼，位于北京最繁华的高级商务区中心地带，内与国贸的商务、办公、会议、饭店、公寓、购物、娱乐等设施连为一体，构成了总面积近50万平方米、服务设施齐全完备的城中这城；总面积达10,000平方米的国贸中心展览大厅由三个展厅及序厅组成，即一号馆（2,000平方米），二号馆（3,500平方米），三号馆（2,100平方米）和可兼作布置并举行展览会开幕式的序厅（2,400平方米）。展览大厅内还设有贵宾室、会议室、咖啡厅等辅助设施，满足接待贵宾、举办专题讲座、召开新闻发布会、展团临时办公、对外联络以及展商、观众休息餐饮等多方面的需要。

展览大厅功能齐全，拥有国内展览场馆中技术最先进的设施，展览现场设立海关办事机构，以协助办理展览物资的报关手续。

地址：北京建国门外大街一号中国国际贸易中心展览部
邮编：100004
电话：010-6505 2288转80448
传真：010-6505 3260
电邮：cwtced@public3.bta.net.cn
网址：www.cwtc.com.cn

### 广东现代国际展览中心

广东现代国际展览中心GDE，位于广东省东莞市厚街镇－著名的加工制造产业基地。室内展览面积为10 万平方米， 室外广场面积为11万平方米；

引入ISO9000质量管理认证体系；一站式A+服务；

2003，2004年；分别获“会展综合服务最佳场馆、中国会展业最佳场馆”称号；

先后成为香港展览厅会议业协会海外成员、中国展览馆协会会员、2004年加人全球展览业协会（UFI）；

2010年会展信息：
广东（厚街）茶业博览会
第二十三届国际名家具（东莞）展览会
第十一届中国（东莞）国际纺织制衣工业技术展览会
第十一届中国（东莞）国际鞋机鞋材工业技术展览会
励华国际瓦楞展2010中国展/2010励华国际彩盒展
2010中国东莞国际鞋类、皮革制品、配件与生产技术展览会
第十九届华南(东莞)国际电子制造采购博览会
第十届东莞国际印刷造纸胶粘带及广告展览会
广东外商投资企业产品（内销）博览会
第二十四届国际名家具（东莞）展览会
第十五届国际集成电路研讨会暨展览会
2010中国东莞国际鞋类、皮革制品、配件与生产技术展览会
第十二届东莞国际模具展及金属加工展
第十二届东莞国际橡塑胶、包装、压铸和铸造展
2010第十届东莞嘉年华时尚生活用品购物节

地址：广东省东莞市厚街镇家具大道广东现代国际展览中心
邮编：523952
电话：0769-8598 1885
传真：0769-8590 9318
邮箱：Dickson@deexpo.com
网址：www.gdeexpo.com

## 澳门威尼斯人®酒店-会展中心

澳门威尼斯人®度假村-酒店-会展中心，拥有先进设施，占地100,000平方米之大型会议展览场地，适合举行商务聚会或国际会议。这里，拥有3000间豪华套房、逾300家国际名店、35家寰宇食府，照顾您各式所需。更提供各式精采表演及体育盛事等，都能令您的各项计划，轻松落实。

澳门威尼斯人®-度假村-酒店-会展中心，时刻以商务旅客为本，所有套房均配备传真机、打印机、复印机、安全高速上网系统，及足可容纳手提电脑之保险箱。还有，澳门地理位置优越，是亚洲交通枢纽，邻近各大城市人口更高达世界总人口的一半，提供前所未有的商业契机。

齐备设施于一身：

100,000平方米会议展览场地

3,000间至少70平方米豪华套房，配备传真机、打印机、复印机及专用数据线

6,500平方米无柱宴会厅、108间会议室

35家寰宇食府，1,000雅座之美食坊

逾300家国际品牌名店

15,000座位之威尼斯人综合馆、1,800座位之威尼斯人剧院拓展无限商机，请即登入 www.venetianmacao.com

电话：853-2882 8800

## 上海新国际博览中心

上海新国际博览中心(SNIEC)由上海陆家嘴(集团)有限公司、德国汉诺威展览公司、德国杜塞尔多夫展览公司、德国慕尼黑展览有限公司联合投资建造。

自2001年11月2日正式开业以来，上海新国际博览中心(SNIEC)已取得了快速的增长，每年举办约60余场知名展览会，并正吸引着越来越多的展会在此举行。位于上海浦东中国的商业中心，SNIEC凭借其方便的交通地理位置、单层无柱式为特点的展馆设施以及多种多样的现场服务，已博得世界的广泛关注。作为一个多功能的场馆，SNIEC也是举办各种社会、公司活动的理想场地。

目前，SNIEC拥有9个无柱展厅，面积达103,500平方米，室外展览面积100,000平方米。

SNIEC的全面扩建将于2010年完成，届时室内面积将达到200,000平方米，室外面积130,000平方米。SNIEC的扩建将进一步巩固其在中国市场的领导地位，并确保上海作为东亚地区会展中心的领导地位。

地址：上海市浦东新区龙阳路2345号

邮编：201204

电话：021-3876 0488

传真：021-6856 6089

网址：www.sniec.ne

## 郑州国际会展中心

郑州国际会展中心由郑州市人民政府投资建造，集会议、展览、商务、餐饮、娱乐演出和旅游观光为一体，功能齐备、设施一流的会展场馆，是郑州市的地标性建筑之一。

郑州国际会展中心由国际著名建筑设计大师黑川纪章规划设计，主体建筑由会议中心和展览中心两部分组成。2003年元月20日开工建设，2005年10月21日投入试运营。于2006年6月1日引入国际化管理，由中外合资的专业场地管理公司 — 郑州香港会展管理有限公司专责管理。

郑州国际会展中心占地面积68.6万平方米，建筑面积达22.68万平方米，其设施包括会议中心、展览中心、3.8万平方米的室外展场及4.5万平方米的室外停车场。

会议中心主体建筑共六层，建筑面积6.08万平方米。其中轩辕堂剧院式会议可容纳5000人，课桌式会议可容纳3,160人，10人台圆桌宴会可容纳1,660人；剧院式九鼎厅可容纳1,090人、大河厅、太室厅分别可容纳400人。另外，还有17个大中小型会议室、贵宾接待室和中餐厅、西餐厅、咖啡厅。轩辕堂、九鼎厅拥有8+1路同声传译系统，大河厅、太室厅拥有4+1路同声传译系统。

展览中心主体建筑两层，辅楼六层，建筑面积16.68万平方米。由两个展馆、68个会议室、餐饮间、洽谈间办公室及各类服务商店等组成。室内展览面积6.5万平方米，可设3,394个国际标准展位。一号展馆和二号展馆内均有推拉式活动隔断，可将每个展馆分隔成4个6,000平方米和2个4,500平方米的独立展厅。一号展馆层高14米，地面承重5吨/平方米；二号展馆层高17.6米，地面承重1.5吨/平方米。

地址：郑州市郑东新区商务内环路中央公园1号

网址：www.zzicec.com

## 亚洲国际博览馆

亚洲国际博览馆位处香港国际机场旁，坐拥完善的海陆空运输网络，交通四通八达，是香港首屈一指的展览及活动场馆，提供超过70,000平方米的可租用面积。

博览馆10个展览馆均采用单层地面无柱式的灵活设计，备有新世代的资讯及通讯科技服务，可独立或打通连接使用，切合不同类型展览活动的需要。自2005年年底开幕以来，已举行众多不同主题的大型国際展览及活动，当中包括：香港有史以来最大型的国际商贸展览暨会议—“国际电信联盟2006世界电信展”、2007年9月更首次举行由新加坡移师至香港的全球最大型民用航天及航空业务及产品展览会暨论壇—“亚洲国际航空展览会暨论坛”及每年4月及10月的“环球资源系列采购交易会”，均吸引大量海内外买家及参展商参与，足证博览馆提供一个有效的商贸平台促进中外贸易交流，让内地企业毋须远涉重洋便能有效地开拓全球市场，同时亦是外商进入中国市场的门槛，发挥双向跳板的作用。

除此之外，博览馆拥有香港规模最大的室内多用途场馆，可容纳多达13,500位观众，至今已举行了几十个国际级大型演唱会及会议。

地址：香港大屿山香港国际机场
电话：852-3606 8888
传真：852-3606 8889
电邮：info@asiaworld-expo.com
网址：www.asiaworld-expo.com

## 香港会议展览中心

香港会议展览中心座落于香港金融商业区中心，19年来，一直是无数项尖国际商贸展会及大型会议的首选场地，先后成功举办多项国际盛事，包括全球和亚洲至具规模的展会、1997香港回归庆典、1997年世界银行／国际货币基金组织理事会年会、世界贸易组织“第六次部长级会议”。

香港会议展览中心总面积达222,000平方米，其中70,000平方米可供租用，备有6个展览厅、2个宽敞雄伟的会议厅、2个环境高雅的前厅、2个国际级演讲厅、52间可容纳28　至640人不等的会议室及餐厅，提供一系列先进且高质素的技术支持设施及专业服务，适合举办各类型展会、国际会议、商务及文娱活动。自1988年开幕至今，共举行了超过34,000项活动。

香港会议展览中心屡获殊荣，其专业服务水平，蜚声国际，赢尽全球组展商的信心，自然成为举办展览会不作他想的选择。

香港会议展览中心扩建展览厅1、2、3的工程已于2006年7月动工，预算需2009年完成。扩建工程将会为香港会议展览中心增加20,000平方米的实用面积，配合积极现代化及设施提升和翻新工程，继续为用家提供信心的保证。

地址：中国香港湾仔博览道一号
电话：852-2582 8888
传真：852-2802 7384
电邮：info@hkcec.com
网址：www.hkcec.com

# 行业先锋

## 酒店

## 上海新苑宾馆

上海新苑宾馆是锦江集团下属的一家庭院式酒店。座落于外籍人士集聚的古北新区，毗邻世贸商城和国际展览中心。中环和延安路高架近在咫尺，交通便捷。宾馆拥有设施完备的各式客房310间套和10-20人大小不等的会议室多个。

步入竹海映衬中的新苑，宛如走进了江南庭院。迟尺之间，移步换景，组合建筑错落有致，假山回廊迂回曲折。推开窗户，没有车水马龙的闹市喧嚣，有的是翠竹幽幽、小桥流水，令人充分领悟到“人与自然的和谐”。

新苑餐饮与其园林景观一样独特，崇尚最好的并非最贵的，将自然、绿色、养生作为菜肴之根本，将中国文化融入其中。以“药膳”闻名的餐饮，带给您的不仅仅是色、香、味的感官体验，更让您感受到触及心灵的愉悦。

地址：中国上海虹桥路1900号
邮编：200336
电话：021-6242 6688
传真：021-6242 3256

# 行业先锋

## 展览运输

## 全球国际货运有限公司

全球国际货运有限公司在全世界约有1500个办事处，55,000名员工。作为世界领先的综合物流服务供应商之一，全球货运能为您提供一系列物流和运输服务，包括：海运，空运和陆运，展览物品运输，移民搬迁运输，特殊项目运输以及为全球体育赛事提供物流服务。全球货运于1979年开始进军中国大陆，目前已在全中国拥有33家办事处和物流中心，4,300多名员工，可为您提供全方位的卓越的物流解决方案。

全球货运有限公司是德国铁路股份公司下属运输和物流子公司。

对于展览会相关的需求，Schenker公司专业的展览队伍会提供给您最合适的解决方案，我们的服务包括：

透过环球网络协调有关方面，以确保世界各地的货物通过空运，海运，陆运的方式安抵展览场地
多样展览品的统一安排
就一切报关文件及清关手续提供专业意见
策划和及时周到的运输服务
专业有素的现场督导服务
专业的仓储服务及包装箱处理
在展览会结束后，安排货物和设备退返原地或续往下一个展览地点
安排座谈会、会议及舞台所需之设备和物料
专业的艺术品运送服务

SCHENKER中国已被指定为2008年奥运会货运代理和清关服务供应商。

华南区－全球国际货运有限公司
香港湾仔港湾道26号华润大厦38楼
电话：852-2585 9688
传真：852-2824 0328
电邮：fairs.hk@schenker.com

华中区－全球国际货运代理（中国）有限公司
上海西藏中路268号来福士广场3802-3806室
邮编：200001
电话：021-6122 5888,2890 6226
传真：021-5292 5194,2890 6223
电邮：fairs.sha@schenker.com

华北区－全球国际货运代理（中国）有限公司北京分公司
北京顺义区天竺空港工业区天纬四街5号
邮编：101312
电话：010-8048 0099
传真：010-8048 0077
电邮：fairs.bjs@schenker.com

### 泛联展览物流香港有限公司

Agility是业内公认的领先国际性企业，在全球100多个国家和地区内设有超过550家办事处，员工总数超过32,000人。我们是一间每年营业收入达60亿美元的上市公司，主要业务包括全球综合物流(GIL)、国防与政府服务事务(DGS)及投资项目。Agility(GIL)是我们商业的一部份，从科技及零售到国防及政府服务事务、化工、石油及汽油等行业，为客户提供综合物流方案。

The Agility DGS 业务包括为全球性政府及非政府机构提供全面性的全球综合物流方。可为客户在全球的交易会，博览会和贸易展会运输提供端到端的全方位管理服务。我们敬业的专业人员布遍亚太、中东、欧洲、非洲和美洲等地区各重要展会地点的办事处。我们为客户提供方便的专人联络方式，并根据您的需要为您量身提供一揽子灵活的展会选项－从规划、包装和货运代理到清关、展品就位、仓储和运返，一应俱全。我们是一间有规模的国际物流和运输管理公司，Agility的全球网络可以确保客户的展品及时地送运、展品就位和运作，并且保证有关产品的印刷品和参展材料按照计划抵达。

泛联展览物流香港有限公司
香港湾仔洛克到33号中央广场福利商业中心29楼
电话：852-2866 2505
传真：852-2866 2421
电邮：fairs-china@agilitylogistics.com
网址：www.agilitylogistics.com

泛联展览物流香港有限公司
香港湾仔骆克道33号中央广场福利商业中心29楼
电话：852-2594 9233
联络人：曾浩婷小姐

泛联国际货运代理(上海)有限公司
上海市延安西路2299号上海世贸商城1606室
邮编：200336
电话：13911992219 / 021-6236 6060
联络人：张维聪先生

泛联国际货运代理(上海)有限公司　北京分公司
北京市朝阳区朝外大街22号泛利大厦　1211室
邮编 100020
电话：13911992219 / 010-6588 1961/1962/1963/1964
联络人：张维聪先生

泛联国际货运代理(上海)有限公司　广州分公司
中国广州市东风东路726号704/706室
邮编：510080
电话：020-37655886
联络人：叶岭阳先生

# The Industry Leaders

## Exhibition Management and Conference Planners

### Koelnmesse GmbH

Koelnmessn GmbH was found in 1922. More than 60 international trade fairs and over 2,000 conferences make us the largest organizer of trade fairs on our own exhibition grounds. And Koelnmesse is also the Number 1 trade-fair location for more than 25 economic sectors. For these sectors, Koelnmesse organizes the leading global trade fairs, which present around 90 percent of the export goods produced throughout the world.

Our trade fairs and other events provide crucial momentum in the following sectors:Food/ House, Garden and Leisure/ Health, Lifestyle and Facilities/ Communications, New Media and Fashion/ Furniture,Interior Design and Textiles/ Technology and Enviroment/ Art and Culture/ IT and Digital Entertainment.

Koelnmesse Co Ltd China
Add: Unit 1018 Landmark Tower II, No. 8 Dongsanhuan N.Road, Beijing 100004, PR China
Tel: 010-6590 7766
Fax: 010-6590 6139
E-mail: info@koelnmesse.cn
Web: www.Koelnmesse.cn

Koelnmesse Shanghai Branch
Add: Unit 1202 (South) No283 Huahai (M) Rd.
Shanghai 200021
PR China
Tel: 021-6390 6161
Fax: 021-6390 6858
E-mail: info2@koelnmesse.cn

Koelnmesse Guangzhou Branch
Add: Room3311 Metro Plaza, 183 Tianhe Road (North), Tianhe District, Guangzhou 510620, PR China
Tel: 020-8755 2467
Fax: 020-8755 2970
E-mail: info3@koelnmesse.cn

### China World Trade Center Co Ltd

CWTC Exhibition Division under China World Trade Center Co., Ltd. is specially engaged in exhibition organization, who put under several subordinated departments, namely the Marketing Development Management Department. A full range of exhibition services are provided, including planning an exhibition, gaining approvals from governmental authorities concerned, inviting exhibitors and promoting campaign, stand-fitting, on-site management, hall maintenance, and leasing facilities etc. The Exhibition D1ivision has successfully involved itself in hosting, organizing, and co organizing a large number of significant exhibitions, and won favora blecomments from all its counterparts and exhibitors home and abroad, with its experiences, language capabilities, well-established management system, widespread contacts inside and outside the country and also the support from the Ministry of Foreign Trade and Economic Cooperation and other state departments and administrations.

Add: Exhibition Division, China World Trade Center Co Ltd,
1 Jian Guo Men Wai Avenue, Beijing 100004, China
Tel: 010-6505 2288ext 80448
Fax: 010-6505 3260
E-mail: cwtced@public3.bta.net.cn
Web: www.cwtc.com.cn

## CMP Asia
## Asia's Leading Trade Fair Organizer

CMP Asia is a leading organizer of trade fairs throughout Asia and a provider of high-quality business information through its publications and websites. It is part of United Business Media, one of the world's leading business-to-business media and market information companies.

CMP Asia operates in 12 market sectors through its regional headquarters in Hong Kong with 600 staff in 13 major cities in Asia and the USA. It has more than 100 media products comprising over 80 trade shows held in 12 countries/ regions and 20 publications with associated B2B websites.

Every year, over 30,000 exhibiting companies and 1,270,000 professional visitors from 150 countries and regions come to CMP Asia's trade fairs.

CMP Asia Ltd - Regional Head Office:
Add: 17/F China Resources Building, 26 Harbour Road,
Wanchai, Hong Kong
Tel: 852-2827 6211
Fax: 852-2827 7831
Email: info@cmpasia.com
Web: www.cmpasia.com

Shanghai CMP Sinoexpo International Exhibition Co Ltd:
Add: 10 Fl. Xian Dai Mansion, 218 Xiang Yang Road (S),
Shanghai 200031, China
Tel: 021-6437 1178
Fax: 021-6437 0982
E-mail: info@cmpsinoexpo.com
Web: www.cmpsinoexpo.com

CMP China (Guangzhou) Co Ltd:
Add: Room1151, China Hotel Office Tower, Liuhua Road,
Guangzhou 510015, China
Tel: 020-8666 0158ext 11
Fax: 020-8667 7120
E-mail: info@cmpchina.com
Web: www.cmpchina.com

## Hong Kong Trade Development Council

Established in 1966, the Hong Kong Trade Development Council (HKTDC) is the international marketing arm for Hong Kong-based traders, manufacturers and service providers. With more than 40 global offices, including 11 in the Chinese mainland, the HKTDC promotes Hong Kong as a platform for doing business with China and Asia.

The HKTDC connects millions of international buyers and sellers through a variety of integrated services, namely its trade fairs, online marketplace and product magazines.

One of the world's major trade fair organisers, the HKTDC puts on more than 30 international trade fairs annually in Hong Kong. Eight of these are the biggest of their kind in Asia.

The HKTDC website, www.hktdc.com, features about 900,000 registered buyers and more than 120,000 quality suppliers from Hong Kong, the Chinese mainland and beyond. Users can browse through more than 7,000 clearly defined product categories to find products and services quickly and efficiently.

With 15 product magazines and industry supplements and more than five million readers, the HKTDC is a major publisher. The HKTDC also produces about 150 trade reports, sector-specific updates and business newsletters a year, providing timely market intelligence on Hong Kong, the Chinese mainland and international markets.

Supporting these services is HKTDC Business Matching, which helps companies find the right partners. Its global databank includes about 1.2 million business contacts.

The HKTDC also produces more than 160 seminars, conferences, workshops and forums a year to help Hong Kong companies develop new markets for their products and services. As well, it organises about 600 Hong Kong promotional events around the world, reaching nearly 100,000 business people in key markets each year, and receives about 600 international business missions a year.

The HKTDC's international reach is reflected in the six bilateral committees it serves. These high-level business forums promote economic ties between Hong Kong and the European Union, France, Japan, Korea, the United Kingdom and the United States. The HKTDC also serves as Secretariat for the Federation of Hong Kong Business Associations Worldwide.

For more information about the HKTDC, visit www.hktdc.com.

Tel: 852-183 0668
Fax: 852-2824 0249
E-mail: hktdc@tdc.org.hk

## Top Repute Company Limited

Top Repute Company Limited, established in 1989, is a rapid growing professional exhibition and conference organizer based in Hong Kong. We expertise in organizing international exhibitions, conferences and events in Mainland China and South East Asia.

Our business scope covers Mainland China and South East Asia markets. Every year, we organize numerous of large-scale international exhibitions in Shanghai, Guangzhou, Vietnam and Cambodia such as: "Shoes & Leather", "Medical Equipment & Technology", "Metalworking & Industrial Machinery", "Rubber & Plastics", "Print & Pack","Food Packaging Machinery & Technology", "Construction, Building Industry & Materials", "Refrigeration, Air-conditioning, Heating & Ventilation System", and "International Trade Fair" etc.

With over 20 years of experience and expertise in the exhibition industry, we have maintained good contacts and have a wide consultancy network with the related industry. We have organised numerous leading events each year, such as the largest and most reputable fairs in China, "Shoes & Leather - Guangzhou" and "Medical - Shanghai" as well as the "International Industrial Machinery Exhibition (IIME)" in Vietnam. All our exhibitions have already gained international reputations in their respective fields of industry.

Whether you plan to tap into new markets, expand existing markets, or enhance your corporate communication, Top Repute Company Limited is always your reliable working partner. We and our well-trained energetic staff will, at all times, assure the best services to our worldwide clients.

Add: Room 2403, Fu Fai Commercial Centre, 27 Hillier Street, Sheung Wan, Hong Kong
Tel: 852-2851 8603
Fax: 852-2851 8637
E-mail: topreput@top-repute.com
Web: www.toprepute.com.hk

## Shanghai Neon Exhibition Ltd

Neon Group was established in January, 2001, and it has subsidiaries: Shanghai Neon Exhibition Ltd, Neon Exhibition (Hong Kong) Ltd, Shanghai Neon Construction & Decorate Ltd, Korea Chengdu Design Ltd. With our understanding of trends in the industry and modern exhibition forms, we are growing to be a comprehensive and professional exhibition enterprise. We are a member of Shanghai Convention & Exhibition Industries Association,Beijing Exhibition Center. Meanwhile, we are the Shanghai office of Busan Exhibition and Convention Center. Our services include: organizing, undertaking and co-organizing large scale international exhibitions; organizing exhibitors and visitors to participate overseas exhibitions; planning business activities; booth construction and showcase design. At present, we are the organizer of Kids Education Expo Shanghai, the overseas agent of 28 well-known exhibitions, and we take part in the design and construction of special stands for about 400 exhibitions. We establish cooperating relations with many famous international enterprises, such as SAMSUNG, INTEL, MICROSOFT, GOODYEAR, Hyundai Motor, HITACHI, SIEMENS, China Telecommunication and so on. As a result, Neon appeal to many talents from China and Korea.

Tel: 021-6113 9515, 6113 9516
Fax: 021-6113 9511
E-mail: simon@neon-expo.com

## Reed Exhibitions Greater China

Reed Exhibitions, the world's leading events organiser, first began operating in China in the early 1980s and has since grown into one of the most dynamic events organisers in China. To date, Reed Exhibitions Greater China boasts 5 member companies, namely Reed Exhibitions China, Reed Sinopharm Exhibitions Co Ltd, Reed Huabo Exhibitions (Shenzhen) Co Ltd, Reed Huaqun Exhibitions Co Ltd and Reed Huayin (Shanghai) International Exhibitions Co Ltd. In total, these companies employ 450 staff and have offices in Beijing, Shanghai, Shenzhen and Hong Kong. Reed Exhibitions seeks to attain sustainable development in China through organic growth, new show launches and forging strategic partnerships of joint ventures. By doing so, it aims to deliver even more premium quality events in China.

Reed Exhibitions Greater China serves an array of China's fast growing specialized sectors including Aerospace and aviation, Electronics manufacturing & assembly, Machine Tools, metalworking and industrial Materials, Converting, Pharmaceutical, medical and health care, Gifts and houseware, and Lifestyle, travel, gaming and property via more than 40 market-leading events per year.

In 2009, the Reed Exhibitions Greater China organised over 40 events, bringing together over 20,000 suppliers and about 700,000 visitors for face to face business meetings, exchanges and negotiations.

Apart from continuously expanding its business in China and contributing to the prosperity of related industries and areas, Reed Exhibitions is also committed to its other industrial and social responsibilities in China. It has been promoting the sustainable development of the Chinese conference and exhibition industry and giving back to local community through the following initiatives:

Endorsing and effecting IPR protection at its events;

Advocating exhibition statistics auditing, transparency and verifiable reporting of statistics;

Creating green exhibitions by raising the environmental awareness of the participants and partners and taking green initiatives;

Training its local employees through the Reed Exhibitions China University;

Implementing the scholarship program to promote exhibition education and talent development;

Making donation to those in need of help;

Organising the annual Reed Exhibitions China Summit and joining hands with leading exhibition organizers in China to promote the development of the industry.

For more information on Reed Exhibitions' business in Greater China, please visit www.reedexpo.com.cn

## Macao Trade and Investment Promotion Institute

Always at Your Service

As the trade and investment promotion institute in Macau, IPIM's mission is to promote Macau's externaltrade and attract investment, to develop and strengthen economic and trade relationship between Macao and other parts of the world.

### One-Stop Service

IPIM provides a personal service "One-Stop Service" for investors, including information enquiries, project assessment, company registration assistance by our notary, guidance on administrative application procedures for licenses, looking for partnership, project follow-up, and assistance in the implementation project. In order to facilitate this service, an independent notary and an investment committee, compose of senior officials from nine different government departments have been established.

### Offshore Services

IPIM is responsible for the issuing of licenses, technical assistance and supervision for nonfinancial offshore institutions, and to promote offshore development through various activities. A lot of incentives are offered to offshore businesses, while there is only a set-up fee, and an operating fee every six months.

### Economic and Trade Promotional Activities

IPIM annually organized or co-organzized and participated different kinds of local and international trade exhibition and investment cooperation promotional activities, namely: Macao Trade and Investment Fair (MIF), China and Portuguese Speaking Countries Economic Forum and Business Environment Presentation of different parts of the world. Moreover, we organize annually various finding tour for local entrepreneurs and welcome overseas delegation, thus creating a cooperation exchange between Maao and Overseas enterprises.

Besides, for international trade and investment fairs, we actively give subsidies for local enterprises: participation and the printing of promotional materials, to provide international information on Exhibition and Convention Industry.

### Macao Business Support Centre

The Centre serves to reduce the initial setup costs for foreign investors, enabling the enterprisesto be familiar with Macao's business environment and the relevant administrative procedures in a relatively short time and to facilitate the implementation of their investment projects, as well as providing a service platform for cooperation exchange between local and overseas enterprises and business association. The center offers the following:Facilities/equipments --- inclue modern offices, meeting rooms, Display Gallery, computers and broad-band Internet services. Apart, there are chargeable fees on multi-functional conference rooms, printing and facsimile services among others business facilities.

Business Service - include "Consultation Service Counter", "Mainland China Business Advisory Service", Secretarial Service and provide administrative procedures and statistical information of local enterprises, business associations stationed in the Centre and Government Services. Moreover, is frequently the organization of Trade and Economic Presentation and Exchange Activities in cooperation with Business Association.

Platform of mutual co-operation between Enterprises and stationed repseresentative offices - several local and overseas business associations/organizations/ institutions/ representative offices, such as Chongqing-Macao Economic Promotion Association-Macao Office, World Federation of Chinese Entrepreneurs Organization, Portuguese - Chinese Chamber of Commerce and Industry, International Lusophone Markets Business Association, China Council for the Promotion of International Trade Hong Kong and Macau Representative Office, German Macau Business Association, Australian Trade Commission- Austrade, Euro-Info Centre, Macau, Macao-Portuguese Businesse Center, Macau British Business Association and Japan Business Service Centre are stationed at MBSC. Enterprises can either contact these offices directly or through the assistances of MBSC to arrange for various business exchanges or cooperations.

### Small and Medium Enterprises Service Centre (SMEC)

In order to enhance the comprehensive competitiveness of local Small and Medium Enterprises (SMEs) and assist them to grasp the opportunities brought about by Macao's economic development and in accordance withto Macao government policies to support SMEs, the Macao Trade and Investment Promotion Institute (IPIM) will launch a series of services to assist local SMEs, which includes the setting-up of the Small and Medium Enterprises Service Centre (SMEC) in the Macao Business Support Centre (MBSC). SMEC will help local SMEs to develop overseas and local markets and provide exchanges between enterprises and cooperation in accordance with overseas and local market's demands. Thus, it will give Macao's

SMEs guidance to grasp the business opportunities brought about by the service, conventions and exhibition industries.

### Information Services and Information Centre

In order to promote Macau's business environment and to furnish the business community with the most up-to-date information, we publish "Newsletter", "Macao Image","Investor's Guide"and related promotional CD-Roms or printing materials.The website is our chief means to deliver quality information service. All our major publications have now an on-line version.Not only general information about Macao and our Institute can be found in the site, a business database of all manufacturers and exporterss also open to free access. Moreover, a free "Etrade" service is provided, helping users in their search for suitable trade or investment partners around the globe.

### Information Centre

There is an Information Centre located on the 2nd floor of World Trade Center. The Information Centre is one of the means by which we provide information enquiry services. The public can read, search for information by computer or by direct enquiry and borrow some of the materials. Reference materials available at the Information Centre include:

General information on local and worldwide economic and trade situation

Local economic and trade policies and regulations

Local and overseas statistical data, updated information on imports and exports

Local and overseas trade directories

Application for the Right of Residence

Those who have submitted investment projects or made a significant investment; or managerial staff and specialist technicians hired by local employers, who due to their qualifications or professional experience, are considered beneficial to Macao may apply to our Residence Application and Legal Affairs Division for a temporary residency in Macao.

Add: Av. Amizade no 918, Edif. World Trade Centre,
1-4 andares, Macau
Tel: 853-2871 0300
Fax: 853-2859 0309, 2871 0304
E-mail: ipim@ipim.gov.mo
Web: www.ipim.gov.mo
24-hour enquiry hotline 853-28 881212

## China Commodities City Exhibition Co Ltd

Yiwu China Commodities City Exhibition Co Ltd (hereinafter referred as "CCC Exhibition" below) is a holding company of Zhejiang China Commodities City Group Co Ltd with registered capital of 8 million Yuan, professional teams composed of over 50 well-educated young people, specially engaging in dometic and overseas exhibition organizing service, as a member of UFI (The Global Association of the Exhibition Industry ) & IAEE ( International Association of Exhibitions and Events ).

As the first exhibition enterprise in Yiwu district, the company was founded in 1998, and was the only execution agency of the past China Yiwu International Commodities Fairs. Dominantly government-guided but specifically hosted by Yiwu China Commodities City Exhibition Co Ltd China Yiwu International Commodities Fair has become the third biggest export commodities exhibition following Caton Fair and East China Fair, and is the sole large international fair for daily consumer goods approved by State Council.

Since the foundation, the company has hosted many national or provincial large convention & exhibition projects, such as National General Merchandise Conference, National Cosmetics & Lavation Conference, China Convention & Exhibition Fortune Forum, Zhejiang Tourism Trade Fair, and Zhejiang Agriculture Fair, Yiwu Sourcing Fair: Consumer Goods, Yiwu International Knitting & garment Machinery Exhibition, China Crystal & Glass industry Fair, China International Woodon Products Fair, and organized the exhibitors' participation in the overseas well-known exhibitions like Frankfurt, LasVegas, Birmingham, Macef, Dubai, achieving the organizing right of part of the overseas well-known exhibitions.

In the newround important economic develepment of China, we'll continue to function as the bridge between industrial economy and commercial economy, with the aim of "build exhibition platform, and promote trade opportunities". We would like to tighten the cooperation with the company in the same industry, improve the service quality, and build an elite team, gradually close to the international first-class modem exhibition service company, under the support of friends from all walks of life.

Add: 3/F, China Commodities City Exhibition (Meihu) Centre, Binwang road 301#, Yiwu, Zhejiang.
Tel: 0579-8541 5888
Fax: 0579-8541 5777

### Shanghai International Exhibition Co Ltd

Shanghai International Exhibition Co Ltd was found in 1984 as the first state enterprise specialized in international exhibitions, which is now jointly invested by Shanghai World Expo (Group) Co., Ltd and CCPIT Shanghai Sub Council. SIEC has held 500 international exhibitions of various themes in China since its founding. SIEC is a full member of Union des Foires International (UFI). Die & Mould China, Auto Shanghai and China Interdye are the approved events of UFI. The five of its show are among the first eight exhibitions awarded as High Quality Trade Show by the Evaluation Committee of Shanghai Convention & Exhibition Industries. The affiliated organizations of SIEC providing a comprehensive solution on exhibition services including Freight Forwarding, Venue Management, Booth Fitting, Advertisement,Trade Liaison and etc.

Add: 8/F, OOCL Plaza, 841 Yan An Zhong Rord,
Shanghai 200040, China
Tel: 021-6279 2828
Fax: 021-6545 5124
E-mail: info@siec-ccpit.com
Web: www.siec-ccpit.com

### China Foreign Trade Guangzhou Exhibition Corporation

Subordinated to China Foreign Trade Center, which is affiliated to the Ministry of Commerce of the People's Republic of China, and the host of the famous China Import and Export Fair (known as the "Canton Fair"), China Foreign Trade Guangzhou Exhibition Corporation (CFTGEC) is one of the most reputable specialized exhibition companies in China. With over 50 years' rich experience in holding the "Canton Fair", CFTGEC now holds more than 10 international exhibitions and trade fairs in China every year, and organizes Chinese enterprises to participate in more than 80 famous fairs abroad.

The Trade Leaders' Club in Spain granted CFTGEC the "29th International Award For The Best Trade Name", for the whole joint ofproducts, activities and services provided by the company, as well as the "Global Quality Management" awarded to the president of the company.

Add: 117 Liu Hua Road, Guangzhou 510014, China
Tel: 020-8667 2120, 2608 1605, 2608 1608
Fax: 020- 8666 3416
Beijing Office Tel: 010-6559 9082
Shanghai Office Tel: 021-6360 5188
Web: www.fairwindow.com

### Younage Exhibition Co Ltd

7/F, No. 650 Baizhang East Road Ningbo, China
Tel: 0574-2771 6625, 2771 6618
Fax: 0574-8784 9306, 2771 6616
E-mail: younage@younage.com
Web: www.meonline.com.cn

### Jinjiang Exhibition Affairs Co Ltd, Fujian

3F Foreign Economy & Trade Building Qingyang, Jinjiang, Fujian. 362200 China
Tel: 0595-8566 4572, 8567 1572
Fax: 0595-8567 4572, 8560 0610
E-mail: jif@cn-jif.com
Web: www.cn-jif.com

### International China Harbin Fair for Trade and Economic Cooperation

35, Meishun Street, Nangang District, Harbin 150090
Tel: 0451-8234 0100
Fax: 0451-8234 0226
E-mail: zhanlanchu@00615.com.cn
E-mail: qying@00615.com.cn
Web: www.00615.com.cn

### Guangdong Research Council of Toy Cultural & Economic Development

2/F, 1 Zhengping Street South, Taojin Road North, Guangzhou 510095, China
Tel: 020-8358 7012, 8358 7037
Fax: 020-8358 7016
E-mail: ex@ctoy.com.cn
Web: www.ctoy.com.cn

### China Entertainment Technology Association (Formally China Theatrical Equipment Association)

No.1 Xilou Alley,Yonghegong Str., Beijing 100007, China
Tel: 010-8402 9994, 6403 3098 ext 201/ 203
Fax: 010-8401 0152
E-mail: zhao@calmexpo.com.cn
Web: www.calmexpo.com.cn

### CCPIT Sub-council of Light Industry

22B, Fuwai Dajie, Beijing 100833 China
Tel: 010-6839 6330
Fax: 010-6839 6422
E-mail: ccpitsli@public3.bta.net.cn
Web: www.fi-c.com

### China Food Additives & Ingredients Association

Rm.1402 Tower C Vantone No. 6A Chaowai St., Beijing 100020 China
Tel: 010-5979 5833
Fax: 010-5907 1335
E-mail: cfaa1990@yahoo.com.cn
Web: www.fi-c.com

### China Foundry Association

A32 Zizhuyuan Rd, Beijing, China
Tel: 010-8851 4541
Fax: 010-8851 4541
E-mail: wangkunyi@foundry.com.cn
Web: www.foundry.com.cn

### China Industrial Association of Power Sources

No.18, Lingzhuangzi Road, Nankai District, Tianjin 300381, China
Tel: 022-2395 9049, 2395 9268
Fax: 022-2338 0938
E-mail: CIAPS@public.tpt.tj.cn
Web: www.cibf.org.cn

### Urumqi foreign Economic Relations and Trade Fair

Urumqi Fair Office, No. 1292, South Xinhua Road, Urumqi, Xinjiang
Tel: 0991-285 0497, 287 9890
Fax: 0991-287 9890
E-mail: urumqifairoffice@163.com
Web: www.urumqifair.com

### Chinese Mechanical Engineering Scociety

2-5-1607 Lianhuaxiaoqu, Haidian District, Beijing 100036, China
Tel: 010-6397 2404, 6398 2928
Fax: 010-6398 0554
E-mail: Whj@cmes.org/ Fanx@cmes.org
Web: essen.cmes.org

### China National Machine Tool Corp Capital Exhibition Services

Unit 01-03,05, 15th Floor, Tower A, Ping An International Finance Center, No.1-3, Xinyuan South Road, Chaoyang District, Beijing 100027, China
Tel: 010-5933 9075, 5933 9078
Fax: 010-5933 9099
E-mail: Jenny.chen@reedces.com.cn
Web: www.cimes.net.cn

### China National Postal and Telecommunications Applicances Corporation

F106A Beijing Ocean Plaza, No. 158 Fu Xing Men Nei Street, Xi Cheng District, Beijing 100031 China
Tel: 010-6642 6288
Fax: 010-6642 6556
E-mail: zhangbaolin@ptac.com.cn
Web: www.ptexpo.com.cn

# Exhibit Designers and Producers

### OCTANORM® Group Great China - OCTANORM System Technology (Suzhou) Co Ltd

It was in 1968 that a great idea matured into a concept and the concept was transformed into an ingenious product - the OCTANORM® exhibition system. After 40 years development, OCTANORM® has been recognised as the world leader in the manufacture and distribution of aluminium profiles and systems for the exhibition, retail and display industries. Recommended and appreciated by designers to contractors, our range of products has represented the benchmark of quality.

With the years of experience and hard work, OCTANORM® System Technology (Suzhou) Co Ltd (www.octanorm.cn), subsidiary of OCTANORM®-Vertriebs-GmbH, was funded in SIP China in May 2003. We inherit the global standardization of produce and service from Germany. The need to implement exhibit designs more efficiently, more logically and considerably more professionally fired the imagination that eventually resulted in the world of systems.

Boasting over 2,000 product innovations, OCTANORM® is not only the original exhibition system but is also the world market leader in system construction. From the very start OCTANORM® set about identifying and consistently applying the latest developments in both technology and design. Also, from the outset, OCTANORM® pursued a marketing strategy that was based on a partnership concept.

The secret of our success has always been in our innovative ideas, experienced staff, state-of-the-art production methods and meticulous quality control. With the increasing development of exhibition in China, OCTANORM® has got great progress and we have opened the offices in Beijing and Shanghai. We are always focusing on research and development in order to create the most scientific system solutions. Every year, we bring surprising products to the public. Meanwhile, with the support of accumulated experience from thousands experiments and more than 158 OSPI members all over the world, OCTANORM® is providing the most professional exhibition service everywhere.

Add: 3A, 428 Xinglong Street, Suzhou Industrial Park, Jiangsu, China
Tel: 0512-6283 3338
Fax: 0512-6283 3330
E-mail: info@octanorm.cn
Web: www.octanorm.cn

### Shanghai New Trend Medium Co Ltd

Shanghai New Trend Medium Co Ltd, located at the east of Shanghai, is a professional service company with more than 10-year experience of booth design, international exhibitions, conferences, publicizing activities, indoor decoration, and exclusive store image. We have a workshop of about 10000m$^2$ and over 150 team workers. Further more, there are excellent designers with the ability of combining 3D art and commerce perfectly. They try the best to make every design a masterpiece by their special creativity. With their sensitivity to the market and the understanding to the clients, they turn the original ideas of clients into great works.With the modern management and operation, international standard service, reasonable price, from the original design to the construction of booths, no doubt that we'll provide you effective and high quality service. Therefore, we win the applause and trust from our clients. Our business covers all over China, and our co-operators expand all over the world. With our staff's effort and our unique advantage, Shanghai New Trend Medium is becoming the leader in Shanghai exhibition and show field. we always devote to the customer needs. We want to be their indispensable partner. We are ambitious to create better works than our customers's expectation. We are committed to providing high quality products and loyal services.we are honored to be one of the appointed booth contractors during the 2010 Shanghai Expo.

Tel: 021-6891 1200
Fax: 021-6891 1211
E-mail: xiaozi1980@126.com

### Shanghai Neon Exhibition Ltd

Neon Group was established in January, 2001, and it has subsidiaries: Shanghai Neon Exhibition Ltd, Neon Exhibition(Hong Kong) Ltd, Shanghai Neon Construction & Decorate Ltd, Korea Chengdu Design Ltd. With our understanding of trends in the industry and modern exhibition forms, we are growing to be a comprehensive and professional exhibition enterprise. We are a member of Shanghai Convention & Exhibition Industries Association,Beijing Exhibition Center. Meanwhile, we are the Shanghai office of Busan Exhibition and Convention Center. Our services include: organizing, undertaking and co-organizing large scale international exhibitions; organizing exhibitors and visitors to participate overseas exhibitions; planning business activities; booth construction and showcase design. At present, we are the organizer of Kids Education Expo Shanghai, the overseas agent of 28 well-known exhibitions, and we take part in the design and construction of special stands for about 400 exhibitions. We establish cooperating relations with many famous international enterprises, such as SAMSUNG, INTEL, MICROSOFT, GOODYEAR, Hyundai Motor, HITACHI, SIEMENS, China Telecommunication and so on. As a result, Neon appeal to many talents from China and Korea.

Tel: 021-6113 9515, 6113 9516
Fax: 021-6113 9511
E-mail: simon@neon-expo.com

## Convention and Exhibition Centers

### China International Exhibition Center Group Corporation (CIEC)

China international exhibition center group corporation (CIEC) , subordinate to China council for the promotion of international trade (CCPIT) , chairs the China association of exhibition centers (CAEC) and is a member of the global association of the exhibition industry (UFI) and the international association for exhibitors and events (IAEE). CIEC business scope covers venue operation and management, domestic and overseas show organization and various relevant exhibition services.

China international exhibition center, located at 6 east beisanhuan road, Chaoyang District, Beijing, covers an area of 136, 000m$^2$ with over 60,000 m$^2$ of indoor exhibiting space. More than 100 shows and exhibitions take place in CIEC venue annually with exhibiting space totaling over 1,000,000 m$^2$ .

New China international exhibition center (NCIEC) , put into operation in early 2008, is located in Tianzhu Airport industrial Zone, Shunyi District, Beijing, close to Beijing capital international Airport. Being the largest exhibition venue with integrated and modern facilities in Beijing, the first phase of NCIEC covers an area of 240,000 m$^2$ with 100,000 m$^2$ of indoor exhibiting space.

Tel: 010-8460 0000
Web: www.ciec-expo.com

### China World Trade Center Exhibition Hall

The CWTC Exhibition Hall as part of China World Trade Center-China's biggest Sino-foreign joint venture providing business service was finished and came into operation in 1989. Up to the end of 2001, it had hosted more than 460 exhibitions of various kinds during these 12 years, and become one of the most prestigious and the most frequency used fair grounds with the most international exhibitions.

Situated at the east of China World Trade Center, which is at the center of the most flourishing high-class business area, the Exhibition Hall is on the one hand, in conjunction with the CWTC business, office area, conference rooms, hotels, apartment buildings, shopping and recreational facilities etc. thus forming a 500,000 m$^2$ well-equipment complex called "A city within a city?"

With a gross area of 10, 000 m$^2$, the CWTC Exhibition Hall is composed of 3 halls and the lobby, namely Hall One (2,000m$^2$), Hall Two (3,500m$^2$), Hall Three (2,100m$^2$) and the Lobby (2,400m$^2$) which can be used either for exhibiting or for holding opening ceremony. The Exhibition Hall has auxiliary facilities like VIP rooms, meeting rooms, offices, and coffee shop so as to meet the exhibitors and the visitors needs of receiving distinguished guests,holding seminars and press conference, handing office work, maintaining contact with the outside, as well as lounge, food and beverage services etc. This poly-functional exhibition hall is an equipped with most technologically advanced facilities in China. A Chinese Customs office is established right at the exhibition site to facilities clearance of exhibition materials.

Address: Exhibition Division, China World Trade Center Co Ltd
1 Jian Guo Men Wai Avenue, Beijing 100004, China
Tel: 010-6505 2288 ext 80448
Fax: 010-6505 3260
E-mail: cwtced@public3.bta.net.cn
Web: www.cwtc.com.cn

## Shanghai New International Expo Center

Shanghai New International Expo Center (SNIEC) is China's leading expo center, boasting state-of-the-art facilities. Situated in Shanghai's Pudong district, the heart of Chinese business, SNIEC has attracted worldwide attention since its opening in November, 2001. Featuring a prime, easily accessible location, a pillar-free, single story structure and a wide array of expert on-site services, SNIEC has been experiencing rapid growth. It now hosts more than 60 world-class exhibitions each year and this number is set to grow in the future.

Currently, SNIEC has 9 exhibition halls with 103500 square meters of indoor exhibition space and 100000 square meters of outdoor exhibition space.

SNIEC plans to complete of all its facilities and reach full exhibition capacity by 2010. By then, the Center will contain 200,000 square meters of indoor floor area and 130,000 square meters of outdoor area. SNIEC's future expansions will cement its market leadership in China and secure Shanghai's position on the forefront of East Asian exhibition destinations.

SNIEC is a multi-functional venue that also caters to a diverse range of both social and corporate events.

Shanghai New International Expo Centre (SNIEC) opened on November 2, 2001, and is jointly owned by Shanghai Lujiazui Development (Group) Co Ltd, Deutsche Messe AG, Messe Duesseldorf GmbH and Messe Muenchen GmbH.

Tel: 021-3876 0488
Fax: 021-6856 6089
Web: www.sniec.net

## Guangdong Modern International Exhibition Center (GDE)

Located at the middle of Canton-Hong Kong Golden corridor - HouJie Dong Guan, the acknowledged base of processing and manufacturing.

100,000 $m^2$ indoor space, 110,000$m^2$ outdoor.
ISO900 quality management system
"One-stop " services
The Best Exhibition Venue of year 2003 & 2004 in China.
A member of HKECIA, CAEC, UFI

2010 Exhibition Program:
Guangdong (Houjie) Tea Expo
The 23th International Famous Furniture Fair (Dongguan)
The 11th China (Dongguan) Int'l Textile & Clothing Industry fair
The 11th China (Dongguan) Int'l Footwear Machinery &Material Industry
The 10th Dongguan Shoes/ China Shoetes
The 19th (Dongguan) south China Eletronic Fair
The 10th Dongguan International Printing and Packaging and paper advertising, adhesive tape, protective film exhibition
Guangdong Foreign-invested Enterprises Commodities Fair
The 24th International Famous Furniture Fair (Dongguan)
The 15th International IC-China Conference & Exhibition
The 11th Dongguan Shoes/ China Shoetes
The 12th China Dongguan International Mould and Metalworking Exhibition
12th China Dongguan International Plastics Packing Rubber Diecasting & Foundry Exhibition

## Hong Kong Convention and Exhibition Centre

As one of the world's freest economies, Hong Kong is renowned for its favourable business environment. Right at the heart of Hong Kong's vibrant and central business district stands the Hong Kong Convention and Exhibition Centre (HKCEC), with a worldwide reputation for service excellence and stringent international standards in management and technology. The HKCEC is highly functional and versatile. Six large exhibition halls, two convention halls, two large foyers, 52 meeting rooms and other function areas offer a total rentable space of 70,000 square metres including the state-of-the-art conference and seminar facilities. The HKCEC plays the leading role in strengthening Hong Kong's position as the Trade Fair Capital of Asia.

Since its opening in 1988, there are more than 34,000 events hosted in HKCEC. The annual attendance of the HKCEC has now reached over five million including exhibitors and delegates along with top buyers and decision makers from more than 150 countries and regions from around the world.

Totally international in outlook and yet fully in tune with Mainland Chinese needs, the HKCEC hosts a wide ranging fair portfolio. This is headed by Asia's largest and world-leading trade fairs for watches and clocks, toys and games, gifts and housewares, jewellery, fashion, textiles, leather, beauty, lighting goods, travel, optical goods, electronics and more. With the expansion of 20,000 square metre exhibition space now underway, and a policy of continues upgrades and modernisation, this is a reputation that is set to endure.

Add: 1 Expo Drive, Wanchai, Hong Kong, China
Tel: 852-2582 8888
Fax: 852-2802 7284
E-mail: info@hkcec.com
Web: www.hkcec.com

## AsiaWorld-Expo

AsiaWorld - Expo is Hong Kong's leading exhibition and events venue offering over 70,000 square metres of rentable space. It is fully integrated with the Hong Kong International Airport and located at the centre of an extensive and efficient air, land and marine transport network.

AsiaWorld-Expo has 10 ground-level, column-free, high specification halls. All of the halls are equipped with advanced ICT services, and can be used either separately or in conjunction with each other to provide one continuous space for events. Since its opening in 2005, AsiaWorld-Expo has already staged a lot of large-scale international events, including "ITU TELECOM WORLD 2006" the largest-ever trade exhibition cum forum in Hong Kong; "Asian Aerospace International Expo and Congress" the world's largest dedicated commercial aviation and aerospace event which has moved to AsiaWorld-Expo since September 2007 after 25 years held in Singapore; "China Sourcing Fairs" in April and October each year, which attracted lots of overseas and local exhibitors and visitors; and also act as an excellent platform for Mainland Chinese enterprises to venture into the global marketplace.

In addition, AsiaWorld-Expo includes the Hong Kong's largest indoor seated venue: AsiaWorld-Arena, which accommodates a maximum capacity of 13,500. The venue has already hosted various world-class concerts and conferences.

Tel: 852-3606 8888
Fax: 852-3606 8889
E-mail: info@asiaworld-expo.com
Web: www.asiaworld-expo.com

## The Venetian® Macao - Resort-Hotel

The ultimate convention and exhibition destination awaits.

The Venetian® Macao offers world - class entertainment, high - tech meeting facilities, suite accommodations, exquisite shopping and dining all under one roof. The 100,000 square meter state-of-the-art convention and exhibition center can comfortably accommodate an event on any scale, from intimate corporate meetings to international conventions. As a truly integrated resort, The Venetian Macao boasts 3,000 hotel suites, a massive shopping mall featuring over 300 of the world's most exclusive brands and 35 acclaimed restaurants. Other attractions include gondola rides down 3 beautiful Venetian canals, spa facilities beyond compare, plus top international shows and exhibitions from the stars of music, stage and sport.

The Venetian® Macao is built with the business traveler in mind. Luxury and convenience go hand in hand. Every hotel room is a luxury suite 70 square meters or larger, complete with every facility to conduct business, including fax/ printer/ copier, high speed Internet access and a safe large enough for a laptop. Macao's cultivated road, air and sea transportation network also means The Venetian Macao is easily accessible to much of the region. And with more than half of the world's population living within a five hour flight from the enclave, visiting Macao has never been easier for travelers and business executives.

MICE features at a glance:
Over 100,000 square meters of Convention & Exhibition space
3,000 suites over 70 square meters, with fax/copier/printer and dedicated data lines
6,500 square meters of pillarless ballroom and 108 meeting rooms
Over 35 acclaimed restaurants and 1,000 seat food court
Over 300 specialty stores
15,000 seat The Venetian-Arena and 1,800 seat The Venetian-Theater
For further inquiries or to book your next event today, simply visit www.venetianmacao.com or call +853 2882 8800

## Zhengzhou International Convention & Exhibition Center

Zhengzhou International Convention & Exhibition Center (ZZICEC) is a fully integrated convention & exhibition facility. It is invested by Zhengzhou Municipal Government, and it integrates convention rooms, exhibition halls, business centres, restaurants, entertainments and performance and tourism facilities all into one. It is one of the signature buildings in Zhengzhou.

Zhengzhou International Convention & Exhibition Centre (ZZICEC) is designed by an internationally acclaimed architect Kisho Kurokawa. The main body of the building is consisted of convention center and exhibition center. ZZICEC has been built since January 20th,2003 and started its operation in October 21st2005 and is managed by Hong Kong - Shanghai Venue Management (Zhengzhou) Limited since June 1st 2006.

ZZICEC covers an area of 686,000 square meters, with a construction area of 226,800 square meters. It consists of a convention centre, an exhibition centre, an outdoor exhibition area of 38,000 square meters and 45,000 square meters of parking space.

The Convention Centre offers 6 levels of multi-purposed function space, with a total construction area of 60,800 square meters. The Grand Hall is an ideal venue for meetings of theatre type up to 5, 000 people, meetings of classroom type up to 3,160 people and seated banquets of up to 1,660 guests, the International Theatre can accommodate 1,090 audiences and two theatres seat 400 audiences each. Also included are 17 meeting rooms of varied sizes, VIP reception rooms, a Chinese restaurant, a western restaurant, and a cafe. Simultaneous interpretation can be provided for up to 8 languages plus 1 within the Grand Hall and International Theatre, while the two theatres can provide 4 languages plus 1 simultaneous interpretation.

The Exhibition Centre offers 2 levels multi-purposed function space of the main body and 6 levels of the secondary body. It was built on a construction area of 166,800 square meters. It consists of two exhibition halls and a variety of auxiliary support facilities, including 68 meeting rooms, food concessions, offices and shops.

The inner exhibition space is 65,000 square meters which could set 3,394 international standard booths. Hall 1 and Hall 2 can be divided into 4 6,000 square meters sections and 2 4,500 square meter sections by floor-to-ceiling operable walls, for independent exhibition use. The ceiling height of Hall 1 is 14 meters and floor loading capacity is 5 tons per square meter. The ceiling height of Hall 2 is 17.6 meters and the floor loading capacity is 1.5 tons per square meter.

# Exhibition Transportation

## Schenker

With a network of around 55,000 people in about 1,500 offices around the world, Schenker is one of the world's leading providers of integrated logistics services, offering air, ocean freight and land concepts as well as logistics services for fairs, relocations, projects and global sports events.

Schenker first entered Mainland China in 1979 and subsequently expanded its presence to nowadays more than 35 locations throughout China with over 4,300 employees working on advanced logistics solutions from one single source.

Schenker is part of DB Logistics, the Transportation and Logistics Division of Deutsche Bahn AG. For all your Fairs & Exhibitions requirements, Schenker's dedicated team of specialists will develop the most efficient and suitable solution.

We offer a full range of exhibition services:

Worldwide coordination of shipments-multimodal transports by air, sea and land

Consolidated shipments of stand building materials, exhibits and promotional materials

Expertise in documentation and customs clearance procedures

Planning and execution of time-defined transports

On-site handling by experienced and trained staff

Professional storage at state-of-the-art facilities and handling of "empties"

Return shipments of complete equipment to the point of origin or to the next fair site

Arrangements of seminar and conference materials as well as stage equipment

Professional transport of art material

Most recently Schenker China has been appointed Official Freight Forwarding & Customs Clearance

Exclusive Supplier of the Beijing 2008 Olympic Games.

Schenker is a part of DB Logistics, the Transportation and Logistics Division of Deutsche Bahn AG.

Our contacts:

South China office-Schenker Intl (H.K.) Ltd.
Add: 38/F, China Resources Building No. 26 Harbour RoadWanchai, Hong Kong
Tel: 852-2585 9688
Fax: 852-2827 5363
E-mail: fairs.hk@schenker.com

Central China office-Schenker China Ltd.
Add: Rm.3802-3806, Raffles City (Office Tower) No.268 Xi Zhang Zhong Road, Shanghai 200001, P.R. China
Tel: 021-6122 5888, 2890 6226
Fax: 021-5292 5194, 2890 6223
E-mail: fairs.sha@schenker.com

North China office-Schenker China Ltd., Beijing Branch
5 Tianwei Sijie
Tianzhu Airport Industrial Area A Beijing 101312, P.R. China
Tel: 010-8048 0099
Fax: 010-8048 0077
E-mail: fairs.bjs@schenker.com

## Agility

Agility is a leading emerging market multinational with more than 32,000 employees, and over 550 offices in 100 countries around the world. A publicly traded company, with over $6 billion in annual revenue, we have three key business groups - Global Integrated Logistics (GIL), Defense & Government Services (DGS) and Investments. Agility GIL is our commercial division, providing integrated logistics solutions to customers spanning a range of industries from technology and retail to defense and government, chemical and oil and gas.

The Agility DGS business group provides comprehensive logistics solutions to various government entities and non governmental organizations on a global basis. With three business divisions - Real Estate, Private Equity and Trade Facilitators, Agility Investments utilizes the local insights from our global network to invest in specialized opportunities in the emerging markets.

AGILITY FAIRS & EVENTS LOGISTICS LIMITED
29/F Fook Lee Comm Centre, Town Place,
33 Lockhart Road, Wanchai, Hong Kong
Tel: 852-2594 9233
Contact: Ms Kenly Tsang

AGILITY FAIRS & EVENTS LOGISTICS (SHANGHAI) CO. LTD
Room 1606, Shanghai Mart, No. 2299, Yan'an Road (West),
Shanghai 200336, P. R. China
Tel: 021-6236 6060, 13911992219
Contact: Mr Mitch Zhang

AGILITY FAIRS & EVENTS LOGISTICS (SHANGHAI) CO. LTD
Beijing Branch
Room 1211 Prime Tower, No.22 Chaowai Street,
Chaoyang District, Beijing 100020, PR China
Tel: 010-6588 1961 / 1962 / 1963 / 1964
Mobile: 13911992219
Contact: Mr Mitch Zhang

AGILITY FAIRS & EVENTS LOGISTICS (SHANGHAI) CO. LTD
Guangzhou Branch
Rm.704/706,7F, No 726 Dong Feng Road East,
Guangzhou 510080 PR China
Tel: 020-3765 5886
Contact: Mr Eric Ye